Main Cities
of Europe
2006

Commitments

"This volume was created at the turn of the century and will last at least as long".

This foreword to the very first edition of the MICHELIN Guide, written in 1900, has become famous over the years and the Guide has lived up to the prediction. It is read across the world and the key to its popularity is the consistency of its commitment to its readers, which is based on the following promises.

THE MICHELIN GUIDE'S COMMITMENTS :

Anonymous inspections: our inspectors make regular and anonymous visits to hotels and restaurants to gauge the quality of products and services offered to an ordinary customer. They settle their own bill and may then introduce themselves and ask for more information about the establishment. Our readers' comments are also a valuable source of information, which we can then follow up with another visit of our own.

Independence: Our choice of establishments is a completely independent one, made for the benefit of our readers alone. The decisions to be taken are discussed around the table by the inspectors and the editor. The most important awards are decided at a European level. Inclusion in the Guide is completely free of charge.

Selection and choice: The Guide offers a selection of the best hotels and restaurants in every category of comfort and price. This is only possible because all the inspectors rigorously apply the same methods.

Annual updates: All the practical information, the classifications and awards are revised and updated every single year to give the most reliable information possible.

Consistency: The criteria for the classifications are the same in every country covered by the Michelin Guide.

... and our aim: to do everything possible to make travel, holidays and eating out a pleasure, as part of Michelin's ongoing commitment to improving travel and mobility.

Contents

COUNTRIES

Classification & Awards

CATEGORIES OF COMFORT

The Michelin Guide selection lists the best hotels and restaurants in each category of comfort and price. The establishments we choose are classified according to their levels of comfort and, within each category, are listed in order of preference.

🏨🏨🏨🏨	🍴🍴🍴🍴🍴	Luxury in the traditional style
🏨🏨🏨	🍴🍴🍴🍴	Top class comfort
🏨🏨	🍴🍴🍴	Very comfortable
🏨🏨	🍴🍴	Comfortable
🏨	🍴	Quite comfortable
	🍴	Traditional pubs serving good food
	🍴	Tapas bars
⌂		Other recommended accommodation
without rest.		This hotel has no restaurant
with rm		This restaurant also offers accommodation

THE AWARDS

To help you make the best choice, some exceptional establishments have been given an award in this year's Guide. They are marked ✿ or 🍴 and **Rest**.

THE BEST CUISINE

Michelin stars are awarded to establishments serving cuisine, of whatever style, which is of the highest quality. The cuisine is judged on the quality of ingredients, the skill in their preparation, the combination of flavours, the levels of creativity, the value for money and the consistency of culinary standards.

✿✿✿	**Exceptional cuisine, worth a special journey** One always eats extremely well here, sometimes superbly.
✿✿	**Excellent cooking, worth a detour**
✿	**A very good restaurant in its category**

RISING STARS

These establishments, listed in red, are the best in their present catregory. They have the potential to rise further, and already have an element of superior quality; as soon as they produce this quality consistently, and in all aspects of their cuisine, they will be hot tips for a higher award. We've highlighted these promising restaurants so you can try them for yourselves; we think they offer a foretaste of the gastronomy of the future.

GOOD FOOD AT MODERATE PRICES

Bib Gourmand
Establishments offering good quality cuisine at reasonable prices (the actual price limit varies from country to country according to the relative costs).

PLEASANT HOTELS AND RESTAURANTS

Symbols shown in red indicate particularly pleasant or restful establishments: the character of the building, its décor, the setting, the welcome and services offered may all contribute to this special appeal.

🏠 to 🏠🏠🏠🏠	**Pleasant hotels**
✗ to ✗✗✗✗✗	**Pleasant restaurants**

OTHER SPECIAL FEATURES

As well as the categories and awards given to the establishment, Michelin inspectors also make special note of other criteria which can be important when choosing an establishment.

LOCATION

If you are looking for a particularly restful establishment, or one with a special view, look out for the following symbols:

🐾	**Quiet hotel**
🐾	**Very quiet hotel**
≤	**Interesting view**
≤	**Exceptional view**

WINE LIST

If you are looking for an establishment with a particularly interesting wine list, look out for the following symbol:

Particularly interesting wine list
This symbol might cover the list presented by a sommelier in a luxury restaurant or that of a simple restaurant where the owner has a passion for wine. The two lists will offer something exceptional but very different, so beware of comparing them by each other's standards.

Facilities
& Services

30 rm	Number of rooms
🛗	Lift (elevator)
A/C	Air conditioning (in all or part of the establishment)
⊁	Establishment with areas reserved for non-smokers.
♿	Establishment at least partly accessible to those of restricted mobility
🍴	Meals served in garden or on terrace
SAT	Satellite TV
📶	Wireless Internet access
Spa	Wellness centre: an extensive facility for relaxation and well-being
🔥 ⅃⅃	Sauna – Exercise room
⅃ ⅃	Swimming pool: outdoor or indoor
🪑	Garden
🎾 ⅃18	Tennis court – Golf course and number of holes
🧍 150	Equipped conference room: maximum capacity
⇔ 4/40	Private dining rooms (minimun and maximum capacity)
🚗 🏠 P P	Valet parking – Garage – Car park, enclosed parking
🐕	No dogs allowed (in all or part of the establishment)
May - October	Dates when open, as indicated by the hotelier
Ⓜ	Nearest metro station

Prices

These prices are given in the currency of the contry in question. Valid for 2006 the rates shown should only vary if the cost of living changes to any great extent.

SERVICE AND TAXES

Except in Greece, Hungary, Poland and Spain, prices shown are inclusive, that is to say service and V.A.T. included. In the U.K. and Ireland, s = service included. In Italy, when not included, a percentage for service is shown after the meal prices, eg. (16 %).

MEALS

Meals 40/56	Set meal prices
Meals à la carte 🎭	"à la carte" meal prices Restaurants offering lower priced pre and/or post theatre menus

HOTEL

86 ch 🛏 650/750	Lowest and highest price for a comfortable single
🛏🛏 750/890	and a best double room
☕ 60/120	Prices include breakfast

BREAKFAST

☕ 20	Price of breakfast

CREDIT CARDS

AE ⓓ ⓜ VISA	Credit cards accepted by the establishment: American Express – Diners Club – MasterCard – Visa

How to use this guide

PRACTICAL & TOURIST INFORMATION

Pages with practical information on every country and city: public transport, tourist information offices, main sites and attractions (museums, monuments, theatres, etc), with a directory of shop addresses and examples of local specialities to take home.

RESTAURANTS

XXXXX à X

The most pleasant : in red.

STARS

❀❀❀ Worth a special journey.

❀❀ Worth a detour.

❀ A very good restaurant.

Establishment named in red : "Rising Star".

RESTAURANTS & HOTELS

The country is indicated by the coloured strip down the side of the page: dark for restaurants, light for hotels.

HOTELS

Âㅔㅔㅔ à 🏠

The most pleasant : in red.

BIB GOURMAND ⊛

Good food at moderate prices.

BELGIQUE BELGIUM

BRUSSELS

• **TAXIS**
Taxis bear an illuminated sign on the car roof. They may be hailed in the street, called by telephone, hired at taxi ranks. ℰ 02 349 49 49 (Taxis Verts) ; ℰ 02 349 43 43 (Taxis Orange) ; ℰ 02 268 00 00 (Taxis Bleus). Minimum pick-up charge is €2,40;

USEFUL ADDRESSES

• **TOURIST OFFICES**
BI-TC (Bruxelles International - Tourisme & Congrès) Plan II C3, Hôtel de Ville, Grand-Place, 1000 Bruxelles. ℰ 02 513 89 40. Open 9am-6pm (2pm Sunday in winter).
OPT (Office de Promotion du Tourisme Wallonie-Bruxelles) Plan II C3, 63 rue du Marché-aux-Herbes, 1000 Bruxelles. ℰ 02 504 03 90. Open 9am-6pm (7pm July-August).

BUSY PERIODS
It is may be difficult to find
reasonable

a journey inside the urban centre (agglomeration) costs €1,15/km and €2,30 outside urban centre. It is customary to round up taxi fares. A night tariff (daytime tariff + €2/km) is applicable from 10pm to 6am.

• **POST OFFICES**
Opening times 9am to 4-5pm. The post office on the first floor of **Centre Monnaie**, Place de la Monnaie Plan II B5 is open on Friday evenings and Saturday mornings, that at **Gare du Midi** is open from 7am to 11pm (7pm for financial operations).

• **EMERGENCIES**
Dial **100 / 112** if calling on a mobile phone) for Ambulance and F
101 for Poli

PARIS - ÉTOILE-CH

Le Petit Four (Martin)
2 rue François 1ᵉʳ (1st) Ⓜ Palais-Royal – ℰ 01 12 96 ⊘
– petit.four@wanadoo.fr – Fax 01 12 96 46 28
Rest (closed in august) 75 €, 185/240 € and a la c

Spec. Foie gras chaud au vinaigre de cidre. Sai
Colvert rôti au miel.
✦ Luxury ✦ Inventive ✦
In the gardens of the Palais-Royal, sumptuo
rated with splendid "pictures under glass"
worthy of this historic monument.

XX **Au Pied de Porc**
15 bd Voltaire (11th) Ⓜ République – ℰ 0
– Pieddeporc@gmw.net – Fax 01 42 13 7
Rest – 29 €, 32/72 € and a la carte 37/⊘
✦ Classic ✦ Trendly ✦
Pigs trotters are the speciality of th
late into the night since opened ir
fruits designs.

ÉTOILE – CHAMPS-ÉLYSÉES

Rond-point des Cham

Palazzo Amédée
25 av. Rabelais (8th) Ⓜ Mar
– ℰ 01 45 12 24 24 – reserv
– Fax 01 45 12 23 23
145 rm ⌂ ✦ ♦ 350 € ⊘⊘ 5
Rest – See **Le jardin** be
Rest *La Cour* – a la car
Spec. Tartare de bar e
chocolats grands cru
✦ Palace ✦ Stylic
Classic style in the l
gallery, stunning ◆
ming, green-filled
when the weath

Le Faubourg
15 r. des Écurie
– reservation
174 rm ⌂ - ⊘
Rest *Café* ✦
carte 60/9
✦ Busin
This "Fa
tech ro

LOCATION

The city, the district, the
map.

ADDRESS

All the information you need
to make a reservation and
find the establishment.

FACILITIES
& SERVICES

See also p.12.

DESCRIPTION OF
THE ESTABLISHMENT

Atmosphere, style and
character.

CLASSIFICATION
BY DISTRICT

With the corresponding
plan number.

PRICES

See also p.13.

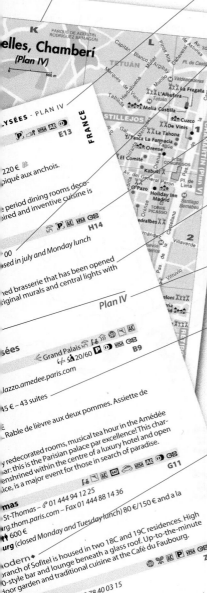

elles, Chamberí
(Plan IV)

YSÉES - PLAN IV

E13

FRANCE

220 € ⁂
piqué aux anchois.

e period dining rooms deco-
bired and inventive cuisine is

H14

00
sed in july and Monday lunch

hed brasserie that has been opened
iginal murals and central lights with

Plan IV

sées

◁ Grand Palais

B9

lazzo.amedee.paris.com

5 € – 43 suites

. Rable de lièvre aux deux pommes. Assiette de

y redecorated rooms, musical tea hour in the Amédée
ar: this is the Parisian palace par excellence! This char-
enshrined within the centre of a luxury hotel and open
ice, is a major event for those in search of paradise.

G11

mas
St-Thomas – ☎ 01 444 94 12 25
rg.thom.paris.com – Fax 01 444 88 14 36
600 €
urg (closed Monday and Tuesday lunch) 80 €/150 € and a la

odern♦
ranch of Sofitel is housed in two 18C and 19C residences. High
0-style bar and lounge beneath a glass roof. Up-to-the-minute
door garden and traditional cuisine at the Café du Faubourg.

Z3

rest)   ☎ 03 78 40 03 15

on the top

KEY WORDS

If you're looking for a specific
type of establishment, look
out for these words. They aim
to encapsulate the key 'theme'
of the hotel or restaurant
– the type of cooking, style
of establishment, décor or
atmosphere – in no more than
three words, guiding you quickly
to the type of hotel or restaurant
that you are looking for.

11

Eurozone : €

 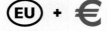 (EU) + €

 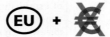 (EU) + €̸

 EU states

Schengen Countries

Area of free movement between member states

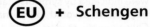 **(EU)** + Schengen

 (EU) + Schengen ✗

 (EU) + Schengen

The Michelin Guide and Europe

Whether it be for business or pleasure, travellers throughout Europe know that they can rely on the Michelin Guide. For over a century, it has been their companion, first in France and then beyond the dotted borderlines printed on the Michelin maps.

Over the last hundred years, the boundaries of Europe have been extended and the circle of gold stars on the European flag has had to adjust in order to welcome other nations. The Michelin Guide has always kept abreast of these profound changes on the ground, in keeping with its goal and its motto: *serving the traveller*. Indeed, in its coverage of Europe, it has witnessed the history of the continent as it unfolded. Year after year, the guide's publication, or absence from the market, has reflected the great upheavals experienced during the 20th century, with its vicissitudes, crises, eras of prosperity and peace.

THE MICHELIN GUIDE: MULTILINGUAL AND INTERNATIONAL

Inspired by its success in France and encouraged by the development of the automobile industry throughout Europe, the Michelin Guide started to spread the concept to neighbouring countries: *Belgique* appeared in 1904 – the second volume in what would quickly become a true European-wide collection. The following year, a third guide – *Benelux* – was published. The collection began to adopt an approach which would include **tourist information**, with new sections covering sights and excursions not to be missed, in addition to the advice and practical information already in the guides. At the same time, the Michelin Guide collection started to espouse Michelin's international ambitions: every new title was published in the language(s) of the country, services and main facilities were indicated by **symbols** that everyone could understand, and several pages were devoted to **international regulations** useful for travellers. Consequently readers could refer to a page dedicated to «General European Traffic Rules», for example, with specific information regarding

which side of the road to drive on in every European country. It is interesting to note that, at the time, the Michelin Guide included Turkey as part of Europe, with information about traffic in that country.

MICHELIN TRAVELS ABROAD

The Michelin Guide began to expand throughout Europe and use other languages. In 1908 *The Michelin Guide to France* was published, an **adaptation in English** of the original French guide, and two years later two new titles were published: *Deutschland und Schweiz* and *España y Portugal*. The following year (1911)

three more guides were published, expanding the collection still further: *British Isles, Alpes et Rhin*, and the exotic *Les pays du Soleil*, covering not only the Côte d'Azur, Corsica and Italy, but also North Africa and Egypt! And that same year, all of these guides were translated into English.

This unprecedented expansion marked the start of the company's desire to spread throughout Europe and North Africa. Proof of the successful formula of the Michelin Guides was summed up in an advertising poster of the era showing Bibendum – the Michelin Man – proudly demonstrating that the total number of copies of the Michelin guide collection, if piled up, would be equivalent to 60 times the height of St Paul's Cathedral in London!

Success was then interrupted in 1939, with the start of the **Second World War**. From 1940 to 1944, the absence of the guide revealed the torment which Europe was going through. When the guide finally reappeared, it was «*for official use only*», printed in Washington to accompany the officers of the Allied forces during the Normandy Landings.

FROM A
EUROPEAN COLLECTION...

The 1950s brought new growth, with Michelin maps now covering all of Western Europe. But it was in the 1960s that the Michelin Guide collection really started to take on a **European dimension**, taking a step by step approach to expansion. In 1964, after a half century's absence, *Deutschland* reappeared (without the GDR and East Berlin), followed ten years later by *Great Britain & Ireland*. Meanwhile, the shorter *Paris* and *London* guides appeared on the shelves, based on information taken from the national guides, and revealing an interest in large **European capital cities**. In order to remain the indispensable companion for travellers throughout Europe, the guides would from then on follow the model of *France*: enhanced with more information, including a **rigorous selection of fine restaurants**.

MICHELIN IN EUROPE

...TO A GUIDE FOR EUROPE

Means of transport were becoming more and more diversified and journey times were shortening considerably, encouraging faster travel and trips made more often and over longer distances than ever before. Michelin needed to bring tourists and business travellers alike a guide which covered the relevant areas, and at the same time cross the borders of the new Europe to the north and to the east.

1982 saw the chance to do this. The first guide devoted to Europe was born of a **partnership** with *Times-Life Magazine* and appeared under the title *20 Cities/Villes EUROPE*. The guide was written in English and twenty thousands copies were published. The selection of establishments adopted for the guide took the best hotel and restaurant addresses in each category from the «country» guides, following the criteria guaranteeing **a constant level of quality**, above and beyond specific national considerations.

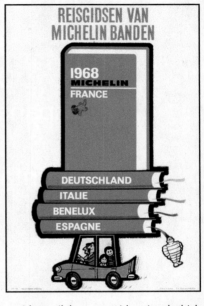

The huge success of this first edition led the company to repeat the experience. The following year, Copenhagen and Vienna were included in the guide: until then, no guide existed which covered these cities, and the more global title *Main Cities of Europe* was adopted in 1984 with more than 50 towns and cities – some of them capitals, but also the other large influential cities in **15 countries**.

Who does not recognise the famous red cover of the Michelin Guide today? Since the beginning of the 20th century, the Guide has established itself throughout Europe thanks to quality service and up-to-date selection. From Oslo to Athens, Lisbon to Budapest, the 12 titles in the collection (not including the latest, *New York City*) suggest nearly 30 700 hotels and 18 200 restaurants, including nearly 1 400 starred restaurants, and 1 200 town plans. With new introductions and practical information on every country and every town and city selected, the 2006 vintage of *Main Cities of EUROPE* offers you the very best. Happy reading and bon voyage with Michelin!

Also in the
Michelin Guide collection

AUSTRIA
ÖSTERREICH

PROFILE

- **AREA:**
  83 853 km² (32 376 sq mi).

- **POPULATION:**
  8 150 000 inhabitants (est. 2005), density = 97 per km².

- **CAPITAL:**
  Vienna (conurbation 1 892 000 inhabitants).

- **CURRENCY:**
  Euro (€); rate of exchange: € 1 = US$ 1.17 (Nov 2005).

- **GOVERNMENT:**
  Parliamentary republic and federal state (since 1955). Member of European Union since 1995.

- **LANGUAGE:**
  German.

- **SPECIFIC PUBLIC HOLIDAYS:**
  Epiphany (6 January); Corpus Christi (late May/June); National Day (26 October); Immaculate Conception (8 December); St. Stephen's Day (26 December).

- **LOCAL TIME:**
  GMT + 1 hour in winter and GMT + 2 hours in summer.

- **CLIMATE:**
  Temperate continental with cold winters – high snow levels – and warm summers (Vienna: January: 0°C, July: 20°C).

- **INTERNATIONAL DIALLING CODE:**
  00 43 followed by area code without initial 0 and then the local number.

- **EMERGENCY:**
  Police: ✆ 133; Medical Assistance: ✆ 144; Fire Brigade: ✆ 122.

- **ELECTRICITY:**
  220 volts AC, 50Hz; 2-pin round-shaped continental plugs.

Vienna

FORMALITIES

Travellers from the European Union (EU), Switzerland, Iceland and the main countries of North and South America need a national identity card or passport (America: passport required) to visit Austria for less than three months (tourism or business purpose). For visitors from other countries a visa may be required, in addition to a passport, especially for those wishing to stay for longer than three months. We advise you to check with your embassy before travelling.

A valid driving licence is essential. An international driving licence is required for drivers from 80 countries, mainly in South America, Africa, Asia, Middle East and Pacific Islands. Third party insurance is the minimum cover required by Austrian legislation but it is advisable to take out fully comprehensive cover (Green Card).

MAJOR NEWSPAPERS

For Austria and Vienna the daily newspapers with the widest distribution are *Neue Kronenzeitung, Die Presse, Der Standard, Die Wiener Zeitung* and *Kurier*.

USEFUL PHRASES

ENGLISH	GERMAN
Yes	**Ja**
No	**Nein**
Good morning	**Guten Morgen**
Goodbye	**Auf Wiedersehen**
Thank you	**Danke**
Please	**Bitte**
Excuse me	**Verzeihung**
I don't understand	**Ich verstehe nicht**

HOTELS

◆ CATEGORIES

Accommodation ranges from luxurious 5-star international hotels and well-appointed first class hotels to smaller, family-run guesthouses (pensions), which are frequently part of a residential building, and bed and breakfast establishments.

◆ PRICE RANGE

The price is per room. Between April and October and in December it is advisable to book in advance.

◆ TAX

Included in the room price.

◆ CHECK OUT TIME

Usually between 11am and noon.

◆ RESERVATIONS

By telephone or by Internet. A credit card number may be required.

◆ TIP FOR LUGGAGE HANDLING

At the discretion of the customer (about €1 per bag).

◆ BREAKFAST

It is often not included in the price of the room and is generally served between 7am and 10am. Most hotels offer a self-service buffet but usually it is possible to have continental breakfast served in the room.

Reception	**Empfang**
Single room	**Einzelzimmer**
Double room	**Doppelzimmer**
Bed	**Bett**
Bathroom	**Bad**
Shower	**Dusche**

RESTAURANTS

In addition to formal restaurants, you will also find a range of establishments for eating and drinking in a pleasant, relaxed atmosphere. **Keller**, similar to German beer cellars, are lively and informal and serve cold meals or a daily special with white wine or beer. **Gasthäuser** or **Weinhäuser**, known as **Beisel** in Vienna, offer regional cuisine at reasonable prices. **Weinstuben** are charming taverns where you can enjoy local wine and light meals. In wine-growing villages around Vienna (Grinzing, Nussdorf, Sievering, Gumpoldskirchen), the **Heurigen** offer cold snacks or complete meals and sometimes feature traditional **Schrammelmusik**. The **Buschenschenken** are similar establishments in Styria.

Breakfast	**Frühstück**	7am – 10am
Lunch	**Mittagessen**	11.30pm – 2pm
Dinner	**Abendessen**	6.30pm – 10-11pm, sometimes later

◆ RESERVATIONS

Reservations are usually made by phone, fax or Internet. For famous restaurants (including Michelin starred restaurants), it is advisable to book several days, even weeks, in advance. A credit card number or a phone number may be required as guarantee.

◆ THE BILL

The bill (check) includes a service charge (10-15%) and VAT in hotels and restaurants. If you are pleased with the service, it is customary to add a tip (5-10%).

Drink or aperitif	**Getränk oder aperitif**
Meal	**Mahlzeit**
Appetizer, first course, starter	**Vorspeise**
Main dish	**Hauptgericht**
Main daily special	**Tagesgericht**
Dessert	**Nachtisch**
Water	**Wasser**
Wine (red, white, rosé)	**Wein (rot, weiss, rosé)**
Beer	**Bier**
Bread	**Brot**
Meat (rare, medium, well-done)	**Fleisch(blutig, mittel, gut durchgebraten)**
Fish	**Fisch**
Salt/pepper	**Salz/Pfeffer**
Cheese	**Käse**
Vegetables	**Gemüse**
Hot/cold	**Heiss/Kalt**
The bill (check) please	**Die Rechnung bitte**

LOCAL CUISINE

The blend of the culinary traditions from countries of the former Austro-Hungarian Empire gives a special distinction to Austrian cooking. Fresh products and regional specialities from lowland and mountain areas are also notable features. Meals are substantial: soup (sometimes with Frittaten – pancake strips, or Leberknödel – liver dumplings) is followed by a main dish, almost always consisting of meat, fried in breadcrumbs or boiled, accompanied by salad and stewed fruit. Dumplings (Knödel) may be served instead of vegetables. The liberal use of spices in many dishes reveals Middle Eastern influences. The most famous dish, Wiener Schnitzel – breaded fillet of veal – is served with sautéed potatoes or potato salad. There are several types of goulash: Rindsgulasch, a paprika-flavoured stew of Hungarian origin; Erdäpfelgulasch, a potato stew served with frankfurters. Tafelspitz is a classic dish of boiled beef with horseradish sauce.

In **Carinthia**, game is accompanied by fresh cranberries picked in the mountains, wild mushrooms from the forests and full-bodied red wine. Among its special dishes are Saure Suppe – soup made with several meats and herbs, sweet and soured cream, flavoured with fennel, aniseed and saffron; Kasnudel – ravioli with curds and mint, meat, spinach, potatoes, mushroom or prunes; and Schlikkrappen – pastry pockets with a filling of offal and fresh herbs. The lake district of Salzkammergut in **Upper Austria** is famous for its freshwater fish – trout, carp, pike-perch and other varieties found nowhere else. **Salzburg** makes the most of its rural and sophisticated traditions: exquisite cheeses, home-cured pork, cured brook trout. **Styria** is well known for its 'black gold' – oil made from pumpkin seeds. Styrian lamb dishes and duck or chicken fried in egg and breadcrumbs are particularly tasty. The food of the **Tyrol** shows the influence of neighbouring Swabia, Carinthia and Friuli. Liver and bacon dumplings (Tirolerleberknödel or Speckknödel) are typical. In **Vorarlberg**, follow the Bregenzerwald Cheese Route which takes in hill farms and alpine dairy farms producing Bergkäse. There are 30 varieties including Emmentaler, spicy Rässkäse, cheeses made from sheep's and goat's milk, tangy green 'Alpzieger' with 40 herbs, beer and wine cheeses and 'Gsieg', a caramel-like cheese. Käsespätzle are gnocchi with grated cheese and topped with fried onion rings.

Austria is famous for the great variety of cakes, sweets and desserts **(Mehlspeisen)** accompanied by lashings of whipped cream. Sachertorte is a rich chocolate cake with a thin layer of apricot jam and covered with chocolate icing; Linzertorte is made with almonds and apricot or raspberry jam filling; Kaiserschmarren are morsels of raisin pancakes served with plum preserve. Other favourites are Strudel, turnover filled with apples or cream cheese and currants; plum or apricot fritters; apricot dumplings; Palatschinken, thin pancake filled with apricot jam or chocolate sauce; and a sweet soufflé (Salzburger Nockerl).

◆ DRINK

Vineyards cultivated in Lower Austria, Weinviertel, Burgenland and Styria produce excellent wines. White wines include **Grüner Veltliner, Sauvignon blanc, Riesling, Welschriesling**. The district of **Wachau** in the Danube Valley produces wines with a delicate bouquet – Spitz, Dürnstein, Weissenkirchen, Krems, Langenlois. New wine called Heuriger is drunk in typical establishments known as Heurigen in Vienna and Buschenschenken in Styria. Red wines, especially the **Pinot Noir**, the **Zweigelt,** the **St. Laurent** and the **Blaufränkischer,** are of high quality. The best-known red wines come from **Burgenland**.

Beer is also drunk with meals. Austrians enjoy a variety of fruit and herbal spirits – **Slivovitz** (plums), **Kirsch** (cherries), **Himbeergeist** (raspberries).

VIENNA
WIEN

Population (est. 2005): 1 573 000 (conurbation 1 892 000) – Altitude: 156m

P. Bénet/MICHELIN

Vienna, an imperial city for over six centuries, epitomises elegance and sophistication. The profusion of splendid Baroque palaces and churches, interesting buildings in a variety of styles, ornate fountains and decorative sculpture creates an overwhelming aura of opulence. The elegant shops, fashionable coffee-houses and restaurants, pedestrian areas and grand avenues entice visitors to browse and while away the time pleasantly.

The Emperors and aristocratic families were discerning patrons of the arts and attracted the luminaries of the time – composers, musicians, artists and architects – to the city. Over the centuries Vienna has retained its considerable prestige as a leading artistic centre as evidenced by its magnificent art collections, excellent museums, and prestigious opera house and concert halls.

Vienna, which was an outpost of the Roman Empire and later withstood countless Turkish onslaughts, remained the easternmost centre of European culture until the collapse of the communist ideology. The city has found an international role as the permanent seat of OPEC, the organisation of petroleum-exporting countries, and as the third permanent centre of the United Nations after New York and Geneva.

WHICH DISTRICT TO CHOOSE

In the historic part of the city graced by the elegant patrician mansions around **the Hofburg** *Plan II* **D2** and the area near **Stephansdom** *Plan II* **E2** you will find luxurious establishments and stylish hotels. There are excellent hotels near the main station in **Landstrasse** *Plan I* **B3**; hotels of a good standard and comfortable pensions with all amenities near the Rathaus *Plan I* **A3**, in the University district, the Museums Quartier *Plan II* **C3**, Mariahilferstrasse *Plan II* **C3**, Währingerstrasse *Plan II* **C1** and near the Prater in Lassalle Strasse *Plan I* **B2**. For sophisticated cuisine look no further than the historic centre, in the streets around

23

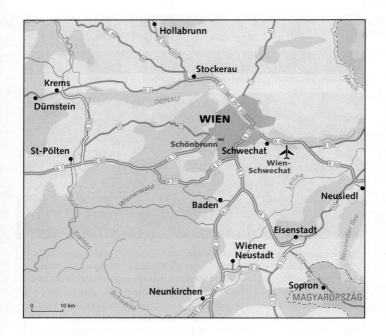

Graben *Plan II* **D2**, **Kohlmarkt** *Plan II* **D2**, **Kärntner Strasse**. Fashionable establishments are numerous in the **Fleischmarkt** *Plan II* **E2** and **Freyung** *Plan II* **D2** districts. There are plen-ty of simple, traditional eateries in the **Spittelberg**, in the University district, in **Stubenring** *Plan II* **E2**, **Praterstr.** *Plan II* **F1**, at **Copa Cagrana** in Donau City.

PRACTICAL INFORMATION

ARRIVAL – DEPARTURE

Wien-Schwechat Airport – 19 km (12 mi) from the city centre. ✆ 01 70 07 22 233 (24hr). www.viennaairport.com

From the airport to the city centre – By **express train** to Wien Mitte: every 30min, time: 16min. €9 single, €16 return trip (reduction with Vienna Card). Check-in including boarding card possible (up to 24hr prior to departure) – except for travel to the USA – and separate CAT platform at Wien Mitte. ✆ 01 25 250, www.cityairporttrain.com

There are also regular train services to/from Wien Mitte, Praterstern/ Wien Nord and Handelskai which all link up with the metro. By taxi: about €30; ask about special airport rates. By express bus: to/from Schwedenplatz/Rotenturmstr.– Postgasse, every 30 min, time: 20min; to/from Südbahnhof, every 30min, time: 20min; to/from

Westbahnhof, every 30min, time: 35min; to/from Vienna International Centre (Donau City), every 90min, time: 25min; fare €6 single, €11 return trip (reduction with Vienna Card). ℰ 05 17 17, www.postbus.at (bus); www.oebb.at (express train).

Railway Stations – Westbahnhof *Plan I* **A3**: trains for Hungary, western Austria and most of Western and Northern Europe. **Südbahnhof** *Plan I* **B3**: trains to Berlin, Italy and Eastern Europe. www.oebb.at

TRANSPORT

♦ BUS, METRO AND TRAM

The **Vienna Card** (Wien-Karte), which allows unlimited travel on the whole of the city's public transport network for 72hr and gives a discount to sights, cafés and restaurants, shops and heurigers, can be purchased from the Tourist Office, at your hotel or from ticket offices of the Vienna Transport Authority. €16.90. There are Rover tickets €5 (24hr), €12 (72hr), €1.50 single. ℰ 05 17 17, www.oebb.at

♦ TAXIS

Allow €7-10 for a short journey. It is customary to give a tip. Radio Taxis ℰ 31 300, 40 100, 60 160. The base fare is €2.50 during the day, Sunday and public holidays (€2.60 at night; radio taxi surcharge €2).

USEFUL ADDRESSES

♦ TOURIST INFORMATION

Albertinaplatz 1 *Plan II* **D3**. ℰ 01 24 555, www.vienna.info. at; open 9am-7pm daily. Also at Rathaus, Westbahnhof, Südbahnhof, Airport, Nordeinfahrt/Florisdorfer Brücke (Donauinsel exit).

♦ POST OFFICES

Opening times Mon-Fri 8am-noon and 2pm-6pm. Some open longer hours: the main post office in Fleischmarkt 19 *Plan II* **E2** (24hr), those at Franz-Joseph-Bahnhof, Althahnstr.10 6am (7am Sat, Sun and holidays) to 10pm, Südbahnhof, Wiedner Gürtel 1a Mon-Sat 7am-10pm, and Westbahnhof, Europaplatz 1/Mariahilferstr. 132 daily 6am-11pm.

♦ BANKS/CURRENCY EXCHANGE

Banks open Mon-Fri, 8am-12.30pm and 1.30pm-3pm (5.30pm Thur). There are cash dispensers, which require a PIN, all over the city. Credit cards are widely accepted. Bureaux de change often charge high commissions.

♦ EMERGENCY

Police ℰ **133;** Fire Brigade ℰ **122;** Ambulance Service ℰ **144.**

EXPLORING VIENNA

It is possible to visit the main sights and museums in three to four days.

Museums and other sights are usually open from 9-10am to 5-6pm. Some close on Mondays or Tuesdays and at lunchtime.

VISITING

Hofburg *Plan II* **D2** – The sumptuous residence of the Habsburgs:

imperial apartments, porcelain and silver collections. Do not miss the **Winter Riding School** (Spanische Reitschule) and the **Treasury** (Schatzkammer).

Stephansdom *Plan II* **E2** – The magnificent Gothic cathedral is the symbol of Vienna. Views from the towers.

Schloss Schönbrunn – The imperial summer palace with ornate rococo decoration and fine gardens. View form the Gloriette.

Karlskirche – A splendid domed Baroque church with harmonious interior and decoration.

Kunsthistorisches Museum *Plan II* **C3** – The outstanding collections of fine arts of the Habsburg dynasty presented in a splendid building.

Secessiongebäude *Plan II* **D3** – An avant-garde building topped by a gilded dome (Beethoven frieze by Klimt).

Belvedere *Plan I* **B3** – Two magnificent Baroque palaces, built for Prince Eugene of Savoy, house excellent museums: **Baroque art** (Lower Belvedere), **Medieval art** (Orangery), **19C-20C Austrian and international art** (Upper Belvedere). French-style gardens with ornate fountain.

Tour of the Ring – Take circular tram Lines 1, 2 from Schottenring/Dr.K.-Lueger Ring: Votivkirche, University, Rathaus, Parliament, Burgtheater, Volksgarden, Heldenplatz, Neue Burg colonnade, Maria Theresien Platz, Burggarten, Opera House, Stadtpark, Museum of Applied Arts, Post Office Savings Bank.

Jugendstil buildings – Examples of modern European architecture. **Secession building** *(see above)*. **Wagner Pavillons** (Karlsplatz *Plan II* **E3**). Linke Wienzeile apartments (Majolikahaus, Medallionhaus) *Plan II* **D3**, Postsparkasse *Plan II* **E2**, Looshaus, 3 Michaelerplatz *Plan II* **D2**. Kirche an Steinhof and Wagner Villas (Penzing).

Boat trips on the Danube from Schwedenplatz *Plan II* **E1**.

Views from Donauturm (Danube Tower), the Ferris Wheel in the Prater, heights of Kahlenberg, and Leopoldsberg.

GOURMET TREATS

If you feel peckish during the day, stop at a typical Würstel-Stand (sausage stand): *Albertina*, 1 Albertinaplatz, *Hoher Markt*, 1 Hoher Markt/Marc-Aurelstr., *Zur Oper*, Kärtner Str. 42. Try *Trzesniewski*, Dorotheergasse 1, a traditional snack bar where the waitresses wear lace bonnets.

Be sure to visit a traditional Viennese coffee house to sample the speciality coffees and cakes or have a drink and a meal. Some are genuine institutions: *Demel*, Kohlmarkt 14, *Central*, Herrengasse 14, *Sacher*, Philarmonikerstr. 4, *Landtmann*, Dr.-Karl-Leuger-Ring 4, *Dommayer*, Dommayergasse 2, *Diglas*, Wollzeile 10, *Café Museum*, Friedrichstr. 6, *Kleines Café*, Franziskanerplatz 3.

Head for the pubs and bars around **Ruprechstkirche** and **Rudolfplatz** *Plan II* **E1** should you wish to go out **for a drink or for the evening.** The in-crowd frequents *Blaustern*, Döblinger Gürtel 2, *Casablanca*, Rabensteig 8, *Loos-Bar*, Kärtner Str.10. Other popular venues are *Cantino*, Seilerstätte 30, *Fischerbräu*, Billrothstr. 17, *Krah Krah*, Rabensteig 8. *Spittelberg* is another lively area. You can also visit the Heuriger district – **Grinzing** *Plan I* **A1**, **Heiligenstadt** *Plan I* **A1**, **Neustift**, **Nussdorf** or **Sievering** – or the 'city Heuriger' such as *Esterházykeller*, Haarhof 1, and *Zwölf Apostelkeller*, Sonnenfelgasse 3.

SHOPPING

Shops and malls usually open Mon-Fri, 9am-6.30pm, Sat 9am-5pm; many are open until 9pm on Thur and 7.30pm on Fri.

For luxury and designer shops visit **Kärntner Strasse** *Plan II* **D2**, **Graben** *Plan II* **D2**, **Kohlmarkt** *Plan II* **D2**, **Neuer Markt** *Plan II* **D2** and

Tuchlauben *Plan II* **D2**. Viennese fashion designers are located in **Seilergasse** *Plan II* **D2** (no 7 *Helmut Lang*), **Singerstrasse** *Plan II* **E2** (no 7 *Michel Meyer*, no 4 *Schellakann*), **Jasomirgottstrasse** (no 5 *Doris Ainedeter*), **Spiegelgasse** *Plan II* **D2** (no 19 *Wiener Blut* – knitwear). The major department stores are: *Steffl*, 1 Kärntner Strasse, *Braum am Graben*, 8 Kärntner Ring, *Ringstrassen Galerien*, 5-7 Kärntner Ring, *Peek und Cloppenburg*, Mariahilferstr. 26-30. The lively **Mariahilferstrasse** *Plan II* **C3** and the side streets are famous for trendy fashions and accessories. Visit *Meinl am Graben*, Graben 19, for fine foods and wines.

MARKETS – **Naschmarkt,** Linke Wienzeile *Plan II* **D3** (Mon-Sat, 6.30am-6pm; flea market Sat 6am-6pm). **Karmelitermarkt,** Krummbaumgasse / Leopoldgasse/Haidgasse *Plan II* **D1** – the Orient in Vienna (Mon-Fri 6am-6.30pm, Sat 6am-2pm). **Am Hof** (Mar-Christmas, Fri-Sat 10am-8pm). **Craft market** at Spittelberggasse *Plan II* **C3**, Sat Apr-Nov, also **Christmas market**, late Nov-Christmas.

WHAT TO BUY – Porcelain, glass, Loden coats, Dirndl, leather goods, jewellery, confectionery and cakes (Sachertorte, Demel Torte, Imperialtorte).

ENTERTAINMENT

Vienna lives up to its cultural reputation with a number of prestigious venues:

Staatsoper *Plan II* **D3**: opera.

Burgtheater *Plan II* **C2**: concerts and shows.

Volksoper *Plan II* **C1**: opera and operettas sung in German, musical comedies.

Volkstheater *Plan II* **C2**: contemporary plays.

Theater an der Wien *Plan II* **D3**: Viennese operettas, ballets.

Wiener Konzerthaus *Plan II* **E3**: international orchestras and soloists.

NIGHTLIFE

Explore the **Bermuda triangle** (around Judengasse *Plan II* **D2**) for bars and nightclubs; listen to live music at *Arena*, Baumgasse 80, *Passage*, Burgring 1, venues under the arches – metro stops Thaliastrasse to Nussdorfer Strasse; dance the night away at *Wuk*, Währingerstr. 59, *Flex*, 1 Donaukanal/Augartbrücke, *Volksgarten Clubdisco*, Burgring 1. Try your luck at *Casino Wien*, Kärntner Strasse 41.

AUSTRIA

HISTORICAL CENTRE Plan II

Imperial
rm rest 120 VISA

Kärntner Ring 16 ✉ 1015 – Ⓜ Karlsplatz – ☏ (01) 50 11 03 56
– hotel.imperial@luxurycollection.com – Fax (01) 50 11 04 10
– www.starwoodhotels.com/imperial **E3**

138 rm – 703 € 703 €, 35 € – 30 suites

Rest *Imperial* *(closed July)* (dinner only) (booking advisable) a la carte 41/74 €

Rest *Café Imperial* a la carte 30/45 €

♦ Palace ♦ Grand Luxury ♦ Historic ♦

The former residence of the Prince of Württemberg is the epitome of a luxury hotel: impressive architecture, furnishings of the highest quality and unique service. A restaurant with refined and exclusive ambience. Viennese coffee-house atmosphere in the "Café'-Imperial".

Grand Hotel
rm 200 VISA

Kärntner Ring 9 ✉ 1010 – Ⓜ Karlsplatz – ☏ (01) 51 58 00
– sales@grandhotelwien.com – Fax (01) 5 15 13 12
– www.grandhotelwien.com **E3**

205 rm – 330/410 € 400/480 €, 29 € – 11 suites

Rest *Le Ciel*, *☏ (01) 5 15 80 91 00 (closed Sunday)* 40 €/58 € and a la carte 45/72 €

Rest *Unkai*, *☏ (01) 5 15 80 91 10 (closed Monday lunch)* 22 € (lunch)/95 €

Rest *Grand Café*, *☏ (01) 5 15 80 91 20* – a la carte 25/45 €

♦ Grand Luxury ♦ Historic ♦ Classic ♦

The glittering world of the Belle Epoque is revived here, in a luxurious hotel with tastefully elegant and refined interiors. "Le Ciel" makes a grand impression, sitting above the roof-tops of Vienna. Sushi and sashimi at "Unkai".

Palais Coburg
rm 150 VISA

Coburgbastei 4 ✉ 1010 – Ⓜ Stubentor
– ☏ (01) 51 81 80 – hotel.residenz@palais-coburg.com – Fax (01) 51 81 81
– www.palais-coburg.com **E2**

35 suites – 460/1920 € 460/1920 €

Rest see ***Restaurant Coburg*** below

Rest *Gartenpavillon*, *☏ (01) 51 81 88 70* – 33 € and a la carte 17/25 €

♦ Grand Luxury ♦ Historic ♦ Modern ♦

This impressive, carefully restored palace from 1840, offers tastefully luxurious lobbies and halls and individual, sumptuously furnished and equipped suites. Pleasantly bright: a garden pavilion in the form of a conservatory, with rattan chairs.

Sacher
rm rest 50 VISA

Philharmonikerstr. 4 ✉ 1010 – Ⓜ Karlsplatz – ☏ (01) 51 45 60
– wien@sacher.com – Fax (01) 51 45 68 10 – www.sacher.com **D3**

152 rm – 306/539 € 368/601 €, 29 € – 7 suites

Rest a la carte 38/65 €

♦ Grand Luxury ♦ Traditional ♦ Classic ♦

A Viennese institution since 1876. A collection of valuable paintings and antiques creates a high-class atmosphere and emphasises its historic charm. Classically elegant restaurant.

Bristol
rm rest 80 VISA

Kärntner Ring 1 ✉ 1015 – Ⓜ Karlsplatz – ☏ (01) 51 51 60
– hotel.bristol@westin.com – Fax (01) 51 51 65 50
– www.westin.com/bristol **D3**

140 rm – 525 € 525 €, 30 € – 10 suites

Rest see ***Korso*** below

Rest *Sirk* a la carte 30/56 €

♦ Grand Luxury ♦ Traditional ♦ Classic ♦

Oh so British: courteous service and a luxurious ambience are ever-present in this establishment. Gracious rooms with well-chosen period furniture. The suites radiate exclusivity! "Sirk": decorated in understatedly elegant tones. With views of the Opera.

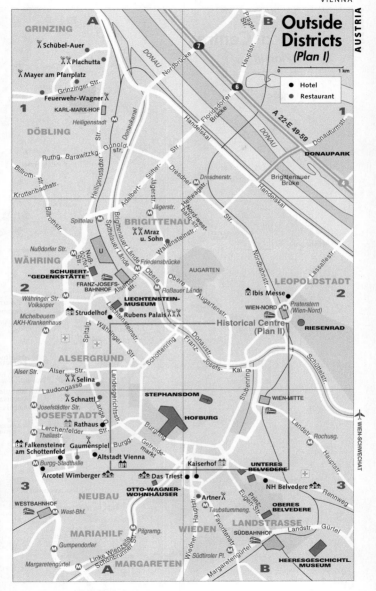

Outside Districts
(Plan I)

AUSTRIA

0   1 km

● Hotel
● Restaurant

GRINZING

X Schübel-Auer

XX Plachutta

X Mayer am Pfarrplatz

Feuerwehr-Wagner X

KARL-MARX-HOF

Heiligenstadt

DÖBLING

Ruthg. Barawitzkg.

Billroth-str.

Krottenbachstr.

DONAU

DONAUPARK

A 22-E 49-59

Donauturmstr.

Brigittenauer Brüke

Spittelau

BRIGITTENAU

XX Mraz u. Sohn

Nußdorfer Str.

WÄHRING

SCHUBERT-"GEDENKSTÄTTE"

FRANZ-JOSEFS-BAHNHOF

Währinger Str. Volksoper

Michelbeuern AKH-Krankenhaus

LIECHTENSTEIN-MUSEUM

Strudelhof

Rubens Palais XXX

AUGARTEN

Roßauer Lände

LEOPOLDSTADT

Ibis Messe ●

WIEN-NORD (Wien-Nord)

Praterstern

RIESENRAD

Historical Centre (Plan II)

ALSERGRUND

Alser Str.

XX Selina

Laudongasse

X Schnattl

Josefstädter Str.

JOSEFSTADT

Rathaus

Lerchenfelder Thaliastr.

Falkensteiner am Schottenfeld

Gaumenspiel

Burgg-Stadthalle

Arcotel Wimberger ●●

STEPHANSDOM

HOFBURG

Burgring

Getreidemarkt

Altstadt Vienna

Das Triest ●

Kaiserhof

WIEN-MITTE

Landstr. Rochusg.

WIEN-SCHWECHAT

UNTERES BELVEDERE

NH Belvedere ●●

Rennweg

WESTBAHNHOF

West-Bhf.

NEUBAU

OTTO-WAGNER-WOHNHÄUSER

Artner X

Taubstummeng.

WIEDEN

OBERES BELVEDERE

MARIAHILF

Pilgramg.

Gumpendorfer

Margaretengürtel

Linke Wienzeile

Schönbrunner Str.

MARGARETEN

SÜDBAHNHOF

LANDSTRASSE

Landstr. Gürtel

Südtiroler Pl.

Margaretengürtel

HEERESGESCHICHTL. MUSEUM

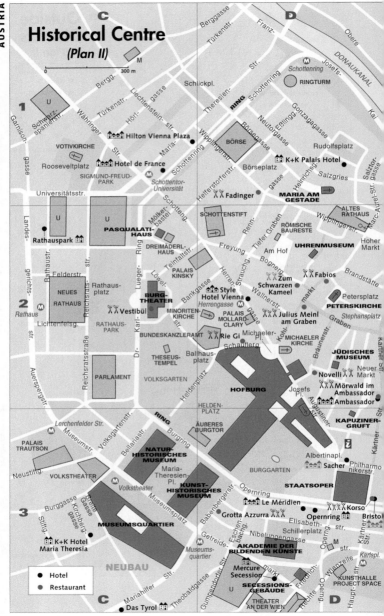

Historical Centre
(Plan II)

0 — 300 m

● Hotel
● Restaurant

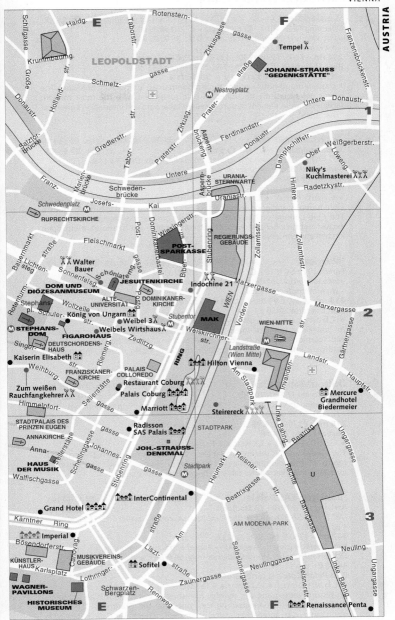

Schillgasse
Haidg-
Rotenstern-
E
Taborstr.
gasse
Zirkusgasse
F
Franzensbrückenstr.
Krummbaumg.
LEOPOLDSTADT
Tempel
JOHANN-STRAUSS
"GEDENKSTÄTTE"
str.
Große
Donaustr.
Holland-
str.
Schmelz-
gasse
Nestroyplatz
Untere Donaustr.
1
Salzbör-
brücke
Gredlerstr.
Praterstr.
Zirkusg.
Prater-
Ferdinandstr.
Donaustr.
Tabor-
Dampfschiffstr.
Ober Weißgerberstr.
Franz-
Marien-
brücke
Untere
Aspern-
brückeng.
Niky's
Kuchlmasterei
Löweng.
Radetzkystr.
Schweden-
brücke
Josefs-
Kai
URANIA-
STERNWARTE
Uraniastr.
Aspern-
brücke
Hintere
Zollamtsstr.
Schwedenplatz
RUPRECHTSKIRCHE
Fleischmarkt
Post-
Wiesingerstr.
POST-
SPARKASSE
REGIERUNGS-
GEBÄUDE
Stubenring
Zollamtsstr.
Marxergasse
Bauernmarkt
straße
Lichten-
steig
Walter
Bauer
Sonnenfelsg.
Schönlate-
Biberstr.
JESUITENKIRCHE
Indochine 21
WIEN
Marxergasse
2
DOM UND
DIÖZESANMUSEUM
Roten-
turm-
Stephans-
Wollzeile
ALTE
UNIVERSITÄT
Schuler-
DOMINIKANER-
KIRCHE
MAK
Vordere
WIEN-MITTE
str.
pl.
König von Ungarn
Stubentor
STEPHANS-
DOM
Singer-
FIGAROHAUS
DEUTSCHORDENS-
HAUS
Weibel 3
Weibels Wirtshaus
RING
Weiskirchner-
str.
Landstraße
(Wien Mitte)
Landstr.
Gärtnergasse
Hauptstr.
Kaiserin Elisabeth
Weihburg-
str.
Riemerg.
Zedlitzg.
Hilton Vienna
Am Stadtpark
Mercure
Grandhotel
Biedermeier
Zum weißen
Rauchfangkehrer
FRANZISKANER-
KIRCHE
PALAIS
COLLOREDO
Restaurant Coburg
Palais Coburg
Invaliden-
Himmelpfort-
Seilerstätte
gasse
Marriott
Steirereck
Linke Bahng.
Beatrixg.
Ungargasse
STADTPALAIS DES
PRINZEN EUGEN
ANNAKIRCHE
Anna-
Seilerstätte
Johannes-
Radisson
SAS Palais
STADTPARK
HAUS
DER MUSIK
Schellinggasse
gasse
gasse
JOH.-STRAUSS-
DENKMAL
Stadtpark
Stubenring
Heumarkt
Reisner-
Rechte
Beatrixgasse
str.
Bahng.
U
Baumgasse
Walfischgasse
InterContinental
Grand Hotel
Kärntner
Ring
AM MODENA-PARK
3
Imperial
Bösendorferstr.
Canovag.
Liszt-
Am
Salesianergasse
Neuling-
Ungargasse
KÜNSTLER-
HAUS
MUSIKVEREINS-
GEBÄUDE
Karlsplatz
Sofitel
straße
Neulinggasse
Reisnerstr.
Linke Bahng.
WAGNER-
PAVILLONS
Lothringer-
Schwarzen-
Bergplatz
Zaunergasse
Rennweg
F
Renaissance Penta
HISTORISCHES
MUSEUM
E

AUSTRIA

Le Méridien ⬚ ⬚ ⬚ ⬚ ⬚ ⬚ ⬚ ⬚rest ⬚ ⬚180 ⬚ VISA ⬚ ⬚ ⬚
Opernring 13 ⊠ 1010 – Ⓜ Karlsplatz – ℰ (01) 58 89 00
– info.vienna@lemeridien.com – Fax (01) 5 88 90 90 90
– www.lemeridien.com   **D3**
294 rm – †305/435 € ††305/435 €, � 23 € – 17 suites
Rest Shambala, ℰ (01) 5 88 90 70 00 – a la carte 33/48 €
♦ Chain hotel ♦ Luxury ♦ Stylish ♦
A classical grand-hotel exterior, but a modern smart interior with bold lines. The
rooms are pleasantly decorated in pale tones and with the most modern
facilities. Simple, elegant design, excellent tableware and interesting lighting at
"Shambala".

InterContinental ⬚ ⬚ ⬚ ⬚ ⬚ ⬚ ⬚rm ⬚rest ⬚ ⬚470
Johannesgasse 28 ⊠ 1037 – Ⓜ Stadtpark   ⬚ VISA ⬚ ⬚ ⬚
– ℰ (01) 71 12 20 – vienna@ichotelsgroup.com – Fax (01) 7 13 44 89
– www.vienna.intercontinental.com   **E3**
453 rm – †280/365 € ††280/365 €, ⊆ 25 € – 61 suites
Rest a la carte 31/47 €
♦ Chain hotel ♦ Luxury ♦ Classic ♦
Light furniture and good technical facilities in rooms geared to business guests.
The Club Lounge on the 10th floor offers both a spectacular view and an
exclusive atmosphere. A touch of the Mediterranean at this restaurant with open
kitchen and conservatory.

Marriott ⬚ ⬚ ⬚ ⬚ ⬚ ⬚rm ⬚rest ⬚ ⬚300 ⬚ VISA ⬚ ⬚ ⬚
Parkring 12a ⊠ 1010 – Ⓜ Stadtpark – ℰ (01) 51 51 80
– vienna.marriott.info@marriotthotels.com – Fax (01) 5 15 18 67 36
– www.marriott.com/vieat   **E2**
313 rm – †280 € ††280 €, ⊆ 24 € – 5 suites
Rest a la carte 26/56 €
♦ Chain hotel ♦ Luxury ♦ Functional ♦
An inner-city hotel devoted to the "American way of life", it impresses
with comfort and professional service. Many rooms have views of the
Stadtpark. Integrated into the lobby is the Garten-Café, offering international
dishes.

Hilton Vienna Plaza ⬚ ⬚ ⬚ ⬚ ⬚rm ⬚rest ⬚ ⬚
Schottenring 11 ⊠ 1010 – Ⓜ   ⬚60 ⬚ VISA ⬚ ⬚
Schottentor-Universität – ℰ (01) 31 39 00 – info.vienna-plaza@hilton.com
– Fax (01) 31 39 02 20 09 – www.hilton.at   **C1**
218 rm – †170/370 € ††170/370 €, ⊆ 25 € – 10 suites
Rest a la carte 27/40 €
♦ Chain hotel ♦ Luxury ♦ Functional ♦
The "Grandhotel" is devoted to Art Deco and classic modernism. The generous
rooms of this designer hotel impress with simple luxury. Contemporary
atmosphere and attractive table settings in the restaurant.

Radisson SAS Palais ⬚ ⬚ ⬚ ⬚ ⬚rm ⬚rest ⬚ ⬚ ⬚190
Parkring 16 ⊠ 1010 – Ⓜ Stadtpark   ⬚ VISA ⬚ ⬚ ⬚
– ℰ (01) 51 51 70 – sales.vienna@radissonsas.com – Fax (01) 5 15 17 33 30
– www.radissonsas.com   **E3**
247 rm – †260 € ††260 €, ⊆ 22 € – 39 suites
Rest Le siècle (closed 2 weeks July - August and Sunday - Monday,
October - December Monday) (dinner only) 54 €/68 € and a la carte
44/58 €
Rest Palais Café a la carte 23/44 €
♦ Chain hotel ♦ Luxury ♦ Classic ♦
An historic setting and the stylishly furnished rooms make this an attractive
destination. Two connected palaces opposite the Stadtpark. "Le siècle"
restaurant has an agreeable classical atmosphere. The "Palais Café" is located in
the conservatory.

AUSTRIA

Hilton Vienna
≤ 🍴 ⅃ゟ 🏠 ⅄ 🏦 ⅍rm 🔲 🕻 ⛊475

Am Stadtpark 3 ✉ 1030 – Ⓜ *Landstraße* 🚬 𝗩𝗜𝗦𝗔 ⓂⓄ 𝖠𝖤 ⓪
– ℰ (01) 71 70 00 – reservation.vienna@hilton.com – Fax (01) 7 13 06 91
– www.hilton.de/vienna **F2**
579 rm – ♦150/380 € ♦♦150/380 €, � 24 € – 36 suites
Rest a la carte 28/40 €
♦ Chain hotel ♦ Luxury ♦ Modern ♦
A spacious lobby atrium and bright, modern rooms are features of this
meeting-oriented hotel. A fantastic view of the city from the top floor.
Contemporary and welcoming atmosphere.

Hotel de France
🏦 ⅍rm 🔲 ⛊100 𝗩𝗜𝗦𝗔 ⓂⓄ 𝖠𝖤 ⓪

Schottenring 3 ✉ 1010 – Ⓜ *Schottentor-Universität – ℰ (01) 31 36 80*
– defrance@austria-hotels.at – Fax (01) 3 19 59 69 – www.hoteldefrance.at
203 rm ⊇ *–* ♦250/270 € ♦♦285/305 € **C1**
Rest *(closed Saturday - Sunday)* a la carte 31/43 €
♦ Luxury ♦ Classic ♦
A classic city hotel. Guests enjoy well-presented rooms, some decorated with
Viennese period furniture, some with modern furnishings. Spacious maisonettes
on the top floor. The "Belle Etage" is a luxurious restaurant. A simpler option: the
"Bistro".

Ambassador
🏦 ⅍ 🔲 ⛊80 𝗩𝗜𝗦𝗔 ⓂⓄ 𝖠𝖤 ⓪

Kärntner Str. 22 ✉ 1010 – Ⓜ *Stephansdom – ℰ (01) 96 16 10*
– office@ambassador.at – Fax (01) 5 13 29 99 – www.ambassador.at
86 rm – ♦228/418 € ♦♦289/524 €, ⊇ 20 € **D2**
Rest see *Mörwald im Ambassador* below
♦ Business ♦ Classic ♦
A successful symbiosis of beautiful period furniture, some antique, with hi-tech.
Themed rooms are named after famous characters.

Renaissance Penta
🍴 ⅃ゟ 🏠 🔲 🚗 ⅄ 🏦 ⅍rm 🔲 ⛊260

Ungargasse 60 ✉ 1030 – ℰ (01) 71 17 50 🚬 𝗩𝗜𝗦𝗔 ⓂⓄ 𝖠𝖤 ⓪
– renaissance.penta.vienna@renaissancehotels.com – Fax (01) 7 11 75 81 43
– www.renaissancehotels.com/viese **F3**
339 rm – ♦135/270 € ♦♦135/270 €, ⊇ 21 €
Rest a la carte 23/35 €
♦ Chain hotel ♦ Functional ♦
Even non-riders are welcome in the neo-classicist, historically listed building of
the former imperial military riding school. Bright, functional rooms with burl
wood furniture. The elegant restaurant "Borromäus" awaits your visit.

Style Hotel Vienna
⅃ゟ 🏠 ⅄ ⅍rm 🎆rest 🕻 ⛊10

Herrengasse 12 ✉ 1010 – Ⓜ *Herrengasse* 🚬 𝗩𝗜𝗦𝗔 ⓂⓄ 𝖠𝖤 ⓪
– ℰ (01) 22 78 00 – info@stylehotel.at – Fax (01) 2 27 80 77
– www.stylehotel.at **D2**
78 rm – ♦208/285 € ♦♦208/285 €, ⊇ 22 €
Rest *Sapori*, *ℰ (01) 2 27 80 78 (closed 1 - 15 August and Sunday,*
June - August Saturday lunch, sunday) a la carte 38/48 €
♦ Business ♦ Stylish ♦
Fine modern interiors are evident from the rotunda-like hall, through to the
elegant rooms of this former bank building. A former basement vault is home to
the Sapori. Italian cuisine.

Das Triest
🍴 🏠 🏦 ⅍rm 🔲 🕻

Wiedner Hauptstr. 12 ✉ 1040 – Ⓜ *Karlsplatz* ⛊60 𝗩𝗜𝗦𝗔 ⓂⓄ 𝖠𝖤 ⓪
– ℰ (01) 58 91 80 – office@dastriest.at – Fax (01) 5 89 18 18
– www.dastriest.at *Plan I* **B3**
72 rm ⊇ *–* ♦200 € ♦♦258 € – 4 suites
Rest *(closed early - mid August and Saturday lunch, Sunday)* 40 €/46 €
and a la carte 28/41 €
♦ Business ♦ Design ♦
The rooms, designed by Terence Conran, feature blue armchairs and desks with
modem connection. Functional, yet homely, without clutter. A modern
ambience of mirrors welcomes you to the Italian cuisine in the restaurant.

NH Belvedere without rest 🏠 🤏 ♿ 📶 ⇔ 📺 📞 VISA 🏧 ⓘ

Rennweg 12a ⊠ 1030 – 𝒞 (01) 2 06 11 – nhbelvedere@nh-hotels.com
– Fax (01) 2 06 11 15 – www.nh-hotels.com Plan I **B3**
114 rm – †117/175 € ††117/175 €, ⊵ 14 €
♦ **Chain hotel** ♦ **Modern** ♦
A modern hotel in the classicist building of the former State Printing Office.
Impressive rooms, some with views of the Botanic Gardens, bistro with snacks.

Arcotel Wimberger 🏠 🤏 ♿ 📶 rm ⇔rm 📺 💰650

Neubaugürtel 34 ⊠ 1070 – Ⓜ Burgg 🚗 VISA 🏧 ⓘ
Stadthalle – 𝒞 (01) 52 16 50 – wimberger@arcotel.at – Fax (01) 52 16 58 11
– www.arcotel.at/wimberger Plan I **A3**
225 rm – †179 € ††219 €, ⊵ 15 € – 7 suites
Rest 22 € (buffet lunch)/25 €
♦ **Business** ♦ **Functional** ♦
After it was destroyed by fire, the old "Hotel Wimberger Opfer" was reborn as a
modern hotel for business travellers, with rooms furnished in attractive natural
wood. The restaurant "Maskerade" is decorated with items from a former ballroom.

Kaiserhof without rest 🏠 🤏 📶 ⇔ 📺 💰30 🚗 VISA 🏧 ⓘ

Frankenberggasse 10 ⊠ 1040 – Ⓜ Karlsplatz – 𝒞 (01) 5 05 17 01
– info@hotel-kaiserhof.at – Fax (01) 5 05 88 75 88
– www.hotel-kaiserhof.at Plan I **B3**
74 rm ⊵ – †125/175 € ††155/250 € – 3 suites
♦ **Traditional** ♦ **Art Deco** ♦
In this building from 1896, the historic charm of the spacious high-ceilinged
rooms has been successfully combined with elegant modern interiors.

K+K Hotel Maria Theresia without rest 🤏 📶 ⇔ 📺 💰40

Kirchberggasse 6 ⊠ 1070 – Ⓜ Volkstheater 🚗 VISA 🏧 ⓘ
– 𝒞 (01) 5 21 23 – kk.maria.theresia@kuk.at – Fax (01) 5 21 23 70
– www.kkhotels.com **C3**
123 rm ⊵ – †175 € ††230 €
♦ **Business** ♦ **Modern** ♦
Located in the artists' quarter of Spittelberg, this hotel also has especially nice
rooms with views of Vienna. The bar in the spacious lobby offers a small menu.

Kaiserin Elisabeth without rest 📶 📺 💰20 VISA 🏧 ⓘ

Weihburggasse 3 ⊠ 1010 – Ⓜ Stephansdom – 𝒞 (01) 51 52 60 – info@
kaiserinelisabeth.at – Fax (01) 51 52 67 – www.kaiserinelisabeth.at **E2**
63 rm ⊵ – †119/160 € ††204/225 €
♦ **Traditional** ♦ **Classic** ♦
Both Mozart and Wagner were guests at this hotel near the Stephansdom, in
operation since 1809. Elegant, dark timber furniture in a style from the turn of the
last century.

Mercure Grandhotel Biedermeier without rest 📶 ⇔ 📺

Landstraßer Hauptstr. 28, (at Sünnhof) 💰60 🚗 VISA 🏧 ⓘ
⊠ 1030 – Ⓜ Landstraße – 𝒞 (01) 71 67 10 – h5357@accor.com
– Fax (01) 71 67 15 03 – www.mercure.com **F2**
203 rm – †147/190 € ††175/220 €, ⊵ 15 € – 12 suites
♦ **Chain hotel** ♦ **Classic** ♦
This hotel is located in a town house with a delightful arcade. All of the rooms are
tastefully decorated with Biedermeier-style cherry-wood furniture.

König von Ungarn 📶 rm ⅌rest 📺 💰15 VISA 🏧 ⓘ

Schulerstr. 10 ⊠ 1010 – Ⓜ Stephansdom – 𝒞 (01) 51 58 40 – hotel@kvu.at
– Fax (01) 51 58 48 – www.kvu.at **E2**
33 rm ⊵ – †138 € ††198 €
Rest (dinner only) a la carte 24/36 €
♦ **Traditional** ♦ **Classic** ♦
Located behind the Stephansdom is this classically decorated 16C building, with
lots of style and warm colours. Don't miss the attractive courtyard! Follow
Mozart's footsteps: This establishment is located in the house where Mozart
once lived.

Das Tyrol without rest
🏠 🏧 ♿ 🖾 🚗 *VISA* 🅜🅢 🅐🅔 ⓞ

Mariahilfer Str. 15 ☒ 1060 – ⓜ Museumsquartier – ℰ (01) 5 87 54 15
– reception@das-tyrol.at – Fax (01) 58 75 41 59 – www.das-tyrol.at   **C3**
30 rm ☷ – ♦109/209 € ♦♦149/259 €
♦ **Family** ♦ **Modern** ♦
This lovingly restored corner building is home to tastefully decorated rooms with modern furnishings. Paintings by Viennese artists adorn the walls.

Altstadt Vienna without rest
♿ 🖾 *VISA* 🅜🅢 🅐🅔 ⓞ

Kirchengasse 41 ☒ 1070 – ⓜ Volkstheater – ℰ (01) 5 26 33 99
– hotel@altstadt.at – Fax (01) 5 23 49 01 – www.altstadt.at   *Plan I* **A3**
37 rm ☷ – ♦109/139 € ♦♦129/159 € – 7 suites
♦ **Traditional** ♦ **Stylish** ♦
Each room in this patrician house has its own character. Well-appointed rooms with high ceilings, parquet, and select objets d'art.

Sofitel
🏧 ♿rm ♨60 🚗 *VISA* 🅜🅢 🅐🅔 ⓞ

Am Heumarkt 35 ☒ 1030 – ⓜ Stadtpark – ℰ (01) 71 61 60 – h1276@accor.com
– Fax (01) 71 61 68 44 – www.sofitel.com   **E3**
211 rm – ♦130/251 € ♦♦150/276 €, ☷ 18 €
Rest *(closed Saturday lunch, Sunday and Bank Holidays lunch)* a la carte 19/39 €
♦ **Chain hotel** ♦ **Functional** ♦
Elements of art nouveau and Gustav Klimt reproductions lend the rooms an agreeable ambience. Timeless natural wood and modern technical facilities. Lovely: the Pullmann Bar. International and Viennese dishes are served in the restaurant.

Rathauspark without rest
♿ 🖾 ♨30 *VISA* 🅜🅢 🅐🅔 ⓞ

Rathausstr. 17 ☒ 1010 – ⓜ Rathaus – ℰ (01) 40 41 20 – rathauspark@
austria-trend.at – Fax (01) 40 41 27 61 – www.austria-trend.at/rhw   **C2**
117 rm ☷ – ♦137/172 € ♦♦197/246 €
♦ **Business** ♦ **Classic** ♦
An attractive stuccoed entrance welcomes guests to this smart hotel from 1880. The mostly high-ceilinged rooms are decorated with modern elegance. An original lift.

Falkensteiner Am Schottenfeld without rest
🏠 🏧 ♿ ♨100

Schottenfeldgasse 74 ☒ 1070 – ⓜ Burgg   🚗 *VISA* 🅜🅢 🅐🅔 ⓞ
Stadthalle – ℰ (01) 5 26 51 81 – schottenfeld@falkensteiner.com
– Fax (01) 52 65 18 11 60 – www.falkensteiner.com   *Plan I* **A3**
95 rm ☷ – ♦129/144 € ♦♦164/185 €
♦ **Business** ♦ **Modern** ♦
Modern interiors from the large lobby through to the pleasantly decorated rooms, with light furnishings and good facilities. The hotel is integrated into a row of houses.

K+K Palais Hotel without rest
🏧 ♿ 🖾 *VISA* 🅜🅢 🅐🅔 ⓞ

Rudolfsplatz 11 ☒ 1010 – ⓜ Schwedenplatz – ℰ (01) 5 33 13 53
– kk.palais.hotel@kuk.at – Fax (01) 5 33 13 53 70
– www.kkhotels.com   **D1**
66 rm ☷ – ♦175 € ♦♦230 €
♦ **Traditional** ♦ **Functional** ♦
Functional, yet homely rooms and warm breakfast room at this historic city villa. The Stephansdom and the underground are close by.

Rathaus without rest
♿ 🖾 ♨20 *VISA* 🅜🅢 🅐🅔 ⓞ

Lange Gasse 13 ☒ 1080 – ⓜ Rathaus – ℰ (01) 4 00 11 22
– office@hotel-rathaus-wien.at – Fax (01) 4 00 11 22 88
– www.hotel-rathaus-wien.at   *Plan I* **A3**
33 rm – ♦118/138 € ♦♦148/198 €, ☷ 13 €
♦ **Family** ♦ **Design** ♦
This Wilhelminian-period house is completely dedicated to the world of wine. The tasteful and modern rooms are each named after an Austrian wine-grower. Wine lounge.

Strudlhof without rest 🔊 ও 🗚 ⇔ 📺 🎰150 🚗 🅿 𝘝𝘐𝘚𝘈 ⓂⓈ 🗚 ①
Pasteurgasse 1 ⊠ 1090 – Ⓜ Währinger Str.-Volksoper – ℰ (01) 3 19 25 22
– seminarhotel@strudlhof.at – Fax (01) 31 92 52 28 00
– www.strudlhof.at Plan I **A2**
84 rm � – ♦135/169 € ♦♦179/199 €
♦ **Business** ♦ **Functional** ♦
This former palace, set back from the street, offers comfortable, well-equipped rooms. A stylish setting for your business function.

Opernring without rest ⇔ 📺 📞 𝘝𝘐𝘚𝘈 ⓂⓈ 🗚 ①
Opernring 11 ⊠ 1010 – Ⓜ Karlsplatz – ℰ (01) 5 87 55 18
– hotel@opernring.at – Fax (01) 5 87 55 18 29
– www.opernring.at **D3**
35 rm ⊠ – ♦140/215 € ♦♦155/280 €
♦ **Business** ♦ **Classic** ♦
Opposite the Opera is this hotel with its pretty art nouveau façade. Spacious rooms combine homeliness with the functionality of modern hotels.

Mercure Secession without rest 🗚 ⇔ 📺 🎰30
Getreidemarkt 5 ⊠ 1060 🚗 𝘝𝘐𝘚𝘈 ⓂⓈ 🗚 ①
– Ⓜ Museumsquartier – ℰ (01) 5 88 38 – h3532@accor.com
– Fax (01) 58 83 82 12 – www.mercure.com **D3**
70 rm ⊠ – ♦141 € ♦♦176 €
♦ **Chain hotel** ♦ **Functional** ♦
Thanks to its central location, this residence is a great base for discovering the city. The rooms are homely and comfortable. Apartments also available.

Ibis Messe ও 🗚 ⇔rm 📺 🎰100 🚗 𝘝𝘐𝘚𝘈 ⓂⓈ 🗚 ①
Lassallestr. 7a ⊠ 1020 – Ⓜ Praterstern – ℰ (01) 21 77 00
– h2736@accor.com – Fax (01) 21 77 05 55
– www.ibishotels.com Plan I **B2**
166 rm – ♦64 € ♦♦79 €, ⊠ 9 €
Rest a la carte 16/25 €
♦ **Chain hotel** ♦ **Functional** ♦
Contemporary, functional rooms with light-coloured furnishings, close to the Prater park. Guests enjoy spacious desks and excellent modern technology.

XXXX **Restaurant Coburg** – Hotel Palais Coburg 🍽 ⅔ 𝘝𝘐𝘚𝘈 ⓂⓈ 🗚 ①
🕸 *Coburgbastei 4 ⊠ 1010 – Ⓜ Stubentor – ℰ (01) 51 81 88 00 – restaurant@*
palais-coburg.com – Fax (01) 51 81 88 18 – www.palais-coburg.com
closed Sunday - Monday, Bank Holidays **E2**
Rest (dinner only) 68 €/98 € and a la carte 39/62 € ⅜
Spec. Salat vom Kalbskopf mit grünem Spargel. Jakobsmuscheln mit Artischocken, Fenchel und Fleckerln. Kutteln mit Vongole.
♦ **French** ♦ **Formal** ♦
An elegant restaurant with attractive vaulted ceiling and fine table settings. Christian Petz's classic cuisine is served by friendly and competent staff.

XXXX **Steirereck** (Reitbauer) 🍽 🗚 ⇅40 𝘝𝘐𝘚𝘈 ⓂⓈ 🗚 ①
🕸 *Am Heumarkt 2, (Stadtpark) ⊠ 1030 – Ⓜ Stadtpark – ℰ (01) 7 13 31 68*
– wien@steirereck.at – Fax (01) 71 33 16 82 – www.steirereck.at
closed Saturday - Sunday, Bank Holidays **F2**
Rest (dinner only) (booking advisable) 95 € ⅜
Rest *Steirereck Light* (closed Saturday - Sunday, Bank Holidays) (lunch only)
a la carte 31/44 €
Spec. Gelierte Backerbsensuppe mit Liebstöckl. Rahmgurke mit lauwarmen Flusskrebsen. Gebratenes und Geschmortes vom Almochsen mit wilden Bohnen und Gänseleber.
♦ **Contemporary** ♦ **Design** ♦
This unusual restaurant in the Stadtpark, on the Wien River, offers large set menus each evening in an exclusive setting. Light meals for lunch. The basement "Meierei" offers pastries, cheeses and breads all day.

XXXX
£3
Korso – Hotel Bristol
🕭 🏧 🍴 **VISA** ⓂⓈ 🅰🅴 ⓞ
Kärntner Ring 1 ✉ *1015 –* Ⓜ *Karlsplatz –* ℰ *(01) 51 51 65 46*
– restaurant.korso@westin.com – Fax (01) 51 51 65 75 – www.westin.com/bristol
closed August and Saturday lunch **D3**
Rest 38 € (lunch)/84 € and a la carte 47/73 €
Spec. Zitronen-Nudeln mit Beluga Kaviar. Riesling-Kalbsbeuscherl mit Semmelflan. Medaillon vom Seeteufel mit Kräutern gebraten.
♦ Austrian ♦ Formal ♦
The epitome of tasteful elegance, the illuminated onyx wall is quite literally a "highlight". A menu of both classical and regional dishes.

XXX
Mörwald im Ambassador
🏧 **VISA** ⓂⓈ 🅰🅴 ⓞ
Kärntner Str. 22, (1st floor) ✉ *1010 –* Ⓜ *Stephansdom*
– ℰ *(01) 96 16 11 61 – ambassador@moerwald.at – Fax (01) 96 16 11 60*
– www.moerwald.at
closed Sunday and Bank Holidays **D2**
Rest (booking advisable) 35 € (lunch)/80 € and a la carte 41/58 € 🥢
♦ Contemporary ♦ Friendly ♦
You enter the elegant restaurant through a bar in the atrium. The large glass window-front is opened in the summer. Creative cuisine.

XXX
Ruben's Palais
🕭 **VISA** ⓂⓈ 🅰🅴 ⓞ
Fürstengasse 1, (Palais Liechtenstein) ✉ *1090 –* Ⓜ *Roßauer Lände*
– ℰ *(01) 3 19 23 96 13 – office@rubens.at – Fax (01) 3 19 23 96 96*
– www.rubens.at
closed Sunday - Tuesday Plan I **A2**
Rest 56 € and a la carte 31/48 € 🥢
Rest *Ruben's Brasserie* *(closed Tuesday)* a la carte 20/34 €
♦ International ♦ Formal ♦
In a building from 1711, next to the "Palais Lichtenstein", is this elegant restaurant with intimate atmosphere and competent service. An attractive forecourt. A more modest alternative to "Ruben's Palais" is the modern "Brasserie".

XXX
Niky's Kuchlmasterei with rm
🕭 🕸 🏧 rm ⇆rm 🍴rm 🛏
Obere Weissgerberstr. 6 ✉ *1030* ⇔30 **VISA** ⓂⓈ 🅰🅴 ⓞ
– ℰ *(01) 7 12 90 00 – office@kuchlmastererei.at – Fax (01) 7 12 90 00 16*
– www.kuchlmasterei.at
closed Sunday and Bank Holidays except December **F1**
5 suites – 🛏240 € 🛏🛏240 €, ☕ 13 €
Rest 30 € (lunch)/51 € and a la carte 34/53 € 🥢
♦ International ♦ Cosy ♦
The rooms of this special restaurant captivate with their rich décor and numerous original artworks. An attractive terrace and enormous wine cellar. Individual, exclusive suites.

XXX
Julius Meinl am Graben
🏧 **VISA** ⓂⓈ 🅰🅴 ⓞ
Graben 19 (1ˢᵗ floor) ✉ *1010 –* Ⓜ *Stephansdom –* ℰ *(01) 5 32 33 34 60 00*
– julius.meinl@restaurant.com – Fax (01) 5 32 33 34 12 90
– www.meinlamgraben.at
closed Sunday and Bank Holidays **D2**
Rest (booking essential) 29 € (lunch)/78 € and a la carte 47/67 € 🥢
♦ International ♦ Friendly ♦
Classic cuisine in an exclusive delicatessen, rich in tradition. The window seats provide a lovely view of the Graben and Pestsäule.

XXX
Grotta Azzurra
VISA ⓂⓈ 🅰🅴 ⓞ
Babenbergerstr. 5 ✉ *1010 –* Ⓜ *Museumsquartier –* ℰ *(01) 5 86 10 44*
– office@grotta-azzurra.at – Fax (01) 5 86 10 44 15
– www.grotta-azzura.at **D3**
Rest a la carte 27/41 €
♦ Italian ♦ Friendly ♦
Austria's oldest Italian restaurant has been in existence since the beginning of the Fifties. Artistic Murano glass and mosaics create a special atmosphere.

XX **Mraz & Sohn** ⌂ P VISA ❶❷ ❶
❀

Wallensteinstr. 59 ✉ 1200 – Ⓜ Friedensbrücke – ℰ (01) 3 30 45 94
– Fax (01) 3 50 15 36 – www.mraz-sohn.at Plan I **A2**
closed 1 - 20 August, 24 December - 7 January and Saturday - Sunday, Bank Holidays
Rest (booking advisable) 35 €/87 € and a la carte 35/48 € ⌕
Spec. Gebratene Gänseleber mit Heidelbeermarmelade und Pofesen. Oxenfilet
mit Rinderbäckchen. Topfen-Kirschauflauf mit Chili-Schokoeis.
♦ **Contemporary** ♦ **Fashionable** ♦
A unique family-run restaurant, with modern ambience, highly creative menu,
and young well motivated staff. The wine cellar is worth a visit.

XX **Selina** VISA ❶❷ AE ❶

Laudongasse 13 ✉ 1080 – Ⓜ Rathaus – ℰ (01) 4 05 64 04
– Fax (01) 4 08 04 59
closed Saturday lunch, Sunday, Bank Holidays, June - August Saturday, Sunday,
Bank Holidays Plan I **A2**
Rest 44 € (lunch)/81 €
♦ **Seasonal cuisine** ♦ **Friendly** ♦
Located on the edge of the inner-city, refined cuisine is served in a modern
atmosphere, with pictures and classic elements setting the scene.

XX **Novelli** ⌂ VISA ❶❷ AE ❶

Bräunerstr. 11 ✉ 1010 – Ⓜ Herrengasse – ℰ (01) 5 13 42 00 – novelli@
haslauer.at – Fax (01) 51 34 20 01 – www.novelli.at **D2**
closed Sunday
Rest (booking advisable) 25 € (lunch)/49 € and a la carte 33/53 €
♦ **Mediterranean** ♦ **Trendy** ♦
In a congenial atmosphere, Italian lifestyle can be experienced here. A
Mediterranean ambience accompanies the classic Mediterranean delights with
strong Italian influences.

XX **Vestibül** VISA ❶❷ AE ❶

Dr. Karl-Lueger-Ring 2, (at Burgtheater) ✉ 1010 – Ⓜ Herrengasse
– ℰ (01) 5 32 49 99 – restaurant@vestibuel.at – Fax (01) 5 32 49 99 10 **C2**
– www.vestibuel.at
closed Saturday lunch, Sunday and Bank Holidays, July - August also Saturday
dinner
Rest a la carte 31/45 €
♦ **International** ♦ **Friendly** ♦
In a side wing of the "Burgtheater", once the emperor's private entrance, is now
a restaurant stylishly deocrated with marble and stucco. Regional and
Mediterranean cuisine.

XX **Walter Bauer** AE ❀ VISA ❶❷ AE ❶
❀

Sonnenfelsgasse 17 ✉ 1010 – Ⓜ Stubentor – ℰ (01) 5 12 98 71
– restaurant.walter.bauer@aon.at – Fax (01) 5 12 98 71
closed Holy week, mid July - mid August and Saturday - Monday lunch,
Bank Holidays **E2**
Rest (booking advisable) 59 € and a la carte 45/54 €
Spec. Carpaccio vom Angusrind mit Senfsauce. Hummerkrautfleisch. Pyramide
von der Valrhona Schokolade.
♦ **International** ♦ **Cosy** ♦
Diners in this Old Town building from the 14th century will be impressed by the
professional service and the regional and international cuisine. Attractive
cross-vaulting adorns the restaurant.

XX **Zum weißen Rauchfangkehrer** AE ⇔ VISA ❶❷

Weihburggasse 4 ✉ 1010 – Ⓜ Stephansdom – ℰ (01) 5 12 34 71
– rauchfangkehrer@utanet.at – Fax (01) 5 12 34 71 28
– www.weisser-rauchfangkehrer.at
closed 2 weeks January, July - August and Sunday - Monday **E2**
Rest (dinner only) (booking advisable) a la carte 41/70 € ⌕
♦ **Austrian** ♦ **Cosy** ♦
One of most attractive traditional Viennese inns, divided into small, nicely
decorated lounges with seating alcoves. Of note is the selection of digestives.

XX **Fabios**   AC ⅀ VISA ⚫ AE ⚫
Tuchlauben 6 ✉ 1010 – Ⓜ Stephansdom – ☏ (01) 5 32 22 22 – fabios@fabios.at
– Fax (01) 5 32 22 25 – www.fabios.at
closed Sunday except Bank Holidays   **D2**
Rest (booking advisable) a la carte 40/55 €
♦ Mediterranean ♦ Trendy ♦
Warm wood tones and bold lines set the scene in this modern restaurant at the
end of the pedestrian zone. Mediterranean cuisine.

XX **Indochine 21**   🍴 AC ⅀ VISA ⚫ AE ⚫
Stubenring 18 ✉ 1010 – Ⓜ Stubentor – ☏ (01) 5 13 76 60
– restaurant@indochine.at – Fax (01) 5 13 76 60 16 – www.indochine.at
Rest 40 €/75 € and a la carte 31/62 €   **F2**
♦ Asian influences ♦ Fashionable ♦
A trendy city location, where a piece of colonial Indo-China is recreated.
High-class fusion cooking, Asiatic with French accents.

XX **Zum Schwarzen Kameel**   🍴 AC ⇔25 VISA ⚫ AE ⚫
Bognergasse 5 ✉ 1010 – Ⓜ Herrengasse – ☏ (01) 5 33 81 25
– info@kameel.at – Fax (01) 5 33 81 25 23
– www.kameel.at
closed Sunday and Bank Holidays   **D2**
Rest (booking advisable) 28 € (lunch)/62 € and a la carte 30/47 €
♦ International ♦ Friendly ♦
You enter this unusual trendy restaurant through a delicatessen. Beautiful art
nouveau details combine with Viennese charm to make this location something
special.

XX **RieGi**   🍴 VISA ⚫ AE ⚫
Schauflergasse 6 ✉ 1010 – Ⓜ Herrengasse – ☏ (01) 5 32 91 26
– world@barbaro.at – Fax (01) 5 32 91 26 20 – www.riegi.at
closed 1 week early January, 3 weeks end July - mid August and Sunday, Bank
Holidays   **D2**
Rest 35 €/65 € and a la carte 32/48 €
♦ International ♦ Friendly ♦
Next to the Sisi Museum, this bright modern restaurant decorated with colourful
pictures offers international fare with a Mediterranean touch.

XX **Fadinger**   VISA ⚫ AE ⚫
😊 Wipplingerstr. 29 ✉ 1010 – Ⓜ Schottentor-Universität – ☏ (01) 5 33 43 41
– restaurant@fadinger.at – Fax (01) 5 32 44 51 – www.fadinger.at
closed Saturday, Sunday and Bank Holidays   **D1**
Rest (booking advisable) 18 € (lunch)/48 € and a la carte 22/46 €
♦ Viennese cuisine ♦ Friendly ♦
An attractive, centrally located establishment, close to the stock exchange.
Colourful watercolours complement the lively, vibrant atmosphere. The menu is
both regional and classical.

X **Schnattl**   🍴 AE ⚫
Lange Gasse 40 ✉ 1080 – Ⓜ Rathaus – ☏ (01) 4 05 34 00 – Fax (01) 4 05 34 00
closed 2 weeks after Easter, 2 weeks end August and Saturday, Sunday, Bank
Holidays   Plan I **A3**
Rest a la carte 33/48 €
♦ Austrian ♦ Cosy ♦
This small, well-presented restaurant with a simple but pleasant ambience is
located on the edge of the inner city. The courtyard deck is particularly nice.

X **Weibels Wirtshaus**   VISA ⚫ AE
Kumpfgasse 2 ✉ 1010 – Ⓜ Stephansdom – ☏ (01) 5 12 39 86
– Fax (01) 5 12 39 86 – www.weibel.at   **E2**
Rest (booking advisable) a la carte 25/39 €
♦ Regional ♦ Cosy ♦
Small booths typify the very cosy atmosphere at this centrally located inn. The
regional menu is enhanced by a number of Viennese dishes.

AUSTRIA

X **Weibel 3** `VISA` `MC` `AE`
Riemergasse 1 ⊠ 1010 – Ⓜ Stubenring – ℰ (01) 5 13 31 10 – Fax (01) 5 13 31 10
– www.weibel.at
closed Saturday lunch, Sunday - Monday and Bank Holidays **E2**
Rest (booking advisable) 36 €/44 € and a la carte 24/44 €
♦ Regional ♦ Rustic ♦
The small, almost intimate tavern with a pleasant atmosphere, serving regional
and international cuisine. The picture display adorns the room.

X **Artner** `VISA` `MC` `①`
Floragasse 6 ⊠ 1040 – Ⓜ Taubstummengasse
– ℰ (01) 5 03 50 33 – restaurant@artner.co.at – Fax (01) 5 03 50 34
– www.artner.co.at
closed Christmas, Saturday lunch, Sunday and Bank Holidays lunch Plan I **B3**
Rest 25 € (lunch)/48 € and a la carte 24/41 €
♦ International ♦ Minimalist ♦
Dark wooden floors and smart lines characterise the simple, modern décor in this
restaurant. International cuisine, with some regional dishes. Good-value lunch
menu.

X **Tempel** `VISA` `MC` `AE` `①`
⊠ 1020 – Ⓜ Nestroyplatz – ℰ (01) 2 14 01 79 – restaurant.tempel@utanet.at
– Fax (01) 2 14 01 79
closed 2 weeks August, 23 December - 8 January and Saturday lunch, Sunday -
Monday **F1**
Rest 14 € (lunch)/37 € and a la carte 23/34 €
♦ Regional ♦ Friendly ♦
This small, simple bistro style restaurant is somewhat concealed in the courtyard.
Regional and at times refined cuisine. A small terrace at the back.

X **Gaumenspiel** `VISA` `MC`
Zieglergasse 54 ⊠ 1070 – Ⓜ Burgg Stadthalle – ℰ (01) 5 26 11 08
– essen@gaumenspiel.at – Fax (01) 5 26 11 08 30
– www.gaumenspiel.at
closed 3 weeks June and Saturday lunch, Sunday Plan I **A3**
Rest (booking advisable) 30 €/35 € and a la carte 27/35 €
♦ International ♦ Bistro ♦
A simply decorated bistro with friendly, competent service. Wooden floors and
a warm red hue underscore the pleasant atmosphere.

OUTER DISTRICTS
Plan I

🏠 **Landhaus Fuhrgassl-Huber** without rest `VISA` `MC` `AE` `①`
*Rathstr. 24 (by Krottenbachstr. **A 1**) ⊠ 1190*
– ℰ (01) 4 40 30 33 – landhaus@fuhrgassl-huber.at – Fax (01) 4 40 27 14
– www.fuhrgassl-huber.at
38 rm ⊒ – �KM85/88 € ♛♛125/128 €
♦ Family ♦ Cosy ♦
The country house atmosphere of this family-run establishment is an attractive
feature, along with the very comfortable, pretty guestrooms and an
appetising, copious breakfast buffet.

XX **Eckel** ♤ ⟲35 `VISA` `MC` `AE` `①`
*Sieveringer Str. 46 (by Billrothstr. **A 1**) ⊠ 1190 – ℰ (01) 3 20 32 18*
– restaurant.eckel@aon.at – Fax (01) 3 20 66 60 – www.restauranteckel.at
closed 2 weeks August, 24 December - mid January and Sunday - Monday
Rest a la carte 24/45 €
♦ Austrian ♦ Rustic ♦
This country house is a combination of bright and welcoming décor and more
traditional dark wood-panelling. Regular guests enjoy the regional and classical
cuisine, and the pretty terrace.

XX **Plachutta** with rm 🛜 📶 *VISA* 🐽 AE ①
Heiligenstädter Str. 179 ⊠ 1190 – ℰ (01) 3 70 41 25 – nussdorf@plachutta.at
– Fax (01) 3 70 41 25 20 – www.plachutta.at
closed end July - early August **A1**
4 rm – ♦55 € ♦♦85 €, ⌿ 8 €
Rest a la carte 25/44 €
♦ Viennese cuisine ♦ Friendly ♦
This friendly establishment is devoted to the joys of beef: hearty soups are served in copper pots, with "Schulterscherzel", "Hüferschwänzel", and other fine cuts.

X **Schübel-Auer** 🛜 *VISA* 🐽 AE ①
Kahlenberger Str. 22, (Döbling) ⊠ 1190 – ℰ (01) 3 70 22 22
– daniela.somloi@schuebel-auer.at – Fax (01) 3 70 22 22
– www.schuebel-auer.at
closed 23 December - 31 January and Sunday - Monday **A1**
Rest (dinner only) 12 € (buffet)
♦ Buffet ♦ Cosy ♦
Built in 1642 as a wine-grower's house with mill, this traditional building was carefully renovated in 1972 and then lovingly furnished. Courtyard terrace.

X **Feuerwehr-Wagner** 🛜 *VISA* 🐽 AE
Grinzingerstr. 53, (Heiligenstadt) ⊠ 1190 – ℰ (01) 3 20 24 42
– heuriger@feuerwehrwagner.at – Fax (01) 3 20 91 41
– www.feuerwehrwagner.at
open from 4pm **A1**
Rest 12 € (buffet)
♦ Buffet ♦ Cosy ♦
This typical "Heurige" (traditional Austrian wine tavern) is greatly appreciated by regulars. Cosy, rustic décor with dark wood and simple tables. Particularly nice: the terraced garden.

X **Mayer am Pfarrplatz** 🛜 *VISA* 🐽 ①
Pfarrplatz 2, (Heiligenstadt) ⊠ 1190 – ℰ (01) 3 70 12 87 – mayer@pfarrplatz.at
– Fax (01) 3 70 47 14 – www.mayer.pfarrplatz.at
closed 22 December - 15 January **A1**
Rest (weekdays dinner only) 15 € (buffet)
♦ Buffet ♦ Cosy ♦
A textbook "Heurige" (traditional Austrian wine tavern): rustic furnishings, traditional Viennese folk music, and an attractive courtyard terrace. Of note: Beethoven lived here in 1817!

AT THE AIRPORT *by Schüttelstr.* **B2** *Plan I*

 NH Vienna Airport 🛎 📶 ⇖rm ✎rest 📶 📞 ♨300 *VISA* 🐽 AE ①
Hotelstr. 1, ⊠ 1300 Wien – ℰ (01) 70 15 10 – nhviennaairport@nh-hotels.com
– Fax (01) 7 01 51 95 39 – www.nh-hotels.com
500 rm – ♦160/280 € ♦♦160/280 €, ⌿ 18 €
Rest a la carte 26/40 €
♦ Chain hotel ♦ Functional ♦
The clean, elegant design of the spacious foyer and the tasteful, modern, well-equipped rooms, some in classic style, are attractive features. The open plan of the restaurant "nhube" is smartly presented. With buffet.

- *Discover the best restaurant ?*
- *Find the nearest hotel ?*
- *Find your bearings using our maps and guides ?*
- *Understand the symbols used in the guide...*

Follow the red Bibs !

Advice on restaurants from Chef Bib.

Advice on hotels from Bellboy Bib.

Tips and advice from Clever Bib **on finding your way around the guide and on the road.**

BELGIUM
BELGIQUE - BELGIË

PROFILE

♦ **AREA:**
30 513 km²
(11 781 sq mi)

♦ **POPULATION:**
10 710 000 inhabitants
(est. 2005), nearly
55% Flemish, 33%
Walloons and about
10% foreigners.
Density = 351 per km².

♦ **CAPITAL:**
Brussels (conurbation
4 477 000 inhabitants).

♦ **CURRENCY:**
Euro (€); rate of
exchange: € 1 = US$
1.17 (Nov 2005).

♦ **GOVERNMENT:**
Constitutional
parliamentary
monarchy
(since 1830) and a
federal state (since
1994). Member of
European Union
since 1957 (one of the
6 founding countries).

♦ **LANGUAGES:**
French (Wallonia),
Flemish (Flanders),
German (Eastern
cantons); most
Belgians also speak
English.

♦ **SPECIFIC PUBLIC
HOLIDAYS:**
National Day (21 July),
Armistice Day 1918
(11 November).

♦ **LOCAL TIME:**
GMT + 1 hour in
winter and GMT + 2
hours in summer.

♦ **CLIMATE:**
Temperate maritime
with cool winters
and mild summers
(Brussels: January:
2°C, July: 18°C); more
continental towards
the Ardennes. Rainfall
evenly distributed
throughout the year.

•Antwerp
•
Brussels

♦ **INTERNATIONAL
DIALLING CODE:**
00 32 followed by
local number without
the initial 0.
Electronic directories:
www.skynet.be,
www.belgacom.be

♦ **EMERGENCY:**
Police: ℰ **101**; Medical
Assistance and Fire
Brigade: ℰ **100**; Police
or Medical Assistance
from cellular phones:
ℰ **112**.

♦ **ELECTRICITY:**
220 volts AC, 50Hz;
2-pin round-shaped
continental plugs.

FORMALITIES

Travellers from the European Union (EU), Switzerland, Iceland and the main countries of North and South America need a national identity card or passport (America: passport required) to visit Belgium for less than three months (tourism or business purpose). For visitors from other countries a visa may be required, in addition to a passport, especially for those wishing to stay for longer than three months. We advise you to check with your embassy before travelling.

A valid driving licence is essential. International driving licence is required for drivers from 80 countries, mainly in South America, Africa, Asia, Middle East and Pacific Islands. Third party insurance is the minimum cover required by Belgian legislation but it is advisable to take out fully comprehensive cover (Green Card).

MAJOR NEWSPAPERS

The main French-language dailies are *Le Soir, La Libre Belgique, La Dernière Heure - Les Sports, La Capitale, La Meuse* and *La Nouvelle Gazette*. The main Dutch-language dailies: *Het Laatste Nieuws, De Morgen, De Standaard, Het Nieuwsblad, Het Volk, De Gentenaar*. Daily German-language paper: *Grenz-Echo*.

USEFUL PHRASES

ENGLISH	FRENCH	DUTCH
Yes	**Oui**	**Ja**
No	**Non**	**Nee**
Good morning	**Bonjour**	**Goedemorgen**
Goodbye	**Au revoir**	**Tot ziens**
Thank you	**Merci**	**Dank u, bedankt**
Please	**S'il vous plaît**	**Alstublieft**
Excuse me	**Excusez-moi**	**Neemt U mij niet kwalijk**
I don't understand	**Je ne comprends pas**	**Ik begrijp het niet**

HOTELS

◆ CATEGORIES

Accommodation ranges from luxurious 5-star international hotels, to smaller, family-run guesthouses and bed and breakfast establishments. The Benelux star rating is conferred on the application of the owner.

◆ PRICE RANGE

The price is per room. There is little difference between the price of a single and a double room.

Between April and October it is advisable to book in advance. From November to March prices may be slightly lower, some hotels offer special cheap rates and some may be closed. In Brussels hotel chains offer lower weekend rates in the low season.

◆ TAX

Included in the room price.

◆ CHECK OUT TIME

Usually between 11am and noon.

◆ RESERVATIONS

By telephone or by Internet. A credit card number may be required.

◆ TIP FOR LUGGAGE HANDLING

At the discretion of the customer (about €1 per bag).

◆ BREAKFAST

It is often not included in the price of the room and is generally served between 7am and 10am. Most hotels offer a self-service buffet but usually it is possible to have continental breakfast served in the room.

Reception	**Reception**	Receptie
Single room	**Chambre simple**	Eenpersoonskamer
Double room	**Chambre double**	Kamer met tweepersoonsbed
Bed	**Lit**	Bed
Bathroom	**Salle de bains**	Badkamer
Shower	**Douche**	Douche

RESTAURANTS

Besides the traditional **restaurants** there are **brasseries, bistros, 'estaminets'** (typical popular cafés serving beer mainly), **taverns, cafés** and **'friteries'** which serve simpler fare.

Breakfast	**Petit-déjeuner**	Het ontbijt	7am – 10am
Lunch	**Déjeuner**	Middagmaal	12.30pm – 2-3pm
Dinner	**Dîner**	Avondeten	6.30pm – 10-11pm sometimes later

NB: in French-speaking regions in Belgium and Luxembourg it is common practice to use the term 'déjeuner' for breakfast, 'dîner' for the midday meal and 'souper' for the evening meal.

Belgian restaurants offer fixed price menus (starter, main course and dessert) or à la carte. Menus are usually printed in French, Dutch and sometimes in English. A fixed price menu is usually less expensive than a meal with the same number of courses selected from the à la carte menu.

It is not uncommon for restaurants to offer a combined food and wine selection in addition to their usual menus ; wine is served by the glass and usually as much as you can drink. There is a shorter or simpler menu on offer at lunchtime than in the evening and sometimes two different menus: one for lunch and another for dinner.

♦ RESERVATIONS

Reservations are usually made by phone, fax or Internet. For famous restaurants (including Michelin starred restaurants), it is advisable to book several days – or weeks in some instances – in advance. A credit card number or a phone number may be required as guarantee.

♦ THE BILL

The bill (check) includes service charge and VAT. Tipping is optional but, if you are particularly pleased with the service, it is customary to round up the total to an appropriate figure – 10% in larger restaurants and the value of the small change elsewhere.

Drink or aperitif	**Apéritif**	Aperitief
Appetizer	**Mise en bouche**	Hapje
Meal	**Repas**	Maaltijd
First course, starter	**Entrée**	Voorgerecht
Main dish	**Plat principal**	Hoofdgerecht
Main dish of the day	**Plat du jour**	Dagschotel
Dessert	**Dessert**	Nagerecht
Water	**Eau**	Water
Wine (red, white, rosé)	**Vin (rouge, blanc, rosé)**	Wijn (rode, witte, rosé)
Beer	**Bière**	Bier
Bread	**Pain**	Brood

Meat (rare, medium, well done)	Viande (bleu, saignant, à point)	Vlees (rood, saignant, gaar)
Fish	Poisson	Vis
Salt/pepper	Sel/poivre	Zout/peper
Cheese	Fromages	Kaas
Vegetables	Légumes	Groenten
Hot/cold	Chaud/froid	Heet/koud
The bill (check) please	L'addition s'il-vous-plaît	De rekening alstublieft

LOCAL CUISINE

Belgium's culinary traditions are among the finest in Europe and while in many respects Belgian cuisine is similar to that of France, its regional specialities lend it a special distinction. Typical dishes include **waterzooi** (chicken or fish stew), **Flanders hochepot** (casserole of pork, beef or mutton), **oie à la mode de Visé** (goose with a garlic sauce), **anguilles au vert** (eel sautéed in butter with chopped herbs), **boulets liégeois** (meatballs in a sauce with sirop de Liège), **carbonades flamandes** (beef braised in beer), **lapin aux pruneaux** (rabbit stewed with prunes) **or à la Gueuze** (with particular beer). **Potée** (stew with potatoes and vegetables served with pork chops, knuckle of ham or sausages) and **stoemp**, a Brussels variant, are very popular home-cooked dishes. Ardennes ham, shrimp rissoles, hop shoots in a mousseline sauce, chicory or Brussels **witloof** (endive) with ham, au gratin or braised, Flanders asparagus served with parsley and chopped hardboiled eggs are also delicious. **Zeeland mussels** and **schrimps** served with a plate of chips fried to perfection are particularly tasty. In the shooting season venison from the Ardennes is served with a medley of wild mushrooms as accompaniment.

The country produces an amazing variety of **cheese** (Herve, Maredsous, Chimay, Orval, Brussels). Delicious cheesy snacks include **doubles** (pancakes filled with cheese), **potkès** or boulettes de Huy (salty cheese from Huy). There are also plenty of delicious tarts to savour, among them **Lierse vlaaikens** (from Lier), **tarte au maton** (fromage frais, buttermilk and almonds), **flamiche** (with local cheese), **djote** (with whitebeet, cheese, eggs, lardons) and **tarte au stofé** (fromage frais, eggs, almonds and potato). Pralines (chocolates), **waffles** from Brussels and Liège, marzipan and sirop de Liège spread are great treats.

♦ DRINK

Beer is the national drink though most restaurant meals are accompanied by wine. There is an extensive variety of local beers known as **'spéciales'**, as a general term, as distinct from ordinary lagers or 'Pils'.

Among the special beers, you should sample the abbey beers (**bières d'abbaye** – Maredsous, Affligem, Floreffe, Corsendonk, Val Dieu, St-Feuillien, Grimbergen, Leffe, etc.) and in particular an authentic Trappist beer (**bière trappiste**, appellation contrôlée reserved for the production of 6 abbeys – the most famous are Orval, N.-D. de Scourmont at Chimay, N.-D. de Saint-Rémy at Rochefort and Westmalle).

The famous speciality of the Brussels region, **lambics**, **gueuzes** and **krieks** (cherry-flavoured) are the same type of refreshing, slightly sour beer, which is naturally fermented without the addition of yeast (cork stoppers are used for the best bottles).

Fruit and plain **gin** (genever) are widely available as well as a variety of spirits and liqueurs (Elixir d'Anvers, Mandarine Napoléon, etc.)

BRUSSELS
BRUXELLES/BRUSSEL

Population (est. 2005): 133 000 (conurbation 4 477 000) – Altitude: about 100m

Brussels is a cosmopolitan city famous for its warm and friendly atmosphere. The Belgian capital is a place of contrasts reflecting its rich and turbulent history and multicultural influences as well as its pivotal role as the seat of NATO, WEU, the European Union institutions and several multinational companies. Brussels comprises 19 local districts or communes with vibrant local communities and their own distinctive charm. The majority of the population speaks French and some 15% are Dutch (Flemish) speakers.

From the historic city centre, wide avenues and boulevards lead to the surrounding areas which have been extensively redeveloped. Major building projects symbolize the dynamism of the city which is known as the capital of Art Nouveau. The delightful parks and gardens are tranquil havens from the bustling pace of life.

The people enjoy the good life and the reputation of Belgian artists and designers grows apace. An endearing aspect of the national character is revealed in the originality and quirky humour of the comic strips.

WHICH DISTRICT TO CHOOSE

The various districts of Brussels are well-endowed with places to stay, restaurants, sights and attractions.

A great concentration of **hotels**, **restaurants** and **brasseries** is located in the Grand'Place area, known as the "Îlot sacré" *Plan IV* **M2**. This quartier is particularly charming and the small streets all around recall the quarter's history. Rue des Bouchers and Petite rue des Bouchers *Plan IV* **M1** are lined with many popular restaurants.

Beware, however, many tourists traps also exist in this area, and we suggest you stick to those restaurants listed in the following pages.

For a gourmet meal with fresh seafood direct from the North Sea, choose one of the many restaurants in the quartier Ste-Catherine *Plan IV* **M1** where fish shops are located. Shrimp rissoles, croquettes de crevettes grises (starter), and succulent soles Meunière (main dish) are some of the tasty offerings.

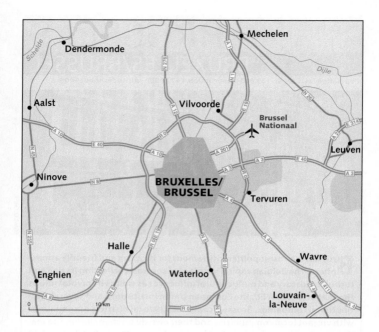

Quartier Louise *Plan III* **K3**, a busy commercial district with luxury shops, has many comfortable hotels and restaurants. Those who prefer simple cooking and a convivial atmosphere will be well served in quartier des Marolles

Plan IV **M3**, a working-class district and in the adjacent quartier des Sablons where antique shops are to be found. Restaurants near Halles St-Géry *Plan IV* **L1**, the latest fashionable area, welcome a young and trendy crowd.

PRACTICAL INFORMATION

ARRIVAL – DEPARTURE

Brussels-National Airport in Zaventem – About 14 km (8 mi) from the city centre. ℘ 02 753 77 53; 0900 70 000 (7am-10pm); info@brusselsairport.be; www.brusselsairport.be

From the airport to the city centre – By **taxi**: €30 + charge for luggage. By **train**: Airport City Express to Bruxelles-Nord, Bruxelles-Centrale and Bruxelles-Midi every 20min. Time: 25min. ℘ 02 753 24 40, 02 555 25 25. Fares €2.60-€3.70. By **bus** B12. Fare €2.50. ℘ 02 515 20 20.

Main Stations – Bruxelles-Midi *Plan II* **E3** is the main interchange for international services. ℘ 02 528 28 28 (8am-8pm; Sat-Sun 9am-5.30pm); www.sncb.be; www.b-rail.be

TRANSPORT

◆ METRO, BUS AND TRAM

Tickets are available from metro stations, STIB/MIVB offices, selected newsagents and tourist information centres. All tram and bus stops are request stops. A single short distance ticket costs €1.50; 5-10 journey cards and one-day travelcards are available (€6.50, €10.00, €3.80 respectively); www.stib.irisnet.be

◆ TAXIS

Taxis bear an illuminated sign on the car roof. They may be hailed in the street, called by telephone, hired at taxi ranks. *Taxis Verts* ℰ 02 349 49 49; *Taxis Orange* ℰ 02 349 43 43; *Taxis Bleus* ℰ 02 268 00 00. Minimum pick-up charge is €2.40; a journey inside the urban centre (agglomeration) costs €1.15/km and €2.30 outside urban centre. It is customary to round up taxi fares. A night tariff (double the daytime tariff) is applicable from 10pm to 6am.

USEFUL ADDRESSES

◆ TOURIST OFFICES

BI-TC (Bruxelles International – Tourisme & Congrès) *Plan IV* **M2**, Hôtel de Ville, Grand-Place, 1000 Bruxelles. ℰ 02 513 89 40. Open 9am-6pm (2pm Sunday in winter).

OPT (Office de Promotion du Tourisme Wallonie-Bruxelles) *Plan IV* **M2**, 63 rue du Marché-aux-Herbes, 1000 Bruxelles. ℰ 02 504 03 90. Open 9am-6pm (7pm July-August).

◆ POST OFFICES

Opening times 9am to 4-5pm. The post office on the first floor of Centre Monnaie, Place de la Monnaie *Plan IV* **M1** is open on Friday evenings and Saturday mornings; that at Gare du Midi is open from 7am to 11pm (7pm for financial operations).

◆ BANKS/CURRENCY EXCHANGE

Banks open Monday to Friday, 9am-4pm. There are cash dispensers all over the city.

◆ EMERGENCY

Dial ℰ **100** (ℰ **112** if calling on a mobile phone) for Ambulance and Fire Brigade and ℰ **101** for Police and Gendarmerie.

BUSY PERIODS

It may be difficult to find a room at a reasonable price (except during weekends) when special events are held in the city:

Sea-Food Expo: end of April or early March.

Labelexpo: September – Stickers show.

Decosit: September – Tissues show.

European Summits: two times a year.

EXPLORING BRUSSELS

DIFFERENT FACETS OF THE CITY

It is possible to visit the main sights and museums in two to three days.

Museums and sights are usually open from 10am to 5pm. Some close on Mondays.

HISTORIC CITY – Grand'Place *Plan IV* **M2**: this splendid square is lined with the ornate Baroque facades of the guildhalls which were built in the 18C and restored in the 19C and are adorned with scrolled gables, sculptures, gilded motifs and flame ornaments. A stunning architectural ensemble at its best during the early morning flower market or floodlit at night. You may also include visits to the **Musée de la Brasserie** (No 10) and the **Musée du Cacao et du Chocolat** (No 13). **Cathédrale des Saints Michel-et-Gudule** *Plan IV* **N1**: a beautiful Gothic building with additions in various styles; wonderful stained glass windows and furnishings.

ARTISTIC CITY – Do not miss **Musées Royaux des Arts de Belgique** *Plan IV* **N2** including **Musée d'Art Ancien** with its outstands collections of

Flemish masters (Bruegel, Rubens, Hieronymus Bosch, Memling). **Musée d'Art Moderne**: Highlights of the 20C collections include Belgian paintings – works by Delvaux and Magritte – and sculpture by Belgian and international artists. **Musée du Cinquantenaire** *Plan II* **H2**: ethnographical and decorative art collections.

ART NOUVEAU CAPITAL – Musée des Instruments de Musique *Plan IV* **N2**: The Art Nouveau buildings of Old England house a prestigious collection of musical instruments – section devoted to Adolphe Sax, Brussels tavern piano, lutemaker's workshop. **Centre Belge de la Bande Dessinée** *Plan IV* **N1**. **Saint-Gilles district**, in particular **Musée Horta** *Plan III* **J2** and **Hotel Hannon** *Plan II* **F3**. **Maison Cauchie** *Plan II* **H2**. The squares around the **Quartier des Institutions Européennes** *Plan II* **G2**. Trail around the lakes at **Ixelles** *Plan III* **K1**.

LOCAL COLOUR – Manneken Pis *Plan IV* **M2**: the mascot of the city. **Underground Art** – 40 stations of the Brussels Metro decorated by famous Belgian artists (*L'Art dans le métro* brochure – in French – from tourist offices). Trail tracing buildings decorated with characters from comic strips (brochure from tourist offices). **Galeries Saint-Hubert** *Plan IV* **M1**: elegant covered arcade with shops, restaurants, tea shops, theatre and cinema.

Lively **markets** are great attractions at weekends: **Place du Grand Sablon** *Plan IV* **M3** and surrounding area; **Place du Jeu de Balle** (flea market) *Plan II* **E3**; **Gare du Midi** *Plan II* **E3**.

To enjoy Brussels-style **'zwanze'** (zwanzer, meaning joking in local dialect, a favourite pastime of the people of Brussels), listen to the people talking around you and try to join in, in particular in the cafés, boutiques and markets in the lower town.

OUTSKIRTS – Basilique du Sacré-Cœur in Koekelberg *Plan I* **A2**, in the Art Deco style. **Atomium in Heysel** *Plan I* **B1**: view from the top sphere at a height of 102m/332ft above ground level, a glittering steel structure consisting of nine spheres represents an iron crystal molecule expanded 165 billion times.

GOURMET TREATS

As you amble along the streets around the **Grand'Place** *Plan IV* **M2** or in the **quartier des Marolles** *Plan IV* **M3** treat yourself to **'caricoles'**, whelks cooked in a peppery broth, or a Belgian waffle, **gaufre de Bruxelles**, a crispy, light pastry, covered with whipped cream (*crème chantilly*).

For a bag of thick, golden chips (**cornet de frites**) served with a variety of sauces, stop at one of the many popular chip shops. The *Maison Antoine*, place Jourdan 1, is one of the best in town.

To sample a thirst-quenching **Gueuze**, a spontaneously fermented regional beer, with a sharp, natural or fruity flavour, such as the delightful **Kriek** (with cherries), or a full-bodied abbey or Trappist beer, take a break in one of the typical **bars (estaminets), cafés, taverns** or **bistros** : *À la Mort Subite*, rue Montagne-Aux-Herbes-Potagères 7; *Au Roy d'Espagne*, Grand'Place 1; *Au Bon Vieux Temps*, rue du Marché-aux-Herbes 12; *L'Imaige de Nostre-Dame*, Impasse des Cadeaux 6; *La Bécasse*, rue Tabora 11; *Le Cirio*, rue de la Bourse 18.

Estaminets and **tavernes-restaurants** (*see listing in the Guide*) are open all day and serve **mussels** (mostly from Zeeland) tasting of the sea and presented in a traditional enamel pot, with a copious helping of chips.

For **pralines** (chocolates), **masse-pain** (marzipan sold mostly in winter), **speculoos** (sweet, spicy biscuits) and other delicacies visit *Wittamer*, pl. du Grand-Sablon 6; *Dandoy*, rue au Beurre 31; *Planète Chocolat*, rue du Lombard 24; *Mary*, rue Royale 73; *Godiva*, Grand'Place 22; *Marcolini*, pl. du Grand-Sablon 39; *Neuhaus*, galerie de la Reine 25.

SHOPPING

Stores are usually open from 10am to 6-7pm. On Friday some department stores close at 8-9pm. In many districts, some shops also open on Sunday and/or in the evening.

Galeries Saint Hubert *Plan IV* **M2**: 3 shopping arcades under one roof: luxury stores and boutiques, book-shops. **Boulevard Anspach, place de Broukère, boulevard A. Max** *Plan IV* **M1**. **Rue Neuve** *Plan IV* **M2**: boutiques, department stores. **Rue Dansaert** *Plan IV* **L1**: trendy fashion bouti-ques. **Avenue Louise, avenue de la Toison d'Or** *Plan II* **F3**. **Boulevard de Waterloo** *Plan II* **F3**: luxury shops, couture houses. **Porte de Namur, rue de Namur** *Plan IV* **N3**: upmarket off-the-peg boutiques. **Rue du Midi** *Plan IV* **M2**: stamps, coins, musical instruments and other items. **Place du Grand Sablon and surroundings** *Plan IV* **M3**: antique shops and art gal-leries.

MARKETS *– See above "Different facets of the city".*

WHAT TO BUY – Brussels lace, fine glassware, earthenware, pewter, silver, diamonds, Tintin memorabilia, almond bread (marzipan), speculoos, Belgian pralines and chocolates, beers.

ENTERTAINMENT

The Bulletin, a weekly publication *(Thursdays)* in English, is a good source of information. *MAD*, the weekly sup-plement to *Le Soir*, and the monthly magazines *Kiosque* and *Tram 81* pub-lish complete entertainment listings for Brussels.

CONCERT HALLS – **Théâtre Royal de la Monnaie** *Plan IV* **M1**. **Palais des Beaux-Arts** *Plan IV* **N2**. **Conservatoire royal de musique** *Plan IV* **M3**.

OTHER VENUES – **Ancienne Belgique** *Plan IV* **M1**. **Cirque Royal** *Plan IV* **N1**. **Forest National** *Plan I* **A3**. **Halles de Schaerbeek** *Plan I* **C2**. **Le Botanique** *Plan II* **F1**.

NIGHTLIFE

Brussels by Night available from the tourist offices lists clubs and disco-theques near the **Grand'Place** *Plan IV* **M2**, **Marolles** *Plan IV* **M3**, **Sablons** and **Midi-Lemonnier** districts, near the **Atomium** *Plan I* **B1** and in the **Upper Town** and university dis-tricts.

Quartier de la Bourse, the focal point for the local youth, in particular around **Halles-St-Géry** *Plan IV* **L1** and in **Rue Dansaert** *Plan IV* **L1**, is very lively late into the night.

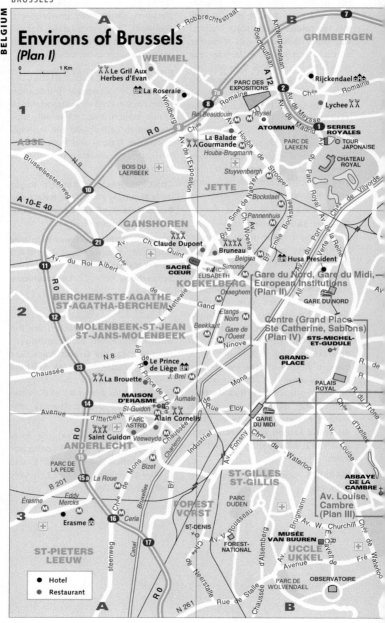

Environs of Brussels
(Plan I)

0   1 Km

R 0

N 209

6

Indringingsweg

MACHELEN

Woluwelaan
R 22

A 1-E 19

N 21

5

12

Haechtsesteenweg

BRUSSEL NATIONAAL
BRUXELLES NATIONAL

Sheraton Airport

A 201

3

Novotel Airport

NH Brussels
Airport

4

Crowne Plaza
Airport

Rainbow Airport

Woluwelaan

Holiday str.

Sofitel Airport

Haechtsesteenweg

Holiday Inn
Airport

A 201

3

Vilvorde

de

Verdun

de

R 0

N 2

EVERE

Chée

Canal

de

Av.

de

Vilvorde

Rue

de

Woluwesteenweg

ZAVENTEM

OTAN

Evere-   straat

N 21

Chaussée

de

Haecht

Leopold III

SCHAERBEEK
SCHAARBEEK

Leuvensesteenweg

20

Woluwe

KRAAINEM

Av. d Deschanel

N 2

Bd

de

Louvain

A 3 - E 40

19

Wezembeek

2

Rogier

Chaussée

WOLUWE-ST-LAMBERT
ST-LAMBRECHTS-WOLUWE

Roodebeek

Vandervelde

Alma

2

Av.   de   Mai

Av.   Hymans

Av. E. Vandervelde

Rue

Tomberg

MARIE
LA MISÉRABLE

Kraainem

la   Loi

PARC DU
CINQUANTENAIRE

N 226

Gribaumont

Chée   de   Stockel

Stokkel

Belliard

Montgomery

J. Charlotte
N 3

Boulevard

Av.   Edmond   Parmentier

Av.   Orban

Av.   Baron   Albert   d'Huart

R 0

N 221

PARC
LEOPOLD

Chée

Avenue

Montgomery

M

Schmidt

ETTERBEEK

Boileau

Petillon

Bd

de

Hankar

PARC
DE
WOLUWE

Av.   Edmond

M

WOLUWE-ST-PIERRE
ST-PIETERS-WOLUWE

Tervuren

de

Tervuren

1

N 3

IXELLES
ELSENE

U

Delta

M

Demey

Beaulieu

Wavre

Souverain

Hermann
Debroux

Chaussée

Chée

AUDERGHEM
OUDERGEM

M

U

Av. F. Roosevelt

BOIS
DE LA
CAMBRE

ST-CLÉMENT

du

de

Wavre

FORÊT

DE

SOIGNES

3

Mont

Saint

Jean

Villa Lorraine

Chaussée   de   la   Hulpe

Av. Delleur

WATERMAEL-BOITSFORT
WATERMAAL-BOSVOORDE

1

A 4 - E 411

R 0
Route

de

Bd

C

D

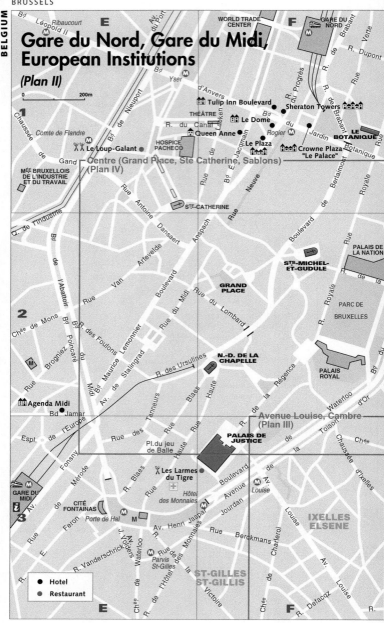

Gare du Nord, Gare du Midi, European Institutions

(Plan II)

0 ————— 200m

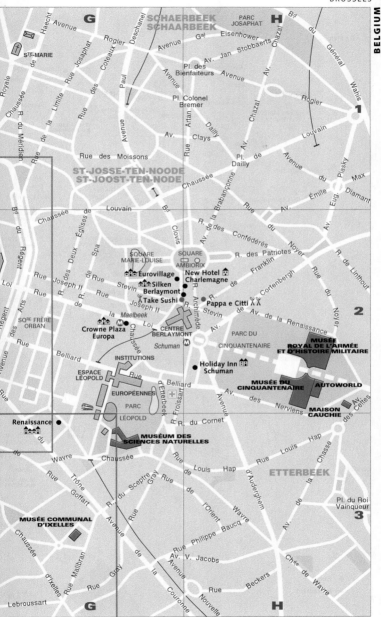

55

Map legend:
- ● Hotel
- ● Restaurant

Labeled features on the map:

Noga
Da Piero
La Marée
Rue de Flandre
Laeken
NH Atlanta
Bd. Adolphe Max
Neuve
Bd. Jacqmain
Welcome
Ste-Catherine
Rue de
Métropole
L'Alban Chambon
Place de Brouckère
Viva M'Boma
Rue du Houblon
Rue Antoine
La Belle Maraîchère
Pl. Ste-Catherine
Rue Ste-Catherine
François
Samourai
Rue du Fossé aux Loups
Pl. du Nouveau Marché aux Grains
STE-CATHERINE
Novotel Centre-Tour Noire
THÉÂTRE DE LA MONNAIE
Atlas
Rue N.-D. du Sommeil
Dansaert
Rue des Fripiers
R. de l'Ecuyer
La Manufacture
Rue des Chartreux
Marriott
Matignon
Vincent
R. des Fabriques
In 't Spinnekopke
Arteveide
Rue Van Arteveide
Pl. de la Bourse
BOURSE
ST-NICOLAS
de l'Ogenblik
Rue T'Kint
RICHES CLAIRES
R. des Riches Claires
Halles St-Géry
HALLES ST-GÉRY
Aux Armes de Bruxelles
GALERIES ST-HUBERT
Rue des Six Jetons
Boulevard
La Maison du Cygne
GRAND-PLACE
Carrefour de l'Europe
Rue de Vautour
Amigo
Bocconi
Le Cerf
Rue du Midi
N.-D. DU BON SECOURS
La Roue d'Or
Le Dixseptième
Pl. Fontainas
MANNEKEN PIS
Royal Windsor
MADELEINE
R. de l'Etuve
Rue du Chêne
Lombard
Place de l'Albertine
Rue de la Verdure
Lemonnier
Bedford
Anneessens
Re-Source
Jaloa
Rue des Alexiens
Boulevard de l'Empereur
Rue des Foulons
Maurice
Neuve
Comme Chez Soi
Rue Terre Neuve
Ursulines
La Clef des Champs
N.-D. DE LA CHAPELLE
Jolly du Grand Sablon
Pl. du Gd Sablon
Boulevard Lemonnier
Stalingrad
Rue des
Rue Haute
Blaes
L'Herbe Rouge
Lola
N.-D. DU SABLON
Avenue de
L'Idiot du village
Rue du Miroir
Rue des Tanneurs
CONSERVATOIRE
R. de la Régence
Bd Poincaré
Rue Terre
Midi
Rue Blaes
Rue Haute
Rue des Capucins
Pl. Poelaert
Ernest Allard
PALAIS DE JUSTICE
JB

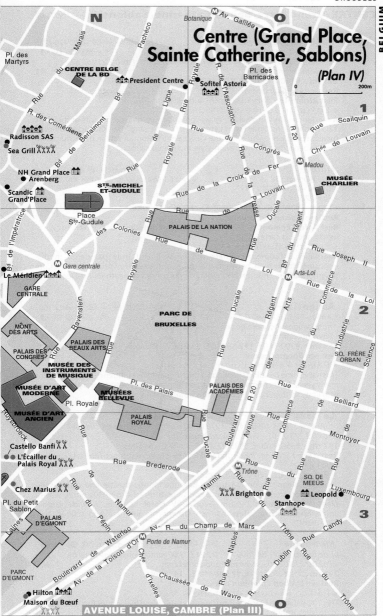

Centre (Grand Place, Sainte Catherine, Sablons)
(Plan IV)

0   200m

N

Pl. des
Martyrs

Botanique   Av. Galilée

CENTRE BELGE
DE LA BD   President Centre   Sofitel Astoria

Pl. des
Barricades

Marais   Pachéco

Rue des Comédiens   Bd   de   Berlaimont   Rue   Ligne   de   Royale   R. d'Association

Scailquin

Rue   Chée   de   Louvain

Radisson SAS
Sea Grill XXX

NH Grand Place
Arenberg

Scandic
Grand'Place

Rue   du   Congrès

R 20   Madou

STS-MICHEL-
ET-GUDULE

Rue   de la   Croix de   de   Fer

Rue   de   Louvain

MUSÉE
CHARLIER

Place
Ste-Gudule   des   Colonies

PALAIS DE LA NATION

de   l'Impératrice

R.   Royale

Rue   de   la   Presse   Rue   Ducale   du   Régent   Rue   Joseph II

Gare centrale

Le Méridien

GARE
CENTRALE

Ravenstein

MONT
DES ARTS

PALAIS DES
CONGRÈS

PALAIS DES
BEAUX ARTS

MUSÉE DES
INSTRUMENTS
DE MUSIQUE

MUSÉE D'ART
MODERNE

MUSÉES
BELLEVUE

Pl. Royale

MUSÉE D'ART
ANCIEN

Huysbroeck

Castello Banfi XX

L'Écailler du
Palais Royal XXX

Chez Marius XX

Pl. du Petit
Sablon

Laines

PALAIS
D'EGMONT

PARC
D'EGMONT

Hilton

Maison du Bœuf
XXXX

Bd   Loi   Arts-Loi   Rue de la   Loi

PARC DE
BRUXELLES

Rue   Ducale   Boulevard   du   Régent   Rue   des   Arts   Rue   du   Rue   de   l'Industrie   SO. FRÈRE
ORBAN   la   Science

2

Pl. des Palais

PALAIS DES
ACADÉMIES

R 20   Rue   Rue   de   Belliard

PALAIS
ROYAL

Rue   Ducale   Boulevard   Avenue   Rue   Commerce   Rue   Montoyer

Rue   Brederode

Rue   Marnix   Rue   Trône   Rue   du   SQ. DE
MEEUS   Luxembourg

XXX Brighton   Stanhope   Leopold

Rue   de   Pépin   Av. R. du Champ de Mars   Candy   3

Boulevard de Waterloo   Porte de Namur   Rue   de   Naples   Rue   de   Dublin   Rue   du   Trône

Av. de la Toison d'Or   Chée   d'Ixelles   Chaussée   de   Wavre

AVENUE LOUISE, CAMBRE (Plan III)

57

BELGIUM

CENTRE (Grand Place, Sainte-Catherine, Sablons) *Plan IV*

Radisson SAS Royal 🖴 🕉 🕭 🏧 ⇘ 🖭 🔳25/420 🗢
r. Fossé-aux-Loups 47 ✉ 1000 ⇨ **VISA** ⦿ 🖭 ⦿
– ✆ 0 2 219 28 28 – guest.brussel@radissonsas.com – Fax 0 2 219 62 62
– www.radissonsas.com **N1**
271 rm – †210/1450 € ††210/1450 €, 🖙 25 € – 10 suites
Rest see *Sea Grill* below
Rest *Atrium* 18 € (weekday lunch) and a la carte 40/57 €
♦ Luxury ♦ Business ♦ Modern ♦
A modern luxury hotel whose glass-roofed atrium bears remnants of the city's
12C fortifications. Four room categories. "Comic strip" bar. Classic, traditional
meals served while you enjoy the view over the Roman wall in the atrium. The
house speciality is Scandinavian-style marinated salmon.

Hilton ≼ town, 🖴 🕉 🕭rest 🏧 ⇘
bd de Waterloo 38 🕉rest 🖭 🔳45/650 🗢 ⇨ **VISA** ⦿ 🖭 ⦿
✉ 1000 – ✆ 0 2 504 11 11
– Fax 0 2 504 21 11 **N3**
417 rm – †145/565 € ††175/595 €, 🖙 32 € – 15 suites
Rest see *Maison du Bœuf* below
Rest *Café d'Egmont*, ✆ 0 2 504 13 33 (open until midnight) 35 € (weekday
lunch) and a la carte 36/58 €
♦ Luxury ♦ Business ♦ Classic ♦
International business clientele will be well and truly pampered in this
imposing Hilton built between the upper and lower towns. The hotel's Café
d'Egmont offers an intercontinental menu, served beneath its Art Deco glass
roof.

Amigo 🖴 🏧 ⇘ 🕉 🖭 🕾 🔳25/160
r. Amigo 1 ✉ 1000 – ✆ 0 2 547 47 47 🗢 **VISA** ⦿ 🖭 ⦿
– hotelamigo@hotelamigo.com – Fax 0 2 513 52 77
– www.hotelamigo.com **M2**
156 rm – †200/600 € ††220/630 €, 🖙 28 € – 18 suites
Rest see *Bocconi* below
♦ Palace ♦ Grand Luxury ♦ Stylish ♦
This handsome building showing Spanish Renaissance influence was a prison for
many years. Collection of works of art on display, chic, contemporary rooms and
proximity to the Grand-Place are this hotel's strong points.

Le Plaza 🏧 ⇘ 🖭 🔳25/600 🗢 ⇨ **VISA** ⦿ 🖭 ⦿
bd. A. Max 118 ✉ 1000 – ✆ 0 2 278 01 00 – admin@leplaza-brussels.be
– Fax 0 2 278 01 01 – www.leplaza-brussels.be *Plan II* **F1**
187 rm – †350/1100 € ††354/1127 €, 🖙 27 € – 6 suites
Rest (closed Saturday lunch and Sunday) 29 € (weekday lunch) and a la carte
37/61 €
♦ Palace ♦ Luxury ♦ Classic ♦
Spacious, elegant rooms, a superb Baroque lounge-theatre and classic-style
public areas are among the noteworthy features of this 1930s hotel, whose
plans were inspired by the Georges V Hotel in Paris. A wide cupola
embellished with a celestial fresco crowns the intimate and refined bar-
restaurant.

Métropole 🕭 🏧 ⇘ 🖭 🕾 🔳25/500 🗢 ⇨ **VISA** ⦿ 🖭 ⦿
pl. de Brouckère 31 ✉ 1000 – ✆ 0 2 217 23 00 – info@metropolehotel.be
– Fax 0 2 218 02 20 – www.metropolehotel.be **M1**
291 rm 🖙 – †299/399 € ††349/449 € – 14 suites
Rest see *L'Alban Chambon* below
♦ Palace ♦ Luxury ♦ Historic ♦
This 19C palace on place de Brouckère was eulogised by Jacques Brel. Impressive
foyer, sumptuous period lounges and delicate Art Nouveau frescoes discovered
in 2004.

BELGIUM

Sofitel Astoria
🗓️ 🅰️ ⇕ 📧 🍴25/210 🅿️ 📶 ⚫⚫ 🅰️ ⓪

r. Royale 103 ⊠ 1000 – 𝒫 0 2 227 05 05 – H1154@accor.com
– Fax 0 2 217 11 50 – www.sofitel.com

O1

106 rm – ♦100/240 € ♦♦120/340 €, � 25 € – 12 suites
Rest *Le Palais Royal (closed 15 July-15 August, Friday dinner,
Saturday and Sunday)* 40 € (weekday lunch) and a la carte 45/62 €
♦ Palace ♦ Luxury ♦ Historic ♦
Emperor Hiro Hito, Churchill and Dali have all stayed at this elegant Belle Époque
palace. Sumptuous lounges, bedrooms adorned with period furniture, and a bar
with an "Orient Express" atmosphere. Meals for the modern palate and classic,
refined decor at Le Palais Royal restaurant.

Royal Windsor
🗓️ 🎎 ⛓️rm 🅰️ ⇕ ✂️rest 📧 ⟲ 🍴25/200 🏨 🅿️

r. Duquesnoy 5 ⊠ 1000 – 𝒫 0 2 505 55 55　　　　⟲ 📶 ⚫⚫ 🅰️ ⓪
– resa.royalwindsor@warwickhotels.com – Fax 0 2 505 55 00
– www.royalwindsorbrussels.com

M2

249 rm – ♦345/440 € ♦♦345/440 €, � 25 € – 17 suites
Rest a la carte 33/46 €
♦ Luxury ♦ Business ♦ Stylish ♦
Luxury, comfort and refinement characterise this grand hotel in the historic
centre, which tends to attract Belgium's fashion victims (you have been warned).
Impeccable service. Contemporary bar-restaurant striving for a colonial
ambience. Modern cuisine.

Marriott
🗓️ 🎎 ⛓️rm 🅰️ ⇕ 📧 ⟲ 🍴25/450 🏨 🅿️ ⟲ 📶 ⚫⚫ 🅰️ ⓪

r. A. Orts 7 (opposite the Stock Exchange) ⊠ 1000 – 𝒫 (0 2) 516 90 90
– Fax (0 2) 516 90 00

M1

214 rm – ♦99/309 € ♦♦99/309 €, � 25 € – 4 suites
Rest 𝒫 02 516 91 00 *(closed Sunday lunch)* 17 € (weekday lunch) and a la carte
26/42 €
♦ Chain hotel ♦ Business ♦ Functional ♦
Luxurious hotel situated in front of the Stock Exchange. Its imposing
turn-of-the-century façade, interior public areas and rooms were given a facelift
in 2002. Modern brasserie where the usual international fare is served with a
contemporary touch. Kitchens and rotisserie opening onto the dining area.

Le Méridien
🗓️ ⛓️rm 🅰️ ⇕ ✂️ 📧 ⟲ 🍴25/200 🏨 ⟲ 📶 ⚫⚫ 🅰️ ⓪

Carrefour de l'Europe 3 ⊠ 1000 – 𝒫 0 2 548 42 11 – info.brussels@
lemeridien.com – Fax 0 2 548 40 80 – www.brussels.lemeridien.com

N2

216 rm – ♦450 € ♦♦450 €, � 25 € – 8 suites
Rest *L'Épicerie (closed 17 July-21 August, Saturday lunch and Sunday dinner)*
52 € (weekday lunch) and a la carte 53/73 €
♦ Chain hotel ♦ Business ♦ Stylish ♦
The hotel's majestic neo-Classical façade stands opposite the Gare Centrale.
Gleaming interior decor, with elegant bedrooms boasting the very latest in
facilities. The restaurant menu is distinctly modern, and offers a cuisine inspired
by the New World and its spices.

Le Dixseptième without rest
🅰️ ⇕ ✂️ 📧 🍴25 📶 ⚫⚫ 🅰️ ⓪

r. Madeleine 25 ⊠ 1000 – 𝒫 0 2 517 17 17 – info@ledixseptieme.be
– Fax 0 2 502 64 24 – www.ledixseptieme.be

M2

18 rm � – ♦170/300 € ♦♦170/300 € – 6 suites
♦ Family ♦ Luxury ♦ Stylish ♦
As its name indicates, this old town house dates from the 17C, when the Spanish
Ambassador occupied its rooms. Elegant lounges and large bedrooms furnished
with antiques from different periods.

NH Atlanta
🗓️ 🎎 ⛓️rest 🅰️ ⇕ 📧 ⟲ 🍴25/180 🏨

bd A. Max 7 ⊠ 1000 – 𝒫 0 2 217 01 20　　　　⟲ 📶 ⚫⚫ 🅰️ ⓪
– nhatlanta@nh-hotels.com – Fax 0 2 217 37 58 – www.nh-hotels.com

M1

234 rm – ♦84/325 € ♦♦84/325 €, � 19 € – 7 suites
Rest *(closed lunch Saturday and Sunday)* a la carte 25/43 €
♦ Chain hotel ♦ Business ♦ Modern ♦
This neo-Classical 1930s building just a stone's throw from the nostalgic passage
du Nord and place de Brouckère has huge rooms and a panoramic breakfast room
on the 6th floor. The modern brasserie serves a range of French and Italian cuisine.

BELGIUM

Bedford 🌜 🔥 rest 🔟 rest ⇞ 🛂 🚬 ♨25/450 🚗 💳 ⓂⒸ 🅰🅴 ①
r. Midi 135 ⊠ 1000 – 𝒞 0 2 507 00 00 – info @ hotelbedford.be
– Fax 0 2 507 00 10 – www.hotelbedford.be   **L2**
318 rm � – ♦230/290 € ♦♦275/340 € – 8 suites
Rest 36 €/46 € and a la carte 39/55 €
♦ Traditional ♦ Business ♦ Classic ♦
Just a short walk from the Manneken Pis and 500m/550yd from the Grand-Place, this hotel houses major seminar facilities and well-appointed rooms. Franco-Belgian cuisine served in a large dining area with British-inspired decor.

Jolly du Grand Sablon 🔥 🔟 ⇞ 🛂rest 🚬 💬 ♨25/150 🚗
r. Bodenbroek 2 ⊠ 1000 – 𝒞 0 2 518 11 00 ⇲ 💳 ⓂⒸ 🅰🅴 ①
– jollyhotelsablon @ jollyhotels.be – Fax 0 2 512 67 66
– www.jollyhotels.com   **M3**
187 rm ⊆ – ♦260/310 € ♦♦285/335 € – 6 suites
Rest *(closed 21 July-18 August, 25 December-5 January and Sunday)*
a la carte 26/45 €
♦ Chain hotel ♦ Business ♦ Stylish ♦
This Italian-owned hotel is located just a stone's throw from the city's prestigious royal museums. Spacious lobby area, well-appointed rooms, plus meeting rooms with all the facilities. The restaurant offers Italian cuisine, buffets and Sunday brunch accompanied by music.

President Centre without rest 🔟 ⇞ 🛂 🚬 🚗 💳 ⓂⒸ 🅰🅴 ①
r. Royale 160 ⊠ 1000 – 𝒞 0 2 219 00 65 – gm @ presidentcentre.be
– Fax 0 2 218 09 10 – www.presidentcentre.be   **N1**
73 rm ⊆ – ♦140/220 € ♦♦165/240 €
♦ Chain hotel ♦ Business ♦ Classic ♦
This hotel near to the EU institutions has a marble entrance hall and reception area, comfortable living room and contemporary-style rooms of varying sizes housed on eight floors.

Carrefour de l'Europe without rest 🔟 ⇞ 🚬 💬
r. Marché-aux-Herbes 110 ⊠ 1000
– 𝒞 0 2 504 94 00 – info @ carrefoureurope.net – Fax 0 2 504 95 00 ♨25/200 💳 ⓂⒸ 🅰🅴 ①
                                                    M2
58 rm – ♦265 € ♦♦265 €, ⊆ 21 € – 5 suites
♦ Traditional ♦ Business ♦ Functional ♦
This modern hotel just off the Grand-Place is in keeping with the harmony of the city's architecture. Bedrooms slightly on the drab side, but of a good standard nonetheless.

NH Grand Place Arenberg 🔟 ⇞ 🛂rm 💬 ♨25/80
r. Assaut 15 ⊠ 1000 – 𝒞 0 2 501 16 16 🚗 💳 ⓂⒸ 🅰🅴 ①
– nhgrandplace @ nh-hotels.com – Fax 0 2 501 18 18   **N1**
155 rm – ♦69/220 € ♦♦69/270 €, ⊆ 19 €
Rest 10 € (weekday lunch) and a la carte 22/37 €
♦ Chain hotel ♦ Business ♦ Modern ♦
This hotel is well-placed for exploring the heart of the city around the Grand-Place. The modern bedrooms are functional yet welcoming, and typical of the NH chain. Contemporary-style restaurant serving international cuisine with modern overtones.

Scandic Grand'Place 🛁 🔥rm 🔟 ⇞ ♨25/70 💳 ⓂⒸ 🅰🅴 ①
r. Arenberg 18 ⊠ 1000 – 𝒞 0 2 548 18 11 – grand.place @ scandic-hotels.com
– Fax 0 2 548 18 20 – www.scandic-hotels.com   **N1**
100 rm ⊆ – ♦95/259 € ♦♦125/289 €
Rest *(closed lunch Saturday and Sunday)* 16 € (weekday lunch) and a la carte 22/34 €
♦ Chain hotel ♦ Business ♦ Functional ♦
This new hotel close to the Grand-Place and accessible via the luxurious Galeries St-Hubert has public areas decorated with wood and an atrium giving onto rooms with a Scandinavian feel. A soberly-designed, yet welcoming and light modern brasserie.

Michelin in the Nordics

o Long Term Presence

Michelin has been established in the Nordic countries for more than 80 years. Accomplishing our mission to improve people's mobility by bringing more safety, more efficiency, more freedom and pleasure by meeting the special challenges of the tough Nordic winter conditions.

o Extreme Expertise

The challenge of the Nordic winter has made it possible for Michelin to develop a real expertise in winter tyres specifically conceived for the Nordic market. Both studded and Non-studded winter tyres are constantly tested in the extreme conditions of Lapland.

o Leading Actors on the Nordic markets

The wide range of Michelin tyres available in the Nordic markets and the experience of local conditions have made Michelin the leading actor on the Nordic tyre markets.

o Nordic Organisation

Michelin's Nordic headquarters are located in Stockholm, Sweden. In Denmark, Finland and Norway our local commercial agencies ensure proximity with each market.

o Efficient Logistics

Michelin's ultra-modern logistics centre in Gothenburg, Sweden serves the Nordic markets, with deliveries going well beyond the Arctic Circle.

o Highly Qualified Staff

The Nordic staff amounts to some 1500 employees, including Michelin's distribution chain Euromaster, which is widely present in Sweden, Finland and Denmark. The Local Michelin Sales Force in each country offers both technical and business expertise to a large number of customers.

MICHELIN
A better way forward

BELGIUM

Novotel Centre-Tour Noire
r. Vierge Noire 32 ⊠ 1000
– ☎ 0 2 505 50 50 – H2122@accor.com – Fax 0 2 505 50 00
– www.accorhotels.com/be **M1**
217 rm – †165/180 € ††165/180 €, ☐ 15 €
Rest a la carte 25/40 €
♦ Chain hotel ♦ Business ♦ Functional ♦
This chain hotel is built around the remains of the city's first defensive walls, including a tower restored in the spirit of Eugène Viollet-le-Duc. The rooms are being overhauled in stages. Contemporary-style brasserie serving good basic cuisine

Welcome without rest
quai au Bois à Brûler 23 ⊠ 1000 – ☎ 0 2 219 95 46 – info@hotelwelcome.com
– Fax 0 2 217 18 87 – www.hotelwelcome.com **M1**
16 rm ☐ – †85/130 € ††95/180 €
♦ Traditional ♦ Stylish ♦
A hotel with charming rooms, each of which has a decor inspired by an exotic land, such as Egypt, Kenya, Congo, China, Bali, Tibet, Japan and India.

Atlas without rest
r. du Vieux Marché-aux- Grains 30 ⊠ 1000
– ☎ 0 2 502 60 06 – info@atlas.be – Fax 0 2 502 69 35
– www.atlas.be **L1**
88 rm ☐ – †75/160 € ††85/239 €
♦ Traditional ♦ Business ♦ Classic ♦
This 18C hotel (modernised inside) stands on a small square in a festive neighbourhood full of Belgian fashion boutiques. Most of the rooms look onto an inner courtyard.

Agenda Midi without rest
bd Jamar 11 ⊠ 1060 – ☎ 0 2 520 00 10 – midi@hotel-agenda.com
– Fax 0 2 520 00 20 – www.hotel-agenda.com *Plan II* **E2**
35 rm ☐ – †72/86 € ††82/114 €
♦ Traditional ♦ Business ♦ Classic ♦
This hotel building is just a short distance from the Gare du Midi TGV railway station. Reliable accommodation at bargain prices. Breakfast buffet served in an inviting room decorated in warm tones.

Noga without rest
r. Béguinage 38 ⊠ 1000 Brussel – ☎ 0 2 218 67 63 – info@nogahotel.com
– Fax 0 2 218 16 03 – www.nogahotel.com **L1**
19 rm ☐ – †65/85 € ††80/100 €
♦ Family ♦ Retro ♦
A friendly hotel in a fine townhouse in a quiet area of the city. A pleasant lounge, bar with a nautical decor, attractive rooms and a stairway decorated with portraits of Belgian royalty.

Queen Anne without rest
bd E. Jacqmain 110 ⊠ 1000 – ☎ 0 2 217 16 00 – Fax 0 2 217 18 38
– www.queen-anne.be *Plan II* **F1**
60 rm ☐ – †70/170 € ††75/205 €
♦ Traditional ♦ Family ♦ Minimalist ♦
This glass-fronted hotel is located on a main road. Ask for one of the small, recently refurbished rooms: sober, fresh and discreet designer features.

Matignon without rest
r. Bourse 10 ⊠ 1000 – ☎ 0 2 511 08 88 – hotelmatignon@skynet.be
– Fax 0 2 513 69 27 – www.hotelmatignon.be **M1**
37 rm ☐ – †75/102 € ††85/150 €
♦ Traditional ♦ Family ♦ Classic ♦
This hotel next to the Stock Exchange has well-maintained rooms, including a dozen junior suites. Mainly popular with tourists.

BELGIUM

Sea Grill – Hotel Radisson SAS Royal   🕭 🎴 🛋 VISA ⓒ⓪ AE ①
r. Fossé-aux-Loups 47 ⊠ 1000 – ℰ 0 2 217 92 25 – seagrill@radissonsas.com
– Fax 0 2 227 31 27
closed 25 February-5 March, 8 to 17 April, 27 July-15 August,
28 October-5 November, Saturday, Sunday and Bank Holidays   **N1**
Rest 49 € (weekday lunch), 75/170 € and a la carte 91/126 € 🎇
Spec. Saint-Jacques cuites à la vapeur d'algues, crème légère au cresson
(15 Sept.-30 April). Bar de ligne cuit en croûte de sel. Manchons de crabe de la mer
de Barents tiédis au beurre de persil plat.
◆ Seafood ◆ Cosy ◆
A warm, Scandinavian-influenced ambience, ambitious fish-dominated menu,
excellent wine cellar, plus a lounge offering a good choice of cigars. Impeccable,
friendly service.

La Maison du Cygne   🎴 ⅍ 🅿 🛋 VISA ⓒ⓪ AE ①
r. Charles Buis 2 ⊠ 1000 – ℰ 0 2 511 82 44 – info@lamaisonducygne.be
– Fax 0 2 514 31 48 – www.lamaisonducygne.be
closed 31 July-20 August, 23 December-2 January,
Saturday lunch and Sunday   **M2**
Rest 40 € (weekday lunch)/80 € and a la carte 63/127 € 🎇
◆ French traditional ◆ Formal ◆
This 17C house on the Grand-Place was originally the headquarters of the
Butchers' Guild. Roasting spit on view, traditional cuisine concocted with
modern flourishes and excellent wine list.

Maison du Bœuf – Hotel Hilton, first floor   ≼ 🕭 🎴
bd de Waterloo 38 ⊠ 1000 – ℰ 0 2 504   ⅍ 🅿 🛋 VISA ⓒ⓪ AE ①
13 34 – maisonduboeuf.brussels@hilton.com
– Fax 0 2 504 21 11   **N3**
Rest 55 € (weekday lunch)/68 € and a la carte 60/128 € 🎇
Spec. Côte de bœuf rôtie en croûte de sel. Bar rôti au thym frais, crème
d'échalotes. Tartare maison au caviar.
◆ French traditional ◆ Formal ◆
The Hilton's gourmet restaurant proposes a resolutely traditional à la carte menu
in keeping with its opulent decor. Extensive wine-list. Views over the Parc
d'Egmont.

Bruneau   🎇 🎴 🛋 (dinner) VISA ⓒ⓪ AE ①
av. Broustin 75 ⊠ 1083 – ℰ 0 2 421 70 70 – restaurant_bruneau@skynet.be
– Fax 0 2 425 97 26 – www.bruneau.be
closed 1 to 10 February, August, Tuesday,
Wednesday and Thursday holidays   Plan I **B2**
Rest 45 € (weekday lunch), 75/135 € b.i. and a la carte 75/280 € 🎇
Spec. Fondant de bar, salade d'herbes à l'huile d'argan. Croustillant de
langoustines au basilic. Galette de pigeon de Vendée, cuisses caramelisées au
soja.
◆ Contemporary ◆ Cosy ◆
This renowned restaurant has achieved a perfect balance of innovation and
tradition while at the same time maintaining its commitment to local products.
Prestigious wine-list. Summer terrace.

L'Alban Chambon – Hotel Métropole   🎴 ⅍ 🅿 VISA ⓒ⓪ AE ①
pl. de Brouckère 31 ⊠ 1000 – ℰ 0 2 217 23 00 – info@metropolehotel.be
– Fax 0 2 218 02 20 – www.metropolehotel.com
closed 17 July-15 August, Saturday, Sunday and Bank Holidays   **M1**
Rest 39 € (weekday lunch)/70 € and a la carte 56/99 €
◆ French traditional ◆ Retro ◆
This restaurant is named after the architect who designed it. Light, classic cuisine
served in a former ballroom embellished with period furniture.

BELGIUM

XXX
ひ ひ ひ

Comme Chez Soi (Wynants)   [AK] 📶 **VISA** 🐄 AE ①
pl. Rouppe 23 ⊠ 1000 – ℰ 0 2 512 29 21 – info @ commechezsoi.be
– Fax 0 2 511 80 52 – www.commechezsoi.be
closed 28 February, 11 April, 2 May, 23 July-21 August, 1 November,
24 December-8 January, Sunday, Monday and Wednesday   **L2**
Rest (booking essential) 67 €/166 € and a la carte 82/281 € ॐ
Spec. Filet de sole, mousseline au riesling, crevettes grises. Grillons de ris de veau
à la truffe d'été, sauté de légumes en vinaigrette. Damier de fraises des bois, glacé
à la frangipane (in season).
◆ French traditional ◆ Retro ◆
The Belle Époque atmosphere, recreated in this Horta-inspired decor, is the
perfect foil for the superb cuisine and magnificent wine list. Unfortunately the
tables are ever-so-slightly cramped.

XXX
ひ ひ

Claude Dupont   **VISA** 🐄 AE ①
av. Vital Riethuisen 46 ⊠ 1083 – ℰ 0 2 426 00 00 – claudedupont @ resto.be
– Fax 0 2 426 65 40 – www.resto.be/claudedupont
closed July, Monday and Tuesday   *Plan I* **A2**
Rest 45 € (weekday lunch), 70/110 € and a la carte 59/115 €
Spec. Sashimi de saumon et bar au caviar. Barbue en écailles de Saint-Jacques au
vin de Chinon. Canette de barbarie au cidre bouché et petites reinettes
caramélisées.
◆ French traditional ◆ Friendly ◆
A master-class in culinary invention. The accolades and awards on display in the
entrance hall are thoroughly deserved. Classic dining area.

XXX

L'Écailler du Palais Royal   [AK] 🍴 **VISA** 🐄 AE ①
r. Bodenbroek 18 ⊠ 1000 – ℰ 0 2 512 87 51 – Fax 0 2 511 99 50
closed August, Christmas-New Year, Sunday and Bank Holidays   **N3**
Rest a la carte 61/137 €
◆ Seafood ◆ Cosy ◆
A cosy and elegant oyster bar where both classic and inventive seafood dishes
are created. A choice of seating: benches, chairs or the bar-counter on the
ground floor, or round tables upstairs.

XX
☺

Aux Armes de Bruxelles   [AK] **VISA** 🐄 AE ①
r. Bouchers 13 ⊠ 1000 – ℰ 0 2 511 55 98 – arbrux @ beon.be – Fax 0 2 514 33 81
– www.armesdebruxelles.be   **M1**
Rest (open until 11 p.m.) 23 € b.i. (weekday lunch), 30/45 € and a la carte
26/70 €
◆ Traditional ◆ Brasserie ◆
A veritable Brussels institution at the heart of the historic centre, this family-run
restaurant established in 1921 focuses on the resolutely Belgian. Rooms in
contrasting styles.

XX

Bocconi – Hotel Amigo   🍴 📶 **VISA** 🐄 AE ①
r. Étuve 9 ⊠ 1000 – ℰ 0 2 547 47 15 – bocconi @ hotelamigo.com
– Fax 0 2 547 47 67 – www.ristorantebocconi.com   **M2**
Rest 34 € (weekday lunch)/50 € and a la carte 40/57 €
◆ Italian ◆ Design ◆
This fine Italian restaurant is in a luxury hotel near the Grand-Place. Inside, the
design is that of a modern brasserie. The cuisine features appetising Italian
classics.

XX

François   🏡 [AK] 📶 **VISA** 🐄 AE ①
quai aux Briques 2 ⊠ 1000 – ℰ 0 2 511 60 89 – Fax (0 2) 512 06 67
– www.restaurantfrancois.be
closed Sunday and Monday   **L1**
Rest 24 € (weekday lunch), 33/37 € and a la carte 34/73 €
◆ Seafood ◆ Friendly ◆
Seafood restaurant and fishmonger run by the same family since the 1930s. The
maritime interior is enlivened with nostalgic photos.

BELGIUM

XX La Belle Maraichère

🗚🗚   AK VISA ⬤⬤ AE ⬤

pl. Ste-Catherine 11 ✉ 1000 – ℰ 0 2 512 97 59 – Fax 0 2 513 76 91
closed 2 weeks carnival, mid July-early August, Wednesday and Thursday
Rest 32 €/50 € and a la carte 37/83 € ❁   **M1**
♦ Seafood ♦ Family ♦
This convivial restaurant with a slightly dated charm is without a doubt one of the most reliably good-value eats in the neighbourhood. Tasty classic cuisine with a penchant for fish and seafood.

XX Castello Banfi

                             ⓺ AK VISA ⬤⬤ AE ⬤

r. Bodenbroek 12 ✉ 1000 – ℰ 0 2 512 87 94 – castellobanfi@hotmail.com
– Fax 0 2 512 87 94
closed first week Easter, last 3 weeks August, Christmas-New Year,
Sunday and Monday   **N3**
Rest 27 € (weekday lunch)/49 € and a la carte 36/79 €
♦ Italian ♦ Fashionable ♦
The menu at this gastronomic restaurant, hidden behind a 1729 façade, encompasses culinary and viticultural specialities from both France and Italy. The name refers to a large Tuscan wine estate.

XX JB

                                 🕮 AK VISA ⬤⬤ AE ⬤

r. Grand Cerf 24 ✉ 1000 – ℰ 0 2 512 04 84 – restaurantjb@vt4.net
– Fax 0 2 511 79 30 – www.restaurantjb.be
closed Saturday lunch, Sunday and Bank Holidays   **M3**
Rest 20 €/30 € and a la carte 35/60 €
♦ Traditional ♦ Family ♦
This friendly, family-run restaurant has nothing to do with the famous Scottish whisky! Appetising classic menu including good set menus.

XX Chez Marius

                            🕮 🗱 VISA ⬤⬤ AE ⬤

pl. du Petit Sablon 1 ✉ 1000 – ℰ 0 2 511 12 08 – info@chez.marius.be
– Fax 0 2 512 27 89
closed 20 July-20 August, Saturday, Sunday and Bank Holidays   **N3**
Rest 25 € (weekday lunch)/43 € and a la carte 46/84 €
♦ Traditional ♦ Friendly ♦
This restaurant opposite the Petit Sablon opened in 1965. Provençal cuisine is served in three classically arranged and very spruce rooms. Small terrace in front.

XX Le Loup-Galant

                                 AK VISA ⬤⬤ AE

quai aux Barques 4 ✉ 1000 – ℰ 0 2 219 99 98 – loupgalant@swing.be
– Fax 0 2 219 99 98 – www.resto.be/leloupgalant
closed 1 week May, 2 weeks August, Christmas week,
Sunday and Monday   *Plan II* **E1**
Rest 19 € (weekday lunch), 25/60 € b.i. and a la carte 40/52 €
♦ Traditional ♦ Rustic ♦
You can spot this old house at one end of the Vismet thanks to its yellow walls and the gold statue of St Michel on the façade of the next house. Classic meals served in a rustic decor of chimney piece and exposed beams.

X La Manufacture

                           🕮 🗱 VISA ⬤⬤ AE ⬤

r. Notre-Dame du Sommeil 12 ✉ 1000 – ℰ 0 2 502 25 25 – info@manufacture.be
– Fax 0 2 502 27 15 – www.manufacture.be
closed Saturday lunch and Sunday   **L1**
Rest (open until 11 p.m.) 13 € (weekday lunch), 29/50 € and a la carte 30/51 €
♦ Contemporary ♦ Brasserie ♦
Metal, wood, leather and granite have all been used to decorate this trendy brasserie occupying the workshop of a renowned leather manufacturer. Contemporary cuisine.

X **de l'Ogenblik** 🍴 VISA ⦿ AE ⦿

Galerie des Princes 1 ⊠ *1000 – ℰ 0 2 511 61 51 – ogenblik @ tiscalinet.be*
– Fax 0 2 513 41 58 – www.ogenblik.be
closed Sunday and lunch holidays **M1**
Rest (open until midnight) 51 €/58 € and a la carte 45/65 €
♦ Traditional ♦ Bistro ♦

This restaurant housed in an old café is known for its classic cuisine and
bistro-style. Popular with the local business community. The same chef has
worked here since 1975.

X **Samourai** AC 🍴 VISA ⦿ AE ⦿

r. Fossé-aux-Loups 28 ⊠ *1000 – ℰ 0 2 217 56 39 – Fax 0 2 771 97 61*
– www.restaurant-samourai.be
closed 15 July-16 August, Tuesday and Sunday lunch **M1**
Rest 22 € (weekday lunch), 46/69 € and a la carte 42/84 €
♦ Japanese ♦ Exotic ♦

A Japanese restaurant established more than 30 years ago near the Théâtre de
la Monnaie. Authentic, varied menu. Rooms with Japanese decor on several
floors.

X **La Roue d'Or** 🍴 VISA ⦿ AE ⦿

r. Chapeliers 26 – ℰ 0 2 514 25 54 – Fax 0 2 512 30 81
closed 10 August-10 August **M2**
Rest (open until midnight) 10 € (weekday lunch) and a la carte 25/52 €
♦ Traditional ♦ Brasserie ♦

A typical old café with a convivial atmosphere where the culinary emphasis is on
staple Belgian brasserie fare. Surrealist wall paintings in the genre of Magritte
and a superb clock in the dining area.

X **Jaloa** 🍴 VISA ⦿ AE

pl. de la Vieille Halle aux Blés 31 ⊠ *1000 – ℰ 0 2 512 18 31 – contact @ jaloa.com*
– Fax 0 2 512 18 31 – www.jaloa.com
closed Saturday lunch and Sunday **M2**
Rest (open until 11 p.m.) 16 € (weekday lunch), 33/60 € and a la carte 43/73 €
♦ Contemporary ♦ Wine bar ♦

A long, narrow dining room in an old house near the Brel Museum with
minimalist modern decor and a view of the kitchen. Contemporary cuisine and
background music.

X **Re-Source** AC P VISA ⦿ AE

r. Midi 164 ⊠ *1000 – ℰ 0 2 5 14 32 23 – info @ restaurantresource.be*
– Fax 0 2 5 14 07 38 – www.restaurantresource.be
closed 23 July-14 August, Sunday, Monday and holiday lunch **L2**
Rest 15 € (weekday lunch), 38/53 €
♦ Contemporary ♦ Trendy ♦

A "hip" restaurant with a trendy decor of brickwork, modern paintings and little
wooden tables laid out side by side and set with a distinctly contemporary
simplicity.

X **Da Piero** ⅖ AC VISA ⦿

r. Antoine Dansaert 181 ⊠ *1000 – ℰ (0 2) 219 23 48 – Fax (0 2) 219 23 48*
closed 8 to 20 August and Sunday **L1**
Rest (open until 11 p.m.) 16 € (weekday lunch) and a la carte 29/43 €
♦ Italian ♦ Rustic ♦

A pleasant family-run "ristorante" serving antipasti, a classic Italian à la carte
menu, and reasonably-priced lunch and fixed menus.

X **In 't Spinnekopke** 🍴 AC VISA ⦿ AE ⦿

pl. du Jardin aux Fleurs 1 ⊠ *1000 – ℰ 0 2 511 86 95 – info @ spinnekopke.be*
– Fax 0 2 513 24 97 – www.spinnekopke.be
closed Sunday **L1**
Rest 14 € b.i. (weekday lunch) and a la carte 25/38 €
♦ Regional ♦ Bistro ♦

This charming, typical tavern is esteemed for its good bistro-style atmosphere
and regional cuisine which does justice to the Belgian tradition.

X **Le Cerf**   AC VISA ◍ AE ◍

Grand'Place 20 ⊠ 1000 – ℰ 0 2 511 47 91 – Fax 0 2 546 09 59
closed July, Saturday and Sunday   **M2**
Rest (open until 11.30 p.m.) 23 € b.i. (weekday lunch), 46 € b.i./54 € b.i.
and a la carte 35/53 €
♦ Traditional ♦ Cosy ♦
The decor of this grand old residence (1710) is a mix of wood, stained glass,
fireplace and warm fabrics, giving an overall intimate and hushed feel. Two
tables overlooking the Grand-Place.

X **Vincent**   ⴢ AC VISA ◍ AE ◍

r. Dominicains 8 ⊠ 1000 – ℰ 0 2 511 26 07 – info@restaurantvincent.com
– Fax 0 2 502 36 93 – www.restaurantvincent.com
closed 2 to 12 January and first 2 weeks August   **M1**
Rest (open until 11.30 p.m.) 18 € (weekday lunch), 25/36 € and a la carte
25/60 €
♦ Taverne/bistro ♦ Retro ♦
Savour the typical Brussels atmosphere of this nostalgic rotisserie adorned with
painted ceramic-tile frescoes. Local dishes to the fore, with meat and mussels
specialities.

X **La Marée**   AC VISA ◍ AE ◍

r. Flandre 99 ⊠ 1000 – ℰ 0 2 511 00 40 – Fax 0 2 511 86 19
– www.lamaree-sa.com
closed 15 June-15 July, Christmas, New Year, Monday and Tuesday   **L1**
Rest a la carte 22/52 €
♦ Seafood ♦ Family ♦
The friendly atmosphere and unpretentious cuisine and decor of this restaurant
account for its popularity. Open kitchen, where the chef prepares freshly
delivered fish and seafood.

X **Viva M'Boma**   ⴢ VISA ◍ AE

☻ *r. Flandre 17 ⊠ 1000 – ℰ 0 2 512 15 93 – Fax 0 2 469 42 84*
closed 1 to 8 January, 1 to 16 August, Wednesday and Thursday   **L1**
Rest 10 € (weekday lunch) and a la carte approx. 31 €
♦ Regional ♦ Bistro ♦
This small restaurant in rue de Flandre near place Sainte-Catherine is well worth
a visit for those wishing to sample typical Belgian/Brussels specialities.

X **Lola**   AC ⴢ VISA ◍ AE

pl. du Grand Sablon 33 ⊠ 1000 – ℰ 0 2 514 24 60 – restaurant.lola@skynet.be
– Fax 0 2 514 26 53 – www.restolola.be   **M3**
Rest (open until 11.30 p.m.) a la carte 30/55 €
♦ Contemporary ♦ Trendy ♦
This convivial brasserie with its contemporary decor devotes its energies to
the latest culinary trends. Choose between sitting on benches, chairs or at
the bar.

X **La Clef des Champs**   🍴 VISA ◍ AE ◍

☻ *r. Rollebeek 23 ⊠ 1000 – ℰ 0 2 512 11 93 – Fax 0 2 502 42 32*
closed Sunday dinner and Monday   **M3**
Rest 15 € (weekday lunch), 30/51 € b.i. and a la carte 41/50 €
♦ Regional ♦ Friendly ♦
This pleasant family-run restaurant with rustic decor celebrated its 20th birthday
in 2005. Regional cuisine from around France. Cheerful, friendly service.

X **L'Herbe Rouge**   VISA ◍ AE

r. Minimes 34 ⊠ 1000 – ℰ 0 2 512 48 34
closed Monday   **M3**
Rest (open until 11 p.m.) 15 € (weekday lunch) and a la carte 29/43 €
♦ Japanese ♦ Fashionable ♦
A reasonably authentic and well-compiled Japanese menu is on offer in this
simply furnished, contemporary-style restaurant. Temporary exhibitions by
Japanese artists.

BELGIUM

X **L'Idiot du village**   `VISA` `MO` `AE` `O`

r. Notre Seigneur 19 ✉ *1000 –* ✆ *0 2 502 55 82*
closed 20 July-20 August, 23 December-3 January, Saturday and Sunday
Rest (open until 11 p.m.) 15 € (weekday lunch) and a la carte 37/58 €   **M3**
♦ Traditional ♦ Bistro ♦
Service with a smile, eclectic, pleasingly kitsch decor, a warm ambience, bistro-style
cuisine with an original, modern touch, astute wine-list and friendly service.

X **Les Larmes du Tigre**   `🍴` `VISA` `MO` `AE` `O`

r. Wynants 21 ✉ *1000 –* ✆ *0 2 512 18 77 – Fax 0 2 502 10 03*
– www.leslarmesdutigre.be
closed Tuesday and Saturday lunch   *Plan II* **E3**
Rest 11 € (weekday lunch), 34/40 € and a la carte 25/36 €
♦ Thai ♦ Exotic ♦
Thai cuisine has been served in this mansion close to the Palais de Justice for 20
years. Parasols adorn the ceiling. Sunday buffet (lunch and dinner).

QUARTIER LOUISE-CAMBRE   *Plan III*

🏨 **Conrad**   `🍴` `⊕` `Ƚⱷ` `ʓ` `▤` `▨` `↳` `☎` `⛫` `🔊` `♨️`25/450 `⌂` `⌂` `VISA` `MO` `AE` `O`

av. Louise 71 ✉ *1050 –* ✆ *0 2 542 42 42 – brusselsinfo@conradhotels.com*
– Fax 0 2 542 42 00 – www.conradhotels.com   **J1**
254 rm – ♦205/595 € ♦♦230/620 €, ⌷ 32 € – 15 suites
Rest *Loui (closed lunch Saturday, Sunday and Monday)* a la carte 39/64 €
Rest *Café Wiltcher's* (lunch only) 28 € (weekday lunch)/40 € and a la carte
38/62 €
♦ Grand Luxury ♦ Business ♦ Classic ♦
An upmarket hotel brilliantly arranged inside a 1900s mansion. Excellent bedrooms with classic furnishings; full range of seminar and leisure facilities. The
trendy restaurant Loui has a contemporary menu showing a variety of culinary
influences, and a "lounge" ambience. The café serves popular lunch buffets.

🏨 **Bristol Stephanie**   `Ƚⱷ` `ʓ` `▤` `&rm` `AK` `↳` `▨` `♨️`25/400 `⌂`

av. Louise 91 ✉ *1050 –* ✆ *0 2 543 33 11*   `⌂` `VISA` `MO` `AE` `O`
– hotel_bristol@bristol.be – Fax 0 2 538 03 07 – www.bristol.be   **J1**
139 rm – ♦340/400 € ♦♦365/425 €, ⌷ 27 € – 3 suites
Rest *(closed 15 July-3 September, 16 December-7 January, Saturday and Sunday)*
40 € b.i. (weekday lunch) and a la carte 41/62 €
♦ Luxury ♦ Business ♦ Classic ♦
The very pleasant guestrooms of this luxury property occupy two interlinked buildings. Three superb suites adorned with typical Norwegian furniture. Contemporary
dining in a Scandinavian-inspired ambience. Buffet options also available.

🏨 **Le Châtelain** ⌕   `🍴` `Ƚⱷ` `&` `AK` `↳` `▨` `☎` `♨️`25/280 `⌂`

r. Châtelain 17 ✉ *1000 –* ✆ *0 2 646 00 55*   `⌂` `VISA` `MO` `AE` `O`
– info@le-chatelain.net – Fax 0 2 646 00 88   **J2**
106 rm – ♦175/310 € ♦♦175/340 €, ⌷ 25 € – 2 suites
Rest *(closed Saturday and Sunday lunch)* 19 € (weekday lunch) and a la carte
35/48 €
♦ Luxury ♦ Business ♦ Functional ♦
A new hotel with large, modern rooms featuring the very latest equipment and
facilities. Superb reception area, well-equipped fitness room and a small garden.
The restaurant offers a range of continental dishes, as well as Asian specialities.

 Warwick Barsey   `🍴` `&rest` `AK` `↳` `%` `▨` `♨️`25/50 `⌂`

av. Louise 381 ✉ *1050 –* ✆ *0 2 641 51 11*   `⌂` `VISA` `MO` `AE` `O`
– res.warwickbarsey@warwickhotels.com – Fax 0 2 640 17 64
– www.warwickbrussels.com   **K3**
94 rm – ♦327/362 € ♦♦327/362 €, ⌷ 22 € – 5 suites
Rest a la carte 35/54 €
♦ Luxury ♦ Business ♦ Stylish ♦
A characterful hotel near the Bois de la Cambre skilfully refurbished in a style
inspired by the Second Empire. Elegant public areas and plush, well-appointed
rooms. Personalised service. Neo-classical decor in the Jacques Garcia-designed
restaurant-lounge.

BELGIUM

Porte de Namur **CENTRE (Plan IV)**

Avenue Louise, Cambre
(Plan III)

J

K

PARC LÉOPOLD

**MUSÉUM DES
SCIENCES NATURELLES**

Rue

Chaussée

M

M

R. de la Paix

Chaussée
d'Ixelles

de

Wavre

Louise

Argus

Beverly Hills

Avenue

Charleroi

R. du Prince Royal

Keyerveld

Rue

Rue

Sans

Trône

Goffart

Sq.
Sans Souci

Conrad

Floris Louise

Louise

Rue

de

l'Arbre

Bénit

Souci

**MUSÉE COMMUNAL
D'IXELLES**

Manos
Stephanie

R. Berkmans

Bristol Stephanie

Meliá

Avenue Louise

Rue

de

Rue

The Avenue

De la Vigne...
à l'Assiette

R. de la Croix

MAISON COMMUNALE
D'IXELLES

Chaussée

Rue

du

College

Maes

Beau-Site

Chaussée

**IXELLES
ELSENE**

Rue

Maliran

R. Marie-Henriette

d'Ixelles

Rue

Agenda Louise

Veyat

R. de l'Ermitage

Graÿ

Manos Premier

Chaussée

Rue

Faider

Rue

de

Livourne

Louise

Avenue

Rue

Lesbroussart

Vleurgat

Pl. E.
Flagey

Rue
Lanfray

**ST-GILLES
ST-GILUS**

STE-TRINITÉ

Le Châtelain

du

Bailli

Rue du Châtelain

Dautzenberg

de

Sq. de
Biarritz

Av. de l'Eperon d'Or

Washington

Rue

A. Campenhout

de

Louise

Chaussée

Vallée

Av. de l'Hippodrome

**MUSÉE
HORTA**

Rue

du

Tabellion

Rue

de

Page

l'Aqueduc

Américaine

L'Atelier de
la Truffe Noire

Tenbosch

Rue Vilain XIII

Chaussée

Rue

de

Tagawa

Vleurgat

Avenue

de

Brussels

R. de Neuray

R. de la Réforme

Chaussée

Rue

Rue

de

Washington

R. Américaine

Waterloo

Sq. H.
Michaux

Warwick Barsey

**MUSÉE CONSTANTIN
MEUNIER**

de

l'Abbaye

Louise

ABBAYE
DE LA CAMBRE

All. du Cloître

Av. Louis

R. E. Lepoutre

Rue

C.

Lemonnier

J.B.

Colyns

Rue

Chaussée

de

Rue J. Lejeune

La Porte des Indes

Av. E. de Mot

Avenue Louise

Rue

Mignot Delstanche

Rue

Molière

Avenue

de

Waterloo

Avenue Louise

Pl. Guy
d'Arezzo

Rue

Lincoln

Rue

Vanderkindere

Rue Legrand

Av. Lloyd Georges

J

K

● Hotel
● Restaurant

0   100 m

Manos Premier 🛏 ﾑ 🕍 ⇌ 🅰🅺 🎬 🕽 🔥25/100 🅿

chaussée de Charleroi 102 ⇌🍴(dinner) **VISA** 🅒🅒 🄰🄴
– 🕻 0 2 537 96 82 – manos@manoshotel.com – Fax 0 2 539 36 55
– www.manoshotel.com **J2**
45 rm ⬚ – ♦295 € ♦♦320 € – 5 suites
Rest Kolya *(closed 24 December-2 January, Saturday lunch, Sunday and holiday lunch)* 15 € *(weekday lunch)*/35 € and a la carte 34/55 €
♦ Luxury ♦ Business ♦ Stylish ♦
A graceful late-19C town house adorned with sumptuous Louis XV and Louis XVI furniture. Ask for a room overlooking the garden. Authentic Turkish baths. Veranda restaurant, chic yet cosy lounge-bar, and an appealing patio.

Manos Stephanie without rest ↳ 🎬 🕽 🅿 **VISA** 🅒🅒 🄰🄴 🅞

chaussée de Charleroi 28 ⊠ *1060 – 🕻 0 2 539 02 50 – manos@manoshotel.com*
– Fax 0 2 537 57 29 – www.manoshotel.com **J1**
50 rm ⬚ – ♦245 € ♦♦270 € – 5 suites
♦ Luxury ♦ Business ♦ Stylish ♦
A hotel offering inviting rooms in a classic style with modern touches and white-leaded wood furnishings. Breakfast room crowned with a cupola.

Meliá Avenue Louise without rest ⊗ ↳ 🍽 🎬 🕽 🔥25

r. Blanche 4 ⊠ *1000 – 🕻 0 2 535 95 00* 🛏 **VISA** 🅒🅒 🄰🄴 🅞
– karin.jongman@solmelia.com – Fax 0 2 535 96 00
– www.solmelia.com **J1**
80 rm – ♦80/260 € ♦♦90/260 €, ⬚ 22 €
♦ Chain hotel ♦ Business ♦ Functional ♦
This hotel is recommended for its cosy atmosphere and the elegantly British feel of its rooms, as well as its public areas, which include a snug, wood-panelled lounge.

Floris Louise without rest ↳ 🍽 🎬 🕽 **VISA** 🅒🅒 🄰🄴 🅞

r. Concorde 59 ⊠ *1000 – 🕻 0 2 515 00 60 – florislouise@busmail.net*
– Fax 0 2 503 35 19 – www.grouptorus.be **J1**
36 rm ⬚ – ♦70/204 € ♦♦75/214 €
♦ Traditional ♦ Business ♦ Cosy ♦
This hotel occupying two grand houses offers good, comfortable rooms. A breakfast buffet is served in a cheerful, light room or on the mini terrace.

Brussels without rest ↳ 🍽 🎬 🔥30 🛏 **VISA** 🅒🅒 🄰🄴 🅞

av. Louise 315 ⊠ *1050 – 🕻 0 2 640 24 15 – brussels-hotel@skynet.be*
– Fax 0 2 647 34 63 – www.brussels-hotel.be **K2-3**
68 rm ⬚ – ♦185/205 € ♦♦205/225 € – 1 suite
♦ Business ♦ Modern ♦
A "flat-hotel" offering two room categories for tourists and those on business - spacious standard rooms and large split-level rooms with a kitchenette.

Agenda Louise without rest ↳ 🎬 🕽 🛏 **VISA** 🅒🅒 🄰🄴 🅞

r. Florence 6 ⊠ *1000 – 🕻 0 2 539 00 31 – louise@hotel-agenda.com*
– Fax 0 2 539 00 63 – www.hotel-agenda.com **J2**
37 rm ⬚ – ♦114 € ♦♦126 €
♦ Traditional ♦ Business ♦ Functional ♦
This recently renovated hotel offers guests reasonably-sized rooms, many of which have standard mahogany-coloured furnishings and are decorated with warm-toned, colour-coordinated fabrics.

Beau-Site without rest 🎬 🛏 **VISA** 🅒🅒 🄰🄴 🅞

r. Longue Haie 76 ⊠ *1000 – 🕻 0 2 640 88 89 – beausite@coditel.net*
– Fax 0 2 640 16 11 – www.hotelbeausite.be **J1-2**
38 rm ⬚ – ♦65/165 € ♦♦75/175 €
♦ Traditional ♦ Business ♦ Functional ♦
100m/110yd from the city's most elegant avenue. This family-run hotel occupies a small corner building and is simple, functional and welcoming. Fairly spacious rooms.

BELGIUM

Beverly Hills without rest   🔥 🕸 🖥 **VISA** 🐄 💳 ⓪
r. Prince Royal 71 ⊠ 1050 – 𝒞 0 2 513 22 22 – beverlyhills@infonie.be
– Fax 0 2 513 87 77 – www.hotelbeverlyhills.be   **J1**
40 rm ⊡ – †109/119 € ††119/139 €
♦ Traditional ♦ Business ♦ Functional ♦
This hotel is situated in a quiet road close to avenue de la Toison d'Or and avenue Louise. The rooms are functional and well kept. Fitness room and sauna.

Argus without rest   🅰🅲 🖥 🕻 **VISA** 🐄 💳 ⓪
r. Capitaine Crespel 6 ⊠ 1050 – 𝒞 0 2 514 07 70 – reception@hotel-argus.be
– Fax 0 2 514 12 22 – www.hotel-argus.be   **J1**
42 rm ⊡ – †65/110 € ††70/160 €
♦ Traditional ♦ Business ♦ Functional ♦
Located in the upper town, this hotel has simple, standard, rooms with soundproofing. The breakfast room is decorated with Art Deco-style stained glass. Good value for money.

XXXX **Villa Lorraine**   🏡 🅰🅲 �ं 🄿 🛋 **VISA** 🐄 💳 ⓪
av. du Vivier d'Oie 75 ⊠ 1000 – 𝒞 0 2 374 31 63 – info@villalorraine.be
– Fax 0 2 372 01 95 – www.villalorraine.be
closed last 3 weeks July and Sunday   Plan I **C3**
Rest 55 € (weekday lunch)/150 € b.i. and a la carte 85/170 € 🍷
♦ French traditional ♦ Formal ♦
A fine restaurant established in 1953 on the edge of the Bois de la Cambre woods. Classic setting and a prestigious wine cellar. Gorgeous terrace in the shade of a chestnut tree.

XXX **The Avenue**   �ं **VISA** 🐄 💳 ⓪
av. Louise 156 ⊠ 1050 Brussel – 𝒞 0 2 642 22 22 – info@andre-dhaese.be
– Fax 0 2 642 22 25 – www.andre-dhaese.be
closed 1 week after Easter, 30 July-20 August, late December, Saturday lunch and Sunday   **J1**
Rest 37 € (weekday lunch), 65/90 € and a la carte 56/90 € 🍷
♦ Innovative ♦ Retro ♦
Inventive cuisine is served in three comfortable, classic rooms on the first floor of this fine hotel. Wine tasting is organised in the prestigious cellar, which houses a fine selection.

XX **Tagawa**   🅰🅲 �ं 🄿 **VISA** 🐄 💳 ⓪
av. Louise 279 ⊠ 1050 – 𝒞 0 2 640 50 95 – o.tagawa@tiscali.be
– Fax 0 2 648 41 36 – www.restaurant-tagawa.be
closed Saturday lunch, Sunday and Bank Holidays   **K2**
Rest 11 € (weekday lunch), 38/65 € and a la carte 22/51 €
♦ Japanese ♦ Minimalist ♦
This simply furnished Japanese restaurant is worth tracking down inside one of the city's shopping galleries. Western and Oriental (tatami mats) seating, plus a sushi bar. Private parking.

XX **La Porte des Indes**   🅰🅲 �ं **VISA** 🐄 💳 ⓪
av. Louise 455 ⊠ 1050 – 𝒞 0 2 647 86 51 – brussels@laportedesindes.com
– Fax 0 2 640 30 59 – www.laportedesindes.com
closed Sunday lunch   **K3**
Rest 20 € (weekday lunch) and a la carte 22/59 €
♦ Indian ♦ Exotic ♦
If your taste-buds fancy a change, head for La Porte des Indes, with its exotic, deliciously flavoured cuisine. The restaurant interior is decorated with Indian antiques.

X **L'Atelier de la Truffe Noire**   🅰🅲 **VISA** 🐄 💳 ⓪
av. Louise 300 ⊠ 1050 – 𝒞 0 2 640 54 55 – luigi.ciciriello@truffenoire.com
– Fax 0 2 648 11 44 – www.atelier.truffenoire.com
closed Sunday and Monday dinner   **K2**
Rest (open until 11 p.m.) a la carte 40/57 €
♦ Brasserie ♦ Fashionable ♦
A modern bistro whose originality and success lie in its fast service and truffle-based gourmet menu. Varied à la carte dishes showing Italian influence. Small terrace.

BELGIUM

✕ De la Vigne... à l'Assiette   _VISA_ ◍ AE

r. Longue Haie 51 ⊠ *1000 – ℰ 0 2 647 68 03 – Fax 0 2 647 68 03*
closed 21 July-20 August, Saturday lunch, Sunday and Monday   **J2**
Rest 12 € (weekday lunch), 20/32 € and a la carte 34/46 € ⠿
♦ Contemporary ♦ Bistro ♦
Wine-lovers will enjoy this lively restaurant, where the decor is plain and simple, the
bistro-style menu respectable, and the advice from the wine-waiter invaluable.

EUROPEAN INSTITUTIONS   *Plan II*

Stanhope   ⅃⌂ 𝕊 ♿ AC ⊠ ✆ ⇌ P _VISA_ ◍ AE ⓪

square de Meëus 4 ⊠ *1000 – ℰ 0 2 506 91 11 – Fax 0 2 512 17 08*
– www.stanhope.be   *Plan IV* **O3**
99 rm – ♟155/275 € ♟♟195/375 €, ⇌ 25 € – 9 suites
Rest see Rest **Brighton** below
♦ Grand Luxury ♦ Traditional ♦ Stylish ♦
Relive the splendour of the Victorian era in this town house with a distinctly
British feel. Choose from a variety of room categories: the suites and split-level
rooms are superb.

Renaissance   ⅃⌂ 𝕊 ▢ AC ↯ ✻ ⊠ ⅏25/360 ⇌ ⇌ _VISA_ ◍ AE ⓪

r. Parnasse 19 ⊠ *1050 – ℰ 0 2 505 29 29 – rhi.brubr.renaissance@*
renaissancehotels.com – Fax 0 2 505 22 76 – www.renaissancehotels.com
256 rm – ♟65/369 € ♟♟65/369 €, ⇌ 18 € – 6 suites   **G3**
Rest *Symphonie (closed Saturday lunch)* 19 € (weekday lunch)/34 €
and a la carte 29/46 €
♦ Chain hotel ♦ Business ♦ Modern ♦
This hotel enjoys a good location on the edge of the European institutions
district. Modern, well-appointed rooms, excellent business, conference and
leisure facilities, plus a full range of hotel services. Good service. The brasserie
offers a traditional choice, including a lunch menu served over three sittings.

Montgomery   ⅃⌂ 𝕊 AC ↯ ✻ ⊠ ✆ ⅏35 ⇌ _VISA_ ◍ AE ⓪

av. de Tervuren 134 ⊠ *1150 – ℰ (0 2) 741 85 11 – hotel@montgomery.be*
– Fax (0 2) 741 85 00 – www.montgomery.be   *Plan I* **C2**
61 rm – ♟140/360 € ♟♟140/360 €, ⇌ 20 € – 2 suites
Rest *(closed 1 to 8 January, 23 December-7 January, Saturday lunch, Sunday and
Bank Holidays)* 18 € b.i. (weekday lunch)/39 € b.i. and a la carte 34/56 €
♦ Luxury ♦ Stylish ♦
An elegant, discreet hotel with theme-based rooms (Asian, nautical or romantic
decor), lovely penthouses, lounge-library, fitness room and sauna. Attentive
service. The cuisine in the snug restaurant will find favour with aficionados of
modern cuisine.

Crowne Plaza Europa   ⌂ ⅃⌂ ♿ AC ↯ ✻ ⊠ ✆ ⅏25/350

r. Loi 107 ⊠ *1040 – ℰ 0 2 230 13 33*   ⇌ _VISA_ ◍ AE ⓪
– brussels@ichotelsgroup.com – Fax 0 2 230 03 26   **G2**
238 rm – ♟70/290 € ♟♟100/320 €, ⇌ 25 € – 2 suites
Rest *The Gallery (closed mid July-August and lunch Saturday and Sunday)* 21 €
(weekday lunch) and a la carte 29/53 €
♦ Chain hotel ♦ Business ♦ Functional ♦
A twelve-storey hotel, located a few steps from the main European institutions.
Comfortable rooms, modern lobby, business centre and full conference facilities.
The Gallery offers a choice of classic and contemporary cuisine as well as buffets.

Silken Berlaymont   ⅃⌂ 𝕊 ♿ rm AC ↯ ⅏25/130 ⇌ _VISA_ ◍ AE ⓪

bd Charlemagne 11 ⊠ *1000 – ℰ 0 2 231 09 09 – hotel-berlaymont@*
hoteles-silken.com – Fax 0 2 230 33 71 – www.hoteles-silken.com   **G2**
210 rm – ⇌ – ♟79/260 € ♟♟79/260 € – 2 suites
Rest *L'Objectif* 20 € (weekday lunch)/34 € and a la carte 34/48 €
♦ Luxury ♦ Business ♦ Design ♦
This newly built chain hotel comprises two modern, inter-connected buildings
with fresh, well-kept contemporary rooms. The interior decor follows a theme of
contemporary photography. The menu is varied and the appetisers original.

BELGIUM

Eurovillage
🏡 *Lⓑ* 🛖 Ⓐ ⇄ ⅍rest ⚏ 🕾 🔬 25/130
bd Charlemagne 80 ☒ 1000 – 𝒞 0 2 230 85 55 🚗 VISA Ⓦⓞ ᴀᴇ ①
– sales@eurovillage.be – Fax 0 2 230 52 05 – www.eurovillage.be **G2**
100 rm – ♦150/200 € ♦♦160/225 €, ⌨ 17 € – 4 suites
Rest *(closed August, Saturday and Sunday lunch)* a la carte 28/48 €
♦ Traditional ♦ Functional ♦
A modern hotel building alongside a verdant park offering three room categories and good seminar and business facilities. Spacious lounge areas. Classic, traditional cuisine served in the modern setting of the restaurant.

Leopold
🛖 & rest Ⓐ ⇄ ⚏ 🕾 🔬 25/80 🚗 VISA Ⓦⓞ ᴀᴇ ①
r. Luxembourg 35 ☒ 1050 – 𝒞 0 2 511 18 28 – reservations@hotel-leopold.be
– Fax 0 2 514 19 39 *Plan IV* **O3**
110 rm ⌨ – ♦135/218 € ♦♦153/386 €
Rest *Salon Les Anges (closed Saturday lunch and Sunday)* (lunch only in July and August) 35 € (weekday lunch) and a la carte 49/61 €
♦ Traditional ♦ Business ♦ Classic ♦
This continually expanding and improving hotel boasts well-appointed bedrooms, smart public areas, a winter garden where breakfast is served. A classic menu is on offer in the hushed Salon Les Anges restaurant; a variety of dishes served in the relaxed brasserie.

Holiday Inn Schuman
Lⓑ & Ⓐ ⇄ ⅍rm 🔬 45 🚗 VISA Ⓦⓞ ᴀᴇ ①
r. Breydel 20 ☒ 1040 – 𝒞 0 2 280 40 00 – hotel@
holiday-inn-brussels-schuman.com – Fax 0 2 282 10 70
– www.holiday-inn.com/brusselsschuman **H2**
56 rm ⌨ – ♦78/510 € ♦♦85/510 € – 2 suites
Rest *(closed Saturday and Sunday)* a la carte 26/51 €
♦ Chain hotel ♦ Business ♦ Functional ♦
Hotel named after a renowned pro-European politician, who would surely have appreciated this hotel offering rooms with a high level of comfort, perfect for those on European business. Traditional meals served in a simple room with parquet floors and bare wooden tables.

New Hotel Charlemagne
⇄ ⅍ ⚏ 🕾 🔬 30/50
bd Charlemagne 25 ☒ 1000 – 𝒞 0 2 230 21 35 🚗 VISA Ⓦⓞ ᴀᴇ ①
– brusselscharlemagne@new-hotel.be – Fax 0 2 230 25 10
– www.new-hotel.be **H2**
68 rm – ♦99/350 € ♦♦99/350 €, ⌨ 19 €
Rest (residents only)
♦ Traditional ♦ Business ♦ Functional ♦
This practical small hotel between Square Ambiorix and the Centre Berlaymont is popular with EU staff. Reception, lounge-bar and breakfast room on the same floor.

Brighton – H. Stanhope
🏡 & Ⓐ ⅍ 🅿 ⌨ VISA Ⓦⓞ ①
r. Commerce 9 ☒ 1000 – 𝒞 0 2 506 91 11 – brighton@stanhope.be
– Fax 0 2 512 17 08 – www.stanhope.be
closed 24 July-18 August, 18 December-6 January,
Saturday and Sunday *Plan IV* **O3**
Rest 39 € (weekday lunch)/55 € and a la carte 53/98 €
An elegant hotel whose dining room with a refined English-style decor is inspired by Brighton's Royal Pavilion. Pleasant patio with a terrace open in fine weather.

Pappa e Citti
🏡 ⅍ VISA Ⓦⓞ ①
r. Franklin 18 ☒ 1000 – 𝒞 0 2 732 61 10 – pappaecitti@skynet.be
– Fax 0 2 732 57 40 – www.pappaecitti.be
closed August, 20 December-6 January, Saturday,
Sunday and Bank Holidays **H2**
Rest 28 € b.i. (weekday lunch) and a la carte 35/100 €
♦ Italian ♦ Friendly ♦
Popular with EU employees who head for this small, friendly Italian restaurant to enjoy Sardinian specialities and wines. Set lunch menu (including drinks) served at two sittings. Terrace.

✗ Take Sushi
✤ VISA ⓒⓄ ΛΞ ①

bd Charlemagne 21 ✉ 1000 – ✆ 0 2 230 56 27 – Fax 0 2 231 10 44
closed 25 to 31 December, Saturday and Sunday lunch   **G2**
Rest 14 € (weekday lunch), 29/55 € and a la carte 22/70 €
♦ Japanese ♦ Exotic ♦
This corner of Japan has existed at the heart of the city's European institutions district for more than 20 years. Japanese decor, background music and small garden. Sushi bar and fixed menus.

GARE DU NORD
Plan II

🏛🏛🏛🏛 Sheraton Towers
₤ᖦ 🕅 🖭 ᡱ 🕅 ᪲ 🕾 ᴥ25/600

pl. Rogier 3 ✉ 1210 – ✆ 0 2 224 31 11   ᗺ VISA ⓒⓄ ΛΞ ①
– reservations.brussels@sheraton.com – Fax 0 2 224 34 56   **F1**
489 rm – ♦105/295 € ♦♦105/295 €, ☲ 25 € – 44 suites
Rest 31 € (weekday lunch), 40/55 € and a la carte 35/63 €
♦ Grand Luxury ♦ Business ♦ Modern ♦
With its full range of facilities, the imposing Sheraton has won over a business clientele, international travellers and conference-goers. Spacious standard rooms, plus club rooms and numerous suites. Attractive contemporary bar. Classic, traditional meals in the dining area facing the place Rogier. Lunch buffet.

🏛🏛🏛 Crowne Plaza "Le Palace"
₤ᖦ 🕅 🕅 ᡱ 🖭 🕾 ᴥ25/600

r. Gineste 3 ✉ 1210 – ✆ 0 2 203 62 00   ᗺ(dinner)
– info@cpbxl.be – Fax 0 2 203 55 55   **F1**
355 rm – ♦320 € ♦♦320 €, ☲ 26 € – 1 suite
Rest *(closed lunch Saturday, Sunday and Bank Holidays)* 18 € (weekday lunch), 30/35 € and a la carte approx. 40 €
♦ Luxury ♦ Art Deco ♦
A Belle Époque-style palace embellished with period furniture in which several rooms have preserved the spirit of the 1900s. Attractive, opulent-looking public areas and contemporary, Art Nouveau-inspired rooms. Restaurant with a modern take on 1900s-style decor; international cuisine.

🏛🏛 Husa President
₤ᖦ 🕅 ᗒ ᡱrm ᡱ 🖭 🕾 ᴥ25/350

bd du Roi Albert II 44 ✉ 1000 – ✆ 0 2 203   ᗙ VISA ⓒⓄ ΛΞ ①
20 20 – info.president@husa.es – Fax 0 2 203 24 40 – www.husa.es
286 rm – ♦95/250 € ♦♦95/260 €, ☲ 21 € – 16 suites   *Plan I* **B2**
Rest *(closed Sunday)* 20 € (weekday lunch) and a la carte 20/47 €
♦ Traditional ♦ Business ♦ Classic ♦
An imposing hotel at one end of Brussels' "Manhattan", close to the Gare du Nord (North Station) and the World Trade Center. The public areas are spacious and the rooms very comfortable. The relaxed restaurant classic menu includes several fixed options and good daily suggestions.

🏛🏛 Le Dome (annex Le Dome II)
ᗜ 🕅 rm ᡱ ᪲rm 🖭 ᴥ25/80 VISA

bd du Jardin Botanique 12 ✉ 1000 – ✆ 0 2 218 06 80   ⓒⓄ ΛΞ ①
– dome@skypro.be – Fax 0 2 218 41 12 – www.hotel-le-dome.be
125 rm ☲ – ♦80/218 € ♦♦95/350 €   **F1**
Rest 16 € (weekday lunch) and a la carte 24/52 €
♦ Traditional ♦ Business ♦ Retro ♦
The dome crowning the 1900s-style façade overlooks the lively place Rogier. Art Nouveau-inspired decor in the hotel's public areas and rooms. A modern brasserie with mezzanine serving traditional Belgian fare, including salads and snacks.

🏛🏛 Tulip Inn Boulevard
₤ᖦ 🕅 ᡱ 🕅 ᡱ ᴥ25/450 ᗙ VISA ⓒⓄ ΛΞ ①

av. du Boulevard 17 ✉ 1210 – ✆ 0 2 205 15 11 – infohotel@tulipinnbb.be
– Fax 0 2 201 15 15   **F1**
450 rm ☲ – ♦89/219 € ♦♦99/229 € – 4 suites
Rest (dinner only) a la carte 21/37 €
♦ Chain hotel ♦ Business ♦ Functional ♦
Opened in 2000, this hotel is the second largest in the city in terms of capacity. Attractive, well-appointed small rooms with wood or carpeted floors. Spacious marble lobby area on basement level. A choice of traditional meals is on offer in the restaurant.

Le Prince de Liège AC rm ⁴⁄₊ ▦ ☏ ♨25 🚗

chaussée de Ninove 664 ⊠ 1070 ➔🍴(lunch) VISA ⓞⓞ AE ⓞ
– ☏ 0 2 522 16 00 – reception.princedeliege@coditel.be
– Fax 0 2 520 81 85 **A2**
32 rm ⊇ – †73/100 € ††93/115 €
Rest *(closed 1 to 15 August, Saturday lunch and Sunday dinner)* 18 € (weekday lunch), 25/45 € and a la carte 32/51 €
♦ Family ♦ Inn ♦ Functional ♦
The rooms at this family-run hotel located alongside a major road junction are functional, double-glazed and offer good value for money. The third-floor rooms are more recent. Bar-restaurant serving simple, classic à la carte choices, with menus and seasonal suggestions highlighted on boards.

Erasme ☆ Ⅰ₅ ᕼ AC rm ⁴⁄₊ ▦ ♨25/80 P VISA ⓞⓞ AE ⓞ

rte de Lennik 790 ⊠ 1070 – ☏ 0 2 523 62 82 – comfort@skynet.be
– Fax 0 2 523 62 83 – www.comfort.com **A3**
74 rm ⊇ – †62/98 € ††62/249 €
Rest *(closed 30 July-15 August and 20 December-3 January)* 17 € (weekday lunch) and a la carte 19/39 €
♦ Chain hotel ♦ Business ♦ Functional ♦
A chain hotel on the outskirts of the city, 1km/0.6mi beyond the ring road, with a choice between standard (small) and executive rooms (bigger). Fitness facilities and seminar rooms. Tavern-style restaurant with a varied international menu.

XXX Saint Guidon AC ⅍ P

av. Théo Verbeeck 2, 2nd floor, in the R.S.C. Anderlecht VISA ⓞⓞ ⓞ
football stadium ⊠ 1070 – ☏ 0 2 520 55 36
– saint-guidon@skynet.be – Fax 0 2 523 38 27
closed 23 June-25 July, Saturday, Sunday, Bank Holidays and at Home
matches **A3**
Rest (lunch only) 57 € b.i. and a la carte 56/88 €
♦ Contemporary ♦ Formal ♦
This restaurant is situated on the second floor of Anderlecht's football stadium draws in supporters of the famous football club. The plus dining area is next to the stands but overlooks the car park.

XX Alain Cornelis ☆ ⅍ VISA ⓞⓞ AE ⓞ

av. Paul Janson 82 ⊠ 1070 – ☏ 0 2 523 20 83 – alaincornelis@skynet.be
– Fax 0 2 523 20 83 – www.alaincornelis.be
closed 1 week Easter, first 2 weeks August, 24 December- 3 January, Wednesday
dinner, Saturday lunch and Sunday **A3**
Rest 30 €/60 € b.i. and a la carte 30/39 €
♦ Traditional ♦ Friendly ♦
A classically bourgeois restaurant with a traditional wine-list. The terrace to the rear is embellished with a small garden. Fixed menus, à la carte and dishes of the month.

XX La Brouette VISA ⓞⓞ AE ⓞ

bd Prince de Liège 61 ⊠ 1070 – ☏ 0 2 522 51 69 – info@labrouette.be
– Fax 0 2 522 51 69 – www.labrouette.be
closed 24 July-20 August, Saturday lunch,
Sunday dinner and Monday **A2**
Rest 25 € (weekday lunch), 40/45 € and a la carte approx. 37 € 🎴
♦ Contemporary ♦ Design ♦
This restaurant's grey and burgundy interior has given it a more modern feel. The flower arrangements on the tables are exhibited on the walls in photos. The owner is also the sommelier.

ATOMIUM QUARTER   *Plan I*

BELGIUM

🏠 Rijckendael ⚜   🛜 🕭 📺 rm ↻ 🖃 🕻 25/40 🕭 🅿 VISA 🕭 AE ⓪
J. Van Elewijckstraat 35 ⊠ 1853 – ℰ 0 2 267 41 24 – rijckendael@vhv-hotels.be
– Fax 0 2 267 94 01 – www.rijckendael.be   **B1**
49 rm ⌂ – ♥45/165 € ♥♥60/180 €
Rest *(closed last 3 weeks July-first week August)* 23 € (weekday lunch), 36/42 €
and a la carte 32/61 €
♦ Traditional ♦ Business ♦ Functional ♦
This hotel of modern design is located in a residential area a short walk from the
Atomium and Heysel stadium. Well-appointed rooms. Private car park.
Restaurant with a rustic feel housed in a small former farmhouse (1857). Classic,
traditional meals.

🏠 La Roseraie   🛜 📺 🕻 🅿 VISA 🕭 AE ⓪
Limburg Stirumlaan 213 ⊠ 1780 – ℰ 0 2 456 99 10 – hotel@laroseraie.be
– Fax 0 2 460 83 20 – www.laroseraie.be   **A1**
8 rm ⌂ – ♥107/125 € ♥♥130/180 €
Rest *(closed Saturday lunch, Sunday dinner and Monday)* 22 € (weekday
lunch)/29 € and a la carte 39/54 €
♦ Family ♦ Personalised ♦
A warm welcome awaits you at this 1930s villa transformed into a family-run
hotel offering impeccably maintained rooms decorated along different themes:
African, Japanese, Roman etc. Traditionally furnished dining room with a piano
which is home to lobsters!

✗✗ Le Gril Aux Herbes d'Evan   🛜 🅿 VISA 🕭 AE ⓪
Brusselsesteenweg 21 ⊠ 1780 – ℰ 0 2 460 52 39 – Fax 0 2 461 19 12
closed 24 December- 2 January, Saturday lunch and Sunday   **A1**
Rest 35 € (weekday lunch)/45 € and a la carte 67/92 € 🕭
♦ Traditional ♦ Fashionable ♦
This small villa perched on a hilltop has a terrace and a large garden. Classic
cuisine and a wine-list that does justice to the reputation of French vineyards.

✗✗ Lychee   📺 VISA 🕭 AE ⓪
r. De Wand 118 ⊠ 1020 – ℰ 0 2 268 19 14 – Fax 0 2 268 19 14
closed Monday except Bank Holidays   **B1**
Rest 15 € and a la carte 18/68 €
♦ Chinese ♦ Exotic ♦
This Chinese restaurant between the Chinese Pavilion and the Roman road has
been serving its Cantonese dishes for more than 25 years. A wide choice of fixed
menus and a very reasonably-priced lunch.

✗✗ La Balade Gourmande   🛜 🕭 VISA 🕭 ⓪
😊
av. Houba de Strooper 230 ⊠ 1020 – ℰ 0 2 478 94 34 – Fax 0 2 479 89 52
*closed 2 weeks carnival, 15 to 31 August, Wednesday dinner, Saturday lunch and
Sunday*   **B1**
Rest 17 € (weekday lunch)/32 €
♦ Contemporary ♦ Friendly ♦
The à la carte and fixed-menu options at this local restaurant cover a
cross-section of traditional dishes prepared with a modern eye. Decor
dominated by red fabrics.

AIRPORT & OTAN   *Plan I*

🏠 Sheraton Airport   🗗 🕭 📺 ↻ 🖃 🕻 🕻 25/600 🕭 🅿
at airport ⊠ 1930 Zaventem – ℰ 0 2 710 80 00   🖃 VISA 🕭 AE ⓪
– info@sheraton.be – Fax 0 2 710 80 80   **D1**
292 rm – ♥105/359 € ♥♥105/359 €, ⌂ 25 € – 2 suites
Rest *Concorde (closed Saturday lunch)* 55 € b.i. (weekday lunch) and a la carte
33/77 €
♦ Chain hotel ♦ Business ♦ Modern ♦
The closest luxury hotel to the airport, offering comfort and numerous services,
this is a popular choice with business customers from around the world.
Contemporary international à la carte menu at the Concorde, which shares a vast
atrium with a bar serving buffets.

BELGIUM

Crowne Plaza Airport 🍴 ⅙ 🍸 🐾 🔟 💆 ⌨ 📞 🔑25/400 **P**
Da Vincilaan 4 ⊠ 1831 Diegem   ⌨ **VISA** ⓪ 🆎 ⓪
– 𝒞 02 416 33 33 – cpbrusselsairport @ ichotelsgroup.com
– Fax 0 2 416 33 44 – www.crowneplaza.com/cpbrusselsarpt   **D1**
311 rm – ♦110/355 €, ♦♦110/355 €, ⊑ 21 € – 4 suites
Rest 21 € (weekday lunch), 35/42 € and a la carte 27/41 €
♦ Chain hotel ♦ Business ♦ Modern ♦
Part of the Crowne Plaza chain, this hotel is located in a business park close to the airport. Central atrium, comfortable, well-equipped rooms as well as good conference facilities and neat gardens. The restaurant offers a choice of contemporary dishes including a buffet lunch option.

Sofitel Airport ⅙ 🝙 🔟 💆 ⌨ 📞 🔑25/300 **P** ⌨ **VISA** ⓪ 🆎 ⓪
Bessenveldstraat 15 ⊠ 1831 Diegem – 𝒞 02 713 66 66 – H0548 @ accor.com
– Fax 0 2 721 43 45 – www.sofitel.com   **C1**
125 rm – ♦330/360 € ♦♦330/440 €, ⊑ 21 €
Rest La Pléiade (closed Friday dinner, Saturday and Sunday lunch) 35 €
(weekday lunch) and a la carte 34/47 €
♦ Chain hotel ♦ Business ♦ Functional ♦
A top-of-the-range chain hotel alongside a motorway 4km/2.5mi from Zaventem airport with quiet, inviting rooms, seven meeting rooms and some leisure facilities. Friendly bar and a restaurant decked out like a luxury brasserie.

NH Brussels Airport ⅙ 🝙 ⅙ 🔟 💆 ⌨ 📞 🔑25/80 🕿
De Kleetlaan 14 ⊠ 1831 Diegem – 𝒞 0 2 203   **P** **VISA** ⓪ 🆎 ⓪
92 52 – nhbrusselsairport @ nh-hotels.be – Fax 0 2 203 92 53
– www.nh-hotels.com   **D1**
234 rm – ♦99/260 € ♦♦99/260 €, ⊑ 19 €
Rest (closed Friday dinner, Saturday and Sunday) 30 € (weekday lunch)
and a la carte 34/44 €
♦ Chain hotel ♦ Business ♦ Functional ♦
A distinctly modern-looking business hotel in the business district close to the airport. Rooms well soundproofed against the nearby railway. Contemporary-style lounge bar and restaurant serving cuisine from around the world as well as fixed buffet menus.

Holiday Inn Airport 🍴 ⅙ 🝙 🔲 💆 ⅙ 🔟 ⅙ 🍽rest
Holidaystraat 7 ⊠ 1831 Diegem – 𝒞 0 2   🔑25/400 **P** **VISA** 🆎 ⓪
720 58 65 – hibrusselsairport @ ichotelsgroup.comm
– Fax 0 2 720 41 45 – www.holiday-inn.com/bru-airport   **D1**
310 rm – ♦100/230 € ♦♦100/230 €, ⊑ 21 €
Rest (open until 11 p.m.) 30 € (weekday lunch), 34/56 € and a la carte 33/42 €
♦ Chain hotel ♦ Business ♦ Functional ♦
A 1970s hotel close to the airport. The rooms are due an overhaul. Comprehensive range of facilities for business or for pleasure. International cuisine is served at the restaurant on the first floor, and simple meals and snacks at the bar downstairs.

Novotel Airport 🍴 ⅙ 🝙 🔳 ⅙ 🔟 rest ⅙ 🍽rest ⌨ 🔑25/100
Da Vincilaan 25 ⊠ 1831 Diegem   **P** **VISA** ⓪ 🆎 ⓪
– 𝒞 0 2 725 30 50 – H0467 @ accor.com – Fax 0 2 721 39 58   **D1**
209 rm – ♦90/220 € ♦♦90/220 €, ⊑ 15 €
Rest (open until midnight) a la carte 30/41 €
♦ Chain hotel ♦ Business ♦ Functional ♦
Ideal for those with an early flight to catch. No surprises in the identical bedrooms, which conform to the Novotel's usual criteria. Seminar rooms and outdoor pool.

Rainbow Airport 🍴 ⅙ rm 🔟 rest ⅙ 🔟 📞 🔑25/100
Berkenlaan 4 ⊠ 1831 Diegem – 𝒞 0 2 721 77 77   **P** **VISA** ⓪ 🆎 ⓪
– reservations @ rainbowhotel.be – Fax 0 2 721 55 96 – www.rainbowhotel.be
100 rm – ♦89/193 € ♦♦99/233 €, ⊑ 16 €   **D1**
Rest (closed 25 July-8 August, Saturday and Sunday) 20 € (weekday lunch)
and a la carte 32/43 €
♦ Chain hotel ♦ Business ♦ Functional ♦
The delightful rooms are well-maintained and spotlessly clean. Modern decor in the restaurant, where the emphasis is on conventional dishes. A haven of peace and quiet for stopover or transit passengers.

ANTWERP
ANVERS - ANTWERPEN

Population (est. 2004): 455 300 – Altitude: sea level

J.Malburet/MICHELIN

Antwerp is Belgium's largest port, its main trading city and a major industrial centre but it remains in many ways a typical old Flemish town with narrow streets, spacious squares, imposing guildhalls and fine old buildings.

The vibrant city is a shoppers' paradise; its fashion designers have made their mark on the international scene. It is also renowned as the world diamond centre which has attracted a large Jewish population over the centuries. The members of the orthodox community in traditional dress are a common sight in the city. People of various origins (India, Lebanon, Armenia, Asia and Africa) working in the diamond trade create a mosaic of cultures.

Its name is said to be derived from the word *handwerpen* meaning 'to throw a hand' from the legend of a giant slain by a Roman soldier who cut off the former's hand and threw it into the river. From the 13C Antwerp flourished as a trading and cultural centre which attracted famous painters, sculptors, architects as well as the intellectual élite. Decline set in owing to political and religious struggles whilst under Austrian and French occupation and it was only in the 20C that Antwerp experienced steady economic growth and regained its prestige.

WHICH DISTRICT TO CHOOSE

For elegant **accommodation** you may choose to stay around Grote Markt *Plan II* **D1** and the area near the cathedral in the old town where charming 16C houses have been beautifully converted. You will also find comfortable hotels in De Keyserlei *Plan II* **F2** near Central Station and in the Diamond district. Het Zuid (South Quarter) with its lovely Art Nouveau buildings offers pleasant hotels in a vibrant district. There are also business hotels in the port area to the north of the city.

For **cafés**, **brasseries** and **restaurants** visit the areas around Grote Markt, Meir *Plan II* **E2**, Central Station *Plan II* **F2**, the Quartier Latin *Plan II* **E2** and Het Zuid *Plan II* **C3** which is the trendy district of Antwerp.

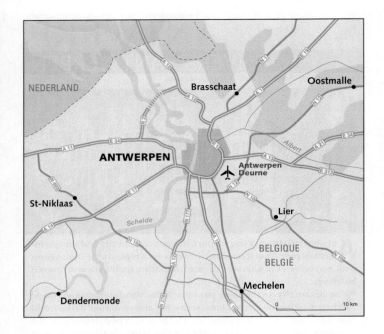

PRACTICAL INFORMATION

ARRIVAL – DEPARTURE

Via Zaventem airport (Brussels) – Take the SN Brussels Airlines shuttle to Central Station (Keyserlei 45). Approx. 45min; departure from Zaventem each precise hour from 7am to 11pm; from Antwerpen each precise hour from 5.30am to 10pm. Single ticket €8, return ticket €15; tickets sold in shuttle bus. ℰ 070 35 11 11; www.flysn.com

Via the airport of Antwerpen-Deurne – Take bus No 16 to Pelikaanstraat, next to Central Station.

Railway Stations – Both international and inter-city trains stop in **Antwerpen-Centraal** *Plan II* **F2** and **Antwerpen-Berchem** stations; www.sncb.be

TRANSPORT

◆ BUS AND TRAM

The **Dagpas Stadt** (city day pass), which gives unlimited travel on the whole of the city's public transport network, is obtainable on board buses and trams and from De Lijn kiosks. Information: De Lijn, ℰ 03 218 14 11; www.delijn.be

◆ TAXIS

Allow €7-10 for a short journey. It is customary to round up taxi fares. *Antwerp Taxi* ℰ 03 238 38 38; *Antwerpse Taxicentrale* ℰ 03 216 16 16.

USEFUL ADDRESSES

◆ TOURIST OFFICES

Tourism Antwerp, Grote Markt 13 *Plan II* **D1**; ℰ 03 232 01 03; www.visi tantwerpen.be; open 9am to 5.45pm

(4.45pm Sundays and public holidays); closed 1Jan and 25 Dec. **Centraal Station** (hall 2) *Plan II* **F2**. **Tourism Federation of the Province of Antwerp**, Koningin Elisabethlei 16 *Plan III* **G1** ℰ 03 240 63 73; www.tpa.be

♦ POST OFFICES

Main Post Office: corner of Schoenmarkt and Nationalestraat *Plan II* **D2**, open Monday to Friday, 9am to noon and 2 to 5pm.

♦ BANKS / CURRENCY EXCHANGE

Banks open Monday to Friday, 9am-4pm. There are cash dispensers all over the city.

♦ EMERGENCY

Police ℰ **101**. Fire Brigade and Medical Emergency Service ℰ **100** (ℰ **112** when calling from a mobile phone).

EXPLORING ANTWERP

It is possible to visit the main sights and museums in two days.

Museums and other sights are usually open from 9-10am to 5pm. Some close on Mondays.

VISITING

Boat trips on the Schelde (Escaut) starting from Steenplein *Plan II* **C1**.

Grote Markt *Plan II* **D1** – A charming square lined with the splendid 16C Town Hall and 16C-17C guildhalls.

Kathedraal *Plan II* **D2** – The largest cathedral in Belgium (14C-16C), crowned by a soaring tower, contains several works by Rubens.

Museum Plantin-Moretus *Plan II* **C2** – The house and printing works built by the famous 16C printer Christophe Plantin, complete with antique furnishings, engravings, manuscripts and early editions.

Rubenshuis *Plan II* **E2** – The home and studio of Antwerp's greatest painter.

Koninklijk Museum voor Schone Kunsten *Plan II* **C3** – The collections of the Royal Museum of Fine Art: European painting from the 14C to the present day, including Flemish Primitives, Rubens, the Belgian School, Expressionists and Surrealists.

Modemuseum (MOMU) *Plan II* **D2** – An innovative display on the evolution of fashion will delight admirers of fashion and design.

Nationaal Scheepvaartmuseum (Het Steen) *Plan II* **C1** – A fascinating exhibition traces maritime and river life with a collection of boats on display in the maritime park. It is housed in a fortress which is the oldest building in Antwerp.

Museum van Hedendaags Kunst Antwerpen (MuKHA) *Plan II* **D2** – A collection of contemporary art by Belgian and international artists housed in a converted grain silo and warehouse.

Provinciaal Diamantmuseum *Plan II* **F2** – An illuminating presentation on the use and transformation of diamonds and the history of diamonds in Antwerp. Diamond workshop and dazzling collection of precious jewels.

Brouwershuis (Brewers' Hall) *Plan I* **A1** – The 16C seat of the brewers' guild: horse treadmill, water-raising system, reservoirs, workshop, Council chamber with walls clad with 17C gilded leather.

Wijk Zurenborg *Plan III* **H1** – An impressive array of town houses built in revival, eclectic and Art Nouveau styles in several streets around Cogels-Osylei.

GOURMET TREATS

Most restaurants serve classic **French cuisine** but Antwerp is a cosmopolitan city where you will find a whole range of European and exotic dishes and the latest food trends. Typical **Flemish specialities** include stewed eel in chervil sauce, mussels in various sauces, dishes with rabbit or beef stew and chicory. To enjoy **frites with mayonnaise**, visit *Fritkot Max*, Groenplaats 12, a traditional 'frituur' (chip shop) which serves golden chips in a paper cone as in the old days. For all you need to know about 'frying' do not miss the tiny museum (photos, lithographs, cartoons, etc. – first floor) which celebrates this Belgian tradition. **Worstenbrood** (sausage rolls), **appelbollen** (apple balls), **roggeverdommeke** (rye/raisin bread), **waffels** and **smoutebollen** (fried dough balls) are delicious snacks.

Beer drinkers will enjoy **'bolleke'**, a special amber-coloured brew, produced by the De Koninck brewery. It is a time-honoured custom to sample a 'bolleke' or a 'keuninkske' at Café *De Pelgrim*, Boomgaardstraat 8.

SHOPPING

Diamonds are forever! Visit *Diamondland Plan II* **F2** and the numerous jewellers in the **diamond district** for that special gift. Look for the logo of the Antwerp Diamond and Jewellery Association (ADJA). More affordable specialities are Antwerpse handjes, small chocolates with filling and also available in biscuit form, Antwerps gebak (a biscuit or cake with almonds, apricot jam and sugar icing) and Semini biscuit (a sweet biscuit with sesame seed and a marzipan image of the Antwerp fertility symbol Semini). Antwerp Elixir is a sweet liqueur made with herbs.

Luxury and designer shops – The pedestrian avenue **Meir** *Plan II* **E2**, **De Keyserlei** *Plan II* **E2**, **Frankrijklei** *Plan II* **E2**, **Huisdevetterstraat** *Plan II* **D2** and adjoining streets (Wiegstraat, Groendalstraat, Korte Gasthuisstraat). You will find the shops of the fashion designers *Chris Mesdagh*, *Ann De Meulemeester*, *Dirk Bikkembergs* in **Lombardenvest** *Plan II* **D2** and **Steenhouwersvest** *Plan II* **D2**. *Dries van Noten* has a shop in Modepaleis, **Nationalestraat** *Plan II* **D2**.

Antiques – Kloosterstraat *Plan II* **C2**, Steenhouwersvest *Plan II* **D2**, Hoogstraat *Plan II* **C1**, Hopland *Plan II* **E2**, Leopoldstraat *Plan II* **D2**, Mechelsesteenweg *Plan II* **E3**.

MARKETS – **Vogelenmarkt** (Bird Market, on Sunday morning) and **Exotic Market** (on Saturdays) on Theaterplein *Plan II* **E2**. **Vrijdagmarkt** (antiques and rare objects) *Plan II* **D2** on Wednesday and Friday mornings.

ENTERTAINMENT

Antwerp has a rich concert and theatre tradition.

Bourla Theatre *Plan II* **D2** – Classical concerts and theatre.

Koningin Elisabethzaal *Plan II* **F2** – Concerts and shows.

Arenberg Cultural Centre (Antwerpsesteenweg 59) – Cabaret and chanson productions.

De Muze *Plan II* **D2** – Live jazz in a converted warehouse.

NIGHTLIFE

Consult the publication *Weekup* (in French and Flemish) available in bars and other public places.

Bars with terraces, cafés with live music, pubs, clubs, discotheques, karaoke bars abound around **Groenplaats** *Plan II* **D2**, **Grote Markt** *Plan II* **D1** and along **Jordaenskaai** *Plan II* **D1** and **Ernest Van Dijckkaai** *Plan II* **C1** on the **banks of the Scheldt**, along **Koningin Astridplein** *Plan II* **F2**, in the neighbourhood of the **Centraal Station** (Franklin Rooseveltplaats, De Coninckplein, Statiestraat, Offerandestaat) and in bustling **Het Zuid** *Plan II* **C3** which boasts literary cafés.

The Grand Horta Café, Hopland 2 is a stylish designer café and *Den Engel*, Grote Markt 3, is a city institution.

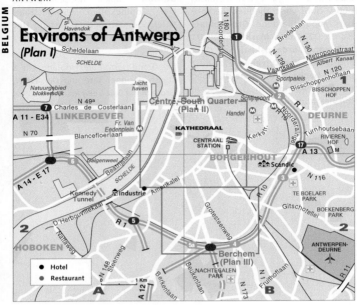

CENTRE (Old Town and Mainstation) *Plan II*

Hilton ⌂⌂⌂   🛗 👿 ⅙ 🅰 ⅙ ♨30/1000 ⌂ ⌂ 🖭 ℡ **VISA** 🅜🅒 🅐🅔 ①

Groenplaats – ☎ 0 3 204 12 12 – fb-antwerp @ hilton.com – Fax 0 3 204 12 13
– www.hilton.com   **D2**
199 rm – ♦139/369 € ♦♦139/369 €, ☲ 25 € – 12 suites
Rest see *Het Vijfde Seizoen* below
Rest *Terrace-Café* 27 € (weekday lunch) and a la carte 29/59 €
◆ Chain hotel ◆ Luxury ◆ Stylish ◆
This luxury hotel occupies a fine early-20C building which started life as a
department store. Large, well-appointed rooms, plus pleasant public areas.
Views of the cathedral and lively Groenplaats from the Terrace Café with its
comprehensive menu.

Astrid Park Plaza ⌂⌂⌂   ⇐ 🛗 👿 🖸 🅰 ⅙ 🖭 ℡ ♨25/500 ⌂
Koningin Astridplein 7 ⊠ 2018 – ☎ 0 3 203 12 34   **VISA** 🅜🅒 🅐🅔 ①
– appsales @ parkplazahotels.be – Fax 0 3 203 12 75
– www.parkplaza.com   **F2**
225 rm – ♦125/220 € ♦♦145/240 €, ☲ 20 € – 3 suites
Rest 30 € and a la carte 28/38 €
◆ Chain hotel ◆ Business ◆ Design ◆
This four-star hotel, its original architectural design the work of Michael Graves,
is on a busy square near the central railway station. Impeccable, spacious and
well-appointed rooms and modern public areas. Bright restaurant serving
contemporary recipes.

Radisson SAS Park Lane ⟨≤ ƒ5 🕉 🖂 ⅋rest 🔼 ↩ ⅋rest 🕽
Van Eycklei 34 ⊠ 2018 🔏 25/600 ⟨⟨ ⤻ *VISA* 🐵 🔼 ⓪
– 𝒞 0 3 285 85 85 – guest.antwerp@radissonsas.com
– Fax 0 3 285 85 86 – www.antwerp.radissonsas.com **E3**
160 rm – ♦121/185 € ♦♦121/185 €, ⊆ 24 € – 14 suites
Rest *(closed August and Sunday)* 30 € *(weekday lunch)* and a la carte 35/53 €
♦ Chain hotel ♦ Traditional ♦ Stylish ♦
This luxury hotel is well-located on a main road away from the centre, opposite
a public park. Full range of tailored facilities and services for its mainly business
clientele. Small dining room serving classic international cuisine.

 De Witte Lelie without rest ⌂ 🔠 ⟨⟨ *VISA* 🐵 🔼 ⓪
Keizerstraat 16 – 𝒞 0 3 226 19 66 – hotel@dewittelelie.be – Fax 0 3 234 00 19
closed 20 December-15 January **D1**
7 rm ⊆ – ♦195/425 € ♦♦265/495 € – 3 suites
♦ Family ♦ Luxury ♦ Personalised ♦
Quiet and full of charm, this small "grand hotel" is spread across several 17C
houses. Cosy, elegantly decorated rooms, in addition to an inviting patio.

 't Sandt 🔼 ⅋ 🕽 🔏 25/100 ⟨⟨ *VISA* 🐵 🔼 ⓪
Het Zand 17 – 𝒞 0 3 232 93 90 – reservations@hotel-sandt.be
– Fax 0 3 232 56 13 – www.hotel-sandt.be **C2**
27 rm ⊆ – ♦135/265 € ♦♦150/280 € – 2 suites
Rest see Rest **de Kleine Zavel** below
♦ Family ♦ Luxury ♦ Stylish ♦
The fine Rococo façade of this impressive 19C residence contrasts starkly with
the sober, contemporary decor of its interior. Delightful, Italianate winter garden
and roomy, elegant guest accommodation.

 Theater 🕉 🔼 ↩ ⅋rest 🔠 🕽 🔏 25/50 *VISA* 🐵 🔼 ⓪
Arenbergstraat 30 – 𝒞 0 3 203 54 10 – info@theater-hotel.be – Fax 0 3 233 88 58
– www.vhv-hotels.be **E2**
122 rm – ♦110/220 € ♦♦130/240 €, ⊆ 20 € – 5 suites
Rest *(closed 21 July-14 August, 22 December- 3 January, Saturday, Sunday and
Bank Holidays)* 17 € *(weekday lunch)* and a la carte approx. 39 €
♦ Business ♦ Classic ♦
A modern, comfortable hotel with an ideal location at the heart of the old city,
just a short distance from the Bourla theatre and Rubens' house. Spacious
bedrooms decorated in warm tones. Characterful restaurant featuring a small
menu from around the world.

 Rubens without rest ⌂ 🔼 🔠 🕽 ⟨⟨ *VISA* 🐵 🔼 ⓪
Oude Beurs 29 – 𝒞 0 3 222 48 48 – hotel.rubens@glo.be – Fax 0 3 225 19 40
– www.hotelrubensantwerp.be **D1**
35 rm ⊆ – ♦145/230 € ♦♦145/230 € – 1 suite
♦ Traditional ♦ Business ♦ Classic ♦
A quiet and friendly renovated hotel near the Grand-Place and cathedral. Some
rooms overlook the inner courtyard, which is flower-decked in summer.

Hyllit without rest ƒ5 🕉 🖂 🔼 ↩ ⅋ 🔠 🔏 25/150 ⟨⟨ *VISA* 🐵 🔼 ⓪
De Keyserlei 28 (access by Appelmansstraat) ⊠ 2018 – 𝒞 0 3 202 68 00
– info@hyllithotel.be – Fax 0 3 202 68 90 – www.hyllithotel.be **E2**
123 rm – ♦100/171 € ♦♦120/196 €, ⊆ 17 € – 4 suites
♦ Business ♦ Modern ♦
Intimate public areas, spacious bedrooms and junior suites, and a good view of
Antwerp's rooftops from the bright breakfast room and two large terraces.

De Keyser without rest ƒ5 🕉 🖂 🔼 ↩ 🔠 🕽
De Keyserlei 66 ⊠ 2018 – 𝒞 0 3 206 🔏 25/120 *VISA* 🐵 🔼 ⓪
74 60 – reservations@dekeyserhotel.be
– Fax 0 3 232 39 70 – www.vhv-hotels.be **F2**
120 rm – ♦90/160 € ♦♦105/160 € – 3 suites
♦ Chain hotel ♦ Business ♦ Classic ♦
Easily accessible and advantageously located close to the railway station and a
metro line. Cosy, modern bedrooms.

Centre, (old town and main station) South Quarter
(Plan II)

C — Waaslandtunnel — D

Oude Leeuwenrui
Oude Leeuwenrui
Pazzo

Falconpl.
Falconrui

0   200m

1

Thonetlaan

Jordenskaai

St.-Paulusstr.

Dock's Café
He Petit Zinc
ST.-PAULUSKERK

Klapdorp
Mutsaertstr.

Stadswaag

Antigone
Veemarkt
Le Zoute Zoen

Minderbroedersrui

Blindestraat

HET STEEN (MUSEUM)

Zirkstr.
Hofstr.

ROCKOXHUIS
Keizerstraat

Steenplein

Van Dijckkaai

VLEESHUIS

Rubens

Neuze Neuze

De Manie
Kipdorp

De Witte Lelie

ETNOGRAFISCH MUSEUM

Orso D'oro
De Gulden Beer
H

ST.- CAROLUS BORROMEUSKERK

Maritime

Suikerrui

Grote Markt

Hendrik Consciencepl.

't Silveren Claverblat

Gin-Fish

Villa Mozart

De Reddende Engel

Julien

Lange

Vlaaikensgang

KATHEDRAAL

't Sandt

Ej.

't Fornuis

Groenpl.
Hilton
Het Vijfde Seizoen

De Kleine Zavel

Groenpl. M

HANDELSBEURS

SCHELDE

Het Nieuwe Palinghuis

MUSEUM PLANTIN-MORETUS

Vrijdagmarkt

Schoenmarkt

Korte Gasthuisstr.

Meir M

Huidevetterstr.

2

Plantinkaai

Kloosterstraat

Lange Ridderstr.

MODEMUSEUM

straat

Lambardenvest

Kammenstr.

Schuttershofstr.

Hecker

St. Andriespl.

Sint-Antoniusstr.

Nationalestraat

P'tit Vatelli

Oudaan

BOURLA-SCHOUWBURG

Huis De Colvenier

MUSEUM MAYER VAN DEN BERGH

Schoyte Str.

Aalmoezenierstr.

Rosier

Vleminckveld

Lange Gasthuisstr.

M

Arenbergstr.

Sint-Michielskaai

Scheldestraat

Kloosterstraat

Sint-Rochusstraat

Kronenburgstraat

Geuzenstr.

Begijnenstr.

Terninckstr.

Schermersstr.

Louizastr.

Begijnenvest

Cockerilkaai

M

Waalsekaai

Kommilfoo

Kaai

Graaf Van Egmontstr.

Volksstr.

de Vriesestr.

Marnixplaats

Kasteelpleinstr.

Tolstraat

Britselei

Justitiestraat

3

Verlatstraat

Karel Rogierstr.

Vlaamse Burburstr.

Gillisplaats

Leopold de Waelpl.

KONINKLIJK MUSEUM VOOR SCHONE KUNSTEN

Amerikalei

Paleisstraat

Kasteelstr.

Gijzelaarsstr.

Lambermontplaats

C — D

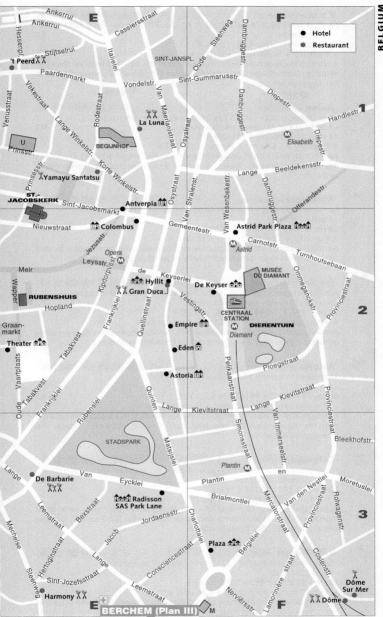

BELGIUM

Plaza without rest   🎞 ↳ 🕾 ♨25 🚗 _VISA_ 🐠 🖭 ①
Charlottalei 49 ⊠ 2018 – ℰ 0 3 287 28 70 – book@plaza.be – Fax 0 3 287 28 71
– www.plaza.be   **F3**
81 rm ⊡ – ♦112/290 € ♦♦112/305 €
♦ Family ♦ Business ♦ Cosy ♦
A warm, friendly atmosphere is the hallmark of this old-style hotel on the edge
of the city centre. Large, elegant rooms, a grand English-style lobby and Victorian
bar. Luggage service.

Julien without rest   🎞 ⌘ 🖂 🕾 _VISA_ 🐠 🖭
Korte Nieuwstraat 24 – ℰ 0 3 229 06 00 – info@hotel-julien.com
– Fax 0 3 233 35 70 – www.hotel-julien.com   **D2**
11 rm ⊡ – ♦160/250 € ♦♦160/250 €
♦ Family ♦ Luxury ♦ Personalised ♦
An intimate hotel with a carriage entrance opening onto a tramlined street. Cosy
interior decor blending classical, rustic and design features. Attractive modern
bedrooms.

Antverpia without rest   ⌘ 🚗 _VISA_ 🐠 🖭 ①
Sint-Jacobsmarkt 85 – ℰ 0 3 231 80 80 – antverpia@skynet.be
– Fax 0 3 232 43 43   **E1**
18 rm ⊡ – ♦99/124 € ♦♦112/175 €
♦ Family ♦ Traditional ♦ Classic ♦
A small, pleasant hotel with attractive, meticulously maintained rooms located
between the railway station and the city's main shopping streets.

Empire without rest   🎞 ↳ 🖂 🕾 _VISA_ 🐠 🖭 ①
Appelmansstraat 31 ⊠ 2018 – ℰ 0 3 203 54 00 – info@empirehotel.be
– Fax 0 3 233 40 60 – www.vhv-hotels.be   **E2**
70 rm – ♦85/135 € ♦♦100/160 €, ⊡ 15 €
♦ Traditional ♦ Business ♦ Functional ♦
Nestled at the heart of the diamond district, the Alfa Empire offers 70 large rooms
ensuring a good night's sleep. Interesting breakfast room decor.

Astoria without rest   ↳6 🎞 ↳ 🕾 🚗 _VISA_ 🐠 🖭 ①
Korte Herentalsestraat 5 ⊠ 2018 – ℰ 0 3 227 31 30
– Fax 0 3 227 31 34   **E2**
66 rm – ♦140/150 € ♦♦165/175 €, ⊡ 13 €
♦ Traditional ♦ Business ♦ Functional ♦
Although slightly away from the action, the Astoria is in a reasonable location
near the diamond district and Stadtspark. Granite lobby and façade, and
well-appointed rooms.

Colombus without rest   ↳6 🖾 ⌘ 🖂 🚗 _VISA_ 🐠 🖭 ①
Frankrijklei 4 – ℰ 0 3 233 03 90 – colombushotel@skynet.be – Fax 0 3 226 09 46
– www.columbushotel.com   **E2**
32 rm ⊡ – ♦97 € ♦♦117 €
♦ Family ♦ Traditional ♦ Retro ♦
Behind the classical façade of this city-centre hotel are rooms with good
soundproofing and attractively decorated public areas. An excellent location
just opposite the city's opera house.

Villa Mozart without rest   ≤ 🕸 ↳ _VISA_ 🐠 🖭 ①
Handschoenmarkt 3 – ℰ 0 3 231 30 31 – info@villamozart.be
– Fax 0 3 231 56 85   **D1**
25 rm – ♦89/139 € ♦♦99/350 €, ⊡ 13 €
♦ Traditional ♦ Family ♦ Classic ♦
Superbly located in the bustling heart of Antwerp between the Grand-Place and
the cathedral (views from some rooms), this small hotel is a pleasant and highly
practical option.

🏠 **Antigone** without rest   🕮 🖃 🕻 🅿 _VISA_ 🐵 🆎 ⓪
Jordaenskaai 11 – ℰ 0 3 231 66 77 – info@antigonehotel.be – Fax 0 3 231 37 74
– www.antigonehotel.be   **D1**
21 rm ⌾ – ♦75/110 € ♦♦85/125 €
♦ Traditional ♦ Family ♦ Classic ♦
A simple, but perfectly comfortable and adequate hotel housed in a
bourgeois-style building near the Schelde River and Steen Museum. Individually
decorated rooms.

🏠 **Eden** without rest   ⅋ 🚗 _VISA_ 🐵 🆎
Lange Herentalsestraat 25 ⊠ 2018 – ℰ 0 3 233 06 08 – hotel.eden@skynet.be
– Fax 0 3 233 12 28   **E2**
66 rm ⌾ – ♦70/100 € ♦♦75/110 €
♦ Traditional ♦ Functional ♦
A refurbished and well-maintained hotel with a prime location in the middle of
the diamond district, close to the railway station. Identical, functional bedrooms.

𝕏𝕏𝕏 **'t Fornuis** (Segers)   ⅋ _VISA_ 🐵 🆎 ⓪
❀ *Reyndersstraat 24 – ℰ 0 3 233 62 70 – fornuis@skynet.be – Fax 0 3 233 99 03*
closed August, Christmas-New Year, Saturday, Sunday and Bank Holidays   **D2**
Rest (booking essential) 88 € and a la carte 65/95 € 🏵
Spec. Salade de crabe frais. Barbue pochée avec œuf et caviar. Langue d'agneau,
grands haricots blancs et sauce madère.
♦ Traditional ♦ Rustic ♦
This restaurant, occupying a fine 17C residence, offers an ambitious menu that
is highly personalised and presented in theatrical fashion by the feisty chef!
Rustic decor.

𝕏𝕏𝕏 **Huis De Colvenier**   🍴 🕮 🅢25/90 🅿 ⌂ _VISA_ 🐵 🆎 ⓪
Sint-Antoniusstraat 8 – ℰ 0 3 226 65 73 – info@colvenier.be – Fax 0 3 227 13 14
closed carnival, August, Saturday lunch, Sunday and Monday   **D2**
Rest 65 € b.i. (weekday lunch)/75 € b.i. and a la carte 60/85 € 🏵
♦ Traditional ♦ Retro ♦
This restaurant is housed in an elegant townhouse dating from 1879. It offers
spruce dining areas embellished with attractive wall paintings, a charming
winter garden and fine wines. Attentive service.

𝕏𝕏𝕏 **Het Vijfde Seizoen** – Hotel Hilton   ⅋ 🕮 ⌂ _VISA_ 🐵 🆎 ⓪
– ℰ 0 3 204 12 12 – fb-antwerp@hilton.com – Fax 0 3 204 12 13
– www.hilton.com   **D2**
Rest *(closed 16 July-21 August, Sunday and Monday)* 39 € (weekday lunch)/70 €
and a la carte 43/91 €
♦ Traditional ♦ Cosy ♦
This comfortable restaurant, popular with the business community, is part of a
chain hotel. Refined decor and a resolutely traditional menu.

𝕏𝕏𝕏 **De Barbarie**   🍴 🕮 ⅋ _VISA_ 🐵 🆎 ⓪
Van Breestraat 4 ⊠ 2018 – ℰ 0 3 232 81 98 – Fax 0 3 231 26 78
– www.barbarie.be
closed first week Easter holidays, 2 weeks September, late December, Saturday
lunch, Sunday and Monday   **E3**
Rest 40 € (weekday lunch)/65 € and a la carte 58/98 € 🏵
♦ Traditional ♦ Fashionable ♦
The creative menu here includes several duck specialities, accompanied by an
attractive wine list. Fine collection of silver tableware. Outdoor restaurant.

𝕏𝕏 **Neuze Neuze**   _VISA_ 🐵 🆎 ⓪
Wijngaardstraat 19 – ℰ 0 3 232 27 97 – neuzeneuze@pandora.be
– Fax 0 3 225 27 38 – www.neuzeneuze.be
closed first week January, 2 weeks August, Sunday and lunch Wednesday and
Saturday   **D1**
Rest 25 € (weekday lunch), 50/58 € and a la carte 34/78 €
♦ Traditional ♦ Rustic ♦
An intimate setting where the clientele ranges from business people to couples
on dates. Separate banqueting rooms. Copious cuisine and refined service.

La Luna
AC ⌂(dinner) VISA ⓜ AE ①

Italeïlei 177 – ℰ 0 3 232 23 44 – info@laluna.be – Fax 0 3 232 24 41
– www.laluna.be
closed 1 week Easter, 24 July-15 August, Christmas-New Year, Saturday lunch,
Sunday and Monday **E1**
Rest 33 € and a la carte 47/73 € ⌂
♦ Contemporary ♦ Trendy ♦
The American brasserie-style atmosphere and cosmopolitan menu are popular with the city's upwardly mobile clientele. A refined, reasonably priced menu and excellent wine list.

Orso D'oro - De Gulden Beer
⇐ ☆ AC ⅍ VISA ⓜ AE ①

Grote Markt 14 – ℰ 0 3 226 08 41 – Fax 0 3 232 52 09 – www.guidenbeer.be **D1**
Rest (open until 11 p.m.) 25 € (weekday lunch), 37/75 € and a la carte 45/65 €
♦ Italian ♦ Friendly ♦
This old house with its crow-step gables stands on the Grand-Place. Inviting Italian menu and pleasant views from the terrace and the bay windows on the first floor.

Harmony
AC P ⌂ VISA ⓜ AE ①

Mechelsesteenweg 169 ⊠ 2018 – ℰ 0 3 239 70 05 – info@diningharmony.com
– Fax 0 3 257 16 09 – www.diningroomharmony.com
closed 23 July-7 August, Wednesday and Saturday lunch **E3**
Rest 23 € (weekday lunch), 30/50 € and a la carte 43/60 €
♦ Contemporary ♦ Fashionable ♦
The contemporary cuisine on offer here is in harmony with the decor of modern filtered lighting, fluted pilasters, lattice-work chairs and plain table setting.

Het Nieuwe Palinghuis
AC ⅍ VISA ⓜ AE ①

Sint-Jansvliet 14 – ℰ 0 3 231 74 45 – hetnieuwepalinghuis@scarlet.be
– Fax 0 3 231 50 53 – www.hetnieuwepalinghuis.be
closed 2 weeks January, June, Monday and Tuesday **C2**
Rest 33 € (weekday lunch)/65 € and a la carte 60/80 €
♦ Seafood ♦ Family ♦
Eel takes pride of place in this fish and seafood restaurant, whose walls are adorned with nostalgic images of old Antwerp. Good choice of affordable wines.

Gran Duca
☆ AC P VISA ⓜ AE ①

6 th floor, De Keyserlei 28 ⊠ 2018 – ℰ 0 3 202 68 87 – granduca@pandora.be
– Fax 0 3 225 51 99 – www.granduca.be
closed Saturday lunch and Sunday **E2**
Rest 25 € (weekday lunch) and a la carte 31/58 €
♦ Italian ♦ Fashionable ♦
The extensive glass frontage of this Italian restaurant above the Hyllit Hotel opens onto three panoramic terraces. Bright, spacious dining room furnished with rattan chairs.

't Silveren Claverblat
⅍ VISA ⓜ AE ①

Grote Pieter Potstraat16 – ℰ 0 3 231 33 88 – Fax 0 3 231 31 46
closed 2 weeks August, Tuesday, Wednesday and lunch Thursday and Saturday **C1**
Rest 40 € (weekday lunch)/65 € and a la carte 58/72 €
♦ Traditional ♦ Rustic ♦
A well-established and renowned restaurant in a typical 16C building in the old quarter. A limited number of tables and concise menu of classic à la carte choices.

Dôme (Burlat)
AC ⅍ VISA ⓜ AE ①

Grote Hondstraat 2 ⊠ 2018 – ℰ 0 3 239 90 03 – info@domeweb.be
– Fax 0 3 239 93 90 – www.domeweb.be
closed 2 weeks August, 24 December-3 January, Monday and lunch Tuesday
and Saturday **F3**
Rest 28 € (weekday lunch)/59 € and a la carte 50/66 € ⌂
Spec. Ravioli de sardines au basilic. Pigeon rôti aux petits pois et fèves de marais. Tarte au chocolat.
♦ Contemporary ♦ Retro ♦
Ambitious contemporary cuisine is served in this restaurant with an impressive neo-Baroque dome and circular dining area, which was once a chic café (19C). Excellent sommelier.

BELGIUM

XX **'t Peerd** 🛋 AC VISA ⦿ AE ⦿

Paardenmarkt 53 – ℰ 0 3 231 98 25 – resto_t_peerd@yahoo.com
– Fax 0 3 231 59 40 – www.tpeerd.be
closed 2 weeks Easter, 2 weeks September, Tuesday and Wednesday **E1**
Rest 38 € (weekday lunch)/50 € and a la carte 44/76 €
♦ Traditional ♦ Friendly ♦
This characterful small restaurant is embellished with equestrian decor, providing a hint of the house specialities. Studied wine list, attentive service and local ambience.

XX **P'tit Vatelli** AC ⦿ VISA ⦿ AE ⦿

Kammenstraat 75 – ℰ 0 3 226 96 46 – info@petitvatelli.be – Fax 0 3 226 96 46
– www.petitvatelli.be
closed first week January, last 2 weeks July, Saturday lunch, Sunday,
Monday and Bank Holidays **D2**
Rest (open until 11 p.m.) 22 € (weekday lunch), 30/57 € and a la carte
45/63 €
♦ Traditional ♦ Cosy ♦
A pleasantly arranged dining room and friendly ambience await guests behind the attractive façade dating from 1577. Classic dishes based on ingredients of the highest quality.

X **De Manie** 🛋 ⇥ VISA ⦿ AE ⦿

H. Conscienceplein 3 – ℰ 0 3 232 64 38 – restaurant.demanie@scarlet.be
– Fax 0 3 232 64 38
closed 14 August-3 September, Wednesday and Sunday dinner **D1**
Rest 27 € (weekday lunch)/50 € and a la carte 38/68 €
♦ Traditional ♦ Cosy ♦
On a pleasant square near the St-Charles-Borromée church, the De Manie's old façade is fronted by a summer terrace. Modern-rustic interior with mezzanine. Contemporary cuisine.

X **Dock's Café** AC ⦿ ⇥ VISA ⦿ AE

Jordaenskaai 7 – ℰ 0 3 226 63 30 – info@docks.be – Fax 0 3 226 65 72
– www.docks.be
closed Saturday lunch **D1**
Rest (open until 11 p.m.) 15 € (weekday lunch)/22 € and a la carte 31/61 €
♦ Brasserie ♦ Trendy ♦
A sense of travel pervades this seafood bar-cum-brasserie with its futurist, maritime decor. Dining room with mezzanine and neo-Baroque staircase. Reservation recommended.

X **de Kleine Zavel** – Hotel 't Sandt VISA ⦿ AE

Stoofstraat 2 – ℰ 0 3 231 96 91 – Fax 0 3 231 79 01
closed Saturday lunch **C2**
Rest 18 € (weekday lunch) and a la carte 37/62 €
♦ Contemporary ♦ Bistro ♦
Modern cooking served in a typical bistro setting, with bare tables, bar and panelled walls. Friendly atmosphere and attractively priced set lunch menu.

X **De Reddende Engel** 🛋 VISA ⦿ AE ⦿

Torfbrug 3 – ℰ 0 3 233 66 30 – de.reddende.engel@telenet.be
– Fax 0 3 233 73 79
closed mid August-mid September, Tuesday, Wednesday and Saturday lunch
Rest 26/32 € and a la carte 28/49 € **D1**
♦ Regional ♦ Rustic ♦
A 17C house close to the cathedral is the setting for this friendly, rustic restaurant serving classic French cuisine with southern influence. Bouillabaisse a speciality.

X **Le Petit Zinc** (Grootaert) 🛋 ⦿ AE ⦿
❀
Veemarkt 9 – ℰ 0 3 213 19 08 – Fax 0 3 213 19 08
closed 1 week Easter, 16 to 31 August, Saturday and Sunday **D1**
Rest 20 € (weekday lunch), 56/76 € and a la carte 46/91 €
Spec. Salade d'artichaut aux truffes. Curry d'agneau. Tarte fine aux pommes.
♦ Traditional ♦ Bistro ♦
A convivial local bistro with closely packed small tables, slate menus featuring tasty, traditional dishes, and attentive service.

BELGIUM

Le Zoute Zoen ⚐ 🍴 VISA ◎ AE
Zirkstraat 17 – ℰ 03 226 92 20 – Fax 03 231 01 30
closed Monday and Saturday lunch **D1**
Rest 16 € (weekday lunch), 27 € b.i./60 € b.i. and a la carte 27/41 €
♦ Traditional ♦ Bistro ♦
The menu in this cosy, intimate "gastro-bistro" offers unique value for money in Antwerp. A range of copious contemporary dishes served by efficient, friendly staff.

Gin-Fish (Garnick) ⚐ AC 🍴 VISA ◎ AE ◎
Haarstraat 9 – ℰ 03 231 32 07 – dematelote@telenet.be
closed first 2 weeks January, first 3 weeks June, Sunday and Monday **D1-2**
Rest (booking essential) (lunch by arrangement)60 € and a la carte 49/64 €
Spec. Ravioli de homard. Bar sauvage aux palourdes. Poêlée de nectarines et glace vanille
♦ Seafood ♦ Friendly ♦
Good seafood dishes prepared before you, behind the counter where guests dine. As the chef is working in full view, he errs on the side of caution by offering only one fixed menu. Lovely staff.

Maritime ⚐ AC VISA ◎ AE ◎
Suikerrui 4 – ℰ 03 233 07 58 – restaurant.maritime@pandora.be
– Fax 03 233 07 58 – www.maritime.be
closed lunch Monday and Thursday July-December, Thursday January-June and Wednesday **C1**
Rest a la carte 36/50 € ⚐
♦ Seafood ♦ Friendly ♦
As its name would suggest, fish and seafood reign supreme here with some of the city's best mussels and eel in season. A good choice of Burgundies and attentive service.

Hecker ⚐ VISA ◎ AE ◎
Kloosterstraat 13 – ℰ 03 234 38 34 – info@hecker.be – www.hecker.be
closed 23 July-7 August, 23 December-2 January, Monday lunch and Wednesday
Rest 17 € (weekday lunch)/48 € and a la carte 31/51 € **C2**
♦ Contemporary ♦ Bistro ♦
This modern bistro sharing its walls with an antiques shop offers a small menu which is both original and enticing. A good choice of wines from around the world.

Pazzo ⚐ AC VISA ◎ AE ◎
Oude Leeuwenrui 12 – ℰ 03 232 86 82 – pazzo@skynet.be – Fax 03 232 79 34
– www.pazzo.be **D1**
closed 21 July-16 August, Christmas-New Year, Saturday, Sunday and Bank Holidays
Rest (open until 11 p.m.) 20 € (weekday lunch) and a la carte 30/69 €
♦ Contemporary ♦ Wine bar ♦
A lively dockside restaurant occupying a former warehouse converted into a modern brasserie, where the emphasis is on contemporary dishes and wines chosen to complement the cuisine.

Dôme Sur Mer ⚐ 🍴 VISA ◎
Arendstraat 1 ⊠ 2018 – ℰ 03 281 74 33 – info@domeweb.be
– Fax 03 239 93 90 – www.domeweb.be **F3**
Rest *(closed late December, Monday and Saturday lunch)* (October-June dinner only until 1 a.m.) a la carte 34/69 €
♦ Seafood ♦ Brasserie ♦
This grand residence has been transformed into an "über-trendy" seafood brasserie with designer decor of bright white set off by the blue of a row of aquariums containing goldfish.

Yamayu Santatsu ⚐ AC VISA ◎ AE ◎
Ossenmarkt 19 – ℰ 03 234 09 49 – Fax 03 234 09 49
closed 1 to 15 August, 24 December-4 January, Sunday lunch and Monday
Rest 13 € (weekday lunch)/47 € and a la carte 24/52 € **E1**
♦ Japanese ♦ Minimalist ♦
This compact and constantly reliable Japanese restaurant and sushi bar is well known to aficionados of Asian cuisine. Quality products and an extensive menu choice.

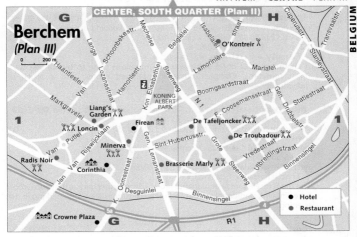

SOUTH QUARTER AND BERCHEM   *Plan III*

Crowne Plaza
G. Legrellelaan 10 ⊠ 2020 – ℰ 0 3 259 75 00
– web.antwerp @ ichotelgroup.com – Fax 0 3 216 02 96
– www.antwerp.crowneplaza.com   **G1**
256 rm – ♦114/245 € ♦♦114/245 €, ⌷ 21 € – 6 suites
Rest *Plaza One for two* 28 € (lunch) and a la carte 34/47 €
♦ Chain hotel ♦ Business ♦ Modern ♦
This international hotel close to a motorway exit offers pleasantly decorated, well-appointed rooms with a contemporary feel. Good conference facilities and 24-hour service. Full à la carte menu available in the restaurant and snacks are served in the lively lounge bar.

Corinthia
Desguinlei 94 ⊠ 2018 – ℰ 0 3 244 82 11 – antwerp @ corinthia.be
– Fax 0 3 216 47 12 – www.corinthiahotels.com   **G1**
208 rm – ♦79/209 € ♦♦79/209 €, ⌷ 20 € – 5 suites
Rest *(closed Saturday lunch and Sunday)* 15 € (weekday lunch), 29/35 €
and a la carte 32/57 €
♦ Business ♦ Modern ♦
This glass-fronted hotel is located close to the city's ring road with links to the Brussels motorway and historical centre. Sleek and spacious foyer, bright and spacious bedrooms, plus a contemporary-style dining room with appealing à la carte/menu options.

Firean ⌂
Karel Oomsstraat 6 ⊠ 2018 – ℰ 0 3 237 02 60 – info @ hotelfirean.com
– Fax 0 3 238 11 68 – www.hotelfirean.com
closed 23 July-16 August and 23 December-8 January   **G1**
12 rm ⌷ – ♦135/171 € ♦♦157/228 €
Rest see *Minerva* below
♦ Luxury ♦ Family ♦ Art Deco ♦
A charming, quiet hotel with a patio occupying an Art Deco-style residence close to the Koning Albert Park. Rooms decorated with stylish antique furniture. Attentive service.

Industrie without rest   ⌖ 🚗 VISA ⓂⓈ AE ①
Emiel Banningstraat 52 – ℰ 0 3 238 66 00 – info @ hotelindustrie.be
– Fax 0 3 238 86 88 – www.hotelindustrie.be   Plan I **A2**
12 rm ⌲ – ✝60/75 € ✝✝80/87 €
♦ Family ♦ Business ♦ Classic ♦
A charming small hotel occupying two mansions close to two of the city's finest museums. Compact but well-appointed rooms with a touch of individuality.

Minerva – Hotel Firean   AC ⌂⌐ VISA ⓂⓈ AE ①
Karel Oomsstraat 6 ⊠ 2018 – ℰ 0 3 216 00 55
– restaurantminerva @ skynet.be – Fax 0 3 216 00 55   **G1**
– www.hotelfirean.com
closed 24 July-16 August, 23 December-9 January,
Sunday and Monday
Rest 50 € (weekday lunch) and a la carte 43/88 €
♦ Traditional ♦ Formal ♦
This modern, elegant restaurant has replaced the former garage that once stood here. Enticing traditional cuisine and seasonal suggestions. Easy parking in the evening.

Loncin   🏠 AC P VISA ⓂⓈ AE ①
Markgravelei 127 ⊠ 2018 – ℰ 0 3 248 29 89 – info @ loncinrestaurant.be
– Fax 0 3 248 38 66 – www.loncinrestaurant.be   **G1**
closed late February- early March, 2 weeks July, Saturday lunch
and Sunday
Rest 35 € (weekday lunch), 50/78 € and a la carte 45/145 € ⌘
♦ Traditional ♦ Family ♦
A soberly elegant bourgeois restaurant serving a classic choice of quality dishes. Wine list featuring prestigious names, fine vintages and a good choice of half-bottles.

De Tafeljoncker   🏠 AC VISA ⓂⓈ AE ①
Frederik de Merodestraat 13 ⊠ 2600 Berchem – ℰ 0 3 281 20 34
– restaurant.de-tafeljoncker @ pandora.be – Fax 0 3 281 20 34   **H1**
– www.resto.be
closed Carnival holidays, 2 weeks July, Sunday dinner,
Monday and Tuesday
Rest 50 € (weekday lunch), 60/75 €
♦ Traditional ♦ Cosy ♦
This cosy restaurant occupying a bourgeois mansion offers guests two menus from which dishes can be ordered separately. Elegant table settings.

Liang's Garden   AC VISA ⓂⓈ AE ①
Markgravelei 141 ⊠ 2018 – ℰ 0 3 237 22 22 – Fax 0 3 248 38 34
closed 10 July-6 August and Sunday   **G1**
Rest 24 € (weekday lunch)/40 € and a la carte 35/62 €
♦ Chinese ♦ Exotic ♦
This attractive mansion houses one of Antwerp's oldest Chinese restaurants. A bourgeois setting with a few Asian touches. Menu featuring Peking duck specialities.

Kommilfoo   AC ⌖ VISA ⓂⓈ AE ①
Vlaamse Kaai 17 – ℰ 0 3 237 30 00 – kommilfoo @ resto.be – Fax 0 3 237 30 00
– www.resto.be/kommilfoo
closed Saturday lunch, Sunday and Monday   Plan II **C3**
Rest 30 € (weekday lunch), 48/50 € and a la carte 45/65 €
♦ Traditional ♦ Rustic ♦
Located opposite a large, free car park a stone's throw from three museums, this former warehouse has been transformed into a restaurant that is sober yet modern in design, with a menu that is equally contemporary.

BELGIUM

XX **Radis Noir** 🍴 VISA ⓪ AE ①
Desguinlei 186 ⊠ 2018 – ℰ 0 3 238 37 70 – radisnoir @ skynet.be
– Fax 0 3 238 39 07 – www.radisnoir.be
closed 1 to 8 February, 1 to 15 August, Saturday, Sunday and Bank Holidays
Rest 30 € (weekday lunch) and a la carte 51/66 € **G1**
♦ Traditional ♦ Fashionable ♦
This bourgeois house on a busy street near the new Palais de Justice has been
transformed into a restaurant with designer-influenced decor. Concise yet
regularly updated menu.

XX **Brasserie Marly** 🍴 P VISA ⓪ AE ①
(😊)
Generaal Lemanstraat 64 ⊠ 2600 Berchem – ℰ 0 3 281 23 23 – info @ marly.be
– Fax 0 3 281 33 10 – www.marly.be
closed 17 July-14 August, Saturday and Sunday **G-H1**
Rest 25 € b.i./50 € b.i. and a la carte 28/65 €
♦ Brasserie ♦ Fashionable ♦
A welcoming brasserie located on the fringes of the city. Imaginative choices in
which fish, oysters and Bresse poultry take centre-stage.

XX **De Troubadour** AK P VISA ⓪ AE ①
(😊)
Driekoningenstraat 72 ⊠ 2600 Berchem – ℰ 0 3 239 39 16
– info @ detroubadour.be – Fax 0 3 230 82 71
closed last week July- mid August, Sunday and Monday **H1**
Rest 25 € (weekday lunch)/33 € and a la carte 38/66 €
♦ Contemporary ♦ Friendly ♦
Intelligently composed menus are a strongpoint of this pleasantly modern res-
taurant where the charismatic owner ensures a warm and friendly atmosphere.

X **O'Kontreir** AK VISA ⓪ AE
Isabellalei 145 ⊠ 2018 – ℰ 0 3 281 39 76 – info @ okontreir.com
– Fax 0 3 237 92 06 – www.okontreir.com
closed 1 to 15 August, 24 December- 2 January, Monday, Tuesday
and lunch Saturday and Sunday **H1**
Rest 45 € and a la carte 35/54 €
♦ Contemporary ♦ Trendy ♦
The O'Kontrier serves creative, contemporary and well-presented dishes in a
distinctly modern setting in the city's Jewish quarter. Japanese tableware and
background music.

AT THE AIRPORT *Plan I*

Scandic 🍴 Ⅰⅻ 🏠 🔲 & AK ↯ 🍴rest 🖭 ✆ Ꮺ25/230
Luitenant Lippenslaan 66 ⊠ 2140 Borgerhout P VISA ⓪ AE ①
– ℰ 0 3 235 91 91 – Fax 0 3 235 08 96 – www.scandic-hotels.com/antwerp
200 rm ⊑ – †80/220 € ††98/238 € – 4 suites **B2**
Rest 30 € (weekday lunch) and a la carte 25/43 €
♦ Chain hotel ♦ Business ♦ Functional ♦
A renovated chain hotel with a good location along the ring road, close to
Borgerhout railway station, the Sterchshof Museum (Zilvercentrum) and a golf
course. Business centre. Modern brasserie with an equally contemporary menu
and attractive teak terrace.

Ter Elst 🍴 Ⅰⅻ 🏠 ℀ & AK ↯ ℀ Ꮬ25/500 🍃 P VISA ⓪ AE ①
Terelststraat 310 (by N173) ⊠ 2650 Edegem – ℰ 0 3 450 90 00 – info @ terelst.be
– Fax 0 3 450 90 90 – www.terelst.be
53 rm ⊑ – †105/120 € ††120/135 €
Rest *Couvert Classique* (closed 2 July-10 August and Sunday) 38 € (weekday
lunch), 35/55 € and a la carte 37/48 € 🍷
♦ Family ♦ Business ♦ Functional ♦
In a slightly isolated location to the south of Antwerp, the Ter Elst is a hotel of
recent design linked to a sports centre. Modern auditorium and large, simply
furnished rooms. Neo-rustic-style dining room serving traditional fare. Attractive
wine list.

CZECH REPUBLIC
ČESKÁ REPUBLIKA

PROFILE

◆ **AREA:**
78 864 km² (30 449 sq mi).

◆ **POPULATION:**
10 241 000 inhabitants (est. 2005), density = 130 per km².

◆ **CAPITAL:**
Prague (population 1 141 000 inhabitants).

◆ **CURRENCY:**
Crown (Kč or CZK); rate of exchange: CZK 100 = € 3.42 = US$ 4.01 (Nov 2005).

◆ **GOVERNMENT:**
Parliamentary republic (since 1993). Member of European Union since 2004.

◆ **LANGUAGE:**
Czech; also German and English.

◆ **SPECIFIC PUBLIC HOLIDAYS:**
Liberation Day (8 May); St. Cyril and St. Methodius Day (5 July); Martyrdom of Jean Hus (6 July); Czech Statehood Day (28 September); Independence Day (28 October); Freedom and Democracy Day (17 November); Boxing Day (26 December).

◆ **LOCAL TIME:**
GMT + 1 hour in winter and GMT + 2 hours in summer.

◆ **CLIMATE:**
Temperate continental with cold winters and warm summers (Prague: January: 0°C, July: 20°C).

Prague

◆ **INTERNATIONAL DIALLING CODE:**
00 420 followed by area code (Prague: 2, Brno: 5, etc.) and then the local number.

◆ **EMERGENCY:**
Police: ℘ 158; Ambulance: ℘ 155; Fire Brigade: ℘ 150.

◆ **ELECTRICITY:**
220 volts AC, 50Hz; 2-pin round-shaped continental plugs.

FORMALITIES

Travellers from the European Union (EU), Switzerland, Iceland and the main countries of North and South America need a national identity card or passport (America: passport required) to visit Czech Republic for less than three months (tourism or business purpose). For visitors from other countries a visa may be required, in addition to a passport, especially for those wishing to stay for longer than three months. We advise you to check with your embassy before travelling.

Driving licences of most countries are recognized in the Czech Republic. If in doubt it is advisable to obtain an international driving licence. Third party insurance is the minimum cover required by Czech legislation but it is advisable to take out fully comprehensive cover (Green Card). To use motorways and similar roads in the Czech Republic you must buy a sticker (vignette) at a border crossing and display it on the car windscreen.

MAJOR NEWSPAPERS

The most important daily newspapers of the Czech Republic are *Mladá fronta Dnes, Právo, Hospodárské noviny, Lidové noviny, Slovo* and *ZN Zemské noviny.*

Popular press: *Blesk*. *Prague Post* is a paper printed in English and *Prager Zeitung* a weekly newspaper printed in German.

USEFUL PHRASES

ENGLISH	CZECH
Yes	**Ano**
No	**Ne**
Good morning	**Dobré jitro**
Goodbye	**Na shledanou**
Thank you	**Děkuji**
Please	**Prosím**
Excuse me	**S dovolením**
I don't understand	**Nerozumím**

HOTELS

◆ CATEGORIES

The range of accommodation in the Czech Republic has improved considerably over the past decade. Large towns and resorts and in particular Prague now offer luxury class and comfortable modern hotels as well as traditional hotels which have been renovated to a good standard. Pensions are usually family-run. Private accommodation (residence) is also available.

◆ PRICE RANGE

The price is per room. There are few single rooms and a supplement is charged for single occupancy of a double room. Prices are 20% cheaper off season and rates in de luxe hotels can be negotiated down by 10-20%. In Prague it is advisable to book in advance in the high season.

◆ TAX

Taxes (19%) and service charges included in the room price.

◆ CHECK OUT TIME

Usually between 10am and noon.

◆ RESERVATIONS

By telephone or fax or by Internet. Make sure you obtain a written confirmation by letter, fax or email.

◆ TIP FOR LUGGAGE HANDLING

At the discretion of the customer.

◆ BREAKFAST

It is often not included in the price of the room and is generally served between 6am and 10.30am. Most hotels offer a self-service continental buffet but hot dishes are charged extra. It is usually possible to have continental breakfast served in the room.

Reception	**recepce**
Single room	**jednolůžkový pokoj**
Double room	**droulůžkový pokoj**
Bed	**postolí**
Bathroom	**koupelnou**
Shower	**sprcha**

RESTAURANTS

Besides the conventional restaurants **(restaurace)**, look out for **vinárny** (wine restaurants) which have an intimate, often traditional, old time atmosphere and where the emphasis is on the wine list. **Pivnice**, **hospody** or **hostinec** are pubs and taverns serving draught beer and traditional meat platters, with a friendly ambience and informal service. **Kavárny** (cafés) serve snacks, sweet pastries and some hot dishes. In less expensive restaurants and in pubs it is normal to share a table if the place is busy (but ask first). Often there are long communal tables for 10-12 people. It is increasingly common for restaurants to offer a set menu **(standardní menu)** as well as à la carte meals at lunchtime and in the evening.

Breakfast	**snídaňů**	6am – 10.30am
Lunch	**oběd**	noon – 2-3pm
Dinner	**večeře**	7pm – 9-11pm, sometimes later

◆ RESERVATIONS

It is not generally necessary to make a reservation unless the place is very popular. However it is advisable to phone in advance for smart restaurants.

◆ THE BILL

The bill (check) does not include a service charge in restaurants. However be wary of hidden charges – cover charge and items like bread, condiments and the little tit-bits at the start of the meal which you may have thought were complimentary. Tipping is not mandatory but it is customary to round up the bill to a reasonable amount or add a 10% tip if you are pleased with the service. Credit cards are accepted in an increasing number of restaurants but it is better to make sure before you order a meal.

Drink or aperitif	**Aperitiv**
Meal	**jídlo**
Appetizer, starter	**předkrm**
Main dish	**hlavní chod**
Main dish of the day	**nabídka dne**
Dessert	**moučník**
Water	**voda**
Mineral water (still, sparkling)	**Minerálka (nešumivá, šumivá)**
Wine (red, white, rosé)	**víno (červené, bílé, rosé)**
Beer	**pivo**
Bread	**chleba**
Meat (rare, medium, well-done)	**maso (krvavý, středně udělaný, dobře udělaný)**
Fish	**ryby**
Salt/pepper	**sůl/pepř**
Cheese	**sýr**
Vegetables	**zeleniny**
Hot/cold	**teplý/studený**
The bill (check) please	**učet prosím**

LOCAL CUISINE

Although the robust Czech cooking is the antithesis of healthy eating with its emphasis on meat dishes, dumplings and cream, with few overcooked vegetables, some effort is being made towards a healthier lifestyle. Some traditional dishes are likely to find favour with most diners. A meal often starts with soup **(polévka)** as a light broth or thick with potatoes, vegetables and meat. Some of the favourites are: **bramborová polévka s houbami** (potatoes, mushrooms, bacon, cabbage, spices), **česneková polévka or česnečka** (garlic), **kuřeci polévka s nudlemi** (chicken noodle), **hovězí polévka s játrovými knedličky** (beef with liver dumplings), **zelná polévka or zelňačka** (sauerkraut), **koprová polévka or koprovka** (dill and sour cream). Tasty starters may be smoked pork **(uzené)**, eggs (vejce), **Prážká Šunka** (thin slices of ham garnished with cucumber and horseradish), ham and cheese in a sandwich, ham stuffed with cream or cheese and horseradish.

Popular meats are chicken (kuře), pork (vepřové), beef (hovězí), duck (kachna), goose (husa) which are either roasted (na rostu), fried (smažený) or breaded (řísek) and served with a garnish **(oblaha** – pickled cabbage, carrots, beets and lettuce) and side dishes – boiled/roasted potatoes **(vařené/opékané brambory)**, mashed potatoes **(bramborová kaše)**, potato salad **(bramborový salát)**, rice **(rýže)**, bread dumplings **(houskové knedlíky)** or potato dumplings **(bramborové knedlíky)**. Although fish is not very common, trout (pstruh), cod (treska) and mackerel (makrela) are well worth trying. Carp (kapr) is a traditional Christmas dish.

Classic main dishes include **hovězí pečeně** (roast beef stuffed with diced ham, peas, onion, spices), **svíčková pečeně na smetaně** (beef in a cream sauce), **Šunka po stavočesku** (boiled beef Bohemian style), **gulaš** (goulash with dumplings), **smažený/vepřové řísek** (veal/pork Wiener schnitzel), **vepřová s knedlíkem a se zelím** (loin of pork with dumplings and sauerkraut).

For dessert you can sample **palačinky**, pancakes filled with fruit and cream or ice cream **(zmrzlina)**; **jablečný závin** (apple strudel); **jablka v županu** (baked apple in flaky pastry with cinnamon and raisins) and **Švestokové/borůvkové knedlíky** (plum/blueberry dumplings).

◆ DRINK

The Czech Republic is the land of beer **(pívo)** and several types of beer are usually on offer. The most common are draught light beer **(svělte)** and dark blends **(tmave)** which are sweeter. The best known are **Plzensky Prazdroj** (Pilsner Urquell) and **Budejovicky Budvar** (Budweiser) but Gambrinus, Krusovice, Radegast, Velkopopovicky kozel or Staropramen are equally good.

The main wine-growing area is Moravia but wine is also produced around Mělník, north of Prague, in Bohemia. Moravian wines are perfectly acceptable. Riesling, Müller-Thurgau or Veltliner grapes are used for white wines (*polusuché* – medium dry, *suché* – dry). **Rulandsé** is a good dry white made from the Pinot grape. Red wines tend to be light-bodied **(Frankovka, Vavřinecké)**. **Burčak** is a young, sweet white wine drunk in Prague in the autumn.

Czech spirits are very popular. **Becherovka** is a bitter-sweet herbal liqueur, which is served as an aperitif or with tonic water. **Borovička** and **Slivovice** (plum brandy) are firm favourites.

PRAGUE
PRAHA

Population (est. 2005): 1 141 000 – Altitude: 250m

P. Bénet/MICHELIN

Prague, the capital of the Czech Republic, has been aptly described as 'Stověžatá Praha', hundred-spired Prague, and the skyline is punctuated by countless towers and turrets, spires and belfries, cupolas and pinnacles, often of extraordinary exuberance in design. The city has transformed itself into a European metropolis and has recaptured its vibrancy. It boasts an array of romantic monuments evocative of its long history and set in beautiful natural surroundings.

The site on the banks of the River Vltava was settled by a prehistoric people, followed by Slav tribes. In the 9C, a princely seat was built on the rocky promontory which became known as Hradčany. After the first timber bridge spanned the river in the 10C, the city developed apace. Malá Strana grew in the 13C and in mid-14C Emperor Charles IV gave Prague its present character as the city spread to the Nové Mèsto (New Town). Splendid palaces were built in a variety of styles in 16-18C. In the 19C the population expanded rapidly as industrial activity grew and by the turn of the 20C Prague was a prosperous city full of gaiety. The war years and communism brought many vicissitudes which came to an end with the Velvet Revolution of 1989. After the birth of the Czech Republic in 1992, Prague regained its proud status as capital.

WHICH DISTRICT TO CHOOSE

For a central location choose Staré Mèsto *Plan II* **G2** where there is a good selection of luxury and medium-priced hotels. In the delightful surroundings of Malá Strana *Plan II* **F2** romantic old houses have been converted into elegant establishments and if you prefer a quiet area there are some smart hotels in Hradčany *Plan II* **E1**. Expensive new hotels in the Jewish Quarter enjoy a view of the Vltava. Modern hotels are located near Wenceslas Square. If you choose to stay in the business hotels on the outskirts make sure you are near a metro station for convenience.

Staré Mèsto is the area for lively **cafés and restaurants** but prices are fairly high. There are excellent restaurants in Malá Strana which take full advanta-

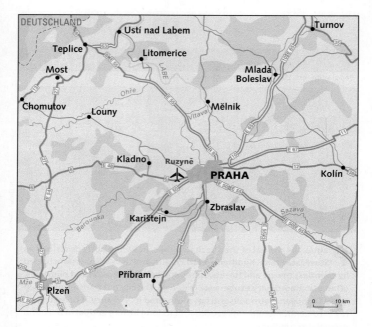

ge of the riverside location and views and with prices to match. Explore the backstreets north of Celetná *Plan II* **G2**, south of Karlova *Plan II* **G2** and south of Národní *Plan II* **G2** for moderately-priced eateries. Vinohrady *Plan II* **H2** is a residential area with cosy neighbourhood restaurants.

Prague's café culture is a great experience when going out **for a drink or for the evening**: *Obecní dům*, Náměstí Republicky 5 *Plan II* **H1**; *Café Europa*, Václavské náměsti 25 *Plan II* **H2**; *Slavia*, Smetanovo nábřeží 2 *Plan II* **G2**; *Café Milena*, Staroměstské náměsti 22 *Plan II* **G2**.

PRACTICAL INFORMATION

ARRIVAL – DEPARTURE

Ruzyně (Prague Airport) – 20 km (12.5 mi) west of the city. ℰ 220 113 314.

From the airport to the city centre – By **taxi**: taxis display the 'Airport Cars' sign. Fare about Kč650. FIX registered taxis: ℰ 02 2056 1788. By **shuttle bus**: operated by *Cedaz* Bus to Terminal Náměstí Republicky every 30min. Fare Kč90; or directly to your hotel (1-4 pas-

sengers). Information desk for both taxis and shuttle bus in Arrivals Hall. ℰ 220 114 296. Or by **bus** nos. 119 and 254 to Dejvická metro station. **Night bus** services operated by *DP Praha*, ℰ 220 115 404.

Main Stations – International trains stop at **Hlavní nádraží** *Plan II* **H2** but some stop at the suburban stations at **Holešovice** *Plan I* **C1** and **Smíchov** *Plan I* **B3**, both with metro stations.

TRANSPORT

◆ BUSES, TRAMS AND METRO

Public transport is convenient and inexpensive. Tourist passes are available for 1, 3, 7 and 15 days: Kč80 to Kč320. Passes are sold at ticket offices at some metro stations and from the Tourist Offices.

◆ TAXIS

Although regulations specify rates, it is not uncommon to be overcharged. Make sure you establish the fare before getting into the car. It is advisable to order a taxi by phone from a reputable taxi firm. *AAA Radiotaxi* ✆ 140 14; *Citytaxi* ✆ 257 257 257; *Credit Taxi* ✆ 235 300 300; *Dimotaxi* ✆ 800 513 306; *Halotaxi* ✆ 244 114 411.

USEFUL ADDRESSES

◆ TOURIST OFFICES

PIS Pražská Informační služba, entrance of Old Town Hall, Staroměstské Náměstí *Plan II* **G2**. ✆ 1244. There are other offices at Lucerna Passage Vodickova 36, main railway station (Hlavni Nadrazi Wilsonovo) and seasonally on the ground floor of the Mala Straná end of Charles Bridge. www.pis.cz

◆ POST OFFICES

Open Mon-Fri 8am-5pm. Main Post Office, Jindříšská 14 *Plan II* **H2**, Mon-Fri 7am-8pm. There is a 24-hr post office at Masaryk Station (Masarykovo nádraží) *Plan II* **H1**.

◆ BANKS/CURRENCY EXCHANGE

Banks are usually open Mon-Fri, 8am-5pm. There are exchange offices in convenient locations in Prague but their charges are fairly high; some in the old city are open 24hr a day. It is strongly advised against changing money other than at banks, exchange offices or authorised offices such as large hotels, tourist offices etc. Credit cards are becoming more widely accepted.

◆ PHARMACY

Several open 24hr. The most central is at Belgická 37. ✆ 2251 9731.

◆ EMERGENCY

Police ✆ **158** (National Police); ✆ **156** (City Police); Fire Brigade ✆ **150**; Ambulance ✆ **155**.

EXPLORING PRAGUE

It is possible to visit the main sights and museums in three days.

Museums and other sights are usually open from 9-10am to 5-6pm. Most close on Mondays and some may also close on public holidays, for long lunch hours and early in the afternoon.

VISITING

Boat trip on the River Vltava starting from Čech Bridge (Čechův most) *Plan II* **G1** and from the quayside at Rašínovo nábřeží *Plan II* **G3**.

Hradčany *Plan II* **E1** – The castle district with a vast square, palaces, churches and small streets. St Vitus Cathedral (**Katedrála sv. Vita**) – 14C-20C. Treasures of Bohemian art: silver reliquary, the Gothic St Wenceslas' Chapel, Crown Jewels. Royal Palace (**Královský Palác**) – 11C-16C. Residence of the Lords of Bohemia: Vladislav Chamber and equestrian staircase. The Church of St George (**Bazilika sv.Jiří**): Baroque west front and fine Romanesque sanctuary. The convent (**Jiřský klášter**) houses the National Gallery of Ancient Czech Art. Picturesque Gold Alley (**Zlatá Wlička**). Belvedere (**Královský Letohrádek**) –

views. **Schwarzenberg Palace** – frescoes, soaring gables, Museum of Army History. National Gallery **(Národní Galérie)** – collection of European art. **Loreta** church. Strahov Monastery **(Strahovský Klášter)** – Literature Museum: Philosophy Room and Theology Room.

Malá Strana *Plan II* **F2** – Picturesque lower town with medieval network of narrow streets and squares. 14C Charles Bridge **(Karlův Most)**. St Nicholas' Church **(Sv. Mikuláš)** with ornate interior. The charming **Nerudova** lined with Renaissance, Baroque and Rococo mansions. The splendid 17C Wallenstein Palace **(Valdštejnský Palác)**. Vrtba Palace and Baroque gardens **(Vrtbovsky Palác-Vrtbovská Zahrada)**.

Staré Město *Plan II* **G2** – A maze of streets and squares with the Town Hall **(Staroměstská radnice)** dominating Staroměstskě Náměstí (astronomical clock, Jan Hus monument, market). Panoramic views from the tower of the former town hall. Around Náměstí Jana Palacha stand the **Rudolfinium** concert hall and a museum of decorative arts **(Uměleckoprůmyslové muzeum – UPM)**. The imposing **Klementinum** houses the University of Prague. On the attractive Celetná Ulice stand the Cubist Black Madonna House **(Dúm U černé Matky boži)** and the 14C Powder Tower (Prašná Brána). The Gothic St Agnes Convent **(Anežský klášter)** – collection of medieval art.

Nové Město *Plan II* **G2** – Gold Cross on the tree-lined Wenceslas Square **(Václavské Náměstí)**. Jan Palach Memorial. Model of Prague in the City Museum **(Muzeum hlavního města Prahy)**.

Josefov *Plan II* **G1** – The oldest Jewish ghetto in Europe. Solemn, inspiring synagogues **(Staronová and Pinkasova Synagóga)**, Old Jewish Cemetery **(Starý židovský hřbitov)**. Pařížská Boulevard lined with Art Nouveau buildings.

Environs – Imperial Karlštejn Castle **(Hrad Karlštejn** – *30km/19mi SW*). Early-14C Konopiště Castle **(Zámek Konopiště** – *40km/25mi SW*).

SHOPPING

Shops are generallly open Mon-Fri, 8-9am to 6-7pm, Sat 8-9am to 6-8pm and Sun 10-6, possibly with a break at lunchtime.

Nearly all the shops of interest to visitors, including major department stores, are concentrated in the city centre, particularly in the pedestrian streets like **Celetná** *Plan II* **G2**, **Na příkopě** *Plan II* **G2**, **Melantrichova**, **Krapova** *Plan II* **G2** and **Nerudova** *Plan II* **F2**.

Craft shops – Bohemian garnets: *Granát*, Dlouhá 30. Glass and porcelain: *Skio Bohemia*, Na příkopě 17; *Dana Bohemia*, Staroměstskě náměstí 16; *Bohemia Crystal*, Celetná 5 and Parížská 12; *Celetná Crystal*, Celetná 15; *Moser*, Na příkopě 12 and shops along **Karlova** and side streets. Wooden toys and marionettes: *Pohádka*, Celetná 32; *Fantasia Kubénova*, Rytířská 19; *Česká lidová řemesia*, Melantichova 17.

Boutiques, perfumeries, fashion shops – Visit the shopping arcades (pasáž): *Darex obchodní dům*, Václavské náměstí 11; *Lucerna pasáž*, Štěpánská 61, Vodičkova 36; *Černá růže*, Na příkopě 12.

Antiques – There are antique shops all over the city. For quality goods, visit the auction house *Dorotheum*, Ovocný trh 2. For antiquarian books, maps and prints: *Antikvariát Galerie Můstek*, 28 října 13; *Antikvariát Karel Křenek*, Celetná 31.

Gourmet shops – For Czech specialities and wines: *Dům lahůdek*, Malé náměstí 3.
MARKETS – Open-air market in **Havelská** (Mon-Fri 7.30am-6pm, Sat-Sun 8.30pm-6pm) and by Národní třída metro station (daily 7.30am-7pm).
WHAT TO BUY – Embroidery, Bohemian garnets, Bohemian glass, ceramics, craft goods, food and wine.

ENTERTAINMENT

Venues for musical events include the great concert halls, gardens, churches and many other places. Consult *Cultural Events* published by the Prague Tourist Office and the weekly *The Prague Post* for listings of events.

Státní Opera Praha *Plan II* **H2**: State Opera – opera and ballet.

Národní divadlo *Plan II* **G2**: National Theatre – drama, opera and ballet.

Stavovské divadlo *Plan II* **G2**: Drama, opera and ballet.

Hudební divadlo v Karlíně *Plan 1* **C1**: Operettas, musicals.

Rudolfinum *Plan II* **G1** and **Obecní dům** *Plan II* **H1**: Classical music.

Klub Lávka *Plan II* **G2**: Music by Mozart in period costume.

Divadlo v Celetné *Plan II* **G2**: Black Theatre performances.

National Marionette Theatre *Plan II* **G2**: Puppet shows for adults and children.

NIGHTLIFE

There are great pubs and bars with live music and entertainment in Staré Město, along the riverside and on both sides of Charles Bridge such as *Pivnice U Sv. Tomáše*, Letenská 12; *U Fleků*, Křemencová 9/11; *U Medvicků*, Na Perštýně 7; *U kalicha*, Na bojišti 12; *U zlatého tygra*, Husova 17. Jazz fans will enjoy *Agharta Jazz Centre*, Zelená 16; *Batalion Music Club*, 28 října 3; *Lávka Club*, Novotného lávka 1; *Lucerna Music Bar*, Vodickova 3-6; *Metropolitan Jazz Club*, Jungmannova 14. You should be aware that Prague has become very popular with stag and hen parties which can become quite boisterous as the night wears on.

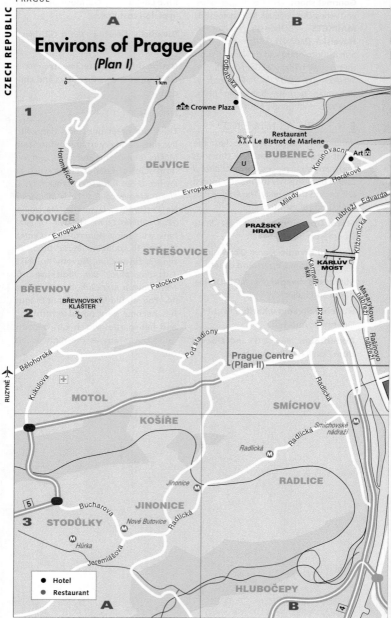

Environs of Prague
(Plan I)

CZECH REPUBLIC

0 ___ 1 km

A   **B**

1

Horoměřická

Podbabská

🏨 Crowne Plaza

Restaurant
🍴 Le Bistrot de Marlene

DEJVICE

BUBENEČ

Korunovační

Art 🏛

U

Evropská

Milady

Horákové

Edvarda

náb. Edvarda

VOKOVICE

Evropská

STŘEŠOVICE

**PRAŽSKÝ
HRAD**

Křižovnická

Masarykovo
nábřeží

2

BŘEVNOV

Patočkova

KARLŮV
MOST

Karmelit-
ská

Újezd

**BŘEVNOVSKÝ
KLÁŠTER**

Pod stadiony

Bělohorská

Prague Centre
(Plan II)

Rašínovo
nábřeží

RUZYNĚ ✈

Kukulova

MOTOL

KOŠÍŘE

SMÍCHOV

Radlická

Radlická Ⓜ

Smíchovské
nádraží Ⓜ

Radlická

RADLICE

Jinonice Ⓜ

5

Bucharova

JINONICE

Nové Butovice Ⓜ

Radlická

3   **STODŮLKY**

Hůrka Ⓜ

Jeremiášova

● Hotel
● Restaurant

A   **HLUBOČEPY**   **B**

4

CZECH REPUBLIC

C LIBEŇ **D**

TRÓJA

Kolbenova
Vysočanská

VLTAVA

Sokolovská VYSOČANY

Nádraží
Holešovice

Českomoravská

Podĕbrad-
ská

HOLEŠOVICE

Palmovka

Českomoravská

1

Libeňsky
most

Invalidovna

Sokolovská

Spojovací

Veletržní

Vltavská

VELETRŽNÍ
PALÁC

KARLÍN

Beneše

Křižíkova

Koněvova

Českobrodská

Křižíkova

Jana Želivského

Wilsonova

ARMÁDNÍ
MUZEUM

MASARYKOVO
NÁDRAŽÍ

ŽIŽKOV

SV. ROCHA

OLŠANSKÉ
HRBITOVY

Černokostelecká

HLAVNÍ
NÁDRAŽÍ
WILSONOVO

Jiřího z
Poděbrad

Flora

Želivského

STRAŠNICE

V olšinách

Aromi

Slezská

Strašnická

Žitná

Náměstí
Miru

Korunní

2

Ječná

Francouzská

VRŠOVICE

Průběžna

Vršovická

VYŠEHRAD

E 48- E55- E65

Vyšehrad

29

VLTAVA

NUSLE

ZÁBĚHLICE

Pražského
povstání

MICHLE

Spořilovská

Pankrác

Modřanská

PODOLÍ

Na
Budějovická

E50- E55- E65

Jeremenkova

Kačerov

1

3

strží

Roztyly

Ryšavého

Chodov

29

E48- E50

KRČ

Vídeňská

C **D**

CZECH REPUBLIC

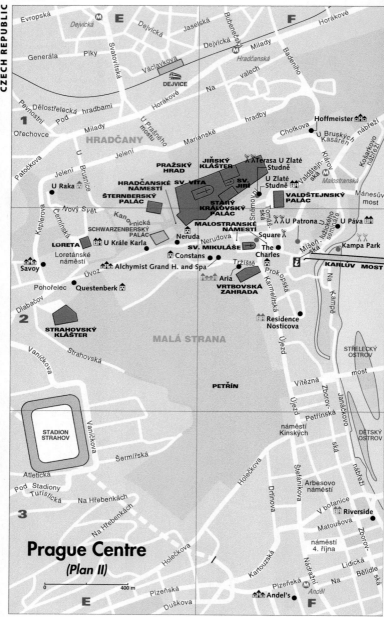

Prague Centre
(Plan II)

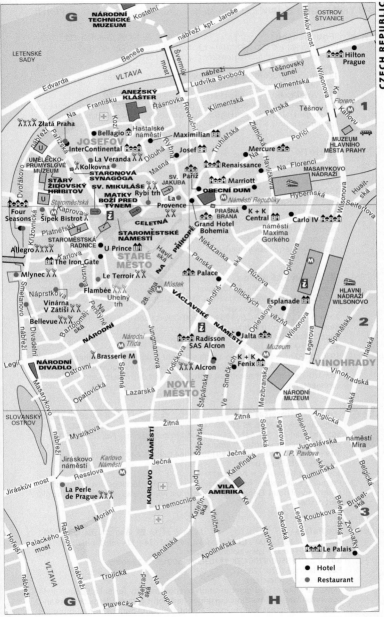

ON THE RIGHT BANK (Old Town, Staroměstské Námesti)   *Plan II*

Four Seasons   Fá ⋒ 🖃 & ⏱ ⅙ 🖭 ⏏80 VISA ❶ 🅰 ①

Veleslavínova 1098/2a ⊠ 110 00 – ⓜ Staroměstská – 𝒞 221 427 0 00
– prg.reservations@fourseasons.com – Fax 221 426 0 00
– www.fourseasons.com/prague   **G2**
141 rm ⌑ – ♦7000/9900 CZK ♦♦7900/11400 CZK – 20 suites
Rest see **Allegro** below
♦ Grand Luxury ♦ Modern ♦
Four houses - modern, neo-Classical, Baroque and neo-Renaissance - make up
this elegant riverside hotel. High standard of service. Basement spa. Luxuriously
appointed rooms.

Carlo IV   Fá ⋒ 🖃 & ⏱ ⅙rm 🖭 ⏏220 ⇐ VISA ❶ 🅰 ①

Senovážné Nám. 13 ⊠ 110 00 – ⓜ Náměsti Republiky – 𝒞 224 593 1 11
– reservation@carloiv.boscolo.com – Fax 224 593 0 00
– www.boscolohotels.com   **H2**
150 rm – ♦9100 CZK ♦♦22800 CZK, ⌑ 724 CZK – 2 suites
Rest Box Block a la carte 1320/2210 CZK
♦ Grand Luxury ♦ Stylish ♦
Unabashed luxury personified: very impressive former bank with stunning
marble lobby, ornate ceiling and pillars, excellent health centre and rooms
exuding luxurious comforts. A stylish restaurant serving modern dishes with a
strong Mediterranean influence.

Radisson SAS Alcron   ⇞ Fá ⋒ 🖃 & ⏱ ⅙rm 🍽 🖭 📞

Štěpánská 40 ⊠ 110 00 – ⓜ Muzeum   ⏏150 ⇐ VISA ❶ 🅰
– 𝒞 222 820 0 00 – sales.prague@radissonsas.com – Fax 222 820 1 00
– www.prague.radissonsas.com   **H2**
205 rm – ♦5100/7000 CZK ♦♦6400/8200 CZK, ⌑ 666 CZK – 6 suites
Rest see also **Alcron** below
Rest La Rotonde a la carte 890/1480 CZK
♦ Luxury ♦ Business ♦ Modern ♦
1930s building refurbished to a high standard. Original art deco theme carried
through to include the spacious, comfortable, well-equipped bedrooms.
Immaculately laid out restaurant with a stylish art deco theme and an outdoor
summer terrace.

InterContinental   ⇐ Fá ⋒ 🖃 & ⏱ ⅙ 🖭 📞 ⏏500

Nám. Curieových 43-45 ⊠ 110 00 – ⓜ   ⇐ VISA ❶ 🅰 ①
Staroměstská – 𝒞 296 631 1 11 – prague@interconti.com – Fax 226 631 2 16
– www.intercontinental.com/prague   **G1**
349 rm – ♦8500/10650 CZK ♦♦9130/11264 CZK, ⌑ 640 CZK – 23 suites
Rest see Zlatá Praha below
♦ Grand Luxury ♦ Modern ♦
Prague's first luxury hotel provides all of the facilities expected of an
international hotel. Elegant bedrooms, most enjoy views of the river or the old
part of the city.

Le Palais   ⋒ Fá ⋒ & ⏱ ⅙ 🖭 ⏏40 ⇐ VISA ❶ 🅰 ①

U Zvonarki 1 ⊠ 120 00 – ⓜ I.P. Pavlova – 𝒞 234 634 1 11 – info@palaishotel.cz
– Fax 234 634 6 35 – www.palaishotel.cz   **H3**
60 rm ⌑ – ♦8500/9700 CZK ♦♦10300/11500 CZK – 12 suites
Rest a la carte 1070/1280 CZK
♦ Luxury ♦ Modern ♦
Elevated, affluent and quiet location overlooking city for Belle Epoque style
converted late 19C mansion. Luxurious bedrooms with modern comforts and
equipment. Original cooking in restaurant; delightful outlook from sumptuous
terrace.

CZECH REPUBLIC

Marriott 🕭 🎵 🖻 ♿ 🅰 📶rm 🖭 📞 🔧700 🚗 VISA 🐵 AE

V Celnici 8 110 00 – 🕅 *Náměsti Republiky – 𝒞 222 888 8 88*
– prague.marriott@marriotthotels.com – Fax 222 888 8 23
– www.marriott.com **H1**
258 rm – 👤6100/7600 CZK 👥👥6100/7600 CZK, ☲ 600 CZK – 35 suites
Rest a la carte 500/1000 CZK
♦ Business ♦ Classic ♦
International hotel, opened in 1999. First-class conference and leisure facilities. Committed service and modern, smart bedrooms with all the latest facilities. Brasserie offers a wide selection of cuisine from American, French to traditional Czech.

Hilton Prague ⇐ 🕭 🕙 🕭 🎵 🖻 ♿ 🅰 📶rm 🖭 🔧1350 🚗 🅿

Pobřežni 1 ⊠ 186 00 – 🕅 *Florenc – 𝒞 222 841 1 11*
– sales.prague@hilton.com – Fax 224 842 3 78 – www.prague.hilton.com
761 rm – 👤4900/9300 CZK 👥👥4900/9300 CZK, ☲ 640 CZK – 27 suites **H1**
Rest *Czech House Rotisserie* (dinner only) a la carte 300/1420 CZK
Rest *Café Bistro* a la carte 830/1560 CZK
♦ Business ♦ Modern ♦
Expansive modern glass edifice by the river. Spectacular atrium befitting largest hotel in the country. Comprehensive facilities; well-equipped rooms with varied vistas. Relaxed rotisserie with wide range of global and Czech dishes. Informal Café Bistro.

Renaissance 🕭 🎵 🖻 ♿ 🅰 📶rm 🖭 📞 🔧240 🚗 VISA 🐵 AE 🛈

V Celnici 7 ⊠ 111 21 – 🕅 *Náměsti Republiky – 𝒞 221 822 1 00*
– renaissance.prague@renaissancehotels.com – Fax 221 822 2 00
– www.renaissancehotels.com **H1**
307 rm – 👤4900/6100 CZK 👥👥4900/6100 CZK, ☲ 600 CZK – 3 suites
Rest *Seven* a la carte 500/1000 CZK
Rest *U Korbele* a la carte 500/1000 CZK
♦ Business ♦ Modern ♦
World brand hotel in the heart of the City. Geared to the modern corporate traveller; well-equipped bedrooms, particularly those on the 'Renaissance Club' floor. Seven specialises in grills and seafood. Czech specialities in casual, relaxing U Korbele.

Palace 🎵 ♿ 🅰 📶rm 📞 🔧150 VISA 🐵 AE 🛈

Panská 12 ⊠ 111 21 – 🕅 *Můstek – 𝒞 224 093 1 11 – info@palacehotel.cz*
– Fax 224 221 2 40 – www.palacehotel.com **H2**
121 rm ☲ – 👤9900 CZK 👥👥10500 CZK – 3 suites
Rest *Gourmet Club* (dinner only) a la carte 1260/1900 CZK
♦ Traditional ♦ Classic ♦
Original Viennese art nouveau style façade dating back to 1906. Elegant interior; bedrooms combine period furniture with modern facilities and services. Brasserie and bar with all-day menu. Classic club ambience and fine dining off broad global carte.

Paříž 🕭 🎵 🅰 📶rm 🖭 🔧30 VISA 🐵 AE 🛈

U obecniho domu 1 ⊠ 110 00 – 🕅 *Náměsti Republiky – 𝒞 222 195 1 95*
– booking@hotel-pariz.cz – Fax 224 225 4 75 – www.hotel-pariz.cz **H1**
80 rm – 👤9700 CZK 👥👥15000 CZK, ☲ 650 CZK – 6 suites
Rest *Sarah Bernhardt* a la carte 980/1650 CZK
♦ Traditional ♦ Classic ♦
Culturally and historically, a landmark famed for its neo-Gothic, art nouveau architecture. Original staircase with preserved window panels. Sound-proofed rooms. Fine example of art nouveau in Sarah Bernhardt restaurant.

Jalta 🕭 ♿ 🅰 📶rm 🖭 🔧150 VISA 🐵 AE 🛈

Václavské Nám. 45 ⊠ 110 00 – 🕅 *Muzeum – 𝒞 222 822 1 11 – booking@*
hoteljalta.com – Fax 222 822 8 33 – www.hoteljalta.com **H2**
89 rm ☲ – 👤4600 CZK 👥👥7000 CZK – 5 suites
Rest *Hot* a la carte 800/1000 CZK
♦ Traditional ♦ Classic ♦
Classic 1950s façade overlooking Wenceslas Square. Bedrooms recently modernised and soundproofed: they are now spacious, well equipped with a pleasant contemporary style. Stylish modern dining room with Asian/Mediterranean menus.

CZECH REPUBLIC

Grand Hotel Bohemia
       💧 AC ↻rm 🖥 🛗140 VISA ⓶ AE ①

Králodvorská 4 ☒ 110 00 – **Ⓜ** *Náměstí Republiky – ✆ 234 608 1 11*
– office@grandhotelbohemia.cz – Fax 222 329 5 45
– www.grandhotelbohemia.cz   **H1**
78 rm – 🛏5200 CZK 🛏🛏5800 CZK, 🍽 430 CZK
Rest a la carte 580/1010 CZK
◆ Traditional ◆ Classic ◆
Classic 1920's hotel, in an ideal location for tourists, with a splendid neo-Baroque ballroom. Comfortable bedrooms are generously proportioned and service professional. Large, classic restaurant with a menu of Czech/international dishes.

Mercure
          🏨 💧 AC ↻rm 🖥 📞 VISA ⓶ AE ①

Na Poříčí 7 ☒ 110 00 – **Ⓜ** *Náměsti Republiky – ✆ 221 800 8 00*
– h3440@accor-hotels.com – Fax 221 800 8 01
– www.accorhotels.com   **H1**
173 rm – 🛏4300/6000 CZK 🛏🛏4700/6400 CZK, 🍽 430 CZK – 1 suite
Rest *Felice* a la carte 660/1080 CZK
◆ Business ◆ Functional ◆
Modern hotel behind ornate 19C façade: many original features remain. Kafka worked here for seven years when insurance offices. Ask for more spacious deluxe room. Named after one of Kafka's lovers: modern Parisian brasserie; pleasant terrace.

Josef
without rest   💧 AC ↻ 🖥 🛗70 🍽 VISA ⓶ AE ①

Rybná 20 ☒ 110 00 – **Ⓜ** *Náměsti Republiky – ✆ 221 700 1 11*
– reservation@hoteljosef.com – Fax 221 700 9 99
– www.hoteljosef.com   **G1**
110 rm 🍽 – 🛏6200 CZK 🛏🛏9000 CZK
◆ Townhouse ◆ Stylish ◆
Stylish boutique hotel with light glass lobby, bar and breakfast room. Design-led bedrooms; deluxe rooms have ultra modern glass bathrooms.

Maximilian
without rest   💧 AC ↻ 🖥 🛗30 🍽 VISA ⓶ AE ①

Haštalská 14 ☒ 110 00 – **Ⓜ** *Náměsti Republiky – ✆ 225 303 1 11*
– reservations@maximilianhotel.com – Fax 225 303 1 21
– www.maximilianhotel.com   **G1**
70 rm 🍽 – 🛏5700 CZK 🛏🛏7500 CZK – 1 suite
◆ Business ◆ Classic ◆
Converted apartment block in quiet area near St Agnes Convent. Designer boutique style prevails. Glass and steel breakfast room. Basement Thai massage spa. Contemporary rooms.

K + K Central
              🛗 🎵 💧 AC ↻rm 🖥 🛗60 🍽 VISA ⓶ AE ①

Hybernská 10 ☒ 110 00 – **Ⓜ** *Náměsti Republiky – ✆ 225 022 0 00*
– hotel.central@kkhotels.cz – Fax 225 022 9 99 – www.kkhotels.com   **H2**
126 rm 🍽 – 🛏8000 CZK 🛏🛏8300 CZK – 1 suite
Rest (in bar) a la carte 440/1110 CZK
◆ Business ◆ Modern ◆
Beautifully restored hotel; combination of elegant art nouveau and ultra modern décor. Glass and steel breakfast gallery in old theatre. Modish rooms. Light dishes in lounge.

U Prince
            ≪ 🏨 AC ↻rm 🖥 VISA ⓶ AE ①

Staroměstské Nám. 29 ☒ 110 00 – **Ⓜ** *Staroměstská – ✆ 224 213 8 07*
– reserve@hoteluprince.cz – Fax 224 213 8 07
– www.hoteluprince.cz   **G2**
23 rm 🍽 – 🛏4300/6300 CZK 🛏🛏4600/6600 CZK – 1 suite
Rest a la carte 397/937 CZK
◆ Traditional ◆ Classic ◆
Restored 17C town house on main square with atmospheric rooms blending with mod cons and antique furnishings. Roof terrace with marvellous city views. Choose the half-panelled bar-restaurant for International cooking or the brick vaulted cellars for seafood.

CZECH REPUBLIC

The Iron Gate

Michalská 19 ⊠ 110 00 – **Ⓜ** *Staroměstská – ℰ 225 777 7 77*
– hotel@irongate.cz – Fax 225 777 7 78 – www.irongate.cz   **G2**
13 rm – ⃗7000/9900 CZK ⃗⃗7000/9900 CZK – **30 suites**, 11100/14250
⌷ 375 CZK
Rest *Zelezna Brata* (live gypsy music) (dinner only) a la carte
700/1300 CZK
♦ Traditional ♦ Classic ♦
Hidden away in Old Town's cobbled street maze. 14C origins; attractive central courtyard. Large rooms with antique furniture or painted beams; some duplex suites. Zelezna Brata in basement for Czech cuisine; gypsy music.

K + K Fenix

Ve Smečkách 30 ⊠ 110 00 – **Ⓜ** *Muzeum – ℰ 225 012 0 00*
– hotel.fenix@kkhotels.cz – Fax 222 212 1 41
– www.kkhotels.com   **H2**
128 rm ⌷ – ⃗8100 CZK ⃗⃗8700 CZK
Rest (in bar) a la carte 440/1110 CZK
♦ Business ♦ Modern ♦
Located off Wenceslas Square; up to date interior behind a classic façade. Bedrooms vary in size and shape but all are smart, clean and comfortable. Light dishes in lounge.

Esplanade

Washingtonova 1600-19 ⊠ 110 00 – **Ⓜ** *Muzeum – ℰ 224 501 1 11*
– esplanade@esplanade.cz – Fax 224 229 3 06
– www.esplanade.cz   **H2**
74 rm – ⃗2900/3700 CZK ⃗⃗4600/7500 CZK, ⌷ 430 CZK
Rest 630 CZK and a la carte 380/980 CZK
♦ Traditional ♦ Classic ♦
Charming and atmospheric; this art nouveau building is something of an architectural gem. Original features abound; bedrooms enjoy style and a timeless elegance. Menu of traditional Czech and French specialities offered in friendly surroundings.

Bellagio

U Milosrdných 2 ⊠ 110 00 – **Ⓜ** *Staroměstská – ℰ 221 778 9 99*
– info@bellagiohotel.cz – Fax 221 778 9 00
– www.bellagiohotel.cz   **G1**
45 rm ⌷ – ⃗4600/6000 CZK ⃗⃗5200/6700 CZK – 1 suite
Rest *Isabella* (dinner only) a la carte 695/1275 CZK
♦ Business ♦ Stylish ♦
Quiet, converted apartment block near the river. Basement vaulted bar/ breakfast room. Airy, attractive bedrooms, well equipped in warm colours. Impressive bathrooms.

XXXX Allegro – at Four Seasons H.

Veleslavínova 1098/2a ⊠ 110 00 – **Ⓜ** *Staroměstská*
– ℰ 221 426 8 80 – Fax 221 426 0 00
– www.fourseasons.com/prague   **G2**
Rest 1200 CZK (lunch) and a la carte 1640/2400 CZK
♦ Italian ♦ Formal ♦
Fine dining restaurant with lovely wood-panelled terrace and modern Czech art on the walls. Accomplished Italian cooking with originality and flair: truffle menu in season.

XXXX Zlatá Praha – at InterContinental H.

≤ Prague,
Nám. Curieových 43-45 ⊠ 110 00
– **Ⓜ** *Staroměstská – ℰ 296 631 1 11 – prague@interconti.com*
– Fax 224 811 2 16 – www.zlatapraharestaurant.cz   **G1**
Rest a la carte 1290/1950 CZK
♦ Modern ♦ Formal ♦
Stunning views of the city skyline provide a backdrop to this elegant room. Modern gourmet cooking with fine wines on an extensive menu. Detailed service; piano accompaniment.

CZECH REPUBLIC

XXX **Alcron** – at Radisson SAS Alcron H.   AC P VISA CO AE O
Štěpánská 40 ⊠ 110 00 – Ⓜ Muzeum – ℰ 222 820 0 38
– sales.prague@radissonsas.com – Fax 222 820 1 00
– www.prague.radissonsas.com
closed Sunday   **H2**
Rest (booking essential) (dinner only) a la carte 1790/1830 CZK
♦ Seafood ♦ Design ♦
An Art Deco mural after de Lempicka dominates this intimate, semi-circular restaurant. Creative and classic seafood served by friendly, professional staff.

XXX **Flambée**   AC VISA CO AE O
Husova 5 ⊠ 110 00 – Ⓜ Můstek – ℰ 224 248 5 12 – flambee@flambee.cz
– Fax 224 248 5 13 – www.flambee.cz   **G2**
Rest 490 CZK (lunch) and a la carte 1830/2300 CZK
Rest *Cafe Bistro 'F'* a la carte 363/813 CZK
♦ Traditional ♦ Formal ♦
Elegant fine dining in established cellar restaurant dating from 11C. Formal yet friendly service and well-judged classics - fine selection of clarets. Café Bistro F - above the restaurant - is a little modern eatery serving simpler international dishes.

XXX **Bellevue**   ⇐ 斎 AC VISA CO AE
Smetanovo Nábřeží 18 ⊠ 110 00 – Ⓜ Staroměstská
– ℰ 222 221 4 43 – bellevue@zatisigroup.cz – Fax 222 220 4 53
– www.zatisigroup.cz
closed 24 December   **G2**
Rest 1490 CZK and a la carte 1230/1970 CZK
♦ Traditional ♦ Formal ♦
Elegant 19C building, affording views of river and royal palace. Classic style and surroundings; serious and formal dining writ large as the nightly piano plays.

XXX **La Perle de Prague**   ⇐ Prague, 斎 AC ⇔25 VISA CO AE O
Dancing House (7 th floor), Rašínovo Nábřeží 80 ⊠ 120 00
– Ⓜ Karlovo Náměstí – ℰ 221 984 1 60 – info@laperle.cz – Fax 221 984 1 79
– www.laperle.cz
closed 24-26 December, Monday lunch and Sunday   **G3**
Rest 490 CZK/900 CZK and a la carte 1200/2000 CZK
♦ French ♦ Fashionable ♦
Eye-catching riverside building: seventh floor restaurant has simply stunning views of city, river and castle. Comfortable, strikingly modern décor. French-inspired menu.

XX **Le Terroir**   斎 AC VISA CO AE O
😊 *Vejvodova 1 ⊠ 110 00 – Ⓜ Můstek – ℰ 602 889 1 18 – rezervace@leterroir.cz*
– www.leterroir.cz   **G2**
Rest a la carte 950/1140 CZK 🍷
♦ Innovative ♦ Rustic ♦
Cobbled courtyard and steps descending past wine store to atmospheric vaulted 10C cellar. Personally run; superb wine list. Good value, accomplished, Pan-European cooking.

XX **La Veranda**   AC VISA CO AE O
Elišky Krásnohorské 2/10 ⊠ 110 00 – Ⓜ Staroměstská – ℰ 224 814 7 33
– office@laveranda.cz – Fax 224 814 5 96 – www.laveranda.cz   **G1**
Rest a la carte 825/1380 CZK
♦ Innovative ♦ Design ♦
Stylish modern restaurant in the old Jewish district. Modern menu in keeping with the décor, fusing East and West to produce light dishes with interesting flavours.

CZECH REPUBLIC

XX **Vinárna V Zátiši**   AC 4⁄ VISA ◯◯ AE

Liliová 1, Betlémské Nám. ⊠ *110 00 –* ◯ *Můstek –* ℰ *222 221 1 55*
– vzatisi@zatisigroup.cz – Fax 222 220 6 29 – www.zatisigroup.cz
closed 24 December, lunch 31 December and lunch 1 January   **G2**
Rest (booking essential at dinner) a la carte 895/1590 CZK
♦ Modern ♦ Cosy ♦
Well run, slick and dependable restaurant offering modern, well-priced cuisine within a range of four rooms which are intimate in places, and more stylish in others.

XX **Mlynec**   ⟵ Charles Bridge, 🍴 VISA ◯◯ AE ◯

Novotného Lávka 9 ⊠ *110 00 –* ◯ *Staroměstská –* ℰ *221 082 2 08*
– mlynec@zatisigroup.cz – Fax 221 082 3 91 – www.zatisigroup.cz
closed 24 December   **G2**
Rest a la carte 812/1490 CZK
♦ Modern ♦ Brasserie ♦
Spacious and contemporary; popular with tourists because of setting. Modern dishes combined with Czech classics. Terrace views of Charles Bridge on fine summer evenings.

XX **Rybí trh**   🍴 AC 🍴 VISA ◯◯ AE ◯

Tânskâ dvůr 5 ⊠ *110 00 –* ◯ *Námĕsti Republiky –* ℰ *224 895 4 47*
– info@rybitrh.cz – Fax 224 895 4 49 – www.rybitrh.cz   **G1**
Rest 590 CZK (lunch) and a la carte 580/1570 CZK
♦ Seafood ♦ Friendly ♦
Modern restaurant which lives up to its name - Fish Market - with fresh seafood on crushed ice before open plan kitchen; fish tanks, adjacent wine shop and tasting cellar.

XX **La Provence**   AC 4⁄ VISA ◯◯ AE ◯

Štupartská 9 ⊠ *110 00 Praha –* ◯ *Námĕsti Republiky –* ℰ *224 816 6 92*
– kontakt@laprovence.com – Fax 224 819 5 70 – www.kampagroup.com
Rest 600 CZK (lunch) and a la carte 625/1560 CZK   **G1**
♦ French ♦ Brasserie ♦
Tucked down a central side street. Classic French brasserie with real 1920s feel: etched mirrors, tile mosaics, Gallic scenes. Menus, too, never stray from classics of France.

X **Šípek Bistrot**   AC 4⁄ VISA ◯◯ AE ◯

Valentinská 9/57 ⊠ *110 00 –* ◯ *Staroměstská –* ℰ *775 155 5 05*
– bistrot@sipekbistrot.com – Fax 222 323 9 48 – www.sipekbistrot.com
closed 24 December and Sunday   **G2**
Rest a la carte 470/1220 CZK
♦ Contemporary ♦ Design ♦
Bland façade but an interior full of glass, original lighting structures, light and shade, boldness and subtlety. Modish cooking with stimulating, if unusual, combinations.

X **Brasserie M**   🍴 AC VISA ◯◯ AE ◯
☺

Vladislavova 17 ⊠ *110 00 –* ◯ *Národni Třída –* ℰ *224 054 0 70*
– info@brasseriem.cz – Fax 224 054 4 40 – www.brasseriem.cz
closed dinner 24 December   **G2**
Rest 199 CZK/665 CZK and a la carte 375/1080 CZK
♦ French ♦ Bistro ♦
Central, but away from touristy main streets. Big, high ceilinged room with dominant open-plan kitchen and French accent to décor. Well-priced Gallic favourites on menu, too.

X **Kolkovna**   🍴 AC 4⁄ VISA ◯◯ AE ◯

V Kolkovně 8 ⊠ *110 00 –* ◯ *Staroměstská –* ℰ *224 819 7 01*
– info@kolkovnagroup.com – Fax 224 819 7 00 – www.kolkovna.cz   **G1**
Rest a la carte 315/645 CZK
♦ Traditional ♦ Inn ♦
Atmospheric Czech Pilsner Urquell bar/restaurant: old pictures, tools and advertisements line green walls under vaulted ceilings. Huge traditional dishes and excellent beers.

CZECH REPUBLIC

ON THE LEFT BANK *(Castel District, Lesser town)* Plan II

Aria   🖼 ⅃⅍ ⅖ 🅰 ⅍rm ⅏ ⅍⅄30 🅿 🆅🆂🅰 ⅏ ⅍ ⅈ

Trziste 9 ⅏ 118 00 – ⓜ Malostranská – 𝒞 225 334 1 11 – stat@aria.cz
– Fax 225 334 1 31 – www.aria.cz   **F2**
43 rm ⌑ – ♦5900/10300 CZK ♦♦5900/10300 CZK – 9 suites
Rest *Coda* a la carte 975/1345 CZK
♦ Luxury ♦ Design ♦
Stylishly overlooking lovely castle gardens; boasts strong music orientation,
including library and rooms themed individually to different music genres.
Personable service. Choose from the stylish menu in intimate Coda or eat on the
stunning roof top terrace.

Alchymist Grand H. and Spa   🖼 ⅏ ⅃⅍ ⅍ ⅖ 🅰 ⅍ 🖾 ⅍⅄30

Tržiště 19 ⅏ 118 00 – ⓜ Malostranská   ⅏ 🆅🆂🅰 ⅏ ⅍ ⅈ
– 𝒞 257 286 0 11 – info@alchymisthotel.com – Fax 257 286 0 17
– www.alchymisthotel.com   **F2**
37 rm ⌑ – ♦7000/8100 CZK ♦♦7000/8100 CZK – 9 suites
Rest *Alchymist Aquarius* 750 CZK (lunch) and a la carte 900/1600 CZK
♦ Luxury ♦ Classic ♦
Four 15C Renaissance and Baroque houses on UNESCO street. Sympathetically
restored and offering sumptuous style. Beautiful spa; enchanting rooms with
16C-19C artefacts. Formal restaurant - and café - opening into a courtyard.

Savoy   ⅃⅍ ⅍ ⅖ 🅰 ⅍rm 🖾 ⅍⅄30 ⅏ 🆅🆂🅰 ⅏ ⅍ ⅈ

Keplerova 6 ⅏ 118 00 – 𝒞 224 302 4 30 – info@hotel-savoy.cz
– Fax 224 302 1 28 – www.hotel-savoy.cz   **E2**
60 rm ⌑ – ♦10500 CZK ♦♦10500 CZK – 1 suite
Rest *Hradčany* 725 CZK (lunch) and a la carte 1020/1850 CZK
♦ Luxury ♦ Classic ♦
Timeless charm; popular with statesmen. Strength lies in its classically styled
bedrooms, which are spacious, tasteful, well equipped and benefit from high
levels of service. Bright formal dining room with glass ceiling and distant city view.

Andel's   ⅃⅍ ⅍ ⅖ 🅰 ⅍rm 🖾 ⅍⅄350 ⅏ 🆅🆂🅰 ⅏ ⅍ ⅈ

Stroupeznického 21 ⅏ 150 00 – ⓜ Anděl – 𝒞 296 889 6 88
– info@andelshotel.com – Fax 296 889 9 99 – www.andelshotel.com   **F3**
257 rm ⌑ – ♦6800 CZK ♦♦7400 CZK – 33 suites
Rest *Oscar's* a la carte 550/925 CZK – **Rest *Nagoya*,** 𝒞 251 511 7 24 (closed
Sunday) (dinner only) a la carte approx. 900 CZK
♦ Business ♦ Modern ♦
Stylish modern hotel with distinctively minimalist appeal; luxurious apartments
in adjacent block. Conference and fitness centres. Well-equipped rooms with all
mod cons. Informal dining in Oscar's brasserie; simple menu. Nagoya offers
traditional Japanese dishes.

Hoffmeister   🖼 ⅖ 🅰 ⅍rm 🖾 ⅍⅄30 ⅏ 🆅🆂🅰 ⅏ ⅍ ⅈ

Pod Bruskou 7 ⅏ 118 00 – ⓜ Malostranská – 𝒞 251 017 1 11
– hotel@hoffmeister.cz – Fax 251 017 1 20 – www.hoffmeister.cz   **F1**
42 rm ⌑ – ♦4760/7280 CZK ♦♦5600/8400 CZK – 5 suites
Rest *Ada* a la carte 1000/1900 CZK
♦ Traditional ♦ Classic ♦
Unprepossessing façade, but inside full of artworks by Adolf Hoffmeister: son
owns hotel. Eclectic range of bedrooms; plus 15C steam room.
Elegant restaurant with original Adolf Hoffmeister cartoons. Attentive service;
French and Italian influenced cooking.

Riverside without rest   ⅏ 🅰 ⅍ ⅏ 🖾 🆅🆂🅰 ⅏ ⅍ ⅈ

Janáčkovo Nábřeži 15 ⅏ 150 00 – ⓜ Anděl – 𝒞 225 994 6 11
– info@riversideprague.com – Fax 225 994 6 15 – www.riversideprague.com
42 rm ⌑ – ♦5500/8800 CZK ♦♦10700/12200 CZK – 3 suites   **F3**
♦ Business ♦ Modern ♦
An early 20C riverside façade conceals relaxing modern hotel with castle view.
Efficient service. Very well appointed bedrooms with luxurious bathrooms;
many with views.

Residence Nosticova 🕭   🖼 🕻 🅿 VISA 🐵 AE ①

Nosticova 1, Malá Strana ✉ *118 00 –* Ⓜ *Malostranská –* ℰ *257 312 5 13*
– info@nosticova.com – Fax 257 312 5 17
– www.nosticova.com   **F2**
6 rm – **†**6200/7100 CZK **††**6200/7100 CZK – **7 suites**, ☲ 350 CZK
Rest Alchymist, ℰ *257 312 5 18 (closed Sunday)* 450 CZK (lunch) and a la carte
940/1475 CZK
♦ Townhouse ♦ Classic ♦
Tastefully refurbished 17C town house in a quiet, cobbled side street. Stylish
suites - all with their own kitchen - combine modern and antique furnishings and
works of art.

U Zlaté Studně 🕭   ≼ 🖽 🖼 🕻 VISA 🐵 AE ①

U Zlaté Studně 166/4 ✉ *118 00 –* Ⓜ *Malostranská –* ℰ *257 011 2 13*
– hotel@zlatastudna.cz – Fax 257 533 3 20
– www.zlatastudna.cz   **F1**
17 rm ☲ – **†**4400/6100 CZK **††**5000/6900 CZK – 3 suites
Rest see **Terasa U Zlaté Studně** below
♦ Historic ♦ Classic ♦
16C Renaissance building in quiet spot between the castle and Ladeburg
Gardens. Inviting bedrooms - most boasting city views - are richly furnished but
uncluttered.

U Krále Karla   🖼 VISA 🐵 AE ①

Úvoz 4 ✉ *118 00 –* ℰ *257 531 2 11 – ukrale@iol.cz – Fax 257 533 5 91*
– www.romantichotels.cz   **E2**
19 rm ☲ – **†**3400/5000 CZK **††**4900/6900 CZK
Rest a la carte 630/850 CZK
♦ Historic ♦ Classic ♦
Below the castle: rebuilt in 1639 into a Baroque house; the style of furniture
endures. Bags of character: every bedroom features stained glass and a
stencilled wood ceiling. Romantic dining room with murals and ambience of Old
Prague.

U Páva   🕉 🖼 VISA 🐵 AE ①

U lužického semináře 32 ✉ *118 00 –* Ⓜ *Malostranská –* ℰ *257 533 3 60*
– hotelupava@iol.cz – Fax 257 530 9 19 – www.romantichotels.cz   **F2**
27 rm ☲ – **†**4600/6700 CZK **††**4800/7200 CZK
Rest a la carte 600/980 CZK
♦ Townhouse ♦ Classic ♦
Converted 17C houses in quiet square: comfort with character. Original features
aplenty, especially in new rooms overlooking square. Nutwood furniture and
ornate décor abound. Vaulted basement dining room has a warm and romantic
feel.

U Raka without rest   🛲 🖽 🕉 🖼 🅿 VISA 🐵 AE

Černínská 10 ✉ *118 00 –* ℰ *220 511 1 00 – info@romantikhotel-uraka.cz*
– Fax 233 358 0 41 – www.romantikhotel-uraka.cz   **E1**
6 rm ☲ – **†**4600/5800 CZK **††**5200/7500 CZK
♦ Family ♦ Cosy ♦
Tucked away, two timbered cottages in a rustic Czech style creating a charming
little hotel. Cosy, comfy and inviting. Clean-lined rooms in warm brick and
wood.

Neruda   🏠 🖽 ↔rm 🖼 🚗 VISA 🐵 AE ①

Nerudova 44 ✉ *1187 00 –* ℰ *257 535 5 57 – info@hotelneruda.cz*
– Fax 257 531 4 92 – www.hotelneruda.cz   **E2**
20 rm ☲ – **†**6300/7000 CZK **††**7000/8600 CZK
Rest a la carte 520/1080 CZK
♦ Business ♦ Modern ♦
Castle dominates views from roof-top terrace. Modern style complements 14C
ceiling and architecture; poet Neruda's quotes decorate walls. Spacious, well
sound-proofed rooms. Simple but attractive café/restaurant offering popular
dishes.

CZECH REPUBLIC

The Charles without rest   ⚡ 📷 *VISA* ◉ Æ

Josefská 1 ⊠ 118 00 – ⓜ Malostranská – ℰ 257 532 9 13 – thecharles@bon.cz
– Fax 257 532 9 10 – www.thecharlesprague.com   **F2**
31 rm ⊇ – ♥2600/3900 CZK ♥♥3000/4300 CZK
♦ Traditional ♦ Cosy ♦
Elegant and ideally situated little hotel. Spacious bedrooms decorated with
stripped floorboards, hand-painted ceilings and Baroque style furnishings.
Listed.

Constans   📷 ⅗↓70 ⌂ *VISA* ◉ Æ ◉

Břetislavova 309 ⊠ 118 00 – ⓜ Malostranská – ℰ 234 091 8 18
– hotel@hotelconstans.cz – Fax 234 091 8 60 – www.hotelconstans.cz
31 rm ⊇ – ♥4500/6000 CZK ♥♥4800/6200 CZK   **F2**
Rest a la carte 290/490 CZK
♦ Family ♦ Classic ♦
Small hotel tucked away in a quiet narrow cobbled street in the castle district.
Good sized, light and airy bedrooms with locally made furniture. Simple
café-style restaurant/breakfast room/bar serving basic menu of international
dishes.

Questenberk without rest   ⪡ 📷 *VISA* ◉ Æ ◉

Úvoz 15/155 ⊠ 110 00 – ℰ 220 407 6 00 – hotel@questenberk.cz
– Fax 220 407 6 01 – www.questenberk.cz   **E2**
30 rm ⊇ – ♥3200/4300 CZK ♥♥3700/5500 CZK
♦ Historic ♦ Classic ♦
Converted 17C monastic hospital with ornate façade at the top of the Castle
district. Arched corridors leading to sizeable bedrooms with good facilities
overlooking the city.

𝕏𝕏 **Terasa U Zlaté Studně** – at U Zlaté Studně H.   ⪡ Prague, 🍴

U Zlaté Studně 4 ⊠ 118 00 – ⓜ Malostranská   🅰️🅲 *VISA* ◉ Æ ◉
– ℰ 257 011 2 13 – restaurant@zlatestudne.cz – Fax 257 533 3 20
– www.terasauzlatestudne.cz   **F1**
Rest a la carte 1250/1600 CZK
♦ Modern ♦ Design ♦
Beautiful skyline views from a clean-lined top-floor restaurant and terrace,
reached by its own lift. Affable staff; full-flavoured modern dishes.

𝕏𝕏 **Kampa Park**   ⪡ Charles Bridge, 🍴 *VISA* ◉ Æ ◉

Na Kampě 8b ⊠ 118 00 – ⓜ Malostranská – ℰ 257 532 6 85 – kontakt@
kampapark.com – Fax 257 533 2 23 – www.kampapark.com   **F2**
Rest (booking essential at dinner) a la carte 1360/2190 CZK
♦ Modern ♦ Fashionable ♦
Celebrity heavy; stunningly located at water's edge by Charles Bridge. Book for
riverside table. Capacious interior; heated terraces: good view likely. Modern
global menus.

𝕏𝕏 **U Patrona**   ⚡ *VISA* ◉ Æ ◉

Dražického Nám. 4 ⊠ 118 00 – ⓜ Malostranská – ℰ 257 530 7 25
– upatrona@seznam.cz – Fax 257 530 7 23 – www.upatrona.cz   **F2**
Rest 290 CZK/1050 CZK and a la carte 870/1280 CZK
♦ Traditional ♦ Cosy ♦
Charming period house near Charles Bridge. Small ground floor restaurant or
larger upstairs room with window into kitchen. French-influenced classics and
Czech specialities.

𝕏 **Square**   🍴 *VISA* ◉ Æ ◉

Malastranské Nám. 5/28 ⊠ 118 00 – ⓜ Malostranská – ℰ 296 826 1 04
– kontakt@squarerestaurant.cz – Fax 257 532 1 07 – www.kampagroup.cz
closed 24 December   **F2**
Rest a la carte 455/975 CZK
♦ International ♦ Brasserie ♦
Simple modern eatery with contemporary décor in good position on a popular
bustling square. Summer terrace and additional basement room. Menus have a
global range.

ENVIRONS OF PRAGUE

Plan I

Crowne Plaza ⌂ 𝄭 𝄡 ⌂ 丩 rm ⊞ 🅓 380 🅟 *VISA* ◍◉ ℅ ⓪

Koulova 15 ⊠ 160 45 – ℰ 296 537 1 11 – hotel @ crowneplaza.cz
– Fax 296 537 5 35 – www.crownepla.cz **B1**
250 rm – ⬩7600/10600 CZK ⬩⬩7600/10600 CZK, ⌇ 464 CZK – 4 suites
Rest 580 CZK (buffet lunch) and a la carte 810/930 CZK
◆ Business ◆ Classic ◆
Stunning example of Socialist Realism architecture: built for Stalin in '50s, but he never showed up! Softened interior retains grandeur. Refurbished, well-equipped bedrooms. Ornate decoration lends a period feel to the restaurant.

Art *without rest* 🄰🄲 丩 🄳 *VISA* ◍◉ ℅ ⓪

Nad Královskou oborou 53 ⊠ 170 00 – ⓂHradčanská – ℰ 233 101 3 31
– booking @ arthotel.cz – Fax 233 101 3 11 – www.arthotel.cz **B1**
24 rm ⌇ – ⬩4600 CZK ⬩⬩5200 CZK
◆ Family ◆ Modern ◆
Stylish design in the shadow of Sparta Prague FC! Artists celebrated on each floor, including owner's father and grandfather. Sleek rooms: two attic suites with balconies.

Restaurant Le Bistrot de Marlene *with rm* ⌂ 𝄡 ⌇ 🄳

Hotel Villa Schwaiger, Schwaigerova 59/3 �14 🅟 *VISA* ◍◉ ℅
⊠ 160 00 – Ⓜ Hradčanská – ℰ 224 921 8 53 – info @ bistrotdemarlene.cz
– Fax 224 920 7 43 – www.bistrotdemarlene.cz
closed Sunday in winter **B1**
22 rm ⌇ – ⬩2000/2600 CZK ⬩⬩2900/4000 CZK
Rest 800 CZK (lunch) and a la carte 1070/1740 CZK
◆ French ◆ Formal ◆
Well renowned restaurant in a small residential villa. Dine in restaurant, Sunshine room, garden or terrace on accomplished, French based and original dishes. Comfy bedrooms.

Aromi ⌂ 丩 *VISA* ◍◉ ℅ ⓪

Mánesova 78/1442 ⊠ 120 00 – Ⓜ Jiřiho z Poděbrad – ℰ 222 713 2 22 – info @
aromi.cz – Fax 222 713 4 44 – www.aromi.cz
closed 24-26 December **C2**
Rest (booking essential at dinner) 750 CZK (lunch) and a la carte 505/1065 CZK
◆ Italian ◆ Rustic ◆
A couple of metro stops to the east, this buzzy restaurant is well worth the journey. Spacious interior with big, chunky wood tables. Great value, authentic Italian dishes.

DENMARK
DANMARK

PROFILE

- **AREA:**
  43 069 km² (16 629 sq mi) excluding the Faroe Islands and Greenland.

- **POPULATION:**
  5 432 000 inhabitants (est. 2005), density = 126 per km².

- **CAPITAL:**
  Copenhagen (conurbation 1 426 000 inhabitants).

- **CURRENCY:**
  Danish Krone (DKK) divided into 100 øre; rate of exchange: DKK 1 = € 0.13 = US$ 0.16 (Nov 2005).

- **GOVERNMENT:**
  Constitutional parliamentary (single chamber) monarchy (since 1849). Member of European Union since 1973.

- **LANGUAGES:**
  Danish; many Danes also understand and speak English.

- **SPECIFIC PUBLIC HOLIDAYS:**
  Maundy Thursday (the day before Good Friday); Good Friday (Friday before Easter); Common Prayer Day (4th Friday after Easter); Constitution Day (5 June); Boxing Day (26 December).

- **LOCAL TIME:**
  GMT + 1 hour in winter and 2 GMT + 2 hours in summer.

- **CLIMATE:**
  Temperate northern maritime with cold winters and mild summers Copenhagen: January: 1°C, July: 18°C).

- **INTERNATIONAL DIALLING CODE:**
  00 45 followed by full local number. Directory Enquiries: ☏ **118**; International Directory Enquiries: ☏ **113**.

- **EMERGENCY:**
  Dial ☏ **112** for Police, Ambulance and Fire Brigade.

- **ELECTRICITY:**
  220 volts AC, 50Hz; 2-pin round-shaped continental plugs.

FORMALITIES

Travellers from the European Union (EU), Switzerland, Norway, Iceland and the main countries of North and South America need a national identity card or passport (America: passport required) to visit Denmark for less than three months (tourism or business purpose). For visitors from other countries a visa may be required, in addition to a passport, especially for those wishing to stay for longer than three months. If you plan to visit Greenland or Faroe Islands while in Denmark, you must purchase a visa in advance in your own country. We advise you to check with your embassy before travelling.

MAJOR NEWSPAPERS

The main national daily Danish newspapers are *B.T. and Jydske Vestkysten*. The Copenhagen area is covered by *Berlingske Tidende, Børsen, Ekstra Bladet, Information* and *Politiken*. The Aarhus area is covered by *Arhus Stiftstidende*; the Bornholm/Ronne area is covered by *Bornholms Tidende*; Viby is covered by *Jyllands-Posten*. *The Copenhagen Post* is a weekly newspaper published in English.

USEFUL PHRASES

ENGLISH	DANISH
Yes	**Ja**
No	**Nej**
Good morning	**God morgen, God dag, Hej**
Goodbye	**Farvel**
Thank you	**Tak**
Please	**Vaer så god**
Excuse me	**Undskyld**
I don't understand	**Jeg forstår ikke**

HOTELS

◆ CATEGORIES

From international luxury to cosy, family-run hotels and inns; castles and manor houses; bed & breakfast, farmhouse holidays, holiday cottages by the beach and in the country.

◆ PRICE RANGE

The price is per room. There is little difference between the price of a single and a double room.

Between April and October it is advisable to book in advance. From November to March prices may be slightly lower, some hotels offer special cheap rates and a few may be closed. In Copenhagen hotel chains offer lower weekend rates in the low season.

◆ TAX

Included in the room price.

◆ CHECK OUT TIME

Usually between 10.30am and noon.

◆ RESERVATIONS

By telephone or by Internet. A credit card number may be required.

◆ TIP FOR LUGGAGE HANDLING

At the discretion of the customer (about Kr 10-15 per bag).

◆ BREAKFAST

It is usually included in the price of the room and is generally served between 7am and 10am. Most hotels offer a self-service buffet, including smørrebrød or something similar; generally it is possible to have breakfast served in the room.

Reception	**Reception**
Single room	**Erkelt vaerelse**
Double room	**Dobbelt vaerelse**
Bed	**Seng**
Bathroom	**Bade vaerelse**
Shower	**Brusebad**

RESTAURANTS

In the last few years Copenhagen has developed into a foodies' paradise, even attracting diners from other countries. The locals dine out a lot and spend all evening at table for the pleasure of savouring the chefs' specialities. Many of the **restaurants** are very stylish, contemporary and minimalist in decor and design. The **brasseries** offer a more homely ambience. At lunchtime the choice is less varied as many of the restaurants, particularly the expensive ones with stars, are open for dinner only.

◆ MEALS

Breakfast	**Morgenmad**	7am – 10am
Lunch	**Forkost**	12pm – 2-3pm
Dinner	**Middag, aftensmad**	6.30pm – 10-11pm, sometimes later

In the evening many restaurants offer **fixed priced set menus** without choice or **tasting menus** with a different glass of wine with each course. Lunch menus are mostly à la carte. Menus are usually printed in Danish and English. A fixed price menu is usually less expensive than a meal with the same number of courses selected from the à la carte menu. The Danish open sandwich, **smørrebrød**, is served mostly at lunch in specialist restaurants.

◆ RESERVATIONS

It is essential to reserve in the evening, usually by phone, fax or Internet. For famous restaurants (including Michelin starred restaurants), it is advisable to book several days – or weeks in some instances – in advance. A credit card number or a phone number may be required as guarantee.

◆ THE BILL

The bill (check) includes service charge and VAT. Tipping is optional but, if you are particularly pleased with the service, it is customary to round up the total to an appropriate figure.

Drink or aperitif	**Drink / drik / aperitif**
Appetizer Meal	**Måltid**
First course, starter	**Forret**
Main dish	**Holvedret**
Main dish of the day	**Dagens ret**
Dessert	**Dessert**
Water	**Vand**
Wine (red, white, rosé)	**Vin (rød, hvid, rosé)**
Beer, draught beer	**Øl, Fadøl**
Bread	**Brød**
Meat (medium, well done)	**Kød (medium, gennemstegt)**
Fish	**Fisk**
Salt/pepper	**Salt / Peber**
Cheese	**Ost**
Vegetables	**Grøntsager**
Hot/cold	**Varm / kold**
The bill (check)	**Regningen**

LOCAL CUISINE

The traditional feature of Danish culinary culture, the cold buffet *(det store kolde bord)*, is generally served at lunchtime in specialist restaurants. A great variety of hot and cold fish and meat dishes is presented, including the famous **smørrebrød**, an open sandwich of sliced buttered rye bread topped with fish (marinated herring), shellfish, liver pate *(leverpostej)*, meat balls *(frikadeller)*, usually accompanied by a glass of lager beer or a tot of aquavit.

At dinner the accent is on innovation. The modern chefs use only the best local and seasonal produce, combining the different elements with flair and originality to produce highly individual dishes. Seafood is always on the menu. Fusion gourmet restaurants offer dishes such as roasted zander served with lemongrass froth and parsnip crisps; Danish blue lobster with wild watercress; wild rabbit with allspice; marinated blueberries with blueberry sherbet. Less exotic dishes are breaded plaice and fish cakes. Classic lunchtime restaurants offer cold dishes such as **Christiansøsild**, herring marinated in herbs or spices and served on a slice of buttered wholemeal rye bread.

Danish **specialities** include smoked salmon and smoked eel, lobster, herring marinated with herbs or spices. Veal is very popular in summer, also veal sweetbreads. There is plenty of home-raised pork (sausages and bacon) and also game. Herbs, spices (carroway), rye bread and berries are frequent ingredients. The Danish have a reputation for their dairy produce, including a few well known cheeses: **Danish blue**, **Jarlsberg**, **Toma**. For dessert there are honey cakes and the more famous Danish pastries and chocolates; berries are served in tarts and brulées or made into sorbets.

◆ DRINK

Denmark is famous for **lager** - Tuborg and Carlsberg. The Carlsberg Brewery, which has been in the same building since 1878 and is open to visitors, also produces 'real ale' in the semper Ardens range as well as the Jacobsen range. Wine is expensive, as it has to be imported, but wine lists are eclectic, offering a worldwide selection. Cocktails are also popular, particularly champagne cocktails. The traditional spirit is **aquavit**, which is often drunk as a chaser

COPENHAGEN
KØBENHAVN

Population (est. 2005): 514 000 (conurbation 1 426 000) – Altitude: about 13 m above sea level

B. Pérousse / MICHELIN

Copenhagen covers the northeast coast of Sjaelland Island. It is a city of contrasts where tradition is preserved beside the ultramodern. The city is gracious, with red-brick walls and green copper roofs. The huge, busy harbour is a sign of economic importance but first impression is that of a friendly and dynamic city. The town carries its 800 years of history lightly and its architectural heritage is well preserved.

The Danish capital does not enjoy any expansive vistas; yet there is a sense of spaciousness created by impressive squares, parks, gardens and lakes.

The name København (port of merchants) reminds the commercial traditions of the city founded by the bishop Absalon in 1167. During the reign of Christian IV (1588-1648) the city enjoyed its golden age, with huge development, particularly in its architecture. Most beautiful monuments and the picturesque Christianshavn district date from this period. Since 2000, the refurbishment of the waterfront and docks is spurred on by Øresund Crossing, a combination of tunnel and bridge, carrying road and rail traffic between Copenhagen and Malmö in Sweden. Another stunning modern building is the 'Black Diamond' extension to the 18C Royal Library.

Famous writers such as Ludvig Holberg, Søren Kierkegård, Hans Christian Andersen and Karen Blixen lived in Copenhagen.

WHICH DISTRICT TO CHOOSE

Most **hotels** and **restaurants** are located in the Old Town and adjacent districts, although there are one or two near the Little Mermaid *Plan I* **D1** and by the canal west of the Old Town; there are also a few in Christianshavn *Plan I* **D3**.

Copenhagen boasts an impressive range of **restaurants**: some classic establishments with long, proud traditions, some modern with fusion themes, a few ethnic, some small and cosy.

The city also has a vibrant café culture with everything from coffee bars to brunch concepts; at the fusion cafés you can buy books, fashion items, ornaments or flowers, or even wash your clothes.

123

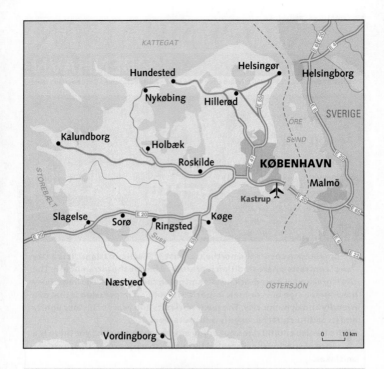

PRACTICAL INFORMATION

ARRIVAL – DEPARTURE

Copenhagen Airport – In Kastrup, about 9 km (5.5 mi) southeast of Copenhagen. ℰ 32 31 32 31, ℰ 32 31 23 60 (service information); www.cph.dk

From the airport to the city centre – By **train**: Airport City Express (13min) to Central Station every 20min. Single fare Kr25.50. By **bus** nos 9, 250S and 500S to city centre (30min). Fare Kr22. By **taxi**: Kr175-195.

Sea Services – **Car and passenger ferries** to Copenhagen from England, Norway, Sweden, Germany, the Netherlands, single and return fares. ℰ 08705 333 000 (8.30am-8pm, Sat 8.30am-5pm, Sun 10am-4pm); www. dfdsseaways.co.uk

Railway Station – **Hovedbanegård**, Bernstorffsgade. ℰ 70 13 14 15

(domestic), ℰ 70 13 14 16 (international); www.dsb.dk, www. rejseplanen.dk

Øresund Bridge – A combination of bridge and tunnel (10 miles/16km long) linking Copenhagen (via the airport) with Malmö in Sweden. Toll: Kr 225 (one way by car); Kr 65 (one way by train 35min).

TRANSPORT

✦ METRO AND BUS

Tickets valid for metro, buses (HUR) and S-train are sold at HUR ticket offices and at DSB stations with ticket outlets. 24hr-ticket Kr100 valid for the entire Greater Copenhagen Region; 7-day Flexcard valid for selected zones; 10-journey punch cards (Klippekort) are valid for all zones. Discounts available for senior citizens and children under 16. The Metro and the S-trains link inner and outer Copenhagen (www. m.dk) (www.hur.dk) (www.dsb.dk/s-tog) (www.dsb.dk).

◆ TAXIS

Vacant taxis carry a yellow light and a sign with the word FRI (free) on display. Credit cards are usually accepted; receipts given on request. Basic fare Kr19 (hailed), Kr32 (phone-booking); Kr10 pkm (6am-4pm) and Kr11 pkm (4pm-7am) and Kr13 Fri-Sat 11pm-7am; no need to tip in addition to the amount shown on the meter. ✆ 38 10 10 10 (Taxa Motor), ✆ 35 35 35 35 (Københavns Taxa), ✆ 70 25 25 25 (Codan Taxa). Taxi tours with foreign-language-speaking driver or guide can be arranged for a max of 4 persons at a fixed price. ✆ 38 10 10 10 (Taxa Motor), ✆ 35 35 35 35 (Taxa), ✆ 32 51 51 51 (Amager-Øbro Taxi).

◆ COPENHAGEN CARD

Valid for unlimited transport by train, bus and metro, free entry to more than 60 museums and sights, as well as discounts on many attractions and on car rental throughout the Greater Copenhagen region. 24hr-card €29 (child €19); 72hr-card €58 (child €33) on sale at the airport, major railway stations and at tourist information offices throughout Denmark.

◆ FREE CYCLES

Brightly painted bicycles, lined up in racks, are available to citizens and tourists for the deposit of a Dkr20 coin. The coin will release a cycle from a stand for an unlimited period and is retrieved when the cycle is returned to any of the 150 stands in the city.

USEFUL ADDRESSES

◆ TOURIST INFORMATION

Copenhagen Right Now: Vesterbro-gade 4A *Plan I* **B3**, ✆ 70 222 442. Open May-June, Mon-Sat, 9am-6pm; Jul-Aug, Mon-Sat 9am-8pm, Sun 10am-6pm; Jan-Apr and Sep-Dec, Mon-Fri 9am-4pm, Sat 9am-2pm (www.visitco penhagen.com) (www.visitdenmark. com).

◆ POST OFFICES

Opening times Mon-Sat 9/10am to 5/6pm (12/2pm Sat). Longer hours at the post office at the **Central Station**.

◆ BANKS/CURRENCY EXCHANGE

Opening times Mon-Fri 10am-4pm (6pm Thurs). Exchange facilities available outside these hours in the centre of Copenhagen, at the Central Railway Station and at the Airport. ATMs available at most banks and at metro stations.

◆ EMERGENCY

Dial ✆ **112** for Police, Fire Brigade, Ambulance.

BUSY PERIODS

It may be difficult to find a room at a reasonable price when special events are held in the city:

Copenhagen Fashion and Design Festival: February and mid August.

Copenhagen Jazz Festival: early July.

Copenhagen International Film Festival: August-September.

Christmas Market: mid November to December.

DIFFERENT FACETS OF THE CITY

It is possible to visit the main sights and museums in two to three days.

Museums and sights are usually open from 10/12am to 3/6pm. Many are closed on Monday.

OLD TOWN – **Slotsholmen**: Island surrounded by a canal on which stands **Christiansborg Slot**, fifth castle built on the site since 1167, housing the Danish Parliament *(Folketing)*, the Supreme Court and royal reception halls; **Marmorbroen**, rococo marble bridge as western entrance to castle courtyard. **Børsen** *Plan I* **C3**: Stock Exchange in the Dutch Renaissance style, founded by Christian IV in 1619. North of the island is a network of narrow streets and charming squares, mostly pedestrianised, lined with 18C terraced houses, cafés and boutiques, and bisected by **Strøget**, the main shopping street. **Vor Frue Kirke** *Plan I* **C2**: Neo-Classical cathedral designed in 1829 with sculptures by Thorwaldsen. Just north of the Old Town is **Rosenborg Slot** *Plan I* **C2**: Fine example of Dutch Renaissance style, built by Christian IV in 1633 as a summer pavilion, now housing the personal collections of the royal family.

NEW TOWN – **Kongens Nytorv** *Plan I* **C2**: the square, lined by impressive buildings, was the first feature of the New Town to be built. **Nyhavn** *Plan I* **D2**: 17C canal lined with warehouses and wharves, now restored or converted into restaurants, bars and cafés. **Amalienborg Palace** *Plan I* **D2**: Royal residence since 1794; changing of the guard daily at noon. **Marmorkirken** *Plan I* **D2**: 18C domed marble church, also called Frederiks Kirke.

MUSEUMS AND GALLERIES – **Nationalmuseet** *Plan I* **C3**: Denmark's history from prehistoric times to AD 1000. **Ny Carlsberg Glyptotek** *Plan I* **C3**: French art from 19C and 20C, Impressionist and Post-Impressionist works, sculptures by Degas and Rodin. **Statens Museum for Kunst** *Plan I* **C1**: Danish Fine Arts Museum displaying the royal art collections: foreign (20C French paintings) and Danish art (Edvard Munch). **Thorvaldsens Museum** *Plan I* **C3**: Memorial to Denmark's most famous sculptor, Bertel Thordvaldsen (1170-1844). **Hans Christian Andersen Museum** *Plan I* **D2**: The author's study and personal effects, photos, letters and a manuscript.

LOCAL COLOUR – **Tivoli Gardens** *Plan I* **B3**: one of the oldest and most prestigious amusement parks, lit at night by 1000 Venetian lanterns in the trees – carousels and crazy rides, concerts and restaurants; also site of the Copenhagen Christmas Market. **Den Lille Havfrue** *Plan I* **D1**: the Little Mermaid statue by Evard Eriksen perches on a rock gazing at the harbour entrance; behind her is the **Citadel of Kastellet**, an 18C fortification. **Waterfront**: experience the view from the water on the HUR waterbus or a guided harbour and canal cruise.

GOURMET TREATS

There are several excellent restaurants serving fish or seafood in the canal district near **Højbro Plads** *Plan I* **C2** and **Gammel Strand** *Plan I* **C2**. The place for the in-crowd is the **Kongens Nytorv** district : trendy cafés in the French or modern Scandinavia style. In **Nyhavn** *Plan I* **D2** popular restaurants and cafés, with tables on the waterside pavements in summer, have replaced the former sailors' taverns;

many serve traditional Danish dishes, including the famous **smørrebrød**, but tend to charge for location as much as for food. The neighbouring streets offer better value. There are several good restaurants and cafés in **Gråbrødre Torv** *Plan I* **C2**. Ethnic restaurants are to be found in the **Vesterbro** district *Plan I* **A3**; **Nørrebro** *Plan I* **A1** will be more to the taste of those on a slim budget.

If you fancy real ale, try **Brewpub**, Copenhagen's new microbrewery, where there is new beer on draught every week.

SHOPPING

Stores are usually open from 9.30/10am to 5.30/7pm (Sat 9/10am-4pm) but they can stay open from 6am-8pm. Alcohol sales are forbidden after 8pm.

Strøget *Plan I* **C2** and **Købmagergade** *Plan I* **C2** are the two main shopping streets: for department stores (Magasin du Nord, Illum) **Strøget**; for fashion and knitwear **Kronprinsensgade**, **Adelgade** and **Ny Østergade**; for art, antiques and cutting edge design **Bredgade**; for avant-garde, underground and up-and-coming boutiques **Larsbjørnsstraede**; for sweaters **Nytorv**; for antiques **Kompagnistraede** *Plan I* **C3** and **Ravnsborggade** and neighbouring streets in the Nørrebro district.

The Danish flair for style is also on show at the **Danish Design Centre** (Dansk Design Center, H C Andersens Bld 27), the **Royal Copenhagen Welcome Centre** (Søndre Fasanvey 5), the **House of Amber** (6 Nygade and 34 Frederiksberggade) and various hand-made glass studios: **Glasseriet** (Jenagade 27); **Hagenglas** (Slotsgade 52E).

WHAT TO BUY – Royal Copenhagen porcelain, Holmegaard glassware, Georg Jensen silver, Bang & Olufsen stereo equipment, jewellery (amber), embroidery, linen, children's toys.

ENTERTAINMENT

Copenhagen This Week, published in English, is a good source of information on shopping, sightseeing, museums, music, theatre and films (www.ctw.dk).

CONCERT HALLS – Opera House. Tivoli Gardens Concert Hall *Plan I* **B3**. Black Diamond Radiohusets Koncertsal.

OTHER VENUES – Royal Danish Theatre Det Ny Teater *Plan I* **D2**. Dansescenen. Kanonhallen. Filmhuset. IMAX Tycho Brahe Planetarium.

NIGHTLIFE

Copenhagen This Week, published in English, prints a good selection. The most trendy bars and cafés are to be found in **Vesterbro** *Plan I* **A3** and **Nørrebro** *Plan I* **A1**, two districts which are transformed at night when DJ's change stylish brasseries into lively bars. There are also one or two night clubs round **Kongens Nytorv** *Plan I* **C2** and in the **Old Town**. For gambling there is the **Casino Copenhagen** (Amager Bld 70).

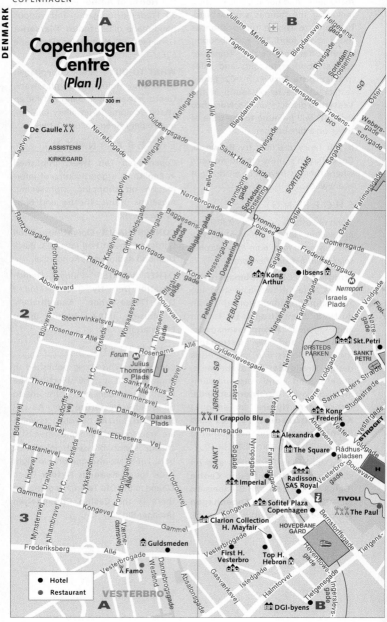

Copenhagen Centre
(Plan I)

DENMARK

NØRREBRO

0   300 m

De Gaulle

ASSISTENS
KIRKEGARD

NØRREBRO

Kong
Arthur   Ibsens

Nørreport

Israels
Plads

ØRSTEDS
PARKEN

Skt. Petri

SANKT
PETRI

Forum
Julius
Thomsens
Plads

Il Grappolo Blu

Kong
Frederik

STRØGET

Danas
Plads

Alexandra

The Square

Rådhus-
pladsen

Imperial

Radisson
SAS Royal

Sofitel Plaza
Copenhagen

TIVOLI

The Paul

Clarion Collection
H. Mayfair

HOVEDBANE-
GÅRD

Guldsmeden

First H.
Vesterbro

Top H.
Hebron

Frederiksberg

Famo

VESTERBRO

DGI-byens

● Hotel
● Restaurant

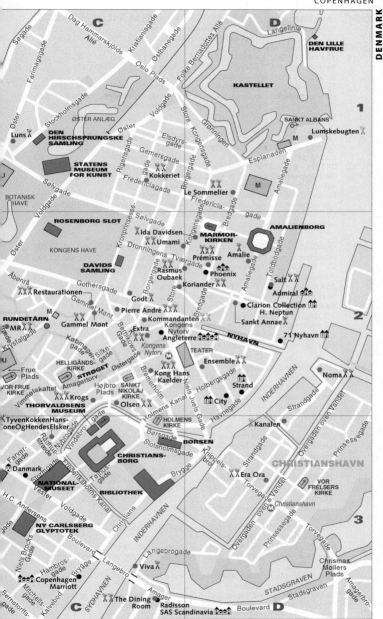

Angleterre 🏨🏨🏨   ⊛ ℩ᴓ 🕉 ⛒ 🗚 ᷧrm ⅍ 🎬 ꝯ ⅏400 ᗢ P VISA ◍ ᴁ ➀
Kongens Nytorv 34 ⊠ *1021 K* – **Ⓜ** *Kongens Nytorv*   ➀
– 𝒞 *33 12 00 95* – *angleterre @ remmen.dk* – *Fax 33 12 11 18*
– *www.remmen.dk*   **C2**
105 rm – †2280 DKK ††2600 DKK, ☲ 155 DKK – 18 suites
Rest *Wiinblad*, 𝒞 *33 37 06 45* – 380 DKK and a la carte 514/705 DKK
 ◆ Grand Luxury ◆ Traditional ◆ Classic ◆
Elegant 18C grand hotel overlooking New Royal Square. Luxury in lobby sets
tone throughout. Spacious rooms enjoy classic décor and antique furniture.
Grand ballroom. Popular afternoon teas. Restaurant in marine blue décor;
Danish and French dishes.

Skt.Petri 🏨🏨🏨   🏖 ⅒ 🗚 ᷧrm ⅍rest 🖂 ꝯ 250 VISA ◍ ᴁ ➀
Krystalgade 22 ⊠ *1172 K* – **Ⓜ** *Nørreport* – 𝒞 *33 45 91 00* – *reservation @*
hotelsktpetri.com – *Fax 33 45 91 10* – *www.hotelsktpetri.com*   **B2**
241 rm – †1395 DKK ††2395 DKK, ☲ 150 DKK – 27 suites
Rest *Brasserie Blu* a la carte 330/575 DKK
 ◆ Luxury ◆ Business ◆ Design ◆
Former department store in central Copenhagen near old St Peter's Church.
Large open plan atrium. Bright, stylish contemporary rooms with design features
by Per Arnoldi. Informal restaurant; international menu of classic brasserie dishes
with Danish theme.

Radisson SAS Royal 🏨🏨🏨   ⩽ Copenhagen, ⊛ ℩ᴓ 🕉 ⅒ 🗚 ᷧrm ⅍ 🖂
Hammerichsgade 1 ⊠ *1611 V*   ꝯ ꝯ400 ᗢ P VISA ◍ ➀
– 𝒞 *33 42 60 00* – *copenhagen @ radissonsas.com* – *Fax 33 42 61 00*
– *www.radissonsas.com*   **B3**
258 rm ☲ – †1295 DKK ††2294 DKK – 2 suites
Rest *Alberto K,* 455 DKK and a la carte 241/386 DKK
Rest *Café Royal*, 𝒞 *33 42 60 53* – 198 DKK and a la carte 241/386 DKK
 ◆ Luxury ◆ Business ◆ Modern ◆
Large international hotel block dominating the skyline west of Tivoli and offering
superb views. Scandinavian bedroom décor. Italian-influenced cuisine on 20th
floor. Popular ground floor brasserie style café.

Copenhagen Marriott 🏨🏨🏨   ⩽ 🏖 ℩ᴓ 🕉 ⅒ 🗚 ᷧrm ⅍ 🖂 ꝯ570
Kalvebod Brygge 5 ⊠ *1560* – 𝒞 *88 33 99 00*   ᗢ VISA ◍ ᴁ ➀
– *mhrs.cphdk.reservations @ marriott.com* – *Fax 88 33 99 99*
– *www.marriott.com/cphkd*   **C3**
386 rm – †2695 DKK ††2695 DKK, ☲ 150 DKK – 9 suites
Rest *Terraneo* 395/425 DKK and a la carte 325/440 DKK
 ◆ Luxury ◆ Business ◆ Modern ◆
Striking, glass-fronted hotel, its handsomely appointed rooms face the water or
overlook the city and Tivoli. Top-floor executive rooms share a stylish private
lounge. Lunchtime buffet and Mediterranean cuisine in the evening.

Radisson SAS Scandinavia 🏨🏨🏨   ⩽ Copenhagen, ℩ᴓ 🕉 ⛒
🖾 ⅒ 🗚 rest ᷧrm ⅍rest 🖂 ꝯ ꝯ1200 P VISA ◍ ᴁ ➀
Amager Boulevard 70 ⊠ *2300 S* – 𝒞 *33 96 50 00*
– *copenhagen @ radissonsas.com* – *Fax 3396 55 00*
– *www.radissonsas.com*   **C3**
542 rm – †1295 DKK ††1595 DKK, ☲ 150 DKK – 19 suites
Rest see *The Dining Room* below
Rest 150/245 DKK (lunch) and a la carte approx. 330 DKK
Rest *Blue Elephant*, 𝒞 *33 95 59 70* (dinner only) 280/800 DKK and a la carte
250/650 DKK
Rest *Kyoto* (dinner only) 300/500 DKK and a la carte 220/430 DKK
 ◆ Business ◆ Classic ◆
Tower-block hotel with spectacular views. Shops, casino and bar in busy lobby.
Original bright bedrooms themed in six different styles. Traditional Danish to
Italian dishes in dining room. Blue Elephant for authentic Thai cuisine. Kyoto for
Japanese menu.

DENMARK

Sofitel Plaza Copenhagen   AC ⇔rm ☑ ⅏30 VISA ⬤ AE ①
Bernstorffsgade 4 ☒ 1577 V – ℰ 33 14 92 62 – sofitel@accorhotel.dk
– Fax 33 93 93 62 – www.sofitel.com   **B3**
87 rm – ♦1859 DKK **♦♦**2059 DKK, ☐ 135 DKK – 6 suites
Rest *Brasserie Flora Danica (closed Sunday)* (dinner only) 245 DKK/845 DKK
♦ Business ♦ Classic ♦
Venerable hotel commissioned in the early 20C by King Frederik VIII and
overlooking Tivoli Gardens. Classic style room décor and atmospheric library bar.
A modern, welcoming brasserie with a French-based menu.

Admiral   ⇐ ⋒ ⇔ ⅏rest ☑ ⅏180 P VISA ⬤ AE ①
Toldbodgade 24-28 ☒ 1253 – ⓜ Kongens Nytorv – ℰ 33 74 14 14
– admiral@admiralhotel.dk – Fax 33 74 14 16 – www.admiralhotel.dk
366 rm – ♦1165 DKK **♦♦**1565 DKK, ☐ 115 DKK   **D2**
Rest see *Salt* below
♦ Business ♦ Design ♦
Converted 18C dockside warehouse, with some rooms facing passing
liners. Maritime theme throughout. Bedrooms complement the rustic charm.

Imperial   ₺ AC rest ⇔rm ⅏ ☑ ⓒ ⅏200 VISA ⬤ AE ①
Vester Farimagsgade 9 ☒ 1606 V – ℰ 33 12 80 00 – imperial@arp-hansen.dk
– Fax 33 93 80 03 – www.imperialhotel.dk   **B3**
214 rm – ♦1055 DKK **♦♦**1735 DKK, ☐ 125 DKK – 1 suite
Rest *Imperial Garden* (dinner only) 270 DKK/425 DKK and a la carte
275/435 DKK
Rest *Imperial Brasserie*, ℰ 33 43 20 83 – 270 DKK (lunch) and a la carte
252/364 DKK
♦ Traditional ♦ Classic ♦
Large mid 20C hotel located on a wide city thoroughfare. Well serviced rooms
range in size and are richly furnished in 1950s Danish designer style. Fine dining
in attractive indoor "winter garden". Less formal dining in ground floor brasserie.

Kong Frederik   ⇔rm ⅏ ☑ ⅏40 VISA ⬤ AE ①
Vester Voldgade 25 ☒ 1552 V – ℰ 33 12 59 02 – kongfrederik@remmen.dk
– Fax 33 93 59 01 – www.remmen.dk
closed 25 December   **B3**
108 rm – ♦1040 DKK **♦♦**1840 DKK, ☐ 125 DKK – 2 suites
Rest *Le Coq Rouge*, ℰ 33 42 48 48 – a la carte 295/375 DKK
♦ Traditional ♦ Classic ♦
Classic elegant old building in good location. Traditional style décor with dark
wood panelling. Comfortable rooms with old-fashioned furniture. Atrium style
banquet hall. Wood-panelled, atmospheric brasserie offering traditional Danish
cooking.

Kong Arthur   ⌂ ⋒ ⇔rm ⅏ ☑ ⅏50 P VISA ⬤ AE ①
Nørre Søgade 11 ☒ 1370 K – ⓜ Nørreport – ℰ 33 11 12 12 – hotel@
kongarthur.dk – Fax 33 32 61 30 – www.kongarthur.dk   **B2**
117 rm ☐ – **♦**900 DKK **♦♦**1085 DKK
Rest *Sticks 'n' Sushi*, ℰ 33 11 14 07 – 250 DKK and a la carte 225/265 DKK
♦ Traditional ♦ Family ♦ Classic ♦
Pleasant family run hotel on elegant late 19C residential avenue by Peblinge lake.
Classic rooms equipped with modern facilities. Sticks 'n' Sushi for Japanese dishes.

First H. Vesterbro   AC ⇔rm ⅏ ☑ ⊜ VISA ⬤ AE ①
Vesterbrogade 23-29 ☒ 1677V – ℰ 33 78 80 00
– reception.copenhagen@firsthotels.dk – Fax 33 78 80 80
– www.firsthotels.com
closed Sunday   **B3**
403 rm – ♦1125 DKK **♦♦**1425 DKK, ☐ 125 DKK
Rest *(closed Sunday)* (dinner only) 95 DKK/150 DKK
♦ Business ♦ Modern ♦
Large modern hotel with metal and glass façade on busy avenue. All bedrooms
have good modern facilities in a contemporary style; superior rooms are larger.
Informal dining in front bar from International menu.

Phoenix
🔲 ⇔rm ✑rest 🖾 🏛110 ☕ VISA ⬤❸ AE ⓪

Bredgade 37 ⊠ 1260 K – ⓶ Kongens Nytorv – ☏ 33 95 95 00
– phoenixcopenhagen@arp-hansen.dk – Fax 33 33 98 33
– www.phoenixcopenhagen.dk
closed Sunday   **D2**
210 rm – ⛟1585 DKK ⛟⛟2585 DKK, � 135 DKK – 3 suites
Rest *Von Plessen* (buffet lunch) 298/300 DKK and a la carte 310/495 DKK
◆ Traditional ◆ Classic ◆
Parts of this elegant hotel, located in the lively modern art and antiques district, date from the 17C. It features a grand marbled lobby and comfortable high ceilinged rooms. Elegant basement dining room with discreet décor in neutral tones.

The Square without rest
🔲 ⇔ ✑ 🖾 VISA ⬤❸ AE ⓪

Rådhuspladsen 14 ⊠ 1550 K – ☏ 33 38 12 00 – thesquare@arp-hansen.dk
– Fax 3338 12 01 – www.thesquare.dk   **B3**
268 rm ⊊ – ⛟1395 DKK ⛟⛟3290 DKK
◆ Business ◆ Design ◆
Ideally located hotel in Town Hall Square. Breakfast room on 6th floor with view of city roofs. Good sized modern bedrooms with square theme in décor and fabrics.

71 Nyhavn
⬉ ⇔rm ✑rest 🖾 VISA ⬤❸ AE ⓪

Nyhavn 71 ⊠ 1051 K – ⓶ Kongens Nytorv – ☏ 33 43 62 00
– 71nyhavnhotel@arp-hansen.dk – Fax 33 43 62 01 – www.71nyhavnhotel.dk
closed Sunday and Bank Holidays   **D2**
142 rm – ⛟1550 DKK ⛟⛟2420 DKK, ⊊ 130 DKK – 8 suites
Rest *Pakhus Kaelder* 335 DKK (dinner) and a la carte approx. 424 DKK
◆ Business ◆ Stylish ◆
Charming converted warehouse by the canal. Interior features low ceilings with wooden beams throughout. Compact comfortable bedrooms, many with views of passing ships. Cellar restaurant with low wood-beamed ceiling. Interesting, seasonal menus.

Alexandra
🏠 ⇔rm ✑rest 🖾 ✆ VISA ⬤❸ AE ⓪

H.C. Andersens Boulevard 8 ⊠ 1553 V – ☏ 33 74 44 44
– reservations@hotel-alexandra.dk – Fax 33 74 44 88 – www.hotel-alexandra.dk
closed 24-26 December   **B3**
61 rm ⊊ – ⛟1265 DKK ⛟⛟1365 DKK
Rest *Mühlhausen*, ☏ 33 74 44 66 – 285 DKK (dinner) and a la carte
295/415 DKK
◆ Traditional ◆ Classic ◆
Classic 19C hotel conveniently located for city centre. Some special design rooms feature Danish style furniture and fittings and an original painting in each. Banquettes and crisp linen in a stylish brasserie with a Mediterranean tone.

Strand without rest
⇔ 🖾 VISA ⬤❸ AE ⓪

Havnegade 37 ⊠ 1058 K – ⓶ Kongens Nytorv – ☏ 33 48 99 00
– copenhagenstrand@arp-hansen.dk – Fax 33 48 99 01
– www.copenhagenstrand.com   **D2**
172 rm ⊊ – ⛟1360 DKK ⛟⛟1670 DKK – 2 suites
◆ Business ◆ Modern ◆
Modern warehouse conversion on waterfront and a useful central location. Smart modern rooms with dark wood furniture and bright colours. Business centre.

DGI-byens
🏠 ♨ 🏊 ⇔rm ✑ 🖾 🏛80 🅿 VISA ⬤❸ AE ⓪

Tietgensgade 65 ⊠ 1704 V – ☏ 33 29 80 00 – info@dgi-byen.dk
– Fax 33 29 80 80 – www.dgi-byen.dk   **B3**
104 rm ⊊ – ⛟1395 DKK ⛟⛟1595 DKK
Rest *Vestauranten*, ☏ 33 29 80 30 – a la carte approx. 295 DKK
◆ Business ◆ Modern ◆
Turn of Millennium hotel, part of huge, modern leisure complex with all the facilities. Minimalist bedrooms with simple, clean style and up-to-date facilities. Bright restaurant in original building offering a varied menu; pleasant terrace.

City without rest ⇔ 🖭 📞 VISA ⓄⓈ 🄰🄴 ⓪

Peder Skrams Gade 24 ⊠ 1054 K – Ⓜ Kongens Nytorv – ℰ 33 13 06 66
– hotelcity@hotelcity.dk – Fax 33 13 06 67
– www.hotelcity.dk   **D2**
81 rm ⌑ – ♦995 DKK ♦♦1465 DKK
♦ Business ♦ Functional ♦
Well situated modern hotel between city centre and docks. Modern Danish style interior décor. Good technical facilities. Superior rooms are larger.

Clarion Collection H. Mayfair without rest ⇔

Helgolandsgade 3 ⊠ 1653 V – ℰ 70 12   ⅌ 🖭 VISA ⓄⓈ 🄰🄴 ⓪
17 00 – info.mayfair@comfort.choicehotels.dk – Fax 33 23 96 86
– www.choicehotels.dk
closed 21 December-2 January   **B3**
103 rm – ♦1330 DKK ♦♦1630 DKK, ⌑ 95 DKK – 3 suites
♦ Business ♦ Functional ♦
Large well run hotel usefully located near station. Interior décor and furniture in classic English style. Neat rooms, well equipped with mod cons. Relaxing bar.

Clarion Collection H. Neptun ⇔rm ⅌ 🖭 📞 ♨60 VISA ⓄⓈ 🄰🄴 ⓪

Sankt Annae Plads 18-20 ⊠ 1250 K – Ⓜ Kongens Nytorv – ℰ 33 96 20 00
– cc.neptun@choice.dk – Fax 33 96 20 66
– www.choicehotels.dk   **D2**
133 rm – ♦1525 DKK ♦♦1925 DKK, ⌑ 125 DKK
Rest *Gendarmen*, ℰ 33 93 66 55 *(closed Sunday)* (dinner only)195/410 DKK
and a la carte approx. 310 DKK
♦ Business ♦ Functional ♦
Converted from two characterful neighbouring houses in the popular Nyhavn district. Rooms are fitted with light wood furniture and offer good range of facilities. Rustic restaurant with wooden tables. Traditional Danish, seasonal menu.

Ibsens 🍽 ⇔rm ⅌ 🖭 📞 VISA ⓄⓈ 🄰🄴 ⓪

Vendersgade 23 ⊠ 1363 K – Ⓜ Nørreport – ℰ 33 13 19 13
– hotel@ibsenshotel.dk – Fax 33 13 19 16
– www.ibsenshotel.dk   **B2**
118 rm – ♦695 DKK ♦♦865 DKK
Rest *La Rocca (closed 24-26 December and Bank Holidays)* 295 DKK and a la carte 189/360 DKK
Rest *Pintxos (closed Sunday)* (dinner only) 295 DKK and a la carte 189/360 DKK
♦ Business ♦ Classic ♦
Large characterful converted apartment block next to sister hotel Kong Arthur. Variety of neat rooms with good facilities. Superior top floor bedrooms. Modern La Rocca for formal Italian dining. Pintxos offers authentic Spanish tapas dinner menu.

Danmark without rest ⇔ ⅌ 🖭 ➔ VISA ⓄⓈ 🄰🄴 ⓪

Vester Voldgade 89 ⊠ 1552 V – ℰ 33 11 48 06 – hotel@hotel-danmark.dk
– Fax 33 14 36 30 – www.hotel-danmark.dk   **C3**
88 rm ⌑ – ♦760 DKK ♦♦945 DKK
♦ Business ♦ Classic ♦
Centrally located close to Tivoli Gardens, offers well kept functional rooms with traditional Scandinavian style décor. Newer rooms in older building are the best.

Top H. Hebron without rest ⇔ ♨50 VISA ⓄⓈ 🄰🄴 ⓪

Helgolandsgade 4 ⊠ 1653 – ℰ 33 31 69 06 – tophotel@hebron.dk
– Fax 33 31 90 67 – www.hebron.dk   **B3**
93 rm ⌑ – ♦780 DKK ♦♦1075 DKK – 6 suites
♦ Traditional ♦ Classic ♦
When it opened in 1900 it was one of the biggest hotels in the city and some of the original features remain. Bedrooms are surprisingly spacious for the price.

Guldsmeden without rest 🆑 🕻 VISA ◑ AE ⓘ
Vesterbrogade 66 ✉ *1620 –* ℰ *33 22 15 00*
– reception@hotelguldsmeden.dk – Fax 33 22 15 55
– www.hotelguldsmeden.dk **A3**
64 rm ⌑ **– ♦970 DKK ♦♦1375 DKK**
♦ Family ♦ Personalised ♦
Family owned, with a relaxing bohemian atmosphere. Extensive, mouthwatering organic breakfasts. Rooms are in a French colonial style: some are in annex, some with balconies.

🍴🍴🍴 Prémisse ⧉ ⇔16 VISA ◑ AE
Dronningens Tvaergade 2 ✉ *1302 –* Ⓜ *Kongens Nytorv –* ℰ *33 11 11 45*
– mail@premisse.dk – Fax 33 11 11 68 – www.premisse.dk
closed 13-17 April, 3-30 July and 23 December-3 January **D2**
Rest (dinner only) 300 DKK/650 DKK and a la carte 645/905 DKK
♦ Innovative ♦ Formal ♦
17C vaulted cellar restaurant further enhanced by modern décor. Wine cellar on view. Open plan kitchen serving uncompromisingly adventurous menu with original flavours.

🍴🍴🍴 Kong Hans Kaelder ⧉ VISA ◑ AE ⓘ
❀
Vingårdsstraede 6 ✉ *1070 K –* Ⓜ *Kongers Nytorv –* ℰ *33 11 68 68*
– konghans@mail.tele.dk – Fax 33 32 67 68 – www.konghans.dk
closed Easter, 3 weeks Summer, last week December
and Bank Holidays **C2**
Rest (booking essential) a la carte 695/775 DKK
Spec. Oysters with caviar, smoked oil and caramelised lemon. Danish beef in three preparations. Quince and pumpkin dessert, sheep's milk yoghurt ice cream.
♦ Modern ♦ Formal ♦
Discreetly located side street restaurant in vaulted Gothic cellar with wood flooring. Fine dining experience; classically based cooking. Friendly and dedicated service.

🍴🍴🍴 Pierre André ⧉ VISA ◑ AE ⓘ
Ny Østergade 21 ✉ *1101 K –* Ⓜ *Kongers Nytorv –* ℰ *33 16 17 19 – Fax 33 16*
17 72 – www.pierreandre.dk
closed Easter, 3 weeks summer, 23-26 December, 1 January, Sunday, Monday,
Saturday lunch and Bank Holidays **C2**
Rest (booking essential) 395 DKK/795 DKK and a la carte 470/725 DKK
♦ French ♦ Formal ♦
Elegant, comfortable dining room with stylish décor in an attractive old building. Full-flavoured cuisine on a classical French base. Efficient and attentive service.

🍴🍴🍴 Restaurationen ⧉ VISA ◑ AE ⓘ
Møntergade 19 ✉ *1116 K –* Ⓜ *Kongens Nytorv –* ℰ *33 14 94 95 – Fax 33 14 85 30*
– www.restaurationen.com
closed 9-17 April, 12-15 May, 2 July-28 August, 21 December-3 January, Sunday
and Monday **C2**
Rest (booking essential) (dinner only except Christmas - set menu only)
650 DKK
♦ Modern ♦ Friendly ♦
A stylish and personally run restaurant. Accomplished modern Danish cooking using well sourced ingredients, accompanied by a comprehensive wine list.

🍴🍴🍴 Krogs 🅰🅒 ⧉ VISA ◑ AE ⓘ
Gammel Strand 38 ✉ *1202 K –* ℰ *33 15 89 15 – krogs@krogs.dk*
– Fax 33 15 83 19 – www.krogs.dk
closed 18-30 December and Sunday **C2**
Rest (booking essential) (dinner only) a la carte 730/840 DKK
♦ Seafood ♦ Formal ♦
Characterful 18C house pleasantly located by canal. Classic room with high ceiling, well lit through large end window. Formal service; seafood dishes attractively presented.

XX ✧
Kommandanten ⅍ ⅗ VISA ⱺⱺ 座 ⓞ
Ny Adelgade 7 ⊠ 1104 K – Ⓜ Kongens Nytorv – ℰ 33 12 09 90
– kommandanten@kommandanten.dk – Fax 33 93 12 23
– www.kommandanten.dk
closed Easter, last 2 weeks July, 22 December-4 January
and Bank Holidays   C2
Rest (booking essential) (dinner only) a la carte 650/840 DKK
Spec. Danish oysters. Chocolate desserts.
 ◆ Modern ◆ Rustic ◆
Distinctive 18C town house: flowers, fine china, stylish contemporary décor and wrought-iron furniture. Exemplary service and original Danish and French cuisine.

XX ✧
MR ⅍ ✧30 VISA ⱺⱺ 座 ⓞ
Kultorvet 5 ⊠ 1175 – ℰ 33 91 09 49 – mr@mr-restaurant.dk
– www.mr.restaurant.dk
closed Easter, 16 July-7 August, 22 December-2 January, lunch Saturday
and Sunday   C2
Rest (set menu only) 300 DKK/425 DKK
 ◆ Modern ◆ Fashionable ◆
Red-painted 18C three-storey townhouse on paved square. Stylish ground-floor lounge with squashy sofas. First floor restaurant serves accomplished, original dishes. Knowledgeable service.

XX ✧
Formel B (Jochumsen/Møller) ⍟ Ⓚ ⅗ VISA ⱺⱺ 座 ⓞ
Vesterbrogade 182, Frederiksberg (via Vesterbrogade) ⊠ 1800 C – ℰ 33 25 10 66
– info@formel-b.dk – www.formel-b.dk
closed Christmas and Sunday
Rest (booking essential) (dinner only) 700 DKK and a la carte approx. 645 DKK
Spec. Turbot and lobster with pumpkin and orange. Pigeon with truffles and foie gras. Chocolate soufflé with vanilla ice cream.
 ◆ Innovative ◆ Neighbourhood ◆
Chic restaurant on the ground floor of an attractive period house. Sleek interior with sandstone and granite. Set menu: precise cooking with well chosen accompanying wines.

XX ✧
Era Ora ⍟ ⅗ VISA ⱺⱺ 座 ⓞ
Overgaden Neden Vandet 33B ⊠ 1414 K
– Ⓜ Christianshavn – ℰ 32 54 06 93 – era-ora@era-ora.dk
– Fax 32 96 02 09
closed Sunday   D3
Rest (booking essential) 280 DKK/425 DKK and a la carte 680/880 DKK
Spec. Antipasti selection. Home-made pasta.
 ◆ Italian ◆ Intimate ◆
Stylish, discreetly located canalside restaurant offers an excellent overview of the best of Italian cuisine, by offering diners a large array of small dishes. Good wine list.

XX ✧
Ensemble (Schou/Egebol) ⅗ VISA ⱺⱺ 座 ⓞ
Tordenskjoldsgade 11 ⊠ 1055 K – Ⓜ Kongens Nytorv – ℰ 33 11 33 52
– kontakt@restaurantensemble.dk – Fax 33 11 33 92
– www.restaurantensemble.dk
closed July, 22 December-3 January, Sunday and Monday   D2
Rest (set menu only) (dinner only) 550 DKK
Spec. Fried turbot with pumpkin and cardamom. Baked salt cod, quail eggs and beetroot. Danish lamb with onions, lemon soubise.
 ◆ Innovative ◆ Minimalist ◆
Whites, greys and bright lighting add to the clean, fresh feel. Open-plan kitchen. Detailed and refined cooking from a set menu, with attentive and courteous service.

Noma (Redzepi) 🛒 🍴 VISA ⊕⊙ AE ⊙
✉ 1401 K – Ⓜ Christianshavn – ✆ 32 96 32 97 – noma@noma.dk
– Fax 32 95 97 22 – www.noma.dk
closed Easter, 3 weeks July, Christmas, Saturday lunch and Sunday　**D2**
Rest 290 DKK/625 DKK and a la carte 415/650 DKK
Spec. Oat wafer and oyster with wild chives. Musk ox and onions in different textures, salad of woodruff. Hazelnut "mayonnaise" and Mutzo apples.
◆ Innovative ◆ Design ◆
Converted 19C harbour warehouse with designer fittings. Talented chefs producing original and innovative dishes with ingredients from Iceland, Greenland and the Faroe Islands.

Kokkeriet 🍴 VISA ⊕⊙ AE
Kronprinsessegade 64 ✉ 1306 K – ✆ 33 15 27 77 – info@kokkeriet.dk
– Fax 33 15 27 75 – www.kokkeriet.dk
closed last 2 weeks July, 24-27 December, 1-5 January, Sunday,
Monday and Bank Holidays　**C1**
Rest (set menu only) (dinner only) 485/585 DKK
Spec. Pumpkin with foie gras and pumpernickel. Monkfish with endive and Cabernet Sauvignon. Chocolate dessert with banana.
◆ Modern ◆ Neighbourhood ◆
Smart, intimate restaurant with neighbourhood feel and stylish furnishings. Inventive modern menu offering 5-7 courses with wine to match. Enthusiastic service.

Koriander Ⓐ 🍴 VISA ⊕⊙ AE ⊙
Store Kongensgade 34 ✉ 1264 – Ⓜ Kongens Nytorv – ✆ 33 15 03 15
closed Sunday　**C2**
Rest (dinner ony) 120 DKK/340 DKK and a la carte 410/665 DKK
◆ Indian ◆ Exotic ◆
Centrally located; charming both without and within: interior is totally white with cream banquettes, pristine chairs and beautifully ornate décor that includes eye-catching lampshades, swags and curtains. Smooth, unobtrusive service. French menus with distinct Indian overlay.

Il Grappolo Blu 🍴 VISA ⊕⊙ AE ⊙
Vester Farimagsgade 35 ✉ 1606 V – ✆ 33 11 57 20 – ilgrappoloblu@
ilgrappoloblu.com – Fax 33 12 57 20 – www.ilgrappoloblu.com
closed Easter, July, Christmas and Sunday　**B3**
Rest (dinner only) 320 DKK/680 DKK
◆ Italian ◆ Friendly ◆
Behind the unpromising façade lies this friendly restaurant, personally run by the owner. Ornate wood panelling and carving. Authentic Italian dishes that just keep on coming.

De Gaulle VISA ⊕⊙ AE ⊙
Kronborggade 3 ✉ 2200 – ✆ 35 85 58 66 – info@de-gaulle.dk – Fax 35 85 58 69
– www.de-gaulle.dk
closed 13-17 April, 16 July-14 August, Christmas, Sunday,
Monday and Bank Holidays　**A1**
Rest (dinner only - set menu only) 390 DKK/500 DKK
◆ French ◆ Friendly ◆
In the Nørrebro area, an intimate personally-run restaurant where young chef delivers some dishes to the table. Choice of 3-6 courses from set menu of modern French dishes.

Umami Ⓐ VISA ⊕⊙ AE ⊙
Store Kongensgade 59 ✉ 1264 – Ⓜ Kongens Nytorv – ✆ 33 38 75 00
– mail@restaurantumami.dk – Fax 33 38 75 15 – www.restaurantumami.dk
closed 27 December-7 January, Saturday and Sunday lunch　**C-D2**
Rest 785 DKK and a la carte 275/430 DKK
◆ Japanese ◆ Fashionable ◆
Elegant and contemporary, with stylish wood tables and eating options on two floors: sushi bar, ancillary dining area or spacious main dining room. Authentic Japanese dishes.

χχ **Olsen** 🍴 VISA ⊕ AE ⊕
Ved Stranden 18 ⊠ 1061 – ℰ 33 14 64 00 – Fax 33 14 64 01
– www.restaurantolsen.com
closed Sunday **C2**
Rest 195 DKK and a la carte 225/345 DKK
♦ Modern ♦ Fashionable ♦
Centrally located restaurant boasts relaxing, though buzzy, vibe with terrace and
canal views. Intimate, popular bar. Tightly packed dining tables: the place to be
seen! Interesting seasonal menus with a Norwegian base.

χχ **The Dining Room** – at Radisson SAS Scandinavia H.
≤ Copenhagen, AK ⅙ P VISA ⊕ AE ⊕
25th Floor, Amager Boulevard 70 – ℰ 33 96 58 58 – info @ thediningroom.dk
– Fax 3396 55 00 – www.thediningroom.dk
closed Sunday-Monday **C3**
Rest (dinner only)300/800 DKK and a la carte 350/570 DKK
♦ Modern ♦ Design ♦
Situated on the 25th floor of the hotel, but run independently, and provi-
ding diners with wonderful panoramic views of the city. Original and modern
menu.

χχ **Extra** 🍴 VISA ⊕ AE ⊕
Østergade 13 ⊠ 1100 – ⊕ Kongens Nytorv – ℰ 35 26 09 52 – extra @
restaurant-extra.dk – Fax 35 26 09 54 – www.restaurant-extra.dk
closed 1 week Christmas and Sunday **C2**
Rest 98 DKK/450 DKK and a la carte 235/385 DKK
♦ Modern ♦ Trendy ♦
Set on very busy, well known pedestrianised shopping street. Basement
restaurant below bar. Chic décor. Artistic modern dishes with some unusual
combinations and flavours.

χχ **Frederiks Have** 🍴 VISA ⊕ AE ⊕
Smallegade 41 (West: 1 1/2 km via Gammel Kongevej) ⊠ 2000 Frederiksberg
– ⊕ Frederiksberg – ℰ 38 88 33 35 – info @ frederikshave.dk
– Fax 38 88 33 37 – www.frederikshave.dk
closed Easter and 22 December-5 January
Rest (dinner only) 188 DKK/718 DKK
♦ Modern ♦ Neighbourhood ♦
Established restaurant in leafy residential district. Homely ambience and
delightful terrace. Monthly menus offer traditional and modern Danish
cooking.

χχ **VB Square** 🍴 VISA ⊕ ⊕
Øster Søgade 114 (via Øster Søgade at junction with Oslo Plads) ⊠ 2100
– ℰ 35 42 22 77 – Fax 35 42 22 70 – www.vbsquare.dk
closed Christmas, New Year, Sunday and Monday
Rest (dinner only) 325 DKK and a la carte 370/430 DKK
♦ Modern ♦ Fashionable ♦
Relatively compact restaurant with a genuine neighbourhood feel.
Contemporary colour scheme of browns and pastels. Knowledgeable service
and modern Danish cooking.

χχ **Gammel Mønt** 🍴 VISA ⊕ AE ⊕
Gammel Mønt 41 ⊠ 1117 K – ⊕ Kongens Nytorv – ℰ 33 15 10 60
– info @ gammel-moent.dk – Fax 33 15 10 60 – www.gammel-moent.dk
closed Easter, 23 June-15 August, Christmas, Bank Holidays,
Saturday and Sunday **C2**
Rest 285 DKK/600 DKK and a la carte 445/590 DKK
♦ Traditional ♦ Family ♦
Half-timbered house from 1732 with striking red façade in smart commercial
district. Traditional cuisine with seasonal variations and interesting range of
herring dishes.

XX ⚕ Rasmus Oubaek   🕏 VISA 🐵 AE ①

Store Kongensgade 52 ⊠ 1264 – Ⓜ Kongens Nytorv – ℰ 33 32 32 09
– rasmus-oubaek@mail.dk – www.rasmusouaek.dk   **C-D2**
closed mid July-mid August, Christmas-New Year, Sunday and Monday
Rest (set menu only) (dinner only) 650 DKK

Spec. Pigeon and foie gras with Jerusalem artichoke, apple and white Alba truffles. Turbot and lobster with carrots and tarragon. Apple tart and rosemary ice cream.

♦ Innovative ♦ Minimalist ♦

Unpretentious restaurant with simple but stylish décor offering accomplished classic dishes; large and comprehensive list of quality wines; pleasant and professional service.

XX 😊 Le Sommelier   🕏 VISA 🐵 AE ①

Bredgade 63-65 ⊠ 1260 K – ℰ 33 11 45 15 – mail@lesommelier.dk
– Fax 33 11 59 79 – www.lesommelier.dk
closed 22 December-3 January and lunch Saturday and Sunday   **D1**
Rest 260 DKK/425 DKK and a la carte 340/455 DKK ⅋

♦ Modern ♦ Brasserie ♦

Popular brasserie in the heart of the old town. The owners' passion for wine shows in posters, memorabilia and an excellent "by glass" list. Modern Danish cooking.

XX Salt – at Admiral H.   ⟨ 🛱 P VISA 🐵 AE ①

Toldbodgade 24-28 – Ⓜ Kongens Nytorv – ℰ 33 74 14 44
– info@saltrestaurant.dk – Fax 33 74 14 16   **D2**
Rest (buffet lunch) 150/345 DKK and a la carte 335/420 DKK

♦ Modern ♦ Design ♦

Conran-designed restaurant in 18C warehouse; outdoor summer tables. Only sea salt is used. Danish buffet and modern a la carte at midday; more extensive modern dinner menu.

X 😊 Kanalen   ⟨ 🛱 🕏 P VISA 🐵 AE ①

Christianshavn Wilders Plads 2 ⊠ 1403 K – Ⓜ Christianshavn – ℰ 32 95 13 30
– info@restaurant-kanalen.dk – Fax 32 95 13 38 – www.restaurant-kanalen.dk
closed 9-17 April, 24-30 December, Sunday and Bank Holidays   **D3**
Rest (booking essential) (set menu only at dinner) 230/490 DKK and lunch a la carte approx. 265 DKK

♦ Modern ♦ Intimate ♦

Delightfully located former Harbour Police office on canalside. Simple elegant décor, informal yet personally run. Well balanced menu of modern Danish cooking.

X Lumskebugten   🛱 VISA 🐵 AE ①

Esplanaden 21 ⊠ 1263 K – ℰ 33 15 60 29 – Fax 33 32 87 18
– www.lumskebugten.dk
closed Christmas, Sunday, Saturday lunch and Bank Holidays   **D1**
Rest a la carte 330/880 DKK

♦ Traditional ♦ Cosy ♦

Mid 19C café-pavilion near quayside and Little Mermaid. Interesting 19C maritime memorabilia and old paintings. Good traditional cuisine. Possibility of dining on boat.

X ⚕ Godt (Rice)   🕏 VISA 🐵 ①

Gothersgade 38 ⊠ 1123 K – Ⓜ Kongens Nytorv – ℰ 33 15 21 22
– restaurant.godt@get2net.dk – www.restaurant-godt.dk
closed Christmas-New Year, Easter, 2 July-7 August, 15-23 October,
Sunday, Monday and Bank Holidays   **C2**
Rest (booking essential) 480 DKK and a la carte 480/600 DKK

Spec. Danish lobster soup with quenelles of lobster and truffle. Turbot with wild herbs and seasonal vegetables. Game with wild forest mushrooms.

♦ Modern ♦ Design ♦

Small stylish modern two floor restaurant with grey décor, ceiling fans and old WWII shells as candle holders. Personally run. Excellently conceived daily menu of modern fare.

M/S Amerika ☆ VISA ◉◉ AE ◉

Dampfaergerej 8 (Pakhus 12, Amerikakaj) (via Folke Bernadottes Allée) ☒ 2100 K
– ℰ 35 26 90 30 – info @ msamerika.dk – Fax 35 26 91 30
– www.msamerika.dk
closed 24 December-2 January, Sunday and Bank Holidays
Rest 236 DKK/345 DKK and a la carte 360/475 DKK
♦ Modern ♦ Brasserie ♦
Characterful 19C former warehouse in attractive quayside location, with popular terrace in the summer. Open plan kitchen provides fresh, appealing, modern Danish fare.

Famo ↳ VISA ◉◉ AE ◉

Saxogade 3 ☒ 1662 – ℰ 33 23 22 50
closed Christmas, Saturday and Sunday **A3**
Rest (booking essential) (Set menu only) 250 DKK/350 DKK
♦ Italian ♦ Bistro ♦
Simple, personally run Italian eatery that feels like an osteria; opened in 2005. No written menus: owners propose the day's good value, authentic regional dishes. Chatty, attentive service completes the picture.

TyvenKokkenHansKoneOgHendesElsker

Magstraede 16 ☒ 1204 K – ℰ 33 16 12 92 ℱ VISA ◉◉ AE ◉
– post @ tyven.dk – www.tyven.dk
closed 10-17 April, 10 July-6 August, 23 December-5 January
and Sunday **C3**
Rest (dinner only) 595 DKK and a la carte 530/605 DKK
♦ Modern ♦ Rustic ♦
18C part timbered house in cobbled street. Named after the Peter Greenaway film. Set menu (5 courses) with small a la carte. French based dishes with Danish influence.

Viva ⪡ ☆ ℱ VISA ◉◉ ◉

Langebrogade Kaj 570 ☒ 1411 K – ⓜ Christianhavn – ℰ 27 25 05 05
– viva @ restaurantviva.dk – www.restaurantviva.dk
closed Christmas-New Year **C3**
Rest 160/330 DKK and a la carte 310/500 DKK
♦ Modern ♦ Minimalist ♦
Converted German tug boat moored on the river; stylish minimalist interior and top deck terrace. Eclectic menu with strong Danish note at lunch.

Fiasco VISA ◉◉ AE ◉

Gammel Kongevej 176, Frederiksberg (via Gammel Kongevej)
☒ 1850 C – ℰ 33 31 74 87 – fiasco @ tiscali.dk
– Fax 33 31 74 87
closed 22 December-10 January and Sunday
Rest 188 DKK/255 DKK and a la carte approx. 255 DKK
♦ Italian ♦ Friendly ♦
Modern Italian restaurant to the west of the city centre. Bright room with fresh feel and large picture windows. Friendly young owners. Carefully prepared, authentic cuisine.

Luns VISA ◉◉

Øster Farimagsgade 12 ☒ 2100 – ℰ 35 26 33 35
– www.restaurantluns.dk
closed Christmas, Easter, July, and Sunday-Tuesday **C1**
Rest (set menu) (booking essential) (dinner only) 275 DKK
♦ Home cooking ♦ Rustic ♦
Opened in 2005: simple rustic neighbourhood eatery that's quickly become locally renowned. Owner cooks and serves set menus of good value rural French fare: you can eat from two to five courses in totally relaxed surroundings.

DENMARK

IN TIVOLI *Vesterbrogade 3 - ⊠1620 V (entrance fee payable):* **Plan I**

✗✗✗ The Paul (Cunningham) 🛗 AC ⅃⁄ ⅏ ✪12 VISA ⑩⓪ AE ①
✿
Vesterbrogade 3 ⊠ 1630 K – ℰ 33 75 07 75 – info@thepaul.dk – Fax 33 75 07 76
– www.thepaul.dk
closed October, Christmas Eve-April and Sunday   **B3**
Rest (dinner only Wednesday-Saturday 15 November-22 December) (set
menu only) 450 DKK/700 DKK
Spec. Foie gras with caramelised pineapple sorbet and sherry vinegar. Pigeon
pot au feu with Danish shrimps. White asparagus, almond foam, wild woodruff
and dark chocolate soup.
◆ Innovative ◆ Formal ◆
Elegant glass-domed 20C structure by the lake in Tivoli Gardens. Open-plan
kitchen with chef's table. Set menu (3-7 courses); elaborate cooking using local
produce.

✗ Amalie 🛗 ⅏ VISA ⑩⓪ AE ①
☺
Amaliegade 11 ⊠ 1256 – Ⓜ Kongens Nytorv – ℰ 33 12 88 10 – Fax 33 12 88 10
closed Sunday   **D2**
Rest (booking essential) (lunch only) 188 DKK/198 DKK and a la carte approx.
206 DKK
◆ Traditional ◆ Friendly ◆
Located in a pretty 18C town house. Wood panelled walls and a clean,
uncluttered style. Helpful service and ideal for those looking for an authentic,
traditional Danish lunch.

✗ Ida Davidsen ⅏ VISA ⑩⓪ AE ①
Store Kongensgade 70 ⊠ 1264 K – Ⓜ Kongens Nytorv – ℰ 33 91 36 55
– ida.davidsen@cirque.dk – Fax 33 11 36 55 – www.idadavidsen.dk
closed 5 June, 3 July-28 July, 22 December-15 January,
Saturday and Sunday   **D2**
Rest (lunch only) 45 DKK/160 DKK
◆ Traditional ◆ Family ◆
Family run for five generations, this open sandwich bar, on a busy city-centre street,
is almost a household name in Denmark. Offers a full range of typical smørrebrød.

✗ Sankt Annae ⅏ VISA ⑩⓪ AE ①
Sankt Annae Plads 12 ⊠ 1250 K – Ⓜ Kongens Nytorv – ℰ 33 12 54 97
– Fax 33 15 16 61 – www.restaurantsanktannae.dk
closed Sunday and Bank Holidays   **D2**
Rest (lunch only) 45 DKK/158 DKK
◆ Traditional ◆ Friendly ◆
Pretty terraced building in popular part of town. Simple décor with a rustic feel
and counter next to kitchen. Typical menu of smørrebrød. Service prompt and
efficient.

SMØRREBRØD *The following list of simpler restaurants and
cafés/bars specialize in Danish open sandwiches and are generally open
from 10.00am to 4.00pm.*

ENVIRONS OF COPENHAGEN

at Nordhavn North: 3 km by Østbanegade and Road 2:

✗✗✗ Paustian at Bo Bech AC P VISA ⑩⓪ ①
Kalkbraenderiløloskaj 2 ⊠ 2100 – ℰ 39 18 55 01 – mail@restaurantpaustian.dk
– www.restaurantpaustian.dk
closed 9 July-1 August, 22 December-6 January and Sunday
Rest 150 DKK/295 DKK and a la carte 500/640 DKK ⅏
◆ Innovative ◆ Design ◆
Stylish quayside restaurant adjoining Paustian, a famous furniture store not far
from city centre by train. Choice of menus offering original creations. Impressive
wine list.

at Hellerup North: 7.5 km by Østbanegade and Road 2 - ⊠ 2900 Hellerup:

DENMARK

Hellerup Parkhotel 🗟 *Là* 🕥 ½⁄ ⊠ 📞 🔌150 **P** *VISA* 🐵 🖭 ⑩
Strandvejen 203 ⊠ *2900 – 𝒞 39 62 40 44 – info@hellerupparkhotel.dk*
– Fax 39 45 15 90 – www.hellerupparkhotel.dk
71 rm ⊆ – 🍴925 DKK 🍴🍴1930 DKK
Rest see **Saison** below
Rest Wine and Dine (dinner only) a la carte 250/455 DKK
♦ Business ♦ Classic ♦
Attractive classic hotel located in affluent suburb north of the city. Rooms vary in size and colour décor but offer same good standard of facilities and level of comfort. Popular local Italian restaurant on side of hotel with terrace.

✗✗ **Saison**   **P** *VISA* 🐵 🖭 ⑩
Strandvejen 203 – 𝒞 39 62 48 42 – saison@saison.dk – Fax 39 62 20 30
– www.saison.dk
closed Easter, 3 weeks July, Christmas and Bank Holidays
Rest 225 DKK/590 DKK and a la carte 410/550 DKK
♦ Modern ♦ Formal ♦
Run separately from the hotel in which it is located. Enjoys a bright and airy feel with high ceiling and large windows. Carefully prepared cooking using quality ingredients.

at Søllerød North: 20 km by Tagensvej (take the train to Holte then taxi)
- ⊠ 2840 Holte:

✗✗✗ **Søllerød Kro** 🗟 ⅌ **P** *VISA* 🐵 🖭 ⑩
Søllerødvej 35 ⊠ *2840 K – 𝒞 45 80 25 05 – mail@soelleroed-kro.dk*
– Fax 45 80 22 70 – www.soelleroed-kro.dk
closed 1 week February, Easter, July, 24 December, 1 January and Monday
Rest 475 DKK/555 DKK and a la carte 534/1044 DKK 🕸
♦ Modern ♦ Inn ♦
Characterful 17C thatched inn with attractive courtyard terrace and stylish Danish rustic-bourgeois décor. Classically based cooking with modern notes and excellent wine list.

at Kastrup Airport Southeast: 10 km by Amager Boulevard:

Hilton Copenhagen Airport ⟨ *Là* 🕥 🖾 ⅊ 🖾 ½⁄rm ⅌rest ⊠
Ellehammersvej 20, Kastrup ⊠ *2770* 🔌450 ⟨⟩ *VISA* 🐵 🖭 ⑩
– 𝒞 32 50 15 01 – res_copenhagen-airport@hilton.com – Fax 32 52 85 28
– www.hilton.com
382 rm – 🍴2250 DKK 🍴🍴2250 DKK, ⊆ 145 DKK
Rest Hamlet, *𝒞 32 44 53 53 (closed Sunday and Bank Holidays)* 545 DKK/745 DKK and a la carte 405/535 DKK
Rest Horizon, *𝒞 32 44 53 53* – 245 DKK/450 DKK and a la carte 145 DKK
♦ Business ♦ Modern ♦
Glass walkway leads from arrivals to this smart business hotel. Bright bedrooms with light, contemporary Scandinavian furnishings and modern facilities. Hamlet is a formal open-plan restaurant with eclectic menu. Relaxed dining in Horizon beneath vast atrium.

Quality Airport H. Dan 🗟 *Là* 🕥 🖾 rest ½⁄rm ⊠ 🔌60
Kastruplundgade 15, Kastrup (North : **P** *VISA* 🐵 🖭 ⑩
2 ½ km by coastal rd) ⊠ *2770 – 𝒞 32 51 14 00 – q.dan@choice.dk*
– Fax 32 51 37 01 – www.choicehotels.dk
228 rm – 🍴1295/1995 DKK, ⊆ 95 DKK
Rest (buffet dinner only) 98 DKK
♦ Business ♦ Functional ♦
Airport hotel not far from beach and countryside, popular with business travellers. All rooms with modern facilities; some with views of canal. Traditional Danish cuisine in the restaurant.

141

FINLAND
SUOMI

PROFILE

- **AREA:**
  338 145 km² (130 558 sq mi).

- **POPULATION:**
  5 225 000 inhabitants (est. 2005), density = 15 per km².

- **CAPITAL:**
  Helsinki (conurbation 1 151 000 inhabitants).

- **CURRENCY:**
  Euro (€); rate of exchange: € 1 = US$ 1.17 (Nov 2005).

- **GOVERNMENT:**
  Parliamentary republic (since 1917). Member of European Union since 1995.

- **LANGUAGES:**
  Finnish (a Finno-Ugric language related to Estonian) spoken by 92% of Finns, Swedish (6%) and Sami (some 7 000 native speakers). English is widely spoken.

- **SPECIFIC PUBLIC HOLIDAYS:**
  Epiphany (6 January); Good Friday (Friday before Easter); Midsummer's Day (25 June); Independence Day (6 December); Boxing Day (26 December).

- **LOCAL TIME:**
  GMT + 2 hours in winter and GMT + 3 hours in summer.

- **CLIMATE:**
  Temperate continental with very cold winters and mild summers (Helsinki: January: -7°C, July: 17°C). Midnight sun: the sun never sets for several weeks around Midsummer in the north. Snow settles in early December to April in the south and centre of the country. Northern Lights

(Aurora Borealis) visible in the north on clear, dark nights; highest frequency in Feb-Mar and Sep-Oct.

- **INTERNATIONAL DIALLING CODE:**
  00 358 followed by area code (Helsinki: 9) and then the local number.

- **EMERGENCY:**
  Fire Brigade, Ambulance, Police: ☎ 112.

- **ELECTRICITY:**
  220 volts AC, 50Hz; 2-pin round-shaped continental plugs.

FORMALITIES

Travellers from the European Union (EU), Switzerland, Iceland and the main countries of North and South America need a national identity card or passport (America: passport required) to visit Finland for less than three months (tourism or business purpose). For visitors from other countries a visa may be required, in addition to a passport, especially for those wishing to stay for longer than three months. If you plan to visit Russia while in Finland, you must purchase an appropriate visa in advance in your own country. We advise you to check with your embassy before travelling.

Nationals of EU or EEA countries require a national driving licence, other travellers should have an international driving licence. Third party insurance is compulsory and a green card is recommended. Laws on drink-driving are strictly enforced. Headlights should be switched on at all times outside built-up areas. In winter, snow tyres are required from December to February and engine heaters recommended.

MAJOR NEWSPAPERS

The main national newspapers are: *Helsingin Sanomat* (Finnish, English), *Hufvudstadtsbladet* (Swedish), *Ilta Sanomat*, *Iltalehti* and *Kauppelehti*.

USEFUL PHRASES

ENGLISH	FINNISH
Yes	**Kyllä**
No	**Ei**
Good morning	**Huomenta**
Goodbye	**Näkemin**
Thank you	**Kütos**
Please	**Olkaa hyvä**
Excuse me	**Anteeksi**
I don't understand	**En ymmärä**

HOTELS

◆ CATEGORIES

The standard of accommodation in Finland is very high from international luxury hotels, elegant manor house and spa hotels to reasonably priced establishments, comfortable motels, guesthouses and bed and breakfast accommodation in the countryside and wilderness lodges. A night in a snow hotel is a memorable experience. Several hotel chains operate throughout Finland.

◆ PRICE RANGE

The price is per room and includes breakfast. Special rates are available during the holiday season. Most hotels have special weekend and summer offers. **Finncheque** and other hotel vouchers which offer special rates can be bought from travel agents.

◆ TAX

Taxes and service are included in the hotel rate.

◆ CHECK OUT TIME

Between 11am and noon.

◆ RESERVATIONS

Bookings can be made by phone, on the Internet or via travel agencies.

◆ TIPS FOR HANDLING LUGGAGE

Gratuities are not compulsory but a small tip is welcome.

◆ BREAKFAST

Breakfast is a copious meal, a self-service buffet of porridge, cereals, pancakes, eggs, ham, sausage, yoghurt, jams and several types of bread.

Reception	**Vastaanottohuone**
Single room	**Yhden hengen huone**
Double room	**Kahden hengen huone**
Bed	**Vuode**
Bathroom	**Kylpy**
Shower	**Suikhu**

RESTAURANTS

The term **ravintola** is used for small intimate restaurants to grand establishments with music and dance floor. A **grilli** or **krouvi** is a small informal restaurant with a hearty menu. Other kinds of eating places include **kahvio** (self-service cafeteria), **kahvila** (café, snack-bar serving cakes, patisseries and light meals), **baari** (snack-bar offering light food and mild beer or coffee) and pubs (for meals with waitress-service). **Yökerho** are nightclubs in big hotels which also serve food.

◆ MEALS

Breakfast	**Aamianen**	7/8am-10am
Lunch	**Lounas**	11am-1pm
Dinner	**Päivällinen**	7-8pm-10pm

Restaurants in Finland offer moderately priced set menus as well as a comprehensive à la carte menu. The menus include traditional Finnish dishes as well as classic international cuisine. The Finnish cold buffet **(voileipäpöytä)** is a good lunch alternative. Menus in English are usually available in large towns.

◆ RESERVATIONS

It is advisable to book in advance if you intend to visit a restaurant prized for its culinary expertise. Reservations should be made by telephone or by Internet. You will usually be asked for a credit card number as guarantee.

◆ THE BILL

The bill (check) includes service and tax. If you are particularly pleased with the service you may wish to give an additional tip.

Appetizer	**Cocktailpala**
Meal	**Ateria**
Starter	**Alkuruokia**
Main dish	**Paaruokalaji**
Main dish of the day	**Päivän tarjous/annos**
Dessert	**Jälkiruoka**
Water/ mineral water	**Vesi/ kivennäisvesi**
(still, sparkling)	**(vielä, hel meilevä)**
Wine (red, white, rosé)	**Vïnïa (puna, valko, rosé)**
Beer	**Olut**
Bread	**Leipää**
Meat	**Liha**
Fish	**Kala**
Salt/pepper	**Suolaa/pippuria**
Cheese	**Juusto**
Vegetables	**Vihannes**
Hot/cold	**Kuuma/kylmä**
The bill (check) please	**Saisinko, laskun**

LOCAL CUISINE

The culinary traditions of Finland reflect its location at the crossroads of Europe and Russia. The abundance and quality of fresh products from land and sea are outstanding and every season brings its own delicacies on offer at the many indoor and outdoor markets.

The Finnish **voileipäpöytä** (meaning 'bread and butter table') comprises a mouthwatering array of dishes: pickled and salted fish (herring, salmon), cold meats, sausages, salads, cheese and a variety of breads: whole wheat, white, black and rye. The dark sour rye **Ruislêipa** is a great favourite. **Rosolli** is a typical salad of beetroot, carrots, potatoes, cucumber, onion and apple.

Thick soups made with peas, fish, meat, mushrooms, rhubarb and summer vegetables are warming in the cold climate. Every region produces tasty sausages: bologna-type sausage, **mustamakkara** (blood sausage), **lenkkimakkara** (loop sausage), black pudding from Tampere, 'raisin' or 'onion' sausage from Turku. Finnish hors-d'œuvre include red Finnish caviar, white fish and herring roe and blini with sour cream and chopped onion; **vorschmack** (chopped herring with garlic, onion and lamb).

The icy waters and rivers of Finland abound in very fine fish: salmon (lohi), burbot, lamprey, vendace, muikku fritti (similar to salmon), pike perch (kuha), perch (ahven), rainbow trout (kirjolohi). **Silakka** (Baltic herring) is pickled, fried, grilled or baked with potatoes and cheese sauce. The crayfish **(rapu)** season in August is a gastronomic highlight.

Among regional specialities are: **karjalanpaisti** (Karelian hotpot), **karjalan piirakka** (Karelian pasties – a thin rye crust filled with rice), **kalakukko** (Karelian pasties filled with fish and fatty pork), lamb and cabbage stew, stuffed cabbage rolls, roast reindeer with cranberry sauce, sauteed reindeer **(poronkäristys)**, smoked reindeer **(savustettua poronlihaa)**, reindeer tongue **(poronkieli)**, meatballs **(lihapulla)**. Game is on the menu in season.

You can indulge in delicious pastries: **pikkupullat** (cardamon buns), **laskiaispulla** (buns filled with marzipan and cream), **korrapuusti** (cinnamon buns), **rahkapulla** (lemon and quark tarts), **tippaleipä** (pastry like brown crunchy spaghetti), **pannukakku** (thick pancakes with jam), **torttu** (fruit tarts). **Mämmi** is a malt-flavoured pudding.

The most popular cheeses (juusto) are **Finlandia** similar to Emmental, the Cheddar-like **juhlajuusto**, the blue-veined **aurajuusto**, the mild **Turunna**. **Uunijuusto** is a fresh soft cheese. **Juustoleipä** or **leipäjuusto** is a cheese bread which is warmed in the oven and eaten with cloudberry jam.

DRINK

Beer is the most popular drink: the secret of Finnish lager is the high quality water, good barley and a long brewing tradition. Koff and Lapinkulta and the malty sahti beer are worth tasting. Try the delicious fruit liqueurs: Lakka (cloudberry), Polar (cranberry), Mesimarja (Arctic raspberry).

The Finns are partial to a glass of schnapps. Mead and sparking wine made from white currants and gooseberries are drunk during carnival on 1 May in Vappu. Glögg, spicy mulled wine, is served at Christmas. Buttermilk is a popular drink with meals.

HELSINKI
HELSINGFORS

Population (est. 2005): 583 000 (conurbation 1 151 000) – Altitude: sea level

R. Mattes / MICHELIN

Helsinki 'Daughter of the Baltic' is located on a peninsula and is Europe's northernmost capital. The compact city has a unique character defined by its history and architectural heritage. Its formal neo-Classical showpieces, the imaginative volumes and decoration of the Art Nouveau period and the pure lines of modern architecture are set against a backdrop of sea and forest. It is a lively university town and a commercial centre with five busy harbours.

The city built in 16C by the King of Sweden was relocated to its present site by the sea in 1640. It was twice occupied by Russia in the 18C. It reverted to the Swedish kingdom from 1746 to 1809 but after the 1808-9 war, Finland broke with Sweden; after unification with Russia, it became an autonomous Grand Duchy while retaining the Swedish constitution and Lutheran religion. Helsinki became the capital in 1812 and prospered under the reign of Alexander II; by the end of the 19C it had become the cultural and political centre of Finland. Since 1917 it has been the capital of an independent state; it has acquired a new status for its bold, modern, post-war architectural achievements and as the Geneva of the North for hosting international conferences.

WHICH DISTRICT TO CHOOSE

Accommodation in Helsinki is of the highest standard with prestigious hotels in the city centre, near the railway station, in the Kampi district *Plan I* **B2**, near the harbours; business hotels in Mannerheimintie *Plan I* **B1**, Pohjoisesplanadi *Plan I* **C2**, Kalastajatorpantie, Messauaukio Eteläranta *Plan I* **C2**; and friendly comfortable hotels in the Länsi-Pasila district.

Restaurants to suit all tastes are to be found in the city centre. There are restaurants in a pleasant setting on the islands. Restaurants with The Helsinki Menu sign offer high-quality Finnish dishes prepared with seasonal products.

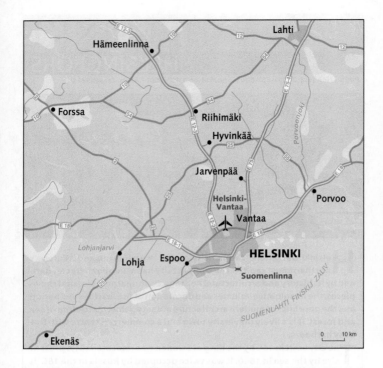

PRACTICAL INFORMATION

ARRIVAL – DEPARTURE

Helsinki-Vantaa Airport – 19 km (12 mi) north of the city. ℰ 0200 14636; www.ilmailulaitos.fi

From the airport to the city centre – By **taxi**: €20-30 or **shuttle minibus**: €20-55 (2-9 persons), time 20-30min. ℰ 0600 555 555; www.airporttaxi.fi; www.yellowline.fi. By **Finnair City Bus** (with request stops): every 20min, €5.20, time 30-40min. By **bus**: Lines 415, 451, 615 to Central Bus Station; time 40min, approx. €3.50.

◆ MAIN STATIONS

Central Railway Station (Rautatieasema) *Plan I* **B2**. ℰ 0600 41 902 (daily 7am-10pm); www.vr.fi

148

Central Bus Station (Linja-autoasema) *Plan I* **B2**. ℰ 0200 4000; www.matkahuolto.fi

TRANSPORT

◆ BUS, TRAM, METRO, TRAIN, FERRY

The public transport system is practical and efficient. Single tram ticket €1.80; single City ticket €2; Regional Travel card '2' €3.40. HKL tourist tickets *(matkakortti)* €5.40 (1 day), €10.80 (3 days), €16.20 (5 days). Single tickets are valid 1hr and transfers are allowed. Tickets can be purchased from the driver, ticket machines, R-kiosks, metro stations, ferry terminal. Prepaid tickets are slightly cheaper. Sightseeing Trams 3T, 3B hop-on hop-off. Helsinki

Card (24, 48, 72hr): approx. €25, 35, 45 gives unlimited transport, free entry to museums and various discounts.

◆ TAXIS

Taxis (yellow vehicles with Taxis/Taxi sign) can be hailed in the streets at taxi stands, near stations and at the airport or can be ordered by phone. An average ride in the city is about €25 and there are evening, Sunday and luggage surcharges. Taxi Helsinki ℰ 09 700 700, 0100 0700; www.taxishelsinki.fi

USEFUL ADDRESSES

◆ TOURIST OFFICE

Helsinki Tourist & Convention Bureau – Pohjoisesplanadi 19 *Plan I* **C2**. Open May-Sept, Mon-Fri 9am-8pm, Sat-Sun 9am-6pm; Oct-Apr, Mon-Fri 9am-6pm, Sat-Sun 10am-4pm. ℰ 09 169 3757; www hel.fi/tourism

A smaller office is located at the Central Railway Station. From June to August 'Helsinki Helpers' in green overalls patrol the streets offering free advice and help to visitors.

◆ BANKS / CURRENCY EXCHANGE

Banks open Mon-Fri 9.15am-4.15pm. ATMs are available all over the city. Credit cards are widely accepted. Exchange offices at the Central Railway Station and at the airport have longer opening hours.

◆ POST OFFICES

Opening times Mon-Fri 9am-6pm. Post boxes are yellow. Main Post Offfice, Elielinaukio 2F *Plan I* **B1** open Mon-Fri 7am-9pm and Sat-Sun 10am-6pm. ℰ 0200 71000. Stamps are also available from book and paper shops, R-kiosks, stations and hotels.

◆ PHARMACY

Look for the sign 'apteekki'. Opening times 9am-5.30pm. There is a 24hr pharmacy at Mannerheimintie 96 *Plan I* **B1**.

EXPLORING HELSINKI

VISITING

It is possible to visit sights and museums in Helsinki in two days.

Museums and other sights are usually open10-11am to 5-6pm; some close on Mondays.

Neo-Classical Helsinki – Imposing monumental ensemble: **Senaatintori** *Plan I* **C2**, a vast square (statue of Czar Alexander II) dominated by the domed **Tuomiokirkko** *Plan I* **C2**, with its stark interior; behind stands the delightful **Pyhää Kolminaisuuden kirkko** *Plan I* **C2**. Around the square are **Valtionneuvoston linna** (Senate House), the University and the domed library, **Yliopiston kirjasto** *Plan I* **C2**, and fine burghers' houses (**Sederholmin talo** *SE*). **Kauppatori**

Plan I **C2**: In Market Square, the Empire frontage includes from east to west: **Presidentinlinna** (Presidential Palace) *Plan I* **C2**, **Korkein Oikeus** (Supreme Court), **Kaupungintalo** (Town Hall). **Esplanadi** *Plan I* **C2** is lined with ornate neo-Renaissance buildings.

New City Centre – **Rautatieasema** (station) *Plan I* **B2** in Art Nouveau style. **Euskuntatalo** (Parliament House) *Plan I* **B2** in red granite. **Finlandiatalo** (Finlandia Hall) *Plan I* **B1** in white marble. **Kansallisooppera** *Plan I* **A1** clad in Finnish granite and white ceramic tiles. **Temppeliaukion kirkko** *Plan I* **A2**: the circular Church in the rock combines ingenious engineering and architectural flair. The red-roofed

Suomen Kansallisteatteri *Plan l C2* in grey granite. The **Lasipalatsi** cultural centre *Plan l B2*.

Museums – Ateneum, The Museum of Finnish Art *Plan l B2*: excellent introduction to Finnish art (18C-1960s). **Kiasma** *Plan l B2*: housed in a striking building, the Museum of Contemporary Art presents an overview of contemporary trends. **Kansallismuseo** *Plan l B1*: interesting architectural style. Frescoes depicting the legends of the *Kalevala*. The museum presents the development of Finnish life from prehistory to the present. **Taideteollisuusmuseo** *Plan l C2*: Museum of Art and Design presents a survey of the famous names of Finnish design from 19C to the present day (Walter Jung, Alvar and Aino Alto, Tappio Wirkkala). **Seurasaari**: open-air museum devoted to traditional ways of life.

Katajanokka *Plan l D2* – Art Nouveau buildings (Nos 1, 5 Luotsikatu). **Icebreaker fleet** and frontage of former naval headquarters. **Uspenskin katedraali**: 19C cathedral, evidence of the city's Russian heritage, ornate interior.

Suomenlinna *Plan l D3* – The Fortress built on a group of six islands is a World Heritage Site: museums, art exhibitions.

Views – Stroll along the waterfront, watch the activity in the harbour and enjoy the view of the rocky islands, of the ferries, Market Square and the two cathedrals as well as the lively atmosphere. View of the bay from the **Sibelius-monumentti** *Plan l A1*.

Boat trips – Excursions around offshore islands from Market Square *Plan l C2*, and to the original site of Helsinki and the archipelago departing from Pohjoisranta *Plan l D1* and Meritullintori *Plan l C2*.

150

SHOPPING

Shops usually open Mon-Fri 9/10am-5/6pm, Sat 9/10am-1/2pm. Shopping centres and department stores open Mon-Fri 9am-9pm, Sat 9am-6pm.

The main shopping streets are **Mannerheimintie** *Plan l B1*, **Aleksanterinkatu** *Plan l C2*, both sides of **Esplanadi** *Plan l C2*, **Fredrikinkatu** *Plan l B2* and **Bulevardi** *Plan l C2*. The main department stores and shopping centres are *Kämp Galleria* on Esplanadi, *Kluuvi, Kiseleff House* (handmade items) on Aleksanterinkatu; *Forum, Stockmann* and *Sokos* on Mammerheimintie, *Itäkestus* (by metro going east). Visit *Design Forum*, Erottaja and along Esplanadi, the *Pentik* gift shop at Mannerheimintie 5 and *Arabia Factory Outlet*, Hämeentie 135A for stylish ceramics, gifts, interior decorations. Antique shops in **Kruununhaka** and **Ullanlinna** districts.

MARKETS – The Market Square on South Harbour for food, handicrafts, souvenirs – **Eteläsatama** *Plan l C2* daily 6.30am (10am Sun) to 6pm (4pm Sat-Sun). **Hakaniemi Market**, Siltasaarenkatu-Hakaniemenranta *Plan l C1* (Mon-Sat 6.30am-3pm, first Sun of each month 10am-4pm): fresh produce and baked goods; **Hakaniemi Hall**, Siltasaarenkatu-Hämeentie *Plan l C1* (Mon-Fri 8am-6pm, Sat 8am-4pm): 100 tiny shops selling delicacies, souvenirs, handicrafts, Finnish design. On the corner of Bulevardi and Hietalahdenkatu *Plan l B3* are held **Hietalahti Flea market** – Mon-Fri 8am-7pm (4pm Sat). **Hietalahti Antique and Art Hall** – Mon-Fri 10am-5pm (3pm Sat), Evening flea market – Jun-Aug, Mon-Fri 3.30pm-8pm. Sunday flea market – May-Sep, 10am-4pm.

WHAT TO BUY – Finnish design (jewellery, wood, glass and ceramic gifts), handicrafts, furs, smoked meats and other specialities.

ENTERTAINMENT

You should obtain a copy of *Helsinki this Week* to find out about events in the city. It is available free from hotels and Tourist Information Offices.

Finlandia-talo *Plan I B1*: Finlandia Hall hosts concerts.

Kansallisoopera *Plan I A1*: The National Opera presents classical and modern opera and ballet.

Suomen Kansallisteatteri *Plan I C1*: The National Theatre presents plays in Finnish.

Hall of Culture: concerts.

Sibelius Academy of Music: classical music.

Kaupunginteatteri: The Municipal Theatre puts on plays, dance and musicals.

Hartwall Arena, Olympiastadion, Helsinki Ice Hall: pop concerts, sporting events.

Kaapelitehdas *Plan I A3*: The former Cable Factory is now a cultural centre.

NIGHTLIFE

Popular restaurants, pubs, bars and cafés are located on the seafront, **Esplanadi**, at **Tennisplasti** *Plan I B2* and **Lasipalatsi** *Plan I B2*. Helsinki has a fine café culture: *Café Engel*, Aleksanterinkatu 26; *Café Ekberg*, Bulevardi 9; *Café Strindberg* and *Café Esplanad*, Pohjoisesplanadi 33/37; *Café Ursula*, Ehrenströmintie 3. There are elegant cafés in museums (City museum, Kiasma) and hotels. Stylish places to visit are *Moskva Bar* and *Corona Baari* (no 11), *Helmi* (no 14), Eerikinkatu; *Bar 9*, Uudenmaankatu 9. For live music go to *Memphis*, Kluuvikatu 8; *Eats* and *On the Rocks*, Mikonkatu 15; *Tavastia Klubi* and *Semi Final*, Urho Kekkosenkatu 4/6; *Klaus Kurki Bar & Klubi*, Bulevardi 2; *Zetor*, Mannerhiemintie 3-5. Trendy nightclubs include *Helsinki Club*, Yliopistonkatu 8; *Studio 51*, Fredrikinkatu 51-53; *La Tour Night Club Premier*, Mannerhiemintie 5. Jazz fans will enjoy *Storyville Jazz Club*, Museokatu 8; *Umo Jazz House*, Pursimiehenkatu 6. The *Grand Casino Helsinki*, Mikonkatu 19 is the place for those who wish to try their luck.

FINLAND

A   B

Mannerheimintie
Runeberginkatu
Topeliuksenkatu
Töölönkatu
Mechelininkatu
Eläintarhanhantie

Lyon
SUOMEN KANSALLISOOPERA

ELAINTARHAN-LAHTI

TÖÖLÖNLAHTI

1   SIBELIUS-MONUMENTTI

Crowne Plaza

Töölöntori

Hesperiankatu
Töölönkatu
Runeberginkatu

FINLANDIA-TALO

Mannerheimintie

KANSALLISMUSEO

HELSINGIN KAUPUNGINMUSEO

Pohjoinen
Eteläinen
Museokatu

Holiday Inn Helsinki City Centre

RAUTATIESEMA

TEMPPELIAUKION KIRKKO

EDUSKUNTATALO

Rautatientori

Vaakuna

Kaivo-katu

Mechelininkatu
Runeberginkatu
Arkadiankatu
Rautatiekatu
Eteläinen Rautatiekatu

LASI-PALATSI

AMOS ANDERSININ TAIDEMUSEO

2   Hietaniemenkatu

Radisson SAS Royal

Simonkenttä

TENNIS-PALATSI

Annankatu

Torni

Kamppi

Kampintori

Pohjoinen

George

Malminkatu

Fredrikinkatu

LAPINLAHTI

Lapinlahdenkatu

Ruoholahdenkatu

Rivoli

Albertinkatu

Bulevardi

Kalevankatu

Lönnrotinkatu

Serata

51

Holiday Inn Helsinki City West

SINEBRYCHOFFIN TAIDEMUSEO

Porkkalankatu

Itämerenkatu

Radisson SAS Seaside

Hietalahdenranta

Punavuoren-

Ruoholahti

Telakkakatu

3   HIETALAHTI

LÄNSISATAMA

RUOHOLAHTI

A   B

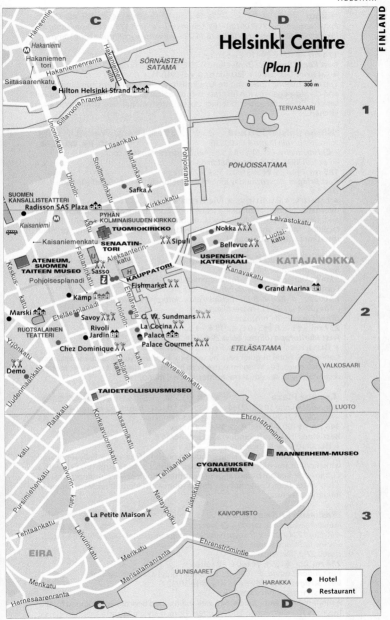

Helsinki Centre

(Plan I)

0   300 m

Hämeentie

Hakaniemi

Hakaniemen tori

Siltasaarenkatu

Hakaniemenranta

SÖRNÄISTEN SATAMA

● Hilton Helsinki Strand

Siltavuorenranta

Unioninkatu

Liisankatu

Marïankatu

Pohjoisranta

TERVASAARI

POHJOISSATAMA

Shellmanninkatu

● Safka

Kirkkokatu

Laivastokatu

SUOMEN KANSALLISTEATTERI

Radisson SAS Plaza

Kaisaniemi

PYHÄN KOLMINAISUUDEN KIRKKO

TUOMIOKIRKKO

Kaisaniemenkatu

SENAATIN-TORI

● Nokka

● Bellevue

Luotsi-katu

KATAJANOKKA

USPENSKIN-KATEDRAALI

Fabianinkatu

Sipuli

Aleksanterin-katu

ATENEUM, SUOMEN TAITEEN MUSEO

● Sasso

Kanavakatu

Keskus-katu

Pohjoisesplanadi

H

KAUPPATORI

Eteläranta

Grand Marina

Marski

● Kämp

Etelaesplanadi

Savoy

Rivoli Jardin

● Fishmarket

G. W. Sundmans

La Cocina

ETELÄSATAMA

VALKOSAARI

RUOTSALAINEN TEATTERI

Chez Dominique

● Palace

Palace Gourmet

LUOTO

Yrjönkatu

Demo

Uudenmaankatu

Laivasillankatu

TAIDETEOLLISUUSMUSEO

Ratakatu

Korkeavuorenkatu

Kasarmikatu

Ehrenströmintie

MANNERHEIM-MUSEO

katu

Pursimiehenkatu

Laivurin-katu

Tehtaankatu

CYGNAEUKSEN GALLERIA

Tehtaankatu

Laivurinkatu

● La Petite Maison

Neitsytpolku

Puistokatu

KAIVOPUISTO

EIRA

Merikatu

Merisatamanranta

UUNISAARET

HARAKKA

Merikatu

Hernesaarenranta

●	Hotel
●	Restaurant

153

Kämp
⌂⌂⌂⌂ 🏠 ⅃ᴃ ᡐ & ᴀᴄ ⅃⁄ ☆ ⌨ ⌂130 ⬡ **VISA** ❻❸ ᴀᴇ ⓪

Pohjoisesplanadi 29 ✉ *00100 –* **Ⓜ** *Kaisaniemi – ℰ (09) 576 1 11 – hotelkamp@*
luxurycollection.com – Fax (09) 576 11 22 – www.luxurycollection.com/kamp
closed Christmas **C2**
174 rm – 🛏169 € 🛏🛏410 € – 5 suites
Rest Kämp Brasserie (buffet lunch) 30 €/45 € and a la carte 27/52 €
♦ Grand Luxury ♦ Business ♦ Stylish ♦
Top class historic hotel with de luxe British style décor. Rooms combine luxury
and classic elegance with first rate technological facilities. Superb professional
service. Sleek restaurant offering classic international fare from open plan
kitchen.

Hilton Helsinki Strand
⌂⌂⌂⌂ ⪡ ⅃ᴃ ᡐ 🖳 & ᴀᴄ ☆rest ⌨ ℄ ⌂180

John Stenbergin Ranta 4 ✉ *00530* ⬡ **VISA** ❻❸ ᴀᴇ ⓪
– **Ⓜ** *Hakaniemi – ℰ (09) 39 3 51 – helsinkistrand@hilton.com*
– Fax (09) 3935 32 55 – www.hilton.com **C1**
185 rm – 🛏142 € 🛏🛏353 €, ⌑ 15 € – 7 suites
Rest Bridges *(closed Sunday dinner)* (buffet lunch) 29 €/45 € and a la carte
30/55 €
♦ Luxury ♦ Business ♦ Modern ♦
International hotel overlooking waterfront. Contemporary Finnish architecture
and décor. Atrium style lobby. Comfortable spacious rooms with hi-tech
facilities. Muted maritime themed restaurant, game a speciality, or main
restaurant with central buffet.

Hilton Helsinki Kalastajatorppa
⌂⌂⌂⌂ 🏠 ⅃ᴃ ᡐ 🖳 ꒰ & ᴀᴄ ☆ ⌨

Kalastajatorpantie 1 (Northwest: ℄ ⌂550 ⬡ **P** **VISA** ❻❸ ᴀᴇ ⓪
5 km by Mannerheimintie, Tukholmankatu,
Paciusgatan off Ramsaynranta)
✉ *00330 – ℰ (09) 45 8 11 – helsinkikalastajatorppa@hilton.com*
– Fax (09) 4581 22 11 – www.hilton.com
closed Easter and Christmas
237 rm – 🛏115 € 🛏🛏310 €, ⌑ 15 € – 1 suite
Rest Meritorppa *(dinner only)* 29 €/45 € and a la carte 26/45 €
♦ Business ♦ Luxury ♦ Functional ♦
Conference hotel in quiet park by sea, 5km by tram. Nordic style rooms; many
with balconies; Sea Wing for suites with hi-tech facilities and sea view. Modern
restaurant with seaside terrace; international menu.

Crowne Plaza
⌂⌂⌂⌂ ⪡ ❀ ⅃ᴃ ᡐ ⅃ ᴀᴄ ⅃⁄ ⌨ ⌂550 ⬡ **VISA** ❻❸ ᴀᴇ ⓪

Mannerheimintie 50 ✉ *00260 – ℰ (09) 2521 00 00 – helsinki-cph@rest.fi*
– Fax (09) 2521 39 99 – www.crowneplaza-helsinki.fi **A1**
345 rm – 🛏190 € 🛏🛏280 €, ⌑ 19 € – 4 suites
Rest Macu *(bar meals Sunday)* a la carte 40/44 €
♦ Business ♦ Modern ♦
Well located for the Opera House and also boasting lake views. Fully renovated
with modern amenities in all public areas. Stylish, relaxed bar; gastro-pub with a
Cuban edge. Spa has broad range of treatments. Rooms over nine floors: best are
'Club' on top floor. Contemporary dining room with Oriental feel. Mediterranean
influenced menus.

Radisson SAS Royal
⌂⌂⌂ ᡐ & ᴀᴄ ⅃⁄rm ☆ ⌨ ℄ ⌂300

Runeberginkatu 2 ✉ *00100 –* **Ⓜ** *Kamppi* ⬡ **VISA** ❻❸ ᴀᴇ ⓪
– ℰ (20) 1234 7 01 – info.royal.helsinki@radissonsas.com – Fax (20) 1234 7 02
– www.radissonsas.com
closed 22-27 December **B2**
254 rm ⌑ – 🛏105 € 🛏🛏160 € – 8 suites
Rest Johan Ludvig, *ℰ (09) 69 5 80 (dinner only)* a la carte 40/47 €
Rest Ströget, *ℰ (09) 69 5 80* – a la carte 30/32 €
♦ Business ♦ Modern ♦
A modern hotel with good-sized, well-maintained bedrooms, equipped for the
business traveller. Johan Ludvig offers Finnish-style a la carte menu in classic
comfort. Glass-fronted Ströget for Scandinavian-Danish dishes.

FINLAND

 Holiday Inn Helsinki City Centre　　Là 🕍 ᴃ 🅰 ⁴⁄₋rm
Elielinaukio 5 ⌧ *00100*　　　　　　⅍ rest 🖭 𝘝𝘐𝘚𝘈 ⓂⓄ 🄰🄴 ①
– Ⓜ *Rautatientori* – ℰ *(09) 5425 50 00 – helsinki.hihcc@restel.fi*
– Fax (09) 5425 52 99 – www.hi-helsinkicity.com　　　　**B2**
174 rm – ♦123 € ♦♦224 €, ⌑ 15 €
Rest *Verde* *(closed Saturday lunch and Sunday)* 9 €/19 € (lunch) and a la carte
27/44 €
♦ Business ♦ Functional ♦
Modern city centre hotel near railway station, post office and all main shopping
areas. Modern well-equipped bedrooms; good city view from 8th floor. Open
style dining room serving popular menu using Finnish produce; lighter dishes
available at lunchtime.

 Radisson SAS Plaza　　Là 🕍 ᴃ 🅰 ⁴⁄₋rm ⅍ 🔏100 𝘝𝘐𝘚𝘈 ⓂⓄ 🄰🄴 ①
Mikonkatu 23 ⌧ *00100* – Ⓜ *Kaisaniemi* – ℰ *(20) 1234 7 03*
– info.plaza.helsinki@radissonsas.com – Fax (20) 1234 7 04
– www.radissonsas.com　　　　　　　**C1-2**
301 rm ⌑ – ♦105 € ♦♦310 € – 1 suite
Rest a la carte 29/47 €
♦ Business ♦ Functional ♦
Near the station, this sizeable modern business hotel maintains the reputation of
this international group. Well-equipped rooms, in "Nordic", "Classic" or "Italian"
style. Modern informal brasserie; striking, painted windows.

 Radisson SAS Seaside　　🕍 ᴃ ⁴⁄₋rm ⅍ 🖭 ℰ 🔏100
Ruoholahdenranta 3 ⌧ *00180*　　　　🕍 𝘝𝘐𝘚𝘈 ⓂⓄ 🄰🄴 ①
– Ⓜ *Ruoholahti* – ℰ *(20) 1234 7 07 – info.seaside.helsinki@radissonsas.com*
– Fax (20) 1234 7 08 – www.radissonsas.com
closed 2 weeks Christmas　　　　　　**B3**
358 rm ⌑ – ♦140 € ♦♦165 € – 6 suites
Rest *Viola*, ℰ *69 3 60* – a la carte 30/40 €
♦ Business ♦ Modern ♦
Large contemporary hotel in quiet area; view of harbour. Caters for business
people and individuals; also for groups. Modern rooms in three categories; some
with kitchenette. Modern restaurant offering mostly Mediterranean oriented
dishes from open kitchen.

 Holiday Inn Helsinki　　Là 🕍 ᴃ 🅰 ⁴⁄₋ ⅍ rest 🔏120
Messuaukio 1 (near Pasila Railway Station)　　　🕍 𝘝𝘐𝘚𝘈 ⓂⓄ 🄰🄴 ①
(North : 4 km by Mannerheimintie,
Nordenskiöldink, Savonkatu off Ratapihantie)
⌧ *00520* – ℰ *(09) 150 9 00 – holiday-inn@holidayinnhelsinki.fi*
– Fax (09) 150 9 01 – www.helsinki.holiday-inn.com
239 rm ⌑ – ♦95 € ♦♦260 € – 5 suites
Rest *Terra Nova* 26/30 € (lunch) and a la carte 30/47 €
♦ Business ♦ Functional ♦
Modern hotel in same building as congress centre; popular for conferences. Take
breakfast in the winter garden style atrium. Spacious well equipped rooms with
modern décor. Cheerful modern brasserie-style restaurant, popular
international cooking.

 Simonkenttä　　Là 🕍 ᴃ 🅰 ⁴⁄₋rm ⅍ 🖭 ℰ 🔏80 𝘝𝘐𝘚𝘈 ⓂⓄ 🄰🄴 ①
Simonkatu 9 ⌧ *00100* – Ⓜ *Kamppi* – ℰ *(09) 68 3 80*
– simonkentta@scandic-hotels.com – Fax (09) 683 81 11
– www.scandic-hotels.com　　　　　　**B2**
357 rm ⌑ – ♦97 € ♦♦240 € – 3 suites
Rest *Simonkatu* *(closed Sunday)* 20 €/30 € and a la carte 24/54 €
♦ Business ♦ Modern ♦
Ultra modern well located hotel with imposing glazed façade. Stylish designer
décor with colourful fabrics and parquet flooring in all rooms. Some rooms with
a view. Stylish restaurant offers range of popular traditional dishes.

FINLAND

Palace
≤ 🕍 🎖 ⅄ 🍴350 🍷 VISA ⓪ 🅰 ①

Eteläranta 10 ⊠ 00130 – Ⓜ Kaisaniemi – 𝒞 (09) 1345 66 61
– reception@palacehotel.fi – Fax (09) 654 7 86
– www.palacehotel.fi
closed Christmas   **C2**
37 rm ⊆ – ♣130 € ♣♣350 € – 2 suites
Rest see *Palace Gourmet* and *La Cocina* below
♦ Business ♦ Classic ♦
1950s hotel by harbour, occupying upper floors of building with street level
reception. Spacious comfortable rooms with tasteful décor and modern facilites.
Some views.

Marski
🛏 🕍 ♿ 🎖 ⅄rm 🍴 🖭 📞 🍷20 🍷 VISA ⓪ 🅰 ①

Mannerheimintie 10 ⊠ 00100 – Ⓜ Rautatientori – 𝒞 (09) 68 0 61
– marski@scandic-hotels.com – Fax (09) 642 3 77 – www.scandic-hotels.com
closed Christmas   **C2**
283 rm ⊆ – ♣116 € ♣♣229 € – 6 suites
Rest *(closed Saturday lunch and Sunday)* a la carte 19/40 €
♦ Business ♦ Functional ♦
Large well run central hotel with imposing façade. Bright lobby with
cosmopolitan coffee shop. Room styles are early and late 1990s, modern with
good facilities. Welcoming bar and restaurant for traditional fare designed to
appeal to all tastes.

Vaakuna
🍴 🕍 ♿ 🎖 ⅄rm 🍴 🖭 🍷20 VISA ⓪ 🅰 ①

Asema-aukio 2 ⊠ 00100 – Ⓜ Rautatientori – 𝒞 (20) 1234 6 10
– reception-vaakunahelsinki@sok.fi – Fax (09) 4337 71 00
– www.sokoshotels.fi
closed Christmas-New Year and 23-26 June   **B2**
258 rm ⊆ – ♣211 € ♣♣241 € – 12 suites
Rest *(closed Saturday lunch and Sunday)* 8 €/14 €
♦ Business ♦ Classic ♦
Modern accommodation, spacious, colourful and well-appointed, in this
sizeable hotel, built for 1952 Olympics. Convenient for station. 10th-floor
restaurant; terrace for armchair dining - good view of station court and roofs;
lighter meals in coffee shop.

Torni
🕍 ⅄rm 🍴rest 📞 🍷35 VISA ⓪ 🅰 ①

Yrjönkatu 26 ⊠ 00100 – Ⓜ Rautatientori – 𝒞 (20) 1234 6 04 – torni.helsinki@
sok.fi – Fax (09) 4336 71 00 – www.sokoshotels.fi   **B2**
152 rm ⊆ – ♣138 € ♣♣218 €
Rest *(closed Saturday lunch and Sunday)* 30 €/54 € and a la carte 41/64 €
♦ Business ♦ Classic ♦
Traditional hotel in converted row of 1920s town houses in city centre. Rooms
vary in size but all feature standard modern décor and facilities. Panoramic
bar on 13th floor. Inviting restaurant overlooking street offering a traditional
menu.

Pasila
🍴 🕍 📺 ♿ 🎖 ⅄rm 🖭 📞 🍷90 🍷 Ⓟ VISA ⓪ 🅰 ①

Maistraatinportti 3 (near Pasila Railway Station)
(North : 4 km by Mannerheimintie, Nordenskiöldink off Vetuvitie) ⊠ 00240
– 𝒞 (20) 123 46 13 – pasila.helsinki@sokoshotels.fi – Fax (09) 143 7 71
– www.sokoshotels.fi
closed 22-31 December
172 rm ⊆ – ♣78/147 € ♣♣101/175 € – 6 suites
Rest *Sevilla* 7 €/20 € and a la carte 16/25 €
♦ Business ♦ Modern ♦
Large, modern business hotel in tranquil district out of town, a short tram ride
from city centre. Rooms feature contemporary local décor and furnishings.
Informal Spanish-influenced restaurant; popular menu with grills.

FINLAND

Holiday Inn Helsinki City West   ⟨ 🕼 🕅 🖾 ↳ 🖵

Sulhasenkuja 3 ✉ *00180 –* 🅜 *Ruoholahti*   🕾 *VISA* 🚯 *AE* ①

– 𝒞 (09) 4152 10 00 – Fax (09) 4152 12 99 – www.hi-helsinkiwest.fi

closed Christmas   **A3**

256 rm ☐ – ♦128/208 € ♦♦128/208 €

Rest *(closed lunch Saturday and Sunday)* a la carte 34/40 €

♦ Business ♦ Modern ♦

Opened in 2005, and well located for the business parks west of the city. Situated two metro stops from centre. Purpose-built corporate hotel, though conference facilities are rather small. Most of the well-equipped rooms have showers; ask for one with lake view. Ground floor bar and restaurant with global menus.

Grand Marina   🔊 🕼 🕅 ᗜ 🕅 ↳rm 🖾 🕾 🖧500 ⇔

Katajanokanlaitari 7 ✉ *00160 – 𝒞 (09) 16 6 61*   P *VISA* 🚯 *AE* ①

– grandmarina@scandic-hotels.com – Fax (09) 664 7 64

– www.scandic-hotels.com   **D2**

446 rm ☐ – ♦201 € ♦♦221 € – 16 suites

Rest *Makasiim* *(closed Sunday and lunch Bank Holidays)* 27 €

and a la carte 24/38 €

♦ Business ♦ Functional ♦

Large harbourside hotel in converted warehouse opposite Marina Congress Centre. Practical rooms, functional fittings. Pub and coffee shop. Vast restaurant, modern Scandinavian décor. Extensive selection of international fare.

Rivoli Jardin without rest   🕼 ᗜ ↳ 🖾 🕾 *VISA* 🚯 *AE* ①

Kasarmikatu 40 ✉ *00130 –* 🅜 *Rautatientori – 𝒞 (09) 681 5 00*

– rivoli.jardin@rivoli.fi – Fax (09) 656 9 88 – www.rivoli.fi   **C2**

55 rm ☐ – ♦207 € ♦♦237 €

♦ Business ♦ Classic ♦

Well run traditional hotel in a quiet location close to city centre. Rooms are functional and comfortable, two on top floor have terrace. Winter garden style breakfast area.

Olympia   🕼 🕅 ↳rm 🕾 🖧40 *VISA* 🚯 *AE* ①

Läntinen Brahenkatu 2 (North : 2 km by Siltasaarenkatu) ✉ *00510*

– 𝒞 (09) 69 1 51 – olympia.cumulus@restel.fi – Fax (09) 691 52 19

– www.cumulus.fi

closed 12-18 April and 17-26 December

101 rm ☐ – ♦128/176 € ♦♦178/208 €

Rest (dinner only) a la carte 17/37 €

♦ Business ♦ Functional ♦

Situated in a residential area near the amusement park 10 min by tram from city centre. Modern bedrooms with standard décor and furnishings. Night club and Irish Pub. International menu in the restaurant.

G. W. Sundmans   ⟨ 🕅 ↳ 🎭 ⟷50 *VISA* 🚯 *AE* ①

Eteläranta 16 (Ist floor) ✉ *00130 –* 🅜 *Kaisaniemi – 𝒞 (09) 622 64 10*

– myyntipalvelu@royalravintolat.com – Fax (09) 661 3 31

– www.royalravintolat.com

closed Easter, 23-30 December, 1 January, Sunday, Saturday lunch and Bank Holidays   **C2**

Rest *(closed lunch in July)* 45 €/74 € and a la carte 62/78 €

Rest *Krog (ground floor)* 37 €/42 € and a la carte 32/47 €

Spec. Slightly salted lavaret with crayfish salad. Fillet of reindeer with herbs. Apple soufflé with Bourbon vanilla ice cream.

♦ Traditional ♦ Formal ♦

19C sea captain's Empire style mansion opposite harbour. Five classically decorated dining rooms with view. Elegant tables. Classically-based cuisine. Informal ground floor restaurant. Menu features local seafood and international dishes.

XXX Nokka 🕮 AK ⅀ VISA ⬤⬤ AE ⬤

Kanavaranta 7F ⊠ 00160 – Ⓜ Kaisaniemi – ℰ (09) 687 73 30
– Matti.lempinen @ royalravintolat.com – Fax (09) 6877 33 30
– www.royalravintolat.com
closed 14-17 April, 24-25 June, 24 December-7 January, Saturday lunch and Sunday
Rest (booking essential) 27 €/69 € and dinner a la carte 36/61 €   **D2**
 ♦ Modern ♦ Design ♦
Converted warehouse divided into two striking rooms; glazed wine cellar;
waterfront terrace. Watch the chefs prepare appealing, modern Finnish cuisine.
Good service.

XXX Palace Gourmet – at Palace H.   ≼ Helsinki and harbour, 🕮

Eteläranta 10 (10th floor) ⊠ 00130   ⅀ VISA ⬤⬤ ⬤
– Ⓜ Kaisaniemi – ℰ (09) 1345 67 15 – ilkka.rantanen @ palaceravintolat.com
– Fax (09) 657 4 74 – www.palace.fi
closed Saturday, Sunday and Bank Holidays   **C2**
Rest 41/58 € (lunch) and dinner a la carte 73/81 €
 ♦ Traditional ♦ Formal ♦
10th-floor restaurant with open view of harbour and sea; splendid roof terrace.
Local style décor and spacious layout. Serves traditional Finnish cuisine with hint
of France.

XXX Savoy   ≼ 🕮 AK ⅀ VISA ⬤⬤ AE ⬤

Eteläesplanadi 14 (8th floor) ⊠ 00130 – Ⓜ Kaisaniemi – ℰ (09) 684 40 20
– terhi.oksanen @ royalravintolat.com – Fax (09) 628 7 15
– www.royalravintolat.com
closed Easter, Midsummer, 2 weeks Christmas, Saturday and Sunday
Rest 50 €/115 € and dinner a la carte 56/87 €   **C2**
 ♦ Traditional ♦ Formal ♦
Panoramic restaurant in city centre with typical Finnish design dating from 1937.
Classic traditional menu of local specialities. Ask for a table in the conservatory.

XX Chez Dominique (Valimaki)   ↳⊬ ⅀ VISA ⬤⬤ AE ⬤
❀❀

Ludviginkatu 3-5 ⊠ 00130 – Ⓜ Rautatientori – ℰ (09) 612 73 93
– info @ chezdominique.fi – Fax (09) 6124 42 20 – www.chezdominique.fi
closed 23-27 December, Easter, July, Sunday, Monday, Saturday lunch and Bank
Holidays   **C2**
Rest (booking essential) 39 € (lunch) and dinner a la carte 75/99 €
Spec. Lobster poached in vanilla butter with avocado cannelloni. Pigeon filled with
foie gras, white beans and lemon confit sauce. Coffee fondant, cardamom foam.
 ♦ Contemporary ♦ Minimalist ♦
Cosy restaurant with discreet ambience. Plain minimalist décor. Refined modern
cuisine: attention to detail includes smooth service and innovative style; special
lunch menu.

XX George (Aremo)   🕮 ↳⊬ ⅀ ⟷12 VISA ⬤⬤ AE ⬤
❀

Kalevankatu 17 ⊠ 00100 – Ⓜ Kamppi – ℰ (09) 647 6 62 – george @ george.fi
– Fax (09) 647 1 10 – www.george.fi
closed 14-17 April, 24-25 June, 23-27 December, Saturday lunch and Sunday
Rest 32 €/49 € and dinner a la carte 56/64 €   **B2**
Spec. Fried scallops with salsify and onion sauce. Breast of pigeon with raspberry
ginger sauce. Dark chocolate mousse, fig compote and Calvados ice cream.
 ♦ Traditional ♦ Friendly ♦
19C town house in central location. Chilled chocolate truffle cabinet in bar. Elegant
tableware. Classically based cooking, using local produce with seasonal interest.

XX Sipuli   ≼ ⅀ ⟷60 VISA ⬤⬤ AE ⬤

Kanavaranta 3 (2nd floor) ⊠ 00160 – Ⓜ Kaisaniemi – ℰ (09) 6229 2 80
– myyntipalvelu @ royalravintolat.com – Fax (09) 6229 28 40
– www.royalravintolat.com/sipuli
closed 22 June-6 August, 23 December-7 January, Saturday and Sunday
Rest (dinner only) a la carte 45/67 €   **D2**
 ♦ Modern ♦ Design ♦
Converted warehouse with view of Uspensky Orthodox cathedral through a
picture window. Waterfront terrace bar. Serves selection of French-inspired
modern Finnish dishes.

FINLAND

✗✗ **La Cocina** – at Palace H.   ⪅ Helsinki Harbour, 🅰🄲 ⅀ **VISA** 🆂🅾 🅰🄴 🅾
Etelärantä 10, (1st floor) ✉ *00130 Helsinki* – Ⓜ *Kaisaniemi* – ℰ *(09) 1345 67 49*
– Fax (09) 1345 67 50 – www.palace.fi
closed 23 December-9 January, July, Saturday lunch and Sunday   **C2**
Rest 48 € (dinner) and a la carte 38/57 €
◆ Spanish ◆ Minimalist ◆
Fashionable, original restaurant - take modern staircase up to first floor. Trendy,
vivid 'splattered art' on walls; enjoy pleasant views of harbour. Spanish music
accompaniment blends perfectly with the earthy, powerful and
authentic Basque dishes on offer, all presented with finesse.

✗✗ **Bellevue**   🅰🄲 **VISA** 🆂🅾 🅰🄴 🅾
Rahapajankatu 3 ✉ *00160* – Ⓜ *Kaisaniemi* – ℰ *(09) 179 5 60 – info@*
restaurantbellevue.com – Fax (09) 636 9 85 – www.restaurantbellevue.com
closed 23 December-1 January, lunch July,
Saturday lunch and Sunday   **D2**
Rest 25 €/58 € and dinner a la carte 38/63 €
◆ Russian ◆ Cosy ◆
Near Orthodox cathedral, restaurant in old town house with fairly sombre
traditional Russian décor and cosy intimate atmosphere. Menu features Russian
delicacies.

✗✗ **Rivoli**   🅰🄲 ↮ ⅀ **VISA** 🆂🅾 🅰🄴 🅾
Albertinkatu 38 ✉ *00180* – Ⓜ *Kamppi* – ℰ *(09) 643 4 55*
– kala.cheri@rivoli.inet.fi – Fax (09) 647 7 80 – www.rivolirestaurants.fi
closed Christmas and Bank Holidays   **B2**
Rest 35 € (dinner) and a la carte 43/69 €
◆ Traditional ◆ Brasserie ◆
Two different style dining rooms: smokers' is cosy with wood panelling;
non-smokers' is brasserie-style. Menu offers fusion of traditional, Finnish and
French influences.

✗✗ **Sasso**   🅰🄲 ⅀ **VISA** 🆂🅾 🅰🄴 🅾
Pohjoisesplanadi 17 ✉ *00170 Helsinki* – Ⓜ *Kaisaniemi* – ℰ *(09) 1345 62 40*
– tables@palace.fi – Fax (09) 1345 62 42 – www.palace.fi
closed 24-27 December and Sunday   **C2**
Rest 52 € (dinner) and a la carte 35/43 €
◆ Italian ◆ Fashionable ◆
Spacious, open-plan restaurant overlooking market place and harbour. Stylish
bar and lounge open all day. Shimmering fabrics typical of smart, contemporary
interior with earthy and olive hues. Italian dishes created with delicacy using top
Finnish ingredients.

✗✗ **Demo**   ⅀ **VISA** 🆂🅾 🅰🄴
Uudenmaankatu 11 ✉ *00120 Helsinki* – Ⓜ *Rautatientori* – ℰ *(09) 228 9 08 40*
– restaurantdemo@kolumbus.fi – Fax (09) 228 9 08 41 – www.restaurantdemo.fi
closed Sunday-Monday   **C2**
Rest (booking essential) (dinner only) a la carte 44/54 €
◆ Modern ◆ Trendy ◆
Locally renowned restaurant run by talented young team. A compact interior
houses trendy red fabric and chrome chairs with a warm candle-lit atmosphere.
Modern, seasonal dishes with Gallic overtones, freshly prepared using local
produce.

✗✗ **FishMarket**   🅰🄲 ↮ ⅀ **VISA** 🆂🅾 🅰🄴 🅾
Pohjoisesplanadi 17 ✉ *00170 Helsinki* – Ⓜ *Kaisaniemi* – ℰ *(09) 1345 62 20*
– tables@palace.fi – Fax (09) 1345 62 22 – www.palace.fi
closed 24-27 December and Sunday   **C2**
Rest a la carte 37/48 €
◆ Seafood ◆ Design ◆
Basement restaurant on the market place, with small, enclosed terrace. Stylish,
modern nautical décor complemented by attentive, friendly service. Seafood
menus change seasonally, highlighted by exciting, original combinations. Prime
local produce to the fore.

✗
☺

Lyon 📠 🕉 **VISA** 🆑 🆎 ①

Mannerheimintie 56 ⊠ 00260 – ℰ (09) 408 1 31 – ravintola.lyon@kolumbus.fi
– Fax (09) 422 0 74 – www.ravintolaopas.net/lyon
restricted opening in summer, closed Sunday,
Saturday lunch and Bank Holidays   **A1**
Rest (booking essential for dinner) 25 €/62 € and a la carte 46/64 €
♦ French ♦ Bistro ♦
Traditional, well established restaurant near the Opera. Menu has varied choice:
seasonal, vegetarian or Helsinki, as well as the main à la carte serving French-style
dishes.

✗

La Petite Maison 🕉 **VISA** 🆑 🆎 ①

Huvilakatu 28A ⊠ 00150 – ℰ (09) 260 96 80 – sales@henrix.fi
– Fax (09) 727 50 58 – www.henrix.fi
closed Sunday   **C3**
Rest (booking essential) (dinner only) 40 €/80 € and a la carte 51/68 €
♦ French ♦ Cosy ♦
Cosy restaurant popular with local clientele in a quiet street known for its Art
Deco architecture. Traditional décor with strong French note. Good French-
influenced classic fare.

✗
☺

Serata 🕉 **VISA** 🆑 🆎 ①

Bulevardi 32 ⊠ 00120 – Ⓜ Kamppi Kampen – ℰ (09) 680 13 65
– serata@serata.net – www.serata.net
closed 17 December-2 January, Easter, 10-29 July, Sunday, Monday dinner,
Saturday lunch and Bank Holidays   **B3**
Rest (booking essential) 25 € and a la carte 27/50 €
♦ Italian ♦ Friendly ♦
Converted shop in residential district. Open kitchen with some counter seating.
Authentic Italian cooking with good value set menus including wine.

✗
☺

Safka 📠 **VISA** 🆑 🆎 ①

Vironkatu 8 ⊠ 00170 – Ⓜ Kaisaniemi – ℰ (09) 135 72 87 – safka@safka.fi
– www.safka.fi
closed Christmas, July, Sunday and Monday   **C1**
Rest (booking essential) 30/45 € (dinner) and a la carte 33/53 €
♦ Traditional ♦ Neighbourhood ♦
Modest, personally run local restaurant in converted shop near the cathedral in city centre. Cosy layout. Unfussy, fresh and seasonal, traditional Finnish
cuisine.

at Helsinki-Vantaa Airport North: 19 km by A 137:

🏨

Vantaa 🛎 🕉 �havndicap 📠 ⊬rm 🕉 🕲 🛄 280 🚗 **VISA** 🆑 🆎 ①

Hertaksentie 2 (near Tikkurila Railway Station) ⊠ 01300
– ℰ (20) 1234 6 18 – hotelvantaa@sokoshotels.fi – Fax (09) 8578 55 55
– www.sokoshotels.fi
closed 23-27 December
265 rm ⊊ – †136/165 € ††167/197 €
Rest *Sevilla* a la carte approx. 35 €
♦ Business ♦ Functional ♦
Beside the railway station and convenient for the airport; a busy corporate hotel.
Well equipped rooms in a modern Scandinavian style. Night club and pub.
Modern restaurant, Spanish-influenced cooking and grills.

🏨

Holiday Inn Garden Court Helsinki Airport ₭ 🕉 ⅙ ⊬rm

Rälssitie 2 ⊠ 01510 – ℰ (09) 870 9 00   🛄 🛄25 **P** **VISA** 🆑 🆎 ①
– airport.higc@restel.fi – Fax (09) 8709 01 01
– www.holiday-inn.com/hel-airport
280 rm ⊊ – †125/185 € ††140/200 €
Rest *(closed Saturday and Sunday lunch)* 28 €/38 € and a la carte 28/38 €
♦ Business ♦ Functional ♦
Modern international hotel, suitable for business people. Standard bedrooms
with modern décor and fittings in local style. Friendly, modern restaurant serves
a simple range of traditional International dishes.

FRANCE

PROFILE

- **AREA:**
  551 500 km²
  (212 934 sq mi).

- **POPULATION:**
  60 656 000 inhabitants
  (est. 2005), density
  = 110 per km².

- **CAPITAL:**
  Paris (conurbation
  9 928 000 inhabitants).

- **CURRENCY:**
  Euro (€); rate
  of exchange: € 1
  = US$ 1.17 (Nov 2005).

- **GOVERNMENT:**
  Parliamentary republic
  (since 1946). Member
  of European Union
  since 1957 (one of the
  6 founding countries).

- **LANGUAGE:**
  French.

- **SPECIFIC PUBLIC HOLIDAYS:**
  Victory Day 1945
  (8 May), Bastille
  Day-National Day
  (14 July), Armistice
  Day 1918
  (11 November).

- **LOCAL TIME:**
  GMT + 1 hour
  in winter and GMT
  + 2 hours in
  summer.

- **CLIMATE:**
  Temperate with cool
  winters and warm
  summers (Paris:
  January: 3°C, July:
  20°C). Mediterranean
  climate in the south
  (mild winters, hot
  and sunny summers,
  occasional strong
  wind called the
  mistral).

- **INTERNATIONAL DIALLING
  CODE:**
  00 33 followed by
  regional code without
  the initial 0 and then
  the local number.

- **EMERGENCY:**
  Police: ☏ 17;
  Ambulance: ☏ 15;
  Fire Brigade: ☏ 18.

- **ELECTRICITY:**
  220 volts AC, 50Hz.
  2-pin round-shaped
  continental plugs.

FORMALITIES

Travellers from the European Union (EU), Switzerland, Iceland and the main countries of North and South America need a national identity card or passport (America: passport required) to visit France for less than three months (tourism or business purpose). For visitors from other countries a visa may be required, in addition to a passport, especially for those wishing to stay for longer than three months. We advise you to check with your embassy before travelling.

Nationals of EU member countries require a valid national driving licence. Nationals of non-EU countries should obtain an international driving licence. Insurance cover is compulsory and although it is no longer a legal requirement in France, it is advisable to have an international insurance certificate (Green Card).

MAJOR NEWSPAPERS

The national daily papers with widest distribution are *Le Monde*, *Le Figaro* and *Libération*. *Le Parisien* covers Paris and the surrounding regions. *Ouest-France* (all of northwest France, including Brittany, Normandy and the Loire region) is the main regional daily. Weekly papers: *Le Point*, *L'Express*, *Le Nouvel Observateur*.

USEFUL PHRASES

ENGLISH	FRENCH
Yes	**Oui**
No	**Non**
Good morning	**Bonjour**
Goodbye	**Au revoir**
Thank you	**Merci**
Please	**S'il vous plaît**
Excuse me	**Excusez-moi**
I don't understand	**Je ne comprends pas**

HOTELS

♦ CATEGORIES

Accommodation ranges from the most prestigious hotels to simple guesthouses, and include comfortable hotels for family and business travellers.

♦ PRICE RANGE

The price is per room. There is no great difference between the charge for single and double rooms.

♦ TAX

Included in the room rate.

♦ CHECK OUT TIME

Usually between 11am and noon.

♦ RESERVATIONS

By telephone or by Internet; a credit card number is required.

♦ TIP FOR LUGGAGE HANDLING

At the discretion of the client (about €1 per item).

♦ BREAKFAST

It is often not included in the room rate and is usually served from 7am to 10am. Most hotels offer a self-service buffet, but you may ask for continental breakfast to be served in the room.

Reception	**Réception**
Single room	**Chambre simple**
Double room	**Chambre double**
Bed	**Lit**
Bathroom	**Salle de bains**
Shower	**Douche**

RESTAURANTS

France is home to every imaginable type of restaurant, whether Michelin starred establishments or neighbourhood eateries where one can enjoy a delicious meal in pleasant surroundings. **Brasseries** serve hearty, traditional and regional fare such as seafood, cassoulet, choucroute and pigs' trotters. **Bistros** are small eating-places with no frills serving simple dishes in a cheerful atmosphere. A **bouchon** is a typical small establishment in Lyon and the **Winstub** is a winebar in Alsace .

Breakfast	**Petit-déjeuner**	7-10am
Lunch	**Déjeuner**	12.30-2pm
Dinner	**Dîner**	7.30-10pm;
		some places close later

Restaurants offer both a fixed menu (starter, main course and dessert) or a menu à la carte.

◆ RESERVATIONS

Reservations can be made by phone. Some places may require a credit card number as guarantee. In the case of Michelin starred or other famous restaurants, it is advisable to book several days, or even weeks, in advance.

◆ THE BILL

The bill (check) includes a service charge and VAT. However, if you are particularly happy with the service it is usual to leave a tip at your discretion (often 5% of the bill).

Aperitif	**Apéritif**
Meal	**Repas**
First course, starter	**Entrée**
Main dish	**Plat principal**
Main dish of the day	**Plat du jour**
Dessert	**Dessert**
Mineral water/	
sparkling water	**Eau minérale/gazeuse**
Wine (rosé, red, white)	**Vin (rosé, rouge, blanc)**
Beer	**Bière**
Bread	**Pain**
Meat (medium, rare, blue)	**Viande (à point, saignant, bleu)**
Fish	**Poisson**
Salt/pepper	**Sel/poivre**
Cheese	**Fromages**
Vegetables	**Légumes**
Hot/cold	**Chaud/froid**
The bill (check) please	**L'addition s'il vous plaît**

LOCAL CUISINE

France is the land of good food and good living and each region takes great pride in its specialities. Some of the most famous dishes rely on **foie gras** and **seafood.** Of course the celebrated **cheeses** of France are an important part of the culinary experience. It is possible to give only an introduction to the delicious fare to savour in the country. In Paris you can sample the cuisine of all the regions of France.

◆ Starters

A meal typically begins with soup or consommé: velouté d'asperges/de champignons (cream of asparagus/mushroom), soupe de poireaux-pommes de terre (leek and potato soup), soupe/gratinée à l'oignon (onion soup), bisque de homard (cream of lobster), garbure (a thick cabbage soup), cotriade (Breton fish soup). A tasty starter or light meal may consist of salade niçoise (tomatoes, anchovies, tuna, olives), salade lyonnaise (green salad with cubed bacon and soft-cooked eggs), salade cauchoise (celery, potatoes, ham). You can also choose a flamiche (leek quiche), a ficelle (ham pancake with mushroom sauce), **quiche lorraine** (ham and cheese flan), flammeküche (thin-crusted savoury tart covered with cream, onions and bacon), pissaladière (Provençal quiche with onions, tomatoes, anchovies) or tapenade (black olives, capers, anchovies). A seafood platter is a glorious dish – oysters, shrimps, prawns, clams, etc.

♦ Main courses

Meat and fish courses are accompanied by seasonal vegetables or served with gratin dauphinois (potatoes, eggs and milk) or gratin savoyard (potatoes, eggs and stock). **Bouillabaisse** is the famous fish stew from Marseilles made with several types of fish and seasoned with saffron, garlic, fennel and herbs. A speciality from Nîmes is **brandade**, a creamy blend of cod mashed with olive oil, milk and garlic cloves. From Brittany come homard à l'armoricaine (lobster with tomatoes, Cayenne pepper, white wine, cognac and herbs), moules à la crème (mussels with cream) and brochet au beurre blanc (shad or pike with Nantes-style butter sauce). Shrimps and cockles are delicious when cooked fresh from the sea in Normandy, which is also well known for its sole dieppoise (sole in a creamy sauce). Loup grillé au fenouil ou au sarment de vigne (seabass grilled with fennel or baked on a fire with vine twigs) are popular dishes in Provence and on the Riviera.

Other favourite regional specialities are: **choucroute** (sauerkraut – cabbage, potatoes, pork, sausage and ham) and baeckeoffe (lamb, beef, pork, vegetables, white wine) from Alsace; **cassoulet** (bean stew, goose or duck pieces, pork) from Toulouse or Castelnaudary; tripes à la mode de Caen (tripe cooked with carrots, celery, herbs, calf's foot); canard au sang (pressed duck) from Rouen; sauce meurette (wine sauce) from Burgundy to accompany poached eggs. Also worth a mention are potée (thick cabbage stew with pork, bacon, turnips or with Morteau or Montbéliard sausage) from Auvergne or Franche-Comté; aligot (a creamy blend of fresh Tomme cheese and mashed potato seasoned with garlic) from Chaudes-Aigues; tripoux (stuffed tripe) from Aurillac; poulet basquaise (chicken with tomatoes, peppers and black olives).

♦ Cheeses

France produces an amazing variety of cheeses with a delicate or pungent flavour. The **cheese platter** is an essential part of a French meal. There are soft, bloomy-rind cheeses such as Brie de Meaux, Brie de Melun, Camembert, Chaource; washed-rind cheeses – Livarot, Pont L'Évêque, Maroilles, Époisses, Reblochon, Munster, Vacherin; natural-rind cheeses – Saint-Marcellin, Cendrés de Bourgogne, de l'Orléanais, de Champagne. Most hard cheeses – Cantal, Beaufort, Comté, Emmental – are non-pasteurized. Some blue cheeses have a natural rind, or no rind at all; varieties include Bleu de Bresse, Fourme d'Ambert, Roquefort (ewe milk), Bleu d'Auvergne, Bleu des Causses.

Goat cheese is made in many regions, especially Touraine (Sainte-Maure, Valençay), Poitou (Chabichou, Bougon), Berry (Crottin de Chavignol), Quercy (Rocamadour), Haute Provence (Banon) and the Cévennes (Picodon).

They can be enjoyed soft (frais) or cured (sec); the textures vary greatly according to the time of aging. The best known cheeses made from ewe milk, besides Roquefort, are Corsican cheeses and Ossau-Iraty made in the Pyrenees.

◆ Desserts

To round off a meal, the choice of **desserts** is mouth-watering. Besides a platter of fresh fruit, fruit salad or fruit stewed in red wine, there are all sorts of delicious cakes. One traditional favourite is **tarte Tatin** (caramelised upside-down apple tart); others are the **baba au rhum** (sponge cake soaked in rum syrup) and the **Paris-Brest** (a praline cream pastry). Of course, the regions all have their dessert specialities, too: gâteau aux noix (walnut cake) from Grenoble, far (baked custard) from Brittany, gâteau basque (chewy sweet cake filled with pastry cream), gâteau de Savoie (a fluffy bundt cake), pain d'épice (gingerbread) from Dijon, clafoutis (oven-baked fruit and custard tart) from Auvergne and Limousin, and Kougelhopf (a sweet crown-shaped yeast cake) from Alsace. Cream caramel, crème brûlée and île flottante (soft meringue with custard sauce) are popular in nearly every region of France.

WINE

Touring the wine-growing regions of France ranks among the great attractions of the country. Wine is the perfect complement to French culinary delights. A 'terroir' is a group of vineyards (or even vines) from the same region, belonging to a specified appellation, and sharing the same type of soil, weather conditions, grapes and wine making savoir-faire, which contribute to give its specific personality to the wine.

◆ Burgundy

Red Burgundy is made of one grape, Pinot noir. The Burgundy area comprises Côte de Nuits, which boasts outstanding full-bodied wines – Gevrey-Chambertin, Chambolle-Musigny, Vosne-Romanée – and Côte de Beaune which also produces very attractive wines – Aloxe-Corton, Savigny-lès-Beaune, Chorey-lès-Beaune, Pommard, Volnay. Some of the famous white wines of the region are Chablis, Meursault, Puligny-Montrachet and Chassagne-Montrachet. The Côte Châlonnaise has some well-known names – Rully, Mercurey, Givry, Montagny while the Mâconnais produces Pouilly-Fuissé, St-Vérand and Mâcon Villages.

◆ Beaujolais

Beaujolais is preferably drunk young but the best vintages, which include Fleurie, Morgon and Moulin-à-Vent, gain greater depth with age.

◆ Bordeaux

Red Bordeaux are made from several grapes: Cabernet-Sauvignon, Cabernet Franc, Petit Verdot... This famous wine-producing area yields superb clarets: St-Estèphe, Pauillac, Pomerol, St-Émilion, St-Julien, Margaux and pleasant dry white wines – Graves, Entre-deux-Mers.

◆ Rhône-Valley

The elegant wines of Côte-Rôtie, Hermitage, Châteauneuf-du-Pape, Gigondas and Condrieu are among the best of Côtes du Rhône, made with Syrah, Grenache, Viognier grapes.

◆ Loire Valley

Loire wines – Muscadet, Anjou, Saumur, Touraine – are made from Muscadet, Chenin blanc, Cabernet Franc while the delicious Sancerre and flinty Pouilly-Fumé are made from Sauvignon blanc and Pinot Noir.

◆ Alsace

The fragrant wines of Alsace are Riesling, Gewurztraminer, Tokay-Pinot-Gris and Sylvaner.

◆ Champagne

Champagne, which is known as the 'nectar of the gods' and the 'wine of kings', brings a festive note to any occasion. The most celebrated champagnes are from the Côte des Blancs (Épernay, Ay, Chouilly terroirs). Only the best years are labelled with the vintage year.

◆ Other sparking wines

There are also some excellent sparkling wines such as Crémant de Bourgogne, Crémant d'Alsace, Crémant de Loire, Blanquette de Limoux and Clairette de Die.

◆ Dessert wines

The best dessert wines are Sauternes (especially Château d'Yquem, a pure nectar and in a class of its own), Monbazillac, Muscat de Beaumes-de-Venise and Muscat de Rivesaltes. Banyuls and Maury are also delicious and accompany chocolate particularly well.

Beyond these famous wines, there are a multitude of regional wines available everywhere you travel in France (Languedoc-Roussillon, Provence, Jura, South-West…) and we hope this brief introduction will whet your appetite.

Population (est. 2005): 2 107 000 (conurbation 9 928 000) - Altitude: 60 m

J. Guillard / SCOPE

The architectural harmony of Paris is striking with its wide avenues lined with elegant 19C buildings, its mediaeval centre and Renaissance and Classical additions which have been remodelled over the centuries. From its origins as the small Gallo-Roman settlement known as Lutetia, Paris grew along the banks of the Seine. The splendid monuments, Notre-Dame, the Louvre, the Place de la Concorde, the Eiffel Tower, with the book stalls, cafés, art galleries and smart shops lining the banks are best admired on a leisurely boat trip by day or when lit up at night. For typically Parisian scenes, explore the maze of alleyways leading to the boulevards and watch the world go by as you savour an espresso or a cool beer at a café terrace where waiters wear the traditional long, white aprons and black waistcoats.

Paris is known as the City of Light. It has a reputation for elegance owing to its fashion designers, perfumers and jewellers and it is a vibrant artistic and intellectual capital with many theatres, concert halls, music halls, museums and bookshops. Its numerous attractions make it an ever popular tourist destination.

WHICH DISTRICT TO CHOOSE

It is useful to understand the layout of the city to avoid confusion over the names of the districts (quartiers) and the 20 arrondissements. The right bank takes in the north and west while the left bank comprises the south. The Île de la Cité *Plan V* **T2** is the nucleus around which the city grew and the oldest quarters around this site are the 1st, 2nd, 3rd, 4th arrondissements on the right bank and 5th, 6th on the left bank *(see the Plan I)*.

Accommodation is plentiful in Paris. Prestigious **hotels** with luxurious amenities are located in the fashionable districts – 1st, 2nd and 8th arrondissements – in the city centre and there are business and moderately

167

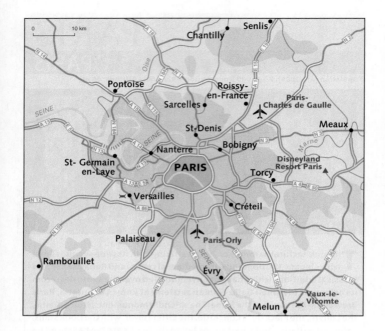

priced hotels in the 5th, 6th, 7th, 14th, 15th arrondissements. Charming small establishments are also to be found in various districts such as the Marais *Plan VII* **X1** and Saint-Germain-des-Prés *Plan V* **S2**.

The city takes great pride in the quality of food available in establishments of all kinds from the simple bistro to the gastronomic temples. You will find the finest **restaurants** in the 1st, 2nd, 5th, 6th, 8th, 16th and 17th arrondissements and excellent restaurants at reasonable prices in the 7th, 14th and 17th arrondissements. There are also cafés, bistros, crêperies, brasseries, tables d'hôte, winebars, tearooms and ethnic eateries for you to enjoy all over the city.

PRACTICAL INFORMATION

ARRIVAL – DEPARTURE

Roissy-Charles-de-Gaulle Airport – 23 km (14 mi) northeast of Paris. ℰ 01 48 62 22 80; www.adp.fr

Orly Airport – 14 km (9 mi) south of Paris. ℰ 01 49 75 15 15; www.adp.fr

From Roissy airport to Paris – By **taxi**: about €50 (+ €1 per item of luggage), time 30min-1hr according to the time of day and the traffic. By **RER**: via Gare du Nord, Châtelet-Les-Halles, Luxembourg and Port-Royal to the city centre, €8. By **Air France bus**: to Invalides or Porte Maillot every 15min and to Gare de Lyon or Montparnasse every 30min. Fares €12 one-way, €18 round trip.

From Orly airport to Paris – By **taxi**: about €30, time 20-45min depending on the traffic. By **Orlyval shuttle-train** from the airport to Antony connecting with the RER and to other stations in Paris: €7.20-€9.05. By **Orly bus** to Denfert-Rochereau €5.80 or **Air France bus** to Invalides or Porte Maillot, every 15min, €8,40 one way, €12 round trip.

Main Stations – **Gare de Lyon** *Plan I* **C2**: trains from southeast France, Italy, Switzerland. **Gare d'Austerlitz** *Plan I* **C3**: trains from southwest France and Spain. **Gare du Nord** *Plan I* **C1**: trains from the United Kingdom, Belgium, The Netherlands. **Gare de l'Est** *Plan I* **C1**: trains from Germany.

TRANSPORT

◆ TAXIS

Taxis may be hailed in the streets, at taxi ranks or called by phone. Average trip: €15-25 during the day and €20-30 at night. For a tip, add up to 10% although this is not compulsory. *Taxis Bleus* ℘ 0891 70 10 10; *Alpha Taxis* ℘ 01 45 85 85 85.

◆ BUS AND METRO

Paris has an excellent and inexpensive public transport system. Fares: €1.40 single ticket; €10.70 carnet (book of 10 tickets). **Paris Visite**: €8.35 (1-day pass 3 zones) to €45.70 (5-day pass 5 zones). **Mobilis** is a one-day pass giving unlimited travel in zones selected: €5.40 (Zones 1-2) to €18.40 (Zones 1-8). The weekly or monthly **Carte Orange** is valid from the first of the month or Mon-Sun and offers an advantageous rate; photograph required.

USEFUL ADDRESSES

◆ TOURIST INFORMATION

Office du tourisme et des congrès de Paris, 25-27 Rue des Pyramides *Plan III* **K3**. ℘ 08 92 68 31 12. Open 9am-8pm; Nov-Mar, Sun and holidays 11am-6pm. Closed 1 May. www.paris-touristoffice.com

There are also welcome points at **Gare de Lyon**, **Gare du Nord**, **Tour Eiffel**, **Opéra** (11 Rue Scribe), **Montmartre** (21 Place du Tertre) and **Carrousel du Louvre** (99 Rue de Rivoli).

◆ POST OFFICES

Open Mon Fri, 8am-7pm; Sat 8am-noon. The main post office at 52 Rue du Louvre opens 24 hours 7 days a week.

◆ BANKS/CURRENCY EXCHANGE

Open Mon-Fri, 4.30pm. Some branches open Sat mornings. Credit cards may be used to withdraw cash from ATMs which require a PIN. Bureaux de change have high charges.

◆ EMERGENCY

Medical assistance (SAMU): ℘ **15**, police: ℘ **17**, Fire Brigade: ℘ **18**.

BUSY PERIODS

It may be difficult to find a room or prices may go up when certain events are held in the city:

Salon de l'Agriculture: late February-March.

Foire de Paris: May.

Mondial de l'Automobile: late September-October – every other year (next: 2006).

DIFFERENT FACETS OF THE CITY

It is possible to visit the main sights and museums in Paris in four to five days.

Museums and other sights are usually open from 10am to 6pm. Most close on Tuesdays.

ROMANTIC CITY – A tour in a **bateau-mouche** on the Seine to admire the splendid cityscape. Take the lift to the top of the **Tour Eiffel** *Plan IV* **O1**. Walk down the **Champs-Élysées** *Plan II* **G32** to the **Arc de Triomphe** *Plan II* **F2**, then explore **Montmartre** *Plan VIII* **AA1** for one of the finest vistas in Paris.

HISTORIC CITY – Walk round the **Île de la Cité** and visit **Notre-Dame de Paris** *Plan V* **U2**. Then cross to the right bank of the Seine past the **Hôtel de Ville** *Plan V* **U1** and on to the **Marais** *Plan VII* **X1**, the oldest quarter with its splendid mansions.

ARTISTIC CITY – A visit to the **Musée du Louvre** *Plan V* **S1** is a must for art lovers, then explore the gardens of the **Palais Royal** *Plan III* **K3** behind the **Comédie Française**. The Musée d'Art Moderne at **Centre Georges-Pompidou** *Plan V* **U1** in the Beaubourg district is of interest for those keen on modern architecture and contemporary art.

LOCAL COLOUR – To capture the flavour of life in the city, spend some time on the left bank where the intellectuals frequent the cafés of the **Quartier Latin** *Plan V* **T2** and the Sorbonne, the **Quartier Saint-Germain-des-Prés** *Plan IV* **S2** where the major publishers are located. The trendy places for the young are near the Bastille and beyond towards **Oberkampf**. To go back in time visit the charming **galleries and arcades**: Passage des Panoramas *Plan III* **L2**, Passage de

Choiseul *Plan III* **K3**, Passage Colbert *Plan III* **K3**, Passage Véro-Dodat *Plan III* **L3**, Passage Vivienne *Plan III* **L3**.

GREEN CITY – The **Jardin des Tuileries** *Plan III* **J3**, **Jardin du Luxembourg** *Plan IV* **S3**, **Buttes-Chaumont** *Plan I* **D1**, **Parc Monceau** *Plan II* **G1** and **Parc André-Citroën** *Plan I* **A3** are havens in central Paris. The **Bois de Boulogne** *Plan I* **A2** and **Bois de Vincennes** *Plan I* **D3** are on the outskirts.

MARKETS – The colourful and lively scene of **open-air markets** is a delight: Marché d'Aligre (near Gare de Lyon) *Plan I* **D2**, Rue Cler *Plan IV* **P2**, Rue de Levis *Plan II* **H1**, Rue Montorgueil *Plan I* **C2**, Boulevard Raspail *Plan VI* **W1**, Rue de Buci *Plan V* **S2**. The **flea markets** at Porte de Clignancourt *Plan I* **C1** and Porte de Vanves *Plan I* **A3** are famous for antiques. Also of interest are: the **flower markets** at Place Louis-Lépine *Plan V* **T1**, Place de la Madeleine *Plan III* **J2** and Place des Ternes *Plan III* **F1**; the **Bird Market**, Place Louis-Lépine *Plan V* **T1**; the **Stamp Market**, Carré Marigny *Plan II* **H3**.

VISITING

Notre-Dame de Paris *Plan V* **U2** – One of the major Gothic cathedrals in France. Nearby is the **Sainte-Chapelle**, a masterpiece of Gothic architecture celebrated for its pure lines and its sumptuous stained glass windows.

Tour Eiffel *Plan IV* **O1** – The soaring tower, which is the symbol of Paris, is a daring architectural achievement. The nightly illumination turns it into a sparkling jewel.

Musée du Louvre *Plan IV* **S1** – One of the world's greatest museums displaying masterpieces: *Mona Lisa*, The *Winged Victory of Samothrace*, *Venus de Milo* among others. The glass pyramid by Pei is remarkable.

Butte Montmartre and Basilique du Sacré-Cœur *Plan VIII* **AA1** – A Romano-Byzantine basilica crowns the heights of Montmartre. From the terrace and from the dome one can enjoy the best views of the city. Do not miss the bustling Place du Tertre where artists offer their paintings or portraits.

Musée National d'Art moderne *Plan V* **U1** – Housed in **Centre Georges-Pompidou**, the museum traces the evolution of art from fauvism and cubism to contemporary trends.

Musée d'Orsay *Plan I* **R1** – Collection of 19C art including many Impressionist works.

Place des Vosges *Plan VII* **X2** – A wonderful, shady square, the oldest in Paris (17C), at the heart of the Marais district. Nearby is the fine **Place des Victoires** dominated by a statue of Louis XIV.

Château de Versailles – *20 km-12.5 mi southwest.* A glorious monument to the French monarchy combining a splendid palace and harmonious gardens.

Disneyland Resort – *30 km-19 mi east.* A world of fun at Disneyland in Europe.

Viewpoints – **Sacré Cœur** *Plan VIII* **AA1**; **Tour Eiffel** *Plan IV* **O1**; **Tour Montparnasse** *Plan VI* **V1**; **Arc de Triomphe** *Plan II* **F2**; **Notre-Dame** towers.

Vistas – From the Rond-Point on the Champs-Élysées *Plan II* **F2** (Arc de Triomphe, Champs-Élysées, Place de la Concorde); from the obelisk on Place de la Concorde *Plan III* **J2** (Madeleine church, Place de la Concorde, Palais Bourbon); from the terrace of the Palais de Chaillot *Plan IV* **N1** (Trocadéro, Eiffel Tower, École Militaire); from Pont Alexandre-III *Plan IV* **Q1** (Invalides, Grand and Petit-Palais).

GOURMET TREATS

The centre of the capital city offers an enticing array of shops selling treats both savoury and sweet. Enjoy the scent and texture of a golden brown **baguette**; have the most typical of Parisian sandwiches, the "**jambon beurre**", made with fresh bread, ham and butter, available at all of the good bakeries (*Kayser*, 8 Rue Monge, to name but one) and in some bistros, cafés and brasseries.

Tasty delights spill out of the cornucopia of Place de la Madeleine, in shops whose names evoke the pleasures of the palate. *Fauchon, Hédiard, La Maison de la Truffe,* and the tea room *Ladurée* (around the corner at 16 Rue Royale) are among the most famous. Another charming tea room, *Angélina* (226 Rue de Rivoli), is known for serving the creamiest **hot chocolate** in town.

Near the Place des Victoires, in the beautiful covered passage Galerie Vivienne, *Legrand* sweet shop also offers a selection of 3 500 vintage **wines**, which you can enjoy with an assortment of cold meats. A different atmosphere prevails at *Père Louis* (38 Rue Monsieur-le-Prince), an authentic wine bar with wine casks for tables, and a friendly, relaxed ambience.

In the St-Germain-des-Prés neighbourhood, the *Pierre Hermé* pastry shop (72 Rue Bonaparte) is the place to go for chewy **macaroons**. Although the shop is unpretentious, it is a local favourite and known around the world. The nearby *Poilâne* bakery (8 Rue du Cherche-Midi) is famous as well for its shortbread biscuits (**sablés**) and many different varieties of **bread**. It is also well worth looking in at the *Fromagerie 31* (64 Rue de Seine), to take advantage of the tasting area and admire the tempting display of **cheeses** from all over France.

End your epicurean adventures on a note of freshness and colour on the island of Saint Louis, with a visit to the famous **ice cream** maker *Berthillon* (Rue St-Louis-en-l'Île). There is a flavour to please everyone, including exotic litchi, thyme or gingerbread.

SHOPPING

Department stores – Boulevard Haussmann *Plan III* **K2** *(Galeries Lafayette, Printemps)*, Rue de Rivoli *Plan V* **U1** *(Samaritaine, Bazar de l'Hôtel de Ville)*, Rue de Sèvres *Plan IV* **Q3** (the elegant *Bon Marché*).

Luxury and designer shops – Rue du Faubourg-St-Honoré *Plan II* **G2**, Rue de la Paix **T2** Rue Royale *Plan III* **J3**, Avenue Montaigne *Plan II* **G3** Place des Victoires *Plan I* **C2**. Famous jewellers' shops are to be found in Place Vendôme *Plan III* **K3**.

Boutiques – Rue des Francs-Bourgeois *Plan VII* **X1**, Forum des Halles *Plan V* **T1**, Rue Étienne-Marcel *Plan I* **C2**, Rue Montorgueil *Plan I* **C2**.

Antiques – Louvre des Antiquaires *Plan IV* **S1**, Village Suisse (Avenue de La Motte-Picquet), Carré Rive Gauche, Village St-Paul *Plan VII* **X2**, flea market, Porte de Clignancourt (Sat, Sun).

Art galleries – The Marais and Bastille districts, Avenue Matignon *Plan II* **H3**, the area around Rue de Seine to St-Germain-des-Prés.

Gourmet shops *(see more addresses in Gourmet Treats chapter)* – Fine foods and wines: *Hédiard* (No 21) and *Fauchon* (No 26) Place de la Madeleine. Chocolates: *La Maison du Chocolat*, 225 Rue du Faubourg-St-Honoré; *La Fontaine de Chocolat*, 201 Rue St-Honoré; *Christian-Constant*, 37 Rue d'Assas; *Jean-Paul Hévin*, 3 Rue Vavin; *Debauve et Gallais*, 30 Rue des Saints-Pères; *Michel Chaudun*, 149 Rue de l'Université; *Richart*, 238 Boulevard St-Germain. Cheeses: *Androuet*, 83 Rue St-Dominique; *Barthélemy*, 151 Rue de Grenelle; *Fil'O Fromage*, 4 Rue Poirier-de-Narçay; *La Ferme La Fontaine*, 75 Rue La Fontaine. Fine wines: *Les Caprices de l'Instant*, 12 Rue Jacques-Cœur; *Les Caves Taillevent*, 199 Rue du Faubourg-St-Honoré. Caviar: *Petrossian*, 18 Boulevard de Latour-Maubourg. Jams: *Furet*, 63 Rue de Chabrol.

ENTERTAINMENT

Several weekly publications (available at newsstands) publish entertainment listings – exhibitions, shows, festivals, concerts and theatres. The best known ones are *Pariscope, L'Officiel des Spectacles* and *Zurban*.

Theatre tickets can be bought at the kiosk at Place de la Madeleine Plan III J2.

Opera and dance – Opéra Bastille *Plan VII* **Y2**, Palais Garnier *Plan III* **K2**, Théâtre de la Ville *Plan VIII* **Z2**.

Classical and contemporary concerts – Théâtre du Châtelet *Plan V* **T1**, Cité de la Musique *Plan I* **D1**, Salle Pleyel *Plan II* **G2**, Salle Gaveau *Plan II* **H2**, Théâtre des Champs-Élysées *Plan II* **G3**.

Theatre – Comédie Française *Plan III* **K3**, Théâtre National de Chaillot *Plan IV* **N1**, Théâtre du Rond-Point *Plan II* **H3**, Odéon Théâtre de l'Europe *Plan IV* **S2**, Théâtre Marigny *Plan II* **H3**, Théâtre des Variétés *Plan III* **L2**.

Cabarets and revues – Lido *Plan II* **G2**, Moulin-Rouge *Plan VIII* **Z2**, Folies-Bergère *Plan III* **L2**, Crazy-Horse *Plan II* **F3**.

Variety shows – Olympia *Plan III* **K2**, Zénith *Plan I* **D1**, Palais Omnisports de Bercy *Plan I* **D3**, Casino de Paris *Plan III* **K1**, La Cigale *Plan VIII* **AA2**, Le Bataclan *Plan VII* **Y1**.

NIGHTLIFE

There is a profusion of bars and cafés to choose from when **going out for a drink or for the evening**, in particular in the districts of St-Germain-des-Prés, Bastille, Montparnasse, Pigalle. Some famous names are: *Café de Flore, Les Deux Magots, Brasserie Lipp* (Boulevard St-Germain), *La Coupole, La Rotonde, Le Dôme, Le Sélect* (Boulevard du Montparnasse), *Bar Hemingway* at the Ritz, 15 Place Vendôme, *Bar de l'hôtel Costes*, 239 Rue St-Honoré.

Hit the high spots of Paris in the bustling districts of: **St-Germain-des-Prés, Montparnasse, Pigalle, Bastille, Oberkampf** and **République**

where discotheques and nightclubs are legion: *Les Bains-Douches*, 7 Rue du Bourg-l'Abbé; *Le Balajo*, 9 Rue de Lappe; *La Locomotive*, 90 Boulevard de Clichy; *Le Queen*, 102 Avenue des Champs-Élysées; *La Rive Gauche*, 1 Rue du Sabot, *Le Batofar*, Quai François-Mauriac.

If you are a jazz fan, some jazz clubs are veritable institutions: *Caveau de la Huchette*, 5 Rue de la Huchette, *Le Duc des Lombards*, 42 Rue des Lombards, *Petit Journal Montparnasse*, 13 Rue du Commandant-Mouchotte, *LeBilboquet*, 13 Rue Saint-Benoît, *Jazz Club Lionel Hampton* at Méridien Etoile, 81 Rue Gouvion-Saint-Cyr, *Le Petit Opportun*, 15 Rue des Lavandières.

RESTAURANTS – ALPHABETIC LIST

City of Paris
(Plan I)

COURBEVOIE **A**

B CLICHY

SEINE

Pte de St-Ouen

D 909

D 911

D 19

D 912

1

LA DÉFENSE

Pte de Clichy

LEVALLOIS-PERRET

Bessières

D 906

Pte d'Asnières

Berthier

Av. de Clichy

Av. de St-Ouen

● Novotel La Défense

NEUILLY-S-SEINE

Av. Ch. de Gaulle

N 13

Pte de Champerret

Bd du Mal Juin

Pl. du Mal Juin

17E

BATIGNOLLES

CIMETIÈRE DE MONTMARTRE

Pte Maillot

Champs-Elysées, Etoile Palais des Congrès (Plan II)

Villiers

Av. de Wagram

Bd de Courcelles

PARC MONCEAU

Malesherbes

Concorde,

GARE ST-LAZARE

Clichy

Longchamp

Av. de la Gde Armée

ARC DE TRIOMPHE

Bd Haussmann

8E

Pl. de la Madeleine

Pte Dauphine

Avenue

R. Pierre

Pl. Ch. de Gaulle

Foch

Av. des Champs Elysées

Av. Marceau

Allée

de

Bd Lannes

Av. Bugeaud

Av. Poincaré

St-James Paris

Pl. de la Concorde

Pré Catelan

Pte de la Muette

Av.

Mandel

Pl. du Trocadéro

Av. de New-York

Quai d'Orsay

BOIS DE BOULOGNE

Suchet

Av. Ingres

Rue de Passy

TOUR EIFFEL

Av. Bosquet

7E

Boulevard

Rue de Rennes

Chez Géraud

PARC DU CHAMP DE MARS

LES INVALIDES

2

16E

Bd de Grenelle

Av. de Breteuil

Bd des Invalides

Pte d'Auteuil

Boulevard

Versailles

Q. Citroën

SEINE

Av. de Suffren

Bd Garibaldi

Av. de

Sèvres

6E

A

13

Benkay

Novotel Tour Eiffel

Rue du

Montparnasse

Relais d'Auteuil

Square ●

BEAUGRENELLE

Tour Eiffel, Invalides (Plan IV)

Bd

Bd Murat

Av. A. Citroën

de

Lecourbe

GARE MONTPARNASSE

CIM. DU MONTPARNASSE

D 907

PARC A. CITROËN

de la Convention

de

Vaugirard

Raspail

N 10

Av.

Quai d'Issy

Bd

15E

Rue

R. de Vouillé

Pl. Denfert Rochereau

Pte de St-Cloud

Pte de Sèvres

Porte de Versailles

Victor

Mercure Porte de Versailles

Montparnasse (Plan VI)

BOULOGNE-BILLANCOURT

Relais de Sèvres

PARIS EXPO

Bd Lefebvre

R.

3

D 1

Sofitel Porte de Sèvres

Boulevard

Brune

Av. J. Moulin

14E

D 7

D 989

VANVES

Bd

Périphérique

Bd

Pte de Châtillon

ISSY-LES-MOULINEAUX

MALAKOFF

Pte d'Orléans

D 906

Av. Pierre Brossolette

N 20

● Hotel

● Restaurant

0   1km

A

B MONTROUGE

ST-OUEN **C** ST-DENIS

N 2 Pte de la Villette **D**

Boulevard Périphérique

Pte de Clignancourt Bd Ney

Pte de la Chapelle Bd Macdonald

PANTIN

CITÉ DES SCIENCES ET DE L'INDUSTRIE

Flandre

N 3

18E

PARC DE LA VILLETTE

Pte de Pantin

1

LE PRÉ-ST-GERVAIS

Montmartre, Pigalle (Plan VIII)

Cube

Bd Barbès

Av.

Jaurès

Bd d'Indochine

Holiday Inn

SACRÉ-CŒUR

Bd de la Chapelle

Jean

Av.

LES LILAS

Opéra, Gare du Nord (Plan III)

GARE DU NORD

19E

Fayette

PARC DES BUTTES CHAUMONT

Bd Sérurier

D 117

9E

R. de Maubeuge

La

GARE DE L'EST

Villette

Rue de

Belleville

Bd des Lilas

Pte des Lilas

10E

Haussmann

Pl. de la République

BELLEVILLE

Mortier

2E

Av. de la République

Av. Gambetta Rue Belgrand

Pte de Bagnolet

A 3

1ER

Holiday Inn

LOUVRE

Murano

3E

Bd Beaumarchais

R. du Fg. du Temple

Boulevard

R. Lenoir

11E

CIMETIÈRE DU PÈRE LACHAISE

20E

Davout

2

MONTREUIL-BAGNOLET

NOTRE-DAME

4E

Rivoli

Bd Henri IV

Pl. de la Bastille

R. de Lyon

Voltaire

Av. Ph. Auguste

Marais, Bastille Gare de Lyon (Plan VII)

Mansouria

St-Antoine

Pl. de la Nation

Crs de Vincennes

Pte de Vincennes

N 34

JARDIN DU LUXEMBOURG

Germain

5E

Bd Bourdon

du Fg

Diderot

ST-MANDÉ

St-Germain-des-Prés, Quartier Latin, Hôtel de Ville (Plan V)

JARDIN DES PLANTES

Boulevard

Novotel Gare de Lyon

GARE DE LYON

12E

Av.

Pl. Félix Eboué

Bd de Port-Royal

GARE D'AUSTERLITZ

Q. de la Râpée

de Bercy

Bd de Reuilly

Daumesnil

Pte Dorée

BOIS DE VINCENNES

3

Av. des Gobelins

13E

Vincent Auriol

Novotel Bercy

Rue de Charenton

BERCY

Bd St-Jacques Bd A. Blanqui

Pl. d'Italie

BIBLIOTHÈQUE F. MITTERRAND

Tolbiac

Quai de Bercy

SEINE

Sofitel Paris Bercy

Pte de Bercy

CHARENTON-LE-PONT

Alésia

Rue

de

Holiday Inn Bibliothèque de France

Masséna

Quai d'Ivry

A 4

PARC MONTSOURIS

Jourdan Bd Kellermann

Pte de Gentilly

Pte d'Italie

Av. d'Italie Bd

Pte de Choisy

IVRY-S-SEINE

N 19

A 6a A 6b

GENTILLY

C

D

Champs-Élysées, Étoile, Palais des Congrès
(Plan II)

E

F

Magellan

Quality Pierre

Michel Rostang

Caves Petrissans

Flaubert

L'Huîtrier

la Pte des Ternes

Av. de Pershing

Ballon des Ternes

Villa des Ternes

Concorde La Fayette

PALAIS DES CONGRÈS DE PARIS

Neuilly - Porte Maillot Palais des Congrès

Méridien Étoile

Les Béatilles

Regent's Garden

Villa Alessandra

Pl. Tristan Bernard

Pl. des Ternes

Porte Maillot Pl. de la Pte Maillot

R. du Débarcadère

St-Ferdinand

Caïus

Petit Colombier

Star Hôtel Étoile

Élysées Céramic

Étoile Résidence Impériale

Timgad

Astrid

Graindorge

Guy Savoy

Mercure Wagram, Arc de Triomphe

Balmoral

Sormani

Étoile Park Hôtel

La Villa Maillot

Pergolèse

Pergolèse

Splendid Étoile

Le Pergolèse

Argentine

Grande Armée

ARC DE TRIOMPHE

Napoléon

Stella Maris

2

Pl. Charles de Gaulle

Chiberta

Foch

Copenhague

Avenue

Hugo

Radisson SAS Champs Élysées

Vernet

16e

Du Bois

Kléber

Les Élysées

Raphael

Amarante Champs Élysées

Table de Joël Robuchon

Le Vinci

Majestic

Chambellan Morgane

Victor Hugo Pl. V. Hugo

Bugeaud

Copernic

La Résidence Bassano

Élysées Régencia

Le Relais du Parc

Sofitel Baltimore

Pl. des États-Unis

Sofitel Le Parc

3

La Table du Baltimore

Cristal Room Baccarat

Boissière

Trocadero Dokhan's

Floride Étoile

Oscar

Didier

Pl. de Mexico

Paul Chêne

Au Palais de Chaillot

Jamin

Pl. d'Iéna

Hiramatsu

Passiflore

Longchamp

Président Wilson

PALAIS DE TOKYO

Iéna

6 New-York

Costes K.

Port Alma

E

F

TOUR EIFFEL / INVALIDES (Plan IV)

182

CHAMPS-ÉLYSÉES, ÉTOILE, PALAIS DES CONGRÈS *Plan II*

FRANCE

Plaza Athénée 🖼 ᴵ⬝ 🅐 ⅏rm ♨20/60 VISA ⓒ AE ①

25 av. Montaigne (8th) – Ⓜ *Alma Marceau –* ℰ *01 53 67 66 65*
– reservation @ plaza-athenee-paris.com – Fax 01 53 67 66 66 **G3**
145 rm – †565 € ††770 €, ⌸ 46 € – 43 suites
Rest see *Alain Ducasse au Plaza Athénée* and *Relais Plaza* below
Rest *La Cour Jardin,* ℰ *01 53 67 66 02 (closed mid-September-mid-May)*
a la carte 85/100 €
◆ Palace ◆ Grand Luxury ◆ Personalised ◆
Classic or Art Deco-style in the luxuriously redecorated rooms, musical tea hour
in the Gobelins gallery, stunning designer bar: This is the Parisian palace par
excellence! The charming, greenery-filled terrace of La Cour Jardin opens when
the weather turns nice.

Four Seasons George V ⓒ ᴵ⬝ ⬚ ᵹrm 🅐 ⅏rm ♨rest ☏

31 av. George V (8th) – Ⓜ *George V* ♨30/240 VISA ⓒ AE ①
– ℰ 01 49 52 70 00 – par.lecinq @ fourseasons.com – Fax 01 49 52 70 10
– www.fourseasons.com **G3**
186 rm – †665/900 € ††695/780 €, ⌸ 47 € – 59 suites
Rest see *Le Cinq* below
Rest *Terrasse d'Été (open May-September)* a la carte 70/91 €
◆ Palace ◆ Grand Luxury ◆ Personalised ◆
Completely renovated in 18C-style, the "Fifth" (le Cinq) has luxurious and
enormous rooms (by Paris standards, in any case), beautiful artwork collections
and a superb spa. The tables at the Terrasse d'Été are set out in the delightful
interior courtyard.

Bristol ⓒ ᴵ⬝ ⬚ ⛟ 🅐 ♨ ♨30/100 ⌸ VISA ⓒ AE ①

112 r. Fg St-Honoré (8th) – Ⓜ *Miromesnil –* ℰ *01 53 43 43 00*
– resa @ lebristolparis.com – Fax 01 53 43 43 01
– www.lebristolparis.com **H2**
126 rm – †580/650 € ††750 €, ⌸ 49 € – 38 suites
Rest see *Bristol* below
◆ Palace ◆ Grand Luxury ◆ Personalised ◆
1925 luxury hotel set around a magnificent garden. Sumptuous rooms, mainly
Louis XV or Louis XVI-style with an exceptional "boat" swimming pool on the top
floor.

Royal Monceau ⓒ ᴵ⬝ ⬚ ᵹ 🅐 ⅏ 🖵 ♨15/200 VISA ⓒ AE ①

37 av. Hoche (8th) – Ⓜ *Charles de Gaulle-Etoile –* ℰ *01 42 99 88 00*
– reservations @ royalmonceau.com – Fax 01 42 99 89 90
– www.royalmonceau.com **G2**
158 rm – †550/750 € ††550/750 €, ⌸ 45 € – 47 suites
Rest see *Jardin* and *Carpaccio* below
◆ Palace ◆ Grand Luxury ◆ Stylish ◆
This luxury hotel, dating from 1928, has nearly completed its renovations, with
decor designed by Jacques Garcia. Magnificent hall-lounge, elegant rooms and
fine fitness centre with pool.

Raphael 🖼 ᴵ⬝ 🅐 ⅏rm ♨50 VISA ⓒ AE ①

17 av. Kléber (16th) ✉ *75116 –* Ⓜ *Kléber –* ℰ *01 53 64 32 00*
– reservation @ raphael-hotel.com – Fax 01 53 64 32 01
– www.raphael-hotel.com **F2**
61 rm – †325 € ††560 €, ⌸ 35 € – 25 suites
Rest *Jardins Plein Ciel –* (7th floor), ℰ *01 53 64 32 30 (open May-October)* 75 €
(lunch)/100 €
Rest *Salle à Manger,* ℰ *01 53 64 32 11 (closed Saturday and Sunday)* 50 € b.i.
(lunch)/65 € b.i.
◆Stylish ◆ Grand Luxury ◆ Personalised ◆
The Raphael, built in 1925, offers a superb wood-panelled gallery, refined rooms,
a rooftop terrace with a panoramic view and a trendy English bar. A lovely view
of Paris and a buffet set menu can be found at the Jardins Plein Ciel (7th floor).
Superb "Salle à Manger" dining room in Grand Hotel style.

FRANCE

Sofitel Le Parc ⌂   ⅃ᴃ 🄰🄲 ⅏ ₷⚁40/250 *VISA* 🆖 🄰🄴 ⓪
55 av. R. Poincaré (16th) ⊠ 75116 – **Ⓜ** Victor Hugo – ℰ 01 44 05 66 66
– h2797@accor.com – Fax 01 44 05 66 00   **E3**
95 rm – †400/550 € ††550 €, � 26 € – 21 suites
Rest see **59 Poincaré** below
♦ Grand Luxury ♦ Modern ♦
The rooms are elegant and pleasingly British in atmosphere. All are well
equipped (with wifi) and distributed around a garden terrace. Part of the bar
decor is by Arman.

Hilton Arc de Triomphe   🏠 ⅃ᴃ � rm 🄰🄲 ⅏ ℛrest ₷⚁15/800
51 r. Courcelles (8th) – **Ⓜ** Courcelles   🚗 *VISA* 🆖 🄰🄴 ⓪
– ℰ 01 58 36 67 00 – info_adt@hilton.com
– Fax 01 58 36 67 77   **G2**
438 rm – †230/630 € ††230/680 €, ⊃ 30 € – 25 suites
Rest Safran, ℰ 01 58 36 67 96 – a la carte 35/78 €
♦ Luxury ♦ Modern ♦
This new hotel, inspired by the liners of the 1930s, has successfully created their
luxurious and refined atmosphere. Elegant Art Deco rooms, patio with fountain,
fitness centre, etc. At the Safran the food reflects current tastes, influenced by the
flavours and perfumes of Asia.

Lancaster   ⅃ᴃ 🄰🄲 ⅏ *VISA* 🆖 🄰🄴 ⓪
7 r. Berri (8th) – **Ⓜ** George V – ℰ 01 40 76 40 76
– reservations@hotel-lancaster.fr – Fax 01 40 76 40 00
– www.hotel-lancaster.fr   **G2**
49 rm – †350 € ††410/520 €, ⊃ 32 € – 11 suites
Rest see **Table du Lancaster** below
♦ Luxury ♦ Personalised ♦
B. Pastoukhoff paid for his lodging with paintings, adding richly to this old
townhouse's elegant decor once so appreciated by Marlene Dietrich.

Sofitel Baltimore   ⅃ᴃ 🄰🄲 ⅏ ℛrest ₷⚁15/50 🚗 *VISA* 🆖 🄰🄴 ⓪
88 bis av. Kléber (16th) ⊠ 75116 – **Ⓜ** Boissière – ℰ 01 44 34 54 54
– welcome@hotelbaltimore.com – Fax 01 44 34 54 44
– www.sofitel.com   **E3**
103 rm – †395/495 € ††395/1015 €, ⊃ 27 €
Rest see **Table du Baltimore** below
♦ Luxury ♦ Modern ♦
Simple furniture, trendy fabrics, old photos of the city of Baltimore: the
contemporary decor of the rooms contrasts with the architecture of this 19C
building.

Vernet   🄰🄲 ℛrest *VISA* 🆖 🄰🄴 ⓪
25 r. Vernet (8th) – **Ⓜ** Charles de Gaulle-Etoile – ℰ 01 44 31 98 00
– reservations@hotelvernet.com – Fax 01 44 31 85 69
– www.hotelvernet.com   **F2**
42 rm – †290/390 € ††330/550 €, ⊃ 35 €
– 9 suites
Rest see **Les Élysées** below
♦ Luxury ♦ Personalised ♦
The building dating from the twenties has a beautiful dressed-stone façade
embellished with wrought-iron balconies. Empire - or Louis XVI-style rooms.
Fashionable bar and grill room.

Costes K. without rest   ⅃ᴃ ⅆ 🄰🄲 ⅏ 🚗 *VISA* 🆖 🄰🄴 ⓪
81 av. Kléber (16th) ⊠ 75116 – **Ⓜ** Trocadéro – ℰ 01 44 05 75 75
– costes.k@wanadoo.fr – Fax 01 44 05 74 74   **E3**
83 rm – †300/250 € ††350/500 €, ⊃ 20 €
♦ Luxury ♦ Modern ♦
This hotel by Ricardo Bofill is ultra-modern. It invites you to enjoy the
discreet calm of its vast rooms with their pure lines, laid out around a
Japanese-style patio.

FRANCE

San Régis   🏧 ✆ 🛜 VISA 🆖 AE ①
12 r. J. Goujon (8th) – Ⓜ *Champs-Elysées Clemenceau –* ✆ *01 44 95 16 16*
– message@hotel-sanregis.fr – Fax 01 45 61 05 48
– www.hotel-sanregis.fr   **G3**
33 rm – 🛏320/425 € 🛏🛏425/575 €, ⚏ 22 € – 11 suites
Rest *(closed August)* a la carte 47/77 €
♦ Luxury ♦ Personalised ♦
1857 town house recently and tastefully redone. Superb rooms filled with furniture picked up here and there. Haute couture fashion shops a step away. The exquisitely appointed restaurant of the San Régis is set in the subdued atmosphere of a luxurious private reading room.

Sofitel Arc de Triomphe   🖧 🏧 ⇆ 🖧40 VISA 🆖 AE ①
14 r. Beaujon (8th) – Ⓜ *Charles de Gaulle-Etoile –* ✆ *01 53 89 50 50*
– h1296@accor.com – Fax 01 53 89 50 51   **G2**
134 rm – 🛏570/440 € 🛏🛏630 €, ⚏ 27 €
Rest see *Clovis* below
♦ Luxury ♦ Modern ♦
Typical late-19C Parisian building, with 18C-inspired decoration but fitted up to 21C standards. Elegant rooms. Try and book the amazing "Concept Room".

Méridien Étoile   🖧rm 🏧 ⇆rm 🖧50/1200 VISA 🆖 AE ①
81 bd Gouvion St-Cyr (17th) – Ⓜ *Neuilly-Porte Maillot –* ✆ *01 40 68 34 34*
– guest.etoile@lemeridien.com – Fax 01 40 68 31 31
– www.etoile-lemeridien.com   **E1**
1008 rm – 🛏385/450 € 🛏🛏430/495 €, ⚏ 24 € – 17 suites
Rest *L'Orenoc (closed 25 July-25 August, Christmas Holidays, Sunday and Monday)* a la carte 40/68 €
Rest *La Terrasse ,* ✆ *01 40 68 30 85 (closed Saturday)* 38 €
♦ Business ♦ Chain hotel ♦ Modern ♦
This gigantic hotel across from the Palais des Congrès convention centre, containing a jazz club, bar and shops, has been fully renovated. Black granite and shades of beige in the rooms. The Orenoc reflects current tastes in food, and has warm, colonial-style decor. A simple menu and buffets are on offer at La Terrasse.

Concorde La Fayette   ≤ 🖧 🏧 ⇆rm 🖧40/2000 VISA 🆖 AE ①
3 pl. Gén. Koenig (17th) – Ⓜ *Porte Maillot –* ✆ *01 40 68 50 68*
– booking@concorde-hotels.com – Fax 01 40 68 50 43
– www.concorde-lafayette.com   **E1**
931 rm – 🛏169 € 🛏🛏338 €, ⚏ 24 € – 19 suites
Rest *La Fayette ,* ✆ *01 40 68 51 19* – 31/45 € and a la carte 37/55 €
♦ Business ♦ Modern ♦
This 33-floor tower, built into the convention centre offers an unrestricted view of Paris from most of its fully-renovated rooms and panoramic bar. Buffet meals are served in the La Fayette restaurant.

De Vigny   🏧 rm ⇆rm ✆ 🖧 VISA 🆖 AE ①
9 r. Balzac (8th) – Ⓜ *Charles de Gaulle-Etoile –* ✆ *01 42 99 80 80 – reservation@hoteldevigny.com – Fax 01 42 99 80 40 – www.hoteldevigny.com*   **G2**
26 rm – 🛏250/415 € 🛏🛏290/725 €, ⚏ 28 € – 11 suites
Rest *Baretto (closed 14 to 20 August)* a la carte 52/83 €
♦ Luxury ♦ Personalised ♦
This discreetly distinctive hotel is close to the Champs-Élysées; cosy and personalised rooms. Elegant, well-appointed dining hall with snug fireplace. The Baretto serves traditional cuisine in a stylish and low key atmosphere and an Art Deco setting.

Champs-Élysées Plaza *without rest*   🖧 🏧 ⇆ ✂ VISA 🆖 AE ①
35 r. Berri (8th) – Ⓜ *George V –* ✆ *01 53 53 20 20*
– info@champselyseesplaza.com – Fax 01 53 53 20 21
– www.champselyseesplaza.com   **G2**
32 rm – 🛏390/890 € 🛏🛏390/890 €, ⚏ 22 € – 11 suites
♦ Traditional ♦ Personalised ♦
The spacious and elegant rooms of this opulent hotel near the Champs-Élysées all have fireplaces and Art Deco-style bathrooms.

FRANCE

Marriott
☆ *IⒶ* ⅁rm ⒶⒸ ⅄rm ✻ ♨15/165 ⌘ 𝑽𝑰𝑺𝑨 ⓄⓄ ⒶⒺ Ⓞ
70 av. Champs Élysées (8th) – Ⓜ *Franklin D. Roosevelt* – ℰ *01 53 93 55 00*
– *mhrs.pardt.ays@marriotthotels.com*
– *Fax 01 53 93 55 01*   G2
174 rm – 🛉775 € 🛉🛉815 €, ☖ 29 € – 18 suites
Rest *Pavillon*, ℰ *01 53 93 55 44 (closed Sunday dinner and Saturday)* 40/75 €
♦ Business ♦ Modern ♦
An American in Paris - Stateside efficiency, and cosy-as-a-quilt comfort in the
rooms, most of which look out onto the Champs-Élysées. Cross the impressive
atrium to find yourself in this "Pavilion" where the decor (lampposts and
frescoes) brings back memories of an imagined Paris of old.

Balzac
ⒶⒸ 𝑽𝑰𝑺𝑨 ⓄⓄ ⒶⒺ Ⓞ
6 r. Balzac (8th) – Ⓜ *George V* – ℰ *01 44 35 18 00*
– *reservation@hotelbalzac.com* – *Fax 01 44 35 18 05*
– *www.hotelbalzac.com*   G2
55 rm – 🛉405 € 🛉🛉405/520 €, ☖ 32 € – 14 suites
Rest see *Pierre Gagnaire* below
♦ Traditional ♦ Personalised ♦
The writer died at No. 22 in the same street. Elegant rooms, glassed-in lounge. Put
down your bags and like Eugène de Rastignac, go out and conquer Paris!

Warwick
ⒶⒸ ⅄⅄ ✻rest ♨30/110 𝑽𝑰𝑺𝑨 ⓄⓄ ⒶⒺ Ⓞ
5 r. Berri (8th) – Ⓜ *George V* – ℰ *01 45 63 14 11*
– *resa.whparis@warwickhotels.com* – *Fax 01 43 59 00 98*   G2
146 rm – 🛉450 € 🛉🛉900 €, ☖ 28 € – 3 suites
Rest see *Le W* below
♦ Traditional ♦ Modern ♦
The hotel opened its doors in 1981 and has recently had a facelift to offer
rooms with warm fabrics, contemporary furniture and material stretched over
the walls.

Napoléon
ⒶⒸ ⅄rm ℭ♨ ♨15/80 𝑽𝑰𝑺𝑨 ⓄⓄ ⒶⒺ Ⓞ
40 av. Friedland (8th) – Ⓜ *Charles de Gaulle-Etoile* – ℰ *01 56 68 43 21*
– *napoleon@hotelnapoleon.com* – *Fax 01 56 68 44 40*   F2
77 rm – 🛉350/490 € 🛉🛉590 €, ☖ 22 € – 24 suites
Rest *(closed August, dinner, Saturday and Sunday)* a la carte 44/64 €
♦ Historic ♦ Personalised ♦
A step from the Étoile and its Arc de Triomphe so dear to the Emperor. Here one
finds autographs, figurines and paintings recalling the Napoleonic era, and
striking just the right note. Directoire- or Empire-style rooms. Traditional menu
served in the cosy, subdued atmosphere (fine wood panels) of this restaurant.

California
☆ ⒶⒸ ⅄rm ℭ♨ ♨20/100 𝑽𝑰𝑺𝑨 ⓄⓄ ⒶⒺ Ⓞ
16 r. Berri (8th) – Ⓜ *George V* – ℰ *01 43 59 93 00* – *cal@hroy.com*
– *Fax 01 45 61 03 62* – *www.hotel-california-paris.com*   G2
158 rm – 🛉440 € 🛉🛉440/540 €, ☖ 25 € – 16 suites
Rest *(closed August, Saturday and Sunday)* 53 € b.i. (lunch), 70 € b.i./80 € b.i.
♦ Traditional ♦ Personalised ♦
Aesthetes will be thrilled: several thousand paintings ornament the walls of this
old luxury hotel dating from the 1920s. There's another collection, of 200
whiskies in the piano-bar. The restaurant room has a stunning patio-terrace
extension (fountain, mosaics, and greenery).

Trémoille
IⒶ ⅁rm ⒶⒸ ⅄rm ✻ ℭ♨ ♨15 𝑽𝑰𝑺𝑨 ⓄⓄ ⒶⒺ Ⓞ
14 r. Trémoille (8th) – Ⓜ *Alma Marceau* – ℰ *01 56 52 14 00*
– *reservation@hotel-tremoille.com* – *Fax 01 40 70 01 08*
– *www.hotel-tremoille.com*   G3
88 rm – 🛉315/420 € 🛉🛉315/495 €, ☖ 22 € – 5 suites
Rest *(closed Sunday)* 60 € b.i. (weekday lunch), 75 € b.i./90 € b.i.
♦ Traditional ♦ Personalised ♦
The hotel has been successfully refurbished with contemporary decor,
combining old and ultramodern. Latest equipment and marble bathrooms with
Portuguese tiles. An elegant dining room with a cosy atmosphere; cuisine in
keeping with current taste.

FRANCE

Mélia Royal Alma without rest ⬛ ⇥ 🛗15 *VISA* 🌐 🆎 ①
35 r. J. Goujon (8th) – Ⓜ *Alma Marceau* – ☎ 01 53 93 63 00
– melia.royal.alma@solmelia.com – Fax 01 53 93 63 01 **G3**
64 rm – ♦335 € ♦♦392/543 €, ⌷ 25 €
◆ Business ◆ Stylish ◆
Refined decoration and antique furniture – with a penchant for Empire style – in
recently decorated rooms. Suites with panoramic terraces on the top floor.

Trocadero Dokhan's without rest ⬛ ⇥ ⅍ 🕯 *VISA* 🌐 🆎 ①
117 r. Lauriston (16th) ✉ 75116 – Ⓜ *Trocadéro* – ☎ 01 53 65 66 99
– welcome@dokhans.com – Fax 01 53 65 66 88 – www.dokhans.com
41 rm – ♦400/480 € ♦♦430/500 €, ⌷ 28 € – 4 suites **E3**
◆ Townhouse ◆ Personalised ◆
One cannot help but be charmed by this elegant townhouse (1910) with its
Palladian architecture and neo-Classical decor. Pastoral 18C wood panels in the
lounge.

De Sers 🍽 🛁 🐾 🛗rm ⬛ ⇥rm ⅍ 🛗35 *VISA* 🌐 🆎 ①
41 av. Pierre 1ᵉʳ de Serbie (8th) – Ⓜ *George V* – ☎ 01 53 23 75 75
– contact@hoteldesers.com – Fax 01 53 23 75 76 – www.hoteldesers.com
closed 31 July-27 August **G3**
45 rm – ♦350/500 € ♦♦390/600 €, ⌷ 30 € – 6 suites
Rest (closed 31 July-27 August) 50/70 €
◆ Townhouse ◆ Modern ◆
Successfully refurbished late-19C townhouse. While the hall has kept its original
character, the rooms are resolutely contemporary. The food reflects current
tastes and is served in a designer dining room or, in summer, on the pleasant
terrace.

Montaigne without rest 🛗 ⬛ 🕯 *VISA* 🌐 🆎 ①
6 av. Montaigne (8th) – Ⓜ *Alma Marceau* – ☎ 01 47 20 30 50 – contact@hotel-
montaigne.com – Fax 01 47 20 94 12 – www.hotel-montaigne.com **G3**
29 rm – ♦200/230 € ♦♦300/450 €, ⌷ 19 €
◆ Traditional ◆ Cosy ◆
The wrought-iron grilles, beautiful flower-decked façade and graciously cosy
interior all contribute to this hotel's attractiveness. The avenue has been taken
over by haute couture fashion designers.

La Villa Maillot without rest 🛁 🛗 ⬛ ⇥ 🕯 🛗15 *VISA* 🌐 🆎 ①
143 av. Malakoff (16th) ✉ 75116 – Ⓜ *Porte Maillot* – ☎ 01 53 64 52 52
– resa@lavillamaillot.fr – Fax 01 45 00 60 61 **E2**
39 rm – ♦250/330 € ♦♦250/380 €, ⌷ 25 € – 3 suites
◆ Business ◆ Modern ◆
A step away from Porte Maillot. Soft colours, a high level of comfort and good
soundproofing in the rooms. Glassed-in space for breakfasts, opening onto the
greenery.

Amarante Champs Élysées without rest ⬛ ⇥ 🕯
19 r. Vernet (8th) – Ⓜ *George V* – ☎ 01 47 20 41 73 🛗30 *VISA* 🌐 🆎 ①
– amarante-champs-elysees@jjwhotels.com – Fax 01 47 23 32 15
– www.jjwhotels.com **F2**
42 rm – ♦300/360 € ♦♦300/710 €, ⌷ 25 €
◆ Business ◆ Modern ◆
A pretty canopy embellishes this neat-as-a-pin corner building. Period furniture
in the rooms. Elegant yet cosy feel to the lounge, with a piano bar and a fireplace
to provide atmosphere.

François 1ᵉʳ without rest ⬛ ⇥ 🛗15 *VISA* 🌐 🆎 ①
7 r. Magellan (8th) – Ⓜ *George V* – ☎ 01 47 23 44 04
– hotel@hotel-francois1er.fr – Fax 01 47 23 93 43 **G3**
40 rm – ♦320/390 € ♦♦350/800 €, ⌷ 21 €
◆ Traditional ◆ Personalised ◆
Mexican marble, mouldings, knick-knacks picked up here and there, a mass of
old furniture and paintings - a luxurious decor designed by French architect
Pierre-Yves Rochon. Generous breakfast (buffet).

FRANCE

Daniel without rest   🕭 AC ⅍ ⅍ ☏ VISA ⍟ AE ①
8 r. Frédéric Bastiat (8th) – Ⓜ St-Philippe du Roule – 𝒞 01 42 56 17 00
– hoteldanielparis @ hoteldanielparis.com – Fax 01 42 56 17 01
– www.hoteldanielparis.com   **G2**
22 rm – †320/380 € ††380/440 €, � 20 € – 4 suites
♦ Luxury ♦ Personalised ♦
This hotel likes travel! Furniture and objects brought back from all over the world combined with the Liberty print create a refined and welcoming decor for Parisian globetrotters.

Sofitel Champs-Élysées   🏡 AC ⅍rm ⅍rm 🕭15/150
8 r. J. Goujon (8th) – Ⓜ Champs-Elysées Clemenceau   🖙 VISA ⍟ AE ①
– 𝒞 01 40 74 64 64 – h1184-re @ accor.com – Fax 01 40 74 79 66
– www.sofitel.com   **G-H3**
40 rm – †355/420 € ††460/580 €, ⊆ 25 € – 2 suites
Rest *Les Signatures*, 𝒞 01 40 74 64 94 (closed 1 to 20 August, 25 December-1 January, Saturday, Sunday and Bank Holidays) (lunch only) 45 €
♦ Chain hotel ♦ Modern ♦
Second Empire townhouse shared with the Maison des Centraliens. The rooms have a new contemporary look, furnished with the very latest equipment. Business centre. Simple decor and lovely terrace at Les Signatures, a restaurant which is frequented by those working in the press.

Majestic without rest   AC ⅍ ☏ VISA ⍟ AE ①
29 r. Dumont d'Urville (16th) ⊠ 75116 – Ⓜ Kléber – 𝒞 01 45 00 83 70
– management @ majestic-hotel.com – Fax 01 45 00 29 48
– www.majestic-hotel.com   **F3**
27 rm – †255 € ††355 €, ⊆ 16 € – 3 suites
♦ Traditional ♦ Classic ♦
A step away from the Champs-Élysées, this discreet building dating from the 1960s has quiet rooms, with an 'old-money' comfort, well-proportioned and impeccably well-maintained.

Splendid Étoile without rest   AC 🕭18 VISA ⍟ AE ①
1bis av. Carnot (17th) – Ⓜ Charles de Gaulle-Etoile – 𝒞 01 45 72 72 00
– hotel @ hsplendid.com – Fax 01 45 72 72 01
– www.hsplendid.com   **F2**
50 rm – †265 € ††265/295 €, ⊆ 23 € – 7 suites
♦ Business ♦ Classic ♦
Beautiful classic façade with wrought-iron balconies. Spacious rooms with character, Louis XV furnishings; some open onto the Arc de Triomphe.

Pergolèse without rest   🕭 AC ⅍ ☏ VISA ⍟ AE ①
3 r. Pergolèse (16th) ⊠ 75116 – Ⓜ Argentine – 𝒞 01 53 64 04 04
– hotel @ pergolese.com – Fax 01 53 64 04 40
– www.hotelpergolese.com   **E2**
40 rm – †190/250 € ††250/380 €, ⊆ 18 €
♦ Business ♦ Design ♦
A restrained 16th arrondissement chic on the outside, but a surprising blue door that sets the tone: inside, designer interior, combining mahogany, glass bricks, chromes and bright colours.

Radisson SAS Champs Élysées   🏡 🕭rm AC ⅍rm ☏
78 av. Marceau (8th) – Ⓜ Charles de Gaulle-Etoile   🖙 VISA ⍟ AE ①
– 𝒞 01 53 23 43 43 – reservations.paris @ radissonsas.com
– Fax 01 53 23 43 44   **F2**
46 rm – †250/345 € ††250/650 €, ⊆ 20 €
Rest (closed 29 July-20 August, 25 December-2 January, Saturday and Sunday) a la carte 58/79 €
♦ Business ♦ Modern ♦
A brand new hotel in a building that once belonged to Louis Vuitton. Contemporary rooms, high-tech equipment (plasma screen TV) and high-quality soundproofing. Customers can sit in the bar, or on the terrace in summer. Short menu with a Provençal flavour.

FRANCE

Élysées Régencia without rest   🗚 ↳ 🕲 🖒 ⚿20 _VISA_ 🐵 🝙 ⓞ
41 av. Marceau (16th) – ⊠ 75116 – ⓜ George V – ℰ 01 47 20 42 65
– info@regencia.com – Fax 01 49 52 03 42 – www.regencia.com   **F3**
43 rm – †180/260 € ††200/500 €, � 18 €
♦ Traditional ♦ Personalised ♦
Three styles of rooms are offered behind this gracious facade: Louis XVI,
Napoleon "just-home-from-Egypt" and contemporary. Elegant lounge, bar and
library.

Regent's Garden without rest   🚿 🗚 ↳ ⚿ 🕲 🅿 _VISA_ 🐵 🝙 ⓞ
6 r. P. Demours (17th) – ⓜ Ternes – ℰ 01 45 74 07 30
– hotel.regents.garden@wanadoo.fr – Fax 01 40 55 01 42   **F1**
39 rm – †138/285 € ††150/285 €, ⊑ 13 €
♦ Business ♦ Cosy ♦
Attractive, elegant townhouse commissioned by Napoleon III for his doctor. Vast
period rooms, some giving onto the garden, which is very pleasant in summer.

Balmoral without rest   🗚 🕲 _VISA_ 🐵 🝙 ⓞ
6 r. Gén. Lanrezac (17th) – ⓜ Charles de Gaulle-Etoile – ℰ 01 43 80 30 50
– hotel@hotelbalmoral.fr – Fax 01 43 80 51 56
– www.hotel-balmoral.com   **F2**
57 rm – †120/130 € ††145/175 €, ⊑ 10 €
♦ Traditional ♦ Personalised ♦
Personalized welcome and general calm characterize this old hotel (1911) a step
away from the Étoile. Bright colours in the rooms; beautiful wood panels in the
lounge.

Pershing Hall   & rm 🗚 🕲 ⚿60 _VISA_ 🐵 🝙 ⓞ
49 r. P. Charron (8th) – ⓜ George V – ℰ 01 58 36 58 00
– info@pershinghall.com – Fax 01 58 36 58 01   **G3**
20 rm – †312/390 € ††312/500 €, ⊑ 26 € – 6 suites
Rest a la carte approx. 70 €
♦ Townhouse ♦ Personalised ♦
Once the home of General Pershing, then a veterans club and finally a charming
hotel designed by Andrée Putman. Chic interior, original and enchanting
hanging garden. Behind the curtain of glass beads, the decor is trendy and the
cuisine very fashionable. Lounge parties.

Chambiges Élysées without rest   & 🗚 ↳ 🕲 _VISA_ 🐵 🝙 ⓞ
8 r. Chambiges (8th) – ⓜ Alma Marceau – ℰ 01 44 31 83 83
– reservation@hotelchambiges.com – Fax 01 40 70 95 51
– www.hotelchambiges.com   **G3**
26 rm ⊑ – †250/265 € ††265/360 € – 8 suites
♦ Townhouse ♦ Personalised ♦
Wood panelling, select drapes and fabrics, period furniture. A romantic, cosy
atmosphere reigns in this fully renovated hotel. Comfy rooms and a pretty
interior garden.

Le A without rest   & 🗚 ↳ 🕲 _VISA_ 🐵 🝙 ⓞ
4 r. Artois (8th) – ⓜ St-Philippe du Roule – ℰ 01 42 56 99 99
– hotel-le-a@wanadoo.fr – Fax 01 42 56 99 90   **G-H2**
16 rm – †329/450 € ††329/450 €, ⊑ 21 € – 10 suites
♦ Townhouse ♦ Design ♦
F. Hybert, a visual artist, and F. Méchiche, an interior designer, have designed this
trendy hotel (or museum, perhaps?) in black and white. Relaxing lounge-library
and bar-lounge.

La Résidence Bassano without rest   🗚 ↳ 🕲 _VISA_ 🐵 🝙 ⓞ
15 r. Bassano (16th) – ⊠ 75116 – ⓜ George V – ℰ 01 47 23 78 23 – info@
hotel-bassano.com – Fax 01 47 20 41 22 – www.hotel-bassano.com   **F3**
28 rm – †160/230 € ††180/280 €, ⊑ 18 € – 3 suites
♦ Family ♦ Personalised ♦
Cosy atmosphere, wrought-iron furniture, sunny fabrics: this place that feels like
a friend's home recalls Provence but is just a few hundred metres from the
Champs-Élysées.

FRANCE

Monna Lisa
AC VISA MO AE O

97 r. La Boétie (8th) – **Ⓜ** St-Philippe du Roule – *ℰ* 01 56 43 38 38
– contact@hotelmonnalisa.com – Fax 01 45 62 39 90 **G-H2**
22 rm – †180/380 €, ††190/380 €, ⇆ 17 €
Rest *Caffe Ristretto* (closed August, Saturday and Sunday) a la carte 34/58 €
♦ Townhouse ♦ Design ♦
This fine hotel built in 1860 is a showpiece for audacious Italian design. Larger rooms on the street side. The Caffe Ristretto offers a delicious journey through the specialities of the Italian peninsula in a wonderfully modern setting.

Quality Pierre without rest
& AC ⇎ ℣ 🐾 30 VISA MO AE O

25 r. Th.-de-Banville (17th) – **Ⓜ** Pereire – *ℰ* 01 47 63 76 69
– amarante-arcdetriomphe@jjwhotels.com – Fax 01 43 80 63 96 **F1**
50 rm – †190/210 €, ††210/240 €, ⇆ 22 €
♦ Business ♦ Stylish ♦
This recent hotel welcomes you in Directoire-style rooms recently redone and favoured by the business clientele. Some rooms open onto the patio.

Étoile Résidence Impériale without rest
AC ⇎ ℀rest

155 av. de Malakoff (16th) ⊠ 75116 VISA MO AE O
– **Ⓜ** Porte Maillot – *ℰ* 01 45 00 23 45 – res.imperiale@wanadoo.fr
– Fax 01 45 01 88 82 – www.bestwestern-etoile-imperiale.com **E2**
37 rm – †130/160 €, ††150/225 €, ⇆ 13 €
♦ Traditional ♦ Personalised ♦
Recently-renovated and well-soundproofed hotel, with theme rooms (Africa, Asia, etc.). Some have retained their exposed beams, while others (ground floor) open onto the patio.

Villa Alessandra without rest ⌘
AC ⊜ VISA MO AE O

9 pl. Boulnois (17th) – **Ⓜ** Ternes – *ℰ* 01 56 33 24 24
– alessandra@leshoteldeparis.com – Fax 01 56 33 24 30
– www.leshotelsdeparis.com **F1**
49 rm – †226/271 €, ††278 €, ⇆ 18 €
♦ Business ♦ Classic ♦
This Ternes quarter hotel is on a delightful quiet little square and is appreciated for its calm. Colours of southern France in the rooms, with wrought-iron beds and painted wood furniture.

Élysées Céramic without rest
AC ℣ VISA MO AE O

34 av. Wagram (8th) – **Ⓜ** Ternes – *ℰ* 01 42 27 20 30 – info@elysees-ceramic.com
– Fax 01 46 22 95 83 **F2**
57 rm – †145/175 €, ††160/225 €, ⇆ 10 €
♦ Traditional ♦ Art Deco ♦
The Art Nouveau façade (1904) with its glazed stoneware is an architectural marvel. The interior lives up to the same standard, with furniture and decor inspired by the same style.

Mercure Wagram Arc de Triomphe without rest
& AC ⇎ ℀

3 r. Brey (17th) – **Ⓜ** Charles de Gaulle-Etoile ℣ VISA MO AE O
– *ℰ* 01 56 68 00 01 – h2053@accor.com – Fax 01 56 68 00 02 **F2**
43 rm – †140/230 €, ††150/240 €, ⇆ 15 €
♦ Chain hotel ♦ Functional ♦
This new Mercure between Étoile and Ternes offers a warm welcome and cosy little rooms with pale wood panels and pretty fabrics that make for a marine feel.

Villa des Ternes without rest
& AC VISA MO AE O

97 av. Ternes (17th) – **Ⓜ** Neuilly-Porte Maillot – *ℰ* 01 53 81 94 94
– hotel@hotelternes.com – Fax 01 53 81 94 95
– www.villadesternes.com **E1**
39 rm – †140/170 €, ††170/260 €, ⇆ 13 €
♦ Business ♦ Stylish ♦
Next to the Palais des Congrès convention centre, this recent hotel is perfect for the business clientele. Warm tones in the rooms, all equipped with modern bathrooms.

FRANCE

Chambellan Morgane without rest   🏧 ⓦ 🛁 20 𝘝𝘐𝘚𝘈 ⓐⓞ 🄰🄴 ⓞ
6 r. Keppler (16th) ⊠ 75116 – Ⓜ George V – ℰ 01 47 20 35 72
– chambellan-morgane@wanadoo.fr – Fax 01 47 20 95 69   **F3**
20 rm – ✦152 € ✦✦168 €, � 12 € ✦
✦ Family ✦ Personalised ✦
Small hotel with character, with the rooms decorated in Provence colours, and all
enhanced by the quiet atmosphere. Pleasant Louis XVI lounge decorated with
painted wood panels.

Floride Étoile without rest   🏧 ↔ ⌀ ⓦ 🛁 30 𝘝𝘐𝘚𝘈 ⓐⓞ 🄰🄴 ⓞ
14 r. St-Didier (16th) ⊠ 75116 – Ⓜ Boissière – ℰ 01 47 27 23 36 – floride.etoile@
wanadoo.fr – Fax 01 47 27 82 87 – www.floride-paris-hotel.com   **E3**
63 rm – ✦120/174 € ✦✦145/215 €, � 12,50 €
✦ Traditional ✦ Functional ✦
A stone's throw from Trocadéro. The renovated rooms are comfortable; those on
the courtyard side are smaller but more tranquil. Flowery, stylishly furnished
lounge.

Magellan without rest ⤜   ⌁ ⌀ ⓦ 𝘝𝘐𝘚𝘈 ⓐⓞ 🄰🄴 ⓞ
17 r. J. B. Dumas (17th) – Ⓜ Porte de Champerret – ℰ 01 45 72 44 51 – paris@
hotelmagellan.com – Fax 01 40 68 90 36 – www.hotelmagellan.com   **F1**
72 rm – ✦131 € ✦✦146 €, � 12 €
✦ Traditional ✦ Art Deco ✦
Practical and spacious rooms in a beautiful building dating from 1900,
completed with a small pavilion nestled at the far end of the garden. Lounge
furnished in Art Deco style.

Étoile Park Hôtel without rest   🏧 ⓦ 𝘝𝘐𝘚𝘈 ⓐⓞ 🄰🄴 ⓞ
10 av. Mac Mahon (17th) – Ⓜ Charles de Gaulle-Etoile
– ℰ 01 42 67 69 63 – ephot@easynet.fr – Fax 01 43 80 18 99
– www.etoileparkhotel.com   **F2**
28 rm – ✦93/139 € ✦✦143/159 €, � 12 €
✦ Business ✦ Functional ✦
This freestone structure has a prime location, close to Étoile. Nicely renovated,
contemporary-style interior. Pleasant breakfast room.

Le 123   ⅙rm 🏧 ↔rm 𝘝𝘐𝘚𝘈 ⓐⓞ 🄰🄴 ⓞ
– Ⓜ St-Philippe-du-Roule – ℰ 01 53 89 01 23 – hotel.le123@astotel.com
– Fax 01 45 61 09 07 – www.le123.fr   **H2**
40 rm – ✦420 € ✦✦468 €, � 22 €
Rest a la carte approx. 30 €
✦ Townhouse ✦ Design ✦
Contemporary decor and a mix of styles, materials and colours: the rooms,
decorated with fashion sketches, are personalised, often original and truly
stunning. Simple, contemporary meals are available at lunchtime.

Pavillon Montaigne without rest   🏧 𝘝𝘐𝘚𝘈 ⓐⓞ 🄰🄴 ⓞ
34 r. J. Mermoz (8th) – Ⓜ Franklin D. Roosevelt – ℰ 01 53 89 95 00
– hotelpavillonmontaigne@wanadoo.fr – Fax 01 42 89 33 00   **H2**
18 rm – ✦131/145 € ✦✦147/160 €, � 8 €
✦ Traditional ✦ Functional ✦
Two buildings connected with one another by the glass-roofed breakfast room.
Old or contemporary furniture in the rooms, many of which have exposed
beams.

Du Bois without rest   ⓦ 𝘝𝘐𝘚𝘈 ⓐⓞ 🄰🄴 ⓞ
11 r. Dôme (16th) ⊠ 75116 – Ⓜ Kléber – ℰ 01 45 00 31 96
– reservations@hoteldubois.com – Fax 01 45 00 90 05
– www.hoteldubois.com   **E-F2**
41 rm – ✦115/169 € ✦✦139/195 €, � 13 €
✦ Traditional ✦ Cosy ✦
This cosy hotel is in the most Montmartre-type street of the whole 16th district,
where Baudelaire passed away. Charming and bright rooms. Georgian-style
lounge.

Star Hôtel Étoile without rest   Ⓐ🄲 ⅍18 VISA ⓌⒸ AE ⓄⒹ

18 r. Arc de Triomphe (17th) – Ⓜ Charles de Gaulle-Etoile – 𝒞 01 43 80 27 69
– star.etoile.hotel @ wanadoo.fr – Fax 01 40 54 94 84
– www.paris-hotel-staretoile.com   **F1-2**
62 rm – 🛉110/150 € 🛉🛉140/220 €, ⬜ 12 €
♦ Traditional ♦ Functional ♦
The reception area, lounge and breakfast room have recently been decorated in
a medieval style. The bedrooms are small but bright and quite quiet.

Astrid without rest   Ⓐ🄲 VISA ⓌⒸ AE ⓄⒹ

27 av. Carnot (17th) – Ⓜ Charles de Gaulle-Etoile – 𝒞 01 44 09 26 00
– paris @ hotel-astrid.com – Fax 01 44 09 26 01
– www.hotel-astrid.com   **F2**
40 rm – 🛉96/119 € 🛉🛉136/152 €, ⬜ 10 €
♦ Family ♦ Functional ♦
This hotel has been run by the same family since 1936, and has a prime location
100m from the Arc de Triomphe. Every bedroom has a different style, such as
Louis XVI, Tyrolean, or Provençal.

Flaubert without rest   ⅊ VISA ⓌⒸ AE ⓄⒹ

19 r. Rennequin (17th) – Ⓜ Ternes – 𝒞 01 46 22 44 35
– paris @ hotelflaubert.com – Fax 01 43 80 32 34
– www.hotelflaubert.com   **F1**
41 rm – 🛉95/96 € 🛉🛉111 €, ⬜ 9 €
♦ Business ♦ Traditional ♦ Functional ♦
The main attraction of this family hotel is its peaceful green patio, which some of
the bedrooms look onto. Light, modern decor; winter garden-style breakfast
room.

Au Palais de Chaillot without rest   ⅍ VISA ⓌⒸ AE ⓄⒹ

35 av. R. Poincaré (16th) ⊠ 75116 – Ⓜ Trocadéro – 𝒞 01 53 70 09 09
– palaisdechaillot-hotel @ magic.fr – Fax 01 53 70 09 08
– www.palaisdechaillot-hotel.com   **E3**
23 rm – 🛉105 € 🛉🛉120/140 €, ⬜ 9 €
♦ Family ♦ Traditional ♦ Classic ♦
Beautiful location near Trocadéro, for this hotel renovated in the colours of
southern France. Fresh and practical little rooms. Breakfast-room furnished in
cane.

XᵡXᵡX **Le "Cinq"** – Hôtel Four Seasons George V   🍴 Ⓐ🄲 ⅍ ⇕8/40
🎄🎄🎄 *31 av. George V (8th) – Ⓜ George V – 𝒞 01 49 52 71 54*   ⊟♀ VISA ⓌⒸ AE ⓄⒹ
– par.lecinq @ fourseasons.com – Fax 01 49 52 71 81
– www.fourseasons.com   **G3**
Rest 75 € (lunch), 120/210 € and a la carte 135/350 € 🕸
Spec. Gaspacho de laitue à la mozzarella et aux girolles. Turbot de ligne rôti au
melon d'eau. Côte de veau de lait fermier aux câpres de Pantelleria.
♦ Innovative ♦ Luxury ♦
Superb dining room - a majestic reference to the Grand Trianon - opening onto
a delightful garden inside. Refined atmosphere and classic cuisine created with
great talent.

XᵡXᵡX **Ledoyen**   Ⓐ🄲 ⅍ ⇕10/80 🅿 ⊟♀ VISA ⓌⒸ AE
🎄🎄🎄 *Carré des Champs-Elysées (1st floor) (8th) – Ⓜ Champs-Elysées Clemenceau*
– 𝒞 01 53 05 10 01 – pavillon.ledoyen @ ledoyen.com – Fax 01 47 42 55 01
– www.ledoyen.com
closed 31 July-27 August, Monday lunch, Saturday and Sunday   **H3**
Rest 73 € (lunch), 188/274 € b.i. and a la carte 145/200 € 🕸
Spec. Grosses langoustines bretonnes croustillantes, émulsion d'agrumes à
l'huile d'olive. Blanc de turbot de ligne braisé, pommes rattes truffées. Noix de ris
de veau en brochette de bois de citronnelle, jus d'herbes.
♦ Innovative ♦ Luxury ♦
A neo-Classical lodge built on the Champs-Elysées in 1848. Magnificent
Napoleon III-style decor, view of the gardens designed by Hittorff and delicious
surf'n'turf cuisine.

FRANCE

FRANCE

XxXxX
දියදියදිය

Alain Ducasse au Plaza Athénée – Hôtel Plaza Athénée

25 av. Montaigne (8th) – Ⓜ *Alma Marceau*   Ⓐ Ⓒ VISA ⑩ Ⓐ ①
– ℰ 01 53 67 65 00 – adpa@alain-ducasse.com – Fax 01 53 67 65 12
closed 13 July-22 August, 22 to 31 December, Saturday, Sunday, lunch Monday,
Tuesday and Wednesday   **G3**
Rest 200/300 € and a la carte 195/255 € ⅏
Spec. Langoustines rafraîchies, nage réduite, caviar osciètre royal. Volaille de Bresse, sauce albuféra aux truffes d'Alba (15 October-31 December). Coupe glacée de saison.
♦ Innovative ♦ Luxury ♦
The sumptuous regency decor has been enhanced in "design and organza"; creative menus ideated by a talented team overseen by Alain Ducasse. 1001 selected wines available!

XxXxX
දියදියදිය

Bristol – Hôtel Bristol   🛏 Ⓐ ⅏ ⌂ VISA ⑩ Ⓐ ①

112 r. Fg St-Honoré (8th) – Ⓜ *Miromesnil* – ℰ *01 53 43 43 00*
– resa@lebristolparis.com – Fax 01 53 43 43 01 – www.lebristolparis.com
Rest 80 € (lunch)/175 € and a la carte 115/240 € ⅏   **H2**
Spec. Macaroni truffés farcis d'artichaut et foie gras, gratinés au parmesan. Filets de sole poudrés à la chapelure de mousserons. Poularde de Bresse cuite en vessie au vin jaune.
♦ Contemporary ♦ Luxury ♦
The winter dining room resembles a small theatre, given its oval shape and splendid wood panels. The summer dining room opens generously onto the hotel's magnificent garden.

XxXxX
දියදියදිය

Taillevent   Ⓐ ⅏ ⇔5/36 VISA ⑩ Ⓐ ①

15 r. Lamennais (8th) – Ⓜ *Charles de Gaulle-Etoile* – ℰ *01 44 95 15 01*
– mail@taillevent.com – Fax 01 42 25 95 18
closed 29 July-28 August, Saturday, Sunday and Bank Holidays   **G2**
Rest (number of covers limited, pre-book) 70 € (lunch), 140/190 €
and a la carte 130/195 € ⅏
Spec. Royale de homard au fenouil. Pastilla de lapin rex du Poitou. Craquant au chocolat et au caramel.
♦ Contemporary ♦ Luxury ♦
The Duke of Morny's former 19C townhouse has become a historical icon of the best French gastronomy. Exquisite cuisine and sumptuous wine list.

XxXxX
දියදිය

Apicius (Vigato)   🚗 Ⓐ ⇔10/25 Ⓟ ⌂ VISA ⑩ Ⓐ ①

20 r. Artois (8th) – Ⓜ *St-Philippe du Roule* – ℰ *01 43 80 19 66*
– restaurant-apicius@wanadoo.fr – Fax 01 44 40 09 57
closed August, Saturday and Sunday   **G2**
Rest 140/150 € and a la carte 100/150 € ⅏
Spec. Foie gras de canard aux radis noirs confits. Compote de cèpes et sabayon à la truffe blanche d'Alba (Automn-Winter). Soufflé au chocolat noir et chantilly sans sucre.
♦ Innovative ♦ Friendly ♦
This elegant restaurant, in a townhouse, is adorned with 19C Flemish paintings and 17C Indian sculptures. Up-to-date cuisine and superb wine list.

XxXxX
දියදිය

Lasserre   Ⓐ ⅏ ⇔6/55 ⌂ VISA ⑩ Ⓐ ①

17 av. F.-D.-Roosevelt (8th) – Ⓜ *Franklin D. Roosevelt* – ℰ *01 43 59 53 43*
– lasserre@lasserre.fr – Fax 01 45 63 72 23 – www.restaurant-lasserre.com
closed August, Sunday, lunch Saturday, Monday,
Tuesday and Wednesday   **H3**
Rest 75 € (weekday lunch)/185 € and a la carte 140/215 € ⅏
Spec. Macaroni aux truffes noires et foie gras. Rouget croustillant à la marjolaine et courgette-fleur (May-December.). Fraises des bois à l'eau de rose, granité à la chartreuse.
♦ Traditional ♦ Luxury ♦
For Parisian gourmets, this is an institution. The neo-Classical dining hall's ceiling, decorated with a saraband of dancing females opens astonishingly. Superb wine list.

FRANCE

XXXXX
£3£3

Laurent ⌂ ✿6/60 ⌒ ✦ VISA ⓒⓄ AE ①
41 av. Gabriel (8th) – Ⓜ Champs Elysées Clemenceau – ☏ 01 42 25 00 39
– info@le-laurent.com – Fax 01 45 62 45 21 – www.le-laurent.com
closed lunch Saturday, Sunday and Bank Holidays   H3
Rest 75/160 € and a la carte 133/208 € ⅗

Spec. Araignée de mer dans ses sucs en gelée, crème de fenouil. Grosses langoustines "tandoori" poêlées, copeaux d'avocat à l'huile d'amande. Flanchet de veau braisé, blettes à la moelle et au jus.
♦ Contemporary ♦ Luxury ♦
This pavilion with its Antique inspiration was built by Hittorff, offering elegant tables outside in the shade and highly traditional cuisine. A little bit of paradise in the Champs-Élysées gardens.

XXXX
£3£3£3

Guy Savoy ⓀⒸ ✿4/12 ⌒ VISA ⓒⓄ AE ①
18 r. Troyon (17th) – Ⓜ Charles de Gaulle-Etoile – ☏ 01 43 80 40 61
– reserv@guysavoy.com – Fax 01 46 22 43 09 – www.guysavoy.com
closed August, 24 December-2 January, Saturday lunch,
Sunday and Monday   F2
Rest 230/285 € and a la carte 125/235 € ⅗

Spec. Soupe d'artichaut à la truffe noire, brioche feuilletée aux champignons et truffes. "Côte" de gros turbot à l'oeuf en salade et soupe. Ris de veau rissolés, "petits chaussons" de pommes de terre et truffes.
♦ Inventive ♦ Trendy ♦
Glass work, leather and Wenge, works by great names in contemporary art, African sculptures and inventive cuisine make this "the hotel of the 21C" par excellence.

XXXX
£3£3

Michel Rostang ⓀⒸ ✿6/20 ⌒ VISA ⓒⓄ AE ①
20 r. Rennequin (17th) – Ⓜ Ternes – ☏ 01 47 63 40 77
– rostang@relaischateaux.fr – Fax 01 47 63 82 75
– www.michelrostang.com
closed 1 to 21 August, Monday lunch, Saturday lunch and Sunday   F1
Rest 70 € (lunch)/175 € and a la carte 120/185 € ⅗

Spec. "Menu truffes" (15 December-15 March). Soufflé de quenelle de brochet sauce homard, façon Jo Rostang. Palet chocolat pur Caraïbes, gelée des Pères Chartreux.
♦ Contemporary ♦ Friendly ♦
Wood panelling, Robj statuettes, works by Lalique and Art Deco stained-glass combine to create a luxurious and original setting. Fine cuisine and a splendid wine list.

XXXX
£3

Les Élysées – Hôtel Vernet ⓀⒸ ✸ ⌒ VISA ⓒⓄ AE ①
25 r. Vernet (8th) – Ⓜ Charles de Gaulle-Etoile – ☏ 01 44 31 98 98
– reservations@hotelvernet.com – Fax 01 44 31 85 69 – www.hotelvernet.com
closed 31 July-28 August, Monday lunch, Saturday and Sunday   F2
Rest 62 € (lunch)/130 € and a la carte 105/160 €

Spec. Tourteau breton, crème froide au vin jaune. Homard bleu cuit sur sel aux aromates, jus au naturel, fenouil, artichaut, gnocchi. Epaule d'agneau de Lozère fondante aux aromates, harissa, figue fraîche.
♦ Contemporary ♦ Friendly ♦
An inventive and masterly cuisine of subtle flavours, to savour in Eiffel's splendid Belle Époque conservatory that bathes the dining room in a soft light.

XXXX
£3£3£3

Pierre Gagnaire – Hôtel Balzac ⓀⒸ ⌒ VISA ⓒⓄ AE ①
6 r. Balzac (8th) – Ⓜ George V – ☏ 01 58 36 12 50 – p.gagnaire@wanadoo.fr
– Fax 01 58 36 12 51
closed 10 to 16 April, 17 to 30 July, 23 to 29 November, 25 to 31 December,
19 to 25 February, Sunday lunch and Saturday   G2
Rest 90 € (lunch), 225/400 € and a la carte 220/330 €

Spec. Langoustines de trois façons. Bar de ligne. Agneau de Lozère.
♦ Innovative ♦ Trendy ♦
The sober and chic contemporary decor (light wood panelling, modern art) fades into the background as you are held spellbound by the jazz musician's wild playing. Music maestro!

XXXX **Hiramatsu**   AC ↳⁄ ⌂⟨lunch⟩ VISA ◐ AE ➀
ಭ 52 r. Longchamp (16th) – Ⓜ Trocadéro – ℰ 01 56 81 08 80
– paris@hiramatsu.co.jp – Fax 01 56 81 08 81
closed 29 July-28 August, 30 December-8 January,
Saturday and Sunday   **E3**
Rest (number of covers limited, pre-book) 70 € (lunch), 130/180 €
and a la carte 110/145 € ❀

Spec. Foie gras de canard aux choux frisés, jus de truffe. Fines lamelles d'agneau, compotée d'oignons blancs, jus de viande. Risotto de riz noir au vin rouge et framboises (dessert).

• Innovative • Fashionable •

Hiramatsu's team have moved from the 4th to the 16th district in Paris. New decor and inventive cuisine, as skilful as ever. High-class Japanese gastronomy!

XXXX **Jardin** – Hôtel Royal Monceau   🏠 AC ❄ ⌂ VISA ◐ AE ➀
ಭ 37 av. Hoche (8th) – Ⓜ Charles de Gaulle-Etoile – ℰ 01 42 99 98 70
– restauration@royalmonceau.com – Fax 01 42 99 89 94
– www.royalmonceau.com
closed 1 to 21 August, Monday lunch, Saturday and Sunday   **G2**
Rest 60 € (lunch)/110 € and a la carte 95/125 € ❀

Spec. Céviche de langoustines au yusu (Spring-Summer). Turbot de nos côtes rôti au café de Birmanie (Winter-Spring). Pigeonneau rôti à la canelle.

• Contemporary • Formal •

This place evokes an elegant Napoleon-style marquee and serves subtle Mediterranean cuisine. The terrace and garden have also been remodelled.

XXXX **Clovis** – Hôtel Sofitel Arc de Triomphe   AC ⌂ VISA ◐ AE ➀
ಭ 14 r. Beaujon (8th) – Ⓜ Charles de Gaulle-Etoile – ℰ 01 53 89 50 50
– h1296@accor.com – Fax 01 53 89 50 51
closed 29 July-28 August, 23 December-2 January, Saturday, Sunday and Bank
Holidays   **G2**
Rest 39 € (lunch), 45/85 € and a la carte 70/110 €

Spec. Queues de langoustines en fritto. Vapeur de sole en impression d'herbes. Ris de veau de lait en fine croûte truffée.

• Contemporary • Trendy •

Classical decor with a modern touch (beige and brown shades), attentive, cheerful service, refined cuisine: the gourmets in the area have made it their "local".

XXX **Jamin** (Guichard)   AC ❄ ✛15 VISA ◐ AE ➀
ಭಭ 32 r. Longchamp (16th) ✉ 75116 – Ⓜ Iéna – ℰ 01 45 53 00 07
– reservation@jamin.fr – Fax 01 45 53 00 15
closed 8 to 17 April, 29 July-21 August, Saturday,
Sunday and Bank Holidays   **E3**
Rest 53 € (lunch), 95/130 € and a la carte 105/150 €

Spec. Ravioli de langoustines de petite pêche. Filet de grosse sole sauce normande. Pigeonneau grillé au foie gras.

• Contemporary • Formal •

Behind a delicately coloured façade, this soberly elegant dining hall provides the setting for an appetising cuisine laying maximum stress on product quality and with a personal touch.

XXX **Table du Lancaster** – Hôtel Lancaster   🏠 AC ❄ ⌂ VISA ◐ AE ➀
ಭ 7 r. Berri (8th) – Ⓜ George V – ℰ 01 40 76 40 18 – restaurant@hotel-lancaster.fr
– Fax 01 40 76 40 00 – www.hotel-lancaster.fr
closed 23 July-23 August, lunch Saturday and Sunday   **G2**
Rest 60 € (lunch)/120 € and a la carte 70/130 €

Spec. Cuisses de grenouilles sautées au tamarin. Bouillon de cabillaud au riz "koshi-hikari". Canon de chevreuil, noisette, sauge frite (October-February).

• Contemporary • Friendly •

Inventive food supervised by Michel Troisgros, and a pleasant, contemporary setting (Chinese prints) opening onto the garden. A fitting restaurant for the Lancaster.

FRANCE

XXX
೫೩ ೫೩

Table de Joël Robuchon   AC ⌂ VISA ❶❷

16 av. Bugeaud (16th) ✉ *75116* – Ⓜ *Victor Hugo* – ☏ *01 56 28 16 16*
– *latabledejoelrobuchon@wanadoo.fr*
– *Fax 01 56 28 16 78*   **E3**
Rest 55 € b.i. (lunch)/150 € and a la carte 56/140 € 🕸
Spec. Oeuf mollet et friand au caviar osciètre. Bar, gros macaroni à la ricotta et basilic, jus à l'olive noire. Chocolat sensation, crème au chocolat araguani, glace chocolat.
♦ Innovative ♦ Trendy ♦
You are sure to enjoy your meal here, with tapas-style snacks, and classic dishes subtly updated by Joël Robuchon, in an elegant setting.

XXX

Maison Blanche   ≤ 🏠 AC ⌂ VISA ❶❷ AE ⓪

15 av. Montaigne (7th floor) (8th) – Ⓜ *Alma Marceau* – ☏ *01 47 23 55 99*
– *info@maison-blanche.fr* – *Fax 01 47 20 09 56*
– *www.maison-blanche.fr*   **G3**
Rest a la carte 77/133 €
♦ Inventive ♦ Trendy ♦
On the roof of the Théâtre des Champs-Élysées, a loft-duplex design with an immense glass canopy facing the golden dome of the Invalides. A Languedoc-inspired cuisine.

XXX

Fouquet's   🏠 ✿10/80 VISA ❶❷ AE ⓪

99 av. Champs-Elysées (8th) – Ⓜ *George V* – ☏ *01 47 23 50 00*
– *fouquets@lucienbarriere.com* – *Fax 01 47 23 60 02*
– *www.lucienbarriere.com*   **G2**
Rest 78 € and a la carte 61/142 €
♦ Brasserie ♦ Retro ♦
This rather famous listed restaurant has been retouched by Jacques Garcia, and continues to please an exclusive clientele as it has since 1899. Popular terrace both in summer and winter.

XXX
೫

La Table du Baltimore – Hôtel Sofitel Baltimore   AC ✿

1 r. Léo Delibes (16th) ✉ *75016* – Ⓜ *Boissière*   ⌂ VISA ❶❷ AE ⓪
– ☏ *01 44 34 54 34* – *latable@hotelbaltimore.com* – *Fax 01 44 34 54 44*
– *www.sofitel.com*
closed 29 July-28 August, 23 December-1 January, Saturday, Sunday and Bank Holidays   **E3**
Rest 45 € b.i. (lunch)/95 € b.i. and a la carte 60/100 €
Spec. Langoustine cuite en feuille de bananier. Épaule d'agneau préparée en petits farcis. Bar rôti en croûte d'épices.
♦ Contemporary ♦ Friendly ♦
Antique wood panelling, modern furnishings, warm colours and a collection of drawings all combine to create the subtle decor of this restaurant. Fine, up-to-date cuisine.

XXX
೫

Sormani (Fayet)   AC ✿10/20 ⌂ VISA ❶❷ AE

4 r. Gén. Lanrezac (17th) – Ⓜ *Charles de Gaulle-Etoile*
– ☏ *01 43 80 13 91* – *sasormani@wanadoo.fr*
– *Fax 01 40 55 07 37*
closed 29 July-21 August, Saturday, Sunday and Bank Holidays   **F2**
Rest 75 € (lunch) and a la carte 70/120 € 🕸
Spec. Tortellini aux cèpes (September-November). Risotto à la truffe blanche (September-January). Oeufs au plat, polenta et truffes noires (November-March).
♦ Italian ♦ Formal ♦
Latin charm predominates in this restaurant near the Place de l'Etoile, with its new decor (red tones and Murano-glass chandeliers), dolce vita atmosphere and carefully-prepared Italian cuisine.

FRANCE

XXX ♧

Le Pergolèse (Gaborieau) AC ⌂ VISA ⓜ AE

40 r. Pergolèse (16th) ⊠ 75116 – Ⓜ *Porte Maillot – 𝒞 01 45 00 21 40*
– le-pergolese@wanadoo.fr – Fax 01 45 00 81 31
closed 5 to 25 August, Saturday and Sunday **E2**
Rest 38/80 € and a la carte 70/90 €

Spec. Moelleux de sardines marinées en filets, fondue de poivrons basquaise. Bar de ligne vapeur, tian de légumes, jus au corail d'oursin. Double côte de veau rôtie en cocotte.

♦ Contemporary ♦ Fashionable ♦

Yellow wall hangings, pale wood panels and surprising sculptures reflect in the mirrors, forming an elegant decor a step away from the select Avenue Foch. A refreshing new take on classic cuisine.

XXX ♧

Le W – Hôtel Warwick AC ❄ ⌂ VISA ⓜ AE ①

5 r. Berri (8th) – Ⓜ *George V – 𝒞 01 45 61 82 08*
– lerestaurantw@warwickhotels.com – Fax 01 43 59 00 98
closed August, Saturday, Sunday and Bank Holidays **G2**
Rest 49 €

Spec. Huîtres Prat ar Coum raidies dans leur jus. Caneton sauvageon désossé et farci. Croustillant caramélisé.

♦ Contemporary ♦ Friendly ♦

W for Warwick: you will taste good cheerful fare in the restaurant's warm contemporary setting, discreetly located in the hotel.

XXX ♧

Chiberta AC VISA ⓜ AE

3 r. Arsène-Houssaye (8th) – Ⓜ *Charles de Gaulle-Etoile*
– 𝒞 01 53 53 42 00 – chiberta@guysavoy.com
– Fax 01 45 62 85 08 – www.lechiberta.com
closed 1 to 21 August, Saturday lunch and Sunday **F2**
Rest 60/100 € and a la carte 65/100 €

Spec. Crême de langoustines et carottes "citronnelle-gingembre". Noix de ris de veau rissolée en brochette. Autour de la rose et de la framboise.

♦ Innovative ♦ Trendy ♦

The Chiberta has been refreshed with decor by J.-M. Wilmotte (dark shades and unusual "bottle" walls) and inventive cuisine supervised by Guy Savoy.

XXX ♧

Carpaccio – Hôtel Royal Monceau AC ⌂ VISA ⓜ AE ①

37 av. Hoche (8th) – Ⓜ *Charles de Gaulle-Etoile – 𝒞 01 42 99 98 90*
– reception@royalmonceau.com – Fax 01 42 99 89 94
closed August **G2**
Rest a la carte 65/120 €

Spec. Macaroni à la tomate pachino et basilic. Risotto au citron et langoustines en ragoût. Côtelettes d'agneau au basilic et aubergines en ragoût.

♦ Italian ♦ Formal ♦

Cross the hall of the Hôtel Royal Monceau to eat in the pleasant Venetian decor among Murano glass chandeliers. Tasty Italian cuisine.

XXX

Marcande ⌂ VISA ⓜ AE

52 r. Miromesnil (8th) – Ⓜ *Miromesnil – 𝒞 01 42 65 19 14*
– info@marcande.com – Fax 01 42 65 76 85
– www.marcande.com
closed 24 December-2 January, 7 to 22 August, dinner Friday
from October-April, Saturday except lunch from May to September
and Sunday **H2**
Rest 19 € (dinner), 40/90 € b.i. and a la carte 79/116 €

♦ Traditional ♦ Friendly ♦

Discreet restaurant frequented by a business clientele. Contemporary dining room facing a pleasant patio with tables outside, which is itself very popular in sunny weather.

FRANCE

XXX
ξ3
Copenhague   🏠 Ⓐ⟦ 🛏️ 𝘝𝘐𝘚𝘈 ⑩ Ⓐ Ⓞ
142 av. Champs-Elysées (1st floor) (8th) – Ⓜ George V – ℰ 01 44 13 86 26
– floradanica@wanadoo.fr – Fax 01 44 13 89 44
– www.restaurantfloradanica.com
closed 29 July-21 August, Saturday and Sunday   **F2**
Rest 51 € (lunch), 70/105 € and a la carte 85/115 €
Rest *Flora Danica* 35 €
Spec. Tartare de Saint-Jacques en écume d'oursin (October-15 April). Dos de
cabillaud demi-sel au bouillon mousseux de palourdes. Noisettes de renne rôties
sauce civet, croustillant de speck à la danoise.
♦ Danish ♦ Design ♦
Scandinavian cuisine, elegant Danish design, view of the Champs-Elysées and a
terrace facing a lovely garden characterise this restaurant located in the Maison
du Danemark. At the Flora Danica, salmon is given pride of place in the shop and
on the menu.

XXX
ξ3
Passiflore (Durand)   Ⓐ⟦ 🛏️ 𝘝𝘐𝘚𝘈 ⑩ Ⓐ
33 r. Longchamp (16th) ✉ 75016 – Ⓜ Trocadéro
– ℰ 01 47 04 96 81 – passiflore@club-internet.fr
– Fax 01 47 04 32 27   **E3**
Rest 35 € (lunch), 38/54 € and a la carte 70/110 €
Spec. Soupe de grenouilles et champignons au galanga (March-September). Riz
noir et langoustines au satay citron. Lièvre à la royale (October-November).
♦ Contemporary ♦ Fashionable ♦
An unassumingly elegant decor of ethnic inspiration (yellow tones and wood
panelling) and a classic, personalised cuisine combine to rejoice the taste buds
of Parisian society.

XXX
Port Alma   Ⓐ⟦ 𝘝𝘐𝘚𝘈 ⑩ Ⓐ Ⓞ
10 av. New York (16th) ✉ 75116 – Ⓜ Alma Marceau – ℰ 01 47 23 75 11
– Fax 01 47 20 42 92
closed August, 24 December-2 January, Sunday and Monday   **F3**
Rest 35 € and a la carte 45/130 €
♦ Seafood ♦ Friendly ♦
On the quays of the Seine, a dining room and veranda with blue beams, where
seafood is the star. Market-fresh ingredients and friendly welcome.

XX
Cristal Room Baccarat   Ⓐ⟦ 𝘝𝘐𝘚𝘈 ⑩ Ⓐ
11 pl. des Etats-Unis (16th) ✉ 75116 – Ⓜ Boissière – ℰ 01 40 22 11 10
– cristalroom@baccarat.fr – Fax 01 40 22 11 99
closed Sunday   **F3**
Rest (pre-book) 59 € (lunch)/120 € and a la carte 50/115 €
♦ Innovative ♦ Design ♦
This mansion was used by M-L de Noailles and now belongs to Baccarat. It offers
a Starck decor and modern dishes at V.I.P. prices. Beauty can be far from
reasonable!

XX
ξ3
Relais du Parc – Hôtel Sofitel Le Parc   🏠 Ⓐ⟦ 🛏️ 𝘝𝘐𝘚𝘈 ⑩ Ⓐ Ⓞ
59 av. R. Poincaré (16th) ✉ 75116 – Ⓜ Victor Hugo
– ℰ 01 44 05 66 10 – le.relaisduparc@wanadoo.fr
– Fax 01 44 05 66 39
closed 15 to 26 August, 26 December-6 January, Saturday lunch, Sunday and
Monday   **E3**
Rest 58 € and a la carte 50/80 € 🍷
Spec. Cocotte de légumes. Tendron de veau aux carottes fondantes. Tarte aux
pralines.
♦ Contemporary ♦ Design ♦
The ground floor of this appealing Belle Époque town house has an elegantly
contemporary dining area opening onto the beautiful courtyard terrace planted
with trees. Seasonal cuisine.

FRANCE

XX **Le Spoon**   AK ⌂⌐ VISA ◍ AE ①

14 r. Marignan (8th) – Ⓜ Franklin D. Roosevelt
– ℰ 01 40 76 34 44 – spoonfood@marignan-elysees.fr
– Fax 01 40 76 34 37
closed 1 to 13 March, 22 July-21 August, 24 December-2 January, Saturday and
Sunday   **G3**
Rest 45/85 € and a la carte 50/82 € ✧
◆ Innovative ◆ Design ◆
Designer-style furniture, exotic wood and an on-view kitchen make for a
contemporary, "zen" setting in which to sample this versatile menu and wines
from five continents.

XX **Relais Plaza** – Hôtel Plaza Athénée   VISA ◍ AE ①

25 av. Montaigne (8th) – Ⓜ Alma Marceau – ℰ 01 53 67 64 00
– reservation@plaza-athenee-paris.com – Fax 01 53 67 66 66
closed August   **G3**
Rest 45 € and a la carte 75/115 €
◆ Contemporary ◆ Friendly ◆
The chic, intimate "local" for the nearby fashion houses. Subtle renovation has
restored lustre to the original Art Deco setting. Classic, refined cuisine.

XX **Fermette Marbeuf 1900**   AK VISA ◍ AE ①

5 r. Marbeuf (8th) – Ⓜ Alma Marceau – ℰ 01 53 23 08 00
– fermettemarbeuf@blanc.net – Fax 01 53 23 08 09   **G3**
Rest 25 € (weekdays)/30 € and a la carte 30/65 €
◆ Brasserie ◆ Retro ◆
One must reserve one's table to enjoy the Art Nouveau decor of this glass dining
hall dating back to 1898 and discovered by chance in the course of renovation.
Classic cuisine.

XX **Marius et Janette**   🛋 AK ⟷ ⌂⌐ VISA ◍ AE ①
❀
4 av. George-V (8th) – Ⓜ Alma Marceau – ℰ 01 47 23 41 88
– Fax 01 47 23 07 19   **G3**
Rest 48 € and a la carte 65/95 €
Spec. Poissons crus en tartare et carpaccio. Merlan de ligne frit, sauce tartare. Bar
de ligne grillé.
◆ Seafood ◆ Friendly ◆
The sign refers to Marseille's Estaque quarter and Robert Guédiguian's films.
Elegant "yacht"-style decor, pleasant outside dining area on the avenue, and the
taste of the sea on your plate.

XX **Stella Maris** (Yoshino)   AK ✧ VISA ◍ AE ①
❀
4 r. Arsène Houssaye (8th) – Ⓜ Charles de Gaulle-Etoile – ℰ 01 42 89 16 22
– stella.maris.paris@wanadoo.fr – Fax 01 42 89 16 01
– www.stellamaris.com
closed 7 to 21 August and Sunday   **F2**
Rest 85/130 € and a la carte 90/120 €
Spec. Millefeuille de thon rouge mariné et aubergine. Tête de veau en
cocotte, crête de coq et oeuf frit. Parfait pina colada, sablé, lait de coco au
tapioca.
◆ Contemporary ◆ Design ◆
A pleasant restaurant with a refined decor near the Arc de Triomphe.
Classic French cuisine with a modern touch added by a skilful Japanese
chef.

XX **Petit Colombier**   AK ⟷8/20 VISA ◍ AE

42 r. Acacias (17th) – Ⓜ Argentine – ℰ 01 43 80 28 54
– le.petit.colombier@wanadoo.fr – Fax 01 44 40 04 29
closed August, lunch Saturday and Sunday   **F2**
Rest 38/80 € and a la carte 66/110 €
◆ Regional ◆ Family ◆
Patinated wood panelling, old clocks and Louis XV chairs lend a provincial charm
to this restaurant which preserves the memory of the great men of State who
have passed through.

FRANCE

XX **Les Béatilles** (Bochaton)   AC VISA MO
ⁿ   *11bis r. Villebois-Mareuil (17th)* – **M** *Ternes* – ℰ *01 45 74 43 80*
     – Fax 01 45 74 43 81
     closed August, Christmas Holidays, Saturday,
     Sunday and Bank Holidays   **F1**
     Rest 45/80 € and a la carte 75/100 €
     Spec. Nems d'escargots et champignons des bois. Pastilla de pigeon et foie gras
     aux épices. La "Saint-Cochon" (November-March).
     ♦ Innovative ♦ Fashionable ♦
     Attentive hospitality, good, simple cuisine, sober and contemporary dining
     room.

XX **Timgad**   AC ⊗ ⌂ VISA MO AE ①
     21 r. Brunel (17th) – **M** *Argentine* – ℰ *01 45 74 23 70*
     – contact@timgad.fr – Fax 01 40 68 76 46 – www.timgad.fr   **E2**
     Rest a la carte 40/75 €
     ♦ Moroccan ♦ Friendly ♦
     Delve into the past splendour of the city of Timgad: the elegant Moresque decor
     of the rooms was carried out by Moroccan stucco-workers. Fragrant Maghrebian
     cuisine.

XX **Stresa**   AC VISA MO AE ①
     7 r. Chambiges (8th) – **M** *Alma Marceau* – ℰ *01 47 23 51 62*
     closed 1 to 8 May, August, 20 December-3 January,
     Saturday and Sunday   **G3**
     Rest (pre-book) a la carte 60/110 €
     ♦ Italian ♦ Family ♦
     Triangle d'Or trattoria frequented by a very jet-set clientele. Paintings by Buffet,
     compressed sculptural art by César... artists also appreciate the Italian cuisine
     here.

XX **Bistrot du Sommelier**   AC ⇄10/12 VISA MO AE
     97 bd Haussmann (8th) – **M** *St-Augustin* – ℰ *01 42 65 24 85*
     – bistrot-du-sommelier@noos.fr – Fax 01 53 75 23 23
     – www.bistrotdusommelier.com
     closed 28 July-22 August, 23 December-2 January,
     Saturday and Sunday   **H2**
     Rest 39 € (lunch), 60 € b.i./100 € b.i. and a la carte 48/70 € ℬℬ
     ♦ Contemporary ♦ Bistro ♦
     This bistro of free-flowing Bacchanalian pleasure belongs to Philippe Faure-Brac,
     elected World's Best Cellarman in 1992.

XX **Kinugawa**   AC VISA MO AE ①
     4 r. St-Philippe du Roule (8th) – **M** *St-Philippe du Roule* – ℰ *01 45 63 08 07*
     – Fax 01 42 60 57 36
     closed 24 December-7 January, lunch Saturday,
     Sunday and Bank Holidays   **G-H2**
     Rest 30 € (lunch), 72/108 € and a la carte 45/95 €
     ♦ Japanese ♦ Minimalist ♦
     Beyond this discreet façade near St-Philippe-du-Roule church is a Japanese
     interior where you will be presented with a long list of specialities from the Land
     of the Rising Sun.

XX **Graindorge**   VISA MO AE
ⁿ   *15 r. Arc de Triomphe (17th)* – **M** *Charles de Gaulle-Etoile*
     – ℰ 01 47 54 00 28 – le.graindorge@wanadoo.fr
     – Fax 01 47 54 00 28
     closed 31 July-20 August, lunch Saturday and Sunday   **F2**
     Rest 28 € (weekday lunch), 32/60 € and a la carte 40/70 €
     ♦ Belgian ♦ Bistro ♦
     Here you can choose between beer and wine, generous Flemish cuisine and
     appealing market dishes in an attractive Art Deco setting.

L'Angle du Faubourg 🗛 ⌖ VISA 🐵 🗛 ①

195 r. Fg St-Honoré (8th) – Ⓜ *Ternes –* ✆ *01 40 74 20 20*
– angledufaubourg@cavestaillevent.com – Fax 01 40 74 20 21
– www.angledufaubourg.com
closed 29 July-28 August, Saturday, Sunday and Bank Holidays　　　**G2**
Rest 35/70 € and a la carte 55/75 € 🕸
Spec. Sablé de thon aux épices. Foie de canard poêlé au banyuls. Macaron aux fruits de saison.
 ♦ Contemporary ♦ Friendly ♦
On the corner of Rue du Faubourg-St-Honoré and Rue Balzac. This modern bistrot serves skilfully updated classic cuisine to suit current tastes. Simple decor.

La Braisière (Faussat) 🗛 VISA 🐵 🗛 ①

54 r. Cardinet (17th) – Ⓜ *Malesherbes –* ✆ *01 47 63 40 37*
– labraisiere@free.fr – Fax 01 47 63 04 76
closed August, Saturday lunch and Sunday　　　**G1**
Rest 30 € (lunch) and a la carte 50/65 €
Spec. Gâteau de pommes de terre au foie gras. Croustillant de lotte aux girolles. Tarte mirliton aux pommes.
 ♦ South-West of France specialities ♦ Friendly ♦
Comfortable restaurant with a modern, refined feel. The menu has appealing overtones of southwest France, although the dishes change according to the market produce available and the mood of the chef.

Paul Chêne 🗛 ⌂(dinner) VISA 🐵 🗛 ①

123 r. Lauriston (16th) ✉ *75116 –* Ⓜ *Trocadéro –* ✆ *01 47 27 63 17*
– Fax 01 47 27 53 18
closed August, Saturday and Sunday　　　**E3**
Rest 38/48 € and a la carte 40/90 €
 ♦ Traditional ♦ Bistro ♦
This restaurant has kept its 1950s soul: an old zinc counter, comfortable bench seats, tables crowded up together, and a lively atmosphere. Traditional dishes including the famous fish, merlan en colère.

Market 🗛 ⌂ VISA 🐵 🗛

15 av. Matignon (8th) – Ⓜ *Franklin D. Roosevelt –* ✆ *01 56 43 40 90*
– prmarketsa@aol.com – Fax 01 43 59 10 87　　　**H3**
Rest 43 € (lunch), 46/87 € and a la carte 53/76 €
 ♦ Fusion ♦ Design ♦
A trendy establishment with a prestigious location. Wood and marble decor, including African masks in niches. Mixed cuisine (French, Italian and Asian).

Le Vinci 🗛 ⌂(dinner) VISA 🐵 🗛

23 r. P. Valéry (16th) ✉ *75116 –* Ⓜ *Victor Hugo –* ✆ *01 45 01 68 18*
– levinci@wanadoo.fr – Fax 01 45 01 60 37
closed 29 July-27 August, Saturday and Sunday　　　**E2-3**
Rest 32 € and a la carte 50/70 €
 ♦ Italian ♦ Family ♦
Tasty Italian cuisine, pleasant colourful interior and friendly service: a highly-prized establishment a step away from the chic shopping in Avenue Victor-Hugo.

6 New-York 🗛 ⌂ VISA 🐵 ①

6 av. New-York (16th) ✉ *75016 –* Ⓜ *Alma Marceau*
– ✆ *01 40 70 03 30 – 6newyork@wanadoo.fr*
– Fax 01 40 70 04 77
closed 31 July-20 August, Saturday lunch and Sunday　　　**F3**
Rest 35 € (lunch) and a la carte 46/62 €
 ♦ Innovative ♦ Design ♦
The sign gives you a clue to the address but does not tell you that this stylish bistro prepares dishes perfectly suited to its modern and refined setting.

XX **Ballon des Ternes** ⇄12/30 *VISA* **⬤⬤** **AE**
103 av. Ternes (17th) – **Ⓜ** *Porte Maillot – ℰ 01 45 74 17 98*
– leballondesternes@fr.oleane.com – Fax 01 45 72 18 84
closed 31 July-21 August **E1**
Rest a la carte 45/70 €
♦ Brasserie ♦ Retro ♦
No, you have not drunk too many "doubles"! The table set upside down on the ceiling is part of the pleasant 1900 decor of this brasserie next to the Palais des Congrès.

XX **Village d'Ung et Li Lam** **AC** *VISA* **⬤⬤** **AE** **⬤**
10 r. J. Mermoz (8th) – **Ⓜ** *Franklin D. Roosevelt – ℰ 01 42 25 99 79*
– Fax 01 42 25 12 06
closed lunch Saturday and lunch Sunday **H2**
Rest 19/35 € and a la carte 38/45 €
♦ Chinese ♦ Exotic ♦
Ung and Li welcome you into a very original Asian setting: suspended aquariums and a flooring of glass-and-sand tiles. Chinese-Thai cuisine.

XX **Al Ajami** **AC** **⅍** *VISA* **⬤⬤** **AE** **⬤**
58 r. François 1er (8th) – **Ⓜ** *George V – ℰ 01 42 25 38 44 – ajami@free.fr*
– Fax 01 42 25 38 39 **G3**
Rest 23 € (weekday dinner), 26/39 € and a la carte 35/45 €
♦ Lebanese ♦ Exotic ♦
This is the embassy of traditional Lebanese cuisine. From father to son, the food has been lovingly prepared here since 1920. Near East decor, family ambiance and a clientele of regulars.

XX **Chez Léon** ⇄18 *VISA* **⬤⬤** **⬤**
32 r. Legendre (17th) – **Ⓜ** *Villiers – ℰ 01 42 27 06 82 – chezleon32@wanadoo.fr*
– Fax 01 46 22 63 67
closed August, 24 December-2 January, 28 July-28 August, Saturday and Sunday **H1**
Rest 19/25 €
♦ Traditional ♦ Family ♦
The bistro has for long been the favourite haunt of discerning Batignolles diners. Fine traditional dishes are served in three rooms, one upstairs.

X **Café Lenôtre-Pavillon Elysée** 🍴 **AC** **P** ⌂ *VISA* **⬤⬤** **AE** **⬤**
10 Champs-Elysées (8th) – **Ⓜ** *Champs-Elysées Clemenceau – ℰ 01 42 65 85 10*
– Fax 01 42 65 76 23 – www.lenotre.fr
closed 1 to 15 August, 1 to 7 February, dinner Sunday and dinner Monday in Winter **H3**
Rest a la carte 40/70 €
♦ Contemporary ♦ Trendy ♦
This elegant building erected for the 1900 World Fair has been renovated and houses a shop, a catering school and a distinctly modern restaurant.

X **Caïus** **AC** **⅍** *VISA* **⬤⬤** **AE**
6 r. Armaillé (17th) – **Ⓜ** *Charles de Gaulle-Etoile – ℰ 01 42 27 19 20*
– Fax 01 40 55 00 93 **F1**
Rest a la carte approx. 38 €
♦ Home cooking ♦ Formal ♦
The contemporary and cosy new decor of this smart bistro goes perfectly with its tasty dishes made with market produce and personal touches.

X **Caves Petrissans** 🍴 ⌂ *VISA* **⬤⬤**
30bis av. Niel (17th) – **Ⓜ** *Pereire – ℰ 01 42 27 52 03 – cavespetrissans@noos.fr*
– Fax 01 40 54 87 56
closed 28 July-29 August, Saturday, Sunday and Bank Holidays **F1**
Rest (pre-book) 34 € and a la carte 38/58 € ⌂
♦ Traditional ♦ Wine bar ♦
Céline, Abel Gance and Roland Dorgelès loved to visit these cellars that are more than a hundred years old, both a wine shop and a restaurant. Good, bistro-style cooking.

FRANCE

X **Daru** AK ⌐⍝(dinner) VISA ⑩ AE
19 r. Daru (8th) – ⓂCourcelles – 𝒞 01 42 27 23 60
– Fax 01 47 54 08 14 – www.daru.fr
closed August and Sunday **G1**
Rest 29/34 € and a la carte 48/190 €
♦ Russian ♦ Formal ♦
Founded in 1918, Daru was Paris' first Russian food shop. Today it is still a treat
for gourmets with its zakouskis, blinis and caviar, offered in a red-and-black
decor.

X **L'Huîtrier** AK VISA ⑩ AE
16 r. Saussier-Leroy (17th) – Ⓜ Ternes – 𝒞 01 40 54 83 44 – Fax 01 40 54 83 86
closed Sunday from May-August and Monday **F1**
Rest a la carte 29/69 €
♦ Seafood ♦ Family ♦
As you enter, the oyster bar will make your mouth water. You can also choose to
eat other seafood, elbow to elbow, in a soberly-modern dining room.

X **Oscar** ⇔ VISA ⑩ AE
☺ 6 r. Chaillot (16th) ⊠ 75016 – Ⓜ Iéna – 𝒞 01 47 20 26 92 – Fax 01 47 20 27 93
closed 7 to 20 August, lunch Saturday and Sunday **F3**
Rest 21 € and a la carte approx. 35 €
♦ Traditional ♦ Bistro ♦
This bistro, with a discreet façade, tables close together and a blackboard with
daily specials, does not need to advertise to attract a clientele from well beyond
the area.

CONCORDE, OPÉRA, BOURSE, GARE DU NORD   Plan III

🏠🏠🏠 **Ritz** 🍴 ⑩ ᵭ 🔲 AK ⅌ ᵴᴬ30/80 VISA ⑩ AE ⑩
15 pl. Vendôme (1st) – Ⓜ Opéra – 𝒞 01 43 16 30 30 – resa@ritzparis.com
– Fax 01 43 16 36 68 – www.ritzparis.com **K3**
106 rm – ♥680 € ♥♥680/770 €, ⊆ 35 € – 56 suites
Rest see **L'Espadon** below
Rest Bar Vendôme, 𝒞 01 43 16 33 63 – a la carte 70/135 €
♦ Grand Luxury ♦ Palace ♦ Historic ♦
In 1898, César Ritz opened the "perfect hotel" of his dreams, boasting Rudolph
Valentino, Proust, Hemingway and Coco Chanel among its guests. Incomparable
refinement. Superb pool. A chic interior and superb terrace can be found at the
Bar Vendôme, which turns into a tearoom in the afternoon.

🏠🏠🏠 **Meurice** ⑩ ᵭ ᵭrm AK ⅌rm ᵴ⁄rest ☏ ᵴᴬ40/70 VISA ⑩ AE ⑩
228 r. Rivoli (1st) – Ⓜ Tuileries – 𝒞 01 44 58 10 10
– reservations@meuricehotel.com – Fax 01 44 58 10 15
– www.lemeurice.com **J3**
121 rm – ♥510/600 € ♥♥610/760 €, ⊆ 65 € – 39 suites
Rest see **Le Meurice** below
Rest Le Jardin d'Hiver, 𝒞 01 44 58 10 44 – 45 € (lunch) and a la carte 55/95 €
♦ Grand Luxury ♦ Palace ♦ Personalised ♦
One of the first luxury hotels, built in 1817 and later converted into a grand hotel
in 1907. Sumptuous rooms and a superb suite on the top floor with a
breathtaking, panoramic view of Paris. Very beautiful Art Nouveau glass roof and
seventy exotic plants at the Jardin d'Hiver.

🏠🏠🏠 **Crillon** ᵭ AK ⅌ ᵴ⁄rest ᵴᴬ30/60 VISA ⑩ AE ⑩
10 pl. Concorde (8th) – Ⓜ Concorde – 𝒞 01 44 71 15 00 – crillon@crillon.com
– Fax 01 44 71 15 02 – www.crillon.com **J3**
103 rm – ♥510/695 € ♥♥630/790 €, ⊆ 47 € – 44 suites
Rest see **Les Ambassadeurs** and **L'Obélisque** below
♦ Grand Luxury ♦ Palace ♦ Personalised ♦
This 18C townhouse has kept its sumptuous, decorative features. The bedrooms,
which are decorated with wood-furnishings, are magnificent. This is a French
style luxury hotel through-and-through.

FRANCE

Park Hyatt 🛋 ⊕ 🕭 ⅙ 🗚 ↔rm ℀ 🏊15/50 ⌬ 𝗩𝗜𝗦𝗔 ⓪ 🆎 ①
5 r. Paix, (2th) – ⓜ Opéra – ✆ 01 58 71 12 34
– vendome@hyattintl.com – Fax 01 58 71 12 35
– www.paris.vendome.hyatt.com   **K3**
143 rm – †580 € ††580/670 €, � 42 € – 35 suites
Rest *Les Orchidées*, ✆ 01 58 71 10 61 – a la carte 50/85 €
Rest *Le Pur' Grill*, ✆ 01 58 71 10 60 – a la carte 55/105 €
♦ Grand Luxury ♦ Modern ♦
Contemporary decor by Ed Tuttle, a collection of modern art, spa and
high-tech equipment: a new lease of life for this group of five
Haussmann buildings transformed into an ultramodern luxury hotel.
Cuisine in keeping with current tastes, to be savoured below Les Orchidées'
glass roof at lunchtime or in the evening in the cosy atmosphere of the
Pur' Grill.

Intercontinental Le Grand Hôtel ⊕ ⅙ 🗚 ↔ ℀ 🏊20/120
2 r. Scribe (9th) – ⓜ Opéra – ✆ 01 40 07 32 32   ⌬ 🅿 𝗩𝗜𝗦𝗔 🆎 ①
– paris.reservations@ichotelsgroup.com – Fax 01 42 66 12 51
– www.paris.intercontinental.com   **K2**
464 rm – †610/900 € ††610/900 €, ⊆ 35 € – 15 suites
Rest see *Café de la Paix* below
♦ Grand Luxury ♦ Personalised ♦
This famous luxury hotel, opened in 1862, reopened after full renovations in
2003. It offers modern comforts, but its French Second Empire spirit has been
judiciously preserved.

The Westin Paris 🛋 🕭 ⅙rm 🗚 ↔rm 🏊15/350 𝗩𝗜𝗦𝗔 ⓪ 🆎 ①
3 r. Castiglione (1st) – ⓜ Tuileries – ✆ 01 44 77 11 11
– reservation.01729@starwoodhotels.com – Fax 01 44 77 14 60
– www.westin.com/paris   **J3**
405 rm – †269/540 € ††269/560 €, ⊆ 32 € – 33 suites
Rest *234 Rivoli*, ✆ 01 44 77 10 40 – 35 € and a la carte 44/72 €
Rest *Terrasse Fleurie*, ✆ 01 44 77 10 40 (open mid May-end September) 35 €
♦ Luxury ♦ Historic ♦
Superb hotel built in 1878. The decor of the rooms evokes the styles of the 19C;
some have views over the Tuileries. Luxurious Napoleon III lounges. Chic and
convivial atmosphere at 234 Rivoli. The courtyard of the Terrasse Fleurie is
secluded from the hustle and bustle of Paris.

Scribe ⅙ 🗚 ↔rm ℀ 🏊20/150 𝗩𝗜𝗦𝗔 ⓪ 🆎 ①
1 r. Scribe (9th) – ⓜ Opéra – ✆ 01 44 71 24 24
– h0663@accor.com – Fax 01 42 65 39 97 – www.sofitel.com   **K2**
208 rm – †450/540 € ††500/735 €, ⊆ 28 € – 5 suites
Rest see *Les Muses* below
Rest *Jardin des Muses*, ✆ 01 44 71 24 19 (closed dinner in August) 26/32 €
and a la carte 39/47 €
♦ Luxury ♦ Cosy ♦
This grand building is home to a hotel appreciated for its discreet luxury. The
public discovered the Lumière brothers' cinematographic art here at their world
premier in 1895. English-style decor and country-style cuisine at the Jardin des
Muses, located in the basement of Scribe.

Costes 🛋 🕭 ▢ 🕭rm 🗚 𝗩𝗜𝗦𝗔 ⓪ 🆎 ①
239 r. St-Honoré (1st) – ⓜ Concorde – ✆ 01 42 44 50 00
– hotel.costes@wanadoo.fr – Fax 01 42 44 50 01   **J-K3**
79 rm – †245/600 € ††400/800 €, ⊆ 30 € – 3 suites
Rest a la carte 55/90 €
♦ Luxury ♦ Palace ♦ Personalised ♦
Napoleon III style revitalised in the purple and gold rooms. Splendid Italian-
style courtyard and lovely fitness centre: an extravagant luxury hotel, popular
with the jet-set. The restaurant of the Hôtel Costes is a shrine to the latest lounge
trend.

FRANCE

J

MONTMARTRE PIGALLE (Plan VIII) K
Blanche Fontaine

Concorde, Opéra, Bourse, Gare du Nord
(Plan III)

Pavillon de Paris

Rome M Bd des Batignolles
Rue d'Amsterdam Rue Pierre Douai Pigalle
Rue de Constantinople
Liège Rue R. Moncey La Petite Sirène de Copenhague
Pl. de l'Europe Rue de Liège Fontaine Baptiste Notre-Dame
Europe M La Bruyère
Rue de Madrid Rue de Vienne Rue Blanche Rue Jean
R. du Rome Rue de Clichy STE-TRINITÉ
Portalis Rochel Rue de Londres Pl. d'Estienne d'Orves M Trinité Rue Saint
GARE ST-LAZARE
Concorde St-Lazare Rue de Mogador Rue de la Provence La
St-Lazare M Saint Rue de Caumartin
ST-AUGUSTIN Rue de la Pépinière Lazare
Pl. St-Augustin M St-Augustin Rue d'Anjou Rue Pasquier Rue Tronchet Boulevard Haussmann Rue de Mogador Chaussée
Bd Malesherbes Lavoisier Rue de l'Arcade Rue Havre Caumartin Rue Mathurins Auber M Auber d'Antin 16 Haussmann
Astor Saint Honoré Queen Mary St-Pétersbourg OPÉRA GARNIER Ambassador
L'Astor Bedford Libertel-Caumartin Les Muses Intercontinental Richmond Opéra
Hyatt Regency L'Arcade Vignon Scribe Le Grand Hôtel
R. de la Ville l'Évêque Pl. de la Madeleine Café de la Paix Quatre Septembre
Rue de Surène MADELEINE Westminster Céladon Noailles du
Madeleine M Bd de la Madeleine L'Horset Opéra États-Unis Fontaine Gaillon
R. du Senderens Le Faubourg Sofitel Demeure Hôtels Castille Paris Mansart Park Hyatt Opéra Mélifère
L'Obélisque Goumard Ritz L'Espadon Stendhal Édouard VII
Crillon Meliá Vendôme Vendôme PLACE VENDÔME Casanova Chez Pauline
Les Ambassadeurs Costes Carré des Feuillants Pyramides Thérèse
PL. DE LA CONCORDE Westin Paris Pinxo Royal St-Honoré Pavillon Louvre Rivoli
Meurice Renaissance Paris Vendôme S¹-ROCH Regina
Le Meurice Tuileries M Pierre au Palais Royal
JARDIN DES TUILERIES Pl. des Pyramides PALAIS ROYAL
Louvre
SEINE Quai des Tuileries

8e 9e 3 1

CHAMPS ÉLYSÉE / ÉTOILE / PALAIS DES CONGRÈS (Plan II)

0 200 m

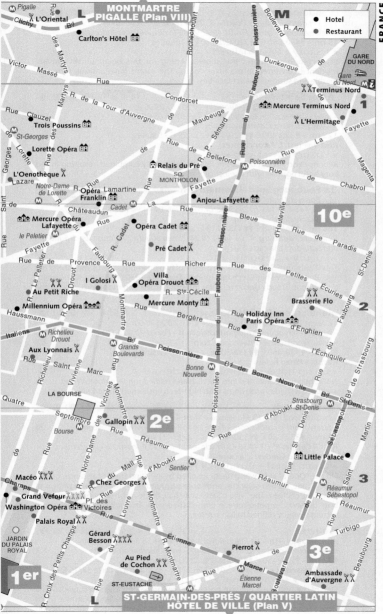

FRANCE

Vendôme without rest   🏧 �winrest 🆅🅸🆂🅰 🆆🅾 🅰🅴 🅾
1 pl. Vendôme (1st) – Ⓜ *Opéra* – ℰ *01 55 04 55 00 – reservations @*
hoteldevendome.com – Fax 01 49 27 97 89 – www.hoteldevendome.com   **K3**
19 rm – †480/550 €, ††720 €, ☑ 30 € – 10 suites
♦ Luxury ♦ Personalised ♦
Place Vendôme creates the superb setting for this beautiful 18C private residence converted into a luxury hotel. The rooms have antique furniture, marble and state-of-the-art facilities.

Astor Saint Honoré   🄵🅐 ᕬ 🏧 ↔ 🆅🅸🆂🅰 🆆🅾 🅰🅴 🅾
11 r. d'Astorg (8th) – Ⓜ *St-Augustin* – ℰ *01 53 05 05 05*
– reservation @astor.3ahotels.com – Fax 01 53 05 05 30
– www.hotel-astorsainthonore.com   **J2**
125 rm – †320/400 €, ††320/510 €, ☑ 25 € – 5 suites
Rest voir rest. *L'Astor* ci-après
♦ Luxury ♦ Art Deco ♦
Regency and Art Deco styles revisited and happily combined, resulting in this cosy hotel popular with a select clientele.

Le Faubourg Sofitel Demeure Hôtels   🄵🅐 ᕬrm 🏧 ↔rm
15 r. Boissy d'Anglas (8th) – Ⓜ *Concorde*   ☁ 🆅🅸🆂🅰 🆆🅾 🅰🅴 🅾
– ℰ 01 44 94 14 14 – h1295@accor.com – Fax 01 44 94 14 28
– www.sofitelfaubourg.com   **J3**
168 rm – †365/438 €, ††435/1213 €, ☑ 28 €
Rest *Café Faubourg*, ℰ *01 44 94 14 24 (closed 30 July-20 August, lunch Sunday and Saturday)* a la carte 53/74 €
♦ Luxury ♦ Design ♦
This "Faubourg" Sofitel is built on the site of two buildings, one 18C and the other 19C. Rooms have high-tech furnishings. There is a 1930s bar and a lounge with a glass roof. Trendy decor, relaxing interior garden and modern cuisine at the Café Faubourg.

Renaissance Paris Vendôme   🄵🅐 ☐ ᕬ 🏧 ↔ 🆅🅸🆂🅰 🆆🅾 🅰🅴 🅾
4 r. Mont Thabor (1st) – Ⓜ *Tuileries* – ℰ *01 40 20 20 00*
– france.reservations @marriotthotels.com – Fax 01 40 20 20 01
– www.renaissanceparisvendome.com   **K3**
85 rm – †330/460 €, ††330/500 €, ☑ 29 € – 12 suites
Rest see *Pinxo* below
♦ Chain hotel ♦ Business ♦ Modern ♦
A 19C building converted into a stylish and refined modern hotel. Wood, beige and brown shades and rooms with high-tech equipment. Fine Chinese bar.

Castille Paris   ☁ 🄵🅐 🏧 ↔rm 🕙 🛀30 🆅🅸🆂🅰 🆆🅾 🅰🅴 🅾
33 r. Cambon (1st) – Ⓜ *Madeleine* – ℰ *01 44 58 44 58*
– reservations @castille.com – Fax 01 44 58 44 00 – www.castille.com   **J3**
86 rm – †330/380 €, ††330/430 €, ☑ 22 € – 21 suites
Rest *Il Cortile*, ℰ *01 44 58 45 67 (closed 31 July-21 August, 25-31 December, Saturday and Sunday)* a la carte 70/95 € ⌘
♦ Chain hotel ♦ Business ♦ Personalised ♦
On the "Opéra" side, warm decor inspired by Italy and the Renaissance; on the "Rivoli" side, French-style chic and sober surroundings, adorned with photos of Paris by Doisneau. The "villa d'Este" style hall, the feverish activity of the piano brigade and the patio-terrace embellished with azulejos create a delightful setting to enjoy refined Italian cuisine.

Louvre   ☁ ᕬrm 🏧 ↔rm ✏rest 🛀20/80 🆅🅸🆂🅰 🆆🅾 🅰🅴 🅾
pl. A. Malraux (1st) – Ⓜ *Palais Royal* – ℰ *01 44 58 38 38 – hoteldulouvre@*
hoteldulouvre.com – Fax 01 44 58 38 01 – www.hoteldulouvre.com   **K3**
132 rm – †230/450 €, ††230/500 €, ☑ 23 € – 45 suites
Rest *Brasserie Le Louvre*, ℰ *01 42 96 27 98 – 33 €* and a la carte 38/75 €
♦ Luxury ♦ Traditional ♦ Classic ♦
One of the first great Parisian hotels, where the painter Pissarro stayed. Some rooms offer a unique view of the Avenue de l'Opéra and the 'Palais Garnier' (Paris Opera House). The Brasserie Le Louvre is traditional both in its 1900s decor and in its cuisine.

Westminster
🛗 🆔 ⟿rm 🛗15/40 ⬡ 🆅🆂🅰 ⓶ 🆑 ⓪

13 r. Paix (2nd) – Ⓜ Opéra – ℰ 01 42 61 57 46 – resa.westminster @
warwickhotels.com – Fax 01 42 60 30 66 – www.hotelwestminster.com
80 rm – ♦270/570 € ♦♦270/570 €, ⤢ 28 € – 21 suites   **K2**
Rest see *Céladon* below
Rest *Petit Céladon*, ℰ 01 47 03 40 42 (closed August) (week-ends only) 51 € b.i.
♦ Luxury ♦ Personalised ♦
It was in 1846 that this elegant hotel, former convent then post house, took the
name of its most regular guest, the Duke of Westminster. Sumptuous rooms,
luxurious apartments. The Céladon becomes the Petit Céladon at the weekend:
Simplified menu and more relaxed service.

Millennium Opéra
🍴 🅰rm 🆔 ⟿rm 📞 🛗80 🆅🆂🅰 ⓶ 🆑 ⓪

12 bd Haussmann (9th) – Ⓜ Richelieu Drouot – ℰ 01 49 49 16 00
– opera @ mill-cop.com – Fax 01 49 49 17 00   **L2**
151 rm – ♦180/400 € ♦♦200/400 €, ⤢ 25 € – 6 suites
Rest *Brasserie Haussmann*, ℰ 01 49 49 16 64 – 40 € b.i./80 € b.i.
♦ Luxury ♦ Business ♦ Modern ♦
This 1927 hotel has lost none of its period lustre. Tastefully appointed rooms with
Art Deco furniture. Modern equipment. Carefully renovated with modern decor,
and typical brasserie fare at the Brasserie Haussmann.

Ambassador
🛗 🆔 ⟿ 🛗15/250 🆅🆂🅰 ⓶ 🆑

16 bd Haussmann (9th) – Ⓜ Richelieu Drouot – ℰ 01 44 83 40 40
– ambass @ concorde-hotels.com – Fax 01 42 46 19 84
– www.hotelambassader-paris.com   **K2**
290 rm – ♦360 € ♦♦360/450 €, ⤢ 22 € – 4 suites
Rest see *16 Haussmann* below
♦ Luxury ♦ Business ♦ Classic ♦
Painted wood panels, crystal chandeliers, antique furniture and decorative
objects in this elegant hotel dating from the 1920s. The renovated rooms offer a
simple, contemporary decor; the others have a more classical style.

Hyatt Regency
🛗 🅰rm 🆔 ⟿rm 🛗10/20 🆅🆂🅰 ⓶ 🆑 ⓪

24 bd Malhesherbes, (8th) – Ⓜ Madeleine – ℰ 01 55 27 12 34 – madeleine @
paris.hyatt.com – Fax 01 55 27 12 35 – www.paris.madeleine.hyatt.com   **J2**
81 rm – ♦515/465 € ♦♦465 €, ⤢ 28 € – 5 suites
Rest *Café M* 55 €
♦ Luxury ♦ Modern ♦
Near the Madeleine, this discreet façade hides a firmly contemporary interior
that is both uncomplicated and welcoming. Spacious rooms, each with an
individual touch. Tasty modern cuisine or brunch (weekends) – either is a good
excuse to home in on Café M.

Concorde St-Lazare
🆔 ⟿rm 🛗250 🆅🆂🅰 ⓶ 🆑 ⓪

108 r. St-Lazare (8th) – Ⓜ St Lazare – ℰ 01 40 08 44 44
– stlazare @ concordestlazare-paris.com – Fax 01 42 93 01 20
– www.concordestlazare-paris.com   **J2**
254 rm – ♦360/450 € ♦♦360/450 €, ⤢ 24 € – 12 suites
Rest *Café Terminus*, ℰ 01 40 08 43 30 – 39/48 € b.i.
♦ Luxury ♦ Art Deco ♦
This "iron palace" (just next to St-Lazare train station) inaugurated in 1889 has
been renovated. Its majestic front hall - an Eiffel School masterpiece - has been
beautifully redone. Brasserie decor with retro charm, and attractive bistro cuisine
at the Café Terminus.

Bedford
🆔 🍴rest 🛗15/50 🆅🆂🅰 ⓶ 🆑

17 r. de l'Arcade (8th) – Ⓜ Madeleine – ℰ 01 44 94 77 77 – reservation @
hotel-bedford.com – Fax 01 44 94 77 97 – www.hotel-bedford.com   **J2**
136 rm – ♦160/182 € ♦♦204/236 €, ⤢ 14 € – 10 suites
Rest (closed 31 July-27 August, Saturday and Sunday) 38 € (lunch)
♦ Luxury ♦ Classic ♦
The hotel, built in 1860 in the elegant Madeleine district, has spacious, comfortable
and fully redecorated rooms. 1900s-style decor with an abundance of decorative,
stucco motifs and a lovely cupola. The restaurant room is the Bedford's real jewel.

FRANCE

FRANCE

Royal St-Honoré without rest   AC VISA OO AE ①

221 r. St-Honoré (1st) – Ⓜ *Tuileries* – ℰ *01 42 60 32 79*
– *rsh@hroy.com* – *Fax 01 42 60 47 44*
– *www.hotel-royal-st-honore.com*   **K3**
65 rm – ♦300/340 € ♦♦340/370 €, ⌷ 21 € – 5 suites
♦ Luxury ♦ Traditional ♦ Personalised ♦
19C building on the site of the former Noailles hotel. Highly elegant, personalised rooms. Louis XVI decor in the breakfast room.

Villa Opéra Drouot without rest   ⅙ AC ⅔ ℅ VISA OO AE ①

2 r. Geoffroy Marie (9th) – Ⓜ *Grands Boulevards* – ℰ *01 48 00 08 08*
– *drouot@leshotelsdeparis.com*
– *Fax 01 48 00 80 60*   **L2**
29 rm – ♦199/289 € ♦♦235/298 €, ⌷ 20 €
♦ Business ♦ Stylish ♦
A surprising and subtle blend of Baroque decor and the latest in elegant comfort in these rooms embellished with wall hangings, velvets, silks and wood panelling.

Regina   🏠 AC ⅙rm ℅ ⅜20/60 VISA OO AE ①

2 pl. Pyramides (1st) – Ⓜ *Tuileries* – ℰ *01 42 60 31 10*
– *reservation@regina-hotel.com* – *Fax 01 40 15 95 16*
– *www.regina-hotel.com*   **K3**
107 rm – ♦340/405 € ♦♦405/465 €, ⌷ 29 € – 13 suites
Rest *(closed August, Saturday, Sunday and Bank Holidays)* 40 € and a la carte 45/68 €
♦ Luxury ♦ Traditional ♦ Art Deco ♦
The superb Art Nouveau reception of this 1900 hotel has been preserved. The rooms, rich in antique furniture, are quieter on the patio side; some offer views of the Eiffel Tower. Dining room with a pretty "Majorelle" fireplace and a courtyard-terrace that is very popular in summer.

Meliá Vendôme without rest   AC ⅙ ⅘ ⅜20 VISA OO AE ①

8 r. Cambon (1st) – Ⓜ *Concorde* – ℰ *01 44 77 54 00*
– *melia.vendome@solmelia.com* – *Fax 01 44 77 54 01*
– *www.solmelia.com*   **J3**
78 rm – ♦165/393 € ♦♦165/493 €, ⌷ 25 € – 5 suites
♦ Chain hotel ♦ Business ♦ Cosy ♦
Cosy, smart decoration, period furniture and a warm atmosphere in the rooms. An elegant lounge with a Belle Époque glass roof, bar and lovely breakfast area.

Édouard VII   AC ⅙rm ⅜15/25 VISA OO AE ①

39 av. Opéra (2nd) – Ⓜ *Opéra* – ℰ *01 42 61 56 90*
– *info@edouard7hotel.com* – *Fax 01 42 61 47 73*
– *www.edouard7hotel.com*   **K3**
64 rm – ♦295/390 € ♦♦390/485 €, ⌷ 23 € – 4 suites
Rest *Angl'Opéra*, ℰ *01 42 61 86 25 (closed 12 to 20 August, Saturday and Sunday)* 20/40 €
♦ Luxury ♦ Traditional ♦ Cosy ♦
Edward VII, Prince of Wales liked to stay here on his trips through Paris. Spacious, luxurious rooms. Dark wood panelling and stained glass decorate the bar. The contemporary and welcoming Angl Opéra restaurant surprises the taste buds with its fusion food.

Mercure Terminus Nord without rest   ⅙ ⅙ ℅

12 bd Denain (10th) – Ⓜ *Gare du Nord*   ⅜30/130 VISA OO AE ①
– ℰ *01 42 80 20 00* – *h2761@accor.com*
– *Fax 01 42 80 63 89*   **M1**
236 rm – ♦135/200 € ♦♦145/200 €, ⌷ 14 €
♦ Chain hotel ♦ Business ♦ Cosy ♦
Thanks to a good renovation, this hotel built in 1865 has recovered its former glory. Art Nouveau stained glass, "British" decor and a cosy atmosphere give it the air of a beautiful Victorian home.

Holiday Inn Paris Opéra &rm 🅰️ ↔rm 📞 🛁45 VISA ⓜⓢ 🄰🄴 ①

38 r. Échiquier (10th) – Ⓜ *Bonne Nouvelle* – ℘ *01 42 46 92 75* – *information @ hi-parisopera.com* – *Fax 01 42 47 03 97* – *www.holiday-inn.com/paris-opera*
92 rm – 🛆150/299 € 🛆🛆249/355 €, ⊑ 19 €   **M2**
Rest 21/37 €
♦ Chain hotel ♦ Business ♦ Retro ♦
A step away from the Grands Boulevards and their string of theatres and brasseries. This hotel offers large rooms decorated in the style of the Belle Époque. The dining room is an authentic gem from the year 1900: mosaics, glass canopy, woodwork and fine Art Nouveau furniture.

Pavillon de Paris without rest &🅰️ ↔ 🚫 📞 🅿️ VISA ⓜⓢ 🄰🄴 ①

7 r. Parme (9th) – Ⓜ *Liège* – ℘ *01 55 31 60 00* – *mail @ pavillondeparis.com*
– *Fax 01 55 31 60 01* – *www.pavillondeparis.com*   **K1**
30 rm – 🛆203/240 € 🛆🛆255/296 €, ⊑ 16 €
♦ Business ♦ Minimalist ♦
Contemporary decor with a Zen twist, and sophisticated technology (Internet access via the TV, fax and answering machine) characterise the rooms in this hotel with its restrained luxury.

Washington Opéra without rest &🅰️ ↔ 🚫 VISA ⓜⓢ 🄰🄴 ①

50 r. de Richelieu (1st) – Ⓜ *Palais Royal* – ℘ *01 42 96 68 06*
– *hotel @ washingtonopera.com* – *Fax 01 40 15 01 12*
– *www.washingtonopera.com*   **L3**
36 rm – 🛆215/245 € 🛆🛆215/335 €, ⊑ 15 €
♦ Traditional ♦ Personalised ♦
Former townhouse of the Marquise de Pompadour. Directoire or 'Gustavian'-style rooms. The 6th floor terrace offers beautiful views over the gardens of the Palais-Royal.

Stendhal without rest 🅰️ VISA ⓜⓢ 🄰🄴 ①

22 r. D. Casanova (2nd) – Ⓜ *Opéra* – ℘ *01 44 58 52 52* – *h1610 @ accor.com*
– *Fax 01 44 58 52 00* – *www.mercure.com*   **K3**
20 rm – 🛆195/235 € 🛆🛆195/285 €, ⊑ 17 €
♦ Luxury ♦ Traditional ♦ Personalised ♦
On the trail of the famous writer, stay in the "Red and Black" suite of this stylish residence. The elegant rooms are all decorated in two colours.

Mansart without rest 🅰️ 🚫 📞 VISA ⓜⓢ 🄰🄴 ①

5 r. Capucines (1st) – Ⓜ *Opéra* – ℘ *01 42 61 50 28* – *mansart @ espritfrance.com*
– *Fax 01 49 27 97 44* – *www.esprit-de-france.com*   **K3**
57 rm – 🛆120/305 € 🛆🛆165/305 €, ⊑ 11 €
♦ Luxury ♦ Traditional ♦ Historic ♦
Renovations in this hotel pay homage to Mansart, architect to Louis XIV. Elegant rooms, adorned with French Empire or Directoire furniture. More modern hall-lounge.

L'Horset Opéra without rest 🅰️ ↔ VISA ⓜⓢ 🄰🄴 ①

18 r. d'Antin (2nd) – Ⓜ *Opéra* – ℘ *01 44 71 87 00*
– *lopera @ paris-hotels-charm.com* – *Fax 01 42 66 55 54*
– *www.paris-hotels-charm.com*   **K2**
54 rm ⊑ – 🛆165/245 € 🛆🛆180/275 €
♦ Traditional ♦ Classic ♦
Colourful wall hangings and warm wood panelling personalise the refurbished rooms of this fine traditional hotel situated a short distance from the Palais Garnier (Paris Opera House). Cosy atmosphere in the lounge.

Mercure Opéra Lafayette without rest &🅰️ ↔

49 r. Lafayette (9th) – Ⓜ *Le Peletier* – ℘ *01 42 85 05 44* 🚫 VISA ⓜⓢ 🄰🄴 ①
– *h2802-gm @ accor.com* – *Fax 01 49 95 06 60*   **L2**
96 rm – 🛆115/199 € 🛆🛆125/259 €, ⊑ 14 € – 7 suites
♦ Traditional ♦ Business ♦ Cosy ♦
The elegance of beige and wood in the hall, rooms in Directoire-style with toile de Jouy wallpaper and a winter-garden setting for breakfasts.

FRANCE

St-Pétersbourg without rest ⬛ 🍴 ♨25 VISA ⓴ AE ⓪

33 r. Caumartin (9th) – Ⓜ *Havre Caumartin –* ℰ *01 42 66 60 38*
– hotel.st-petersbourg@wanadoo.fr – Fax 01 42 66 53 54
– www.hotel-st-petersbourg.com   **J2**
100 rm � – ♦145/184 € ♦♦184/225 €
♦ Traditional ♦ Business ♦ Classic ♦
The Louis XVI-style rooms are often spacious and face the courtyard.
Comfortable lounge, lit by coloured glass.

Richmond Opéra without rest ⬛ 🍴 VISA ⓴ AE ⓪

11 r. Helder (9th) – Ⓜ *Chaussée d'Antin –* ℰ *01 47 70 53 20*
– paris@richmond-hotel.com – Fax 01 48 00 02 10   **K2**
59 rm – ♦132/147 € ♦♦152/223 €, � 10 €
♦ Traditional ♦ Business ♦ Classic ♦
The spacious elegant rooms almost all give onto the courtyard. The lounge is
rather grandly decorated in the Empire style.

L'Arcade without rest ⬛ 📞 ♨25 VISA ⓴ AE

7-9 r. Arcade (8th) – Ⓜ *Madeleine –* ℰ *01 53 30 60 00 – reservation@
hotel-arcade.com – Fax 01 40 07 03 07 – www.hotel-arcade.com*   **J2**
41 rm – ♦142/172 € ♦♦188/226 €, ⊠ 9,50 €
♦ Traditional ♦ Stylish ♦
The marble and wood panels in the hall and lounges, and the soft colours and
carefully-chosen furniture in the rooms, all contribute to the charm of this
elegant and discreet hotel near the Madeleine.

Lavoisier without rest ♿ ⬛ 🍴 📞 VISA ⓴ AE ⓪

21 r. Lavoisier (8th) – Ⓜ *St-Augustin –* ℰ *01 53 30 06 06*
– info@hotellavoisier.com – Fax 01 53 30 23 00 – www.hotellavoisier.com   **J2**
27 rm – ♦175/265 € ♦♦175/265 €, ⊠ 12 € – 3 suites
♦ Business ♦ Modern ♦
Contemporary rooms, cosy little library-cum-lounge also serving as a bar, and a
vaulted breakfast room are the hallmarks of this hotel in the St-Augustin district.

Lorette Opéra without rest ♿ ⬛ ⇟ 📞 VISA ⓴ AE ⓪

36 r. Notre-Dame de Lorette, (9th) – Ⓜ *St-Georges –* ℰ *01 42 85 18 81*
– hotel.lorette@astotel.com – Fax 01 42 81 32 19   **L1**
84 rm – ♦112/204 € ♦♦180/204 €, ⊠ 11 €
♦ Business ♦ Modern ♦
This completely renovated hotel has a decor harmoniously marrying
contemporary style and freestone. Large, pleasant rooms with a modern, refined
feel.

Opéra Cadet without rest ⬛ ⇟ 🍴 📞 ♨50 🛏 VISA ⓴ AE ⓪

24 r. Cadet (9th) – Ⓜ *Cadet –* ℰ *01 53 34 50 50 – infos@operacadet.com*
– Fax 01 53 34 50 60 – www.operacadet.com   **L2**
85 rm ⊠ – ♦120/166 € ♦♦133/298 €
♦ Business ♦ Modern ♦
Leave your car in the garage, settle into this contemporary-style hotel and get to
know the capital on foot. Choose a room facing the garden for more peace and
quiet.

Little Palace ♿ rm ⬛ ⇟rm VISA ⓴ AE ⓪

4 r. Salomon de Caus (3rd) – Ⓜ *Réaumur Sébastopol –* ℰ *01 42 72 08 15*
– info@littlepalacehotel.com – Fax 01 42 72 45 81
– www.littlepalacehotel.com   **M3**
49 rm – ♦148/168 € ♦♦165/185 €, ⊠ 13 € – 4 suites
Rest *(closed 29 July-28 August, dinner Friday, Saturday and Sunday)* a la carte
28/40 €
♦ Family ♦ Traditional ♦ Modern ♦
This 1900s building on a charming small square has had a face-lift. It has pretty,
modern rooms, with the best on the 5th and 6th floors offering a balcony and
view of Paris. Lovely brown, sculpted wood panelling, light tones and minimalist
furniture can be found in the restaurant.

FRANCE

Queen Mary without rest
AC VISA MC AE ①

9 r. Greffulhe (8th) – Ⓜ Madeleine – ℰ 01 42 66 40 50
– reservation@hotelqueenmary.com – Fax 01 42 66 94 92
– www.hotelqueenmary.com
J2
36 rm – †155/195 € ††179/329 €, � 18 €
♦ Chain hotel ♦ Personalised ♦

A refined establishment with a "British" feel to it, where a welcome gift of a carafe of sherry awaits you. Attentive service, pleasant patio, charming breakfast room and hushed bedrooms.

Vignon without rest
ぐ AC ⁴⁄₌ ℃ VISA MC AE ①

23 r. Vignon (8th) – Ⓜ Madeleine – ℰ 01 47 42 93 00
– reservation@hotelvignon.com – Fax 01 47 42 04 60
– www.levignon.com
J2
28 rm – †230/320 € ††240/350 €, ⊿ 23 €
♦ Traditional ♦ Functional ♦

A warm, discreet hotel just a step away from Place de la Madeleine. Cosy rooms – those on the top floor have just been refurbished in a distinctly contemporary style.

États-Unis Opéra without rest
AC ⁹⁄₋ ⁴⁄₌ 25 VISA MC AE ①

16 r. d'Antin (2nd) – Ⓜ Opéra – ℰ 01 42 65 05 05 – us-opera@wanadoo.fr
– Fax 01 42 65 93 70 – www.hotel-paris-opera.com
K3
45 rm – †95/175 € ††135/290 €, ⊿ 11 €
♦ Traditional ♦ Functional ♦

This hotel in a 1930s building offers modern, comfortable, recently renovated rooms. Breakfast is served in the inviting English-style bar.

Noailles without rest
Fõ AC ⁴⁄₌ 20 VISA MC AE ①

9 r. Michodière (2nd) – Ⓜ 4 Septembre – ℰ 01 47 42 92 90
– goldentulip.denoailles@wanadoo.fr – Fax 01 49 24 92 71
K2
58 rm – †225/242 € ††300 €, ⊿ 15 € – 2 suites
♦ Business ♦ Design ♦

Staunchly contemporary elegance behind a sober ancient façade. Japanese-style decor in the spacious rooms most of which open onto an attractive patio.

Thérèse without rest
AC ⁹⁄₋ ℃ VISA MC AE ①

5-7 r. Thérèse (1st) – Ⓜ Pyramides – ℰ 01 42 96 10 01
– info@hoteltherese.com – Fax 01 42 96 15 22
– www.hoteltherese.com
K3
43 rm – †136/220 € ††136/266 €, ⊿ 12 €
♦ Traditional ♦ Business ♦ Personalised ♦

Discreet, refined contemporary decoration, with a few exotic touches. This hotel has been fully renovated, offering rooms with character and a vaulted breakfast room.

Opéra Franklin without rest
⁴⁄₌ ⁹⁄₋ ℃ VISA MC AE ①

19 r. Buffault (9th) – Ⓜ Cadet – ℰ 01 42 80 27 27
– info@operafranklin.com – Fax 01 48 78 13 04
– www.operafranklin.com
L1
68 rm – †139/163 € ††152/208 €, ⊿ 13 €
♦ Family ♦ Traditional ♦ Historic ♦

In a quiet street, this hotel's rooms have elegant furnishings recalling Napoleonic-era military campaigns. Unusual naive trompe-l'oeil at the front desk.

Libertel-Caumartin without rest
⁴⁄₌ ℃ VISA MC AE ①

27 r. Caumartin (9th) – Ⓜ Havre Caumartin – ℰ 01 47 42 95 95
– h2811@accor.com – Fax 01 47 42 88 19
J2
40 rm – †151/180 € ††162/190 €, ⊿ 14 €
♦ Chain hotel ♦ Business ♦ Modern ♦

Prettily-decorated contemporary rooms furnished in pale wood. Pleasant breakfast room decorated with colourful paintings.

Anjou-Lafayette without rest   ⟶ ☏ VISA ⓂⓈ AE ①
4 r. Riboutté (9th) – Ⓜ Cadet – ✆ 01 42 46 83 44 – hotel.anjou.lafayette @
wanadoo.fr – Fax 01 48 00 08 97 – www.hotelanjoulafayette.com   **M1**
39 rm – ♦98/108 € ♦♦118/150 €, ☑ 11,50 €
♦ Business ♦ Modern ♦
Near the leafy Square Montholon with its Second Empire wrought-iron gates,
comfortable, soundproofed and totally renovated, contemporary rooms.

Trois Poussins without rest   & AC ⟶ ☏ VISA ⓂⓈ AE ①
15 r. Clauzel (9th) – Ⓜ St-Georges – ✆ 01 53 32 81 81 – h3p @ les3poussins.com
– Fax 01 53 32 81 82 – www.les3poussins.com   **L1**
40 rm – ♦106/153 € ♦♦119/189 €, ☑ 10 €
♦ Traditional ♦ Business ♦ Cosy ♦
Elegant rooms offering several levels of comfort. View of Paris from the top floors.
Prettily vaulted breakfast room. Small courtyard-terrace.

Mercure Monty without rest   AC ⟶ ☏ ♨50 VISA ⓂⓈ AE ①
5 r. Montyon (9th) – Ⓜ Grands Boulevards – ✆ 01 47 70 26 10
– hotel @ mercuremonty.com – Fax 01 42 46 55 10 – www.mercure.com   **L2**
70 rm – ♦125/195 € ♦♦130/200 €, ☑ 13 €
♦ Chain hotel ♦ Business ♦ Functional ♦
Beautiful façade dating from the 1930s, Art Deco setting at the front desk, and the
hotel chain's standard equipment characterise this Mercure located in view of
the Folies Bergère.

Pavillon Louvre Rivoli without rest   & AC VISA ⓂⓈ AE ①
20 r. Molière (1st) – Ⓜ Pyramides – ✆ 01 42 60 31 20 – louvre @
leshotelsdeparis.com – Fax 01 42 60 32 06 – www.leshotelsdepariscom
29 rm – ♦180/210 € ♦♦225/260 €, ☑ 14 €   **K3**
♦ Traditional ♦ Personalised ♦
Well-placed in the Opéra quarter and the Louvre museum, this
completely refurbished hotel will appeal to art lovers and shoppers. Rooms are
small, but fresh and colourful.

Relais du Pré without rest   ⟨⟩ VISA ⓂⓈ AE ①
16 r. P. Sémard (9th) – Ⓜ Poissonnière – ✆ 01 42 85 19 59 – relais @
duprehotels.com – Fax 01 42 85 70 59 – www.leshotelsdupre.com   **L-M1**
34 rm – ♦82/85 € ♦♦98/112 €, ☑ 10 €
♦ Business ♦ Modern ♦
Near two other older hotels in the same chain, this one offers the same rooms -
modern and neat as a pin. Contemporary, rather cosy bar and lounge.

𝕏𝕏𝕏𝕏𝕏
☸☸   **Le Meurice** – Hôtel Meurice   AC ⟨⟩ ⟳25/120 ⌂ VISA ⓂⓈ AE ①
228 r. Rivoli (1st) – Ⓜ Tuileries – ✆ 01 44 58 10 55 – restauration @
meuricehotel.com – Fax 01 44 58 10 76 – www.lemeurice.com
closed August, 17 February-4 March, Saturday and Sunday   **J-K3**
Rest 75 € (lunch)/190 € and a la carte 142/250 € �
Spec. Langoustines marinées à la gelée de pomme verte (June-September.).
Tarte flammenkuechen aux truffes (December-February). Cœur de poire rôtie à
la vanille (September-December).
♦ Innovative ♦ Luxury ♦
The Grand Siècle-style dining hall has clearly drawn its inspiration from the state
apartments of the Versailles chateau; the cuisine is exceptional and up-to-date
- a palace for gourmets!

𝕏𝕏𝕏𝕏𝕏
☸☸   **Les Ambassadeurs** – Hôtel Crillon   AC ⟨⟩ ⟳20/120 ⌂ VISA ⓂⓈ AE
10 pl. Concorde (8th) – Ⓜ Concorde – ✆ 01 44 71 16 16
– restaurants @ crillon.com – Fax 01 44 71 15 02 – www.crillon.com
closed August, Monday lunch and Sunday   **J3**
Rest 70 € (lunch) and a la carte 140/230 € ⓝative
Spec. Blanc à manger d'oeuf, truffe noire (January-March). Pigeonneau désossé,
foie gras, jus à l'olive. Comme un vacherin, au parfum de saison.
♦ Innovative ♦ Luxury ♦
This splendid dining hall where gold and marble is reflected in immense mirrors
is the ballroom of an 18C mansion. The cuisine is distinctive.

FRANCE

XXXXX
⊗

L'Espadon – Hôtel Ritz   🔲 🈸 ⌨ 𝐕𝐈𝐒𝐀 ⊛ 🄰🄴 ⓪

15 pl. Vendôme (1st) – ⓜ Opéra – ☎ 01 43 16 30 80
– food-bev@ritzparis.com – Fax 01 43 16 33 75
– www.ritzparis.com
closed August   **K3**
Rest 75 € (lunch)/180 € and a la carte 125/185 €
Spec. Araignée de mer en riviera de mangue et jus d'agrumes. Agneau princier
en écrin de truffe, pommes soufflées. Millefeuille "tradition Ritz".
♦ Traditional ♦ Luxury ♦
The restaurant area is weighted in gold and drapery, a dazzling decor
reminiscent of its famous guests, and has a pleasant terrace in a flower garden
and fine, original cuisine. The Ritz in all its splendour!

XXXX
⊗⊗⊗

Grand Vefour   🔲 🈸 ⊷2/20 ⌨ 𝐕𝐈𝐒𝐀 ⊛ 🄰🄴 ⓪

17 r. Beaujolais (1st) – ⓜ Palais Royal – ☎ 01 42 96 56 27
– grand.vefour@wanadoo.fr – Fax 01 42 86 80 71
closed 10 to 17 April, 1 to 31 August, 23 to 31 December, dinner Friday,
Saturday and Sunday   **L3**
Rest 75 € (lunch)/255 € and a la carte 166/230 € ⅏
Spec. Ravioles de foie gras à l'émulsion de crème truffée. Parmentier de queue
de bœuf aux truffes. Palet noisette et chocolat au lait, glace au caramel.
♦ Innovative ♦ Luxury ♦
In the gardens of the Palais-Royal, sumptuous Directoire period dining rooms
decorated with splendid "pictures under glass". The inspired and inventive
cuisine is worthy of this historic monument.

XXXX
⊗⊗

Carré des Feuillants (Dutournier)   🔲 ⊷6/44 ⌨ 𝐕𝐈𝐒𝐀 ⊛ 🄰🄴 ⓪

14 r. Castiglione (1st) – ⓜ Tuileries – ☎ 01 42 86 82 82
– carre.des.feuillants@wanadoo.fr – Fax 01 42 86 07 71
– www.carredesfeuillants.fr
closed August, Saturday and Sunday   **K3**
Rest 65 € (lunch)/150 € and a la carte 125/155 € ⅏
Spec. Gelée d'écrevisses, foie gras et ris de veau (Summer). Carré d'agneau
des Pyrénées au four, gigot d'agneau cuit à l'étouffée dans l'argile (Spring).
Figues caramélisées, gingembre confit, crème glacée aux noix fraîches
(Autumn).
♦ Traditional ♦ Formal ♦
This restaurant, on the site of the former Feuillants convent, has a decisively
modern setting. Up-to-date cuisine with Gascony touches and superb wine
list.

XXXX
⊗

Goumard   🔲 ⊷4/18 ⌨ 𝐕𝐈𝐒𝐀 ⊛ 🄰🄴 ⓪

9 r. Duphot (1st) – ⓜ Madeleine – ☎ 01 42 60 36 07
– goumard.philippe@wanadoo.fr – Fax 01 42 60 04 54
– www.goumard.com   **J3**
Rest 46 € and a la carte 105/160 € ⅏
Spec. Langoustines bretonnes rôties. Bar de ligne rôti, couteaux, racines
maraîchères et jus iodé. Gros capeletti au cacao et liqueur de maracuja.
♦ Seafood ♦ Formal ♦
Small, intimate dining rooms in Art Deco style, enhanced by ocean scenes. The
washrooms, vestige of the original Majorelle decor, are well worth a visit.
Delicious seafood cuisine.

XXXX

Les Muses – Hôtel Scribe   ♿ 🔲 ⌨ 𝐕𝐈𝐒𝐀 ⊛ 🄰🄴 ⓪

1 r. Scribe (9th) – ⓜ Opéra – ☎ 01 44 71 24 26 – h0663-re@accor.com
– Fax 01 44 71 24 64
closed August, 24-31 December, Saturday and Sunday   **K2**
Rest 45 € (lunch), 70/120 € and a la carte 85/150 €
♦ Contemporary ♦ Formal ♦
The dining hall, embellished by a fresco and canvasses evoking the area around
Opéra as it was in the 19C, is located in the basement of the hotel. Enticing menu
for the modern palate.

Gérard Besson
XXXX ⛨ 🔠 ✂ 🚗 VISA ⓜ AE ①

5 r. Coq Héron (1st) – Ⓜ Louvre Rivoli – ☎ 01 42 33 14 74
– gerard.besson4@libertysurf.fr – Fax 01 42 33 85 71
closed 1 to 27 August, Monday lunch, Saturday lunch and Sunday **L3**
Rest 56 € (lunch), 63/105 € and a la carte 105/130 €
Spec. Fricassée de homard "Georges Garin". Carte de truffes (mid-December-late March). Gibier (October-mid-December).
♦ Traditional ♦ Formal ♦
Elegant, low-key restaurant near the Halles decorated in beige tones with still-life paintings and Liberty prints. Subtly reinterpreted classic cuisine.

Senderens
XXX ⛨⛨ 🔠 ✂ ⇔10/12 🚗 VISA ⓜ AE ①

9 pl. Madeleine (8th) – Ⓜ Madeleine – ☎ 01 42 65 22 90
– restaurant@senderens.fr – Fax 01 42 65 06 23 **J2**
Rest a la carte 70/110 € ⸙
Spec. Chipirons à la plancha, artichauts barigoule, tomates confites. Lotte et moules au curry vert. Millefeuille à la vanille, zestes d'orange confite.
♦ Contemporary ♦ Trendy ♦
Contemporary furnishings and Art Nouveau wood panels by Majorelle are artfully combined in this luxurious and ever-lively brasserie. Innovative cuisine; sublime blend of dishes and wines.

Céladon – Hôtel Westminster
XXX ⛨ 🔠 ⇔15/40 🚗 VISA ⓜ AE ①

15 r. Daunou (2nd) – Ⓜ Opéra – ☎ 01 47 03 40 42
– christophemoisand@leceladon.com – Fax 01 42 61 33 78
– www.leceladon.com
closed August, Saturday, Sunday and Bank Holidays **K2**
Rest 55 € b.i. (lunch), 71/110 € and a la carte 95/130 €
Spec. Pâté froid de lapin de garenne (15 September-15 January). Saint-pierre rôti au beurre d'escargot. Soufflé williamine.
♦ Innovative ♦ Cosy ♦
Delightful dining rooms with a high-class decor: Regency-style furniture, "celadon" green walls and a collection of Chinese porcelain. Cooking suited to current tastes.

Café de la Paix – -Intercontinental Le Grand Hôtel
XXX ♿ 🔠 ✂

12 bd Capucines (9th) – Ⓜ Opéra ⇔10/450 🚗 VISA ⓜ AE ①
– ☎ 01 40 07 36 36 – Fax 01 40 07 36 13 **K2**
Rest 39 € (lunch)/44 € and a la carte 60/100 €
♦ Traditional ♦ Brasserie ♦
This famous luxury brasserie, open from 7am to midnight remains popular with the Parisians. Fine murals, gold wainscoting and French Second Empire-inspired furniture.

L'Astor – Hôtel Astor Saint Honoré
XXX 🔠 VISA ⓜ AE ①

11 r. d'Astorg, (8th) – Ⓜ St-Augustin – ☎ 01 53 05 05 20
– restaurant@astor.3ahotels.com
– Fax 01 53 05 05 30 **J2**
Rest (closed 29 July-28 August, 23 to 30 December, Saturday and Sunday)
47 € (weekday lunch), 33 € b.i./76 € and a la carte 65/85 €
♦ Traditional ♦ Formal ♦
An elegant dining room under a glass roof that creates soft lighting effects. The sand-coloured walls are sprinkled with stars, the Directoire-style furniture is dark wood. The menu includes traditional and unique dishes.

Fontaine Gaillon
XXX 🌳 🔠 ⇔12/40 🚗 VISA ⓜ AE

Pl. Gaillon (2nd) – Ⓜ 4 Septembre – ☎ 01 47 42 63 22
– Fax 01 47 42 82 84
closed 5 to 29 August, 13 to 20 February, Saturday and Sunday **K2-3**
Rest 38 € (lunch) and a la carte 50/70 €
♦ Seafood ♦ Fashionable ♦
Elegant dining room in a 17C townhouse. Terrace set up around a fountain. Fish and seafood dishes and wine selection supervised by Gérard Depardieu.

FRANCE

XXX **Macéo** ⚡ ⟷40 *VISA* **MC**
15 r. Petits-Champs (1st) – **M** *Bourse* – ℰ *01 42 97 53 85 – info@*
maceorestaurant.com – Fax 01 47 03 36 93 – www.maceorestaurant.com
closed 5 to 20 August, Saturday lunch and Sunday   **L3**
Rest 30/36 € and a la carte 48/71 € ⌘
♦ Innovative ♦ Friendly ♦
A surprising blend of French Second Empire decor and contemporary furniture.
Up-to-date cuisine, a vegetarian menu and international wine list. Friendly
lounge-bar.

XXX **L'Obélisque** – Hôtel Crillon **AC** ⚡ *VISA* **MC** **AE**
6 r. Boissy d'Anglas (8th) – **M** *Concorde* – ℰ *01 44 71 15 15*
– restaurants@crillon.com – Fax 01 44 71 15 02 – www.crillon.com
closed 16 to 31 July and 7 to 11 February   **J3**
Rest 50 €
♦ Contemporary ♦ Friendly ♦
Dining room ornamented with wood panels, mirrors and engraved glass, where
the number of square feet is almost lower than the number of diners. Not so
surprising, given the tasty and carefully-prepared cuisine!

XX **Pierre au Palais Royal** **AC** *VISA* **MC** **AE** **①**
10 r. Richelieu (1st) – **M** *Palais Royal* – ℰ *01 42 96 09 17*
– pierreaupalaisroyal@wanadoo.fr – Fax 01 42 96 26 40
closed 6 to 27 August, lunch Saturday and Sunday   **K3**
Rest 31/38 €
♦ Seasonal cuisine ♦ Fashionable ♦
Sober and pleasant decor in aubergine shades with prints of the neighbouring
Palais-Royal. Contemporary cuisine based on seasonal market produce.

XX **Palais Royal** ⌂ *VISA* **MC** **AE** **①**
110 Galerie de Valois (1st) – **M** *Bourse* – ℰ *01 40 20 00 27 – palaisrest@aol.com*
– Fax 01 40 20 00 82
closed 18 December-14 January and Sunday   **L3**
Rest a la carte 44/100 €
♦ Traditional ♦ Retro ♦
Beneath the windows of Colette's apartment, an Art Deco-style restaurant with
an idyllic terrace, opening onto the Palais-Royal garden.

XX **16 Haussmann** – Hôtel Ambassador ⌂ **AC** ⌂ *VISA* **MC** **AE**
16 bd Haussman (9th) – **M** *Richelieu Drouot* – ℰ *01 48 00 06 38*
– 16haussmann@concorde-hotels.com – Fax 01 44 83 40 57
– www.hotelambassador-paris.com   **K2**
Rest 40 € and a la carte approx. 45 €
♦ Contemporary ♦ Design ♦
Shades of Paris blue and golden yellow, reddish-brown wood, red seats by Starck
and large bay windows opening onto the boulevard, with the street life adding
to the decor.

XX **Au Petit Riche** **AC** ⇔ ⟷6/50 *VISA* **MC** **AE** **①**
25 r. Le Peletier (9th) – **M** *Richelieu Drouot* – ℰ *01 47 70 68 68*
– aupetitriche@wanadoo.fr – Fax 01 48 24 10 79
closed Sunday   **L2**
Rest 25/30 € and a la carte 35/50 €
♦ Traditional ♦ Brasserie ♦
Gracious lounge-dining rooms dating from the late 19C, decorated with mirrors
and hat-boxes. Perhaps you will be seated at Chevalier's or Mistinguett's
favourite table.

XX **Gallopin** **AC** ⟷8 *VISA* **MC** **AE** **①**
😊
40 r. N.-D.-des-Victoires (2nd) – **M** *Bourse* – ℰ *01 42 36 45 38 – administration@*
brasseriegallopin.com – Fax 01 42 36 10 32 – www.brasseriegallopin.com
Rest 28/34 € b.i. and a la carte 30/60 €   **L3**
♦ Brasserie ♦ Retro ♦
Arletty, Raimu and the exaggerated Victorian decor have brought fame to this
brasserie situated opposite the Palais Brongniart. An attractive glass roof in the
back room.

FRANCE

Luna
🅰️ ✗ 𝘝𝘐𝘚𝘈 ⓦ 🅐🅔
69 r. Rocher (8th) – Ⓜ Villiers – ☎ 01 42 93 77 61 – mchoisnluna@noos.fr
– Fax 01 40 08 02 44
closed 30 July-22 August, Sunday and Bank Holidays   Plan II **H1**
Rest a la carte 65/100 €
Spec. Galette de langoustines aux jeunes poireaux. Cassolette de homard aux petits légumes. Le "vrai baba" de Zanzibar.
♦ Seafood ♦ Friendly ♦
Restrained Art Deco setting and fine cuisine based on fish delivered fresh daily from Atlantic coast waters. And the rum baba cakes for dessert will leave you agog!

Chez Pauline
🅰️ ⟷10/14 𝘝𝘐𝘚𝘈 ⓦ 🅐🅔 ⓞ
5 r. Villédo (1st) – Ⓜ Pyramides – ☎ 01 42 96 20 70 – chez.pauline@wanadoo.fr
– Fax 01 49 27 99 89 – www.chezpauline.fr
closed Saturday except dinner from September-June and Sunday   **K3**
Rest 27 € (lunch), 40/50 € and a la carte 41/75 €
♦ Traditional ♦ Bistro ♦
In a small, quiet street, a discreet restaurant, decorated in the style of an early 20C bistro. The first-floor dining room is more private. Traditional cuisine.

Au Pied de Cochon
🛋 🅰️ ⟷ 🍴 𝘝𝘐𝘚𝘈 ⓦ 🅐🅔 ⓞ
(24 hr service) 6 r. Coquillière (1st) – Ⓜ Châtelet-Les Halles – ☎ 01 40 13 77 00
– de.pied-de-cochon@blanc.net – Fax 01 40 13 77 09   **L3**
Rest a la carte 45/65 €
♦ Brasserie ♦ Retro ♦
Pig's trotters are the speciality of this renowned brasserie that has been open late into the night since it opened in 1946. Original murals and central lights with fruit designs.

Ambassade d'Auvergne
🅰️ ⟷10/40 𝘝𝘐𝘚𝘈 ⓦ 🅐🅔
22 r. du Grenier St-Lazare (3rd) – Ⓜ Rambuteau – ☎ 01 42 72 31 22
– info@ambassade-auvergne.com – Fax 01 42 78 85 47
– www.ambassade-auvergne.com   **M3**
Rest 28 € and a la carte 30/50 €
♦ Traditional ♦ Friendly ♦
True ambassadors of a province rich in flavours and traditions: Auvergne-style furniture and setting offering products, recipes and wines of the region.

Brasserie Flo
🛋 🅰️ ↳ 🍴(dinner) 𝘝𝘐𝘚𝘈 ⓦ 🅐🅔 ⓞ
7 cour Petites-Écuries (10th) – Ⓜ Château d'Eau – ☎ 01 47 70 13 59
– Fax 01 42 47 00 80 – www.floparis.com   **M2**
Rest 25 € b.i./35 € b.i. and a la carte 45/72 €
♦ Traditional ♦ Brasserie ♦
In the heart of the picturesque Petites-Écuries courtyard. The beautiful decor of dark wood panels, coloured glass and painted panels recalls the Alsace of the early 20C.

Terminus Nord
🅰️ ↳ 𝘝𝘐𝘚𝘈 ⓦ 🅐🅔
23 r. Dunkerque (10th) – Ⓜ Gare du Nord – ☎ 01 42 85 05 15
– Fax 01 40 16 13 98 – www.terminusnord.com   **M1**
Rest a la carte 25/57 €
♦ Traditional ♦ Brasserie ♦
High ceilings, frescoes, posters and sculptures are reflected in the mirrors of this brasserie that successfully mixes Art Deco and Art Nouveau. Cosmopolitan clientele.

Pinxo – Hôtel Renaissance Paris Vendôme
🅰️ 🍴 𝘝𝘐𝘚𝘈 ⓦ 🅐🅔
9 r. Alger (1st) – Ⓜ Tuileries – ☎ 01 40 20 72 00 – Fax 01 40 20 72 02
– www.pinxo.fr
closed August   **K3**
Rest a la carte 45/65 €
♦ Innovative ♦ Design ♦
A restaurant with minimalist furniture, black and white shades, an open kitchen and sober but stylish decoration, serving simple, tasty dishes à la Dutournier.

FRANCE

Chez Georges
1 r. Mail (2nd) – Ⓜ *Bourse –* ☎ *01 42 60 07 11*
closed August, Saturday lunch, Sunday and Bank Holidays
Rest a la carte 38/67 €
♦ Traditional ♦ Bistro ♦
The Sentier "institution". This typical Parisian bistro has conserved its original decor: bar, seats, stucco and mirrors. You bathe in the Paris of the 1900s.

VISA ⦿⦿ AE   L3

Aux Lyonnais
32 r. St-Marc (2nd) – Ⓜ *Richelieu Drouot –* ☎ *01 42 96 65 04*
– auxlyonnais@online.fr – Fax 01 42 97 42 95
closed 23 July-21 August, 24 December-1 January, Lunch Saturday,
Sunday and Monday
Rest (pre-book) 28 € and a la carte 40/60 €
♦ Lyonnaise cuisine ♦ Bistro ♦
This bistro founded in 1890 proposes delicious Lyonnais recipes, intelligently brought up to date. A deliciously retro setting: bar counter, bench seating, bevelled mirrors and mouldings.

VISA ⦿⦿   L2

La Petite Sirène de Copenhague
47 r. N.-D. de Lorette (9th) – Ⓜ *St-Georges –* ☎ *01 45 26 66 66*
closed August, 23 December-2 January, lunch Saturday, Sunday and Monday
Rest (pre-book) 28 € (lunch)/32 € and a la carte 46/58 €
♦ Scandinavian ♦ Friendly ♦
One dines here in sober elegance - whitewashed walls, subdued lighting in the Danish style accompany the classical recipes of Andersen's homeland. A warm, attentive welcome.

VISA ⦿⦿   K1

L'Oenothèque
20 r. St-Lazare (9th) – Ⓜ *Notre Dame de Lorette –* ☎ *01 48 78 08 76*
– loenotheque2@wanadoo.fr – Fax 01 40 16 10 27
closed 10 to 31 August, 23 December-2 January, Saturday and Sunday
Rest 20 € and a la carte 35/65 € 🏱
♦ Traditional ♦ Bistro ♦
Neighbourhood establishment combining a simple restaurant with a wine shop. Fine selection of wines to accompany the traditional dishes featured on the chalkboard.

AK VISA ⦿⦿ AE   L1

I Golosi
6 r. Grange Batelière (9th) – Ⓜ *Richelieu Drouot –* ☎ *01 48 24 18 63*
– i.golosi@wanadoo.fr – Fax 01 45 23 18 96
closed 7 to 20 August, dinner Saturday and Sunday
Rest a la carte 25/46 € 🏱
♦ Italian ♦ Minimalist ♦
On the 1st floor, Italian designer decor with a minimalism made up for by the joviality of the service. Café, shop and little spot for tasting things on the ground floor. Italian cuisine.

AK VISA ⦿⦿   L2

Pré Cadet
10 r. Saulnier (9th) – Ⓜ *Cadet –* ☎ *01 48 24 99 64 – Fax 01 47 70 55 96*
closed 1 to 8 May, 1 to 21 August, 24 December-1 January, lunch Saturday and
Sunday
Rest (number of covers limited, pre-book) 29 € and a la carte 40/54 €
♦ Traditional ♦ Friendly ♦
This restaurant-cum-gallery owes its success to its exhibitions – paintings or sculptures shown every month – and its old-fashioned dishes such as veal brawn. Very good coffee list.

AK VISA ⦿⦿ AE ⦿   L2

Pierrot
18 r. Etienne Marcel (2nd) – Ⓜ *Etienne Marcel –* ☎ *01 45 08 00 10*
closed 31 July-21 August, 25 December-2 January and Sunday
Rest a la carte 35/55 €
♦ Traditional ♦ Bistro ♦
Right in the lively Sentier district, this friendly bistro offers a discovery tour of all the savours and specialities of the Aveyron. Small summer terrace on the pavement.

AK VISA ⦿⦿ AE   M3

FRANCE

Mellifère   VISA ⓂⓈ AE

8 r. Monsigny (2nd) – Ⓜ *4 Septembre* – ℰ *01 42 61 21 71*
– Fax 01 42 61 31 71   **K3**
Rest 28 € (lunch)/32 €
♦ French traditional ♦ Bistro ♦
A colony of bees frequents this beehive that is as busy as the neighbouring
Théâtre des Bouffes Parisiens. Bistrot cuisine and Basque dishes.

L'Hermitage   AK VISA ⓂⓈ AE ①

5 bd Denain (10th) – Ⓜ *Gare du Nord* – ℰ *01 48 78 77 09*
– restaurantlhermitage@wanadoo.fr – Fax 01 42 85 17 27
closed 1 to 20 August, Monday, Saturday lunch and Bank Holidays   **M1**
Rest 26 €
♦ Traditional ♦ Friendly ♦
The name evokes the famous vineyard of the Rhône Valley, the region from where
the owners hail. Red and orange interior and tasty cuisine with a modern bent.

TOUR EIFFEL, INVALIDES   *Plan IV*

Mercure Tour Eiffel Suffren   🕊 ᴸᵃ AK 📞 🛁 30/100

20 r. Jean Rey (15th) – Ⓜ *Bir-Hakeim* – ℰ *01 45 78 50 00*   P VISA ⓂⓈ AE ①
– h2175@accor.com – Fax 01 45 78 91 42 – www.mercure.com   **N2**
405 rm – †150/300 € ††250/415 €, � 21 €
Rest a la carte 32/50 €
♦ Business ♦ Functional ♦
A complete, careful renovation has been carried out in this perfectly
soundproofed hotel, and the new decor has a "nature and garden" theme. Some
rooms have a view of the Eiffel Tower. A dining room opening directly onto a
pleasant terrace surrounded by trees and greenery.

Mercure Tour Eiffel without rest   ᴸᵃ & AK ⇔ 🛁 25/40

64 bd Grenelle (15th) – Ⓜ *Dupleix* – ℰ *01 45 78 90 90*   🚗 VISA ⓂⓈ AE ①
– hotel@mercuretoureiffel.com – Fax 01 45 78 95 55
– www.mercuretoureiffel.com   **N-O3**
76 rm – †190/300 € ††200/360 €, ⊝ 19 €
♦ Business ♦ Functional ♦
The main building houses rooms designed to the standards of the chain. Those
in the new wing are more comfortable and have many little extras.

Bourgogne et Montana without rest   AK VISA ⓂⓈ AE ①

3 r. Bourgogne (7th) – Ⓜ *Assemblée Nationale* – ℰ *01 45 51 20 22 – bmontana@*
bourgogne-montana.com – Fax 01 45 56 11 98 – bourgogne-montana.com
28 rm ⊝ – †150/260 € ††170/220 € – 4 suites   **Q1**
♦ Traditional ♦ Business ♦ Classic ♦
Elegance and beauty fill every room of this discreet 18C hotel. The top floor rooms
offer superb views over the "Palais-Bourbon" (French Parliament buildings).

Tourville without rest   AK ⇔ VISA ⓂⓈ AE

16 av. Tourville (7th) – Ⓜ *Ecole Militaire* – ℰ *01 47 05 62 62 – hotel@tourville.com*
– Fax 01 47 05 43 90 – hoteltourville.com   **P2**
30 rm – †150/330 € ††330 €, ⊝ 12 €
♦ Business ♦ Traditional ♦ Cosy ♦
Sharp colours, pleasant combination of modern and period furniture and
paintings create the decor of the elegant rooms. Lounge decorated by the David
Hicks studio. Excellent service.

Eiffel Park Hôtel without rest   AK ⇔ 🍽 VISA ⓂⓈ AE ①

17bis r. Amélie (7th) – Ⓜ *La Tour Maubourg* – ℰ *01 45 55 10 01 – reservation@*
eiffelpark.com – Fax 01 47 05 28 68 – www.eiffelpark.com   **P1**
36 rm – †125/185 € ††125/199 €, ⊝ 12 €
♦ Traditional ♦ Family ♦ Personalised ♦
The furniture, painted in old-fashioned style, and the Indian and Chinese objects,
create an exotic atmosphere in this hotel. Summer terrace and cosy lounge with
a fireplace. Attentive service.

FRANCE

Walt without rest   🖼 AC ↺ VISA 🌐 AE ①
37 av. La Motte Picquet (7th) – Ⓜ Ecole Militaire – ✆ 01 45 51 55 83
– lewalt@inwoodhotel.com – Fax 01 47 05 77 59
– www.inwoodhotel.com   **P2**
25 rm – ♦250 € ♦♦270/290 €, ☑ 12 €
♦ Business ♦ Luxury ♦ Modern ♦
This new hotel near the École Militaire offers original rooms with an imposing
Renaissance-style portrait at the head of the bed and modern furniture.

Les Jardins d'Eiffel without rest   AC ↺ ⌀ 🕻 ➰ VISA 🌐 AE ①
8 r. Amélie (7th) – Ⓜ La Tour Maubourg – ✆ 01 47 05 46 21
– paris@hoteljardinseiffel.com – Fax 01 45 55 28 08
– www.hoteljardineiffel.com   **P1**
81 rm – ♦140/200 € ♦♦180/200 €, ☑ 13,50 €
♦ Family ♦ Traditional ♦ Functional ♦
The two buildings of the hotel, in a quiet street, are linked by a patio where
breakfast is served in summer. Gaily-coloured rooms; some with a balcony.

Relais Bosquet without rest   AC VISA 🌐 AE ①
19 r. Champ-de-Mars (7th) – Ⓜ Ecole Militaire – ✆ 01 47 05 25 45
– hotel@relaisbosquet.com – Fax 01 45 55 08 24
– www.hotelrelaisbosquet.com   **P2**
40 rm – ♦106/130 € ♦♦122/170 €, ☑ 11 €
♦ Traditional ♦ Business ♦ Classic ♦
This discreet hotel has a prettily-furnished Directoire-style interior. Renovated
rooms, all decorated with the same attention to detail, with thoughtful little
touches.

Tour Eiffel Invalides without rest   AC ↺ VISA 🌐 AE ①
35 bd La Tour Maubourg (7th) – Ⓜ La Tour Maubourg – ✆ 01 45 56 10 78
– invalides@my-paris-hotel.com – Fax 01 47 05 65 08
– www.my-paris-hotel.com   **P1**
30 rm – ♦89/209 € ♦♦99/309 €, ☑ 13 €
♦ Traditional ♦ Family ♦ Cosy ♦
Predominant red brick and white decor, Louis XVI-style furniture, and
reproductions of Impressionist paintings characterise the rooms of this 19C
building.

Muguet without rest   AC ↺ ⌀ 🕻 VISA 🌐
11 r. Chevert (7th) – Ⓜ Ecole Militaire – ✆ 01 47 05 05 93
– muguet@wanadoo.fr – Fax 01 45 50 25 37
– www.hotelmuguet.com   **P2**
43 rm – ♦95 € ♦♦110/165 €, ☑ 9 €
♦ Traditional ♦ Family ♦ Functional ♦
Hotel nestling in a quiet road. Modern hall and rooms adorned with Louis
Philippe-style furniture (seven of which offer views of the Eiffel tower or
Invalides).

Londres Eiffel without rest   AC 🕻 VISA 🌐 AE ①
1 r. Augereau (7th) – Ⓜ Ecole Militaire – ✆ 01 45 51 63 02
– info@londres-eiffel.com – Fax 01 47 05 28 96
– www.londres-eiffel.com   **O2**
30 rm – ♦99/120 € ♦♦110/175 €, ☑ 12 €
♦ Traditional ♦ Family ♦ Cosy ♦
Cosy hotel done up in warm colours near the Champ-de-Mars' leafy paths. The
second building, reached through a small courtyard, has quieter rooms.

Du Cadran without rest   AC ↺ ⌀ 🕻 VISA 🌐 AE ①
10 r. Champ-de-Mars (7th) – Ⓜ Ecole Militaire – ✆ 01 40 62 67 00
– info@cadranhotel.com – Fax 01 40 62 67 13 – www.hotelducadran.com   **P2**
42 rm – ♦120/165 € ♦♦120/178 €, ☑ 10 €
♦ Traditional ♦ Business ♦ Modern ♦
A stone's throw from the lively rue Cler market. The modern, recently refurbished
rooms are enhanced by a number of Louis XVI-style touches. Fine 17C fireplace
in the lounge-cum-library.

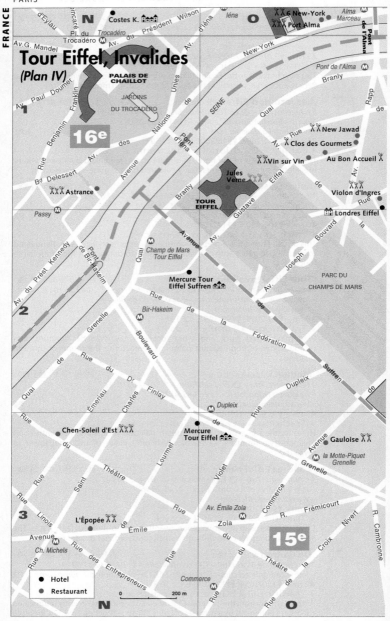

Tour Eiffel, Invalides
(Plan IV)

16e

15e

Costes K.
N
Pl. du Trocadéro
Av. du Président Wilson
Iéna
O
6 New-York
Port Alma
Alma Marceau
Pont de l'Alma

PALAIS DE CHAILLOT

JARDINS DU TROCADÉRO

Pont de l'Alma
Branly

New Jawad
Clos des Gourmets
Vin sur Vin
Au Bon Accueil
Violon d'Ingres
Londres Eiffel

TOUR EIFFEL

Jules Verne

Astrance

Passy

Mercure Tour Eiffel Suffren

Champ de Mars Tour Eiffel

PARC DU CHAMPS DE MARS

Bir-Hakeim

Fédération

Dupleix

Chen-Soleil d'Est

Mercure Tour Eiffel

Dupleix

Gauloise
la Motte-Piquet Grenelle

L'Épopée

Av. Émile Zola

| ● | Hotel |
| ● | Restaurant |

0   200 m

N   O

222

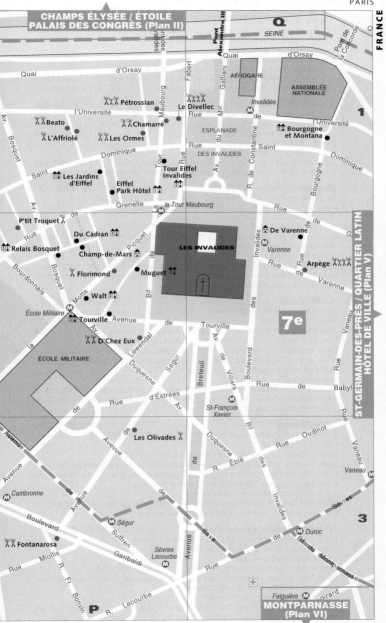

FRANCE

De Varenne without rest   AC ✗ ☎ VISA MO AE

44 r. Bourgogne (7th) – Ⓜ Varenne – ℰ 01 45 51 45 55
– info@hoteldevarenne.com – Fax 01 45 51 86 63
– www.hoteldevarenne.com   **Q2**
24 rm – ♦130/150 € ♦♦150/170 €, ☲ 10 €
♦ Traditional ♦ Family ♦ Functional ♦
A fully renovated, rather quiet hotel adorned with French Empire and Louis XVI-style furniture. In summer, breakfast is served in a small, verdant courtyard.

Champ-de-Mars without rest   ✗ VISA MO

7 r. Champ-de-Mars (7th) – Ⓜ Ecole Militaire – ℰ 01 45 51 52 30
– reservation@hotelduchampdemars.com – Fax 01 45 51 64 36
– www.hotelduchampdemars.com   **P2**
25 rm – ♦78 € ♦♦84/88 €, ☲ 7 €
♦ Family ♦ Traditional ♦ Cosy ♦
Small hotel with an English atmosphere, between the Champ-de-Mars and Invalides. Dark green façade, cosy rooms and neat Liberty-style decor.

Arpège (Passard)   AC ⇔8/14 VISA MO AE ⓪

84 r. Varenne (7th) – Ⓜ Varenne – ℰ 01 45 51 47 33 – arpege.passard@wanadoo.fr – Fax 01 44 18 98 39 – www.alain-passard.com
closed Saturday and Sunday   **Q2**
Rest 140 € (lunch)/340 € (dinner) and a la carte 168/306 €
Spec. Légumes du potager. Aiguillettes de homard des îles Chausey au vin jaune. Millefeuille au miel du jardin.
♦ Innovative ♦ Formal ♦
Choose the elegant modern dining room, with rare wood and glass decorations by Lalique, rather than the basement. Savour dazzling vegetable garden-based cuisine by a master chef and poet of the land.

Le Divellec   AC ✗ ⌛ VISA MO AE ⓪

107 r. Université (7th) – Ⓜ Invalides – ℰ 01 45 51 91 96 – ledivellec@noos.fr
– Fax 01 45 51 31 75
closed August, 24 December-2 January, Saturday and Sunday   **P-Q1**
Rest 55 € (lunch)/70 € (lunch) and a la carte 120/195 €
Spec. Ecrevisses en millefeuille, vinaigrette de carapace. Crème moussante aux fèves et pois, brunoise de Saint-Jacques. Blanc épais de cabillaud aux bâtons dorés de seiche, jus noir au beurre salé.
♦ Seafood ♦ Formal ♦
A chic nautical setting with waves on frosted glass, a lobster tank, and a blue and white colour scheme. Fine seafood cuisine using only the freshest produce directly from the Atlantic.

Jules Verne   ≤ Paris, AC ✗ VISA MO AE ⓪

Eiffel Tower : 2nd platform, lift in south leg (7th) – ℰ 01 45 55 61 44
– Fax 01 47 05 29 41   **O1**
Rest 57 € (weekday lunch)/128 € and a la carte 110/165 €
Spec. Saint-Jacques au jus de volaille, brunoise de seiche et bigorneaux foie gras poêlé (October-March). Dos de bar de ligne au salpicon d'huîtres. Poitrine de canard sauvage aux Saint-Jacques (October-February).
♦ Contemporary ♦ Formal ♦
The Slavik decor is easily upstaged by the Ville lumière show. For the trip to be truly memorable, reserve a table near the windows.

Violon d'Ingres (Constant)   AC VISA MO AE ⓪

135 r. St-Dominique (7th) – Ⓜ Ecole Militaire – ℰ 01 45 55 15 05
– violondingres@wanadoo.fr – Fax 01 45 55 48 42
– www.leviolondingres.com   **O1**
Rest 50 € b.i. (weekday lunch), 80/110 € and a la carte 80/110 €
Spec. Foie gras de canard poêlé au pain d'épice. Suprême de bar croustillant aux amandes. Tatin de pied de porc caramélisée.
♦ Contemporary ♦ Formal ♦
Wood-furnishings enliven the atmosphere of this dining room which is an elegant meeting point for gourmets attracted by the very individual cuisine of the master chef.

FRANCE

Astrance (Barbot)

4 r. Beethoven (16th) ⊠ 75016 – **Ⓜ** Passy
– ℰ 01 40 50 84 40
*closed 28 July-28 August, 27 October-7 November, 26 February-4 March,
Saturday, Sunday and Monday*   **N1**
Rest (number of covers limited, pre-book) 70 € (lunch), 150/250 € b.i.
and a la carte 105/150 €
Spec. Foie gras mariné au verjus, galette de champignons de Paris. Langoustines
dorée, coulis de peau de tomate, jus de roquette (Summer). Pigeon cuit au
sautoir, pâte de chocolat fumé.
◆ Contemporary ◆ Fashionable ◆
The Astrance (from the Latin Aster, a star-like flower) boasts delicious,
inventive cuisine, a surprise evening menu, choice wines and attractive modern
decor.

Pétrossian

144 r. Université (7th) – **Ⓜ** Invalides – ℰ 01 44 11 32 32
– Fax 01 44 11 32 35   **P1**
Rest 35 € (weekday lunch)/45 € and a la carte 70/130 €
◆ Seafood ◆ Formal ◆
The Petrossians have treated Parisians to caviar from the Caspian sea since 1920.
On the upper floor of the shop, elegant restaurant room and inventive
cuisine.

Chen-Soleil d'Est

15 r. Théâtre (15th) – **Ⓜ** Charles Michels – ℰ 01 45 79 34 34
– Fax 01 45 79 07 53   **N3**
closed August and Sunday
Rest 40 € (weekday lunch)/75 € and a la carte 60/150 €
Spec. Fleurs de courgettes aux corps de tourteaux. Pigeonneau aux cinq
parfums. Tan Yuang aux fleurs de laurier.
◆ Chinese ◆ Exotic ◆
Delve beneath the buildings overlooking the Seine to discover an authentic little
corner of Asia; steamed dishes and wok cuisine. Furnishings and wood panels
imported from China.

Chamarré

13 bd La Tour Maubourg (7th) – **Ⓜ** Invalides
– ℰ 01 47 05 50 18 – chantallaval @ wanadoo.fr
– Fax 01 47 05 91 21
closed Saturday lunch, Sunday and Monday   **P1**
Rest 28 € (weekday lunch), 60/80 €
Spec. Carpaccio de haut bar et marlin fumé. Cochon de lait. Savarin punché au
rhum.
◆ French-Mauritian cuisine ◆ Friendly ◆
Elegantly modern decor (exotic wood panelling), friendly environment and a
delightful cuisine combining French and Mauritian specialities (one of the chefs
is from the island).

Les Ormes (Molé)

22 r. Surcouf (7th) – **Ⓜ** La Tour Maubourg – ℰ 01 45 51 46 93
– molestephane @ noos.fr – Fax 01 45 50 30 11
*closed 30 July-23 August, 7 to 15 January,
Sunday and Monday*   **P1**
Rest 36 € (weekday lunch)/44 € and a la carte 60/75 €
Spec. Filet de Saint-Pierre à la pistache. Jarret de veau braisé à la cuiller. Lièvre à
la royale (mid October-mid December).
◆ Contemporary ◆ Cosy ◆
Goodbye Bellecour, hello Les Ormes! Stéphane Molé has left the 16th
district to take over this restaurant near Invalides. Elegant setting. Traditional
cuisine.

XX ❀ **Vin sur Vin**   AC VISA ◐◉
20 r. de Monttessuy (7th) – ◍ *Pont de l'Alma –* ☏ *01 47 05 14 20*
closed 21 to 29 May, August, 23 December-6 January, Monday except dinner hom
mid September-late March, Saturday lunch and Sunday   **O1**
Rest (number of covers limited, pre-book) a la carte 65/100 € 🍷
Spec. Les légumes. Agneau de Lozère. Millefeuille chocolat.
♦ Traditional ♦ Cosy ♦
Warm welcome, elegant decor, delicious traditional dishes and extensive wine
list (600 vintages) – full marks for this restaurant close to the Eiffel Tower!

XX **New Jawad**   AC 🍴 VISA ◐◉ AE ◑
12 av. Rapp (7th) – ◍ *Ecole Militaire –* ☏ *01 47 05 91 37*
– Fax 01 45 50 31 27   **O1**
Rest 16/40 € and a la carte 35/46 €
♦ Indian-Pakistani cuisine ♦ Friendly ♦
Pakistani and Indian specialities, attentive service and an elegant
setting characterise this restaurant in the immediate vicinity of the Pont de
l'Alma.

XX **Beato**   AC VISA ◐◉ AE
8 r. Malar (7th) – ◍ *Invalides –* ☏ *01 47 05 94 27 – beato.rest @ wanadoo.fr*
– Fax 01 45 55 64 41
closed 15 July-15 August, 24 December-1 January, Saturday lunch and
Sunday   **P1**
Rest 23 € (weekday lunch) and a la carte 35/60 €
♦ Italian ♦ Friendly ♦
This chic restaurant has a bourgeois Italian decor with frescoes, Pompeii
columns and neo-classical seats. Dishes from Milan, Rome and other Italian
regions.

XX **D'Chez Eux**   AC VISA ◐◉ AE ◑
2 av. Lowendal (7th) – ◍ *Ecole Militaire –* ☏ *01 47 05 52 55*
– contact @ chezeux.com – Fax 01 45 55 60 74 – www.chezeux.com
closed 29 July-27 August and Sunday   **P2**
Rest a la carte 55/110 €
♦ South-West of France specialities ♦ Bistro ♦
For 40 years customers have been seduced by this restaurant where hearty
dishes from Auvergne and southwest France are served in a "provincial auberge"
atmosphere by waiters in smocks.

XX **Gauloise**   🍴 ✿16 VISA ◐◉ AE
59 av. La Motte-Piquet (15th) – ◍ *La Motte Picquet Grenelle –* ☏ *01 47 34 11 64*
– Fax 01 40 61 09 70   **O3**
Rest a la carte 30/57 €
♦ Traditional ♦ Bistro ♦
This 1900 brasserie must have seen many celebrities pass through, judging from
the signed photos on the walls. A pleasant, kerbside terrace.

XX **Fontanarosa**   🍴 AC VISA ◐◉
28 bd Garibaldi (15th) – ◍ *Cambronne –* ☏ *01 45 66 97 84*
– Fax 01 47 83 96 30   **P3**
Rest 30 € and a la carte 38/72 € 🍷
♦ Italian ♦ Family ♦
This authentic trattoria takes you far away from the bustle of Paris. Delightful
patio and terrace and a good choice of wine and dishes from Sardinia.

XX **L'Épopée**   VISA ◐◉ AE ◑
89 av. É. Zola (15th) – ◍ *Charles Michels –* ☏ *01 45 77 71 37*
– Fax 01 45 77 71 37
closed 24 July-23 August, lunch Saturday and Sunday   **N3**
Rest 32/41 € 🍷
♦ Traditional ♦ Bistro ♦
Despite the grandeur its name (The Epic) might suggest, this is a small, convivial
restaurant. Regulars keep coming back for its excellent wine list and traditional
cuisine.

FRANCE

Au Bon Accueil

14 r. Monttessuy (7th) – Ⓜ *Pont de l'Alma*
– 𝄢 *01 47 05 46 11*
closed Saturday and Sunday   O1
Rest 27 € (lunch)/31 € and a la carte 21/52 €
♦ Contemporary ♦ Friendly ♦
Beneath the shadow of the Eiffel Tower, this modern restaurant and small adjacent room offer delicious up-to-date dishes pleasantly reflecting the changing seasons.

Les Olivades

41 av. Ségur (7th) – Ⓜ *Ségur –* 𝄢 *01 47 83 70 09*
– Fax 01 42 73 04 75
closed August, lunch Saturday, lunch Monday and Sunday   P3
Rest 32 € (lunch), 40/60 €
♦ Mediterranean ♦ Friendly ♦
A restaurant where olive oil flows freely, with appetising dishes based on Provençal cuisine. Simple, pleasant decor in pastel shades, with modern paintings and rustic furniture.

Clos des Gourmets

16 av. Rapp (7th) – Ⓜ *Alma Marceau –* 𝄢 *01 45 51 75 61*
– Fax 01 47 05 74 20
closed 10 to 25 August, Sunday and Monday   O1
Rest 29 € (weekday lunch)/33 €
♦ Contemporary ♦ Friendly ♦
Many regulars love this discreet restaurant decorated in warm colours. The tempting menu varies according to the availability of market produce.

Florimond

19 av. La Motte-Picquet (7th) – Ⓜ *Ecole Militaire –* 𝄢 *01 45 55 40 38*
– Fax 01 45 55 40 38
closed 1 to 8 May, 29 July-20 August, 25 December-7 January,
lunch Saturday and Sunday   P2
Rest 20 € (weekday lunch)/35 € and a la carte 48/53 €
♦ Traditional ♦ Bistro ♦
Sun-drenched colours and wood panelling decorate this tiny restaurant (for non-smokers) named after Monet's gardener in Giverny. The cuisine is redolent of market freshness.

P'tit Troquet

28 r. l'Exposition (7th) – Ⓜ *Ecole Militaire –* 𝄢 *01 47 05 80 39*
– Fax 01 47 05 80 39
closed 1 to 28 August, lunch Saturday, lunch Monday and Sunday P2
Rest (number of covers limited, pre-book) 27 € (lunch)/30 €
♦ Traditional ♦ Retro ♦
This bistro is certainly as small as its name suggests! But it has so much going for it, with its charming setting enlivened by old advertisements, its friendly atmosphere and its tasty market cuisine. No-smoking restaurant.

L'Affriolé

17 r. Malar (7th) – Ⓜ *Invalides –* 𝄢 *01 44 18 31 33*
– Fax 01 44 18 91 12
closed August, 24 December-3 January, Saturday and Sunday   P1
Rest 29 € (lunch), 33/40 €
♦ Contemporary ♦ Bistro ♦
This bistro's chef prepares seasonal dishes with fresh market produce, which are announced as daily specials on the blackboard or in a set menu that changes every month.

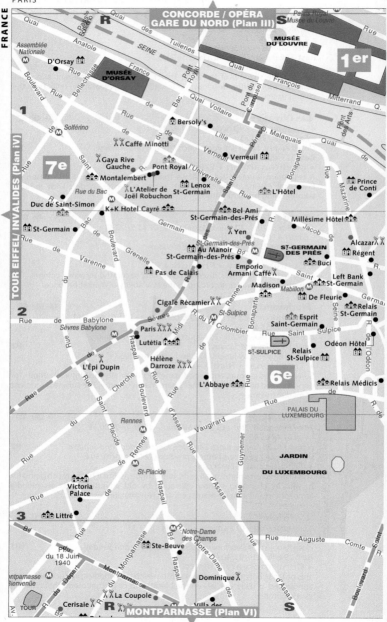

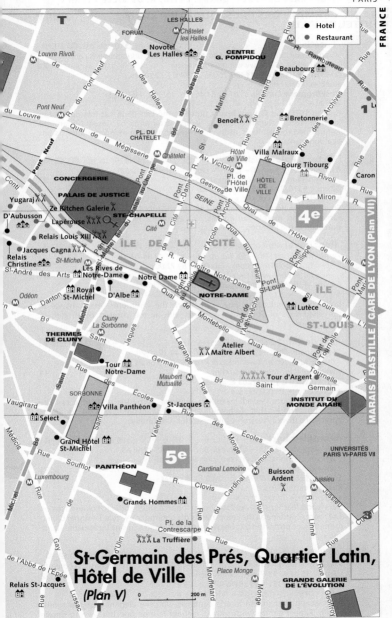

St-Germain des Prés, Quartier Latin,
Hôtel de Ville
(Plan V)

SAINT-GERMAIN DES PRES, QUARTIER LATIN, *Plan V*
HOTEL DE VILLE

FRANCE

Lutétia
45 bd Raspail (6th) – ℰ 01 49 54 46 46 – lutetia-paris @ lutetia-paris.com
– Fax 01 49 54 46 00 – www.lutetia-paris.com **R2**
219 rm – ♦400/750 € ♦♦400/750 €, ☲ 24 € – 12 suites
Rest see *Paris* below
Rest *Brasserie Lutétia*, ℰ 01 49 54 46 76 – 36/39 €
♦ Palace ♦ Historic ♦
Built in 1910, this famous luxury hotel on the Left Bank has lost none of its
sparkle: "retro" elegance, Lalique lamps, sculptures by César, Arman, etc.
Refurbished rooms. Paris' most chic come to the Brasserie Lutétia for its fine
seafood menu.

Victoria Palace without rest
6 r. Blaise-Desgoffe (6th) – Ⓜ St-Placide – ℰ 01 45 49 70 00
– info @ victoriapalace.com – Fax 01 45 49 23 75 – www.victoriapalace.com **R3**
62 rm – ♦310/372 € ♦♦310/595 €, ☲ 18 €
♦ Luxury ♦ Historic ♦
Small luxury hotel with undeniable charm: toiles de Jouy, Louis XVI-style
furniture and marble bathrooms in the rooms. Paintings, red velvet and
porcelain in the lounges.

Pont Royal without rest
7 r. Montalembert (7th) – Ⓜ Rue du Bac – ℰ 01 42 84 70 00
– hpr @ hotel-pont-royal.com – Fax 01 42 84 71 00
– www.hotel-pont-royal.com **R1**
64 rm – ♦380/430 € ♦♦380/430 €, ☲ 26 € – 11 suites
♦ Luxury ♦ Stylish ♦
Bold colours and mahogany walls adorn the bedrooms: the romance of
the salad days of St-Germain-des-Prés with all the comfort of an elegant
"literary hotel"!

Duc de Saint-Simon without rest
14 r. St-Simon (7th) – Ⓜ Rue du Bac – ℰ 01 44 39 20 20
– duc.de.saint.simon @ wanadoo.fr – Fax 01 45 48 68 25
– www.hotelducdesaintsimon.com **R1**
29 rm – ♦220 € ♦♦245/265 €, ☲ 15 € – 5 suites
♦ Luxury ♦ Business ♦ Stylish ♦
Cheerful colours, wood panelling, antique furniture and objects. The
atmosphere here is that of a beautiful house of olden times, with the additional
appeal of a friendly welcome and peaceful surroundings.

Montalembert
3 r. Montalembert (7th) – Ⓜ Rue du Bac – ℰ 01 45 49 68 68
– welcome @ montalembert.com – Fax 01 45 49 69 49
– www.montalembert.com **R1**
56 rm – ♦260 € ♦♦260/380 €, ☲ 20 € – 8 suites
Rest a la carte 35/65 €
♦ Luxury ♦ Modern ♦
Dark wood, leather, glass, and steel, with tobacco, plum and lilac-coloured decor.
The rooms combine all the components of contemporary style. Designer dining
room, terrace protected by a boxwood partition, and a cuisine for appetites large
and small!

K+K Hotel Cayré without rest
4 bd Raspail (7th) – Ⓜ Rue du Bac – ℰ 01 45 44 38 88 – reservations @ kkhotels.fr
– Fax 01 45 44 98 13 – www.kkhotels.com **R1-2**
125 rm – ♦306/351 € ♦♦351/630 €, ☲ 23 €
♦ Luxury ♦ Business ♦ Modern ♦
The discreet Haussmann façade contrasts with the elegant designer rooms
within. Fitness centre (with sauna), elegant lounge and bar serving simple
bistro-style dishes.

FRANCE

D'Aubusson without rest   🖐 🕭 🛠 📶 15/35 🖵
33 r. Dauphine (6th) – 🅜 Odéon – 🕽 01 43 29 43 43   🅿 VISA ❿ AE ①
– reservations@hoteldaubusson.com – Fax 01 43 29 12 62
– www.hoteldaubusson.com   **T2**
68 rm – ♦280/425 € ♦♦280/425 €, � 23 €
◆ Luxury ◆ Traditional ◆ Historic ◆
A 17C town house with character, offering elegant rooms with Versailles parquet, Aubusson tapestries and jazz evenings at the Café Laurent on weekends.

Relais Christine without rest 🐾   ⺄ 🕭 🛠 20 🖵 VISA ❿ AE ①
3 r. Christine (6th) – 🅜 St-Michel – 🕽 01 40 51 60 80 – contact@
relais-christine.com – Fax 01 40 51 60 81 – www.relais-christine.com   **T2**
35 rm – ♦355 € ♦♦405/750 €, ⊆ 25 €
◆ Luxury ◆ Traditional ◆ Historic ◆
Beautiful private hotel built on the site of a 13C convent (the breakfast room occupies the former arched kitchen). Pretty, well-kept rooms with a personal touch.

Bel Ami St-Germain-des-Prés without rest   ⺄ 🕭 🛠 🛠
7 r. St-Benoît (6th) – 🅜 St-Germain des Prés   📶 10/30 VISA ❿ AE ①
– 🕽 01 42 61 53 53 – contact@hotel-bel-ami.com – Fax 01 49 27 09 33
– www.hotel-bel-ami.com   **S2**
115 rm – ♦270/330 € ♦♦270/520 €, ⊆ 22 €
◆ Business ◆ Luxury ◆ Design ◆
Attractive 19C building near Café Flore and Les Deux Magots. A distinctly contemporary setting and "zen" decor with high-tech facilities: a designer look and very trendy.

Buci without rest   🖐 🕭 🛠 🕭 VISA ❿ AE ①
22 r. Buci (6th) – 🅜 Mabillon – 🕽 01 55 42 74 74 – hotelbuci@wanadoo.fr
– Fax 01 55 42 74 44 – www.bucihotel.com   **S2**
21 rm – ♦195/250 € ♦♦215/335 €, ⊆ 22 € – 3 suites
◆ Luxury ◆ Personalised ◆
The hotel overlooks the busy market held in this picturesque street. Canopies on the beds, English period furniture and refurbished, perfectly soundproofed rooms. Piano-bar.

L'Abbaye without rest 🐾   🕭 🛠 🕭 VISA ❿ AE
10 r. Cassette (6th) – 🅜 St-Sulpice – 🕽 01 45 44 38 11 – hotel.abbaye@
wanadoo.fr – Fax 01 45 48 07 86 – www.hotel-abbaye.com   **S2**
40 rm ⊆ – ♦199/214 € ♦♦296/458 € – 4 suites
◆ Luxury ◆ Traditional ◆ Stylish ◆
Hotel in a former 18C convent combining old-world charm with modern comfort. Pleasant veranda, duplex apartment with a terrace, and stylish rooms. Some overlook a delightful patio.

Littré without rest   🕭 🛠 🛠 📶 8/20 🖵 VISA ❿ AE ①
9 r. Littré (6th) – 🅜 Montparnasse Bienvenüe – 🕽 01 53 63 07 07
– hotellittre@hotellittreparis.com – Fax 01 45 44 88 13
– www.hotel-liettre-paris.com   **R3**
79 rm – ♦255/360 € ♦♦255/360 €, ⊆ 17 € – 11 suites
◆ Luxury ◆ Business ◆ Stylish ◆
Classic building, halfway between Saint-Germain-des-Prés and Montparnasse, whose rather spacious rooms have been elegantly furnished. Comfortable English bar.

L'Hôtel   ⺄ 🕭 🛠 VISA ❿ AE ①
13 r. Beaux Arts (6th) – 🅜 St-Germain des Prés – 🕽 01 44 41 99 00
– reservation@l-hotel.com – Fax 01 43 25 64 81 – www.l-hotel.com   **S1**
16 rm – ♦280/345 € ♦♦370/640 €, ⊆ 17 € – 4 suites – **Rest Le Bélier**,
🕽 01 44 41 99 01 (closed August, Sunday and Monday) a la carte 50/70 €
◆ Luxury ◆ Personalised ◆
Lofty atrium and extravagant decor by Garcia (Baroque, French Empire and Oriental). L'Hôtel is unique, combining nostalgia with pleasure. Oscar Wilde passed away here. Green and gold hues with old lanterns and glasswork make up the sumptuous setting of this restaurant.

FRANCE

Esprit Saint-Germain without rest   🕍 🕭 AC ⇘ VISA 🐮 AE ①
22 r. St-Sulpice (6th) – Ⓜ Mabillon – ℰ 01 53 10 55 55
– contact@espritsaintgermain.com – Fax 01 53 10 55 56
– www.espritsaintgermain.com   **S2**
31 rm – 🛏350 € 🛏🛏350/550 €, ⊡ 26 € – 1 suite
♦ Luxury ♦ Design ♦
Elegant and contemporary rooms pleasantly combining red, chocolate and beige colours with modern paintings and furniture; bathrooms with slate walls.

Relais St-Germain without rest   AC ⇘ VISA 🐮 AE ①
9 carrefour de l'Odéon (6th) – Ⓜ Odéon – ℰ 01 43 29 12 05
– hotelrsg@wanadoo.fr – Fax 01 46 33 45 30   **S2**
22 rm ⊡ – 🛏210 € 🛏🛏275/420 €
♦ Luxury ♦ Traditional ♦ Historic ♦
Elegant hotel comprising three 17C buildings. Polished beams, shimmering fabrics and antique furniture.

Madison without rest   ⩽ AC VISA 🐮 AE ①
143 bd St-Germain (6th) – Ⓜ St-Germain des Prés – ℰ 01 40 51 60 00
– resa@hotel-madison.com – Fax 01 40 51 60 01   **S2**
54 rm – 🛏158/213 € 🛏🛏215/390 €, ⊡ 15 €
♦ Luxury ♦ Family ♦ Cosy ♦
This hotel was popular with Albert Camus. Some of its elegant rooms offer views of the church of St-Germain-des Prés. Attractive Louis Philippe lounge.

Relais Médicis without rest   AC ⅍ VISA 🐮 AE ①
23 r. Racine (6th) – Ⓜ Odéon – ℰ 01 43 26 00 60
– reservation@relaismedicis.com – Fax 01 40 46 83 39   **S2**
16 rm ⊡ – 🛏138/168 € 🛏🛏168/245 €
♦ Traditional ♦ Family ♦ Stylish ♦
A hint of Provence enhances the rooms of this hotel near the Odeon theatre; those overlooking the patio are quieter. Interesting antique furniture.

Villa Panthéon without rest   🕭 AC ⇘ VISA 🐮 AE ①
41 r. Ecoles (5th) – Ⓜ Maubert Mutualité – ℰ 01 53 10 95 95
– pantheon@leshotelsdeparis.com – Fax 01 53 10 95 96
– www.villa-pantheon.com   **T2**
59 rm – 🛏280/310 € 🛏🛏280/710 €, ⊡ 18 €
♦ Traditional ♦ Townhouse ♦ Stylish ♦
Parquet, colourful hangings, exotic wood furniture and Liberty-style lights. The reception, rooms and bar (good selection of whiskies) have a British feel.

Left Bank St-Germain without rest   🕭 AC ⇘ 📞 VISA 🐮 AE ①
9 r. Ancienne Comédie (6th) – Ⓜ Odéon – ℰ 01 43 54 01 70
– lb@paris-hotels-charm.com – Fax 01 43 26 17 14
– www.paris-hotels-charm.com   **S2**
31 rm ⊡ – 🛏165/220 € 🛏🛏185/353 €
♦ Traditional ♦ Family ♦ Classic ♦
Damask, Liberty print, Louis XIII period furniture and half-timbered walls create the decor in this 17C building. Some rooms offer views over Notre-Dame.

Millésime Hôtel without rest ⤳   AC VISA 🐮 AE ①
15 r. Jacob (6th) – Ⓜ St-Germain des Prés – ℰ 01 44 07 97 97
– reservation@millesimehotel.com – Fax 01 46 34 55 97   **S2**
22 rm – 🛏185/155 € 🛏🛏205 €, ⊡ 16 €
♦ Traditional ♦ Family ♦ Cosy ♦
Colours of the South and selected furniture and fabrics create a warm atmosphere in the splendid rooms of this recently refurbished hotel. Superb 17C staircase.

FRANCE

Novotel Les Halles 🏠 👤 📺 ↩rm ♨15/80 ⚛ 𝑽𝑰𝑺𝑨 ⓜⓔ 𝔸𝔼 ⓜ
8 pl. M.-de-Navarre (1st) – ⓜ *Châtelet* – 𝒞 *01 42 21 31 31 – h0785@accor.com*
– Fax 01 40 26 05 79 – www.novotelparisleshalles.com **T1**
271 rm – 🛇159/233 € 🛇🛇159/288 €, ⚏ 16 € – 14 suites
Rest a la carte 24/31 €
♦ Chain hotel ♦ Business ♦ Functional ♦
The hotel near the Forum des Halles has good seminar facilities. The renovated rooms are attractive and contemporary and some look out onto the church of St-Eustache. When the restaurant is closed you can eat in the bar (traditional cuisine and grilled meat.

Bourg Tibourg without rest 👤 📺 ℀ 📞 𝑽𝑰𝑺𝑨 ⓜⓔ 𝔸𝔼 ⓜ
19 r. Bourg Tibourg (4th) – ⓜ *Hôtel de Ville* – 𝒞 *01 42 78 47 39 – hotel@bourgtibourg.com – Fax 01 40 29 07 00 – www.hotelbourgtibourg.com* **U1**
30 rm – 🛇160/220 € 🛇🛇220/350 €, ⚏ 14 €
♦ Family ♦ Luxury ♦ Personalised ♦
This charming hotel has pleasant, newly-decorated, personalised rooms in different styles: neo-Gothic, Baroque or oriental. A small gem set in the heart of the Marais quarter.

Les Rives de Notre-Dame without rest ≤ 📺 📞 𝑽𝑰𝑺𝑨 ⓜⓔ 𝔸𝔼 ⓜ
15 quai St-Michel (5th) – ⓜ *St-Michel* – 𝒞 *01 43 54 81 16*
– hotel@rivesdenotredame.com – Fax 01 43 26 27 09
– www.rivesdenotredame.com **T2**
10 rm – 🛇130/243 € 🛇🛇130/500 €, ⚏ 14 €
♦ Traditional ♦ Family ♦ Classic ♦
Splendidly preserved 16C residence with spacious Provençal-style rooms all overlooking the Seine and Notre-Dame. Penthouse.

Royal St-Michel without rest 📺 ↩ 𝑽𝑰𝑺𝑨 ⓜⓔ 𝔸𝔼 ⓜ
3 bd St-Michel (5th) – ⓜ *St-Michel* – 𝒞 *01 44 07 06 06*
– hotelroyalstmichel@wanadoo.fr – Fax 01 44 07 36 25
– www.hotelroyalsaintmichel.com **T2**
39 rm – 🛇170/225 € 🛇🛇180/290 €, ⚏ 18 €
♦ Family ♦ Traditional ♦ Modern ♦
On the Boulevard St Michel, opposite the fountain of the same name, take in the Latin quarter atmosphere around this hotel, which houses modern and renovated rooms.

Au Manoir St-Germain-des-Prés without rest 📺 ↩
153 bd St-Germain (6th) – ⓜ *St-Germain des Prés* 📞 𝑽𝑰𝑺𝑨 ⓜⓔ 𝔸𝔼 ⓜ
– 𝒞 01 42 22 21 65 – msg@paris-hotels-charm.com – Fax 01 45 48 22 25
– www.paris-hotels-charm.com **S2**
33 rm ⚏ – 🛇150/180 € 🛇🛇183/260 €
♦ Traditional ♦ Stylish ♦
Elegant hotel, opposite the Flore and Deux Magots (famous St-Germain-des-Prés cafés), with period furniture, murals, wood panelling and Liberty prints.

Grands Hommes without rest ≤ 📺 ♨20 𝑽𝑰𝑺𝑨 ⓜⓔ 𝔸𝔼 ⓜ
17 pl. Panthéon (5th) – ⓜ *Luxembourg* – 𝒞 *01 46 34 19 60*
– reservation@hoteldesgrandshommes.com – Fax 01 43 26 67 32
– www.hoteldesgrandshommes.com **T3**
31 rm – 🛇180/235 € 🛇🛇210/255 €, ⚏ 12 €
♦ Traditional ♦ Historic ♦
Facing the Panthéon, a pleasant hotel renovated in Directoire style (antique furnishings). Over half the rooms overlook the last resting place of the "great men of France".

Villa Malraux without rest 📺 ↩ ℀ 📞 𝑽𝑰𝑺𝑨 ⓜⓔ 𝔸𝔼 ⓜ
6 r. des Archives , (4th) – ⓜ *Hôtel de Ville* – 𝒞 *01 53 01 90 90 – resa@villamalraux.com – Fax 01 53 01 90 91 – www.villamalraux.com* **U1**
26 rm – 🛇300 € 🛇🛇350 €, ⚏ 12 €
♦ Business ♦ Design ♦
High-tech equipment (wi-fi, flat screen TV), modern and period furniture: this comfortable hotel close to the Hôtel de Ville subtly brings together tradition and modernity.

FRANCE

Tour Notre-Dame without rest   AK ℭ VISA ⑯ AE ①
20 r. Sommerard (5th) – Ⓜ Cluny la Sorbonne – ℰ 01 43 54 47 60
– tour-notre-dame@magic.fr – Fax 01 43 26 42 34
– www.la-tour-notre-dame.com   **T2**
48 rm – ♦125/217 € ♦♦133/231 €, ☲ 12 €
♦ Traditional ♦ Family ♦ Stylish ♦
This hotel is very well situated, almost adjoining the Cluny museum. Comfortable, recently-renovated rooms. Those at the back are quieter.

Relais St-Sulpice without rest ⌂   & AK ⇜ ℅ ♨20 VISA ⑯ AE ①
3 r. Garancière (6th) – Ⓜ St-Sulpice – ℰ 01 46 33 99 00 – relaisstsulpice@wanadoo.fr – Fax 01 46 33 00 10 – www.relais-saint-sulpice.com   **S2**
26 rm – ♦175/210 € ♦♦175/210 €, ☲ 12 €
♦ Traditional ♦ Personalised ♦
Appealing hotel with 19C facade housing exotically decorated rooms, combining both African and Asian styles. Those at the back are very quiet.

Grand Hôtel St-Michel without rest   & AK VISA ⑯ AE ①
19 r. Cujas (5th) – Ⓜ Luxembourg – ℰ 01 46 33 33 02 – grand.hotel.st.michel@wanadoo.fr – Fax 01 40 46 96 33 – www.grand-hotel-st-michel.com   **T3**
40 rm – ♦105/170 € ♦♦130/170 €, ☲ 12 € – 5 suites
♦ Family ♦ Traditional ♦ Classic ♦
This renovated Haussmann creation offers luxurious rooms with painted furniture. Napoleon III-style lounge; breakfast is served in an arched room.

De Fleurie without rest   AK ℅ ℭ VISA ⑯ AE ①
32 r. Grégoire de Tours (6th) – Ⓜ Odéon – ℰ 01 53 73 70 00 – bonjour@hotel-de-fleurie.tm.fr – Fax 01 53 73 70 20 – www.hotel-de-fleurie.fr   **S2**
29 rm – ♦135/150 € ♦♦170/270 €, ☲ 12 €
♦ Family ♦ Functional ♦
Spruce 18C façade adorned with statues in niches. Elegant rooms with soft tones, enhanced by woodwork. Choose the quieter rooms overlooking the courtyard.

Notre Dame without rest   < AK ⇜ ℅ VISA ⑯ AE ①
1 quai St-Michel (5th) – Ⓜ St-Michel – ℰ 01 43 54 20 43
– hotel.lenotredame@libertysurf.fr – Fax 01 43 26 61 75   **T2**
23 rm – ♦150/199 € ♦♦199 €, ☲ 7 €
♦ Traditional ♦ Family ♦ Cosy ♦
The cosy little rooms in this hotel have all been refurbished and are air-conditioned and well appointed. Most rooms have a view over Notre-Dame cathedral.

Relais St-Jacques without rest   & AK ℅ ℭ ♨10 VISA ⑯ AE ①
3 r. Abbé de l'Épée (5th) – Ⓜ Luxembourg – ℰ 01 53 73 26 00
– nevers.luxembourg@wanadoo.fr – Fax 01 43 26 17 81
– www.paris-hotal-saintjacques.com   **T3**
22 rm – ♦170/255 € ♦♦170/480 €, ☲ 17 €
♦ Traditional ♦ Family ♦ Stylish ♦
Rooms of various styles (Directoire, Louis Philippe, etc.), a glass-roofed breakfast room, Louis XV lounge and 1920s bar, make this a stylish hotchpotch hotel!

Prince de Conti without rest   & AK ⇜ ℅ VISA ⑯ AE ①
8 r. Guénégaud (6th) – Ⓜ Odéon – ℰ 01 44 07 30 40 – princedeconti@wanadoo.fr – Fax 01 44 07 36 34 – www.prince-de-conti.com   **S1**
26 rm – ♦165/280 € ♦♦165/280 €, ☲ 13 €
♦ Traditional ♦ Family ♦ Stylish ♦
18C building adjoining the Hotel de la Monnaie : an ideal location to explore the famous germanopratin art galleries. English-style decoration in the bedrooms and lounges

Odéon Hôtel without rest   AK ⇜ ℅ ℭ VISA ⑯ AE ①
3 r. Odéon (6th) – Ⓜ Odéon – ℰ 01 43 25 90 67 – odeon@odeonhotel.fr
– Fax 01 43 25 55 98 – www.odeonhotel.fr   **S2**
33 rm – ♦130/170 € ♦♦170/270 €, ☲ 12 €
♦ Family ♦ Classic ♦
The façade along with the exposed stone and beams in the rooms are a clue to the age of this building - (17C). Bathrooms are decorated with azulejos.

FRANCE

Régent without rest   AC ⌧ ☎ VISA ◐ AE ⊙
61 r. Dauphine (6th) – Ⓜ Odéon – 𝒞 01 46 34 59 80 – hotel.leregent @
wanadoo.fr – Fax 01 40 51 05 07 – www.regent-paris-hotel.com   **S2**
25 rm – ♦150/225 € ♦♦150/225 €, ⌑ 12 €
♦ Traditional ♦ Family ♦ Classic ♦
Tall façade dating from 1769. The rooms are cosy and well equipped. Breakfast
room with exposed stone walls, located in the basement.

Verneuil without rest   AC ⌧ ☎ VISA ◐ AE ⊙
8 r. de Verneuil (7th) – Ⓜ Rue du Bac – 𝒞 01 42 60 82 14 – info @
hotelverneuil.com – Fax 01 42 61 40 38 – www.hotelverneuil.com   **S1**
26 rm – ♦130 € ♦♦155/200 €, ⌑ 12 €
♦ Traditional ♦ Family ♦ Classic ♦
Old building on the Left bank, decorated in the style of a private house. Elegant
rooms with prints on the walls. N°5 bis, the house with graffiti on it, was where
singer Serge Gainsbourg lived.

Lenox Saint-Germain without rest   AC ⌧ VISA ◐ AE ⊙
9 r. Université (7th) – Ⓜ St-Germain des Prés – 𝒞 01 42 96 10 95
– hotel @ lenoxsaintgermain.com – Fax 01 42 61 52 83   **R-S1**
32 rm – ♦120/125 € ♦♦145/205 €, ⌑ 14 € – 2 suites
♦ Traditional ♦ Business ♦ Functional ♦
Rooms are a little on the small side, but attractively decorated and with an air of
tasteful luxury. "Egyptian" frescos adorn the breakfast room. Art deco-style bar.

D'Orsay without rest   & AC ⌧ ☎ ⚞5/12 VISA ◐ AE ⊙
93 r. Lille (7th) – Ⓜ Solférino – 𝒞 01 47 05 85 54 – orsay @ espritfrance.com
– Fax 01 45 55 51 16 – www.esprit-de-france.com   **R1**
41 rm – ♦129/148 € ♦♦170/320 €, ⌑ 10 €
♦ Traditional ♦ Business ♦ Modern ♦
The hotel occupies two handsome, late-18C buildings that have been
painstakingly renovated. Attractive individualised rooms and welcoming
lounge overlooking a charming, green patio.

St-Germain without rest   AC ☎ VISA ◐ AE
88 r. Bac (7th) – Ⓜ Rue du Bac – 𝒞 01 49 54 70 00 – info @ hotel-saint-germain.fr
– Fax 01 45 48 26 89   **R2**
29 rm – ♦150/190 € ♦♦150/210 €, ⌑ 12 €
♦ Traditional ♦ Family ♦ Functional ♦
Empire, Louis-Philippe, high tech design, antique objects, contemporary
paintings - the charm of variety. Comfortable library, patio pleasant in summer.

Pas de Calais without rest   AC VISA ◐ AE ⊙
59 r. Saints-Pères (6th) – Ⓜ St-Germain des Prés – 𝒞 01 45 48 78 74 – infos @
hotelpasdecalais.com – Fax 01 45 44 94 57 – www.hotelpasdecalais.com
38 rm – ♦125/140 € ♦♦145/300 €, ⌑ 15 €   **R2**
♦ Traditional ♦ Family ♦ Functional ♦
This discreet hotel, along a busy street, offers stylish, gradually renovated rooms
with personal touches. Exposed beams on the top floor.

Select without rest   AC ⌧ ☎ VISA ◐ AE ⊙
1 pl. Sorbonne (5th) – Ⓜ Cluny la Sorbonne – 𝒞 01 46 34 14 80
– info @ selecthotel.fr – Fax 01 46 34 51 79 – www.selecthotel.fr   **T3**
67 rm – ♦149/189 € ♦♦149/189 €, ⌑ 6 €
♦ Traditional ♦ Family ♦ Functional ♦
Staunchly contemporary hotel in the heart of the student quarter of Paris. Bar
and lounges disposed around a patio with a cactus garden. Some rooms offer
views over the rooftops.

D'Albe without rest   AC ⥂ ⌧ ☎ VISA ◐ AE ⊙
1 r. Harpe (5th) – Ⓜ St-Michel – 𝒞 01 46 34 09 70 – albehotel @ wanadoo.fr
– Fax 01 40 46 85 70 – www.albehotel.com   **T2**
45 rm – ♦120/160 € ♦♦145/170 €, ⌑ 12 €
♦ Traditional ♦ Family ♦ Functional ♦
Attractive, modern hotel with smallish, yet nicely-arranged and cheerful rooms.
With the Latin quarter and the Île de la Cité close by, Paris is at your doorstep!

FRANCE

Bretonnerie without rest   *VISA* ⚈⊜

22 r. Ste-Croix-de-la-Bretonnerie (4th) – Ⓜ Hôtel de Ville – ℰ 01 48 87 77 63
– hotel@bretonnerie.com – Fax 01 42 77 26 78   **U1**
22 rm – ♦116 € ♦♦116/149 €, � 9,50 € – 4 suites
♦ Traditional ♦ Family ♦ Stylish ♦
Some of the rooms of this elegant, private hotel in the Marais (17C) include
four-poster beds and exposed beams. Vaulted ceiling in the breakfast room.

Beaubourg without rest   ⚿ *VISA* ⚈⊜ ⚈ ⓪

11 r. S. Le Franc (4th) – Ⓜ Rambuteau – ℰ 01 42 74 34 24 – htlbeaubourg@
hotellerie.net – Fax 01 42 78 68 11 – www.htlbeaubourg.com   **U1**
28 rm – ♦112/140 € ♦♦115/140 €, ⊃ 8 €
♦ Traditional ♦ Business ♦ Classic ♦
Nestled in a tiny street behind the Georges-Pompidou Centre. Some of the friendly,
well-soundproofed rooms have exposed stone walls and wooden beams.

Lutèce without rest   ⚿ ⚿ ⚈ *VISA* ⚈⊜ ⚈

65 r. St-Louis-en-l'Ile (4th) – Ⓜ Pont Marie – ℰ 01 43 26 23 52 – hotel.lutece@
free.fr – Fax 01 43 29 60 25 – www.hoteldelutece.com   **U2**
23 rm – ♦170 € ♦♦170 €, ⊃ 11 €
♦ Traditional ♦ Family ♦ Retro ♦
On the Ile St-Louis, the rustic charm of this country inn is particularly popular with
an American clientele. Welcoming and restful rooms. Fine ancient woodwork in
the lounge.

Bersoly's without rest   ⚿ *VISA* ⚈⊜ ⚈ ⓪

28 r. Lille (7th) – Ⓜ Musée d'Orsay – ℰ 01 42 60 73 79 – hotelbersolys@
wanadoo.fr – Fax 01 49 27 05 55 – closed August   **R-S1**
16 rm – ♦100/115 € ♦♦130 €, ⊃ 10 €
♦ Traditional ♦ Business ♦ Personalised ♦
Impressionist nights in this 17C building - each bedroom honours a different
artist and you can see some of their paintings at the nearby musée d'Orsay
(Renoir, Gauguin...).

St-Jacques without rest   ⚿ *VISA* ⚈⊜ ⚈ ⓪

35 r. Ecoles (5th) – Ⓜ Maubert Mutualité – ℰ 01 44 07 45 45 – hotelsaintjacques@
wanadoo.fr – Fax 01 43 25 65 50 – www.paris-hotel-stjacques.com   **T2**
38 rm – ♦55/84 € ♦♦95/124 €, ⊃ 8,50 €
♦ Traditional ♦ Family ♦ Stylish ♦
Modern comfort allies with old-style charm in the rooms of this hotel. Library with
18C and 19C works. Breakfast room with Roaring Twenties cabaret-style decor.

Tour d'Argent   ≤ Notre-Dame, ⚿ ⚙15/55 ⊐⚿ *VISA* ⚈⊜ ⚈ ⓪

15 quai Tournelle (5th) – Ⓜ Maubert Mutualité – ℰ 01 43 54 23 31
– resa@latourdargent.com – Fax 01 44 07 12 04
closed 1 to 28 August, Thuesday and Monday   **U2**
Rest 70 € (lunch)/230 € and a la carte 130/230 € ⚙⚙
Spec. Quenelles de brochet "André Terrail". Canard "Tour d'Argent". Poire "Vie
parisienne".
♦ Traditional ♦ Luxury ♦
The open-air dining room offers a splendid view of Notre-Dame. Exceptional
wine-cellar, exquisite Challans duck and famous clientele since the 16C. An
institution!

Jacques Cagna   ⚿ ⊐⚿(dinner) *VISA* ⚈⊜ ⚈ ⓪

14 r. Grands Augustins (6th) – Ⓜ St-Michel – ℰ 01 43 26 49 39 – jacquescagna@
hotmail.com – Fax 01 43 54 54 48 – www.jacques-cagna.com
closed 29 July-24 August, Saturday lunch, Monday lunch and Sunday   **T2**
Rest 42 € (weekday lunch)/90 € and a la carte 90/145 €
Spec. Foie gras de canard poêlé aux fruits de saison caramélisés. Coquilles
Saint-Jacques (October-March). Gibier (Season).
♦ Traditional ♦ Rustic ♦
Located in one of the oldest homes in the old Paris, the comfortable dining hall
is embellished by massive rafters, 16C woodwork and Flemish paintings. Refined
cuisine.

FRANCE

XXX ☆

Paris – Hôtel Lutetia   ৬ AK ➡ VISA ⑩ AE ①
45 bd Raspail (6th) – Ⓜ Sèvres Babylone – ℰ 01 49 54 46 46 – lutetia-paris @
lutetia-paris.com – Fax 01 49 54 46 00 – www.lutetia-paris.com
closed 29 July-28 August, Saturday, Sunday and Bank Holidays   **R2**
Rest 52 € (weekday lunch), 68/130 € and a la carte 85/125 €
Spec. Homard à l'huile de pistache. Turbot de ligne cuit sur le sel de Guérande
dans le wakamé. Ananas Victoria.
◆ Traditional ◆ Retro ◆
In keeping with the style of the hotel, the Sonia Rykiel art deco dining room is a
recreation of one of the lounges from the ship The Normandy. Versatile
contemporary cuisine.

XXX ☆☆

Relais Louis XIII (Martinez)   AK ↳ ✿12/20 ➡ VISA ⑩ AE
8 r. Grands Augustins (6th) – Ⓜ Odéon – ℰ 01 43 26 75 96
– contact @ relaislouis13.com – Fax 01 44 07 07 80 – www.relaislouis13.com
closed August, 25 December-3 January, Sunday, Monday and Bank Holidays   **T2**
Rest 45 € (lunch), 68/89 € and a la carte 115/155 €
Spec. Ravioli de homard, foie gras et crème de cèpes. Caneton challandais aux
épices douces et fortes. Millefeuille, crème légère à la vanille bourbon.
◆ Traditional ◆ Cosy ◆
The building dates from the 16C and there are three Louis XIII-style dining rooms
with balustrades, tapestries and open stonework. The cuisine is subtle and
up-to-date.

XXX ☆☆

Hélène Darroze   AK ↳ ➡ VISA ⑩ AE
4 r. d'Assas (6th) – Ⓜ Sèvres Babylone – ℰ 01 42 22 00 11
– reservation @ helenedarroze.com – Fax 01 42 22 25 40
closed Monday except dinner from 24 July -26 August and Sunday   **R2**
Rest (dinner only from 24 July-26 August) 68 € (lunch), 172/215 € and a la carte
115/150 € ⅋ – **Rest Salon** 89/125 € b.i. ⅋
Spec. Foie gras de canard des Landes grillé au feu de bois. Cochon de lait de race
basque sous toutes ses formes (May-October). Chocolat, coriandre, chicorée et
vanille bourbon.
◆ South-West of France specialities ◆ Cosy ◆
Close to the Bon Marché, the decor is modern and rich in colour; here one can
enjoy delicious cuisine and the fine wines of southwest France. On the ground
floor of the restaurant, Hélène Darroze presides over the Salon and serves tapas
and small dishes with a rustic flavour of the Landes.

XXX

Lapérouse   AK ✿2/50 ➡ VISA ⑩ AE ①
51 quai Grands Augustins (6th) – Ⓜ St-Michel – ℰ 01 43 26 68 04
– restaurantlaperouse @ wanadoo.fr – Fax 01 43 26 99 39 – closed August   **T2**
Rest 45 € b.i. (weekday lunch)/90 € b.i. and a la carte 70/100 €
◆ Traditional ◆ Retro ◆
Founded in 1766, and frequented by the Parisians from the late 19C thanks to its
reputation for small discreet salons. The spirit of this elegant restaurant is
carefully maintained.

XXX

La Truffière   AK ↳ VISA ⑩ AE ①
4 r. Blainville (5th) – Ⓜ Place Monge – ℰ 01 46 33 29 82
– restaurant.latruffiere @ wanadoo.fr – Fax 01 46 33 64 74 – www.latruffiere.com
closed 1-27 August, 23-30 December, Sunday and Monday   **T3**
Rest 20 € (weekday lunch), 32 € b.i./55 € and a la carte 70/110 € ⅋
◆ Innovative ◆ Cosy ◆
A 17C house with three dining rooms. One is rustic with exposed beams and the
two others have a vaulted ceiling. Traditional cuisine from southwest France and
fine wine selection.

XX

Cigale Récamier   🍽 AK VISA ⑩
4 r. Récamier (7th) – Ⓜ Sèvres Babylone – ℰ 01 45 48 86 58
closed Sunday – **Rest** a la carte 30/53 €   **R2**
◆ Traditional ◆ Friendly ◆
A literary establishment where writers and editors often meet up. Original menu
with soufflés and sweet and savoury dishes renewed every month. Pleasant
peaceful terrace.

FRANCE

XX Caffé Minotti (Vernier) ☞(dinner) VISA ⊕ AE

33 r. Verneuil (7th) – Ⓜ *Rue du Bac – ℰ 01 42 60 04 04 – caffeminotti@ wanadoo.fr – Fax 01 42 60 04 05*

closed 31 July-23 August, 24 December-1 January, Sunday and Monday

Rest 32 € (lunch) and a la carte 60/85 € **R1**

Spec. Gamberoni-fritti, Lasagne-Minotti, Risotto-langoustines.

♦ Italian ♦ Design ♦

Italian caffè with elegant modern-style decor (unusual red chandelier in Murano glass), offering a full taste of Italy, minus the Vespa fumes!

XX Benoît AC ✧10/20 VISA ⊕ AE

20 r. St-Martin (4th) – Ⓜ *Châtelet – ℰ 01 42 72 25 76 – restaurant.benoit@ wanadoo.fr – Fax 01 42 72 45 68 – www.alain-ducasse.com*

Closed August **U1**

Rest 38 € (lunch) and a la carte 55/90 €

Spec. Tête de veau ravigote. Escargots en coquille, beurre d'ail, fines herbes. Cassoulet aux cocos de Paimpol.

♦ Traditional ♦ Bistro ♦

Alain Ducasse is now in charge of this lively and stylish bistro. You will savour his traditional cuisine, which is in keeping with the spirit of this fine, authentic old building.

XX Yugaraj AC VISA ⊕ AE ①

14 r. Dauphine (6th) – Ⓜ *Odéon – ℰ 01 43 26 44 91 – contact@yugaraj.com – Fax 01 46 33 50 77*

closed 7 to 31 August, 1 to 4 January, lunch Thursday and Monday **T1**

Rest 34 € and a la carte 44/60 €

♦ Indian ♦ Exotic ♦

Wood panelling, ornamental panels, silks and antique objets d'art give an almost museum-style air to this highly acclaimed Indian restaurant with its very well researched menu.

XX Atelier Maître Albert AC ☞ VISA ⊕ AE ①

1 r. Maître Albert (5th) – Ⓜ *Maubert Mutualité – ℰ 01 56 81 30 01 – ateliermaitrealbert@guysavoy.com – Fax 01 53 10 83 23 – www.ateliermaitrealbert.com*

closed Christmas Holidays, lunch Saturday and Sunday **U2**

Rest 28 € (weekday lunch), 40/50 € and a la carte 42/58 €

♦ Meat specialities ♦ Bistro ♦

Guy Savoy has a winning team, serving carefully-prepared dishes in a sober modern setting that also includes a huge medieval fireplace, a rotisserie (meat on the spit) and exposed beams.

XX Alcazar ⅖ AC ✧10/42 VISA ⊕ AE ①

62 r. Mazarine (6th) – Ⓜ *Odéon – ℰ 01 53 10 19 99 – contact@alcazar.fr – Fax 01 53 10 23 23 – www.alcazar.fr* **S2**

Rest 19 € (weekday lunch), 29 € b.i./39 € and a la carte 40/70 €

♦ Fusion ♦ Trendy ♦

The famous cabaret has been transformed into a huge, trendy, designer restaurant with photos of artists. The cooking ranges are visible from the tables, and the cuisine is contemporary.

X L'Atelier de Joël Robuchon AC ⅔ ☞ VISA ⊕

7 r. de Montalembert (7th) – Ⓜ *Rue du Bac – ℰ 01 42 22 56 56 – latelierdejoelrobuchon@wanadoo.fr – Fax 01 42 22 97 91*

Service 11.30 am to 3.30 pm and 6.30 pm to midnight. Reservations for certain sittings only: call for details **R1**

Rest 98 € and a la carte 60/115 € 🕮

Spec. Oeuf cocotte et crème aux girolles. Aile de pigeon au chou et foie gras. Chocolat sensation.

♦ Innovative ♦ Design ♦

An original concept in a chic decor designed by Rochon: no tables, just high stools in a row facing the counter where you can sample a selection of the fine, modern dishes, tapas style. Car parking service at lunchtime and on Saturday and Sunday evenings.

FRANCE

Yen

⟋ **VISA** **MO** **AE**

22 r. St-Benoît (6th) – **M** *St-Germain des Prés* – ☎ *01 45 44 11 18*
– restau.yen@wanadoo.fr – Fax 01 45 44 19 48
closed 5 to 20 August and Sunday lunch **S2**
Rest 55 € (weekdays) and a la carte 47/76 €
♦ Japanese ♦ Minimalist ♦
Two dining rooms with highly refined Japanese decor, the one on the first floor
is slightly warmer in style. Pride of place on the menu for the chef's speciality:
soba (buckwheat noodles).

Gaya Rive Gauche par Pierre Gagnaire

⟋ 15/20

44 r. du Bac (7th) – **M** *Rue du Bac* – ☎ *01 45 44 73 73* **VISA** **MO** **AE**
– p.gagnaire@wanadoo.fr – Fax 01 45 44 73 73
– www.pierre-gagnaire.com **R1**
Rest a la carte 50/100 €
Spec. Pressé de tourteau au chou-fleur, oseille fondue. Riz noir crémeux,
gambas de Madagascar au saté. Pavé de bar sauvage poché au beurre
clarifié.
♦ Contemporary ♦ Design ♦
A new lease of life has been given to this Left Bank restaurant thanks to Pierre
Gagnaire. In a lovely Ghion-designed decor, innovative dishes based on seafood
will delight your taste buds.

L'Épi Dupin

⟋ **VISA** **MO**

11 r. Dupin (6th) – **M** *Sèvres Babylone* – ☎ *01 42 22 64 56*
– lepidupin@wanadoo.fr – Fax 01 42 22 30 42
closed 31 July-26 August, Monday lunch, Saturday and Sunday **R2**
Rest (number of covers limited, pre-book) 31 €
♦ Innovative ♦ Friendly ♦
Beams and stonework for character, closely-packed tables for conviviality and
delicious cuisine to delight the palate: this pocket-handkerchief-sized restaurant
has captivated people in the Bon Marché area.

Buisson Ardent

⟋ **VISA** **MO**

25 r. Jussieu (5th) – **M** *Jussieu* – ☎ *01 43 54 93 02*
– Fax 01 46 33 34 77
closed August, Saturday lunch and Sunday **U3**
Rest 16 € (weekday lunch), 29/45 € and a la carte approx. 45 €
♦ Traditional ♦ Bistro ♦
A friendly atmosphere reigns in this small, local restaurant frequented by
students from nearby Jussieu university at lunchtime. Traditional cuisine.
Original frescoes dating back to 1923.

Emporio Armani Caffé

⟋ **VISA** **MO** **AE**

149 bd St-Germain (6th) – **M** *St-Germain des Prés* – ☎ *01 45 48 62 15*
– Fax 01 45 48 53 17 **S2**
Rest a la carte 44/82 €
♦ Italian ♦ Fashionable ♦
Stylish, comfortable and attractively-redecorated Italian-style "caffé", on the
first floor of this renowned designer's boutique. Trendy clientele and Italian
cuisine.

Ze Kitchen Galerie

⟋ **VISA** **MO** **AE**

4 r. Grands Augustins (6th) – **M** *St-Michel* – ☎ *01 44 32 00 32*
– zekitchen.galerie@wanadoo.fr – Fax 01 44 32 00 33
– www.zekitchengalerie.fr
closed lunch Saturday and Sunday **T1-2**
Rest 33 € (lunch) and a la carte 29/64 €
♦ Fusion ♦ Design ♦
Ze Kitchen is "ze" hip place to be on the Left Bank. Works of art by modern artists,
designer furniture and trendy cuisine prepared in front of your eyes.

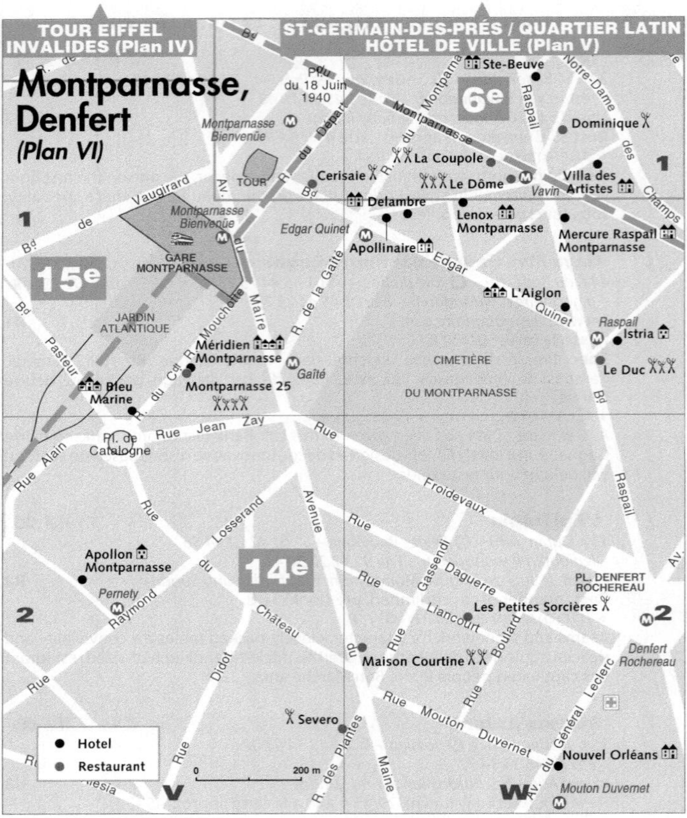

MONTPARNASSE-DENFERT *Plan VI*

Méridien Montparnasse

19 r. Cdt-Mouchotte (14th) 25/2000 VISA
– Montparnasse Bienvenüe – 01 44 36 44 36 – meridien.montparnasse@lemeridien.com – Fax 01 44 36 49 00 – www.montparnasse.lemeridien.com
918 rm – 360/455 € 360/455 €, 25 € – 35 suites **V1**
Rest see ***Montparnasse 25*** below – **Rest *Justine***, *01 44 36 44 00* – 38/46 €
♦ Chain hotel ♦ Business ♦ Modern ♦
Most of the rooms in this glass-and-concrete building have been redone; they are large and very modern. Beautiful view of the capital from the top floors. At Justine's, winter garden decor, green terrace and buffet menus.

Bleu Marine

rm rm 80 VISA
40 r. Cdt Mouchotte (14th) – Gaîté – 01 56 54 84 00 – restauration.montparnasse@bleumarine.fr – Fax 01 56 54 84 84 **V1**
354 rm – 250 € 250 €, 13 € – **Rest** *(closed 15 July-15 August)* 26 €
♦ Chain hotel ♦ Business ♦ Modern ♦
This completely new hotel, set on the Place de Catalogne has many advantages: calm and refined rooms, interior garden, fitness centre, and bar. This restaurant, with rare wood and coloured fabrics, offers buffets and à la carte dishes.

LOUIS ROEDERER
CHAMPAGNE

Little Red Riding Hood

But Little Red Riding Hood had her regional map with her, and so she did not fall into the trap. She did not take the path through the wood and she did not meet the big bad wolf. Instead, she chose the picturesque touring route straight to Grandmother's house, and arrived safely with her cake and her little pot of butter.

The End

FRANCE

L'Aiglon without rest   AC ⌂ VISA ●● AE ①
232 bd Raspail (14th) – Ⓜ *Raspail –* ℰ *01 43 20 82 42*
– aiglon@espritfrance.com – Fax 01 43 20 98 72   **W1**
38 rm – †115/153 € ††135/153 €, ⊆ 9,50 € – 9 suites
♦ Traditional ♦ Classic ♦
The discreet façade hides a beautiful Empire-style interior. The effectively double-glazed rooms are pleasant, if sometimes on the small side.

Ste-Beuve without rest   AC ⌖ VISA ●● AE ①
9 r. Ste-Beuve (6th) – Ⓜ *Notre-Dame des Champs –* ℰ *01 45 48 20 07*
– saintebeuve@wanadoo.fr – Fax 01 45 48 67 52
– www.parishotelcharme.com   **W1**
22 rm – †135/240 € ††135/280 €, ⊆ 14,50 €
♦ Family ♦ Traditional ♦ Cosy ♦
This establishment resembles a private house : cosy atmosphere, soft sofas, glowing fire... the rooms are a blend of old-fashioned and contemporary styles.

Villa des Artistes without rest ⌖   AC ⇆ ⌖ VISA ●● AE ①
9 r. Grande Chaumière (6th) – Ⓜ *Vavin –* ℰ *01 43 26 60 86*
– hotel@villa-artistes.com – Fax 01 43 54 73 70   **W1**
59 rm – †129/149 € ††129/225 €, ⊆ 13 €
♦ Family ♦ Traditional ♦ Stylish ♦
The name pays tribute to the artists who embellished the history of the Montparnasse district. Pleasant rooms, most overlooking the courtyard. Glass-roofed breakfast room.

Lenox Montparnasse without rest   AC ⌖ VISA ●● AE ①
15 r. Delambre (14th) – Ⓜ *Vavin –* ℰ *01 43 35 34 50*
– hotel@lenoxmontparnasse.com – Fax 01 43 20 46 64   **W1**
58 rm – †135 € ††135/290 €, ⊆ 14 €
♦ Traditional ♦ Cosy ♦
Establishment frequented by elegant people, many from the fashion world. Period rooms, charming bathrooms, pleasant suites on the 6th floor. Nice bar and lounges.

Nouvel Orléans without rest   AC ⇆ ⌖ VISA ●● AE ①
25 av. Gén. Leclerc (14th) – Ⓜ *Mouton Duvernet –* ℰ *01 43 27 80 20*
– nouvelorleans@aol.com – Fax 01 43 35 36 57
– www.hotelnouvelorleans.com   **W2**
46 rm – †90/120 € ††90/175 €, ⊆ 10 €
♦ Traditional ♦ Modern ♦
The name comes from the Porte d'Orléans, 800 m away. In the entirely renovated hotel, modern furniture and warm colourful materials decorate the rooms.

Delambre without rest   ὅ AC ⌖ ⌖ VISA ●● AE
35 r. Delambre (14th) – Ⓜ *Edgar Quinet –* ℰ *01 43 20 66 31*
– delambre@club-internet.fr – Fax 01 45 38 91 76
– www.hoteldelambre.com   **W1**
30 rm – †85/105 € ††90/160 €, ⊆ 9 €
♦ Traditional ♦ Modern ♦
André Breton stayed over in this hotel located in a quiet street close to the Gare de Montparnasse railway station. The decor is modern; the rooms are simple but bright and many are spacious.

Mercure Raspail Montparnasse without rest   ὅ AC
207 bd Raspail (14th) – Ⓜ *Vavin –* ℰ *01 43 20 62 94*   ⇆ VISA ●● AE ①
– h0351@accor.com – Fax 01 43 27 39 69
– www.mercure.com   **W1**
63 rm – †145/160 € ††150/190 €, ⊆ 13,50 €
♦ Chain hotel ♦ Business ♦ Functional ♦
Stay overnight in this Haussmann building near the famous Montparnasse brasseries. Modern rooms with contemporary, light wood furniture.

FRANCE

Apollinaire without rest
`AC VISA MO AE O`

39 r. Delambre (14th) – Ⓜ *Edgar Quinet – ℰ 01 43 35 18 40 – infos @ hotel.apollinaire.com – Fax 01 43 35 30 71*
– www.hotel-apollinaire.com
W1
36 rm – ♦105 € ♦♦125/135 €, ⌴ 7,50 €
♦ Traditional ♦ Functional ♦

The hotel is named after the poet who was a friend of the writers and artists living in Montparnasse. The colourful rooms are well-kept and functional. Comfortable lounge.

Istria without rest
`AC ⅍ VISA MO AE O`

29 r. Campagne Première (14th) – Ⓜ *Raspail – ℰ 01 43 20 91 82*
– hotel.istria @ wanadoo.fr – Fax 01 43 22 48 45
W1
26 rm – ♦96/140 € ♦♦96/149 €, ⌴ 10 €
♦ Traditional ♦ Functional ♦

Aragon immortalised this hotel in "Il ne m'est Paris que d'Elsa". Small, simple bedrooms, a pleasant lounge and a breakfast room in a pretty vaulted cellar.

Apollon Montparnasse without rest
`AC 📞 VISA MO AE O`

91 r. Ouest (14th) – Ⓜ *Pernety – ℰ 01 43 95 62 00*
– apollonm @ wanadoo.fr – Fax 01 43 95 62 10
– www.apollon-montparnasse.com
V2
33 rm – ♦69/79 € ♦♦85/91 €, ⌴ 7 €
♦ Traditional ♦ Functional ♦

Near Montparnasse station and the Air France airport shuttle, a courteous welcome and stylish rooms are the main assets of this hotel on a rather quiet street.

Montparnasse 25 – Hôtel Méridien Montparnasse
`AC ⅍`

19 r. Cdt Mouchotte (14th)
`P VISA MO AE O`
– Ⓜ *Montparnasse Bienvenüe – ℰ 01 44 36 44 25*
– meridien.montparnasse @ lemeridien.com – Fax 01 44 36 49 03
– www.montparnasse.lemeridien.com
Closed 1 to 7 May, 10 July-27 August, 25 December-7 January, Saturday, Sunday and Bank Holidays
V1
Rest 49 € (lunch)/108 € and a la carte 90/120 € 🕮

Spec. Langoustines au galanga (Spring-Summer). Pâté chaud de colvert (season). Canard au tamarin.
♦ Contemporary ♦ Formal ♦

The modern setting based around black lacquer may surprise you, but this restaurant turns out to be comfortable and warm. Contemporary cuisine, superb cheese boards.

Le Duc
`AC 🍴 VISA MO AE O`

243 bd Raspail (14th) – Ⓜ *Raspail – ℰ 01 43 20 96 30 – Fax 01 43 20 46 73*
closed 29 July-21 August, 24 December-3 January, Monday and lunch Saturday
W1
Rest 46 € (weekday lunch) and a la carte 60/100 €

Spec. Poissons crus. Queues de langoustines aux épices. Lotte aux endives caramélisées (October-May).
♦ Seafood ♦ Retro ♦

Fish and seafood cuisine - a blend of quality and simplicity - served in a comfortable yacht cabin with mahogany panelling, wall lights with a marine theme and gleaming brasses.

Le Dôme
`AC VISA MO AE O`

108 bd Montparnasse (14th) – Ⓜ *Vavin – ℰ 01 43 35 25 81 – Fax 01 42 79 01 19*
closed Sunday and Monday in August
W1
Rest a la carte 75/95 €
♦ Brasserie ♦ Retro ♦

One of the temples to the literary and artistic bohemian lifestyle of the Twenties has been turned into a stylish and trendy Left-Bank brasserie, with its Art Deco style intact. Fish and seafood.

FRANCE

XX
&

Maison Courtine (Charles) AC VISA MO

157 av. Maine (14th) – M *Mouton Duvernet*
– ℰ 01 45 43 08 04 – yves.charles @ wanadoo.fr
– Fax 01 45 45 91 35
closed August, Saturday lunch, Monday lunch and Sunday **W2**
Rest 38 €
Spec. Escalopes de foie gras de canard poêlées aux raisins. Canard sauvage rôti entier au poivre long (October-February). Médaillon de veau de lait et lentilles blondes de la Planèze.
◆ Traditional ◆ Cosy ◆
Here one can enjoy a culinary Tour de France; the brightly- coloured interiors are modern and the furnishing is in the Louis-Philippe style. An assiduously frequented establishment.

XX

La Coupole AC ⇔ VISA MO AE ①

102 bd Montparnasse (14th) – M *Vavin – ℰ 01 43 20 14 20*
– lejeune @ groupeflo.fr – Fax 01 43 35 46 14
– www.flobrasseries.com **W1**
Rest 35 € b.i. and a la carte 45/60 €
◆ Brasserie ◆ Retro ◆
The spirit of Montparnasse lives on in this immense Art Deco brasserie, first opened in 1927. The 32 pillars were decorated by artists of the period. A lively atmosphere.

X
☺

Les Petites Sorcières VISA MO AE

12 r. Liancourt (14th) – M *Denfert Rochereau – ℰ 01 43 21 95 68*
– Fax 01 43 21 95 68
closed mid-July-mid-August, lunch Saturday, lunch Monday and Sunday **W2**
Rest 30 €
◆ Contemporary ◆ Cosy ◆
A "bewitching" bistro full of gourmet charms. Prepare to be enchanted!

X
☺

Cerisaie VISA MO

70 bd E. Quinet (14th) – M *Edgar Quinet – ℰ 01 43 20 98 98*
– Fax 01 43 20 98 98
closed 1 to 8 May, 25 July-25 August, Saturday, Sunday and Bank Holidays **V1**
Rest (pre-book) 29/34 €
◆ South-West of France specialities ◆ Bistro ◆
A tiny restaurant in the heart of the Breton quarter. Every day, the owner marks the carefully-prepared dishes of the southwest on a blackboard.

X
☺

Severo VISA MO

8 r. Plantes (14th) – M *Mouton Duvernet – ℰ 01 45 40 40 91*
closed 22 July-21 August, 23 December-2 January, 19 to 26 February, Saturday and Sunday **V2**
Rest a la carte 27/45 € 🍷
◆ Meat specialities ◆ Bistro ◆
Products from Auvergne (meat, charcuterie) take centre stage on the daily slate menu of this friendly bistro. The wine list is enticingly eclectic.

X

Dominique AC VISA MO AE ①

19 r. Bréa (6th) – M *Vavin – ℰ 01 43 27 08 80*
– restaurant.dominique @ mageos.com
– Fax 01 43 27 03 76 **W1**
Rest 35 € (dinner) and a la carte 45/73 €
◆ Russian ◆ Musical ◆
Vodka bar, grocery and restaurant all rolled into one : location renowned in Paris for its Russian cuisine. Sample zakouskis in the bistro or enjoy a candlelit dinner in the rear dining room.

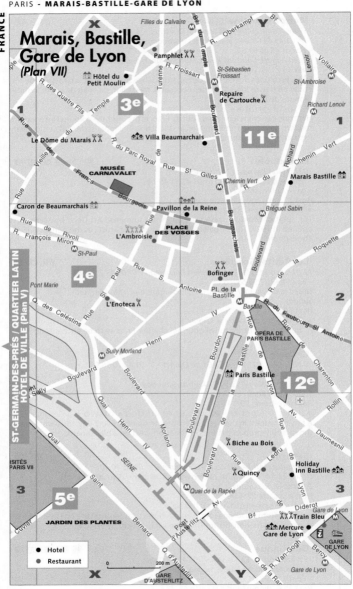

FRANCE

Marais, Bastille, Gare de Lyon
(Plan VII)

X

Filles du Calvaire

Pamphlet XX

🏛 Hôtel du Petit Moulin

3e

R. des Quatre Fils

Temple

R. des Quatre Fils

Le Dôme du Marais XX

R. du Parc Royal

🏠 Villa Beaumarchais

MUSÉE CARNAVALET

Rue St-Gilles

des

Francs

Bourgeois

Caron de Beaumarchais 🏠

Rue de Rivoli

R. François Miron

🚇 St-Paul

Pavillon de la Reine 🏠

XXX **L'Ambroisie**

PLACE DES VOSGES

4e

Rue

Paul

S

Antoine

Pont Marie

Q. des Célestins

Rue

L'Enoteca X

Henri

🚇 Sully Morland

Boulevard

Boulevard

Morland

Boulevard

Quai Henri IV

SEINE

Q. d'Austerlitz

ISITÉS PARIS VII

3

5e

JARDIN DES PLANTES

Cuvier

Saint

Bernard

Pont d'Austerlitz

XXX Bofinger

Pl. de la Bastille

🚇 Bastille

IV

OPÉRA DE PARIS BASTILLE

🏛 Paris Bastille

Bourdon

Boulevard

de

la

Boulevard

de

Quai de la Rapée

Av.

Pont d'Austerlitz

🚇 Oberkampf

Y

Lenoir

Voltaire

St-Sébastien Froissart

St-Ambroise

R. Froissart

Turenne

Boulevard

Repaire de Cartouche X

Richard Lenoir

11e

Chemin Vert

🚇 Chemin Vert

du

Marais Bastille 🏠

🚇 Bréguet Sabin

Beaumarchais

Boulevard

de

la

Roquette

2

R. du Faubourg St Antoine

Charenton

Rue

de

Lyon

12e

Av.

Rollin

Daumesnil

X Biche au Bois

Rue

Ledru

X Quincy

Holiday Inn Bastille 🏠

Rue de Lyon

3

Diderot

Bd

Gare de Lyon

XXX **Train Bleu**

🏠 Mercure Gare de Lyon

Bercy

GARE DE LYON

🚇 Gare de Lyon

Q. de la R. Van-Gogh

ST-GERMAIN-DES-PRÉS / QUARTIER LATIN / HÔTEL DE VILLE (Plan V)

● Hotel
● Restaurant

0   200 m

X

GARE D'AUSTERLITZ

Y

MARAIS-BASTILLE-GARE DE LYON   *Plan VII*

Pavillon de la Reine without rest ⌂   AK ☎ ⅍25
28 pl. Vosges (3rd) – Ⓜ Bastille – ℰ 01 40 29 19 19   🚗 VISA ⓂⓄ AE ①
– contact@pavillon-de-la-reine.com – Fax 01 40 29 19 20   **Y2**
41 rm – ♥350/405 € ♥♥395/450 €, ⌑ 25 € – 15 suites
♦ Grand Luxury ♦ Stylish ♦
Behind one of the 36 brick houses lining the Place des Vosges stand two
buildings, one dating from the 17C, housing refined guest rooms on the
courtyard or garden side (private garden).

Villa Beaumarchais without rest ⌂   ⅙ AK ⅏ ⅍15 VISA ⓂⓄ AE ①
5 r. Arquebusiers (3rd) – Ⓜ Chemin Vert – ℰ 01 40 29 14 00 – beaumarchais@
leshotelsdeparis.com – Fax 01 40 29 14 01   **X-Y1**
50 rm – ♥380 € ♥♥480 €, ⌑ 26 €
♦ Luxury ♦ Stylish ♦
Set back from the hustle and bustle of the boulevard Beaumarchais. Refined
rooms graced with gold-leafed furniture; all rooms overlook a pretty winter
garden.

Holiday Inn Bastille without rest   ⅙ AK ⅏ ℱrest
11 r. Lyon (12th) – Ⓜ Gare de Lyon – ℰ 01 53 02 20 00   ☎ VISA ⓂⓄ AE
– resa.hinn@guichard.fr – Fax 01 53 02 20 01 – www.parisholidayinn.com
125 rm – ♥159/199 € ♥♥159/269 €, ⌑ 15 €   **Y3**
♦ Business ♦ Functional ♦
The façade of this hotel dates from the 19C. In the wood-panelled rooms with
their beautiful wall hangings, modern and period pieces of furniture can be
found side by side. Attractive Baroque-influenced lounge.

Mercure Gare de Lyon without rest   ⅙ AK ⅏ ☎
2 pl. Louis Armand (12th) – Ⓜ Gare de Lyon   ⅍15/90 VISA ⓂⓄ AE ①
– ℰ 01 43 44 84 84 – h2217@accor.com – Fax 01 43 47 41 94
– www.mercure.com   **Y3**
315 rm – ♥140/185 € ♥♥150/215 €, ⌑ 15 €
♦ Business ♦ Functional ♦
The glass façade of this recently built hotel stands in contrast to the adjacent
belfry of the Gare de Lyon. The soundproofed rooms have been redecorated and
are furnished in ceruse wood. Wine bar.

Du Petit Moulin without rest   AK VISA ⓂⓄ AE ①
26 r. du Poitou (3rd) – Ⓜ St-Sébastien Froissart – ℰ 01 42 74 10 10
– contact@hoteldupetitmoulin.com – Fax 01 42 74 10 97
– www.hoteldupetitmoulin.com   **X1**
17 rm – ♥350 € ♥♥350 €, ⌑ 15 €
♦ Luxury ♦ Stylish ♦
For this hotel in the Marais, Christian Lacroix has designed a unique and refined
decor, playing on the contrasts between traditional and modern. Each room has
a different design. Cosy bar.

Caron de Beaumarchais without rest   AK ☎ VISA ⓂⓄ AE
12 r. Vieille-du-Temple (4th) – Ⓜ Hôtel de Ville – ℰ 01 42 72 34 12
– hotel@carondebeaumarchais.com – Fax 01 42 72 34 63
– www.carondebeaumarchais.com   **X2**
19 rm – ♥122/142 € ♥♥152/162 €, ⌑ 10 €
♦ Traditional ♦ Business ♦ Historic ♦
Figaro's father lived in the historic rue du Marais – the bourgeois decoration in
this charming hotel faithfully pays tribute to him. Small, comfortable rooms.

Paris Bastille without rest   AK ℱ ⅍25 VISA ⓂⓄ AE ①
67 r. Lyon (12th) – Ⓜ Bastille – ℰ 01 40 01 07 17 – infosbastille@wanadoo.fr
– Fax 01 40 01 07 27 – www.hotelparisbastille.com   **Y2**
37 rm – ♥155 € ♥♥163/200 €, ⌑ 12 €
♦ Business ♦ Modern ♦
Up-to-date comfort, modern furnishings and carefully chosen colour schemes
characterise the rooms in this hotel facing the Opéra.

FRANCE

Marais Bastille without rest
36 bd Richard Lenoir (11th) – Ⓜ *Bréguet Sabin*
– 𝒞 01 48 05 75 00 – maraisbastille@wanadoo.fr
– Fax 01 43 57 42 85
VISA **◍◎** **AE** **①**
Y1
36 rm – †145 € ††130/145 €, ☐ 10 €
♦ Family ♦ Functional ♦
The hotel runs along the boulevard and gardens that have covered the St-Martin canal since 1860. Renovated interior - entrance-lounge with leather armchairs and oak furniture in the rooms.

L'Ambroisie (Pacaud)
9 pl. des Vosges (4th) – Ⓜ *St-Paul* – 𝒞 01 42 78 51 45
closed 1 to 21 August, February Holidays, Sunday and Monday
AC � ⇔12 ☐♦ **VISA** **◍◎** **AE**
X2
Rest a la carte 180/225 €
Spec. Feuillantine de langoustines aux graines de sésame, sauce curry. Navarin de homard et pommes de terre fondantes au romarin. Tarte fine sablée au chocolat, glace vanille.
♦ Contemporary ♦ Luxury ♦
Under the arcades of the Place des Vosges, a royal decor and a subtle cuisine, close to perfection: Was not ambrosia the food of the Greek gods?

Train Bleu
Gare de Lyon (12th) – Ⓜ *Gare de Lyon* – 𝒞 01 43 43 09 06
– reservation.trainbleu@ssp.fr – Fax 01 43 43 97 96
– www.le-train-bleu.com
VISA **◍◎** **AE** **①**
Y3
Rest 43 € b.i./84 € b.i. and a la carte 50/88 €
♦ Traditional ♦ Retro ♦
This superb, extraordinary station buffet dating from 1901 is a must-see: a profusion of gilt, stucco and murals recalling the legendary PLM line. Brasserie-style dishes.

Bofinger
5 r. Bastille (4th) – Ⓜ *Bastille* – 𝒞 01 42 72 87 82 – eberne@groupeflo.fr
– Fax 01 42 72 97 68
AC ⇔15/30 ☐♦(dinner) **VISA** **◍◎** **AE**
Y2
Rest 25 € b.i. (weekday lunch)/35 € b.i. and a la carte 35/70 €
♦ Brasserie ♦ Retro ♦
The famous clients and remarkable decor have bestowed enduring renown on this brasserie created in 1864 an unforgettable location. The interior boasts a finely worked cupola, and a room on the first floor decorated by Hansi.

Pamphlet
38 r. Debelleyme (3rd) – Ⓜ *Filles du Calvaire* – 𝒞 01 42 72 39 24
– Fax 01 42 72 12 53
AC **VISA** **◍◎**
closed 1 to 8 May, 7 to 27 August, 1 to 15 January, lunch Saturday, lunch Monday and Sunday
X1
Rest 34/50 €
♦ Traditional ♦ Friendly ♦
Charming address smack in the middle of the Marais: rustic decor brightened with pretty colours, bullfight posters, carefully-prepared traditional cuisine and some dishes from the southwest region.

Le Dôme du Marais
53bis r. Francs-Bourgeois (4th) – Ⓜ *Rambuteau*
– 𝒞 01 42 74 54 17 – ledomedumarais@hotmail.com
– Fax 01 42 77 78 17
VISA **◍◎** **AE**
closed 13 August-4 September, Sunday and Monday
X1
Rest 32/45 €
♦ Contemporary ♦ Friendly ♦
Tables are laid under the pretty dome in the old sales room of the Crédit Municipal and in a second dining room that ressembles a winter garden. Modern cuisine.

FRANCE

✗ Quincy   🗚

28 av. Ledru-Rollin (12th) – Ⓜ *Gare de Lyon – ℰ 01 46 28 46 76*
– Fax 01 46 28 46 76 – www.lequincy.fr
closed 12 August-12 September, Saturday, Sunday and Monday   **Y3**
Rest a la carte 50/75 €
♦ Traditional ♦ Family ♦
A warm atmosphere in this rustic bistrot where you are served a hearty cusine
that, like "Bobosse", the jovial owner, has plenty of character.

✗ L'Enoteca   𝑉𝐼𝑆𝐴 ⓂⒺ

25 r. Charles V (4th) – Ⓜ *St-Paul – ℰ 01 42 78 91 44 – enoteca@enoteca.fr*
– Fax 01 44 59 31 72
closed 10 to 20 August, 24 to 27 December and lunch in August   **X2**
Rest (pre-book) a la carte 25/50 € 🕮
♦ Italian ♦ Friendly ♦
A 16C building housing a restaurant whose superb wine list of about 500 Italian
wines is its main asset. Italian dishes and very lively atmosphere.

✗ Repaire de Cartouche   𝑉𝐼𝑆𝐴 ⓂⒺ

99 r. Amelot (11th) – Ⓜ *St-Sébastien Froissart – ℰ 01 47 00 25 86*
– Fax 01 43 38 85 91
closed August, February Holidays, one week in May, Sunday and Monday   **Y1**
Rest 25 € (lunch) and a la carte 35/62 € 🕮
♦ Traditional ♦ Bistro ♦
Cartouche, the impetuous yet honourable bandit, took refuge here between
two bad adventures; the restaurant murals recall his epic life. Attractive wine
list.

✗ Biche au Bois   𝑉𝐼𝑆𝐴 ⓂⒺ 🇦🇪 ⓪

45 av. Ledru-Rollin (12th) – Ⓜ *Gare de Lyon – ℰ 01 43 43 34 38*
closed 23 July-23 August, 24 December-2 January, lunch Monday,
Saturday and Sunday   **Y3**
Rest 24 € and a la carte 32/50 €
♦ Traditional ♦ Family ♦
Restaurant with a simple decor and a noisy, smoky atmosphere, but there
is attentive service and the generous traditional cuisine favours game in
season.

MONTMARTRE, PIGALLE   *Plan VIII*

🏨 Terrass'Hôtel   🍽 🗚 ⅙rm 🕽 ⅍25/100 𝑉𝐼𝑆𝐴 ⓂⒺ 🇦🇪 ⓪

12 r. J. de Maistre (18th) – Ⓜ *Place de Clichy – ℰ 01 46 06 72 85*
– reservation@terrass-hotel.com – Fax 01 42 52 29 11
– www.terrass-hotel.com   **Z1**
85 rm – ♦248/334 € ♦♦334 €, ⌑ 14 € – 15 suites
Rest *Terrasse* , ℰ 01 44 92 34 00 (closed August and dinner Sunday) 28 €
and a la carte 37/59 €
♦ Traditional ♦ Family ♦ Modern ♦
At the foot of Sacré-Cœur. Stunning view over Paris from the bedrooms on the
upper floors on the street side. Elegant and welcoming interior; lounge with a
beautiful fireplace. Refined contemporary decor (shades of beige, grey and
black) and an area specially dedicated to wine.

🏨 Mercure Montmartre without rest   ⅍ 🗚 ⅙

1 r. Caulaincourt (18th) – Ⓜ *Place de Clichy*   ⅍20/70 𝑉𝐼𝑆𝐴 ⓂⒺ 🇦🇪 ⓪
– ℰ 01 44 69 70 70 – h0373@accor.com – Fax 01 44 69 70 71
– www.mercure.com   **Z2**
305 rm – ♦160/185 € ♦♦170/195 €, ⌑ 14 €
♦ Chain hotel ♦ Business ♦ Functional ♦
The hotel is not far from the famous Moulin Rouge. Opt for one of the
rooms on the top three floors so as to fully enjoy the view over the Paris
rooftops.

FRANCE

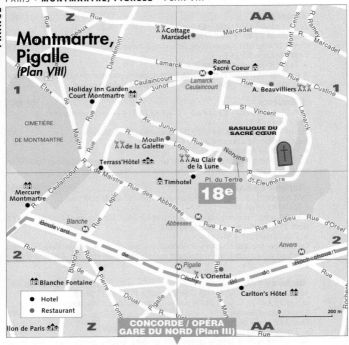

Montmartre, Pigalle *(Plan VIII)*

CIMETIÈRE DE MONTMARTRE

× × Cottage Marcadet
Roma Sacré Coeur
Holiday Inn Garden Court Montmartre
Lamarck Caulaincourt
A. Beauvilliers × × ×
× × de la Galette
Moulin
Terrass'Hôtel
× × Au Clair de la Lune
Timhotel
Pl. du Tertre
BASILIQUE DU SACRÉ CŒUR
Mercure Montmartre

18e

Blanche Fontaine
Pigalle
× L'Oriental
Carlton's Hôtel
Ilon de Paris

● Hotel
● Restaurant

0   200 m

CONCORDE / OPÉRA
GARE DU NORD (Plan III)

Carlton's Hôtel without rest 🕸 VISA ⓂⓈ AE ⓪
55 bd Rochechouart (9th) – Ⓜ Anvers – ℰ 01 42 81 91 00
– *carltons@club-internet.fr* – Fax 01 42 81 97 04   **AA2**
111 rm – †122/130 € ††130/179 €, � 9 €
♦ Business ♦ Functional ♦
This establishment's strong point is its position offering a panorama of the roofs of Paris. Comfortable rooms, with good soundproofing on the street side.

Holiday Inn Garden Court Montmartre without rest ♿ AC
23 r. Damrémont (18th)   ↯ 📞 🛁20 VISA ⓂⓈ AE ⓪
– Ⓜ Lamarck Caulaincourt – ℰ 01 44 92 33 40
– *hiparmm@aol.com* – Fax 01 44 92 09 30
– *www.holiday-inn.com/parismontmart*   **Z1**
54 rm – †130/221 € ††130/221 €, ⊃ 13 €
♦ Chain hotel ♦ Business ♦ Functional ♦
In a steep Montmartre street, a recently created hotel with cool and functional bedrooms. Breakfast room decorated with a pretty trompe-l'œil.

Blanche Fontaine without rest 🌿 AC ↯ 🕸 rest
34 r. Fontaine (9th) – Ⓜ Blanche – ℰ 01 44 63 54 95   📠 VISA ⓂⓈ AE ⓪
– *tryp.blanchefontaine@solmelia.com* – Fax 01 42 81 05 52
– *www.solmelia.com*   **Z2**
66 rm – †105/188 € ††105/209 €, ⊃ 16 € – 5 suites
♦ Business ♦ Functional ♦
This hotel, an oasis of calm in the busy city, has spacious well-maintained rooms. Pleasant breakfast room.

FRANCE

Timhôtel without rest 🔲 🔄 VISA ⓜ AE ①
11 r. Ravignan (18th) – ⓜ *Abbesses* – ℰ *01 42 55 74 79*
– montmartre@timhotel.fr – Fax 01 42 55 71 01
– www.my-paris-hotel.com **AA2**
59 rm – †160 € ††160 €, ⊑ 8,50 €
♦ Chain hotel ♦ Functional ♦
On one of the most charming squares in the neighbourhood stands this smartly renovated hotel. The rooms on the 5th and 6th floors offer unbeatable views of the capital.

Roma Sacré Cœur without rest VISA ⓜ AE ①
101 r. Caulaincourt (18th) – ⓜ *Lamarck Caulaincourt* – ℰ *01 42 62 02 02*
– hotel.roma@wanadoo.fr – Fax 01 42 54 34 92
– www.hotelroma-fr **AA1**
57 rm – †75/85 € ††85/105 €, ⊑ 7,50 €
♦ Traditional ♦ Family ♦ Classic ♦
Here one finds all the charm of Montmartre – a garden in front and stairways on either side leading to the Sacré-Cœur. Vivid colours enliven the renovated rooms.

A Beauvilliers 🔲 VISA ⓜ AE
52 r. Lamarck (18th) – ⓜ *Lamarck Caulaincourt*
– ℰ 01 42 55 05 42 **AA1**
Rest 35 € (weekday lunch)/45 € and a la carte 48/83 €
♦ Traditional ♦ Romantic ♦
There is change in the air at this Montmartre institution: delicious contemporary cuisine with a personal touch and an elegant decor. Pleasant terrace for fine weather.

Cottage Marcadet 🔲 VISA ⓜ
151bis r. Marcadet (18th) – ⓜ *Lamarck Caulaincourt* – ℰ *01 42 57 71 22*
– Fax 01 42 57 71 22
closed 14 to 24 April, August and Sunday **AA1**
Rest 29/39 € and a la carte 45/86 €
♦ Traditional ♦ Retro ♦
An intimate ambiance awaits you in this classic dining room with comfortable Louis XVI furnishings. Carefully-prepared traditional cuisine.

Moulin de la Galette 🔲 VISA ⓜ AE
83 r. Lepic (18th) – ⓜ *Abbesses* – ℰ *01 46 06 84 77*
– Fax 01 46 06 84 78 **Z1**
Rest 25 €, 45/45 €
♦ Traditional ♦ Retro ♦
A windmill in 1622, then a popular dance hall painted by Renoir and Toulouse-Lautrec, this place is now a pleasant restaurant with a charming terrace.

Au Clair de la Lune VISA ⓜ AE
9 r. Poulbot (18th) – ⓜ *Abbesses* – ℰ *01 42 58 97 03*
– Fax 01 42 55 64 74
closed 15 August-15 September, Monday lunch and Sunday **AA1**
Rest 30 € and a la carte 40/65 €
♦ Traditional ♦ Rustic ♦
"Mon ami Pierrot" of the beloved nursery tune would feel at home in this tavern bearing the song's name, behind Place du Tertre. Convivial atmosphere with murals representing old Montmartre.

L'Oriental 🔲 VISA ⓜ AE
76 r. Martyrs (18th) – ⓜ *Pigalle* – ℰ *01 42 64 39 80* – *Fax 01 42 64 39 80*
– www.loriental-restaurant.com
closed 22 July-23 August, Sunday and Monday **AA2**
Rest 14,50 € (weekday lunch)/34 € and a la carte 30/46 €
♦ Couscous specialities ♦ Exotic ♦
Very warm welcome and a pretty Near East setting (tables decorated with Moroccan enameled tiles, and latticework screens) in this North African restaurant in the heart of cosmopolitan Pigalle.

OUTSIDE CENTRAL AREA

Plan I

Murano
13 bd Temple (3rd) – **Ⓜ** Filles du Calvaire – ℰ 01 42 71 20 00
– paris@muranoresort.com – Fax 01 42 71 21 01
– www.muranoresort.com

C2

42 rm – ♦350 € ♦♦400/650 €, ⌑ 28 € – 9 suites
Rest 30 € (weekday lunch) and a la carte 43/81 €
♦ Grand Luxury ♦ Design ♦
The Murano is a new trendy hotel that stands out from the others with its immaculate designer decor, play of colours, high-tech equipment, pop-art bar (150 types of vodka), etc. The restaurant has a colourful contemporary style, international food and a D.J. at the decks.

St-James Paris
43 av. Bugeaud (16th) ⌂ 75116
– **Ⓜ** Porte Dauphine – ℰ 01 44 05 81 81
– contact@saint-james-paris.com – Fax 01 44 05 81 82
– www.saint-james-paris.com

A2

38 rm – ♦360 € ♦♦470/510 €, ⌑ 28 € – 10 suites
Rest (closed Saturday, Sunday and Bank Holidays) (residents only) 47 €
♦ Grand Luxury ♦ Personalised ♦
Beautiful private townhouse built in 1892 by Mme Thiers, in the heart of a shady garden. Majestic staircase, spacious rooms and a bar-library with the atmosphere of an English club.

Sofitel Paris Bercy
1 r. Libourne (12th) – **Ⓜ** Cour St-Emilion – ℰ 01 44 67 34 00
– h2192@accor.com – Fax 01 44 67 34 01
– www.sofitel.com

D3

376 rm – ♦370/475 € ♦♦370/475 €, ⌑ 25 € – 10 suites
Rest Café Ké (closed Saturday and Sunday) 33 €
♦ Chain hotel ♦ Business ♦ Functional ♦
A beautiful glass façade, contemporary interior in shades of brown, beige and blue and all the latest equipment. Some of the rooms have a view across Paris. The Café Ké with its new decor makes for a pleasant stop in the middle of Bercy "village"; modern cuisine.

Sofitel Porte de Sèvres
8 r. L. Armand (15th) – **Ⓜ** Balard – ℰ 01 40 60 30 30
– h0572@accor.com – Fax 01 40 60 30 00
– www.accorhotels.com/sofitel_paris_porte_de_sevres.htm

A3

608 rm – ♦310/390 € ♦♦310/440 €, ⌑ 25 € – 12 suites
Rest see Relais de Sèvres below
Rest Brasserie , ℰ 01 40 60 33 77 (closed Saturday lunch and Sunday lunch) a la carte 35/60 €
♦ Business ♦ Chain hotel ♦ Functional ♦
Opposite the heliport, this hotel offers soundproofed rooms, some of which have been refurbished in an elegantly modern style. The upper floors have a lovely view over western Paris. Brasserie with a setting from the Roaring Twenties: Mosaics, cupola, benches, etc...

Square
3 r. Boulainvilliers (16th) ⌂ 75016 – **Ⓜ** Mirabeau – ℰ 01 44 14 91 90
– hotel.square@wanadoo.fr
– Fax 01 44 14 91 99

A2

22 rm – ♦260 € ♦♦260/340 €, ⌑ 20 € – 2 suites
Rest Zébra Square, ℰ 01 44 14 91 91 – 50/65 €
♦ Luxury ♦ Business ♦ Design ♦
A flower of contemporary architecture across from the Maison de la Radio. Curves, colours, high-tech equipment and abstract paintings: A hymn to modern art! Trendy decor with striped theme in the restaurant, a cellar-library and contemporary cuisine on the menu.

Holiday Inn ⓘ &rm 🄰🄲 ↩rm ﹪rest 🛗25/150 𝗩𝗜𝗦𝗔 ⓜⓞ 🄰🄴 ⓞ
10 pl. République (11th) – Ⓜ *République* – ℰ *01 43 14 43 50*
– pardl.reservations@ichotelsgroup.com – Fax 01 47 00 32 34
– www.paris-republique.holiday-inn.com **C2**
318 rm – ♦152/247 € ♦♦152/397 €, ⌑ 22 €
Rest *(closed 15 July-15 August)* 17/30 €
♦ Business ♦ Chain hotel ♦ Functional ♦
In this 19C building, a fine (listed) wrought-iron stairway leads to comfortable,
well-furnished rooms; opt for one overlooking the inner, Napoleon III-style
courtyard. Belle Epoque-style restaurant extended by a veranda-terrace.
Friendly atmosphere.

Holiday Inn ⌂ ⓘ &rm 🄰🄲 ↩rm 🛗15/140 🄿 𝗩𝗜𝗦𝗔 ⓜⓞ 🄰🄴 ⓞ
216 av. J. Jaurès (19th) – Ⓜ *Porte de Pantin* – ℰ *01 44 84 18 18*
– hilavillette@alliance-hospitality.com – Fax 01 44 84 18 20
– www.holidayinn-parisvillette.com **D1**
182 rm – ♦205/600 € ♦♦205/600 €, ⌑ 17 €
Rest *(closed Saturday, Sunday and Banks Holidays)* 25 €
♦ Chain hotel ♦ Business ♦ Functional ♦
Modern construction across from the Cité de la Musique. Spacious and
soundproofed rooms, offering modern comfort. Métro station a few metres
away. Simple brasserie-style restaurant and small terrace protected from the
street by a curtain of plants.

Holiday Inn Bibliothèque de France without rest &🄰🄲 ↩ ﹪
21 r. Tolbiac (13th) – Ⓜ *Bibliothèque F. Mitterrand* 🛗25 ⌂ 𝗩𝗜𝗦𝗔 ⓜⓞ 🄰🄴 ⓞ
– ℰ 01 45 84 61 61 – hibdf@wanadoo.fr
– Fax 01 45 84 43 38 **C3**
71 rm – ♦87/187 € ♦♦87/187 €, ⌑ 13 €
♦ Chain hotel ♦ Business ♦ Functional ♦
In a busy street 20m from the métro station, this hotel offers comfortable, well-kept rooms with double glazing. Simple dishes available in the
evening.

Kube without rest ⓘ 🄰🄲 ↩ ☏ ⌂ 𝗩𝗜𝗦𝗔 ⓜⓞ 🄰🄴 ⓞ
1 passage Ruelle (18th) – Ⓜ *La Chapelle* – ℰ *01 42 05 20 00*
– paris@kubehotel.com – Fax 01 42 05 21 01 – www.kubehotel.com **C1**
41 rm – ♦250 € ♦♦300 €, ⌑ 25 €
♦ Business ♦ Design ♦
The 19C façade belies the firmly designer, high-tech interior of this hotel. The
bar – built entirely with ice (-5°C) – makes for an unusual but unmissable
experience.

Mercure Porte de Versailles without rest 🄰🄲 ↩ 🛗50/250
69 bd Victor (15th) – Ⓜ *Porte de Versailles* ⌂ 𝗩𝗜𝗦𝗔 ⓜⓞ 🄰🄴 ⓞ
– ℰ 01 44 19 03 03 – h1131@accor.com – Fax 01 48 28 22 11
– www.accorhotels.com/mercure_paris_porte_de_versailles.htm **A3**
91 rm – ♦90/270 € ♦♦90/400 €, ⌑ 15 €
♦ Chain hotel ♦ Business ♦ Functional ♦
A hotel in a 1970s building opposite the Parc des Expositions exhibition
centre. Opt for one of the renovated rooms; the others are functional but
plain.

Novotel Bercy ⌂ &rm 🄰🄲 ↩rm 🛗80 𝗩𝗜𝗦𝗔 ⓜⓞ 🄰🄴 ⓞ
85 r. Bercy (12th) – Ⓜ *Bercy* – ℰ *01 43 42 30 00 – h0935@accor.com*
– Fax 01 43 45 30 60 **D3**
150 rm – ♦105/175 € ♦♦105/203 €, ⌑ 14 €
Rest 24 €
♦ Chain hotel ♦ Functional ♦
The rooms in this Novotel have recently adopted the chain's standards.
At your feet: Bercy Park which succeeded the old wine merchants'
quarter. In good weather, the dining room veranda and terrace are in great
demand.

FRANCE

Novotel Gare de Lyon
〒 ☒ ᕇrm Ⓚ 4⁄rm 🛎75
2 r. Hector Malo (12th) – Ⓜ *Gare de Lyon* ☜ **VISA** **⁵** **AE** **①**
– 𝓒 *01 44 67 60 00 – h1735@accor.com – Fax 01 44 67 60 60*
– *www.novotel.com* **D2**
253 rm – ♥155/185 € ♥♥165/250 €, ☲ 13,50 €
Rest (dinner only Saturday and Sunday) a la carte 23/37 €
♦ Chain hotel ♦ Business ♦ Functional ♦
A modern building giving onto a peaceful square offering practical rooms,
some with a little terrace on the 6th floor. 24-hour swimming pool and
well-designed children's area. Coté Jardin: traditional cuisine in a contemporary
restaurant.

Novotel Tour Eiffel
≼ ᕇ₅ ☒ ᕇrm Ⓚ 4⁄rm 🛎500
61 quai Grenelle (15th) – Ⓜ *Charles Michels* ☜ **VISA** **⁵** **AE** **①**
– 𝓒 *01 40 58 20 00 – h3546@accor.com – Fax 01 40 58 24 44* **A2**
752 rm – ♥260/450 € ♥♥290/450 €, ☲ 20 € – 12 suites
Rest *Café Lenôtre*, 𝓒 *01 40 58 20 75* – a la carte 30/50 €
♦ Chain hotel ♦ Business ♦ Functional ♦
This fully renovated hotel offers comfortable modern rooms (wood, light
shades). Most of them overlook the Seine. High-tech conference centre. The
Café Lenôtre offers pleasant, refined decor, modern cuisine and a delicatessen
area.

XXXX
£₃

Grande Cascade
〒 ⇆6/47 **P** ⊶ **VISA** **⁵** **AE** **①**
allée de Longchamp (opposite the hippodrome) (16th) ⊠ *75016*
– Ⓜ *Porte d'Auteuil* – 𝓒 *01 45 27 33 51 – grandecascade@wanadoo.fr*
– *Fax 01 42 88 99 06*
closed Christmas Holidays
Rest 70/165 € and a la carte 130/175 €
Spec. Chair de tourteau et avocat au caviar d'Aquitaine, crème de langoustines.
Homard bleu à la vanille. Déclinaison de gourmandises en deux services.
♦ Traditional ♦ Retro ♦
A Parisian paradise at the foot of the Grande Cascade (10m!) in the Bois de
Boulogne. Delicately distinctive cuisine served in the 1850 pavilion or on the
splendid terrace.

XXXX
£₃£₃

Pré Catelan
〒 ⇶ Ⓚ **P** ⊶ **VISA** **⁵** **AE** **①**
rte Suresnes (16th) ⊠ *75016* – Ⓜ *Porte Dauphine* – 𝓒 *01 44 14 41 14*
– *leprecatelan-restaurant@lenotre.fr – Fax 01 45 24 43 25*
– *www.lenotre.fr*
*closed 26 October-7 November, 4 to 28 February, Sunday except lunch from
May-October and Monday* **A2**
Rest 70 € (weekday lunch), 135/175 € and a la carte 160/210 € 🕸
Spec. L'os à moelle en deux façons. L'étrille en coque, fine gelée de corail et
caviar, soupe au parfum de fenouil. Le café "expresso" en sabayon, ganache
fouettée, crème glacée brûlée, amandes écrasées.
♦ Innovative ♦ Luxury ♦
Elegant Napoleon III pavilion is in the centre of the wood, near the unusual
Shakespeare theatre. Caran d'Ache decor, refreshing terrace and creative
cuisine.

XXXX
£₃

Relais de Sèvres
– Hôtel Sofitel Porte de Sèvres
Ⓚ **P**
8 r. L. Armand (15th) – Ⓜ *Balard* – 𝓒 *01 40 60 33 66* ⊶ **VISA** **⁵** **AE** **①**
– *h0572@accor.com – Fax 01 40 60 30 00*
*closed 29 July-28 August, 23 December-2 January, 17 to 26 February, Friday
dinner, Saturday, Sunday and Bank Holidays* **A3**
Rest (lunch only Friday) 55/72 € and a la carte 75/105 €
Spec. Pied de cochon en ballotine à la truffe et foie gras de canard. Carré
d'agneau du Limousin rôti, darphin aux olives et champignons. Dégustation de
grands crus de chocolat.
♦ Traditional ♦ Formal ♦
An appealing restaurant for business clients and gourmets. Contemporary
cuisine and fine wine list with elegant and plush decor highlighting "Sèvres Blue"
porcelain.

FRANCE

XXX **Benkay** ⪡ 🆎 🍴 ⇔6/32 ⊡ 𝗩𝗜𝗦𝗔 ⓄⓄ 🆎 Ⓞ
61 quai Grenelle (4th floor) (15th) – Ⓜ *Bir-Hakeim –* ☎ *01 40 58 21 26*
– h3546@accor.com – Fax 01 40 58 21 30 **A2**
Rest 26 € (lunch), 60/125 € and a la carte 60/125 €
♦ Japanese ♦ Exotic ♦
On the top floor of a small building, a restaurant with a fine view of the River
Seine. Sober decor (wood and marble), a sushi and teppanyaki bar.

XXX **Relais d'Auteuil** (Pignol) 🆎 ⊡ 𝗩𝗜𝗦𝗔 ⓄⓄ 🆎 Ⓞ
❀❀ *31 bd Murat (16th)* ⊠ *75016 –* Ⓜ *Michel Ange Molitor –* ☎ *01 46 51 09 54*
– pignol-p@wanadoo.fr – Fax 01 40 71 05 03 **A2**
closed August, Christmas Holidays, Monday lunch, Saturday lunch and Sunday
Rest 49 € (weekday lunch), 115/145 € and a la carte 105/140 € ❀
Spec. Petits chaussons de céleri-rave et truffes (November to February). Ris de
veau à la cardamome. Beignets de chocolat bitter.
♦ Contemporary ♦ Fashionable ♦
A pleasant setting combining a touch of the modern with period furniture. As for
the menus, refinement of taste vies with culinary virtuosity. An exceptional wine
list.

XX **Chez Géraud** 𝗩𝗜𝗦𝗔 ⓄⓄ
☺ *31 r. Vital (16th)* ⊠ *75016 –* Ⓜ *La Muette –* ☎ *01 45 20 33 00 – Fax 01 45 20 46 60*
closed 28 July-28 August, 22 December-2 January, Saturday and Sunday
Rest a la carte 50/75 € **A2**
♦ Traditional ♦ Bistro ♦
The facade and then the inside mural, both in Longwy faience, draw the eye. Chic
bistrot setting with a cuisine that features game in season.

XX **Mansouria** 🆎 🍴 𝗩𝗜𝗦𝗔 ⓄⓄ
☺ *11 r. Faidherbe (11th) –* Ⓜ *Faidherbe Chaligny –* ☎ *01 43 71 00 16*
– Fax 01 40 24 21 97 **D2**
Rest 30/46 € b.i. and a la carte 33/50 €
♦ Moroccan ♦ Exotic ♦
Run by a former ethnologist, well-known in Paris in the field of Moroccan cuisine.
The delicate, aromatic dishes are prepared by women and served in a Moorish
decor.

LA DÉFENSE

🏨 **Sofitel Grande Arche** 🛋 🕴 ♿rm 🆎 🍴rm 🕏rest 🎱10/100
11 av. Arche (exit Défense 6) ⊠ *92081* 🌐 𝗩𝗜𝗦𝗔 ⓄⓄ 🆎 Ⓞ
– ☎ *01 47 17 50 00 – h3013@accor.com – Fax 01 47 17 55 66 – www.sofitel.com*
352 rm – ♦345 € ♦♦397/431 €, ⊡ 25 € – 16 suites
Rest *Avant Seine,* ☎ *01 47 17 59 99 (closed 1 to 20 August, 23 December-*
1 January, Friday diner, Saturday and Sunday) a la carte approx. 46 €
♦ Chain hotel ♦ Luxury ♦ Stylish ♦
Beautiful architecture, resembling a ship's hull, a combination of glass and ochre
stonework. Spacious, elegant rooms, lounges and very well equipped
auditorium (with simultaneous translation booths). The Avant Seine offers you
quality designer décor and spit-roast dishes.

🏨 **Renaissance** 🛋 🕴rm 🆎 🍴rm 🕏 🎱160 🌐 𝗩𝗜𝗦𝗔 ⓄⓄ 🆎 Ⓞ
60 Jardin de Valmy (by ring road, exit La Défense 7) ⊠ *92918 –* ☎ *01 41 97 50 50*
– rhi.parld.exec.sec@renaissancehotels.com – Fax 01 41 97 51 51
– www.renaissancehotels.com/parld
closed Saturday, Sunday and lunch bank holidays
324 rm – ♦195/315 € ♦♦195/340 €, ⊡ 24 € – 3 suites
Rest 29 € (weekday lunch), 43/65 €
♦ Chain hotel ♦ Luxury ♦ Cosy ♦
At the foot of the Carrare marble Grande Arche, this contemporary hotel has
well-equipped rooms, with refined decoration. Good fitness facilities. In the
restaurant, all-wood features with a "retro" brasserie atmosphere and a view of
the gardens of Valmy.

Hilton La Défense 🛜 &rm 📺 ↔rm ℅ 🕽 ♨5/60 🚗
2 pl. Défense ✉ 92053 – ℰ 01 46 92 10 10   P VISA 🅼🅾 AE ⓘ
– parldhirm @ hilton.com – Fax 01 46 92 10 50
– www.hilton.com
139 rm – ∮240/540 € ∮∮240/540 €, ☲ 26 € – 9 suites
Rest Les Communautés, ℰ 01 46 92 10 30 – 57 €
Rest L'Échiquier, ℰ 01 46 92 10 35 – 26 € (lunch) and a la carte 35/60 €
♦ Chain hotel ♦ Business ♦ Modern ♦
The completely refurbished hotel is situated within the CNIT complex. The welcoming designer rooms cater particularly to a business clientele. Les Communautés restaurant offers modern cuisine and a fine view. The Échiquier offers a traditional menu.

Sofitel Centre 🛜 ∱& &rm 📺 ↔rm 🕽 ♨10/80 🚗 VISA 🅼🅾
34 cours Michelet (by ring road, exit La Défense 4) ✉ 92060 Puteaux – ℰ 01 47 76 44 43 – h0912 @ accor.com – Fax 01 47 76 72 10
– www.sofitel.com
150 rm – ∮345/510 € ∮∮395/560 €, ☲ 25 € – 1 suite
Rest Les Deux Arcs, ℰ 01 47 76 72 30 (closed 14 July-22 August, 25 December-3 January, Saturday, Sunday and Bank Holidays) 68 €
Rest Le Botanic, ℰ 01 47 76 72 40 (closed dinner Friday, Saturday and Bank Holidays) a la carte 37/52 €
♦ Chain hotel ♦ Business ♦ Design ♦
The scalloped façade of this hotel stands out amid the skyscrapers of La Défense. Spacious, well-equipped rooms, which are gradually being refurbished in a more trendy style. Italian cuisine served in a modern setting. A relaxed atmosphere pervades the Italian Lounge.

Novotel La Défense ∱& &rm 📺 ↔rm ♨130 🚗 VISA 🅼🅾 AE ⓘ
2 bd Neuilly (exit Défense 1) – ℰ 01 41 45 23 23 – h0747 @ accor.com
– Fax 01 41 45 23 24 – www.novotel.com   Plan I **A1**
280 rm – ∮190/225 € ∮∮200/235 €, ☲ 15 €
Rest a la carte 27/49 €
♦ Chain hotel ♦ Business ♦ Classic ♦
Sculpture and architecture: La Défense, a veritable open-air museum, is right at the foot of this hotel. Practical rooms, some overlooking Paris. The bar has a trendy new decor. Contemporary decor in the dining room, which also has a buffet area.

PARIS AIRPORTS

Orly – Airport South 16 km

Hilton Orly ∱& & 📺 ↔rm 🕽 ♨10/280 P VISA 🅼🅾 AE ⓘ
✉ 94544 – ℰ 01 45 12 45 12 – rm.orly @ hilton.com – Fax 01 45 12 45 00
– www.hilton.com
351 rm – ∮141/195 € ∮∮210 €, ☲ 18 €
Rest a la carte 28/45 €
♦ Chain hotel ♦ Business ♦ Functional ♦
This 1960s hotel has discreet, elegant rooms. It offers high-quality facilities for meetings and offers full service for business people. Modern decor, brasserie-style dishes or buffet option at this restaurant.

Mercure & 📺 ↔rm ♨15/40 P VISA 🅼🅾 AE ⓘ
✉ 94547 – ℰ 01 49 75 15 50 – h1246 @ accor.com – Fax 01 49 75 15 51
192 rm – ∮145/175 € ∮∮205 €, ☲ 13,50 €
Rest 24 €
♦ Chain hotel ♦ Business ♦ Functional ♦
Convenient for travellers in need of a full-service hotel when they are between flights. Well-kept rooms. Trendy bistro setting, brasserie-style dishes and Mercure wine list.

Roissy-Charles de Gaulle Airport *North East 26 km*

Commercial Area Z. I. Paris Nord II

Hyatt Regency ⊗   🕵 ◻ ❋ 👶rm 🅰🅲 ⟵⟶rm ♨300 🅿 *VISA* ◕◉ 🅐🅔 ◑
351 av. de la Pie – ✆ 01 48 17 12 34 – cdg@hyattintl.com – Fax 01 48 17 17 17
376 rm – 🛏130/330 € 🛏🛏130/395 €, ⬚ 25 € – 12 suites
Rest 53/59 €
♦ Chain hotel ♦ Business ♦ Modern ♦
Spectacular, contemporary architecture on the edge of the airport complex: a vast atrium links the two wings containing large, comfortable rooms. The Hyatt Regency dining area has a large glass-roof; buffets or classical menu.

at Terminal 2

Sheraton ⊗   ≤ 🍽 🕵 👶rm 🅰🅲 ⟵⟶rm ♨2/65 🅿, *VISA* ◕◉ 🅐🅔 ◑
– ✆ 01 49 19 70 70 – Fax 01 49 19 70 71 – www.sheraton.com/parisairport
242 rm – 🛏229/499 € 🛏🛏229/569 €, ⬚ 28 € – 12 suites
Rest *Les Étoiles* *(closed Saturday, Sunday and Bank Holidays)* 57 €
Rest *Les Saisons* a la carte approx. 46 €
♦ Chain hotel ♦ Business ♦ Modern ♦
Leave your plane or train and take a trip on this "luxury liner" with its futuristic architecture. Decor by Andrée Putman, a view of the runways, absolute quiet and refined rooms. Les Étoiles offers modern cuisine and beautiful contemporary setting. Brasserie dishes at Les Saisons.

at Roissypole

Hilton   🕵 ◻ 👶 🅰🅲 ⟵⟶rm ♨15/500 🚗 *VISA* ◕◉ 🅐🅔 ◑
– ✆ 01 49 19 77 77 – cdghitwsal@hilton.com – Fax 01 49 19 77 78
383 rm – 🛏149/519 € 🛏🛏149/600 €, ⬚ 24 €
Rest *Le Gourmet*, ✆ 01 49 19 77 95 *(closed July-August, 23 to 31 December, Saturday and Sunday)* 47 €
Rest *Les Aviateurs*, ✆ 01 49 19 77 95 – 37 € b.i./55 €
♦ Chain hotel ♦ Business ♦ Modern ♦
Daring architecture, space and light are the main features of this hotel. Its ultra-modern facilities make it an ideal place in which to work and relax. Modern food is to be found at Le Gourmet. Les Aviateurs, small choice of brasserie dishes.

Sofitel   🕵 🍽 ◻ ❋ 👶rm 🅰🅲 ⟵⟶rm ♨ 10/100 🅿 *VISA* ◕◉ 🅐🅔 ◑
West central zone – ✆ 01 49 19 29 29 – h0577@accor.com – Fax 01 49 19 29 00 – www.sofitel.com
344 rm – 🛏275/550 € 🛏🛏275/550 €, ⬚ 24 € – 4 suites
Rest *L'Escale* a la carte 45/65 €
♦ Chain hotel ♦ Business ♦ Modern ♦
A personal welcome, comfortable atmosphere, conference rooms, an elegant bar and well-looked-after rooms are the advantages of this hotel between two airport terminals. A restaurant with a nautical flavour and seafood. This is a nice place to stop, dedicated to the sea.

at Roissy-Ville

Courtyard Marriott   🍽 🕵 👶 🅰🅲 ⟵⟶rm ♨12/230 🚗
allée du Verger – ✆ 01 34 38 53 53   🅿 *VISA* ◕◉ 🅐🅔 ◑
– jerome.bourdais@courtyard.com – Fax 01 34 38 53 54
300 rm – 🛏135/300 € 🛏🛏155/300 €, ⬚ 19 € – 4 suites
Rest 40 € b.i. (weekday lunch), 35 € b.i. (dinner)/55 € b.i.
♦ Business ♦ Modern ♦
Behind its colonnaded white façade, this establishment has modern facilities perfectly in tune with the requirements of businessmen transiting through Paris. Classic cuisine served in a decor based on the brasseries of the "Ville Lumière"

FRANCE

Millennium ⌗ ƒ ⊡ ⅙ rm 🆑 ⅙ rm 🛋18/150 ➰ 𝘝𝘐𝘚𝘈 ◑◑ 🅐🅔 ⓪
allée du Verger – ℰ 01 34 29 33 33 – sales.cdg @ mill-cop.com
– Fax 01 34 29 03 05
239 rm – ♦115/280 € ♦♦115/700 €, � 20 €
Rest 32 € b.i.
♦ Business ♦ Modern ♦
Bar, Irish pub, fitness centre, an attractive swimming pool, conference rooms, and spacious bedrooms with one floor specially equipped for businessmen: a hotel with good facilities. International cuisine and brasserie buffet or fast food served at the bar.

Dorint by Novotel ◑ ƒ ⊡ ⅙ 🆑 ⅙ rm ⓦ 🛋8/200
– ℰ 01 30 18 20 00 – h5418 @ accor.com ➰ 🅿 𝘝𝘐𝘚𝘈 ◑◑ 🅐🅔
– Fax 01 34 29 95 60
282 rm – ♦250 € ♦♦350 €, ⊏ 18 € – 7 suites
Rest a la carte 26/40 €
♦ Business ♦ Chain hotel ♦ Modern ♦
The latest arrival in the hotel zone at Roissy offers impressive services: extensive seminar facilities, kids' corner and comprehensive wellness centre.

Country Inn and Suites ⌗ ƒ ⅙ 🆑 ⅙ rm 🛋15/95 ➰
allée du Verger – ℰ 01 30 18 21 00 – info @ countryinns.de 🅿 𝘝𝘐𝘚𝘈 ◑◑ 🅐🅔 ⓪
– Fax 01 30 18 21 12
180 rm – ♦100/175 € ♦♦100/220 €, ⊏ 13 €
Rest 20 € b.i. and a la carte 30/45 €
♦ Business ♦ Modern ♦
The former Château de Roissy, burnt down during the Revolution, provided the model for this hexagonal building with an interior garden. English-style bar. This restaurant offers a tasty combination of French and American dishes.

Mercure ⌗ ⅙ 🆑 ⅙ rm 🛋30/90 🅿 𝘝𝘐𝘚𝘈 ◑◑ ⓪
allée des Vergers – ℰ 01 34 29 40 00 – h1245 @ accor.com – Fax 01 34 29 00 18
– www.mercure.com
203 rm – ♦135/180 € ♦♦145/240 €, ⊏ 13 €
Rest 23 €
♦ Chain hotel ♦ Business ♦ Modern ♦
This hotel has a meticulous decor comprising Provençal style in the hall, old-fashioned zinc in the bar and spacious rooms in light wood. The dining room of the Mercure has been completely revamped and now offers amusing mock bakery decor.

LYONS
LYON

Population (est. 2005): 468 000 (conurbation 1 449 000) – Altitude: 175m

Its favourable location at the confluence of two great waterways, the Rivers Saône and Rhône, gives Lyons, France's second city, a unique character. It is an industrial city specialising in metalworking and chemistry. It is also a university town and a world famous centre in the field of medicine. Its cuisine is renowned and it has a well-deserved reputation as one of the gastronomic centres in France. The city is a popular tourist destination.

Lyons has always been a prosperous city. Trade flourished during the Roman Empire and the Renaissance. The city took full advantage of its geographical situation as it lies on the road to Italy, between Central and Eastern France, and midway between northern France and the southern provinces. Christianity took hold in the 2C and several martyrs were put to death. In the Middle Ages, Lyons came under royal rule and the workers rebelled against the elected consuls. From the end of the 15C the city prospered with the organisation of fairs and the development of the banking sector. Artists, poets, writers and printers gave impetus to its social, intellectual and cultural life. In the 16C silk weaving was the major activity.

The spirit of the local people is embodied by the puppets, Guignol, his wife Madelon and his sparring partner Gnafron; the puppet shows are a Lyons tradition.

WHICH DISTRICT TO CHOOSE

The **city centre** from Place Bellecour to Place des Terreaux *Plan II* **F2** and the **old town** *Plan II* **F2** are the areas to choose for luxury accommodation. There are chain hotels around La Part-Dieu and Perrache stations and comfortable establishments in Rue Victor-Hugo *Plan II* **F3**, Rue de la Charité *Plan II* **F3**, along the quays near Place Bellecour and near the Opera *Plan II* **F1**.

It is unusual not to eat well in Lyons. The famous establishments in the city centre, in the old town and on the outskirts are the places to visit for a gastronomic experience. A meal at

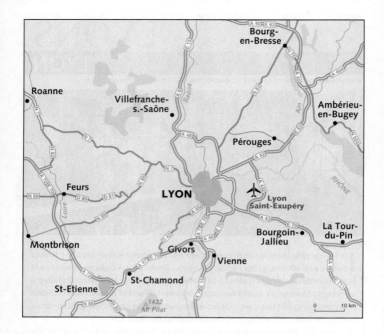

one of the typical '**bouchons**' is a must to enjoy the hearty local specialities. **Brasseries** are also favourite haunts.

When going out **for a drink or for the evening**, make for the terraces lining Rue Ste-Catherine *Plan II* **F1**.

PRACTICAL INFORMATION

ARRIVAL – DEPARTURE

Lyon-Saint-Exupéry Airport – 27km (12mi) east of the city centre. ℰ 0826 800 826; www.lyon.aéroport.fr

From the airport to the city centre – By **express bus**: time: 20 min; fare €8.40 single, €14.90 return trip. ℰ 04 72 68 17. By **taxi**: approx. €35-40 (€50-55 between 7pm to 7am and Sun). GIE Aéroport ℰ 04 72 22 70 90.

Main Stations – **La Part-Dieu** Station *Plan II* **H3**: TGV high-speed trains ; **Lyon-Perrache** *Plan II* **E3** TGV high-speed trains and regional destinations.

TRANSPORT

◆ BUS, METRO, TRAM AND FUNICULAR

The 'Liberty' ticket (€4.20) is valid for 1 day for travel on the city's public transport network. A single ticket costs €1.50 and a book of 10 tickets €11.90.

◆ TAXIS

Allow €10-15 for a short journey. Some taxis accept payment by Credit card. Tips are not compulsory. *Espace Taxi* ℰ 04 78 27 31 31; *Lyon International Taxi* ℰ 04 78 88 16 16; *Allo Taxi* ℰ 04 78 28 23 23; *Taxi Lyonnais* ℰ 04 78 26 81 81.

Place Bellecour *Plan II* **F2**. ☏ 04 72 77 69 69; www.lyon-france.com; open 9am-7pm daily.

◆ POST OFFICES

Opening times Mon-Fri 8am-noon and 2pm-6pm.

◆ BANKS/CURRENCY EXCHANGE

Banks open Mon-Fri, 9am-noon and 2-5pm. There are cash dispensers (ATM), which require a PIN number, all over the city. Credit cards are widely accepted. Bureaux de change often charge high commissions.

◆ EMERGENCY

Police ☏ **17,** Fire Brigade ☏ **18,** Medical assistance ☏ **15**.

EXPLORING LYONS

It is possible to visit the main sights and museums in two days.

Museums and other sights are usually open from 9-10am to 5.30-6pm. Some close on Mondays or Tuesdays and at lunchtime.

VISITING

Tour of the town centre (Péninsule) – The core of the city: from the shady Place Bellecour *Plan II* **F2** along Rue de la République to Place des Terreaux *Plan II* **F1**. Do not miss the **Musée des Tissus** devoted to the weaver's art and silk production in Lyons.

Musée des Beaux-Arts *Plan II* **F1** – Housed in Palais St-Pierre, the museum presents an excellent survey of art through the centuries.

Château Lumière *Plan I* **C2** – An elegant mansion, the former residence of the Lumière brothers: Institut Lumière, exhibition, performances.

Musée d'Art Contemporain *Plan IiI* **H1** – A display of modern art in a striking building.

Musée de l'Automobile Henri-Malartre – *At La Rochetaillée-sur-Saône*. A remarkable collection of vintage and racing cars, cycles, motor cycles and public transport vehicles.

Fourvière heights *Plan II* **E2** – **Basilique Notre-Dame**, Tour Métallique, archaeological site, museums, Roman theatres, aqueducts, mausoleums. Viewpoints from esplanade and observatory.

Tour of Old Lyons *Plan II* **E2** – Explore the St-Jean, St-Paul and St-Georges districts: the **'traboules' passageways**, squares and courtyards, fountains, **15-17C period mansions**, 12C church – Place St-Jean, Rue St-Jean, Rue des Trois-Maries, Place du Gouvernement, Place du Change, Rue Lainerie, Rue Juiverie, Rue du Bœuf, Place de la Trinité, Rue St-Georges, Montée du Gourguillon.

Tour of Croix-Rousse district *Plan II* **F1** – The **'traboules'**, the silk trade workshops (Maison des Canuts), Cour des Voraces, Amphithéâtre des Trois Gaules, Fresque des Lyonnais, Gros Caillou. View from Place Rouville.

Boat trips – On the Rhône and Saône from Quai des Célestins *Plan II* **F2**.

SHOPPING

Shops and malls usually open Mon-Fri, 9am-6.30pm, Sat 9am-5pm; many are open until 9pm on Thur and 7.30pm on Fri.

Le **Carré d'Or** between Place Bellecour *Plan II* **F2** and Place des Cordeliers *Plan II* **F2** is the area for **luxury and designer shops** (local designers Nathalie Chiaze, Max Chaoul, Azuleros). If you are keen on **antiques**, explore the **Quartier Auguste Comte** (Rue Auguste Comte *Plan II* **F3**, Rue de la Charité *Plan II* **F3**) and *Cité des Antiquaires*, 117 Boulevard Stalingrad. **Old-fashioned shops** (knives, hats etc.) are to be found in the arcade, **Le Passage de l'Argue**, between Rue de la République *Plan II* **F2** and Rue Édouard-Herriot *Plan II* **F1**. The pedestrian avenue running from Rue Victor-Hugo to Rue de la République is also worth a visit for **clothes and other goods**.

L'Atelier de Soierie, 33 Rue Romarin (silk and velvet fabric); *Chez Disagn' Cardelli*, 6 Rue St-Jean (music boxes, masks and puppets); *Bonnard*, 36 Rue Granette; *Reynon*, 13 Rue des Archers; *Pignol*, 8 Place Bellecour (Lyonnais specialities). *Voisin*, 28 Rue de la République (chocolates, candied fruit, confectionery).

MARKETS – **Marché de la Création**, Quai Romain Rolland *Plan II* **F2** (Sun 6am-1pm) – paintings, sculpture jewellery; **Marché de l'Artisanat**, Quai Fulchiron *Plan II* **E3** (Sun 7am-1pm) – crafts. **Puces du Canal**, 1 Rue du Canal *Plan I* **B1** (Thu-Sat 8am-noon, Sun 6am-1pm) – antiques. **Book sellers**, Quai de la Pêcherie *Plan II* **F2** (daily 9am-9pm). **Stamp market**, Place Bellecour *Plan II* **F2** (Sun). There are also traditional markets: **Halles de Lyon**, 102 Cours Lafayette *Plan III* **G3** (regional products and small taverns), Boulevard de la Croix-Rousse *Plan II* **F1** (Tue-Sun mornings), Quai St Antoine-Célestins *Plan II* **F2** (Tue-Sun mornings).

WHAT TO BUY – Silk goods, marionnettes and music boxes, fine foods, confectionery (coussins, cocons, quenelles, palets d'or).

ENTERTAINMENT

For listings of shows and entertainment consult *Lyon Poche*; www.lyon poche.com

Opéra National de Lyon *Plan II* **F2**: opera, ballet, classical, jazz and world music.

Auditorium-Orchestre National de Lyon *Plan II* **F2**: concerts.

Théâtre National Populaire *Plan I* **C1**: contemporary plays.

Maison de la Danse *Plan I* **C2**: classical and modern dance.

Halle Tony-Garnier *Plan II* **B2**: shows and events.

Le Guignol de Lyon *Plan II* **F2**: shows for children and adults.

Au Pied dans l'Plat *Plan II* **E2**: cabaret.

NIGHTLIFE

Rue Ste-Catherine *Plan II* **F1** and **Rue Mercière** *Plan II* **F2** are particularly lively in the evenings. Jazz lovers should visit *Hot Club*, 26 Rue Lanterne, *Bar de la Tour Rose*, 22 Rue du Bœuf. *Le Cintra*, 43 Rue de la Bourse, is a smart piano-bar. Popular venues for dancing are *BC Blues*, 25 Place Carnot, *Fish Club*, 21 Quai Victor-Augagneur. *Ninkasi Ale House*, 267 Rue Marcel-Mérieux, is a trendy place with a micro-brewery, café, DJ evenings. Or while away the evening at *Casino Le Pharaon*, 70 Quai Charles-de-Gaulle or *Casino Le Lyon Vert*, 200 Avenue du Casino, La Tour-de-Salvagny.

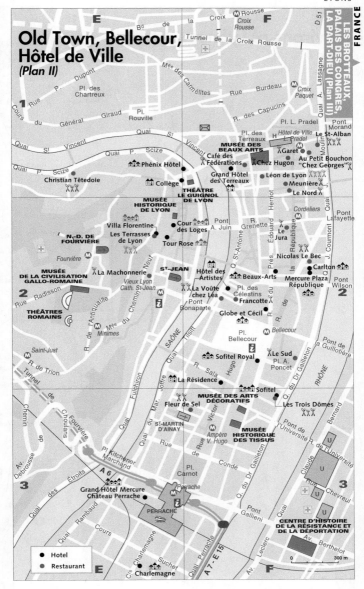

Old Town, Bellecour, Hôtel de Ville
(Plan II)

Bd de la Croix
Croix Rousse
M Rousse

Tunnel de la Croix Rousse

D 51

Quai A. Lassagne

Rue P. Dupont

Pl. des Chartreux

Rue du Général Giraud

Pl. Rouville

Rue Burdeau

M Croix Paquet

R. des Capucins

Pl. L. Pradel

Pont Morand

Cours du Quai St Vincent

Quai St Vincent

Pl. des Terreaux

Hôtel de Ville L. Pradel

Le St-Alban

Quai P. Scize

MUSÉE DES BEAUX ARTS

Au Petit Bouchon "Chez Georges"

Quai P. Scize

Phénix Hôtel

Café des Fédérations

Garet

Chez Hugon

Christian Têtedoie

Collège

Grand Hôtel des Terreaux

Léon de Lyon

Meunière

MUSÉE HISTORIQUE DE LYON

Herriot

Le Nord

THÉÂTRE LE GUIGNOL DE LYON

Cordeliers

Pont Lafayette

Villa Florentine

Cour des Loges

Pont A. Juin

R. Grenette

Le Jura

N.-D. DE FOURVIÈRE

Les Terrasses de Lyon

Tour Rose

R. Édouard Herriot

R. de la République

Nicolas Le Bec

J. Courmont

Fourvière

M

Prés.

Carlton

MUSÉE DE LA CIVILISATION GALLO-ROMAINE

La Machonnerie

ST-JEAN

Hôtel des Artistes

Q. St-Antoine

Beaux-Arts

Mercure Plaza République

Pont Wilson

Rue Radisson

Vieux Lyon Cath. St-Jean

R. de l'Antiquaille

Mée du Chemin Neuf

La Voûte chez Léa

Pl. des Célestins

Francotte

R. du

THÉÂTRES ROMAINS

Saint-Just

Pont Bonaparte

Globe et Cécil

R. de Trion

Tunnel de Fourvière

Mée des Minimes

SAÔNE

Quai Tilsitt

Pl. Bellecour

M Bellecour

Pont de la Guillotière

Sofitel Royal

Le Sud

Pl. A. Poncet

RHÔNE

Quai Fulchiron

Quai du Mar. Joffre

R. Sala

R. Victor Hugo

La Résidence

Sofitel

Pont de l'Université R. de l'Université

MUSÉE DES ARTS DÉCORATIFS

Fleur de Sel

Les Trois Dômes

Av. Debrousse

Chemin de Choulans

ST-MARTIN D'AINAY

Ampère V. Hugo

MUSÉE HISTORIQUE DES TISSUS

Q. du Dr Gailleton

Pont Gallieni

Quai Claude Bernard

U

Av. des Étroits

Pl. Kitchener Marchand

Rue

Rue V. Hugo

Condé

Pl. Carnot

Rue Chevreul

U

A 6

Grand Hôtel Mercure Château Perrache

Perrache

PERRACHE

U

Quai Rambaud

Cours

PERRACHE

Pont Gallieni

Quai Perrache

CENTRE D'HISTOIRE DE LA RÉSISTANCE ET DE LA DÉPORTATION

Av. Berthelot

● Hotel
● Restaurant

C's Charlemagne

Charlemagne

Suchet

A 7 - E 15

Av. Leclerc

0   300 m

Environs of Lyons
(Plan I)

CHAMPAGNE-
AU-MONT-D'OR

CALUIRE

Auberge de l'Ile

FORT DE
MONTESSUY

Tunnel de Calluire et Cuire

Lyon
Métropole

Auberge
de Fond Rose

Palais
La Part

Cuire

Hénon

LA CROIX-ROUSSE

Gare
de Vaise

ÉCULLY

Old Town, Bellecour,
Hôtel de Ville (Plan II)

Valmy

Q. St. Vincent

H

Gorge
de Loup

Q. P. Scize

FORT DE
LOYASSE

N.-D. DE
FOURVIÈRE

TASSIN-LA-
DEMI-LUNE

Buyer

Pl.
Bellecour

Av. du Point du Jour

Guillotière

Pl.
Carnot

Saxe Gambetta

Charcot

PERRACHE

STE-FOY-
LÈS-LYON

R. Châtelain

HALLE
T. GARNIER

U

Delbourg

Pl. J.
Jaurès

FRANCHEVILLE

LA MULATIÈRE

Av. T. Garnier

ARCHES DE
CHAPONOST

D 50

Stade de Gerland

GERLAND

PORT E.
HERRIOT

CHAPONOST

OULLINS

A 7

PIERRE-
BÉNITE

FORT DE
COTE LORETTE

A 450

ST-GENIS-
LAVAL

● Hotel

● Restaurant

0   1 km

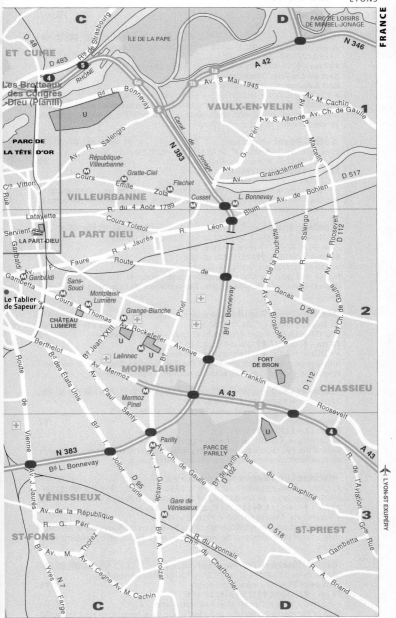

Sofitel ⬳ ⬳ rm 🅰️ ⬳rm ⬳15/200 ⬳ 🆅🅸🆂🅰️ 🆖 🅰️🅴 ⓞ
20 quai Gailleton ⬳ *69002 –* ☏ *04 72 41 20 20 – h0553@accor.com*
– Fax 04 72 40 05 50 **F3**
137 rm – ⬳275/420 € ⬳⬳305/420 €, ⬳ 24 € – 29 suites
Rest see *Les Trois Dômes* below
Rest *Sofishop*, ☏ *04 72 41 20 80 –* 24 € b.i./26 € b.i.
♦ Chain hotel ♦ Business ♦ Modern ♦
The cubic, somewhat sober exterior contrasts with the luxurious interior. Opt for the renovated rooms with mahogany or light wooden furniture. Brasserie atmosphere and fare at the Sofishop.

Sofitel Royal without rest 🅰️ ⬳ ⬳ 🆅🅸🆂🅰️ 🆖 🅰️🅴 ⓞ
20 pl. Bellecour ⬳ *69002 –* ☏ *04 78 37 57 31 – h2952@accor.com*
– Fax 04 78 37 01 36 – www.sofitel.com **F2**
78 rm – ⬳185 € ⬳⬳200/400 €, ⬳ 20 €
♦ Chain hotel ♦ Stylish ♦
A 19C building facing the most famous square in Lyon. A choice of the mahogany and brass furnishings of the small "clipper" rooms, large Louis XV-style rooms or functional rooms.

Carlton without rest 🅰️ ⬳ ⬳ 🆅🅸🆂🅰️ 🆖 🅰️🅴 ⓞ
4 r. Jussieu ⬳ *69002 –* ☏ *04 78 42 56 51 – h2950@accor.com*
– Fax 04 78 42 10 71 – www.mercure.com **F2**
83 rm – ⬳78/158 € ⬳⬳103/158 €, ⬳ 12 €
♦ Traditional ♦ Family ♦ Retro ♦
Purple and gold are the two predominant colours in this traditional hotel, decorated with old-fashioned style. The venerable lift cage has a charm of its own.

Mercure Plaza République without rest ⬳ 🅰️ ⬳ ⬳
5 r. Stella ⬳ *69002 –* ☏ *04 78 37 50 50* ⬳20/35 🆅🅸🆂🅰️ 🆖 🅰️🅴 ⓞ
– h2951-gm@accor.com – Fax 04 78 42 33 34 – www.mercure.com **F2**
78 rm – ⬳76/122 € ⬳⬳118/154 €, ⬳ 12,50 €
♦ Chain hotel ♦ Business ♦ Modern ♦
A mascaron crowns each window of this 19C building. The exterior contrasts dramatically and surprisingly with the resolutely modern interior.

Globe et Cécil without rest 🅰️ ⬳ ⬳25 🆅🅸🆂🅰️ 🆖 🅰️🅴 ⓞ
21 r. Gasparin ⬳ *69002 –* ☏ *04 78 42 58 95*
– accueil@globeetcecilhotel.com – Fax 04 72 41 99 06
– www.globeetcecilhotel.com **F2**
60 rm ⬳ – ⬳120 € ⬳⬳155 €
♦ Family ♦ Traditional ♦ Personalised ♦
Behind the 19C façade is a hotel with character. Rooms with a personal touch, antique furniture and a wood-panelled breakfast room.

Mercure Lyon Beaux-Arts without rest 🅰️ ⬳ ⬳
75 r. Prés. E. Herriot ⬳ *69002 –* ☏ *04 78 38 09 50* ⬳15 🆅🅸🆂🅰️ 🆖 🅰️🅴 ⓞ
– h2949@accor.com – Fax 04 78 42 19 19 – www.mercure.com **F2**
75 rm – ⬳104/131 € ⬳⬳112/157 €, ⬳ 12,50 € – 4 suites
♦ Family ♦ Traditional ♦ Functional ♦
Beautiful building from 1900, most of the bedrooms are furnished in Art Deco style. Four of the bedrooms, the most unique, were decorated by contemporary artists.

Grand Hôtel des Terreaux without rest ⬳ ⬳ 🆅🅸🆂🅰️ 🆖 🅰️🅴 ⓞ
16 r. Lanterne ⬳ *69001 –* ☏ *04 78 27 04 10 – ght@hotel-lyon.fr*
– Fax 04 78 27 97 75 – www.hotel-lyon.fr **F1**
53 rm – ⬳85/130 € ⬳⬳115/130 €, ⬳ 11 €
♦ Family ♦ Traditional ♦ Personalised ♦
Most of the rooms behind this graceful façade have been renovated. Colourful materials and various styles of furniture. Enjoy the indoor pool.

La Résidence without rest   [AC] [☎] [VISA] [MO] [AE] [①]

18 r. V. Hugo ⊠ *69002 – ℰ 04 78 42 63 28*
– hotel-la-residence@wanadoo.fr – Fax 04 78 42 85 76
– www.hotel-la-residence.com   **F2**
67 rm – ♦73 € ♦♦73 €, ⊑ 6,50 €
♦ Family ♦ Traditional ♦ Functional ♦
In a pedestrian street near the Bellecour square, this hotel provides rooms and a
lounge in 1970s style. The renovated rooms are more lively.

Des Artistes without rest   [AC] [⅍] [VISA] [MO] [AE] [①]

8 r. G. André ⊠ *69002 – ℰ 04 78 42 04 88 – hartiste@club-internet.fr*
– Fax 04 78 42 93 76 – www.hoteldesartistes.fr   **F2**
45 rm – ♦75/110 € ♦♦85/115 €, ⊑ 9 €
♦ Traditional ♦ Stylish ♦
The hotel is named after the "artistes" of the neighbouring Célestins
theatre. Light, stylish rooms. A Cocteau style fresco adorns the breakfast
room.

Léon de Lyon (Lacombe)   [AC] [½] [⊑ₜ] [VISA] [MO] [AE]

1 r. Pleney ⊠ *69001 – ℰ 04 72 10 11 12 – leon@relaischateaux.com*
– Fax 04 72 10 11 13 – www.leondelyon.com
closed 9 to 17 July, 30 July-21 August, Sunday and Monday   **F1**
Rest 59 € (lunch), 115/150 € and a la carte 95/130 € ⅋
Spec. Cochon fermier du Cantal, foie gras et oignons confits. Traditionnelle
quenelle de brochet lyonnaise "revue et corrigée". Cinq petits desserts sur le
thème de la praline de Saint-Genix.
♦ Lyonnais cuisine ♦ Formal ♦
The great Lyon tradition for food is alive and well in these wood-panelled
dining rooms, decorated with paintings in honour of the kitchen boy.
Splendid!

Les Trois Dômes – Hôtel Sofitel   ≼ Lyon, [AC] [P] [⊑ₜ] [VISA] [MO] [AE] [①]

20 quai Gailleton (at 8th floor) ⊠ *69002 – ℰ 04 72 41 20 97 – h0553@accor.com*
– Fax 04 72 40 05 50
closed 22 July-22 August, 17 to 27 February, Sunday and Monday   **F3**
Rest 52 € (weekday lunch), 72/121 € b.i. and a la carte 80/115 €
Spec. Millefeuille de crabe et avocat. Quenelle de brochet soufflée. Volaille de
Bresse.
♦ Regional ♦ Fashionable ♦
This restaurant offers a fine panoramic view from the top floor of the Sofitel hotel,
where you can also enjoy delicious cuisine with regional touches.

Le St-Alban   [AC] [VISA] [MO] [AE]

2 quai J. Moulin ⊠ *69001 – ℰ 04 78 30 14 89 – Fax 04 72 00 88 82*
closed 22 July-21 August, 2 to 10 January, Saturday lunch, Sunday and Bank
Holidays   **F1**
Rest 28 € (weekdays)/66 € and a la carte 53/71 €
♦ Traditional ♦ Friendly ♦
Silk squares depicting Lyon monuments enliven the chic interior of this
vaulted dining room near the opera house. Classical cuisine with a contemporary
touch.

Nicolas Le Bec   [ﺩ] [AC] [VISA] [MO] [AE] [①]

14 r. Grolée ⊠ *69002 – ℰ 04 78 42 15 00 – restaurant@nicolaslebec.com*
– Fax 04 72 40 98 97
closed 1 to 8 May, 14 to 21 August, 30 October-6 November, 1 to 8 January,
Sunday, Monday and Bank Holidays   **F2**
Rest 45 € (weekday lunch), 85/125 € and a la carte 85/120 € ⅋
Spec. Galette de cèpes au jus de poulet rôti (September-October). Lapereau aux
raisins blonds, fèves et amandes (July-Sept). Mousse de chocolat chaude et
crème glacée aux pistaches (July-September).
♦ Contemporary ♦ Trendy ♦
Restaurant in a modern setting decorated in shades of toffee and chocolate,
serving refined and inventive cuisine. Wine list glorifying French wine.

XX **Fleur de Sel** · *VISA* · ⑩⑤

3 r. Remparts d'Ainay ⊠ 69002 – ℰ 04 78 37 40 37 – Fax 04 78 37 26 37
closed August, Sunday and Monday **F3**
Rest 19 € (weekdays), 29/49 €
♦ Mediterranean ♦ Formal ♦

The light gently filters through the green and yellow curtains of this vast dining
area. Well-spaced tables and modern seats. Personalised cooking, inspired by
the flavours of Provence.

XX **La Voûte - Chez Léa** · *AC* *VISA* ⑩⑤ *AE*

11 pl. A. Gourju ⊠ 69002 – ℰ 04 78 42 01 33 – Fax 04 78 37 36 41
closed Sunday **F2**
Rest 18 € (weekdays)/38 €
♦ Lyonnais cuisine ♦ Retro ♦

The unchanging menu leads us to the era, not so long ago, when the Mères
reigned over the Lyon gastronomic scene. "Retro" decor on the ground floor,
more refined on the first floor.

X **Le Nord** · 🍴 *AC* *VISA* ⑩⑤ *AE* ⑩

18 r. Neuve ⊠ 69002 – ℰ 04 72 10 69 69 – Fax 04 72 10 69 68 **F1**
Rest 21/26 €
♦ Traditional ♦ Formal ♦

"The North" is proud of its speciality - Alsatian choucroute from eastern France.
Authentic 1900s brasserie decor: wine-coloured banquettes, colourful tile floors,
wood panelling and ball lamps.

X **Le Sud** · 🍴 *AC* *VISA* ⑩⑤ *AE* ⑩

11 pl. Antonin Poncet ⊠ 69002 – ℰ 04 72 77 80 00 – Fax 04 72 77 80 01
Rest 21/26 € **F2**
♦ Mediterranean ♦ Brasserie ♦

"The South" is another of chef Paul Bocuse's cardinal points, this one specialising
in "sunny cuisine", in a bright and youthful ambience. Almost like being there...

X **Francotte** · *AC* *VISA* ⑩⑤ *AE*

8 pl. des Célestins ⊠ 69002 – ℰ 04 78 37 38 64 – infos @ francotte.fr
– Fax 04 78 38 20 35 – www.francotte.fr
closed 1 to 15 August, Sunday and Monday **F2**
Rest 19 € (lunch), 23/27 €
♦ Lyonnais cuisine ♦ Brasserie ♦

This restaurant next to the Célestins theatre in a bistro setting serves brasserie-
style cuisine. Breakfasts served in the morning; tea room in the afternoon.

BOUCHONS *Regional wine tasting and local cuisine in a typical
Lyonnais atmosphere*

X **Au Petit Bouchon "Chez Georges"** · *VISA* ⑩⑤
☺
8 r. Garet ⊠ 69001 – ℰ 04 78 28 30 46
closed August, Saturday, Sunday and Bank Holidays **F1**
Rest 17 € (lunch)/24 € (a la carte dinner) and a la carte 25/36 €
♦ Lyonnais cuisine ♦ Bistro ♦

In an informal atmosphere, savour this typical "bouchon": the famous Lyonnais
"tablier de sapeur (breaded, grilled tripe), quenelles (dumplings) and more, with
a carafe of Beaujolais.

X **Garet** · *AC* *VISA* ⑩⑤ *AE*
☺
7 r. Garet ⊠ 69001 – ℰ 04 78 28 16 94 – legaret @ wanadoo.fr
– Fax 04 72 00 06 84
closed 21 July-21 August, 12 to 18 February, Saturday and Sunday **F1**
Rest (pre-book) 18 € (lunch)/22 €
♦ Lyonnais cuisine ♦ Retro ♦

Locals in shirtsleeves, coveralls, or business suits mingle here to enjoy the
traditional dishes ... and never count the calories!

Chez Hugon
VISA MC

12 r. Pizay ✉ 69001 – ✆ 04 78 28 10 94 – Fax 04 78 28 10 94
closed 22 to 28 May, August, Saturday and Sunday **F1**
Rest (pre-book) 23/33 €
◆ Lyonnais cuisine ◆ Bistro ◆
You can watch the chef stirring the blanquette de veau in this warm and lively "bouchon". Plenty of good cheer for all!

Café des Fédérations
A/C VISA MC

8 r. Major Martin ✉ 69001 – ✆ 04 78 28 26 00 – yr@lesfedeslyon.com – Fax 04 72 07 74 52
closed 23 July-21 August, Saturday and Sunday **F1**
Rest (pre-book) 20 € (lunch)/24 €
◆ Lyonnais cuisine ◆ Bistro ◆
Checked tablecloths, tables and guests close together, giant sausages hanging above the counter and copious regional cooking: a genuine "bouchon" for sure!

Le Jura
VISA MC

25 r. Tupin ✉ 69002 – ✆ 04 78 42 20 57
closed 1 to 20 August, Monday from September to April, Saturday from May to September and Sunday **F2**
Rest (pre-book) 20 €
◆ Lyonnais cuisine ◆ Retro ◆
Do not be misled by the sign: this is an authentic "bouchon", the 1930s setting scrupulously preserved, serving typical dishes of Lyon.

La Meunière
A/C VISA MC

11 r. Neuve ✉ 69001 – ✆ 04 78 28 62 91 – Fax 04 78 28 62 91 – www.la-meuniere.fr
closed 14 July-15 August, 24 December-2 January, Sunday, Monday and Bank Holidays **F1**
Rest (pre-book) 18 € (weekday lunch), 22/29 €
◆ Lyonnais cuisine ◆ Retro ◆
This "bouchon" is in the rue Neuve: the 1920s decor has not changed one iota and the menu is appetising, so inevitably, at meal times, the line of hungry patrons stretches round the block.

OLD TOWN
Plan II

Villa Florentine
< Lyon, 15
P VISA MC AE

25 montée St-Barthélémy ✉ 69005 – ✆ 04 72 56 56 56 – florentine@relaischateaux.com – Fax 04 72 40 90 56 **E2**
20 rm – 🚹150/350 € 🚹🚹150/350 €, ☕ 16 € – 8 suites
Rest see ***Les Terrasses de Lyon*** below
◆ Grand Luxury ◆ Traditional ◆ Personalised ◆
This former convent with its Renaissance adornments, on "the hill that prays" (Michelet), rivals the most sumptuous Tuscan villas.

Cour des Loges
A/C 15/50
VISA MC AE

6 r. Boeuf ✉ 69005 – ✆ 04 72 77 44 44 – contact@courdesloges.com – Fax 04 72 40 93 61 – www.courdesloges.com **E2**
52 rm – 🚹230 € 🚹🚹280/590 €, ☕ 22 € – 10 suites
Rest ***Les Loges*** *(open October-April)* (dinner only) 55/75 €
◆ Grand Luxury ◆ Traditional ◆ Historic ◆
The astonishing decoration of a group of 14C and 18C houses set around a splendid galleried courtyard was designed by contemporary designers and artists. At Les Loges, in the winter, creative cuisine and decor with a personal touch.

FRANCE

Tour Rose ⊛   AC ⁙rest ♨25 ⌂ VISA ⚫ AE ①
22 r. Boeuf ⊠ 69005 – ℰ 04 78 92 69 10 – contact @ latour-rose.com
– Fax 04 78 42 26 02 – www.tour-rose.com   **E2**
6 rm – ♦230 € ♦♦200/290 €, ⊊ 18 € – 6 suites
Rest (closed Sunday) 53/106 €
♦ Luxury ♦ Traditional ♦ Classic ♦
These typical houses of historic Lyons have characteristic staircases and terraced
gardens. Remarkable bedrooms decorated in the best Lyon silks. Attractive
windows at the foot of the pink tower and an elegant dining room where creative
cuisine with a touch of spice is served.

Phénix Hôtel without rest   & AC ⊬ ℰ♨30 ⌂ VISA ⚫ AE ①
7 quai Bondy ⊠ 69005 – ℰ 04 78 28 24 24
– reception @ hotel-le-phenix.fr – Fax 04 78 28 62 86
– www.hotel-le-phenix.fr   **E1**
36 rm – ♦120/124 € ♦♦156/166 €, ⊊ 12 €
♦ Traditional ♦ Family ♦ Functional ♦
An old building on the Saône quayside. Large rooms with modern decor, some
with a fireplace. Pleasant breakfast room under a glass roof.

Collège without rest   & AC ⊬ ℰ♨20 ⌂ VISA ⚫ AE ①
5 pl. St-Paul ⊠ 69005 – ℰ 04 72 10 05 05 – contact @ college-hotel.com
– Fax 04 78 27 98 84 – www.college-hotel.com   **E1**
39 rm – ♦105/135 € ♦♦120/135 €, ⊊ 11 €
♦ Traditional ♦ Business ♦ Personalised ♦
The Collège offers a trip down memory lane, with old-fashioned school desks, a
pommel horse and geography maps.

Les Terrasses de Lyon – Hôtel Villa Florentine   ≤ Lyon, ⌖ ⌖ AC
25 montée St-Barthélémy ⊠ 69005   P ⌖ VISA ⚫ AE ①
– ℰ 04 72 56 56 56 – lesterrassesdelyon @ villaflorentine.com
– Fax 04 72 40 90 56 – www.villaflorentine.com
closed Sunday and Monday   **E2**
Rest 45 € (weekday lunch), 70/120 € and a la carte 100/150 €
Spec. Cannelloni de tourteau, crémeux de petits pois et caviar. Homard cuit
minute, fricassée d'escargots, cocotte de légumes et jus de crustacés. Selle de
veau poêlée, cocotte de ris de veau braisés et morilles
♦ Innovative ♦ Formal ♦
Choose between the former nun's dining hall, stunning glass roof and
panoramic terrace: three elegant settings offering lovely, modern food.

Christian Têtedoie   AC ⌖ VISA ⚫ AE
54 quai Pierre Scize ⊠ 69005 – ℰ 04 78 29 40 10 – restaurant @ tetedoie.com
– Fax 04 72 07 05 65 – www.tetedoie.com
closed 31 July-20 August, 19 to 25 February, Monday lunch, Saturday lunch and
Sunday   **E1**
Rest 40/75 € and a la carte 65/85 €
Spec. Marinière de coquillages et homard (October-March). Anguille farcie au
bœuf carottes (October-March). Tuile dentelle à l'olive, crème mascarpone et
mousseux cacao.
♦ Contemporary ♦ Family ♦
Behind this elegant façade is a dining room with modern decor of subtle yellow
tones. Some tables have a view of the Saône River. Contemporary cuisine and
wine display cabinet.

La Machonnerie   AC VISA ⚫ AE ①
36 r. Tramassac ⊠ 69005 – ℰ 04 78 42 24 62
– felix @ lamachonnerie.com – Fax 04 72 40 23 32
– www.lamachonnerie.com
closed Sunday and lunch except Saturday   **E2**
Rest (pre-book) 20/43 € b.i.
♦ Lyonnais cuisine ♦ Bistro ♦
The tradition of the Lyon "mâchon" has been respected in this restaurant:
informal service, a friendly atmosphere and authentic cuisine.

PERRACHE

Plan II

Grand Hôtel Mercure Château Perrache

AC 4/rm ℡

12 cours Verdun ✉ *69002* ♨20/200 ☞ **P** **VISA** **CO** **AE** **①**
– 𝒞 04 72 77 15 00 – h1292@accor.com – Fax 04 78 37 06 56
– www.mercure.com **E3**
109 rm – ♦98/167 € ♦♦112/182 €, � 13,50 € – 2 suites
Rest *Les Belles Saisons* *(closed 31 July-21 August and lunch Saturday)* 32 €
♦ Chain hotel ♦ Business ♦ Historic ♦
This former hotel of the PLM group has partially conserved its Art nouveau
setting, with its intricately sculpted wood-furnishings in the lobby. An incredible
period. The full effect of the Majorelle style is reflected in this superb restaurant,
Les Belles Saisons.

Charlemagne

🏠 AC ℡ ♨15/120 ☞ **P** **VISA** **CO** **AE** **①**

23 Cours Charlemagne ✉ *69002 – 𝒞 04 72 77 70 00 – charlemagne@
hotel-lyon.fr – Fax 04 78 42 94 84 – www.hotel-lyon.fr* **E3**
116 rm – ♦80/135 € ♦♦85/135 €, ⊂ 10 €
Rest *(closed 29 July-27 August, Saturday and Sunday)* 19/23 €
♦ Family ♦ Business ♦ Modern ♦
Two buildings separated by a courtyard; the rooms in the second building are
more spacious and pleasant. Winter-garden style breakfast room. Modern
restaurant with a pleasant terrace in summer and unpretentious, standard fare.

LES BROTTEAUX - LA PART-DIEU

Plan III

Hilton

🏠 £ᶀ ♿rm AC 4/rm ℡ ♨15/400 ☞ **VISA** **CO** **AE** **①**

70 quai Ch. de Gaulle ✉ *69006 – 𝒞 04 78 17 50 50 – rm-lyon@hilton.com
– Fax 04 78 17 52 52 – www.hilton-lyon.com* **H1**
186 rm – ♦139/404 € ♦♦139/914 €, ⊂ 24 € – 13 suites
Rest *Blue Elephant* , 𝒞 *04 78 17 50 00 (closed 20 July-20 August, Saturday lunch
and Sunday)* 23 € (lunch), 40/50 €
Rest *Brasserie* , 𝒞 *04 78 17 51 00 –* 17 € (lunch) and a la carte 36/50 €
♦ Chain hotel ♦ Business ♦ Design ♦
Modern hotel for the international city bringing together a convention centre, a
casino and a museum of contemporary art. Spacious bedrooms facing the Tête
d'Or park or the Rhône. Thai specialities and decor at the Blue Elephant.
Traditional food is to be found at the Brasserie.

Radisson SAS ⌖

≼ Lyon and Rhône valley, AC 4/rm ℡ ♨15/110

129 r. Servient (32 nd floor) ✉ *69003 – 𝒞 04* ☞ **VISA** **CO** **AE** **①**
78 63 55 00 – info.lyon@radissonsas.com – Fax 04 78 63 55 20 **H3**
245 rm – ♦110/250 € ♦♦110/270 €, ⊂ 19 €
Rest *L'Arc-en-Ciel* *(closed 15 to 25 July, Saturday lunch and Sunday)* 44 €
(lunch), 56 € b.i./74 € b.i. ⌘
Rest *Bistrot de la Tour* *–* (ground floor) *(closed Sunday lunch and Saturday)*
19 € and a la carte 24/42 €
♦ Luxury ♦ Business ♦ Functional ♦
At the top of the "Crayon" (100m high), panoramic view and interior layout
inspired by the houses of old Lyons: interior courtyards and superimposed
galleries. You are guaranteed a view at the Arc-en-Ciel, located on the 32nd floor
of the tower! The Bistrot is situated on the ground floor.

Novotel La Part-Dieu

♿rm AC 4/rm ♨15/70 ☞ **VISA** **CO** **AE** **①**

47 bd Vivier-Merle ✉ *69003 – 𝒞 04 72 13 51 51 – h0735@accor.com
– Fax 04 72 13 51 99 – www.novotel.com* **H3**
124 rm – ♦114/138 € ♦♦122/146 €, ⊂ 13 €
Rest *(closed Friday dinner, Saturday and Sunday)* 23 €
♦ Chain hotel ♦ Business ♦ Functional ♦
A vast lounge-bar with an Internet area, rooms in line with the chain's latest
standards - a practical place for an overnight stay quite close to the station. This
Novotel restaurant is practical for business travellers with a train to catch or
between meetings.

Les Brotteaux, Palais des Congrès, La Part-Dieu

(Plan III)

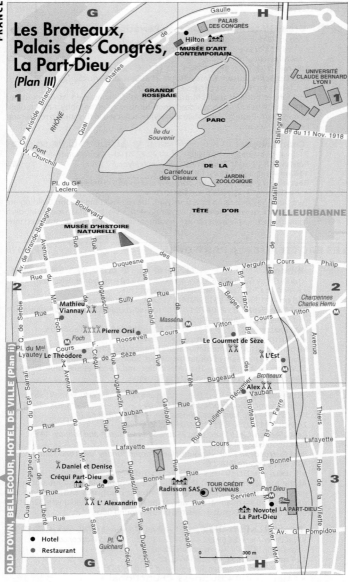

Créqui Part-Dieu &rm 🖭 ⇆rm 📞 ⚙30 VISA ⓪◎ 🅰 ①

37 r. Bonnel ⊠ 69003 – ℰ 04 78 60 20 47 – inforesa@hotel-crequi.com
– Fax 04 78 62 21 12   **G3**
46 rm – ∲69/144 € ∲∲79/154 €, � 11 € – 3 suites
Rest *(closed 31 July-21 August, Saturday and Sunday out of season)*
a la carte approx. 35 €
♦ Traditional ♦ Business ♦ Design ♦
The establishment is located opposite the court area. The layout of the bedrooms is inspired by Provençal colours and materials, while a new wing offers a distinctly modern setting.

Pierre Orsi 🏠 & 🖭 ﹪ ⊸ VISA ⓪◎ 🅰

3 pl. Kléber ⊠ 69006 – ℰ 04 78 89 57 68 – orsi@relaischateaux.com
– Fax 04 72 44 93 34
closed Sunday and Monday except Bank Holidays   **G2**
Rest 45 € (weekday lunch), 80/110 € and a la carte 80/120 € ⅏
Spec. Ravioles de foie gras de canard au jus de porto et truffes. Homard acadien en carapace. Pigeonneau en cocotte aux gousses d'ail confites.
♦ Lyonnais cuisine ♦ Formal ♦
This old building is home to an elegant restaurant and rose garden terrace. Serves good cuisine from Lyon. With a fine, 200-year old vaulted cellar.

L' Alexandrin (Alexanian) 🏠 🖭 VISA ⓪◎ 🅰

83 r. Moncey ⊠ 69003 – ℰ 04 72 61 15 69 – lalexandrin@lalexandrin.com
– Fax 04 78 62 75 57 – www.lalexandrin.com
closed 25 to 29 May, 1 to 22 August, 29 October-1 November,
23 December-3 January, Sunday and Monday   **G3**
Rest 38 € (lunch), 60/80 € ⅏
Spec. Fritots de carpe royale de la Dombes. Mousseline de brochet en quenelle. Fricassée de volaille de Bresse.
♦ Innovative ♦ Friendly ♦
Modern, chic decor with friendly service, a good selection of Côtes-du-Rhône wines and original cuisine that gives a new lease of life to traditional recipes. Popular with Lyon's jet set.

Le Gourmet de Sèze (Mariller) 🖭 ⇆ VISA ⓪◎ 🅰

129 r. Sèze ⊠ 69006 – ℰ 04 78 24 23 42 – legourmetdeseze@wanadoo.fr
– Fax 04 78 24 66 81
closed 1 to 8 May, 23 July-22 August, 1 to 3 January, 18 to 26 February, Sunday
and Monday   **H2**
Rest (number of covers limited, pre-book) 35/66 €
Spec. Croustillants de pieds de cochon. Cannelloni de langoustines à la truffe blanche (April-July). Grand dessert du gourmet.
♦ Contemporary ♦ Family ♦
Smart, small restaurant and classical cooking intelligently brought up-to-date : the gourmets of the Rue de Sèze are not the only ones to be beguiled.

Mathieu Viannay 🖭 VISA ⓪◎ 🅰

47 av. Foch ⊠ 69006 – ℰ 04 78 89 55 19 – Fax 04 78 89 08 39
closed 29 July-27 August, 10 to 18 February, Saturday and Sunday   **G2**
Rest 32 € (weekday lunch), 46/80 € and a la carte 55/85 €
Spec. Pâté de volaille de Bresse et foie gras en croûte. Fricassée d'ormeaux et champignons des bois (September-April). Madeleines tièdes au miel, glace au fromage blanc.
♦ Contemporary ♦ Minimalist ♦
Resolutely modern dining room, with parquet flooring, colourful seats and an original chandelier created by the Lyon designer, Alain Vavro. Delicious contemporary cuisine.

Alex 🛋 AC ⌧ VISA ⚫ AE

44 bd Brotteaux ⊠ 69006 – 𝒞 04 78 52 30 11 – chez.alex@club-internet.fr
– Fax 04 78 52 34 16
closed August, Sunday and Monday **H3**
Rest 20 € (weekday lunch), 24/52 €
♦ Innovative ♦ Trendy ♦
Restaurant in a smart, refined setting boldly allying colours, designer furniture and contemporary artworks. Fine cuisine for the modern palate.

L'Est 🛋 AC VISA ⚫ AE ⓪

Gare des Brotteaux, 14 pl. J. Ferry ⊠ 69006 – 𝒞 04 37 24 25 26
– Fax 04 37 24 25 25 – www.bocuse.fr **H2**
Rest 21/26 €
♦ Brasserie ♦ Fashionable ♦
Old station converted into a trendy brasserie. Electric train circuits and cooking from the continents: gourmet globe-trotters, all aboard!

Le Théodore 🛋 AC VISA ⚫ AE ⓪

34 cours Franklin Roosevelt ⊠ 69006 – 𝒞 04 78 24 08 52
– le.theodore@wanadoo.fr – Fax 04 72 74 41 21
closed 6 to 20 August, Sunday and Bank Holidays **G2**
Rest 20 € (weekday lunch), 22/35 €
♦ Traditional ♦ Bistro ♦
Behind a subtle painted facade, a bistro atmosphere and Belle Époque setting is more than enough to beguile you. Pleasant summer terrace. Traditional cooking.

Daniel et Denise AC VISA ⚫ AE ⓪

156 r. Créqui ⊠ 69003 – 𝒞 04 78 60 66 53 – Fax 04 78 60 66 53
closed 27 July-29 August, 24 December-3 January, Saturday, Sunday and Bank Holidays **G3**
Rest 27/39 €
♦ Lyonnais cuisine ♦ Bistro ♦
The former delicatessen provides an attractive setting – smooth, time-worn surfaces, old posters and photographs, chequered tablecloths. Generous helpings of tasty Lyon specialities.

ENVIRONS OF LYONS *Plan I*

Lyon Métropole 🛋 ⊕ ⚊ ▣ ※ ⌖rm AC ♨15/300 ⌂ ℙ

85 quai J. Gillet ⊠ 69004 – 𝒞 04 72 10 44 44 **ℙ VISA ⚫ AE ⓪**
– metropole_lyonmetropole_concorde.com – Fax 04 72 10 44 42
– www.lyonmetropole-concorde.com **B1**
117 rm – ♦160/190 € ♦♦160/250 €, ⊇ 23 € – 1 suite
Rest *Brasserie Lyon Plage*, 𝒞 04 72 10 44 30 – 24 €
♦ Business ♦ Traditional ♦ Art Deco ♦
This 1980s hotel, reflected in the Olympic swimming pool, offers varied leisure and sports facilities, including a large spa, a fitness room, tennis and squash courts, as well as golf practice areas. Renovated rooms. A blue interior and terrace by the water at the Brasserie Lyon Plage.

Auberge de Fond Rose (Vignat) 🛋 ⊜ AC ⌖ ℙ VISA ⚫ AE

23 quai G. Clemenceau ⊠ 69300 – 𝒞 04 78 29 34 61
– contact@aubergedefondrose.com – Fax 04 72 00 28 67
– www.aubergedefondrose.com
closed 2 to 20 November, 19 February-5 March, Sunday dinner and Monday except Bank Holidays **B1**
Rest 38 € b.i. (weekday lunch), 48/69 € and a la carte 80/100 €
Spec. Rémoulade de grenouilles et fritot d'escargots. Féra argentée au jus d'oignons nouveaux. Selle d'agneau farcie rôtie.
♦ Traditional ♦ Friendly ♦
This grand 1920s house is surrounded by a shady garden with flowers. Dining area with fireplace and peaceful terrace, serving good traditional cuisine.

FRANCE

XX
$$$$ **Auberge de l'Ile** (Ansanay-Alex)   ⅙ 🅿 ⌂ (dinner) 𝗩𝗜𝗦𝗔 ⚫⚫ 🄰🄴 ⓞ
sur l'Ile Barbe ⊠ *69009 – ℰ 04 78 83 99 49 – info @ aubergedelile.com*
– Fax 04 78 47 80 46
closed 30 July-21 August   **B1**
Rest 60 € (weekday lunch), 90/120 €
Spec. Figue rôtie et homard, beurre de corail à la vendange tardive (Summer).
Omble chevalier au beurre de mousserons (Spring). Crème glacée à la réglisse,
cornet de pain d'épices.
♦ Contemporary ♦ Fashionable ♦
This charming restaurant is set in a 17C building on an island in the middle of the
Saône River. Refined, modern cuisine is served in the characterful (non-smoking)
dining area.

X
 Le Tablier de Sapeur   🄰🄲 ⅙ 𝗩𝗜𝗦𝗔 ⚫⚫ 🄰🄴
16 r. Madeleine ⊠ *69007 – ℰ 04 78 72 22 40 – Fax 04 78 72 22 40*
*closed August, 25 December-2 January, Monday from October-June, Saturday
from July-September and Sunday*   **C2**
Rest 20/36 €
♦ Lyonnais cuisine ♦ Bistro ♦
Family welcome, cool setting, traditional dishes - including the famous tablier de
sapeur, a Lyonnais speciality made with tripe - and a choice of wines by the
carafe.

Collonges-au-Mont-d'Or *North 12 km by D 51 –* **B 1**

XXXXX
 Paul Bocuse   🄰🄲 🅿 ⌂ 𝗩𝗜𝗦𝗔 ⚫⚫ 🄰🄴 ⓞ
bridge of Collonges (N : 12 km by the banks of River Saône (D 433, D 51) ⊠ *69660
– ℰ 04 72 42 90 90 – paul.bocuse @ bocuse.fr – Fax 04 72 27 85 87
– www.bocuse.fr*
Rest 110/190 € and a la carte 95/155 € ⌘
Spec. Soupe aux truffes noires VGE. Rouget barbet en écailles de pommes de
terre. Volaille de Bresse en vessie "Mère Fillioux".
♦ Traditional ♦ Family ♦
The colourful and elegant Paul Bocuse restaurant serves historic dishes to an
international clientele. Paintings of the great chefs adorn the courtyard.

Charbonnières-les-Bains *West 8 km by N 7 –* **A 1**

🏨 **Le Pavillon de la Rotonde** ⌘   ⚫ ▣ 🄿 🔥 🄰🄲 ⅙ 🕭 ♨️ 15/25 🅿
au Casino Le Lyon Vert – ℰ 04 78 87 79 79   𝗩𝗜𝗦𝗔 ⚫⚫ 🄰🄴 ⓞ
– contact @ pavillon-rotonde.com – Fax 04 78 87 79 78
– www.pavillon-rotonde.com
16 rm – ♦295 € ♦♦525 €, ⊡ 19 €
Rest see *La Rotonde* below
♦ Grand Luxury ♦ Personalised ♦ Stylish ♦
A stone's throw from the casino, a luxurious hotel with contemporary decor and
discreet Art Deco touches. Spacious rooms with terrace giving onto the gardens.
Heated indoor swimming pool and spa.

XXXX
 La Rotonde   🄰🄲 𝗩𝗜𝗦𝗔 ⚫⚫ 🄰🄴 ⓞ
*au Casino Le Lyon Vert – ℰ 04 78 87 79 79 – contact @ pavillon-rotonde.com
– Fax 04 78 87 79 78 – www.pavillon-rotonde.com*
closed 22 July-23 August, Sunday and Monday
Rest 40 € (weekday lunch), 85/140 € and a la carte 100/130 € ⌘
Spec. Il était une fois... quatre foies pressés. Tajine de homard entier aux petits
farcis. Cannelloni de chocolat amer à la glace de crème brûlée.
♦ Innovative ♦ Romantic ♦
A renowned gourmet restaurant on the first floor of the famous casino, under the
sign of Lady Luck since 1882. An elegant Art Deco-style dining room enlivened
with superb flower arrangements, opening onto the gardens.

STRASBOURG

STRASBOURG

Population (est. 2004) : 273 100 (conurbation 427 300) – Altitude: 143m

R. Mattès/MICHELIN

Strasbourg's favourable location as a major communications hub linking the Mediterranean with the Rhineland, Central Europe, the North Sea and the Baltic, has shaped its character. It is an outgoing city as befits its role as the seat of the Council of Europe and other European institutions. Visitors will be charmed by the attractive historic district with its elegant old houses and mansions surrounded by the canal and the River Ill. Strasbourg is also famous as a gastronomic centre.

From its beginnings as a small Roman town, it rapidly became a prosperous city and a meeting-point of different peoples. It remained a free city within the Holy Roman Empire but was annexed to France in 1681. It is famous for the Strasbourg Oaths of 842; this is considered to be the oldest document in a Romance language which was to evolve into modern French. Strasbourg has suffered a varied fate during the wars but now the institutions set up in the city champion reconciliation and human rights. Its famous sons inlude Frédéric de Dietrich, the mayor who commissioned the French national anthem, La Marseillaise; Gustave Doré, the caricaturist and illustrator; Jean Arp, the avant-garde painter.

WHICH DISTRICT TO CHOOSE

In the old city, you will find elegant **accommodation** in period houses and mansions which have been turned into hotels in the cathedral area *Plan II* **G2** and in the Petite France *Plan II* **F2**. There are comfortable modern, business hotels near the Palais de l'Europe *Plan I* **C1** and Palais des Droits de l'Homme *Plan I* **D1**.

There are highly-prized **restaurants** around the cathedral, in the Petite France district and on the outskirts of

the city *(see listings in the guide)* and numerous excellent establishments along the canal and river banks. To sample the hearty Alsatian cuisine – Baeckeoffe, flammekueche, pot-au-feu with bacon and sausages, potato pancakes, quenelles – and delightful Alsatian wines – Riesling, Sylvaner, Muscat, Pinot Blanc, Gewurztraminer – beers and fruit-flavoured liqueurs in the convivial atmosphere of the typical **Winstubs** (wine bars), large **brasseries** and **bierstubs**, try *Maison Kammerzell*, 16 Place de la Cathédrale, *La Maison des Tanneurs*, 42 Rue du Bain-aux-Plantes, *À l'Ancienne Douane*, 6 Rue de la Douane, *Le Clou*, 3 Rue du Chaudron, *Gurtlerhof*, 13 Place de la Cathédrale. Tea rooms and cake shops serve delicious cakes such as kougelhopf.

PRACTICAL INFORMATION

ARRIVAL – DEPARTURE

Strasbourg-Entzheim International Airport – 12 km (7.5 mi) from the city centre. ℰ 03 88 64 67 67; www.strasbourg.aeroport.fr

From the airport to the city centre – By **train** to Central Station: from Entzheim Station (5min on foot from airport) regular services, time: 15min. €5 single. By **taxi**: about €30. By **shuttle bus** and **tram**: bus to Baggersee (Tram Line A), every 20min, time: 12min; fare €5 single, €9.30 round trip.

Railway Station – Central Station *Plan II* **E1**: good train service to many European destinations and major cities in France.

TRANSPORT

♦ BUS AND TRAM

Tickets are valid for the whole transport network. €1.20 single; €5.30 carnets (Multipass). Tour-Pass gives unlimited travel for 24hr: €3.20. Family Pass: €4.30

♦ TAXIS

Taxis can be hailed at taxi ranks at the Central railway station and at Place de l'Homme-de-Fer *Plan II* **F1**. Allow €10-15 for a short journey. Payment by credit card is accep-

ted and tipping is not expected. *France Taxis* ℰ 03 88 22 19 19; *Taxi 13* ℰ 03 88 36 13 13. The base fare is €1.20/km during the day, €1.80/km at night and weekends. There is an extra charge of €0.50 per item of luggage.

USEFUL ADDRESSES

◆ TOURIST OFFICES

17 Place de la Cathédrale *Plan II* **G2** ℰ 03 88 52 28 28; Place de la Gare *Plan II* **E1** ℰ 03 88 32 51 49; Pont de l'Europe ℰ 03 88 61 39 23; www.ot-strasbourg.fr; open 9am-7pm daily.

◆ POST OFFICES

Opening times Mon-Fri 8am-7pm, Sat 8am-noon. Some branches close between noon and 2pm and may finish for the day at 4pm.

◆ BANKS/CURRENCY EXCHANGE

Banks open Mon-Fri, 9am-noon and 2-5pm. There are cash dispensers all over the city. Credit cards are widely accepted. Bureaux de change often charge high commissions.

◆ EMERGENCY

Police: ℰ **17**, Fire Brigade: ℰ **18**, Medical services: ℰ **15**.

EXPLORING STRASBOURG

It is possible to visit the main sights and museums in two days.

Museums and other sights are usually open from 9-10am to 6-7pm. Some close on Mondays or Tuesdays and at lunchtime.

VISITING

Cathédrale Notre-Dame *Plan II* **G2** – A splendid Gothic cathedral with a Romanesque east end: facade, steeple, astronomical clock. Spectacular view from platform. Proceed to the **cathedral museum** and then to the fine 18C **Palais Rohan**, which houses the **Musée des Arts décoratifs** (arts and crafts from Strasbourg and Eastern France).

Musée des Beaux-Arts *Plan II* **G2** – An interesting collection of paintings from the Middle Ages to the 18C.

Musée alsacien *Plan II* **G2** – A museum dedicated to the history and traditions of Alsace is housed in three 16-17C houses.

Musée d'Art moderne et contemporain *Plan II* **E2** – A collection of modern art (works by Arp) presented in a striking building.

Tour of the old city *Plan II* **G2** – The area around the cathedral boasts charming squares.

Petite France *Plan II* **F2** – A medieval quarter by the canal with typical old houses, in particular in Rue du Bain-aux-Plantes.

Boat trips – On the Ill from the quay near the Palais Rohan *Plan II* **G2**.

Views from Quai de la Petite-France *Plan II* **F2**, Barrage Vauban *Plan II* **E2**, Pont St-Martin *Plan II* **F2**.

SHOPPING

Shops usually open Mon-Fri, 9am-8pm, Sat 9am-7pm; department stores open 10am-7pm.

The main commercial centre is at **Place des Halles** *Plan II* **F1** with 120 shops. For **designer shops** visit **Rue des Orfèvres** *Plan II* **G2** and **Rue de la Mésange** *Plan II* **G1**. Smart outlets are to be found in **Rue des Hallebardes** *Plan II* **G2** and **Rue du Vieux-Marché** *Plan II* **F1**. *Galeries Lafayette* is at Rue du 22 Novembre, *Printemps* at 1-5 Rue de la Haute-Montée and *FNAC* at Place Kléber. You will find Alsatian costumes at *Maison du Costume Alsacien*,

11b Quai de Turckheim, Christmas decorations at *Un Noël en Alsace*, 10 Rue des Dentelles, English and American books at *The Bookwork*, 3 Rue de Pâques. Visit *Edouard Artzner*, 7 Rue de la Mésange and *Souvenirs et Foie Gras d'Alsace*, 7 Rue d'Austerlitz for foie gras and other delicacies. Au *Millésime Sárl*, 7 Rue du Temple Neuf are suppliers of fine wines. For traditional products go to *Dietrich d'Obernai*, 4 Rue Merdère, *La Cure Gourmande*, 5 Rue Merdère, *Biscuiterie St-Thomas*, 9 Rue des Serruriers, and *Vitrines d'Alsace*, 18 Place de la Cathédrale.

WHAT TO BUY – Christmas decorations, loden coats, Alsatian wines and fruit liqueurs, foie gras, biscuits, chocolates.

MARKETS – There is a **flea market** in Rue du Vieil-Hôpital *Plan II* **G2** and Place de la Grande-Boucherie (Wed, Sat, 9am-6pm); a **book market**, Place and Rue Gutenberg *Plan II* **G2** (Wed, Sat 6am-6pm). **Traditional markets** are held at Place de Broglie *Plan II* **G1** and Quai de Turckheim *Plan II* **E2** (Wed, Fri 7am-1pm), Boulevard de la Marne *Plan I* **D2** (Tue, Sat 7am-1pm) and Rue de Zurich *Plan II* **H2** (Wed) as well as a **farmers' market** at Place du Marché-aux-Poissons *Plan II* **G2** (Sat 7am-1pm). There is also a **Christmas market** (Christkindelsmärkt).

ENTERTAINMENT

National Theatre of Strasbourg *Plan II* **G1**: contemporary works.

Palais de la Musique et des Congrès *Plan I* **C1**.

Opéra National du Rhin *Plan II* **G1**: opera, chamber music, dance, concerts.

La Laiterie *Plan I* **A3**: 'New Music' venue.

La Choucrouterie *Plan II* **F2**: Cabaret-theatre.

NIGHTLIFE

There are plenty of lively places to visit in the historic centre and on the river banks when going out **for a drink or for the evening**: *Les 3 Brasseurs*, 22 Rue des Veaux; *Les Aviateurs*, 12 Rue des Sœurs; *L'Opéra-Café*, Place Broglie; *Bar des Glacières*, 5 Rue des Moulins; *Key West*, 9 Quai des Pêcheurs.

The area around the cathedral, the covered markets and the districts of St-Étienne, Krutenau, Petite France come to life in the evening. *Le Chalet*, 376 Route de la Wantzenau, is a giant complex with restaurants, bars and discos. The disco *Le Retro* is at 24 Place des Halles. For a smart venue, choose *Le Bateau Ivre*, Quai des Alpes, a bar-disco in a huge barge. You can also venture further afield to try your luck at *Casino de Niederbronn*, 10 Place des Thermes.

FRANCE

STRASBOURG-INTERNATIONAL

A A 4

B

Rte du Gal de Gaulle

Rue de Bischwiller

R. L. Pasteur

R.

1

Rue de

R. de Dettwiller

Rte de Mittelhausbergen

Route d'Oberhausbergen

Rue du Marché Gare

Hochfelden

Rue de l'Église Rouge

A 350

Canal de dérivation

Hilton

Jacques

Kablé

Avenue

Clemenceau

R. Oberlin

Rue

Pl. de Haguenau

A 35 · E 25

2

A 351

des

Fossé

Remparts

Bd du Prést. Wilson

Bd de Metz

R. du Travail

Kléber

Q. St-Jean

Q. de Paris

Quai

R. du Fg de Pierre

Q. J. Sturm

Q. Schoepflin

Bd

R. du

Historical Centre (Plan II)

Pl. de la République

HÔTEL DE VILLE

GARE CENTRALE

Pl. de la Gare

Pl. de la Madeleine

Pl. Broglie

Rue Brûlée

R. du Dôme

Pl. St-Étienne

R. de Kœnigshoffen

Bd de Nancy

Pl. Hans Jean Arp

R. du 22 Novembre

Grand' Rue

Pl. Kléber

CATHÉDRALE

ILL

Quai des

Q. St-Nicolas

R. de la

Rue de Molsheim

Rue de Lyon

Humann

Diana-Dauphine

Rte de l'Hôpital

3

Rte de Schirmeck

R. de la Montagne Verte

4

A 35

Plaine des

Bouchers

Quai Louis Pasteur

Rte de l'Armée

0   300 m

A   **B**

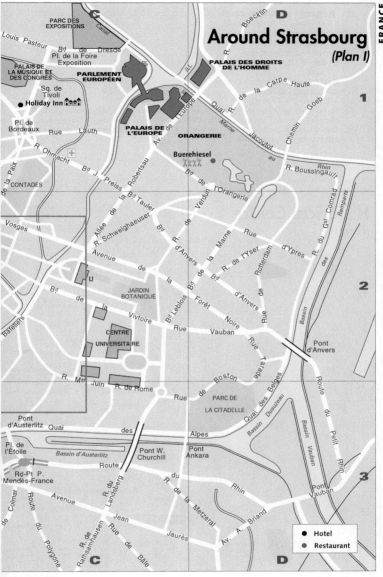

Around Strasbourg
(Plan I)

PARC DES
EXPOSITIONS

C

Boecklin

D

Louis Pasteur

Bd   de   Dresde

Pl. de la Foire
Exposition

PALAIS DE
LA MUSIQUE ET
DES CONGRÈS

Canal

PARLEMENT
EUROPÉEN

PALAIS DES DROITS
DE L'HOMME

R.

Sq. de
Tivoli

● Holiday Inn 🏨

de la Carpe   Haute

Goeb

Pl. de
Bordeaux

Rue   Lauth

PALAIS DE
L'EUROPE

Av. de l'Europe

Quai

Marne

Jacoutot

Chemin

1

R Ohmacht

✚

ORANGERIE

Buerehiesel 🍴🍴🍴🍴 ●

au

Rhin

R. Boussingault

R. du Gal. Conrad

de la Paix

CONTADES

Bd J. Preiss

la   Robertsau

Bd   de   l'Orangerie

Rhin

Remparts

Vosges

Allée   de   la   Bd Tauler

R. Schweighaeuser

Bd   de   Verdun

R.   de   la   Marne

Rue

d'Ypres

Rotterdam

des

Avenue   de   la

R.
d'Anvers

de   la   Bd

R. de l'Yser

Rue

d'Anvers

de

Bassin

2

U

JARDIN
BOTANIQUE

Bd

de

Bd Leblois   Forêt

Noire

Rue

Bateliers

Bd

Vivtoire

Rue   Vauban

Rue Tarade

Route   du   Petit   Rhin

Pont
d'Anvers

CENTRE
UNIVERSITAIRE

R. Mal   Juin

R. de Rome

Rue   de   Boston

PARC DE
LA CITADELLE

Quai   des   Belges

Bassin   Dusuzeau

Bassin   Vauban

Pont
d'Austerlitz   Quai

des

Alpes

Pl. de
l'Étoile

Bassin d'Austerlitz

Pont W.
Churchill

Pont
Ankara

Pont
Vauban

3

Rd-Pt P.
Mendès-France

Route

du

R. de la Metzeral

Rhin

Av. A. Briand

de Colmar

Route   du   Polygone

Avenue

R. du Landsberg

R. de Rathsamhausen

Jean

Rue   de   Bâle

Jaurès

C

D

● Hotel
● Restaurant

Régent Petite France ⌂   ← 🛋 ⅙ & 🎦 ⅙rm 📞 🛁30/80

5 r. Moulins – 🕿 03 88 76 43 43   🚗 **VISA** **MC** **AE** **①**
– rpf@regent-hotels.com
– Fax 03 88 76 43 76
– www.regent-hotels.com   **F2**
61 rm – †235/280 € ††255/305 €, ⊆ 20 €
– 7 suites
Rest *(closed Sunday from October-April, and Monday from May-September)*
(dinner only) 25/45 €
♦ Luxury ♦ Design ♦
Metal, glass, designer and high-tech furnishings make up the very contemporary
decor of this hotel set in the old ice factory on the banks of the Ill. The elegant,
fashionable decor and pretty view over the river and old town are the two main
attractions of this restaurant.

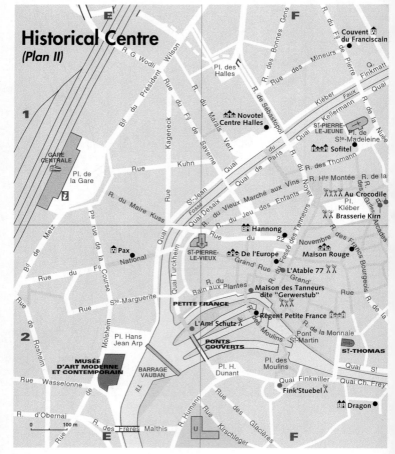

FRANCE

Hilton ⚨ &rm 🅰🅲 ↩rm 🗊 ♨25/350 ☕ 🅿 𝚅𝙸𝚂𝙰 ⓪⓪ 🅰🅴 ⓪
av. Herrenschmidt – ℰ *03 88 37 10 10*
– contact@hilton-strasbourg.com
– Fax 03 88 36 83 27
– www.hilton-strasbourg.com   *Plan I* **B1**
237 rm – †150/235 € ††150/235 €, � 22 € – 6 suites
Rest *La Table du Chef*, ℰ *03 88 37 41 42 (closed July-August, Saturday, Sunday and Bank Holidays)* (lunch only) 38 €
Rest *Le Jardin du Tivoli*, ℰ *03 88 35 72 61* – 29 €
◆ Chain hotel ◆ Business ◆ Modern ◆
This glass and steel hotel has renovated its rooms and fitted them out most fashionably. Lobby with shops, a multimedia centre and bars. La Table du Chef offers a British ambience: traditional food at lunchtime and wine bar in the evening. A fine terrace is to be found at the Jardin du Tivoli (buffets).

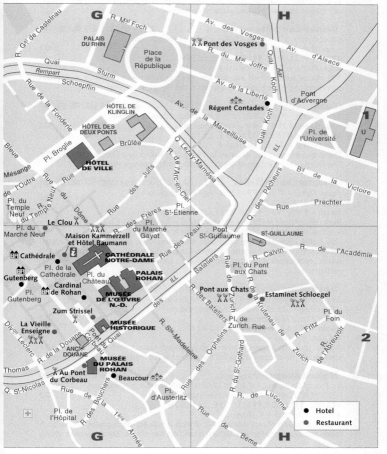

FRANCE

Sofitel 🛋 AK ⑯rm 📞 🏊100 ⌖ VISA ⓪ AE ①
pl. St-Pierre-le-Jeune – ℰ 03 88 15 49 00 – h0568@accor.com
– Fax 03 88 15 49 99 – www.sofitel.com   **F1**
155 rm – ♦195/295 € ♦♦225/1300 €, ⌒ 20 €
Rest 29 € (weekday lunch) and a la carte 40/60 €
♦ Chain hotel ♦ Business ♦ Modern ♦
The first Sofitel built in France (1964) still provides modern comfort and many
services. Lobby leading onto patio. Cosy rooms. Restaurant with dark woodwork
and contemporary cuisine inspired by the region.

Holiday Inn 🗚 🖃 ⑯rm AK ⑯rm 🏊300 P VISA ⓪ ①
20 pl. Bordeaux – ℰ 03 88 37 80 00 – histrasbourg@alliance-hospitality.com
– Fax 03 88 37 07 04   Plan I **C1**
170 rm – ♦205/230 € ♦♦205/290 €, ⌒ 17 €
Rest (closed Saturday lunch and Sunday lunch) 26 €
♦ Chain hotel ♦ Business ♦ Modern ♦
Near the European courts and Congressional palaces, a building perfectly suited
to a conference clientele. Well equipped rooms. Traditional cooking with a taste
of Provence served in a Louisiana-style decor.

Régent Contades without rest AK ⑯ 📞 🏊15 VISA ⓪ AE ①
8 av. Liberté – ℰ 03 88 15 05 05 – rc@regent-hotels.com
– Fax 03 88 15 05 15   **H1**
47 rm – ♦175/415 € ♦♦195/435 €, ⌒ 18 €
♦ Luxury ♦ Traditional ♦
19C manor with refined interior: low-key bar, splendid woodwork, numerous
paintings and Belle Epoque breakfast room. Spacious rooms.

Beaucour without rest & AK 🏊25 VISA ⓪ AE ①
5 r. Bouchers – ℰ 03 88 76 72 00 – info@hotel-beaucour.com
– Fax 03 88 76 72 60 – www.hotel-beaucour.com   **G2**
49 rm – ♦66/118 € ♦♦135/181 €, ⌒ 12 €
♦ Luxury ♦ Traditional ♦
These two elegant 18C Alsatian buildings are linked by a flower-decked patio.
The rooms are a mixture of regional rustic and contemporary decor.

Novotel Centre Halles &rm AK ⑯rm 📞 🏊15/80 VISA ⓪ AE ①
4 quai Kléber – ℰ 03 88 21 50 50 – h0439@accor.com
– Fax 03 88 21 50 51   **F1**
98 rm – ♦109/149 € ♦♦109/159 €, ⌒ 12,50 €
Rest (closed Bank Holidays lunch and Sunday lunch) 22/31 € b.i.
♦ Chain hotel ♦ Business ♦ Modern ♦
This hotel, located in the Les Halles shopping mall, provides well-equipped
rooms, some overlooking the old town. Cinema decor in the bar. The original and
warm, contemporary decor are different from those of the usual Novotel
restaurant.

De l'Europe without rest AK ⑯ 🏊30 ⌖ VISA ⓪ AE ①
38 r. Fossé des Tanneurs – ℰ 03 88 32 17 88 – info@hotel-europe.com
– Fax 03 88 75 65 45 – www.hotel-europe.com
closed 23 to 29 December   **F2**
60 rm – ♦61/130 € ♦♦92/184 €, ⌒ 12 €
♦ Traditional ♦ Classic ♦
Rather spacious rooms, some with exposed beams and half-timbering. A
spectacular small-scale model of the cathedral is on display in the reception.

Maison Rouge without rest & 📞 🏊15/30 VISA ⓪ AE ①
4 r. Francs-Bourgeois – ℰ 03 88 32 08 60 – info@maison-rouge.com
– Fax 03 88 22 43 73 – www.maison-rouge.com   **F2**
142 rm – ♦69/160 € ♦♦111/313 €, ⌒ 13,50 €
♦ Traditional ♦ Classic ♦
Behind a façade of red stone, a hotel with a refined atmosphere where each
room has a personal touch and each landing has a superbly decorated sitting
room.

FRANCE

Cathédrale without rest   *VISA* **MO** **AE** **①**
12 pl. Cathédrale – ℰ 03 88 22 12 12 – reserv@hotel-cathedrale.fr
– Fax 03 88 23 28 00 – www.hotel-cathedrale.fr   **G2**
47 rm – †55/110 € ††100/150 €, � 10 €
♦ Family ♦ Classic ♦
This century-old residence enjoys an ideal location opposite the cathedral
that you can admire from the breakfast room and some of the comfortable
rooms.

Hannong without rest   **AC** ♿ 20/40 *VISA* **MO** **AE** **①**
15 r. 22 Novembre – ℰ 03 88 32 16 22 – info@hotel-hannong.com
– Fax 03 88 22 63 87
closed 2 to 7 January   **F2**
72 rm – †76/182 € ††114/182 €, ⊠ 13 €
♦ Family ♦ Classic ♦
The fresco in the elegant Horn living room recalls the history of this hotel built in
1920 on the site of the old Hannong (18C) pottery works. Parquet floors and
warm colours in the rooms.

Diana-Dauphine without rest   **AC** ☎ ⌂ *VISA* **MO** **AE** **①**
30 r. 1ᵉ Armée – ℰ 03 88 36 26 61 – info@hotel-diana-dauphine.com
– Fax 03 88 35 50 07 – www.hotel-diana-dauphine.com
closed 23 December-2 January   *Plan I* **B3**
45 rm – †85 € ††85/100 €, ⊠ 10 €
♦ Traditional ♦ Modern ♦
The tram passes in front of this hotel, leading you quickly to the old town. Rooms
with beautiful Louis XV and Louis XVI furniture; renovated bathrooms.
Well-prepared breakfast.

Dragon without rest   ♿ ↔ ⌘ *VISA* **MO** **AE** **①**
2 r. Ecarlate – ℰ 03 88 35 79 80 – hotel@dragon.fr – Fax 03 88 25 78 95
– www.dragon.fr   **F2**
32 rm – †69/106 € ††83/115 €, ⊠ 10,50 €
♦ Traditional ♦ Business ♦ Modern ♦
17C building around a small quiet courtyard with a firmly contemporary air.
Shades of grey, designer furniture and art exhibitions.

Cardinal de Rohan without rest   **AC** ↔ *VISA* **MO** **AE** **①**
17 r. Maroquin – ℰ 03 88 32 85 11 – info@hotel-rohan.com
– Fax 03 88 75 65 37   **G2**
36 rm – †59/66 € ††89/129 €, ⊠ 10 €
♦ Traditional ♦ Classic ♦
Hotel near the cathedral in the pedestrian part of town, providing comfortable rooms furnished in Louis XV style with good soundproofing. Cosy
lounges.

Gutenberg without rest   *VISA* **MO**
31 r. Serruriers – ℰ 03 88 32 17 15 – hotel.gutenberg@wanadoo.fr
– Fax 03 88 75 76 67 – www.hotel-gutenberg.com   **G2**
42 rm – †55/85 € ††75/115 €, ⊠ 8,50 €
♦ Traditional ♦ Classic ♦
This building dating back to 1745 is home to rather spacious and comfortable
rooms. Those on the top floor are somewhat smaller. Breakfast room under a
glass roof.

Couvent du Franciscain without rest   ♿ **AC** ☎
18 r. Fg de Pierre – ℰ 03 88 32 93 93 – info@   ♿ 15 **P** *VISA* **MO** **AE**
hotel-franciscain.com – Fax 03 88 75 68 46 – www.hotel-franciscain.com
closed 24 December-7 January   **F1**
43 rm – †37/38 € ††64/68 €, ⊠ 9 €
♦ Traditional ♦ Functional ♦
Two buildings, nestled at the far end of a cul-de-sac. Opt for the rooms in the
new wing. Breakfast served in a basement room brightened by an amusing
mural.

FRANCE

Pax   🛱 ⚐rm AC rest ⚐rm ♨15/60 VISA ⓜ AE ①

24 r. Fg National – ☏ 03 88 32 14 54 – info@paxhotel.com – Fax 03 88 32 01 16
– www.paxhotel.com
closed 24 December-8 January   **E2**
106 rm – ♦56/71 € ♦♦71 €, ⊇ 8 €
Rest 13,50/18 €
♦ Traditional ♦ Functional ♦
This hotel is on a street restricted to Strasbourg tramway traffic. Simply-furnished
rooms. On fine days, dining is outside on the pretty terrace-patio under the
Virginia creeper. Regional cuisine.

Buerehiesel (Westermann)   ⚐ AC P VISA ⓜ AE ①

set in the Orangery Park – ☏ 03 88 45 56 65 – westermann@buerehiesel.fr
– Fax 03 88 61 32 00 – www.buerehiesel.com
closed 1 to 23 August, 31 December-18 January, dinner Sunday, dinner Tuesday
and lunch Monday to Friday   Plan I **D1**
Rest 136/158 € and a la carte 140/175 € ⌂
Spec. Foie gras d'oie frais des Landes truffé en croûte. Schniederspaetle et
cuisses de grenouilles poêlées au cerfeuil. Poularde de Bresse cuite entière
comme un baeckeoffa (15 December-15 March).
♦ Contemporary ♦ Formal ♦
The authentic, half-timbered farmhouse, restored in 1904, and its modern glass
roof nestle under the foliage of Orangery park. A paradise of Alsatian gastronomy!

Au Crocodile (Jung)   AC ⚐ VISA ⓜ AE ①

10 r. Outre – ☏ 03 88 32 13 02 – info@au-crocodile.com – Fax 03 88 75 72 01
– www.au-crocodile.com
closed 9 to 31 July, 24 December-8 January, Sunday and Monday   **F1**
Rest 58 € (weekday lunch), 86/132 € and a la carte 95/130 € ⌂
Spec. Pistache fermière au foie de canard, en croûte de pommes de terre. Sandre
et laitance de carpe au persil et beurre fumé. Variation d'orange à l'écume de
blanc d'œuf, tuile croquante.
♦ Alsatian cuisine ♦ Formal ♦
Splendid wood panelling, classical paintings and the famous crocodile brought
back from the Egyptian campaign by an Alsatian captain: The decor is as refined
as the cuisine.

La Vieille Enseigne   AC VISA ⓜ AE ①

9 r. Tonneliers – ☏ 03 88 32 58 50 – info@la-vieille-enseigne.com
– Fax 03 88 75 63 80 – www.la-vieille-enseigne.com
closed Saturday lunch and Sunday   **G2**
Rest 30/41 € and a la carte 43/70 € ⌂
♦ Contemporary ♦ Formal ♦
This restaurant, housed in a splendid 17C Alsatian residence, offers
contemporary menus, an excellent choice of wines and elegantly restful decor.

Estaminet Schloegel   AC VISA ⓜ AE

19 r. Krütenau – ☏ 03 88 36 21 98 – Fax 03 88 36 21 98
closed 1 to 31 August, Saturday lunch, Sunday and Monday   **H2**
Rest 25 € (weekday lunch), 37/50 €
♦ Contemporary ♦ Friendly ♦
Away from the historic centre, a pretty colourful former inn distinguished by its
tasteful contemporary decoration. A wooden spiral stairway leads to the two
sitting rooms.

Maison Kammerzell et Hôtel Baumann with rm   AC

16 pl. Cathédrale – ☏ 03 88 32 42 14   ♨80/100 VISA ⓜ AE ①
– info@maison-kammerzell.com – Fax 03 88 23 03 92
– www.maison-kallerzell.com
hotel : closed February   **G2**
9 rm – ♦67/102 € ♦♦94/113 €, ⊇ 10 €
Rest 30/45 € and a la carte 30/70 €
♦ Alsatian cuisine ♦ Retro ♦
With its wall paintings, stained-glass windows, sculptures on wood and Gothic
arches, this 16C Strasbourg institution resembles a museum. Regional dishes.

XXX **Maison des Tanneurs dite "Gerwerstub"**   VISA MO AE OD

FRANCE

42 r. Bain aux Plantes – ℰ 03 88 32 79 70 – maison.des.tanneurs@wanadoo.fr
– Fax 03 88 22 17 26
closed 31 December-25 January, Sunday and Monday   **F2**
Rest a la carte 44/64 €
◆ Alsatian cuisine ◆ Rustic ◆
Ideally located by the Ill, this typical Alsatian house in La Petite France is the place
to go if you love sauerkraut.

XX **L'Atable 77**   AC VISA MO AE OD

77 Grand'Rue – ℰ 03 88 32 23 37 – Fax 03 88 32 50 24
– www.latable77.com
closed 30 April-8 May, 14 July-7 August, 21 to 29 January, Sunday, Monday and
lunch Bank Holidays   **F2**
Rest 28/70 €
◆ Contemporary ◆ Trendy ◆
Deliberately sparse and contemporary decor, with paintings displayed.
Appetising modern dishes served in this attractive restaurant.

XX **Serge and Co** (Burckel)   AC VISA MO

ॐ
14 r. Pompiers ✉ 67300 Schiltigheim – ℰ 03 88 18 96 19 – serge.burckel@
wanadoo.fr – Fax 03 88 83 41 99
closed Saturday lunch, Monday lunch and Sunday
Rest 46/78 €
Spec. Thon rouge mariné. Grenouilles "clin d'oeil aux escargots". "Cigare" au
chocolat.
◆ Innovative ◆ Trendy ◆
The chef, Serge, is back home after a long trip through Asia and America.
Appetising cuisine, inspired by his travels, served in a pleasant, contemporary
restaurant.

XX **Pont des Vosges**   🛱 VISA MO AE OD

15 quai Koch – ℰ 03 88 36 47 75 – pontdesvosges@noos.fr
– Fax 03 88 25 16 85
closed Sunday   **H1**
Rest a la carte 38/52 €
◆ Brasserie ◆ Retro ◆
In a semi-circular room on the ground floor of an old building, this restaurant has
a mix of old-fashioned and modern decor in the dining room. Brasserie-style
menu.

XX **Brasserie Kirn**   AC VISA MO AE OD

6/8 r. de l'Outre – ℰ 03 88 52 03 03 – Fax 03 88 52 01 00
– www.brasserie-kirn.fr
closed Sunday dinner   **F1**
Rest 23 € (weekday lunch)/30 €
◆ Brasserie ◆ Retro ◆
This former butcher's shop contains a large 1900s-style dining room lit by a
beautiful central cupola and decorated with stained glass windows. Brasserie
dishes.

XX **Le Pont aux Chats**   🛱 ⅄ VISA MO AE

42 r. Krutenau – ℰ 03 88 24 08 77 – Fax 03 88 24 08 77   **H2**
Rest 19 € (weekday lunch), 40 € b.i./65 € b.i.
◆ Innovative ◆ Friendly ◆
This small restaurant on the right bank successfully marries contemporary
furnishings with old half-timbering. Delightful terrace nestled in the interior
courtyard. Innovative cuisine.

FRANCE

WINSTUBS *Regional specialities and wine tasting in a typical alsatian atmosphere*

X **L'Ami Schutz**   ⌇ ⇔ ⅋ 𝗩𝗜𝗦𝗔 ◐⊙ 𝖠𝖤 ⓪

1 r. Ponts Couverts – ℰ 03 88 32 76 98 – info@ami-schutz.com
– Fax 03 88 32 38 40 – www.ami-schutz.com
closed 25 December-6 January   **E-F2**
Rest 25 € b.i./47 € b.i.
♦ Alsatian cuisine ♦ Inn ♦
Between the meanders of the Ill, a typical bierstub extended by a terrace shaded by lime trees. Charming dining area with a warm atmosphere and beautiful old wood panelling.

X **Le Clou**   𝖠𝖢 𝗩𝗜𝗦𝗔 ◐⊙ 𝖠𝖤

3 r. Chaudron – ℰ 03 88 32 11 67 – Fax 03 88 21 06 43
closed Wednesday lunch, Sunday and Bank Holidays   **G1-2**
Rest a la carte 29/56 €
♦ Alsatian cuisine ♦ Inn ♦
Traditional decor and a friendly atmosphere characterise this winstub (wine bar) situated near the cathedral, frequented by passing celebrities whose photos are displayed.

X **Au Pont du Corbeau**   𝖠𝖢 𝗩𝗜𝗦𝗔 ◐⊙

21 quai St-Nicolas – ℰ 03 88 35 60 68 – corbeau@reperes.com
– Fax 03 88 25 72 45
closed August, February Holidays, Sunday lunch and Saturday except in December   **G2**
Rest a la carte 23/44 €
♦ Alsatian cuisine ♦ Inn ♦
On the banks of the Ill, next to the Alsatian Museum (folk art), a house with its original decoration inspired by the regional Renaissance style. Regional specialities.

X **Fink'Stuebel**   𝗩𝗜𝗦𝗔 ◐⊙

26 r. Finkwiller – ℰ 03 88 25 07 57 – finkstuebel@noos.fr – Fax 03 88 36 48 82
closed 5 to 28 August, Sunday and Monday   **F2**
Rest a la carte 28/55 €
♦ Alsatian cuisine ♦ Inn ♦
Half timbering, bare parquet floor, painted wood, regional furniture and floral tablecloths: this place is the epitome of the traditional winstub. Regional cooking, foie gras has pride of place.

X **Zum Strissel**   𝗩𝗜𝗦𝗔 ◐⊙ 𝖠𝖤 ⓪

5 pl. Gde Boucherie – ℰ 03 88 32 14 73 – Fax 03 88 32 70 24
closed 3 to 31 July, 28 January-5 February, Sunday and Monday   **G2**
Rest 11 € (weekdays)/24 €
♦ Alsatian cuisine ♦ Inn ♦
Authentic winstub held by the same family since 1920. Pretty rustic setting (especially on the first floor) brightened by artistic wrought iron work and stained glass windows depicting the Alsace wine industry.

TOULOUSE

TOULOUSE

Population (est. 2004): 390 350 (conurbation 761 100) – Altitude: 146m

J. Sierpinski /TOP

Toulouse is a pleasant university town, known as the 'ville rose' or pink city. The historic city is bounded on three sides by the Canal du Midi, the Canal de Brienne and the Garonne. The squares and gardens and the cultural and leisure amenities add to its charm.

Over the centuries the city has been the focus of diverse influences, as it is linked to the Mediterranean via the low Lauraguais Pass and with the Atlantic via the Garonne, while the valleys running down from the Pyrenees keep it in touch with Spain. Great movements of populations since Roman times have left their mark. Toulouse has a stormy history; it was the capital of the Visigoths in the 5C and then came under the rule of the Franks. From the 9C to the 13C it was the fief of the Counts of Toulouse and it became part of the French kingdom in the 13C. Europe's oldest literary society to celebrate the 'Langue d'oc', the language of southern France, was founded here in 1323. In the 16C the city flourished as the cultivation of woad, which yielded a blue-black colour for use in dyestuff, boomed. It is now a major industrial centre dominated by the aeronautical and other high-tech industries.

WHICH DISTRICT TO CHOOSE

There are elegant **hotels** around Place du Capitole *Plan II* **E1**, Place Wilson *Plan II* **F1** and Avenue Jean-Jaurès *Plan II* **F1**. For comfortable accommodation at reasonable rates look near the Matabiau station *Plan II* **F1** and in the Pont-Neuf area. You will find modern business hotels near the Centre des Congrès *Plan I* **C2**.

The southwest is famous for its hearty fare: cassoulet, sausages, foie gras, confits, ham, salami, bouillinade to list but a few of its specialities. **Restaurants** with a gastronomic reputation are to be found around Place du Capitole, near Place St-Sernin as well as in the environs of the city *(see listings in the guide)*. There are brasseries, bistros and other charming establishments in the old town and along the quays.

If you prefer a light meal with a glass of wine try *Au Père Louis*, 45 Rue des Tourneurs; *Le Petit Bacchus*, 16 Rue Pharaon. For a quick bite, go to *L'Autre Salon de Thé*, 45 Rue des Tourneurs, for pastries to *Jean Chiche*, 3 Rue St-Pantaléon.

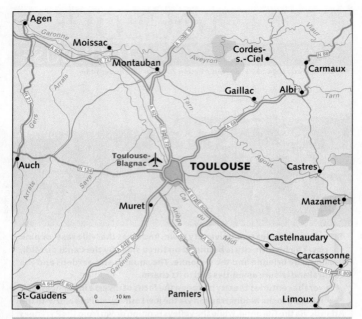

PRACTICAL INFORMATION

ARRIVAL – DEPARTURE

Toulouse-Blagnac Airport – 7 km (4 mi) from the city centre. ☎ 0825 38 00 00; www.toulouse.aeroport.fr

From the airport to the city centre – By **express bus**: to the city centre Gare Matabiau SNCF terminus, time: 20min; €3.90 single, €5.90 return trip. By **taxi**: approx. €25. *Taxi aéroport* ☎ 05 61 30 02 54, 06 09 30 84 35.

Main Station – Gare **Matabiau** SNCF *Plan II* **F1**: High-speed trains to Paris and the regions of France.

TRANSPORT

◆ BUS AND METRO

A red ticket €1.30 one trip allows you to travel anywhere on the network for 1hr. A round trip ticket €2.40, a Day ticket €4.60 and 10-12 trip tickets are also available. Information: Tisseo-Connex, 9 rue Michel-Labrousse. ☎ 05 61 41 70 70; www.tisseo.fr

◆ TAXIS

There are taxi stands around the main squares and at the Station. Allow €10-15 for a short journey. Tips are not compulsory. *Taxi*

Radio Toulousain ☎ 05 61 42 38 38; *Association Taxis Toulouse* ☎ 05 61 35 89 00, 06 09 33 25 83, *Capitole Taxi* ☎ 05 34 25 02 50.

USEFUL ADDRESSES

◆ TOURIST OFFICE

Donjon du Capitole *Plan II* **E1**. ☎ 05 61 11 02 22; www.ot-toulouse.fr

◆ POST OFFICES

Main Post Offfice, 9 Rue Lafayette. Open Mon-Fri 8am-7pm, Sat 8am-noon. Other post offices close noon-2pm and in the afternoon at 4pm.

◆ BANKS/CURRENCY EXCHANGE

Banks open Mon-Fri, 9am-noon and 2-5pm. Branches at the airport open 7am-7pm on weekdays. There are cash dispensers (ATM), which require a PIN number, all over the city. Credit cards are widely accepted.

◆ EMERGENCY

Police: ☎ **17**, Fire Brigade: ☎ **18**, First Aid: ☎ **15**.

It is possible to visit the main sights and museums in two days.

VISITING

Basilique St-Sernin *Plan II* **E1** – A great Romanesque pilgrimage church (12C) – octagonal bell-tower.

Les Jacobins *Plan II* **E2** – An architectural masterpiece with ribbed vaulting, 'palm-tree' pillars and radiating arches (13C).

Cathédrale St-Étienne *Plan II* **F2** – An interesting building with an unusual plan – vast 12C hall and Gothic chancel.

Musée des Augustins *Plan II* **E2** – A splendid collection of Romanesque sculpture and French paintings.

Hôtel d'Assezat *Plan II* **E2** – The magnificent mansion is home to the Bemberg Foundation – paintings and works of art from the Renaissance to the 20C.

Musée St-Raymond *Plan II* **E1** – Interesting collections of archaeology and ancient art.

Cité de l'Espace *Plan I* **D3** – Interactive presentation of the evolution of the universe and space travel.

Boat trips – On the Garonne from Quai de la Daurade *Plan II* **E2**.

Views from Quai de la Daurade *Plan II* **E2**, Pont St-Michel *Plan II* **E3**, Rue de Metz (near Musée des Augustins) *Plan II* **E2**.

SHOPPING

The main shopping streets (*Plan II* **E2-F2**) are **Rue de l'Alsace-Lorraine, Rue Croix-Baragnon, Rue St-Antoine-du-T., Rue Boulbonne, Rue des Arts** and the pedestrian sections of **Rue St-Rome, Rue des Filatiers, Rue Baronie** and **Rue de la Pomme**.

Specialist shops include *Atelier du Chocolat de Bayonne*, 1 Rue du Rempart Villeneuve; *Olivier Confiseur-Chocolatier*, 20 Rue Lafayette; – fine chocolates; *Busquets*, 10 Rue Rémusat – regional specialities and wines from the southwest; *La Maison de la Violette*, Boulevard de Bonrepos-Canal du Midi, *Violette & Pastels*, 10 Rue St-Pantaléon – confectionery, liqueurs, cosmetics.

WHAT TO BUY – Foie gras, cassoulet, confits, candied violets and other violet-based products, wine and liqueurs ; chocolates *(capitouls* – almonds in dark chocolate, *Clémence Isaure* – Armagnac-soaked grapes in dark chocolate, *brindilles* – nougatine in chocolate praline, *Péché du Diable* – dark chocolate ganache with orange peel and ginger).

MARKETS (*Plan II* **E1 à E3**) – **Flea markets**: L'**Inquet**, around Basilique St-Sernin (Sun mornings); Allée Jules-Guesde (first weekend of each month). **Farmers markets** are held around Église St-Aubin (Sun mornings), Place du Capitole (organic products, Sun mornings) and Place du Salin (foie gras, etc. Wed-Fri, Nov-Mar).

ENTERTAINMENT

Théâtre du Capitole *Plan II* **E2**: opera, operetta. **Théâtre de la Cité**: music, theatre, entertainment. **Théâtre Garonne** 6 Av Château d'Eau: plays. **Auditorium St-Pierre-des-Cuisines** 12, place Saint-Pierre: music, plays. **Café-Théâtre des 3T**: shows. **Halle aux Grains**, Place Dupuy *Plan II* **F2**: pop and classical concerts. **Zénith**, 11 Avenue Raymond-Badiou *Plan I* **B2**: rock concerts, variety acts, musical comedies.

NIGHTLIFE

The café terraces lining **Place du Capitole** *(Le Bibent, Le Café des Arcades, Brasserie de l'Opéra, Mon Caf)* are ideal places to visit when going out **for a drink or for the evening**.

For a lively scene with music and dancing explore the **areas around Place du Capitole, Place St-Georges, Place St-Pierre** and just off **Rue St-Rome** and **Rue des Filatiers**. *Bar La Loupiote*, 39 Rue Réclusane; *Bar One*, 27 Boulevard de Strasbourg; *La Bodega Bodega*, 1 Rue Gabriel-Péri; *Monsieur Carnaval*, 34 Rue Bayard; *La Tantina de Bourgos*, 27 Rue de la Garonette are very popular. Also worth a visit are *Disco Cockpit*, 1 Rue du Puits-Vert; *Disco La Strada*, 4 Rue Gabriel-Péri; *Le New Shangai*, 12 Rue de la Pomme.

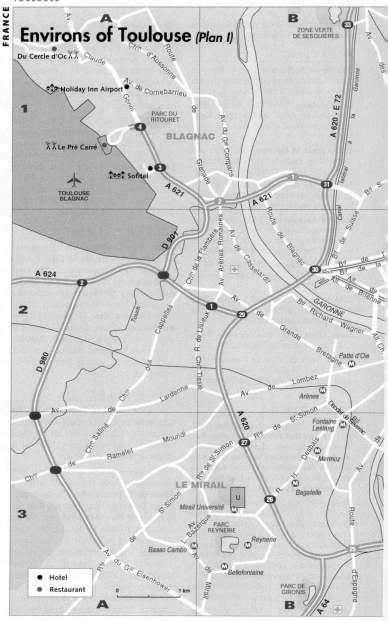

Environs of Toulouse (Plan I)

Du Cercle d'Oc ✕✕ Claude

Holiday Inn Airport

Le Pré Carré ✕✕

Sofitel

TOULOUSE
BLAGNAC

ZONE VERTE
DE SESQUIÈRES

BLAGNAC

PARC DU
RITOURET

LE MIRAIL

Mirail Université

PARC
REYNERIE

Basso Cambo

Bellefontaine

PARC DE
GIRONIS

● Hotel
● Restaurant

0   1 km

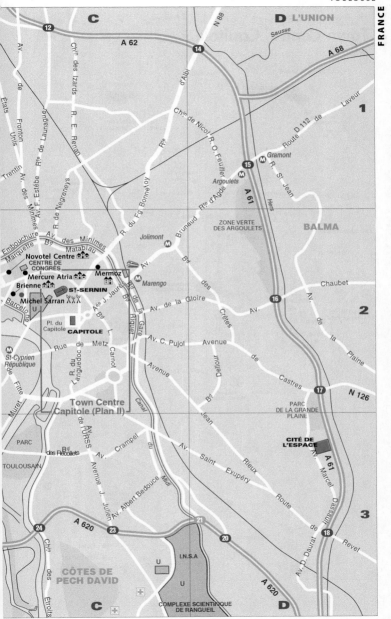

FRANCE

Town Centre, Capitole
(Plan II)

Pl. Arnaud Bernard

E

F

Président

IV

MATABIAU

R. Matabiau

R. Raymond

Bayard

Bd. P. Sémard

R. de la Chaîne

R. Merly

Bd

7 Place St-Sernin

BASILIQUE ST-SERNIN

Pl. Jeanne-d'Arc

Rue

de

R. B. de Born

Pl. de Belfort

Belfort

Bonnepos

Jaurès

Sofitel Centre

1

MUSÉE ST-RAYMOND

Pl. St-Sernin

R. du Périgord

R. de Rémusat

Lorraine

Strasbourg

R. Denfert-Rochereau

Grand Hôtel Jean Jaurès "Les Capitouls"

Rue

U

Pl. A. France

R. Déville

Rue

des

Lois

N.-D.-DU-TAUR

Albert 1er

d'Alsace

Pl. V. Hugo

Jean Jaurès

Allées

R. des Sept Troubadours

Gabriel

Périer

Pierre

R. Pargaminières

CAPITOLE

R. de la Fayette

Pl. la Capitole

Holiday Inn Centre

Pl. Wilson

Rue

Chez Laurent Orsi "Bouchon Lyonnais"

R. de la Colombette

Pl. St-Aubin

Crowne Plaza

Pl. du Capitole

Brasserie de l'Opéra

R. M. Fonvielle

R. d'Abuisson

LES JACOBINS

HÔTEL DE BERNUY

Lakanal

Gambetta

St-Rome

Grand Hôtel de l'Opéra

de la Pomme

Lorraine

Pl. Occitane

R. du Rempart St-Étienne

Lazare

Pl. de la Daurade

R. Peyrolières

R. Cujas

R. Peyras

Émile

Pl. St-George

Carnot

R. des Frères Lion

2

Brasserie Flo "Les Beaux Arts"

Pont Neuf

HÔTEL D'ASSÉZAT

de

Esquirol

M

Metz

des Arts

Rue

MUSÉE DES AUGUSTINS

de

Metz

Riquet

Allées

Beaux Arts

Le 19

Garonne

Pl. Rouaix

Croix

Baragnon

R. Riguepels

CATHÉDRALE ST-ÉTIENNE

R. Fermat

Allées François Verdier

Poitiers

Rue des

Tounis

Quai

Rue

de

la

Garonnette

des

Filatiers

Languedoc

R. Tolozane

R. St-Jacques

Nihau

Rue

GARONNE

N.-D. LA DALBADE

Pl. des Carmes

Cosi Fan Tutte

R. Mage

R. Perchepinte

R. V. éliane

Pl. Montoulieu

MUSÉE PAUL DUPUY

R. Espinasse

Ozenne

Av. M. Hauriou

Rue

de

la

Dalbade

Pharaon

Grde Rue Nazareth

Pl. du Salin

JARDIN ROYAL

GRAND ROND

Guesde

3

Pont Saint-Michel

All. P. Feuga

Pl. A. Lafourcade

Allées

Jules

R. Lamarck

Rue

Alfred

Duméril

U

MUSÉUM D'HISTOIRE NATURELLE

JARDIN DES PLANTES

Ail. Frédéric Mistral

● Hotel
● Restaurant

0   200 m

E

F

TOWN CENTRE   *Plan II*

FRANCE

Sofitel Centre   &rm ⚙ ↔rm ⅍ ♨150 ⛯ 🆅🅸🆂🅰 ⓜⓢ 🄰🄴
84 allées J. Jaurès – ℰ 05 61 10 23 10 – h1091@accor.com
– Fax 05 61 10 23 20   **F1**
119 rm – ♛260/280 € ♛♛299/322 €, ☲ 22 € – 14 suites
Rest *S W Café* a la carte 30/70 €
♦ Chain hotel ♦ Business ♦ Modern ♦
The hotel occupies eight floors of an imposing red-brick and glass building. Discreetly luxurious rooms, with good soundproofing. Business centre and good seminar facilities. At SW Café, you will find a contemporary setting and recipes combining regional products and international spices.

Crowne Plaza   🏠 🖪 &rm ⚙ ↔rm ☏ ♨60 🆅🅸🆂🅰 ⓜⓢ 🄰🄴 ⓞ
7 pl. Capitole – ℰ 05 61 61 19 19 – hicptoulouse@alliance-hospitality.com
– Fax 05 61 23 79 96 – www.crowne-plaza-toulouse.com   **E2**
162 rm – ♛260/325 € ♛♛260/435 €, ☲ 22 € – 10 suites
Rest *(closed August)* 23/39 €
♦ Luxury ♦ Traditional ♦ Classic ♦
This luxury hotel enjoys a prestigious location on the famous Place du Capitole. Pleasant, renovated rooms, some of which look out onto the town hall. An intimate atmosphere in the dining room opening onto a pleasant interior courtyard

Grand Hôtel de l'Opéra without rest   🖪 & ⚙ ☏
1 pl. Capitole – ℰ 05 61 21 82 66   ♨15/40 🆅🅸🆂🅰 ⓜⓢ 🄰🄴 ⓞ
– contact@grand-hotel-opera.com – Fax 05 61 23 41 04
– www.grand-hotel-opera.com   **E2**
49 rm – ♛175/310 € ♛♛175/460 €, ☲ 22 €
♦ Luxury ♦ Traditional ♦ Stylish ♦
This hotel in a 17C convent has an air of serenity and charm. Beautiful rooms with wood panels and red and yellow velvet. Pleasant bar lounge.

Holiday Inn Centre   🏠 &rm ⚙ ↔rm ☏ ♨50 🆅🅸🆂🅰 ⓜⓢ 🄰🄴 ⓞ
13 pl. Wilson – ℰ 05 61 10 70 70 – hicapoul@guichard.fr – Fax 05 61 21 96 70
– www.hotel-capoul.com   **F1**
130 rm – ♛140/160 € ♛♛140/195 €, ☲ 15 €
Rest *Brasserie le Capoul*, ℰ 05 61 21 08 27 – 24 €
♦ Chain hotel ♦ Business ♦ Functional ♦
An old hostelry on a busy and pretty square, distinguished by its superb glass-paned hall and contemporary rooms, each with an original bathroom. Toulouse's smart brasserie serving seafood, daily specials and dishes of southwest France.

Brienne without rest   & 🖪 ♨25 ⛯ 🅿 🆅🅸🆂🅰 ⓜⓢ 🄰🄴 ⓞ
20 bd Mar. Leclerc – ℰ 05 61 23 60 60 – hoteldebrienne@wanadoo.fr
– Fax 05 61 23 18 94 – www.hoteldebrienne.com   *Plan I* **C2**
71 rm – ♛77/91 € ♛♛77/135 €, ☲ 10 €
♦ Traditional ♦ Functional ♦
A brick and glass construction named after the nearby canal. The refurbished rooms are colourful and impeccably maintained. Verdant hall opening onto the patio.

Mercure Atria   🏠 &rm 🖪 ↔rm ☏ ♨200 ⛯ 🆅🅸🆂🅰 ⓜⓢ 🄰🄴 ⓞ
8 espl. Compans Caffarelli – ℰ 05 61 11 09 09 – h1585@accor.com
– Fax 05 61 23 14 12   *Plan I* **C2**
134 rm – ♛105/133 € ♛♛115/143 €, ☲ 12,50 € – 2 suites
Rest a la carte 24/37 €
♦ Chain hotel ♦ Business ♦ Modern ♦
Business clientele appreciate this modern hotel directly linked to the convention centre. Large quiet modern rooms. The restaurant dining room offers a soothing view of the public park, and another, busier one of the work in the kitchen.

Novotel Centre 🐾   🔊 🗌 🕭 rm 🅐🅒 ↔rm 🕭 🏛100
5 pl. A. Jourdain – ℰ 05 61 21 74 74   🛏 **VISA** 🅒🅞 🅐🅔 🅞
– h0906@accor.com – Fax 05 61 22 81 22 – www.novotel.com   *Plan I* **C2**
135 rm – 🛏120/145 € 🛏🛏125/195 €, ⌷ 12,50 €
Rest a la carte 18/37 €
◆ Chain hotel ◆ Business ◆ Functional ◆
This regional-style building adjacent to a Japanese garden has spacious rooms and renovated, some with a terrace. A festival of colours in this dining room opening onto the greenery. Traditional and local cuisine.

Garonne without rest   🕭 🅐🅒 🕊 **VISA** 🅒🅞 🅐🅔 🅞
22 descente de la Halle aux Poissons – ℰ 05 34 31 94 80
– contact@hotelgaronne.com – Fax 05 34 31 94 81
– www.hotelsdecharmetoulouse.com   **E2**
14 rm – 🛏155/180 € 🛏🛏155/259 €, ⌷ 20 €
◆ Traditional ◆ Modern ◆
An old building in an alley in Old Toulouse. A contemporary interior: dyed oak parquet, ultramodern furniture, silky drapes and the odd little Japanese touch.

Beaux Arts without rest   🗲 🅐🅒 🕊 🕭 **VISA** 🅒🅞 🅐🅔 🅞
1 pl. Pont-Neuf – ℰ 05 34 45 42 42 – contact@hoteldesbeauxarts.com
– Fax 05 34 45 42 43 – www.hoteldesbeauxarts.com   **E2**
20 rm – 🛏92/210 € 🛏🛏138/210 €, ⌷ 16 €
◆ Traditional ◆ Cosy ◆
Tastefully done 18C establishment with cosy refined rooms, some with a view of the Garonne. Venture into the Occitan lifestyle...

Grand Hôtel Jean Jaurès "Les Capitouls" without rest   🕭
29 allées J. Jaurès – ℰ 05 34 41 31 21   🅐🅒 ↔ 🏛20 **VISA** 🅒🅞 🅐🅔 🅞
– info@hotel-capitouls.com – Fax 05 61 63 15 17   **F1**
53 rm – 🛏115/168 € 🛏🛏120/168 €, ⌷ 13,50 € – 2 suites
◆ Traditional ◆ Classic ◆
Just at the metro station, this former private residence has a distinctive foyer with red brick vaulting. The rooms provide Internet access via the TV.

Mermoz without rest 🐾   🕭 🅐🅒 🏛30 🛏 **VISA** 🅒🅞 🅐🅔
50 r. Matabiau – ℰ 05 61 63 04 04 – reservation@hotel-mermoz.com
– Fax 05 61 63 15 64   *Plan I* **C2**
52 rm – 🛏115 € 🛏🛏115/135 €, ⌷ 10 €
◆ Traditional ◆ Retro ◆
This hotel's spare decor recalls the Aeropostale's heroic pilots. Bright, candy-coloured rooms. Flower-decked glassed-in area or tree-shaded outside tables for breakfast.

Président without rest   🅐🅒 🛏 **VISA** 🅒🅞 🅐🅔
43 r. Raymond IV – ℰ 05 61 63 46 46 – hotel-president@wanadoo.fr
– Fax 05 61 62 83 60
closed 1 to 7 May, 25 December-2 January   **F1**
31 rm – 🛏55/58 € 🛏🛏58/75 €, ⌷ 9 €
◆ Traditional ◆ Functional ◆
The hotel has rooms (some with air-conditioning) in a unique arrangement on the ground floor around verdant patios. Modern decor.

Albert 1er without rest   🅐🅒 🏛15 **VISA** 🅒🅞 🅐🅔
8 r. Rivals – ℰ 05 61 21 17 91 – toulouse@hotel-albert1.com – Fax 05 61 21 09 64
– www.hotel-albert1.com   **E1**
49 rm – 🛏49/87 € 🛏🛏59/87 €, ⌷ 10 €
◆ Traditional ◆ Classic ◆
A very practical address for discovering the "pink city" by foot. Ask for one of the refurbished rooms, or one at the rear for optimum peace and quiet. A pretty mural decorates the hall.

FRANCE

XXX
✿✿

Michel Sarran　　　　　　　🖼 AC ⇆ VISA ⦿ AE
21 bd A. Duportal – ℰ 05 61 12 32 32 – restaurant @ michel-sarran.com
– Fax 05 61 12 32 33 – www.michel-sarran.com
closed 29 July-30 August, 28 December-5 January, Wednesday lunch, Saturday
and Sunday　　　　　　　　　　　　　　　　　　　　Plan I **C2**
Rest (pre-book) 45 € b.i. (weekday lunch), 75/140 € b.i. and a la carte
75/145 €
Spec. Soupe tiède de foie gras à l'huître. Liégeois de bar. Pigeon fermier en kadaïf,
cuisses confites à l'encre de seiche.
◆ Innovative ◆ Fashionable ◆
This charming large 19C residence invites gourmets to enjoy savoury cuisine of
southern specialities in purposely minimalist decor.

XX

7 Place St-Sernin　　　　　　　　　　　AC VISA ⦿ AE
7 pl. St-Sernin – ℰ 05 62 30 05 30 – Fax 05 62 30 04 06
closed Saturday lunch and Sunday　　　　　　　　　　**E1**
Rest 24 € b.i. (lunch), 34/60 € b.i.
◆ Contemporary ◆ Fashionable ◆
A flamboyantly coloured restaurant in a typical Toulouse house, elegantly done
and brightened with contemporary paintings. Modern dishes.

XX

Brasserie Flo " Les Beaux Arts"　　　🖼 VISA ⦿ AE ⦿
1 quai Daurade – ℰ 05 61 21 12 12 – Fax 05 61 21 14 80
– www.brasserie-lesbeauxarts.com　　　　　　　　　**E2**
Rest 25 € b.i. (weekdays), 39/50 € b.i.
◆ Brasserie ◆ Retro ◆
This brasserie at the Garonne's edge was once frequented by Ingres, Matisse and
Bourdelle, and is appreciated by the locals. Pretty retro decor. Highly varied
menu.

XX

Le 19　　　　　　　　　　　　　🍸 VISA ⦿ AE ⦿
19 descente de la Halle aux Poissons – ℰ 05 34 31 94 84
– contact @ restaurant le19.com – Fax 05 34 31 94 85
– www.restaurantle19.com　　　　　　　　　　　　**E2**
closed 22 December-8 January, lunch Monday, lunch Saturday and Sunday
Rest 35/55 €
◆ Contemporary ◆ Fashionable ◆
Welcoming dining rooms, one with a superb 16C rib vaulted ceiling, an open
wine cellar and smoking room in a resolutely modern style. Dishes with an
international flavour.

XX

Chez Laurent Orsi "Bouchon Lyonnais"　　　🍸
13 r. Industrie – ℰ 05 61 62 97 43　　　　　🖼 VISA ⦿ AE ⦿
– orsi.le-bouchon-lyonnais @ wanadoo.fr – Fax 05 61 63 00 71
– www.lebouchonlyonnais.free.fr
closed Saturday lunch and Sunday except Bank Holidays　　**F1**
Rest 20/33 €
◆ Lyonnais cuisine ◆ Bistro ◆
A large bistro whose imitation leather benches, end-to-end tables and mirrors
are reminiscent of the brasseries of the 1930s. The menu oscillates between
southwest France and Lyon.

XX

Émile　　　　　　　　　　🍸 AC VISA ⦿ AE ⦿
13 pl. St-Georges – ℰ 05 61 21 05 56 – restaurant-emile @ wanadoo.fr
– Fax 05 61 21 42 26 – www.restaurant-emile.com
closed 25 December-8 January, Monday except dinner October to April and
Sunday　　　　　　　　　　　　　　　　　　**F2**
Rest 18 € (lunch), 35/48 € ⌂
◆ Contemporary ◆ Friendly ◆
This restaurant created in the 1940s is prized for its wonderful wine list and
cuisine of hearty local food and fish. The outside dining area is invaded in
summer.

FRANCE

XX   **Brasserie de l'Opéra**   🛆 AC VISA ⓜⓞ AE ⓞ

1 pl. Capitole – ℰ 05 61 21 37 03 – Fax 05 62 27 16 49

closed August and Sunday   **E2**

Rest 25 € b.i. (weekday lunch), 35 € b.i./55 € b.i.

♦ Brasserie ♦ Retro ♦

Chic 1930s style brasserie where you meet everyone in Toulouse, along with stars who leave their photo to mark their visit. The veranda is turned into an outside dining area in fine weather.

X   **Cosi Fan Tutte** (Donnay)   VISA ⓜⓞ

ⓢ   8 r. Mage – ℰ 05 61 53 07 24 – cosi-fan-tutte @ wanadoo.fr – Fax 05 61 52 27 92

Closed 18 to 30 June, 1 to 22 August, Sunday and Monday   **F2**

Rest (number of covers limited, pre-book) 44/79 € and a la carte 60/80 € ᵇ

Spec. Cappelli à l'encre de seiche et crevettes. Selle d' agneau aux cornes d'abondance. Cannoli à la ricotta et fruits confits.

♦ Italian ♦ Fashionable ♦

The cuisine is deliciously market fresh, prepared in the Italian tradition, accompanied by Italian wines. Decor of red tints, imitation leopard-skin carpets and original paintings.

BLAGNAC   *Plan I*

🏚   **Sofitel**   🛆 ▢ ✗ 🚗 AC ⅙rm 📞 ♨90 P VISA ⓜⓞ AE ⓞ

2 av. Didier Daurat (by road of airport, exit nr 3) – ℰ 05 34 56 11 11

– h0565 @ accor.com – Fax 05 61 30 02 43   **A1**

100 rm – ♦225/275 € ♦♦225/290 €, ⌹ 21 €

Rest *Caouec* (closed Saturday, Sunday and Bank Holidays) 32 €

♦ Chain hotel ♦ Business ♦ Modern ♦

Prestigious establishment linked to the airport by a free shuttle. Elegantly renovated rooms, in predominantly yellow shades. Pool and tennis court for relaxing between flights. The Caouec offers traditional cuisine and some specialities of southwest France.

🏢   **Holiday Inn Airport**   🛆 ⅙ 🏊 ⅙rm AC ⅙rm ♨15/150

pl. Révolution – ℰ 05 34 36 00 20 – tlsap @

ichotelsgroup.com – Fax 05 34 36 00 30

– www.toulouseairport.holiday-inn.com   **A1**

150 rm – ♦125/215 € ♦♦125/250 €, ⌹ 20 €

Rest 21/34 €

♦ Chain hotel ♦ Business ♦ Modern ♦

Both peaceful and welcoming shades characterise the rooms decorated with modern furniture. A well-appointed seminar area. A shuttle links the hotel to the airport. A pleasant brasserie-style restaurant decorated with frescoes depicting olive trees.

XX   **Du Cercle d'Oc**   🛆 🚗 AC P VISA ⓜⓞ AE ⓞ

6 pl. M. Dassault – ℰ 05 62 74 71 71 – cercledoc @ wanadoo.fr

– Fax 05 62 74 71 72

closed 31 July-20 August, 25 December-2 January, Saturday, Sunday and Bank

Holidays   **A1**

Rest 32 € b.i. (weekday lunch)/50 €

♦ Contemporary ♦ Inn ♦

This pretty 18C farm is in an island of greenery in the middle of a business area. English club atmosphere in the lounge and elegant dining room. Pleasant outside tables.

XX   **Le Pré Carré**   ⪡ VISA ⓜⓞ AE ⓞ

Toulouse-Blagnac airport, (2ⁿᵈ flour) – ℰ 05 61 16 70 40

– opta.gestion @ wanadoo.fr – Fax 05 61 16 70 50

closed 14 July-15 August, Sunday dinner and Saturday   **A1**

Rest 27 € b.i./46 €

♦ Traditional ♦ Design ♦

Pleasant airport restaurant facing the runways, inside a brasserie. Design decor in red tones and wood furnishings.

GERMANY
DEUTSCHLAND

FORMALITIES

Travellers from the European Union (EU), Switzerland, Iceland and the main countries of North and South America need a national identity card or passport (America: passport required) to visit Germany for less than three months (tourism or business purpose). For visitors from other countries a visa may be required, in addition to a passport, especially for those wishing to stay for longer than three months. We advise you to check with your embassy before travelling.

A valid national or international driving licence is required. Valid insurance cover is compulsory. To hire a car the driver must be over 23 and have held a driving licence for more than one year.

MAJOR NEWSPAPERS

Die Welt, Frankfurter Allgemeine Zeitung, Frankfurter Rundschau and *Süddeutsche Zeitung* are distributed nationally; Regional newpapers: in Berlin: *Berliner Morgenpost, Tagesspiegel, Berliner Zeitung, taz, BZ*; in Frankfurt: *Frankfurter Neue Presse*; in Hamburg: *Hamburger Morgenpost, Hamburger Abendblatt*; in Munich: *Münchner Merkur, AZ*.

USEFUL PHRASES

ENGLISH	GERMAN
Yes	**Ja**
No	**Nein**
Good morning	**Guten Tag**
Goodbye	**Auf Wiedersehen**
Thank you	**Danke**
Please	**Bitte**
Excuse me	**Entschuldigung**
I don't understand	**Ich verstehe nicht**

HOTELS

◆ CATEGORIES

Accommodation ranges from luxurious 5-star international hotels, via smaller, family-run guesthouses to bed-and-breakfast establishments *(Zimmer frei)*. The German Hotel Reservation Service (HRS) makes reservations in all hotels, inns and pensions – www.hrs.de

◆ PRICE RANGE

The price is per room. In summer hotels in Berlin and Frankfurt may offer cheaper rates.

◆ TAX

Included in the room price.

◆ CHECK OUT TIME

Usually between 11am and noon.

◆ RESERVATIONS

By telephone or by Internet; a credit card number may be required.

◆ TIP FOR LUGGAGE HANDLING

At the discretion of the customer (about €1 per bag).

◆ BREAKFAST

Breakfast is usually included in the price of the room and is served between 7am and 10am. Most hotels offer a buffet meal but usually it is possible to have continental breakfast served in the room.

Reception	**Rezeption**
Single room	**Einzelzimmer**
Double room	**Doppelzimmer**
Bed	**Bett**
Bathroom	**Badezimmer**
Shower	**Dusche**

RESTAURANTS

Restaurants serve lunch from noon to 2pm and dinner from 7pm to 10pm, although some restaurants continue to serve after 10pm.

Besides the traditional **restaurants** there are small fast-food concerns (**Imbiss)** in towns, at the roadside and on motorways, and which are good for a light lunch of grilled sausage *(Bratwurst)* with potato salad or chips.

Breakfast	**Frühstück**	7am – 10am
Lunch	**Mittagessen**	12 noon – 2pm
Dinner	**Abendessen**	7pm – 10pm

Restaurants offer fixed price menus (starter, main course and dessert) or à la carte. A fixed price menu is usually less expensive than the same dishes chosen à la carte. Menus are printed in German and sometimes in English.

◆ RESERVATIONS

Reservations are usually made by phone. For famous restaurants (including Michelin starred restaurants), it is advisable to book several days – in some instances weeks – in advance. A credit card number or a phone number may be required to guarantee the booking.

◆ THE BILL

The bill (check) includes service charge and VAT. It is customary to leave a tip of about 5-10% of the total bill.

Drink or aperitif	**Getränk oder Aperitif**
Appetizer	**kleine Vorspeise**
Meal	**Mahlzeit**
Starter	**Vorspeise**
Main dish	**Hauptgericht**
Main dish of the day	**Tagesgericht**
Dessert	**Nachspeise**
Water, mineral water	**Wasser, Wasser mit Kohlensäure**
Wine (red, white, rosé)	**Rotwein, Weisswein, Roséwein**
Beer	**Bier**
Bread	**Brot**
Meat	**Fleisch**
Fish	**Fisch**
Salt/pepper	**Salz/Pfeffer**
Cheese	**Käse**
Vegetables	**Gemüse**
Hot/cold	**heiss/kalt**
The bill (check) please	**Die Rechnung, bitte**

LOCAL CUISINE

German food is more varied and better balanced than is generally supposed, and the composition and presentation of meals are in themselves original.

Breakfast includes cold meats and cheese with some of Germany's 300 varieties of breads and rolls, and often a soft-boiled egg. Lunch usually begins with soup, followed by a fish or meat main course always accompanied by a salad (lettuce, cucumber, shredded cabbage). For the evening meal, there will be a choice of cold meats (**Aufschnitt**), delicatessen and cheeses, with a selection of different types of bread and/or rolls.

Certain dishes are served all over the country: the most popular are **Wiener Schnitzel** (veal cutlet fried in bread crumbs), **Eisbein** (salted knuckle or shin of pork), **Sauerbraten** (beef in a brown sauce) and **Gulasch** (either in the form of soup or as a stew).

Certain specialities are regional: in Hessen and Westphalia you may find **Töttchen** (ragout of brains and calf's head, cooked with herbs). Lower Saxony and Schleswig-Holstein are known for **Aalsuppe** (sweet-and-sour soup, made of eels, prunes, pears, vegetables, bacon and seasoning) and **Labskaus** (a favourite sailor's dish of beef, pork and salted herrings with potatoes and beetroot, the whole topped with gherkins and fried egg). The specialities in Bavaria and Franconia include **Leberknödel** (large dumplings of liver, bread and chopped onion, served in a clear soup), **Leberkäs** (minced beef, pork and liver, cooked as a galantine), **Knödel** (dumplings of potato or soaked bread), **Haxen** (veal or pork trotters), **Schlachtschüssel** (breast of pork, liver sausage and black pudding, served with pickled cabbage and dumplings) and **Rostbratwürste** (small sausages grilled over beechwood charcoal).

◆ DRINK

The national beverage is **beer**, of which the Germans are justifiably proud. There are nearly 1,200 breweries in Germany, still brewing in accordance with a purity law *(Reinheitsgebot)* decreed in 1516 which forbids the use of anything but barley, hops and plain water, although nowadays yeast may be added.

German vineyards produce a great variety of wine from a wide range of grapes – as the visitor may discover in most bars and restaurants, sampling them by the glass *(offene Weine)*. Notable among the **white wines** (80% of production) are the vigorous Rieslings of the Middle Rhein and those of the Mosel, Saar and Ruhr rivers, aromatic and refreshing; the high quality, delicate wines of the Rheingau; full-bodied and elegant Nahe wines; the potent wines of Franconia, verging sometimes on the bitter; and the many and varied wines of Baden and Württemberg. Among the **red wines**, particularly choice examples come from Rheinhessen and Württemberg, not forgetting the vigorous, well-balanced reds of the Palatinate and, above all, the wines of the Ahr, paradise of the Spätburgunder. **Sekt**, German sparkling wine is popular for special occasions. Germany also bottles a good range of mineral waters

In Germany the favourite spirit, for an after-dinner drink, is **Schnapps**, the generic term for all spirits, whether they are clear or coloured, bitter or sweet; generally they are clear. In the northern and eastern part of Germany Schnapps is mostly distilled from grain, such as Doppelkorn (corn spirit); in the south, however, fruits from the orchards of the Rhine Valley and the Lake Constance area are distilled to obtain fruit-flavoured spirits, and the berries from the Black Forest are used to create fine, scented spirits, such as Kirschwasser (cherry brandy).

L'infini pluriel

Route du Fort-de-Brégançon - 83250 La Londe-les-Maures - Tél. 33 (0)4 94 01 53 53
Fax 33 (0)4 94 01 53 54 - domaines-ott.com - ott.particuliers@domaines-ott.com

BERLIN
BERLIN

Population (est. 2005): 3 373 000 (conurbation 3 761 000) – Altitude: 40m

N. Hautemanière / SCOPE

Berlin, once symbol of two opposing ideologies, is a modern metropolis with a lively economic and cultural life. It owes its dynamism to the fact that for 30 years both Federal Republic and former East Germany made the city a showcase for their respective ways of life.

Berlin was first mentioned in 1244 and in 1359 joined the Hanseatic League. In 1871 the city became the German Empire's capital. Industrialisation began in the early 19C and by 1929 it was the largest commercial city in continental Europe. The Allies (France, UK, USA, USSR) administered Berlin after 1945. During the 1950s the disparity in the standard of living between East and West Berlin caused important immigration to the West.

In August 1961 the crossing points were closed and the wall was built. West Berlin became an enclave in East Germany, linked to West Germany by a road, a rail and an air corridor. In 1990 the wall was demolished and the city and the country reunified.

During division period, West Berlin was embellished with the work of famous architects such Le Corbusier and provided with many cultural facilities to keep the town alive: numerous first-class museums, universities, concert and opera halls, Schiller Theatre and Kulturforum. The city has had a great reputation for music, maintained in the post-war years especially by H. von Karajan.

WHICH DISTRICT TO CHOOSE

Berlin offers a great selection of **hotels** in all categories. Most of the established hotels are located in the western part of the city near Kurfürstendamm *Plan III* **K2**. Several new hotels have been opened in the last 10 years, mostly in the eastern part of the city – near Sony Center *Plan III* **K2**, Unter den Linden *Plan II* **G1** and Gendarmenmarkt *Plan II* **G2**.

The best cooking in the city is usually found in the grand hotels but there are a good many interesting **restaurants** in the town centre, which is also a focal point for shopping and sightseeing. Many of these restaurants are located near Gendarmenmarkt, Unter den Linden and Brandenburger Tor *Plan II* **F1**. In the last few

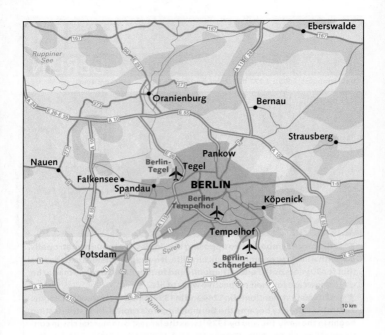

years several small restaurants have been opened in the Kreuzberg district *Plan I* **C3** offering a casual atmosphere and good value. An interesting selection of cosy restaurants also exists in the western part of the city not far from Kurfürstendamm and Europacenter *Plan III* **K2**.

PRACTICAL INFORMATION

ARRIVAL – DEPARTURE

Berlin-Tegel Airport (TXL) about 12 km (8 mi) northwest of the city centre – **Transport to the city centre**: by **taxi** (€18), by **U-Bahn** and **S-Bahn** trains.

Berlin-Tempelhof Airport (THF) about 7 km (4 mi) south of the city centre – **Transport to the city centre**: by **U-Bahn** train.

Berlin-Schönefeld Airport (SXF) about 21 km (13 mi) southeast of the city centre – **Transport to the city centre**: by **S-Bahn** trains; by **taxi** to the Zoo station (approx. €30-35).

Buses operate between Tegel Airport and Schönefeld Airport every 30min. ✆ 01 805 000 186.

Railway Stations – Bahnhof Zoologischer Garten (Bahnhof Zoo) in Charlottenburg for trains to the west, ✆ (030) 19 44 9 (5.30am-11pm); **Spandau Station** for trains to the north; **Wannsee Station** for trains to the south and west; **Ostbahnhof** for trains to the east; **Bahnhof Lichtenberg** for regional trains and trains to the north; ✆ 01 80 599 66 33 (passenger information service).

TRANSPORT

♦ BUSES, TRAMS AND METRO

Buses operate between 4.30am and 1am (entrance is at the front - exit in the middle); the metro (**U-Bahn**) operates between 4am and midnight/1am; **S-Bahn** trains run every 10min.

Berlin and its environs (eg Potsdam) are divided into 3 fare zones; Zone AB for journeys within the city. Tickets are available in all U-Bahn and S-Bahn stations, at yellow and orange ticket vending machines, on trams and from bus drivers; the ticket must be punched in the red box on the bus or in front of the escalators. Normal fare €2.20 (valid 2hr); short journey *(Kurzstreckentarif)* €1.20 valid for 3 U-Bahn or S-Bahn stations and for 6 bus stations without changing line; weekly pass *(Wochenkarte)* €22; day ticket €5.80; group day ticket (2 adult and up to 3 children) €14.80 – day cards are valid from the time of punching until 3am next morning.

Buses, **trams** and **metro** are controlled by the **BGV** (Berliner Verkehrs-Betriebe); ✆ (030) 1 94 49 (Mon-Fri 5.30am-10.30pm and Sat 8.45am-4.15pm); the **S-Bahn** and the region round Berlin are controlled by the **VBB** (Verkehrsverbund Berlin-Brandenburg) in conjunction with the BGV, ✆ (030) 25 41 41 41 (Mon-Fri 8am-8pm, Sat 9am-6pm). Information available at the BGV-Pavilion in Hardenbergplatz (Bahnhof Zoo) (6.30am-8.30pm) and at many U-Bahn and S-Bahn stations.

The **Berlin–Potsdam Welcome Card** €19 (valid 3 days) for an adult with up to three children (under 14yrs) on the entire VBB network; it also gives discounts for selected theatres, museums, attractions and city tours. The card is available at public transport ticket desks, in many hotels and at the information offices of the Berlin Tourismus Marketing.

Bus number 100, which shuttles between Bahnhof Zoo and Alexanderplatz, connecting the two city centres, passes many of Berlin's sights.

♦ TAXIS

There are taxi ranks dispersed all over the western part of Berlin, in particular at the **Zoo Station** (Hardenbergplatz in Charlottenburg) and at **Savignyplatz** (in Charlottenburg too); in the east the taxi ranks are concentrated in **Alexanderplatz**, at the entrance to the S-Bahn station, in front of the Palasthotel, on **Unter den Linden**, to the south of the **Weidendammerbrücke**, in **Rosenthaler Platz** and near the **Volksbühne**. Basic fare €8 (+ €3 for a taxi called by telelephone); many taxis accept credit cards. ✆ (030) 690 22; 691 50 59; 26 10 26; 21 01 01; 21 02 02; 96 44; www.funktaxi-berlin.de

USEFUL ADDRESSES

♦ TOURIST INFORMATION

Berlin Tourismus Marketing: Mon-Fri 8am-7pm, Sat-Sun 9am-6pm; ✆ (030) 25 00 25. **Europa Center** *Plan III K2*: Mon-Sat 8.30am-8.30pm, Sun 10am-6.30pm. **Brandenburg Gate** *Plan II F1*, south wing: Mon-Sat 10am-6pm. **Tegel Airport** *Plan I A1*, opposite Gate 0: daily, 5am-10.30pm. **KaDeWe**, Reisecenter (travel centre) ground floor: Mon-Fri 8.30am-8pm, Sat 9am-4pm.

♦ POST OFFICES

Mon-Fri 8am-6pm, Sat 8am-12 noon. **Postamt 120**, Zoologischer Garten Station: Mon-Sat 8am-midnight, Sun and public holidays 10am-midnight; **Postamt 519**, Tegel Airport, Main Hall: Mon-Fri 7am-9pm, Sat-Sun 8am-8pm ✆ (030) 417 84 90, (Deutsche Post AG ✆ (030) 62 78 10).

◆ BANKS/CURRENCY EXCHANGE

Mon-Fri 8.30am-12.30pm and 2.30-4pm (6pm Thursday); closed Sat-Sun and public holidays. Foreign exchange offices generally offer better rates than banks and some are open until late in the evening and at the weekend.

◆ EMERGENCY

Police : ✆ **110**; Fire Brigade: ✆ **112**; Medical Emergencies: ✆ **1 00 31**.

BUSY PERIODS

It may be difficult to find a room at a reasonable price (except during week- ends) when special events are held in the city as hotel prices may be raised substantially:

Berlin Fair: January.

Berlinale: February – International Film Festival.

Internationale Tourismus-Börse (ITB): March – International Tourism Fair.

Berlin Festival: September – Opera, ballet, theatre, concerts, artistic exhibitions.

Jazz Festival: November.

EXPLORING BERLIN

DIFFERENT FACETS OF THE CITY

It is possible to visit the main museums and sights of Berlin in four to five days.

Museums and sights are usually open from 10am to 5pm. Most close on Mondays and public holidays.

Bus number 100 which shuttles between Bahnhof Zoo and Alexanderplatz, connecting the two city centres, passes by many of Berlin's sights.

HISTORIC CENTRE – **Brandenburg Gate** Plan II **F1**. Once part of the wall dividing the city but now restored to its role as triumphal arch. **Unter den Linden** Plan II **G1**. Famous avenue 'under the lime trees'. **Gendarmenmarkt** Plan II **G2**. The most beautiful square in Berlin, bordered by the **Schauspielhaus** Plan II **G2** and two 18C churches – **Deutscher Dom** and **Französischer Dom** – which now house museums. **Zeughaus** Plan II **H1**. Baroque edifice housing the German Historical Museum.

MUSEUM SELECTION – **Gemäldegalerie** Plan II **F2**. Comprehensive collection of European painting from 13C to 18C. **Neue Nationalgalerie** Plan II **F2**. 20C paintings and sculpture housed in a steel and glass structure by Mies van der Rohe. **Pergamonmuseum** Plan II **G1**. Greek and Roman Antiquities, Middle Eastern antiquities and Islamic Art. **Egyptian Museum** Plan III **I1**. Collections from the time of the Pharaohs, including the bust of Queen Nefertiti. **Museum of Ethnography**. **Alte Nationalgalerie** Plan II **H1**. 19C paintings and sculptures. **Bode-Museum** Plan II **G1**. Sculpture and numismatic collections. **Altes Museum** Plan II **H1**. Antique jewellery (Hildesheimer Silberfund) and Greek and Roman antiquities. **Deutsches Historisches Museum** Plan II **H1**. German Historical Museum. **Kunstgewerbemuseum** Plan II **F2**. Museum of decorative art. **Museum Haus am Checkpoint Charlie** Plan II **G2**. Berlin Wall Museum illustrating the construction of the Berlin Wall and attempts to climb over it.

CHARLOTTENBURG – **Schloss Charlottenburg** Plan III **I1**. Royal summer residence named after Sophie-Charlotte, wife of Frederick I, and its English landscaped garden. **Kaiser-Wilhelm-Gedächtniskirche** Plan III **K2**. Ruined neo-Romanesque church preserved as a reminder of the horrors of conflict. **Kurfürstendamm**. The prestigious Ku'damm, the centre of Berlin cosmopolitan life (cafés, restaurants, theatres, cinemas, galleries and fashion boutiques).

OUTDOOR BERLIN – Boat trips. Through the **historic centre** (1hr) beginning in the Nikolaiviertel *Plan II* **H1**; through the **inner city** on the Spree and the Landwehr canals (3hr 30min) beginning at the Jannowitzbrücke and Schlossbrücke; on the **Havel** from Wannsee to Potsdam/Lange Brücke (1hr 15min); ℰ (030) 5 36 36 00.

GOURMET TREATS

A great variety of international cuisine is on offer together with traditional Brandenburger specialities such as **Eisbein** (pig's knuckles with sauerkraut and pease-pudding). Berliners call a tankard of lager beer a **Berliner Molle**; a light beer with a dash of raspberry syrup or woodruff is a **Berliner Weisse mit Schuss**. In summer the **beer** tastes better in a beer garden. For **Kaffee und Kuchen** (coffee and cake) try one of the cafés in the Kurfürstendamm or Unter den Linden; the **Tele-Café** (Panoramastrasse 1) in the Television Tower (200m/640ft) turns on its axis every 30min and offers a fine view.

SHOPPING

Shops are usually open from 9am/10am to 6.30pm/8pm. They are closed on Sunday.

Good shopping streets are **Tauentzienstrasse/Kurfürstendamm** *Plan III* **K2** and the **Potsdamer Platz Arkaden** *Plan II* **G2**. Berlin's most famous **department stores** are the *KaDeWe* (Tauentzienstrasse 221), a gigantic selection in a luxurious setting, and *Galeries Lafayette* (Friedrichstrasse 207), a reasonably priced shop in an amazing architectural setting. **Exclusive shops** are located in **Fasanenstrasse** *Plan III* **K2** and **Friedrichstrasse** *Plan II* **G1**. **Off-beat shops** are to be found in **Kreuzberg** *Plan I* **C3** and **Prenzlauer Berg** *Plan I* **D1**. *Hackesche Höfe* (Rosenthalerstrasse/Sophienstrasse) is a special shopping address, offering 8 floors of arcades, fashion boutiques, antiques shops, restaurants and bars, a cinema and even a cabaret (www.hackesche-hoefe.com).

For **antiques** the best streets are around **Eisenacher Strasse/ Kalckreuthstrasse** and **Keithstrasse**, in **Fasanenstrasse**, around **Bleibtreustrasse**, **Pestalozzistrasse**, and **Knesebeckstrasse** and under the arches of the S-Bahn in **Friedrichstrasse**.

MARKETS – There is a twice-weekly market in **Winterfeldplatz** *Plan III* **L3** (Wed and Sat 8am-1pm) and a **Turkish** weekly market in **Maybachufer** *Plan I* **D3** (Tue and Fri noon-6.30pm). The Great Berlin **flea and art** market is held in **Charlottenburg** (Strasse des 17 Juni – Sat-Sun 11am-5pm). There are other flea markets in **Wilmersdorf** (Fehrbelliner Platz – Sat-Sun 7am-4pm). Berlin **art and nostalgia** market in **Museumsinsel** *Plan II* **H1** (Sat-Sun 11am-5pm).

WHAT TO BUY – Porcelain, crystal glass, fashion, music recordings, children's toys, Cold War souvenirs (Red Army clothes and symbols etc.).

ENTERTAINMENT

Zitty and *Tip*, published fortnightly and the *Berlin-Programm*, published monthly, provide information on events of all kinds. Berlin's major dailies have a weekly insert featuring a calendar of events. Tickets are available up to 3 weeks before the performance at *Berlin Tourismus Marketing*. The numerous theatre box offices are the best place to buy tickets when in town.

Deutsche Oper Berlin *Plan III* **I1** – Charlottenburg Opera House rebuilt after the war.

Staatsoper Unter den Linden *Plan II* **G1** – The oldest and most magnificent opera house in Berlin.

Komische Oper *Plan II* **G1** – Theatre founded in 1947.

Theater des Westens *Plan III* **K2** – Musical productions.

Konzerthaus Berlin *Plan II* **G1** – Berlin's most beautiful concert hall.

Philharmonie und Kammermusiksaal *Plan II* **F2** – Home of the Berlin Philharmonic Orchestra.

Berliner Ensemble *Plan II* **G1** – Home base of the company founded by Bertolt Brecht who staged the *Threepenny Opera* here in 1928.

Deutsches Theater *Plan II* **G1** – With 3 stages and repertory ranging from classical to contemporary.

Friedrichstadtpalast *Plan II* **G1** – The most important revue theatre in Europe.

Wintergarten Variété *Plan II* **F2** – Variety, acrobats, magicians and illusionists.

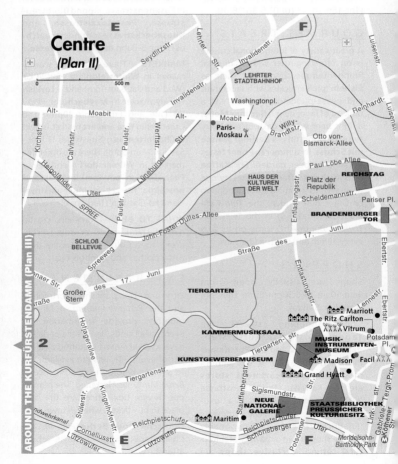

NIGHTLIFE

Berlin's night-life has a great reputation with countless bars, discotheques, pubs and clubs of all styles. All the 'in' shops sell magazines, such as *030*, which publishes information about all the latest trends and clubs. The night-life on the **Kreuzberg Hill** has a cosmopolitan, anti-establishment flavour but many other districts have plenty going on. *Dorian Gray*, Marlene-Dietrich-Platz 4, Mitte provides 3 floors of music and partying. *Knaack Klub Berlin*, Greifswalder Strasse 224, **Prenzlauer Berg**, for every type of music and karaoke. In **Charlottenburg** for a traditional atmosphere try *Schwarzes Café*, Kantstrasse 148; *Zillemarket*, Bleibtreustrasse 48a or *Hardtke*, Meineckestrasse 27. In **Schöneberg** *Slumberland*, Goltzstrasse 24, plays reggae. In **Tiergarten** try the elegant cocktails served at the very long bar in *Bar am Lützowplatz*, Lützowplatz 7. German's most modern casino is the *Spielbank Berlin*, Marlene-Dietrich-Platz 1, Mitte.

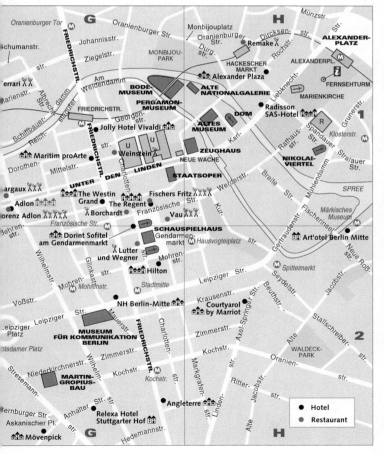

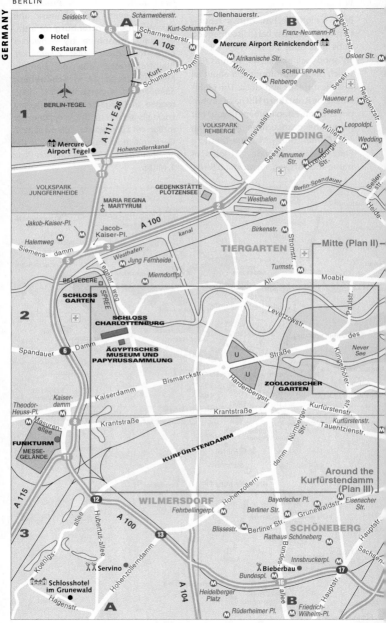

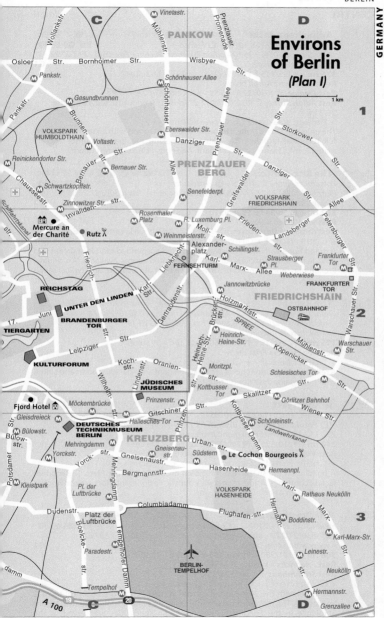

Environs of Berlin
(Plan I)

0   1 km

1

Vinetastr.

PANKOW

Prenzlauer Promenade

Osloer   Str.   Bornholmer   Str.   Wisbyer   Str.

Mühlenstr.

Pankstr.

Schönhauser Allee

Gesundbrunnen

Schönhauser Allee

Brunnen-

VOLKSPARK HUMBOLDTHAIN

Voltastr.

Eberswalder Str.

Storkower

Str.

Reinickendorfer Str.

Schwartzkopffstr.

Bernauer Str.

Str.

Bernauer Str.

Danziger

Prenzlauer

PRENZLAUER BERG

Allee

Danziger

Str.

Str.

Chausseestr.

Schiffartskanal

Zinnowitzer Str.

Invaliden-

str.

Senefelderpl.

Greifswalder

Str.

VOLKSPARK FRIEDRICHSHAIN

Landsberger

Allee

Petersburger Str.

Rosenthaler Platz

Friedrich-

Friedrich-

R. Luxemburg Pl.

Moll-

str.

Mercure an der Charité   Rutz ✕

Weinmeisterstr.

Alexander- platz

Schillingstr.

Strausberger Pl.

Frankfurter Tor

Liebknecht-

Karl-

Marx-

Allee

Weberwiese

FRANKFURTER TOR

Warschauer Str.

REICHSTAG

UNTER DEN LINDEN

Juni

BRANDENBURGER TOR

17.

TIERGARTEN

Karl-

Str.

FERNSEHTURM

Gertraudenstr.

Jannowitzbrücke

Holzmarktstr.

Brücken-

str.

SPREE

FRIEDRICHSHAIN

OSTBAHNHOF

2

Leipziger   Str.

Koch-

str.

KULTURFORUM

Wilhelm-

Lindenstr.

Oranien-

JÜDISCHES MUSEUM

Prinzenstr.

Heinrich-Heine-Str.

Heinrich-Heine-Str.

Moritzpl.

str.

Kottbusser Tor

Skalitzer

Köpenicker

Str.

Mühlenstr.

Schlesisches Tor

Görlitzer Bahnhof

Warschauer Str.

Fjord Hotel

Möckernbrücke

Gleisdreieck

Bülowstr.

Bülow-str.

Yorckstr.

Potsdamer

Kleistpark

Gitschiner

DEUTSCHES TECHNIKMUSEUM BERLIN

Hallesches Tor

Prinzen-

KREUZBERG

Mehringdamm

Gneisenau-

str.

Yorck-

str.

Gneisenaustr.

Bergmannstr.

Pl. der Luftbrücke

Dudenstr.

Platz der Luftbrücke

Boelcke-

Columbiadamm

Paradestr.

damm

Tempelhof

A 100

19

20

Mehringdamm

Urban-

Südstern

Kottbusser Damm

Schönleinstr.

Landwehrkanal

Wiener Str.

Str.

Le Cochon Bourgeois ✕

Hasenheide

Hermannpl.

VOLKSPARK HASENHEIDE

Flughafen-str.

BERLIN-TEMPELHOF

Tempelhofer Damm

str.

Karl-

Rathaus Neukölln

Hermann-

Boddinstr.

Marx-

Str.

Karl-Marx-Str.

Leinestr.

Neukölln

Hermannstr.

Grenzallee

3

C

D

C

D

GERMANY

Adlon Kempinski 🚗 🌐 🖪 🕭 🖵 🛦 🖾 ⇆rm ⅍rest 🖾 🕻 🔊300

Unter den Linden 77 ⊠ 10117 – **Ⓜ** *Franzö-* 🚗 **VISA** **ⓞⓞ** **ⒶⒺ** **①**
sische Str. – ℰ (030) 2 26 10 – adlon@kempinski.com – Fax (030) 22 61 22 22
– www.hotel-adlon.de **G1**
375 rm – ♦355/475 € ♦♦405/525 €, � 32 € – 68 suites
Rest see *Lorenz Adlon* below
Rest *Quarré*, ℰ *(030) 22 61 15 55 –* a la carte 33/62 €
Rest *Adlon Stube*, ℰ *(030) 22 61 11 27 (closed Monday - Tuesday)* a la carte
25/31 €
◆ **Palace** ◆ **Grand Luxury** ◆ **Classic** ◆
The ultimate "Grand hotel"! Handsome, elegant rooms with luxury features and
full technical facilities. The suites overlooking the Brandenburger Tor are
magnificent. Quarré: classic, elegant. An English club style restaurant.

The Ritz-Carlton 🚗 🖪 🕭 🖵 🛦 🖾 ⇆rm 🖾 🔊450

Potsdamer Platz 3 ⊠ 10785 – **Ⓜ** *Potsdamer* 🚗 **VISA** **ⓞⓞ** **ⒶⒺ** **①**
Platz – ℰ (030) 33 77 77 – berlin@ritzcarlton.com – Fax (030) 3 37 77 55 55
– www.ritzcarlton.com **F2**
302 rm – ♦250/280 € ♦♦280/310 €, � 28 € – 33 suites
Rest see *Vitrum* below
Rest *Brasserie Desbrosses*, ℰ *(030) 3 37 77 63 40 –* a la carte 30/46 €
◆ **Chain hotel** ◆ **Grand Luxury** ◆ **Classic** ◆
A grand hotel with an impressive lobby with suspended marble staircase and
gold leaf décor. Spacious, tastefully decorated rooms available. An original
French brasserie, founded in 1875 with a light atmosphere and typical meals
available.

The Regent 🖪 🕭 🛦 🖾 ⇆ ⅍rest 🔊70 🚗 **VISA** **ⓞⓞ** **ⒶⒺ** **①**

Charlottenstr. 49 ⊠ 10117 – **Ⓜ** *Französische Str. – ℰ (030) 2 03 38*
– info.berlin@rezidorregent.com – Fax (030) 20 33 61 19
– www.theregentberlin.com **G1**
195 rm – ♦265/325 € ♦♦300/360 €, � 27 € – 39 suites
Rest see *Fischers Fritz* below
◆ **Grand Luxury** ◆ **Classic** ◆
A refined and luxurious hotel providing elegant and spacious rooms and suites,
with personalised service for guests.

Grand Hyatt 🚗 🌐 🖪 🕭 🖵 🛦 🖾 ⇆rm ⅍ 🖾 🔊320

Marlene-Dietrich Platz 2 ⊠ 10785 🚗 **VISA** **ⓞⓞ** **ⒶⒺ** **①**
– **Ⓜ** *Potsdamer Platz – ℰ (030) 25 53 12 34 – berlin@hyatt.de – Fax (030)*
25 53 12 35 – www.berlin.grand.hyatt.com **F2**
342 rm – ♦210/325 € ♦♦240/355 €, � 24 € – 12 suites
Rest *Vox*, ℰ *(030) 25 53 17 72 –* a la carte 25/55 €
◆ **Chain hotel** ◆ **Grand Luxury** ◆ **Design** ◆
A building in the shape of a trapezium on the Potsdamer Platz. The modern
façade continues inside: rooms with puristic designer interiors are convincing.
Vox offers an Asian atmosphere.

The Westin Grand 🚗 🖪 🕭 🖵 🛦 🖾 ⇆rm ⅍rest 🖾 🔊160

Freidrichstr. 158 ⊠ 10117 – **Ⓜ** *Französische Str.* **VISA** **ⓞⓞ** **ⒶⒺ** **①**
– ℰ (030) 2 02 70 – info@westin-grand.com – Fax (030) 20 27 33 62
– www.westin.com/berlin **G1**
358 rm – ♦131/380 € ♦♦156/405 €, � 23 € – 18 suites
Rest *Friedrichs* a la carte 29/46 €
Rest *Stammhaus* a la carte 23/35 €
◆ **Chain hotel** ◆ **Luxury** ◆ **Classic** ◆
This hotel with the 30m high glass roof in the heart of the historical town is
impressive. The residence radiates pure elegance and nostalgic charm. Elegant
ambience in the Friedrichs. Regional Berlin specialities are served in the
Stammhaus.

GERMANY

Hilton 🛜 📶 ℉₅ 🕱 🖵 ﹠ 🞐 ↯rm 🖃 📞 ⅏300 🚗 𝖵𝖨𝖲𝖠 🆖 🆎 ⓪

Mohrenstr. 30 ⊠ 10117 – 🛈 Stadtmitte – 𝒞 (030) 2 02 30
– info.berlin@hilton.com – Fax (030) 20 23 42 69
– www.hilton.de   **G2**
589 rm – 🛉144/309 € 🛉🛉144/329 €, ⊑ 23 € – 14 suites
Rest Fellini (dinner only) a la carte 29/40 €
Rest Mark Brandenburg a la carte 29/41 €
Rest Trader Vic's (dinner only) a la carte 31/50 €
♦ Chain hotel ♦ Luxury ♦ Functional ♦
A splendid reception hall welcomes you to this luxurious hotel. All rooms
overlooking the street offer a magnificent view of the Gendarmenmarkt! A
spacious modern Wellness area. Fellini – Italian cuisine. Mark Brandenburg – with
typical regional interiors. Polynesian cuisine served.

Marriott ℉₅ 🕱 🖵 ﹠ 🞐 ↯rm 🎗rest 🖃

Inge-Beisheim-Platz 1 ⊠ 10785   ⅏420 🅿 𝖵𝖨𝖲𝖠 🆖 🆎 ⓪
– 🛈 Potsdamer Platz – 𝒞 (030) 22 00 00 – berlin@marriotthotels.de
– Fax (030) 2 20 00 10 00 – www.berlinmarriott.com   **F2**
379 rm – 🛉150/230 € 🛉🛉150/230 €, ⊑ 22 €
Rest a la carte 20/42 €
♦ Chain hotel ♦ Luxury ♦ Modern ♦
A modern business hotel with spacious atrium style lobby and comfortable
rooms with American cherry wooden furnishings. Bistro style restaurant with
open kitchen and large window façade.

Radisson SAS-Hotel 🛜 ℉₅ 🕱 🖵 ﹠ 🞐 ↯rm 🎗rest 🖃 📞 ⅏220

Karl-Liebknecht-Str. 3 ⊠ 10178   🚗 𝖵𝖨𝖲𝖠 🆖 🆎 ⓪
– 🛈 Alexanderplatz – 𝒞 (030) 23 82 80 – info.berlin@radissonsas.com
– Fax (030) 2 38 28 10 – www.berlin.radissonsas.com   **H1**
427 rm – 🛉140/380 € 🛉🛉140/380 €, ⊑ 21 €
Rest Heat a la carte 25/39 €
Rest Noodles (dinner only) a la carte 25/40 €
♦ Chain hotel ♦ Business ♦ Stylish ♦
A purist style atrium lobby with an impressive 25m high cylindrically shaped
aquarium. Smartly designed rooms. International cuisine in a modern bistro
atmosphere. South-east Asian cuisine.

Maritim 🕱 🖵 ﹠ 🞐 ↯ 🎗rest 🖃 📞 ⅏1200

Stauffenbergstr. 26 ⊠ 10785   🚗 𝖵𝖨𝖲𝖠 🆖 🆎 ⓪
– 🛈 Mendelssohn-Bartholdy-Park – 𝒞 (030) 2 06 50 – info.ber@maritim.de
– Fax (030) 20 65 10 10 – www.maritim.de   **F2**
505 rm – 🛉159/275 € 🛉🛉178/294 €, ⊑ 21 €
Rest a la carte 24/36 €
Rest Grandrestaurant M a la carte 36/45 €
♦ Chain hotel ♦ Luxury ♦ Modern ♦
An exclusive style lobby and refined rooms with all modern technical fittings, as
well as a function room. The presidential suite is an impressive 350 sq.m. A 1920s
style restaurant.

Mövenpick 🕱 ﹠ 🞐 ↯rm 🖃 📞 ⅏175 🚗 𝖵𝖨𝖲𝖠 🆖 🆎 ⓪

Schönebergerstr. 3 ⊠ 10963 – 𝒞 (030) 23 00 60
– hotel.berlin@moevenpick.com – Fax (030) 23 00 61 99
– www.moevenpick-berlin.com   **G2**
243 rm – 🛉180/245 € 🛉🛉200/265 €, ⊑ 17 €
Rest a la carte 21/32 €
♦ Chain hotel ♦ Modern ♦
Formerly a Siemens building, now listed, providing a mixture of modern design
and historical touches to create an unusual interior. Restaurant with
glass-covered interior courtyard.

Maritim proArte
Lⳇ ℑ ☒ ⅋ ᵹᴋ ⅋rm ▥ ℃ ⌘600

Freidrichstr. 151 ✉ *10117 –* Ⓜ *Friedrichstr.*   ☕ **VISA** ⓪ AE ⓪
– 𝒞 (030) 2 03 35 – info.bpa@maritim.de – Fax (030) 20 33 42 09
– www.maritim.de   **G1**
403 rm ☷ – ♥153/263 € ♥♥172/282 €
Rest *Atelier* (dinner only) 41 €/85 €
Rest *Bistro media* (lunch only) a la carte 18/28 €
◆ Chain hotel ◆ Business ◆ Modern ◆
An avant-garde hotel near the lime tree-lined Pracht blvd. Providing well-appointed rooms with Jungen Wilden art on display. A modern designer style restaurant.

Jolly Hotel Vivaldi
Lⳇ ℑ ᵹ ᴋ ⅋rm ℀rest ▥ ⌘60 ☕ **VISA**

Freidrichstr. 96 ✉ *10117 –* Ⓜ *Friedrichstr. – 𝒞 (030) 2 06 26 60*   ⓪ AE ⓪
– vivaldi.jhb@jollyhotels.de – Fax (030) 2 06 26 69 99 – www.jollyhotels.de
254 rm – ♥155/230 € ♥♥175/250 €, ☷ 18 €   **G1**
Rest 32 €/40 € and a la carte 31/41 €
◆ Business ◆ Stylish ◆
When entering this modern, well-run hotel you will notice the spacious hall. High-quality wooden furniture and agreeable colours make the rooms a pleasant place to stay. Light, open-plan restaurant with Italian cuisine.

Madison
Lⳇ ℑ ᵹ ℀ ▥ ℃ ⌘20 ☕ **VISA** ⓪ AE ⓪

Potsdamer Str. 3 ✉ *10785 –* Ⓜ *Potsdamer Platz – 𝒞 (030) 5 90 05 00 00*
– welcome@madison-berlin.de – Fax (030) 5 90 05 05 00
– www.madison-berlin.de   **F2**
166 rm – ♥140/315 € ♥♥190/350 €, ☷ 21 € – 17 suites
Rest see *Facil* below
◆ Business ◆ Stylish ◆
In the media and communications area, not far from Sony, the cinema and the shopping mall. The apartment hotel combines hotel and boarding house. Rooms with kitchens and shopping service.

Dorint Sofitel am Gendarmenmarkt
⌂ Lⳇ ℑ ᵹ ᴋ ⅋rm ▥

Charlottenstr. 50 ✉ *10117*   ℃ ⌘80 **VISA** ⓪ AE ⓪
– Ⓜ *Französische Str. – 𝒞 (030) 20 37 50 – info.bergen@dorint.com*
– Fax (030) 20 37 51 00 – www.sofitel.com   **G1-2**
92 rm – ♥240/255 € ♥♥270/285 €, ☷ 23 €
Rest *Aigner* a la carte 30/43 €
◆ Chain hotel ◆ Business ◆ Design ◆
Directly opposite the French cathedral in the Gendarmenmarkt. Renovated panelled building, the history of which is not instantly apparent. Furnished in a straightforward designer style. The Aigner was built from original parts of a Viennese coffeehouse.

Courtyard by Marriott
⌂ ℑ ᵹ ᴋ ⅋ ▥ ⌘120

Axel-Springer-Str. 55 ✉ *10117*   ☕ **VISA** ⓪ AE ⓪
– Ⓜ *Spittelmarkt – 𝒞 (030) 8 00 92 80 – berlin.mitte@courtyard.com*
– Fax (030) 8 00 92 81 00 – www.marriott.com   **H2**
267 rm – ♥119/169 € ♥♥129/179 €, ☷ 16 € – 4 suites
Rest a la carte 19/26 €
◆ Chain hotel ◆ Business ◆ Functional ◆
A centrally located business hotel providing homely, well-equipped rooms with functional furnishings. A Mediterranean bistro style restaurant with bar.

Alexander Plaza
⌂ Lⳇ ℑ ⅋rm ▥ ℃ ⌘70 ☕ **VISA** ⓪ AE ⓪

Rosenstr. 1 ✉ *10178 –* Ⓜ *Alexanderplatz – 𝒞 (030) 24 00 10*
– info@hotel-alexander-plaza.de – Fax (030) 24 00 17 77
– www.hotel-alexander-plaza.de   **H1**
92 rm – ♥110 € ♥♥120 €, ☷ 15 €
Rest (closed 17 July - 14 August and Sunday) (dinner only) a la carte 18/29 €
◆ Business ◆ Functional ◆
Between the Marienkirche and the market, this restored old building provides modern rooms and apartments with small kitchen facilities. International dishes are served in the restaurant with conservatory.

GERMANY

NH Berlin-Mitte
Leipziger Str. 106 ⊠ *10117* – Ⓜ *Stadtmitte*
– ℰ *(030) 20 37 60* – *nhberlinmitte@nh-hotels.com* – *Fax (030) 20 37 66 00*
– *www.nh-hotels.com*   **G2**
392 rm – †86/196 € ††86/196 €, � 16 €
Rest a la carte 19/37 €
♦ Chain hotel ♦ Functional ♦
This residence with its spacious hall and rooms, which are modern, functional and comfortable, is well situated in the centre of Berlin. Leisure area on the 8th floor. The bistro-style restaurant is open to the lobby.

Angleterre
Friedrichstr. 31 ⊠ *10969* – Ⓜ *Kochstr.* – ℰ *(030) 20 21 37 00*
– *info.berang@gold-inn.de* – *Fax (030) 20 21 37 77*
– *www.gold-inn.de*   **G2**
155 rm – †81/185 € ††91/195 €, ⊑ 15 € – 3 suites
Rest *Speakers' Corner* a la carte 21/35 €
♦ Business ♦ Modern ♦
A modern, elegant hotel including a palatial building from 1891, providing comfortable rooms and suites. Features a lovely old stairwell. Named after Speaker's Corner in Hyde Park, London.

relexa Hotel Stuttgarter Hof
Anhalter Str. 8 ⊠ *10963* – Ⓜ *Kochstr.*
– ℰ *(030) 26 48 30* – *berlin@relexa-hotel.de* – *Fax (030) 26 48 39 00*
– *www.relexa-hotels.de*   **G2**
206 rm ⊑ – †130/195 € ††160/225 € – 10 suites
Rest a la carte 26/32 €
♦ Business ♦ Functional ♦
This hotel has a large reception area and provides rooms with light beech wood furniture and warm décor. A charming restaurant.

Art'otel Berlin Mitte
Wallstr. 70 ⊠ *10179* – Ⓜ *Märkisches Museum* – ℰ *(030) 24 06 20*
– *aobminfo@artotels.de* – *Fax (030) 24 06 22 22* – *www.artotels.com*   **H2**
109 rm – †130/190 € ††160/210 €, ⊑ 14 €
Rest a la carte 25/35 €
♦ Business ♦ Design ♦
Listed building on the Mark Brandenburg bank that is an interesting link with the modern architecture of the hotel. Exclusively designed interior.

Mercure an der Charité
Invalidenstr. 38 ⊠ *10115* – Ⓜ *Zinnowitzer Str.*
– ℰ *(030) 30 82 60* – *h5341@accor.com* – *Fax (030) 30 82 61 00*
– *www.mercure.com*   *Plan I* **C2**
246 rm – †77/106 € ††86/116 €, ⊑ 13 €
Rest a la carte 19/29 €
♦ Chain hotel ♦ Functional ♦
Next to the National History Museum. Modern hotel especially designed for business guests. Large postcards decorate the passageways and rooms.

Fjord Hotel without rest
Bissingzeile 13 ⊠ *10785* – Ⓜ *Mendelssohn-Bartholdy-Park*
– ℰ *(030) 25 47 20* – *fjordhotelberlin@t-online.de* – *Fax (030) 25 47 21 11*
– *www.fjordhotelberlin.de*   *Plan I* **C2**
57 rm ⊑ – †95 € ††115 €
♦ Business ♦ Functional ♦
Hotel on the octagonal Leipziger Platz. Welcoming light rooms of standard design with cherry coloured furnishings. In fine weather breakfast is served on the roof terrace!

GERMANY

Lorenz Adlon – Hotel Adlon 🔲 ✂ VISA 🕮 AE ①

Unter den Linden 77 ✉ *10117 –* Ⓜ *Französische Str. –* ℰ *(030) 22 61 19 60*
– adlon@kempinski.com – Fax (030) 22 61 22 22
– www.hotel-adlon.de
closed 20 July - 20 August and Sunday - Monday   **G1**
Rest (dinner only) 105 €/160 €
Spec. Parfait von der Gänsestopfleber mit Birnenchutney. Atlantik Steinbutt mit grünem Spargel und Perigord Trüffel. Caneton à la presse mit Pommes Maximes und Sauce Rouennaise.
♦ French ♦ Formal ♦
Stylish atmosphere and excellent service featured in this restaurant serving traditional cuisine, located in Berlin's Pracht boulevard.

Fischers Fritz – The Regent 🔲 VISA 🕮 AE ①

Charlottenstr. 49 ✉ *10117 –* Ⓜ *Französische Str. –* ℰ *(030) 20 33 63 63*
– fischersfritz.berlin@rezidorregent.com – Fax (030) 20 33 61 19
– www.theregentberlin.com   **G1**
Rest 29 € (lunch) and a la carte 74/86 € ⌀
Spec. Langostinos und geröstetes Kalbsbries mit weißer Rosmarincreme. Darne vom Steinbutt mit Sauce Choron (2 pers.). Halbflüssiger Schokoladenkuchen mit Zichorienrahmeis.
♦ Seafood ♦ Formal ♦
A stylish, elegant restaurant in the Regent hotel serving creative cuisine based on classic recipes.

Vitrum – Hotel The Ritz Carlton 🔲 ✂ VISA 🕮 AE ①

Potsdamer Platz 3 ✉ *10785 –* Ⓜ *Potsdamer Platz –* ℰ *(030) 3 37 77 63 40*
– ccr.berlin@ritzcarlton.com – Fax (030) 3 37 77 53 41 – www.ritzcarlton.com
closed 2 weeks January, 4 weeks July - August and Sunday - Monday   **F2**
Rest (dinner only) 58 €/98 € and a la carte 52/74 €
♦ Contemporary ♦ Formal ♦
The traditional-style Grand hotel restaurant offers luxurious and even ostentatious surroundings. The cuisine is served in a lavish and creative manner.

Margaux (Hoffmann) 🔲 🔲 ✂ VISA 🕮 AE

Unter den Linden 78 (entrance Wilhelmstraße) ✉ *10117 –* Ⓜ *Französische Str.*
– ℰ *(030) 22 65 26 11 – hoffmann@margaux-berlin.de – Fax (030) 22 65 26 12*
– www.margaux-berlin.de
closed Sunday - Monday   **G1**
Rest 50 € (lunch)/110 € and a la carte 64/90 € ⌀
Spec. Glattbutt mit Badoitgelée und geeistem Olivenöl. Bar de Ligne à la vapeur mit Langustinentartar, weiße Mandelsauce. Poulet de Bresse à la Barigoule.
♦ Contemporary ♦ Fashionable ♦
Amber toned onyx, black marble décor in this restaurant serving Hoffmann's "avant garde classique" cuisine.

FACIL – Hotel Madison 🔲 🔲 ✂ VISA 🕮 AE ①

Potsdamer Str. 3 (5th floor) ✉ *10785 –* Ⓜ *Potsdamer Platz*
– ℰ *(030) 5 90 05 12 34 – welcome@facil.de – Fax (030) 5 90 05 05 00*
– www.facil.de
closed 1 - 22 January, 22 July - 6 August and Saturday - Sunday   **F2**
Rest 36 € (lunch)/100 € and a la carte 66/75 € ⌀
Spec. Gänseleberterrine mit Sonnenblumenkrokant und Taubensalat. Carabineiro mit lauwarmem Kalbskopfsandwich. Saibling mit Wacholder gedämpft, chinesischer Senfkohl und Saiblings-Kaviar.
♦ French ♦ Design ♦
An elegant, simple styled restaurant in Asian design with inner courtyard. Creative cuisine with much finesse.

GERMANY

VAU 🛋 ⚄ VISA ⏣ AE ①
Jägerstr. 54 ✉ 10117 – Ⓜ Französische Str. – ℰ (030) 2 02 97 30 – restaurant@
vau-berlin.de – Fax (030) 20 29 73 11 – www.vau-berlin.de
closed Sunday **G1**
Rest 36 € (lunch)/110 € and a la carte 64/80 € ⁂
Spec. Soufflierter Kartoffelschmarrn mit Imperial Kaviar. Sautierter St.Pierre mit
Ochsenmark und Pfifferlingen. Ente aus der Röhre mit Kopfsalat, Erbsen und
jungem Knoblauch.
◆ Contemporary ◆ Fashionable ◆
A bistro style restaurant in modern design. Serving creative cuisine on standard
recipes. Nice inner courtyard.

Ferrari 🛋 VISA ⏣ AE
Rheinhardtstr. 33 ✉ 10117 – Ⓜ Friedrichstr. – ℰ (030) 27 58 26 08
– info@ferrari-ristorante.de – Fax (030) 27 58 26 10 – www.ferrari-ristorante.de
closed Saturday lunch, Sunday **G1**
Rest 64 €/82 € and a la carte 39/51 €
◆ Italian ◆ Friendly ◆
Restaurant with Mediterranean, elegant atmosphere and friendly service. North
Italian cuisine.

Rutz 🛋 ⚄ VISA ⏣ AE ①
Chausseestr. 8 ✉ 10115 – Ⓜ Oranienburger Tor – ℰ (030) 24 62 87 60 – info@
rutz-weinbar.de – Fax (030) 24 62 87 61 – www.rutz-weinbar.de
closed Sunday *Plan I* **C2**
Rest (dinner only) a la carte 41/47 € ⁂
◆ Contemporary ◆ Trendy ◆
A modern, pure atmosphere serving creative Mediterranean cuisine and
featuring an excellent wine selection. Charming vine covered terrace.

Remake 🛋 VISA ⏣ AE
Große Hamburger Str. 32 ✉ 10115 – ℰ (030) 20 05 41 02 – restaurantremake@
aol.com – Fax (030) 97 89 48 60 – www.restaurant-remake.de
closed Saturday lunch, Sunday **H1**
Rest 39 €/59 € and a la carte 35/43 €
◆ Contemporary ◆ Fashionable ◆
A long restaurant with modern décor and a light atmosphere, serving creative
Mediterranean cuisine.

Paris-Moskau 🛋
Alt-Moabit 141 ✉ 10557 – ℰ (030) 3 94 20 81 – restaurant@paris-moskau.de
– Fax (030) 3 94 26 02 – www.paris-moskau.de
closed Saturday lunch, Sunday lunch **F1**
Rest (booking advisable) 58 € and a la carte 35/45 €
◆ International ◆ Rustic ◆
Not far from Lehrt town station is this old timber-framed hotel in the former border
region. Timeless interiors, international cuisine with well- priced midday meals.

Borchardt 🛋 VISA ⏣ AE
Französische Str. 47 ✉ 10117 – Ⓜ Französische Str. – ℰ (030) 81 88 62 62
– borchardt@gastart.de – Fax (030) 81 88 62 55 **G1**
Rest a la carte 30/46 €
◆ International ◆ Trendy ◆
Columns with gold-plated chapters and stucco ceilings impress guests. It is no
wonder at this fine address. Here you have to "see and be seen"! Courtyard
terrace.

Weinstein 🛋 VISA ⏣ AE ①
Mittelstr. 1 ✉ 10117 – Ⓜ Friedrichstr. – ℰ (030) 20 64 96 69 – weinstein-mitte@
gmx.de – Fax (030) 20 64 96 99
closed end July - early August and Saturday lunch, Sunday **G1**
Rest 29 €/41 €
◆ Mediterranean ◆ Bistro ◆
An interior that combines an exclusive Paris bistro ambience with a touch of Art
Deco. The kitchen serves dishes with a Mediterranean touch.

315

X **Lutter und Wegner** 🛜 *VISA* 🐠

Charlottenstr. 56 ⊠ *10117 –* Ⓜ *Französische Str. –* ℰ *(030) 2 02 95 40 – info @ l-w-berlin.de – Fax (030) 20 29 54 25 – www.l-w-berlin.de* **G2**
Rest a la carte 30/43 € 🏵
♦ **Austrian ♦ Wine bar ♦**
E.T.A. Hoffmann lived just round the corner. Three large columns painted by contemporary artists set the motto: Wine, women and song. Cosy wine bar.

X **Le Cochon Bourgeois** 🛜

Fichtestr. 24 ⊠ *10967 –* Ⓜ *Südstern –* ℰ *(030) 6 93 01 01 – Fax (030) 6 94 34 80 – www.le-cochon.de*
closed 1 week early January and Sunday - Monday *Plan I* **D3**
Rest (dinner only) 37 €/48 € and a la carte 28/40 €
♦ **French ♦ Cosy ♦**
With a character all its own, this unique establishment successfully combines boldly rustic décor with fine French cuisine.

AROUND THE KURFÜRSTENDAMM *Plan III*

🏨🏨🏨 **Palace** 🌐 🛋 🕍 🏊 ⅗ 🄰🄲 ↔ ⅔rest 🖭 📞 �350 🛆 *VISA* 🐠 🄰🄴 ⓪
Budapester Str. 45 ⊠ *10787 –* Ⓜ *Zoologischer Garten –* ℰ *(030) 2 50 20 – hotel @ palace.de – Fax (030) 25 02 11 19 – www.palace.de* **K2**
282 rm – 🛏225/495 € 🛏🛏225/495 €, ⊆ 20 € – 19 suites
Rest see *First Floor* below
♦ **Grand Luxury ♦ Classic ♦**
Guests at this private hotel enjoy modern, smart rooms with extensive technical facilities, luxurious suites and an elegant Mediterranean 800 m² spa area.

🏨🏨🏨 **Grand Hotel Esplanade** 🌐 🛋 🕍 🖵 🄰🄲 ↔rm ⅔rest �260
Lützowufer 15 ⊠ *10785 –* ℰ *(030) 25 47 80* 🛆 *VISA* 🐠 🄰🄴 ⓪
– info @ esplanade.de – Fax (030) 2 54 78 82 22 – www.esplanade.de **L2**
385 rm – 🛏230/280 € 🛏🛏255/305 €, ⊆ 20 € – 23 suites
Rest see *Vivo* below
Rest *Eckkneipe,* ℰ *(030) 25 47 86 20* – a la carte 18/37 €
♦ **Grand Luxury ♦ Modern ♦**
A fine example of modern design, this grand hotel also displays Jungen Wilden art. Ideal for conference guests. Down-to-earth Berlin fare served at wooden tables in this rustic corner pub.

🏨🏨 **Swissôtel** 🛋 🕍 🏊 🄰🄲 ↔ ⅔rest 🖭 📞 �220 🛆 *VISA* 🐠 🄰🄴 ⓪
Augsburger Str. 44 ⊠ *10789 –* Ⓜ *Kurfürstendamm –* ℰ *(030) 22 01 00*
– ask-us @ swissotel.com – Fax (030) 2 20 10 22 22
– www.swissotel-berlin.com **K2**
316 rm – 🛏120/225 € 🛏🛏140/245 €, ⊆ 21 €
Rest see *44* below
♦ **Luxury ♦ Modern ♦**
An international style, modern and luxurious hotel with spacious lobby, well-equipped rooms and a spa area.

🏨🏨 **Kempinski Hotel Bristol** 🛜 🛋 🕍 🖵 🏊 ↔rm ⅔rest 🖭 📞
Kurfürstendamm 27 ⊠ *10719 –* Ⓜ �280 🛆 *VISA* 🐠 🄰🄴 ⓪
Uhlandstr. – ℰ *(030) 88 43 40 – reservations.bristol @ kempinski.com – Fax (030) 8 83 60 75 – www.kempinski.com* **K2**
301 rm – 🛏270/350 € 🛏🛏330/420 €, ⊆ 23 € – 21 suites
Rest *Kempinski Grill* (closed Sunday - Monday, Saturday lunch) a la carte 48/67 €
Rest *Kempinski-Eck* a la carte 26/31 €
♦ **Luxury ♦ Classic ♦**
A red carpet leads directly from the renowned Kudamm to the elegant luxury hotel built in the 1950's. Distinguished guests such as John F. Kennedy and Sophia Loren have stayed here. Legendary Kempinski Grill with a carefully chosen interior. Brasserie-style Kempinski-Eck.

GERMANY

InterContinental 🏠🏠🏠 🛉 ⚙ 🛵 🏊 🖥 ⚕ 🎬 ⚿rm ⚔rest 🎦 🛋860

Budapester Str. 2 ⊠ 10787 – ℰ (030) 2 60 20   🚗 **VISA** 🅿️ 🆎 ⓘ
– berlin@ichotelsgroup.com – Fax (030) 26 02 26 00
– www.berlin.intercontinental.com   **L2**
584 rm – 🛉199/269 € 🛉🛉254/319 €, ⌷ 22 € – 42 suites
Rest see *Hugos* below
Rest *L. A. Cafe*, ℰ *(030) 26 02 12 50* – a la carte 25/24 €
  ♦ Chain hotel ♦ Luxury ♦ Classic ♦
An impressive hotel, from the lobby to the conference room. Some rooms are
tastefully elegant while those in the eastern wing are simple and modern. The
Vitality Club is also worth a visit. American-style L.A. Café under a pretty glass cupola.

Dorint Sofitel Schweizerhof 🏠🏠🏠 🛉 ⚙ 🛵 🏊 🖥 ⚕ 🎬 ⚿rm ⚔rest

Budapester Str. 25 ⊠ 10787 – ℰ (030)   🎦 🛋460 🚗 **VISA** 🅿️ 🆎 ⓘ
2 69 60 – info.bersch@dorint.com – Fax (030) 26 96 10 00
– www.schweizerhof.com   **L2**
384 rm – 🛉185/230 € 🛉🛉210/255 €, ⌷ 20 € – 10 suites
Rest 29 €/41 € and a la carte 31/38 €
  ♦ Chain hotel ♦ Business ♦ Design ♦
The modern hall can be seen through the glass frontage. Perfect technology for
the businessman. Recuperate in the Health centre with its 25m pool. Warm
colours and large paintings in this bistro restaurant.

Steigenberger 🏠🏠🏠 🛉 🏊 🖥 ⚕ 🎬 ⚿rm 🎦 ☎ 🛋300 🚗

Los-Angeles-Platz 1 ⊠ 10789 – 🅜 Augsburger Str.   **VISA** 🅿️ 🆎 ⓘ
– ℰ (030) 2 12 70 – berlin@steigenberger.de – Fax (030) 2 12 71 17
– www.berlin.steigenberger.de   **K2**
397 rm – 🛉199/395 € 🛉🛉199/395 €, ⌷ 21 € – 11 suites
Rest *Louis* (closed 4 weeks July - August and Sunday - Monday) (dinner only)
a la carte 36/53 €
Rest *Berliner Stube* a la carte 21/31 €
  ♦ Business ♦ Classic ♦
A spacious lobby in modern style greets the guest in this luxurious hotel. An
executive floor with club lounge on the 6th floor. Several bars also feature. In the
Louis: exclusive interior and creative cuisine. Rustic flair in the Berliner Stube.

Brandenburger Hof 🏠🏠 🏊 ⚿rm ⚔rest ☎ 🛋30 🚗

Eislebener Str. 14 ⊠ 10789 – 🅜 Augsburger Str.   **VISA** 🅿️ 🆎 ⓘ
– ℰ (030) 21 40 50 – info@brandenburger-hof.com – Fax (030) 21 40 51 00
– www.brandenburger-hof.com   **K3**
72 rm ⌷ – 🛉170/260 € 🛉🛉245/295 € – 8 suites
Rest see *Die Quadriga* below
Rest *Quadriga-Lounge*, ℰ *(030) 21 40 56 50* – 22 €/66 € and a la carte 29/37 €
  ♦ Traditional ♦ Design ♦
A distinctive ambience in this Wilhelmine city palace. The Bauhaus fixtures and
fittings are in exciting contrast to the architecture of this fine residence. Pure
elegance: the Quadriga Lounge extending into the Bar area.

Louisa's Place without rest 🏊 🖥 ⚕ ⚿ ⚿rm 🎦 ☎ 🚗 **VISA** 🅿️ 🆎 ⓘ

Kurfürstendamm 160 ⊠ 10709 – 🅜 Adenauerplatz – ℰ (030) 63 10 30 – info@
louisas-place.de – Fax (030) 63 10 31 00 – www.louisas-place.de   **J3**
47 suites – 🛉145/275 € 🛉🛉145/275 €, ⌷ 18 €
  ♦ Business ♦ Personalised ♦
Tasteful, spacious suites with kitchens, providing friendly service in this exclusive
hotel. Also with a stylish breakfast room and library.

Ramada Plaza 🏠🏠 🛵 ⚕ 🎬 ⚿rm ⚔rest 🎦 🛋70 🚗 **VISA** 🅿️ 🆎 ⓘ

Pragerstr. 12 ⊠ 10779 – 🅜 Güntzelstr. – ℰ (030) 2 36 25 00 – berlin.plaza@
ramada-treff.de – Fax (030) 2 36 25 05 50 – www.ramada-plaza-berlin.de
184 rm – 🛉139/189 € 🛉🛉139/189 €, ⌷ 17 € – 60 suites   **K3**
Rest a la carte 24/31 €
  ♦ Chain hotel ♦ Modern ♦
A business hotel providing elegant rooms and suites with American cherry wood
furnishings and the latest technical facilities. With executive décor and paintings
by suites on the sixth floor. A classic style restaurant.

SCHLOSS-
GARTEN

SCHLOSS
CHARLOTTENBURG

SAMMLUNG
BERGGRUEN-
PICASSO UND
SEINE ZEIT

BRÖHAN-
MUSEUM

ÄGYPTISCHES
MUSEUM UND
PAPYRUSSAMMLUNG

Tegeler Weg

Quedlinburger Str.

SPREE

Otto-   Suhr-   Allee
Richard-Wagner-Pl.
Alt-Lietzow
Guerickestr.
Einsteinufer
Salzufer
Helmholtz-

Christstr.

CHARLOTTENBURG

Knobelsdomstr.

Zillestr.

Sophie-
Charlotte-Pl.

Sophie-Charlotte-Pl.

Kaiserdamm

Wundt-

LIETZENSEE
PARK

Lietzen
see

Seehof

Neue   Kant-

Lietzen
see

Richard-   Wagner-   Str.

Zillestr.

Deutsche Oper

Bismarckstr.

Bismarck-   str.

Schillerstr.

Ernst-Reuter-Pl.

Bismarckstr.

Ernst-Reuter Platz

Schillerstr.

Goethe-

Pestalozzistr.

Kaiser-Friedrich-Str.

Windscheidstr.

Pesta-   lozzi-

Alt Luxemburg

str.

Amtsgerichtspl.

Leonhardtstr.

Kantstr.

Domicil   Wilmersdorfer Str.

SAVIGNYPLATZ

Bleibtreustr.

Holtzendorff-
str.

Rönnestr.

Stuttgarter
Pl.

CHARLOTTENBURG

Mommsenstr.

Mommsenstr.

Suarezstr.

Holtzendorffpl.

Damaschkestr.

Droysenstr.

Dahlmannstr.

Lewishamstr.

Lietzow
Gisebrecht-
str.

Kurfürstendamm
am Adenauerplatz

Bleibtreu
Str.

KURFÜRSTEN-

Hellbronner Str.

Wolters am Kurfürstendamm

Adenauerpl.

Louisa's Place

Paderborner
Olivaer Pl.

Pariser
Str.

Ku'Damm 101

Georg-Wilhelm-   Str.

Joachim-

Friedrich-   Str.

KURFÜRSTENDAMM

Nestorstr.

Xantener Str.

Albrecht-
Achilles-

Pader-
borner
Str.

Brandenburgische Str.

Düsseldorfer   Str.

Kronprinz

HALENSEE

Westfälische   Str.

Hochmeisterpl.

Paulsborner   Str.

Eisenzahnstr.

Konstanzer   Str.

Konstanzer Str.

Württembergische   Str.

Sächsische   Str.

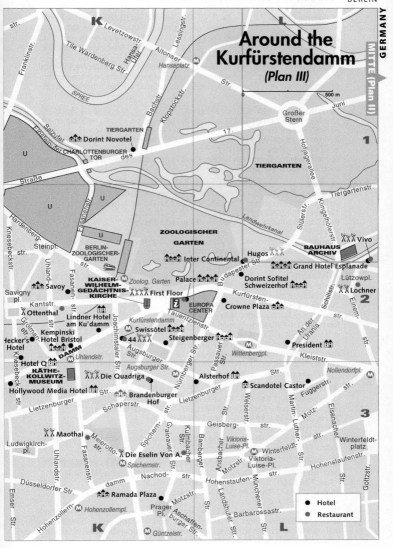

Around the Kurfürstendamm
(Plan III)

GERMANY

Crowne Plaza
🏠 🏗 🛏 🚫 ☒ 🍴rm ☒rest 🖾 ☎ ♨350 ⛵ **P** VISA 🐾 AE ⊙

Nürnberger Str. 65 ⊠ 10787 – 🚇 Wittenbergplatz – 🖉 (030)
21 00 70 – info@cp-berlin.com – Fax (030) 2 13 20 09 – www.cp-berlin.com **L2**
423 rm – 🛏135/265 € 🛏🛏165/295 €, ☐ 18 € – 10 suites – **Rest** a la carte 25/37 €
◆ Chain hotel ◆ Functional ◆
Good starting point for a stroll over the Kudamm or to the KaDeWe. Practical, individual furnishings. Conference area, complete with all the necessary technical equipment and new Conference Centre. International repertoire in the simple restaurant.

Dorint Novotel am Tiergarten
🏗 🏛 🛏 ☒ ♨300 ⛵

Straße des 17. Juni 106 ⊠ 10623 – 🖉 (030) 60 03 50
– h3649@accor.com – Fax (030) 60 03 56 60 – www.accorhotels.com **K1**
274 rm – 🛏139/219 € 🛏🛏154/234 €, ☐ 17 € – 6 suites – **Rest** a la carte 28/44 €
◆ Chain hotel ◆ Modern ◆
Located near the Tiergarten station, this business hotel provides well-equipped rooms in modern design.

Savoy
🌳 🏗 🍴rm ☒rest 🖾 ☎ ♨40 VISA 🐾 AE ⊙

Fasanenstr. 9 ⊠ 10623 – 🚇 Zoologischer Garten – 🖉 (030) 31 10 30
– info@hotel-savoy.com – Fax (030) 31 10 33 33 – www.hotel-savoy.com
125 rm – 🛏142/292 € 🛏🛏152/295 €, ☐ 15 € – 18 suites **K2**
Rest (closed Sunday) 13 € (lunch) and a la carte 24/36 €
◆ Business ◆ Modern ◆
Charming town hotel with 70 years of experience, mentioned in the writings of Thomas Mann, and where even today celebrities continually come and go. Cigar-lounge. Modern interior with red upholstered armchairs in the restaurant.

Alsterhof
🏗 🏛 🍴rm 🖾 ☎ ♨120 ⛵ VISA 🐾 AE ⊙

Augsburger Str. 5 ⊠ 10789 – 🚇 Augsburger Str. – 🖉 (030) 21 24 20
– info@alsterhof.com – Fax (030) 2 18 39 49 – www.alsterhof.com **L3**
200 rm – 🛏100 € 🛏🛏120 €, ☐ 16 €
Rest (closed Sunday dinner) a la carte 25/34 €
Rest Zum Lit-Fass (dinner only) a la carte 22/31 €
◆ Business ◆ Functional ◆
An attractive corner building with a glass roof pavilion. Very comfortable rooms and a small, but inviting leisure area on the 6th floor. Internet terminal. There is a hotel restaurant located in the basement. Go rustic at the Zum Lit-Fass with the lovely beer garden.

Hotel Q
🏗 🏛 🍴rm ☒rest 🖾 ☎ ♨15 ⛵ VISA 🐾 AE ⊙

Knesebeckstr. 67 ⊠ 10623 – 🚇 Uhlandstr. – 🖉 (030) 8 10 06 60 – q-berlin@
loock-hotels.com – Fax (030) 8 10 06 66 66 – www.loock-hotels.com **K2**
77 rm ☐ – 🛏130 € 🛏🛏150 € – **Rest** (residents only)
◆ Business ◆ Stylish ◆
Minimalist design, dark tones and modern atmosphere with simply equipped rooms. "Members bar".

Seehof
≤ 🌳 ☒ 🍴rm 🖾 ☎ ♨30 ⛵ VISA 🐾 AE

Lietzensee-Ufer 11 ⊠ 14057 – 🖉 (030) 32 00 20 – info@hotel-seehof-berlin.de
– Fax (030) 32 00 22 51 – www.hotel-seehof-berlin.de **I2**
75 rm ☐ – 🛏135/180 € 🛏🛏150/220 € – **Rest** a la carte 25/36 €
◆ Business ◆ Classic ◆
This hotel with its lovely lakeside terrace is situated on the green banks of the Lietzen lake. The rooms are comfortable and elegant, some furnished in mahogany, others with antiques. Restaurant with classic ambience and beautiful terrace overlooking the lake.

President
🏗 🏛 ☒ 🍴rm 🖾 ☎ ♨70 ⛵ **P** VISA 🐾 AE ⊙

An der Urania 16 ⊠ 10787 – 🚇 Wittenbergplatz – 🖉 (030) 21 90 30 – info@
president.bestwestern.de – Fax (030) 2 18 61 20 – www.president.bestwestern.de
178 rm – 🛏123/149 € 🛏🛏141/167 €, ☐ 14 € – **Rest** a la carte 24/42 € **L2**
◆ Business ◆ Functional ◆
Choose from functional Economy and Business rooms with Internet access or Club rooms with extra large desks and comfortable leather armchairs. Wicker chairs and contemporary design in the restaurant.

Lindner Hotel am Ku'damm

🏠 🗚 ↔rm ⅀rest ➁

Kurfürstendamm 24 ⊠ *10719*　　　　　　　　🛗140 VISA ⚫ ஊ ➀

– Ⓜ *Kurfürstendamm* – ✆ *(030) 81 82 50* – *info.berlin@lindner.de*

– *Fax (030) 8 18 25 11 88* – *www.lindner.de*　　　　　　　　**K2**

146 rm ⌂ – †99/189 € ††119/219 €

Rest a la carte 20/35 €

♦ Chain hotel ♦ Modern ♦

Located on a lively shopping promenade in the heart of the city, this hotel is sophisticated, modern and elegant. En-suite bathrooms. Restaurant serving international cuisine.

Hollywood Media Hotel without rest

♿ ↔ 🗚 ➁ 🛗90

Kurfürstendamm 202 ⊠ *10719*　　　　　　　　➁ VISA ⚫ ஊ ➀

– Ⓜ *Uhlandstr.* – ✆ *(030) 88 91 00* – *info@filmhotel.de* – *Fax (030) 88 91 02 80*

– *www.filmhotel.de*　　　　　　　　**K3**

185 rm ⌂ – †95/182 € ††115/202 € – 12 suites

♦ Business ♦ Modern ♦

This residence is devoted to the world of film. The tasteful, contemporary rooms are decorated with numerous film posters and photos of stars. The hotel has its own small cinema.

Domicil

🏠 ♿ ↔rm 🗚 ➁ 🛗50 VISA ⚫ ஊ ➀

Kantstr. 111a ⊠ *10627* – Ⓜ *Wilmersdorfer Str.* – ✆ *(030) 32 90 30*

– *info@hotel-domicil-berlin.de* – *Fax (030) 32 90 32 99*

– *www.hotel-domicil-berlin.de*　　　　　　　　**J2**

70 rm ⌂ – †118/143 € ††145/184 € – 3 suites

Rest 20 € and a la carte 22/36 €

♦ Business ♦ Modern ♦

In this hotel high above the city you will stay in attractive rooms in Italian style, in which the highlights are contemporary art and Tuscan fabrics. Rooftop restaurant with a roof garden. Cuisine with international influences.

Hecker's Hotel

♿ 🗚 ↔rm 🛗25 ➁ P VISA ⚫

Grolmanstr. 35 ⊠ *10623* – Ⓜ *Uhlandstr.* – ✆ *(030) 8 89 00*

– *info@heckers-hotel.de* – *Fax (030) 8 89 02 60*

– *www.heckers-hotel.de*　　　　　　　　**K2**

69 rm – †120/250 € ††140/280 €, ⌂ 16 €

Rest *Cassambalis*, ✆ *(030) 8 85 47 47* – a la carte 31/42 €

♦ Business ♦ Design ♦

A hotel which values individuality and service. The rooms, some cosy and functional, some in modern designer style or tastefully fitted out as themed rooms. Mediterranean flair on offer in the Cassambalis.

Bleibtreu

🏠 🕌 ♿ ↔rm ⅀rest 🛗 ➁ P VISA ⚫ ஊ ➀

Bleibtreustr. 31 ⊠ *10707* – Ⓜ *Uhlandstr.* – ✆ *(030) 88 47 40*

– *info@bleibtreu.com* – *Fax (030) 88 47 44 44*

– *www.bleibtreu.com*　　　　　　　　**J3**

60 rm – †122/222 € ††132/232 €, ⌂ 15 €

Rest a la carte 26/35 €

♦ Business ♦ Design ♦

Restored Gründerzeit town house. From the bedrooms to the bathrooms, Italian and German manufacturers have made the modern furniture especially for the hotel. The chic, bistro-style restaurant is open to the lobby.

Ku'Damm 101 without rest

🕌 ♿ ↔ ⅀ 🛗 ➁ 🛗60 ➁ VISA

Kurfürstendamm 101 ⊠ *10711* – ✆ *(030) 5 20 05 50*　　　　　　⚫ ஊ ➀

– *info@kudamm101.com* – *Fax (030) 5 20 05 55 55*

– *www.kudamm101.com*　　　　　　　　**I3**

170 rm – †101/161 € ††118/178 €, ⌂ 13 €

Deliberately understated designer style. Rooms with modern colour schemes, large windows and modern facilities. The breakfast room on the seventh floor offers a view over the town.

GERMANY

Kronprinz without rest
                ⅙ ⅙ ♨25 VISA ⦿⦾
Kronprinzendamm 1 ✉ 10711 – ℰ (030) 89 60 30
                   AE ⓪
– reception @ kronprinz-hotel.de – Fax (030) 8 93 12 15
– www.kronprinz-hotel.de   **I3**
76 rm ☞ – †115/130 € ††145/165 €
♦ Traditional ♦ Cosy ♦
A late 19th century building is home to light, homely rooms and a charming
"Romantic room". Convention centre within walking distance. Terrace shaded
by chestnut trees.

Scandotel Castor without rest
            ⅙ 🖭 **P.** VISA ⦿⦾ AE ⓪
Fuggerstr. 8 ✉ 10777 – ⓜ Nollendorfplatz – ℰ (030) 21 30 30
– scandotel @ t-online.de – Fax (030) 21 30 31 60
– www.scandotel-castor.de   **L3**
78 rm ☞ – †90/107 € ††100/135 €
♦ Business ♦ Functional ♦
Whether you want to visit the Ku'damm or KaDeWe, the cinema or pub: this
contemporary hotel with its functionally furnished rooms and full technical
facilities is close to it all!

Kurfürstendamm am Adenauerplatz without rest
           🖭 ♨30
Kurfürstendamm 68 ✉ 10707 – ⓜ   **P.** VISA ⦿⦾ AE ⓪
Adenauerplatz – ℰ (030) 88 46 30 – info @ hotel-kurfuerstendamm.de
– Fax (030) 8 82 55 28 – www.ibhotel-berlin-kurfuerstendamm.de   **J3**
34 rm ☞ – †95 € ††145 €
♦ Business ♦ Functional ♦
Standard rooms with functional cherry wood furnishings. The hotel is also a
training centre for trainee chefs.

First Floor – Hotel Palace
               🆔 ⅍ VISA ⦿⦾ AE ⓪
XXXX   *Budapester Str. 45 ✉ 10787 – ⓜ Zoologischer Garten*
✓3   *– ℰ (030) 25 02 10 20 – hotel @ palace.de – Fax (030) 2 50 21 19*
– www.firstfloor.palace.de
closed 17 July - 14 August and Saturday lunch   **K2**
Rest 40 € (lunch)/105 € and a la carte 58/72 € 🕮
Spec. Gratinierte Jakobsmuscheln mit gebratener Lauchterrine. Geschmorte
Lammschulter mit Kräuterknusper und Petersilienpürree. Kalbskotelett mit
Kalbsbries und Gänseleber gefüllt.
♦ French ♦ Formal ♦
A classically elegant restaurant with luxurious interior, serving French cuisine.
Interesting wine menu.

Hugos – Hotel InterContinental
        ⩽ Berlin, 🆔 ⅍ VISA ⦿⦾ AE ⓪
XXX   *Budapester Str. 2 (14th floor) ✉ 10787 – ℰ (030) 26 02 12 63*
✓3   *– mail @ hugos-restaurant.de – Fax (030) 26 02 12 39 – www.hugos-restaurant.de*
closed 2 weeks January, 4 weeks July - August and Sunday   **L2**
Rest (dinner only) 78 €/127 € and a la carte 65/80 € 🕮
Spec. Krosser Spanferkelbauch auf asiatische Art. In Olivenöl konfierter Kabeljau
mit Steinpilz-Gemüsevinaigrette. Geschmortes Schulterscherzel mit Rotwein-
Schalottensauce.
♦ French ♦ Design ♦
The restaurant on the 14th floor of the InterContinental has an elegant, modern
design, affording a view over the city. Serves classic and creative cuisine.

Die Quadriga – Hotel Brandenburger Hof
       ⅍ VISA ⦿⦾ AE ⓪
XXX   *Eislebener Str. 14 ✉ 10789 – ⓜ Augsburger Str. – ℰ (030) 21 40 56 50 – info @*
✓3   *brandenburger-hof.com – Fax (030) 21 40 51 00 – www.brandenburger-hof.com*
closed 2 - 13 January, 17 July - 18 August and Saturday - Sunday   **K3**
Rest (dinner only) 85 €/105 € and a la carte 61/80 € 🕮
Spec. Confierte Gänseleber mit grünem Pfeffer und Rosinenbrioche. Bresse
Poularde à la Perigourdine. Buttermilch, Himbeere und tasmanischer Pfeffer.
♦ French ♦ Formal ♦
A fine, stylish atmosphere in this restaurant serving creative cuisine. Sea-blue
tone décor and paintings by expressionist artist Lovis Corinth on display.

XXX   **Vivo** – Grand Hotel Esplanade   🛎 🃏 ✘ **VISA** 🆎 🆎 ①
ಜಿ
Lützowufer 15 ⊠ 10785 – ℰ (030) 2 54 78 86 30 – vivo@esplanade.de
– Fax (030) 2 54 78 86 17 – www.esplanade.de
closed 18 July - 15 August and Sunday - Monday   **L2**
Rest (dinner only) 60 €/78 € and a la carte 53/71 €
Spec. Steinbutt mit Chicorée und gehobelter Gänseleber. Wolfsbarsch mit Rinderhaxenscheiben und Champagnersauce. Schokoladensoufflé mit Bananensorbet.
♦ Mediterranean ♦ Fashionable ♦
Warm, earthy tones give this modern restaurant a Latin feel. The young waiters are very attentive, the cuisine is good with Mediterranean influences.

XXX   **44** – Swissôtel   🛎 🃏 **VISA** 🆎 🆎 ①
Augsburger Str. 44 ⊠ 10789 – Ⓜ Kurfürstendamm – ℰ (030) 22 01 00 – ask-us@swissotel.com – Fax (030) 2 20 10 22 22 – www.swissotel-berlin.com   **K2**
Rest 20 € (lunch)/88 € and a la carte 37/61 €
♦ Innovative ♦ Fashionable ♦
A simple, elegant restaurant with large window front. Creative and traditional cuisine served.

XX   **Alt Luxemburg**   🃏 **VISA** 🆎 🆎 ①
Windscheidstr. 31 ⊠ 10627 – Ⓜ Wilmersdorfer Str. – ℰ (030) 3 23 87 30 – info@altluxemburg.de – Fax (030) 3 27 40 03 – www.altluxemburg.de
closed Sunday   **I2**
Rest (dinner only) (booking advisable) 65 €/72 € and a la carte 47/56 €
♦ French ♦ Family ♦
Enjoy the sophisticated atmosphere and classic cuisine in this restaurant run since 1982 by the Wannemacher family.

XX   **Lochner**   🛎 **VISA** 🆎
Lützowplatz 5 ⊠ 10785 – Ⓜ Nollendorfplatz – ℰ (030) 23 00 52 20 – info@lochner-restaurant.de – Fax (030) 2 30 04 21 – www.lochner-restaurant.de
closed Monday   **L2**
Rest (dinner only) 58 €/76 € and a la carte 33/48 €
♦ International ♦ Friendly ♦
A pleasant, light atmosphere and subdued décor in this restaurant serving international cuisine. Small terrace in front.

XX   **Maothai**   🛎 **VISA** 🆎 🆎
Meierottostr. 1 ⊠ 10719 – Ⓜ Spichernstr. – ℰ (030) 8 83 28 23 – Fax (030) 88 67 56 58 – www.maothai-am-fasanenplatz.de   **K3**
Rest (Monday - Friday dinner only) a la carte 19/44 €
♦ Thai ♦ Exotic ♦
An intimate, candle-lit atmosphere in this restaurant near the Fasanen square, serving Thai cuisine. Charming terrace dining area.

X   **Bieberbau**   🛎
😊
Durlacher Str. 15 ⊠ 10715 – Ⓜ Bundesplatz – ℰ (030) 8 53 23 90
– webmaster@bieberbau-berlin.de – Fax (030) 81 00 68 65
– www.bieberbau-berlin.de
closed Sunday - Monday   *Plan I* **B3**
Rest (dinner only) 29 €/47 €
♦ International ♦ Cosy ♦
Half-timbered building with wooden panelling in the restaurant. A friendly young staff serving set menu dishes.

X   **Ottenthal**   **VISA** 🆎 🆎
😊
Kantstr. 153 ⊠ 10623 – Ⓜ Uhlandstr. – ℰ (030) 3 13 31 62
– restaurant@ottenthal.com – Fax (030) 3 13 37 32
– www.ottenthal.com   **K2**
Rest (dinner only) (booking advisable) a la carte 25/40 €
♦ Austrian ♦ Bistro ♦
This restaurant is named after a wine estate in Austria. Serving food from that country, and featuring décor inspired by the old church.

Die Eselin von A.

Kulmbacher Str. 15 ⊠ 10777 – ⓜ Spichernstr. – ℰ (030) 2 14 12 84 – info@
die-eselin-von-a.de – Fax (030) 21 47 69 48 – www.die-eselin-von-a.de
closed 2 weeks early January, 2 weeks August **K3**
Rest (dinner only) 38 €/43 € and a la carte 31/38 €

♦ International ♦ Bistro ♦

Friendly service, relaxed atmosphere and modern international cuisine using
fresh ingredients make this bistro-style restaurant popular with its many regular
customers.

ENVIRONS OF BERLIN

at Berlin-Grunewald   *Plan I*

 Schlosshotel im Grunewald ❧

Brahmsstr. 10 ⊠ 14193
– ℰ (030) 89 58 40 – info@schlosshotelberlin.com – Fax (030) 89 58 48 00
– www.schlosshotelberlin.com – closed 1 - 15 January **A3**
54 rm – †169/285 € ††198/305 € – 12 suites
Rest (lunch only, Tuesday - Wednesday and dinner) a la carte 36/46 €
Rest Vivaldi (closed Tuesday - Wednesday) (dinner only) a la carte 58/78 €

♦ Castle ♦ Luxury ♦ Design ♦

Not a dream: a palace with an intimate atmosphere! Nestling in parkland this
hotel, with its lavish furnishings and décor, is an inspiration. The Vivaldi offers
sumptuous elegance

 Servino

Flinsberger Platz 8 ⊠ 14193 – ℰ (030) 89 73 86 28 – servino@servino.de
– Fax (030) 89 73 53 02 – closed Tuesday **A3**
Rest (dinner only) a la carte 31/46 €

♦ International ♦ Friendly ♦

This villa belonging to a tennis club is home to a restaurant serving international
and creative cuisine. The terrace affords a view of the courts.

at Berlin-Tegel (Airport)   *Plan I*

 Mercure Airport

Gotthardstr. 96 ⊠ 13403 – ℰ (030) 49 88 40 – h5348@accor.com
– Fax (030) 49 88 45 55 – www.mercure.de **B1**
303 rm – †59/109 € ††59/119 €, ⊑ 12 € – **Rest** a la carte 17/27 €

♦ Chain hotel ♦ Functional ♦

The bus for Tegel airport stops on the doorstep. There are also good connections
to the extensive transport system. Rooms are furnished in functional and
contemporary style. Restaurant serving international cuisine.

 Sorat Hotel Humboldt-Mühle ❧

An der Mühle 5 (by Seidelstraße A 1)
⊠ 13507 – ℰ (030) 43 90 40 – humboldt-muehle@sorat-hotels.com
– Fax (030) 43 90 44 44 – www.sorat-hotels.com
120 rm ⊑ – †109/179 € ††134/204 € – **Rest** a la carte 28/41 €

♦ Chain hotel ♦ Functional ♦

The rooms of this distinctive hotel are shared over the former grain silo, a modern
building with glass façade and a villa. Cross a narrow bridge over the Tegelersee
side canal to get to the restaurant.

Mercure Airport

Kurt-Schumacher-Damm 202 (by airport approach) ⊠ 13405
– ⓜ Kurt-Schumacher-Platz – ℰ (030) 4 10 60 – h0791@accor.com
– Fax (030) 4 10 67 00 – www.mercure.com **A1**
184 rm – †45/136 € ††45/136 €, ⊑ 14 €
Rest a la carte 22/33 €

♦ Chain hotel ♦ Functional ♦

This functional hotel near the airport is ideal for business guests. New design
planned for spring 2006.

FRANKFURT
FRANKFURT AM MAIN

Population (est. 2005): 649 000 (conurbation 1 489 000) – Altitude: 40m

ALLOVERCOLORISE

Frankfurt is set on the banks of the River Main at the crossing point of Germany's north-south and east-west roads. It is the commercial capital of Germany and a truly cosmopolitan city with a rich tradition.

The city centre is Cathedral Hill (Domhügel), once the site of Roman fortifications and a Carolingian palace; the election of the Holy Roman Emperors first took place in the cathedral in 1356. Germany's first freely elected parliament met in Frankfurt in 1848 in St Paul's Church.

In 16C the city was granted the right to mint money leading to a flourishing money market and foundation of the stock exchange. In the 18C the economy was dominated by German banks, which in 19C acquired a worldwide reputation thanks to financiers such as Rothschild (1744-1812). Frankfurt is now home to the Federal Bank and the European Central Bank. Modern high-rise office blocks in the commercial district – the German Manhattan – dwarf the medieval historic centre.

Frankfurt is the birthplace of J. W. von Goethe, who described his native town in his memoirs; here he wrote several great works as Die Leiden des jungen Werthers (1744), written in one month. The university founded in 1914, research institutes, the opera, theatres and museums have made the city the scientific and cultural metropolis of the Hessen Land.

WHICH DISTRICT TO CHOOSE

Most **hotels** and **restaurants** are in the city centre, around the railway station *Plan III* **H2** and near the exhibition centre *Plan III* **G2**. There are also several attractive small restaurants in the Westend *Plan III* **H1** and in side-streets of the Fressgass (Eatery Alley) *Plan II* **F2** as well as near the opera house *Plan II* **E2** and the stock exchange *Plan II* **E2**. Round the station there are cafés, cabarets, bars and various exotic places. Popular with tourists and local people are the **Äppelwoilokale** in the Sachsenhausen district *Plan II* **F2**; they have a casual and lively atmosphere where you can try *Handkäs' mit Musik* (a small yellow cheese with vinegar, oil and onions), *Frankfurter Grüne Sauce* (a herb sauce) and – of course – *Apfelwein*.

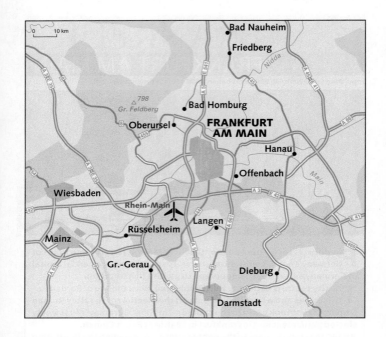

ARRIVAL – DEPARTURE

Frankfurt Airport, about 9 km (5 mi) southwest of the city centre, ℰ (069) 69 00.

From the airport to the city centre – By **taxi**: approx. €20-25. By **train**: the S-Bahn trains S8 and S9 leave every 15min for Frankfurt Station in the city centre (journey time: 11min; ticket tariff is rate 4).

By rail – There are regular national and international train services from **Frankfurt Station**.

TRANSPORT

METRO, BUSES AND TRAMS

Normal fare is €3.25 (between 9am and 4pm); day ticket €7.20, group day ticket (max 5 people) €12.50 (valid until the last ride of the day). Tickets are available at vending machines and from bus drivers but **not** on tram-cars, the U-Bahn and S-Bahn. Local public transport within the city of Frankfurt is managed by the **VGF** (Verkehrsgesellschaft Frankfurt am Main); ℰ (069) 1 94 49 (Mon-Thu 8am-5pm, Fri 8am-1pm); buses, trams, the U-Bahn (metro) and S-Bahn and regional trains in the greater Frankfurt region are managed by the **RMV** (Rhein-Main-Verkehrsbund); ℰ (069) 2 73 07 62 (daily 8am-6pm, Sat 9am-4pm). Information on the traffic island of the Hauptwache (Mon-Fri 9am-8pm, Sat 9am-4pm); also at Konstablerwache, Passage B level and other U-Bahn and S-Bahn stations. www.rmv.de; www.vgt-ffm.de

FRANKFURT CARD

The **Frankfurt Card** is valid for the RMV network within city limits, including the airport, and also discounts at 15 museums and other attractions; also 25-30% for selected boat rides. The card is available in many travel agencies, at tourist information offices and in both terminals at the airport. 1-day ticket €7.80; 2-day ticket €11.50.

TAXIS

Taxis are cream-coloured, numerous and relatively cheap. They can be hailed in the street, hired at taxi ranks and called by telephone. The initial charge is €2 (€1.38 per km); night rate €2.50 (€1.53 per km). ☎ (069) 25 00 01 (Taxi Zentrale).

USEFUL ADDRESSES

TOURIST INFORMATION

Tourismus + Congress GmbH, *Plan III* **G2**; Mon-Fri 8.30am-5pm; ☎ (069) 21 23 88 00. **Railway Station Entrance Hall** *Plan III* **H1**; Mon-Fri 8am-9pm, Sat-Sun 9am-6pm; ☎ (069) 21 23 88 49. **Römer** *Plan II* **E1**, Römerberg 7; Mon-Fri 9.30am-5.30pm, Sat-Sun 10am-4pm. **City Info Zeil**, Mon-Fri 10am-6pm, Sat 19am-4pm. www.frankfurt-tourismus.de

POST OFFICES

Mon-Fri 8am-6pm, Sat 8am-12 noon. **Zeil Post Office**: Mon-Fri 9.30am-8pm, Sat 9am-4pm; **Railway Station**: Mon-Fri 7am-7.30pm, Sat 8am-4pm; **Airport**: daily 7am-9pm.

BANKS

Mon-Fri, 8.30am-12.30pm and 2-4pm (sometimes later); closed Sat-Sun and public holidays.

EMERGENCY

Dial ☎ **110**; Fire Brigade ☎ **112**.

BUSY PERIODS

It may be difficult to find a room at a reasonable price (except during weekends) when special events are held in the city as hotel prices may be raised substantially:

Frankfurt International Fair: February and August.

Dippemess: end March to early April and September – Pottery fair.

Mainfest: end July to early August – Festival of the river Main.

Apfelwein Festival: early August – Apple wine festival on the Römerberg.

Museumsuferfest: August – Museum Embankment Festival of art and culture beside the river.

International Motor Show: September (alternate years) – 10 days with cars in the limelight.

Buchmesse: October – Frankfurt Book Fair, one of the biggest in the world.

Traditional Christmas Market: late November to 22 December.

EXPLORING FRANKFURT

It is possible to visit the main sights and museums in two days.

Museums and sights are usually open between 10am and 5pm. Most are closed on Mondays and public holidays.

VISITING

Dom *Plan II* **F1** – Gothic Cathedral (13C-15C), where the emperors were crowned.

Goethe-Haus und Goethe-Museum *Plan II* **E1** – Goethe's birthplace and adjoining art gallery of his era.

Städtisches Kunstinstitut und Städtische Galerie *Plan II* **E2** – Art Museum displaying an important collection of works by Old Masters, 18C German works and German Expressionists.

Zoo *Plan I* **D2** – One of the leading zoos in Europe, famous for its rare species, living in their natural habitat.

Palmengarten *Plan III* **G1** – The Tropical Gardens are a lush oasis of calm in the heart of the city with plants from nearly every climatic region.

SHOPPING

Shops are usually open from 9am/10am to 6.30pm/8pm. They are closed on Sunday.

In Frankfurt the main street for **shops and department stores** is **Zeil**, including among others the passage called *les facettes*. Nearby are the more **exclusive shops** in the streets around the **Grosse Bockenheimer Strasse** *Plan II* **E1** and **Goethestrasse** *Plan II* **E1**. **Schillerstrasse** *Plan II* **E1** has upmarket shops selling porcelain and household goods. There are interesting shops in Schweizer Strasse in **Sachsenhausen** *Plan II* **F2** and in Leipziger Strasse in **Bockenheim** *Plan I* **A1**.

Most **art galleries** are concentrated in **Braubachstrasse** *Plan II* **F1**, although they are to be found throughout the city; the **antique dealers** have settled in Pfarrgasse in the **cathedral (Dom) district**.

MARKETS – The **flea market** is always held **along the Main** on Sat 9am-2pm. Other markets are a **farmers' market** in **Konstablerwache** every Sat; in Berger Strasse, **Bornheim**, Wed 7am-6pm and at the Südbahnhof in **Sachsenhausen** (South Bank) Fri 8am-6pm.

ENTERTAINMENT

Journal Frankfurt (in newsagents), *Fritz* (no charge) and *Welcome to Frankfurt* (in German) provide information on all events. Ticket sales (only on location) at the Tourismus + Congress GmbH.

Oper und Ballett Frankfurt *Plan II* **E1** – Daring staging and modern choreography under the direction of William Forsythe have earned the ensemble admiration and fame. www.oper-frankfurt.de

Alte Oper Frankfurt *Plan II* **E1** – Concert and conference centre opened in 1981 in the Old Opera House. www.alte-oper-frankfurt.de

Jahrhunderthalle Hoechst, Pfaffenwiese – Venue for classical concerts and other entertainment events.

Schauspiel Frankfurt *Plan II* **E2** – Home of the Schauspielhaus (Theatre), the Kammerspiele (Chamber Theatre), opera and ballet.

Die Komödie *Plan II* **E2** – Comedies and variety theatre.

Künstlerhaus Mousonturm *Plan I* **D2** – Cultural Centre, in converted soap factory, offering professional free theatre and also a stage for various local and guest ensembles. www.mousonturm.de

Schirn Kunsthalle *Plan II* **F1** – Prestigious art gallery.

NIGHTLIFE

The main centre for nightlife is around **Frankfurt Station**, where there is a selection of cabarets, bars, cafés and restaurants, and other exotic places.

Steigenberger Frankfurter Hof   🛜 🕉 🐾 AC ⁄rm 🕉 rest 🔲

Am Kaiserplatz ✉ 60311 – Ⓜ *Willy-*   🕻 🖪 300 *VISA* ⓂⓈ ⒶⒺ ⓪
Brandt-Platz – 𝒞 *(069) 2 15 02 – frankfurter-hof@steigenberger.de*
– Fax (069) 21 59 00 – www.frankfurter-hof.steigenberger.de   **E1**
332 rm – 🛉395 € 🛉🛉445 €, ⌷ 26 € – 10 suites
Rest *Français* *(closed 1 week January, 1 week April, 5 weeks July - August and Saturday - Sunday)* 98 €/108 € and a la carte 48/83 €
Rest *Oscar's* a la carte 30/49 € – **Rest *Iroha*** 35 €/87 €
♦ Grand Luxury ♦ Business ♦ Classic ♦
The magnificence of the traditional Steigenberg ancestral seat, the Grand Hotel, which dates back to 1876, can be seen everywhere – especially after the lavish renovation of the " Weißfrauen" wing. Oscar's is in the bistro style. The Iroha offers Far Eastern specialities.

A 66

21

B

Hansa-

Eschersheimer

Adickesallee

Miquelallee

Miquel- /
Adickesallee

allee

Eysseneckstr.

Landstr.

1

Ginnheimer Landstr.

Franz Rücker Allee

Frauenlobstr.

Zeppelinallee

Miquelallee

Zeppelinallee

Villa Merton

GRÜNEBURG PARK

Holzhausenstr.

U

Bremer

Str.

Hansaallee

Str.

Eschersheimer

Sophienstr.

BOCKENHEIM

PALMEN-GARTEN

Fürstenberger

La Trattoria

Around the Exhibition
Centre (Plan III)

Grüneburgweg

Grüneburg-

Leipziger Str.

Leipziger

Str.

Sophienstr.

Zeppelinallee

Siesmayerstr.

Friedrich-vom-Stein-Str.

Leibigstr.

Leibigstr.

weg

Eschersheimer

Schloß-

Adalbert-

Gräfstr.

Bockenheimer

Landstr.

Bockenheimer

Landstr.

Reuterweg

Bockenheimer

Hochstr.

SENKENBERG-
MUSEUM

Senckberganlage

Gräf-

str.

Robert Mayer Str.

Kettenhofweg

Mendelssohnstr.

Westendstr.

Feuerbachstr.

Ulmenstr.

Kettenhofweg

str.

Neue

Junghofstr.

L. Meitner
Str.

Hamburger

Allee

Emil

Sulzbach Str.

2

Dorint Novotel
Frankfurt City

Theodor

Heuss

Allee

Friedrich Ebert Anlage

Rheinstr.

Westendstr.

Mainzer

Land-

Taunusanlage

Taunusstr.

Weserstr.

Taunustor

Gallus
anlage

Große
Gallusstr.

Mainzer

Str.

Emser

CONGRESS
CENTER

MESSE FRANKFURT

Europa

Allee

Düsseldorfer

Str.

Wesserstr.

Brücke

Kölner

Str.

Frankenallee

Mainzer

Landstr.

Hafenstr.

HAUPTBAHNHOF

Baseler

Str.

Leuschner Str.

Untermainkai

STÄDELSCHES
KUNSTINSTITUT

Idstainer Str.

Frankenallee

Gutleut

Str.

Wilhelm

Unter der
Friedensbrücke

Schaumainkai

Hölbein-

str.

Allee

3

Mainzer

Kleyerstr.

Camberger Str.

Landstr.

Manheimer

Hafen-

str.

Friedens-
brücke

Stresemannallee

Oskar
Sommer
Str.

Gutleutstr.

MAIN

Stern

Kai

Garten-

Kennedy

Express by
Holiday Inn

A

Theodor

B

RHEIN-MAIN

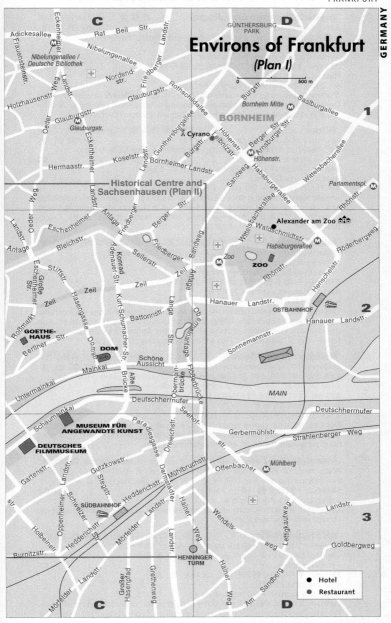

Environs of Frankfurt
(Plan I)

GERMANY

ArabellaSheraton Grand Hotel
🏛️ ℔ 🏛️ 🔲 🗚 ⇖rm 🚪 🛎️280

Konrad-Adenauer Str. 7 ✉ 60313 🚗 **VISA** **MO** **AE** **①**
– **M** *Konstablerwache* – ℰ *(069) 2 98 10 – grandhotel.frankfurt@*
arabellasheraton.com – Fax (069) 2 98 18 10
– *www.starwoodhotels.com/frankfurt* **F1**
378 rm – ♦275/515 € ♦♦300/540 €, ⇆ 24 € – 12 suites
Rest a la carte 29/46 €
♦ Chain hotel ♦ Luxury ♦ Modern ♦
Modern Grand Hotel with rooms and suites in various décors ranging from Art
Deco, Arabic and Asian to a Bavarian "Balneum Romanum" bathing setting An
atrium restaurant with a Mediterranean-influenced open kitchen.

Hilton
🏛️ ℔ 🏛️ 🔲 🕭 🗚 ⇖rm 🚪 🛎️300 🚗

Hochstr. 4 ✉ 60313 – **M** *Eschenheimer Tor* **VISA** **MO** **AE** **①**
– ℰ *(069) 1 33 80 00 – sales.frankfurt@hilton.com – Fax (069) 13 38 20*
– *www.hilton.de* **E1**
342 rm – ♦229/449 € ♦♦229/449 €, ⇆ 26 € – 3 suites
Rest a la carte 32/50 €
♦ Chain hotel ♦ Luxury ♦ Modern ♦
The old town swimming pool, a listed building, has been completely renovated
and is now part of the extensive modern hotel. It also includes a unique fitness
department. "The fine American style" is the motto of the "Pacific Colors
Restaurant".

InterContinental
🏛️ ℔ 🏛️ 🔲 🕭 🗚 ⇖rm 🚪 🛎️400 **VISA** **MO** **AE** **①**

Wilhelm-Leuschner-Str. 43 ✉ 60329 – ℰ *(069) 2 60 50 – frankfurt@*
ichotelsgroup.com – Fax (069) 25 24 67
– *www.frankfurt.intercontinental.com* **E2**
770 rm – ♦405 € ♦♦425 €, ⇆ 21 € – 35 suites
Rest Signatures a la carte 24/45 €
♦ Chain hotel ♦ Luxury ♦ Functional ♦
This hotel, which is situated on the river Main, is notable for its period furniture,
warm colours and beautiful fabrics. If you happen to be here for a conference on
the 21st floor, take a look out of the window at the skyline. All elegance and warm
tones – this is "Signatures ". Plus a chic conservatory.

Holiday Inn City-South
℔ 🏛️ 🗚 ⇖rm 𝒳rest 🚪 🕭 🛎️200 🚗

Mailänder Str. 1 (by Darmstädter Landstr. C 3) **P** **VISA** **MO** **AE** **①**
✉ 60598 – ℰ *(069) 6 80 20 – info.hi-frankfurt-citysouth@queensgruppe.de*
– Fax (069) 6 80 23 33 – www.frankfurt-citysouth-holiday-inn.de
435 rm – ♦175/380 € ♦♦195/400 €, ⇆ 19 €
Rest a la carte 27/45 €
♦ Chain hotel ♦ Functional ♦
Light rooms with cherry wood furniture await you opposite the Henninger
tower. The rooms on the 25th floor offer breathtaking views of the city. Elegant
hotel restaurant "Le Chef" with international dishes.

Alexander am Zoo without rest
🏛️ ⇖ 🛎️30 🚗 **VISA** **MO** **AE** **①**

Waldschmidtstr. 59 ✉ 60316 – **M** *Habsburgerallee* – ℰ *(069) 94 96 00 – info@*
alexanderamzoo.de – Fax (069) 94 96 07 20 – www.alexanderamzoo.de
66 rm ⇆ – ♦125 € ♦♦150 € – 9 suites *Plan I* **D2**
♦ Business ♦ Modern ♦
A modern hotel with light, modern furnished rooms. Ideal for conference guests.
Terrace with view over the town.

NH Frankfurt-City
🏛️ 🕭 🗚 ⇖rm 🚪 🛎️120 **VISA** **MO** **AE** **①**

Vilbelerstr. 2 ✉ 60313 – **M** *Konstablerwache* – ℰ *(069) 9 28 85 90*
– nhfrankfurtcity@nh-hotels.com – Fax (069) 9 28 85 91 00
– *www.nh-hotels.com* **F1**
256 rm – ♦99/170 € ♦♦99/170 €, ⇆ 18 € – 8 suites
Rest a la carte 23/34 €
♦ Chain hotel ♦ Functional ♦
Centrally located, this well run hotel is right in the pedestrian zone of town.
Providing modern comfortable rooms with all mod cons. Restaurant on the first
floor with a large buffet.

GERMANY

Villa Orange without rest
Hebelstr. 1 ⊠ 60318 – ℰ (069) 40 58 40 – contact@villa-orange.de
– Fax (069) 40 58 41 00 – www.villa-orange.de
38 rm � – ♦120/140 € ♦♦140/150 €
F1
♦ Business ♦ Personalised ♦
You can tell that this residence is run with warmth and common sense. Tasteful, comfortable rooms create an atmosphere of well-being. Vintage baths in some bathrooms.

Steigenberger Frankfurt-City
Lange Str. 5 ⊠ 60311 – ℰ (069) 21 93 00
– frankfurt-city@steigenberger.de – Fax (069) 21 93 05 99
– www.frankfurt-city.steigenberger.de
149 rm – ♦140/261 € ♦♦170/296 €, ⊒ 16 €
F1
Rest a la carte 21/33 €
♦ Business ♦ Functional ♦
Business guests especially value this hotel, which was opened mid-2001. It offers tastefully decorated rooms, with the most up-to-date technical facilities. Some have a view of the skyline. Restaurant with a show kitchen.

Memphis without rest
Münchener Str. 31 ⊠ 60329 – Ⓜ Willy-Brandt-Platz – ℰ (069) 2 42 60 90
– memphis-hotel@t-online.de – Fax (069) 24 26 09 99
– www.memphis-hotel.de
E2
42 rm ⊒ – ♦65/130 € ♦♦75/160 €
♦ Business ♦ Design ♦
A charming designer hotel close to the theatre and in the heart of a lively arts scene. It combines clear shapes with strong colours. Some rooms overlooking the inner courtyard are very peaceful.

Miramar without rest
Berliner Str. 31 ⊠ 60311 – ℰ (069) 9 20 39 70
– info@miramar-frankfurt.de – Fax (069) 92 03 97 69
– www.miramar-frankfurt.de
closed 23 - 31 December
E-F1
39 rm ⊒ – ♦92/130 € ♦♦105/150 €
♦ Business ♦ Functional ♦
Located between the Zeil and the Römer this hotel offers comfortable, cheerful rooms with dark grained root wood furniture – functional fittings include internet access.

Scala without rest
Schäfergasse 31 ⊠ 60313 – Ⓜ Konstablerwache – ℰ (069) 1 38 11 10
– info@scala.bestwestern.de – Fax (069) 28 42 34
– www.scala.bestwestern.de
F1
40 rm – ♦90/97 € ♦♦113/125 €, ⊒ 11 €
♦ Business ♦ Functional ♦ A centrally located hotel in modern style with well-appointed rooms available.

Tiger-Restaurant
Heiligkreuzgasse 20 ⊠ 60313 – Ⓜ Konstablerwache
– ℰ (069) 92 00 22 25 – info@tigerpalast.de – Fax (069) 92 00 22 17
– www.tigerpalast.de
closed 1 - 9 January, 9 - 24 April, 25 - 29 May, 15 - 19 June, 23 July - 21 August,
24 - 30 December and Sunday - Monday
F1
Rest (dinner only) (booking essential) 62 €/98 € and a la carte 59/91 €
Rest *Palast-Bistrot* (closed 26 - 28 February, 23 July - 21 August and Monday)
(dinner only) 38 €/46 € and a la carte 34/45 €
Spec. Cannelloni von roter und gelber Paprika mit Oliventapenade. Rückenfilet vom Pauillac Lamm im Foccaciamantel gebacken. Glaciertes Törtchen von Baby-Bananen mit Bananen-Passionsfruchtkompott und Kokos-Chili-Eis.
♦ French ♦ Fashionable ♦
This restaurant shares its address with a variety theatre, and serves creative seasonal cuisine. An affinity for the arts is also apparent in the paintings on display. An historic brick-vaulted ceiling in this bistro style restaurant

XX **Opéra** 🛱 *VISA* 🐼 🔤 ⓞ
Opernplatz 1 ⊠ 60313 – Ⓜ Alte Oper – ℰ (069) 1 34 02 15 – info @
opera-restauration.de – Fax (069) 1 34 02 39 – www.opera-restauration.de
Rest a la carte 35/48 €   **E1**
♦ International ♦ Formal ♦
Extensively renovated former foyer of the Old Opera House with parquet floor,
stucco ceilings, wall decorations and original Art Nouveau candelabra. Terrace
with a view of Frankfurt's skyline.

XX **Aubergine** *VISA* 🐼 🔤
Alte Gasse 14 ⊠ 60313 – Ⓜ Konstablerwache – ℰ (069) 9 20 07 80 – info @
aubergine-frankfurt.de – Fax (069) 9 20 07 86 – www.aubergine-frankfurt.de
closed 3 weeks July - August and Saturday lunch, Sunday   **F1**
Rest (booking advisable) 28 € (lunch)/58 € and a la carte 41/57 € ⊯
♦ International ♦ Cosy ♦
Enjoy the Italian-based cuisine, served among modern art and on Versace dishes,
in this historic townhouse with the red sandstone walls and coloured lead-glass
windows.

XX **Maingaustuben** *VISA* 🐼 🔤 ⓞ
Schifferstr. 38 ⊠ 60594 – ℰ (069) 61 07 52 – maingau @ t-online.de
– Fax (069) 61 99 53 72 – www.maingau.de
closed 2 weeks end July - early August and Saturday lunch, Sunday dinner
- Monday   **F2**
Rest 14 € (lunch)/58 € and a la carte 21/43 €
♦ International ♦ Friendly ♦
Tasteful décor and stylish ambience characterise this restaurant, which offers
international and some classic cuisine.

X **Main Tower Restaurant** ⋖ Frankfurt, 🍴 *VISA* 🐼 🔤
Neue Mainzer Str. 52 (53th floor) ⊠ 60311 – Ⓜ Alte Oper – ℰ (069) 36 50 47 77
– maintower.restaurant @ compass-group.de – Fax (069) 36 50 48 71
– www.maintower-restaurant.de
closed Sunday - Monday   **E1**
Rest (dinner only) (booking advisable) 55 €/98 € and a la carte 60/71 €
♦ Contemporary ♦ Trendy ♦
Dine in a simple, modern atmosphere, 200 metres over the city. The
glass-enclosed semi-circular restaurant offers the best views.

X **Cyrano** 🛱 🍴 *VISA* 🐼
Leibnizstr. 13 ⊠ 60385 – Ⓜ Höhenstr. – ℰ (069) 43 05 59 64 – info @
cyrano-restaurant.de – Fax (069) 43 05 59 65 – www.cyrano-restaurant.de
closed 24 December - 5 January   Plan I **D1**
Rest (dinner only) a la carte 41/52 €
♦ Contemporary ♦ Minimalist ♦
Stone floors, dark wood benches and chairs, and small but nicely laid tables
contribute to a simple modern ambience. Friendly and well-trained staff take
good care of you.

X **Klaane Sachsehäuser** 🛱
Neuer Wall 11 ⊠ 60594 – ℰ (069) 61 59 83 – klaanesachse @ web.de
– Fax (069) 62 21 41 – www.klaane-sachsehaeuser.de
closed 22 December - 8 January and Sunday   **F2**
Rest (open from 4pm) a la carte 12/20 €
♦ Regional ♦ Rustic ♦
The home-brewed "Stöffche" and good Frankfurt food have been served in this
traditional pub since 1876. And no one ever has to sit alone!

X **Zum gemalten Haus** 🛱 *VISA* 🐼
Schweizer Str. 67 ⊠ 60594 – Ⓜ Schweizer Platz – ℰ (069) 61 45 59
– Fax (069) 6 03 14 57 – www.zumgemaltenhaus.de
closed mid July - mid August, 25 December - 3 January and Monday   **F2**
Rest a la carte 11/20 €
♦ Regional ♦ Rustic ♦
Huddle up, talk shop and chat in the midst of these wall murals and mementoes
from bygone days. The main thing is the "Bembel" is always full!

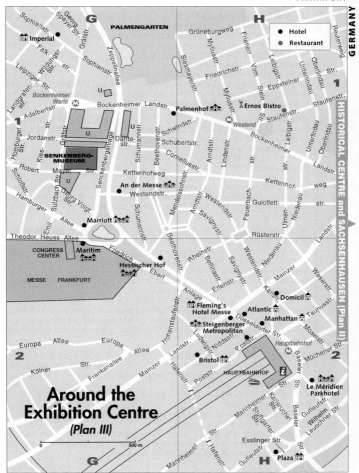

Around the Exhibition Centre
(Plan III)

0 _____ 500 m

WESTEND, EXHIBITION-CENTRE AND STATION   *Plan III*

🏨🏨🏨   **Hessischer Hof**   AK ✦rm ⅍rest 🖥 ☏ 🔧120 🚗 P VISA ⨂ AE ①
Friedrich-Ebert-Anlage 40 ⊠ 60325 – ℰ (069) 7 54 00
– info@hessischer-hof.de – Fax (069) 75 40 29 24
– www.hessischer-hof.de   **G2**
117 rm – †218/363 € ††268/313 €, � 20 € – 3 suites
Rest a la carte 43/53 €
  ◆ Luxury ◆ Traditional ◆ Classic ◆
Exclusive antiques that once belonged to the Prince of Hesse help to make a visit
here something memorable. The rooms are of contemporary comfort and
elegance, and appeal to the most discerning guest. Sèvres porcelain and trompe
l'oeil paintings set the scene in the restaurant.

GERMANY

Le Méridien Parkhotel 🕾 🖾 🕅 ↔rm 🔤 🛦180 🖾

Wiesenhüttenplatz 28 🖂 *60329 –* **Ⓜ** *Haupt-*   **P** **VISA** **◍◍** **AE** **①**
bahnhof – 𝒞 (069) 2 69 70 – info.frankfurt@lemeridien.com
– Fax (069) 2 69 78 84 – www.frankfurt.lemeridien.com   **H2**
297 rm – †360/420 € ††380/420 €, ⌷ 21 €
Rest 35 € and a la carte 22/43 €
♦ Chain hotel ♦ Luxury ♦ Design ♦
An historical town house with sandstone façade and a modern extension.
Well-appointed rooms and technically well-equipped rooms available. Art
nouveau style. Bistro style restaurant.

Marriott ≤ Frankfurt, 🖾 🕅 🕅 ↔rm 🔤 🛦600

Hamburger Allee 2 🖂 *60486 – 𝒞 (069) 7 95 50*   🖾 **VISA** **◍◍** **AE** **①**
– info.frankfurt@marriotthotels.com – Fax (069) 79 55 24 32
– www.marriott.com/fradt   **G1**
588 rm – †129 € ††129 €, ⌷ 22 € – 10 suites
Rest a la carte 28/39 €
♦ Chain hotel ♦ Luxury ♦ Modern ♦
Situated opposite the trade fair site, this skyscraper reaches up towards the sky.
Boasting high-speed internet access in all rooms, it also has the city's biggest ball
room (700m²). The Arizona restaurant serves specialities from the American
Southwest.

Maritim 🖾 🕅 🔲 ଐ 🕅 ↔rm 🍽rest 🔤 🛦210 🖾 **VISA** **◍◍** **AE** **①**

Theodor-Heuss-Allee 3 🖂 *60486 – 𝒞 (069) 7 57 80 – info.fra@maritim.de*
– Fax (069) 75 78 10 00 – www.maritim.de   **G2**
543 rm – †240/312 € ††285/359 €, ⌷ 23 € – 8 suites
Rest *Classico* a la carte 32/42 €
Rest *SushiSho* (closed 25 July - 21 August and Saturday - Sunday, except during
exhibitions) 30 €/90 € and a la carte 19/50 €
♦ Chain hotel ♦ Business ♦ Modern ♦
As a direct neighbour of the festival hall and trade fair tower, the upper floors
afford fantastic views of the city. With extra-long beds for tall people. The elegant
"Classico" offers international cuisine. "SushiSho" will seduce you in Japanese
style.

Steigenberger Metropolitan 🖾 🕅 ଐ 🕅 ↔rm 🍽rest 🔤 🕾

Poststr. 6 🖂 *60329 –* **Ⓜ** *Hauptbahnhof*   🛦220 🖾 **VISA** **◍◍** **AE** **①**
– 𝒞 (069) 5 06 07 00 – metropolitan@steigenberger.de – Fax (069) 5 06 07 05 55
– www.metropolitan.steigenberger.de   **H2**
131 rm – †220/445 € ††245/445 €, ⌷ 19 €
Rest a la carte 20/32 €
Rest *Fine Dining* (closed Saturday lunch, Sunday lunch) a la carte 34/51 €
♦ Chain hotel ♦ Modern ♦
This 19th century city manor house with a sumptuous façade is home to a
luxurious hotel providing modern, well furnished elegant rooms. A modern
hotel and restaurant. A classic fine dining restaurant.

An der Messe without rest 🚄 🕅 🔤 🖾 **VISA** **◍◍** **AE** **①**

Westendstr. 104 🖂 *60325 – 𝒞 (069) 74 79 79 – hotel.an.der.messe@web.de*
– Fax (069) 74 83 49 – www.hotel-an-der-messe.de   **G1**
45 rm ⌷ – †125/290 € ††150/320 €
♦ Business ♦ Personalised ♦
Choose your own residence! Rooms individually designed – from rustic to
elegant, some with Asian or African highlights.

Palmenhof without rest 🔤 🕾 **P** **VISA** **◍◍** **AE** **①**

Bockenheimer Landstr. 89 🖂 *60325 –* **Ⓜ** *Westend – 𝒞 (069) 7 53 00 60*
– info@palmenhof.com – Fax (069) 75 30 06 66 – www.palmenhof.com
closed 23 December - 2 January   **G1**
46 rm – †110/140 € ††150/170 €, ⌷ 15 €
♦ Business ♦ Classic ♦
Stay the night in an individually furnished room, comprised of period furniture, some exquisite bureaux with inlaid work, brass beds and stylish fitted
furniture.

Imperial
*Sophienstr. 40 ⊠ 60487 – **M** Leipziger Str. – ℰ (069) 7 93 00 30 – info @*
imperial.bestwestern.de – Fax (069) 79 30 03 88 – www.imperial.bestwestern.de
closed 22 December - 2 January   **G1**
68 rm ⊑ – ♦125 € ♦♦155 €
Rest (dinner only) a la carte 16/28 €
♦ Business ♦ Functional ♦
Mahogany furnishings and bold coloured décor in this comfortable, homely
hotel. Peaceful rooms available towards the back. Restaurant with an
international menu.

Fleming's Hotel Messe
*Mainzer Landstr. 87 ⊠ 60329 – **M** Hauptbahnhof – ℰ (069) 8 08 08 00*
– frankfurt @ flemings-hotels.com – Fax (069) 8 08 08 04 99
– www.flemings-hotel.com   **H2**
96 rm – ♦144/285 € ♦♦175/315 €, ⊑ 14 €
Rest a la carte 15/32 €
♦ Business ♦ Modern ♦
A business hotel in the centre of town with modern, functional rooms with all
technical facilities. Bistro style restaurant with international cuisine.

Dorint Novotel Frankfurt City
Lise-Meitner-Str. 2 ⊠ 60486 – ℰ (069) 79 30 30
– h1049 @ accor.com – Fax (069) 79 30 39 30 – www.novotel.com
235 rm – ♦130/180 € ♦♦145/195 €, ⊑ 15 €   *Plan I* **A2**
Rest a la carte 20/28 €
♦ Chain hotel ♦ Functional ♦
Behind a modern façade, this hotel in an industrial area near the conference
centre provides functional rooms.

Bristol without rest
*Ludwigstr. 15 ⊠ 60327 – **M** Hauptbahnhof – ℰ (069) 24 23 90*
– info @ bristol-hotel.de – Fax (069) 25 15 39 – www.bristol-hotel.de   **H2**
145 rm ⊑ – ♦70/105 € ♦♦80/130 €
♦ Business ♦ Modern ♦
Close to the main railway station in the centre of town, this modern hotel
provides contemporary, well-equipped rooms. Summer lounge area.

Plaza without rest
Esslinger Str. 8 ⊠ 60329 – ℰ (069) 2 71 37 80
– info @ plaza-frankfurt.bestwestern.de – Fax (069) 23 76 50
– www.plaza-frankfurt.bestwestern.de   **H2**
45 rm – ♦89/99 € ♦♦115/128 €, ⊑ 11 €
♦ Business ♦ Modern ♦
A former admin. building, now with a homely atmosphere and modern
furnishings in light-wood, as well as a warm décor.

Express by Holiday Inn without rest
Gutleutstr. 296 ⊠ 60327 – ℰ (069) 50 69 60
– express.frankfurtmesse @ ichotelsgroup.com – Fax (069) 50 69 61 00
– www.hiexpress.com   *Plan I* **A3**
175 rm ⊑ – ♦99 € ♦♦99 €
♦ Chain hotel ♦ Functional ♦
Ideal for business travellers, this modern well-equipped hotel is conveniently
located near the exhibition centre and the local station.

Atlantic without rest
*Düsseldorfer Str. 20 ⊠ 60329 – **M** Hauptbahnhof – ℰ (069) 27 21 20 – info @*
atlantic.pacat.com – Fax (069) 27 21 21 00 – www.hotel-atlantic-frankfurt.de
closed 23 December - 1 January   **H2**
60 rm ⊑ – ♦55/99 € ♦♦70/110 €
♦ Business ♦ Functional ♦
The blue-white façade of this city hotel is a welcoming sight on the way from the
main station to the trade fair site. Guests are accommodated in light,
contemporary rooms with solid furnishings.

GERMANY

Domicil without rest ✓ ⌨ 📠 VISA 🅒 🅐 🅞

Karlstr. 14 ⊠ 60329 – Ⓜ Hauptbahnhof – ℰ (069) 27 11 10
– info@domicil-frankfurt.bestwestern.de – Fax (069) 25 32 66
– www.domicil-frankfurt.bestwestern.de   **H2**
68 rm – 🛏88/98 €, 🛏🛏112/122 €, ⌖ 11 €
   ◆ Business ◆ Functional ◆

Thanks to the underground and fast train, this hotel has ideal links to the airport. The trade fair site and main station are just a few minutes' walk away.

Manhattan without rest ✓ ⌨ 📠 VISA 🅒 🅐 🅞

Düsseldorfer Str. 10 ⊠ 60329 – ℰ (069) 2 69 59 70
– manhattan-hotel@t-online.de – Fax (069) 2 69 59 77 77
– www.manhattan-hotel.com   **H2**
60 rm ⌖ – 🛏80/110 €, 🛏🛏90/130 €
   ◆ Business ◆ Modern ◆

Here, modern design is carried through from the bright lobby, with its parquet floors, to the chic boudoir-style rooms. Churches, banks, art and culture are on your doorstep.

۩۩۩ Villa Merton ⌂ ⌨

Am Leonhardsbrunnen 12 ⊠ 60487 – ℰ (069) 70 30 33
– jp@kofler-company.de – Fax (069) 7 07 38 20
– www.kofler-company.de
closed 19 December - 8 January and Saturday - Sunday,
Bank Holidays   *Plan I* **A1**
Rest (booking advisable) 28 € (lunch)/96 € and a la carte 54/68 €
Spec. St. Pierre in Madras-Curryjus mit Limettenfilets und Koriandersalat. Lamm mit geschmortem Fenchel und Kreuzkümmel-Gnocchi. Sorbet-Impressionen.
   ◆ Contemporary ◆ Formal ◆

In the diplomatic quarter of town, this villa is home to an elegant restaurant offering good service and creative cuisine with a traditional basis.

۩۩ La Trattoria ⌂ VISA 🅒 🅐 🅞

Fürstenberger Str. 179 ⊠ 60322 – Ⓜ Holzhausenstr.
– ℰ (069) 55 21 30 – info@latrattoria-ffm.de – Fax (069) 55 21 30
– www.latrattoria-ffm.de
closed Saturday - Sunday and Bank Holidays,
except during exhibitions   *Plan I* **B1**
Rest (booking advisable) 63 €/67 € and a la carte 49/57 €
   ◆ Italian ◆ Family ◆

Beautifully prepared tables, dedicated staff and Italian cuisine await you in this restaurant with the rustic Mediterranean touch, which is in a corner house from the Turn of the century.

۩ Ernos Bistro ⌂ VISA 🅒 🅐

Liebigstr. 15 ⊠ 60323 – Ⓜ Westend – ℰ (069) 72 19 97
– Fax (069) 17 38 38
closed Christmas - early January, mid July - mid August and Saturday - Sunday,
Bank Holidays   **H1**
Rest (booking advisable) 31 € (lunch)/90 € and a la carte 55/74 €
Spec. Tartar vom Rinderfilet mit Osietra Kaviar und Wodka-Vinaigrette. Zanderfilet mit Speck auf elsässischem Sauerkraut und Blutwurstsauce. Rosette vom Lammrücken und Curry-Süßkartoffeln mit Schwarzwurzeln.
   ◆ French ◆ Bistro ◆

In the Westend, this charming bistro style restaurant serves French cuisine with charming, friendly service.

ENVIRONS OF FRANKFURT

at Franfurt-Fechenheim by Hanauer Landstr. D 2

XX **Silk** ♿ ❄ VISA ⓜⓞ AE
Carl-Benz-Str. 21 ✉ 60386 – ℰ (069) 90 02 00 – reservierung@cocoonclub.net
– Fax (069) 90 02 05 90 – www.cocoonclub.net
closed August and Sunday - Monday
Rest (dinner only) 76 €
Rest Micro (dinner only) a la carte 26/48 €
♦ Innovative ♦ Trendy ♦
A modern, elegant restaurant with mostly white décor. Serves creative cuisine.
Restaurant serving micro-fusion cuisine in an electronic atmosphere!

at Frankfurt-Rödelheim by Theodor Heuss Allee A 2

XX **Osteria Enoteca** ☕ ❄
✿ Arnoldshainer Str. 2 (corner of Lorscher Straße) ✉ 60489 – ℰ (069) 7 89 22 16
– Fax (069) 7 89 22 16
closed 22 December - 6 January and Saturday lunch, Sunday, Bank Holidays
Rest 48 €/108 € and a la carte 47/56 €
Spec. Auberginentörtchen mit Tomatenvelouté. Rotbarbe mit Zwiebel-
Kartoffel-Pizza und Kohlrabimousse. Schweinebauch mit Cannelloni von
Salsiccia und Gänseleber.
♦ Italian ♦ Friendly ♦
Restaurant serving creative Italian cuisine. Light décor and modern artwork on
display, providing a colourful touch.

at the Rhein-Main Airport by Kennedy Allee B 3

🏨 **Sheraton Frankfurt Hotel & Towers** 🛗 🛁 ♿ AC ♿rm ❄rest
Hugo-Eckener-Ring 15, (terminal 1) ⌨ ⚒700 VISA ⓜⓞ AE ⓞ
✉ 60549 Frankfurt – ℰ (069) 6 97 70 – reservationsfrankfurt@sheraton.com
– Fax (069) 69 77 22 09 – www.sheraton.com/frankfurt
1008 rm ⌂ – ♦310/575 € ♦♦345/610 € – 28 suites
Rest Flavors , ℰ (069) 69 77 12 46 – a la carte 34/53 €
Rest Taverne , ℰ (069) 69 77 12 59 (closed Saturday - Sunday) a la carte 33/50 €
♦ Chain hotel ♦ Business ♦ Modern ♦
From breakfast to boarding or from the plane straight to bed – this elegant hotel
with the impressive hall opposite Terminal 1 makes it possible! Modern ambience
and good choice of international cuisine in the Flavors. Rural charm in the Taverne.

🏨 **Kempinski Hotel Gravenbruch** ☕ 🛁 ⚊ (heated) ⬜ ❄ 🚗 🐾
AC ♿rm ❄rest ⌨ ☎ ⚒180 🌳 P VISA ⓜⓞ AE ⓞ
Graf zu Ysenburg und Büdingen-Platz 1 ✉ 63263 Neu-Isenburg-Gravenbruch
– ℰ (069) 38 98 80 – reservations.gravenbruch@kempinski.com
– Fax (069) 38 98 89 00 – www.kempinski-frankfurt.com
283 rm – ♦132/165 € ♦♦132/165 €, ⌂ 24 € – 15 suites
Rest a la carte 34/44 €
Rest L'Olivo (closed Saturday - Sunday) (dinner only) a la carte 22/36 €
♦ Chain hotel ♦ Classic ♦
A former estate in the midst of an attractive, small park, rooms in classic style and
luxurious suites. Leisure area with beauty farm, hairdresser and cosmetics studio.
A fine restaurant with garden views. L'Olivo is in the Italian style.

🏨 **Steigenberger Airport** 🛗 🛁 ⬜ AC ♿rm ❄rest 🚗 ⚒270 🌳
P VISA ⓜⓞ AE 🚗
Unterschweinstiege 16 ✉ 60549 Frankfurt
– ℰ (069) 6 97 50 – info@airporthotel.steigenberger.de – Fax (069) 69 75 25 05
– www.airporthotel.steigenberger.de
573 rm – ♦139/219 € ♦♦159/239 €, ⌂ 21 € – 10 suites
Rest Waldrestaurant Unterschweinstiege a la carte 30/51 €
Rest Faces (closed Sunday - Monday) (dinner only) 42 € and a la carte 47/65 €
♦ Chain hotel ♦ Modern ♦
A spacious, elegant reception with light marble décor, and luxurious well-
equipped rooms, some with designer bathrooms. Rustic and cosy atmosphere in
the historic "Schweinstiege" restaurant. "Faces" has a fine bistro atmosphere.

InterCityHotel Frankfurt Airport 余 & ⅍rm 🖭 🕾 ⚩150
Cargo City Süd ✉ *60549 Frankfurt* – 🕾 *(069)* **P** 𝖵𝖨𝖲𝖠 ⓐ 🆎 ⓞ
69 70 99 – frankfurt-airport@intercityhotel.de – Fax (069) 69 70 94 44
– www.frankfurt-airport.intercityhotel.de
360 rm – 🛉145/235 € 🛉🛉165/255 €, ⌓ 16 €
Rest a la carte 24/33 €
♦ **Chain hotel** ♦ **Functional** ♦
Rooms come in two varieties as regards space, standard and comfort, but all have
coloured and functional furnishings. Modern restaurant with international
cuisine and buffet.

HAMBURG
HAMBURG

Population (est. 2005): 1 750 000 (conurbation 2 290 000) – Altitude: at sea level

Comnet/COLORISE

Hamburg, the second largest city in Germany after Berlin, is one of the most important ports in Europe. Its old title of 'Free and Hanseatic Town' and its status as a 'City State' (Stadtstaat) testify to its eminence and influence over the centuries.

Each year, in May, there is an anniversary celebration in the port of Hamburg (Hafengeburtstag), commemorating the concession granted by Frederick Barbarossa in 1189 of the right to free navigation on the lower Elbe. The exercise of this right, menaced by piracy and the feudal pretensions of neighbouring states, especially Denmark, demanded a continual watch by the city fathers until the 17C.

As a port Hamburg enjoys a large recreational lake, the Alster, at its centre and the Speicherstadt district contains one of the largest former warehouse complexes.

Hamburg is the birthplace of Johannes Brahms, where he composed many of his works, and has a strong musical tradition.

WHICH DISTRICT TO CHOOSE

The highest concentration of **hotels** and **restaurants** is to be found around the Binnenalster *Plan I* **C2** and the Aussenalster *Plan I* **C2**. Hamburg is well-known for its good fish restaurants located in the harbour district *Plan I* **B3**; here you will find eel in all its forms as well as the famous *Labskaus*, a local dish of herring, beet-root, salt meat and pickled gherkins. The numerous scenic restaurants recently opened by the harbour offer a great view of the passing shipping. The Altona *Plan I* **B3** and Eppendorf *Plan I* **C1** districts are also known for very good restaurants but some of the best restaurants are out of town along the Elbe.

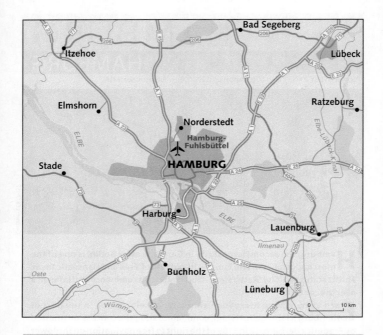

PRACTICAL INFORMATION

ARRIVAL – DEPARTURE

Hamburg Airport about 15 km (10 mi) from the city centre. ✆ (040) 5 07 50; info@ham.airport.de; www. ham.airport.de

From the airport to the city centre – By **taxi**: €17 (20min). By **public transport**: Airport buses leave for Hamburg Hauptbahnhof every 15-20min and Altona Station every 30min (journey time for both: 30min).

Railway Stations – Hauptbahnhof Nord and Hauptbahnhof Süd for international and national services. ✆ 0190 50 70 90 (€1.49 per min) (24hr); www. bahnhof-hamburg.de

River Boat and Ferry Stations – Tours of Hamburg Harbour depart from the Landungsbrücken 1-9 in St Pauli (every hour Apr-Oct

Mon-Fri 10am-5pm, Sat 11am-5pm (less often in winter). Tours of the Alster, Fleet and canal depart from Jungfernstieg.

TRANSPORT

♦ METRO AND BUSES

All buses and underground trains are controlled by the **HVV** (Hamburger Verkehrsverbund); the lines reach into the surrounding region of Schleswig-Holstein. Tickets are available from vending machines and from bus drivers. Single ticket for rides into the town centre from €1.40; 1-day ticket €5.50; 3-day ticket €13.30; group day ticket for up to 5 people €7.75 (the 2 latter tickets are valid from 9am until the last ride). Information available at many V- and S-Bahn stations and at the HVV office at the Railway Station (Hauptbahnhof), Mon-Fri 6am-10pm,

Sat-Sun 7am-10pm; ☏ 1 94 49 (24hrs) – www.hvv.de

The **Hamburg Card** is valid for the **HVV** network, free entrance to 11 state-run museums, discounts on other activities and on tours on water and on land. The card is available at the Tourist Information Offices, at vending machines, in many hotels and travel agents and in the HVV Customer Offices. Single person €6.54; group card for up to 5 people €12.56 (both are valid on the date of issue and from 6pm onward on the previous day); 3 day card €13.55 or €21.99.

◆ TAXIS

Taxis are cream-coloured. They can be hailed in the street, hired at taxi ranks and called by telephone. Initial charge €2.10 (€1.60 per km for first 11km, €1.28 per km thereafter). *Taxi Hamburg* ☏ 040 66 66 66.

USEFUL ADDRESSES

◆ TOURIST INFORMATION

Hamburg Tourismus GmbH, Steinstrasse 7 *Plan II* **G3**; daily 8am-8pm; ☏ 40 30 05 13 00. **Main Railway Station** (Hauptbahnhof) *Plan II* **H2**; daily 7am-11pm. **Harbour**, St Pauli Landungsbrücken (between piers 4 and 5) daily 10am-7pm (5.30pm Oct-Mar) – info@hamburg-tourismus.de; www.hamburg-tourismus.de

◆ **POST OFFICES**
Mon-Fri 8am-6pm, Sat 8am-12 noon.
Railway Station, Hachmannplatz: Mon-Fri 8am-8pm, Sat 9am-6pm.

◆ BANKS

Mon-Fri 8.30am-12.30pm and 2-4pm (sometimes later); closed Sat-Sun and public holidays.

◆ EMERGENCY

Dial ☏ **110**; Fire Brigade ☏ **112**.

BUSY PERIODS

It may be difficult to find a room at a reasonable price when special events are held in the city as hotel prices may be raised substantially:

Volksfest Dom: mid March to mid April, mid July to mid August, early Nov to Dec – Folk festival near the cathedral with the biggest funfair in north Germany.

Hafengeburtstag: early May – Harbour anniversary.

Hamburger Ballettage: July – Ballet days.

Alstervergnügen: end of August – Alster Fair offering art, culture and fun around the Inner Alster.

Hamburg Christmas Market: late November to 23 December – Traditional Christmas market in the city centre and Town Hall Square.

EXPLORING HAMBURG

It is possible to visit the main sights and museums in two days.

Museums and sights are usually open between 9am/10am and 5pm/6pm (some later on Thursday). Most are closed on Mondays and public holidays.

VISITING

Views of Hamburg – Take a boat trip around the Harbour *(Hafenrundfahrt)* from the quayside in St Pauli. Take a boat trip on the **Aussenalster** *Plan I* **C2**. Make a circuit by road of the **Alster** *Plan II* **E3**.

Hauptkirche St Michaelis *Plan II* **E3** – A fine brick-built church (1762) in the Baroque tradition with a tower, known locally as *Michel* which is the emblem of the city; view from the platform of the town centre and the river.

Hamburger Kunsthalle *Plan II* **H2** – Fine Art Museum housing one of the largest art collections in Germany.

Altonaer Museum in Hamburg – Norddeutsches Landesmuseum *Plan III* **I1** – Art, culture and daily life in Schleswig-Holstein including an exceptional collection of **ships' figureheads** from 18C-19C.

SHOPPING

Shops are usually open between 9am/10am and 6.30pm/8pm. They are closed on Sunday.

The wealth of pedestrianised areas and old-established stores makes Hamburg a shoppers' paradise. **Jungfernstieg**, **Mönckebergstrasse** *Plan II* **G2** and **Spitalerstrasse** are the big shopping streets with department stores. The many shopping arcades in the inner city are especially attractive, with over 300 speciality stores and boutiques. **Exclusive stores** can be found in **Neuer Wall** *Plan II* **F3**. The shopping streets between **Neuer Wall** and **Colonnaden** *Plan II* **F2** are lined with luxurious arcades.

For **antiques** try the **Quartier Satin** in ABC-Strasse *Plan II* **F2** and the **Antik-Center** of the market hall in Klosterwall *Plan II* **H3**.

MARKETS – Hamburg's most famous market is the **fish market** (Sun 5am (7am winter) to 10am). **Weekly markets** are held in all districts of the city. Particularly recommended is the especially beautiful market held on the covered central strip of the elevated train at the U-bahn station Eppendorfer Baum (Mon-Fri). Regular **flea markets** are held on Saturdays in Barmbek (Hellbrockstrasse – 7am-

5pm) and in Eppendorf (Nedderfeld/Parkhaus – 4.30-7.30pm). For information about more spontaneous flea markets in Hamburg consult the *Menschen & Märkte* brochure.

WHAT TO BUY – *Harry's Hamburger Hafenbasar*, Balduinstrasse 18 St Pauli, for worldly souvenirs.

ENTERTAINMENT

Prinz, published every 2 weeks, *Szene Hamburg*, published every 4 weeks, and the *Hamburger Vorschau* (available at the Tourist Information Offices) provide information on events of all sorts. Tickets for select events are on sale at the Tourist Information Office.

Hamburgische Staatsoper *Plan II* **F2** – Opera and ballet – www.hamburg ische-staatsoper.de; www.hamburgb allett.de

Allee-Theater *Plan III* **J1** – Hamburg chamber opera and children's theatre – www.theater-fuer-kinder.de

Neue Flora *Plan III* **I1** – Musicals.

Operettenhaus *Plan II* **F2** – Musicals.

Musikhalle *Plan II* **E2** – Baroque concert hall at the centre of the musical life of Hamburg, where all three Hamburg orchestras play.

NIGHTLIFE

The famous nightclub district is **Sankt Pauli** *Plan III* **J1** with cabarets, bars and various exotic places. In the side streets flanking the **Reeperbahn** and the **Grosse Freiheit**, bars, discotheques, exotic restaurants, clubs and the Eros Centre function day and night in the gaudy illumination of multicoloured neon signs.

CENTRE

Raffles Hotel Vier Jahreszeiten
⫨ Binnenalster, *Fá* ⑥ AC

Neuer Jungfernstieg 9 ⁴⁄rm ⑯ 🖾 🕾 *Fá* 110 ⇔ **VISA** **MO** AE ⑨
✉ 20354 – **M** *Jungfernstieg* – ℰ (040) 3 49 40 – emailus.hvj@raffles.de
– Fax (040) 34 94 26 00 – www.raffles-hvj.de **F2**
156 rm – ✦220/295 € ✦✦270/345 €, ⚏ 24 € – 11 suites
Rest see *Haerlin* below
Rest *Doc Cheng's*, ℰ (040) 3 49 43 33 (closed Saturday lunch, Sunday lunch,
Monday) a la carte 34/46 €
Rest *Jahreszeiten Grill*, ℰ (040) 34 94 33 12 – a la carte 33/64 €
♦ Grand Luxury ♦ Traditional ♦ Classic ♦
Luxurious rooms with a classic modern level of comfort await you in the last
"genuine" Grand Hotel on the Binnenalster. Exclusive AmritaSpa. Doc Cheng's
successfully combines Western and Far Eastern fare. In the Grill: classic
elegance.

Atlantic Kempinski
⫨ Außenalster, 🏠 ⑥ ▢ ⁴⁄rm ⑯rest 🖾 🕾

An der Alster 72 ✉ 20099 *Fá* 220 ⇔ **VISA** **MO** AE ⑨
– ℰ (040) 2 88 80 – hotel.atlantic@kempinski.com – Fax (040) 24 71 29
– www.kempinski.atlantic.de **H1**
252 rm – ✦230/430 € ✦✦270/470 €, ⚏ 23 € – 11 suites
Rest (closed Sunday lunch) a la carte 47/71 €
♦ Grand Luxury ♦ Traditional ♦ Classic ♦
The "Weisse Riese" has been a renowned meeting point for society since 1909.
The rooms have high stucco ceilings and period furniture; some rooms with a
view of the Alster. This restaurant boasts a tastefully elegant atmosphere and an
indoor terrace.

Park Hyatt
🏠 ⑨ *Fá* ⑥ ▢ 🕭 AC ⁴⁄rm ⑯ 🖾 *Fá* 120 ⇔ **VISA** **MO** AE

Bugenhagenstr. 8 ✉ 20095 – **M** *Mönckebergstr.* – ℰ (040) 33 32 12 34
– hamburg@hyatt.de – Fax (040) 33 32 12 35
– www.hamburg.park.hyatt.com **H2**
252 rm – ✦160/290 € ✦✦185/325 €, ⚏ 23 € – 5 suites
Rest *Apples*, ℰ (040) 33 32 15 11 (closed Saturday lunch, Sunday lunch)
a la carte 31/51 €
♦ Chain hotel ♦ Grand Luxury ♦ Stylish ♦
This historic brick-built, former office building opens up a world of simple
elegance with high quality fabrics, Canadian cherry and bathrooms by Philipp
Starcke. Stylish contemporary decoration gives "Apples" its unmistakable charm.

Le Royal Méridien
Fá ⑥ ▢ 🕭 AC ⁴⁄rm ⑯rest 🖾 *Fá* 200

An der Alster 52 ✉ 20099 – ℰ (040) 2 10 00 ⇔ **VISA** **MO** AE ⑨
– info.lrmhamburg@lemeridien.com – Fax (040) 21 00 11 11
– www.hamburg.lemeridien.com **H1**
284 rm – ✦149/279 € ✦✦169/299 €, ⚏ 20 € – 7 suites
Rest 53 € (dinner) and a la carte 32/46 €
♦ Chain hotel ♦ Luxury ♦ Modern ♦
A touch of exclusivity will follow you from the spacious hall through to the "Art
+ Tech Design" rooms equipped with the most modern facilities. The restaurant
Le Ciel, on the 9th floor, offers a fantastic view over the Aussenalster.

Dorint Sofitel
🏠 ⑨ *Fá* ⑥ ▢ 🕭 AC ⁴⁄rm ⑯rest *Fá* 250

Alter Wall 40 ✉ 20457 – **M** *Rödingsmarkt* ⇔ **VISA** **MO** AE ⑨
– ℰ (040) 36 95 00 – info.hamalt@dorint.com – Fax (040) 36 95 10 00
– www.sofitel.com **F3**
241 rm – ✦190/280 € ✦✦190/280 €, ⚏ 20 € – 10 suites
Rest a la carte 33/45 €
♦ Chain hotel ♦ Luxury ♦ Design ♦
This modern designer hotel is in the former post office on an Alster canal. The
interior is marble and exposed concrete, elegant wood and modern art. The
"opulent minimalism" of the restaurant is pleasing to the eye.

Environs of Hamburg
(Plan I)

A 26 STELLINGEN

B

Kieler
Koppel- str.
Hagenbecks Tierpark

Julius Vosseler

Str.

Lutterothstr.

Hotelluftchaussee

Gartnerstr.

1

Schnackenburgallee

VOLKSPARK

27

A7-E45

Schnackenburgallee

Müggenkampstr.

Osterstr. Osterstr.

Osterstr.

Im Gehölz

Bundesstr.

EIMSBÜTTEL

BAHRENFELD

Holstenkamp

Emilienstr. Frucht-

Doormanns-

weg

Christskirche allee

Schlump

2

Bahrenfelder
Chaussee

Das Kleine Rote

Kieler

Str.

Alsen-
str.

Sternschanze

Altonaer Str.

FERNS

28

Pfitznerstr.

Stresemannstr.

Daimler str.

Holstenstr.

Allee

Stresemannstr.

Schanzen-
str.

Feldstr.

Friedensallee

Barner

Str.

Julius
Leber Str. Brauer

Holstenstr.

Budapester Str.

29

Behringstr.

Behringstr.

Hohenzollernring

Max

ALTONA

ST-
PAULI

East

Simon von

OTHMARSCHEN

NORDDEUTSCHES
LANDESMUSEUM

Ehrenberg-
str.

Louise
Schroeder
Str.

Königstr.

Utrecht Str.

Reeperbahn

3

Elbchaussee

Königstr.

Palmaille

Breite Str.

St Pauli
Fischmarkt

Elbchaussee

Harbour and
Altona (Plan III)

ELBE

A7-E45

Süderelbe

0   1 km

A

B

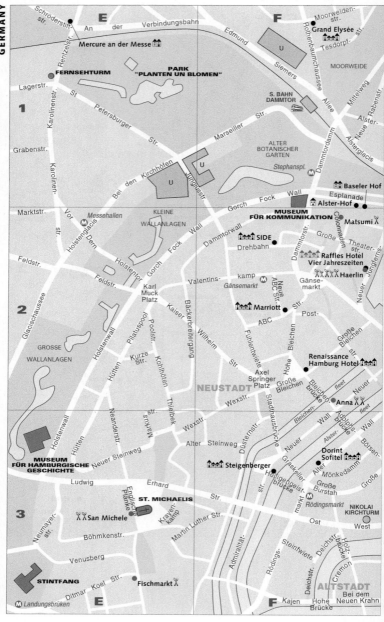

Schröderstift str.
An der Verbindungsbahn
Rentzelstr.
Edmund
Moorweiden- str.
Rothenbaumchaussee
Grand Elysée
Tesdorpf-
MOORWEIDE
Mercure an der Messe
Lagerstr.
FERNSEHTURM
PARK "PLANTEN UN BLOMEN"
Karolinenstr.
St
Petersburger Str.
Siemers Allee
S. BAHN DAMMTOR
Alsterglacis
Neue Rabenstr.
Mittelweg
Alster-
Dammtordamm
1
Grabenstr.
Karolinen-
Bei den Kirchhöfen
Jungiusstr.
Marseiller Str.
ALTER BOTANISCHER GARTEN
Stephanspl.
Alsterglacis
Baseler Hof
Esplanade
Marktstr.
Vor str.
Messehallen
Holstenglacis
Dem
KLEINE WALLANLAGEN
Gorch Fock Wall
MUSEUM FÜR KOMMUNIKATION
Alster-Hof
Colonnaden
Matsumi
Feldstr.
Holstenfor
Feldstr.
Holstenwall
Dammtorwall
Drehbahn
SIDE
Große Theater- str.
Colonnaden
Dammtorstr.
Raffles Hotel Vier Jahreszeiten
Haerlin
2
Glacischaussee
GROSSE
WALLANLAGEN
Karl Muck Platz
Pilatuspool
Poolstr.
Backerbreitergang
Kaiser
Wilhelm
Valentins- kamp
Gänsemarkt
Neue ABC Str.
Gänse- markt
ABC
Neuer Jungfernst.
Post-
Marriott
Holstenwall
Hütten
Kurze Str.
Kohlhöfen
Thielbek
Str.
Fuhlentwiete
Hohe Bleichen
Große Bleichen
Große Bleichen str.
Renaissance Hamburg Hotel
NEUSTADT
Axel Springer Platz
Bleichen- brücke
fleet
Neuer Wall
Anna
Markus- str.
Neanderstr.
Wexstr.
Stadthausbrücke
Bleichen-
Adolphs- brücke
Alster-
fleet
3
MUSEUM FÜR HAMBURGISCHE GESCHICHTE
Holstenwall
Hütten
Neuer Steinweg
Alter Steinweg
Wexstr.
Düsternstr.
Neuer Wall
Adolphs-
Boisen-
Dorint Sofitel
Ludwig
Erhard
Str.
Steigenberger
Heiligengeist- brücke
Graskeller
Alter
Große Burstah
Mönkedamm
Große
ST. MICHAELIS
Englisch Planke
Kraven- kamp
Martin Luther Str.
Heiligengeist- brücke
Rödingsmarkt
NIKOLAI KIRCHTURM
West
San Michele
Neumayer- str.
Böhmkenstr.
markt
Ost
Steinwiete
Deichstr.
Holz- brücke
STINTFANG
Venusberg
Ditmar Koel Str.
Fischmarkt
Admiralität-
Rödings-
Steinwiete
Deichstr.
Deichtor
Cremon
ALTSTADT
Bei dem Neuen Krahn
Landungsbrücken
E
Kajen
Hohe Brücke
F

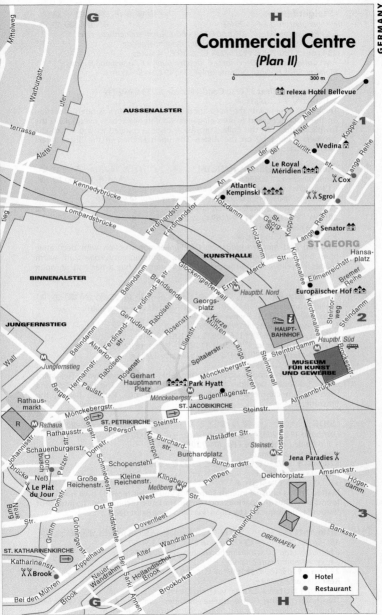

Commercial Centre
(Plan II)

0   300 m

relexa Hotel Bellevue

AUSSENALSTER

Wedina

Le Royal Méridien

Cox

Atlantic Kempinski

Sgroi

Senator

ST-GEORG

Hansaplatz

KUNSTHALLE

Bremer Reihe

Europäischer Hof

BINNENALSTER

Hauptbf. Nord

Georgsplatz

HAUPT-BAHNHOF

JUNGFERNSTIEG

Jungfernstieg

Hauptbf. Süd

MUSEUM FÜR KUNST UND GEWERBE

Gerhart Hauptmann Platz

Park Hyatt

Rathausmarkt

Rathaus

ST. PETRIKIRCHE

ST. JACOBIKIRCHE

Jena Paradies

Le Plat du Jour

ST. KATHARINENKIRCHE

Brook

OBERHAFEN

● Hotel
● Restaurant

GERMANY

Steigenberger 🍴 & 🅰 ⫷rm ⅋rest 📺 ☎ ⚓180

Heiligengeistbrücke 4 ⊠ 20459
– ⓜ Rödingsmarkt – ℰ (040) 36 80 60 – hamburg@steigenberger.de ⚓ **VISA** 🆗 🆎 ⓪
– Fax (040) 36 80 67 77 – www.hamburg.steigenberger.de **F3**
234 rm – †180/225 € ††206/251 €, ⊊ 19 € – 4 suites
Rest *Calla* *(closed 23 December - 6 January, 6 July - 8 August and Sunday -*
Monday, Bank Holidays) (dinner only) 37 €/49 € and a la carte
31/47 €
Rest *Bistro am Fleet* 27 €/30 € and a la carte 22/38 €
♦ Luxury ♦ Classic ♦
This establishment with the Hanseatic red-brick façade is in a wonderful location
on the Alsterfleet, and is pure elegance. Conference rooms overlooking the
town's rooftops. In the Calla: Euro-Asian dishes, enjoyed as you watch the
steamers gliding by on the Alster. The open kitchen in the Bistro offers
international dishes.

Renaissance Hamburg Hotel 🍴 🔼 🐾 🅰 ⫷rm ⅋rest 📺 ☎

Große Bleichen ⊠ 20354 ⚓80 🅿 **VISA** 🆗 🆎 ⓪
– ⓜ Jungfernstieg – ℰ (040) 34 91 80
– rhi.hamrn.info@renaissancehotels.com – Fax (040) 34 91 89 19
– www.renaissancehotels.com/hamrn **F2**
205 rm – †129/159 € ††139/169 €, ⊊ 19 €
Rest a la carte 26/40 €
♦ Luxury ♦ Classic ♦
Tradition and modern elegance: the clinker construction with decorative
blue balcony railings houses spacious, contemporary rooms in warm
shades of yellow, orange and red. This restaurant has a bar and an open
kitchen.

Grand Elysée 🍴 🔼 🐾 🖥 🅰 ⫷rm ☎ ⚓325 ⚓ **VISA** 🆗 🆎 ⓪

Rothenbaumchaussee 10 ⊠ 20148 – ℰ (040) 41 41 20 – info@elysee.de
– Fax (040) 41 41 27 33 – www.elysee.de
(additional 215 rooms by Spring 2006) **F1**
305 rm – †136/186 € ††156/206 €, ⊊ 18 € – 4 suites
Rest *Piazza Romana*, *ℰ (040) 41 41 27 34* – a la carte 32/45 €
Rest *Brasserie*, *ℰ (040) 41 41 27 24* – a la carte 22/31 €
♦ Luxury ♦ Classic ♦
Classic elegance and spacious, comfortable rooms await you. The spirit
of the boulevard pervades the palatial hall with café. The Piazza Romana
serves Italian cuisine in a Mediterranean ambience. Parisian flair in the
Brasserie.

SIDE 🌐 🔼 🐾 🖥 & 🅰 ⫷rm 📺 ☎ ⚓160 ⚓ **VISA** 🆗 🆎 ⓪

Drehbahn 49 ⊠ 20354 – ⓜ Stephansplatz – ℰ (040) 30 99 90
– info@side-hamburg.de – Fax (040) 30 99 93 99
– www.side-hamburg.de **F2**
178 rm – †190/250 € ††215/275 €, ⊊ 22 € – 10 suites
Rest a la carte 30/46 €
♦ Luxury ♦ Design ♦
Matteo Thun's unusual interior surrounds you in this recently built hotel. The
rooms and suites are spacious and contain the latest technology. The interior of
"Fusion" is distinguished by clean lines and minimalist décor.

Marriott 🍴 🔼 🐾 🖥 & 🅰 ⫷rm 📺 ⚓160 ⚓ **VISA** 🆗 🆎 ⓪

ABC-Str. 52 ⊠ 20354 – ⓜ Gänsemarkt – ℰ (040) 3 50 50
– hamburg.marriott@marriotthotels.com – Fax (040) 35 05 17 77
– www.hamburgmarriott.com **F2**
277 rm – †169/189 € ††169/189 €, ⊊ 19 € – 5 suites
Rest a la carte 19/48 €
♦ Chain hotel ♦ Luxury ♦ Modern ♦
This hotel on the Gänse square provides comfortable rooms with fine
furnishings. Hair dresser and beauty studio in house. Modern designs and an
abundance of light wood in Restaurant Speicher 52.

350

GERMANY

 Europäischer Hof 🏵 ♨ 🐾 📺 📠 rest ⇆rm ⅋ 🖭 🛁200 ☕

Kirchenallee 45 ⊠ *20099 –* Ⓜ *Hauptbahnhof Süd* 🖭 VISA 🐵 ⁄Æ ⓪
– ℰ *(040) 24 82 48 – info @ europaeischer-hof.de – Fax (040) 24 82 47 99*
– www.europaeischer-hof.de **H2**
320 rm ⊑ *–* �105/153 € ♦♦135/183 €
Rest (Tuesday - Wednesday dinner only) a la carte 20/30 €
Rest *Paulaner's* a la carte 19/27 €
♦ Business ♦ Classic ♦
Elegant woods and warm colours are key features of our wellbeing rooms. The highlight in the leisure section is the six-level waterslide down to the swimming pool. Paulaner's: rustic and relaxed.

 Dorint Novotel Hamburg Alster ♨ 🕭 📠 ⇆ 🖭 🛁160

Lübecker Str. 3 ⊠ *22087 –* Ⓜ *Lübecker Str.* ☕ VISA 🐵 ⁄Æ ⓪
– ℰ *(040) 39 19 00 – h3737@ accor.com – Fax (040) 39 19 01 90*
– www.novotel.com **D2**
210 rm *–* ♦69/120 € ♦♦69/120 €, ⊑ 16 €
Rest a la carte 28/39 €
♦ Chain hotel ♦ Modern ♦
A modern hotel providing well-equipped rooms in comfortable, modern style. Conferences facilities available. Restaurant accessed from the hotel lobby.

 relexa Hotel Bellevue ⇆rm ⅋rest 🖭 🛁45 ☕

An der Alster 14 ⊠ *20099 –* ℰ *(040) 28 44 40* 🅿 VISA 🐵 ⁄Æ ⓪
– hamburg @ relexa-hotel.de – Fax (040) 28 44 42 22
– www.relexa-hotels.de **H1**
92 rm ⊑ *–* ♦80/110 € ♦♦111/145 €
Rest a la carte 24/31 €
♦ Business ♦ Functional ♦
Classic, white hotel building. Rooms in the guesthouse are very pretty; the single rooms are quite small, but satisfactory, and most have a view of the Alster - in St. Georg. During the day diners can eat overlooking the Alster, and in tasteful lounges in the basement in the evenings.

 Mercure an der Messe 🕭 📠 ⇆rm 🕻 🛁70 ☕ VISA 🐵 ⁄Æ ⓪

Schröderstiftstr. 3 ⊠ *20146 –* ℰ *(040) 45 06 90*
– h5394@ accor.com – Fax (040) 4 50 69 10 00
– www.mercure.com **E1**
180 rm *–* ♦85/115 € ♦♦85/135 €, ⊑ 14 €
Rest (closed Sunday dinner) a la carte 24/32 €
♦ Business ♦ Functional ♦
Business hotel next door to the exhibition centre and a few minutes' walk from the TV tower. Rooms with a modern design and functional equipment.

 Vorbach without rest ⇆ 🖭 🛁20 ☕ VISA 🐵 ⁄Æ

Johnsallee 63 ⊠ *20146 –* ℰ *(040) 44 18 20*
– info @ hotel-vorbach.de – Fax (040) 44 18 28 88
– www.hotel-vorbach.de *Plan I* **C2**
116 rm ⊑ *–* ♦85/135 € ♦♦105/150 €
♦ Traditional ♦ Classic ♦
Three townhouses from the turn of the century are home to this hotel providing modern, well-kept rooms.

 Senator without rest ⇆ 🖭 🕻 ☕ VISA 🐵 ⁄Æ ⓪

Lange Reihe 18 ⊠ *20099 –* Ⓜ *Hauptbahnhof Nord –* ℰ *(040) 24 12 03*
– info @ hotel-senator-hamburg.de – Fax (040) 2 80 37 17
– www.hotel-senator-hamburg.de **H2**
56 rm ⊑ *–* ♦99/179 € ♦♦99/179 €
♦ Business ♦ Functional ♦
Pale wood and pastel tones create a harmonious atmosphere in the rooms, some of which have a waterbed for a perfect night's sleep.

Baseler Hof
🔊 ⇄rm 🎦 🖵 ✆ 🕻55 VISA ⓪ AE ①

Esplanade 11 ⊠ 20354 – Ⓜ Stephansplatz – ℰ (040) 35 90 60
– info@baselerhof.de – Fax (040) 35 90 69 18
– www.baselerhof.de **F1**
167 rm ☷ – ✝85/115 € ✝✝115/135 €
Rest Kleinhuis, ℰ (040) 35 33 99 – a la carte 21/30 €
♦ Traditional ♦ Functional ♦

Smart rooms with furnishings varying from mahogany to rattan, this hotel is located between the Aussenlaster and the Botanical Gardens, and is a member of the Association of Christian Hotels. The Kleinhuis is a nice bistro-style restaurant.

Arcadia
🔊 ⅋ 🔟 ⇄rm 🖵 ✆ 🕻40 🅿 VISA ⓪ AE ①

Spaldingstr. 70 (by Nordkanalstraße) ⊠ 20097 – ℰ (040) 23 65 04 00
– arcadiahotel@compuserve.com – Fax (040) 23 65 06 29
– www.arcadiahotel.de Plan I **D2**
98 rm ☷ – ✝76/99 € ✝✝86/129 €
Rest (closed Sunday dinner) a la carte 19/34 €
♦ Business ♦ Functional ♦

This former office block was converted into a hotel in 2000. In a central location with practical and functional accommodation. The "Aquarius" restaurant is simply decorated.

Mercure City
🔊 ⅋ ⇄rm 🎦rest 🖵 🕻60 🅿 VISA ⓪ AE ①

Amsinckstr. 53 ⊠ 20097 – ℰ (040) 23 63 80 – h1163@accor.com
– Fax (040) 23 63 81 45 – www.mercure.de Plan I **D3**
187 rm – ✝64/129 € ✝✝64/129 €, ☷ 15 €
Rest a la carte 25/33 €
♦ Chain hotel ♦ Functional ♦

Modern functional rooms in this inner city hotel, ideal for business guests. A restaurant where the chef works in front of diners.

Wedina without rest
🚗 🎦 🖵 🅿 VISA ⓪ ①

Gurlittstr. 23 ⊠ 20099 – ℰ (040) 2 80 89 00
– info@wedina.de – Fax (040) 2 80 38 94
– www.wedina.de **H1**
59 rm ☷ – ✝90/130 € ✝✝110/160 €
♦ Family ♦ Cosy ♦

The different buildings which make up this hotel are aglow in Bauhaus colours. The interior is also attractively designed featuring natural materials.

Alster-Hof without rest
🖵 ✆ VISA ⓪ AE ①

Esplanade 12 ⊠ 20354 – Ⓜ Stephansplatz – ℰ (040) 35 00 70
– info@alster-hof.de – Fax (040) 35 00 75 14
– www.alster-hof.de **F1**
113 rm ☷ – ✝81/96 € ✝✝105/131 €
♦ Traditional ♦ Functional ♦

This centrally located hotel provides functional rooms with a refined atmosphere.

Haerlin – Hotel Vier Jahreszeiten
≤ Binnenalster, 🔟 VISA ⓪ AE ①

Neuer Jungfernstieg 9 ⊠ 20354 – Ⓜ Jungfernstieg – ℰ (040) 34 94 33 10
– emailus.hvj@raffles.com – Fax (040) 34 94 26 08
– www.raffles-hvj.de
closed end December - early January, 2 weeks mid March, 4 weeks July - August
and Sunday - Monday **F2**
Rest (dinner only) 60 €/94 € and a la carte 59/71 € ❀
Spec. Dorade in der Salzkruste. Rücken und geschmorte Schulter vom Eiderstädter Lamm mit Tomatencrèmepolenta. Etouffé Taubenbrust mit Karotten-Koriandertörtchen und Petersilienpüree.
♦ French ♦ Formal ♦

Stylish atmosphere in this restaurant with excellent service and classic cuisine on offer. The large window affords pleasant views.

XXX **Insel am Alsterufer**　　　　　　　　　🛗 ⟨⟩40 VISA ⦿◎ ᴀᴇ ❶
Alsterufer 35 (1ˢᵗ floor) ⊠ 20354 – ℰ (040) 4 50 18 50
– Fax (040) 45 01 85 11 – www.insel-am-alsterufer.de
info@insel-am-alsterufer.de – closed Sunday - Monday　　　　　　*Plan I* **C2**
Rest 38 €/49 € and a la carte 37/63 €
◆ French ◆ Trendy ◆
The white façade of this villa is beautifully lit up at night. An elegant Mediterranean style interior with warm décor, serving classic dishes.

XX **Sgroi**　　　　　　　　　　　　　　　　🛗 VISA ⦿◎
✿ *Lange Reihe 40 ⊠ 20099 – ℰ (040) 28 00 39 30 – Fax (040) 28 00 39 31*
– www.sgroi.de – closed Saturday lunch, Sunday - Monday　　　　　　**H1**
Rest 58 €/68 € and a la carte 47/59 €
Spec. Gedünstete Jakobsmuscheln mit jungen Artischocken. Spaghetti alla Chitarra con le Sarde. Römische Abbacchio von Milchlammkeule mit Rosmarinkartoffeln.
◆ Italian ◆ Minimalist ◆
A light and modern atmosphere in this restaurant serving Italian cuisine prepared with excellent produce.

XX **Anna**　　　　　　　　　　　　　　　　🛗 VISA ⦿◎ ᴀᴇ
Bleichenbrücke 2 ⊠ 20354 – Ⓜ Rathaus – ℰ (040) 36 70 14
– Fax (040) 37 50 07 36
closed Sunday, Bank Holidays　　　　　　　　　　　　　　　　**F2**
Rest a la carte 34/43 €
◆ International ◆ Friendly ◆
Designed in colourful Mediterranean style this restaurant arranged on two floors offers a wide range of international cuisine. Pretty terrace by the canal.

XX **San Michele**　　　　　　　　　　　　　　VISA ⦿◎ ᴀᴇ ❶
Englische Planke 8 ⊠ 20459 – Ⓜ Landungsbrücken – ℰ (040) 37 11 27
– info@san-michele.de – Fax (040) 37 81 21 – www.san-michele.de
closed Monday　　　　　　　　　　　　　　　　　　　　　**E3**
Rest a la carte 39/51 €
◆ Italian ◆ Friendly ◆
The "most Italian of all Italians" is directly opposite the "Michel"! Enjoy traditional Neapolitan cuisine in a cheerful Mediterranean ambience. Small bistro on the ground floor.

XX **Brook**　　　　　　　　　　　　　　　　⦿◎ ᴀᴇ
☺ *Bei den Mühren 91 ⊠ 20457 – ℰ (040) 37 50 31 28 – Fax (040) 37 50 31 27*
– www.restaurant-brook.de
closed Sunday　　　　　　　　　　　　　　　　　　　　　**G3**
Rest 29 €/33 € and a la carte 31/39 €
◆ Contemporary ◆ Minimalist ◆
A modern and deliberately simple restaurant, with good, friendly service. In the evening there is a pretty view of the illuminated Speicherstadt (warehouses) opposite.

X **La Mirabelle**　　　　　　　　　　　　　　VISA ⦿◎ ᴀᴇ
Bundesstr. 15 ⊠ 20146 – ℰ (040) 4 10 75 85 – Fax (040) 4 10 75 85
– www.la-mirabelle-hamburg.de – closed Sunday　　　　　　*Plan I* **C2**
Rest (dinner only) 30 € and a la carte 32/41 €
◆ French ◆ Bistro ◆
Small, friendly restaurant with relaxed atmosphere and a touch of France. The chef personally recommends the specialities of the day to his guests.

X **Fischmarkt**　　　　　　　　　　　　　　🛗 VISA ⦿◎ ᴀᴇ
Ditmar-Koel-Str. 1 ⊠ 20459 – Ⓜ Landungsbrücken – ℰ (040) 36 38 09
– Fax (040) 36 21 91 – www.restaurant-fischmarkt.de
closed Saturday lunch　　　　　　　　　　　　　　　　**E3**
Rest (booking advisable) 26 €/44 € and a la carte 27/51 €
◆ Seafood ◆ Bistro ◆
Close to the harbour, this fine restaurant with Mediterranean décor and a bistro atmosphere with open kitchen serves many fish specials.

GERMANY

✗
😊 **Le Plat du Jour** $\quad$ VISA ⓜ AE ①
Dornbusch 4 ⊠ 20095 – Ⓜ Rathaus – ℰ (040) 32 14 14 – jacqueslemercier@
aol.com – Fax (040) 4 10 58 57- Sunday $\quad$ **G3**
closed 23 December - 7 January, Sunday, July - August Saturday
Rest (booking advisable) 26 € (dinner) and a la carte 26/34 €
♦ French ♦ Bistro ♦
A pleasant French style bistro with wooden seats and black & white photos on
the walls. Good value for money.

✗
Cox $\quad$ ⓜ③
Lange Reihe 68 ⊠ 20099 – ℰ (040) 24 94 22 – info@restaurant-cox.de
– Fax (040) 28 05 09 02 – www.restaurant-cox.de
closed Saturday lunch, Sunday lunch $\quad$ **H1**
Rest (dinner booking essential) a la carte 25/35 €
♦ Modern ♦ Bistro ♦
Diners are served international cuisine with a Mediterranean touch in this
charming, warm bistro near the city's principal theatre.

✗
Matsumi $\quad$ VISA ⓜ③ AE ①
Colonnaden 96 (1st floor) ⊠ 20354 – Ⓜ Stephansplatz – ℰ (040) 34 31 25
– Fax (040) 34 42 19 – www.matsumi.de
closed 23 December - 8 January and Sunday, Bank Holidays lunch $\quad$ **F2**
Rest 43 €/50 € and a la carte 22/40 €
♦ Japanese ♦ Minimalist ♦
You will find this classic Japanese restaurant in the pedestrian zone. The
authentic fare is served at the table, at the sushi bar or in the tatami rooms (for
groups).

✗
😊 **Jena Paradies**
Klosterwall 23 ⊠ 20095 – Ⓜ Steinstr. – ℰ (040) 32 70 08 – jena-paradies@
t-online.de – Fax (040) 32 75 98 – www.restaurant-jenaparadies.de $\quad$ **H3**
Rest 25 €/32 € and a la carte 22/31 €
♦ International ♦ Bistro ♦
The high-ceilinged rooms of this former part of the art academy now house a
bistro in the Bauhaus style that serves international dishes. Plain fare at good
prices served at midday.

NORTH OF THE CENTRE $\qquad$ *Plan I*

InterContinental $\quad$ ⬉ Hamburg and Alster, 🏵 ⓦ ⅃⒮ 🛁 🖃 ㎹ ↩rm
Fontenay 10 ⊠ 20354 $\quad$ 🖵 ⚒300 ⌂ P̲ VISA ⓜ③ AE ①
– ℰ (040) 4 14 20 – hamburg@interconti.com – Fax (040) 41 42 22 99
– www.hamburg.intercontinental.com $\quad$ **C2**
281 rm – ♦195/245 € ♦♦195/245 €, � 20 € – 11 suites
Rest *Windows*, ℰ (040) 41 42 25 31 *(closed Sunday - Monday)* (dinner only)
39 €/70 € and a la carte 40/59 €
Rest *Signatures*, ℰ (040) 41 42 25 20 – a la carte 35/44 €
♦ Chain hotel ♦ Luxury ♦ Functional ♦
This hotel located on the Alster will charm guests thanks to its extravagant
appearance, international flair and contemporary, functional rooms. Fabulous:
the views from the elegant Windows restaurant on the 9th floor. Bright: the
Signatures conservatory restaurant.

Garden Hotel without rest ⌂ $\quad$ 🚿 ↩ ⚒15 ⌂ VISA ⓜ③ AE
Magdalenenstr. 60 ⊠ 20148 – ℰ (040) 41 40 40
– garden@garden-hotels.de – Fax (040) 4 14 04 20
– www.garden-hotels.de $\quad$ **C2**
58 rm – ♦125/155 € ♦♦145/175 €, ⊆ 12 €
♦ Business ♦ Functional ♦
Everything chic in Hamburg practically starts at this door – and what's behind it?
Imaginatively furnished, modern and elegant rooms in three delightful
establishments.

GERMANY

Abtei   ⌂ ⟿ 🅰️ rest ❄️rest 🚪 **VISA** **MC** **AE**

Abteistr. 14 ⊠ 20149 – ℰ (040) 44 29 05 – abtei@relaischateaux.com
– Fax (040) 44 98 20 – www.abtei-hotel.de
closed 24 - 27 December   C1
11 rm � – ♦135/180 € ♦♦180/260 €
Rest (closed Sunday - Monday) (dinner only) (booking essential) 69 €/79 €
and a la carte 56/74 €
Spec. Gebratene Jakobsmuscheln mit Zuckerschoten. Loup de mer mit
geschmolzener Gänsestopfleber und Rotweinbutter. Schokoladenvariation.
♦ Townhouse ♦ Personalised ♦
A lovely building with high stucco ceilings with an intimate atmosphere and
tastefully decorated, elegant rooms. An intimate atmosphere in the restaurant.

Nippon   ↯rm 🍽️ 🚪 📞 🚗20 ⟿ **VISA** **MC** **AE** **①**

Hofweg 75 ⊠ 22085 – ℰ (040) 2 27 11 40 – reservations@
nippon-hotel-hh.de – Fax (040) 22 71 14 90
– www.nippon-hotel-hh.de
closed 23 December - 1 January   D1
42 rm – ♦95/118 € ♦♦113/146 €, � 10 €
Rest (closed Monday) (dinner only) a la carte 25/38 €
♦ Business ♦ Minimalist ♦
Furnished in a modern, purist Japanese style with light colours and clear
shapes: tatami floors, shoji walls and futons. A Japanese restaurant and sushi
bar.

Piment (Nouri)   ⌂ **VISA** **MC** **AE** **①**

Lehmweg 29 ⊠ 20251 – ℰ (040) 42 93 77 88 – Fax (040) 42 93 77 89
closed 6 - 18 March and Sunday   C1
Rest (dinner only) 40 €/68 € and a la carte 53/62 €
Spec. Gänsestopfleberschnitte mit orientalischem Kalbsfilettatar und
Chicoréesalat. Geschmortes Kalbsbäckchen gratiniert in Schalotten mit
Kartoffelcrème. Variation vom Topfen mit Holunderblütenaufguss.
♦ Contemporary ♦ Friendly ♦
North African influences in this restaurant serving classic cuisine. Charming
jugendstil style, with a homely atmosphere.

Poletto   ⌂

Eppendorfer Landstr. 145 (by Breitenfelder Str. C 1) ⊠ 20251 – ℰ (040) 4 80 21 59
– Fax (040) 41 40 69 93 – www.poletto.de
closed 1 week July and Saturday lunch, Sunday - Monday, Bank Holidays
Rest (booking advisable) 29 € (lunch)/72 € (dinner) and a la carte 51/73 €
Spec. Handgemachte Tortelloni alla Carbonara mit Tiroler Speck. Geangelter
Loup de mer in Olivenöl gegart mit Fenchelmousse und geschmolzenen
Tomaten. Das Beste vom Müritz Lamm mit Bohnentörtchen.
♦ Italian influences ♦ Friendly ♦
Restaurant with a modern interior of light tones and a relaxed atmosphere.
Mediterranean and Italian cuisine served.

Allegria   ⌂ **AE**

Hudtwalckerstr. 13 (by Sierichstr. C 1) ⊠ 22299 – ℰ (040) 46 07 28 28 – info@
allegria-restaurant.de – Fax (040) 46 07 26 07 – www.allegria-restaurant.de
closed 2 - 8 January, Monday
Rest (weekdays dinner only) 46 €/65 € and a la carte 30/45 €
♦ International ♦ Fashionable ♦
Directly adjacent to the Winterhuder Fährhaus Theater, you'll dine in a modern,
colourful and light-flooded ambience, and enjoy delicious cuisine with a hint of
Felix Austria.

Tirol   ⌂ **VISA** **MC** **AE**

Milchstr. 19 ⊠ 20148 – ℰ (040) 44 60 82 – Fax (040) 44 80 93 27
closed Sunday   C2
Rest a la carte 28/40 €
♦ Austrian ♦ Cosy ♦
For anyone who is homesick for Austria! The rustic ambience will help you to forget
north Germany's drizzle. A cosy environment and delightful Austrian treats!

HARBOUR AND ALTONA   *Plan III*

 East   🏛 🏵 ఉ ⇔ 🖬 🔏100 ⇔ 𝗩𝗜𝗦𝗔 ⬤⑩ 🄰🄴 ⓪

Simon-von-Utrecht-Str. 31 ⊠ *20359 –* ⓜ *St. Pauli –* ℰ *(040) 30 99 30*
– info@east-hamburg.de – Fax (040) 30 99 32 00
– www.east-hamburg.de   *Plan I* **B2**
103 rm – ♦150/170 € ♦♦170/190 €, ⊑ 12 €
Rest *(closed Saturday lunch, Sunday lunch)* a la carte 26/44 €
♦ Business ♦ Design ♦
In a former iron smelting factory, stands this stunning designer hotel providing rather modern rooms with all mod cons and large bar area on the 2nd floor. Restaurant with brick vaulted ceiling in a converted factory shop.

 Domicil without rest   ⇔ 🖬 📞🖢 ⇔ 𝗩𝗜𝗦𝗔 ⬤⑩ 🄰🄴 ⓪

Stresemannstr. 62 ⊠ *22769 –* ⓜ *Sternschanze –* ℰ *(040) 4 31 60 26*
– info@domicil-hamburg-mitte.de – Fax (040) 4 39 75 79
– www.domicil-hamburg-mitte.de   **J1**
75 rm – ♦55/150 € ♦♦70/250 €, ⊑ 13 €
♦ Business ♦ Functional ♦
This hotel is enlivened by strong colours, especially black and lilac. Original details emphasise the individuality of the spacious rooms.

 InterCityHotel Hamburg Altona   ఉ ⇔rm 🖬 📞🖢

Paul-Nevermann-Platz 17 ⊠ *22765*   🔏60 𝗩𝗜𝗦𝗔 ⬤⑩ 🄰🄴 ⓪
– ℰ (040) 38 03 40 – hamburg-altona@intercityhotel.de – Fax (040) 38 03 49 99
– www.hamburg-altona.intercityhotel.de   **I1**
133 rm – ♦79/110 € ♦♦79/120 €, ⊑ 12 €
Rest *(closed Sunday and Bank Holidays)* a la carte 17/20 €
♦ Chain hotel ♦ Functional ♦
Right by the ICE-train station, this hotel provides modern, spaciously furnished rooms. The use of local transport is included in the room price. Bistro style restaurant.

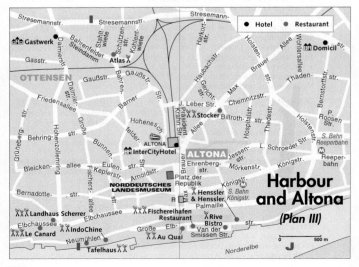

XXX

ε3

Landhaus Scherrer   AC P VISA MO AE ①

Elbchaussee 130 ⊠ 22763 – ℰ (040) 8 80 13 25 – info@landhausscherrer.de
– Fax (040) 8 80 62 60 – www.landhausscherrer.de
closed Easter, Whitsun and Sunday   **I1**
Rest 108 € and a la carte 54/88 € ⅏
Rest *Bistro* a la carte 34/38 €
Spec. Bouillabaisse von Nordseefischen. Gebratener Hummer mit
Graupenrisotto. Krosse Vierländer Ente im Ganzen gebraten (2 pers.).
◆ French ◆ Formal ◆
A lovely country house built in 1827, home to an elegant restaurant. Serves
French cuisine. Paintings on display. Pleasant, friendly Bistro with light wood
panelling.

XXX

Le Canard   ≼ 🏠 ⚄ P VISA MO

Elbchaussee 139 ⊠ 22763 – ℰ (040) 88 12 95 31
– info@lecanard-hamburg.de – Fax (040) 88 12 95 33
– www.lecanard-hamburg.de
closed Monday, Saturday lunch, Sunday lunch   **I1**
Rest 24 € (lunch)/90 € (dinner) and a la carte 33/47 € ⅏
◆ International ◆ Fashionable ◆
Set above the Elbe is this round shaped restaurant with a modern, chic
atmosphere and large window façade affording harbour views. Classic dishes
served.

XXX

Fischereihafen Restaurant   ≼ 🏠 P VISA MO AE ①

Große Elbstr. 143 ⊠ 22767 – ℰ (040) 38 18 16 – info@
fischereihafenrestaurant.de – Fax (040) 3 89 30 21
– www.fischereihafenrestaurant.de   **J1**
Rest (booking advisable) 19 € (lunch)/50 € and a la carte 26/54 €
◆ Seafood ◆ Formal ◆
This Hamburg institution is a restaurant serving regional cuisine, specialising in
fish. Terrace overlooking the Elbe.

XX

Au Quai   ≼ 🏠 VISA MO AE ①

Große Elbstr. 145 b ⊠ 22767 – ℰ (040) 38 03 77 30
– info@au-quai.com – Fax (040) 38 03 77 32
– www.au-quai.com
closed 1 - 8 January, Saturday lunch, Sunday   **J1**
Rest 18 € (lunch) and a la carte 29/47 €
◆ Modern ◆ Trendy ◆
This popular establishment is situated close to the harbour and has a terrace
facing the water. The modern interior is complemented by designer items and
holographs.

XX

IndoChine   ≼ 🏠 P VISA MO AE

Neumühlen 11 ⊠ 22763 – ℰ (040) 39 80 78 80 – info@indochine.de
– Fax (040) 39 80 78 82 – www.indochine.de   **I1**
Rest a la carte 28/49 €
◆ Asian ◆ Trendy ◆
A fantastic view from this modern, elegant restaurant situated on the 2nd and
3rd floors. Cambodian, Laotian, Vietnamese cuisine. Riverside terrace, lovely
ground-floor bar.

XX

ε3

Tafelhaus   ≼ 🏠 VISA MO AE

Neumühlen 17 ⊠ 22763 – ℰ (040) 89 27 60 – anfrage@tafelhaus.de
– Fax (040) 8 99 33 24 – www.tafelhaus.de
closed Saturday lunch, Sunday   **I1**
Rest 37 € (lunch)/65 € and a la carte 53/68 € ⅏
Spec. Gedämpfter Kabeljau im Bananenblatt. Rehschulter mit Holundersauce
und kleinem Pilzcroissant. Pochierter Pfirsich mit Zitronen-Thymianeis und
Himbeeren.
◆ Modern ◆ Fashionable ◆
A modern, pure design restaurant with glass façade affording a view of the Elbe.
Creative cuisine with French influences. 'Elbe' terrace.

GERMANY

XX **Stocker**   ⌂ *VISA* ⑩ AE ⓞ

Max-Brauer-Allee 80 ⊠ 22765 – ℰ (040) 38 61 50 56
– info@restaurant-stocker.de – Fax (040) 38 61 50 58
– www.restaurant-stocker.de
closed 2 weeks early January, Saturday lunch, Sunday lunch, Monday   **J1**
Rest 42 €/64 € and a la carte 30/44 €
♦ Austrian ♦ Friendly ♦
Playful frescoes and stucco ornamentation are the backdrop for Manfred Stocker's Austrian cooking, which also offers typical Viennese dishes.

X **Henssler Henssler**   ⌂ AE

Große Elbstr. 160 ⊠ 22767 – ⓜ Königstr. – ℰ (040) 38 69 90 00
– Fax (040) 38 69 90 55 – www.hensslerhenssler.de
closed Christmas - early January, July and Sunday   **J1**
Rest 34 €/41 € and a la carte 26/37 €
♦ Japanese ♦ Minimalist ♦
Very modern, deliberately simple restaurant in an old fishmonger's: Japanese-inspired interior, sushi bar and Japanese cuisine with Californian highlights.

X **Rive Bistro**   ⬿ ⌂ AE

Van-der-Smissen Str. 1 (Cruise-Centre) ⊠ 22767 – ⓜ Königstr.
– ℰ (040) 3 80 59 19 – info@rive.de – Fax (040) 3 89 47 75
– www.rive.de   **J1**
Rest (booking advisable) a la carte 26/53 €
♦ International ♦ Fashionable ♦
Enjoy the views of the harbour close to the fish market – and the international cuisine with the emphasis very much on fish. Original décor consisting of metal leaves. Fresh oysters available at the bar.

ELBE-WESTERN DISTRICTS

🏨 **Louis C. Jacob**   ⬿ port and Elbe River, ⌂ 🐾 ⟨ᴋ⟩ ⫩rm ✗rest ⬜ ☏
*Elbchaussee 401 (by Elbchaussee **A 3**)*   ♨120 ⟨ᴐ⟩ *VISA* ⑩ AE ⓞ
⊠ 22609 – ℰ (040) 82 25 50 – jacob@hotel-jacob.de – Fax (040) 82 25 54 44
– www.hotel-jacob.de
85 rm – ♦185/225 € ♦♦235/385 €, � 20 € – 8 suites
Rest see *Weinwirtschaft Kleines Jacob* below
Rest (booking advisable) 57 € (lunch)/98 € and a la carte 54/85 € ▩
Spec. Sautierte Jakobsmuscheln mit Orangenblütensauce und gehobeltem grünem Spargel. Junge Vieländer Ente in zwei Gängen serviert. Coulant von der Bitterschokolade mit Eis von gerösteten Kakaobohnen.
♦ Luxury ♦ Traditional ♦ Personalised ♦
Luxury hotel with understated style. The rooms have modern, yet classic furnishings with smooth, elegant lines. Lovely: the location overlooking the Elbe. A stylish restaurant with subtle cream tone décor. Serves French cuisine. Lovely tree-shaded terrace.

🏨 **Gastwerk**   🐾 ⫩rm ⬜ ☏ ♨100 P *VISA* ⑩ AE ⓞ
Beim Alten Gaswerk 3 (corner of Daimlerstraße) ⊠ 22761
– ℰ (040) 89 06 20 – info@gastwerk-hotel.de – Fax (040) 8 90 62 20
– www.gastwerk-hotel.de   *Plan I* **I1**
135 rm – ♦125/165 € ♦♦125/165 €, � 15 € – 3 suites
Rest (closed Saturday lunch, Sunday lunch) a la carte 34/40 €
♦ Business ♦ Stylish ♦
From the gasworks to a guest work: the impressive industrial memorial has been turned into a loft-style designer hotel with spacious rooms, natural materials and lots of tasteful details. A modern restaurant serving Italian cuisine.

Landhaus Flottbek 🛜 🚗 📺 📶 ✨30 🅿 *VISA* 📠 ⅍ ⓘ

Baron-Voght-Str. 179 (by Stresemannstr. **A 2)** ✆ 22607 – 𝒸 *(040) 8 22 74 10*
– info@landhaus-flottbek.de – Fax (040) 82 27 41 51
– www.landhaus-flottbek.de
25 rm – ♦90/120 € ♦♦105/140 €, ☷ 13 €
Rest *(closed Saturday lunch, Sunday)* a la carte 28/43 €
Rest Club-House, 𝒸 *(040) 82 27 41 61 (closed Monday - Friday lunch)* 28 €/48 €
and a la carte 29/37 €
♦ Family ♦ Cosy ♦
A group of 18C farmhouses with a beautiful garden. The lovely, individually furnished, country-style rooms are rustic and elegant. This restaurant, situated in former stables, has lots of atmosphere. Pretty: the Bistro Club-House.

Süllberg-Seven Seas (Hauser) with rm ≼ 🛜 🅰 ✨rest 📺 📶

Süllbergsterrasse 12 (by Elbchaussee **A 3)** ⟳100 ⛶ *VISA* 📠 ⅍
✉ 22587 – 𝒸 *(040) 8 66 25 20 – info@suellberg-hamburg.de*
– Fax (040) 86 62 52 13 – www.suellberg-hamburg.de
closed 2 - 25 January and Monday - Tuesday
11 rm – ♦130/160 € ♦♦160/190 €, ☷ 16 €
Rest *(weekdays dinner only)* 56 €/98 € and a la carte 42/72 € 🕸
Rest Bistro 27 €/37 € and a la carte 28/43 €
Spec. Cassoulette vom spanischen Carabinieros. Getrüffelter Steinbutt im Brotmantel mit weißem Spargel und Kartoffelvinaigrette. St. Petersfisch unter der Pinienkruste mit Ratatouillefumet und Parmesanravioli.
♦ French ♦ Formal ♦
This establishment is set high above the Elbe, with a maritime atmosphere. Also featuring a fine ballroom. The Bistro: friendly and with a modern style.

Das Kleine Rote (Hinz) 🛜 🅿

Holstenkamp 71 ✉ 22525 – 𝒸 *(040) 89 72 68 13 – das-kleine-rote@web.de*
– Fax (040) 89 72 68 14 – www.das-kleine-rote.de
closed early - mid January, 2 weeks July and Saturday lunch,
Sunday - Monday   *Plan I* **A2**
Rest *(booking essential)* 29 € (lunch)/69 € (dinner) and a la carte 45/58 €
Spec. Tartar vom Wolfbarsch mit gebackenen Austern und Meerrettich. Geschmorte Ochsenwade mit Chicorée und gehobelter Entenleber. Gebratene Aprikosen mit Rosmarin und Honig-Weineis.
♦ Contemporary ♦ Friendly ♦
Modern restaurant with a Mediterranean touch housed in a small red house surrounded by a charming garden. Light creative cuisine served.

Atlas 🛜 🅿 *VISA* 📠

Schützenstr. 9a (entrance Phoenixhof) ✉ 22761 – 𝒸 *(040) 8 51 78 10*
– atlas@atlas.at – Fax (040) 8 51 78 11 – www.atlas.at
closed Saturday lunch   *Plan III* **I1**
Rest 28 € and a la carte 28/36 €
♦ International ♦ Bistro ♦
A former fish smokery which has been converted into a well-run restaurant with a modern and simple bistro style. Behind the building there is a small, ivy-covered terrace.

Weinwirtschaft Kleines Jacob – Hotel Louis C. Jacob

Elbchaussee 404 (by Elbchaussee **A 3)** ✉ 22609   *VISA* 📠 ⅍ ⓘ
– 𝒸 (040) 82 25 55 10 – kleines-jacob@hotel-jacob.de – Fax (040) 82 25 54 44
– www.hotel-jacob.de
closed 2 weeks early January, 4 weeks July - August and Tuesday
Rest *(weekdays dinner only)* a la carte 25/35 € 🕸
♦ International ♦ Cosy ♦
This restaurant is a pleasant, comfortable alternative to the Louis C. Jacob Hotel opposite and has been carefully decorated to hone its rustic style.

AT THE AIRPORT

 Courtyard by Marriott   🛜 🗥 🖭 📶 ↔rm 🖾 📶140 🚗
Flughafenstr. 47 ✉ *22415 Hamburg*   **P** **VISA** **◑** **AE** **①**
– 𝒞 (040) 53 10 20 – service@airporthh.com – Fax (040) 53 10 22 22
– www.marriott.com
159 rm – 🛉129/203 € 🛉🛉129/203 €, ⍗ 15 €
Rest a la carte 27/54 €
♦ Business ♦ Functional ♦
A short distance from the airport, this hotel with a country style charm has
pleasant décor and well-furnished rooms. An airy, classic restaurant.

 Mercure-Airport-Nord   🛜 🗥 🖭 🕭 ↔rm %rest 🖾 📶80
Langenhorner Chaussee 183   🚗 **VISA** **◑** **AE** **①**
✉ *22415 Hamburg – 𝒞 (040) 53 20 90 – h5393@accor.com*
– Fax (040) 53 20 96 00 – www.mercure.com
146 rm – 🛉79/103 € 🛉🛉79/103 €, ⍗ 16 €
Rest 24 €/26 € (Buffet) and a la carte 20/30 €
♦ Chain hotel ♦ Business ♦ Functional ♦
The architectural design of glass corridors and landscaped courtyards of this
establishment close to the airport is delightful. The rooms are modern and
functional.

RAMOS PINTO

Est.1880

- [ ] **a.** *Meals served in the garden or on the terrace*
- [ ] **b.** *A particularly interesting wine list*
- [ ] **c.** *Cask beers and ales usually served*

Find out all the answers in the Michelin Guide "Eating Out in Pubs"!

A selection of 500 dining pubs and inns throughout Britain and Ireland researched by the same inspectors who make the Michelin Guide.

- for good food and the right atmosphere
- in-depth descriptions bring out the feel of the place and the flavour of the cuisine.

The pleasure of travel with Michelin Maps and Guides.

MUNICH
MÜNCHEN

Population (est. 2005): 1 205 000 (conurbation 1 656 000) – Altitude: 520m

AGE Carlos/HOA QUI

The Bavarian capital, third largest and one of the most important German towns, lies on River Isar's banks, not far north of the Alps. It is a renowned cultural centre (over 40 theatres, an academy of fine arts, one of Europe's largest film studios, dozens of museums, 10 university colleges) and the most flourishing economic zone in southern Germany. Its commercial influence has increased enormously in recent years, through the rising of high-tech industries allied to the production of motor vehicles (BMW), locomotives, rubber, chemicals and electronics (Siemens).

The choice of Munich as seat of the European Patents Office since 1980 recognises the city's illustrious scientific past, resounding with such famous names as Fraunhofer, Liebig, Ohm and Sauerbruch.

Among writers working in Munich were T. Mann, F. Wedekind and L. Thoma. It is however in the absurd logic of the stand-up comedian K. Valentine that Munich's spirit most popularly expresses itself.

With the foundation of the review Jugend (1896) the city became the centre of the Jugendstil movement; and later, one of the Mecca of modern art.

Munich's cultural wealth, its special atmosphere – blend of gaiety, tolerance and respect for tradition – and the beauty of the surrounding countryside have combined to make it one of the most attractive German cities.

WHICH DISTRICT TO CHOOSE

The greatest concentration of **hotels** is in the immediate neighbourhood of the station. Many of the hotels and restaurants are located in the city centre – near Stachus, Marienplatz, Maximilianstrasse and Frauenkirche. A number of characterful **restaurants** and **inns** are located around the Viktualienmarkt but the best restaurants in Munich are to be found in the city centre and in the Bogenhausen and Schwabing districts. Munich is known for its solid regional cooking and especially for its attractive, lively **brewery-inns** where locals and visitors meet over

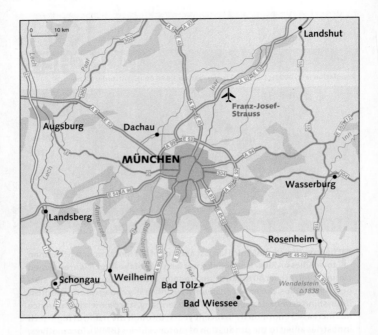

a tankard of the typical Bavarian *Weissbier* and a portion of the famous *Weisswurst* (local sausage). In recent decades so many small intimate **Italian restaurants** have appeared on the scene that Munich has been dubbed "the northernmost city of Italy".

PRACTICAL INFORMATION

ARRIVAL – DEPARTURE

Airport Franz-Josef Strauss about 28 km (17,5 mi) northeast of the city centre. ℰ (089) 9 75 00; info@munich-airport.de; www.munich-airport.de

From the airport to the city centre – By **taxi**: €56. By rapid transit **train** (Line 8) to Railway Station every 20min.

Railway Station – Hauptbahnhof for international routes and trains. ℰ 0190 50 70 90 (24hr - €1.49 per min); www.bahn.de

TRANSPORT

◆ METRO, BUS AND TRAM

Munich and its surroundings are divided into four ring-shaped price zones. Underground trains (U-Bahn) are controlled by the local transport and fare association **MVV** (Münchner Verkehrs- und Tarifverbund); buses and trams (Strassenbahn), railway trains (S-Bahn) and the transport authorities for the surrounding area are controlled by SWM (Stadtwerke München); ℰ (089) 41 42 43 44. Information at the **Hauptbahnhof** on the mezzanine level, Mon-Sat

9am-6pm and Marienplatz mezzanine level, Mon-Fri 9am-8pm, Sat 9am-4pm. Tickets on sale at any underground or railway station, from ticket machines or bus drivers and on trams. Tickets for the central zone (Münchner Innenraum), including Munich city centre: single ticket €2.20, 10-trip ticket *(10er Streifenkarte)* €8.80 (in Munich city centre two strips on this ticket must be validated), 1-day ticket €4.50. 1-day 'Partner' ticket for up to five people €7.20 (both valid from when they are stamped to 6am the following day). There is a 3-day ticket: €11 for 1 person, €18,50 for 2-5 people.

♦ MÜNCHEN WELCOME CARD

The **München Welcome Card** is valid for use on public transport in Munich city centre and for discounts of up to 50% for more than 30 sights, museums, castles and palaces, city tours and bicycle hire; 1-day single €6.50; 3-day single €16; 3-day Partner (2 adults and up to 3 children under 18yrs) €20.

♦ TAXIS

Taxis are cream-coloured and numerous. They can be hailed in the street, hired at taxi ranks and called by telephone. Initial charge €2.70 (€1.45 per km for first 5km, €1.30 per km for next 5km, €1.20 per km thereafter). *Taxi München* ✆ (089) 2 16 10; www.taxi-muenchen-online.de

USEFUL ADDRESSES

♦ TOURIST INFORMATION

Fremdenverkehrsamt München *Plan II* **G2**; Mon-Thu 9am-3pm, Fri 9am-12.30pm; ✆ (089) 2 33 03 00. **Railway Station**; Mon-Sat 9am-8pm, Sun 10am-6pm; ✆ (089) 23 33 02 57/58.

Neues Rathaus, Marienplatz; Mon-Fri 10am-8pm, Sat 10am-4pm, ✆ (089) 23 33 02 72/73, **City Info Zeil**, Mon-Fri 10am-6pm, Sat 19am-4pm. www.muenchen.de

♦ POST OFFICES

Mon-Fri 8am-6pm, Sat 8am-12 noon. **Railway Station** (Postfiliale 32), Bahnhofsplatz: Mon-Fri 7am-8pm, Sat 9am-4pm, Sun 10am-4pm; **Airport** (Postfiliale 24), central area, level 3 in McPaper: Mon-Sat 7.30am-9pm.

♦ BANKS

Mon-Fri 8.30am-12.30pm and 2-4pm (sometimes later); closed Sat-Sun and public holidays.

♦ EMERGENCY

Dial ✆ **110**; Fire Brigade ✆ **112**.

BUSY PERIODS

It may be difficult to find a room at a reasonable price when special events are held in the city as hotel prices may be raised substantially:

Starkbierzeit: March – Festival of strong beers.

Fasching: Carnival is celebrated just before Lent.

Auer Dult: late April to early May, late July and mid October – antiques market.

TollWood Sommerfestival: mid June to mid July.

Opernfestspiele: July – Opera festival.

Feast of the Assumption: 15 August – the Blessed Virgin Mary is the patron of Munich.

Oktoberfest: late September to early October (16 days) – Beer festival.

Christkindlmarket: December.

DIFFERENT FACETS OF THE CITY

It is possible to visit the main sights and museums in two to three days.

Museums and sights are usually open between 9am or 10am and 5pm (later on Thursday). Most are closed on Mondays or Tuesdays and public holidays.

OLD TOWN – Marienplatz *Plan II* **G2**. The heart of Munich where the carillon plays three times a day. **Frauenkirche** *Plan II* **G2**. A hall church with twin onion domes housing the cenotaph of Emperor Ludwig of Bavaria; good view of Munich from the top of the South Tower (lift). **Theatinerkirche** *Plan II* **G1**. 17C Baroque church with a rococo façade.

ROYAL MUNICH – Residenz *Plan II* **G1**. Former royal palace of the Wittelsbach family, comprising the **Schatzkammer** (Treasury) and the state rooms, a very rich example of interior design. **Nymphenburg**, once the summer residence of the Bavarian sovereigns set in a formal park. **Englischer Garten** *Plan I* **C2**. One of the largest and most beautiful town parks, laid out by Prince Elector Karl Theodor in 1789.

ART COLLECTIONS – Deutsches Museum *Plan II* **H3**. History of science and technology from the beginning of time to the present. **Alte Pinakothek** *Plan I* **B2**. Outstanding works by European painters from 14C to 18C collected by the rulers of Bavaria. **Neue Pinakothek** *Plan I* **B2**. 19C art. **Pinakothek der Moderne** *Plan I* **F1**. Modern and contemporary painting and sculpture, jewellery, design, graphic art and the architectural museum collection. **Bayerisches Nationalmuseum** *Plan I* **C2**. Bavarian arts and crafts. **Städtische Galerie im Lenbachhaus** *Plan II* **E1**. The Lenbach Collections are housed in a Florentine villa, devoted mainly to 19C Munich painters but including the avant-garde *Blaue Reiter* works of art.

GOURMET TREATS

Each year five million hectolitres (110 000 000 gallons) of **beer** are brewed in Munich. To sample the locals' favourite drink, visit one of the beer cellars or taverns; in fine weather it tastes best in one of the beer gardens, where you can take your own food. The best-known of the famous beer halls is the *Hofbräuhaus Plan II* **H2**; in the huge vaulted ground-floor Bierschwemme, the rowdiest part of the house, the servers deliver fistfuls of tankards to the tables, while odours of strong tobacco mingle with those of sausages and beer. The arrival of the month of May is celebrated by the drinking of Maibock. Local specialities to sample with the beer are white sausages *(Weisswurst)*, roast knuckle of pork *(Schweinshaxe)* and a meat and offal pâté *(Leberkäs)* which can be bought in slices, hot, from most butchers any time after 11am. Other accompaniments for beer are white radishes *(Radi)*, pretzels and small salt rolls *(Munich Salzstangen)*. A favourite offering at the beer festivals is small fish grilled on a skewer *(Steckerlfisch)*.

SHOPPING

Shops are usually open from 9am/10am to 6.30pm/8pm. They are closed on Sundays.

The **Old Town** has numerous shopping arcades which cater for all budgets. *Beck am Rathauseck* and other department stores are located between **Marienplatz** *Plan II* **G2** and **Stachus** *Plan II* **F2**. **Exclusive boutiques** are to be found in **Residenzstrasse**, **Brienner Strasse** and of course

Maximilianstrasse *Plan II* **H2**. There is also the *Fünf Höfen* shopping centre in stylish **Theatinerstrasse** *Plan II* **G1**. Another good shopping district is **Schwabing** (on and to the west of Leopoldstrasse) *Plan I* **B1**.

Munich covers the whole range of antiques from elegant, exclusive antique dealers' establishments to inexpensive bric-à-brac shops. **Schwabing** boasts a wealth of antique shops in the area around Amalien-, Türken-, Barer-, Kurfürsten- and Hohenzollernstrasse, as does the city centre around Lenbach- and Promenadenplatz.

MARKETS – **Flea markets** are held in Arnulfstrasse by the old container depot (Fri-Sat 7am-6pm) and in Kunstpark Ost behind the Ostbahnhof (Fri 9am-6pm, Sat 7am-6pm). The best market in town is, as it has always been, the **Viktualienmarket** *Plan II* **G2**; small permanent markets are held in Elisabethplatz in **Schwabing** and in Wiener Platz in **Haidhausen**.

WHAT TO BUY – Beer mugs, traditional Bavarian clothes.

ENTERTAINMENT

Prinz and *Münchner* are local newspapers, available from news kiosks, which publish details of events.

Tickets can be booked in advance at the tourist information point in the Neues Rathaus or at the ticket booths.

Nationaltheater *Plan II* **G2** – The main stage venue for the Bavarian State Opera, which also offers ballet performances as part of its programme. From time to time they perform in the rococo treasure, the Cuvilliés-Theater and the Prinzregententheater – www. staatstheater.bayern.de

Staatstheater am Gärtnerplatz *Plan II* **G3** – Opera evenings and also operettas, ballet and musicals – www. staatstheater.bayern.de

Deutsches Theater *Plan II* **F2** – Musical and operettas, in which the Paris Lido also makes an appearance during its tour – www.deutsches-theater.de

Philharmonie im Gasteig *Plan I* **C3** – Modern cultural centre and base of the Munich Philharmonic Orchestra – www.muenchnerphilharmoniker.de

Herkulessaal der Residenz *Plan II* **G1** – Classical music in a classical setting.

Prinzregententheater *Plan I* **C3** – Magnificent concert hall in a converted 1900 theatre – www.prinzregen tentheater.de

Müncher Kammerspiele-Schauspielhaus *Plan II* **H2** – The famous company offers superb spoken theatre – www.muenchner-kam merspiele.de

Residenztheater and the **Altes Residenztheater (Cuvilliés-Theater)** *Plan II* **G2** – The home of the Bayrisches Staatsschauspiel.

Münchner Volkstheater *Plan II* **F1** – High quality popular theatre, a cut above farce – www.muenchner-volk stheatre.de

Muffathalle *Plan I* **C3** – Another place to experience the multicultural scene offering concerts, theatre and dance.

NIGHTLIFE

Kunstpark Ost (Grafinger Strasse 6 - by the Ostbahnhof) has over 30 bars, clubs and restaurants, where people party through the night every weekend from about 11pm onwards. **Nachtwerk** (Landsberger Strasse 185 - continuation of Bayerstrasse, towards Ammersee) is a warehouse converted into a discotheque for young people.

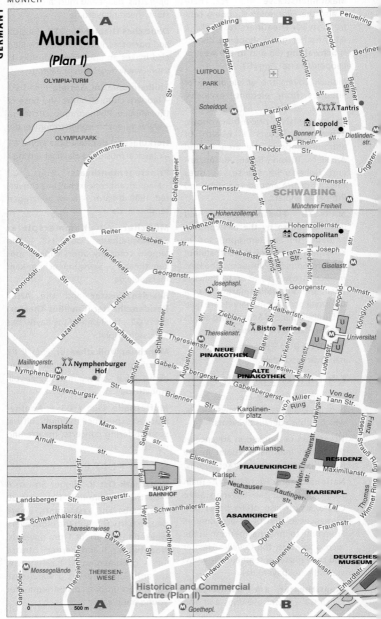

Munich
(Plan I)

OLYMPIA-TURM

1

OLYMPIAPARK

Petuelring

Petuelring

Belgradstr.

Rümannstr.

Isoldenstr.

Leopold.

Berliner

LUITPOLD

PARK

Berliner Str.

Str.

Scheidpl.

Parzival-

str.

Bonner Str.

✕✕✕✕ Tantris

🏠 Leopold

Bonner Pl.

Rhein-

str.

Dietlinden-

str.

Ackermannstr.

Karl

Theodor

Belgrad-

str.

Str.

Ungerer-

Schleißheimer

Clemensstr.

Clemensstr.

SCHWABING

Münchner Freiheit

Hohenzollernpl.

Hohenzollernstr.

Hohenzollernstr.

Cosmopolitan

Reiter

Str.

Dachauer

Schwere

Elisabeth-

str.

Infanteriestr.

Elisabethstr.

Teng-

Kurfürsten-

Nordend-

Franz-

Str.

Friedrichstr.

Joseph

Leonrodstr.

Str.

Georgenstr.

str.

Georgenstr.

Giselastr.

Leopold-

Ohmstr.

Lothstr.

Josephspl.

Arcisstr.

Adalbertstr.

str.

Königinstr.

2

Lazarettstr.

Schleißheimer

Ziebland-

str.

Barer

Str.

Türkenstr.

Bistro Terrine

Universität

Dachauer

str.

Theresienstr.

Theresienstr.

Amalienstr.

Ludwigstr.

Maillingerstr.

✕✕ Nymphenburger

Hof

Sandstr.

Gabels-

bergerstr.

Augusten-

NEUE

PINAKOTHEK

Theresien-

str.

Nymphenburger

Str.

Gabelsbergerstr.

ALTE

PINAKOTHEK

Von der

Tann Str.

Blutenburgstr.

Brienner

Str.

Karolinen-

platz

O. von Miller

Ring

Ludwigstr.

Franz

Joseph Strauß Ring

Marsplatz

Mars-

str.

Seidlstr.

Str.

Maximilianspl.

Wein-Theatinerstr.

RESIDENZ

Arnulf-

Elisenstr.

FRAUENKIRCHE

str.

Maximilianstr.

Landsberger

Str.

Bayerstr.

Grasserstr.

Paul

HAUPT

BAHNHOF

Karlspl.

Neuhauser

Str.

Kaufinger-

str.

MARIENPL.

Thomas

Wimmer Ring

3

Schwanthalerstr.

Heyse

Schwanthalerstr.

Sonnenstr.

ASAMKIRCHE

Tal

Frauenstr.

str.

Theresienwiese

Goethestr.

Oberanger

Blumenstr.

Corneliusstr.

DEUTSCHES

MUSEUM

Bavariaring

Messegelände

THERESIEN-

WIESE

Theresienhöhe

Lindwurmstr.

Erhardtstr.

Ganghofer

0   500 m

A

Historical and Commercial

Centre (Plan II)

B

Goethepl.

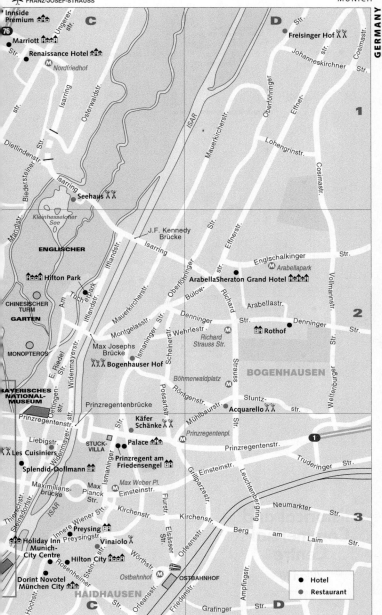

FRANZ-JOSEF-STRAUSS

Innside Premium 🏨

76

Marriott 🏨

Renaissance Hotel 🏨

Nordfriedhof

Ungererstr.

Osterwaldstr.

Isarring

Dietlindenstr.

Biedersteiner

str.

Madlstr.

Freisinger Hof ✗✗

Str.

Johanneskirchner Str.

Oberföhringer str.

Efnerstr.

D

C

Lohengrinstr.

Cosimastr.

1

ISAR

Mauerkircherstr.

Seehaus ✗✗

Kleinhesseloner See

ENGLISCHER

J.F. Kennedy Brücke

Isarring

Iflandstr.

Englschalkinger Str.

Arabellapark

ArabellaSheraton Grand Hotel 🏨

Hilton Park 🏨

CHINESISCHER TURM

GARTEN

Am Tucherpark

Iflandstr.

Mauerkirchstr.

Oberföhringer str.

Bülowstr.

Richard

Arabellastr.

Denninger Str.

Denninger Str.

Rothof 🏨

Vollmannstr.

2

MONOPTEROS

E. Riedel Str.

Widenmayerstr.

Montgelasstr.

Ismaninger Str.

Scheinerstr.

Wehrlestr.

Richard Strauss Str.

Strauss

BOGENHAUSEN

Welfenburger

Max Josephs Brücke

Bogenhauser Hof ✗✗✗

Böhmerwaldplatz

Stuntz-str.

BAYERISCHES NATIONAL-MUSEUM

Oettingenstr.

Prinzregentenstr.

Prinzregentenbrücke

Possartstr.

Röntgenstr.

Mühlbaurstr.

Acquarello ✗✗

Prinzregentenpl.

1

Liebigstr.

Les Cuisiniers ✗✗

Splendid-Dollmann 🏨

STUCK-VILLA

Ismaninger Str.

Käfer Schänke ✗✗

Palace 🏨

Prinzregent am Friedensengel 🏨

Prinzregentenstr.

Truderinger Str.

Widenmayerstr.

Maximilians-brücke

Max Planck Str.

Max Weber Pl.

Einsteinstr.

Grillparzerstr.

Einsteinstr.

Leuchtenbergring

Neumarkter Str.

3

Thierschstr.

Steinsdorfstr.

ISAR

Innere Wiener Str.

Preysing 🏨

Preysingstr.

Kirchenstr.

Flurstr.

Kirchenstr.

Berg

am

Laim

Str.

Holiday Inn Munich-City Centre 🏨

Vinaiolo ✗

Stein str.

Wörthstr.

Elsässer Str.

Orleanstr.

Hilton City 🏨

Rosenheimer

Dorint Novotel München City 🏨

Hochstr.

Ostbahnhof

OSTBAHNHOF

Ampfingstr.

HAIDHAUSEN

Orleanstr.

Friedenstr.

Grafinger Str.

Grafinger Str.

C

D

●	Hotel
●	Restaurant

Stiglmaierplatz
Nymphenburger Str.

E

GALERIE IM LENBACHHAUS

GLYPTOTHEK

U
Luisenstr.
Arcisstr.

F
Gabelsbergerstr.

PINAKOTHEK DER MODERNE

Brienner Str.

Augustenstr.

Königsplatz
Königspl.

PROPYLÄEN

Barer Str.

Brienner Str.

Karolinenpl.

● Hotel
● Restaurant

Karl- str.
Seidlstr.
Dachauer Str.

1

ANTIKENSAMMLUNGEN

Luisenstr.

Meiserstr.

Karl- str.

Max Joseph Str.
Otto-
Str.

Mars- str.
Seidlstr.

Dachauer Str.

ⓜ King's Hotel Center

Hirtenstr.

Elisenstr.

Sophien- str.

Arcostr.

Barer str.
Otto-

╳╳ Hunsinger's Pacific

Maximilianspl.

Lenbach ╳╳

Arnulfstr.

HAUPTBAHNHOF

Prielmayerstr.

Bahnhofpl.

Elisenstr.

Lenbachpl.

Maxburg- str.

Pacellistr.

Kapellen- str.

DEUTSCHES JAGD-UND FISCHEREIMUSEUM

● Meier ⌂

Königshof ⌂⌂⌂

Karlsplatz
Karlspl.

Wilhelm

ⓜ
ℹ
Hauptbahnhof

Schützenstr.
●Excelsior
Bayer- str.
⌂ Anna

str.

Neuhauser Str.

MICHAELS- KIRCHE

2

Le Méridien ⌂⌂⌂
● Drei Löwen ⌂⌂
ⓜ Maritim

Schillerstr.

Adolf Kolping Str.

Sonnenstr.
Sonnenstr.

Herzog Wilhelm

Herzog

Augustiner Gaststätten ╳

Dorint Sofitel Bayerpost ⌂⌂⌂
Paul Heyse str.
Mittererstr.
Goethestr.

Senefelderstr.

Präsident ⌂

Schwanthalerstr.

Herzogspitalstr.

╳╳ Weinhaus Neuner

Damenstiftstr.

● Apollo
Schwanthalerstr.

Landwehrstr.

Mathildenstr.

Josephspitalstr.

Kreuzstr.

Stadthotel Asam ⌂⌂

ASAMKIRCHE

● Atrium ⌂⌂

Pettenkoferstr.
Uhlandstr.
Lessingstr.
Goethe- str.
Schiller- str.

Pettenkofer- str.

Exquisit ⌂⌂

Sendlinger Tor Pl.
ⓜ Sendlinger Tor

Oberanger

3

Nußbaum- str.

Ziemsensstr.

Lindwurmstr.

Riegenstr.
Str.

Blumenstr.

Historical and Commercial Centre *(Plan II)*

Kaiser-Ludwigs-Pl.

0   200 m

E

Reisingerstr.
Malstr.
Frauenlobstr.
Lindwurmstr.
Thalkirchner Str.
Pestalozzistr.
Holzstr.
Müllerstr.

F

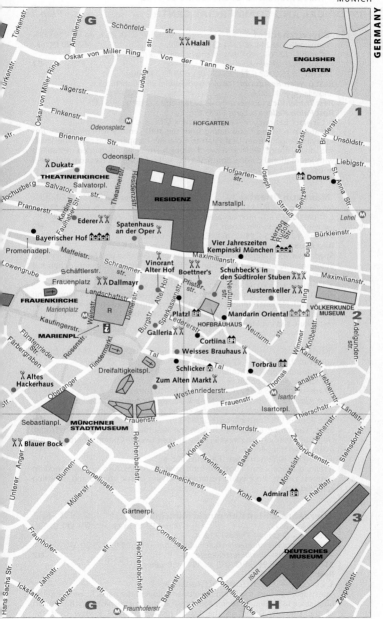

Bayerischer Hof 🛜 🕭 🕅 🔲 ♿ 🅰 ↝rm 📺 🕻 🕍850
Promenadeplatz 2 ✉ *80333* – 🅜 *Marienplatz* 🛏 ⓥⓘⓢⓐ ⓜⓒ ⓐⓔ ⓞ
– 🖉 (089) 2 12 00 – info@bayerischerhof.de – Fax (089) 2 12 09 06
– www.bayerischerhof.de **G2**
395 rm – ♦183/383 € ♦♦290/430 €, ⌷ 23 € – 17 suites
Rest *Garden-Restaurant* (booking advisable) 36 € (lunch)/65 €
and a la carte 41/60 €
Rest *Trader Vic's* (dinner only) 44 €/75 € and a la carte 29/51 €
Rest *Palais Keller* a la carte 17/35 €
♦ Grand Luxury ♦ Traditional ♦ Classic ♦
Privately run Grand Hotel dating from the 19th century with elegant rooms
in styles ranging from Graf Pilati to Colonial. Pamper yourself in the lavish
spa on 3 floors, with a view of Munich. An elegant garden restaurant
with international cuisine. South Sea flair in Trader Vic's. A Bavarian style beer
house.

Mandarin Oriental ⛲ (heated) 🕅 ⅏rest 🕍50
Neuturmstr. 1 ✉ *80331* – 🅜 *Isartor* 🛏 ⓥⓘⓢⓐ ⓜⓒ ⓐⓔ ⓞ
❀ *– 🖉 (089) 29 09 80 – momuc-reservations@mohg.com – Fax (089) 22 25 39*
– www.mandarinoriental.com **H2**
73 rm – ♦305/575 € ♦♦355/645 €, ⌷ 27 € – 6 suites
Rest *Mark's* (closed Sunday - Monday) a la carte 53/71 €
Spec. Salat von Langostinos mit mediterranem Gemüse und Pestovinaigrette.
Steinbutt mit weißem Pfirsich und Pfifferlingen. Ingwerschaumtörtchen mit
Champagnereis.
♦ Palace ♦ Grand Luxury ♦ Modern ♦
This historic palace is now a luxurious hotel providing excellent service and
rooms with elegant interiors. Also features roof-top terrace and swimming pool.
A marble stairway leads the guest up from the lobby to the first floor of this
restaurant, serving Mediterranean cuisine.

Königshof 🕭 🕅 ⅏ ↝rm ⅏rest 📺 🕻 🕍80 🛏 ⓥⓘⓢⓐ ⓜⓒ ⓐⓔ ⓞ
Karlsplatz 25 ✉ *80335* – 🅜 *Karlsplatz (Stachus)* – 🖉 *(089) 55 13 60*
❀ *– koenigshof@geisel-privathotels.de – Fax (089) 55 13 61 13*
– www.geisel-privathotels.de **F2**
87 rm – ♦220/345 € ♦♦270/430 €, ⌷ 21 € – 10 suites
Rest (closed 1 - 17 January, 14 - 17 April, 30 July - 29 August and Sunday -
Monday, Bank Holidays, October - December only Sunday) (booking advisable)
42 € (lunch)/118 € and a la carte 52/84 € 🏵
Spec. Lauwarme Kalbskopfscheiben mit Krautfleckerl und Périgord Trüffel.
Gegrillter Steinbutt mit zweierlei Artischocken. Geeiste Champagnerpraline mit
marinierten Himbeeren.
♦ Luxury ♦ Traditional ♦ Classic ♦
A refined atmosphere in both the lobby and the rooms. Also available: modern
business rooms. An elegant restaurant serving classic cuisine and affording
splendid views.

Vier Jahreszeiten Kempinski München 🕅 🔲 🕅 ↝rm
Maximilianstr. 17 ⅏rest 📺 🕻 🕍230 🛏 ⓥⓘⓢⓐ ⓜⓒ ⓐⓔ ⓞ
✉ *80539* – 🅜 *Lehel* – 🖉 *(089) 2 12 50*
– reservations.vierjahreszeiten@kempinski.com – Fax (089) 21 25 20 00
– www.kempinski-vierjahreszeiten.de **H2**
316 rm – ♦230 € ♦♦230/370 €, ⌷ 29 € – 50 suites
Rest a la carte 39/53 €
♦ Luxury ♦ Traditional ♦ Classic ♦
Guests from all over the world have been enjoying the panache of this grand
hotel since 1858. Elegant rooms combine the charm of the past with the comfort
of the present. Diners in the bistro restaurant have a view over the
Maximilianstrasse.

GERMANY

Dorint Sofitel Bayerpost 〔🛏 ♨ 📺 ⴲ 📠 ⱳrm ♨rest 📶 🛗 450 🚗 VISA ◉◎ AE ①

Bayerstr. 12 ✉ 80335 – Ⓜ Hauptbahnhof
– ℰ (089) 59 94 80 – h5413@accor.com – Fax (089) 5 99 48 10 00
– www.sofitel.com   E2
396 rm ⌿ – †230/425 € ††275/470 € – 26 suites
Rest a la carte 34/45 €
♦ Chain hotel ♦ Luxury ♦ Design ♦
Behind the sandstone façade is a modern hotel, featuring avant-garde design throughout - dark colours and muted light. Close to the main railway station.

Le Méridien 〔♨ ◎ 〔🛏 ♨ 📺 📠 ⱳrm 📶 🛗 160 🚗 VISA ◉◎ AE

Bayerstr. 41 ✉ 80335 – Ⓜ Hauptbahnhof – ℰ (089) 2 42 20 – info.muenchen@
lemeridien.com – Fax (089) 24 22 11 11 – www.munich.lemeridien.com
381 rm – †155/435 € ††155/435 €, ⌿ 21 € – 8 suites   E2
Rest a la carte 32/44 €
♦ Chain hotel ♦ Luxury ♦ Design ♦
Simple elegance is evident throughout - clean lines and exquisite materials. Lovely views from the restaurant of the pretty, plant-filled courtyard.

Hilton Park ♨ 📺 ⴲ 📠 ⱳrm 📶 ☎ 🛗 690 🚗 VISA ◉◎ AE ①

Am Tucherpark 7 ✉ 80538 – ℰ (089) 3 84 50 – info.munich@hilton.com
– Fax (089) 38 45 25 88 – www.hilton.de   Plan I **C2**
479 rm – †169/259 € ††199/284 €, ⌿ 25 € – 3 suites
Rest a la carte 23/33 €
Rest *Tivoli & Club* a la carte 29/45 €
♦ Chain hotel ♦ Luxury ♦ Modern ♦
This hotel offers an attractive location at the English Garden and provides contemporary, well-equipped rooms. Business and executive rooms also available. The bistro-style main restaurant offers international cuisine and a buffet.

Excelsior 🎇 ⱳrm 📶 🛗 25 🚗 VISA ◉◎ AE ①

Schützenstr. 11 ✉ 80335 – Ⓜ Hauptbahnhof – ℰ (089) 55 13 70
– excelsior@geisel-privathotels.de – Fax (089) 55 13 71 21
– www.geisel-privathotels.de   E2
114 rm – †155/250 € ††200/250 €, ⌿ 17 €
Rest *Geisel's Vinothek* *(closed Sunday lunch)* a la carte 27/36 €
♦ Business ♦ Classic ♦
Perhaps the elegant yet rustic ambience of the foyer and the rooms explain the feeling that, amid the pulsing life of the city centre, you are in a quiet country house. Rustic, country wine cellars with painted cross-vaults.

Maritim 🎇 ♨ 📺 📠 ⱳrm 📶 🛗 250 🚗 VISA ◉◎ AE ①

Goethestr. 7 ✉ 80336 – Ⓜ Hauptbahnhof – ℰ (089) 55 23 50
– info.mun@maritim.de – Fax (089) 55 23 59 01 – www.maritim.de   E2
339 rm – †157/265 € ††181/289 €, ⌿ 19 € – 6 suites
Rest a la carte 24/36 €
♦ Business ♦ Functional ♦
Enjoy pleasant comfort in the tastefully elegant rooms in this hotel, which is close to the Deutsches Theater, the "Stachus" and the "Theresienwiese". The grill-room and bistro restaurants serve international cuisine.

Exquisit without rest ♨ ⴲ ⱳ 🛗 25 🚗 VISA ◉◎ AE ①

Pettenkoferstr. 3 ✉ 80336 – Ⓜ Sendlinger Tor – ℰ (089) 5 51 99 00 – info@
hotel-exquisit.com – Fax (089) 55 19 94 99 – www.hotel-exquisit.com   F3
50 rm ⌿ – †129/210 € ††170/250 € – 5 suites
♦ Business ♦ Classic ♦
Not far from the Sendlinger gate, this hotel provides stylish mahogany furnished rooms. Fine, comfortable suites also available.

GERMANY

Anna
       🏧 ↔rm 🖭 📞 🥢 *VISA* 🐵 🖭 ①
Schützenstr. 1 ⊠ 80335 – ⓜ Karlsplatz (Stachus) – ℰ (089) 59 99 40 – anna@
geisel-privathotels.de – Fax (089) 59 99 43 33 – www.geisel-privathotel.de
73 rm � – **†**165/250 € **††**185/300 €   **F2**
Rest 27 € (dinner) and a la carte 26/32 €
♦ Business ♦ Modern ♦
In the old part of Munich, directly next to the Stachus. Attractive hotel with a
modern design, cheerful colours and state of the art technical equipment.
Contemporary bistro-like restaurant with a sushi bar.

Platzl
      🍴 🕏 🛝 🛋 ↔rm 🖭 🛅70 🥢 *VISA* 🐵 🖭 ①
Sparkassenstr. 10 ⊠ 80331 – ⓜ Marienplatz – ℰ (089) 23 70 30 – info@platzl.de
– Fax (089) 23 70 38 00 – www.platzl.de   **G2**
167 rm ⊻ – **†**97/159 € **††**161/245 €
Rest *Pfistermühle* (closed Sunday) a la carte 27/40 €
Rest *Ayingers* a la carte 18/29 €
♦ Traditional ♦ Cosy ♦
Rooms in traditional Bavarian style in the centre of the historic Old Town. Some
quiet rooms facing the courtyard. A recreation area in the style of King Ludwig II's
"Moorish Kiosk". Old Munich flair under the vaults of the Pfistermühle. Ayingers:
tasteful tavern style.

Drei Löwen without rest
     ↔ 🖭 🛅15 *VISA* 🐵 🖭 ①
Schillerstr. 8 ⊠ 80336 – ⓜ Hauptbahnhof – ℰ (089) 55 10 40 – info@
hotel3loewen.de – Fax (089) 55 10 49 05 – www.hotel3loewen.de   **E2**
97 rm ⊻ – **†**116/195 € **††**149/223 € – 3 suites
♦ Business ♦ Classic ♦
In the city centre, close to the station, a congenial place to stay. The modern
rooms are fitted with stylish wooden furniture.

Stadthotel Asam without rest
    🛋 ↔ 🖭 📞 🥢 *VISA* 🐵 🖭 ①
Josephspitalstr. 3 ⊠ 80331 – ⓜ Sendlinger Tor – ℰ (089) 2 30 97 00
– info@hotel-asam.de – Fax (089) 23 09 70 97 – www.hotel-asam.de
closed Christmas   **F2**
25 rm – **†**129/145 € **††**158/174 €, ⊻ 14 € – 8 suites
♦ Business ♦ Personalised ♦
A small hotel with a touch of luxury in the City Centre. The rooms are stylish and
tasteful with very carefully chosen details.

Cortiina without rest
     🏧 ↔ 🖭 🥢 *VISA* 🐵 🖭 ①
Ledererstr. 8 ⊠ 80331 – ⓜ Isartor – ℰ (089) 2 42 24 90 – info@cortiina.com
– Fax (089) 2 42 24 91 00 – www.cortiina.com   **H2**
35 rm ⊻ – **†**126/176 € **††**186 €
♦ Business ♦ Modern ♦
The rooms all have a modern style with clean lines and parquet floors. State of the
art technical equipment. Nice bar with a small menu.

Torbräu
      🍴 🏧rm ↔rm 🖭 🛅30 🥢 🄿 *VISA* 🐵 🖭
Tal 41 ⊠ 80331 – ⓜ Isartor – ℰ (089) 24 23 40 – info@torbraeu.de
– Fax (089) 24 23 42 35 – www.torbraeu.de   **H2**
92 rm ⊻ – **†**138/220 € **††**175/290 € – 3 suites
Rest *La Famiglia*, ℰ (089) 22 80 75 23 – a la carte 34/44 €
♦ Traditional ♦ Classic ♦
Built in the 15C, this hotel must be the oldest in the city. Pleasant spacious rooms,
all with air conditioning. Tuscan flair and Italian cuisine in the terracotta-tiled
"La Famiglia".

Admiral without rest
     ↔ 🖭 📞 🥢 *VISA* 🐵 🖭 ①
Kohlstr. 9 ⊠ 80469 – ⓜ Isartor – ℰ (089) 21 63 50 – info@hotel-admiral.de
– Fax (089) 29 36 74 – www.hotel-admiral.de   **H3**
33 rm ⊻ – **†**160 € **††**190 €
♦ Business ♦ Functional ♦
Just a few minutes by foot from the City Centre this hotel has functional rooms,
some of which are extremely quiet. In fine weather you can enjoy breakfast in the
small garden.

King's Hotel Center without rest   ᕳ ⇆ 𝗩𝗜𝗦𝗔 ⓪⓪ 𝗔𝗘 ⓪
Marsstr. 15 ✉ *80335 – ℰ (089) 51 55 30 – center@kingshotels.de*
– Fax (089) 51 55 33 00 – www.kingshotels.de   **E1**
90 rm – ♥99 € ♥♥125 €, ⴾ 12 €
♦ Business ♦ Classic ♦
Centrally located hotel with inviting wooden lobby and comfortable rooms with
four-poster beds.

Atrium without rest   𝕣 ⇆ 🖭 ㎟20 ⇔ 𝗩𝗜𝗦𝗔 ⓪⓪
Landwehrstr. 59 ✉ *80336 –* Ⓜ *Theresienwiese – ℰ (089) 51 41 90*
– info@atrium-hotel.de – Fax (089) 53 50 66 – www.atrium-hotel.de   **E2**
162 rm ⴾ – ♥109/129 € ♥♥139/175 €
♦ Business ♦ Functional ♦
Marble and mirrors predominate in the foyer of this modern hotel. The rooms are
furnished in natural wood with modern technical facilities. Small, pretty
courtyard with lots of plants.

Splendid-Dollmann without rest   🖭 𝗩𝗜𝗦𝗔 ⓪⓪ 𝗔𝗘 ⓪
Thierschstr. 49 ✉ *80538 –* Ⓜ *Lehel – ℰ (089) 23 80 80 – splendid-muc@*
t-online.de – Fax (089) 23 80 83 65 – www.hotel-splendid-dollmann.de
36 rm – ♥120/150 € ♥♥150/190 €, ⴾ 11 €   *Plan I* **C3**
♦ Traditional ♦ Personalised ♦
A 19C middle-class house with a stylish lobby, presented as a library; individually
decorated rooms, some with antiques, and a pretty breakfast room with arched
ceiling.

Domus   ⇆ ⇔ 𝗩𝗜𝗦𝗔 ⓪⓪
St-Anna-Str.31 ✉ *80538 –* Ⓜ *Lehel – ℰ (089) 2 17 77 30 – reservation@*
domus-hotel.de – Fax (089) 2 28 53 59 – www.domus-hotel.de
closed Christmas   **H1**
45 rm ⴾ – ♥105/140 € ♥♥130/165 €
Rest *facile (closed Saturday lunch - Sunday and Bank Holidays)* 15 € (lunch)/
34 € and a la carte 27/34 €
♦ Business ♦ Functional ♦
Embedded between the Maximilianstrasse and Prinzregentenstrasse, this tastefully furnished establishment is ideal as a base from which to explore the town's
art, culture and shopping. Modern atmosphere and Italian cuisine served.

Apollo without rest   ⇆ 🖭 ⇔ 𝗣 𝗩𝗜𝗦𝗔 ⓪⓪ 𝗔𝗘 ⓪
Mittererstr. 7 ✉ *80336 –* Ⓜ *Hauptbahnhof – ℰ (089) 53 99 31*
– info@apollohotel.de – Fax (089) 53 40 33 – www.apollohotel.de   **E2**
74 rm ⴾ – ♥89 € ♥♥99 €
♦ Business ♦ Classic ♦
This hotel situated in the centre of town offers spacious, comfortable rooms with
mahogany furniture; some of the rooms overlook the quiet back courtyard."

Präsident without rest   ⇆ 🖭 ㎟15 𝗩𝗜𝗦𝗔 ⓪⓪ 𝗔𝗘 ⓪
Schwanthalerstr. 20 ✉ *80336 –* Ⓜ *Hauptbahnhof – ℰ (089) 5 49 00 60*
– hotel.praesident@t-online.de – Fax (089) 54 90 06 28
– www.hotel-praesident.de   **E2**
42 rm ⴾ – ♥79/151 € ♥♥95/181 €
♦ Business ♦ Functional ♦
The location of this fairly central hotel is ideal for theatre-goers and is diagonally
opposite the Deutsche Theater. Contemporary rooms with light-coloured
wooden furniture.

Schlicker without rest   🖭 ℂⁿ 𝗣 𝗩𝗜𝗦𝗔 ⓪⓪ 𝗔𝗘 ⓪
Tal 8 ✉ *80331 –* Ⓜ *Isartor – ℰ (089) 2 42 88 70 – info@hotel-schlicker.de*
– Fax (089) 29 60 59 – www.hotel-schlicker.de
closed 23 December - 7 January   **G2**
68 rm ⴾ – ♥85/115 € ♥♥115/200 €
♦ Family ♦ Classic ♦
Building in the Old Town dating from the 16th century; in sight of the Town Hall
with its world-famous Glockenspiel (carillon). Contemporary hotel with
individually furnished rooms.

Meier without rest   ⇔ VISA ⚫ AE ①
Schützenstr. 12 ⌧ *80335 –* ⓜ *Hauptbahnhof –* ℰ *(089) 5 49 03 40*
– info@hotel-meier.de – Fax (089) 5 49 03 43 40 – www.hotel-meier.de
closed 23 - 27 December   **E2**
50 rm ⌂ – †75/88 € ††95/116 €
♦ Business ♦ Functional ♦
At the end of the 1990s the Etagenhotel was renovated and it now offers its
visitors uniform, functional rooms.

Schuhbeck's in den Südtiroler Stuben   ⇔60 VISA ⚫ AE
Platzl 6 ⌧ *80331 –* ⓜ *Isartor –* ℰ *(089) 2 16 69 00 – info@schuhbeck.de*
– Fax (089) 21 66 90 25 – www.schubeck.de
closed 2 weeks early January and Sunday - Monday lunch, Bank Holidays
Rest 58 € (lunch)/88 €   **H2**
Spec. Salat von der bayerischen Ente mit geschmortem Spitzkraut. Saibling mit
Rahmfrisée auf geröstetem Schwarzbrot. Schubecks Eisvariationen.
♦ Contemporary ♦ Rustic ♦
Rustic and elegant atmosphere in this restaurant serving gourmet regional
cuisine. Also features a spice shop and cooking school.

G   ⇧ AC VISA ⚫ AE
Geyerstr. 52 (by Lindwurmstr. A 3 and Kapuzinerstr.) ⌧ *80469*
– ℰ *(089) 74 74 79 99 – info@g-munich.de – Fax (089) 74 74 79 29*
– www.g-munich.de – closed Sunday - Monday
Rest (dinner only) (booking advisable) a la carte 52/72 €
♦ Modern ♦ Fashionable ♦
The style is modern and minimalist, the cuisine has a creative Mediterranean flair.
Stylish lounge with elegant leather seats.

Blauer Bock   AE
Sebastiansplatz 9 ⌧ *80331 –* ⓜ *Marienplatz –* ℰ *(089) 45 22 23 33*
– mail@restaurant-blauerbock.de – Fax (089) 45 22 23 30
– www.restaurant-blauerbock.de
closed 1 - 10 January and Saturday - Sunday lunch, Bank Holidays   **G3**
Rest 49 € (dinner)/57 € and a la carte 49/58 €
♦ International ♦ Minimalist ♦
Just a few steps from the Viktualienmarkt is this modern restaurant. The
ambience is simple, with warm tones. International cuisine with French roots.

Boettner's   ⇧ AC VISA ⚫ AE ①
Pfisterstr. 9 ⌧ *80331 –* ⓜ *Marienplatz –* ℰ *(089) 22 12 10 – Fax (089) 29 16 20 24*
closed Sunday and Bank Holidays   **H2**
Rest (booking advisable) 32 € (lunch)/78 € and a la carte 35/75 €
Rest *Boettner's Atrium* a la carte 22/31 €
♦ French ♦ Rustic ♦
The "Boettner" institution is in the Orlando block. Dine in rooms with an elegant
classic interior and some old dark wood panelling. Classic cuisine.

Halali   VISA ⚫ AE
Schönfeldstr. 22 ⌧ *80539 –* ⓜ *Odeonsplatz –* ℰ *(089) 28 59 09*
– halali-muenchen@t-online.de – Fax (089) 28 27 86
closed 3 weeks August and Saturday lunch, Sunday, Bank Holidays   **H1**
Rest (booking advisable) 22 € (lunch)/50 € and a la carte 34/45 €
♦ International ♦ Cosy ♦
19C former guesthouse, now a wood-panelled restaurant decorated with
flowers and tasteful, rustic furnishings.

Ederer   ⇧ AC ⇔10 VISA ⚫ AE
Kardinal-Faulhaber-Str. 10 ⌧ *80333 –* ⓜ *Odeonsplatz –* ℰ *(089) 24 23 13 10*
– restaurant-ederer@t-online.de – Fax (089) 24 23 13 12
– www.restaurant-ederer.de
closed 1 week Christmas and Sunday, Bank Holidays   **G2**
Rest (booking advisable) 22 € (lunch) and a la carte 35/62 € ⌘
♦ Contemporary ♦ Fashionable ♦
A chic location for this restaurant with modern, stylish atmosphere. International
cuisine. Nice inner courtyard dining.

GERMANY

XX **Hunsinger's Pacific** ⌖ 🅰 ⇌25 𝗩𝗜𝗦𝗔 ⓐ 🅰🅴 ⓪
Maximiliansplatz 5 (entrance Max-Joseph-Straße) ✉ *80333*
– ✆ (089) 55 02 97 41 – Fax (089) 55 02 97 42
closed Sunday   **F1**
Rest a la carte 30/46 €
♦ International ♦ Friendly ♦
Werner Hunsinger brings the Pacific to the former "Aubergine", its four walls with the airy trompe l'oeil paintings and chandeliers. International with a touch of Asia!

XX **Austernkeller** 𝗩𝗜𝗦𝗔 ⓐ 🅰🅴 ⓪
Stollbergstr. 11 ✉ *80539 –* Ⓜ *Isartor – ✆ (089) 29 87 87 – Fax (089) 22 31 66*
– www.austernkeller.de   **H2**
Rest (dinner only) (booking advisable) a la carte 29/45 €
♦ Seafood ♦ Cosy ♦
If your taste is for crustaceans and freshly-caught fruits de mer, try this listed cellar vault decorated with porcelain plates.

XX **Dallmayr** 🅰 ↵ 𝗩𝗜𝗦𝗔 ⓐ 🅰🅴
Dienerstr. 14 (1st floor) ✉ *80331 –* Ⓜ *Marienplatz – ✆ (089) 2 13 51 00*
– gastro@dallmayr.de – Fax (089) 2 13 54 43 – www.dallmayr.de
closed Monday - Wednesday from 7 pm, Thursday - Friday from 8 pm, Saturday
from 4 pm, Sunday and Bank Holidays   **G2**
Rest 33 €/48 € and a la carte 38/55 €
♦ Contemporary ♦ Friendly ♦
The restaurant run by the well-known delicatessen which has in the past supplied crowned heads has made the freshness and naturalness of its products into a philosophy.

XX **Nymphenburger Hof** ⌖ �"' 𝗩𝗜𝗦𝗔 ⓐ 🅰🅴
Nymphenburger Str. 24 ✉ *80335 –* Ⓜ *Maillingerstr. – ✆ (089) 1 23 38 30*
– Fax (089) 1 23 38 52 – www.nymphenburgerhof.de
closed 24 December - 10 January and Saturday lunch, Sunday, Bank Holidays
Rest (booking advisable) 18 € (lunch)/55 € and a la carte 31/46 €   *Plan I* **A2**
♦ International ♦ Friendly ♦
Bright, informal restaurant with lots of flowers and a lovely terrace in front of the building. Cuisine is international with Austrian highlights.

XX **Lenbach** ⌖ 𝗩𝗜𝗦𝗔 ⓐ 🅰🅴 ⓪
Ottostr. 6 ✉ *80333 –* Ⓜ *Karlsplatz (Stachus) – ✆ (089) 5 49 13 00*
– info@lenbach.de – Fax (089) 54 91 30 75 – www.lenbach.de
closed Sunday and Bank Holidays   **F1**
Rest 26 € (lunch)/64 € and a la carte 31/46 €
♦ Modern ♦ Trendy ♦
Designer Sir Terence Conran was responsible for the décor in the Lenbach palace. Fashionable large-scale gastronomy is the theme, featuring a sushi bar and modern restaurant.

XX **Galleria** 🅰 𝗩𝗜𝗦𝗔 ⓐ 🅰🅴 ⓪
Sparkassenstr. 11 (corner of Ledererstraße) ✉ *80331 –* Ⓜ *Marienplatz*
– ✆ (089) 29 79 95 – ristorantegalleria@yahoo.de – Fax (089) 2 91 36 53
– www.geocities.com/ristorantegalleria
closed Sunday, except during exhibitions and December   **G2**
Rest (booking advisable) a la carte 38/45 €
♦ Italian ♦ Cosy ♦
A small, cosy restaurant in the inner city with Italian cuisine. Temporary art displays in the dining area.

XX **Weinhaus Neuner** 𝗩𝗜𝗦𝗔 ⓐ 🅰🅴
Herzogspitalstr. 8 ✉ *80331 –* Ⓜ *Karlsplatz (Stachus) – ✆ (089) 2 60 39 54*
– weinhaus-neuner@t-online.de – Fax (089) 26 69 33
– www.weinhaus-neuner.de
closed Sunday and Bank Holidays   **F2**
Rest a la carte 25/33 €
♦ International ♦ Rustic ♦
As the "oldest wine bar" in Munich, this building dating back to 1852 stands out with its cross-shaped vaults and lovely wall paintings. International cuisine.

GERMANY

XX
(☺)

Les Cuisiniers

🛋 *VISA* ⓿ ⒶⒺ ⓿

Reitmorstr. 21 ✉ 80538 – Ⓜ Lehel – ℰ (089) 23 70 98 90 – Fax (089) 23 70 98 91
– www.lescuisiniers.de
closed Saturday lunch and Sunday　　　　　　　　　　　　　　Plan I **C3**
Rest a la carte 26/36 €
◆ Mediterranean ◆ Bistro ◆
Light and friendly décor in this bistro-style restaurant - modern pictures adorn
the walls. An uncomplicated Mediterranean menu.

X

Vinorant Alter Hof

🛋 *VISA* ⓿

Alter Hof 3 ✉ 80331 – Ⓜ Marienplatz – ℰ (089) 24 24 37 33
– mail@alter-hof-muenchen.de – Fax (089) 24 24 37 34
– www.alter-hof-muenchen.de　　　　　　　　　　　　　　　　**G2**
Rest a la carte 19/31 €
◆ Regional ◆ Rustic ◆
At the former Wittelsbach residence, one of the oldest buildings in Munich,
guests dine in two halls with attractive vaulted ceilings and simple modern
decoration. Downstairs there are wine cellars and a bar.

X
(☺)

Dukatz

🛋

Salvatorplatz 1 ✉ 80333 – Ⓜ Odeonsplatz – ℰ (089) 2 91 96 00
– info@dukatz.de – Fax (089) 29 19 60 28 – www.dukatz.de
closed Sunday dinner　　　　　　　　　　　　　　　　　　　　**G1**
Rest (booking advisable) a la carte 27/37 €
◆ International ◆ Fashionable ◆
At the Literaturhaus, a former market hall dating from 1870, international cuisine
is served on two levels beneath a fine cross-vault.

X

Zum Alten Markt

🛋

Dreifaltigkeitsplatz 3 ✉ 80331 – Ⓜ Marienplatz – ℰ (089) 29 99 95
– lehner.gastro@zumaltenmarkt.de – Fax (089) 2 28 50 76
– www.zumaltenmarkt.de
closed Sunday and Bank Holidays　　　　　　　　　　　　　　**G2**
Rest (booking essential for dinner) a la carte 22/34 €
◆ Regional ◆ Inn ◆
With lavish wood panelling in the style of a South Tyrolean councillor's parlour,
part of which is authentic and over 400 years old, this establishment on the
Viktualienmarkt is very cosy.

X

Spatenhaus an der Oper

🛋 *VISA* ⓿ ⒶⒺ

Residenzstr. 12 ✉ 80333 – Ⓜ Marienplatz – ℰ (089) 2 90 70 60
– spatenhaus@kuffler.de – Fax (089) 2 91 30 54 – www.kuffler.de　　**G2**
Rest a la carte 22/38 €
◆ Bavarian specialities ◆ Cosy ◆
This town house, more than 100 years old, has a variety of pleasant rooms on the
first floor. The ground floor is in a similar Alpine style.

X

Weisses Brauhaus

🛋 ⟷30 *VISA* ⓿

Tal 7 ✉ 80333 – Ⓜ Isartor – ℰ (089) 2 90 13 80 – info@weisses-brauhaus.de
– Fax (089) 29 01 38 15 – www.weisses-brauhaus.de　　　　　　**G2**
Rest a la carte 16/32 €
◆ Bavarian specialities ◆ Inn ◆
This house in the Old Town, built around 1900, has a fine façade and cosy
furnishings. The restaurant serves authentic regional specialities.

X

Augustiner Gaststätten

🛋 *VISA* ⓿ ⒶⒺ ⓿

Neuhauser Str. 27 ✉ 80331 – Ⓜ Karlsplatz (Stachus) – ℰ (089) 23 18 32 57
– augustinerstammhaus@yahoo.de – Fax (089) 2 60 53 79
– www.augustiner-restaurant.com　　　　　　　　　　　　　　**F2**
Rest a la carte 15/26 €
◆ Bavarian specialities ◆ Inn ◆
Until 1885, beer was still brewed in the Augustinians' "headquarters" on the
Neuhauser Strasse. An arcaded garden and a "Muschelsaal" are among the
monuments of Munich's Art Nouveau period. Lovely beer garden.

GERMANY

Altes Hackerhaus ☐ VISA ◯◯ AE ◯

Sendlinger Str. 14 ☒ 80331 – **◯** *Marienplatz*
– ℰ (089) 2 60 50 26 – hackerhaus@aol.com – Fax (089) 2 60 50 27
– www.hackerhaus.de **G2**
Rest a la carte 12/43 €
♦ Bavarian specialities ♦ Inn ♦
The lovingly decorated rooms of this inn are really cosy with their rustic panelling
and sturdy seating. Extremely pretty inner courtyard terrace. Good home
cooking.

ENVIRONS *Plan I*

ArabellaSheraton Grand Hotel ← ◯ *ᴌᴙ* ஓ ☐ ⅄ AK ⅄rm

Arabellastr. 6 ☒ 81925 – **◯** ⅄rest 🖾 *ᴌ*650 ஸ VISA ◯◯ AE ◯
Arabellapark – ℰ (089) 9 26 40 – grandhotel.muenchen@
arabellasheraton.com – Fax (089) 92 64 86 99
– www.sheraton.com/grandmunich **D2**
643 rm – ♦355 € ♦♦380 €, ☐ 21 € – 28 suites
Rest *(closed Sunday)* (lunch only) 26 € and a la carte 28/34 €
Rest *Die Ente vom Lehel (closed 1 August - 6 September and Sunday, Monday)*
(dinner only) a la carte 38/48 €
Rest *Paulaner's (closed Saturday lunch, Sunday and Bank Holidays lunch)*
a la carte 19/33 €
♦ Chain hotel ♦ Grand Luxury ♦ Modern ♦
Renovated Grand Hotel with an impressive foyer and beautifully furnished
rooms. Opposite: the Arabella Park with boutiques, bistros, cinemas and a night
club. A lively atmosphere welcomes you in the elegant Ente vom Lehel, which is
open to the foyer.

Marriott *ᴌᴙ* ஓ ☐ ⅄ AK ⅄rm ⅄rest *ᴌ*300 ஸ VISA ◯◯ AE ◯

Berliner Str. 93 ☒ 80805 – **◯** *Nordfriedhof – ℰ (089) 36 00 20*
– muenchen.marriott@marriotthotels.com – Fax (089) 36 00 22 00
– www.marriott.com/mucno **C1**
348 rm – ♦135/254 € ♦♦135/254 €, ☐ 20 € – 14 suites
Rest a la carte 28/40 €
♦ Luxury ♦ Traditional ♦ Functional ♦
An establishment in the grand hotel style, with a modern conference
floor. The recently renovated rooms are comfortably decorated in floral
fabrics. An "American-style" restaurant with a lovely large buffet and a show
kitchen.

Hilton City *ᴙ ᴌᴙ* ⅄ AK ⅄rm 🖾 ℰ *ᴌ*180 ஸ VISA ◯◯ AE ◯

Rosenheimer Str. 15 ☒ 81667 – ℰ (089) 4 80 40 – info.munich@hilton.com
– Fax (089) 48 04 48 04 – www.hilton.de **C3**
480 rm – ♦115/275 € ♦♦135/295 €, ☐ 23 € – 3 suites
Rest a la carte 25/37 €
♦ Chain hotel ♦ Functional ♦
Near the cultural centre, this hotel provides functional rooms ideal for business
guests. Exclusive floor. Rustic and elegant restaurant serving regional and
international cuisine.

Palace ஓ *ᴙ* ⅄rm ℰ *ᴌ*20 ஸ VISA ◯◯ AE ◯

Trogerstr. 21 ☒ 81675 – **◯** *Prinzregentenplatz – ℰ (089) 41 97 10*
– palace@kuffler.de – Fax (089) 41 97 18 19
– www.muenchenpalace.de **C3**
74 rm – ♦155/230 € ♦♦200/280 €, ☐ 18 € – 3 suites
Rest a la carte 28/32 €
♦ Luxury ♦ Traditional ♦ Personalised ♦
Elegant building with quality furnishings: all rooms with Louis-XVI-
style furniture, some with parquet flooring. If the sun is shining, a visit
to the roof terrace or the garden will repay itself. Stylish, elegant palace
restaurant.

GERMANY

Innside Premium
🛋 ₤₅ 🕅 🔟 ⅍rm 📺 ☏ 🛁80
Mies-van-der-Rohe-Str. 10 ⊠ 80807 🅿 **VISA** ⓪ 🆎 ⓪
– 𝒞 (089) 35 40 80 – muenchen.schwabing@innside.de – Fax (089) 35 40 82 99
– www.innside.de **C1**
160 rm ⌑ – ♦151/171 € ♦♦185/205 €
Rest (closed Saturday lunch, Sunday lunch) a la carte 28/34 €
♦ Business ♦ Functional ♦
A modern building with a glass façade and contemporary design interior, with well-equipped rooms. Bistro style restaurant with interesting lighting. International cuisine served.

Renaissance Hotel
🛋 🕅 ⅍rm ☏ 🛁30 🅿 **VISA** ⓪ 🆎 ⓪
Theodor-Dombart-Str. 4 (corner of Berliner Straße) ⊠ 80805
– ⓜ Nordfriedhof – 𝒞 (089) 36 09 90 – renaissance.munich.mucbr@
renaissancehotels.com – Fax (089) 3 60 99 65 00
– www.marriott.com/mucbr **C1**
261 rm – ♦155/179 € ♦♦155/179 €, ⌑ 17 € – 40 suites
Rest a la carte 20/33 €
♦ Chain hotel ♦ Modern ♦
Close to the English Garden. Comfortable rooms and elegant suites offer a high level of quality. Relax in the "Oasis of Rest". Modern Bistro in Mediterranean colours. International cuisine with the emphasis on the Mediterranean area.

Dorint Novotel München City
🛋 ₤₅ 🕅 🔲 ⅃ 🔟 ⅍rm 📺
Hochstr. 11 ⊠ 81669 🛁120 🅿 **VISA** ⓪ 🆎 ⓪
– 𝒞 (089) 66 10 70 – h3280@accor.com – Fax (089) 66 10 79 99
– www.novotel.com **C3**
307 rm – ♦71/184 € ♦♦86/199 €, ⌑ 15 €
Rest 26 € and a la carte 25/37 €
♦ Chain hotel ♦ Modern ♦
The well-equipped rooms of this business hotel are presented in pleasant tones and with smart design, some with a lovely view of the inner city. Light, contemporary restaurant.

Holiday Inn Munich - City Centre
🔟 ⅍rm ℅rest 📺 🛁350
Hochstr. 3 ⊠ 81669 – 𝒞 (089) 4 80 30 🅿 **VISA** ⓪ 🆎 ⓪
– muchb@ichotelsgroup.com – Fax (089) 4 48 82 77
– www.holiday-inn.de **C3**
580 rm – ♦180/250 € ♦♦180/250 €, ⌑ 18 €
Rest a la carte 21/34 €
♦ Chain hotel ♦ Functional ♦
A modern hotel intended for business guests attending functions and events, with spacious and functional rooms and a 2,100 square-metre conference area. A bistro-style restaurant with rustic beer lounge.

Cosmopolitan without rest
⅍ 📺 🅿 **VISA** ⓪ 🆎 ⓪
Hohenzollernstr. 5 ⊠ 80801 – ⓜ Münchner Freiheit – 𝒞 (089) 38 38 10
– cosmo@cosmopolitan-hotel.de – Fax (089) 38 38 11 11
– www.cosmopolitan-hotel.de **B2**
71 rm ⌑ – ♦110/160 € ♦♦120/170 €
♦ Business ♦ Modern ♦
Two annexed houses in the heart of Schwabing provide modern rooms with functional furnishings and modern, technical equipment.

Prinzregent am Friedensengel without rest
🕅 ⅍ 📺 🛁35
Ismaninger Str. 42 ⊠ 81675 – ⓜ 🅿 **VISA** ⓪ 🆎 ⓪
Prinzregentenplatz – 𝒞 (089) 41 60 50 – friedensengel@prinzregent.de
– Fax (089) 41 60 54 66 – www.prinzregent.de
closed 23 December - 8 January **C3**
65 rm ⌑ – ♦145/185 € ♦♦165/215 €
♦ Traditional ♦ Cosy ♦
After a night in an Alpine natural-wood bed, breakfast can be eaten amid fine wainscoting or in the winter garden, followed by only five minutes' walk to the English Garden.

Preysing without rest

[icons] 🆔 📠 📞 ♨20 ⬛ **VISA** 🅌 🅰🅴 ⓪

Preysingstr. 1 ✉ 81667 – 𝒞 (089) 45 84 50 – info @ hotel-preysing.de
– Fax (089) 45 84 54 44 – www.hotel-preysing.de
closed 24 December - 6 January
62 rm ⬜ – **†**130/180 € **††**180/215 € – 5 suites
GERMANY **C3**
♦ Family ♦ Functional ♦
The attention to detail in these rooms furnished in modern pale wood furniture makes them comfortable and welcoming. Attractive also is the bright breakfast room with a generous buffet.

Rothof without rest

🚗 🆔 ⬛ **VISA** 🅌 🅰🅴 ⓪

Denninger Str. 114 ✉ 81925 – Ⓜ Richard-Strauss-Str. – 𝒞 (089) 9 10 09 50
– rothof @ t-online.de – Fax (089) 91 50 66 – www.hotel-rothof.de
closed 23 December - 8 January
D2
37 rm ⬜ – **†**121/141 € **††**172/192 €
♦ Family ♦ Functional ♦
The well-run hotel offers light, spacious and friendly rooms with large windows and modern facilities - some well-located rooms at the rear.

Leopold

🏡 🐾 📞 ♨20 ⬛ **P** **VISA** 🅌

Leopoldstr. 119 ✉ 80804 – Ⓜ Dietlindenstr. – 𝒞 (089) 36 04 30
– hotel-leopold @ t-online.de – Fax (089) 36 04 31 50
– www.hotel-leopold.de
closed 23 - 30 December
B1
65 rm ⬜ – **†**95/140 € **††**128/185 €
Rest a la carte 19/29 €
♦ Family ♦ Classic ♦
Hotel rich in tradition, family-run, with a wide range of rooms furnished in different styles. Ask for a room with a view of the idyllic garden.

Tantris

🏡 🆔 🍴 **P** **VISA** 🅌 🅰🅴 ⓪

Johann-Fichte-Str. 7 ✉ 80805 – Ⓜ Dietlindenstr. – 𝒞 (089) 3 61 95 90
– info @ tantris.de – Fax (089) 36 19 59 22 – www.tantris.de
closed 1 - 9 January and Sunday - Monday, Bank Holidays
B1
Rest (booking advisable) 60 € (lunch)/128 € (dinner) and a la carte 58/94 € ❀
Spec. Sautierte Langoustinen mit Corail-Gnocchi und Spinat. Marinierter Thunfisch mit Kaviarcrème. Gefüllter Schweinsfuß mit Spitzkraut und Meerrettich.
♦ French ♦ Retro ♦
This gourmet restaurant is an authentic 1970s style establishment designed by Bruno Weber, serving cuisine prepared by chef Hans Haas.

Bogenhauser Hof

🏡 ♨40 **VISA** 🅌 🅰🅴 ⓪

Ismaninger Str. 85 ✉ 81675 – 𝒞 (089) 98 55 86 – bogenhauser-hof @ t-online.de
– Fax (089) 9 81 02 21 – www.bogenhauser-hof.de
closed 24 December - 9 January, 14 - 23 April and Sunday,
Bank Holidays
C2
Rest (booking advisable) 46 €/98 € and a la carte 41/61 €
♦ International ♦ Rustic ♦
This hunting lodge dating from 1825 is a classic of Munich gastronomy. Superior classical cuisine, which can also be enjoyed in the idyllic summer garden.

Acquarello

🏡 🍴 🅌 🅰🅴

Mühlbaurstr. 36 ✉ 81677 – Ⓜ Böhmerwaldplatz – 𝒞 (089) 4 70 48 48
– info @ acquarello.com – Fax (089) 47 64 64 – www.acquarello.com
closed 1 - 4 January and Saturday lunch, Sunday,
Bank Holidays lunch
D2
Rest 29 € (lunch)/77 € and a la carte 39/65 €
Spec. Vitello Tonnato. Von Kopf bis Fuß vom Kalb. Schokoladenravioli mit Minzeis und Orangensauce.
♦ Italian ♦ Friendly ♦
An elegant restaurant serving creative Italian cuisine. Large wall paintings in subtle tones provide a Mediterranean atmosphere.

GERMANY

XX **Käfer Schänke**   45 VISA MC AE ①
Prinzregentenstr. 73 ⊠ 81675 – Ⓜ Prinzregentenplatz – ℰ (089) 4 16 82 47
– kaeferschaenke@feinkost-kaefer.de – Fax (089) 4 16 86 23
– www.feinkost-kaefer.de
closed Sunday and Bank Holidays   **C3**
Rest (booking essential) a la carte 36/62 €
♦ International ♦ Cosy ♦
The restaurant is comfortable, and the small rooms have been lovingly
decorated, from the "Cutlery Parlour" to the "Tobacco Parlour".

XX **Seehaus**   ≤ 120 P VISA MC AE
Kleinhesselohe 3 ⊠ 80802 – ℰ (089) 3 81 61 30 – seehaus@kuffler.de
– Fax (089) 34 18 03 – www.kuffler.de   **C1**
Rest a la carte 29/41 €
♦ International ♦ Inn ♦
International and local dishes are served in this idyll on the Kleinhesseloh lake.
The pretty lakeside terrace is particularly popular.

XX **Freisinger Hof** with rm   VISA MC AE ①
Oberföhringer Str. 189 ⊠ 81925 – ℰ (089) 95 23 02
– freisinger.hof@t-online.de – Fax (089) 9 57 85 16
– www.freisinger-hof.de
(additional 37 rooms by spring 2006)   **D1**
13 rm ⊇ – ♦98/115 € ♦♦130 €
Rest a la carte 27/45 €
♦ Regional ♦ Inn ♦
This inn dating from 1875 has kept its charm and character in spite of
modernisation. Rustic atmosphere and regional dishes. There are cosy country-
style rooms.

X **Acetaia**   VISA MC AE ①
Nymphenburger Str. 215 (A 2) ⊠ 80639 – ℰ (089) 13 92 90 77
– Fax (089) 13 92 90 78 – www.acetaia.de
closed Saturday lunch
Rest 46 € and a la carte 38/45 €
Spec. Pecorino-Ravioli mit Majoran und Balsamico. Seewolf mit Artischocken
und Tomaten. Schokoladen-Bavarese mit Cafégelee und Himbeeren.
♦ Italian ♦ Cosy ♦
An Italian restaurant with a cosy, elegant atmosphere and mosaic floor.
Charming terrace dining area.

X **Terrine**   VISA MC AE
Amalienstr. 89 (Amalien-Passage) ⊠ 80799 – Ⓜ Universität
– ℰ (089) 28 17 80 – Fax (089) 2 80 93 16
closed 1 - 8 January and Monday lunch, Saturday lunch, Sunday, Bank
Holidays   **B2**
Rest (booking advisable for dinner) 23 € (lunch)/49 € and a la carte
30/38 €
♦ Seasonal cuisine ♦ Bistro ♦
Authentic French bistro style restaurant decorated with Art Nouveau lamps.
Classic French menu based on market produce.

X **Vinaiolo**   VISA MC
Steinstr. 42 ⊠ 81667 – Ⓜ Ostbahnhof – ℰ (089) 48 95 03 56
– Fax (089) 48 06 80 11 – www.vinaiolo.de
closed Saturday lunch   **C3**
Rest (booking essential for dinner) 44 € and a la carte 41/46 €
♦ Italian ♦ Bistro ♦
A restaurant styled as a colonial warehouse. The wines are displayed in
cabinets from the former apothecary, which are still the originals. Italian
cuisine.

AT THE EXHIBITION CENTRE by *Prinzregentenstr. Plan I D 3*

 NH Dornach 🛋 🖙 🕉 🕭 🔞 ≠rm 🛏 🖴350 🚗 **P** **VISA** **◑◉** 🕮 **◑**
Einsteinring 20 (Industrialpark-East) ⊠ *85609 – 𝒞 (089) 9 40 09 60*
– nhmuenchendornach@nh-hotels.com – Fax (089) 9 40 09 61 00
– www.nh-hotels.com
222 rm – †69/99 € ††69/99 €, � 16 €
Rest a la carte 23/38 €
♦ Chain hotel ♦ Functional ♦
This hotel has been especially designed for business travellers, offering modern
functional rooms at a location close to the exhibition centre. This modern
restaurant opens onto the hall. Large glass façade.

 Innside Premium 🛋 🖙 🕉 🔞 rest ≠rm 🕲 🖴80 🚗
Humboldtstr. 12 (Industrialpark-West) ⊠ *85609*   **P** **VISA** **◑◉** 🕮 **◑**
– 𝒞 (089) 94 00 50 – muenchen@innside.de – Fax (089) 94 00 52 99
– www.innside.de
closed 24 December - 1 January
134 rm ⊑ – †157/177 € ††197/217 €
Rest *(closed Saturday lunch, Sunday lunch)* a la carte 21/33 €
♦ Business ♦ Modern ♦
Interestingly designed rooms with unusual features - free-standing glass
showers for instance. Be inspired by the original art works. Bistro-style restaurant
with international cuisine.

 Schreiberhof 🛋 🖙 🕉 🕭 ≠rm 🛏 🕲 🖴90 🚗 **P** **VISA** **◑◉** 🕮 **◑**
Erdinger Str. 2 ⊠ *85609 – 𝒞 (089) 90 00 60 – info@schreiberhof.de*
– Fax (089) 90 00 64 59 – www.schreiberhof.de
87 rm ⊑ – †98/156 € ††126/192 €
Rest *Alte Gaststube* 39 € and a la carte 25/39 €
♦ Family ♦ Classic ♦
Elegant and spacious, functional rooms with tasteful natural-stone baths.
The light-flooded conservatory is an unusual setting for a conference.
Good international and regional dishes are served in the comfortable Alte
Gaststube.

 Prinzregent an der Messe 🛋 🖙 🕉 ≠rm 🛏 🖴40
Riemer Str. 350 ⊠ *81829 – 𝒞 (089) 94 53 90*   🚗 **P** **VISA** **◑◉** 🕮
– messe@prinzregent.de – Fax (089) 94 53 95 66
– www.prinzregent.de
92 rm ⊑ – †129 € ††149 € – 4 suites
Rest a la carte 33/45 €
♦ Traditional ♦ Classic ♦
18C building extended with a modern annexe. Together they offer traditionally
furnished, cosy rooms and a leisure centre. Close to the exhibition centre. The
cosy restaurant is located in the historical part of the building.

 Dorint Novotel München Messe 🛋 🕭 🔞 ≠rm 🛏 🕲 🖴230
Willy-Brandt-Platz 1 ⊠ *81829*   🚗 **VISA** **◑◉** 🕮 **◑**
– 𝒞 (089) 99 40 00 – h5563@accorhotels.com – Fax (089) 99 40 01 00
– www.accor.com
278 rm – †125 € ††135 €, ⊑ 15 €
Rest 25 € and a la carte 26/41 €
♦ Chain hotel ♦ Business ♦ Modern ♦
Located in the former airport grounds next to the convention centre, this hotel
features modern décor from the spacious lobby to the rooms. Light, friendly
restaurant with glass frontage.

GERMANY

AT THE AIRPORT *by Prinzregentenstr. Plan I D 3*

Kempinski Airport München   🛜 ℔ 🐾 ⧉ ☕ 🅰 ↔rm 🖭 🔒280
Terminalstraße Mitte 20 ✉ 85356   🚗 **VISA** ⓂⓄ 🄰🄴 ⓞ
– ☎ *(089) 9 78 20 – info@kempinski-airport.de – Fax (089) 97 82 26 10*
– *www.kempinski-airport.de*
389 rm – ✝188/420 € ✝✝188/420 €, ⌚ 25 € – 18 suites
Rest 25 € and a la carte 24/40 €
Rest *Safran (closed Friday, Sunday-Monday)* (dinner only) 35/69 € and a
la carte 39/62 €
◆ Business ◆ Functional ◆
The huge glass atrium stands out as a pinnacle of modern hotel architecture, with
18m-high palms soaring upwards. Completely up-to-date technical facilities in
the conference area. A discreet elegance and cosmopolitan interior dominate
the restaurant.

GREECE
ELLÁDA

PROFILE

- **AREA:**
  131 944 km²
  (50 944 sq mi).

- **POPULATION:**
  10 668 000 inhabitants
  (est. 2005), density =
  81 per km².

- **CAPITAL:**
  Athens (conurbation
  3 368 000 inhabitants).

- **CURRENCY:**
  Euro (€); rate of
  exchange: € 1 =
  US$ 1.17 (Nov 2005).

- **GOVERNMENT:**
  Parliamentary republic
  (since 1974). Member
  of European Union
  since 1981.

- **LANGUAGE:**
  Greek.

- **SPECIFIC PUBLIC HOLIDAYS:**
  Epiphany (6 January);
  Orthodox Shrove
  Monday (late
  February-March);
  Independence Day
  (25 March); Orthodox
  Good Friday (Friday
  before Easter);
  Orthodox Easter
  Monday; Day of
  the Holy Spirit (late
  May-June); Ochi Day
  (28 October); Boxing
  Day (26 December).

- **LOCAL TIME:**
  GMT + 2 hours in
  winter and GMT +
  3 hours in summer.

- **CLIMATE:**
  Temperate
  Mediterranean, with
  mild winters and

  hot, sunny summers
  (Athens: January: 10°C,
  July: 27°C).

- **INTERNATIONAL DIALLING CODE:**
  00 30 followed by
  local number.

- **EMERGENCY:**
  General Police: ☏ **100**,
  Tourist Police: ☏ **171**,
  Ambulance: ☏ **166.**

- **ELECTRICITY:**
  220 volts AC, 50Hz;
  2-pin round-shaped
  continental plugs.

FORMALITIES

Travellers from the European Union (EU), Switzerland, Iceland and the main countries of North and South America need a national identity card or passport (America: passport required) to visit Greece for less than three months (tourism or business purpose). For visitors from other countries a visa may be required, in addition to a passport, especially for those wishing to stay for longer than three months. We advise you to check with your embassy before travelling.

A valid national driving licence is sufficient for citizens of EU member countries and for US drivers for up to 3 months but an international driving licence is necessary for other drivers. Fully comprehensive insurance cover (Green Card) is compulsory.

MAJOR NEWSPAPERS

The main national newspapers are: *Eleftherotipia, Ethnos, Kathimerini* (Greek, English), *Ta Nea, To Vima, Adesmeytos Typos. Athens News* is the main English language paper in the capital.

USEFUL PHRASES

ENGLISH	GREEK
Yes	**Né**
No	**Óhi**
Good morning	**Kaliméra**
Goodbye	**Andío**
Thank you	**Efharistó**
Please	**Parakaló**
Excuse me	**Signómi**
I don't understand	**Then katalavéno**

HOTELS

◆ CATEGORIES

Greece has a well-developed tourist infrastructure offering everything from luxury hotels to rooms in private houses (**thomátia**). Establishments approved by the GNTO (EOT) display a blue and yellow plaque – details from local tourist offices. Outside large towns and resorts, it is common to take a room in a private house, especially on the Aegean Islands. It is advisable to seek accommodation through the local tourist office.

◆ PRICE RANGE

The price is quoted per room. Prices vary according to category and are often reduced by half out of season.

◆ TAX

Prices include taxes and service charges.

◆ CHECK OUT TIME

Usually between 10.30am and noon.

◆ RESERVATIONS

By telephone or by Internet. Credit card details may be requested. It is advisable to reserve a room well in advance in high season, especially in areas popular with tourists.

◆ TIP FOR LUGGAGE HANDLING

At the discretion of the customer.

◆ BREAKFAST

It is not normally included in the price of the room. It is served between 7.30am and 10am and most hotels offer a buffet. Some budget hotels do not serve breakfast but there are usually cafés nearby.

Reception	**Resepsió**
Single room	**Monóklino thomátio**
Double room	**Thíklino thomátio**
Bed	**Kreváti**
Bathroom	**Bánio**
Shower	**Doús**

RESTAURANTS

There are five types of establishments to be found in Greece. Restaurants (**estiatória**) offer a smart décor and excellent service and serve both Greek and international cuisine. **Tavernas** are popular restaurants serving traditional fare. **Ouzería** and **mezethopólii** are different from tavernas because their menus feature mezédes (small dishes) instead of cooked or meat dishes. **Psistariá** (steakhouses) are small, inexpensive eateries, offering souvlákia (skewers) and grilled meats served with chips and a tomato salad. **Kafenía**, Greek cafés, also serve a variety of mezédes. Cafeterias serving breakfast and simple meals are numerous. For desserts go to a **zaharoplastío** (patisserie).

◆ MEALS

Breakfast	**Proïnó**	7am – 10am
Lunch	**Mesimerianó**	12.30pm – 2.30pm
Dinner	**Thípno**	7-8pm – 10-11pm
		sometimes later

◆ RESERVATIONS

It is generally a good idea to book in advance if you wish to visit a smart or popular restaurant.

◆ THE BILL

The bill (check) includes service charge and tax but it is customary to leave a tip.

Appetizer	**Mezéthes**
Meal	**Yévma**
First course	**Orektiká**
Main dish	**Kírio pyáto**
Dessert	**Gliká, epithórpio**
Water/mineral water (still, sparkling)	**Neró/metalikó neró (apló, aerioúko)**
Wine (red, white, rosé)	**Krasí (kókino, áspro, rosé)**
Beer	**Bíra**
Bread	**Psomí**
Meat	**Kréas**
Fish	**Psári**
Salt/pepper	**Aláti/pipéri**
Cheese	**Tirí**
Vegetables	**Lahaniká**
Hot/cold	**Zestó/krío**
The bill (check) please	**To logariasmó, parakaló**

LOCAL CUISINE

Greek fare is simple but full of flavour. A Greek menu comprises numerous side dishes and starters, which tend to be served all at once (be sure to ask if you want them served one after another). Most dishes are prepared in advance and often served lukewarm. The words **tis oras** next to a dish on the menu mean that it will be freshly cooked (ie while you wait).

Aperitifs are usually accompanied by **mezéthes** which include vine leaves stuffed with meat and rice (**dolmáthes**), spit-roasted offal sausages (**kokorétsi**), aubergine purée with black olives **(melidzánasalata)**, yoghurt with chopped cucumber and garlic **(tzatzíki)**, fish roe puréed with breadcrumbs or potatoes **(taramosaláta)**, rice with tomatoes **(piláfi)**, stuffed tomatoes, peppers and aubergines **(gemistá)**. **Moussaká** is a traditional dish of minced lamb and aubergine with a béchamel sauce. **Psarosoúpa** is a fish soup and **soupa avgo-lémono** is a broth with rice, egg and lemon. **Mayerítsa** is an offal soup served at Easter. For fish **(psári)** dishes, the fish is weighed before cooking and priced per pound and is served boiled (vrastó), fried or grilled (psitó). Prawns (garídes), sole (glóssa), swordfish (ksifías), squid (kalamári), octopus (oktapódi) and sardines (sardéles) are the staple seafood dishes.

Meat – mutton and lamb (arní, arnáki), minced beef (biftéki), pork (hirinó), chicken (kotópoulo), veal (moshári) – can be roasted, grilled (skára), boiled or braised (stifádo). **Soutzoukákia** are meatballs in tomato sauce and **souvlákia** are beef, mutton or goat meat on a skewer served with tomatoes and onions. Vegetables are often stuffed or fried. Cucumbers (angouria), beans (fasolakia), courgettes (kolokinthákia), aubergines (melidzánes), potatoes (patátes) are plen-tiful. **Thomátes gemistés** (tomatoes with rice), **thomatosalata** (tomato salad) are delicious. The classic Greek salad, **saláta horiatikí**, composed of tomatoes, cucumber, oregano, onions, olives, green peppers and féta cheese, is usually ser-ved with pitta bread. Other tasty snacks are **spanakópita** (spinach in filo pastry) and **tirópita** (cheese in filo pastry).

The Greeks are very fond of cheese. The best known are goat's or sheep's milk cheese **(féta)**, a type of Gruyère (graviéra) and a mild cheese similar to Cheddar (kasséri). Kefalotíri is a sweeter version of Parmesan.

Meals often end with fresh fruit. Desserts tend to be eaten separately, often as an afternoon snack. These include millefeuilles with walnuts or almonds and cin-namon **(baklavá)**; rolls of thread-like pastry with honey and walnuts or almonds **(kadaïfi)**, mini doughnuts with honey and sesame or cinnamon **(loukoumádes)**, flaky pastry turnover with cream and cinnamon **(bougátsa)**, rice cake **(rizógalo)** and almond and sesame paste **(halvá)**. To accompany these, try Greek coffee **(Elinikós kafés)** which has a strong aromatic flavour. You should let the grounds settle and then only drink about half the cup. Ask for **skéto** (without sugar), **métrio** (slightly sweet), **glikó** (sweet). Greek coffee is always served with a glass of water.

◆ DRINK

Oúzo is the national drink; aniseed-flavoured, it is either consumed neat or diluted with water. The best-known Greek wine is **retsína**, a white wine to which pine resin has been added as a preservative. Among the unresinated wines (aretsínato), some are reputed: the full-bodied red from Náoussa in Macedonia, the fruity reds from Neméa in the Argolid, the scented rosé from Aráhova near Delphi, the well-rounded dry white wines of Hymettos and Palíni in Attica, the sparkling dry white wine of Zítsa in Epirós, the white wines of Chalcidice, and the popular white wines of Achaia (Demestica, Santa Laura, Santa Helena). In the islands there are the generous reds and rosés from Crete, dry whites from Lindos in Rhodes, the heady and scented wines from the Cyclades, particularly Náxos and Santoríni, and from the Ionian Islands: Zákynthos (Verdéa, Delizia), Kephalloniá (fruity and musky Róbola) and Lévkas (Santa Maura).

Samian wine can be drunk as a liqueur. Métaxa is the brand name of Greek brandy. Cretan **rakí** is a fruit brandy, and **mastíka** a sweet liqueur flavoured with mastic gum.

ATHENS
ATHÍNA

Population (est. 2005): 732 000 (conurbation 3 368 000) – Altitude: 156m

R. Mattès / MICHELIN

Athens spreads out over eight hills and plains planted with vines and olive trees. The attractive site, the brilliant light, the beauty of the Ancient monuments, the quality of the museums and the unique landscape of indented coastline, beaches and mountains of its environs, all contribute to the fascination of Athens, the city of Athena and the cradle of Western civilization. It is, however, a modern metropolis which has been greatly enhanced by recent improvements in the infrastructure. The verve of the Athenians is reflected in the ebullient way of life and the sense of enjoyment and revelry which characterises the city.

The city has a long history with the first settlement dating back to the Neolithic age. In 5C BC, the 'Golden Age of Pericles', its civilisation was at its zenith and its ideas and values have proved to be seminal influences which have enriched western culture. Athens also has many Roman, Byzantine and neo-Classical remains; certain districts, such as the old Bazaar, have a strong and enticing oriental flavour and remarkable monuments of the Ottoman period have been preserved.

WHICH DISTRICT TO CHOOSE

The luxury and design-oriented boutique **hotels** in Athens are located around Síntagma Square *Plan I* **C2** and Odós Panepistimiou *Plan I* **C2**. For comfortable mid-range hotels look around Omonia Square *Plan I* **B2**; hotels near the Acropolis and Philoppapos Hill have a good location and great views. The Plaka *Plan I* **B3** has many budget hotels.

The elegant district of Kolonaki *Plan I* **C2** bounded by Síntagma Square and Vassilisis Sofias Avenue *Plan I* **C2** abounds in fashionable cafés and luxury **restaurants**. You will find cafés, traditional tavernas and first class restaurants around Varnava Square *Plan I* **D3** in the fashionable Metz neighbourhood. In the narrow alleys of Plaka *Plan I* **B3**, Monastiraki *Plan I* **A3**, Psiri there is a multitude of cafés, restaurants and ouzeries with a great atmosphere. Kyfissiá on the outskirts has some excellent restaurants.

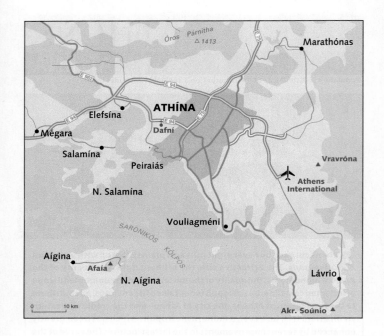

PRACTICAL INFORMATION

ARRIVAL – DEPARTURE

Athens International Airport 'Eleftherios Venizelos' – 33 km (20 mi) east of the city centre. ✆ 210 3530000; www.aia.gr

From the airport to the city centre – By **taxi**: about €20-25 (airport surcharge €3, surcharge for baggage over 10kg €0.30). SATA ✆ 210 5239524, 5221123, 5227986; sataxi@freemail.gr. By **metro**: Line 3 to Monastiraki. Time: 27min. Fare: €6 single (€10 for 2-3 people), €10 round trip (within 48hr). By **express bus**: Line E95 to Síntagma Square 24hr a day, every 10-30min, time: 70-80min, fare: €2.90. By **rail**: to Larissis Station, 6.50am-9.05pm, time: 30min; fare: €6. Express buses also

388

run to the outlying districts and to Piraeus.

Railway stations – Larissis Station (Athens Central Railway Station), 31 Odós Deligiani for northern and eastern Greece. ✆ 210 5297777. **Peloponnese Station** *Plan I* **A1**, 3 Odós Sidirodromon for the southwest of the country. ✆ 210 51 31601; www.ose.gr

TRANSPORT

✦ METRO, BUS AND TROLLEY BUSES

Athens has an excellent, integrated public transport network. Buses and trolley-buses: €0.45 single (carnets of 10 available); metro and ISAB (subway) €0.70 single. A day ticket €2.90 valid

24hr gives unlimited travel on the whole network. Remember to validate your ticket. Tickets can be bought from newsstands, OASA booths and kiosks and at metro or subway stations. www.oasa.gr

◆ TAXIS

Taxis (yellow vehicles with an illuminated sign when free) can be hailed in the street or ordered by phone. Minimum fare: €1.75, €0.85 pick-up charge, €0.30-0.56 per km and luggage surcharge €0.30. There is also a night rate. *Radio Taxis Ikaros* ✆ 210 515 2800; *Express* ✆ 210 994 3000; *Kosmos* ✆ 210 1300.

USEFUL ADDRESSES

◆ TOURIST INFORMATION

Greek National Tourism Organisation (EOT), 26A Amalia St *Plan I* **C3**, ✆ 210 3310392, 210 3310716, 210 3310640; info@gnto.gr, www.gnto. gr; Airport Information Centre, ✆ 210 3530445-448; venizelos@gnto.gr

EXPLORING ATHENS

It is possible to visit the main sights and museums in three days.

Classical sights and the national museum are open 8am-7pm. Other sights and museums open 9am to 4-5pm. Some may be closed on Tuesdays or Thursdays and Sundays.

VISITING

Acropolí *Plan I* **B3** – The upper town crowning the summit of a steep rock platform epitomises Greek civilisation. Pass the Odeon of Herodes Atticus **(Odío Iródou Atikoú)** and Temple of Athena Nike **(Naos Athinás Níkis)** on the way to the monumental entrance **(Propílea)**. The Parthenon **(Parthenónas)** – splendid Doric temple, dedicated to Athena (pedi-

◆ POST OFFICES

Opening times Mon-Fri, 7.30am-2pm. The branches at Mitropoleos St *Plan I* **B2**, 100 Aeolou St *Plan I* **B2** open Mon-Fri 7.30am-8pm, Sat 7.30am-2pm, Sun 9am-1pm. The branch at Mitropoleos Square has similar opening hours but is closed on Sunday.

◆ BANKS/CURRENCY EXCHANGE

Banks open Mon-Thu 8am-2pm, Fri 8am-1.30pm. There are ATMs and exchange offices all over the city. You can also change money at the post office.

◆ EMERGENCY

Police : ✆ **100**; Tourist Police: ✆ **171**; Medical emergencies: ✆ **166**; Fire Brigade: ✆ **199**.

BUSY PERIODS

It may be difficult to find a room when special events are held in the city:

Athens Festival – June to September.

ments, fluted columns, frieze, metopes). Elegant Erechtheum **(Eréthio)** – Caryatid Porch with noble statues dressed in pleated tunics. **Acropolis Museum** – Classical statues, Parthenon pediments, caryatids. **Théatro Dioníssou** – Splendid views.

Thissío *Plan I* **A3** – **Theseion:** 5C BC Doric temple. From the **Hephaisteion:** views of the agora, the Monastiráki district and the Acropolis. **Arhéa Agorá**, the centre of Athenian public life in Antiquity: **Stoa of the Giants, Stoa Atálou**.

Lófos Filopápou *Plan I* **A3** – Cave dwellings, Philopappos monument and theatre. Spectacular views of the Acropolis, Athens, Hymettos and the Attica plain.

Ethnikó Arheologikó Moussío *Plan I* **B2** – Fabulous collection of treasures from Greece's main archaeological sites.

Moussío Benáki *Plan I* **C2** – Ancient Greek and Byzantine art and costumes.

Moussío Kikladikís Téhnis *Plan I* **D2** – The Museum of Cycladic Art presents a superb private collection illustrating the development of Greek art over a period of 3 000 years – magnificent collection of Cycladic marble figurines.

Vizandinó Moussío *Plan I* **D2** – The Byzantine Museum displays a rich collection of icons. Reconstructions of two early churches.

Pláka *Plan I* **B3** – Picturesque narrow streets and alleys, squares and terraces – shops, tavernas famous for the nightlife. **Mikrí Mitrópoli** – 12C Byzantine church. **Romaikí Agorá** (Roman Forum). **Aérides** (Tower of the Winds) – carved winged figures of the winds. **Píli Adrianoú** (Hadrian's Arch). **Naós Olímbiou Diós** (Olympieion) – huge Corinthian marble columns.

Platía Sindágmatos *Plan I* **C2** – Elegant Síntagma Square lined with famous buildings. Parliament **(Voulí)** on the east side: Changing of the guard. **Ethnikós Kípos** (National Garden), **Zápio** (Zappeion Park). Walk up Odós El. Venizélou (Panepistimíou) *Plan I* **C2** past **Schliemann's House**, the Cathedral **Ágios Dionisis Areopagitis**, **Panepistímio** (University), **Akadimía** (Academy) and **Ethnikí Vivliothíki** (National Library).

Views – **Lycabettos** *Plan I* **D1** – Exceptional view of the Acropolis, the whole city and of the sea beyond; from rooftop bar of Hilton Hotel (opposite Megalis Tou Genous Scholi Square). From the terrace of the Pnyx **(Pnílka)** *Plan I* **A3** – view of the Acropolis.

Kessarianí Monastery and **Mount Hymettos** – *9km-5.5mi E.* 11C monastery in a beautiful setting. Continue through the pine woods past 11C Asteri Monastery for fine views of Athens and the Saronic Gulf as far as the Peloponnese to the west, and of the Attic peninsula (Mesógia), its eastern shore and Euboia to the east.

Apollo Coast to Cape Sounion – *65km-41mi round trip.* An unforgettable excursion along the coast road past elegant resorts and beaches (Glyfáda, Voúla, Vouliagméni, Lagoníssi, Anávissos) to Soúnio (view of the cape) and Akri Soúnio (Temple of Poseidon).

Daphní and **Elefsina** – *Around 90km-56mi.* 11C domed Byzantine church – superb mosaics. The Sanctuary at Eleusis was one of the great shrines in Antiquity – acropolis, temples, museum.

SHOPPING

In summer shops are usually open 8am-1.30pm and 5.30pm-8.30pm. They close on Sun and at 2.30pm on Mon, Wed, Sat. In winter they open 9am-5pm on Mon, Wed, 10am-7pm on Tue, Thu, Fri, 8.30am-3.30pm Sat. Department stores in **Odós Patission** *Plan I* **B2** and **Eolou** *Plan I* **B2** open 8.30am-8pm weekdays (3pm Sat).

Fashionable shops featuring Greek and international designers line **Odós Ermou** *Plan I* **A2**. For that special gift visit the jewellery shops around Síntagma Square, in **Letka St** *Plan I* **C2** which connects **Perikleous St** and **Kolokotroni St** and nearby arcades. The elegant districts of **Kolonáki**, **Kyfissia** and **Glyfada** boast luxury shops for fashion, jewellery, antiques. Browse along **Odós Panepistimiou** linking Síntagma and Omónia Squares. The streets around **Omónia** are full of small shops. For handicrafts, souvenirs, leather goods and antiques explore the colourful **Plaka**, **Monastiraki**, **Psiri** districts.

MARKETS – The **flea market** in Monastiraki is an amazing experience. The shops are open all week but it is at weekends that it is particularly busy.

WHAT TO BUY – Jewellery, Kastoria furs, crafts, ceramics, pottery, wool and cotton garments, carpets and rugs, embroidery, embroidered tapestries, cushions and bags, leather goods.

ENTERTAINMENT

For information on cultural events consult *Athens News* on sale at central kiosks or visit www.cultureguide.gr; *Time Out Athens* is another useful source of information.

National Opera House *Plan I* **B3** – Opera, ballet and music in two auditoria (Olympia, Acropol).

Odeon of Herodes Atticus *Plan I* **B3** – Opera, ballet, concerts, traditional dance and Classical tragedies during Athens Festival.

Dora Stratou Theatre *Plan I* **B3** – Traditional dance. Performances at **Philopappos Theatre** during festival.

Athens Concert Hall *Plan I* **D2** – Concerts, opera, ballet.

Likavitós *Plan I* **C1** – Folk dancing.

NIGHTLIFE

Explore the streets around **Síntagma Square** for restaurants, bars clubs and disco bars. The lively venues in **Plaka**, **Monastiraki**, **Psiri**, **Gazi**, **Thissio** (Irakleidon St *Plan I* **A3**) are open late into the night. Some tavernas have live bouzouki music. A young crowd flocks to establishments in **Exarchia Square** and the streets up to Streffi Hill. There are smart clubs with dancing in **Kolonaki**, along **Singrou** and **Poseidonos Avenues** leading to the elegant south coast resorts of **Glyfada**, **Voula** and **Vougliameni**. Casinos on Mount Parnitha and at Loutraki are frequented by a fashionable clientele.

A   B

ΠΛΑΤ. ΑΙΓΥΠΤΟΥ
Pl. Egiptou

Alexandras

Park
H. Athens
ΜΕΤΣΟΒΟΥ

Ioulianou

ΑΧΑΡΝΩΝ

Γ΄ ΣΕΠΤΕΜΒΡΙΟΥ
3 Septemvriou

28 ΟΚΤΩΒΡΙΟΥ
28

ΣΠΥΡ. ΤΡΙΚΟΥΠΗ

Larissis

ΝΕΟΦ. ΜΕΤΑΞΑ
Neof. Metaxa

ΗΠΕΙΡΟΥ

ΛΙΟΣΙΩΝ
Liossion

ΕΘΝΙΚΟ
ARHEOLOGIKÓ
MOUSSÍO

ΤΟΣΙΤΣΑ

Deligiani

1

ΙΩΑΝΝΙΝΩΝ

ΧΙΟΥ

ΨΑΡΩΝ

Museum

PELOPONISSOS

ΣΤΟΥΡΝ ΑΡΑ

Art

ΜΑΡΝΗ
Marni

ΛΕΝΟΡΜΑΝ

Deligiani

ΦΑΒΙΕΡΟΥ

ΜΑΡΝΗ
Marni

ΠΛΑΤ. ΒΑΘΗΣ
Pl. Vathis

H

Γ΄ ΣΕΠΤΕΜΒΡΙΟΥ
3 Septemvriou

ΠΟΛΙΤΕΧΝΙΟΥ

Residence Georgio
ΠΛΑΤ.
ΚΑΝ ΙΓΓΟΣ
Pl. Kaningos

ΟΚΤΩΒΡΙΟΥ
(Patission)

Karolou

Omonia

ΘΕΜΙΣΤΟΚΛΕΟΥΣ

ΑΚΑΔΗΜΙΑΣ
Akadimias

Metaxourghio

ΠΛ.
Karaïskaki

ΑΓ. ΚΩΝΣΤΑΝΤΙΝΟΥ
Ag. Konstandinou

ΜΕΝΑΝΔΡΟΥ

Omonia
Grand

OMONOIA

ΠΑΝ ΕΠΙΣΤΗΜΙΟΥ
Panepistimiou

ΕΘΝΙΚΗ
VIVLIOTHÍKI

Athens Imperial

ΔΕΛΗΓΙΩΡΓΗ

Athens
Acropol

Athens Imperial

ΑΧΙΛΛΕΩΣ
Ahileos

ΚΟΛΟΚΥΝΘΟΥΣ

ΤΣΑΛΔΑΡΗ (Tsaldari)

ΜΕΤΑΞΟΥΡΓΕΙΟ
METAXOURGÍO

Athena
Grand

ΣΤΑΔΙΟΥ
Stadiou

ΠΑΝΕΠΙΣΤΗΜΙΟΥ
Panepistimio

2

ΘΕΡΜΟΠΥΛΩΝ

ΜΥΛΛΕΡΟΥ

H

ΠΛΑΤ.
ΚΟΤΖΙΑ
Pl. Kodzia

ΠΛΑΤ.
ΚΛΑΥΘΜΩΝΟΣ
Pl. Klafthmonos

ΜΕΓ.

ΚΕΡΑΜΕΙΚΟΥ

Sofokleous

ΚΕΝΔΡΙΚΗ
ΑΓΟΡΑ
KENDRIKÍ
AGORÁ

ΕΘΝΙΚΟ
ΙΣΤΟΡΙΚΟ
MOUSSÍO

ΠΑΝΑΓΗ
Panagi

ΠΛΑΤ.
ΕΛΕΥΘΕΡΙΑΣ
Pl. Eleftherias

ΕΥΡΙΠΙΔΟΥ

Arion

ΑΙΟΛΟΥ
Eolou

ΚΟΛΟΚΟΤΡΩΝΗ

Eridanus

Jérôme Serres

Varoulko

ΚΡΙΕΖΗ

ΣΑΡΡΗ

Oraia Penteli

ΑΡΙΣΤΟΦΑΝΟΥΣ

ΑΘΗΝΑΣ
Athinas

ΚΑΡΝΙΚΑΡΕΑ
KARNIKARÉA

Ermou

(ΠΕΙΡΑΙΩΣ)
(Pireos)

Hytra

Mitropoleos
ΜΗΤΡΟΠΟΛΕΩΣ

KERAMIKÓS

ΕΡΜΟΥ

ΠΛ.
ΜΟΝΑΣΤΗΡΑΚΙ
PL.
MONASTIRÁKI

Plaka

ΜΙΚΡΗ
ΜΗΤΡΟΠΟΛΗ
MIKRÍ
MITRÓPOLI

Hermes

Thissio

Monastiraki

ΑΔΡΙΑΝΟΥ

MONASTIRÁKI

THISSÍO

ΑΡΧΑΙΑ ΑΓΟΡΑ
ARHÉA AGORÁ

ΡΟΜΑΙΚΗ
ΑΓΟΡΑ
ROMAÏKÍ
AGORÁ

ΠΛΑΚΑ
PLÁKA

Nileos

ΑΠΟΣΤΟΛΟΥ
Apostolou

ΑΡΕΙΟΣ
ΠΑΓΟΣ
ÁRIOS
PÁGOS

M

Psara`s

3

ΑΣΤΕΡΟΣΚΟΠΕΙΟ
ASTEROSKOPÍO

ΛΟΦΟΣ
ΝΙΜΦΩΝ
LÓFOS
NIMFÓN

ΠΑΥΛΟΥ
Pavlou

ΑΚΡΟΠΟΛΗ
AKRÓPOLI

ΚΕΝΔΡΟ
ΜΕΛΕΤΩΝ
ΑΚΡΟΠΟΛΕΩΣ
KÉNDRO
MELETÓN
AKROPOLEOS

ΠΝΥΚΑ
PNÍKA

ΩΔΕΙΟΝ
ΗΡΩΔΟΥ
ΑΤΤΙΚΟΥ
ODIOU
IRÓDOU
ATIKÚ

ΘΕΑΤΡΟ
ΔΙΟΝΥΣΟΥ
THÉATRO
DIONÍSSOU

Dionissiou

Aeropogitou

M

Akropoli

ΠΑΡΘΕΝΩΝΟΣ
Parthenonos

ΡΟΒ. ΓΚΑΛΛΙ

A   B

ΛΟΦΟΣ FILOPÁPOU
LÓFOS

Divani Palace
Acropolis

ΧΑΤΖΗΧΡΗΣ-
ΤΟΥ

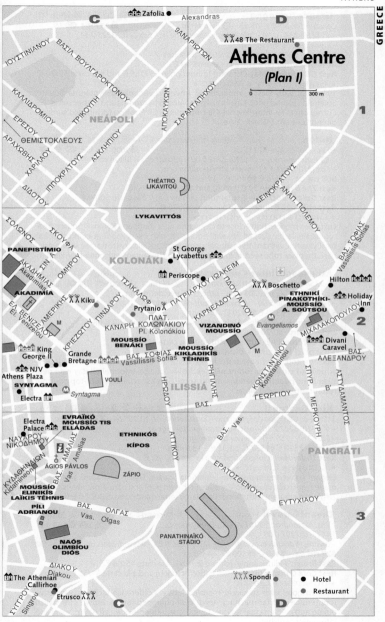

Athens Centre
(Plan I)

0   300 m

Zafolia

Alexandras

ΘΑΝΑΡΙΩΤΩΝ

48 The Restaurant

ΙΟΥΣΤΙΝΙΑΝΟΥ

ΒΑΣΙΛ. ΒΟΥΛΓΑΡΟΚΤΟΝΟΥ

ΚΑΛΛΙΔΡΟΜΙΟΥ

ΤΡΙΚΟΥΠΗ

ΕΡΕΣΟΥ

ΘΕΜΙΣΤΟΚΛΕΟΥΣ

ΑΡΑΧΩΒΗΣ

ΧΑΡΙΛΑΟΥ

ΙΠΠΟΚΡΑΤΟΥΣ

ΔΙΔΟΤΟΥ

ΑΣΚΛΗΠΙΟΥ

ΝΕΑΠΟΛΙ

ΑΠΟΚΑΥΚΩΝ

ΣΑΡΑΝΤΑΠΗΧΟΥ

ΔΕΙΝΟΚΡΑΤΟΥΣ

ΒΑΣ. ΑΝΑΠ. ΠΟΛΕΜΟΥ

ΘΕΑΤΡΟ
ΛΙΚΑΒΙΤΟΥ
THÉATRO
LIKAVITOÚ

LYKAVITTÓS

ΛΥΚΑΒΗΤΤΟΣ

ΣΟΛΩΝΟΣ

ΣΚΟΥΦΑ

ΟΜΗΡΟΥ

ΠΑΝΕΠΙΣΤΙΜΙΟ

KOLONÁKI

St George
Lycabettus

Periscope

ΒΑΣ. ΣΟΦΙΑΣ
Vassilíssis Sofías

ΑΚΑΔΗΜΙΑΣ
Akadimías

ΑΚΑΔΙΜΙΑ

Kiku

ΤΣΑΚΑΛΩΦ

ΠΙΝΔΑΡΟΥ

Prytanio

ΠΑΤΡΙΑΡΧΟΥ ΙΩΑΚΕΙΜ

ΠΛΟΥΤΑΡΧΟΥ

ΚΑΡΝΕΑΔΟΥ

Boschetto

Hilton

ΕΤΝΙΚΙ
ΠΙΝΑΚΟΘΙΚΙ-
MOUSSÍO
A. SOÚTSOU

Holiday
Inn

ΕΛ. ΒΕΝΙΖΕΛΟΥ
Εl. Venizélou

ΚΡΙΕΖΩΤΟΥ

ΚΑΝΑΡΗ

ΠΛΑΤ.
ΚΟΛΩΝΑΚΙΟΥ
Pl. Kolonákiou

MOUSSÍO
BENÁKI

VIZANDINÓ
MOUSSÍO

Evangelismos

MIXAΛΑΚΟΠΟΥΛΟΥ

Divani
Caravel

ΒΑΣ.
ΑΛΕΞΑΝΔΡΟΥ

King
George II

Grande
Bretagne

ΒΑΣ. ΣΟΦΙΑΣ
Vassilíssis Sofías

MOUSSÍO
KIKLADIKÍS
TÉHNIS

ΚΩΝΣΤΑΝΤΙΝΟΥ
Konstandínou

ΑΣΤΥΔΑΜΑΝΤΟΣ

NJV
Athens Plaza

VOULÍ

ΗΡΩΔΟΥ

ILISSIÁ

ΡΗΓΙΛΗΣ

ΣΠΥΡ.

ΜΕΡΚΟΥΡΗ

PANGRÁTI

SYNTAGMA

Electra

Syntagma

ΒΑΣ.

ΒΑΣ. vas.

ΓΕΩΡΓΙΟΥ

Β'

Electra
Palace

ΝΑΥΑΡΧΟΥ
ΝΙΚΟΔΗΜΟΥ

ΕΥΡΑΪΚΟ
MOUSSÍO TIS
ELLÁDAS

ETHNIKÓS
KÍPOS

ΑΤΤΙΚΟΥ

ΕΡΑΤΟΣΘΕΝΟΥΣ

ΕΥΤΥΧΙΟΥ

ΚΥΔΑΘΗΝΑΙΩΝ
Kidathineón

ΑΓΙΟΣ ΠΑΥΛΟΣ
ÁGIOS PÁVLOS

ΒΑΣ. ΑΜΑΛΙΑΣ
Vas Amalías

ΖΑΠΙΟ
ZÁPIO

MOUSSÍO
ELINIKÍS
LAÏKÍS TÉHNIS

ΠΙΛΙ
ADRIANOU

ΒΑΣ. ΟΛΓΑΣ
Vas. Olgas

NAÓS
OLIMBÍOU
DIÓS

PANATHINAIKÓ
STADIO

ΣΥΓΓΡΟΥ
Singrou

ΔΙΑΚΟΥ
Diakou

The Athenian
Callirhoe

Etrusco

Spondi

● Hotel
● Restaurant

⌂⌂⌂⌂⌂ **Grande Bretagne** ⋖ Athens, 🏋 ♨ 🏊 ⊡ ♿ ❄ 🚭rm 🚫
Constitution Sq. ✉ 105 63 – Ⓜ Syntagma 👥380 VISA MC AE DC
– ✆ (210) 3330 0 00 – info@grandebretagne.gr – Fax (210) 3228 0 34
– www.grandebretagne.gr **C2**
262 rm – †280 € ††490 €, ☕ 29 € – 59 suites
Rest *GB Corner* 60 € and a la carte 48/69 €
Rest *GB Rooftop* (May-October) (dinner only) 55 €/65 € and a la carte 52/70 €
◆ Grand Luxury ◆ Modern ◆
19C hotel with classic, modernised interior overlooking Syntagma Square. Splendid spa and pool. Luxuriously-appointed bedrooms and corner suites. GB Corner offers an international à la carte menu. GB Rooftop for alfresco summer dining; authentic Greek dishes.

⌂⌂⌂⌂⌂ **Hilton** ⋖ Athens and Acropolis, ⛱ 🏋 ♨ 🏊 ♿ ❄ 🚭rm 🚫rest
46 Vas. Sofias Ave ✉ 115 28 👥2000 🚗 VISA MC AE DC
– Ⓜ Evangelismos – ✆ (210) 7281 0 00 – info.athens@hilton.com
– Fax (210) 7281 1 11 – www.athens.hilton.com **D2**
508 rm ☕ – †375 € ††464 € – 19 suites
Rest *The Byzantine* 30 € (lunch) and a la carte 45/66 €
Rest *Galaxy BBQ* (May-September) (dinner only) a la carte 50/60 €
Rest *Milo's* 20 € (lunch) and a la carte 42/76 €
◆ Grand Luxury ◆ Modern ◆
Luxurious modern hotel close to city centre near shops and Kolonaki Square. Bedrooms similar in size; all are well-equipped with every modern comfort. Informal Byzantine with an international menu. Rooftop Galaxy with terrace and lounge/bar is the place to be seen. Milo's is large seafood restaurant with open-plan kitchen.

⌂⌂⌂⌂⌂ **Athenaeum Inter-Continental** ⋖ Acropolis, ⛱ 🏋 ♨ 🏊 ♿
89-93 Singrou (Southwest : 2 ¾ km) ❄ 🚭rm 🚫 👥2000 🚗 VISA MC AE DC
✉ 117 45 – ✆ (210) 9206 0 00 – athens@intercontin.com
– Fax (210) 9206 5 00 – www.intercontinental.com
543 rm ☕ – †360 € ††420 € – 60 suites
Rest *Première (9th floor)* (closed Sunday) (dinner only) 50 €/68 € and a la carte 50/70 €
Rest *Cafezoe* 33 € (buffet lunch) and a la carte 42/79 €
◆ Grand Luxury ◆ Business ◆ Modern ◆
Modern, top class corporate hotel, close to business district. Luxuriously-appointed club floor rooms with exclusive lounge. Informal all day café near swimming pool; international menu, some Greek specialities. Roof-top gourmet restaurant; splendid views.

⌂⌂⌂⌂ **King George II** ⛱ 🏋 ♨ ⊡ ♿ ❄ 🚭rm 🚫 👥410 VISA MC AE DC
3 Vasileos Georgiou A, Syntagma (Constitution) Sq ✉ 105 64 – Ⓜ Syntagma
– ✆ (210) 3222 2 10 – reservations@kinggeorge.gr
– Fax (210) 3250 5 04 – www.grecotel.gr **C2**
89 rm – †529 € ††937 €, ☕ 32 € – 13 suites
Rest *Tudor Hall* (closed Sunday) a la carte 62/82 €
◆ Luxury ◆ Classic ◆
Elegant converted mansion in Syntagma Square. Stylish bedrooms with hand-made French furniture; rooftop suite with own pool and panoramic views. Stylish 7th floor restaurant with chandeliers, large terrace and good views. Eclectic menu.

⌂⌂⌂⌂ **Divani Caravel** ⋖ Athens, 🏋 ♨ 🏊 ♿ ❄ 🚭 🚫 👥1000
2 Vas. Alexandrou ✉ 161 21 – Ⓜ Evangelismos 🚗 VISA MC AE DC
– ✆ (210) 7207 0 00
– divanis@divanicaravel.gr – Fax (210) 7236 6 83 – www.divanis.gr **D2**
427 rm ☕ – †400 € ††800 € – 44 suites
Rest *Brown's* (dinner only) (closed Sunday) a la carte 45/68 €
Rest *Café Constantinople* – 28 € (buffet lunch) and a la carte 34/55 €
◆ Business ◆ Classic ◆
Modern hotel with spacious, marbled lobby. Conference facilities. Attractive roof terrace with far-reaching views. Well-equipped rooms. Brown's for stylish dining and elegant cigar lounge. Café Constantinople open all day for local and international dishes.

Metropolitan 🛋 🕼 🕸 ⚒ 🕭 🖼 🏊rm ⅍ 🔥450 **P** 𝖵𝖨𝖲𝖠 ⚍ 🆑 ⑩
385 Singrou (Southwest : 7 km) ⊠ *175 64 – ℰ (210) 9471 0 00*
– metropolitan @ chandris.gr – Fax (210) 9471 0 10
– www.chandris.gr
362 rm – 🛏500 € 🛏🛏800 €, � 20 € – 12 suites
Rest *Trocadero* 25 € (buffet lunch Monday-Friday) and a la carte 29/52 €
♦ Business ♦ Modern ♦
Striking, modern corporate hotel with easy access into and out of the city.
Spacious, comfortable rooms with state-of-the-art facilities. Popular for business
conventions. International or Italian fare can be taken overlooking the garden or
beside the pool.

Ledra Marriott 🕼 🕸 ⚒ ⚒ 🕭 🏊rm ⅍ 🔥650 ⇌ 𝖵𝖨𝖲𝖠 ⚍ 🆑 ⑩
115 Singrou (Southwest : 3 km) ⊠ *117 45 – ℰ (210) 9559 1 53*
– athensledramarriott @ marriotthotels.com – Fax (210) 9559 1 53
– www.marriott.com
300 rm – 🛏480 € 🛏🛏540 €, ⊽ 20 € – 14 suites
Rest *Kona Kai* (closed Sunday) (dinner only) 42 € and a la carte 41/81 €
Rest *Zephyros* 22 € (buffet lunch) and a la carte 31/41 €
♦ Business ♦ Modern ♦
Commercial hotel with panoramic views from rooftop terrace. Executive rooms
have exclusive lounge and high-tech extras. Ornate Kona Kai for authentic Thai
and Polynesian dishes. Zephyros on 1st floor for traditional and international
buffet.

Athens Imperial 🕼 🕸 ⚒ ⚒ 🕭 🏊rm ⅍ 🔥600 ⇌ 𝖵𝖨𝖲𝖠 ⚍ 🆑 ⑩
Karaiskaki Sq ⊠ *104 37 –* ⓜ *Metaxourghio – ℰ (210) 5 20 16 00 – sales_ai @*
grecotel.gr – Fax (210) 5 22 55 21 – www.grecotel.gr   **A2**
244 rm ⊽ – 🛏130 € 🛏🛏145 € – 24 suites
Rest a la carte 30/40 €
♦ Business ♦ Modern ♦
Modern hotel, its impressive atrium boasting an opulent lounge and bar. Lovely
rooftop decked pool area with superb views to Acropolis. Mod cons match smart,
stylish rooms. Views over the square from restaurant; Mediterranean food
served.

Residence Georgio 🛋 🕼 🕸 ⚒ ⚒ 🕭 🏊rm 🖭 🕼
14 Chalkokondili & 28 October ⊠ *106 77*   ⇌ 𝖵𝖨𝖲𝖠 ⚍ 🆑 ⑩
– ⓜ *Omonia – ℰ (210) 3 32 01 00 – info @ residencegeorgio.com*
– Fax (210) 3 32 02 00 – www.residencegeorgio.com   **B1**
126 rm ⊽ – 🛏250 € – 10 suites
Rest *Vivendo* (closed Sunday) (dinner only) (winter only) a la carte 33/46 €
Rest *Captains Bar* (closed Sunday) (dinner only) (summer only) a la carte
33/46 €
♦ Business ♦ Modern ♦
Near National Archaeological Museum; in stylish lounge a perspex piano - one of
only five in the world - is played nightly. Smart rooms with extra touches are a
strong point. Vivendo mezzanine restaurant in winter. Captains Bar for summer
rooftop dining. Italian menus.

St George Lycabettus ≤ Athens, 🛋 🕼 🕸 ⚒ ⅍ 🕼 🔥210
2 Kleomenous ⊠ *106 75 – ℰ (210) 7290 7 12*   ⇌ 𝖵𝖨𝖲𝖠 ⚍ 🆑 ⑩
– Fax (210) 7290 4 39 – www.sglycabettus.gr   **C2**
148 rm ⊽ – 🛏382 € 🛏🛏469 € – 6 suites
Rest *Le Grand Balcon* (closed Sunday and Monday) (dinner only) a la carte
43/60 €
Rest *Frame* a la carte 34/51 €
♦ Business ♦ Classic ♦
Elevated position on Lycabettus Hill. Greek artwork and artifacts throughout.
Roof-top pool. South-facing rooms with balconies, view of Acropolis and Athens
skyline. Le Grand Balcon roof-top restaurant for international menu. All day
Frame for Greek dishes.

Electra Palace ⅃⅚ 🛠 ⌱ ▢ ㏍ ♨rm 🖭 ℡ 🚄 290
18-20 Nikodimou St ✉ *1057 57 –* Ⓜ *Syntagma* 🅿 *VISA* 🆎 ⓪
– ℰ (210) 3370 0 00 – aelectrapalace@ath.forthnet.gr – Fax (210) 3241 8 75
140 rm ⌑ – **♦**206 € **♦♦**527 € – 10 suites **C3**
Rest a la carte 21/29 €
♦ Business ♦ Modern ♦
Modern interior behind a classical façade in Plaka. Ultra modern bedrooms and suites with classical décor; some with view of the Acropolis. Ground-floor restaurant opened in 2005: American buffet breakfast; à la carte lunch and dinner.

NJV Athens Plaza ▢ ♨rm ℀ 🖭 ℡ 🚄 300 *VISA* 🆎 ⓪
2 Vas. Georgiou A, Syntagma Sq ✉ *105 64 –* Ⓜ *Syntagma – ℰ (210) 3352 4 00*
– sales_njv@grecotel.gr – Fax (210) 3235 8 56 – www.grecotel.gr **C2**
159 rm ⌑ – **♦**440 € **♦♦**550 € – 23 suites
Rest *The Parliament* a la carte 51/79 €
♦ Business ♦ Modern ♦
Modern hotel handy for the shopping and business districts. Local stone adorns the contemporary lobby and bar. Boldly decorated, hi-tech bedrooms and luxurious suites. Modern menu of international dishes on first floor.

Stratos Vassilikos ⅃⅚ 🛠 🅶 ▢ ℀ 🖭 ℡ 🚄 180 🅿 *VISA* 🆎 ⓪

Mihalakopoulou 114 (by Mihalakopoulou, beyond Holiday Inn) ✉ *115 27*
– Ⓜ *Megaro Moussikis – ℰ (210) 7706 6 11 – info@airotel.gr*
– Fax (210) 7708 1 37 – www.airotel.gr
82 rm ⌑ – **♦**145 € **♦♦**171 € – 6 suites
Rest a la carte 33/48 €
♦ Business ♦ Modern ♦
Elegant, modern hotel with an interesting décor, set away from the city centre. Spacious well-furnished bedrooms, some with balconies. Riva restaurant in the atrium for lunch or formal dinner.

Park H. Athens ⋞ Athens, ⅃⅚ 🛠 ⌱ 🅶 ▢ ♨rm ℀ 🖭 🚄 700
10 Alexandras Ave ✉ *106 82 –* Ⓜ *Victoria* 🅿 *VISA* 🆎 ⓪
– ℰ (210) 8894 5 15 – sales@athensparkhotel.gr – Fax (210) 8238 4 20
– www.athensparkhotel.gr **B1**
140 rm ⌑ – **♦**190 € **♦♦**450 € – 10 suites
Rest *Alexandra's* a la carte 33/52 €
Rest *Park Café* a la carte 20/35 €
Rest *St'Astra* a la carte 45/78 €
♦ Business ♦ Traditional ♦ Classic ♦
Modern, family owned hotel between the archaeological museum and Pedio Areos Park. Smartly fitted rooms, suites with spa baths. Dine in Alexandra's with piano accompaniment. All day Park Café for a light meal. Enjoy view from St'Astra by rooftop pool: French menu.

Zafolia ⋞ Athens, ⅃⅚ 🛠 ⌱ 🅶 ▢ ♨rm ℀ 🖭 🚄 200

87-89 Alexandras Ave ✉ *114 74* 🅿 *VISA* 🆎 ⓪
– ℰ (210) 6449 0 02 – info@zafoliahotel.gr – Fax (210) 6442 0 42 **C1**
185 rm ⌑ – **♦**105 € **♦♦**/150 € – 7 suites
Rest 22 € (lunch) and a la carte 25/40 €
♦ Business ♦ Modern ♦
Privately owned, commercial hotel on east side of city. Well-equipped rooms with modern amenities, some with private balcony. Excellent views from rooftop bar and pool. Shop-fitted mezzanine level restaurant. Greek and international menu.

Holiday Inn ⋞ ⅃⅚ 🛠 ⌱ ▢ ♨rm ℀ 🖭 ℡ 🚄 650 🅿 *VISA* 🆎 ⓪

50 Mihalakopoulou ✉ *115 28 –* Ⓜ *Megaro Moussikis – ℰ (210) 7278 0 00*
– info@hiathens.com – Fax (210) 7278 6 00 – www.hiathens.com **D2**
192 rm – **♦**420 € **♦♦**580 €, ⌑ 33 €
Rest 45 € (lunch) and a la carte 25/55 €
♦ Chain hotel ♦ Business ♦ Modern ♦
Modern corporate hotel with extensive state-of-the-art conference facilities. All bedrooms are aimed at the commercial traveller. Plaza Restaurant offers international menu; light meals in summer in poolside roof garden commanding far-reaching city views.

Holiday Suites without rest 　　　　🅰 🍴 📺 📞 VISA 🅜🅞 🅐🅔 🅞
4 Arnis St (by Mihalakopoulou) ⊠ *115 28 –* 🅜 *Megaro Moussikis*
– 𝒞 (210) 7278 0 00 – info@hiathens.com – Fax (210) 7278 6 00
– www.holiday-suites.com
34 rm – ♦520 € ♦♦550 €, ⊇18€
Rest see *Holiday Inn* above
♦ Business ♦ Modern ♦
Converted apartments in quiet residential area. Spacious rooms each with
kitchenette and work area, superbly equipped with CD/DVD/fax. Breakfast here
or at Holiday Inn.

 Divani Palace Acropolis 　　　　🗻 🅰 ↳rm 🍴 📺 📞
19-25 Parthenonos ⊠ *117 42 –* 🅜 *Akropolis* 　　　🛗300 VISA 🅜🅞 🅐🅔 🅞
– 𝒞 (210) 9280 1 00 – divanis@divaniacropolis.gr – Fax (210) 9214 9 93
– www.divaniacropolis.gr 　　　　　　　　　　　　　　　　　**B3**
240 rm ⊇ *– ♦260 € ♦♦290 € – 10 suites*
Rest *Aspassia* 26 €/36 € and a la carte 32/56 €
Rest *Roof Garden* 50 € (dinner buffet only)
♦ Traditional ♦ Classic ♦
Near the Parthenon yet fairly quiet with parts of Themistocles' wall in the
basement. Particularly comfortable suites. Aspassia for formal meals. Roof
Garden for barbecue buffet with live music.

 The Athenian Callirhoe 　　　　📻 🐾 🅰 ↳ 🍴 📺 📞
52 Kallirois Ave and Petmeza ⊠ *117 43* 　　　　　🛗100 VISA 🅜🅞 🅐🅔 🅞
– 𝒞 (210) 9215 3 53 – hotel@tac.gr – Fax (210) 9215 3 42
– www.tac.gr 　　　　　　　　　　　　　　　　　　　　**C3**
84 rm ⊇ *– ♦420 € ♦♦700 €*
Rest see *Etrusco* below
♦ Business ♦ Stylish ♦
A bright, contemporary boutique hotel with subtle art deco styling. City views
from the rooftop terrace and balconies of the smartly fitted executive rooms.

 Eridanus 　　　　📻 🐾 🅰 🍴 📺 📞 🛗60 🌿 VISA 🅜🅞 🅐🅔 🅞
78 Pireaus Ave, Keramikos ⊠ *104 35 –* 🅜 *Thissio – 𝒞 (210) 5205 3 60*
– eridanus@eridanus.gr – Fax (210) 5200 5 50 – www.eridanus.gr 　　**A2**
38 rm ⊇ *– ♦190 € ♦♦350 €*
Rest see *Varoulko* and *Jérôme Serres* below
♦ Business ♦ Stylish ♦
Contemporary design hotel on a busy main road. Luxurious bedrooms with
high-tech equipment and hydro massage showers; some with views of the
Acropolis.

 Andromeda 　　　　🅰 ↳ 🍴 📞 🛗100 🌿 VISA 🅜🅞 🅐🅔 🅞
22 Timoleontos Vassou St (via Vas Sofias off Soutsou D.) ⊠ *115 21 –* 🅜 *Megaro*
Moussikis – 𝒞 (210) 6415 0 00 – reservations@andromedaathens.gr
– Fax (210) 6466 3 61 – www.andromedahotels.gr
21 rm ⊇ *– ♦250 € ♦♦350 € – 10 suites*
Rest (room service only) 15 €/25 €
♦ Business ♦ Stylish ♦
Striking glass fronted 'boutique' hotel in a tranquil residential road. Blends
contemporary style and traditional services. Individually designed rooms and
annexe apartments.

 Athena Grand 　　　　🅰 ↳ 📺 📞 🛗30 VISA 🅜🅞 🅐🅔 🅞
65 Athens St ⊠ *105 52 Athens –* 🅜 *Omonia – 𝒞 (210) 3 25 09 00*
– athenagrand@grecotel.gr – Fax (210) 3 25 09 20
– www.grecotel.gr 　　　　　　　　　　　　　　　　　**B2**
67 rm ⊇ *– ♦200 € – 11 suites*
Rest *Meat Me* a la carte 18/36 €
♦ Business ♦ Modern ♦
Totally renovated city centre hotel. Relax in lounge with squashy sofas; take
breakfast at marble tables. Individually designed rooms are well equipped.
Taverna style restaurant serves Greek meze dishes; terrace for al fresco dining.

Alexandros 🕭 ⓕ 🕭 ⴟ 🅰 𝒮 🖾 📞 ꕔ220 𝑽𝑰𝑺𝑨 ⓒⓞ 🅰🅴 ⓘ
8 Timoleontos Vassou St (via Vas Sofias off Soutsou D.) ⌧ 115 21 – Ⓜ *Megaro Moussikis – ℰ (210) 6430 4 64 – alexandros@airotel.gr – Fax (210) 6441 0 84*
– www.airotel.gr
90 rm ⌐ – ♦152 € ♦♦180 € – 3 suites
Rest *Don Giovanni* a la carte 20/32 €
♦ Business ♦ Design ♦
A relaxed, commercial hotel off a very busy avenue in residential area. Simple accommodation is offered in comfortably appointed bedrooms. Don Giovanni is an elegant little restaurant with marble décor offering international/ Mediterranean cuisine with some Greek specialities.

Electra 🅰 ⴟ 🖾 📞 ꕔ60 𝑽𝑰𝑺𝑨 ⓒⓞ 🅰🅴 ⓘ
5 Ermou ⌧ 105 63 – Ⓜ *Syntagma – ℰ (210) 3378 0 00*
– electrahotels@ath.forthnet.gr – Fax (210) 3220 3 10
– www.electrahotels.gr   **C2**
106 rm ⌐ – ♦186 € ♦♦312 € – 3 suites
Rest a la carte 17/29 €
♦ Business ♦ Modern ♦
Popular tourist hotel within the lively pedestrianised shopping area. Soundproofed bedrooms are thoughtfully equipped and well maintained, some have spa baths.

Art 🅰 ⴟ 🖾 📞 ꕔ40 𝑽𝑰𝑺𝑨 ⓒⓞ 🅰🅴 ⓘ
27 Marnis St ⌧ 104 32 Athens – Ⓜ *Omonia – ℰ (210) 5 24 05 01*
– info@arthotelathens.gr – Fax (210) 5 24 33 84
– www.arthotelathens.gr   **B1**
30 rm ⌐ – ♦79 € ♦♦120 €
Rest (room service only) 20 €
♦ Family ♦ Personalised ♦
The name's the clue: artwork in all areas of this family owned 21C boutique hotel behind a classic 1930s façade on busy central street. Simply furnished, unfussy bedrooms.

Periscope without rest ⓕ 🅰 ⴟ 🖾 📞 𝑽𝑰𝑺𝑨 ⓒⓞ 🅰🅴 ⓘ
22 Haritos St., Kolonaki ⌧ 106 75 Athens – Ⓜ *Evangelismos*
– ℰ (210) 6 23 63 20 – info@periscope.gr – Fax (210) 6 23 63 23
– www.periscope.gr   **D2**
22 rm ⌐ – ♦275 € ♦♦375 €
♦ Business ♦ Modern ♦
Minimalism in an area renowned for its smartness; trendy bar has plasma screens and reconditioned Mini Cooper seats! Uniquely styled rooms boast balconies and enlarged Athenian images on ceiling.

Omonia Grand 🅰 𝒮 🖾 𝑽𝑰𝑺𝑨 ⓒⓞ 🅰🅴 ⓘ
2 Pireos, Omonia Sq ⌧ 105 52 – Ⓜ *Omonia – ℰ (210) 5235 2 30*
– salesacr@grecotel.gr – Fax (210) 5282 1 59 – www.grecotel.gr   **B2**
115 rm ⌐ – ♦150 € ♦♦520 €
Rest a la carte 25/36 €
♦ Business ♦ Modern ♦
Beyond the bronze sculptured door and impressive marbled lobby is a bright and up-to-date hotel. Many of the interior-designed bedrooms overlook the bustling square. Appealing, modern first floor restaurant with international menu.

Athens Acropol ⓕ 🕭 🅰 𝒮 🖾 ꕔ350 𝑽𝑰𝑺𝑨 ⓒⓞ 🅰🅴 ⓘ
1 Pireos, Omonia Sq ⌧ 105 52 – Ⓜ *Omonia – ℰ (210) 5282 1 00*
– acr@grecotel.gr – Fax (210) 5282 1 59 – www.grecotel.gr   **B2**
164 rm ⌐ – ♦320 € ♦♦370 € – 3 suites
Rest a la carte 20/23 €
♦ Business ♦ Modern ♦
Sister hotel to Omonia, blending modern and classic styling. Soundproofed bedrooms and suites offer sanctuary from the hustle and bustle of the city centre below. Spacious Acropol restaurant with extensive international menu or lighter snacks in bar.

GREECE

⌂ **Hermes** without rest   AK ⅏ AE VISA ⓂⓈ AE ①
19 Apollonos St ✉ *105 57 –* Ⓜ *Syntagma –* ✆ *(210) 3235 5 14*
– hermes@tourhotel.gr – Fax (210) 3222 4 12
– www.hermes-athens.com   **B3**
45 rm � *–* ❅90 € ❅❅145 €
♦ Family ♦ Modern ♦
Small modern hotel, refurbished in 2005, in Plaka near the shops. Stylish
lobby and breakfast room. Bedrooms have balcony or terrace and all mod
cons.

⌂ **Arion** without rest   AK ⅏ AE VISA ⓂⓈ AE ①
18 Aglou Dimitriou St ✉ *105 54 –* Ⓜ *Monastiraki –* ✆ *(210) 3 24 04 15*
– arion@tourhotel.gr – Fax (210) 3 22 24 12 – www.arionhotel.gr   **B2**
51 rm ⊃ *–* ❅90 € ❅❅145 €
♦ Family ♦ Modern ♦
Opened in 2005, a sensibly priced tourist hotel in lively part of city. Roof-top
terrace with superb views. Compact, impressive rooms - ask for one that
overlooks Acropolis.

⌂ **Plaka** without rest   ⪡ Athens, AK ⅏ AE ℣ VISA ⓂⓈ AE ①
7 Kapnikareas and Mitropoleos St ✉ *105 56 –* Ⓜ *Monastiraki*
– ✆ *(210) 3222 0 96 – plaka@tourhotel.gr – Fax (210) 3222 4 12*
– www.plakahotel.gr   **B3**
67 rm ⊃ *–* ❅95 € ❅❅145 €
♦ Traditional ♦ Family ♦
Privately owned hotel among shops and tavernas, with a rooftop bar
overlooking the old town. Spotless, sensibly priced modern rooms; ask for one
with a view of the Acropolis.

⌂ **Museum** without rest   AK ⅟ ⅏ AE ℣ 🛁80 VISA ⓂⓈ AE ①
16 Bouboulinas St – Ⓜ *Victoria –* ✆ *(210) 3805 6 11*
– reservations30@yahoo.com – Fax (210) 3800 5 07
– www.bestwestern.com/gr/hotelmuseum   **B1**
93 rm ⊃ *–* ❅60 € ❅❅120 €
♦ Family ♦ Functional ♦
Overlooking the National Archaeological Museum and offering comfy facilties:
extension rooms are more stylish and modern. Other rooms all benefit from
balcony views.

✕✕✕ **Spondi**   ⌖ AK P VISA ⓂⓈ AE ①
❀
5 Pyronos, off Varnava Sq., Pangrati ✉ *116 36 –* ✆ *(210) 7564 0 21*
– info@spondi.gr – Fax (210) 7567 0 21
– www.spondi.gr
closed 1 week Easter and 10-16 August   **D3**
Rest 88 €/115 € and a la carte 69/82 € ⅋
Spec. Langoustine with five spice, onion and mango purée flavoured with
coriander. Red mullet in bread crust with basil flavoured tomato. Almond parfait
with caramelised apricot and pineapple.
♦ French ♦ Formal ♦
Attractive converted villa creating an intimate atmosphere in its elegant
rooms and external courtyard and terraces. Outstanding modern French
cooking.

✕✕✕ **Varoulko** (Lefteris)   ⌖ AK ⅏ VISA ⓂⓈ AE ①
❀
80 Pireaus Ave, Keramikos ✉ *104 35 –* Ⓜ *Thissio –* ✆ *(210) 5228 4 00*
– info@varoulko.gr – Fax (210) 5228 8 00 – www.varoulko.gr
closed Sunday   **A2**
Rest (booking essential) (dinner only) a la carte 46/56 €
Spec. Cuttlefish ink soup with grouper. Fried squid with basil pesto. Shrimp with
mashed split peas and truffle.
♦ Seafood ♦ Fashionable ♦
Modern, stylish restaurant in converted house with roof terrace and view of the
Acropolis. À la carte and tasting menu of finest local seafood. Accomplished
cooking.

399

Jérôme Serres – at Eridanus H.   🅰🅲 🅿 𝘝𝘐𝘚𝘈 ⓂⓈ 🄰🄴 ⓞ
78 Pireaus Ave, Keramikos – Ⓜ *Thissio –* ℰ *(210) 5 20 06 30*
– Fax (210) 5 22 88 00
closed June-August, 5 days Easter and Sunday   **A2**
Rest (dinner only) a la carte approx. 80 €
Spec. Sabayon of seasonal mushrooms with tarragon and roast langoustine.
Veal kidneys with polenta, spinach, olives and capers. Cinnamon rice pudding,
red fruits and yoghurt ice cream.
♦ French ♦ Formal ♦
Set in the chic Eridanus, this contemporary restaurant shows off modern Greek
artwork on the walls and offers accomplished classical French cooking with
modern flourishes.

Etrusco   🏠 🅰🅲 ⅗ 𝘝𝘐𝘚𝘈 ⓂⓈ 🄰🄴 ⓞ
32 Kallirois Ave – ℰ *(210) 9223 9 23 – hotel @ tac.gr*
– Fax (210) 9215 3 42
closed Sunday   **C3**
Rest a la carte 52/58 €
♦ Innovative ♦ Trendy ♦
Stylish contemporary restaurant with roof terrace for dining in summer, situated
in the Callirhoe Hotel. Innovative modern Greek cooking and international
fusion cuisine.

Boschetto   🏠 🅰🅲 ⅗ 𝘝𝘐𝘚𝘈 ⓂⓈ 🄰🄴 ⓞ
Evangelismou, off Vas. Sofias ✉ *116 76 –* Ⓜ *Evangelismos*
– ℰ *(210) 7210 8 93 – info @ boschettorestaurant.gr*
– Fax (210) 7223 5 98 – www.boschettorestaurant.gr
closed 25 December, 1 January and Sunday   **D2**
Rest a la carte 51/82 €
♦ Italian ♦ Formal ♦
Attractive summer house secluded within the neatly trimmed hedge of this small
city park. Polished service of an elaborate international menu with strong Italian
influences.

48 The Restaurant   🏠 🅰🅲 𝘝𝘐𝘚𝘈 ⓂⓈ 🄰🄴 ⓞ
48 Armatolon and Klefton ✉ *114 71 –* Ⓜ *Ambelokipi –* ℰ *(210) 6 41 10 82*
– www.48therestaurant.com
closed Sunday   **D1**
Rest (dinner only) a la carte 56/74 € 🈂
♦ Inventive ♦ Design ♦
Trendy, atmospheric restaurant where minimalism holds sway, underpinned by
modern art on the walls. Dishes, accordingly, are an evolving, modish reworking
of Greek classics.

Hytra   🅰🅲 ⅗ 𝘝𝘐𝘚𝘈 ⓂⓈ 🄰🄴 ⓞ
Navarhou Apostoli 7, Psirri – Ⓜ *Monastiraki –* ℰ *(210) 3316 7 67*
– Fax (210) 3316 7 67
closed July-September and Sunday   **B2**
Rest (dinner only) 37 € and a la carte 40/49 €
♦ Inventive ♦ Trendy ♦
Refurbished, vibrant modern restaurant in trendy Psirri. Modish Greek menus,
innovative in places: reworking of Greek classics. Friendly, knowledgable
service.

Kiku   🅰🅲 ⅗ 𝘝𝘐𝘚𝘈 ⓂⓈ 🄰🄴 ⓞ
12 Dimokritou St ✉ *103 45 –* Ⓜ *Syntagma –* ℰ *(210) 3647 0 33*
– Fax (210) 3626 2 39
closed 4 days Easter, August, 25 December, 1 January and Sunday   **C2**
Rest (dinner only) 48 €/58 € and a la carte 42/62 €
♦ Japanese (Okonomi-Yaki) ♦ Minimalist ♦
Stylish and authentic Japanese restaurant. Minimalist interior in shades of
black and white with screens and soft lighting. Extensive selection of sushi and
sashimi.

✗ **Psara's** 🛒 _VISA_ **MO**

16 Erehtheos and Erotskritou St, Plaka ✉ _105 56 –_ **Ⓜ** _Monastiraki_
– 𝒞 (210) 3 21 87 33 – Fax (210) 3 21 87 34 **B3**
Rest a la carte 18/37 €
♦ Traditional ♦ Rustic ♦
Just below the Acropolis; has been a taverna since 1898. Refurbished rustic style
within two yellow-washed houses with terrace. Fresh ingredients enhance
classic taverna menus.

✗ **Prytanio** 🛒 _AC_ ✂ _VISA_ **MO** _AE_ **①**

7 Millioni St, Kolonaki ✉ _106 73 – 𝒞 (210) 3643 3 53 – kolonaki @ prytaneion.gr_
– Fax (210) 8082 5 77 – www.prytaneion.gr **C2**
Rest a la carte 33/72 €
♦ Mediterranean ♦ Bistro ♦
Watch the fashionable shoppers go by from a table on the terrace or choose the
more intimate interior or the garden. Pleasant service and modern Mediterra-
nean-influenced menu.

✗ **Oraia Penteli** 🛒 _VISA_ **MO**

Iroon Sq, Psirri ✉ _105 54 –_ **Ⓜ** _Monastiraki – 𝒞 (210) 3218 6 27_
– Fax (210) 3218 6 27 **B2**
Rest a la carte 12/31 €
♦ Traditional ♦ Rustic ♦
Historic building in the centre of Psirri converted into café-restaurant preparing
traditional Greek recipes; live Greek music mid-week evenings and weekend
afternoons.

ENVIRONS OF ATHENS

at Kifissia _Northeast: 15 km by Vas. Sofias:_

🏨 **Pentelikon** ⌂ 🛒 ⊐ 🚗 ⅏ _AC_ ↵rm ✂ _CD_ ♨350 ⌂

66 Diligianni St, Kefalari (off Harilaou Trikoupi, **P** _VISA_ **MO** _AE_ **①**
follow signs to Politia) ✉ _145 62 –_ **Ⓜ** _Kifissia_
– 𝒞 (210) 6230 6 50 – pentilik @ otenet.gr – Fax (210) 8019 2 23
– www.hotelpentelikon.gr
95 rm – ♦315 € ♦♦410 €, ⊇ 24 € – 7 suites
Rest see **Vardis** below
Rest La Terrasse 40 €/60 €
♦ Grand Luxury ♦ Traditional ♦ Classic ♦
Imposing late 19C mansion in affluent residential suburb. Opulence and
antiques throughout. Most charming and tranquil rooms overlook the gardens.
Traditional service. Conservatory restaurant with a Mediterranean theme
offering full range of dishes.

🏨 **Theoxenia Palace** ₤₅ 🛁 ⊐ _AC_ ↵rm ✂ _CD_ ☎ ♨350

2 Filadelfeos St ✉ _145 62 –_ **Ⓜ** _Kifissia_ ⌂ _VISA_ **MO** _AE_ **①**
– 𝒞 (210) 6233 6 22 – reservations @ theoxeniapalace.com – Fax (210) 6231 6 75
– www.theoxeniapalace.com
69 rm ⊇ – ♦200 € ♦♦420 € – 2 suites
Rest a la carte 31/51 €
♦ Business ♦ Modern ♦
Renovated 1920s hotel with imposing façade. Spacious well-equipped rooms.
Good leisure and large conference/banqueting facilities. Informal dining room.

🏨 **Theoxenia House** without rest _AC_ ✂ _CD_ ☎ ♨80 ⌂

42 Harilaou Trikoupi St and 9 Pentelis St ✉ _145 62_ _VISA_ **MO** _AE_ **①**
_–_ **Ⓜ** _Kifissia – 𝒞 (210) 6233 6 22 – reservations @ theoxeniapalace.com_
– Fax (210) 6231 6 75 – www.theoxeniahouse.com
11 rm ⊇ – ♦180 € ♦♦240 € – 1 suite
♦ Business ♦ Modern ♦
Stylish house in pleasant suburb converted to provide very large, well-equipped
rooms, each with lounge area and cooking facilities, plus full use of Theoxenia
Palace hotel.

The Kefalari Suites without rest   AC ⇄ ⚇ 🖨 🕿 📶 VISA ⓿❾ AE ⓪
1 Pentelis and Kolokotroni St, Kefalari ⊠ 145 62 – Ⓜ Kifissia – 𝒞 (210) 6233 3 33
– info@kefalarisuites.gr – Fax (210) 6233 3 30 – www.kefalarisuites.gr
2 rm ⌧ – †200 € ††280 € – **11 suites** ⌧ – †200 € ††280 €
♦ Townhouse ♦ Stylish ♦
Early 20C villa set in a smart, quiet suburb; stylish, airy, thoughtfully appointed
rooms, each on a subtle, imaginative theme, most with lounge and veranda.
Rooftop spa bath.

Semiramis   Ⅰ⑤ 🕸 ⚓ AC ⇄rm ⚇ 🖨 🕿 ♨160 ⊜ VISA ⓿❾ AE ⓪
48 Charilaou Trikoupi St, Kefalari ⊠ 145 62 – Ⓜ Kifissia – 𝒞 (210) 6 28 44 00
– info@semiramisathens.com – Fax (210) 6 28 44 99 – www.semiramisathens.com
50 rm ⌧ – †180 € ††350 € – 1 suite
Rest a la carte 35/59 €
♦ Business ♦ Modern ♦
Striking 1930s conversion accentuated by lime green balconies, boldly hued
public areas and organic shaped pool. Rooms with no numbers on the doors and
stunning interiors. Dine on soft seats at a mix of tables: Greek dishes meet
mainstream Med style.

Twenty One   🏠 AC ⇄rm 🖨 🕿 VISA ⓿❾ AE ⓪
21 Kolokotroni and Mykonou St, Kefalari ⊠ 145 62 – Ⓜ Kifissia – 𝒞 (210)
6 23 35 21 – info@twentyone.gr – Fax (210) 6 23 38 21 – www.twentyone.gr
21 rm ⌧ – †190 € ††240 €
Rest a la carte 30/40 €
♦ Business ♦ Modern ♦
Converted slate grey 19C former watermill in pleasant suburb. Flowing minimalistic
interior. Standard rooms are well designed, some with balconies; five trendy loft
suites. Informal dining room and expansive terrace; simple international menus.

XXXX **Vardis** – at Pentelikon H.   🏠 AC ⚇ P VISA ⓿❾ AE ⓪
66 Diligianni St, Kefalari (off Harilaou Trikoupi, follow signs to Politia) – Ⓜ Kifissia
– 𝒞 (210) 6230 6 60 – vardis@hotelpentelikon.gr – Fax (210) 8019 2 23
– www.hotelpentelikon.gr
Rest (closed Sunday) (booking essential) (dinner only) a la carte 56/80 €
♦ French ♦ Formal ♦
Elegant, ornately decorated restaurant with extensive terrace. Fine table
settings. Formal and polished service of elaborate classic French/Mediterranean
influenced cuisine.

at Ekali Northeast: 20 km by Vas Sofias:

Life Gallery   🏠 ⚇ Ⅰ⑤ 🕸 ⚓ 🌊 ⛲ AC ⇄rm 🖨 🕿 ♨120
103 Thisseos Ave ⊠ 145 78 – 𝒞 (210) 6 26 04 00   P VISA ⓿❾ AE ⓪
– info-lifegallery@bluegr.com – Fax (210) 6 22 93 53 – www.bluegr.com
30 rm ⌧ – †690 € ††990 €
Rest (residents only Sunday and Monday) a la carte 44/57 €
♦ Luxury ♦ Stylish ♦
Strikingly smart 'glass cube' with discreet yet eye-catchingly contemporary
décor at every turn: don't miss the modern library. Sleek, stylish bedrooms all
boast balconies. Bright, spacious restaurant with capacious outdoor terrace.
Mediterranean influenced menus.

at Athens International Airport East: 35 km by Vas. Sofias:

Sofitel Athens Airport   🏠 Ⅰ⑤ 🕸 ⚓ 🖭 & AC ⇄rm 🖨 🕿 ♨600
⊠ 190 19 – Ⓜ Airport – 𝒞 (210) 3544 0 00   ⊜ VISA ⓿❾ AE ⓪
– h3167@accor.com – Fax (210) 3544 4 44 – www.sofitel.com
332 rm ⌧ – †270 € ††355 € – 13 suites
Rest Karavi (dinner only) a la carte 62/95 €
Rest Mesoghaia a la carte 38/56 €
♦ Business ♦ Modern ♦
First hotel at the new airport. Modern and very well equipped from comfy library
bar to exclusive leisure club. Spacious rooms and impressive bathrooms. French
menus on the 9th floor in Karavi. Informal brightly decorated Mediterranean
themed Mesoghaia.

at Lagonissi *Southeast: 40 km by Singrou:*

 Grand Resort Lagonissi ⟨⟩ ≤ Saronic Gulf, 🍴 *Ⅰ₅* ⬛ (heated) ℀
Sounio Ave ✉ *190 10* 🛏 🌭 🄰🄲 ℀rest 🛁180 🄿 *VISA* 🌐 🄰🄴 🄾
– ☏ *(22) 9107 60 00 – grandresort@grandresort.gr – Fax (22) 9102 45 34*
– *www.grandresort.gr*
closed in winter
182 rm ⌂ – ♜450 € ♜♜500 € – 99 suites
Rest a la carte 35/40 €
Rest Kohylia a la carte 70/100 €
Rest Captain's House (dinner only) a la carte 40/60 €
Rest Ouzeri a la carte 35/50 €
♦ Grand Luxury ♦ Modern ♦
Luxurious, stunning resort on a private peninsula. 16 beaches; suites with private
pools. Service to satisfy the most demanding. Mediterraneo for seafood.
Polynesian and Japanese cuisine in Kohylia. Captain's House for Italian dishes.
Greek cooking in Ouzeri.

at Vouliagmeni *South: 18 km by Singrou:*

 Divani Apollon Palace ≤ Saronic Gulf, 🍴 🌐 *Ⅰ₅* ⬛ ⬛ 🄳 ℀ 🛏
10 Ag. Nicolaou 🄰🄲 ᐸ⁄rm ℀ ✉ 🛁1200 ⬤ *VISA* 🌐 🄰🄴 🄾
and Iliou St (Kavouri) off Athinas ✉ *166 71*
– ☏ *(210) 8911 1 00 – divanis@divaniapollon.gr – Fax (210) 9658 0 10*
– *www.divanis.gr*
279 rm ⌂ – ♜280 € ♜♜440 € – 7 suites
Rest Mythos (dinner only) a la carte 53/111 €
Rest Anemos a la carte 58/75 €
♦ Luxury ♦ Modern ♦
Modern hotel in fashionable resort. Poolside lounge. Spa and thalassotherapy
centre. Every bedroom boasts balcony overlooking the Saronic Gulf. Small
private beach. Dine in Mythos on the beach with local dishes. Anemos is modern
with global fare.

 The Margi 🍴 *Ⅰ₅* 🄳 🄰🄲 ℀ ✉ 🛁500 *VISA* 🌐 🄰🄴 🄾
11 Litous St, off Athinas by Apollonos ✉ *166 71 –* ☏ *(210) 8 92 90 00*
– *themargi@themargi.gr – Fax (210) 8 92 91 43 – www.themargi.gr*
88 rm ⌂ – ♜220 € ♜♜600 €
Rest a la carte 35/57 €
♦ Business ♦ Stylish ♦
A stylish hotel that combines contemporary elegance with a colonial feel.
Breakfast can be taken on the poolside terrace. Bedrooms have antique pieces
and smart marble bathrooms. Informal restaurant with its eclectic menu is
popular with the 'in crowd'.

at Kalamaki *Southwest: 14 km by Singrou:*

℀℀℀ **Akrotiri** 🍴 🄳 🄰🄲 ℀ 🄿 *VISA* 🌐 🄰🄴 🄾
Vas. Georgiou B5, Agios Kosmas, Elliniko ✉ *167 77 –* ☏ *(210) 9859 1 47*
– *akrotiri@enternet.gr – Fax (210) 9859 1 49 – www.akrotirilounge.gr*
closed in winter
Rest (dinner only) a la carte 50/67 €
♦ French ♦ Fashionable ♦
A seaside restaurant combining simplicity and luxury. Candlelit dinners on the
pool terrace; DJ music. Menu of good quality international cuisine with French
influence.

HUNGARY
MAGYARORSZÁG

PROFILE

- **AREA:**
  93 032 km² (35 920 sq mi).

- **POPULATION:**
  10 007 000 inhabitants (est. 2005), density = 108 per km².

- **CAPITAL:**
  Budapest (conurbation 2 232 000 inhabitants).

- **CURRENCY:**
  Forint (Ft or HUF); rate of exchange: HUF 100 = € 0.40 = US$ 0.46 (Nov 2005).

- **GOVERNMENT:**
  Parliamentary republic (since 1989). Member of European Union since 2004.

- **LANGUAGE:**
  Hungarian; many Hungarians also speak English and German.

- **SPECIFIC PUBLIC HOLIDAYS:**
  1848 Revolution Day (15 March); National Day-St. Stephen Day (20 August); Republic Day-1956 Uprising Remembrance Day (23 October); Boxing Day (26 December).

- **LOCAL TIME:**
  GMT + 1 hour in winter and GMT + 2 hours in summer.

- **CLIMATE:**
  Temperate continental with cold winters and warm summers (Budapest: January: -1°C, July: 22°C).

- **INTERNATIONAL DIALLING CODE:**
  00 36 followed by area code and local number. International enquiries: ☎ 199.

- **EMERGENCY:**
  Central emergency line: ☎ 112; Ambulance: ☎ 108, Fire Brigade: ☎ 105, Police: ☎ 107, Roadside breakdown service: ☎ 188.

- **ELECTRICITY:**
  230 volts, 50 Hz; 2-pin round-shaped continental plugs.

• Budapest

FORMALITIES

Travellers from the European Union (EU), Switzerland, Iceland and the main countries of North and South America need a national identity card or passport (America: passport required) to visit Hungary for less than three months (tourism or business purpose). For visitors from other countries a visa may be required, in addition to a passport, especially for those wishing to stay for longer than three months. We advise you to check with your embassy before travelling.

A valid driving licence is essential. The larger car rental companies require that the driver is at least 21 years old with at least one year's driving experience.

MAJOR NEWSPAPERS

The main dailies are *Magyar Nemzet*, *Népszabadság* and *Nepszava*. The *Budapest Sun*, the *Budapest Business Journal* and the *Hungarian Quarterly* are printed in English.

USEFUL PHRASES

ENGLISH	HUNGARIAN
Yes	**Igen**
No	**Nem**
Good morning	**Jo Reggelt**
Goodbye	**Viszlat**
Thank you	**Köszönöm**
Please	**Kerem**
Excuse me	**Bocsanat**
I don't understand	**Nem ertem**

HOTELS

◆ CATEGORIES

In Budapest accommodation ranges from luxurious 5-star international hotels, to smaller, family-run guesthouses and paying-guest rooms.

◆ PRICE RANGE

The price is per room. There is little difference between the price of a single and a double room.

Budapest is a popular resort throughout the year and it is therefore advisable to book in advance. However some hotel chains offer lower weekend rates in low season.

◆ TAX

Included in the room price.

◆ CHECK OUT TIME

Usually between 10am and noon.

◆ RESERVATIONS

By telephone or by Internet. A credit card number may be required.

◆ TIP FOR LUGGAGE HANDLING

At the discretion of the customer (about Ft 500 per bag).

◆ BREAKFAST

It is often not included in the price of the room and is generally served between 7am and 10am. Most hotels offer a self-service buffet but it is usually possible in the more expensive hotels to have continental breakfast served in the room.

Reception	**Recepcio**
Single room	**Egyagyas szoba**
Double room	**Ketaghas szoba**
Bed	**Agy**
Bathroom	**Sürdö szoba**
Shower	**Tusolo**

RESTAURANTS

Most **restaurants (étterem)** are in the traditional Hungarian style, sometimes with live gypsy music; most are also privately owned and reflect the philosophy of the chef/patron. There are also Italian, French and other ethnic restaurants.

◆ MEALS

Breakfast	**Regelli**	7am – 10am
Lunch	**Ebéd**	12.30pm – 2-3pm
Dinner	**Vacsora**	6.30pm – 10-11pm

A traditional Hungarian menu does not list starters but they are offered in most restaurants. The majority of menus are à la carte but there are some fixed price menus.

◆ RESERVATIONS

Reservations are usually made by phone, fax or Internet. For famous restaurants, it is advisable to book several days in advance. A credit card number or a phone number may be required as guarantee.

◆ THE BILL

The bill (check) includes VAT but no service charge. Tipping is optional but, if you are particularly pleased with the service, it is customary to round up to an appropriate figure (10%).

Drink or aperitif	**Rövid ital**
Appetizer	**Etel**
First course, starter	**Elöetel**
Main dish	**Föetel**
Main dish of the day	**Napi ajanlat**
Dessert	**Desszert**
Water	**Viz**
Wine (red, white, rosé)	**Bor (börös, feher, rosé)**
Beer, draught beer	**Sör, csapolt sör**
Bread	**Kenyer**
Meat	**Hus**
Fish	**Hal**
Salt/pepper	**So / Bors**
Cheese	**Sajt**
Vegetables	**Zöldség**
Hot/cold	**Forro / hideg**
The bill (check) please	**A szamlat, kerem**

LOCAL CUISINE

Hungarian chefs are versatile and inventive, making good use of local seasonal produce. Many of the dishes are nourishing and hearty – and portions are generous – but not all are flavoured with **paprika**, although the red powder, hot (*csípős*) or sweet (*édesnemes*), is much in evidence and on sale in all tourist haunts. Other flavourings are herbs and pickles.

There is little saltwater fish but plenty of freshwater **pike-perch (fogas)** from Lake Balaton and also **trout (pisztrang)**. **Halászlé** is a fish soup made of a mixture of sea and freshwater fish poached with tomatoes, green peppers and paprika. The best known dish is probably **goulash (gulyás)**, a thick soup of beef, onions and potatoes, usually served as a main course; other favourite soup ingredients are beans, dumplings and cabbage. In summer there are cold fruit soups. Menus offer beef and pork, chicken and turkey, goose and game in season, but lamb is rare. The accent of paprika is stronger in dishes such as **tötött káposzta**, stuffed cabbage, and **pörkölt**, meat and onion stew, which is known as **paprikás**, when thickened with flour and sour cream. **Lecsó** is a sauce of onions, tomatoes and stewed peppers, served with meat. Some ingredients – beef and salmon – may be served tartar style. Garlic sausage, salami and goose liver are served as starters, as are smoked fish, ham and goose. Cheeses are made from cow's and ewe's milk; curd cheese is a particular favourite.

Pancakes *(palacsinta)*, dumplings and strudels appear frequently, as savoury (herb dumplings, spinach strudel) or sweet dishes. The wide choice of desserts includes such peaks of Hungarian gastronomy as Gundel pancakes, filled with a walnut mixture and served with hot chocolate sauce; golden dumplings, flavoured with ground walnuts and served with vanilla custard; Somlói galuska, layers of sponge cake and custard, smothered in walnuts, sultanas, chocolate sauce, rum syrup and whipped cream; Eszterházy cake made with ground walnuts, layered with a cream filling and white chocolate coating; Vargabéles, a soft sweet sponge cake made with curd cheese and flavoured with vanilla and raisins; strudels filled with apple, plums or cherries.

◆ DRINK

Hungary has 22 wine regions producing both red and white wine. Best known among the reds is the dark and spicy-flavoured **Egri Bikavér** (Bull's Blood of Eger); there are also distinctive reds from **Villány** and **Szekszárd** and **Kéknyelű**. Among the whites **Olaszrixling** (Italian Riesling), with the taste of bitter almonds, is recommended with fish, **Harslevelű** with poultry and dry **Furmint** with desserts; the Eger district also produces reputed white wines. The wines from the Tokay region have the highest alcohol, sugar and acid content of any wines in Hungary. The non-*aszú* Tokay wines generally have a hard, acidic character, with strong body and bouquet. Bottles bearing the words *édes or félszáraz* cater to the local taste for sweet red and white wine.

The most famous Hungarian wine is the dessert wine, **Tokaji aszú**. The grapes are grown on the south and southwest facing slopes of the foothills of the Zemplén range; the volcanic soil is rich in nutrients. In autumn while the grapes are maturing there is often a period of perhaps one week during which a mild, sunny and dry spell takes over from the otherwise drizzly, damp weather. This favours the development of the Botrytis fungus, which causes the 'noble rot' which makes Tokaj aszú so distinctive. Aszú wines are prepared by adding grapes with the famed 'noble rot' to the wine base; the number of baskets *(puttonyok)* of grapes added is signified in the type of wine – ranging from 3-6 puttonyos. Among speciality wines, the dry and sweet **Szamorodni** wines deserve special mention; they are produced by adding small quantities of *aszú* grapes.

Beer is sold by the half-litre *(korsó)* or a smaller glass *(pohár)*. As well as local brands such as Dreher and Borsodi, bars may also offer the products of German, Austrian, Czech or even Belgian breweries.

Hungary produces its own **brandy (pálinka)**; pear brandy *(körtepálinka)*, apricot brandy *(barackpálinka)* and the plum brandy *(szilvapálinka)* of Szatmár are drunk as aperitifs. **Unicum**, a dark brown herb liqueur with a bitter flavour, is a unique Hungarian aperitif to be drunk sparingly.

BUDAPEST

Population (est. 2005): 1 702 000 (conurbation 2 231 000) – Altitude: 102m

R. Mattes/MICHELIN

The Hungarian capital on the River Danube was formed in 1872 by the merger of three towns: Buda, Pest and Obuda (Old Buda), whose Roman remains are still visible.

Budapest has a continental climate, with cold winters and very hot summers. It is a lively, friendly city which has succeeded in integrating modern innovations and architecture with a rich historical heritage, and now offers a wealth of entertainment and cultural activities for visitors. An excellent but inexpensive public transport system of buses, trolleybuses, trams and underground lines covers the city.

Buda and Pest are linked by bridges; the most famous of which are Chain Bridge (Széchenyi Lánchíd), guarded by huge stone lions, and Liberty Bridge (Szabadság híd), a fine metal structure built at the end of the 19C. The city's golden age was in the 19C which has left a rich legacy of Art Nouveau buildings. Passenger craft provide regular trips on the Danube to see the sights, particularly when they are flood-lit at night, or 20km up stream to Szentendre.

Budapest is a great place for 'taking the waters'; the thermal springs developed into a national institution under the Turkish occupation; some Turkish baths are still in use in their original state; the warm open air baths are popular in winter; there are also modern spa hotels and medical treatment centres.

WHICH DISTRICT TO CHOOSE

The majority of **hotels**, particularly the group hotels and the smaller privately-owned ones, are in the commercial district *Plan II* **H2** in Pest on the east bank of the Danube. The castle district *Plan II* **D2** on the west bank of the Danube also has a few hotels. Some of the cheaper smaller hotels are located north of the castle district.

Restaurants are distributed on the same pattern as the hotels, being mostly in the commercial district

409

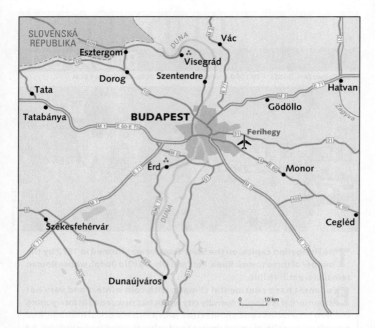

SLOVENSKÁ REPUBLIKA
Esztergom
Dorog
Tata
Tatabánya
BUDAPEST
Vác
Visegrád
Szentendre
Hatvan
Gödöllo
Ferihegy
Monor
Érd
Székesfehérvár
Cegléd
Dunaújváros

0   10 km

Plan II **H2** in Pest, with a few up near the Castle *Plan II* **D2**. There are also some in the Városliget, the City Park next to Heroes Square *Plan I* **B1**. The

floating restaurants moored along the east bank of the Danube provide a splendid view at night of the Castle and the flood-lit bridges.

PRACTICAL INFORMATION

ARRIVAL – DEPARTURE

Ferihegy Budapest National Airport – About 24 km (15 mi) southeast of the city centre. ℰ 296 9696; flight information ℰ 296 7000.

From the airport to the city centre – By **airport minibus** to individual hotels. Fare Ft 2 100. ℰ 296 8555. By **taxi**: 45min-Ft 4 000 to Pest, 1hr 15min-Ft 5 000 to Buda. By **public transport** – bus (20min), BKV Busz (Reptér Busz) which stops between the terminals and **metro** (blue line – 35mins). Fares Ft 190.

Railway Stations – **Eastern Station** (Keleti pályaudvar) *Plan I* **B2**. ℰ 413

4610. **Western Station** (Nyugati Pályaudvar) *Plan I* **A1**. ℰ 349 8503. **Southern Station** (Déli pályaudvar) *Plan II* **C2**. ℰ 375 6593, 461 5400 (domestic services), 461 5500 (international services); www.elvira.hu

River Station – Belgrád Rakpart; **Hydrofoil service** to Budapest from Bratislava (3hr 30min – 6hr) and Vienna (4hr-6hrs 30min) April-October. Ft 19 977.50 (€79). ℰ 318 6042, 484 4000; (passnave@mahartpassnave.hu)

TRANSPORT

◆ METRO, TRAM, TROLLEYBUS AND BUS

The extensive public transport network is composed of three metro lines (yellow, red and blue) intersecting at Deák Square, trams, trolleybuses and buses. Tickets must be purchased in advance and validated in the ticket stampers at the start of the journey; spot checks are made. Tickets are available from metro stations, ticket machines, tobacconists and newsagents. Single Ft 145; different cheaper ticket types are available at metro stations (see also Budapest Card). ℰ 06 80 406 611 (www.bkv.hu).

◆ TAXIS

Authorised taxis display a yellow taxi sign and yellow number plates. It is best to order one through hotel reception (less expensive) or take one waiting outside a hotel. Unauthorised taxis can be very expensive. Maximum basic charge Ft 300 (day), Ft 420 (night); Ft 240 per km (day), Ft 336 per km (night). The larger companies have lower charges. A tip of 10% is generally acceptable. ℰ 233 3333 (Budataxi), 433 3333 (Budapest Taxi), 322 3344 (Central Hotel Taxi), 211 1111 (Citytaxi), 205 5555 (Expo Taxi), 222 2222 (Fötaxi), 377 7777 (Rádiótaxi).

◆ BUDAPEST CARD

Includes unlimited travel on public transport, free or reduced price admission to 60 museums and sights, cultural and folklore programmes, discounts in some shops, restaurants and thermal baths, discounts on car hire. 48hr-card Ft 4 700; 72hr-card Ft 5 900. On sale at the airport, in Tourist Offices and in some hotels.

USEFUL ADDRESSES

◆ TOURIST INFORMATION

Tourinform Main Office, Sütö u.2, Deák Tér. ℰ 438 8080. Open 8am-8pm. **Buda Castle**, Szentháromság tér (Budai Vár) *Plan II* **D2**. ℰ 488 0474/5. Open mid-Jun to mid-Sep 9am-8pm,

otherwise 10am-7pm (Nov-Mar Mon-Fri 10am-7pm, Sat-Sun 10am-4pm). **Western Railway Station** (Nyugati Pályaudvar) *Plan I* **A1**. ℰ 302 8580. Open mid-Jun to mid-Sep 9am-7pm, otherwise Mon-Fri 9am-6pm, Sat-Sun 9am-3pm. **Tourinform Office**, Liszt Ferenc tér 9-11 *Plan II* **E2**. ℰ 342 9390 (liszt@budapestinfo. hu). Open Apr-Oct daily 9am-7pm, Nov-March, daily 10am-6pm. **Ferihegy Airport**, Terminals 2A and 2B. ℰ 438 8080, 488 4661. Open 8am-11pm. **Tourinform Hotline** ℰ (06 80) 630 800; from abroad ℰ (0036 30) 30 30 600; hungary@tourinform.hu; info@budapestinfo.hu; www.hunga rytourism.hu; www.budapestinfo.hu

◆ POST OFFICES

Opening times Mon-Fri 8am-6pm, Sat, 8am-1pm. Longer opening hours at Teréz körút 51, Mon-Sat 7am-9pm, Sun 8am-8pm and at the **Eastern Railway Station**, Baross tér, Mon-Sat 7am-9pm.

◆ BANKS/CURRENCY EXCHANGE

Opening times Mon-Thurs 8.30am to 3pm, Fri 8am-1pm. There are ATMs at most banks and many currency exchange machines.

◆ EMERGENCY

Central emergency line ℰ **112**; Ambulance ℰ **104**; Fire Brigade ℰ **105**; Police ℰ **107**; Roadside breakdown service ℰ **188**.

BUSY PERIODS

It may be difficult to find a room at a reasonable price when special events are held in the city:

Budapest Spring Festival: March – music, opera, ballet and folklore performances.

Budapest Búcsú: June – rock and pop music festival celebrating the departure of the Soviet army.

Sziget Festival: July-August – 8-day multicultural popular music festival on Hajógyári Island.

Formula 1 Grand Prix: August.

Budapest International Wine and Champagne Festival: September.

Budapest Christmas Fair: December.

EXPLORING BUDAPEST

DIFFERENT FACETS OF THE CITY

It is possible to visit the main sights and some museums in three days.

Museums and sights are usually open from 10am to 6pm. Most museums are closed on Monday.

CASTLE HILL – Budavári Palota Plan II **D2**: the Royal Castle *(funicular railway from Chain Bridge)* is the former royal residence, built in Classical and Baroque style. **Mátyás Templom** Plan II **D1**: 13C Gothic church with glazed tile roof. **Várnegyed** Plan II **D2**: charming old streets lined with medieval houses, Baroque mansions, small interior courtyards and other interesting buildings; in summer, horse-drawn carriage rides.

MUSEUMS AND GALLERIES – BUDA: **Magyar Nemzeti Galéria** Plan II **F3**: Hungarian art with medieval sculpture; 19C and 20C paintings and sculptures. **Budapesti Történeti Múzeum** Plan II **D2**: History of Budapest from the Magyar period. **PEST**: **Szépművészeti Múzeum** Plan I **B1**: National Museum of Fine Arts (gallery of Old Masters, paintings from the Spanish School, drawing and print room). **Magyar Nemzeti Múzeum** Plan II **F3**: Hungarian National Museum tracing the country's history from prehistoric times to the 1848 revolution. **Iparművészeti Múzeum** Plan I **B2**: Museum of Applied Arts, housed in an Art Nouveau building; reconstructions of Hungarian and European interiors.

PEST – Országház Plan II **E1**: the Parliament with its pinnacle turrets, arcades and flying buttresses fronting the river, displays St Stephen's crown. **Szent István Bazilika** Plan II **E1**: immense domed basilica dedicated to the first king of Hungary. **Magyar Állami Operaház** Plan II **F1**: impressive Opera House with richly-decorated interior. **À Dohány Utcai Zsinagóga** Plan II **F2**: Great Synagogue in Byzantine-Moorish style with beautiful interior decoration. **Vásárcsarnok** Plan II **F3**: Central Market, an attractive metal structure full of stalls selling fresh food – meat, fish, vegetables, fruit; also linen and crafts *(upper gallery)*.

CITY OF BATHS – Budapest has some 50 thermal baths *(fürdő)*, fed by over 80 active thermal springs and wells. **Király** Plan I **A1, Rácz** and **Rudas** Plan II **E3** are Turkish baths preserved in their original state. The **Gellért Baths** Plan II **E3** opened in 1918; the pool, built in the former greenhouse, is renowned for its mosaics, columns and balconies. **Széchenyi Baths** Plan I **B1** are housed in a huge neo-Classical building with domes, pediments, statues and a late 19C interior; floating chessboards in the open-air pool. **Danubius Thermal Baths** Plan I **A1** part of a luxury modern hotel on Margaret Island.

OUTDOOR BUDAPEST – Hősök tere and Varosliget Plan I **B1**: Heroes Square, marked by the Millennium Monument, a column symbolising 1 000 years of Hungarian history, leads into City Park; zoo, circus and amusement park. **Margit-Sziget** *Plan I* **A1**: a green island of tranquillity; lawns, flower beds, trees, walks, play areas, sports grounds, swimming pools, pump rooms and hotels. **Gyermekvasút**: the Children's (Pioneers') Train, staffed by children, runs mainly through woods (12km/7.5miles) in the Buda Hills; from Janós-Hegy station a path leads up to a viewing tower with a magnificent panorama *(From near Hotel Budapest take the rack railway to the top of Mount Széchenyi; walk to the Children's Train Station).*

GOURMET TREATS

The cafés and tea rooms of Budapest offer a great array of **pastries** and **cakes** – strudels, sponges and layer cakes, chocolate confections and a variety of ice creams. Drinks range from **coffee** (introduced by the Turks), **hot chocolate** and **tea** to freshly pressed **fruit juices** – orange, peach. For refreshment and shade in summer or warmth and shelter in winter, take a seat in a café/tea house: *Gerbeaud Plan II* **E2**; *Zsolnay* in the Béke Hotel *Plan II* **F1**; *Hauer*, Rákóczi Ut; *Mozart*, Erzsébet Bld; *Gellért Hotel Plan II* **E3**.

SHOPPING

Stores are usually open from Mon-Fri 10am to 6pm (7pm Thurs), Sat 9am-1pm; food stores 7am-6pm. Large shopping centres are open daily, 9/10am to 9pm, Sun 9/10am-3pm.

The main shopping area is **Váci utca** *Plan II* **E2**, a pedestrianised street, which links **Vörösmarty Square** *Plan II* **F1** and **Fövam Tér** and is lined, above and below ground, with fashion boutiques, indoor and pavement cafés, jewellers shops, bookstores and street vendors; also some of the side streets, such as **Párizsi Udvar** (the Paris Arcade is worth seeing if only

for its architecture) and **Kígyó ut**. For Hungarian folk art try *Folkart Centrum*, Váci utca 58. *The House of Hungarian Wines*, Szentháromság tér, on Castle Hill, offers wine tasting and a detailed display about Hungarian wine.

WHAT TO BUY – Herend porcelain, Zsolnay porcelain, leather goods, embroidery and lace, Tokay (Tokaij) and other Hungarian wines, paprika, salami, palinka, goose liver, Szamos marzipan, dried fruit, pasta in fancy shapes.

ENTERTAINMENT

Budapest City Guide, published in English and German by the Budapest Tourist Office, is a good source of information about cultural events in Budapest.

CONCERT HALLS – Hungarian State Opera House *Plan II* **F1**: opera and ballet. **Academy of Music** *Plan II* **E2**. **Budai Vigadó** *Plan II* **D1**: Hungarian State Folk Ensemble.

THEATRES – National Theatre *Plan II* **E2**. **Vigszínház Comedy Theatre** *Plan I* **A1**. **Katona József** *Plan II* **E2**. **International Buda Stage (IBS)**. **Merlin International Theatre** *Plan II* **F2**.

OTHER VENUES – Várszínház *Plan II* **D2**. **The National Dance Theatre** *Plan II* **D2**. **Contemporary Dance Theatre Society** *Plan I* **A2**.

NIGHTLIFE

Budapest City Guide, published by the Budapest Tourist Office, lists places for music and dancing. There are a number of addresses in the side streets around **Kalvin tér**. *Plan II* **F3** and also in the side streets off **Andrássy út**. between the Opera and the Octagon *Plan II* **F1**.

HUNGARY

Four Seasons Gresham Palace ⟨ 🏛 🌐 Ⓕ♨ 🗽 ♿ ⚑ ⤒rm 🏊

Roosevelt tér 5-6 ✉ *1051*   📺 📞 ♨90 🚗 **VISA** **⑳** AE ⓪
– Ⓜ *Vörösmarty tér* – ℘ *(01) 268 60 00*
– *budapest.reservations@fourseasons.com – Fax (01) 268 50 00*
– *www.fourseasons.com/budapest*   **E2**
165 rm – ❶87600 HUF ❶❶96900 HUF, ⊑ 6250 HUF – 14 suites
Rest *Páva* (dinner only) (closed Sunday) 10500 HUF and a la carte
8600/11500 HUF
Rest *Gresham Kávénáz* a la carte 7050/8250 HUF
♦ Grand Luxury ♦ Business ♦ Classic ♦
Art Nouveau palace on the Danube in business district converted into an
elegant, modern hotel; excellent service and spa treatments. Riverside
dining room and terrace; seasonal menu of Italian-classic Hungarian dishes with
modish twist. Kávénáz is coffee house renowned for traditional dishes - and its
cakes.

Kempinski H. Corvinus 🏛 🌐 Ⓕ♨ 🗽 🖵 ♿ ⚑ ⤒rm 🏊rest 📺 📞

Erzsébet tér 7-8 ✉ *1051* – Ⓜ *Deák tér*   ♨450 🚗 **VISA** **⑳** AE ⓪
– ℘ *(01) 429 37 77 – hotel.corvinus@kempinski.com – Fax (01) 429 47 77*
– *www.kempinski-budapest.com*   **E2**
337 rm – ❶65000 HUF ❶❶103000 HUF, ⊑ 7250 HUF – 28 suites
Rest *Ristorante Giardino* (dinner only) a la carte 9900/12400 HUF
Rest *Bistro Jardin* (buffet lunch) 7200 HUF and a la carte 7300/11500 HUF
♦ Grand Luxury ♦ Business ♦ Modern ♦
Modern hotel in the heart of the city. Spa boasts panoply of up-to-date
treatments. Rooms provide top class comforts and facilities. Italian Ristorante
Giardino. Bistro Jardin buffet restaurant.

Corinthia Grand H. Royal ♿ 🖾 ⤒rm 📺 📞 ♨400

Erzsébet krt 43-49 ✉ *1073* – Ⓜ *Oktogon*   🚗 **VISA** **⑳** AE ⓪
– ℘ *(01) 479 40 00 – royal@corinthia.hu – Fax (01) 479 43 33*
– *www.corinthia.hu*   *Plan I* **B2**
383 rm – ❶88500 HUF ❶❶88500 HUF, ⊑ 5000 HUF – 31 suites
Rest *Brasserie Royale* a la carte 6500/9200 HUF
Rest *Rickshaw* (closed Monday) (dinner only) 8500 HUF/11500 HUF
and a la carte 5000/8500 HUF
♦ Grand Luxury ♦ Business ♦ Modern ♦
Early 20C grand hotel with impressive atrium. Well appointed bedrooms -
particularly Executive - with modern décor in warm colours. Brasserie Royale for
pleasant atrium dining. Far Eastern dishes and sushi bar in Rickshaw.

Le Meridien 🏛 Ⓕ♨ 🗽 🖵 ♿ 🖾 ⤒rm 📺 📞 ♨200 **VISA** **⑳** AE ⓪

Erzsébet tér 9-10 ✉ *1051* – Ⓜ *Deák tér* – ℘ *(01) 429 55 00 – info@le-meridien.hu*
– *Fax (01) 429 55 55 – www.budapest.lemeridien.com*   **E2**
192 rm – ❶78000 HUF ❶❶78000 HUF, ⊑ 6200 HUF – 26 suites
Rest *Le Bourbon* 6200 HUF and a la carte 5650/10000 HUF
♦ Business ♦ Modern ♦
Top class hotel, ideally located for both business and leisure. Classically
furnished, very comfortable bedrooms and particularly smart bathrooms.
Atrium styled restaurant with Art Deco glass dome and impressive French
influenced desserts.

Sofitel Atrium ⟨ Ⓕ♨ 🗽 🖵 ♿ 🖾 ⤒rm 🏊rest 📺 📞 ♨400

Roosevelt Ter 2 ✉ *1051* – Ⓜ *Vörösmarty tér*   🚗 **VISA** **⑳** AE ⓪
– ℘ *(01) 266 12 34 – h3229-re@accor.com – Fax (01) 235 91 01*
– *www.sofitel.com/hu*   **E2**
328 rm – ❶7200 HUF ❶❶7200 HUF, ⊑ 5750 HUF – 23 suites
Rest *Paris Budapest Café* – 4500 HUF and a la carte 5800/8500 HUF
♦ Business ♦ Modern ♦
Modern hotel near Chain Bridge. 'Bibliotheque' and coffee lounge; bi-plane
suspended from roof. Comfortable, well-equipped rooms. Café has Hungarian
edge to menus: Paris meets Budapest in retro décor.

Inter-Continental 📶 🛗 🛅 🖥 🐾 🅰 ↔rm 📺 ☎ 🚪850 🚗 **VISA** **MC** **AE** **①**

Apáczai Csere János utca 12-14

✉ *1052* – Ⓜ *Vörösmarty tér* – ✆ *(01) 327 63 33*

– budapest @ interconti.com

– Fax (01) 327 63 57

– www.budapest.intercontinental.com

E2

383 rm – 🛏54400 HUF 🛏🛏66000 HUF, ☕ 5600 HUF – 15 suites

Rest a la carte 5400/10100 HUF

♦ Business ♦ Modern ♦

Large hotel tower on river bank with good views from most rooms which have modern décor and all mod cons. Popular with business travellers. Viennese style coffee house.

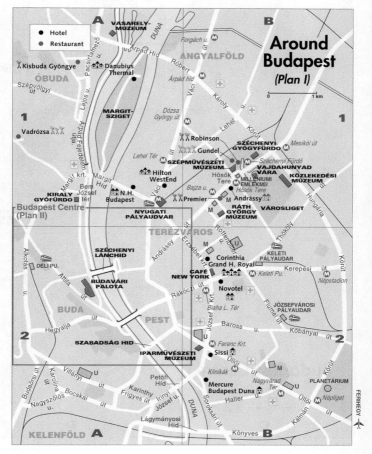

HUNGARY

● Hotel
● Restaurant

C Csalogány u.

Széna tér

Nagy imre tér

Csalogány u. D

Bem rakpart

Krisztina Körút

Logodi u.

Batthyány u.

Moszkva tér

Várfok út

Szabó u.

Batthyány u.

Donáti u.

Batthyány tér M

SZT. ANNA TEMPLOM

Bécsi kapu tér

Hunfalvy u.

Toldy

Ilonka

Ferenc u.

VÍZIVÁROS

Városmajor u.

Lovas út

Kapisztrán tér

1

HADTÖRTÉNETI MÚZEUM

Attila

Országház

Úri

Táncsics Mihály u.

Café Pierrot

Fortuna u.

Janko

M

M

Duna u.

M

Hilton

Art'otel

Bem Fő

DUNA

Alkotás

Logodi u.

Lovas

Alabárdos

Szentháromság tér

Szentháromság u.

MÁTYÁS-TEMPLOM

Hunyadi

Victoria

Kék Golyó u.

Déli pu. M

Krisztina

DÉLI PU.

Tárnok u.

M

VÁRNEGYED

Dísz tér

János u.

Carlton

SZÉCHENYI

Nagyenyed u.

Kosciuszko

Körút

Attila

Tábor u. Palota

Szent György tér

Clark Ádám tér

Lánchid

Várkert

Krisztina tér

Alagút u. út

2

Márvány u.

Alkotás u.

BUDA

Kuny Domokos

Tádé

Naphegy

Lisznyai

Krisztina

Attila

BUDAVÁRI PALOTA

Ybl Miklós tér

U

Avar út

Mészáros

Naphegy tér

Fém u.

Naphegy u.

Derék Dezső u.

SEMMELWEIS ORVOSTÖTENETI MÚZEUM

Győri út

Tigris

TABÁNI PLÉBÁNIA TEMPLOM

Tartsay V. u.

Arcade Bistro

Kereszt u.

TABÁN

Hegyalja

Csörsz u.

Alkotás u.

Csörsz u.

Avar

Aladár u.

Hegyalja

Sánc u.

GELLÉRT-

3

Hegyalja út

Mihály Szirtes

Szirtes út

Budapest Centre
(Plan II)

0   400 m

Somlói út

Kelenhegyi út

Szirtes út

Alsóhegy

Ménesi út

C

D

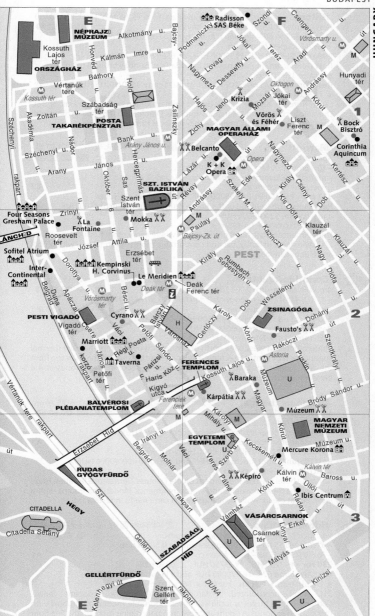

E

NÉPRAJZI
MÚZEUM
Alkotmány u.

Kossuth
Lajos
tér
ORSZÁGHÁZ

Honvéd
Kálmán Imre u.
Báthory
Hold

Vértanúk
tere
Szabadság
tér

Zoltán

Akadémia

Kossuth tér

Zsilinszky

POSTA
TAKARÉKPÉNZTÁR

Bank
Hercegprímás

Arany János u.

Széchenyi u.
Nádor

Arany

János

Október

Sas

Szent
István
tér

SZT. ISTVÁN
BAZILIKA

Révay

Four Seasons
Gresham Palace

LÁNCHÍD

Sofitel Atrium

Inter-
Continental

Zrínyi

Roosevelt
tér

József

Dorottya

Apáca

Duna

Mokka

La
Fontaine

Attila

Erzsébet
tér

Kempinski
H. Corvinus

Le Meridien

Deák
Ferenc tér

Deák tér

Vörösmarty tér

Andrássy

Paulay

Bajcsy-Zs. út

Király

Rumbach
Sebestyén u.

Wesselényi

Dob

PEST

Kazinczy

Klauzál
tér

Nagy Diófa u.

Klauzál

Kis Diófa u.

PESTI VIGADÓ

Cyrano

Vigadó
tér

Váci

Marriott

Régi Posta

Taverna

Pánzsl

Petőfi
tér

Haris Köz

Kígyó
utca

Ferenciek
tere

BALVÉROSI
PLÉBÁNIATEMPLOM

FERENCES
TEMPLOM

Kossuth Lajos u.

Baraka

Kárpátia

Károly

Gerlóczy

ZSINAGÓGA

Dohány

Fausto's

Rákóczi

Astoria

Múzeum

Púskin

U

Bródy Sándor u.

Múzeum

MAGYAR
NEMZETI
MÚZEUM

Radisson
SAS Béke

Szondi

Csengery

Vörösmarty u.

Podmaniczky

Jókai

Teréz

Aradi

Nagymező

Lovag

Dessewffy

Oktogon

Andrássy

Hunyadi
tér

Krizia

Mozsár

Jókai
tér

Körút

Hajós

Jenő

Vörös
és Fehér

Liszt
Ferenc
tér

Bock
Bisztró

Zichy

MAGYAR ÁLLAMI
OPERAHÁZ

Belcanto

Lázár u.

K + K
Opera

Opera

Nagymező

Ede u.

Székely M. u.

Corinthia
Aquincum

Kertész

Király

Csányi u.

Dob

H

Váci

Szerb

Egyetem
TEMPLOM

Kecskeméti u.

Veres

Pálné

Képíró

Kálvin
tér

Károly

Mihály u.

Irányi u.

Belgrád

Molnár

rakpart

RUDAS
GYÓGYFÜRDŐ

CITADELLA

Citadella Sétány

HEGY

Erzsébet Híd

Vámház

VÁSÁRCSARNOK

Csarnok
tér

Lónyai

Erkel

U

Mátyás

Kinizsi

DUNA

SZABADSÁG
HÍD

GELLÉRTFÜRDŐ

Szent
Gellért
tér

Kelenhegyi út

Gellért rakpart

Szt.

E

F

Mercure Korona

Múzeum u.

Kálmán

Ibis Centrum

Baross u.

Üllői

1

2

3

417

HUNGARY

Hilton
⊰ Danube and Pest, 🏨 ⅌ 🄰🄲 ↔rm ℅rest 🖃 📞 🔊650

Hess Andras Ter 1-3 ✉ *1014* – Ⓜ *Batthyány tér* 🚗 **VISA** 💳 🄰🄴 ①
– ℰ *(01) 889 66 00* – *hiltonhu@hungary.net* – *Fax (01) 889 66 44*
– *www.budapest.hilton.com* **D1**
299 rm – ⸙59000 HUF ⸙⸙59000 HUF, ⊊ 6250 HUF – 23 suites
Rest *Dominican* (dinner only and Saturday and Sunday brunch) (pianist)
a la carte 3985/17930 HUF
Rest *Corvina* 5975 HUF/10215 HUF and a la carte 3610/10215 HUF
♦ Traditional ♦ Classic ♦
Large hotel in historic castle district with stunning views. Remains of 13C Dominican church and cellars. Classic rooms. Dominican is fine dining room with superb views. Informal Corvina with traditional Hungarian menu.

Marriott
⊰ Danube and Buda, 🍴 ⅃🄰 🏨 🔲 ⅌ 🄰🄲 ↔rm ℅ 🖃 📞

Apáczai Csere János útca 4 ✉ *1052* 🔊800 🚗 **VISA** 💳 🄰🄴 ①
– Ⓜ *Vörösmarty tér* – ℰ *(01) 266 70 00*
– *marriott.budapest@axelero.hu* – *Fax (01) 266 50 00*
– *www.marriott.com/budhu* **E2**
351 rm – ⸙55200 HUF ⸙⸙55200 HUF, ⊊ 5200 HUF – 11 suites
Rest *Duna Grill* (seafood buffet Friday dinner) (buffet lunch) 4500 HUF
and a la carte 5200/8500 HUF
♦ Traditional ♦ Classic ♦
Huge American-style hotel on river bank where every room has a balcony. Late 20C style décor in lobby, bar and comfortable rooms. Informal grill with global and Hungarian menus.

Corinthia Aquincum
⊰ 🖒 ⅃🄰 🏨 🔲 ⅌ 🄰🄲 ⅌ ℅rest 🖃 🔊300 🚗

Arpád Fejedelem útca 94 ✉ *1036* – Ⓜ *Árpád híd* **P.** **VISA** 💳 🄰🄴 ①
– ℰ *(01) 436 41 00* – *reservation@aqu.hu* – *Fax (01) 436 41 56*
– *www.corinthianhotels.com* *Plan I* **F1**
302 rm ⊊ – ⸙54000 HUF ⸙⸙56500 HUF – 8 suites
Rest *Apicius* a la carte 4000/8500 HUF
♦ Business ♦ Modern ♦
Modern hotel on west bank north of centre with own comprehensive thermal spa and therapy centre. Executive level rooms are best: worth the short trip from the city. Apicius restaurant with smart modern décor in warm tones and a pleasant atmosphere.

Danubius Thermal
⊰ 🍴 🖒 ⅃🄰 🏨 🔲 (heated) 🔲 🚗 ⅌ 🄰🄲 ↔rm

Margitsziget ✉ *1138* ℅rest 🔊300 🚗 **P.** **VISA** 💳 🄰🄴 ①
– Ⓜ *Árpád híd* – ℰ *(01) 889 47 00*
– *resind@margitsziget.danubiusgroup.com* – *Fax (01) 889 49 88*
– *www.danubiushotels.com/thermalhotel* *Plan I* **A1**
259 rm ⊊ – ⸙26000 HUF ⸙⸙50000 HUF – 8 suites
Rest *Platan* (buffet lunch) 5500 HUF and a la carte 4000/9000 HUF
♦ Business ♦ Modern ♦
Concrete hotel set in island gardens on the Danube. Conference facilities. Huge thermal spa: heat, massage and water treatments. Modern bedrooms with a view. Buffet meals available alongside à la carte menu in restaurant.

Hilton WestEnd
🍴 ⅃🄰 🏨 🖒 🄰🄲 ↔rm ℅rest 🖃 🔊350

Váci útca 1-3 ✉ *1062* – Ⓜ *Nyugati pályaudvar* 🚗 **VISA** 💳 🄰🄴 ①
– ℰ *(01) 288 55 00* – *info.budapest-westend@hilton.com*
– *Fax (01) 288 55 88* – *www.hilton.com* *Plan I* **A1**
230 rm – ⸙73750 HUF ⸙⸙73750 HUF, ⊊ 6250 HUF
Rest *Arrabona* 6250 HUF/9000 HUF and a la carte 5100/7200 HUF
♦ Business ♦ Chain hotel ♦ Modern ♦
21C hotel incorporated in large adjoining indoor shopping centre. Comprehensive business facilities. Very comfortable modern bedrooms with roof garden as bonus. A bright and contemporary dining room on the first floor of the hotel, with a Mediterranean theme.

Art'otel ≤ 😊 ₤ 🏠 ⅙ 🎴 ½rm ℅rest �Δ160 🚗 VISA ⓿ 🎴 ①

Bem Rakpart 16-19 ⊠ *1011 –* ⓜ *Batthyány tér –* ℰ *(01) 487 94 87*
– budapest@artotel.hu – Fax (01) 487 94 88 – www.artotel.hu **D1**
156 rm 🖵 – 🛏31000 HUF 🛏🛏62000 HUF – 9 suites
Rest *Chelsea* a la carte 4400/7450 HUF
♦ Business ♦ Design ♦
Half new building, half converted baroque houses. Stylish and original interior in cool shades and clean lines. Features over 600 pieces of original art by Donald Sultan. Bright dining room with vaulted ceiling topped with glass and modern artwork.

Radisson SAS Béke 🏠 🔲 ⅙ 🎴 ½rm ℅rest 📧 📞 �Δ330

Teréz körút 43 ⊠ *1138 –* ⓜ *Nyugati tér* 🚗 VISA ⓿ 🎴 ①
– ℰ (01) 889 39 00 – sales.budapest@radissonsas.com – Fax (01) 889 39 15
– www.radissonsas.com **F1**
239 rm – 🛏29700 HUF 🛏🛏50150 HUF, 🖵 4250 HUF – 8 suites
Rest *Szondi Lugas* (buffet lunch) 4700 HUF and a la carte 4400/8700 HUF
♦ Traditional ♦ Functional ♦
Classic façade with mosaic fronts large international hotel in busy shopping street. Rear bedrooms quieter. Tea salon is their proud feature. Spacious restaurant with tropical paradise theme: Hungarian cuisine to the fore.

Andrássy 😊 🎴 ½rm ℅ 📧 📞 P VISA ⓿ 🎴 ①

Andrássy útca 111 ⊠ *1063 –* ⓜ *Bajza u –* ℰ *(01) 462 21 00*
– reservation@andrassyhotel.com – Fax (01) 322 94 45 *Plan I* **B1**
64 rm – 🛏59000 HUF 🛏🛏80000 HUF, 🖵 3000 HUF – 6 suites
Rest *Zebrano* a la carte 5700/9900 HUF
♦ Business ♦ Stylish ♦
A classical Bauhaus building converted into a hotel in 2001. Stylish lobby of glass and metal filigree, plus stylish water feature. Bright and contemporary bedrooms, most with balconies. Friendly, informal restaurant which doubles as bar and café: Asian influences.

N. H. Budapest ₤ 🏠 ⅙ 🎴 ½rm ℅rest 📧 📞 �Δ100

Vigszinház u. 3 ⊠ *1137* 🚗 VISA ⓿ 🎴 ①
– ⓜ *Nyugati pályaudvar –* ℰ *(01) 814 0 00 – nhbudapest@nh6hotels.com*
– Fax (01) 814 01 00 – www.nh-hotels.com *Plan I* **A1**
160 rm – 🛏47750 HUF 🛏🛏47750HUF, 🖵 4000 HUF
Rest 3200 HUF and a la carte 4420/6880 HUF
♦ Business ♦ Modern ♦
Modern hotel in city suburbs. Conference facilities; gym and sauna. Bright, modern, well-furnished rooms in bold colours with extra touches; some with balconies. Simple restaurant; dishes show modern Hungarian style.

K + K Opera ⅍ ₤ 🏠 ⅙ 🎴 ½rm 📧 �Δ80 🚗 VISA ⓿ 🎴 ①

Révay utca 24 ⊠ *1065 –* ⓜ *Opera –* ℰ *(01) 269 02 22 – kk.hotel.opera@*
kkhotels.hu – Fax (01) 269 02 30 – www.kkhotels.com **F1**
204 rm 🖵 – 🛏45250 HUF 🛏🛏56250 HUF – 2 suites
Rest (dinner only) a la carte 5000/7000 HUF
♦ Business ♦ Modern ♦
Well run hotel in quiet street of business district near opera. Stylish modern interior design. Good size rooms smartly furnished and well equipped. Informal dining in bar with bright modern décor and pale wood furniture; bistro style menu.

Mercure Korona 🏠 🔲 ⅙ 🎴 ½rm ℅rest 📧 📞 �Δ100

Kecskeméti útca 14 ⊠ *1053 –* ⓜ *Kálvin tér* 🚗 VISA ⓿ 🎴 ①
– ℰ (01) 486 88 00 – h1765@accor.com – Fax (01) 318 38 67
– www.mercure-korona.hu **F3**
413 rm – 🛏27000 HUF 🛏🛏38000 HUF, 🖵 3600 HUF – 11 suites
Rest *(closed Saturday and Sunday lunch)* 4600 HUF and a la carte 5500 HUF
♦ Business ♦ Chain hotel ♦ Modern ♦
Well equipped modern business hotel close to Hungarian National Museum. Contemporary rooms with all mod cons. Coffee bar and modish lounge. Buzzy restaurant above lobby: informal, modern with original lighting and contemporary local menus.

HUNGARY

Novotel &6 ⋒ & AC 4≁rm 🎬 ⓒ⁹ ▨350 ⟨⟩ *VISA* ⓸ AE ⓪
Rákóczi út 43-45 ⊠ 1088 – ⓂBlaha tér – ℰ (01) 477 54 00 – h3560@accor.com
– Fax (01) 477 53 53 – www.novotel-bud-centrum.hu Plan I **B2**
227 rm – †30150 HUF ††37695 HUF, ⊇ 3700 HUF
Rest *Palace Garden Brasserie* 6000 HUF and a la carte 5500/1000 HUF
• Business • Chain hotel • Functional •
Early 20C Art Deco hotel with extensions, in the business district. Conference
facilities; basement leisure club. Spacious, well-fitted and modern bedrooms.
The ornate, classic Palace restaurant serves an international menu.

Taverna ⋒ AC 4≁ %rest ⓒ⁹ ▨100 ⟨⟩ *VISA* ⓸ AE ⓪
Váci utca 20 ⊠ 1052 – Ⓜ Ferenciek tere – ℰ (01) 485 31 00 **E2**
– hotel@hoteltaverna.hu – Fax (01) 485 31 11 – www.hoteltaverna.hu
223 rm ⊇ – †42000 HUF ††46500 HUF – 4 suites
Rest *Gambrinus* (dinner only) a la carte approx. 6000 HUF
Rest *Taverna Brasserie* a la carte approx. 2500 HUF
• Traditional • Functional •
Business and tourist hotel located on main pedestrianised shopping street.
Extensive facilities offering something for everyone. Rooms are comfortable.
Classical style at Gambrinus. Convivial ambience at traditional brasserie.

Uhu Villa ⤸ ≤ 🈐 ⋒ ⬚ ⪥ AC 4≁ % 🎬 ⓒ⁹ Ⓟ *VISA* ⓸ AE ⓪
Keselyü I/a (Northwest : 8 km by Szilágyi Erzsébet fasor) ⊠ 1025
– ℰ (01) 275 10 02 – uhuvilla@uhuvilla.hu – Fax (01) 398 05 71 – www.uhuvilla.hu
12 rm ⊇ – †47500 HUF ††47500 HUF– 1 suite
Rest *(closed Sunday)* (dinner only) a la carte 8600/10300 HUF
• Traditional • Cosy •
Friendly, discreet, personally styled early 20C villa with gardens in peaceful Buda
Hills. Smart, contemporary bedrooms with neat décor, some with balconies. Res-
taurant with terrace and view serving Italian dishes: Hungarian and Italian wine list.

Sissi without rest & 4≁ 🎬 ⓒ⁹ ▨25 Ⓟ *VISA* ⓸ AE ⓪
Angyal útca 33 (by Tuzoltó útca) ⊠ 1094 – Ⓜ Ferenc Krt – ℰ (01) 215 00 82
– hsissi@t-online.hu – Fax (01) 216 60 63 – www.hotelsissi.hu Plan I **B2**
44 rm ⊇ – †23500 HUF ††30000 HUF
• Family • Classic •
Bedrooms are decorated in warm yellows and blues; some have balconies
overlooking residential area, and a Scandinavian feel. Breakfast served in
conservatory overlooking neat rear garden.

Carlton without rest AC 4≁ 🎬 ⓒ⁹ ▨25 ⟨⟩ *VISA* ⓸ AE ⓪
Apor Péter útca 3 ⊠ 1011 – Ⓜ Batthyány tér – ℰ (01) 224 09 99 – carltonhotel@
t-online.hu – Fax (01) 224 09 90 – www.carltonhotel.hu **D2**
95 rm ⊇ – †18750 HUF ††26250 HUF
• Traditional • Classic •
Usefully located hotel on Buda side of river, offering straightforward
accommodation for the cost-conscious traveller. Rooms are functional and
comfortable. Small bar.

Victoria without rest ≤ Danube and Pest, ⋒ AC Ⓟ *VISA* ⓸ AE ⓪
Bem Rakpart 11 ⊠ 1011 – Ⓜ Batthyány tér – ℰ (01) 457 80 80
– victoria@victoria.hu – Fax (01) 457 80 88 – www.victoria.hu **D1**
27 rm ⊇ – †22300 HUF ††30200 HUF
• Traditional • Functional •
Family-run hotel, popular with tourists, in a row of town houses just below the
castle. Rooms are spacious, equipped with good range of facilities and all offer
fine views.

Ibis Centrum without rest & AC 4≁ ⓒ⁹ *VISA* ⓸ AE ⓪
Raday utca 6 ⊠ 1092 – Ⓜ Kálvin tér – ℰ (01) 456 41 00 – h2078@accor.com
– Fax (01) 456 41 16 – www.accor.com **F3**
126 rm – †22000 HUF ††22000 HUF, ⊇ 2000 HUF
• Business • Chain hotel • Functional •
Modern hotel well located for city and national museum. Good functional
accommodation with all necessary facilities. Lounge, small bar, bright breakfast
room, roof garden.

Live in Italian

S.PELLEGRINO

At finer restaurants in Paris, London, New York and of course, Milan.

a. **Coteaux de Chiroubles vineyards (Beaujolais) ?**

b. **The vineyards around Les Riceys (Champagne) ?**

c. **Riquewihr and the surrounding vineyards (Alsace) ?**

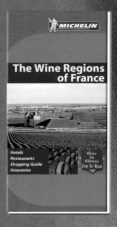

The Wine Regions
of France

Hotels
Restaurants
Shopping Guide
Itineraries

Can't decide ?

Then immerse yourself in the Michelin Green Guide !

- Everything to do and see
- The best driving tours
- Practical information
- Where to stay and eat

The Michelin Green Guide:
the spirit of discovery.

A better way forward

HUNGARY

Mercure Budapest Duna without rest 　　　　🔳 ⅍ ⚒ 📧 📞
Soroksári útca 12 ✉ *1095 –* 🕾 *(01) 455 83 00* 　　　　♨ 50 VISA ⑩ 𝔸𝔼 ⓪
– h2025@accor.com – Fax (01) 455 83 85
– www.mercure-duna.hu 　　　　　　　　　　　　　　　*Plan I* **B2**
130 rm – 🛉19750 HUF 🛉🛉24750 HUF, ⌯ 3000 HUF
♦ Business ♦ Chain hotel ♦ Functional ♦
Modern hotel catering well for business people and tourists, close to river and
city. Fair sized bedrooms offer simple but modern comforts and reasonable level
of mod cons.

XXXX **Gundel** 　　　　　　　🏡 🔳 ⚒ ✧60 🅿 VISA ⑩ 𝔸𝔼 ⓪
Allatkerti útca 2 ✉ *1146 –* Ⓜ *Hösök tere –* 🕾 *(01) 468 40 40 – info@gundel.hu*
– Fax (01) 363 19 17 – www.gundel.hu
closed 24 December 　　　　　　　　　　　　　　　　　　*Plan I* **B1**
Rest (booking essential) 3300 HUF/22500 HUF and a la carte 9000/16500 HUF
Rest *1894* *(closed Sunday-Monday)* (dinner only) 4900 HUF/5600 HUF
and a la carte 3000/7000 HUF
♦ Traditional ♦ Musical ♦
Hungary's best known restaurant, an elegant classic. Spacious main room with
walnut panelling and ornate ceiling. Traditional cuisine. Summer terrace. Live
music at dinner.

XXX **Vadrózsa** 　　　　　　　　　　🏡 🔳 ✧40 VISA ⑩ 𝔸𝔼 ⓪
Pentelei Molnár útca 15 (via Rómer Flóris útca) ✉ *1025 –* 🕾 *(01) 326 58 17*
– vadrozsa@hungary.net – Fax (01) 326 58 09
– www.vadrozsa.hu
closed 24-26 December 　　　　　　　　　　　　　　　　*Plan I* **A1**
Rest 4800 HUF/9900 HUF and a la carte 7700/9800 HUF
♦ Traditional ♦ Formal ♦
Pleasant villa just out of town. Elegant dining room with wood panelling. Display
of raw ingredients presented with the menu. Attractive summer terrace.
Detailed service.

XXX **Alabárdos** 　　　　　　　🏡 🔳 ⅍ ⚒ ✧30 VISA ⑩ 𝔸𝔼 ⓪
Országház útca 2 ✉ *1014 –* Ⓜ *Moszkva tér –* 🕾 *(01) 356 08 51*
– alabardos@t-online.hu – Fax (01) 214 38 14 – www.alabardos.hu
closed Sunday 　　　　　　　　　　　　　　　　　　　　**D1**
Rest (dinner only and Saturday lunch) (booking essential) a la carte
9000/15000 HUF ⌛
♦ Traditional ♦ Formal ♦
Well run restaurant in vaulted Gothic interior of characterful 17C building with
covered courtyard in castle square. Extensive menu of good traditional
Hungarian classics.

XX **Fausto's** 　　　　　　　　　　🔳 ⚒ VISA ⑩ 𝔸𝔼
Dohány útca 5 ✉ *1072 –* Ⓜ *Astoria –* 🕾 *(01) 269 68 06 – faustos@axelero.hu*
– Fax (01) 269 68 06 – www.fausto.hu
closed Easter, 3 weeks August,24-26 December, Sunday and
Bank Holidays 　　　　　　　　　　　　　　　　　　　**F2**
Rest 4000 HUF/15000 HUF and a la carte 6000/17500 HUF
♦ Italian ♦ Fashionable ♦
Popular, personally run restaurant in avenue next to impressive synagogue;
enduringly smart décor and slick service. Attractive menu of Italian classics.

XX **Premier** 　　　　　　　　　　🏡 🔳 VISA ⑩ 𝔸𝔼 ⓪
Andrássy út 101 ✉ *1062 –* Ⓜ *Bajza u –* 🕾 *(01) 342 17 68*
– premier-restaurant@axelero.hu – Fax (01) 322 16 39
– www.premier-restaurant.hu
closed 24 December and Sunday October-April 　　　　　　*Plan I* **B1**
Rest a la carte 4300/8700 HUF
♦ Traditional ♦ Intimate ♦
Early 20C Art Nouveau villa with three basement rooms and a pleasant outdoor
terrace. Attentive service. Traditional or global dishes; look out too for specials on
offer.

✗✗ Robinson ⬚ VISA ⓜⓒ AE ⓞ

Városligeti tó ✉ *1146 –* Ⓜ *Széchenyi Fürdö –* 𝒞 *(01) 422 02 22*
– robinson@axelero.hu – Fax (01) 422 00 72
– www.restaurantguide.hu/robinson
closed 24-26 December   Plan I **B1**
Rest a la carte 4500/7000 HUF
♦ **Traditional** ♦ **Friendly** ♦
Pavilion on tiny island in park; plenty of ducks to watch in lake with fountains. Spacious conservatory with terrace. Extensive menu of traditional and modern fare. Guitar music at dinner.

✗✗ Mokka ⬚ VISA ⓜⓒ AE

Sas u. 4 – Ⓜ *Bajcsy-Zs-út –* 𝒞 *(01) 328 00 81 – mokkar@mokkarestaurant.hu*
– Fax (01) 328 00 82 – www.mokkarestaurant.hu
closed 25 and 31 December   **E2**
Rest (booking essential) a la carte 4840/15650 HUF
♦ **Innovative** ♦ **Trendy** ♦
Trendy, warm and buzzy destination close to the Basilica: booking essential. Decorated with Moroccan lighting and North African artefacts. Totally eclectic menus (French, Asian, African) bursting with spices, exotic combinations and originality.

✗✗ Café Pierrot ⬚ AK ↳ VISA ⓜⓒ AE ⓞ

Fortuna u. 14 ✉ *1014 –* Ⓜ *Moszkva tér –* 𝒞 *(01) 375 69 71 – info@pierrot.hu*
– Fax (01) 375 69 71 – www.pierrot.hu
closed 24 December   **C1**
Rest 4000 HUF (lunch) and a la carte 6000/9500 HUF
♦ **Modern** ♦ **Friendly** ♦
Eye-catching exterior will make you stop and look: trees in pots, twinkling fairy lights. Inside is tasteful Pierrot clown theming with some original artwork by local artists. Hungarian base underpins dishes skilfully concocted with Gallic finesse.

✗✗ Kárpátia ↳ ⬚35 VISA ⓜⓒ AE ⓞ

Ferenciek tere 7-8 ✉ *1053 –* Ⓜ *Ferenciek tere –* 𝒞 *(01) 317 35 96*
– restaurant@karpatia.hu – Fax (01) 318 05 91
– www.karpatia.hu
closed 24 December   **F2**
Rest a la carte 6000/11000 HUF
♦ **Traditional** ♦ **Rustic** ♦
One of the city's oldest restaurants with characterful vaulted Gothic style interior, beautifully painted walls and works of art. Extensive menu of good traditional cuisine.

✗✗ Cyrano ⬚ AK ⬚30 VISA ⓜⓒ AE ⓞ

Kristóf tér 7-8 ✉ *1052 –* Ⓜ *Vörösmarty tér –* 𝒞 *(01) 266 30 96*
– cyrano@citynet.hu – Fax (01) 266 68 18
closed 24 December   **E2**
Rest a la carte 4170/7760 HUF
♦ **Contemporary** ♦ **Trendy** ♦
Popular informal restaurant just off main shopping street with unusual dramatic modern designer style décor. Serves selection of good modern European and Hungarian food.

✗✗ Képiró ⬚ AK VISA ⓜⓒ AE

Képiró u. 3 ✉ *1053 –* Ⓜ *Kálvin tér –* 𝒞 *(01) 266 04 30*
– info@kepirorestaurant.com – Fax (01) 266 04 25
– www.kepirorestaurant.com
closed Saturday lunch and Sunday   **F3**
Rest a la carte 6500/8500 HUF
♦ **Innovative** ♦ **Friendly** ♦
Glass-fronted restaurant, in narrow street near city centre, divided by central bar. Approachable and friendly serice. Modern style cooking with eclectic, seasonal menus.

Janko   🗚 VISA ⓜⓞ

Hess András tér ✉ *1014 –* ⓜ *Batthyány tér –* ✆ *(01) 488 74 16*
– janko@janko.hu – www.janko.hu
closed 2 weeks January   **D1**
Rest 5200 HUF/7200 HUF and a la carte 5000/7100 HUF
♦ **Traditional** ♦ **Design** ♦
Right opposite the Hilton, with a stylish modern interior enhanced by bright red flowers and softly hued table lamps. Gallery for browsing is adjacent. Leather furnished bar with pianist. Authentic Hungarian dishes with an original slant: set menus called 'Tradition and Progress' and 'Taste Test'.

Múzeum   🗚 ⅍ VISA ⓜⓞ 🗛🗉 ①

Múzeum körút 12 ✉ *1088 –* ⓜ *Astoria –* ✆ *(01) 338 42 21*
– muzeum11@axelero.hu – Fax (01) 338 42 21
– www.muzeumkavehaz.hu
closed 25 December and Sunday   **F2**
Rest a la carte 3500/10700 HUF
♦ **Traditional** ♦ **Brasserie** ♦
Founded in 1885, next to National Museum. High ceilings, tiled walls and large windows. Formally attired staff serve large portions of traditional Hungarian cooking.

Belcanto   🗚 ⅍ ⇄35 VISA ⓜⓞ 🗛🗉 ①

Dalszínház útca 8 ✉ *1061 –* ⓜ *Opera –* ✆ *(01) 269 27 86*
– restaurant@belcanto.hu – Fax (01) 311 95 47 – www.belcanto.hu
closed 25 December   **F1**
Rest (booking essential) 4500 HUF/9800 HUF and a la carte 6900/10000 HUF
♦ **Traditional** ♦ **Musical** ♦
Next to the opera and famous for classical and operatic evening recitals, including impromptu performances by waiters! Atmosphere is lively and enjoyable. Hungarian food.

Baraka   🗚 ⅍ VISA ⓜⓞ 🗛🗉

Magyar útca 12-14 ✉ *1053 –* ⓜ *Astoria –* ✆ *(01) 483 13 55*
– desboek@gmail.com – Fax (01) 266 88 08
– www.barakarestaurant.hu
closed 24-25 December, 1 January and Sunday   **F2**
Rest (booking essential) (dinner only) a la carte 5600/9800 HUF
♦ **Asian influences** ♦ **Fashionable** ♦
Modern restaurant with simple décor and original style; quieter tables on mezzanine floor. Modern, eclectic dishes showing French and Asian influences; blackboard specials.

Vörös és Fehér   🗚 VISA ⓜⓞ 🗛🗉

Andrássy út 41 ✉ *1061 –* ⓜ *Oktogon –* ✆ *(01) 413 15 45*
– vorosesfeher@vorosesfeher.com – www.vorosesfeher.com
closed 24-26 December   **F1**
Rest 6000 HUF and a la carte 4300/6500 HUF ⌘
♦ **Contemporary** ♦ **Trendy** ♦
Discreet appearance on fashionable street. More intimate feel to upstairs gallery. Attentive service, particularly vast wine selection. Original menus: honest Hungarian ingredients with a contemporary interpretation - everything from cheese board to full Degustation menu.

Arcade Bistro   🗟 🗚 ⅍ VISA ⓜⓞ

Kiss Janos Alt u. 38 ✉ *1126 –* ⓜ *Déli pu –* ✆ *(01) 225 19 69*
– arcadebistro@freestart.hu – Fax (01) 225 19 68
– www.arcadebistro.hu
closed 24-26 December and Sunday   **C2-3**
Rest (booking essential) a la carte 5000/6700 HUF
♦ **Mediterranean** ♦ **Bistro** ♦
Small local restaurant with central column water feature and colourful modern art décor. Seasonal menu of modern cuisine: daily specials and Mediterranean influences.

✗ **Krizia**   AC VISA ◐◑ AE
Mozsár útca 12 ✉ 1066 – Ⓜ Oktogon – ℰ (01) 331 87 11 – ristorante.krizia@
axelero.hu – Fax (01) 331 87 11 – www.ristorantekrizia.hu
closed 3 weeks July-August, 24-26 December, 1 week January and Sunday
Rest 2600 HUF/10000 HUF and a la carte 3400/8500 HUF   **F1**
 ♦ Italian ♦ Cosy ♦
A pleasant intimate atmosphere, with candlelight and friendly service. Carefully
prepared Italian cooking with the menu supplemented by regularly changing
specials.

✗ **Kisbuda Gyöngye**   🍴 AC VISA ◐◑ AE ①
Kenyeres útca 34 ✉ 1034 – Ⓜ Árpád hid – ℰ (01) 368 64 02
– gyongye@remiz.hu – Fax (01) 368 92 27 – www.remiz.hu
closed 24-26 December, 1 January and Sunday   *Plan I* **A1**
Rest (booking essential) (music at dinner) a la carte 4700/9000 HUF
 ♦ Traditional ♦ Cosy ♦
A genuine neighbourhood restaurant in a residential street. Wood panelling
created by old wardrobes. Attentive service. Good choice menu; international
and authentic food.

✗ **Bock Bisztró**   AC VISA ◐◑
Erzsébet Krt 43-49 ✉ 1073 – Ⓜ Oktogon – ℰ (01) 321 03 40
– bockbisztro@axelero.hu – Fax (01) 321 03 40 – www.bockbisztro.hu
closed Sunday and Bank Holidays   **F1**
Rest a la carte 3500/7000 HUF ⛉
 ♦ Traditional ♦ Bistro ♦
Run independently of Corinthia Grand Hotel Royal, this is a serious wine
establishment, with over 50 by the glass: you can just walk in and buy. Stylish
décor with Art Deco lighting, though the feel is informal bistro. Classic local
recipes with a 21C lift, though tapas and cheese/ham plates are available too.

✗ **Náncsi Néni**   🍴 VISA ◐◑ AE
😊 *Ördögárok útca 80, Hüvösvölgy (Northwest : 10 km by Szilágyi Erzsébet fasor)*
✉ 1029 – ℰ (01) 397 27 42 – info@nancsineni.hu – Fax (01) 397 27 42
– www.nancsineni.hu
closed 24 December
Rest a la carte 2700/6200 HUF
 ♦ Home cooking ♦ Bistro ♦
Interior similar to a Swiss chalet, with gingham tablecloths, convivial atmosphere
and large terrace. Well-priced home-style Hungarian cooking. Worth the drive
from the city.

✗ **La Fontaine**   VISA ◐◑ AE ①
Mérleg útca 10 ✉ 1051 – Ⓜ Bajcsy-Zsilinszky út – ℰ (01) 317 37 15
– restaurant@lafontaine.hu – Fax (01) 318 85 62 – www.lafontaine.hu
closed Sunday   **E2**
Rest (dinner only) a la carte 7000/10000 HUF
 ♦ French ♦ Friendly ♦
Authentic Gallic charm: run by gregarious young owner. High ceiling adds to the
airy feel. Traditional French menu with blackboard specials, all described with
enthusiasm.

Republic of IRELAND
ÉIRE

FORMALITIES

Travellers from the European Union (EU), Switzerland, Iceland and the main countries of North and South America need a national identity card or passport (except for British nationals travelling from the UK; America: passport required) to visit Ireland for less than three months (tourism or business purpose). For visitors from other countries a visa may be required, in addition to a passport, especially for those wishing to stay for longer than three months. We advise you to check with your embassy before travelling.

Nationals of EU countries require a valid national driving licence; nationals of non-EU countries require an International Driving Licence. Third party insurance is essential. Drivers must be at least 21 or 25 to hire a vehicle.

MAJOR NEWSPAPERS

The main daily newspapers in the Irish Republic are *The Irish Times*, *The Independent* and *The Examiner*. Additionally Dublin has three local newspapers: *Northside People, Southside People* and *Fingal Independent*.

SMOKING-NO SMOKING

The laws in the Republic of Ireland prohibit smoking in all restaurants, bars and in the public areas of hotels. Some hotel bedrooms are still available for smokers.

HOTELS

◆ CATEGORIES

Accommodation ranges from luxurious 5-star international hotels, via smaller, family-run guesthouses to bed and breakfast establishments.

◆ PRICE RANGE

The price is per room. There is little difference between the price of a single and a double room.

Between April and October it is advisable to book in advance. From November to March prices may be slightly lower, some hotels offer special cheap rates and some may be closed.

◆ TAX

Included in the room price.

◆ CHECK OUT TIME

Usually between 11am and noon.

◆ RESERVATIONS

By telephone or by Internet. A credit card number may be required.

◆ TIP FOR LUGGAGE HANDLING

At the discretion of the customer (about €1 per bag).

◆ BREAKFAST

It is usually included in the price of the room and is generally served between 7.30am and 9.30am. Most hotels offer a full cooked breakfast as well as a continental breakfast and usually it is possible to have continental breakfast served in the room.

RESTAURANTS

Besides the more formal **restaurants** there are **brasseries, bistros** and pubs, which serve simpler fare, and cafés and fast-food outlets, where one can eat quickly and cheaply.

Breakfast	7.30am – 9.30am
Lunch	12.30pm – 2.30pm
Dinner	7pm – 10-11pm

Restaurants in Ireland offer fixed price menus (starter, main course and dessert) and à la carte. Menus are written in English. A fixed price menu is usually cheaper than the same dishes chosen à la carte.

◆ RESERVATIONS

Reservations are usually made by phone, fax or via the Internet. For famous restaurants (including Michelin starred restaurants), it is advisable to book several days – in some instances weeks – in advance.

A credit card number or a phone number may be required to guarantee the booking.

✦ **THE BILL**

The bill (check) includes VAT and a service charge (12.5%). Tipping is at the client's discretion but, if you are particularly pleased with the service, it is customary to add 10% or to round up the total to an appropriate figure.

LOCAL CUISINE

Ireland is a sociable and hospitable country where the people readily gather in a bar or round a table. There are two culinary traditions: the formal meals served in town and country mansions, and the simple dishes of earlier centuries. As Ireland is an agricultural country, there is an abundance of fresh produce: fruit and vegetables, meat and dairy products and a wide variety of fresh and saltwater fish. The Irish have a great way with the potato, which was introduced at the end of the 16C and became a staple of the national diet.

The traditional cooked breakfast, known as the Irish Fry, consists of some or all of the following: egg, bacon, sausage, black pudding, potato cakes, mushrooms and tomatoes; it is sometimes served as the evening meal. Other breakfast dishes are kippers, kedgeree and smoked salmon omelette.

Salmon, farmed or wild, is rarely off the menu, which may also include trout. Near the coast the menus might feature **shellfish**: crab, lobster, scallops, mussels, Dublin Bay prawns and Galway Bay oysters. From the local fishing grounds come black sole (known also as Dover sole), lemon sole, plaice, monkfish, turbot, brill, John Dory, cod, hake, haddock, mackerel and herring.

Prime **beef** is raised on the lush grass of the lowlands and **lamb** on the uplands; **pigs** are raised everywhere. Chicken is common; duck appears more rarely. There is also game in season.

The most popular traditional dishes are **Irish stew** (neck of mutton layered in a pot with potatoes, onions and herbs); **Colcannon** (mashed potatoes, onions, parsnips and white cabbage, mixed with butter and cream); **champ** (a simpler dish of potatoes mashed with butter and vegetables such as chopped chives, parsley, spring onions, shallots, cabbage, nettles or peas). Nettles are also made into soup. Seaweed is also a culinary ingredient; traditionally it was used to thicken soups and stews: **carrageen** is still used to make a dessert with a delicate flavour and **dulse** is made into a sweet (candy).

The country produces excellent milk and cream, which is served as whipped cream or made into ice cream, a popular dessert, into butter and into a wide variety of **cheeses** – **Cashel Blue** (a soft creamy, blue-veined cow's milk cheese); **Cooleeny** (a Camembert-type soft cheese); **Milleens** (a distinctive spicy cheese, which is washed with salt water as it matures); **Gubbeen** (a soft surface-ripening cheese).

Many different breads and cakes are baked for breakfast and tea. The most well-known is **soda bread**, made of white or brown flour and buttermilk. **Barm brack** is a rich fruit cake made with yeast.

DRINK

Stout or porter, made by Guinness or Murphys is the traditional thirst-quencher in Ireland but the drinking of ales (bitter) and lagers is not uncommon. Black Velvet is a mixture of stout and champagne.

Although there are now only three distilleries in Ireland, there are many different brands of whiskey; their distinctive flavours arise from subtle variations in the production process, in which the spirit is triple distilled. **The Flag** is a patriotic drink, a mixture of crème de menthe, tequila and Southern Comfort representing the green, white and orange of the Republican tricolour.

Irish coffee is a delicious creation, consisting of a measure of whiskey, brown sugar and very hot black coffee mixed in a heated glass and topped with a layer of fresh cream.

DUBLIN
BAILE ÁTHA CLIATH

Population (2002): 495 101 (conurbation 1 004 614) - Altitude: sea level

Ph. Bénet, R. Holzbachova / MICHELIN

Dublin's 'fair city', the capital of Ireland, bestrides the River Liffey and looks seawards to its port and the broad water of Dublin Bay. The Vikings settled on both banks of the Liffey; the Anglo-Normans sited their castle on the mound on the south side. In the relative peace of the Georgian era, after centuries of conflict, the city expanded: public bodies put up handsome buildings; men of property commissioned fine mansions. Under the Wide Streets Commissioners (1758) Dublin developed into an elegant city; the Liffey was embanked between quays and spanned by several bridges. The 19C brought stagnation and the 20C the destruction caused by the Easter Rising and the Civil War; most of it has, however, been made good, and Dublin can claim to be the finest Georgian city in the British Isles.

Something like a third of Ireland's population lives in the greater Dublin area and a disproportionate amount of the country's business is conducted there. The economic success of the 'Celtic tiger' period has resulted in much modernisation and improvement as well as the building of many houses in the suburbs and adjacent towns and villages. The increasingly cosmopolitan life of street, café, restaurant and bar coupled with the city's Georgian architectural heritage make Dublin an attractive destination for a weekend or longer.

WHICH DISTRICT TO CHOOSE

The greatest concentration of **hotels** is in the city centre and the districts south of the Grand Canal; there are also a few near the airport. Cheaper hotels are found near the bus station in Gardiner Street *Plan II* **F1**; guesthouses cluster south of the Grand Canal; there are B&B addresses in most districts and near the airport. Many of the **restaurants** are also found in the city centre and the districts south of the Grand Canal. In Dublin there seems to be a pub in every street, with many of the more popular places in **Temple Bar** *Plan II* **E2**.

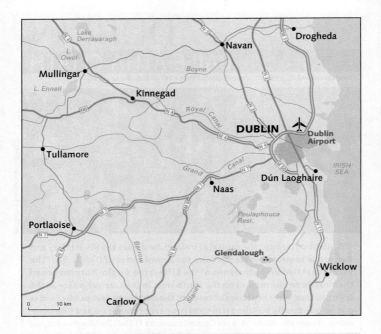

PRACTICAL INFORMATION

ARRIVAL – DEPARTURE

Dublin Airport – About 12 km (7.5 mi) north of the city centre, ✆ 01 814 1111.

From the airport to the city centre – By **taxi**: the cost is approx. €20, including one piece of luggage; €0.50 extra for each additional piece of luggage. By **coach**: Air Coach (30mins) between Dublin Airport and the city centre, every 15min during daytime (24hrs/24 service), stopping at major hotels as far south as Stillorgan; €7, return €12. ✆ 01 844 7118; www. aircoach.ie. By **bus**: Air Link No 747 from Dublin Airport to the bus station *(Busáras)*, €5, return €9; and Air Link No 748 from Dublin Airport via city centre to Heuston Railway Station, €5.50; ✆ 01 873 4222 (Mon-Sat 9am-7pm); info@dublinbus.ie; www.dublinbus.ie

By sea – There are regular ferry services to and from two terminals – Dublin Port and Dún Laoghaire.

TRANSPORT

♦ TAXIS

Taxis can be hailed in the street but the best way is to request them at a taxi rank. They are distinguished by a light on the roof, which is lit when the taxi is occupied. Tariff calculated at approx. €0.15 pkm (approx. €0.20 Sundays, public holidays and at night 10pm-8am).

♦ BUSES

The bus network covers the whole city from the Central Bus Station *(Busáras)* in Store Street *Plan II F1*; any bus bearing the direction An Lár is going to the city centre. The price of a single ticket varies according to the number of stages from €0.90 to €1.65. Dublin Rambler 1-day bus ticket €5; 3-day €10, 5-day €15.50, 7-day €19; 1-day Family ticket €8; 5 1-day €17, 6 5-day €75. ✆ 01 873 4222 (Mon-Sat 9am-7pm); ✆ 01 703 3028 (ticket sales); info@dublinbus.ie; www.dublinbus.ie

✦ TRAMS

The two LUAS tram routes are the Green Line from St Stephen's Green to Sandyford and the Red Line from Connolly Station to Tallaght; Mon-Fri 5.30am-0.30am, every 5 mins (less frequently outside the rush hour and not so early and late at the weekend). Fares vary according to zones from €1.30 to €3.80; 7-day ticket from €10; 30-day ticket from €40; tickets can be bought from ticket vending machines at Luas stops or, more cheaply, from selected retailers. ℰ 1800 300 604; www.luas.ie

✦ DART

The **Dublin Area Rapid Transport (DART)** operates a rail service along the coast (40 km – 25 mi) from Howth in the north to Bray in the south. It serves three stations in central Dublin – Connolly *Plan II* **F1**, Tara Street *Plan II* **F2** and Pearse *Plan II* **F2**. Trains daily between 6am (9am Sun) and 11.45pm every 5-10min during peak times and every 15min off-peak. Tickets available at any station: All-day rail ticket (according to distance) up to €2.15; all-day rail and bus ticket €7.20. ℰ 01 814 1062 or 01 836 6222 (passenger information); www.aerdart.ie

✦ DUBLIN PASS

Free entry to over 30 tourist attractions, free transport with Air Coach from Dublin Airport to the city centre and discounts on purchases and admissions; 1-day €29 (child €17), 2-day €49 (child €29), 3-day €59 (child €34), 6-day €89 (child €44); available at Tourist Information Offices; www.dublinpass.com

USEFUL ADDRESSES

✦ TOURIST OFFICES

Dublin Tourism Centre – Suffolk Street *Plan II* **D2** (Mon-Fri, 9am-5.30 (7pm July and August), Sun and public hols (10.30am-3pm); O'Connell Street *Plan II* **E1** (Mon-Sat; closed bank hols); Dublin Airport,

Arrivals Hall (daily). ℰ 1850 230 330 (Mon-Fri 8am-11pm, Sat 9am-6pm), Reservations ℰ 1800 668 668; information@dublintourism.ie; www.visitdublin.com

✦ BANKS/CURRENCY EXCHANGE

The major banks are to be found in the town centre and at the railway stations, Mon-Fri, 8.30am-4.30pm (closed at lunchtime); some larger banks are open on Sat morning. Bank cash machines (ATMs) are open 24hrs (pin number required).

✦ POST OFFICES

O'Connell Street *Plan II* **E1**, Suffolk Street *Plan II* **D2**. Opening times: Mon-Sat 8am-5pm.

✦ EMERGENCY

ℰ **999** for Fire Brigade, Police, Ambulance, Mountain, Cave, Coastguard and Sea rescue.

BUSY PERIODS

It may be difficult to find a room at a reasonable price when special events are held in the city:

St Patrick's Day: 17 March – Patron saint of Ireland's feast day with processions.

Bloomsday: 16 June – Annual celebration of James Joyce's great novel *Ulysses* reading, re-enactments, music, theatre, street theatre.

Dublin Horse Show: August – International equestrian and social event of the year with team jumping competitions held at the Royal Dublin Society ground in Ballsbridge.

All Ireland Hurling Finals: September – Annual national hurling championships at Croke Park.

All Ireland Football Finals: September – Annual national Gaelic Football championship finals at Croke Park.

Dublin Theatre Festival: September – Best of world theatre and new productions from all the major Irish companies.

DIFFERENT FACETS OF THE CITY

There is time to visit the main sights and museums in two to three days.

Usual opening times 10am-5pm but closed on Mondays and public holidays.

TRINITY COLLEGE – The **Long Room** in the **Old Library** housing the **Book of Kells** and other illuminated medieval manuscripts, as well as a medieval Irish Harp.

OLD DUBLIN – **Dublin Castle** *Plan II* **D2**; formerly the centre of British rule in Ireland: State Appartments, Throne Room, Wedgwood Room, St Patrick's Hall, Church of the Most Holy Trinity. **Christ Church Cathedral** *Plan II* **D2**; Romanesque/Early English building, largely rebuilt in the 19C by George Scott: Romanesque south door, brass eagle lectern, Strongbow monument, 12C crypt. **St Patrick's Cathedral** *Plan II* **D3**; Early-English building: tomb of Jonathan Swift, Dean of the cathedral and author of *Gulliver's Travels*, banners of the knights of the Order of St Patrick, the door of the old Chapter House with the hole through which the Earl of Kildare 'chanced his arm'.

GEORGIAN DUBLIN – **Marsh's Library** *Plan II* **D3**; 18C library with 'cages' where precious books can be consulted behind locked wire screens. **Liffey Bridge** *Plan II* **E2**; cast-iron footbridge (1816) better known as the Ha'penny Bridge owing to the original ½d toll. **Bank of Ireland** *Plan II* **E2**; formerly the Irish Parliament containing the original House of Lords and a display about banking. **Newman House** *Plan II* **E3**; two 18C houses, the smaller by Richard Castle with many original features and plasterwork by the Lafranchini brothers, the larger with rococo plasterwork by Richard West. **Custom House** *Plan II* **F1**; 18C masterpiece designed by James Gandon; the ceremonial vestibules behind the south portico contain a **Visitor Centre** illustrating the work of the government offices which have occupied the building **Number Twenty-Nine** *Plan II* **F3**; vivid picture of 18C life in Dublin; some original furniture. **Marino Casino** *Plan I* **B1**; charming Palladian villa designed by Sir William Chambers.

MUSEUMS AND GALLERIES – **Chester Beatty Library** *Plan II* **D2**; beautiful display of Islamic, Far Eastern and European manuscripts and artworks collected by Sir Alfred Chester Beatty (1875-1968). **National Museum** (Kildare Street) *Plan II* **E3**; outstanding collection of work by Irish artists (Jack B Yeats) as well as by British and other European painters. **National Museum** (Collins Barracks); decorative arts, folk life, history and geology. **National Gallery** *Plan II* **F3**; **Kilmainham Gaol Museum** *Plan I* **A1**; Irish struggle for political independence: souvenirs.

OUTDOOR DUBLIN – **Phoenix Park** *Plan I* **A1**; the largest urban park in Europe was enclosed in 1662 by the Duke of Ormond: herd of fallow deer, Wellington Monument, Papal Cross (1979), Visitor, Zoological Gardens, official residence of the President of Ireland. **National Botanic Gardens** *Plan I* **A1**; 20 000 species growing beside the Tolka River: rose garden, peat garden, bog garden, Victorian glasshouses.

SHOPPING

The smartest shopping district is **Grafton Street** *Plan II* **E2** and its side streets; the **Powerscourt Centre** *Plan II* **E2** comprises a complex of individual boutiques housed in the stables, yard and rooms of an elegant Georgian mansion with decorative plasterwork; **Nassau Street** *Plan II* **E2** contains several shops selling a range of Irish goods from high fashion to modest souvenirs: clothing, craftwork, pottery, Irish music and instruments, family crests; **Dawson Street** is home to the major book shops. **Temple Bar** *Plan II* **E2** offers an eclectic mix of individual little shops and outdoor stalls. The north bank of the Liffey has its own shopping district centred on **O'Connell Street** *Plan II* **E1** and the side streets to the west – Henry Street and Abbey Street. Cobblestones in **Smithfield Village** *Plan II* **C1** offers examples of Irish craftsmanship. **Francis Street** *Plan II* **C2** is a good place to buy **antiques**.

MARKETS – Lovers of markets should visit the **Temple Bar Market** (Sat morning) in Meeting House Square which sells local produce – cheeses, sauces, bread, chocolates, vegetables, drink, pizzas, pies and sausages; **Moore Street Market** (Mon-Sat) *Plan II* **E1**; the Dublin Corporation **Fruit and Vegetable Market** (Sat morning) under a cast-iron roof in **Mary's Lane** *Plan II* **D1**.

WHAT TO BUY – Food (smoked salmon, cheeses), alcohol (whiskey, Guinness and liqueurs), perfumes and soaps, fashion (linen, lace, Donegal tweed and chunky Aran sweaters), linen napkins and tablecloths, crystal from Waterford and other factories, hand-blown glass, porcelain from Belleek, Irish Dresden figures, Celtic inspired jewellery, silverware, hand-turned wooden bowls, bog wood sculptures, musical instruments, CDs of Irish music.

ENTERTAINMENT

Abbey Theatre *Plan II* **E2**: a proud symbol of Irish culture performing plays by Ireland's best-known authors (Shaw, Synge, Yeats, O'Casey) and lesser known playwrights; also experimental Peacock Theatre.

Gate Theatre *Plan II* **E1**: another Dublin institution founded in the 1920s, which includes non-Irish works in its repertoire.

Olympia Theatre *Plan II* **D2** and **Gaiety Theatre** *Plan II* **E3**: opera and musicals.

National Concert Hall *Plan II* **E3**: concerts and recitals.

Bank of Ireland Arts Centre *Plan II* **E2**: evening and lunchtime musical recitals, exhibitions, theatre, poetry readings.

Jurys Irish Cabaret *Plan III* **J1**: 2000 shows a year incorporating music, singing and dancing in both modern and traditional styles (also facilities for a drink and a meal).

Burlington Cabaret *Plan III* **H1**: cabaret venue which describes itself as "a celebration of everything Irish in comedy, music, song and dance".

NIGHTLIFE

The *Event Guide*, published weekly, lists the major entertainments; available free of charge from record shops (www.eventguide.ie). The most central district for night-life is **Temple Bar** *Plan II* **E2**, a medieval network of narrow streets, alleys and courts on the south bank of the Liffey, where traditional pubs and restaurants alternate with ethnic restaurants, alternative shops and hotels. Most of the larger nightclubs are south of the Liffey. Good places include *D Basement* (Fleet Street); *Gaiety Theatre* (South King Street); *The International Bar* (23 Wicklow Street) cosy little bar where assorted blues bands alternate with theatre and comedy club; *O'Donoghue's* (14-15 Merrion Row) where *The Dubliners* came roaring on the music scene in 1962 – traditional Irish music; *Brazen Head* (20 Lower Bridge Street) which claims to be the oldest pub in Dublin – music; *Café Bewley* (Grafton Street) Art deco décor with Café Cabaret in the evening; *Mitchell & Son* (21 Kildare Street) celebrated for its famous 'Green Spot' whiskey, rare malts, spirits and vast range of wines.

IRELAND

CENTRAL DUBLIN   *Plan II*

The Merrion   ⊕ ℔ ⊡ ☞ 🅰 rest ↔ ⚡ 🖭 ℅ 🚗50 ⊖ 🆎 ⓪
Upper Merrion St ⊠ *D2 – ℰ (01) 603 06 00 – info @ merrionhotel.com*
– Fax (01) 603 07 00 – www.merrionhotel.com   **F3**
133 rm – 🛏410 € 🛏🛏515 €, � 27 € – 10 suites
Rest see *The Cellar* and *The Cellar Bar* below
♦ Grand Luxury ♦ Classic ♦
Classic hotel in series of elegantly restored Georgian town houses; many of the
individually designed grand rooms overlook pleasant gardens. Irish art in
opulent lounges.

The Westin   ₺ 🅰 ↔ ⚡ 🖭 ℅ 🚗250 🆅🅸🆂🅰 🆎 ⓪
College Green, Westmoreland St ⊠ *D2 – ℰ (01) 645 10 00*
– reservations.dublin @ westin.com – Fax (01) 645 12 34
– www.westin.com/dublin   **E2**
150 rm – 🛏190/410 € 🛏🛏190/410 €, ⊟ 25 € – 13 suites
Rest *The Exchange* (closed Saturday lunch) a la carte 33/51 €
Rest *The Mint* a la carte 26/60 €
♦ Luxury ♦ Modern ♦
Immaculately kept and consummately run hotel in a useful central location.
Smart, uniform interiors and an ornate period banking hall. Excellent bedrooms
with marvellous beds. Elegant, Art Deco 1920s-style dining in Exchange. More
informal fare at The Mint.

Conrad Dublin   ℔ ₺ 🅰 ↔ ⚡ 🖭 🚗370 ⊖ 🆅🅸🆂🅰 🆎 ⓪
Earlsfort Terrace ⊠ *D2 – ℰ (01) 602 89 00 – dublininfo @ conradhotels.com*
– Fax (01) 676 54 24 – www.conradhotels.com   **E3**
192 rm – 🛏180/250 € 🛏🛏195/535 €, ⊟ 25 €
Rest *Alex* 32 €/39 €
♦ Luxury ♦ Modern ♦
Smart, business oriented international hotel opposite the National Concert Hall.
Popular, pub-style bar. Spacious rooms with bright, modern décor and
comprehensive facilities. Bright pastel and well-run brasserie.

The Westbury   ℔ ₺ 🅰 ↔ ⚡ 🖭 ℅ 🚗220 ⊖ 🆅🅸🆂🅰 🆎 ⓪
Grafton St ⊠ *D2 – ℰ (01) 679 11 22 – westbury @ jurysdoyle.com*
– Fax (01) 679 70 78 – www.jurysdoyle.com   **E2**
196 rm – 🛏401 € 🛏🛏441 €, ⊟ 24 € – 8 suites
Rest *Russell Room* a la carte 34/62 €
Rest *The Sandbank* a la carte approx. 21 €
♦ Luxury ♦ Modern ♦
Imposing marble foyer and stairs leading to lounge famous for afternoon teas.
Huge luxurious bedrooms, most with air-conditioning, offer every conceivable
facility. Russell Room has distinctive, formal feel. Informal, bistro-style Sandbank.

The Clarence   ⪕ ℔ ₺ ↔ ⚡ 🖭 🚗60 🅿 🆅🅸🆂🅰 🆎 ⓪
6-8 Wellington Quay ⊠ *D2 – ℰ (01) 407 08 00 – reservations @ theclarence.ie*
– Fax (01) 407 08 20 – www.theclarence.ie   **D2**
43 rm – 🛏340 € 🛏🛏340 €, ⊟ 28 € – 5 suites
Rest see *The Tea Room* below
♦ Luxury ♦ Design ♦
A discreet, stylish warehouse conversion in Temple Bar overlooking river and
boasting contemporary interior design. Small panelled library. Modern,
distinctive bedrooms.

The Fitzwilliam   ⪕ 🅰 rest ↔ ⚡ 🖭 🚗70 ⊖ 🆅🅸🆂🅰 🆎 ⓪
St Stephen's Green ⊠ *D2 – ℰ (01) 478 70 00 – enq @ fitzwilliamhotel.com*
– Fax (01) 478 78 78 – www.fitzwilliamhotel.com   **E3**
137 rm – 🛏360 € 🛏🛏360 €, ⊟ 25 € – 2 suites
Rest see also *Thornton's* below
Rest *Citron* 30 €/40 € and a la carte 30/45 €
♦ Business ♦ Modern ♦
Rewardingly overlooks the Green and boasts a bright contemporary interior.
Spacious, finely appointed rooms offer understated elegance. Largest hotel roof
garden in Europe. Cheerful, informal brasserie.

Stephen's Green
50 VISA AE

Cliffe St, off St Stephen's Green ✉ D2 – ✆ (01) 607 36 00
– info@ocallaghanhotels.com – Fax (01) 661 56 63
– www.ocallaghanhotels.com
closed 25-27 December **E3**

64 rm – †325 € ††325 €, ☕ 14 € – 11 suites

Rest *The Pie Dish* *(closed lunch Saturday and Sunday)* a la carte 35/60 €

♦ Business ♦ Modern ♦

This smart modern hotel housed in an originally Georgian property is popular with business clients. Bright, relatively compact bedrooms offer a good range of facilities. Bright and breezy bistro restaurant.

Brooks
30 VISA AE

Drury St ✉ D2 – ✆ (01) 670 40 00 – sales@brookshotel.ie – Fax (01) 670 44 55
– www.brookshotel.ie **E2**

98 rm ☕ – †195/240 € ††255/290 €

Rest *Francesca's* (dinner only) a la carte 26/48 €

♦ Business ♦ Stylish ♦

Commercial hotel in modern English town house style. Smart lounges and spacious rooms with tasteful feel and good facilities. Extras in top range rooms, at a supplement. Ground floor Francesca's restaurant with open kitchen for chef-watching.

The Alexander
400 VISA AE

Fienian St, Merrion Sq ✉ D2 – ✆ (01) 607 37 00
– info@ocallaghanhotels.com – Fax (01) 661 56 63
– www.ocallaghanhotels.com **F2**

98 rm ☕ – †195/240 € ††255/290 €

Rest *Caravaggio's* (bar lunch Saturday and Sunday) a la carte 25/35 €

♦ Business ♦ Modern ♦

This bright corporate hotel, well placed for museums and Trinity College, has a stylish contemporary interior. Spacious comfortable rooms and suites with good facilities. Stylish contemporary restaurant with wide-ranging menus.

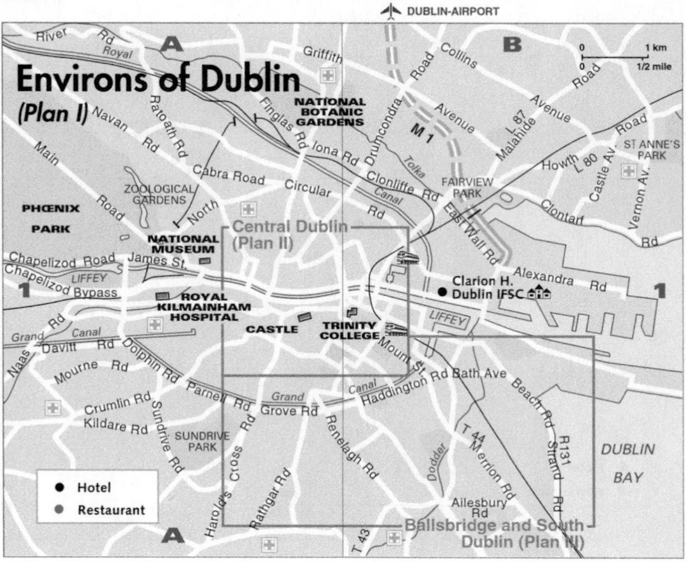

Central Dublin
(Plan II)

BLUECOAT SCHOOL

Manor Street

Blackhall Place

Brunswick Street North

King Street

Queen Street

King Street

Constitution Hill

Dominick Street

King's Inns St.

Bolton Street

Loftus Lane

Capel Street

Jervis Street

Mary St.

Island Street

Arran Quay

Usher's Quay

Church St.

Chancery St.

FOUR COURTS

Inns Quay

Ormond Quay

Morrison

Bridgefoot

Merchants Quay

Wood Q.

Essex Q.

Wellington

LIFFEY

The Clarence

The Tea Room

James Street

Oliver Bond Street

Cook Street

Les Frères Jacques

Eden

Tomas Street West

High St.

Back Lane

CHIRST CHURCH CATHEDRAL

Lord Ed St.

CITY HALL

Mermald Café

TAILORS' HALL

Francis St.

Nicholas St.

CASTLE

Meath Street

Swift's Alley

Ship

CHESTER BEATTY LIBRARY

Jaipur St.

The Coombe

Bull Alley

Golden Lane

Patrick St.

Cork Street

St PATRICK'S CATHEDRAL

Bride St.

Peter St.

Peter Row

Angier

Chamber St.

Newmarket

MARSH'S LIBRARY

Kevin St. Upper

Kevin St.

Cuffe St.

Mill Street

New Row South

Wexford St.

Ocury Road

St Tomas Road

Blackpitts

New Street

Long Lane

Camden Row

Camden Street

Donovan Road

Clanbrassil Street

● Hotel
● Restaurant

0 ___ 300 m
0 ___ 300 yards

Chapter One E F

HUGH LANE MUNICIPAL GALLERY OF MODERN ART

Street

Dermontt

Buckingham Street

North

Cassidys

THEATRE

ROTUNDA HOSPITAL CHAPEL

Parnell Street

Sean

Mac

St.

Parnell Street

O'Connell Street

Marlborough Street

Gardiner Street

CONNOLLY 1

Sheriff St.

The Gresham

PRO-CATHEDRAL

Street

Talbot Street

Amiens Street

Henry Street

Moore St.

Liffey Street

MAIN POST OFFICE

O'Connell Street

Street

Beresford Hall

Abbey Street

THEATRE

CUSTOM HOUSE

IRISH MUSIC HALL OF FAME

Eden Quay

Custom

House Quay

HA'PENNY BRIDGE

Bachelors Walk

Aston Quay

Burgh Quay

George's Quay

LIFFEY

City Quay

MILLENNIUM BRIDGE

The Morgan

Fleet Street

D'Olier St.

Westmoreland St.

Tara Street

TARA

Moss St.

Quay

BAR

The Westin

Pearse

Townsend Street

BANK OF IRELAND

Dame St.

TRINITY COLLEGE

Street

2

Siam Thai

Gt. George's St.

Pearse

The Bistro

La Maison des Gourmets

COLLEGE PARK

PEARSE

Pearse Row

Street

Brooks

POWERSCOURT CENTRE

M

Jacobs Ladder

Westland Row

The Alexander

Cafe Mao

The Westbury

Mont Clare

The Davenport

King St. South

Grafton Street

One Pico

Clare St.

Fenian Street

The Mercer

Bleu

MANSION HOUSE

NATIONAL MUSEUM

NATIONAL GALLERY

West

MERRION SQUARE

North Street

The Fitzwilliam

Peploe's

brownes brasserie

brownes

M

East

Thornton's

West North

The Merrion

Shanahan's on the Green

ST STEPHEN'S GREEN

Bang Cafe

Merrion St.

Patrick Guilbaud

The Cellar

South

Street

Stephen's Green

East

Pearl Brasserie

The Cellar Bar

Dobbin's 3

Saagar

NEWMAN HOUSE

South

Baggot Street

NUMBER TWENTY NINE

Street

Longfield's

Harrington Hall

Hatch Street

Earlsfort Terrace

U

Conrad Dublin

Pembroke Street

Fitzwilliam Lower

L'Ecrivain

Harcourt Street

IRELAND

The Davenport 🏛 🔥 🅰 ⅘ ⅗ 🔲 ⓣ 🔊 275 🚗 **VISA** ⓪ 🅰🅴 ⓪
Lower Merrion St, off Merrion Sq ⊠ D2 – ℰ (01) 607 35 00
– info@ocallaghanhotels.com – Fax (01) 661 56 63
– www.ocallaghanhotels.com **F2**
112 rm – 🛏371 €, 🛏🛏371 €, ☲ 14 € – 2 suites
Rest *Lanyon* a la carte 35/60 €
♦ Business ♦ Modern ♦
Sumptuous Victorian gospel hall façade heralds elegant hotel popular with
business clientele. Tastefully furnished, well-fitted rooms. Presidents bar
honours past leaders. Dining room with formal, Georgian interior.

The Gresham 🔥 🔥 🅰 ⅘rest ⅗ 🔊400 **P** **VISA** ⓪ 🅰🅴 ⓪
23 Upper O'Connell St ⊠ D1 – ℰ (01) 874 68 81
– info@thegresham.com – Fax (01) 878 71 75
– www.gresham-hotels.com **E1**
283 rm – 🛏450 €, 🛏🛏450 €, ☲ 19 € – 6 suites
Rest *23* (dinner only) a la carte 33/52 €
Rest *The Aberdeen* 26 €/45 € and a la carte 31/49 €
♦ Business ♦ Modern ♦
Long-established restored 19C property in a famous street offers elegance
tinged with luxury. Some penthouse suites. Well-equipped business centre,
lounge and Toddy's bar. The Aberdeen boasts formal ambience. 23 is named
after available wines by glass.

Clarion H. Dublin IFSC ⟨ 🔥 🐎 🔲 🔥 🅰 ⅘ ⅗ 🔲
Excise Walk, International Financial Services 🔊120 **VISA** ⓪ 🅰🅴 ⓪
Centre, ⊠ D1 – ℰ (01) 433 88 00 – info@
clarionhotelifsc.com – Fax (01) 433 88 11 – www.clarionhotelifsc.com
closed 25 December Plan I **B1**
154 rm – 🛏265 €, 🛏🛏265 €, ☲ 21 € – 8 suites
Rest *Sinergie* (close Saturday lunch) 15 €/25 € and a la carte 21/28 €
Rest *Kudos* (closed Sunday) a la carte 19/34 €
♦ Business ♦ Modern ♦
In the heart of a modern financial district, a swish hotel for the business person:
smart gym and light, spacious, contemporary rooms, some with balconies. Busy
bar leads to clean-lined Sinergie with glass walls onto the kitchen. Kudos serves
Asian menus.

Morrison 🅰 ⅘rm 🔲 🔊240 **P** **VISA** ⓪ 🅰🅴 ⓪
Lower Ormond Quay, ⊠ D1 – ℰ (01) 887 24 00 – info@morrisonhotel.ie
– Fax (01) 878 31 85 – www.morrisonhotel.ie
closed 24-26 December **D2**
136 rm – 🛏285 €, 🛏🛏285 €, ☲ 22 € – 4 suites
Rest *Halo* a la carte 24/47 €
♦ Luxury ♦ Design ♦
Modern riverside hotel with ultra-contemporary interior by acclaimed fashion
designer John Rocha. Hi-tech amenities in rooms. "Lobo" late-night club and
sushi bar. Ultramodern, minimal, split level restaurant designed by John Rocha,
offering talented Asian and French influenced cuisine featuring interesting and
original dishes.

brownes 🔥 🅰 ⅘ ⅗ 🔲 ⓣ **VISA** ⓪ 🅰🅴 ⓪
22 St Stephen's Green, ⊠ D2 – ℰ (01) 638 39 39
– info@brownesdublin.com – Fax (01) 638 39 00
– www.brownesdublin.com
closed 25-27 December **E3**
11 rm – 🛏200 €, 🛏🛏270 €, ☲ 21 €
Rest see *brownes brasserie* below
♦ Townhouse ♦ Stylish ♦
Restored Georgian town house with original fittings in situ. Combines traditional
charm with modern comfort. Bedrooms are well-appointed and stylish, some
with view.

The Morgan without rest 　　　　　　　AK ⇄ ✄ VISA ⚭ AE ⓪
10 Fleet St ⊠ D2 – ℰ (01) 679 39 39 – reservations @ themorgan.com
– Fax (01) 679 39 46 – www.themorgan.com
closed 23-26 December　　　　　　　　　　　　　　　　　　E2
106 rm – †130 € **††**130 €, ☑ 18 € – 15 suites
♦ Business ♦ Minimalist ♦
Discreet contemporary hotel in vibrant area emphasises style. Simple
elegant foyer contrasts with large, busy bar. Sleek minimalist décor in
well-equipped bedrooms.

Mont Clare　　　　　　　AK ⇄rm ✄ ▥ 🛏120 ⬡ VISA ⚭ AE ⓪
Lower Merrion St, off Merrion Sq ⊠ D2 – ℰ (01) 607 38 00
– info @ ocallaghanhotels.com – www.ocallaghanhotels.com
closed 24-26 December　　　　　　　　　　　　　　　　　　F2
74 rm – †253 € **††**253 €, ☑ 14 €
Rest *Goldsmiths* (closed lunch Saturday and Sunday) a la carte 30/40 €
♦ Business ♦ Modern ♦
Classic property with elegant panelled reception and tasteful comfortable
rooms at heart of Georgian Dublin. Corporate suites available. Traditional pub
style Gallery bar. Formal restaurant with tried-and-tested menus.

Cassidys　　　　　　　AK rest ⇄ ✄ 🛏80 🅿 VISA ⚭ AE ⓪
Cavendish Row, Upper O'Connell St ⊠ D1 – ℰ (01) 878 05 55
– stay @ cassidyshotel.com – Fax (01) 878 06 87 – www.cassidyshotel.com
closed 24-26 December　　　　　　　　　　　　　　　　　　E1
112 rm ☑ – **†**85/160 € **††**150/185 € – 1 suite
Rest *Number Six* (dinner only) 21 €/25 € and a la carte 23/44 €
♦ Business ♦ Stylish ♦
Classic Georgian redbrick town house makes an elegant backdrop for modern
comfort. Cheerful room décor. Limited on-street guest parking. Popular Groomes
bar open to public. Bright, stylish dining room sports a homely ambience.

The Mercer　　　　　⅁ AK ⇄ ✄ 🛏100 ⬡ VISA ⚭ AE ⓪
Mercer Street Lower ⊠ D2 – ℰ (01) 478 21 79 – stay @ mercerhotel.ie
– Fax (01) 478 03 28 – www.mercerhotel.ie
closed 23-29 December　　　　　　　　　　　　　　　　　　E3
41 rm – †185/220 € **††**250 €, ☑ 5 €
Rest *Cusack's* (closed Sunday) a la carte approx. 25 €
♦ Business ♦ Modern ♦
This modern boutique hotel, hidden away next to the Royal College of Surgeons,
is pleasant and stylish. It offers comprehensive amenities including air
conditioning. Smart yet relaxing restaurant.

Beresford Hall without rest 　　　　　　⇄ ✄ 📞 VISA ⚭ ⓪
2 Beresford Pl ⊠ D1 – ℰ (01) 801 45 00 – stay @ beresfordhall.ie
– Fax (01) 801 45 01 – www.beresfordhall.ie
closed 23 December -3 January　　　　　　　　　　　　　　　F1
16 rm ☑ – **†**80/90 € **††**110/160 €
♦ Townhouse ♦ Classic ♦
Georgian townhouse on edge of city centre, exuding a stylish, discreet air. Comfy
lounge with chintz décor. Especially impressive bedrooms: original features in
most.

Longfield's　　　　　　　　⇄rest ✄ VISA ⚭ AE ⓪
10 Lower Fitzwilliam St ⊠ D2 – ℰ (01) 676 13 67 – info @ longfields.ie
– Fax (01) 676 15 42 – www.longfields.ie　　　　　　　　　F3
26 rm ☑ – **†**90 € **††**235 €
Rest @ *Number Ten* (closed Saturday lunch, Sunday and Monday) 25 € (lunch)
and dinner a la carte 26/42 €
♦ Townhouse ♦ Classic ♦
Classic Georgian town house on reputedly Europe's longest Georgian road.
Spacious lounge; stylish, individually furnished rooms of good size, all redolent
of times gone by. This bijou basement establishment with an atmosphere of
understated elegance offers well cooked interesting menus combining
traditional European cuisine with local flair.

IRELAND

🏠 **Harrington Hall** without rest   ⇪ ⅏ 🖾 📞 **P** **VISA** **CO** **AE** **①**
70 Harcourt St ⊠ D2 – ℰ (01) 475 34 97 – harringtonhall@eircom.net
– Fax (01) 475 45 44 – www.harringtonhall.com   **E3**
28 rm ⌷ – **♦**115/173 € **♦♦**173/240 €
• Townhouse • Classic •
Two usefully located mid-terrace Georgian town houses. Friendly and well-run.
Bright, spacious bedrooms with soundproofing, ceiling fans, access to fax and
internet.

⌂ **Kilronan House** without rest   ⇪ ⅏ 🖾 **VISA** **CO** **AE**
70 Adelaide Rd ⊠ D2 – ℰ (01) 475 52 66 – info@dublinn.com
– Fax (01) 478 28 41 – www.dublinn.com   Plan III **G1**
12 rm ⌷ – **♦**45/120 € **♦♦**90/170 €
• Traditional • Classic •
In the heart of Georgian Dublin, a good value, well-kept town house run by
knowledgeable, friendly couple. Individually styled rooms; sustaining
breakfasts.

XXXX **Patrick Guilbaud**   **AC** ⇪ ⇔25 **VISA** **CO** **AE** **①**
🕸🕸 *21 Upper Merrion St ⊠ D2 – ℰ (01) 676 41 92 – restaurantpatrickguilbaud@*
eircom.net – Fax (01) 661 00 52 – www.restaurantpatrickguilbaud.ie
closed 1 week after Christmas, Sunday and Monday   **F3**
Rest 45 € (lunch) and a la carte 83/112 € ⅋
Spec. Oysters and caviar. Calf's sweetbreads and liquorice, parsnip sauce, lemon
confit. Assiette of chocolate.
• Contemporary • Formal •
Top class restaurant run by consummate professional offering accomplished
Irish influenced dishes in elegant Georgian town house. Contemporary Irish art
collection.

XXXX **Thornton's** – at The Fitzwilliam H.   **AC** ⇪ **P** **VISA** **CO** **AE** **①**
🕸 *128 St Stephen's Green ⊠ D2 – ℰ (01) 478 70 08 – thorntonsrestaurant@*
eircom.net – Fax (01) 478 70 09 – www.thorntonsrestaurant.com
closed 1 week Christmas, Good Friday, Sunday and Monday   **E3**
Rest 30/40 € (lunch) and a la carte 91/104 € ⅋
Spec. Sautéed prawns with prawn bisque, truffle sabayon. Suckling pig with
trotter, glazed turnip and poitin sauce. Orange soufflé with mandarin sorbet.
• Modern • Formal •
Stylish modern restaurant on second floor offers interesting culinary ideas
drawing on Irish, French and Italian cuisine, and fine views too. Good value lunch
menus.

XXX **Shanahan's on the Green**   **AC** ⇪ **VISA** **CO** **AE** **①**
119 St Stephen's Green ⊠ D2 – ℰ (01) 407 09 39 – info@shanahans.ie
– Fax (01) 407 09 40 – www.shanahans.ie
closed Christmas-New Year and Good Friday   **E3**
Rest (booking essential) (dinner only and Friday lunch) a la carte 76/99 €
• Beef specialities • Formal •
Sumptuous Georgian town house: upper floor window tables survey the Green.
Supreme comfort enhances your enjoyment of strong seafood dishes and
choice cuts of Irish beef.

XXX **L'Ecrivain** (Clarke)   🖃 **AC** ⇪ ⇔20 **VISA** **CO** **AE**
🕸 *109A Lower Baggot Street ⊠ D2 – ℰ (01) 661 19 19 – enquiries@lecrivain.com*
– Fax (01) 661 06 17 – www.lecrivain.com   **F3**
closed 23 December-4 January, Easter, Saturday lunch, Sunday and Bank Holidays
Rest (booking essential) 45 €/70 € and dinner a la carte 74/98 €
Spec. Loin of wild venison, candied pear, celeriac mousseline and beetroot jus.
Assiette of Dublin Bay prawns. Roast turbot with pea purée, foie gras tart and
girolles.
• Contemporary • Formal •
Soft piano notes add to the welcoming ambience. Robust, well prepared,
modern Irish food with emphasis on fish and game. Private dining room in
glass-enclosed cellar.

IRELAND

XXX   **Chapter One**   AC ⇔ ✿ 14 VISA ●●
The Dublin Writers Museum, 18-19 Parnell Sq ⊠ D1
– ☎ (01) 873 22 66 – info@chapteronerestaurant.com
– Fax (01) 873 23 30 – www.chapteronerestaurant.com
closed first 2 weeks August, 24 December-8 January, Saturday lunch, Sunday and
Monday   **E1**
Rest 31 € (lunch) and dinner a la carte 52/60 €
♦ Modern ♦ Formal ♦
In basement of historic building, once home to whiskey baron. Comfortable
restaurant with Irish art on walls. Interesting menus focus on good hearty food:
sample the oysters.

XX   **The Tea Room** – at The Clarence H.   ⇔ VISA ●● AE ①
6-8 Wellington Quay ⊠ D2 – ☎ (01) 407 08 13
– tearoom@theclarence.ie – Fax (01) 407 08 26
– www.theclarence.ie
closed 24-26 December and Saturday lunch   **D2**
Rest (booking essential) 30 €/55 €
♦ Modern ♦ Fashionable ♦
Spacious elegant ground floor room with soaring coved ceiling and stylish
contemporary décor offers interesting modern Irish dishes with hint of
continental influence.

XX   **brownes brasserie** – at brownes H.   AC ⇔ VISA ●● AE ①
22 St Stephen's Green – ☎ (01) 638 39 39 – info@brownesdublin.com
– Fax (01) 638 39 00 – www.brownesdublin.com
closed Saturday lunch and Bank Holidays   **E3**
Rest (booking essential) 30 € (lunch) and a la carte 43/53 €
♦ Modern ♦ Brasserie ♦
Smart, characterful, with a Belle Epoque feel. On the ground floor of the
eponymous Georgian town house, in central location, with interesting and
appealing classic dishes.

XX   **The Cellar** – at The Merrion H.   AC ⇔ P. VISA ●● AE ①
Upper Merrion St ⊠ D2 – ☎ (01) 603 06 30 – Fax (01) 603 07 00
– www.merrionhotel.com
closed Saturday lunch   **F3**
Rest 25 € (lunch) and dinner a la carte 31/58 €
♦ Mediterranean ♦ Formal ♦
Smart open-plan basement restaurant with informal ambience offering well
prepared formal style fare crossing Irish with Mediterranean influences. Good
value lunch menu.

XX   **One Pico**   AC ⇔ VISA ●● AE ①
5 6 Molesworth Pl ⊠ D2 – ☎ (01) 676 03 00
– eamonnoreilly@ireland.com – Fax (01) 676 04 11
– www.onepico.com
closed 24-31 December, Sunday and Bank Holidays   **E3**
Rest 25 €/35 € and a la carte 40/55 €
♦ Modern ♦ Fashionable ♦
Wide-ranging cuisine, classic and traditional by turns, always with an elaborate,
eclectic edge. Décor and service share a pleasant formality, crisp, modern and
stylish.

XX   **Les Frères Jacques**   AC ⇔ VISA ●● AE
74 Dame St ⊠ D2 – ☎ (01) 679 45 55 – info@lesfreresjacques.com
– Fax (01) 679 47 25 – www.lesfreresjacques.com
closed 24 December-3 January, Saturday lunch,
Sunday and Bank Holidays   **D2**
Rest 22 €/36 € and a la carte 50/62 €
♦ French ♦ Bistro ♦
Smart popular family-run bistro offering well prepared simple classic French
cuisine with fresh fish and seafood a speciality, served by efficient team of French
staff.

IRELAND

XX **Peploe's** · AC · 😳 · *VISA* · ⬤⬤ · AE

16 St Stephen's Green ⊠ D2 – 𝒞 (01) 676 31 44
– reservations @ peploes.com – Fax (01) 676 31 54
– www.peploes.com
closed 25-29 December and Good Friday **E3**
Rest 33 €/45 € and a la carte 29/49 €
♦ Mediterranean ♦ Fashionable ♦
Fashionable restaurant - a former bank vault - by the Green. Irish wall mural, Italian leather chairs, suede banquettes. Original dishes with pronounced Mediterranean accents.

XX **Saagar** · 😳 · *VISA* · ⬤⬤ · AE · ⓞ

16 Harcourt St ⊠ D2 – 𝒞 (01) 475 50 60
– info @ saagarindianrestaurants.com – Fax (01) 475 57 41
– www.saagarindianrestaurants.com
closed 25 December, 1 January, Sunday and Bank Holidays **E3**
Rest a la carte 16/27 €
♦ Indian ♦ Friendly ♦
Well-run restaurant serving subtly toned, freshly prepared Indian fare in basement of Georgian terraced house. Main road setting. Ring bell at foot of stairs to enter.

XX **Locks** · 😳 · *VISA* · ⬤⬤ · AE · ⓞ

1 Windsor Terrace, Portobello ⊠ D8 – 𝒞 (01) 454 33 91
– Fax (01) 453 83 52
closed 1 week Easter, 1 week Christmas-New Year, Saturday lunch, Sunday and
Bank Holidays *Plan III* **G1**
Rest (booking essential at dinner) 29 €/49 € and a la carte 59/75 €
♦ Traditional ♦ Family ♦
Street corner mainstay for 20 years; watch the swans swimming by on adjacent canal. Offers wide range, from simple one course dishes to more elaborate classic French fare.

XX **Jacobs Ladder** · 😳 · *VISA* · ⬤⬤ · AE · ⓞ
😳

4-5 Nassau St ⊠ D2 – 𝒞 (01) 670 38 65 – dining @ jacobsladder.ie
– Fax (01) 670 38 68 – www.jacobsladder.ie
closed 1 week Christmas, 1 week August, 17 March, Sunday, Monday and Bank
Holidays **E2**
Rest (booking essential) 37 €/45 € (dinner) and a la carte 30/57 €
♦ Modern ♦ Fashionable ♦
Up a narrow staircase, this popular small first floor restaurant with unfussy modern décor and a good view offers good value modern Irish fare and very personable service.

XX **Siam Thai** · AC · 😳 · *VISA* · ⬤⬤ · AE

14-15 Andrew St ⊠ D2 – 𝒞 (01) 677 33 63 – siam @ eircom.net
– Fax (01) 670 76 44 – www.siamthai.ie
closed 25-26 December and lunch Saturday and Sunday **E2**
Rest 35 € (dinner) and a la carte 26/35 €
♦ Thai ♦ Exotic ♦
Centrally located restaurant with a warm, homely feel, embodied by woven Thai prints. Basement room for parties. Daily specials; Thai menus with choice and originality.

XX **Jaipur** · 😳 · *VISA* · ⬤⬤ · AE

41 South Great George's St ⊠ D2 – 𝒞 (01) 677 09 99 – dublin @ jaipur.ie
– Fax (01) 677 09 79 – www.jaipur.ie
closed 25-26 December **D2**
Rest (dinner only) 40 € and a la carte 23/43 €
♦ Indian ♦ Minimalist ♦
Vivid modernity in the city centre; run by knowledgeable team. Immaculately laid, linen-clad tables. Interesting, freshly prepared Indian dishes using unique variations.

IRELAND

Bang Café
ⓧⓧ
⊙

11 Merrion Row ✉ *D2 – ℰ (01) 676 08 98 – Fax (01) 676 08 99*
– www.bangrestaurant.com
closed 1 week Christmas, Sunday and Bank Holidays   **E3**
Rest (booking essential) a la carte 26/47 €
♦ Innovative ♦ Fashionable ♦
Stylish, mirror-lined lounge bar, closely set linen-topped tables and an open kitchen lend a lively, contemporary air. Flavourful menu balances the classical and the creative.

Bleu
ⓧ

Dawson St ✉ *D2 – ℰ (01) 676 70 15 – Fax (01) 676 70 27 – www.onepico.com*
closed 25-26 December   **E3**
Rest 20 €/29 € and a la carte 21/38 €
♦ Modern ♦ Fashionable ♦
Distinctive modern interior serves as chic background to this friendly all-day diner. Appealing bistro fare, well executed and very tasty. Good selection of wines by glass.

Dobbin's
ⓧ

15 Stephen's Lane, off Lower Mount St ✉ *D2 – ℰ (01) 676 46 79*
– dobbinswinebistro @ eircom.net – Fax (01) 661 33 31
closed 1 week Christmas-New Year, Sunday, Monday dinner, Saturday lunch and
Bank Holidays   **F3**
Rest (booking essential) 25 €/45 € and a la carte 28/45 €
♦ Traditional ♦ Retro ♦
In the unlikely setting of a former Nissen hut in a residential part of town, this popular restaurant, something of a local landmark, offers good food to suit all tastes.

Pearl Brasserie
ⓧ

20 Merrion St Upper ✉ *D2 – ℰ (01) 661 35 72 – info @ pearl-brasserie.com*
– Fax (01) 661 36 29
closed first week January and lunch Saturday-Monday   **F3**
Rest 25 € (lunch) and dinner a la carte 29/52 €
♦ French ♦ Brasserie ♦
A metal staircase leads down to this intimate, vaulted cellar brasserie and oyster bar. Franco-Irish dishes served at granite-topped tables. Amiable and helpful service.

The Bistro
ⓧ

4-5 Castlemarket ✉ *D2 – ℰ (01) 671 54 30 – info @ thebistro.ie*
– Fax (01) 670 33 79 – www.thebistro.ie
closed 25-26 December, 1 January and Good Friday   **E2**
Rest a la carte 22/44 €
♦ Modern ♦ Bistro ♦
Friendly and buzzing in the heart of the city. Exposed floor boards, coir carpeting and vividly coloured walls. Additional terrace area. Interesting, modern dishes.

Eden
ⓧ

Meeting House Sq, Temple Bar ✉ *D2 – ℰ (01) 670 53 72 – Fax (01) 670 33 30*
– www.edenrestaurant.ie
closed 25 December-3 January and Bank Holidays   **D2**
Rest 20/23 € (lunch) and dinner a la carte 36/49 €
♦ Modern ♦ Minimalist ♦
Modern minimalist restaurant with open plan kitchen serves good robust food. Terrace overlooks theatre square, at the heart of a busy arty district. Children welcome.

Mermald Café
ⓧ

69-70 Dame St ✉ *D2 – ℰ (01) 670 82 36 – info @ mermald.ie*
– Fax (01) 670 82 05 – www.mermaid.ie
closed 24-26 and 31 December, 1 January and Good Friday   **D2**
Rest (booking essential) 24 € (lunch) and a la carte 31/48 €
♦ Modern ♦ Fashionable ♦
This small informal restaurant with unfussy décor and wood floors offers an interesting and well cooked selection of robust modern dishes. Good service.

✕ **Cafe Mao**   AC ⅍ VISA ⓜ⊘ AE

2-3 Chatham Row ✉ D2 – ✆ (01) 670 48 99 – info@cafemao.com
– www.cafemao.com   **E2**
Rest (bookings not accepted) a la carte 28/35 €
♦ South-East Asian ♦ Trendy ♦
Well run trendy modern restaurant serving authentic southeast Asian fusion
cuisine in an informal setting buzzing with action and atmosphere. Tasty food at
tasty prices.

✕ **La Maison des Gourmets**   ⅍ VISA ⓜ⊘ AE ⓪

15 Castlemarket ✉ D2 – ✆ (01) 672 72 58 – lamaison@indigo.ie
– Fax (01) 864 56 72 – www.gourmetmaison.com
closed 25-28 December and Sunday   **E2**
Rest (lunch only) a la carte 19/24 €
♦ French ♦ Cosy ♦
Simple, snug restaurant on the first floor above an excellent bakery offering high
quality breads and pastries. Extremely good value meals using fine local
ingredients.

🍺 **The Cellar Bar** – at The Merrion H.   ⅍ P VISA ⓜ⊘ AE ⓪

Upper Merrion St ✉ D2 – ✆ (01) 603 06 31 – info@merrionhotel.com
– Fax (01) 603 07 00 – www.merrionhotel.com
closed Sunday   **F3**
Rest (lunch only) (carving lunch) a la carte 22/30 €
♦ Traditional ♦ Pub ♦
Characterful stone and brick bar-restaurant in the original vaulted cellars with
large wood bar. Popular with Dublin's social set. Offers wholesome Irish pub
lunch fare.

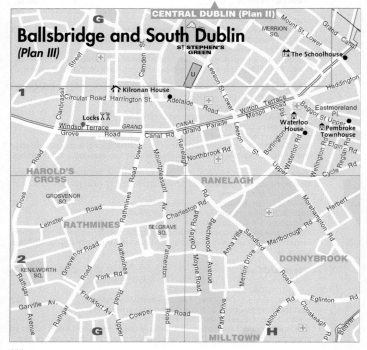

BALLSBRIDGE and SOUTH DUBLIN

Four Seasons ⊗ 𝄞 🕭 🖾 🚗 ᵹ 🅐🅒 ⅙ 🖾 📞 🚗800

Simmonscourt Rd ⊠ *D4 – ℰ (01) 665 40 00* 🚗 P VISA 🅜🅒 🅐🅔
– sales.dublin@fourseasons.com – Fax (01) 665 40 99
– www.fourseasons.com/dublin **J2**
192 rm – 🛏380/425 € 🛏🛏380/425 €, ⍁ 27 € – 67 suites
Rest *Seasons* 28 €/72 € and a la carte 28/38 €
Rest *The Cafe* a la carte 34/48 €
♦ Grand Luxury ♦ Modern ♦
Every inch the epitome of international style - supremely comfortable rooms
with every facility; richly furnished lounge; a warm mix of antiques, oils and soft
piano études. Dining in Seasons guarantees luxury ingredients. Informal
comforts in The Café.

The Berkeley Court ᵹ 🅐🅒 ⅙ ℀ 🖾 🚗450 🚗 P VISA 🅜🅒 🅐🅔 ⓪

Lansdowne Rd ⊠ *D4 – ℰ (01) 665 32 00 – berkeleycourt@jurysdoyle.com*
– Fax (01) 661 72 38 – www.jurysdoyle.com **J1**
182 rm – 🛏338/380 € 🛏🛏380 €, ⍁ 25 € – 4 suites
Rest *Berkeley Room* 30 €/60 €
Rest *Palm Court Café* a la carte 42/71 €
♦ Luxury ♦ Classic ♦
Luxurious international hotel in former botanical gardens; two minutes from the
home of Irish rugby. Large amount of repeat business. Solidly formal feel
throughout. Berkeley Room for elegant fine dining. Breakfast buffets a feature of
Palm Court Café.

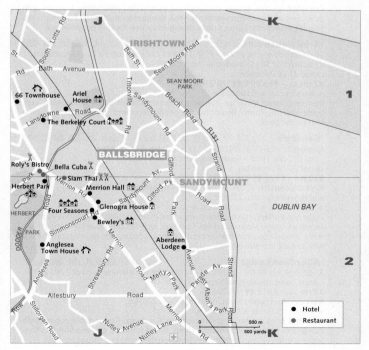

IRELAND

Herbert Park 🔝 ↳ 🖾 ↳ ↗ 🎮 🕮 ⚙100 **P** *VISA* **⓪** 🖭 ⓪
✉ D4 – ℰ (01) 667 22 00 – reservations@herbertparkhotel.ie
– Fax (01) 667 25 95 – www.herbertparkhotel.ie   **J2**
150 rm – ♦230 € ♦♦275 €, ⌷ 19 € – 3 suites
Rest *The Pavilon* (closed dinner Sunday and Monday) 24 € (lunch) and dinner
a la carte 36/53 €
♦ Business ♦ Modern ♦
Stylish contemporary hotel. Spacious, open, modern lobby and lounges.
Excellent, well-designed rooms with tasteful décor. Some offer views of park.
Good business facilities. French-windowed restaurant with al fresco potential;
oyster/lobster specialities.

The Schoolhouse 🚗 🖾 ↳ ↗ 🎮 🕮 **P** *VISA* **⓪** 🖭 ⓪
2-8 Northumberland Rd ✉ D4 – ℰ (01) 667 50 14 – reservations@
schoolhousehotel.com – Fax (01) 667 50 15 – www.schoolhousehotel.com
closed 24-26 December   **H1**
31 rm ⌷ – ♦99/199 € ♦♦199/300 €
Rest *The Canteen* (bar lunch Saturday and Sunday) a la carte 26/51 €
♦ Business ♦ Historic ♦
Spacious converted 19C schoolhouse, close to canal, boasts modernity and
charm. Rooms contain locally crafted furniture. Inkwell bar has impressive split-
level seating area. Old classroom now a large restaurant with beamed ceilings.

Merrion Hall 🔝 🚗 🖾 ↳ ↗ 🎮 📞 ⚙40 *VISA* **⓪** 🖭 ⓪
54-56 Merrion Rd ✉ D4 – ℰ (01) 668 14 26 – merrionhall@iol.ie
– Fax (01) 668 42 80 – www.halpinsprivatehotels.com   **J2**
30 rm ⌷ – ♦109 € ♦♦149 € – 4 suites
Rest (dinner only) a la carte 23/34 €
♦ Family ♦ Classic ♦
Extended ivy-clad house on main road in suburbs. Welcoming lounges with
open fires and homely ornaments. Well-equipped, refurbished bedrooms are
brightly lit and airy. Large, formal dining room overlooking patio/terrace.

Ariel House without rest ↳ ↗ 🎮 **P** *VISA* **⓪**
50-54 Lansdowne Rd ✉ D4 – ℰ (01) 668 55 12 – reservations@ariel-house.net
– Fax (01) 668 58 45 – www.ariel-house.net
closed 23-28 December   **J1**
37 rm ⌷ – ♦69/99 € ♦♦170/210 €
♦ Business ♦ Classic ♦
Restored, listed Victorian mansion in smart suburb houses personally run,
traditional small hotel. Rooms feature period décor and original antiques; some
four poster beds.

Bewley's 🔝 ₼ 🖾 rest ↳ ↗ ⚙30 🍃 *VISA* **⓪** 🖭 ⓪
Merrion Rd ✉ D4 – ℰ (01) 668 11 11 – bb@bewleyshotel.com
– Fax (01) 668 19 99 – www.bewleyshotels.com
closed 24-26 December   **J2**
220 rm – ♦99 € ♦♦99 €, ⌷ 9 €
Rest *O'Connells* , ℰ (01) 647 34 00 (carvery lunch) 28 €/33 € (dinner)
and dinner a la carte 27/39 €
♦ Business ♦ Functional ♦
Huge hotel offers stylish modern accommodation behind sumptuous Victorian
façade of former Masonic school. Location, facilities and value for money make
this a good choice. Informal modern O'Connells restaurant, cleverly constructed
with terrace in stairwell.

Aberdeen Lodge 🚗 ↳ ↗ 🎮 📞 **P** *VISA* **⓪** 🖭 ⓪
53-55 Park Ave ✉ D4 – ℰ (01) 283 81 55 – aberdeen@iol.ie – Fax (01) 283 78 77
– www.halpinsprivatehotels.com   **J2**
17 rm ⌷ – ♦99 € ♦♦140/200 €
Rest (residents only) (light meals) a la carte 23/34 €
♦ Townhouse ♦ Classic ♦
Neat red brick house in smart residential suburb. Comfortable rooms with
Edwardian style décor in neutral tones, wood furniture and modern facilities.
Some garden views. Comfortable, traditionally decorated dining room.

IRELAND

Pembroke Townhouse without rest ⌁ ⌖ ⌂ P VISA ⦿ AE ①

90 Pembroke Rd ⊠ D4 – ℰ (01) 660 02 77 – info @ pembroketownhouse
– Fax (01) 660 02 91 – www.pembroketownhouse.ie
closed 22 December-3 January **H1**
48 rm ☲ – †88/165 € ††120/260 €

♦ Townhouse ♦ Classic ♦

Period-inspired décor adds to the appeal of a sensitively modernised, personally run Georgian terrace town house in the smart suburbs. Neat, up-to-date accommodation.

Waterloo House without rest ⌁ ⌖ ⌂ P VISA ⦿

8-10 Waterloo Rd ⊠ D4 – ℰ (01) 660 18 88 – waterloohouse @ eircom.net
– Fax (01) 667 19 55 – www.waterloohouse.ie
closed 23-28 December **H1**
17 rm ☲ – †59/79 € ††115/155 €

♦ Townhouse ♦ Classic ♦

Pair of imposing Georgian town houses. Elegant breakfast room with conservatory. Large comfortable rooms with coordinated heavy drapes and fabrics in warm modern colours.

Glenogra House without rest ⌁ ⌖ ⌂ ⌂ ⌂ P VISA ⦿ AE ①

64 Merrion Rd ⊠ D4 – ℰ (01) 668 36 61 – info @ glenogra.com
– Fax (01) 668 36 98 – www.glenogra.com
closed 23 December-5 January **J2**
12 rm ☲ – †79/89 € ††109 €

♦ Family ♦ Cosy ♦

Neat and tidy bay windowed house in smart suburb. Personally run guesthouse with bedrooms attractively decorated in keeping with a period property. Modern facilities.

Anglesea Town House without rest ⌁ ⌖ ⌂ VISA ⦿ AE

63 Anglesea Rd ⊠ D4 – ℰ (01) 668 38 77 – helen @ 63anglesea.com
– Fax (01) 668 34 61 – www.63anglesea.com
closed 20 December-5 January **J2**
7 rm ☲ – †70/100 € ††130/140 €

♦ Townhouse ♦ Personalised ♦

Red brick Edwardian residence in smart suburb with many pieces of fine period furniture. Individually styled rooms with good facilities. Parking can be a challenge.

66 Townhouse without rest ⌁ ⌖ ⌂ P VISA ⦿

66 Northumberland Rd ⊠ D4 – ℰ (01) 660 03 33 – Fax (01) 660 10 51
closed 22 December-6 January **J1**
8 rm ☲ – †70/80 € ††100/175 €

♦ Townhouse ♦ Cosy ♦

Attractive Victorian red brick house with extension in smart suburb. Comfortable homely atmosphere. Good size rooms with tasteful décor and modern facilities.

Siam Thai AC ⌖ VISA ⦿ AE ①

Sweepstake Centre ⊠ D4 – ℰ (01) 660 17 22 – siam @ eircom.net
– Fax (01) 660 15 37 – www.siamthai.ie
closed 25-26 December, lunch Saturday and Sunday and Good Friday **J2**
Rest 13 €/32 € and a la carte 31/34 €

♦ Thai ♦ Friendly ♦

Unerringly busy restaurant that combines comfort with liveliness. Smart waiters serve authentic Thai cuisine, prepared with skill and understanding. Good value lunches.

Roly's Bistro AC ⌖ VISA ⦿ AE ①

7 Ballsbridge Terrace ⊠ D4 – ℰ (01) 668 26 11 – ireland @ rolysbistro.ie
– Fax (01) 660 85 35 – www.rolysbistro.ie
closed 25-27 December **J1**
Rest (booking essential) 20 €/39 € and a la carte 36/48 €

♦ Traditional ♦ Bistro ♦

A Dublin institution: this roadside bistro is very busy and well run, with a buzzy, fun atmosphere. Its two floors offer modern Irish dishes and a very good value lunch.

IRELAND

✄

Bella Cuba   ↳ *VISA* **ⓜⓞ** **AE**

11 Ballsbridge Terrace ⊠ D4 – ℰ (01) 660 55 39 – info@bella-cuba.com
– Fax (01) 660 55 39 – www.bella-cuba.com
closed lunch Saturday and Sunday   **J1**
Rest *(booking essential) (dinner only and lunch Thursday-Friday)* 20 € (lunch)
and a la carte 31/37 €
♦ Cuban ♦ Family ♦
Family-owned restaurant with an intimate feel. Cuban memoirs on walls, fine
choice of cigars. Authentic Cuban dishes, employing many of the island's
culinary influences.

---

at **DUBLIN AIRPORT** *North : 6,5 m. by N1 and M1 -* ⊠ *Dublin*

Crowne Plaza   *Fô* **ᴮ** **AC** ↳ *ᴽ* **ᴘ** *ℳ*240 **P** *VISA* **ⓜⓞ** **AE** **①**

Northwood Park, Santry Demesne, Santry ⊠ D9 – ℰ (01) 862 88 88 – info@
crowneplazadublin.ie – Fax (01) 862 88 00 – www.cpdublin-airport.com
202 rm – ♥105/265 € ♥♥105/265 €, � 21 € – 2 suites
Rest *Touzai (closed Saturday and Bank Holidays)* (buffet lunch) dinner
a la carte 32/37 €
Rest *Cinnabar* a la carte 25/30 €
♦ Luxury ♦ Modern ♦
Next to Fingal Park, two miles from the airport. Hotel has predominant Oriental
style, extensive meeting facilities, and modern, well-equipped rooms, some of
Club standard. Touzai for Asian specialities. Stylish Cinnabar has extensive,
eclectic menu range.

Hilton Dublin Airport   *Fô* **ᴮ** **AC** ↳ *ᴽ* ℬ *ℳ*550 **P** *VISA* **ⓜⓞ** **AE**

Northern Cross, Malahide Rd ⊠ D17 – ℰ (01) 866 18 00
– dublinairport@hilton.com – Fax (01) 866 18 66 – www.hilton.com
162 rm – ♥120/320 € ♥♥120/320 €, ⊒ 20 € – 4 suites
Rest *Solas (dinner only and Sunday lunch)* a la carte 31/39 €
♦ Business ♦ Modern ♦
Opened in 2005, just five minutes from the airport, adjacent to busy shopping
centre. Modish feel throughout. State-of-the-art meeting facilities. Airy,
well-equipped rooms. Spacious dining room serves tried-and-tested dishes.

Great Southern   **ᴮ** ↳ *ᴽ* **ᴘ** ℬ *ℳ*450 **P** *VISA* **ⓜⓞ** **AE** **①**

– ℰ (01) 844 60 00 – res@dubairport-gsh.com – Fax (01) 844 60 01
– www.greatsouthernhotels.com
closed 23-27 December
227 rm – ♥270 € ♥♥270 €, ⊒ 15 € – 2 suites
Rest *Potters (closed Sunday and Monday)* (dinner only) 35 €
Rest *O'Deas Bar* (carvery lunch) a la carte 23/37 €
♦ Business ♦ Modern ♦
Modern hotel catering for international and business travellers. Range of guest
rooms, all spacious and smartly furnished with wood furniture and colourful
fabrics. Potters has a spacious, formal feel. O'Deas Bar for intimate carvery
menus.

Clarion H. Dublin Airport   **ᴮ** **AC** rest ↳ *ᴽ* *ℳ*130
                               P *VISA* **ⓜⓞ** **AE** **①**

– ℰ (01) 808 05 00 – reservations@
clarionhoteldublinairport.com – Fax (01) 844 60 02
– www.clarionhoteldublinairport.com
closed 24-26 December
247 rm – ♥250 € ♥♥250 €, ⊒ 19 €
Rest *Bistro (closed Saturday lunch)* a la carte 18/29 €
Rest *Sampans (closed Bank Holidays)* (dinner only) a la carte 18/29 €
♦ Business ♦ Modern ♦
Modern commercial hotel offers standard or Millennium rooms, all with
colourful feel and good facilities. Free use of leisure centre. Live music at
weekends in Bodhran bar.

ITALY
ITALIA

PROFILE

- **AREA:**
  301 262 km²
  (116 317 sq mi).

- **POPULATION:**
  58 103 000 inhabitants
  (est. 2005), density =
  193 per km².

- **CAPITAL:**
  Rome (conurbation
  2 867 000 inhabitants).

- **CURRENCY:**
  Euro (€); rate of
  exchange: € 1 =
  1.17 US$ (Nov 2005).

- **GOVERNMENT:**
  Parliamentary republic
  with two chambers
  (since 1946). Member
  of European Union
  since 1957 (one of the
  6 founding countries).

- **LANGUAGE:**
  Italian.

- **SPECIFIC PUBLIC
  HOLIDAYS:**
  Epiphany (6 January);
  Liberation Day
  (25 April); Anniversary
  of the Republic
  (2 June); Immaculate
  Conception
  (8 December); St.
  Stephen's Day
  (26 December).
  Each town also
  celebrates the
  feast day of its
  patron saint (Rome:
  29 June St. Peter,
  Milan: 7 December
  St. Ambrose, etc
  details from the local
  tourist offices).

- **LOCAL TIME:**
  GMT + 1 hour
  in winter and
  GMT + 2 hours in
  summer.

- **CLIMATE:**
  Temperate
  Mediterranean, with
  mild winters and
  hot, sunny summers
  (Rome: January: 8°C,
  July: 25°C).

- **INTERNATIONAL
  DIALLING CODE:**
  00 39 followed by
  area or city code
  and then the local
  number.

- **EMERGENCY:**
  Police: ℰ 112; Fire
  Brigade: ℰ 115;
  Health services:
  ℰ 118.

- **ELECTRICITY:**
  220 volts AC, 50Hz;
  2-pin round-shaped
  continental plugs.

FORMALITIES

Travellers from the European Union (EU), Switzerland, Iceland and the main countries of North and South America need a national identity card or passport (America: passport required) to visit Italy for less than three months (tourism or business purpose). For visitors from other countries a visa may be required, in addition to a passport, especially for those wishing to stay for longer than three months. We advise you to check with your embassy before travelling.

A valid driving licence is essential. Third party insurance is the minimum cover required by Italian legislation but it is advisable to take out fully comprehensive cover (Green Card).

MAJOR NEWSPAPERS

The main Italian dailies are *Corriere della Sera* and *La Repubblica*, available throughout Italy. There are also many important local papers like *Il Messaggero* in Rome, *La Stampa* in Turin and *La Nazione* in Florence; the main economic newspaper is *Il Sole 24 Ore*. The *Osservatore Romano* is the official paper of the Vatican City.

SMOKING-NO SMOKING

The laws in Italy prohibit smoking in all restaurants, bars and in the public areas of hotels. Some hotel bedrooms are still available for smokers.

USEFUL PHRASES

ENGLISH	ITALIAN	ENGLISH	ITALIAN
Yes	**Si**	Thank you	**Grazie**
No	**No**	Please	**Per favore**
Good morning	**Buon giorno**	Excuse me	**Mi scusi**
Goodbye	**Arrivederci**	I don't understand	**Non capisco**

HOTELS

◆ CATEGORIES

Major towns have **hotels** in all categories from luxury establishments to **guest-houses**. It is not always easy to find value for money accommodation in tourist centres and during the summer months prices may well go up. For regions and cities popular with tourists, it is advisable to book well in advance if you plan to go from April to October.

◆ PRICE RANGE

Price are quoted per room. In general from November to March (with the exception of the art cities such as Florence, Venice and Rome) prices are considerably lower and many hotels offer discounts or special weekend deals.

◆ TAX

Included in the price of the room.

◆ CHECK OUT TIME

Usually between 11am and noon.

◆ RESERVATIONS

By telephone or by Internet. A credit card number may be required.

◆ TIP FOR LUGGAGE HANDLING

At the discretion of the customer (about €1 per item).

◆ BREAKFAST

It is often not included in the price of the room. It is served between 7am and 10am. Most hotels offer a self-service buffet but usually it is possible to have continental breakfast served in the room.

Reception	**Ufficio ricevimento**	Bed	**Letto**
Single room	**Camera singola**	Bathroom	**Bagno**
Double room	**Camera doppia**	Shower	**Doccia**

RESTAURANTS

Besides the traditional **restaurants** which offer elegant cuisine and service, there are various types of places to eat which serve simpler fare. A **trattoria** is a medium-priced, family-run establishment serving home-made dishes, a **taverna** is a more modest type of trattoria and an **osteria** is a local inn serving simple dishes in an informal atmosphere. A **locanda** usually serves local dishes. A **pizzeria** is the place to choose for a tasty, quick and reasonably priced meal; other dishes are often on offer. **Tavola calda** (hot table) is a cafeteria-style restaurant serving hot dishes and a **rosticceria** specialises in grilled meat, chicken and fish. **Enoteche** (wine bars) serve light starters and daily specials with a varied choice of wines by the glass or bottle.

Breakfast	**La colazione**	7am – 10am
Lunch	**Il pranzo**	12.30pm – 2.30pm
Dinner	**La cena**	7.30-11pm sometimes later

Most restaurants offer a fixed price menu (*menù turistico* – a three or four course meal with limited choice), the speciality of the day or the more extensive à la carte menu.

◆ RESERVATIONS

Reservations are usually made by phone. For famous restaurants (including Michelin starred restaurants), it is advisable to book several days, even weeks, in advance.

◆ THE BILL

The bill (check) includes service and VAT (sales tax IVA). Bread and cover charges are usually included in the price but in some trattorie and pizzerie they are calculated separately. It is customary to leave a tip in proportion to customer satisfaction. An appropriate percentage for a tip is suggested on the bill.

Appetizer	**Antipasto**	Bread	**Pane**
Meal	**Pasto**	Meat (rare, medium well done)	**Carne (al sangue, a puntino, ben cotta)**
First course	**Primi piatti**	Fish	**Pesce**
Main dish	**Secondi piatti**	Salt/pepper	**Sale/pepe**
Main dish of the day	**Piatto del giorno**	Cheese	**Formaggio**
Dessert	**Dolce**	Vegetables	**Verdure**
Water/ sparkling/ mineral	**Acqua naturale/ gasata/minerale**	Hot/cold	**Caldo/freddo**
Wine (red, white, rosé)	**Vino (rosso, bianco, rosé)**	The bill (check) please	**Il conto per favore**
Beer	**Birra**		

LOCAL CUISINE

The gastronomic excellence of Italy rates among the pleasures of a visit to the country and the great variety of regional specialities never ceases to delight. The fertile land ensures a plentiful supply of fresh fruits and vegetables and the local markets are a riot of colour. The long coastline and many rivers provide fresh fish in abundance.

Popular dishes of **Piedmont** are fonduta (melted cheese with milk, eggs and white truffles), agnolotti (ravioli), braised beef in Barolo wine, boiled beef, fritto misto alla Piemontese (fried small fish and seafood) and bonèt (chocolate pudding). In **Lombardy**, polenta is a staple in country cooking; minestrone (soup of green vegetables, pasta and bacon), risotto and costoletta (breaded veal fillet) are all prepared *'alla milanese'*. Ossobuco (veal shank with marrow bone) and tortelli di zucca (pumpkin fritters), pizzoccheri (buckwheat tagliatelle), panettone (fruit cake with lemon peel), torrone (nougat) and mostarda (candied fruits in mustard and wine) from Cremona are regional delicacies. Gorgonzola, Grana Padano and Taleggio are well-known cheeses.

The people of **Veneto** in the Po delta eat polenta, bigoli (a type of spaghetti), risi e bisi (rice and peas), risotto with chicory, fegato alla veneziana (calves' liver with onions) and excellent fish dishes including shellfish, eels, sardines in brine and spaghetti with squid ink. Pandoro, a star-shaped Christmas cake, is baked in Verona. Specialities of **Alto Adige** comprise canederli (dumplings), gröstl (meat and potato pie), smoked pork with sauerkraut and delicious pastries (Strüdel) while **Friuli** is famous for cialzons (ravioli), jòta (meat soup), prosciutto di San Daniele (raw ham), scampi, grancèvole (spider crabs), frico (fried cheese) and montasio cheese. **Liguria** enjoys pasta with pesto sauce, lasagne, pansotti (ravioli) with walnut sauce, cima (stuffed meat parcels), buridda and cappon magro (fish and vegetable salad).

Emilia-Romagna is renowned for Bologna salami and mortadella, Parma ham, pasta alla bolognese and Parmesan cheese, and, last but not least, the balsamic vinegar of Modena, aged in traditional oak and chestnut barrels. **Tuscany** is a gourmet heaven with soups (minestrone, ribollita), Florentine specialities: baccalà alla fiorentina (dried cod), bistecca (grilled steak), fagioli all'uccelletto (beans with quails) or 'al fiasco' (with oil, onions and herbs), as well as triglie (red mullet from Livorno), Sienese panforte and pecorino and caciotta cheeses. The glories of **Umbria** include black truffles (tartufo nero) and porchetta (roast suckling pig) while the **Marche** serve vincisgrassi (pasta with a meat and cream sauce), stringozzi (a type of pasta), stuffed olives, brodetto (fish soup) and stocco all'anconetana (dried cod).

Rome sets the standard in **Lazio**: pasta with spicy (all'amatriciana) or creamy (alla carbonara) sauce, saltimbocca alla romana (veal fillet with ham, sage and Marsala), abbacchio al forno (roast lamb), lamb alla cacciatora (with anchovy sauce) and carciofi alla Guidia. In **Campania**, choose spaghetti with shellfish (alle vongole), costata alla pizzaiola (fillet steak with wild marjoram), mozzarella in carrozza (cheese savoury) and especially pizza and calzone (a folded pizza). Typical dishes of **Puglia** are orecchiette con cime di rapa (pasta with turnip tops), rice with mussels, capretto ripieno al forno (roast kid) and oysters from Taranto while in **Basilicata** you will find pasta alla potentina, lamb and mutton dishes and good cheeses (caciocavallo, scamorza, ricotta). In **Sicily** look out for pasta con le sarde (with sardines) or alla Norma (with aubergine, tomato, ricotta), swordfish dishes, couscous with a fish soup as well as cassata and cannoli (pastry with ricotta and candied fruit). **Sardinia** is famous for malloreddus (pasta shells with sausage and tomato), lobster soup and spit-roasted pork.

There is a good choice of desserts: cakes and tarts including zuppa inglese (a kind of trifle), tiramisu, zabaglione. Ice-cream (gelato) is a firm favourite with an amazing choice of flavours.

◆ DRINK

Italy is one of the leading wine-producing countries in Europe. Vineyards grow all over the country and most regions have notable wines. Some establishments offer local wine, mostly drunk young, in carafes at moderate prices.

The most famous wines from **Piedmont** are Barolo, Barbaresco and Barbera and sweet dessert wine Moscato d'Asti. **Tuscany** produces the popular Chianti and good wines such as Brunello di Montalcino, Nobile di Montepulciano (reds), Vernaccia di San Gimignano (white) and Vin Santo (dessert wine). Lambrusco, a fruity, sparkling red wine, and white Albana are to be found in **Emilia-Romagna**.

Red wines from the Pinot, Cabernet, Merlot grapes and white wines such as Soave, Riesling, Sauvignon, Pinot Bianco and Chardonnay are very palatable and are produced in **Trentino-Alto Adige**, **Veneto** and **Friuli Venezia Giulia**. Valpolicella and Bardolino from the **Veneto**, the red wines of Valtellina and Pavia districts in **Lombardy** are pleasant wines. White wines from **Umbria** (Orvieto) and Marche (Verdicchio) and **Lazio** (Montefiascone, Castelli – Frascati) are deliciously fragrant. Wines produced from grapes grown in volcanic soil have a delicate, slightly sulphurous taste: **Lacryma Christi**, Fiano di Avellino, Greco di Tufo, and red Gragnano and Taurasi **(Campania)**, white wines of Etna and Lipari **(Sicily)**. Sicily is best known for Marsala, a dark, strong wine and Malvasia, a dessert wine.

The most popular aperitifs are vermouth (Martini, Americano) and Campari, bitter flavoured with orange peel and herbs, with ice and sparkling water.

ROME
ROMA

Population (est. 2005): 2 480 000 (conurbation 2 867 000) – Altitude: about 100m above sea level

J. Malburet/ MICHELIN

Rome, the Eternal City built on seven hills, never fails to impress by the imposing remains of its ancient civilizations and its lively modern activity. No other city boasts such a wealth of Classical antiquities, Renaissance palaces and Baroque churches, all bathed in the soft, golden light for which Rome is famous. There is a profusion of domes, bell towers and fine palaces. Explore the older districts with ochre-coloured facades to catch a glimpse of small squares with a bustling market, or stairways descending to a fountain; go to the fashionable areas to admire the elegant shops, cafés and buildings but most of all take in the lively character of the people in daily life.

Two centuries of Etruscan settlement were followed by the Republican era when disputes among political rivals led to civil war, which was resolved by the rise of Julius Caesar. Augustus became the first Roman emperor and extended Rome's influence. His successors driven by their qualities and flaws, have all left their mark on the city. As Roman power waned, a new force, Christianity, began to emerge and was to spread its message throughout the world. The popes embellished the city during the Renaissance. Since Rome was proclaimed the capital of Italy in 1870, it has undergone widespread expansion into a sprawling modern city.

WHICH DISTRICT TO CHOOSE

For luxury **accommodation** choose the Via Veneto *Plan II* **G1** and the area around Villa Borghese *Plan II* **G1**. You will find comfortable **pensioni** and hotels in the historical centre with its many shops and tourist sights. Trastevere *Plan II* **E3** is an attractive area but it has limited accommodation. The Vatican *Plan III* **J2** and Prati districts, which are quieter, offer reasonably priced hotels. Via Cavour *Plan II* **H2** (near the

Rione Monti district) between Stazione Termini and the Fori Imperiali has a good selection of mid-range hotels. There is a concentration of pensioni and smaller hotels in the area around Stazione Termini *Plan II* **H2**, which is well served by public transport. For your comfort, choose a hotel with air-conditioning during the summer.

There is an ample choice of **restaurants** to suit all tastes ranging from

453

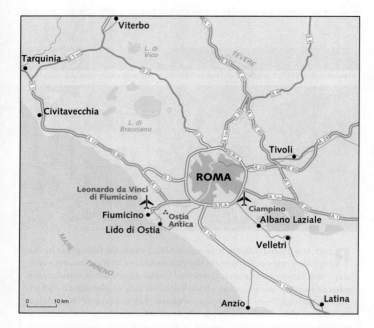

family-run **trattorias** or **osterias**, **pizzerias** to elegant establishments. The historical centre – Piazza Venezia *Plan II* **G3**, Piazza di Spagna *Plan II* **F1**, Piazza Navona *Plan II* **E2**, Corso Vittorio Emanuele II *Plan II* **F3** – is famous for its starred restaurants, Vatican City *Plan II* **J2** also offers a good selection of places serving excellent fare while the area around Stazione Termini *Plan II* **H2** has classic restaurants with good food and atmosphere. For simple, traditional cuisine go to Trastevere *Plan II* **E3**. Restaurants bearing a green logo 'Ristorante tipico' promote traditional Roman cuisine.

PRACTICAL INFORMATION

ARRIVAL – DEPARTURE

Leonardo da Vinci Airport at Fiumicino, 32 km (20 mi) southwest of Rome. ℰ 06 65 951; **Ciampino Airport**, 15 km (10 mi) southeast. ℰ 06 79 49 41.

From the airport to the city centre – By **taxi**: €35-40 (Fiumicino), €25 + additional charge for luggage, night runs and public holidays. By **train**: from Fiumicino Leonardo Express to Stazione Termini – every 30min; time: 32min; ℰ 06 65 951, 06 36 00 43 999; fares €9.50 (€11 on board); from the airport to Tiburtina Station every 15min, fare €5 and from Tiburtina to Roma Termini

every 15min, journey time 40min, fare €5. From Ciampino Railway Station to Termini Station every 10-15min.

By **bus**. From Fiumicino to Stazione Termini every 2hrs, time 40min, fare €9; also to Cornelia metro station (line A), every hour, time 90min, fare €2.80. ℰ 06 65 95 86 46. From Ciampino to Ciampino **rail station** and Anagnina **metro** (line A), every 10-15min.

Main Stations – Stazione Termini or Tiburtina for mainline national and international services; both are linked to the city centre on Lines A and B. ℰ 8488 88 088; www.trenitalia.com

TRANSPORT

♦ METRO, BUS AND TRAM

Tickets are available from metro stations, bus terminals, ticket machines, tobacconists, newsagents, cafés and tourist information centres. A single ticket costs €1; travelcards (1, 3, 7 days) are available (€4, €11, €16 respectively).

♦ TAXIS

Taxis, which are white vehicles, bear an illuminated sign on the car roof. They may be hailed in the street, called by telephone, hired at taxi ranks. Minimum pick-up charge is €2.33 (extra charge for luggage and at night); mileage is charged at €0.78 km. An average taxi ride costs €10-15. Radio Taxis ☎ 06 35 70, 06 66 45, 06 88 22, 06 41 57, 06 55 51.

USEFUL ADDRESSES

♦ TOURIST INFORMATION

APT (Azienda di Promozione Turistica), Via Parigi 11, 00185 Roma *Plan II* **H1** ☎ 06 48 89 91; at Fiumicino Airport ☎ 06 65 95 60 74; www.romaturismo.it; open 9am-6pm (2pm Sunday in winter).

Comune di Roma has information kiosks at Stazione Termini, Castel Sant'Angelo, Fontana di Trevi, Fori Imperiali, Piazza di Spagna, Piazza Navona, Santa Maria Maggiore, Via Nazionale, Piazza Sonnino in Trastevere, Piazza San Giovanni. Open 9am-6pm. www.comune.roma.it

♦ POST OFFICES

Opening times Mon-Sat, 8am to 1.45pm.

♦ BANKS / CURRENCY EXCHANGE

Open Mon-Fri, 8.30am to 1.30pm. Some branches open in the city centre and shopping centres on Saturday mornings.

♦ EMERGENCY

☎ **118** for Ambulance, ☎ **115** for Fire Brigade and ☎ **113** for Police.

BUSY PERIODS

It may be difficult to find a room at a reasonable price (except during weekends) when special events are held in the city as hotel prices may be raised substantially:

Industrial and Commercial Fair: June

Tevere-Expo: June-July

Furniture and Design Show : June

Alta Moda a Roma: February, June

EXPLORING ROME

DIFFERENT FACETS OF THE CITY

It is possible to visit the main sights and museums in four to five days.

Museums and sights are usually open from 10am to 5pm. Some close on Mondays.

ANCIENT ROME – **Campidoglio** *Plan II* **G3**: **Piazza del Campidoglio**, palaces and gardens, views from Via del Campidoglio. **Terme di Caracalla** *Plan I* **C3**, baths decorated with marble, mosaics and statues. Ruins of the **Fori Imperiali** *Plan II* **G3** (Trajan's Column, markets, temples). The **Colosseum** *Plan II* **H3**, an amphithea-

tre for Roman spectacles, and **Arco di Constantino**. **Foro Romano** *Plan II* **G3** (basilicas, temples and arches). The **Palatino** *Plan II* **G3** and imperial residences (Domus Augustana, Casa di Livia). **Pantheon** *Plan II* **F2**. **Aula Ottagona** *Plan II* **H1**, **Ara Pacis Augustae** *Plan II* **F1**, **Area Sacra di Largo Argentina** *Plan II* **F3**.

CHRISTIAN ROME – **Basilica di San Pietro** *Plan III* **K2** (Sistine Chapel, Raphael Rooms, views from the dome); **Chiesa del Gesù** *Plan II* **H3**; **San Giovanni in Laterano** *Plan I* **C3**; **Santa Maria Maggiore** *Plan II* **H2**; **Santa Maria d'Aracoeli** *Plan II* **E3**; **San Paolo fuori le Mura** *Plan I* **B3**; **San**

Luigi dei Francesi *Plan II* **F2** (works by Caravaggio); **Sant'Andrea al Quirinale** *Plan II* **G2**; **San Carlo alle Quattro Fontane** *Plan II* **G2**; **Santa Cecilia in Trastevere** *Plan I* **B3** (*Last Judgement* by Cavallini); **San Clemente** *Plan II* **H3**; **Sant'Ignazio** *Plan II* **F2**; **San Lorenzo Fuori le Mura** *Plan I* **C2**; **Santa Maria degli Angeli** *Plan II* **H2**; **Santa Maria della Vittoria** *Plan II* **H1** (*Ecstasy of St Teresa* by Bernini); **Santa Susanna** *Plan II* **G1**; **Santa Maria in Cosmedin** *Plan I* **B3** (*Bocca della Verita*); **Santa Maria in Trastevere** *Plan II* **E3**; **Santa Maria sopra Minerva** *Plan II* **F2**; **Santa Maria del Popolo** *Plan IV* **L2** (paintings by Caravaggio); **Sant'Andrea della Valle** *Plan II* **F3**; **Sant'Agostino** *Plan II* **F2** (*Madonna of the Pilgrims* by Caravaggio); **San Pietro in Vincoli** *Plan II* **H3** (*Moses* by Michelangelo); **Catacombs** *Plan I* **C3**.

PALACES AND MUSEUMS – **Palazzo Altemps** *Plan II* **E2**; **Castel Sant' Angelo** *Plan II* **E2**; **Villa Borghese** *Plan IV* **M2** (Galleria Borghese); **Palazzo Barberini** *Plan II* **G2**; **Palazzo Senatorio** *Plan*; **Palazzo dei Conservatori and Palazzo Nuovo** *Plan II* **G3** (views); **Palazzo del Quirinale** *Plan II* **G2**; **Palazzo Farnese** *Plan II* **E3**; **Palazzo della Cancelleria** *Plan II* **E3**; **Villa Farnesina** *Plan I* **B2**; **Musei Vaticani** *Plan III* **J1**; **Musei Capitolini** *Plan II* **G3**; **Museo Nazionale di Villa Giulia** *Plan IV* **L2**; **Museo Nazionale Romano** (Palazzo Massimo alle Terme) *Plan II* **H1**; **Galleria Doria Pamphili** *Plan II* **F2**.

SQUARES, PARKS AND GARDENS – **Piazza San Pietro** *Plan III* **K2**; **Giardini Vaticani** *Plan II* **J2**; **Piazza di Spagna** *Plan II* **F1** (Spanish Steps); **Piazza Navona** *Plan II* **E2** (Fontana dei Fiumi); **Piazza del Popolo** *Plan II* **F1**; **Fontana di Trevi** *Plan II* **G2**; **Piazza dell'Esquilino** *Plan II* **H2** (views); **Orti Farnesiani** *Plan II* **E3** (views); **Pincio** *Plan II* **F1** (views); **Gianicolo** *Plan II* **E3** (views); **Borghese Gardens** *Plan IV* **M2**; **Monte Mario** *Plan I* **A1** (views); **Parco Savello** on the **Aventino** *Plan I* **B3** (views).

OUTSKIRTS – **Tivoli** (Villa Adriana, Villa d'Este); **Ostia Antica**; tour of the **Castelli Romani**.

GOURMET TREATS

To enjoy a refreshing **ice cream**, *granita* or *grattachecca*, take a break at *Il Gelato di San Crispino*, Via della Panetteria 42 and Via Acaia 56, *Giolitti*, Via Uffici del Vicario and Via Oceania 90, *Bar Cile*, Piazza Santiago del Cile, *Duse (Da Giovanni)*, Via Duse 1E, *Alberto Pica*, Via della Seggiola 12, *Santa Barbara*, Largo dei Librari 86, *Gelateria Tony*, Largo Nassiroli 15-17, *Chioschi Grattachecca*, Lungotevere Trastevere near Ponte Umberto, which are among the best in the city.

Chocoholics will enjoy *La Bottega del Cioccolato*, Via Leonina 82; *Dolce Idea* – Fabbrica di *Cioccolato* – Via San Francesco a Ripa 27. **Cheese** lovers should visit *Latticini Micocci*, Via Collina 14, *Cooperativa Agricola Stella*, Via Garigliano 68. For traditional Gentilini **biscuits** go to *Latteria Ugolini*, Via della Lungaretta 161. Some of the best **pasticcerias** are *Boccioni*, Via del Portico d'Ottavia 1, *La Dolceroma*, Via del Portico d'Ottavia 20b, *La Deliziosa*, Via Savelli 50, *Dolci Claudio Desideri*, Via Barrilli 66, *Cipriani*, Via C. Botta 21. Typical Roman cakes and pastries include *panpepato* with cystallised fruit and spices, *pangiallo* with walnuts and pine nuts, *torta di ricotta e visciole* (ricotta and sour cherry) and *bignè di San Giuseppe* (puff pastry with cream).

Antica Enoteca, Via della Croce 76b, sells **olive oil** and **wine**; *Enoteca Cavour*, Via Cavour 313, has fine wines, *Divinare*, Via Ostilia 4 for hams, cheese, fine wines. The shops in Via Natale del Grande, *Trimani*, Via Cernaia 37, *Andreoli*, Via del Pellegrino 116 and *Cambi*, Via del Leoncino 30 are also recommended.

SHOPPING

Stores are usually open from 10am to 1pm and from 4pm to 7pm in winter and 5pm to 8pm in summer. In the historic centre shops tend to stay open all day. Clothes stores are closed on Monday morning and food shops on Thursday afternoon. In Rome there are boutiques and small shops to suit all tastes and budgets but few department stores. Luxury stores line **Via Veneto** *Plan II* **G1** and you will find some of the best-known names of the world of fashion (Armani, Gucci, Prada, Valentino) in the area between **Via del Corso** *Plan II* **F2** and **Piazza di Spagna** *Plan II* **F1**, especially in **Via Frattina** *Plan II* **F2**, **Via del Babuino** *Plan II* **F1**, **Via Borgognona** *Plan II* **F1** (*Laura Biagiotti*, *Versace*, *Fendi* etc.), and **Via Bocca di Leone** *Plan II* **F1**. The famous jewellers *Bulgari* is located at the beginning of **Via dei Condotti** *Plan II* **F1** where *Raggi*, a popular shop selling striking jewellery, is also located. Antique and second-hand shops line **Via dei Coronari** *Plan II* **E2**. The shops in Via del Corso, **Via Nazionale** *Plan II* **G2**, **Via del Tritone** *Plan II* **G2** and **Via Cola di Rienzo** *Plan III* **K1** sell a variety of goods at reasonable prices.

For antique shops browse in the area of **Via dei Coronari** *Plan II* **E2** and Via del Babuino.

MARKETS – There is a long-standing flea market in **Via Portuense** (Sun, dawn to 2pm). Visit also **Borgo Parioli**, Via Tirso 14 *Plan IV* **N2**. Catacombe di Priscilla district (Sat-Sun, 9am to 8pm) is famous for antiques. Go to **Mercato di Via Sannio**, Via Sannio *Plan I* **C3**, San Giovanni in Laterano district (Mon-Sat, 10am-1pm) for new and second-hand clothes and shoes sold at factory prices and to *Testaccio*, Piazza di Testaccio *Plan I* **B3** (Mon-Sat) for quality goods. Visit **Mercato dell'Antiquariato**, Piazza Borghese *Plan II* **F2** for books and prints and in Piazza Verdi *Plan IV* **N1** for antiques, arts and crafts.

WHAT TO BUY – The latest fashions, leather goods, design and craft products, high-quality food products, antiques.

ENTERTAINMENT

For listings of venues and programmes see the brochure *L'Evento* published by the tourist office (in Italian, English). It is available from information points throughout the city. www.romatu rismo.it

Auditorium Parco della Musica – Viale Pietro de Coubertin 15/30 *Plan I* **A1**.

Auditorium di Via della Conciliazione – Via della Conciliazione 4 (Vatican) *Plan III* **K2**.

Accademia Filarmonica Romana (Teatro Olimpico) – Piazza Gentile da Fabriano 17 *Plan I* **B1**.

Teatro dell'Opera – Piazza Beniamino Gigli 1 (S. Maria Maggiore) *Plan II* **H2**.

Teatro Eliseo – Via Nazionale 183 (Quirinal) *Plan II* **G2**.

Teatro Sistina – Via Sistina 129 (Piazza di Spagna) *Plan II* **F1**.

NIGHTLIFE

A visit to one of the atmospheric traditional Roman cafés should not be missed when **going out for a drink** or **for the evening**: *Caffè Capitolino*, Piazzale Cafarelli 4 for snacks, drinks, cocktails; *Ciampini*, Viale della Trinità dei Monti and Lucina 29; *Caffè Greco*, Via dei Condotti 86, the oldest literary café in Rome, *Doney*, Via Vittorio Veneto 145. Other pleasant venues include *Bar del Fico*, Piazza del Fico 26, *Vineria*, Piazza Campo dei Fiori, *Trimani*, Via Cernaia 37, *Antica Enoteca*, Via della Croce 76b, *Bar della Pace*, Via della Pace 5, *Bulzoni*, Viale Parioli 36, *Marco e Giancarlo*, Via Monte della Farina 38 and *Bar San Callisto*, Piazza San Callisto.

For **music and dancing**, Rome boasts trendy nightclubs, disco bars and bars with live bands. The district between **Piazza Campo dei Fiori** *Plan II* **E3** and **Piazza Navona** *Plan II* **E2** has a wide choice of pubs and bars, where students, tourists and the theatre crowd congregate. The bars and restaurants in **Trastevere** *Plan II* **E3**, which play live music, have a particular Roman character. The popular nightclubs are in the **Testaccio district** *Plan I* **B3** and in the nearby **Via di Libetta**.

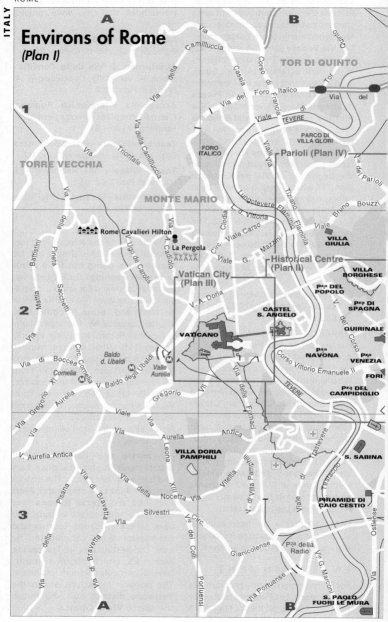

Environs of Rome
(Plan I)

A
B

TOR DI QUINTO

1

TORRE VECCHIA

MONTE MARIO

Rome Cavalieri Hilton
La Pergola

PARCO DI
VILLA GLORI

Parioli (Plan IV)

VILLA
GIULIA

Vatican City
(Plan III)

Historical Centre
(Plan II)

P.za DEL
POPOLO

P.za DI
SPAGNA

QUIRINALE

CASTEL
S. ANGELO

2

VATICANO

Baldo
d. Ubaldi

Valle
Aurelia

P.za
NAVONA

P.za
VENEZIA

FORI

P.za DEL
CAMPIDIGLIO

VILLA DORIA
PAMPHILI

S. SABINA

3

PIRAMIDE DI
CAIO CESTIO

P.za della
Radio

S. PAOLO
FUORI LE MURA

A
B

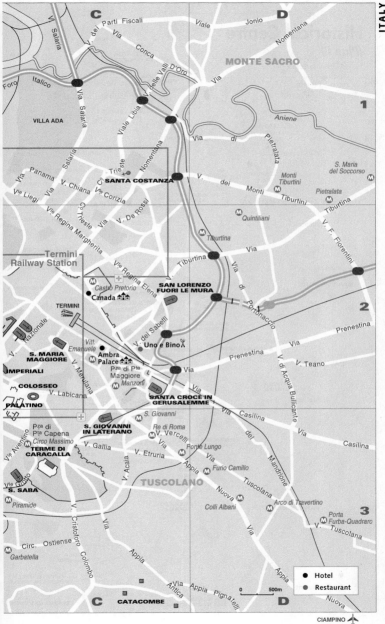

C — V. del Parti Fiscali
Viale — Jonio — D
Via — Conca
Nomentana
Valli D'Oro
MONTE SACRO
Foro — Italico
Salaria
VILLA ADA
Aniene — 1
Via — di — Pietralata
Viale Libia
S. Maria
del Soccorso
Nomentana
Via — Panama
V. Chiana
Salaria
C° Corizia
Trieste
SANTA COSTANZA
Monti
Tiburtini
Pietralata
Tiburtini
V.le Liegi
V.le Regina Margherita
C° Trieste
V. De Rossi
V. dei — Monti
Quintiliani
Tiburtina
Via — V. F. Fiorentini
Tiburtina
Termini
Railway Station
V.le Regina Elena
Tiburtina
Via — di — Portonaccio
2
SAN LORENZO
FUORI LE MURA
Prenestina
Castro Pretorio
Canada
Vitt.
Emanuele
V. dei Sabelli
Uno e Bino
Via — Prenestina
Prenestina
V. Teano
V. di Acqua Bullicante
TERMINI
Nazionale
S. MARIA
MAGGIORE
Ambra
Palace
P.za di P.ta
Maggiore
V. Manzoni
IMPERIALI
COLOSSEO
V. Labicana
SANTA CROCE IN
GERUSALEMME
Via — Casilina
Via — dei
Casilina
PALATINO
S. Giovanni
V. Merulana
S. GIOVANNI
IN LATERANO
P.za di
P.ta Capena
Circo Massimo
TERME DI
CARACALLA
V. Gallia
V. Acaia
Re di Roma
V. Vercelli
Ponte Lungo
Furio Camillo
Via — Tuscolana
Mandrione
V.le Aventino
V.le Giotto
S. SABA
V. Etruria
TUSCOLANO
Appia
Nuova
Colli Albani
Arco di Travertino
3
Piramide
Garbatella
Circ. Ostiense
V. Cristoforo Colombo
Appia
Via — Antica
Appia
Pignatelli
Appia
Nuova
Porta
Furba-Quadraro
Tuscolana

● Hotel
● Restaurant

0 — 500m

C — CATACOMBE — D

CIAMPINO ✈

459

PARIOLI (Plan IV)

Historical Centre
(Plan II)

E

F

FLAMINIO

Flamino

PRINCIO

VILLA

V. del

Via

Beccaria

V. L. di Savoa

Lungotev Michelangelo

da

Brescia

Muro Torto

Vle P. Canonica

Vle d. Magnolia

S. MARIA
DEL POPOLO

PIAZZA DEL
POPOLO

Giulio Cesare

Giulio

Cesare

Farnese

V. degli Scipioni

Pompeo Magno

Gracchi

Pza della
Libertà

Jolly Leonardo
da Vinci

Lungotevere

TEVERE

Dal Bolognese

Antico
Bottaro

De Russie

Piranesi-Palazzo Nainer

Il Valentino

Valadier

Mozart

V. Trinità dei Monti

Margutta

TRINITÀ D.
MONTI

Babuino

Hassler Villa Medici

Spagna

Pza
DI SPAGNA

The Inn at
the Spanish Steps

V. Colonna dei

V. Cicerone

Ennio

Visconti Palace

L'Antico
Porto

Dei Mellini

di Ripetta

del Corso

Arcangelo

L'Arcangelo

ARA PACIS
AUGUSTAE

Grand Hotel
Plaza

D'Inghilterra

Boezio

Virgilio

Il Simposio-
di Costantini

Piazza
Cavour

V. V. Colonna Pte Cavour V.

Ripetta

Tomacelli

di

V. Frattina

Dei Borgognoni

Adriana

Lungotev. Prati

Marzio

Scrofa

El Toulà

del

Via del Tritone

Piazza

CASTEL
SANT'ANGELO

Lungotev. Vaticano

Pte S. Angelo

Lungotev. Castello

Nona

Lungotevere

Mte Brianzo

della

Hostaria dell'Orso
di Gualtiero Marchesi

SANT'AGOSTINO

Pza
Colonna

FONTANA
DI TREVI

Lungotev. Tor di

Il Convivio-Troiani

PALAZZO
ALTEMPS

Pza
Cinque Lune

Myosotis

Quinzi &
Gabrieli

Enoteca Capranica

Nazionale

Federico 1er

V. dei Coronari

SANTA MARIA
DELLA PACE

S. LUIGI
D. FRANCESI

La Rosetta

V. d. Seminario

SANT'
IGNAZIO

L'Altro Mastai

Cso

V. d. Governo Vecchio

Pza
NAVONA

Rinascimento

PANTHEON

Corso

PALAZZO
DORIA PAMPHILI

CHIESA
NUOVA

Il Pagliaccio

Vittorio

Emanuele II

S. MARIA
SOPRA MINERVA

Grand Hotel
dela Minerve

Cso

Via Giulia

V. d. Cappellari

PALAZZO
BRASCHI

Vittorio

Emanuele II

V. d. Plebiscito

GESÙ

PALAZZO
VENEZIA

Lungotevere d. Sangallo

SANTA MARIA
D'ARACOELI

V. Monserrato

SANT'ANDREA
DELLA VALLE

AERA
SACRA

PALAZZO
FARNESE

Da Pancrazio

V. del Giubbonari

VILLA
FARNESINA

PALAZZO
SPADA

Lungotev. dei Tebaldi

Lungara

V. d. Scala

Pte Sisto

L. dei Vallati

Arenula

Lungotev. dei Cenci

TEATRO DI
MARCELLO

L. dei Pierleoni

Via T. di Marcello

ISOLA
TIBERINA

TEMPIO DELLA
FORTUNA VIRILE

Lungotevere Gianicolense

della

TEVERE

Lungotev. Farnesina

L. R. Sanzio

Pza
G. G. Belli

Via d. Lungaretta

Garibaldi

E

S. MARIA
IN TRASTEVERE

F

Pte Palatino

TEMPIO DI VESTA

- Hotel
- Restaurant

VATICAN CITY (Plan III)

viale
Lepanto

Via degli

V. Farnese

Colonna dei

Via

Lungotev. di Mellini

Piazza
Cavour

Pza S.
Angelo

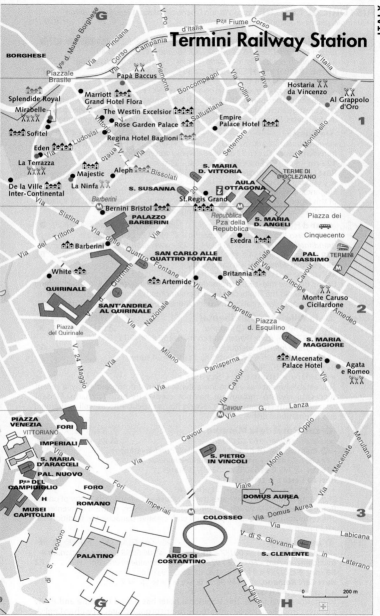

Termini Railway Station

BORGHESE

Piazzale Brasile

Papà Baccus

Splendide Royal
Mirabelle
Sofitel
Eden
La Terrazza
De la Ville Inter-Continental

Marriott Grand Hotel Flora
The Westin Excelsior
Rose Garden Palace
Regina Hotel Baglioni

Majestic
Aleph
La Ninfa

S. SUSANNA

Bernini Bristol

PALAZZO BARBERINI

Barberini

White

QUIRINALE

SANT'ANDREA AL QUIRINALE

Piazza del Quirinale

SAN CARLO ALLE QUATTRO FONTANE

Artemide

Hostaria da Vincenzo
Al Grappolo d'Oro

Empire Palace Hotel

S. MARIA D. VITTORIA

AULA OTTAGONA

TERME DI DIOCLEZIANO

St.Regis Grand

S. MARIA D. ANGELI

Pza della Repubblica

Exedra

Britannia

Piazza dei Cinquecento

PAL. MASSIMO

TERMINI

Monte Caruso Cicilardone

Piazza d. Esquilino

S. MARIA MAGGIORE

Mecenate Palace Hotel

Agata e Romeo

PIAZZA VENEZIA

VITTORIANO

FORI IMPERIALI

S. MARIA D'ARACŒLI

PAL. NUOVO

P²ª DEL CAMPIDIGLIO

MUSEI CAPITOLINI

FORO ROMANO

PALATINO

S. PIETRO IN VINCOLI

DOMUS AUREA

COLOSSEO

ARCO DI COSTANTINO

S. CLEMENTE

0   200 m

ITALY

HISTORICAL CENTRE *(corso Vittorio Emanuele, piazza Venezia, Pantheon e Quirinale, piazza di Spagna, piazza Navona)* *Plan II*

Hassler Villa Medici
100 VISA
piazza Trinità dei Monti 6 ✉ 00187 – Ⓜ Spagna – ✆ 06 69 93 40 – booking@hotelhassler.it – Fax 06 6 78 99 91 – www.hotelhassler.com
86 rm – †410/440 € ††500/790 €, ☕ 45 € – 13 suites **F1**
Rest a la carte 81/111 €
◆ Grand Luxury ◆ Business ◆ Classic ◆
Looking onto the Spanish Steps, this is Rome's most luxurious hotel, where tradition, prestige and elegance merge to create an ambience of unparalleled pampering for guests. Dining in the rooftop restaurant is an unforgettable experience.

De Russie
90 VISA
via del Babuino 9 ✉ 00187 – Ⓜ Flaminio – ✆ 06 32 88 81 – reservations@hotelderussie.it – Fax 06 32 88 88 88 – www.roccofortehotels.com **F1**
123 rm – †470 € ††630/880 €, ☕ 26 € – 23 suites
Rest ***Le Jardin du Russie***, *✆ 06 32 88 88 70* – a la carte 62/92 €
◆ Luxury ◆ Business ◆ Classic ◆
Elegant and eclectic contemporary style in evidence in the pale coloured décor of this legendary cosmopolitan hotel, now with its "secret garden" by Valadier. Smart restaurant with windows opening onto terrace garden.

Grand Hotel Plaza
rm 400 VISA
via del Corso 126 ✉ 00186 – Ⓜ Spagna – ✆ 06 69 92 11 11 – plaza@grandhotelplaza.com – Fax 06 69 94 15 75 – www.grandhotelplaza.com
179 rm ☕ – †298/354 € ††411/539 € – 21 suites **F1**
Rest ***Bistrot-Mascagni*** a la carte 52/80 €
◆ Palace ◆ Business ◆ Stylish ◆
Dating from the mid-19C and remodelled in the Art Nouveau period, this charming hotel overlooks the Trinità dei Monti. The sumptuous lounge area has stucco decoration. The atmosphere of bygone splendour also pervades the charming restaurant.

De la Ville Inter-Continental
rm 100 VISA
via Sistina 69 ✉ 00187 – Ⓜ Spagna – ✆ 06 6 73 31 – rome@interconti.com – Fax 06 6 78 42 13 – www.rome.intercontinental.com **G1**
168 rm – †249/299 € ††299/399 €, ☕ 29 € – 24 suites
Rest a la carte 70/98 €
◆ Luxury ◆ Business ◆ Stylish ◆
This establishment has all the ingredients for an unforgettable stay; a recent successful revamp throughout has not eroded its historic charm. Elegant restaurant with efficient service serving Roman specialities as well as national and international dishes.

Grand Hotel de la Minerve
120 VISA
piazza della Minerva 69 ✉ 00186 – Ⓜ Colosseo – ✆ 06 69 52 01 – minerva@hotel-invest.com – Fax 06 6 79 41 65 – www.grandhoteldelaminerve.it **F2**
118 rm – †375 € ††610 €, ☕ 32 € – 19 suites
Rest ***La Cesta*** a la carte 52/93 €
◆ Luxury ◆ Business ◆ Stylish ◆
The figure of Minerva dominates the Art Nouveau ceiling in the lobby of one of Rome's finest hotels, which combines luxury with every modern convenience. The restaurant offers cuisine prepared with creative panache, yet traditional in inspiration.

D'Inghilterra
rm 55 VISA
via Bocca di Leone 14 ✉ 00187 – Ⓜ Spagna – ✆ 06 69 98 11 – reservation.hir@royaldemeure.com – Fax 06 69 92 22 43 – www.royaldemeure.com **F2**
88 rm – †256/287 € ††385/531 €, ☕ 26 € – 9 suites
Rest ***Cafè Romano***, *✆ 06 69 98 15 00* – a la carte 55/87 €
◆ Luxury ◆ Business ◆ Stylish ◆
In a former royal lodge, this traditional hotel has period furniture and many pictures throughout its elegant interior; rooms of great character with an English feel. The completely renovated restaurant serves international fusion cuisine.

Dei Borgognoni without rest   🔲 🍴 📼 📞 ☎60 🚗 <u>VISA</u> 🐶 🔤 ◑
via del Bufalo 126 ✉ *00187* – **Ⓜ** *Spagna* – 𝒞 *06 69 94 15 05*
– *info@hotelborgognoni.it* – *Fax 06 69 94 15 01*
– *www.hotelborgognoni.it*   **F2**
51 rm ☲ – 🛉260 € 🛉🛉280/320 €
♦ Traditional ♦ Business ♦ Modern ♦
This elegant and distinguished hotel is housed in a restored 19C palazzo,
with spacious public areas, comfortable rooms and unexpected courtyard
garden.

 Piranesi-Palazzo Nainer without rest   ♨ ⋒ 🔲 🍴
via del Babuino 196 ✉ *00187* – **Ⓜ** *Flaminio*   ♨40 <u>VISA</u> 🐶 🔤 ◑
– 𝒞 *06 32 80 41* – *info@hotelpiranesi.com* – *Fax 06 3 61 05 97*
– *www.hotelpiranesi.com*   **F1**
44 rm ☲ – 🛉198/270 € 🛉🛉320/390 €
♦ Palace ♦ Business ♦ Classic ♦
This recently opened hotel is classically elegant in style. The white marble interior
enhances the light, much to the benefit of the handsome furnishings.

 White without rest   🔲 🍴 📼 📞 <u>VISA</u> 🐶 🔤 ◑
via In Arcione 77 ✉ *00187* – **Ⓜ** *Barberini* – 𝒞 *06 6 99 12 42*
– *white@travelroma.com* – *Fax 06 6 78 84 51*
– *www.travelroma.com*   **G2**
44 rm ☲ – 🛉200/250 € 🛉🛉220/300 €
♦ Traditional ♦ Modern ♦
Close to the Trevi fountain and the Quirinale, this comfortable hotel has a
modern interior; rooms with furniture in pale woods.

 Nazionale   🔲 📼 📞 ♨800 <u>VISA</u> 🐶 🔤 ◑
piazza Montecitorio 131 ✉ *00186* – **Ⓜ** *Spagna* – 𝒞 *06 69 50.01*
– *hotel@nazionaleroma.it* – *Fax 06 6 78 66 77*
– *www.nazionaleroma.it*   **F2**
95 rm ☲ – 🛉274/331 € 🛉🛉331/530 € – 2 suites
Rest *31 Al Vicario*, 𝒞 *06 69 92 55 30 (closed 7 August-4 September and Sunday)*
a la carte 37/60 €
♦ Traditional ♦ Business ♦ Classic ♦
Looking onto Piazza Montecitorio, there is a well-presented classical ambience
to this hotel, composed of two separate buildings which have been
harmoniously joined together. The comfortable restaurant offers a traditional
Italian menu.

 Valadier   🏠 🔲 📼 📞 ♨35 <u>VISA</u> 🐶 🔤 ◑
via della Fontanella 15 ✉ *00187* – **Ⓜ** *Flaminio* – 𝒞 *06 3 61 19 98*
– *info@hotelvaladier.com* – *Fax 06 3 20 15 58*
– *www.hotelvaladier.com*   **F1**
53 rm ☲ – 🛉110/240 € 🛉🛉150/370 € – 7 suites
Rest see *Il Valentino* below
Rest *La Terrazza della Luna*, 𝒞 *06 3 61 08 80* – a la carte 37/49 €
♦ Traditional ♦ Modern ♦
An elegant hotel near Piazza del Popolo; smart interior with much attention to
detail as seen in the woodwork and mirrors which feature throughout.
Panoramic roof-garden.

 Barberini without rest   🔲 🍴 📼 ♨50 <u>VISA</u> 🐶 🔤 ◑
via Rasella 3 ✉ *00187* – **Ⓜ** *Barberini* – 𝒞 *06 4 81 49 93*
– *info@hotelbarberini.com* – *Fax 06 4 81 52 11*
– *www.hotelbarberini.com*   **G2**
35 rm – 🛉181/232 € 🛉🛉232/310 €, ☲ 25 € – 4 suites
♦ Traditional ♦ Classic ♦
Near the Barberini palace, this recently opened hotel occupies a restored
period building; the décor features fine marble, elegant fabrics and wooden
fittings.

The Inn at the Spanish Steps without rest $\boxed{AC}$
via dei Condotti 85 ⊠ *00187 –* Ⓜ *Spagna* — $\%$ 🖼 **VISA** **⑩** **AE** **①**
– 🌭 06 69 92 56 57 – spanishstep @ tin.it – Fax 06 6 78 64 70
– www.atspanishsteps.com **F1**
24 rm ☲ – ♦250/580 € ♦♦300/650 €
♦ Inn ♦ Classic ♦
In the same building as the famous Caffè Greco, this hotel fulfils the requirements
of even the most romantic of visitors to the Eternal City.

Mozart without rest $\boxed{AC}$ $\%$ 🖼 **VISA** **⑩** **AE** **①**
via dei Greci 23/b ⊠ *00187 –* Ⓜ *Spagna – 🌭 06 36 00 19 15*
– info @ hotelmozart.com – Fax 06 36 00 17 35
– www.hotelmozart.com **F1**
56 rm ☲ – ♦140/175 € ♦♦196/245 €
♦ Traditional ♦ Classic ♦
Occupying a centrally-located 19C palazzo, this refurbished hotel has elegant
period furnishings throughout; attractive sun terrace.

Hostaria dell'Orso di Gualtiero Marchesi $\boxed{}$ $\boxed{AC}$ $\%$
via dei Soldati 25/c ⊠ *00186 –* Ⓜ *Spagna* ⇄12/28 **VISA** **⑩** **AE** **①**
– 🌭 06 68 30 11 92 – info @ hdo.it – Fax 06 68 21 70 63
– www.hdo.it
closed August and Sunday **E-F2**
Rest (booking essential) (dinner only) a la carte 50/82 € 🕮
Spec. Carciofi alla romana (October-April). Stracci di pasta fresca al ragù fine di
vitello. Agnello da latte arrosto, melanzane alla menta.
♦ Contemporary ♦ Fashionable ♦
Revisit the bygone splendours of Roman high society in this elegant 15C building
decorated in period style: restaurant, piano-bar and disco.

El Toulà $\boxed{AC}$ $\%$ ⇄18 **VISA** **⑩** **AE** **①**
via della Lupa 29/b ⊠ *00186 –* Ⓜ *Spagna – 🌭 06 6 87 34 98*
– toula2 @ libero.it – Fax 06 6 87 11 15 – www.toula.it
closed August, 24 to 26 December, Saturday lunch,
Sunday and Monday **F2**
Rest (booking essential) a la carte 50/94 €
♦ Contemporary ♦ Formal ♦
In Rome's government district, a long-established restaurant with elegant decor;
modern dishes on offer alongside more traditional Venetian fare.

Antico Bottaro $\boxed{AC}$ $\%$ **VISA** **⑩** **AE** **①**
via Passeggiata di Ripetta 15 ⊠ *00186 –* Ⓜ *San Pietro – 🌭 06 3 23 67 63*
– anticobottaro @ anticobottaro.it – Fax 06 3 23 67 63
– www.anticobottaro.it
closed 4 to 25 August and Monday **E-F1**
Rest a la carte 63/94 €
♦ Inventive ♦ Fashionable ♦
This 17C palazzo has terracotta floors and pink stucco walls. In business for
around 130 years, the restaurant is under dynamic new management.

Il Convivio-Troiani $\boxed{AC}$ $\%$ ⇄16/24 **VISA** **⑩** **AE** **①**
vicolo dei Soldati 31 ⊠ *00186 –* Ⓜ *Spagna – 🌭 06 6 86 94 32*
– info @ ilconviviotroiani.com – Fax 06 6 86 94 32
– www.ilconviviotroiani.com
closed 9 to 15 August and Sunday **E2**
Rest (booking essential) (dinner only) a la carte 79/115 € 🕮
Spec. Rigatoni con scampi, fave, trippa di maiale, pecorino e menta. Variazione
di agnello da latte. Tiramisù di fragolini di bosco al pepe verde.
♦ Innovative ♦ Fashionable ♦
A modern creative slant to the meat and fish dishes served in the three
elegant rooms of this restaurant, tucked away in an alley in the old city
centre.

L'Altro Mastai

AK 🕸 VISA 🐵 AE 🕦

via Giraud 53 ang. via dei Bianchi Nuovi ⊠ 00186 – ℰ 06 68 30 12 96
– restaurant@laltromastai.it – Fax 06 6 86 13 03 – www.laltromastai.it
closed 7 to 31 August, 1 week in January, Sunday and Monday **E2**
Rest (dinner only) (booking essential) a la carte 66/90 € 🕮

Spec. Fegato d'oca marinato con salsa di fichi e gelato al miele di lavanda. Pralina di trippa al pecorino romano. Soufflé alle pere con ragù di castagne e frutti di bosco con gelato alla cannella.
   ◆ Inventive ◆ Fashionable ◆
Opened in late 2003, this restaurant looks set to make its mark on the Roman culinary scene in spectacular style. Refined ambience, extensive wine list and top quality service.

Enoteca Capranica

AK 🕸 ⇔25 VISA 🐵 AE 🕦

piazza Capranica 99/100 ⊠ 00186 – Ⓜ Spagna – ℰ 06 69 94 09 92
– Fax 06 69 94 09 89 – www.enotecacapranica.it
closed Saturday lunch and Sunday **F2**
Rest (dinner only in August) (booking essential for dinner) a la carte 44/74 € 🕮
   ◆ Innovative ◆ Fashionable ◆
Close to Montecitorio, this former wine bar has been transformed into an elegantly exclusive restaurant; traditional Mediterranean dishes and an excellent wine list.

Il Valentino – Hotel Valadier

AK 🕸 ⇔15/20 VISA 🐵 AE 🕦

via della Fontanella 14 ⊠ 00187 – Ⓜ Flaminio – ℰ 06 3 61 08 80
– Fax 06 3 20 15 58 – www.ilvalentino.com **F1**
Rest a la carte 39/60 €
   ◆ Seafood ◆ Cosy ◆
Pale woods and warm colours distinguish this sophisticated restaurant. Its well-planned, creative menu is well suited to the elegant ambience; good service.

La Rosetta (Riccioli)

AK 🕸 VISA 🐵 AE 🕦

via della Rosetta 9/8 ⊠ 00186 – Ⓜ Spagna – ℰ 06 6 86 10 02 – larosetta@tin.it
– Fax 06 68 21 51 16 – www.larosetta.com
closed 10-30 August and Sunday **F2**
Rest (booking essential) a la carte 85/126 €

Spec. Spaghetti con scampi, fiori di zucca e pecorino romano. Fritturina di moscardini con nastri di zucchine e menta. Gran zuppa di pesce con crostini.
   ◆ Seafood ◆ Formal ◆
The day's catch is displayed alluringly at the entrance of this restaurant; luckily its popularity has not affected the quality of the cuisine or its pleasant ambience.

Dal Bolognese

🕭 AK 🕸 VISA 🐵 AE

piazza del Popolo 1/2 ⊠ 00187 – Ⓜ Flaminio – ℰ 06 3 61 14 26
– dalbolognese@virgilio.it – Fax 06 3 22 27 99 **F1**
closed 5-25 August, Christmas, New Year and Monday **– Rest** a la carte 49/64 €
   ◆ Seafood ◆ Formal ◆
Taste the finest Emilian cuisine at this establishment, one of the most renowned restaurants in the city. Summer dining out in the piazza.

Il Pagliaccio

AK 🕸 VISA 🐵 AE 🕦

via dei Banchi Vecchi 129 ⊠ 00186 – Ⓜ Spagna – ℰ 06 68 80 95 95
– ilpagliaccio@tiscali.it – Fax 06 68 21 75 04 – www.ristoranteilpagliaccio.it
closed 6-24 August, 9-17 January, Sunday, Monday and Tuesday lunch
Rest (booking essential for dinner) a la carte 44/68 € **E2**
   ◆ Inventive ◆ Formal ◆
A "young", attractively smart restaurant with two dining areas; the tables are laid in simple style, while the cuisine is creative and features local dishes.

Federico I

🕭 AK 🕸 ⇔26 VISA 🐵 AE 🕦

via della Colonna Antonina 48 ⊠ 00186 – Ⓜ Barberini – ℰ 06 6 78 37 17
– info@federicoprimo.com – Fax 06 6 78 78 18 – www.federicoprimo.com
closed 10-30 August, 24 December-1 January, and Sunday **F2**
Rest a la carte 77/95 €
   ◆ Seafood ◆ Formal ◆
Just the right place if you like fish, the standard fare of this well-presented restaurant; there is a pleasant outdoor area for dining in the summer months.

ITALY

XX **Quinzi & Gabrieli** 🛋 AK ⅌ ⟷20/25 VISA ⦿ AE ⓪
via delle Coppelle 6 ⊠ 00186 – ⓂSpagna – ⌀ 06 6 87 93 89 – quinziegabrieli@
tin.it – Fax 06 6 87 49 40 – www.quinziegabrieli.it
closed 7-31 August and 1-7 January **F2**
Rest (dinner only and Sunday lunch) (booking essential) a la carte 80/110 €
♦ Seafood ♦ Trendy ♦
All the tang and taste of the sea in the heart of the city; this top-level restaurant
is always in fashion and full of people.

XX **Da Pancrazio** ⟷15/30 VISA ⦿ AE ⓪
piazza del Biscione 92 ⊠ 00186 – ⓂColosseo – ⌀ 06 6 86 12 46
– dapancrazio@tin.it – Fax 06 97 84 02 35 – www.dapancrazio.com
closed 5-25 August, Christmas and Wednesday **F3**
Rest a la carte 36/53 €
♦ Roman ♦ Formal ♦
Two thousand years of history permeate this charming establishment built on
part of the ruins of the ancient Teatro di Pompeo; a historic taverna serving
local-style cuisine.

XX **Myosotis** AK ⅌ ⟷12 VISA ⦿ AE ⓪
piazza delle Coppelle 49 ⊠ 00186 – ⓂBarberini – ⌀ 06 6 86 55 54
– marsili@libero.it – Fax 06 6 86 55 54 – www.myosotis.it
closed 10-24 August, 2-9 January and Sunday **F2**
Rest (dinner only) a la carte 29/58 € ⌘
♦ Seafood ♦ Formal ♦
In a charming little street between Piazza Navona and Montecitorio, this elegant
country-style restaurant under experienced family management offers meat
and fish dishes.

TERMINI RAILWAY STATION *(via Vittorio Veneto, via Nazionale, Viminale,*
Santa Maria Maggiore, Porta Pia) ***Plan II***

🏨 **St. Regis Grand** ⅙ 🏠 ⅚ AK ⅌rest 🖂 ℃ ⅏300 VISA ⦿ AE ⓪
via Vittorio Emanuele Orlando 3 ⊠ 00185 – ⓂRepubblica – ⌀ 06 4 70 91
– stregisgrandrome@stregis.com – Fax 06 4 74 73 07
– www.stregis.com/grandrome **H1**
138 rm – ♥♥750 €, ⊑ 43 € – 23 suites – **Rest** *Vivendo*, ⌀ 06 47 09 27 36
(closed Saturday lunch and Sunday) a la carte 54/76 € ⌘
♦ Chain hotel ♦ Luxury ♦ Historic ♦
Frescoes, textiles and Empire furniture in the luxurious rooms and opulent public
areas of this hotel, which retains the splendour of its earliest days (opened in
1894). Grand atmosphere of bygone days in the restaurant.

🏨 **The Westin Excelsior** 🛋 ⅙ 🏠 🖻 ⅚ AK ⅌rest 🖂 ℃ ⅏600
via Vittorio Veneto 125 ⊠ 00187 – ⓂBarberini VISA ⦿ AE ⓪
– ⌀ 06 4 70 81 – excelsiorrome@westin.com – Fax 06 4 82 62 05
– www.westin.com/excelsiorrome **G1**
284 rm – ♥525 € ♥♥780 €, ⊑ 42 € – 32 suites – **Rest** *Doney* a la carte 62/74 €
♦ Chain hotel ♦ Luxury ♦ Historic ♦
This large, prestigious hotel is run along traditional lines for a smart, discerning
clientele. The sumptuous interior is well appointed with antique items; Italy's
largest suite is in this hotel. The elegantly modern restaurant also serves light
meals and post theatre snacks.

🏨 **Eden** ≼ ⅙ AK ⅌ 🖂 ℃ ⅏80 VISA ⦿ AE ⓪
via Ludovisi 49 ⊠ 00187 – ⓂBarberini – ⌀ 06 47 81 21
– reservations@hotel-eden.it – Fax 06 4 82 15 84 – www.hotel-eden.it **G1**
121 rm – ♥506/528 € ♥♥748/858 €, ⊑ 50 € – 13 suites
Rest see *La Terrazza* below
♦ Palace ♦ Luxury ♦ Stylish ♦
Stylish simplicity in this hotel where the elegant, distinguished ambience does
not inhibit a warm welcome. Service and accommodation to satisfy even the
most demanding guest.

ITALY

Sofitel
🏨 🅰️ 🍴 🎧 📶 ⚙️45 *VISA* 🆎 🅰️ ⓿

via Lombardia 47 ✉ *00187 –* ⓜ *Barberini –* ☎ *06 47 80 21*
– prenotazioni.sofitelroma@accor-hotels.it – Fax 06 4 82 10 19
– www.sofitel.com   G1
113 rm ⚏ – �352 € ♦♦496 €
Rest a la carte 34/63 €
♦ Luxury ♦ Business ♦ Historic ♦
A historic building on the Via Veneto with a Neo-classical interior including an
abundance of statues and busts. Fine view from the terrace. Elegant restaurant
with vaulted ceilings in the old stable block.

Majestic
🏨 🔲 👌rm 🅰️ 🍴 📧 ⚙️150 *VISA* 🆎 🅰️ ⓿

via Vittorio Veneto 50 ✉ *00187 –* ⓜ *Barberini –* ☎ *06 42 14 41*
– info@hotelmajestic.com – Fax 06 4 88 09 84 – www.hotelmajestic.com   G1
98 rm – ♦390/485 € ♦♦515/640 €, ⚏ 40 € – 8 suites
Rest-bistrot see *La Ninfa* below – **Rest** *La Veranda* (closed January) a la carte
53/68 €
♦ Luxury ♦ Traditional ♦ Classic ♦
Cosmopolitan luxury combines with Italian hospitality in the elegant
atmosphere of this smart hotel, one of the capital's finest. Linen and silverware
in the refined yet welcoming La Veranda restaurant.

Splendide Royal
🏨 🅰️ 🍴 📧 🎧 ⚙️90 *VISA* 🆎 🅰️ ⓿

Porta Pinciana 14 ✉ *00187 –* ⓜ *Barberini –* ☎ *06 42 16 89 – reservations@*
splendideroyal.com – Fax 06 42 16 88 00 – www.splendideroyal.com   G1
60 rm ⚏ – ♦280/450 € ♦♦350/620 € – 9 suites
Rest see *Mirabelle* below
♦ Luxury ♦ Traditional ♦ Stylish ♦
Gilding, damask and fine antique furniture grace the interior of this exclusive
modern hotel, located in a former palazzo.

Regina Hotel Baglioni
👌 🅰️ 🍴 📧 ⚙️80 *VISA* 🆎 🅰️ ⓿

via Vittorio Veneto 72 ✉ *00187 –* ⓜ *Barberini –* ☎ *06 42 11 11 – regina.roma@*
baglionihotels.com – Fax 06 42 01 21 30 – www.baglionihotels.com   G1
137 rm – ♦300/470 € ♦♦405/570 €, ⚏ 25 € – 6 suites
Rest a la carte 60/90 €
♦ Luxury ♦ Traditional ♦ Art Deco ♦
This hotel, occupying a restored building, has a stylish Art Deco ambience
and top quality service; the splendid rooms are elegant in their simplicity.
A refined yet warm atmosphere in the restaurant, serving international
cuisine.

Exedra
🏊 👌 🅰️ 🍴 📧 🎧 ⚙️120 *VISA* 🆎 🅰️ ⓿

piazza della Repubblica 47 ✉ *00185 –* ⓜ *Repubblica –* ☎ *06 48 93 80 20*
– reservation@exedra.boscolo.com – Fax 06 48 93 80 00
– www.boscolo.com   H2
233 rm – ♦♦349/449 €, ⚏ 26 € – 5 suites
Rest *Tazio* , ☎ *06 48 93 81* – a la carte 39/68 €
♦ Luxury ♦ Chain hotel ♦ Classic ♦
Situated in one of Rome's best-known piazzas, this superior hotel is spacious with
comfortable and well-equipped rooms. Its Tazio restaurant can accommodate
business functions; alternatively there is La Frusta, open evenings only.

Marriott Grand Hotel Flora
🔲 👌rm 🅰️ 🍴 📧

via Vittorio Veneto 191 ✉ *00187 –* ⓜ   ⚙️150 *VISA* 🆎 🅰️ ⓿
Spagna – ☎ *06 48 99 29 – info@grandhotelflora.net – Fax 06 4 82 03 59*
– www.hotelfloraroma.com   G1
148 rm – ♦322 € ♦♦478 €, ⚏ 30 € – 8 suites
Rest (buffet lunch) a la carte 41/82 €
♦ Luxury ♦ Business ♦ Classic ♦
Following a complete refit, this hotel at the end of Via Veneto is a harmonious and
functional combination of simple elegance and modern refinement. Parquet
floors and other decorative features in wood lend an ambience of warmth to the
restaurant.

ITALY

Aleph
丘 ℌ ⅙rm 🅰️ ℅ 🔲 📞 ⅙60 🅿️ 𝗩𝗜𝗦𝗔 🆎 🅰🅴 ⓘ

via San Basilio 15 ⊠ 00187 – Ⓜ *Barberini – ℰ 06 42 29 01 – reservation @*
aleph.boscolo.com – Fax 06 42 29 00 00 – www.boscolo.com **G1**
92 rm – ♦♦310/561 €, � 22 € – 7 suites
Rest *Maremoto* a la carte 106/186 €

• Luxury • Design •
A prestigious establishment in the design hotel mould; unusual lobby with
distinctive colour scheme. Innovatively styled rooms and good health spa.
Modern cuisine and minimalist décor in the restaurant.

Bernini Bristol
丘 ℌ 🅰️ ℅ 🔲 📞 ⅙100 𝗩𝗜𝗦𝗔 🆎 🅰🅴 ⓘ

piazza Barberini 23 ⊠ 00187 – Ⓜ *Barberini – ℰ 06 48 89 31 – reservationsbb @*
sinahotels.it – Fax 06 4 82 42 66 – www.berninibristol.com **G2**
127 rm – ♦342 € ♦♦549 €, ⊏ 30 € – 10 suites
Rest *L'Olimpo,* ℰ 06 4 88 93 32 88 – a la carte 78/101 €

• Traditional • Business • Classic •
A perfect balance between bygone glories and modern comforts in one of
Rome's most elegant hotels. Rooftop restaurant offers outside dining and fine
views over the Eternal City.

Empire Palace Hotel
丘 ⅙ 🅰️ ℅ 🔲 📞 ⅙50 𝗩𝗜𝗦𝗔 🆎 ⓘ

via Aureliana 39 ⊠ 00187 – Ⓜ *Repubblica – ℰ 06 42 12 81 – gold @*
empirepalacehotel.com – Fax 06 42 12 84 00 – www.empirepalacehotel.com
109 rm ⊏ – **♦295/351 € ♦♦332/425 € – 5 suites** **H1**
Rest *Aureliano (closed Sunday)* a la carte 42/63 €

• Palace • Business • Design •
A sophisticated hybrid of 19C building and contemporary design, with modern
art displayed in the public areas; simple elegance in the rooms. Red and blue
chandeliers and cherrywood decorate the dining room.

Rose Garden Palace
⅙ 🅰️ ℅ 🔲 ⅙50 𝗩𝗜𝗦𝗔 🆎 🅰🅴 ⓘ

via Boncompagni 19 ⊠ 00187 – Ⓜ *Barberini – ℰ 06 42 17 41*
– info @ rosegardenpalace.com – Fax 06 4 81 56 08 **G1**
65 rm ⊏ – **♦247 € ♦♦385 €**
Rest (residents only)

• Business • Design •
Minimalist design has inspired the interiors of this new hotel, occupying an early
19C palazzo; unusual.

Ambra Palace
⅙rm 🅰️ 🔲 ⅙55 𝗩𝗜𝗦𝗔 🆎 🅰🅴 ⓘ

via Principe Amedeo 257 ⊠ 00185 – Ⓜ *Vittorio Emanuele – ℰ 06 49 23 30*
– booking @ ambrapalacehotel.com – Fax 06 49 23 31 00
– www.ambrapalacehotel.com Plan I **C2**
78 rm ⊏ – **♦170/210 € ♦♦260/300 €**
Rest (residents only) (dinner only) a la carte 43/55 €

• Business • Classic •
Occupying a mid-19C palazzo, this well-appointed hotel is especially popular
with business people.

Canada without rest
🅰️ ℅ 🔲 📞 𝗩𝗜𝗦𝗔 🆎 🅰🅴 ⓘ

via Vicenza 58 ⊠ 00185 – Ⓜ *Castro Pretorio – ℰ 06 4 45 77 70 – info @*
hotelcanadaroma.com – Fax 06 4 45 07 49 – www.hotelcanadaroma.com
70 rm ⊏ – **♦124/134 € ♦♦142/158 €** Plan I **C2**

• Business • Classic •
In a period building near the Termini railway station, this hotel has a simple
elegance. Tastefully furnished, stylish rooms; ask for one with a canopy bed.

Mecenate Palace Hotel without rest
⅙ 🅰️ ℅ 🔲 📞

via Carlo Alberto 3 ⊠ 00185 – Ⓜ *Termini* ⅙45 𝗩𝗜𝗦𝗔 🆎 🅰🅴 ⓘ
– ℰ 06 44 70 20 24 – info @ mecenatepalace.com – Fax 06 4 46 13 54
– www.mecenatepalace.com **H2**
59 rm ⊏ – **♦180/260 € ♦♦280/365 € – 3 suites**

• Business • Classic •
The elegant, stylish interiors are in keeping with the spirit of this 19C building,
recently converted into a hotel offering a high standard of comfort and good
facilities.

ITALY

 Britannia without rest · AC AAT VISA MO AE ①

via Napoli 64 ✉ *00184 –* Ⓜ *Repubblica – ℰ 06 4 88 31 53*
– info@hotelbritannia.it – Fax 06 48 98 63 16 – www.hotelbritannia.it **H2**
33 rm ☲ – ✝140/180 € ✝✝220/290 €
♦ Traditional ♦ Business ♦ Personalised ♦
Competent family management at this small hotel with adequate facilities,
where attention to detail is important. Unusual rooms in eclectic style; very
comfortable.

Artemide · ᴋ rm AC ✵ ⊠ ℰ️ ⋒120 VISA MO AE ①

via Nazionale 22 ✉ *00184 –* Ⓜ *Repubblica – ℰ 06 48 99 11 – hotelartemide@*
hotelartemide.it – Fax 06 48 99 17 00 – www.hotelartemide.it **G-H2**
85 rm ☲ – ✝257 € ✝✝355 €
Rest 38 €/55 €
♦ Traditional ♦ Business ♦ Classic ♦
Occupying an attractively restored Art Nouveau building, this classically stylish
hotel offers all modern comforts; good conference facilities.

ХХХХ **La Terrazza** – Hotel Eden · AC ✵ VISA MO AE ①

via Ludovisi 49 ✉ *00187 –* Ⓜ *Barberini – ℰ 06 47 81 27 52 – reservations@*
hotel-eden.it – Fax 06 47 81 27 18 – www.hotel-eden.it **G1**
Rest (booking essential) a la carte 86/152 € ❀
♦ Contemporary ♦ Fashionable ♦
The focal point of this elegant, modern restaurant with roof garden is the
charming panoramic view of Rome, an ideal backdrop against which to enjoy
memorable cuisine.

ХХХХ **Mirabelle** – Hotel Splendide Royal · ⇗ AC ⇔30 VISA MO AE ①

Porta Pinciana 14 ✉ *00187 –* Ⓜ *Barberini – ℰ 06 42 16 88 38*
– mirabelle@splendideroyal.com – Fax 06 42 16 88 70
– www.mirabelle.it **G1**
Rest (booking essential) a la carte 69/107 €
♦ Mediterranean ♦ Fashionable ♦
A luxurious and historic feel to this charming restaurant overlooking Rome;
dining outside in summer. Modern cuisine with Mediterranean roots.

ХХХ **Agata e Romeo** (Parisella) · AC ✵ VISA MO AE ①
✿
via Carlo Alberto 45 ✉ *00185 –* Ⓜ *Vittorio Emanuele – ℰ 06 4 46 61 15*
– ristorante@agataeromeo.it – Fax 06 4 46 58 42
– www.agataeromeo.it
closed 4-25 August, 1-13 January, Saturday and Sunday **H2**
Rest (booking essential) a la carte 75/105 € ❀
Spec. Raviolini di caprino e asparagi selvatici (spring). Variazione di pomodoro
(summer). Quattro modi di cucinare il baccalà islandese.
♦ Roman ♦ Formal ♦
This small restaurant, elegant and carefully set out, combines traditional cuisine
and creativity. One of the finest wine-lists in Rome.

ХХ **La Ninfa** – Hotel Majestic · AC ✵ VISA MO AE ①

via Vittorio Veneto 50 ✉ *00187 –* Ⓜ *Barberini – ℰ 06 42 14 41* **G1**
Rest (booking essential) a la carte 41/66 €
♦ Mediterranean ♦ Formal ♦
Under the same roof as the Hotel Majestic, this first class restaurant serves
interesting cuisine; carefully prepared dishes, an elegant ambience and leisurely
opening hours.

ХХ **Al Grappolo d'Oro** · ⇗ AC VISA MO AE ①

via Palestro 4/10 ✉ *00185 –* Ⓜ *Castro Pretorio – ℰ 06 4 94 14 41 – info@*
algrappolodoro.it – Fax 06 4 45 23 50 – www.algrappolodoro.it
closed August, Saturday lunch and Sunday **H1**
Rest a la carte 34/46 €
♦ Seafood ♦ Formal ♦
Close to the Baths of Diocletian, this classic restaurant has been improved by
recent refurbishment; it offers an extensive traditional menu.

ITALY

XX **Papà Baccus** 🛍 🎟 🍴 ⟷14/20 VISA ⬤ AE ⓪

via Toscana 32/36 ⊠ 00187 – ⓜ Barberini – ℰ 06 42 74 28 08 – papabaccus@
papabaccus.com – Fax 06 42 01 00 05 – www.papabaccus.com
closed 15 days in August, Saturday lunch and Sunday   **G1**
Rest (booking essential) a la carte 48/65 €
♦ Tuscany ♦ Formal ♦
Near the Via Veneto, this popular traditional restaurant serves seafood
and Tuscan specialities (beef from the Val di Chiana and pork from the Siena
region).

XX **Monte Caruso Cicilardone** 🎟 🍴 ⟷12/20 VISA ⬤ AE ⓪

via Farini 12 ⊠ 00185 – ⓜ Termini – ℰ 06 48 35 49 – cicilardone@tiscali.it
– www.montecaruso.com
closed August, Sunday and Monday lunch   **H2**
Rest a la carte 25/47 €
♦ Regional ♦ Family ♦
The emphasis is on the flavours of the south in this warm and welcoming
family-run restaurant; menu based on dishes from the Basilicata region, simply
and authentically prepared.

XX **Hostaria da Vincenzo** 🎟 VISA ⬤ AE ⓪

via Castelfidardo 6 ⊠ 00185 – ⓜ Termini – ℰ 06 48 45 96
– Fax 06 4 87 00 92
closed August and Sunday   **H1**
Rest a la carte 26/40 €
♦ Seafood ♦ Friendly ♦
A classic restaurant, in terms of atmosphere and cuisine, with an emphasis on
seafood. Pleasant friendly ambience; many regulars and popular with business
people.

X **Uno e Bino** 🎟 VISA ⬤ ⓪

😊 via Degli Equi 58 ⊠ 00185 – ⓜ Manzoni – ℰ 06 4 46 07 02
closed Monday   Plan I **C2**
Rest (dinner only) a la carte 30/49 €
♦ Contemporary ♦ Bistro ♦
This welcoming restaurant's best feature is the excellent value for money which
it represents; its bistro feel makes for a friendly and informal atmosphere.

ST-PETER'S BASILICA (Vatican City and Monte Mario)   *Plan III*

🏨🏨🏨 **Rome Cavalieri Hilton** ⟨ city, 🛍 🎐 ᴸᵟ 🎐 ⤢ 🍴 ❀ 🛗 🎟 🎐

via Cadlolo 101 ⊠ 00136   🖿 📞 🖨2000 ⬤ P VISA ⬤ AE ⓪
– ⓜ Cipro-Musei-Vaticani – ℰ 06 3 50 91
– info@cavalieri-hilton.it – Fax 06 35 09 22 41
– www.cavalieri-hilton.it   Plan I **A2**
345 rm – ♦470/810 € ♦♦525/865 €, � 32 € – 25 suites
Rest see *La Pergola* below
Rest *Il Giardino dell'Uliveto* a la carte 77/82 €
♦ Luxury ♦ Business ♦ Classic ♦
Fine views over the city, sun-terraces and pool with gardens; these are some of
the features of this great hotel which excels in every respect. An informal
poolside restaurant offers dining with cabaret.

🏨🏨 **Visconti Palace** without rest 🛗 🎟 🎐 🖿 📞 🖨150

via Federico Cesi 37 ⊠ 00193 – ⓜ Lepanto   ⬤ VISA ⬤ AE ⓪
– ℰ 06 36 84 – info@viscontipalace.com – Fax 06 3 20 05 51
– www.viscontipalace.com   Plan II **E1**
234 rm ⊑ – ♦280 € ♦♦330 € – 13 suites
♦ Business ♦ Modern ♦
A large 1970s building, this hotel appeals to business people and tourists alike;
it has a new modern-style lobby and conference area; rooms with every modern
convenience.

Dei Mellini without rest   🛁 🕰 🌿 🖭 🕻 🖧70 *VISA* 🆎 🆎 🅾️

via Muzio Clementi 81 ✉ *00193 – Ⓜ Lepanto – 𝒞 06 32 47 71 – info@
hotelmellini.com – Fax 06 32 47 78 01 – www.hotelmellini.com*   *Plan II* **E1**

67 rm ⚬ – ♦300 € ♦♦350 € – 13 suites

♦ Luxury ♦ Classic ♦

This stylish yet simple hotel on the right bank of the Tiber offers excellent
modern facilities and a high standard of service; well-equipped rooms; sun
terrace.

Jolly Leonardo da Vinci   🕰 🌿 🖭 🕻 🖧180 *VISA* 🆎 🆎 🅾️

via dei Gracchi 324 ✉ *00192 – Ⓜ Lepanto –* 𝒞 *06 32 84 81
– roma-leonardodavinci@jollyhotels.com – Fax 06 3 61 01 38
– www.jollyhotels.com*   *Plan II* **E1**

244 rm ⚬ – ♦195/275 € ♦♦225/305 € – 5 suites

Rest a la carte 41/64 €

♦ Chain hotel ♦ Business ♦ Modern ♦

A very comfortable hotel which is equally popular with a business/conference
clientele and tourists. Spacious, elegant lobby and rooms to match. The
traditional style restaurant offers dishes to suit every taste.

Giulio Cesare without rest   🚗 🕰 🌿 🖭 🖧30 *VISA* 🆎 🆎 🅾️

via degli Scipioni 287 ✉ *00192 – Ⓜ Lepanto –* 𝒞 *06 3 21 07 51 – giulioce@
uni.net – Fax 06 3 21 17 36 – www.hotelgiuliocesare.com*   *Plan II* **E1**

80 rm ⚬ – ♦180/280 € ♦♦210/300 €

♦ Luxury ♦ Stylish ♦

Simple elegance, inside and out, is the hallmark of this welcoming hotel, housed
in a villa dating from 1906; courtyard garden and smart Louis XVI-style furniture.

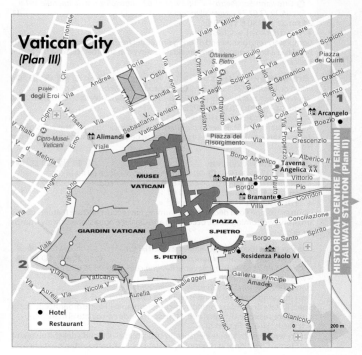

Vatican City
(Plan III)

ITALY

Farnese without rest   🗚 ⌘ 🖭 🅿 *VISA* 🐵 🆎 ①
via Alessandro Farnese 30 ⊠ 00192 – ⓜ Lepanto – 𝒞 06 3 21 25 53 – info@
hotelfarnese.com – Fax 06 3 21 51 29 – www.hotelfarnese.com   Plan II **E1**
23 rm ⌑ – ♦190/230 € ♦♦240/300 €
♦ Luxury ♦ Business ♦ Stylish ♦
In a restored patrician palace, this hotel is situated in the quiet Prati quarter, yet
only 50m from the metro; elegant and well-presented interior.

Residenza Paolo VI without rest   ⋖ 🗚 ⌘ 🖭 *VISA* 🐵 🆎 ①
via Paolo VI 29 ⊠ 00193 – ⓜ Ottaviano-San Pietro – 𝒞 06 68 48 70 – info@
residenzapaoloVI.com – Fax 06 6 86 74 28 – www.residenzapaoloVI.com   **K2**
29 rm ⌑ – ♦210 € ♦♦270 €
♦ Luxury ♦ Stylish ♦
One of the Eternal City's finest and rarest views, looking out over St Peter's, may
be enjoyed from the terrace of this hotel, located in a charming and graceful
former monastery.

Arcangelo without rest   ⋖ St. Peter's Basilica, 🗚
via Boezio 15 ⊠ 00192 – ⓜ Lepanto   ⌘ 🖭 *VISA* 🐵 🆎 ①
– 𝒞 06 6 87 41 43 – hotel.arcangelo@travel.it – Fax 06 6 89 30 50
– www.travel.it/roma/arcangelo   Plan III **K1**
33 rm – ♦100/140 € ♦♦170/211 €
♦ Traditional ♦ Business ♦ Classic ♦
Tasteful decoration and attention to detail in the wood-panelled public areas of
this late-19C villa; sun terrace with view of St Peter's.

Hotel Alimandi Vaticano without rest   ♿ 🗚 ⌘ 🖭
Viale Vaticano 99 ⊠ 00165   ☎ *VISA* 🐵 🆎 ①
– ⓜ Ottaviano-San Pietro – 𝒞 06 39 74 55 62 – hotelali@hotelalimandie.191.it
– Fax 06 39 73 01 32 – www.alimandi.it   **J1**
24 rm ⌑ – ♦140 € ♦♦170 €
♦ Traditional ♦ Classic ♦
Completely refurbished and offering simple yet fresh and functional rooms, this
hotel has a fine terrace where breakfast is served in summer; close to the Musei
Vaticani.

Bramante without rest   🗚 ⌘ 🖭 *VISA* 🐵 🆎 ①
vicolo delle Palline 24 ⊠ 00193 – ⓜ Ottaviano-San Pietro – 𝒞 06 68 80 64 26
– hotelbramante@libero.it – Fax 06 68 13 33 39 – www.hotelbramante.com   **K2**
16 rm ⌑ – ♦140/170 € ♦♦150/220 €
♦ Traditional ♦ Family ♦ Classic ♦
A short walk from St. Peter's colonnade, almost backing on to the walls of the
Vatican, this is a pleasant hotel if you prefer to be at the ecclesiastical heart of the
Holy City.

Sant'Anna without rest   🗚 🖭 *VISA* 🐵 🆎 ①
borgo Pio 133 ⊠ 00193 – ⓜ Ottaviano-San Pietro – 𝒞 06 68 80 16 02
– santanna@travel.it – Fax 06 68 30 87 17 – www.hotelsantanna.com
20 rm ⌑ – ♦130/160 € ♦♦152/200 €   **K1-2**
♦ Traditional ♦ Personalised ♦
Unusual trompe l'oeil décor and a charming inner courtyard are features of this
small and welcoming hotel, occupying a 16C palace not a stone's throw from St
Peter's.

XXXXX **La Pergola** (Beck) – Hotel Rome Cavalieri Hilton   ⋖ city, 🍽 ♿ 🗚 ⌘
🏵🏵🏵 ⊠ 00136 – ⓜ Cipro-Musei Vaticani   ⇌18 🅿 *VISA* 🐵 🆎 ①
– 𝒞 06 35 09 21 52 – lapergola.rome@hilton.com – Fax 06 35 09 21 65
– www.cavalieri-hilton.it
closed 13-28 August, 1-23 January, Sunday and Monday   Plan I **A2**
Rest (booking essential) (dinner only) a la carte 100/154 € ⌛
Spec. Tartare di scampi su brunoise di cetriolo e papaia. Filetto di dentice in crosta
di verdure su brodo di fagioli neri. Mousse di spezie con gelato al mandarino
♦ Inventive ♦ Formal ♦
Luxury tempered by simple elegance, impeccable service, and a delightful view of
the Eternal City; dinner at this rooftop restaurant is an unforgettable experience.

ITALY

XX **L'Arcangelo**   ✗ 𝘝𝘐𝘚𝘈 ⓂⒸ AE ①

via Giuseppe Giocchino Belli 59/61 ⊠ 00193 – Ⓜ Lepanto – ℰ 06 3 21 09 92
– Fax 06 3 21 09 92   Plan II   **E1**
closed August, Saturday lunch (dinner only in July), Sunday and Bank Holidays
Rest (booking essential) 45 €/65 € and a la carte 39/55 € ᪲
♦ Contemporary ♦ Friendly ♦
This cosy, competently managed restaurant has some fine wooden panelling; it
serves traditional meat and fish dishes with a modern twist.

XX **Il Simposio-di Costantini**   AK 𝘝𝘐𝘚𝘈 ⓂⒸ AE ①

piazza Cavour 16 ⊠ 00193 – Ⓜ Lepanto – ℰ 06 32 11 11 31
– Fax 06 3 21 15 02
closed August, Saturday lunch and Sunday   Plan II   **E2**
Rest a la carte 35/68 € ᪲
♦ Contemporary ♦ Wine bar ♦
This restaurant-wine bar offers the choice between a drink at the bar or dining in
the elegant restaurant; hot and cold dishes, and a good cheese selection.

XX **Taverna Angelica**   AK ✗ 𝘝𝘐𝘚𝘈 ⓂⒸ AE

piazza Amerigo Capponi 6 ⊠ 00193 – Ⓜ Ottaviano-San Pietro
– ℰ 06 6 87 45 14 – www.tavernaangelica.it
closed 10-20 August and lunch except Sunday   **K1**
Rest (Post theatre restaurant, open until late) a la carte 34/47 €
♦ Contemporary ♦ Trendy ♦
Modern in feel, a good place to go after a visit to the theatre. The cuisine is
colourful and imaginative, but not lacking in technical proficiency.

XX **L'Antico Porto**   AK ✗ 𝘝𝘐𝘚𝘈 ⓂⒸ AE ①

via Federico Cesi 36 ⊠ 00193 – Ⓜ Lepanto – ℰ 06 3 23 36 61
– boombastik @ alice.it – Fax 06 3 20 34 83
closed August, Saturday lunch and Sunday   Plan II   **E1**
Rest a la carte 35/78 €
♦ Seafood ♦ Family ♦
The reliably professional management here has focused on fish dishes with great
success. Classical style and cosiness combined.

PARIOLI (via Flaminia, Villa Borghese, Villa Glori, via Nomentana,
via Salaria)   **Plan IV**

🏨🏨 **Grand Hotel Parco dei Principi**   ≤ ⅙ ⅃ (heated) 🚗 🕭 ᴓ AK

via Gerolamo Frescobaldi 5   ✗ rest 🖂 ☎ ₰⅄ 900 ⌚ 𝘝𝘐𝘚𝘈 AE ①
⊠ 00198 – Ⓜ Veneto – ℰ 06 85 44 21 – principi @ parcodeiprincipi.com
– Fax 06 8 84 51 04 – www.parcodeiprincipi.com   **M2**
183 rm ⌚ – ♦400/450 € ♦♦540/600 € – 32 suites
Rest Pauline Borghese a la carte 52/71 €
♦ Luxury ♦ Business ♦ Classic ♦
Overlooking the parkland of the Villa Borghese, this hotel is an oasis of verdant
calm in the heart of Rome; elegant warm interiors, with much attention to detail
in evidence and excellent service. Exclusive restaurant offering well-presented
eclectic cuisine.

🏨🏨 **Aldrovandi Palace**   ⅙ ⅃ 🕭 ᴓ rm AK ✗ 🖂 ☎ ₰⅄ 300

via Ulisse Aldrovandi 15 ⊠ 00197 – Ⓜ Flaminio   ℙ 𝘝𝘐𝘚𝘈 ⓂⒸ AE ①
– ℰ 06 3 22 39 93 – hotel @ aldrovandi.com – Fax 06 3 22 14 35
– www.aldrovandi.com   **M2**
121 rm – ♦400/470 € ♦♦500/550 €, ⌚ 30 € – 10 suites
Rest see Baby below
♦ Luxury ♦ Stylish ♦
Occupying an elegant late-19C palazzo with views of the Villa Borghese, this
hotel has a small shaded park with swimming pool, opulent public areas and
stylish bedrooms.

ITALY

Lord Byron ⌨   AC 🍴 📺 📞 VISA 🏧 AE ①
via De Notaris 5 ⊠ 00197 – Ⓜ Flaminio – 𝒞 06 3 22 04 04 – info @
lordbyronhotel.com – Fax 06 3 22 04 05 – www.lordbyronhotel.com   **L-M1**
32 rm ⌷ – ♦275/396 € ♦♦300/528 € – 3 suites
Rest *Sapori del Lord Byron* (closed Sunday) a la carte 45/68 €
♦ Luxury ♦ Stylish ♦
Feeling more like an exclusive private residence than a hotel, this refined establishment has rooms combining luxury with modern comforts and faultless
service. The smart dining room is equally suitable for intimate meals or meetings.

The Duke Hotel   ♿ rm AC 🍴 rest 📺 📞 🏊 80 🚗 VISA 🏧 AE ①
via Archimede 69 ⊠ 00197 – Ⓜ Flaminio – 𝒞 06 36 72 21 – theduke @
thedukehotel.com – Fax 06 36 00 41 04 – www.thedukehotel.com   **L1**
78 rm ⌷ – ♦315 € ♦♦359 € – 7 suites
Rest (residents only) 37 €
♦ Luxury ♦ Business ♦ Stylish ♦
The discreet, well-upholstered ambience of an English club pervades the stylish
interiors of this well-appointed new hotel; afternoon tea served in front of the fire.

Mercure Roma Corso Trieste without rest   🛗 🎡 ♿ AC 🍴 📺
via Gradisca 29 ⊠ 00198 – 𝒞 06 7 00   🏊 30 🚗 VISA 🏧 AE ①
18 74 – mercure.romatrieste @ accor-hotels.it – Fax 06 7 00 57 81   **O1**
97 rm ⌷ – ♦165 € ♦♦200 €
♦ Chain hotel ♦ Business ♦ Modern ♦
Comfortable, spacious and modern rooms in this hotel, unusually situated in a
residential quarter. Gym and sun deck on top floor.

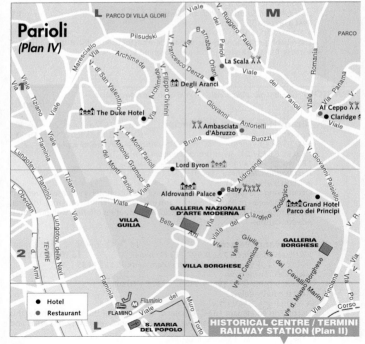

Albani without rest AC ⚡ GB 📶90 VISA CO AE ①
via Adda 45 ⊠ 00198 – Ⓜ Termini – ℰ 06 8 49 91 – hotelalbani@flashnet.it
– Fax 06 8 49 93 99 – www.hotelalbani.it   **N2**
143 rm ⌂ – ♦186/204 € ♦♦260/297 €
♦ Business ♦ Modern ♦
Overlooking the gardens of the Villa Albani near the Via Veneto, this modern-style
hotel has comfortable public areas, especially the fine and airy lobby.

Claridge ⅃ₛ ℛ 忐 AC ⚡rest GB 🕻 📶100 VISA CO AE ①
viale Liegi 62 ⊠ 00198 – ℰ 06 84 54 41 – claridge@rhr.it – Fax 06 8 55 51 71
– www.roscioli.com   **M1**
93 rm ⌂ – ♦169/250 € ♦♦197/290 €
Rest (residents only)
♦ Business ♦ Modern ♦
White predominates in the spacious, airy lobby, but the bedrooms are decorated
in warm colours set off by an abundance of wooden fittings; some have their own
balcony.

Degli Aranci ⅋ 忐rm AC ⚡ GB 📶40 VISA CO AE ①
via Oriani 11 ⊠ 00197 – Ⓜ Flaminio – ℰ 06 8 07 02 02
– hotel.degliaranci@flashnet.it – Fax 06 8 07 07 04   **M1**
54 rm ⌂ – ♦180 € ♦♦250 € – 2 suites
Rest a la carte 37/65 €
♦ Traditional ♦ Modern ♦
Not far from Viale Parioli, this genteel hotel is situated in a quiet, leafy area;
pleasant, stylish public areas and very comfortable rooms. The restaurant looks
out over the grounds.

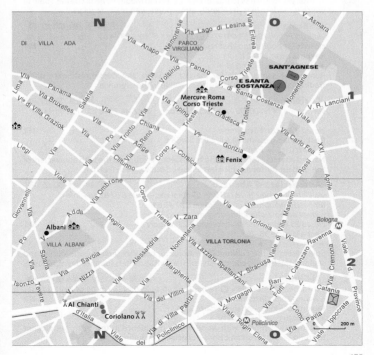

ITALY

Fenix   🛜 🚙 Ⓚ ⅏ 🖳 ℃ 🛗32 𝘷𝘐𝘚𝘈 ⓒⓞ ⒶⒺ ⓞ
viale Gorizia 5 ⊠ 00198 – ⓜ Bologna – ℰ 06 8 54 07 41
– info@fenixhotel.it – Fax 06 8 54 36 32 – www.fenixhotel.it   O1
73 rm ⌑ – ♦110/130 € ♦♦150/200 € – 8 suites
Rest (closed August, Saturday dinner and Sunday) (residents only) a la carte
24/40 €
♦ Traditional ♦ Business ♦ Classic ♦
Close to the parkland of Villa Torlonia, this establishment has smart
well-presented public areas, and comfortable rooms which are tastefully
furnished; pleasant courtyard garden. Understated décor in the restaurant.

🍴🍴🍴🍴 **Baby** – Hotel Aldrovandi Palace   🛜 Ⓚ ⅏ ⓟ 𝘷𝘐𝘚𝘈 ⓒⓞ ⒶⒺ ⓞ
🍃 via Ulisse Aldrovandi 15 ⊠ 00197 – ⓜ Flaminio – ℰ 06 3 21 61 26
closed Monday   M2
Rest a la carte 60/85 €
Spec. Tagliata di tonno al fumo di fieno ed acqarello di sapori. Spiedino di astice
e mozzarella di bufala con raviolo di pesca e barbabietole. Lombetto di vitello
con salvia, mozarella di bufala e verdure al profumo di vaniglia.
♦ Mediterranean ♦ Fashionable ♦
Housed in the de luxe Aldrovandi Palace hotel, this charming contemporary
restaurant overlooks the gardens and swimming pool; high-quality cuisine

🍴🍴 **Al Ceppo**   Ⓚ 𝘷𝘐𝘚𝘈 ⓒⓞ ⒶⒺ ⓞ
via Panama 2 ⊠ 00198 – ℰ 06 8 55 13 79
– info@ristorantealceppo.it – Fax 06 85 30 13 70 – www.ristorantealceppo.it
closed 8-24 August and Monday   M1
Rest (booking essential) a la carte 46/62 € ⅋
♦ Mediterranean ♦ Rustic ♦
A rustic yet stylish feel to this restaurant serving Mediterranean cuisine, some of
which is modern in style; friendly atmosphere with many regulars.

🍴🍴 **La Scala**   🛜 Ⓚ ⅏ 𝘷𝘐𝘚𝘈 ⓒⓞ ⒶⒺ ⓞ
viale dei Parioli 79/d ⊠ 00197 – ⓜ Euclide – ℰ 06 8 08 44 63 – Fax 06 8 08 39 78
closed 6-21 August and Wednesday   M1
Rest a la carte 29/40 €
♦ Roman ♦ Formal ♦
Run by the same family for the last 30 years, this classic restaurant offers
traditional Italian fare; pizzas also available in the evenings.

🍴🍴 **Coriolano**   Ⓚ 𝘷𝘐𝘚𝘈 ⓒⓞ ⒶⒺ ⓞ
via Ancona 14 ⊠ 00198 – ⓜ Castro Pretorio – ℰ 06 44 24 98 63 – Fax 06 44 24
97 24
closed 8 August-1 September   N2
Rest (booking essential) a la carte 39/58 €
♦ Roman ♦ Formal ♦
Named after its proprietor, who has recently celebrated the 50th anniversary of
this elegant trattoria, which has a relaxed but well-run feel to it.

🍴🍴 **Ambasciata d'Abruzzo**   🛜 Ⓚ 𝘷𝘐𝘚𝘈 ⓒⓞ ⒶⒺ ⓞ
via Pietro Tacchini 26 ⊠ 00197 – ⓜ Flaminio – ℰ 06 8 07 82 56 – info@
ambasciatadiabruzzo.com – Fax 06 8 07 49 64
– www.ambasciatadiabruzzo.com
closed 23 August-7 September and 9-23 January   M1
Rest a la carte 33/46 €
♦ Regional ♦ Rustic ♦
Specialising in the cuisine of the Abruzzo, but also serving Lazio dishes and
seafood, this friendly country-style restaurant also offers summer dining alfresco.

🍴 **Al Chianti**   Ⓚ ⅏ ⇔20/30 𝘷𝘐𝘚𝘈 ⓒⓞ ⒶⒺ ⓞ
via Ancona 17 ⊠ 00198 – ⓜ Termini – ℰ 06 44 25 02 42 – Fax 06 44 29 15 34
– www.alchiantiristorante.it   N2
Rest (booking essential) a la carte 37/47 €
♦ Tuscany ♦ Friendly ♦
A warm environment with wood much in evidence in this rustic yet elegant
trattoria-taverna; Tuscan dishes a speciality, including game.

MILAN
MILANO

Population (est. 2005): 1 216 000 (conurbation 3 798 000) – Altitude: 122m

Milan, which has a well-earned reputation for elegance, artistic flair, cultural tradition and gastronomic excellence, enjoys a lively social and political life. It offers a vibrant combination of old and new. It is famous for its historical monuments, outstanding museums, ultra-modern architecture and contemporary art. Although Milan is Italy's second city as regards population, politics and cultural heritage, it proudly claims to be the country's financial heartland owing to its commercial, industrial and banking activities.

Milan has a rich history from Roman occupation when it became the seat of the Western Empire at the end of the 3C. Emperor Constantine granted freedom of worship to Christians by the Edict of Milan (313) and St Ambrose became bishop in 375. Barbarian invasions in 5C and 6C were followed by the creation of the Lombard kingdom. After conquest by the Franks, Charlemagne became King of the Lombards in 774. In the 12C Milan joined the Lombard League against Emperor Frederic Barbarossa and gained independence. During the rule of the Visconti and the Sforza, the city flourished and attracted the geniuses of the time, Leonardo da Vinci and Bramante. Milan became the capital of the Cisalpine Republic in 1797, and later of the Kingdom of Italy (1805) and of the Venetian-Lombard Kingdom (1815).

WHICH DISTRICT TO CHOOSE

You will find a large selection of **hotels** in the luxury category near the Duomo in the historical centre *Plan II* **G2**, and hotels of a good standard near Stazione Centrale *Plan III* **M1**, near Piazza della Repubblica *Plan III* **M2**, in the Montenapoleone district, and in the business district around Corso Buenos Aires *Plan I* **C1**. There are moderately priced hotels in the university area *Plan II* **G2** and in the trade fair district around Viale Certosa *Plan I* **A1**. Business hotels are also to be found on the outskirts. Milan has many **restaurants** with a fine culinary tradition. The historical area abounds in luxury

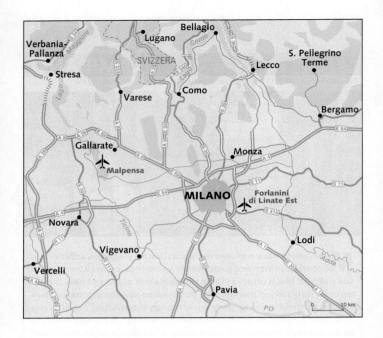

establishments near the Duomo *Plan II* **G2**, Via Manzoni *Plan II* **G1**, Piazza della Scala *Plan II* **G1**. For good food at reasonable prices look in the Romana-Vittoria area – Porta Romana *Plan I* **D3**, Viale Umbria *Plan I* **D3**, Corso Porta Vittoria *Plan II* **H2**. For typical restaurants with a pleasant ambience and trattorias serving seafood, visit the Navigli district – Piazza XXIV Maggio *Plan II* **F3**, Ripa di Porta Ticinese *Plan I* **B3**, Via Solari *Plan I* **B3**.

PRACTICAL INFORMATION

ARRIVAL – DEPARTURE

Malpensa Airport, 45 km (28 mi) northwest of the city centre. **Linate Airport**, 8 km (5 mi) east. ℰ 02 748 52200.

From the airport to the city centre – Taxis are rather expensive as **Malpensa** Airport is some distance from the city. A train connects Malpensa Airport with Stazione Cadorna (every 30min, time: 40min) which in turn connects to the metro system. Fare €9. Malpensa Express, ℰ 02 20 222. There is a shuttle bus service to Stazione Centrale (every 20min, time 45min/1hr depending on the traffic) costing €5.50 (one way). Malpensa Shuttle Express, ℰ 02 58 58 10 64; www.sea-aeroportimilano.it

From **Linate** Airport bus no 73 runs to Piazza San Babila metro station (every 10min, time 25min). Fare €1 (tickets on sale at newsstands). ℰ 800 016 857. There is also a STARFLY bus service to

Stazione Centrale (every 30min, time 30min) which also stops at Stazione Lambrate. Fare €2.50. www.sea-aero portimilano.it

Main station – International and inter-city train services operate from Stazione Centrale *Plan III* **M1**.

TRANSPORT

✦ BUS AND METRO

There are three metro lines. Tickets are valid for 75min on the whole bus/metro network. A single ticket costs €1 (book of 10 tickets €9.20); a 1-day travel card costs €3, 2-day travel card €5.50. Tickets can be purchased at kiosks, bars, tobacconists and ticket machines.

✦ TAXIS

Taxis, which are white vehicles and bear an illuminated sign, can be hired at a taxi stand or hailed in the street. The minimum pick-up charge is €3.10. There is a supplement of €3.10 at night and €1.55 on public holidays. An average taxi ride costs €10-15. *Radio Taxis* ℰ 02 4040, 02 8585, 02 8383.

USEFUL ADDRESSES

✦ TOURIST OFFICE

Via Marconi, 1 – 20123 Milano *Plan II* **G2**. ℰ 02 72 52 43 01/2; www.mila noinfotourist.com

✦ BANKS/CURRENCY EXCHANGE

The major banks and foreign exchange offices are to be found in the town centre and at the main railway stations. Banks open Mon-Fri, 8.30am-1.30pm and 3-4.30pm (some banks open on Saturday morning until 1.30pm); closed national holidays and 7 December (the town's patron Saint's Day). Bank cash machines (ATMs) are open 24hrs (pin number required).

✦ EMERGENCY

Medical emergencies: ℰ **118**; Police: ℰ **113**.

✦ CHEMIST / PHARMACY

The chemist in Galleria delle Partenze, Stazione Centrale *Plan III* **M1** is open 24 hours. ℰ 02 66 90 935.

BUSY PERIODS

It may be difficult to find a room when special events are held in the city:

Milano Internazionale Antiquariato – Antiques Fair: early May.

Naviglio Grande – Antiques Fair: late June.

International Furniture Fair – April.

Milanovendemoda – Fashion: late February (winter fashion), late Sept-early Oct (summer fashion).

MICAM – Footwear Fair: late March and late September.

Moda Prima – International knitwear market: early June. Fashion and accessories show: late November-early December.

Monza – Formula One race: September.

Smau – Electronic Fair: late October.

EXPLORING MILAN

In two days there is time to visit the main sights and museums.

Opening times are usually from 9.30-10am to 5-5.30pm but closed on Mondays and public holidays.

VISITING

Duomo *Plan II* **G2** – A Gothic marvel in white marble with belfries, gables, pinnacles, statues, rose windows and tracery. Do not miss a visit to the roof for stunning views and the cathedral museum. Then go through to the magnificent **Galleria Vittorio Emanuele**, the centre of Milanese political and social life.

Pinacoteca di Brera *Plan II* **G1** – A 17C palace houses masterpieces (*Dead Christ* by Mantegna, *Pietà* by Bellini, *Montefeltro altarpiece* by Piero della Francesca, *Marriage of the Virgin* by Raphael, *Meal at Emmaus* by Caravaggio) and 20C works by Italian Futurists.

Castello Sforzesco *Plan II* **F1** – The former residence of the Dukes of Milan – sculpture museum (*Rondanini Pietà* by Michaelangelo), picture gallery, archaeological museum and musical instruments.

Palazzo Bagatti Valsecchi *Plan II* **G2** – A Renaissance palace with opulent decor: frescoes, sculpture, paintings, furnishings.

Pinacoteca Ambrosiana *Plan II* **F2** – One of the oldest libraries in the world displays outstanding exhibits: drawings and *The Musician* by Leonardo da Vinci, cartoons by Raphael, *Basket of Fruit* by Caravaggio.

Museo della Scienza e della Tecnica Leonardo da Vinci *Plan II* **E2** – Models of Leonardo's inventions and displays tracing scientific advances through the ages.

Chiesa di Santa Maria delle Grazie *Plan II* **E2** – A 15-16C Renaissance church with an impressive dome by Bramante. Leonardo's *Last Supper* in the restored Cenacolo.

Galleria d'Arte Moderna *Plan II* **G2** – An interesting display of contemporary art by Italian and European artists. Marino Marini Museum.

Basilica di Sant'Ambrogio *Plan II* **E2** – A magnificent basilica, founded in 4C by St Ambrose, is in the Lombard-Romanesque (11-12C) – altar front, ambo, mosaics, portico by Bramante.

Monza *(21 km – 13 mi – NE of Milano)* – Attractive town famous for its cathedral (Iron Crown of the Kings of Lombardy in the treasury), and the royal villa Parco di Villa Reale with a vast park where the **Monza racing circuit** is.

GOURMET TREATS

If you fancy a snack or light meal, visit *Bar della Crocetta*, Corso di Porta Romana 67 and the tiny *Crota piemunteisa*, Piazza Cesare Beccaria 10. *Gattullo*, Piazza Porta Ludovica 2, is one of the best places for a freshly baked brioche and a cappuccino. *Taveggia*, Via Visconti di Modrone 2, serves dark and syrupy hot chocolate. *Cova*, Via Monte Napoleone 8, *Panerello*, Via Speronari and Corso di Porta Romana, *Cucci*, Corso di Porta Genova offer delicious pastries.

Gelateria Marghera, Via Marghera 33, *Umberto*, Piazza Cinque Giornate, *Il Massimo del Gelato*, Via Castelvetro 18, *Riva Reno*, Via Col di Lana 8 and *Ruggero*, Piazza Emilia 4 have an excellent selection of ice cream.

SHOPPING

Shops are open daily except Sun and Mon, 9-9.30am to 12.30-1pm and from 3.30-4pm to 7.30-8pm.

For **luxury items** stroll through the fashionable districts – Corso Vittorio Emanuele II *Plan II* **G2**, Piazza San Babila *Plan II* **G1**, Corso Venezia *Plan II* **H1**, Via Monte Napoleone *Plan II* **G1**, Via Dante *Plan II* **F1**, Corso Vercelli *Plan I* **B2**, Corso Buenos Aires *Plan I* **C1** and Via della Spiga (where the couture houses are) *Plan II* **G1**. For **young fashions** browse in Corsa di Porta Ticinese and Via Torino *Plan II* **F2**. Lovers of **antiques** will find a profusion of shops in Corso Magenta *Plan II*

F2 and the narrow streets around Sant'Ambrogio *Plan II* **E2**, Via Lanzone *Plan II* **F2**, Via Caminadella *Plan II* **F3**, Via Santa Marta *Plan II* **F2**, Via Brera *Plan II* **F1** and environs and in Via Bagutta *Plan II* **G1**.

Peck and other shops in Via Spadari *Plan II* **F2**, Via Speronari *Plan II* **G2** and Via Cantù *Plan II* **F2** specialise in delicacies and fine foods.

MARKETS – In Piazza Diaz *Plan II* **G2**, (**old books** – every second Sun), in Via Armorari *Plan II* **F2** (**stamps and postcards** – Sun), in Piazza Gaspari (**objects** – Sat) and in Via Fiori Chiari *Plan II* **F1** (**antiques** – every third Sun). Popular **flea markets** are: Fiera di Senigallia, Piazza Stazione di Porta Genova *Plan II* **E3** (Sat), Mercato di San Donato (Metro San Donato, Sun).

WHAT TO BUY – Latest fashions, leather goods, shirts of the famous football teams Milan AC and Inter Milan, furniture and design.

ENTERTAINMENT

Consult the brochure *Milano Mese* which gives listings of entertainment and venues throughout the city. It is available from the tourist office. www.milanoturismo.com

La Scala *Plan II* **G1** – A world famous venue for opera and ballet. The season starts on St Ambrose Day (7 Dec).

Conservatorio *Plan II* **H2** – Chamber and orchestral music.

Auditorium di Milano *Plan I* **B3** – Classical, jazz and other types of music, literary evenings, events for children and audiences with famous artists.

Teatro Dal Verme *Plan II* **F1** – Plays.

Piccolo Teatro *Plan II* **F2** – Three theatres present drama.

NIGHTLIFE

Milan has lively cafés and bars for **going out for a drink** or **for the evening** in the historical centre and near the station. *Bar Magenta*, Via Carducci 13 is one of the famous bars in Milan and *Bar Basso*, Via Plinio 39 serves delicious cocktails. Other pleasant venues are *Moscatelli*, Corso Garibaldi, *Morigi*, Via Morigi, *Roïalto*, Via Piero della Francesca, *La Belle Aurore*, via Abamonti 1/Via Castel Morrone. *See Entertainment above.*

At night the liveliest part of the city is the picturesque **Brera** district *Plan II* **G1** where there are bars and nightclubs popular with artists. The **Navigli** and **Ticinese** areas and **Corso Como** *Plan III* **L1** are also well worth a visit.

Around of Milan
(Plan I)

La Pobbia 1850 ✕✕✕
Mirage 🏨🏨
Innocenti Evasioni ✕✕
Accademia 🏨🏨🏨
Regency 🏨🏨
Da Stefano il Marchigiano ✕✕
Enterprise Hotel 🏨🏨🏨
Osteria del Borgo Antico ✕✕

Melià Milano 🏨🏨
Atahotel Fieramilano 🏨🏨🏨

FIERA DI MILANO

Astoria 🏨🏨
Domenichino 🏨🏨
Mini Hotel Tiziano 🏨

Rubens 🏨🏨
Al Molo 13 ✕✕
Milan Marriot Hotel 🏨🏨🏨
Capitol World Class 🏨🏨
Pace ✕

Il Luogo di Aimo e Nadia ✕✕✕
Des Etrangers 🏨🏨

Il Torchietto ✕✕
Sadler ✕✕✕

Sempione (Plan III)

Historical Centre (Plan II)

PARCO SEMPIONE

CASTELLO SFORZESCO
NORD
Pza Castello

PORTA GENOVA

S. CRISTOFORO

MONCUCCO

● Hotel
● Restaurant

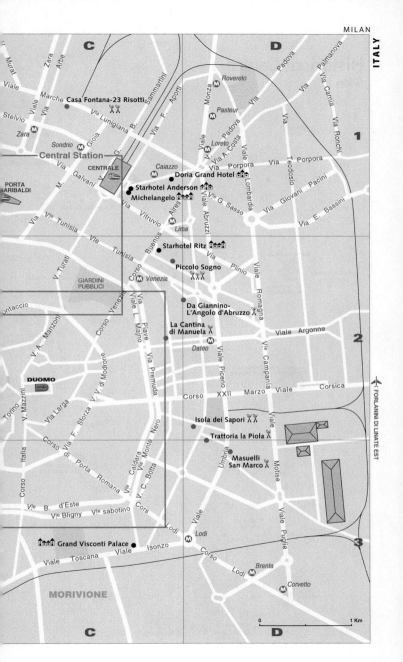

C

D

Viale Murat
Zara
Arbe

Viale
Marche **Casa Fontana-23 Risotti**
V^le Lunigiana

Stelvio
Via
Via

Zara
Ⓜ

Sondrio Ⓜ Gioia

— Central Station —

Via Galvani
CENTRALE

PORTA
GARIBALDI

Viale Tunisia

Via Vitruvio

V. Turati

V^le Tunisia

Buenos Aires

GIARDINI
PUBBLICI

Corso Venezia

ntaccio

V. A. Manzoni

Corso Venezia

Viale L. Majno

Via Plave

Via Premuda

DUOMO

Torino
V. Mazzini

Via Larga

Corso di Porta Romana

Viale Monte Nero

V. V. d. Modrone

V. F. Sforza

Caldara

V. C. Botta

V^le B. d'Este
V^le Bligny
V^le sabotino

Corso

Italia

Corso

Lodi

Grand Visconti Palace ●

Viale Toscana
Viale Isonzo

MORIVIONE

Sammartini

Via F. Aporti

Monza
Rovereto Ⓜ

Pasteur

Padova

Viale Loreto Ⓜ
Via A. Costa

Caiazzo Ⓜ
Via Porpora

Doria Grand Hotel 🏛

V^le G. Sasso

Starhotel Anderson 🏛
Michelangelo 🏛

Lima Ⓜ

Starhotel Ritz 🏛

Via

Piccolo Sogno
✗✗✗

Ⓜ Venezia

**Da Giannino-
L'Angolo d'Abruzzo** ✗

**La Cantina
di Manuela** ✗

Dateo Ⓜ

Viale Piceno

Corso XXII Marzo

Isola dei Sapori ✗✗
Trattoria la Piola ✗

**Masuelli
San Marco** ✗

Lodi Ⓜ

Corso

Lodi

Padova
Via

Via Carnia

Via Palmanova

Via Ronchi

1

Via Teodosio

Via Giovanni Pacini

Via E. Bassini

Viale Lombardia

Viale Plinio

Viale Romagna

Viale Argonne

Viale Campania

Corsica
Viale Corsica

2

FORLANINI DI LINATE EST

Viale Umbria

Viale Motise

Viale Puglie

3

Brenta

Corvetto Ⓜ

0 ————————— 1 Km

C

D

483

Historical Centre
(Plan II)

Piazza Sempione **E**

ARENA

S. SIMPLICIANO

PARCO SEMPIONE

Via M. Pagano

Viale Milton

Viale E.

Gadio

F

Via Solterino

Lanza

Via Pontaccio

Nabucco

Via Mercato

Via Buonaparte

Trattoria Torre di Pisa

1

Via Petrarca

Vincenzo

Settembre

20

Via V. Globreti

Via G. Boccaccio

Alemagna

Via Giacomo Leopardi

Cadorna

NORD

CASTELLO SFORZESCO

Castello

Piazza Cairoli

Via Cusani

UNA Hotel Cusani

Foro

V. M. Campero

Via Dante

Emilia e Carlo

Via dell'Or

La Felicità

Via Brojetto

CENACOLO

Antica Locanda Leonardo

S. MARIA D. GRAZIE

Corso

Bandello

Magenta

V. Fili Ruffini

V. Caradosso

Via V. Monti

Carducci

PAL. LITTA

Corso Magenta

Via Meravigli

King

M

S. MAURIZIO

Piazza Cordusio

Cordusio

M

Via

Cracco-Peck

Spadari al Duomo

Hostaria Borromei

V. Lanni

Via Sta Marta

PINACOTECA AMBROSIANA

Via Nerino

Torino

2

Via

San

Gian

degli

Olivetani

Battista

Vico

Drona

Vittore

MUSEO NAZIONALE LEONARDO DA VINCI

Via

S. AMBROGIO

U

M S. Ambrogio

Via

E.

Lanzone

Via Cappuccio

Via Sta

Carrobbio

Via

Stampa

Piazza Misso

Alla Collina Pistoiese

Via Omelio

Regina

De Via Cesare Correnti

Viale

Viale

Coni

PARCO SOLARI

M

S. Agostino

Via Cesare da Sesto

Via

Aribert

San

Crespi

Vicenzo

Genova

Naviglio

Amicis

Corso di Porta Ticinese

S. LORENZO MAGGIORE

Via Molino delle Armi

PARCO DELLE BASILICHE

V. Calatafimi

3

Via

Cerano

V. Andrea Solari

Zugna

Tortona

Savona

Papiniano

Via

Corso

Via

Alessi

Via

G.

del

Ferrari

G.

Conca

Arena

SANT' EUSTORGIO

Via Sambuco

PORTA GENOVA

Al Porto

PORTA GENOVA

Via Valenza

Porta Genova F. S.

C. C. Colombo

Viale

Tano Passami l'Olio

Via

Vigevano

Gonzla

D'Annunzio

Viale G. Galeazzo

Viale Col di Lana

P.TA TICINESE

Osteria di Porta Cicca

Ripa di Porta Ticinese

Il Navigante

E

F

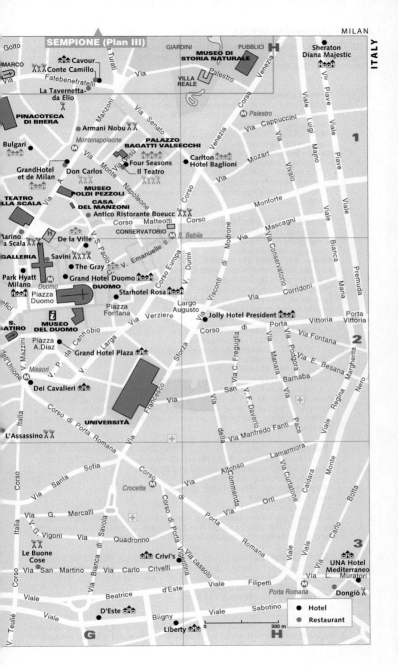

SEMPIONE (Plan III)

Goito

MARCO

Via

Cavour
Conte Camillo
Fatebenefratelli
La Tavernetta-
da Elio

Turati

GIARDINI
PUBBLICI

MUSEO DI
STORIA NATURALE

VILLA
REALE

Palestro

Sheraton
Diana Majestic

Via Senato

PINACOTECA
DI BRERA

Manzoni

Montenapoleone

Bulgari

Armani Nobu

M Palestro

Via Cappuccini

Via Mozart

Vivaio

Corso Venezia

Luigi Majno

Viale Piave

Viale Piave

1

GrandHotel
et de Milan

Don Carlos
Il Teatro

PALAZZO
BAGATTI VALSECCHI

Four Seasons

MUSEO
POLDI PEZZOLI
CASA
DEL MANZONI

Carlton
Hotel Baglioni

Via Monte Napoleone

Via

Monforte

Via

Viale

TEATRO
LLA SCALA

Antico Ristorante Boeucc

Corso Matteotti

Corso

Mascagni

Via Conservatorio

Bianca

Maria

Marino
a Scala

De la Ville

CONSERVATORIO

M S. Babila

V. S. Paolo

Via Modrone

Premuda

GALLERIA

Savini

V. Emanuelle II

Corso Europa

Durini

Porta
Vittoria

Porta
Vittoria

Park Hyatt
Milano

fici

The Gray

Grand Hotel Duomo

Duomo

Piazza
Duomo

DUOMO

Starhotel Rosa

Visconti di Modrone

Corridoni

Maria

Via

Via Conservatorio

2

S.
ATIRO

MUSEO
DEL DUOMO

Piazza
Fontana

Piazza
A.Diaz

da Cannobio

Larga

Via

Verziere

Largo
Augusto

Jolly Hotel President

Porta

Via Fontana

Margherita

V. Mazzini

dell'Unione

Missori

Grand Hotel Plaza

Dei Cavalieri

M

Corso di Porta Romana

Italia

V. P. da

V.

Storza

Francesco

San

Via

Corso

di

Via C. Freguglia

Via Manara

Via Podgora

V. F. Daverio

Barnaba

Via

Via E. Besana

Pace

Regina

Nero

Viale

L'Assassino

UNIVERSITÀ

della

Via Manfredo Fanti

Corso

Santa

Sofia

Corso

Via

Crocetta

Alfonso

Commenda

Via Curtatone

Lamarmora

Monte

Caldara

Botta

Via

G. Mercalli

V.-G. Vigoni

Via

Quadronno

di Savoia

Porta

Ortì

Via

Carlo

Italia

Le Buone
Cose

Crivi's

Via San Martino

Via Bianca di

Via Carlo Crivelli

d'Este

Viale

Romana

Filipetti

Porta Romana

Viale

Viale

UNA Hotel
Mediterraneo

L. Muratori

Dongio

3

Viale

V. Teulié

D'Este

Beatrice

Bligny

Liberty

Sabotino

Viale

0   300 m

● Hotel
● Restaurant

G   H

485

HISTORICAL CENTRE (*Centro Storico Duomo, Scala, Castello Sforzesco, corso Magenta, via Torino, corso Vittorio Emanuele, via Manzoni, corso Porto Vittoria, corso Romana, corso Lodi, Navigli, Ripa di Porta Ticinese*) **Plan II**

Four Seasons   🗗 🚗 🕭rm 🖾 ⅋rest 🆔 🕍280 ⭗ 𝗩𝗜𝗦𝗔 ⓿❾ 🅰🅴 ⓪

via Gesù 6/8 ⊠ *20121* – Ⓜ *Montenapoleone* – ℰ *02 7 70 88*
– *milano@fourseasons.com* – *Fax 02 77 08 50 00*
– *www.fourseasons.com/milan*   **G1**
78 rm – †500/590 € ††570/690 €, � 32 € – 23 suites 1 100 €
Rest see *Il Teatro* below
Rest *La Veranda* a la carte 70/90 €
♦ Chain hotel ♦ Grand Luxury ♦ Stylish ♦
Within Milan's golden triangle, hidden away in a 15C former convent, this hotel retains some of its original features and is the most exclusive and elegant place to stay in the city. Its distinguished restaurant overlooks a leafy courtyard garden.

Grand Hotel et de Milan   🗗 🖾 🕍50 𝗩𝗜𝗦𝗔 ⓿❾ 🅰🅴 ⓪

via Manzoni 29 ⊠ *20121* – Ⓜ *Montenapoleone* – ℰ *02 72 31 41*
– *reservation@grandhoteletdemilan.it* – *Fax 02 86 46 08 61*
– *www.grandhoteletdemilan.it*   **G1**
95 rm – †442/748 € ††544/748 €, ⊏ 35 € – 8 suites
Rest see *Don Carlos* below – **Rest** *Caruso* (dinner only) a la carte 46/63 €
♦ Luxury ♦ Traditional ♦ Stylish ♦
The spirit of Verdi, who lived here, still lingers within this prestigious hotel's sumptuous late-19C interiors. Well-presented rooms with fine antique furniture. Well-lit restaurant dedicated to the maestro.

Carlton Hotel Baglioni   🗗 🕭rm 🖾 ⅋rest 🆔 🕍80

via Senato 5 ⊠ *20121* – Ⓜ *San Babila*   ⭗ 𝗩𝗜𝗦𝗔 ⓿❾ 🅰🅴 ⓪
– ℰ *02 7 70 77* – *carlton.milano@baglionihotels.com* – *Fax 02 78 33 00*
– *www.baglionihotels.com*   **H1**
87 rm – †360 € ††440 €, ⊏ 31 € – 9 suites
Rest *Il Baretto al Baglioni* (closed 5-26 August) a la carte 66/73 €
♦ Chain hotel ♦ Luxury ♦ Personalised ♦
Careful details, from the period furnishings to the fine tapestries, give warmth to the public areas and rooms of this elegant jewel in the heart of fashionable Milan. The elegant yet cosy rooms of the restaurant have wood panelled walls.

Bulgari   ⓢ 🗗 🖾 🚗 🕭 ⅋ 🆔 🕻 𝗩𝗜𝗦𝗔 ⓿❾ 🅰🅴 ⓪

via privata Fratelli Gabba 7/b ⊠ *20121* – Ⓜ *Montenapoleone* – ℰ *02 8 05 80 51*
– *milano@bulgarihotels.com* – *Fax 02 8 05 80 52 22*
– *www.bulgarihotels.com*   **G1**
52 rm – †580/690 € ††690/790 €, ⊏ 30 € – 7 suites
Rest a la carte 65/89 €
♦ Luxury ♦ Stylish ♦
A new star on Milan's hotel scene, remarkable for its understated elegance achieved by the tasteful use of fine furnishings. Charming and unexpected garden; the exclusive restaurants looks out over greenery.

Grand Hotel Duomo   ≤ Duomo, 🍽 🕭rm 🖾 ⅋rest 🆔

via San Raffaele 1 ⊠ *20121* – Ⓜ *Duomo*   🕍100 ⓿❾ 🅰🅴 ⓪
– ℰ *02 88 33* – *bookings@grandhotelduomo.com* – *Fax 02 86 46 20 27*
– *www.grandhotelduomo.com*   **G2**
159 rm ⊏ – †340 € ††540 € – 17 suites
Rest a la carte 56/77 €
♦ Business ♦ Classic ♦
A 1950s feel to the interior of this elegant hotel, situated next to the Duomo; its spires seem almost within reach from the terrace and many of the rooms. The smart dining room has an aura of exclusivity, and overlooks Piazza Duomo.

ITALY

Starhotel Rosa ᵇ₃ &rm 🄰🄲 ⅌ 🄴 📞 ♨130 𝘝𝘐𝘚𝘈 🄰🄴 ①
via Pattari 5 ⊠ 20122 – ⓜ Duomo – ☎ 02 88 31 – rosa.mi@starhotels.it
– Fax 02 8 05 79 64 – www.starhotels.com   **G2**
246 rm ⌂ – ♀385/495 € ♀♀450/495 € – 2 suites
Rest a la carte 38/48 €
♦ Business ♦ Classic ♦
Situated close to the Duomo, this recently refurbished establishment has large
and elegant public areas with much marble and stucco work, and comfortable
rooms. Well-equipped conference centre. The restaurant offers a traditional
dining experience.

Grand Visconti Palace ⊛ ᵇ₃ ♨ ⃞ & 🄰🄲 ⅌ 🄶🄰🄳 ♨250
viale Isonzo 14 ⊠ 20135 – ⓜ Lodi T.I.B.B.   ⌂ 𝘝𝘐𝘚𝘈 🄰🄴 ①
– ☎ 02 54 03 41 – info@grandviscontipalace.com – Fax 02 54 06 95 23
– www.grandviscontipalace.com   Plan I **C3**
172 rm ⌂ – ♀219/400 € ♀♀249/470 € – 6 suites
Rest *Al Quinto Piano* (closed 4-28 August) a la carte 75/95 €
♦ Business ♦ Personalised ♦
This classically elegant hotel occupies the spacious premises of a former factory
building. Excellent health and fitness centre and conference facilities, pleasant
garden. The fifth-floor restaurant offers some imaginative dishes.

Jolly Hotel President &rm 🄰🄲 ⅌rest 🄴 📞 ♨140 𝘝𝘐𝘚𝘈 🄰🄴 ①
Largo Augusto 10 ⊠ 20122 – ⓜ San Babila – ☎ 02 7 74 61 – milano-president@
jollyhotels.com – Fax 02 78 34 49 – www.jollyhotels.com   **H2**
225 rm ⌂ – ♀199/275 € ♀♀259/360 € – 7 suites
Rest *Il Verziere* a la carte 38/55 €
♦ Business ♦ Classic ♦
In a central location, this large international hotel has conference rooms, and
spacious public areas. Every convenience to be expected in a hotel of this
category is apparent. Elegantly genteel restaurant.

UNA Hotel Cusani 🄰🄲 ⅌ 🄴 📞 𝘝𝘐𝘚𝘈 🄰🄴 ①
via Cusani 13 ⊠ 20121 – ⓜ Cairoli – ☎ 02 8 56 01 – una.cusani@unahotels.it
– Fax 02 8 69 36 01 – www.unahotels.it   **F1**
85 rm ⌂ – ♀268/387 € ♀♀315/454 € – 5 suites
Rest (closed Saturday lunch and Sunday) a la carte 47/72 €
♦ Business ♦ Modern ♦
Occupying a fine position opposite the Castello Sforzesco, this comfortable hotel
has large rooms with mahogany furnishings and decorated with pastels. The
small restaurant is light and stylish.

Park Hyatt Milano ᵇ₃ & 🄰🄲 ⅌rest 🄴 📞 ♨60 𝘝𝘐𝘚𝘈 🄰🄴 ①
via Tommaso Grossi 1 ⊠ 20121 – ⓜ Duomo – ☎ 02 88 21 12 34
– milano@hyattintl.com – Fax 02 88 21 12 35
– www.milan.park.hyatt.com   **G2**
91 rm – ♀430/540 € ♀♀480/590 €, ⌂ 26 € – 9 suites
Rest *The Park* (closed August) a la carte 66/88 €
♦ Business ♦ Chain hotel ♦ Modern ♦
Occupying a palace built in 1870 and next to the Galleria Vittorio Emanuele, this
is the flagship of the Hyatt group in Italy. Inside, the feel is contemporary with
ample use of travertine. The elegant modern look is also in evidence in the
restaurant.

De la Ville ᵇ₃ ♨ ⃞ &rm 🄰🄲 ⅌ 🄴 📞 ♨60 𝘝𝘐𝘚𝘈 🄰🄴 ①
via Hoepli 6 ⊠ 20121 – ⓜ Duomo – ☎ 02 8 79 13 11
– reservationsdlv@sinahotels.it – Fax 02 86 66 09
– www.delavillemilano.com   **G2**
108 rm ⌂ – ♀336 € ♀♀374 € – 1 suite
Rest *L'Opera*, ☎ 02 8 05 12 31 (closed Sunday) a la carte 40/52 €
♦ Luxury ♦ Cosy ♦
A warm English drawing room feel with panelling, velvet and wood floors in
evidence. This very central hotel has well-appointed rooms and a smart
restaurant.

The Gray

   ⚙ 🗚 ⚙ 🖴 📞 *VISA* ⓜ 🗚 ⓞ

via San Raffaele 6 ⊠ *20121 –* ⓜ *Duomo – ℰ 02 7 20 89 51*
– info.thegray@sinahotels.it – Fax 02 86 65 26
– www.hotelgray.com　　　　　　　　　　　　　　　　　　**G2**
21 rm – 🛉363 € 🛉🛉528 €, ⊊ 28 €
Rest a la carte 48/72 €
♦ Luxury ♦ Stylish ♦
An exercise in class and style, with each room individually designed and featuring a wealth of fine detail; some rooms have views of the Galleria. Elegant restaurant.

Spadari al Duomo

   🗚 ⚙ 🖴 📞 *VISA* ⓜ 🗚 ⓞ

via Spadari 11 ⊠ *20123 –* ⓜ *Duomo – ℰ 02 72 00 23 71 – reservation@*
spadarihotel.com – Fax 02 86 11 84 – www.spadarihotel.com
closed Christmas　　　　　　　　　　　　　　　　　　**F2**
40 rm ⊊ – 🛉208/258 € 🛉🛉218/288 € – 1 suite
Rest (light meals only)
♦ Business ♦ Functional ♦
Italy's first "art hotel" is ten years old; small, elegant and exclusive in feel, it houses a fine collection of contemporary art and design.

Cavour

   🗚 ⚙ ♨80 *VISA* ⓜ 🗚 ⓞ

via Fatebenefratelli 21 ⊠ *20121 –* ⓜ *Turati – ℰ 02 62 00 01 – booking@*
hotelcavour.it – Fax 02 6 59 22 63 – www.hotelcavour.it　　　　　**G1**
111 rm – 🛉194 € 🛉🛉205 €, ⊊ 21 € – 5 suites
Rest see *Conte Camillo* below
♦ Business ♦ Functional ♦
A large colonnaded lobby welcomes visitors to this establishment, run for decades by the same family of Milanese hoteliers. The well-appointed rooms have recently been refitted.

Dei Cavalieri

   🗚 ↔rm ⚙rest 🖴 📞 ♨250 *VISA* ⓜ 🗚 ⓞ

piazza Missori 1 ⊠ *20123 –* ⓜ *Missori – ℰ 02 8 85 71*
– info@hoteldeicavalieri.com – Fax 02 8 85 72 41
– www.hoteldeicavalieri.com　　　　　　　　　　　　　**G2**
177 rm ⊊ – 🛉229/289 € 🛉🛉309/379 € – 2 suites
Rest a la carte 52/61 €
♦ Traditional ♦ Functional ♦
This hotel celebrated its fiftieth birthday in 1999. Slightly cramped public areas, but a recent refit has created a pleasant space in which to entertain, and there is a fine terrace. The well-proportioned restaurant is traditionally stylish.

Regina

   ⚙ 🗚 🖴 📞 ♨40 *VISA* ⓜ 🗚 ⓞ

via Cesare Correnti 13 ⊠ *20123 –* ⓜ *Sant' Ambrogio*
– ℰ 02 58 10 69 13 – info@hotelregina.it – Fax 02 58 10 70 33
– www.hotelregina.it
closed 23 December-7 January and August　　　　　　　　**F2**
43 rm ⊊ – 🛉139/200 € 🛉🛉176/290 €
Rest (residents only) (light meals only)
♦ Business ♦ Modern ♦
The courtyard of an 18C building covered by a glass pyramid is now the lobby of this modern-style hotel; parquet floors in the well-presented rooms.

Grand Hotel Plaza without rest

   🗚 🖴 📞 ♨100 *VISA* ⓜ 🗚 ⓞ

piazza Diaz 3 ⊠ *20123 –* ⓜ *Duomo – ℰ 02 85 55*
– info@grandhotelplazamilano.it – Fax 02 86 72 40
– www.grandhotelplazamilano.it　　　　　　　　　　**G2**
136 rm ⊊ – 🛉250/300 € 🛉🛉300/353 €
♦ Business ♦ Traditional ♦ Classic ♦
If you want to stay in the heart of Milan, this is the hotel for you, in the same square as the Terrazza Martini; spacious, standardised rooms on six floors.

ITALY

 Carrobbio without rest   🕭 🎬 🖼 ⚒30 *VISA* 🞧 🞧 🞧
via Medici 3 ✉ *20123 –* 🅜 *Duomo – 𝒞 02 89 01 07 40*
– info@hotelcarrobbio.it – Fax 02 8 05 33 34
– www.hotelcarrobbio.it
closed 22 December-6 January and August   **F2**
56 rm ☲ – ♦180 € ♦♦256/436 €
♦ Business ♦ Classic ♦
Central, but in a secluded location, this good quality, if functional, hotel has recently been renovated. Well-appointed rooms with good furnishings.

 D'Este without rest   🎬 🖏 🖼 🕭 ⚒80 *VISA* 🞧 🞧 🞧
viale Bligny 23 ✉ *20136 –* 🅜 *Porta Romana – 𝒞 02 58 32 10 01*
– reception@hoteldestemilano.it – Fax 02 58 32 11 36
– www.hoteldestemilano.it   **G3**
79 rm ☲ – ♦120/150 € ♦♦180/220 €
♦ Business ♦ Functional ♦
A well-lit, 1980s-style lobby and spacious public areas in this hotel; rooms decorated in a variety of styles, but all are equally comfortable and quiet.

 Crivi's without rest   🎬 🖼 🕭 ⚒120 🚗 *VISA* 🞧 🞧 🞧
corso Porta Vigentina 46 ✉ *20122 –* 🅜 *Crocetta*
– 𝒞 02 58 28 91 – crivis@tin.it – Fax 02 58 31 81 82
– www.crivis.com
closed August and Christmas   **G3**
83 rm ☲ – ♦121/170 € ♦♦178/240 € – 3 suites
♦ Business ♦ Functional ♦
Centrally located and near the metro station, an agreeable hotel with pleasant public areas; modern furnishings in the rooms, which are reasonably spacious and comfortable.

 Liberty without rest   🎬 🖏 🖼 *VISA* 🞧 🞧 🞧
viale Bligny 56 ✉ *20136 –* 🅜 *Porta Romana – 𝒞 02 58 31 85 62*
– reserve@hotelliberty-milano.com – Fax 02 58 31 90 61
– www.hotelliberty-milano.com
closed 24 July-20 August and Christmas   **G3**
55 rm ☲ – ♦70/130 € ♦♦99/150 €
♦ Traditional ♦ Personalised ♦
The public areas of this elegant hotel, near the Bocconi University, are Art Nouveau in style with some antique furniture; many rooms with jacuzzi baths.

 UNA Hotel Mediterraneo   🎬 🖏 🖼 🕭 ⚒75 *VISA* 🞧 🞧 🞧
via Muratori 14 ✉ *20135 –* 🅜 *Porta Romana – 𝒞 02 55 00 71*
– una.mediterraneo@unahotel.it – Fax 02 5 50 07 22 17
– www.unahotels.it   **H3**
93 rm ☲ – ♦175/251 € ♦♦206/296 €
Rest (residents only) a la carte 34/53 €
♦ Business ♦ Functional ♦
In the Porta Romana district near the metro station, a completely refurbished hotel with a comfortable modern feel throughout; relaxing, soundproofed rooms.

 King without rest   🎬 🖼 🕭 *VISA* 🞧 🞧 🞧
Corso Magenta 19 ✉ *20123 –* 🅜 *Cadorna FNM – 𝒞 02 87 44 32*
– info@hotelkingmilano.com – Fax 02 89 01 07 98
– www.hotelkingmilano.com   **F2**
48 rm ☲ – ♦110/220 € ♦♦160/300 €
♦ Business ♦ Functional ♦
From the upper floors of this totally refurbished and opulently furnished hotel there are views of the Duomo and the Castello. The rooms are not large but are comfortable.

ITALY

XXXX **Savini**   🄰 ⇔12 𝖵𝖨𝖲𝖠 🄼🄲 🄰🄴 ⓪
Galleria Vittorio Emanuele II ⊠ 20121 – 🄼 *Duomo* – ℰ 02 72 00 34 33
– savini@thi.it – Fax 02 72 02 28 88
closed 6-27 August, 1-6 January and Sunday   **G2**
Rest (booking essential) a la carte 59/88 €
♦ Milanese ♦ Formal ♦
A traditional hotel in the prestigious setting of Milan's historic Galleria. Old-fashioned luxury typified by red velvet, chandeliers and gilt-framed mirrors.

XXXX **Cracco-Peck**   🄰 🕉 𝖵𝖨𝖲𝖠 🄼🄲 🄰🄴 ⓪
😀😀 *via Victor Hugo 4* ⊠ 20123 – 🄼 *Cordusio* – ℰ 02 87 67 67 74 – cracco-peck@peck.it
– Fax 02 86 10 40 – www.peck.it
closed 3 weeks in August, 22 December-10 January, Sunday and Saturday lunch.
Also Saturday dinner from 15 June-August   **F2**
Rest (booking essential) a la carte 80/118 € ▨
Spec. Tuorlo d'uovo marinato con fonduta leggera di parmigiano. Risotto con olio d'acciuga, limone e cacao. Vitello impanato alla milanese con pomodoro, fiori di zucca e zucchine.
♦ Inventive ♦ Fashionable ♦
A legendary name in Milanese cuisine and a famous chef; a winning combination for a new restaurant. Classic elegance, perfect service and excellent food.

XXXX **Il Teatro** – Hotel Four Seasons   🄰 🕉 ⇔14 𝖵𝖨𝖲𝖠 🄼🄲 🄰🄴 ⓪
via Gesù 68 ⊠ 20121 – 🄼 *Montenapoleone* – ℰ 02 77 08 14 35 – milano@
fourseasons.com – Fax 02 77 08 50 00 – www.fourseasons.com/milan
closed August, Christmas, 1-7 January, and Sunday   **G1**
Rest (booking essential) (dinner only) a la carte 71/96 €
♦ Contemporary ♦ Formal ♦
A very elegant and exclusive ambience in this restaurant among the stunning surroundings of the Four Seasons hotel. Creatively prepared cuisine.

XXX **Don Carlos** – Grand Hotel et de Milan   🄰 𝖵𝖨𝖲𝖠 🄼🄲 🄰🄴 ⓪
via Manzoni 29 ⊠ 20121 – 🄼 *Montenapoleone* – ℰ 02 72 31 46 40 – info@
ristorantedoncarlos.it – Fax 02 86 46 08 61 – www.ristorantedoncarlos.it
closed August   **G1**
Rest (booking essential) (dinner only) a la carte 63/102 €
♦ Regional ♦ Cosy ♦
An atmosphere of snug luxury with wooden panelling, red lamps, and a wealth of drawings and photos of the Verdi era; creative seasonal dishes of Piedmontese origin.

XXX **Conte Camillo** – Hotel Cavour   🄰 🕉 𝖵𝖨𝖲𝖠 🄼🄲 🄰🄴 ⓪
via Fatebenefratelli 21 (Galleria di piazza Cavour) ⊠ 20121
– 🄼 Turati – ℰ 02 6 57 05 16 – booking@hotelcavour.it – Fax 02 6 59 22 63
– www.hotelcavour.it
closed August, 24 December-6 January, Saturday and Sunday lunch   **G1**
Rest a la carte 32/43 €
♦ Contemporary ♦ Formal ♦
Good service in elegant surroundings, where the atmosphere is warm and welcoming; traditional cuisine with a modern twist and themed menus available.

XXX **Sadler**   🄰 ⇔16 𝖵𝖨𝖲𝖠 🄼🄲 🄰🄴 ⓪
😀😀 *via Ettore Troilo 14 [angolo via Conchetta (moving to via Ascanio Sforza 77)]*
⊠ 20136 – 🄼 *Romolo* – ℰ 02 58 10 44 51 – sadler@sadler.it
– Fax 02 58 11 23 43 – www.sadler.it
closed 8 August-2 September, 1-12 January and Sunday   *Plan I* **B3**
Rest (booking essential) (dinner only) a la carte 70/115 € ▨
Spec. Fogliette di tonno rosso e lattuga con salsa tonnata (spring-summer). Ravioli di stoccafisso, crema di topinambour e spuma di latte di stoccafisso (winter). Padellata di crostacei con passatina di broccoletti, patate cristallo e trevisana.
♦ Innovative ♦ Trendy ♦
Stylish in both design and cuisine, this elegant modern restaurant is a famous name among its Milanese peers; a carefully thought-out and creative menu.

ITALY

XXX **Antico Ristorante Boeucc**   AC ⌘ ⇔16/26 AE

piazza Belgioioso 2 ✉ 20121 – Ⓜ San Babila – ✆ 02 76 02 02 24
– Fax 02 79 61 73 – www.boeucc.com   **G1**
closed 13-17 April, August, 24 December-2 January, Saturday and Sunday lunch
Rest (booking essential) a la carte 51/67 €
♦ Milanese ♦ Formal ♦
In the stable block of the 18C Palazzo Belgioioso, an elegant and historic
establishment; the choice of Milan's elite for 300 years; traditional cuisine.

XX **Armani Nobu**   AC ⌘ ⇔30 VISA ⦿ AE ①

via Pisoni 1 ✉ 20121 – Ⓜ Montenapoleone – ✆ 02 62 31 26 45
– Fax 02 62 31 26 74
closed August, 25 December-7 January, Sunday and Monday lunch   **G1**
Rest (booking essential) a la carte 53/84 €
♦ Japanese ♦ Fashionable ♦
An exotic marriage of fashion with gastronomy: Japanese fusion cuisine with
South American influences, served in stylishly simple surroundings inspired by
Japanese design.

XX **Nabucco**   AC VISA ⦿ AE ①

via Fiori Chiari 10 ✉ 20121 – Ⓜ Lima – ✆ 02 86 06 63 – info@nabucco.it
– Fax 02 8 36 10 14 – www.nabucco.it   **F1**
Rest (booking essential) a la carte 46/66 €
♦ Milanese ♦ Friendly ♦
In one of the alleyways characteristic of the Brera district, this restaurant offers
some interesting and unusual dishes, both meat and fish; candlelit dining in the
evenings.

XX **L'Assassino**   AC VISA ⦿ AE

via Amedei 8 (angolo via Cornaggia) ✉ 20123 – Ⓜ Missori – ✆ 02 8 05 61 44
– lamberto@ristorantelassassino.it – Fax 02 86 46 73 74
– www.ristorantelassassino.it
closed 23 December-2 January and Monday   **G2**
Rest (booking essential) a la carte 33/64 €
♦ Seafood ♦ Friendly ♦
Located in the Palazzo Recalcati, this classic venue is always very popular. Traditional cuisine, both meat and fish; the fresh, home made pasta is especially good.

XX **Al Porto**   AC VISA ⦿ AE ①

piazzale Generale Cantore ✉ 20123 – Ⓜ Porta Genova – ✆ 02 89 40 74 25
– alportodimilano@acena.it – Fax 02 8 32 14 81
closed August, 24 December-3 January, Sunday and Monday lunch   **E3**
Rest (booking essential) a la carte 42/62 €
♦ Seafood ♦ Retro ♦
Located in the former 19C customs house at Porta Genova, this well-known
restaurant has a harbour-side atmosphere and serves only seafood.

XX **Osteria di Porta Cicca**   AC ⌘ VISA ⦿ AE ①

ripa di Porta Ticinese 51 ✉ 20143 – Ⓜ Porta Genova – ✆ 02 8 37 27 63
– osteriadiportacicca@hotmail.com – Fax 02 8 37 27 63
closed Saturday lunch and Sunday   **E3**
Rest (booking essential) a la carte 35/47 €
♦ Contemporary ♦ Cosy ♦
Opened in 1995, this smart and welcoming restaurant run by a young
management team gives a new spin to traditional cuisine.

XX **Tano Passami l'Olio**   AC ⌘ VISA ⦿ AE ①

via Vigevano 32/a ✉ 20144 – Ⓜ Porta Genova – ✆ 02 8 39 41 39
– info@tanopassamilolio.it – Fax 02 83 24 01 04 – www.tanopassamilolio.it
closed August, 24 December-6 January and Sunday   **E3**
Rest (booking essential) (dinner only) a la carte 60/86 €
♦ Inventive ♦ Cosy ♦
Soft lighting and a romantic atmosphere in this cosy restaurant, with an
imaginative menu of easily digestible meat and fish dishes cooked using extra
virgin olive oil.

ITALY

XX **Il Torchietto**   AC ✵ VISA ⬤⬤ AE ⓞ
via Ascanio Sforza 47 ⊠ 20136 – ⓜ Porta Genova – ℰ 02 8 37 29 10
– info@il.torchietto.com – Fax 02 8 37 20 00 – www.il.torchietto.com
closed August, 26 December-3 January, Saturday lunch and Monday   Plan I **B3**
Rest a la carte 31/49 €
♦ Regional ♦ Friendly ♦
Elegant and spacious trattoria on the Naviglio Pavese which has recently been
refurbished; the menu features seasonal dishes and regional (especially
Mantuan) specialities.

XX **Il Navigante**   AC P. VISA ⬤⬤ AE ⓞ
via Magolfa 14 ⊠ 20143 – ⓜ Porta Genova – ℰ 02 89 40 63 20
– info@navigante.it – Fax 02 89 42 08 97 – www.navigante.it
closed August, Sunday lunch and Monday   **F3**
Rest a la carte 40/66 €
♦ Seafood ♦ Friendly ♦
Close to the Naviglio, this restaurant features live music every night. Run by a
former ship's cook, it has an unusual underfloor aquarium and serves seafood.

XX **Le Buone Cose**   AC VISA
via San Martino 8 ⊠ 20122 – ⓜ Missori – ℰ 02 58 31 05 89 – Fax 02 58 31 05 89
closed August, Saturday lunch and Sunday   **G3**
Rest (booking essential) a la carte 28/59 €
♦ Seafood ♦ Cosy ♦
Small, elegant and welcoming, this family-run establishment has many regular
customers; it serves flavoursome seafood cooked in traditional style.

XX **Alla Collina Pistoiese**   AC VISA ⬤⬤ AE ⓞ
via Amedei 1 ⊠ 20123 – ⓜ Missori – ℰ 02 87 72 48 – Fax 02 87 72 48
closed Easter, 10 to 20 August, 24 December-2 January, Friday and Saturday
lunch   **F2**
Rest a la carte 34/52 €
♦ Tuscany ♦ Friendly ♦
The spirit of old Milan in a historic setting, run by the same family since 1938; the
menu covers all aspects of Italian cuisine but specialises in Tuscan and Milanese
dishes.

XX **Isola dei Sapori**   AC ✵ ⇔16 VISA ⬤⬤ AE
via Anfossi 10 ⊠ 20135 – ⓜ Porta Romana – ℰ 02 54 10 07 08
– Fax 02 54 10 07 08
closed August, 23 December-3 January, Sunday and Monday lunch   Plan I **D2**
Rest (booking essential for dinner) a la carte 31/43 €
♦ Sardinian ♦ Friendly ♦
An innovative seafood restaurant run by three young Sardinians in a
modern-style setting; generous portions with the emphasis on quality.

XX **Emilia e Carlo**   AC ⇔20 VISA ⬤⬤ AE ⓞ
via Sacchi 8 ⊠ 20121 – ⓜ Cairoli – ℰ 02 87 59 48 – andreagalli.chef@tin.it
– Fax 02 86 21 00 – www.andreagalli.com
closed August, Christmas, Saturday lunch and Sunday   **F1**
Rest a la carte 42/55 €
♦ Innovative ♦ Formal ♦
This Tuscan trattoria, occupying an early 19th-century building, was established
in 1966 but has kept up with the times. The cuisine is contemporary in style; good
wine list.

X **La Felicità**   & AC ✵ VISA ⬤⬤ AE ⓞ
via Rovello 3 ⊠ 20121 – ⓜ Cordusio – ℰ 02 86 52 35 – fangleivalerio@
hotmail.com – Fax 02 86 52 35   **F1**
Rest 20 €/25 € and a la carte 19/27 €
♦ Chinese (Canton) ♦ Family ♦
Cantonese cuisine together with Vietnamese, Thai and Korean dishes in this
smart oriental restaurant; the mezzanine floor offers the cosiest and most
romantic ambience.

La Tavernetta-da Elio
AC ♦12 VISA ⓤ AE

via Fatebenefratelli 30 ⊠ 20121 – Ⓜ Montenapoleone
– ℰ 02 65 34 41 – ristorante@tavernetta.it – Fax 02 6 59 76 10
– www.tavernetta.it
closed August, 24 December-2 January, Saturday lunch, Sunday and Bank
Holidays   **G1**
Rest a la carte 32/44 €
♦ Regional ♦ Family ♦
Under the same management for over forty years, this simple, friendly and lively restaurant has a strong local following; classic dishes and Tuscan specialities.

Hostaria Borromei
☆ ❀ ♦20 VISA ⓤ AE ①

via Borromei 4 ⊠ 20123 – Ⓜ Cordusio – ℰ 02 86 45 37 60
– Fax 02 86 45 21 78
closed 8 August-1 September, 24 December-7 January, Saturday lunch and
Sunday   **F2**
Rest (booking essential) a la carte 34/49 €
♦ Mantuan/Regional ♦ Family ♦
Delightful summer dining in the courtyard of a historic building in the city centre; seasonal Lombard cuisine with an emphasis on the Mantova region.

Trattoria Torre di Pisa
AC ♦12/28 VISA ⓤ AE ①

via Fiori Chiari 21/5 ⊠ 20121 – Ⓜ Lanza – ℰ 02 87 48 77 – Fax 02 80 44 83
– www.trattoriatorredipisa.it
closed 3 weeks August, Saturday lunch and Sunday   **F1**
Rest a la carte 37/43 €
♦ Tuscany ♦ Family ♦
A family-run Tuscan trattoria in the heart of the historic Brera district. The flavours of Dante country at affordable prices.

Masuelli San Marco
AC ♦14/16 VISA ⓤ AE ①

viale Umbria 80 ⊠ 20135 – Ⓜ Lodi T.I.B.B. – ℰ 02 55 18 41 38
– masuelli.trattoria@tin.it – Fax 02 54 12 45 12
– www.masuelli-trattoria.com
closed 3 weeks in August, 25 December-6 January,
Sunday and Monday lunch   *Plan I* **D3**
Rest (booking essential for dinner) a la carte 31/41 €
♦ Milanese ♦ Friendly ♦
Rustic but elegant atmosphere in this traditional trattoria, in the same hands since 1921; cuisine solidly anchored in the Lombard-Piedmontese tradition.

Trattoria la Piola
AC VISA ⓤ AE

via Perugino 18 ⊠ 20135 – Ⓜ Lodi T.I.B.B. – ℰ 02 55 19 59 45 – info@lapiola.it
– Fax 02 55 19 59 45 – www.lapiola.it
closed Easter, August, 24 December-2 January,
Saturday lunch and Sunday   *Plan I* **D2**
Rest a la carte 35/66 €
♦ Seafood ♦ Rustic ♦
The great strength of this simple establishment is the freshness of its ingredients; its appealing seafood menu includes many raw fish specialities.

Dongiò
AC VISA ⓤ AE ①

via Corio 3 ⊠ 20135 – Ⓜ Porta Romana – ℰ 02 5 51 13 72
– Fax 02 5 51 03 71
closed August, Saturday lunch and Sunday   **H3**
Rest (booking essential) a la carte 23/35 €
♦ Regional ♦ Family ♦
One of the last authentic trattorias, unfussy and family-run; the specialities are fresh pasta, meat dishes and Calabrian cuisine.

ITALY

CENTRAL STATION *(Stazione Centrale, corso Buenos Aires, via Vittor Pisani, piazza della Repubblica, Centro Direzionale via della Moscova, via Solferino, via Melchiorre Gioia)* *Plan III*

Principe di Savoia   🕲 ⅃ᴤ 🏠 🖂 🎧 🕭 🖭 📞 🏊700 VISA ⵙ AE ⑤

piazza della Repubblica 17 ⊠ *20124 –* Ⓜ *Repubblica – 𝒞 02 6 23 01*
– principe@hotelprincipedisavoia.com – Fax 02 6 59 58 38
– www.hotelprincipedisavoia.com   **M2**
341 rm – ♦580/840 € ♦♦770/1030 €, ⌷ 45 € – 63 suites
Rest see *Galleria* below
♦ Palace ♦ Grand Luxury ♦ Stylish ♦
Opulence on a grand scale throughout this showcase hotel, with its fine furnishings and unparalleled attention to tasteful detail; regal suites with own pool.

The Westin Palace   ⅃ᴤ ᴑ rm 🎧 🕭rest 📞 🏊250 🖀 VISA ⵙ ⑤

piazza della Repubblica 20 ⊠ *20124 –* Ⓜ *Repubblica – 𝒞 0 26 33 61*
– palacemilan@westin.com – Fax 02 65 44 85 – www.westin.com   **M2**
232 rm – ♦205/512 € ♦♦326/847 €, ⌷ 35 € – 7 suites
Rest *Casanova Grill* (booking essential) (dinner only in August) a la carte 83/112 € 🏵
♦ Grand Luxury ♦ Stylish ♦
Modern skyscraper with sumptuous interior of brocades, gilding, panelling and fine details; all the grandeur of a hotel of the highest quality. Well-spaced tables, comfortable seating and soft tones make for a pampered ambience in the restaurant.

Excelsior Gallia   🏠 🎧 🕭 🏊500 VISA ⵙ AE ⑤

piazza Duca d'Aosta 9 ⊠ *20124 –* Ⓜ *Centrale FS – 𝒞 02 6 78 51 – sales@
excelsiorgallia.it – Fax 02 66 71 32 39 – www.lemeridien-excelsiorgallia.com*
237 rm – ♦445 € ♦♦454 €, ⌷ 33 € – 13 suites   **M1**
Rest 39 €
♦ Palace ♦ Classic ♦
Next to the railway station, this giant of the Milanese hotel scene has been a byword for discreet hospitality, uncompromising luxury, and a prestigious clientele since opening in 1932. The sophisticated restaurant is located on the top floor.

Starhotel Ritz   🎧 🕭 🖭 📞 🏊180 VISA ⵙ AE ⑤

via Spallanzani 40 ⊠ *20129 –* Ⓜ *Lima – 𝒞 02 20 55 – ritz.mi@starhotels.it*
– Fax 02 29 51 86 79 – www.starhotels.com   *Plan I* **C2**
195 rm ⌷ – ♦265/500 € ♦♦340/500 € – 6 suites
Rest a la carte 51/87 €
♦ Chain hotel ♦ Functional ♦
Central but quiet, this modern hotel has been refurbished and offers high levels of comfort and attention to detail throughout.

Michelangelo   🕭 🎧 🕭rest 🖭 🏊500 🖀 VISA ⵙ AE ⑤

via Scarlatti 33 (angolo piazza Luigi di Savoia) ⊠ *20124 –* Ⓜ *Centrale FS – 𝒞 02
6 75 51 – michelangelo@milanhotel.it – Fax 02 6 69 42 32 – www.milanhotel.it*
301 rm ⌷ – ♦156/232 € ♦♦183/272 € – 4 suites   *Plan I* **C1**
Rest a la carte 42/54 €
♦ Business ♦ Functional ♦
An unprepossessing façade to a hotel with spacious rooms of a sober elegance offering every modern convenience; excellent well-equipped conference centre. A sophisticated ambience to the dining room.

Jolly Hotel Touring   🎧 🕭 🖭 📞 🏊120 VISA ⵙ AE ⑤

via Tarchetti 2 ⊠ *20121 –* Ⓜ *Repubblica – 𝒞 02 6 33 51 – milano-touring@
jollyhotels.com – Fax 02 6 59 22 09 – www.jollyhotels.com*   **M2**
283 rm ⌷ – ♦180/260 € ♦♦210/310 € – 6 suites
Rest *Amadeus, 𝒞 02 63 35* – a la carte 38/50 €
♦ Chain hotel ♦ Functional ♦
Between Piazza della Repubblica and the Via Palestro gardens, this quality hotel is well suited to conferences; fine rooms, most of which have been recently refurbished. A stylish yet cosy atmosphere to the restaurant, with round tables and fitted carpets.

Sheraton Diana Majestic

🛜 ⅃ぉ 🖅 ％rest 🖭 📞

viale Piave 42 ✉ *20129 –* Ⓜ *Venezia*   ⅃ἀ150 🟦 🟠 🔲 ⑩

– 🕿 *02 2 05 81 – sheraton.diana.majestic@starwood.com – Fax 02 20 58 20 58*

– www.sheraton.com/dianamajestic

closed August   *Plan II* **H1**

107 rm *–* ♛365 € ♛♛465 €, ⚌ 33 € – 4 suites

Rest *Il Milanese Curioso,* 🕿 *02 20 58 20 34* – a la carte 50/66 €

♦ Chain hotel ♦ Palace ♦ Historic ♦

An early 20C feel and all modern comforts combine in this historic city-centre hotel; fine shaded garden with a well-frequented fashionable bar. The elegant restaurant offers outdoor dining in the summer.

Grand Hotel Verdi

க் 🕮 ％rest 🖭 📞 ⅃ἀ25 🍃 🟦 🟠 🔲 ⑩

via Melchiorre Gioia 6 ✉ *20124 –* Ⓜ *Gioia –* 🕿 *02 6 23 71 – reservation.ver@framon-hotels.it – Fax 02 6 23 70 50 – www.framon.hotels.com*

closed 4-22 August   **L1**

96 rm ⚌ *–* ♛180/321 € ♛♛211/399 € – 3 suites

Rest a la carte 35/49 €

♦ Business ♦ Modern ♦

Deep red predominates in the modern interior, which also evokes the decoration of La Scala opera house. Spacious rooms and good quality fittings. Cuisine of high calibre in the elegant restaurant, where large windows admit plenty of light.

Atahotel Executive without rest

க் 🕮 ↳ ％ 🖭 📞

viale Luigi Sturzo 45 ✉ *20154*   ⅃ἀ800 🟦 🟠 🔲 ⑩

– Ⓜ *Porta Garibaldi –* 🕿 *02 6 29 41 – prenotazioni@hotel-executive.com*

– Fax 02 29 01 02 38 – www.atahotels.it   **L1**

414 rm ⚌ *–* ♛196 € ♛♛246 € – 6 suites

♦ Chain hotel ♦ Classic ♦

Opposite the Garibaldi railway station, this large, recently renovated hotel has well-equipped conference facilities (18 meeting rooms); pleasant well-lit rooms.

Holiday Inn Milan Garibaldi Station

⅃ぉ க்rm 🕮 ％ 🖭 📞

via Farini (angolo via Ugo Bassi)   ⅃ἀ50 🍃 🟦 🟠 🔲 ⑩

✉ *20154 –* Ⓜ *Porta Garibaldi –* 🕿 *02 6 07 68 01 – reservations@hmilangaribaldi.com – Fax 02 6 88 07 64 – www.holiday-inn.com*   **K1**

131 rm ⚌ *–* ♛99 € ♛♛380 €

Rest 11 € (lunch)/35 €

♦ Chain hotel ♦ Design ♦

Extensive restoration has created a light and welcoming hotel where minimalist design prevails. Attractive breakfast room with glass roof, and small restaurant serving fusion cuisine.

Jolly Hotel Machiavelli

க் 🕮 🖭 📞 ⅃ἀ70 🟦 🟠 🔲 ⑩

via Lazzaretto 5 ✉ *20124 –* Ⓜ *Repubblica –* 🕿 *02 63 11 41 – machiavelli@jollyhotels.com – Fax 02 6 59 98 00 – www.jollyhotels.com*   **M2**

103 rm *–* ♛185/265 € ♛♛215/315 €, ⚌ 18 €

Rest *Caffè Niccolò,* 🕿 *02 63 11 49 21* – a la carte 29/48 €

♦ Chain hotel ♦ Modern ♦

An airy and harmonious design taking in all the public areas of this modern hotel lends it a contemporary and comfortable style. The rooms are attractively furnished. Smart bistro-style restaurant which also has a wine bar.

Doria Grand Hotel

க் 🕮 🖭 📞 ⅃ἀ120 🟦 🟠 🔲 ⑩

viale Andrea Doria 22 ✉ *20124 –* Ⓜ *Caiazzo –* 🕿 *02 67 41 14 11*

– info.doriagrandhotel@adihotels.com – Fax 02 6 69 66 69

– www.adihotels.com   *Plan I* **C1**

122 rm ⚌ *–* ♛163/310 € ♛♛183/360 € – 2 suites

Rest *(closed 24 December-6 January and 18 July-21 August)* a la carte 43/52 €

♦ Business ♦ Personalised ♦

A caring management at this comfortable new hotel; public areas decorated in an early-20C style, while a warmer, softer look is used in the rooms. Pale wood panelling and mirrors in the stylish restaurant.

ITALY

Manin
🛋 📺 🍴rest 📶 📞 🏊100 *VISA* 💳 🏧 ⓸

via Manin 7 ✉ 20121 – Ⓜ *Turati – ℰ 02 6 59 65 11*
– info@hotelmanin.it – Fax 02 6 55 21 60
– www.hotelmanin.it
closed 4-27 August   **M2**
118 rm ☕ – ♦118/215 € ♦♦156/295 €
Rest *Il Bettolino (closed Saturday)* a la carte 32/44 €
♦ Business ♦ Classic ♦
A garden complete with plane trees is an unexpected pleasure at this hotel, soon to celebrate its centenary and recently refurbished; stylish, well-appointed rooms. A smart yet cosy atmosphere in the excellent restaurant.

Starhotel Anderson
🕭rm 📺 🍴 📶 📞 🏊50 *VISA* 💳 🏧 ⓸

piazza Luigi di Savoia 20 ✉ 20124 – Ⓜ *Centrale FS – ℰ 02 6 69 01 41*
– anderson.mi@starhotels.it – Fax 02 6 69 03 31
– www.starhotels.com   *Plan I* **C1**
106 rm ☕ – ♦♦320/499 €
Rest a la carte 33/43 €
♦ Chain hotel ♦ Traditional ♦ Classic ♦
Modern design is a feature of this elegant but simple hotel, with public areas decorated in dark colours; functional, wood-floored rooms, also suited to single travellers.

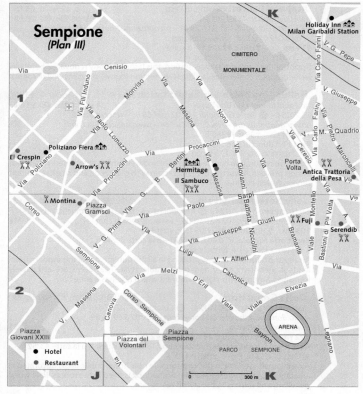

🏨 **Sanpi** without rest   🛴 🚗 🏧 🍸 📺 📞 🏊30 *VISA* 🌐 AE ①

via Lazzaro Palazzi 18 ⊠ 20124 – Ⓜ Venezia – 𝒞 02 29 51 33 41
– info@hotelsanpimilano.it – Fax 02 29 40 24 51
– www.hotelsanpimilano.it
closed 9-25 August and 24 December-2 January   **M2**
79 rm ⌑ – ♦95/295 € ♦♦119/395 €
♦ Business ♦ Classic ♦

Attention to detail is evident in the decoration of the well-lit public areas of this pleasant modern hotel, which overlook a charming garden; rooms decorated in pastel shades.

🏨 **Auriga** without rest   🏧 🛁 🍸 📺 📞 🏊25 *VISA* 🌐 AE ①

via Pirelli 7 ⊠ 20124 – Ⓜ Centrale F.S. – 𝒞 02 66 98 58 51
– auriga@auriga-milano.com
– Fax 02 66 98 06 98
– www.auriga-milano.com
closed 5-28 August and 23 December-1 January   **M1**
52 rm ⌑ – ♦110/210 € ♦♦170/270 €
♦ Business ♦ Personalised ♦

A dramatic mixture of colours and styles in this hotel, from its striking façade to its extravagant public areas and more classically styled bedrooms.

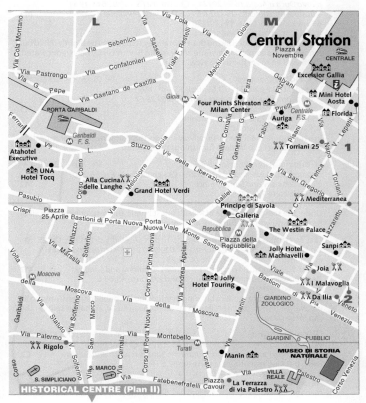

ITALY

UNA Hotel Tocq
🔲 ⚙ 📺 📞 🛗110 *VISA* 🔷 AE ⑩

via A. de Tocqueville 7/D ✉ *20154 –* Ⓜ *Porta Garibaldi –* ☎ *02 6 20 71*
– una.tocq@unahotels.it – Fax 02 6 57 07 80 – www.unahotels.it   **L1**
122 rm ☲ – ♦228/329 € ♦♦268/387 € – 1 suite
Rest a la carte 35/46 €
♦ Chain hotel ♦ Business ♦ Design ♦
Sophisticated design and modern technology are the central themes of
this minimalist-style hotel with a strong contemporary feel. The main area
of the restaurant is brightly decorated with a parquet floor in natural Danish
oak.

Four Points Sheraton Milan Center
🛴 ㅊ 🔲 ⚙rest 📺 📞

via Cardano 1 ✉ *20124 –* Ⓜ *Centrale FS*   🛗180 *VISA* 🔷 AE ⑩
– ☎ *02 66 74 61 – bookin@fourpointsmilano.it – Fax 02 6 70 30 24*
– www.fourpointsmilano.it   **M1**
254 rm ☲ – ♦107/293 € ♦♦117/353 €
Rest 41 € b.i.
♦ Chain hotel ♦ Business ♦ Modern ♦
Inside this modern building is an elegantly decorated interior with restful public
areas; good comfortable rooms, all recently refurbished. Large windows give
plenty of light in the tastefully decorated dining room.

Mini Hotel Aosta without rest
🔲 📺 📞 *VISA* 🔷 AE ⑩

piazza Duca d'Aosta 16 ✉ *20124 –* Ⓜ *Centrale FS –* ☎ *02 6 69 19 51*
– aosta@minihotel.it – Fax 02 6 69 62 15 – www.minihotel.it   **M1**
63 rm ☲ – ♦90/120 € ♦♦130/170 €
♦ Traditional ♦ Classic ♦
The interior of this hotel facing the main railway station may be slightly dated but
is nonetheless comfortable; some of the rooms have recently been redecorated;
the breakfast room has a fine view.

Florida without rest
🔲 📺 📞 *VISA* 🔷 AE ⑩

via Lepetit 33 ✉ *20124 –* Ⓜ *Centrale FS –* ☎ *02 6 70 59 21*
– info@hotelfloridamilan.com – Fax 02 6 69 28 67
– www.hotelfloridamilan.com   **M1**
55 rm ☲ – ♦125 € ♦♦190 € – 1 suite
♦ Family ♦ Classic ♦
In a quiet street near the main railway station, this comfortable hotel appeals to
business travellers. Modern furnishings throughout.

XXX Galleria – Hotel Principe di Savoia
🔲 ⚙ *VISA* 🔷 AE ⑩

piazza della Repubblica 17 ✉ *20124 –* Ⓜ *Repubblica –* ☎ *02 6 23 01*
closed Saturday and Sunday lunch   **M2**
Rest a la carte 77/100 €
♦ International ♦ Formal ♦
Under the same roof as one of Milan's finest hotels, this restaurant has an air of
regal luxury, with fine furniture and antiques.

XXX La Terrazza di via Palestro
← 🏡 🔲 ⚙ ⇔200 *VISA* 🔷 AE ⑩

via Palestro 2 ✉ *20121 –* Ⓜ *Turati –* ☎ *02 76 00 21 86 – terrazzapalestro@*
esperiaristorazione.it – Fax 02 76 00 33 28
closed 8-28 August, 24 December-8 January, Saturday and Sunday   **M2**
Rest (booking essential) 27 € (lunch) and a la carte 45/65 €
♦ Contemporary ♦ Formal ♦
On the top floor of a modern building overlooking the public gardens. Among its
innovative dishes, do not miss the Mediterranean sushi, an Italian spin on the
Japanese classic.

XXX Piccolo Sogno
ㅊ 🔲 ⚙ ⇔15/20 *VISA* 🔷 AE ⑩

via Stoppani 5 angolo via Zambelletti ✉ *20129 –* Ⓜ *Venezia –* ☎ *02 20 24 12 10*
closed 20 days in August, 1 to 10 January, Saturday lunch and Sunday   *Plan I* **C2**
Rest (booking essential) a la carte 46/67 € 🌿
♦ Contemporary ♦ Formal ♦
An unfussy, well-presented restaurant under friendly and competent family
management; traditional meat and fish dishes, and a well-stocked wine cellar.

XX **Casa Fontana-23 Risotti**   ☒ ☒ VISA ⬤❸ 〓 ⓪
piazza Carbonari 5 ☒ 20125 – ⓜ Sondrio – ℰ 02 6 70 47 10
– trattoria@23risotti.it – Fax 02 66 80 04 65 – www.23risotti.it
closed Easter, August, Christmas, 1-6 January, Monday, Saturday lunch and
Saturday dinner-Sunday in July   *Plan I* **C1**
Rest (booking essential) a la carte 30/43 €
◆ Milanese ◆ Cosy ◆
It is worth seeking out this small friendly restaurant, slightly away from the city
centre; be prepared for the ritual 25-minute wait while the chef prepares one of
his trademark risottos.

XX **Alla Cucina delle Langhe**   ☒ ☒ ⬭25 VISA ⬤❸ 〓 ⓪
corso Como 6 ☒ 20154 – ⓜ Porta Garibaldi – ℰ 02 6 55 42 79
– Fax 02 29 00 68 59
closed August, Saturday in July and Sunday   **L1**
Rest a la carte 38/52 €
◆ Regional ◆ Friendly ◆
Attractive traditional-style trattoria, whose local atmosphere is well suited to the
Lombard and Piedmontese specialities on offer; a wide range of salads is also
available.

XX **Rigolo**   ☒ ☒ ☒ ⬭23 VISA ⬤❸ 〓 ⓪
largo Treves ang. via Solferino 11 ☒ 20121 – ⓜ Moscova – ℰ 02 80 45 89
– ristorante.rigolo@tiscalinet.it – Fax 02 86 46 32 20 – www.rigolo.it
closed August and Monday   **L2**
Rest a la carte 32/44 €
◆ Tuscany ◆ Retro ◆
Run by the same family for over 40 years, this recently refurbished restaurant in
a fashionable part of the city centre has many regular customers; it serves both
meat and fish dishes.

XX **Mediterranea**   ☒ VISA ⬤❸ 〓 ⓪
piazza Cincinnato 4 ☒ 20124 – ⓜ Venezia – ℰ 02 29 52 20 76
– ristmediterranea@fastwebnet.it – Fax 02 20 11 56
– www.ristorantemediterranea.it
closed 5-25 August, 27 December-7 January, Sunday and Monday lunch
Rest a la carte 38/66 € ⒝   **M1-2**
◆ Seafood ◆ Formal ◆
A maritime feel here thanks to an illuminated blue glass canopy running
the length of the restaurant and tanks of crustaceans; simple flavoursome
seafood.

XX   **Joia** (Leemann)   ☒ ⬭16/20 VISA ⬤❸ 〓 ⓪
❀   *via Panfilo Castaldi 18 ☒ 20124 – ⓜ Repubblica – ℰ 02 29 52 21 24*
– joia@joia.it – Fax 02 2 04 92 44 – www.joia.it
closed 4-25 August, Saturday lunch and Sunday   **M2**
Rest (booking essential) a la carte 51/71 € ⒝
Spec. Sfera croccante di zucchine, carciofi e piselli, salsa di zafferano e brodo di
funghi. Risotto con zucchine e finferli, tuorlo d'uovo. Carciofi, scorzanera dolce e
altre verdure con la loro salsa.
◆ Inventive ◆ Minimalist ◆
Dark wood floors and skylights in the main dining area; creative vegetarian-
inspired cuisine and some excellent fish dishes, which look and taste great.

XX **Torriani 25**   ☒ ☒ ⬭16 VISA ⬤❸ 〓 ⓪
via Napo Torriani 25 ☒ 20124 – ⓜ Centrale FS – ℰ 02 67 07 81 83
– Fax 02 67 47 95 48 – www.torriani25.it
closed 12-20 August, Saturday lunch and Sunday   **M1**
Rest (booking essential) a la carte 39/52 €
◆ Seafood ◆ Design ◆
A spacious modern restaurant with an open kitchen and a buffet just inside,
to whet the appetite of arriving diners in search of the elaborate cuisine
on offer.

ITALY

XX **I Malavoglia** AC ❄ VISA ⓶ AE ①
via Lecco 4 ⊠ 20124 – Ⓜ Venezia – ℰ 02 29 53 13 87 – www.imalavoglia.com
closed Easter, 1 May, August, 24 December-4 January and Sunday **M2**
Rest (booking essential) (dinner only) a la carte 39/54 €
♦ Sicilian ♦ Family ♦
Run by the same husband and wife team since 1973 (he is the cook), this elegant, tastefully decorated restaurant specialises in Sicilian dishes and seafood with a modern twist.

XX **Da Ilia** 🍴 AC ⟷30 VISA ⓶ AE ①
via Lecco 1 ⊠ 20124 – Ⓜ Repubblica – ℰ 02 29 52 18 95
– mail@ristorante-ilia.it – Fax 02 29 40 91 65 – www.ristorante-ilia.it
closed Easter, August, 26 December-5 January, Friday and Saturday lunch
Rest a la carte 34/52 € **M2**
♦ Tuscany ♦ Friendly ♦
An informal atmosphere to this family-run restaurant, serving classic dishes with a strong Milanese influence.

XX **Antica Trattoria della Pesa** ₺ AC ❄ VISA ⓶ AE ①
via Pasubio 10 ⊠ 20154 – Ⓜ Porta Garibaldi – ℰ 02 6 55 57 41 – Fax 02 29 01 51 57
closed Sunday **K1**
Rest a la carte 49/62 €
♦ Milanese ♦ Rustic ♦
A pleasantly dated ambience in this old Milanese trattoria so typical of bygone Italy, serving dishes native to the city and Lombardy. One room is devoted to Ho Chi Min.

XX **Serendib** AC VISA ⓶
via Pontida 2 ⊠ 20121 – Ⓜ Moscova – ℰ 02 6 59 21 39 – Fax 02 6 59 21 39
– www.serendib.it
closed 10-20 August **K2**
Rest (booking essential) (dinner only) 15 €/20 € and a la carte 20/25 €
♦ Indian ♦ Friendly ♦
Singhalese and Indian cuisine authentically prepared with décor to match in this pleasant restaurant, which bears the ancient name of Sri Lanka (meaning: to make happy).

XX **Fuji** AC ❄ VISA ⓶ ①
viale Montello 9 ⊠ 20154 – Ⓜ Moscova – ℰ 02 6 55 25 17
closed Easter, 1-23 August, 24 December-2 January and Sunday **K2**
Rest (booking essential) (dinner only) a la carte 40/60 €
♦ Japanese ♦ Minimalist ♦
A successful joint venture between an Italian and a Japanese; now approaching its tenth anniversary this no-frills Oriental restaurant also has a sushi bar.

X **Da Giannino-L'Angolo d'Abruzzo** AC VISA ⓶
😊 *via Pilo 20 ⊠ 20129 – Ⓜ Venezia – ℰ 02 29 40 65 26*
– Fax 02 29 40 65 26
closed August and Monday Plan I **D2**
Rest (booking essential for dinner) a la carte 25/32 €
♦ Regional ♦ Friendly ♦
This family-run restaurant, in the same hands for over 45 years, has a welcoming, light and airy ambience; authentic Abruzzo cuisine at modest prices.

X **La Cantina di Manuela** 🍴 AC VISA ⓶ AE
😊 *via Poerio 3 ⊠ 20129 – Ⓜ San Babila – ℰ 02 76 31 88 92 – cantina4@virgilio.it*
– Fax 02 76 31 29 71 – www.lacantinadimanuela.it
closed Sunday Plan I **C2**
Rest a la carte 27/38 € 🍷
♦ Regional ♦ Wine bar ♦
Quality ingredients and interesting choices in a relaxed setting; a varied and attractive menu, featuring pork products, cheeses and traditional dishes.

FIERA-SEMPIONE *(viale Certosa, San Siro, via Novara, corso Sampione, piazza Carlo Magno, via Monte Rosa, via Washington, viale Fulvio Testi, Niguarda, viale Fermi)* *Plan I* **ITALY**

Hermitage &rm 🔟 ⚙ 🖭 📞 🛎180 ⌂ VISA ⑩ 🅰🅴 ⑩
*via Messina 10 ⊠ 20154 – 🅜 Porta Garibaldi – ℰ 02 31 81 70 – hermitage.res@
monrifhotels.it – Fax 02 33 10 73 99 – www.monrifhotels.it*
closed August Plan III **K1**
119 rm � – 🛏273 € 🛏🛏320 € – 8 suites
Rest see *Il Sambuco* below
♦ Business ♦ Stylish ♦
Refinement and comfort are the key words at this hotel which combines a classically stylish interior with every modern convenience; popular with models and VIPs.

Melià Milano 🕍 🏠 & 🔟 🖭 📞 🛎500 VISA ⑩ 🅰🅴 ⑩
*via Masaccio 19 ⊠ 20149 – 🅜 Lotto – ℰ 02 4 44 06 – melia.milano@
solmelia.com – Fax 02 44 40 66 00 – www.solmelia.com* **A2**
288 rm – 🛏🛏145/475 €, � 29 € – 6 suites
Rest *Alacena (closed August)* a la carte 62/94 €
♦ Chain hotel ♦ Modern ♦
A prestigious modern hotel featuring marble, crystal chandeliers and antique tapestries in the lobby, and imposing but very comfortable rooms; excellent-quality Spanish cuisine in the smart "Alacena" restaurant.

Milan Marriott Hotel 🕍 🔟 4⁄rm ⚙ 🖭 📞 🛎1300 VISA ⑩ 🅰🅴 ⑩
*via Washington 66 ⊠ 20146 – 🅜 Wagner – ℰ 02 4 85 21 – milan@
marriothotels.com – Fax 02 4 81 89 25 – www.marriott.com* **A2**
322 rm – 🛏🛏155/450 €, � 26 € – 1 suite
Rest *La Brasserie de Milan*, ℰ 02 48 52 28 34 – a la carte 48/65 €
♦ Chain hotel ♦ Modern ♦
An unusual contrast between the modern façade and the classically elegant interiors in this hotel, which hosts many corporate events. Well-presented functional rooms. Traditional-style dining room with open kitchen.

Atahotel Fieramilano &rm 🔟 ⚙ 🖭 📞 🛎220 VISA ⑩ 🅰🅴 ⑩
*viale Boezio 20 ⊠ 20145 – ℰ 02 33 62 21 – prenotazioni@
grandhotelfieramilano.com – Fax 02 31 41 19 – www.atahotels.it*
closed August **B2**
236 rm � – 🛏145/275 € 🛏🛏185/348 € – 2 suites
Rest *Ambrosiano (dinner only)* a la carte 36/49 €
♦ Chain hotel ♦ Modern ♦
Opposite the Fiera, this recently refitted hotel has every modern convenience and a high level of comfort; in summer breakfast is served in the gazebo outside. Quiet, elegant dining room.

Enterprise Hotel 🕍 & 🔟 4⁄rm 🖭 📞 🛎350 VISA ⑩ 🅰🅴 ⑩
*corso Sempione 91 ⊠ 20154 – 🅜 Lotto – ℰ 02 31 81 81
– info@enterprisehotel.com – Fax 02 31 81 88 11
– www.enterprisehotel.com* **A1**
120 rm � – 🛏239/399 € 🛏🛏259/419 € – 2 suites
Rest *Sophia's* a la carte 50/65 €
♦ Business ♦ Design ♦
A marble and granite exterior, coupled with made-to-measure furnishings give a strong geometrical theme to this elegant hotel where the emphasis is on design and detail. An unusual yet pleasant ambience for lunch or dinner.

Capitol World Class 🕍 🔟 🖭 📞 🛎70 VISA ⑩ 🅰🅴 ⑩
*via Cimarosa 6 ⊠ 20144 – 🅜 Pagano – ℰ 02 43 85 91
– info@capitolmilano.com – Fax 02 4 69 47 24 – www.capitolmilano.com*
61 rm � – 🛏99/260 € 🛏🛏129/385 € – 5 suites **B2**
Rest *(residents only)* a la carte 48/66 €
♦ Business ♦ Personalised ♦
From the near-demolition of its predecessor has emerged this small elegant jewel of a hotel. The decorative detail is outstanding, in both the public areas and the very well-appointed bedrooms.

ITALY

Regency without rest   🏧 ⚄ 🖥 📞 ♨50 VISA 🅾 💳 ①
via Arimondi 12 ⊠ 20155 – ℰ 02 39 21 60 21 – regency@regency-milano.com
– Fax 02 39 21 77 34 – www.regency-milano.com
closed 5-25 August and 24 December-7 January   **A1**
71 rm ⌷ – †160/200 € ††200/300 €
♦ Traditional ♦ Personalised ♦
This late-19C aristocratic residence with its delightful courtyard is charming and
tastefully decorated throughout; it has a particularly pleasant lounge with
roaring fire.

Poliziano Fiera   🛗 🏧 🖥 📞 ♨90 🍽 VISA 🅾 💳 ①
via Poliziano 11 ⊠ 20154 – ℰ 02 3 19 19 11 – info.hotelpolizianofiera@
adihotels.com – Fax 02 3 19 19 31 – www.adihotels.com
closed 25 July-25 August and 18 December-7 January   *Plan III* **J1**
98 rm ⌷ – †137/293 € ††158/337 € – 2 suites
Rest (residents only) a la carte 25/36 €
♦ Business ♦ Modern ♦
This small, modern hotel has been totally refurbished; friendly and attentive
management; well-proportioned bedrooms pleasantly decorated in light
greens and pale yellows. This small, modern hotel has been totally refurbished;
friendly and attentive management; well-proportioned bedrooms pleasantly
decorated in light greens and pale yellows.

Rubens   ⅙ 🏧 ⚄rest 🖥 📞 ♨35 🅿 VISA 🅾 💳 ①
via Rubens 21 ⊠ 20148 – Ⓜ Gambara – ℰ 02 4 03 02
– rubens@antareshotels.com – Fax 02 48 19 31 14
– www.antareshotels.com
closed 4-20 August   **A2**
87 rm ⌷ – †140/225 € ††180/299 €
Rest (residents only)
♦ Business ♦ Personalised ♦
The walls of the public areas and bedrooms of this elegant, functional hotel
have been decorated in fresco by contemporary artists; attention to detail
evident throughout.

Accademia   🏧 ⚄rest 🖥 📞 ♨70 VISA 🅾 💳 ①
viale Certosa 68 ⊠ 20155 – Ⓜ Lotto – ℰ 02 39 21 11 22 – accademia@
antareshotels.com – Fax 02 33 10 38 78 – www.antareshotels.com   **A1**
67 rm ⌷ – †105/230 € ††150/299 €
Rest (residents only) 20 €/50 €
♦ Business ♦ Personalised ♦
Endowed with great character, this hotel mixes modernity with classic style
throughout its comfortable public areas and rooms, decorated with modern
trompe l'œil scenes.

Domenichino without rest   🏧 🖥 ♨60 🍽 VISA 🅾 💳 ①
via Domenichino 41 ⊠ 20149 – Ⓜ Amendola Fiera – ℰ 02 48 00 96 92 – hd@
hoteldomenichino.it – Fax 02 48 00 39 53 – www.hoteldomenichino.it
closed 4-21 August and 22 December-2 January   **A2**
77 rm ⌷ – †70/135 € ††90/195 € – 2 suites
♦ Business ♦ Functional ♦
On a tree-lined street close to the Trade Fair site, this elegant hotel offers good
facilities; the public areas are not spacious, but the bedrooms are comfortable
with modern furnishings.

Mirage   ⅙rm 🏧 ⚄rest 🖥 📞 ♨100 🍽 VISA 🅾 ①
viale Certosa 104/106 ⊠ 20156 – Ⓜ Lotto – ℰ 02 39 21 04 71 – mirage@
gruppomirage.it – Fax 02 39 21 05 89 – www.gruppomirage.it
closed 30 July-22 August   **A1**
86 rm ⌷ – †148/189 € ††208/249 €
Rest *(closed Friday and Saturday)* (residents only) a la carte 34/44 €
♦ Business ♦ Functional ♦
Out of town but not far from the Trade Fair site, ideal for the business traveller;
currently being extended, this hotel has modern public areas and comfortable
rooms.

ITALY

 Astoria without rest 🔟 ⅏ 📺 📞 🛁50 VISA ⚌ AE ①
viale Murillo 9 ⊠ 20149 – Ⓜ *Amendola Fiera – ℰ 02 40 09 00 95*
– info@astoriahotelmilano.com – Fax 02 40 07 46 42
– www.astoriahotelmilano.com   **A2**
69 rm ⊊ – ♦49/130 € ♦♦90/210 €
♦ Business ♦ Functional ♦
Situated on an avenue forming part of the city ring-road, this recently refitted
hotel is popular with tourists and business people alike; modern rooms with
excellent soundproofing.

 Mini Hotel Tiziano without rest 🔊 🔟 📺 📞 🅿 VISA ⚌ AE ①
via Tiziano 6 ⊠ 20145 – Ⓜ *Buonarroti – ℰ 02 4 69 90 35*
– tiziano@minihotel.it – Fax 02 4 81 21 53
– www.minihotel.it   **A-B2**
54 rm ⊊ – ♦115/140 € ♦♦165/190 €
♦ Inn ♦ Classic ♦
Near the Fiera but in a quiet location, this hotel has the advantage of its own
gardens to the rear; comfortable rooms.

 Des Etrangers without rest 🔟 📺 🛁80 VISA ⚌ AE ①
via Sirte 9 ⊠ 20146 – Ⓜ *Wagner – ℰ 02 48 95 53 25 – info@hde.it*
– Fax 02 48 95 53 25 – www.hoteldesetrangers.it   **A3**
96 rm ⊊ – ♦80/95 € ♦♦120/150 €
♦ Family ♦ Classic ♦
On a quiet street, this establishment has been enlarged and totally renovated;
practicality and comfort in evidence throughout. Convenient underground
garage.

 Antica Locanda Leonardo without rest 🚊 🔟 ⅏ 📺
corso Magenta 78 ⊠ 20123 – Ⓜ *Conciliazione* 📞 VISA ⚌ AE ①
– ℰ 02 48 01 41 97 – info@anticalocandaleonardo.com – Fax 02 48 01 90 12
– www.anticalocandaleonardo.com
closed 5-25 August and 31 December-6 January   *Plan II* **E2**
16 rm ⊊ – ♦95 € ♦♦205 €
♦ Inn ♦ Cosy ♦
A combination of genteel surroundings and warm welcome at this hotel, which
looks onto a small courtyard; close by is Leonardo's Last Supper.

XXX **IL luogo di Aimo e Nadia** (Moroni) 🔟 ⅏ VISA ⚌ AE ①
ⅇⅉ *via Montecuccoli 6 ⊠ 20147 –* Ⓜ *Primaticcio – ℰ 02 41 68 86*
– info@aimoenadia.com – Fax 02 48 30 20 05
– www.aimoenadia.com
closed 1-21 August, 1-10 January, Saturday lunch and Sunday   **A3**
Rest (booking essential) 33 € (lunch except Bank Holidays)
and a la carte 75/136 €
Spec. Zupetta di asparagi con buratta e agnoli di gallina (spring-summer).
Paccheri di Gragnano farciti di patate, porcini e parmigiano in guazzetto di
calamaretti (spring-autumn). Cioccolata con scorze di limoni e limoncello in
gelatina
♦ Contemporary ♦ Formal ♦
A leading light of the city's culinary scene, this restaurant, with an
impressive display of modern works of art, has cuisine memorable for its
creativity.

XXX **La Pobbia 1850** 🏠 ♿ 🔟 ⟷12/20 VISA ⚌ AE ①
via Gallarate 92 ⊠ 20151 – Ⓜ *Lampugnano – ℰ 02 38 00 66 41*
– lapobbia@tiscali.it – Fax 02 38 00 07 24 – www.lapobbia.com
closed August and Sunday   **A1**
Rest a la carte 35/45 €
♦ Milanese ♦ Formal ♦
Highly experienced management in this long-established restaurant (opened in
1920), with smart country-style ambience and al fresco dining in summer.
Lombard and international cuisine.

ITALY

XXX **Il Sambuco** – Hotel Hermitage　　　　🔲 🅿 VISA ⓒⓞ AE ⓞ
via Messina 10 ⊠ *20154 –* Ⓜ *Porta Garibaldi – ℰ 02 33 61 03 33*
– info@ilsambuco.it – Fax 02 33 61 18 50 – www.ilsambuco.it　　*Plan III* **K1**
closed Easter, 1-20 August, 25 December-3 January, Saturday lunch and Sunday
Rest a la carte 60/90 € ♨
♦ Seafood ♦ Trendy ♦
Like the hotel in which it is located, this restaurant is elegant and has high service standards; renowned for its seafood cuisine, limited to 'bolliti' (stew) on Mondays.

XX **Arrow's**　　　　　🏡 🔲 ⅀ ✧15/18 VISA AE ⓞ
via Mantegna 17/19 ⊠ *20154 –* Ⓜ *Porta Garibaldi – ℰ 02 34 15 33*
– Fax 02 33 10 64 96 – closed August, Sunday and Monday lunch　　*Plan III* **J1**
Rest (booking essential) a la carte 41/51 €
♦ Seafood ♦ Formal ♦
Packed at lunchtime, largely with business clients, but more friendly and personal during the evenings, this restaurant near Corso Sempione specialises in traditional seafood.

XX **El Crespin**　　　　🔲 ⅀ ✧20/30 ⓒⓞ AE ⓞ
via Castelvetro 18 ⊠ *20154 –* Ⓜ *Porta Garibaldi – ℰ 02 33 10 30 04*
– Fax 02 33 10 30 04
closed August, 26 December-7 January, Saturday lunch and Sunday　*Plan III* **J1**
Rest (booking essential) a la carte 34/43 €
♦ Seasonal cuisine ♦ Friendly ♦
Old photos decorate the entrance area of this tastefully presented restaurant, where the menu is dictated by the changing seasons.

XX **Innocenti Evasioni**　　　🏡 🚗 🔲 ✧14 VISA ⓒⓞ AE ⓞ
via privata della Bindellina ⊠ *20155 –* Ⓜ *Lotto – ℰ 02 33 00 18 82 – ristorante@*
innocentievasioni.com – Fax 02 33 00 18 82 – www.innocentievasioni.com
closed August, 3-9 January and Sunday　　　　　**A1**
Rest (booking essential) (dinner only) a la carte 37/45 €
♦ Contemporary ♦ Cosy ♦
An unpromising exterior in a narrow suburban street hides a pleasant modern restaurant, with soft lighting and large windows overlooking a small garden; inspired creative cuisine.

XX **Al Molo 13**　　　　　🔲 VISA ⓒⓞ AE ⓞ
via Rubens 13 ⊠ *20148 –* Ⓜ *De Angeli – ℰ 02 4 04 27 43 – info@molo13.it*
– Fax 02 40 07 26 16 – closed August, 31 December-9 January, Sunday and
Monday lunch – **Rest** a la carte 47/83 €　　　　**A2**
♦ Seafood ♦ Rustic ♦
This welcoming modern establishment's best advertisement is the fresh fish buffet that diners pass on the way in; seafood and Sardinian specialities.

XX **Da Stefano il Marchigiano**　　🔲 ⅀ VISA ⓒⓞ AE ⓞ
via Arimondi 1 (angolo via Plana) ⊠ *20155 –* Ⓜ *Lotto – ℰ 02 33 00 18 63*　**A1**
closed 3 weeks in August, Friday dinner and Saturday – **Rest** a la carte 35/50 €
♦ Regional ♦ Friendly ♦
For over twenty years this classic restaurant has been a favourite with lovers of traditional cuisine; meat and seafood dishes prepared using quality ingredients.

X **Trattoria Montina**　　　　🔲 VISA ⓒⓞ AE ⓞ
via Procaccini 54 ⊠ *20154 –* Ⓜ *Porta Garibaldi – ℰ 02 3 49 04 98*　*Plan III* **J2**
closed 8 August-1 September, 30 December-9 January, Sunday and Monday lunch
Rest a la carte 17/35 €
♦ Seasonal cuisine ♦ Friendly ♦
Pleasant bistro atmosphere with closely spaced tables and soft lighting in this restaurant run by twin brothers; seasonal cuisine featuring Italian and Milanese dishes.

X **Pace**　　　　　　🔲 ⅀ VISA ⓒⓞ AE ⓞ
☺ *via Washington 74* ⊠ *20146 –* Ⓜ *Wagner – ℰ 02 43 98 30 58 – Fax 02 46 85 67*
closed Easter, 1-24 August, 24 December-5 January, Saturday lunch and
Wednesday – **Rest** a la carte 26/36 €　　　　**A2-3**
♦ Seasonal cuisine ♦ Rustic ♦
This family-run trattoria, simple yet well presented, has been offering diners a warm welcome for over 30 years; traditional meat and fish dishes.

LUXEMBOURG
LËTZEBUERG

PROFILE

- **AREA:**
  2 586 km² (998 sq mi).

- **POPULATION:**
  468 600 inhabitants
  (est. 2005) nearly
  62% nationals,
  38% resident
  foreigners (mostly
  Belgian, French,
  German, Italian and
  Portuguese). Density =
  181 per km².

- **CAPITAL:**
  Luxembourg
  (conurbation
  125 000 inhabitants).

- **CURRENCY:**
  Euro (€); rate of
  exchange: € 1 =
  US$ 1.17 (Nov 2005).

- **GOVERNMENT:**
  Constitutional
  parliamentary
  monarchy (since 1868).
  Member of European
  Union since 1957 (one
  of the 6 founding
  countries).

- **LANGUAGES:**
  The official language

is Lëtzebuergesch, a
variant of German,
similar to the Frankish
dialect of the Moselle
valley; High German
is used for general
purposes and is the
first language for
teaching; French
is the literary and
administrative
language.

- **SPECIFIC PUBLIC
  HOLIDAYS:**
  Carnival (Late
  February-March);
  National Day (23 June);
  Luxembourg City
  Kermesse (early
  September, applies to
  the Luxembourg City
  only); St. Stephen's
  Day (26 December).

- **LOCAL TIME:**
  GMT + 1 hour in winter
  and GMT + 2 hours in
  summer.

- **CLIMATE:**
  Temperate continental
  with cold winters

Luxembourg

and mild summers
(Luxembourg: January:
1°C, July: 17°C).

- **INTERNATIONAL
  DIALLING CODE:**
  00 352 (from USA:
  011352; from Japan:
  001352) followed by
  the local number of 5
  or 6 or (exceptionally)
  8 figures. Online
  telephone directory:
  www.editus.lu

- **EMERGENCY NUMBERS:**
  Police : ☎ **113** ;
  Medical Assistance :
  ☎ **112**.

- **ELECTRICITY:**
  220 volts AC, 50Hz;
  2-pin round-shaped
  continental plugs.

FORMALITIES

Travellers from the European Union (EU), Switzerland, Iceland and the main countries of North and South America need a national identity card or passport (America: passport required) to visit the Grand Duchy of Luxembourg for less than three months (tourism or business purpose). For visitors from other countries a visa may be required, in addition to a passport, especially for those wishing to stay for longer than three months. We advise you to check with your embassy before travelling.

An international driving licence is not required, only the traveller's own national driving licence.

MAJOR NEWSPAPERS

The daily press in Luxembourg reflects the multilingual population and is printed in Lëtzebuergesch, French and German. In some papers more than one language is used. Of the 6 major daily newspapers 4 are mainly in German (*Luxemburger Wort* and *Tageblatt* being the most important) and 2 are in French (*La Voix, Le Quotidien*).

USEFUL PHRASES

ENGLISH	FRENCH
Yes	**Oui**
No	**Non**
Good morning	**Bonjour**
Goodbye	**Au revoir**
Thank you	**Merci**
Please	**S'il vous plaît**
Excuse me	**Excusez-moi**
I don't understand	**Je ne comprends pas**

HOTELS

◆ CATEGORIES

Accommodation ranges from luxurious 5-star international hotels, via smaller, family-run guesthouses and bed and breakfast establishments. The Benelux star rating is conferred on the application of the owner.

◆ PRICE RANGE

The price is per room. There is little difference between the price of a single and a double room.

Between April and October it is advisable to book in advance. From November to March prices may be slightly lower, some hotels offer special cheap rates and some may be closed. At the weekend out of season, chain hotels in the capital often offer reduced rates.

◆ TAX

Included in the room price.

◆ CHECKOUT TIME

Usually between 11am and noon.

◆ RESERVATIONS

By telephone or by the Internet using a credit card.

◆ TIPS FOR HANDLING LUGGAGE

At the discretion of the client (about €1 per suitcase).

◆ BREAKFAST

Breakfast is usually included in the room price, although this may not be so in smaller hotels. Most hotels offer a self service buffet between 7am and 10am but it is often possible to order a continental breakfast in the bedroom.

Reception	**Reception**
Single room	**Chambre simple**

Double room	**Chambre double**
Bed	**Lit**
Bathroom	**Salle de bains**
Shower	**Douche**

✦ RESTAURANTS

As well as the **traditional restaurants** there are **brasseries** which offer a main dish of the day, **bistros** and **cafés** which serve lighter meals. The **Winstub** is principally a wine bar which also serves food. In the commercial districts the **patisseries** serve breakfast as well as tea/coffee and pastries.

Breakfast	**Petit-déjeuner**	7-10am
Lunch	**Déjeuner**	12.30-2pm
Dinner	**Dîner**	7.30-10pm

***NB**: French speakers in Luxembourg usually say «déjeuner» for breakfast, «dîner» for the midday meal and «souper» for the evening meal.*

Restaurants in Luxembourg offer the choice of a menu (starter, main dish and dessert) or à la carte. Menus are usually printed in French and English and sometimes also in Lëtzebuergesch. A fixed-price menu (menu à prix fixe) is usually less expensive than the same number of dishes chosen à la carte.

With some fixed-price menus there is a food and wine suggestion, where the wine is served by the glass.

In some restaurants the lunchtime menu is shorter than the dinner menu or there may be two different menus: one for midday and one for the evening.

✦ RESERVATIONS

Reservations can be made by telephone, Internet or fax. To book a table in a well known restaurant (those with Michelin stars) it is best to phone several days or even weeks in advance. A credit card number or a phone number may be required as a guarantee.

✦ THE BILL

The bill (check) includes service charge and VAT. Tipping is optional but, if you are particularly pleased with the service, it is customary to round up the total to an appropriate figure – 10% in larger restaurants and the value of the small change elsewhere.

Drink or aperitif	**Apéritif**
Appetizer	**Mise en bouche**
Meal	**Repas**
Starter	**Entrée**
Main dish	**Plat principal**
Main dish of the day	**Plat du jour**
Dessert	**Dessert**
Water/ Sparkling water	**Eau/gazeuse**
Wine (red, white, rosé)	**Vin (rouge, blanc, rosé)**
Beer	**Bière**
Bread	**Pain**
Meat (medium, rare, blue)	**Viande (à point, saignant, bleu)**
Fish	**Poisson**
Salt/pepper	**Sel/poivre**

Cheese	**Fromage**
Vegetables	**Légumes**
Hot/cold	**Chaud/froid**
The bill (check) please	**L'addition s'il vous plaît**

LOCAL CUISINE

Luxembourg Grand Duchy's culinary traditions are similar to those of France, its regional specialities lend it a special distinction. Among the gastronomic specialities of the Grand Duchy are sucking pig in aspic, smoked and cured ham from the Ardennes, and other smoked meats. The national dish is **Judd mat Gaardebounen**, smoked neck of pork with broad beans, which makes a hearty meal in itself. Game and mushrooms from Ardennes are eaten in season. Freshwater fish is delicious fried (friture de la Moselle) or poached in Riesling. **Kachkéis** is a soft, cooked cheese. In September plum tart is eaten, and, in season, the little puff-pastry crowns known as Veianer Kränzercher.

◆ DRINK

Although beer is the most popular drink, Luxembourg produces its own dry white wines, from the vineyards which carpet the slopes of the Moselle Valley – the more expensive Auxerrois, the less expensive Rivaner and Elbling, and Pinot Blanc, Pinot Gris, Riesling and Traminer. There are also a few rosé and sparkling wines (crémant). The liqueurs of Luxembourg – made with cherries (kirsch), plums (quetsch), blackcurrants, pears, elderberries and marc – have a good reputation.

LUXEMBOURG
LËTZEBUERG

Population (est. 2004): 77 400 (conurbation 125 000) – Altitude: 300m

SGM/COLORISE

Luxembourg is set high on a sandstone bluff or deep down in the bottom of the deep ravines created by two rivers – the Pétrusse and the Alzette – which divide the city into distinctive districts, linked by spectacular bridges spanning lush green valleys. The city squares, with their elegant facades painted in pastel colours, may suggest a theatrical backdrop but Luxembourg is a lively business centre with all the dignity of a capital city, despite its comparatively small size. In 1994 UNESCO World Heritage status was conferred on the Old Town and its extensive defences; floodlighting in the high season enhances the city and its setting.

Luxembourg first took its name in 963 as an autonomous earldom but, owing to its strategic position at one of the major European crossroads, it was a desirable prize; for four centuries the city was ruled successively by the Burgundians, Spanish, French and Austrians, until its independence was established by the Treaties of London in 1839 and 1867. In 1952 Luxembourg, the birthplace of Robert Schuman who was one of the fathers of EC, became the headquarters of the European Coal and Steel Community (ECSC) and is now the seat of many other European institutions, including the Council of Ministers of the European Union (for 3 months a year) and the General Secretariat of the European Parliament.

WHICH DISTRICT TO CHOOSE

The greatest concentration of **hotels** is near the railway station *Plan I* **B3**; it is not however difficult to find a room in the Old Town *Plan II* **C1**. There are also a few charming places to stay scattered on the outskirts of Luxembourg.

For a **restaurant** it is best to look in the Old town, especially in the pedestrian area bordered by Place d'Armes, Place Guillaume II and Rue Notre-Dame *Plan II* **C1**.

For a **drink only**, choose the shady terraces in Place d'Armes *Plan II* **C1** or try one of the many **brasseries** and **tavernes** in the town centre: eg *Brasserie Mansfeld*, 3 rue de la Tour Jacob *Plan I* **B2**, taverne *Wëlle Man*, 12 rue Wiltheim *Plan II* **D1**, etc.

509

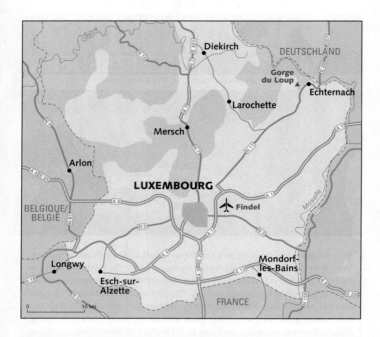

PRACTICAL INFORMATION

ARRIVAL – DEPARTURE

Luxembourg-Findel Airport – About 6 km (4 mi) NE of the city centre, ☎ 24 56 50 50.

From the airport to the city centre – By **taxi** the cost is about €20 including one piece of luggage; €0.75 extra for each additional piece. There is a **bus** service costing €1.20 for the ticket and €1.20 for bulky luggage.

Railway Station – There are regular train services from **Luxembourg Station** *Plan I* **B3** to Namur, Brussels and Liège (Belgium), to Trier (Germany) and to Metz (France); www.cfl.lu

TRANSPORT

◆ BUS

Tickets can be purchased on the bus or at the bus station or at newsagents

and tobacconists. A single short distance ticket (valid for 1hr) costs €1.20 (book of 10 tickets €9.20); a single network ticket (valid for 24 hrs) costs €4.60 (book of 5 tickets €18.50); www.autobus.lu

◆ TAXIS

Taxis, which are distinguished by a yellow light, can be hired only at a taxi stand. The minimum pick up charge is €2, the cost calculated at €2.50 per km; at night the cost increases by between 10% and 35% of the daytime fare. *Colus Taxis* ☎ (352) 48 22 33; www.colux.lu

USEFUL ADDRESSES

◆ TOURIST OFFICE

City Tourist Office, Place d'Armes, Luxembourg, ☎ 22 28 09 – Place de la Gare, Luxembourg. ☎ 42 82 82-20; www.lcto.lu; touristinfo@lcto.lu

♦ BANKS/CURRENCY EXCHANGE

The major banks are to be found in the town centre *Plan II* **C1** and at the railway station *Plan I* **B3**, Mon-Fri, 8.30am-4.30pm (closed at lunchtime); some larger banks are open on Saturday morning. Bank cash machines (ATMs) are open 24hrs (pin number required).

♦ EMERGENCY

Ambulance, Doctor, Dentist *☏* **112**; Police *☏* **113**; also *☏* **999**.

BUSY PERIODS

It may be difficult to find a room at a reasonable price when special events are held in the city as hotel prices may be raised substantially:

Emais'chen: Easter Monday – Traditional folk festival.

Printemps Musical-Festival de Luxembourg: March-May – Classic jazz festival.

April, June and October – Sessions of the Council of Ministers of the European Union.

National Day and the Eve of National Day: 22nd and 23rd June.

Schueberfouer: late August to mid-September – Large fair and market dating from 1340.

EXPLORING LUXEMBOURG

In one day there is time to visit the main sights and museums.

Opening times are usually from 10am-5pm but closed on Mondays and public holidays.

VISITING

Chemin de la Corniche *Plan II* **D1** – Called the most beautiful balcony in Europe for its splendid views of the the Alzette Gorge and the Plateau du Rham.

Le Bock *Plan II* **D1** – Site of ruined fortifications (10C-18C) with a view of the Plateau du Rham.

Casemates du Bock *Plan II* **D1** – Labyrinth of 17C-18C underground defences.

The Pétrusse and Alzette Valleys viewed from the top of the **citadel on the Plateau du St-Esprit** *Plan II* **D1**.

Pont Adolphe (1899-1903) and the Pétrusse Gorge viewed from **Place de la Constitution** *Plan II* **C1**.

Tour of the **Old Town** *Plan II* **C1** from Place d'Armes to **Le Bock** taking in the views listed above.

Musée national d'Histoire et d'Art *Plan II* **D1** – Gallo-Roman collection; Luxembourg Life section: decorative arts, folk art and tradition.

Pétrusse Express – Tour of the historic sights in the lower town and the Pétrusse Valley by motor train starting from Place de la Constitution *Plan II* **C1** (Mar-Oct).

Luxembourg City Tour – Tour of the main city sights by hop-on-hop-off open-top bus starting from Place de la Constitution or Place d'Armes *Plan II* **C1** (Mar-Oct).

SHOPPING

Shops are open daily except Sun, 9am-6pm (Mon 2-6pm) but may close for 1hr at midday; there are some shopping Sundays near Christmas.

The pedestrian streets around Place d'Armes (including **Grand-Rue**, **Rue des Capucins** and **Rue Chimay**) are particularly good for browsing and window-shopping. There are also many opportunities in the district near the railway station. There are a few luxury shops around Place d'Armes in the Old Town *Plan II* **C1**.

MARKETS – There is a **food and flower market** in Place Guillaume II in the Old Town, every Wed and Sat morning (Sat only in winter) and a **flea market** in Place d'Armes, every 2nd and 4th Saturday, mainly in the morning.

WHAT TO BUY – The local specialities are **porcelain** by Villeroy & Boch, **chocolate,** cakes and pastries (try one of the many tea rooms in the city, eg *la Maison Namur*, 27 rue des Capucins); excellent **Moselle wines** and **sparkling wines** (eg on the outskirts of the capital: *Caves vinicoles de Wormeldange*, 115 route du Vin at Wormeldange).

ENTERTAINMENT

Utopolis *Plan I* **B1** – Vast complex with a hi-tech cinema and a range of leisure facilities, including themed bars and restaurants, a 'Bistropolis' and a 'Coyote Café' as well as boutiques.

Conservatoire – Modern concert hall.

Salle de Concerts Grande–Duchesse Joséphine-Charlotte *Plan I* **B1** – Home of the Luxembourg Philharmonic Orchestra (Orchestre Philharmonique de Luxembourg).

Grand Théâtre de la Ville *Plan I* **A1** – Drama in different languages, opera and dance.

Théâtre des Capucines *Plan II* **C1** – Home productions and guest performances.

NIGHTLIFE

There are three sources for details of theatres, concerts, cinemas, shows and exhibitions – *Agenda Lux* (www.agendalux.lu) and *Rendez-vous Lëtzebuerg*, which are published monthly and are available free of charge from hotels and the Tourist Information Office; also *Vademecum*, a monthly listing of cultural events, available from the City Tourist Office in Place d'Armes.

At night the liveliest part of the city is the **Station district** *Plan I* **B3** where there are bars and night clubs. In the lower town – **Grund/Clausen** *Plan II* **D1** – there are bars and music cafés, which are popular with the locals; they have outdoor tables and live music – jazz and folk.

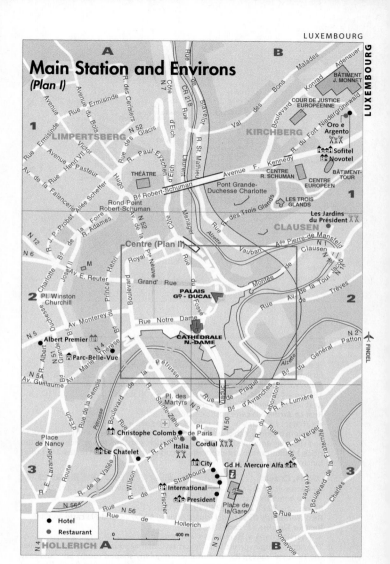

Main Station and Environs
(Plan I)

LUXEMBOURG

A

B

1

LIMPERTSBERG

KIRCHBERG

BÂTIMENT
J. MONNET

COUR DE JUSTICE
EUROPÉENNE

Oro e
Argento

Sofitel
Novotel

THÉÂTRE

Pont Grande-
Duchesse Charlotte

CENTRE
R. SCHUMAN

CENTRE
EUROPÉEN

BÂTIMENT-
TOUR

Rond-Point
Robert-Schuman

Bd Robert-Schuman

LES TROIS
GLANDS

CLAUSEN

Les Jardins
du Président

Centre (Plan II)

PALAIS
Gd - DUCAL

CATHÉDRALE
N-DAME

2

Pl. Winston
Churchill

Albert Premier

Parc-Belle-Vue

M

2

FINDEL

Pl. des
Martyrs

Christophe Colomb

Le Chatelet

Italia

Pl.
de Paris

Cordial

City

Gd H. Mercure Alfa

International

President

Place
de Nancy

Place
de la Gare

3

HOLLERICH

A

B

3

● Hotel
● Restaurant

0   400 m

513

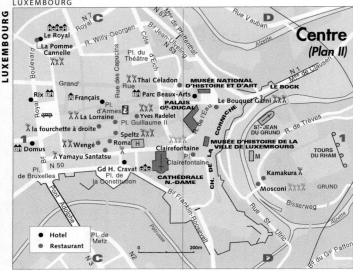

Centre
(Plan II)

Legend:
- ● Hotel
- ● Restaurant

CENTRE

Plan II

Le Royal

🏠 ⊛ Ⅰ♨ 🏊 🖥 & rest 🅰 ✈ 🖂 ℂ⁹ 🈸25/350 🚗
📠 🆅🆁🆂🅰 🆆🆅 🆀🅴 C1

bd Royal 12 ✉ 2449 – ℰ 241 61 61
– reservations @ hotelroyal.lu – Fax 22 59 48 – www.hotelroyal.lu

185 rm – ♦350/480 € ♦♦350/480 €, � 25 € – 20 suites
Rest see *La Pomme Cannelle* below
Rest *Le Jardin* a la carte approx. 42 €

◆ Grand Luxury ◆ Business ◆ Classic ◆

A modern building at the heart of Luxembourg's "Wall Street" with large, modern and superbly equipped bedrooms. Top-notch, personalised service around the clock. Mediterranean atmosphere and cuisine in the Le Jardin restaurant. Buffet lunch served on Sundays.

Gd H. Cravat

🅰 rest ✈ ⊛ 🖂 ℂ⁹ 🈸25 🆅🆁🆂🅰 🆆🆅 🆀🅴 🆔

bd Roosevelt 29 ✉ 2450 – ℰ 22 19 75 – contact @ hotelcravat.lu – Fax 22 67 11
– www.hotelcravat.lu C1

60 rm ⊏ – ♦221/257 € ♦♦330/397 € – 1 suite
Rest *Normandy (first floor)* (closed August) 40 €/72 € and a la carte 36/63 €
Rest *La Taverne* a la carte 31/63 €

◆ Traditional ◆ Business ◆ Classic ◆

This hotel occupies an old building on a panoramic square (affording views over the Pétrusse Valley). Its comfortable, irregularly shaped rooms are classically furnished. Gourmet restaurant at the Normandy (on the first floor). Regional cuisine served at the Taverne on the ground floor.

Parc Belair without rest

≤ Ⅰ♨ 🏊 ✈ 🖂 ℂ⁹ 🈸25/300
🚗 🆅🆁🆂🅰 🆆🆅 🆀🅴 🆔

av. du X Septembre 111 (by N5) ✉ 2551
– ℰ 442 32 31 – paribel @ hpb.lu – Fax 44 44 84 – www.hpb.lu

52 rm ⊏ – ♦230/270 € ♦♦250/290 € – 1 suite

◆ Traditional ◆ Business ◆ Functional ◆

This luxury hotel on the edge of a park is appreciated by guests for its modern, comfortable rooms, including junior suites and rooms with themed decor. Pleasant lounge bar and lovely views.

LUXEMBOURG

Albert Premier without rest 🕸 📧 📞 🚗 **VISA** 🐵 🖭 ①
r. Albert 1er 2a ✉ 1117 – ℰ 442 44 21 – info@albert1er.lu – Fax 44 74 41
– www.albert1er.lu   Plan I **A2**
14 rm – †140/245 € ††140/375 €, ☲ 15 €
♦ Luxury ♦ Business ♦ Stylish ♦
This hotel on the city's outskirts was formerly a grand residence. Guests are won
over by its plush, English-style interior decor, and cosy rooms.

Parc Beaux-Arts without rest 🕸 🅿 🅿 **VISA** 🐵 🖭 ①
r. Sigefroi 1 ✉ 2536 – ℰ 442 32 31 – Fax 44 44 84   **D1**
10 rm ☲ – †330/385 € ††350/405 €
♦ Luxury ♦ Modern ♦
This ancient building close to the history and art museum has been lovingly
restored. Attractive parquet floors in the suites; those at the front offer views of
the Palais Grand-Ducal.

Domus 🏦 🔟 ½ 🕸 📧 🚗 **VISA** 🐵 🖭
av. Monterey 37 ✉ 2163 – ℰ 467 87 81 – info@domus.lu – Fax 46 78 79
– www.domus.lu   **C1**
38 rm – †135/150 € ††135/220 €, ☲ 15 €
Rest *le sot l'y laisse*, ℰ 467 87 88 (closed 3 weeks August, last 2 weeks
December, Saturday, Sunday and Bank Holidays) a la carte 31/45 €
♦ Business ♦ Modern ♦
A contemporary "apartment-hotel" with spacious, modern, meticulously
kept rooms, almost all of which have fully equipped kitchenettes. Bright dining
room with high-tech bistro-style furnishings and a summer restaurant in the
garden.

Rix without rest 🕸 📧 🅿 **VISA** 🐵
bd Royal 20 ✉ 2449 – ℰ 47 16 66 – rixhotel@vo.lu – Fax 22 75 35
– www.hotelrix.lu
closed 5 to 20 August and 22 December-2 January   **C1**
20 rm ☲ – †120/170 € ††135/190 €
♦ Family ♦ Business ♦ Functional ♦
A pleasant family-run hotel offering sober, varied rooms. Impressive
Classical-style breakfast room and priceless private parking.

Parc-Belle-Vue 🦢 ⋘ 🏦 ½ 📧 📞 🖾 25/350 🚗 🅿 **VISA** 🐵 🖭 ①
av. Marie-Thérèse 5 ✉ 2132 – ℰ 456 14 11 – bellevue@hpb.lu
– Fax 456 14 12 22 – www.hpb.lu   Plan I **A2**
58 rm ☲ – †120 € ††135/160 €
Rest *Parc-Belle-Vue* 19 € (weekday lunch) and a la carte approx. 38 €
♦ Business ♦ Functional ♦
This hotel certainly lives up to its name with its park and fine views. The
rooms in the new extension are the most comfortable but here the views are
lacking. The restaurant and tavern serve buffet meals. Panoramic summer
terrace.

Annexe
av. Marie-Thérèse 5 – ℰ 456 14 11 – bellevue@hpb.lu – Fax 456 14 12 22
89 rm – †171 € ††186 €

Français 🏦 📧 📞 🖾 30 **VISA** 🐵 🖭 ①
pl. d'Armes 14 ✉ 1136 – ℰ 47 45 34 – info@hotelfrancais.lu – Fax 46 42 74
– www.hotelfrancais.lu   **C1**
25 rm ☲ – †99/104 € ††127/150 €
Rest 18 € (weekday lunch), 29/45 € and a la carte 34/54 €
♦ Family ♦ Business ♦ Functional ♦
Run by the same family since 1970, the Français overlooks the liveliest
square in the city. Works of art are dotted about the public areas and the
rooms are impeccably kept. Tavern-style restaurant serving classic-traditional
cuisine.

LUXEMBOURG

Clairefontaine (Magnier)   🕏 AK VISA ⓪❸ AE ①
pl. de Clairefontaine 9 ✉ 1341 – ☎ 46 22 11 – clairefo @ pt.lu – Fax 47 08 21
– www.restaurantclairefontaine.lu – closed Easter week, last 2 weeks August, first
week September, Christmas, Saturday and Sunday   **C-D1**
Rest 62 € b.i. (weekday lunch), 73/90 € and a la carte 67/97 € ⬡

Spec. Tartare de langoustine, haricots verts à la truffe, carpaccio de tête de veau.
Poularde de Bresse cuite en vessie, farce au foie gras et riz basmati à la truffe.
Cannelé bordelais, glace à la truffe noire et coulis de truffe blanche.
♦ Innovative ♦ Formal ♦
In the old town, fronting a charming square close to the cathedral, this renowned
restaurant is known for its ever-evolving cuisine, complementary, well-balanced
cellar and quality service.

Mosconi   🕏 ⍟ ⌂ᴅ VISA ⓪❸ AE ①
r. Münster 13 ✉ 2160 – ☎ 54 69 94 – mosconi @ pt.lu – Fax 54 00 43
closed Easter week, 13 August-4 September, Christmas- NewYear,
Saturday lunch, Sunday and Bank Holidays   **D1**
Rest 34 € (lunch), 49/94 € and a la carte 71/87 €

Spec. Pâté de foie de poulet à la crème de truffes blanches. Risotto aux truffes
blanches (Oct-Dec). Entrecôte de veau légèrement panée.
♦ Italian ♦ Cosy ♦
A smart house on the banks of the River Alzette serving fine Italian cuisine. A
romantic setting where the emphasis is on discreet luxury. Attractive terrace by
the water's edge and fine wine list.

Le Bouquet Garni (Duhr)   VISA ⓪❸ AE ①
r. Eau 32 ✉ 1449 – ☎ 26 20 06 20 – bouquetgarni @ pt.lu – Fax 26 20 09 11
closed late December- early January, Sundays and Mondays   **D1**
Rest 48 € b.i./60 € and a la carte 60/93 €

Spec. Salade tiède de pommes de terre de Noirmoutier et homard rôti (May-Oct).
Pied de cochon farci de morilles et ris de veau (autumn and winter). Mousseline
de pomme de terre au caviar, crème fleurette à la ciboulette.
♦ Traditional ♦ Rustic ♦
An elegant, rustic-style restaurant housed in an 18C building in a street running
alongside the Palais Grand-Ducal. Classic fare enlivened by modern touches and
served meticulously.

Speltz   🕏 AK VISA ⓪❸ AE ①
r. Chimay 8 (angle r. Louvigny) ✉ 1333 – ☎ 47 49 50
– info @ restaurant-speltz.lu – Fax 47 46 77 – ww.restaurant-speltz.lu
closed 15-24 April, 25-29 May, 27 July-15 August, 23 December-1 January,
Sunday, Monday and Bank Holidays   **C1**
Rest 43/108 € b.i. and a la carte 61/77 € ⬡
♦ Contemporary ♦ Friendly ♦
Refined, contemporary cuisine served in two rooms with period furniture or, on
sunny days, on the busy front terrace lining one of the city's pedestrian streets.
Well-informed and informative sommelier.

La Pomme Cannelle – Hotel Le Royal   AK ⍟ ⌂ᴅ VISA AE ①
bd Royal 12 ✉ 2449 – ☎ 241 61 61 – reservations @ hotelroyal.lu – Fax 22 59 48
– www.hotelroyal.lu – closed 30 July-21 August, 24 December-2 January,
Saturday, Sunday and Bank Holidays   **C1**
Rest 47 € (weekday lunch)/67 € and a la carte 56/71 € ⬡
♦ Contemporary ♦ Fashionable ♦
Highly original cuisine in which high-quality ingredients, wines and spices from
the New World take pride of place. The chic, yet welcoming interior calls to mind
exotic locations.

Yves Radelet   🕏 VISA ⓪❸ AE ①
r. Curé 20 ✉ 1368 – ☎ 22 26 18 – info @ yvesradelet.lu – Fax 46 24 40
– www.yvesradelet.lu – closed 25 August-2 September, Sunday and Monday
Rest 25 € (weekday lunch), 45/95 € b.i. and a la carte 49/66 €   **C1**
♦ Contemporary ♦ Cosy ♦
You will be handed an appetising menu of classic dishes with a modern twist at
this restaurant whose owner, who is also the chef, produces the cheeses,
charcuterie and cured foods himself.

XX **La Lorraine** 🛜 VISA ⊕❸ AE ⓪

pl. d'Armes 7 (1st floor) ⊠ *1136 –* 𝒫 *47 14 36 – lorraine@pt.lu – Fax 47 09 64*
– ww.lalorraine.lu
closed Sunday and Bank Holidays   **C1**
Rest 52 €/70 € and a la carte 55/74 €
Rest *Bistrot La Lorraine (ground floor)* 39 €/49 € and a la carte 32/54 €
♦ Seafood ♦ Retro ♦
Two main types of cuisine are served in this fine edifice on the place d'Armes:
local cuisine, with oysters (in season) on the bistro-style ground floor, and
contemporary fare in an attractive Art Deco room on the first floor.

XX **Wengé** 🛜 VISA ⊕❸ AE

r. Louvigny 15 ⊠ *1946 –* 𝒫 *26 20 10 58 – wenge@vo.lu*
– Fax 26 20 12 59   **C1**
Rest (lunch only except Wednesday and Friday) 37 €/87 € b.i. and a la carte
40/70 € 🏶
♦ Contemporary ♦ Fashionable ♦
A fashionable restaurant housed at the back of a delicatessen. A calm
atmosphere reigns in the designer dining area embellished with wenge panels
and a mezzanine. Selected wines.

XX **Thai Céladon** 🛜 VISA ⊕❸ AE ⓪

r. Nord 1 ⊠ *2229 –* 𝒫 *47 49 34 – Fax 37 91 73*
closed Sunday dinner and Monday   **C1**
Rest 18 € (weekday lunch), 37/46 € and a la carte approx. 40 €
♦ Thai ♦ Exotic ♦
This central restaurant with two floors serves Thai cuisine and vegetarian dishes
in a simple, contemporary ambience. It takes its name from a glaze used by
Oriental potters.

X **Roma** 🛜 🗚 VISA ⊕❸ AE ⓪

r. Louvigny 5 ⊠ *1946 –* 𝒫 *22 36 92 – Fax 22 04 96*
closed Sunday dinner and Monday   **C1**
Rest a la carte 33/55 €
♦ Italian ♦ Friendly ♦
One of the oldest "ristoranti" in Luxembourg. Relaxed atmosphere and decor to
match the era. Two types of menu: classic and contemporary. Good choice of
Italian wines.

X **La fourchette à droite** 🛜 🗚 VISA ⊕❸ AE ⓪

av. Monterey 5 ⊠ *2163 –* 𝒫 *22 13 60 – Fax 22 24 95*
closed Saturday lunch and Bank Holidays   **C1**
Rest 20 €, 32/43 € and a la carte 45/59 €
♦ Traditional ♦ Bistro ♦
Modern bistro set amid a variety of restaurants in a pedestrian area attracting a
range of clients, including locals, tourists and workers. A second room upstairs.

X **Yamayu Santatsu** VISA ⊕❸ AE ⓪

r. Notre-Dame 26 ⊠ *2240 –* 𝒫 *46 12 49 – Fax 46 05 71*
closed 3 weeks August, Sunday lunch, Monday and Bank Holidays   **C1**
Rest a la carte 18/48 €
♦ Japanese ♦ Minimalist ♦
Japanese restaurant in a minimalist setting about 200m/220yd from the
cathedral. Typical and varied choice, including one fixed menu. You can see the
sushi being made behind the counter in the restaurant.

X **Kamakura** 🍴 VISA ⓪
😊
r. Münster 4 ⊠ *2160 –* 𝒫 *47 06 04 – kamakura@pt.lu – Fax 46 73 30*
– www.kamakura.lu
closed 2 weeks Easter, last 2 weeks August, Bank Holidays, Saturday lunch and
Sunday   **D1**
Rest 11 € (weekday lunch), 28/65 € and a la carte 35/51 €
♦ Japanese ♦ Exotic ♦
The Kamakura makes few concessions to the West with its minimalist ambience
and design. Good sushi-bar and fixed menus which remain loyal to Japanese
customs. A firm favourite.

LUXEMBOURG

MAIN STATION

Plan I

President

AC ↵ 🖾 🖫25 **P** VISA 🕥 AE ①

pl. de la Gare 32 ✉ *1024 –* ℰ *48 61 61 – president@pt.lu – Fax 48 61 80
– www.president.lu*   **B3**

41 rm ➗ – ♦145 € ♦♦150/180 € – 1 suite

Rest see *Les Jardins du President* below at Clausen, 3 km by shuttle

♦ Traditional ♦ Business ♦ Classic ♦

The rooms at this attractive, discreetly luxurious hotel in front of the station are comfortable and frequently refurbished. Personalised service, neo-Classical lobby and an intimate ambience.

Mercure Grand Hôtel Alfa

AC ↵ 🖾 📞 🖫25/55 VISA 🕥 AE ①

pl. de la Gare 16 ✉ *1616 –* ℰ *490 01 11 – h2058@accor.com – Fax 49 00 09
– www.accorhotels.com/lu*   **B3**

140 rm – ♦175/270 € ♦♦175/290 €, ➗ 18 € – 1 suite

Rest 20 € (weekday lunch) and a la carte 31/57 €

♦ Chain hotel ♦ Business ♦ Modern ♦

This completely refurbished chain hotel is a useful address for rail travellers. Behind its imposing façade, typical of the 1930s, are pleasant rooms where a good night's sleep is guaranteed. The atmosphere of a Parisian-style brasserie reigns in the vast Art Deco restaurant.

International

AC ↵ 🖾 📞 🚗 VISA 🕥 AE ①

pl. de la Gare 20 ✉ *1616 –* ℰ *48 59 11 – info@hotelinter.lu – Fax 49 32 27
– www.hotelinter.lu*   **B3**

69 rm ➗ – ♦125/140 € ♦♦145/155 € – 1 suite

Rest *Am Inter* (closed 22 December-7 January and Saturday lunch) 29 €/36 € and a la carte 39/62 €

♦ Family ♦ Business ♦ Classic ♦

Located opposite the railway station, this hotel is gradually being overhauled. Well-maintained rooms, the best being the new junior suites at the front. The restaurant occupies the corner of the building and the large bay windows allow light to flood in. Classic menu with substantial choice.

Le Châtelet without rest

🖪 🏠 🖾 **P** VISA 🕥 AE ①

bd de la Pétrusse 2 ✉ *2320 –* ℰ *40 21 01 – contact@chatelet.lu
– Fax 40 36 36*   **A3**

36 rm ➗ – ♦75/114 € ♦♦85/130 €

♦ Family ♦ Business ♦ Classic ♦

Overlooking the Pétrusse Valley, this hotel is an amalgam of several houses, one of which is crowned by an imposing turret. White-leaded furniture and Oriental carpets in the largest rooms.

City without rest

AC 🖾 🖫25/80 🚗 VISA 🕥 AE ①

r. de Strasbourg 1 ✉ *2561 –* ℰ *291 11 22 – mail@cityhotel.lu – Fax 29 11 33
– www.cityhotel.lu*   **B3**

35 rm ➗ – ♦87/130 € ♦♦120/178 €

♦ Family ♦ Business ♦ Classic ♦

This corner building dating from the inter-war period has fairly spacious rooms decorated in a style reminiscent of the 1980s, each with an individual feel.

Christophe Colomb without rest

🖾 📞 🖫25 🚗 VISA 🕥 AE ①

r. Anvers 10 ✉ *1130 –* ℰ *408 41 41 – mail@christophe-colomb.lu – Fax 40 84 08
– www.christophe-colomb.lu*   **A3**

24 rm ➗ – ♦80/158 € ♦♦90/168 €

♦ Family ♦ Business ♦ Modern ♦

Just 500m/550yd from the station, this pleasant small hotel is ideal for those arriving in the city by train. Standard, reasonably spacious rooms with modern furnishings.

𝙓𝙓𝙓 Cordial ~~VISA~~ ⓂⓈ AE

pl. de Paris 1 (1st floor) ✉ 2314 – ☎ 48 85 38 – Fax 40 77 76
*closed 17-24 April, 5-12 June, 1-22 August, Saturday lunch, Sunday dinner and
Monday* **B3**
Rest 33 € (weekday lunch), 42/70 € and a la carte 43/72 €
♦ French traditional ♦ Formal ♦
A large, comfortable restaurant with a conventional layout and elegant ambience.
Classic culinary options including a combination of menus and daily specials.

𝙓𝙓 Italia with rm 🛏 𝐀𝐂 rest ~~VISA~~ ⓂⓈ ①

r. Anvers 15 ✉ 1130 – ☎ 486 62 61 – italia@euro.lu – Fax 48 08 07 **A3**
20 rm ⌂ – †70/80 € ††80/90 €
Rest a la carte 36/50 €
♦ Italian ♦ Family ♦
A restaurant with classic set-up and a menu strong on Italian specialities and
grilled meats. Terrace hidden at the rear. The best rooms are at the front.

ENVIRONS OF LUXEMBOURG *Plan I*

🏨 Sheraton Aérogolf 🛏 𝐀𝐂 ⚡ ✉ ⚙25/120 **P** ~~VISA~~ ⓂⓈ AE ①

rte de Trèves 1 ✉ 2633 – ☎ 34 05 71 – sheraton.luxembourg@sheraton.com
– Fax 34 02 17 – www.sheraton.com
147 rm – †89/340 € ††89/340 €, ⌂ 20 € – 1 suite
Rest a la carte 29/49 €
♦ Chain hotel ♦ Business ♦ Modern ♦
A full range of creature comforts, sophisticated luxury, triple glazing, views of the
airport and impeccable service are the hallmarks of this recently renovated
1970s-built hotel. Bright, simple brasserie with an international menu and a
summer terrace.

🏨 Hilton 🌀 ⬅🛏 ⚙ ♨ 🛁 🔲 𝐀𝐂 ⚡ ♒rest ✉ ⚙25/360

r. Jean Engling 12 ✉ 1466 – ☎ 4 37 81 **P** ~~VISA~~ ⓂⓈ AE ①
– hilton.luxembourg@hilton.com – Fax 43 60 95
– www.hilton.com
298 rm – †235/285 € ††235/285 €, ⌂ 22 € – 39 suites
Rest *Indigo* a la carte 39/55 €
♦ Chain hotel ♦ Business ♦ Classic ♦
This luxury hotel hugs the side of the valley on the edge of the forest. Rooms with
every creature comfort, attentive service and a full range of conference facilities.
Contemporary brasserie-style restaurant serving buffets and classic à la carte
menu.

🏨 Sofitel 🌀 🛁rm 𝐀𝐂 ⚡ ✉ 📞 ⚙25/75 🌳 **P** ~~VISA~~ ⓂⓈ AE ①

r. Fort Niedergrünewald 6 (European Centre) ✉ 2015 – ☎ 43 77 61
– h1314@accor.com – Fax 42 50 91 **B1**
100 rm – †310/330 € ††310/330 €, ⌂ 20 € – 4 suites
Rest see also **Oro e Argento** below
Rest *Le Stübli* (closed July, Sunday and Monday) a la carte approx. 27 €
♦ Chain hotel ♦ Business ♦ Classic ♦
This bold, oval-shaped hotel with a central atrium is located at the heart of the
European institutions district. Comfortable, spacious rooms with service to
match. Regional cuisine served in a welcoming setting, where waiting staff are
dressed in traditional attire.

🏨 Novotel 🌀 🛏 & 𝐀𝐂 ⚡ ✉ ⚙25/300 **P** ~~VISA~~ ⓂⓈ AE ①

r. Fort Niedergrünewald 6 (European Centre) ✉ 2226 – ☎ 429 84 81
– h1930@accor.com – Fax 43 86 58 – www.accorhotels.com **B1**
260 rm – †160/190 € ††160/195 €, ⌂ 15 €
Rest (open until midnight) a la carte 24/46 €
♦ Chain hotel ♦ Business ♦ Functional ♦
The Novotel is run by the same group as its neighbour, the Sofitel, and offers
business customers a full range of seminar facilities as well as recently
refurbished rooms. Brasserie-style restaurant with an international menu in line
with the Novotel standard.

LUXEMBOURG

Ponte Vecchio without rest   🏧 **P** **VISA** **⑩** **AE** **①**
r. Neudorf 271 ⊠ 2221 – ℰ 424 72 01 – vecchio@pt.lu – Fax 424 72 08 88
– www.vecchio.lu
45 rm – †89 € ††107 €, � 9 €
♦ Traditional ♦ Business ♦ Functional ♦
This old brewery has been skilfully redeveloped into a series of impressive
bedrooms (with and without kitchenettes) - including nine split-level - and
public areas adorned with romantic Italianate frescoes.

Ibis   ≤ 🏡 🕭 & rm 🏧 ⅍ 25/60 **P** **VISA** **⑩** **AE** **①**
rte de Trèves ⊠ 2632 – ℰ 43 88 01 – h0974@accor.com – Fax 43 88 02
122 rm – †63/81 € ††63/96 €, ⊑ 10 € – **Rest** a la carte approx. 25 €
♦ Chain hotel ♦ Business ♦ Functional ♦
A chain hotel with attractive lounge and dining areas plus a cheaper annexe for
the budget-conscious. Although quite small, the bedrooms offer the level of
comfort you would expect from the Ibis name. A glass rotunda provides the
backdrop for the restaurant.

XXX **Oro e Argento** – H. Sofitel   🏧 **P** **VISA** **⑩** **AE** **①**
r. Fort Niedergrünewald 6 (European Centre) – ℰ 43 77 68 70
– h1314@accor.com – Fax 42 50 91 – closed August and Sunday   **B1**
Rest a la carte approx. 51 €
♦ Italian ♦ Cosy ♦
Attractive transalpine restaurant set in a luxury hotel. Seasonal Italian menu,
elegant interior décor in the Venetian style, intimate atmosphere with
well-trained staff.

XXX **Host. du Grünewald** with rm   🏡 🚃 🏧 rest 💎 rest
rte d'Echternach 10 – ℰ 43 18 82 – hostgrun@pt.lu   **P** **VISA** **⑩** **AE** **①**
– Fax 42 06 46 – www.hotel-romantik.com
25 rm – †70/125 ††85/160 – **Rest** (closed 2-17 January, 31 July-22 August,
Saturday lunch, Sunday and Monday lunch) 51 /85 € and a la carte 55/75 €
♦ Traditional ♦ Rustic ♦
We recommend that you reserve a table in the central dining room.
Well-presented classic cuisine. Attentive service. A delightful, traditional-style
hostelry with a hushed, romantic atmosphere.

XX **Les Jardins du President** – H.President with rm 💐   🏡 🚃 & 📠
pl. Ste-Cunégonde 2 ⊠ 1367 – ℰ 260 90 71   **P** **VISA** **⑩** **AE** **①**
– jardins@president.lu – Fax 26 09 07 73 – www.president.lu
closed last week December- first week January   **B2**
7 rm ⊑ – †180/250 € ††250/350 € – **Rest** (closed Saturday lunch and Sunday)
25 € (weekday lunch)/45 € and a la carte 49/68 € ⅋
♦ Contemporary ♦ Fashionable ♦
An elegant restaurant set amid an oasis of greenery producing dishes with a
modern touch. Well-informed sommelier. The terrace overlooks a garden and
waterfall. Individually designed bedrooms.

XX **Le Grimpereau**   🏡 **P** **VISA** **⑩** **AE** **①**
r. Cents 140 ⊠ 1319 – ℰ 43 67 87 – bridard@pt.lu – Fax 42 60 26
– www.legrimpereau.lu – closed Easter week, 2 weeks August, All Saint's week,
Saturday lunch, Sunday dinner and Monday
Rest 50 € b.i./75 € and a la carte 59/82 €
♦ Contemporary ♦ Rustic ♦
A villa reminiscent of a chalet is the setting for this simple and spacious neo-rustic
restaurant with exposed beams and stone fireplace. Contemporary cuisine.

XX **La Mirabelle**   🏡 🏧 **VISA** **⑩** **AE** **①**
pl. d'Argent 9 ⊠ 1413 – ℰ 42 22 69 – Fax 42 22 69 – www.espaces-saveurs.lu
closed Saturday lunch and Sunday
Rest 28 € (weekday lunch)/58 € and a la carte 41/58 € ⅋
♦ Traditional ♦ Brasserie ♦
A restaurant in a smart townhouse offering contemporary cuisine with a
southern bent and a well-stocked wine cellar. Daily specialities, made with local
produce, are announced by the waiting staff. Hidden terrace.

NETHERLANDS
NEDERLAND

- **AREA:**
  41 863 km² (16 163 sq mi).

- **POPULATION:**
  16 407 000 inhabitants (est. 2005), density = 392 per km².

- **CAPITAL:**
  Amsterdam (conurbation 1 193 000 inhabitants); The Hague is the seat of government and Parliament.

- **CURRENCY:**
  Euro (€); rate of exchange: € 1 = US$1.17 (Nov 2005).

- **GOVERNMENT:**
  Constitutional parliamentary monarchy (since 1815). Member of European Union since 1957 (one of the 6 founding countries).

- **LANGUAGE:**
  Dutch; many Dutch people also speak English.

- **SPECIFIC PUBLIC HOLIDAYS:**
  Good Friday (Friday before Easter); Queen's Day (30 April, 2006: 29 April); Liberation Day (5 May); Boxing Day (26 December).

- **LOCAL TIME:**
  GMT + 1hour in winter and GMT + 2 hours in summer.

- **CLIMATE:**
  Temperate maritime with cool winters and mild summers (Amsterdam: January: 2°C, July: 17°C), rainfall evenly distributed throughout the year.

- **INTERNATIONAL DIALLING CODE:**
  00 31 followed by area code without the initial 0 and then the local number. International Directory enquiries: ✆ 06 0418.

- **EMERGENCY:**
  Fire Brigade: ✆ 112; Police, Ambulance, Roadside assistance: ✆ 0900 8418.

- **ELECTRICITY:**
  220 volts AC, 50Hz; 2-pin round-shaped continental plugs.

FORMALITIES

Travellers from the European Union (EU), Switzerland, Iceland and the main countries of North and South America need a national identity card or passport (America: passport required) to visit the Netherlands for less than three months (tourism or business purpose). For visitors from other countries a visa may be required, in addition to a passport, especially for those wishing to stay for longer than three months. We advise you to check with your embassy before travelling.

Nationals of EU member states require a valid national driving licence; nationals of non-EU countries require an international driving licence. Car hire is available in most major towns and resorts. The minimum age for the driver is 21-25, having held a valid licence for at least one year.

MAJOR NEWSPAPERS

The main national newspapers are: *de Telegraaf, NRC Handelsblad, Algemeen Dagblad, de Volkskrant* and *het Nederlands Dagblad*. The main dailies of Amsterdam, Den Haag and Rotterdam are respectively *Het Parool, de Haagsche Courant* and *het Rotterdams Dagblad. Het Financieele Dagblad* deals with financial matters.

USEFUL PHRASES

ENGLISH	DUTCH
Yes	**Ja**
No	**Nee**
Good morning	**Goedemorgen, Dag**
Goodbye	**Dag, Tot ziens**
Thank you	**Dank u, bedankt**
Please	**Alstublieft**
Excuse me	**Excuseer mij / Neemt U mij niet kwalijk**
I don't understand	**Ik begrijp het niet**

HOTELS

◆ CATEGORIES

Accommodation ranges from luxurious 5-star international hotels, via simple hotels and smaller, family-run guesthouses and bed and breakfast establishments. There is also a wide range of rented accommodation – bungalows, log cabins, holiday cottages, flats and apartments. The Benelux star rating is conferred on the application of the owner.

◆ PRICE RANGE

The price is per room. There is little difference between the price of a single and a double room. Between April and October it is advisable to book in advance. From November to March prices may be slightly lower, some hotels offer special cheap rates and some may be closed. In the major towns hotel chains may offer lower weekend rates in the low season.

◆ TAX

Included in the room price.

◆ CHECK OUT TIME

Usually between 11am and noon.

◆ RESERVATIONS

By telephone or by Internet. A credit card number may be required.

◆ TIP FOR LUGGAGE HANDLING

At the discretion of the customer (about €1 per bag).

◆ BREAKFAST

It is often not included in the price of the room in the more expensive hotels and is generally served between 7am and 10am. Most hotels offer a self-service buffet but usually it is possible to have continental breakfast served in the room.

Reception	**Receptie**
Single room	**Eenpersoonskamer**
Double room	**Kamer met tweepersoonsbed /**
	Kamer met twee bedden
Bed	**Bed**
Bathroom	**Badkamer**
Shower	**Douche**

RESTAURANTS

Besides traditional **restaurants** there are **brasseries**, serving less formal meals. Asian cuisines are well represented: Chinese, Japanese, Indian and particularly the famous Indonesian *rijsttafel*.

Breakfast	**Het ontbijt**	7am – 10am
Lunch	**Middagmaal**	11am – 2-3pm
Dinner	**Avondeten**	5.30pm – 10pm

The more formal restaurants are usually open only in the evening and not at mid-day. Menus are usually printed in Dutch and sometimes in English. Some Dutch restaurants offer a 3-course tourist menu, which offers good value but not much choice. A fixed price menu is usually less expensive than a meal with the same number of courses selected from the à la carte menu. The restaurants of the Neerlands Dis chain, displaying a red, white and blue soup tureen emblem, offer a selection of traditional Dutch dishes. Restaurants displaying a blue wall plaque with a white fork offer a tourist menu at a reasonable price – a three course meal (starter, main course and dessert).

◆ RESERVATIONS

Reservations are usually made by phone, fax or Internet. For famous restaurants (including Michelin starred restaurants), it is advisable to book several days – or weeks in some instances – in advance. A credit card number or a phone number may be required as guarantee.

◆ THE BILL

The bill (check) includes service charge and VAT. Tipping is optional but, if you are particularly pleased with the service, it is customary to round up the total to an appropriate figure – 10% in larger restaurants and the value of the small change elsewhere.

Drink or aperitif	**Aperitief**
Appetizer	**Hapje**
Meal	**Maaltijd**
First course, starter	**Voorgerecht**
Main dish	**Hoofdgerecht**
Main dish of the day	**Dagschotel**
Dessert	**Nagerecht**
Water	**Water**
Wine (red, white, rosé)	**Wijn (rood, witte, rosé)**
Beer	**Bier, Pils**
Bread	**Brood**
Meat (rare, medium, well done)	**Vlees (rood, saignant, gaar)**

Fish	**Vis**
Salt/pepper	**Zout/peper**
Cheese	**Kaas**
Vegetables	**Groenten**
Hot/cold	**Heet/koud**
The bill (check) please	**De rekening alstublieft**

LOCAL CUISINE

The Netherlands is the world's third largest exporter of agricultural produce: dairy products from the famous black and white Friesian cattle, vegetables and flowers. This is reflected in the local cuisine. Breakfast is a generous meal consisting of cheese, cold meats, eggs and milk products, as well as cereal, different kinds of breads and pastries, and is accompanied by coffee, tea, hot chocolate and milk. Lunch is usually a cold snack with coffee: a shrimp or eel sandwich; soft bread rolls with various fillings (broodje) ; open sandwiches (uitsmijter) with butter, ham or roast beef and two fried eggs on top; deep-fried balls of spiced mince meat (kroketten).

Dinner is a larger meal starting with soup, kippers (marinated, smoked herrings), a vegetable hors-d'œuvre, followed by a main dish of meat or fish and an abundance of fresh vegetables in gravy, salad with mayonnaise, finishing with dessert (ice-cream or pastries topped with whipped cream).

Fish soup is popular but two more unusual recipes are **Abraham's Mosterdsoep**, mustard soup, and **Erwten Soep**, split-pea soup cooked with pieces of sausage and bacon fat. Owing to their long coastline the Dutch catch a lot of fish: cod, haddock, herring, also oysters, mussels, crab and lobster. A favourite dish is **mussels** (mosselen) served with a white wine Hollandaise sauce and chives, or cooked with celery and onions in white wine and served with French fries (patat). Their speciality is herring; **maatjesharing** is eaten raw with onions in early summer; for **Hollandse Nieuwe** the herrings are caught in the spring when their fat content is high, then gutted, salted, matured, filleted and preserved in brine.

Most menus will feature beef, veal and calves liver; **Friet met Zoervlies** is a dish of beef cooked in a sour vinegar and apple sauce and served with French fries. **Hutspot**, a traditional recipe from Leiden, is steak or brisket boiled with potatoes and carrots in milk and water. In spring asparagus (asperge) will be on the menu, often served with ham and butter.

Both fish and cheese are preserved by smoking; smoked eel (gerookte paling) is a delicacy on the coast.

Cheese is the staple ingredient of breakfast and cold meals. Creamy when fresh (jonge), it becomes dry and pungent when ripe (oude): the cylindrical, flat **Gouda** and spherical **Edam** are both found in the picturesque market of Alkmaar; **Leyden** cheese (Leidse kaas) contains caraway seeds, while **Friesland** (Friese kaas) is flavoured with cloves.

For dessert there is fruit, particularly apples: **Appelbol**, a pastry ball filled with apples and raisins; **appelgebak**, apple and cinnamon pie; **Krudoorntjesbrij**, a gooseberry porridge made with gooseberries, milk, cream and sugar; **Haagse Bluf**, a blackcurrant fool. Other sweet dishes are syrup waffles (siroopwafels), a speciality from Gouda; **Haagse Kakker**, bread pudding flavoured with cinnamon, raisins and almond paste; **Vlaai**, an open tart filled with apples, cherries or strawberries; **Bossche Bol**, a chocolate covered pastry; **Eierkoeken**, large soft pastries made of eggs; **Pannenkoeken**, sweet or spicy pancakes; **Oliebollen**, doughnuts filled with raisins, apple or custard. **Speculaas** are almond biscuits and **pepernoten** are a sort of ginger nut.

◆ DRINK

Beer is the most popular drink. Among the popular brands are Amstel, Grolsch, Heineken and Oranjeboom. There are several smaller breweries: Gulpen, Bavaria, Drie Ringen Leeuw and Utrecht; La Trappe is brewed by Trappist monks. Belgian beers are also popular. There are also seasonal beers: **witbier**, brewed in summer, is served with a slice of lemon or lime, and **bockbier**, rich and fruity appears in autumn.

The only grape-growing area is round Maastricht where there are 12 vineyards, some of which organise tours. To try a local wine at dinner ask for Apostelhoeve for white wine and Thiessen for red. Advocaat is a famous brand of eggnog; in Groningen they drink **Hiet Beer**, another Dutch eggnog. In Noord-Brabant the local tipple is **Brandewijn**, brandy served with sugar.

The Dutch are famous for their **gin** (genever). Starting with distilling grain in about 1600, they narrowed down their production over the years to malt spirit. Finally they specialised in making genever, using the juice of juniper berries to give the spirit its particular flavour. Schiedam, with its five distilleries, is the centre of the industry. Each distillery has its own recipe, which is a closely-guarded secret. They produce young genever - **jong jenever** and old genever - **oude jenever**, the latter having a fuller flavour. **Kopstout** is a glass of beer with a genever chaser.

AMSTERDAM

AMSTERDAM

Population (est. 2005): 750 000 (conurbation 1 193 000) – Altitude: sea level

R. Mattès/MICHELIN

Amsterdam is a magnificent city dominated by water. It is divided into different districts by rivers and numerous canals. It is also famous for its architecture, particularly the stepped façades of its tall, narrow brick houses. The best way to explore the town is on foot, by bicycle or boat.

Apart from its international importance as a port, Amsterdam is a city of great cultural wealth, with prestigious museums and galleries, containing works by some of the great Dutch painters. The first written record of the city dates from 1275, when Count Floris V of Holland granted toll privileges to the herring-fishing village, situated on two dikes joined by a dam, at the mouth of the Amstel River.

In the late 16C a period of great affluence began with the arrival of diamond merchants from Antwerp and the Marranos, Jews from Spain and Portugal. In the 17C the Dutch began a period of overseas expansion, particularly in the Far East. The revival of economic activity in the early 20C is marked by the Amsterdam School of architecture, which favoured asymmetry, differences of level and curved walls. Amsterdam is now a major industrial city; its activities include medical technology, metals, printing, food and tourism. Despite the development of modern suburbs many people live in the numerous houseboats moored along the canals.

WHICH DISTRICT TO CHOOSE

Most **hotels** and **restaurants** are located within the great curve of the Singelgracht canal, although there are a few beyond this line.

The city offers various cuisines – traditional Dutch restaurants and **brasseries**, the famous Indonesian **rijsttafel** and other Asian restaurants. *See also Gourmet Treats chapter.*

526

ARRIVAL – DEPARTURE

Schiphol International Airport
Plan I **A3** – About 18 km (11 mi) south-west of the city centre. ℰ 0900 724 474 65 (from inside The Netherlands); ℰ 0031 (0) 20 794 0800 (from outside the Netherlands); www.schiphol.com

From the airport to the city centre – By **train**: Suburban train (20min) to Amsterdam Central Station every 20min during daytime; €3.70 single, approx. €6.50 return. By **bus**: No 197 Connexion and No 370 Interliner (30min). ℰ 020 653 49 75. By **taxi**: 20min (1hr in the rush hour), approx. €40. ℰ 020 653 10 00. Airport shuttles and KLM shuttle are also available to reach the city centre.

Railway Station – Central Station
Plan II **G1**: regular train services from major towns in the Netherlands, Belgium, France and Germany. ℰ 0900 202 11 63, 0900 92 92; www.ns.nl

Ferry Terminal – Regular ferries to **Amsterdam (IJmuiden)** from Newcastle in England; www.dfds seaways.co.uk

TRANSPORT

◆ TRAM, BUS AND METRO

Most of the trams and buses run from the Central Station. Tram tickets to be punched in the yellow machines; bus tickets to be shown to the driver; metro tickets to be punched in the machines near the platform steps. Tickets are sold at the main information office (opposite Central Railway Station), in ticket vending machine and in many tobacconists' shops. Prices vary according to the number of pricing zones

crossed: 15-stripcard *(strippenkaart)*, approx. €7.00 or 45-stripcard, approx. €20.00, valid throughout the country on buses, trams and metro; one-week pass: between €11 and €27 (according to pricing zones). **Circle-Tram 20** has a circular route (31 stops) which takes in most of the main sights, museums and large hotels in the city (9am-7pm every 10min). ℰ 0900 80 11, 0900 92 92; www.gvb.nl

◆ BOAT

Canal Bus has 3 routes (green, red, blue) with 11 stops; day ticket; ℰ 020 626 55 74; www.canal.nl **Museum Boat** has a single route with 7 stops (10am-5pm); price according to length of journey. **Artis Express** runs regularly from Central Station to Nederlands Scheepvaartmuseum and Artis; ℰ 020 530 10 90; www. lovers.nl Several companies offer boat trips; most from opposite the Central Station. In fine weather the Canal Bike is a good way of touring the canals; 4 landing stages (start at one stage and finish at another). ℰ 020 626 55 74; www.canal.nl

◆ TAXI

Taxis bear blue number plates and an illuminated sign on the roof. They may be called by telephone (ℰ 020 677 77 77) or hired at taxi ranks – airport, railway stations, Dam Square; although they are not supposed to stop, they can also be hailed in the street. Pick-up charge €5.12; price per km €1.94; taxi fares are usually rounded up (5-10%); www.taxi.amsterdam.nl

◆ TAXI-CYCLE

Wieler Taxi €2.50 + €1 per 3 min per person; ℰ 282 475 50.

◆ I AMSTERDAM CARD

This card entitles the holder to free public transport, free admission to major museums, a canal cruise and 25% discounts in some restaurants; 24hr-card €33; 48hr-card €43; 72hr-card €53. Available from the Tourist Office; www.iamsterdam.nl

USEFUL ADDRESSES

◆ TOURIST OFFICES

VVV Amsterdam: Stationsplein 10 *Plan II* **G1**; ℰ 020 201 88 00; open 9am-6pm (2pm Sunday in winter). **Central Station**, platform 2, Leidsestraat1; ℰ 020 551 25 25. **Schipol Airport**, Arrivals Hall 2 (daily 7am-10pm); ℰ 900 400 40 40; www.amsterdam.nl; www.visitams terdam.nl; info@atcb.nl

◆ POST OFFICES

Open Mon-Fri 8.30am-5pm, Sat 8.30am-12 noon. The Main Post Office (Hoofdpostkantoor PTT) is at Singel 250-256 *Plan II* **F1** (open Mon-Fri 8.30am-6pm (8pm Thurs), Sat 10am-1.30pm).

◆ BANKS

Opening times generally are Mon-Fri 9am-4/5pm. Most banks have ATMs.

◆ EMERGENCY

Phone ℰ **112** for Fire Brigade, Police, Ambulance.

BUSY PERIODS

It may be difficult to find a room at a reasonable price (except at weekends) during special events:

Carnival: February.

Nationaal Museumweekend: April (3rd weekend) – Free admission to all museums.

Koninginnedag: April 30 – Queen's Birthday celebrated by young people dressed in orange.

Holland Festival: June – Concerts, opera, ballet, theatre.

Vondelpark Openluchttheater: June-August – Open-air theatre – free concerts in Vondelpark.

Grachtenfestival: August – Classical concert in courtyards, private canal-side houses and on the canals.

Uitmarkt: late August (3 days) – Free concerts and info booths advertising the new cultural season.

Bloemencorso: September (1st Sat) – Floral procession from Aalsmeer to Amsterdam.

Jordaan Festival: September (3 days) – Crooners singing in Westerkerk.

Sinterklaas: December (3rd Sat before 5 Dec) – Official entry of Sinterklaas (St Nicolas) in Prins Hendrikkade.

EXPLORING AMSTERDAM

DIFFERENT FACETS OF THE CITY

It is possible to visit the main sights and museums in three to four days. **Museumjaarkaart** provides free admission to some 440 museums throughout the Netherlands for one year.

Museums and sights are usually open from 10am to 5pm. Some close on Mondays and public holidays.

OLD AMSTERDAM – Grachten *Plan II* **G2**: City centre canals, lined with beautiful 17C and 18C merchants houses, with brick façades and gables of various shapes and decoration, surmounted by carved pediments, some with a small sculptured stone which was the owner's emblem or the symbol of his trade. To the north (near the port) warehouses have characteristic wooden shutters. **Koninklijk Paleis** *Plan II* **F1**: The Royal Palace, formerly the town hall redesigned in 1808 by Louis Bonaparte. **Nieuwe Kerk** *Plan II* **F1**: The New Church (15C Gothic), setting for the coronations of Dutch sovereigns. **Begijnhof** *Plan II* **F2**: Former church of the Beguines, founded in 14C, set in a green meadow, surrounded by lovely sculptured 17C and 18C stone façades – one of the rare surviving church enclosures. **Bloemenmarkt** *Plan II* **F2**: Open-air flower stalls, supplied by barges on the Singel.

MUSEUMS AND GALLERIES

– **Rijksmuseum** *Plan II* **F3**: The National museum, founded by Louis Bonaparte in 1808: exceptional collection of 15C and 17C paintings; sculpture and decorative arts, historical department, print collection, Asian arts section. **Van Gogh Museum** *Plan II* **F3**: Over 200 paintings and 600 drawings by Van Gogh (1853-90): Dutch and Provençal landscapes, peasant portraits, views of Paris and self-portraits. **Stedelijk Museum** *Plan II* **E3**: Municipal museum of modern art (1850 to the present day): Cézanne, Monet, Picasso, Léger, Malevitch, Chagall, Mondrian and Van Doesburg; recent trends in European and American Art. **Nederlands Scheepvaart Museum** *Plan II* **H2**: Maritime Museum in 17C maritime warehouse; exhibits on navigation, replica of 18C merchant ship.

WEST OF CENTRE – Anne Frank Huis *Plan II* **F1**: Narrow 17C house where Anne Frank and her family hid until deported to Auschwitz in 1944. **Westerkerk** *Plan II* **F1**: Stone church (1619-31) with original colours (restored) and bell-tower (85m/280ft) with remarkable carillon; wooden vaulted nave.

SOUTH EAST OF CENTRE – Museum Het Rembrandthuis *Plan II* **F3**: Rembrandt's House (in main street of old Jewish district); collection of his drawings. **Magere Brug** *Plan II* **G3**: Fragile 18C bridge spanning the Amstel. **Artis** *Plan II* **H2**: Zoo with 6000 animals; planetary show at Zeiss Planetarium.

GOURMET TREATS

Amsterdam is the city of a thousand **cafés** *(kroeg)*, renowned for serving drinks in their warm and friendly atmosphere; some *(eetcafé)* also serve snacks and simple meals. Coffee houses serving coffee are not to be confused with **coffeeshops**, which also serve drinks but whose main business is selling legal soft drugs. The area around **Leidseplein** *Plan II* **F3** and **Rembrandtplein** *Plan II* **G2** is particularly busy in the evenings; the latter is mainly known for its large terrace cafés, restaurants and discos – *Café Américain* (Leidsekade 97 and Leidseplein 26): Art Deco brasserie; *Café Dantzig* (Zwanenburgwal 15): terrace on the Amstel and separate reading area; *De Kroon* (Rembrandtplein 17): Amsterdam landmark with terrace overlooking the square; *De Prins* (Prinsengracht 124): pleasant place with a terrace near Anne Frank's House; *Winkel* (Noordermarkt 43) for breakfast and apple cake; *Het Blauwe Theehuis* (Vondelpark) for breakfast; *De Bakkerswinkel* (Warmoestraat 69) for traditional Dutch sandwiches, quiches and cakes; *Lunchcafé 404* (Singel 404) for excellent open sandwiches.

The **brown cafés**, so-called because of their nicotine-stained wooden interiors, are the most typically Dutch; they tend to be small and crowded. Most customers order beer or schnapps but coffee and hot chocolate are also served. The most authentic brown cafés are in the **city centre** and **Jordaan** *Plan II* **F1**. *Café Hoppe* (Spui 18-20): meeting place for writers and journalists, where custo-

mers spill out onto the pavement in summer; *De Admiraal* (Herengracht 563): makes its own gin in one of the city's oldest distilleries; *'t Papeneiland* (Prinsengracht 2): the most romantic with Delft tile decoration, old-fashioned stove and waterside location; *'t Smalle* (Egelantiersgracht 12): tiny café with terrace overlooking the canal.

The **proeflokalen**, tasting places set up in the 17C, still offer the chance to sample the product before buying – Dutch gin and other spirits, many of them distilled on the premises – *De Drie Fleschjes* (Gravenstraat 18), its walls lined with carafes of exotically named drinks; *Wynand Fockink* (Pijlsteeg 31) an attractive courtyard and wide selection of gin and other local spirits.

SHOPPING

Stores are usually open daily from 8.30/9am to 5.30/6pm but close on Monday mornings; Thursday is late-night shopping until 9pm. Supermarkets are open Mon-Sat 8am-8pm (Sat 6pm).

De Bijenkorf (Damrak 1): department store. *Magna Plaza Center* (Nieuwezijds Voorburgwal 182): up-market indoor shopping centre (40 shops). Metz & Co (corner of Keizersgracht and Leidsestraat): design, gifts etc. *Vroom and Dreesmann* (Kalverstraat 201): department store.

The **Museum District** *Plan II* **F3** for exclusive and trendy fashion stores, luxury shoe shops and jewellers, particularly in **P C Hooftstraat** and **Van Baerlestraat**; pedestrianised **Kalverstraat** and **Nieuwendijk** for more down-to-earth clothes shops.

10 **diamond factories** are open to the public; ask at the Tourist Information Centre.

For **antique shops** visit the main canal area (Singel, Herengracht, Keizersgracht and Prinsengracht) and more especially in **Spiegelstraat**, **Nieuwe Spiegelstraat** and **Kerkstraat**.

MARKETS – The **markets** are a delight. **Albert Cuypmarkt** *Plan II* **F2** (Albert Cuypstraat): general goods (Mon-Sat). **Bloemenmarkt** *Plan II* **F2** (Singel between Muntplein and Koningsplein): flower market (Mon-Sat). **Antiques market** *Plan II* **G1** (Nieuwmarkt) (Sun; May-Sep). There are two **flea markets**: one outdoor *Plan II* **G2** (Waterlooplein) (Mon-Sat) and one indoor *Plan II* **E2** (Looiersgracht 38) (Sat-Sun).

WHAT TO BUY – Diamonds, Delft porcelain, Dutch cheese, Dutch gin and other spirits, cigars, clogs.

ENTERTAINMENT

Full listings of music, dance, theatre etc. are published in *Uitkrant* (www.uitkrant.nl) available from theatres, bookshops and cafés, and in *What's On in Amsterdam*, published in English every three weeks and available in tourist offices and some bookshops, and in *Day by Day*, published monthly.

Concertgebouw *Plan I* **B2** (Concertgebouwplein 2-6): home of the world-famous orchestra.

Beurs van Berlage *Plan II* **G1** (Damrak 213) for concerts by the Netherlands Philharmonic Orchestra and others.

Felix Meritis *Plan II* **F2** (Keizersgracht 324): classical concerts in a magnificent 18C auditorium. **Bimhuis** *Plan II* **H1** (Oude Schans 73) for jazz lovers.

Amsterdam ArenA *Plan I* **D3** (Huntum 2): performances by big international names.

Koninklijk Theater Carré *Plan II* **H3** (Amstel 115-125): musicals, variety, circus.

Muziektheater (Stopera) *Plan II* **G2** (Amstel 3): performances by the Nederlandse Opera, the Nationale Ballet and the Nederlands Dans Theater.

Stadsschouwburg *Plan II* **F3** (Leidsplein 26): neo-renaissance building hosting the City Theater; plays some international English-language productions.

NIGHTLIFE

What's On in Amsterdam gives full listings of music, dance, theatre, and other events (see above). Amsterdam has some of the best nightlife anywhere, including the Holland Casino (Max Euweplein 64) and **Walletjes** *Plan II* **G1**, the famous red-light district. Nightclubs operate from about midnight to 3 or 4am; admission €3-€20: *Escape* (Rembrandtplein 11) which is one of the largest clubs; *iT* (Amstelstraat 24), an extravagant venue with go-go girls, drag queens and special gay evenings; *Club II* (Oosterdokskade 3-5), great atmosphere and fabulous DJs; *Club Arena* (in Hotel Arena), popular with Amsterdammers.

Environs of Amsterdam
(Plan I)

0   1 Km

A   **B**

Nieuwe Hemweg   HET IJ

Mercuriushaven

N 202

S 101   S 102

Basisweg

Ⓜ Isolatorweg

● **Tulip Inn Art** 🏨

Ⓜ Transformatorweg

◁ M

Sloterdijk

A 10 - E 22

S 103

WESTERPARK

weg

N 200

Haarlemmer-

weg

Haarlemmer-

Ruys de Beerenbrouckstr.

S 104

Burg. de Vlugtlaan

Bos en Lommerweg

S 104

SLOTERMEER

De Vlugtlaan Ⓜ

Burg. Röeluftstr.

Jan van Galenstr.

S 105

Nassaukade

Nassaukade

Rozengracht

Mauritskade

Marnixstr.

GEUZENVELD SLOTERMEER

J.V. Galenstr.

Jan

Allardtplein

Evertsenstr.

Kinkerstr.

S 106

SPORTPARK

Sloter plas

REMBRANDT PARK

Postjesweg

Hoofd weg

Prest.

Robert-Fruinlaan

Postjesweg

🏛 De Filosoof ●

RIJKSMUSEUM

S 106

Ookmeerweg

Tulip Inn 🏨

● **City West**

Johan-

Postjesweg

Overtoom

🏨 **Museum Square**

Baden Powell

Meer en Vaart

S 106

Cornelis Lelylaan

VONDELPARK

🏛 Villa ● Spring ✕

OSDORP

Tussen Meer

taan

Ⓜ Lelylaan

Borgmann ●

OUD-ZUID

Pieter-

Caland

Huizingalaan

✕ **Brasserie van Baerle**

✕ The Gresham Memphis ●

S 107

S 107

Plesmanlaan

Heemstedestr.

🏨 Hilton ●

Beethovenstr.

Meer

laan

S 107

Henk Sneevlietweg Ⓜ

🏨 **Bilderberg Garden**

✕✕ Mangerie De Kersentuin

weg

🏨 **Le Meridien Apollo**

SLOTERVAART/ OVERTOOMSE VELD

A 10

Stadion-

S 108

S 109

Sloterweg

● **Artemis** 🏨

A 10

Schinkel

Amstelveense-weg

Ⓜ Zuid-W.T.C.

SPORTPARK SLOTEN

A4 - E 19

❶ Mercure Airport 🏨

ZUIDERAMSTEL

De Boelelaan

Ⓤ ● De Boelelaan/VU

Jaagpad

A.J. Ernststr.

BUITENVELDERT

Nieuwe Meer

Van Nijenrodeweg

S 109

N 232

Koenenkade

V. Boshuizenstr.

Koenenkade

Bosbaan

Bosbaanweg

Kalfjeslaan

 Ⓤ

HAARLEMMERMEER

Uilendtede

Schipholweg

❸

Buitenveldertse laan

Ⓜ Kronenburg

AMSTERDAMSE BOS

Zonnestein

Belux

Rembrandtweg

Ⓜ Onderuit

✈

AMSTERDAM-SCHIPHOL

Burg.

AMSTELVEEN

S 108

Amsterdamseweg

Ⓜ Oranjebaan

Zonnestein

baan

| ● | Hotel |
| ● | Restaurant |

Ⓜ Dorint Sofitel Airport

AMSTERDAMSE BOS

Colijnweg

V. Prinstererlaan

COBRA

A 9

Oranjebaan

S 109

De Poel

❺

A   **B**

532

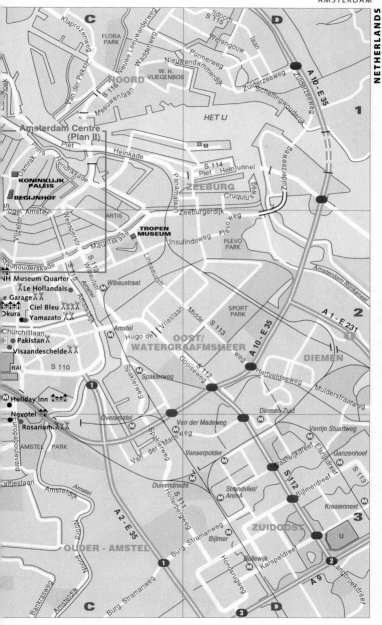

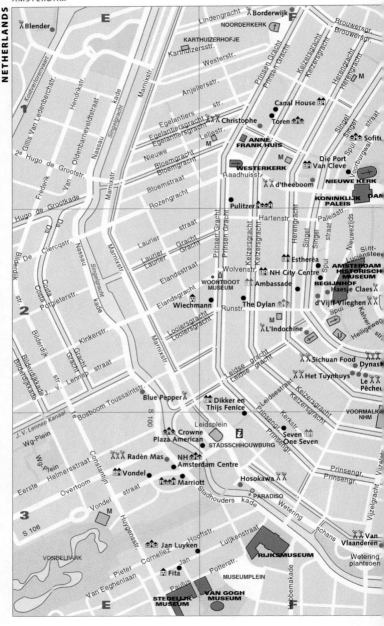

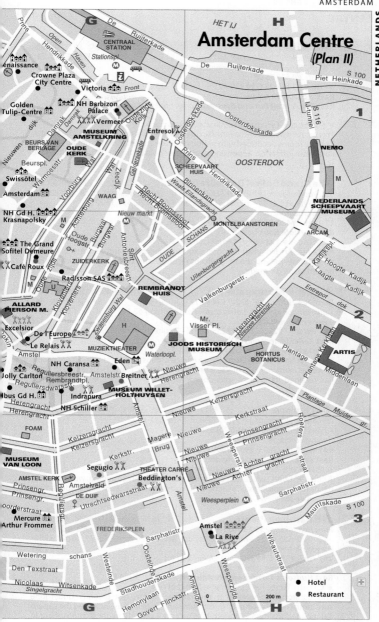

Amsterdam Centre
(Plan II)

HET IJ

De Ruijterkade

Piet Heinkade

S 100

S 116

IJ-tunnel

De Ruijterkade

CENTRAAL
STATION

Stationspl.

enaissance

Crowne Plaza
City Centre

Victoria

Front

Golden
Tulip-Centre

NH Barbizon
Palace

Vermeer

Entresol

OOSTERDOK

NEMO

BEURS VAN
BERLAGE

MUSEUM
AMSTELKRING

OUDE
KERK

Beurspl.

SCHEEPVAART
HUIS

Prins
Hendrikkade

Binnenkant

Swissôtel

Amsterdam

NEDERLANDS
SCHEEPVAART
MUSEUM

WAAG

ARCAM

NH Gd H.
Krasnapolsky

Nieuw markt

MONTELBAANSTOREN

Recht Boomssloot

SCHANS

Hoogte Kadijk

The Grand
Sofitel Demeure

OUDE

Laagte Kadijk

Café Roux

ZUIDERKERK

Uilenburgerstr.

Entrepot

dok

Radisson SAS

REMBRANDT
HUIS

Valkenburgerstr.

ALLARD
PIERSON M.

Herengracht
Nieuwe Herengr.

ARTIS

Excelsior

Mr.
Visser Pl.

De l'Europe

Le Relais

MUZIEKTHEATER

JOODS HISTORISCH
MUSEUM

HORTUS
BOTANICUS

Plantage
Kerklaan

Amstel

Waterloopl.

Middenlaan

NH Caransa

Eden

Nieuwe

Jolly Carlton

Reguliersbreestr.

Amstelstr.

Breitner

Herengracht

Plantage
Mulder
gr.

Rembrandtpl.

Reguliersdwarsstr.

Kerkstraat

bus Gd H.

Indrapura

MUSEUM WILLET-
HOLTHUYSEN

Herengracht

NH Schiller

Nieuwe

Keizersgracht

Weesperstr.

Prinsengracht

Herengracht

FOAM

Keizersgracht

Magere
Brug

Nieuwe

Nieuwe

Achter gracht

Achter
gracht

Keizersgracht

Kerkstr.

Sarphatistr.

MUSEUM
VAN LOON

Segugio

THEATER CARRÉ

Beddington's

Weesperplein

Mauritskade

S 100

AMSTEL KERK

Amstelveld

Prinsengr.

DE DUIF

Prinsengr.

Utrechtsedwarsstraat

Nieuwe

oorderstraat

Mercure

Arthur Frommer

FREDERIKSPLEIN

Amstel

Sarphatistr.

Amstel

La Rive

Wetering

schans

Sarphatistr.

Weesperzijde

Den Texstraat

Westeinde

Oosteinde

Stadhouderskade

Amsteldijk

Wibautstraat

Nicolaas Witsenkade

Singelgracht

Hemonylaan

Govert Flinckstr.

0   200 m

● Hotel
● Restaurant

Amstel ⚓   ≤ 😊 ʃ♨ 俞 ☒ 樋 ⅙ ※ 🎫 📞 ♨ 25/180 ℙ
Prof. Tulpplein 1 ⊠ 1018 GX   ➡ **VISA ⦿ ⌷ ①**
– ℘ (0 20) 622 60 60 – amstel@interconti.com
– Fax (0 20) 622 58 08   **H3**
64 rm – ♥325/625 €, ♥♥325/625 €, ⌷ 23 € – 15 suites
Rest see *La Rive* below
Rest *The Amstel Bar and Brasserie (open until 11.30p.m.)* a la carte
45/59 €
♦ Palace ♦ Grand Luxury ♦ Historic ♦
This palace is a veritable haven of luxury and fine taste on the banks of the Amstel, its huge rooms decorated with period furniture and attention to detail. The cosy library-bar offers an appetising and cosmopolitan menu. Efficient, attentive service.

The Grand Sofitel Demeure ⚓   ʃ♨ 俞 ☒ ⍼ 樋 ⅙ ※ 🎫 📞
O.Z. Voorburgwal 197 ⊠ 1012 EX   ♨25/300 😊 ℙ ⦿ ⌷ ①
– ℘ (0 20) 555 31 11 – h2783@accor.com – Fax (0 20) 555 32 22
– www.thegrand.nl   **G2**
170 rm – ♥420/970 € ♥♥420/970 €, ⌷ 26 € – 12 suites
Rest see *Café Roux* below
♦ Palace ♦ Luxury ♦ Historic ♦
Authentic Art Nouveau lounges, exquisite bedrooms and an interior garden await guests behind the magnificent façade of this building, which in the 16C hosted Maria de' Medici.

NH Gd H. Krasnapolsky   ʃ♨ 樋 ⅙ 🎫 📞 ♨25/750 😊
Dam 9 ⊠ 1012 JS – ℘ (0 20) 554 91 11   ➡ **VISA ⦿ ⌷ ①**
– nhkrasnapolsky@nh-hotels.com – Fax (0 20) 554 62 14
– www.nh-hotels.com   **G2**
461 rm ⌷ – ♥235/429 € ♥♥235/429 € – 7 suites
Rest *Reflet (dinner only)* 41 €
♦ Palace ♦ Business ♦ Historic ♦
This large hotel on the Dam offers a choice of "business" and "executive" rooms as well as apartments in modern or traditional style. The Reflet, created in 1883, has retained its original splendour and refined atmosphere. Delightful 19C winter garden.

De l'Europe ≤ ʃ♨ 俞 ☒ 樋 📞 ♨25/80 ℙ ➡ **VISA ⦿ ⌷ ①**
Nieuwe Doelenstraat 2 ⊠ 1012 CP – ℘ (0 20) 531 17 77
– hotel@leurope.nl – Fax (0 20) 531 17 78
– www.leurope.nl   **G2**
94 rm – ♥295/360 € ♥♥365/505 €, ⌷ 23 € – 6 suites
Rest see *Excelsior* and *Le Relais* below
♦ Palace ♦ Grand Luxury ♦ Historic ♦
A late-19C hotel-palace that combines both charm and tradition, with tastefully decorated bedrooms. Collection of paintings by Dutch landscape artists. Attractive sea views.

NH Barbizon Palace   ʃ♨ ⅚rm 樋 ⅙ 🎫 📞 ♨25/300
Prins Hendrikkade 59 ⊠ 1012 AD   😊 **VISA ⦿ ⌷ ①**
– ℘ (0 20) 556 45 64 – nhbarbizonpalace@nh-hotels.com – Fax (0 20) 624 33 53
– www.nh-hotels.com   **G1**
267 rm – ♥390 € ♥♥390 €, ⌷ 24 € – 3 suites
Rest see *Vermeer* below
Rest *Hudson's Terrace and Restaurant* a la carte 34/44 €
♦ Chain hotel ♦ Luxury ♦ Modern ♦
This comfortable hotel near the railway station has recently undergone substantial renovation in its guestrooms and public areas, including the superb colonnaded main hall. Modern cuisine and a vaguely nautical atmosphere in Hudson's restaurant.

NETHERLANDS

Radisson SAS ⌘   🔥 ⌂ &rm 🅰🅲 ↯ 🖭 ℃ ᔕ 25/180 ⌂
Rusland 17 ✉ *1012 CK – ℰ (0 20) 623 12 31*   🖃 VISA ⚫ AE ①
– reservations.amsterdam@radissonsas.com – Fax (0 20) 520 82 00
– www.radissonsas.com   **G2**
242 rm – †265/295 € ††295/325 €, ⌧ 22 € – 1 suite
Rest *Brasserie De Palmboom* 31 € (weekday lunch) and a la carte 43/64 €
◆ Chain hotel ◆ Business ◆ Modern ◆
A modern chain hotel with an 18C presbytery in the atrium. Good standard and business rooms, decorated in Scandinavian, Dutch, Oriental and Art Deco styles. Modern brasserie with a relaxed atmosphere serving Dutch and international cuisine.

Marriott   🔥 ⌂ &rm 🅰🅲 ↯ ᔕ 25/450 ⌂ 🖃(dinner) VISA ⚫ AE ①
Stadhouderskade 12 ✉ *1054 ES – ℰ (0 20) 607 55 55 – amsterdam@ marriotthotels.com – Fax (0 20) 607 55 11 – www.marriott.com/amsnt*
387 rm – †189/259 € ††189/259 €, ⌧ 24 € – 5 suites   **E3**
Rest *(closed first 3 weeks January and Monday)* 33 € (weekday lunch)/36 € and a la carte 33/49 €
◆ Chain hotel ◆ Business ◆ Classic ◆
Impressive American-style hotel on one of the city's main roads. Huge rooms with a full range of creature comforts. Business centre and conference facilities.

Renaissance   🔥 ⌂ &rm 🅰🅲 ↯ 🍴 🖭 ᔕ 25/400 ⌂
Kattengat 1 ✉ *1012 SZ – ℰ (0 20) 621 22 23*   🖃 VISA ⚫ AE ①
– renaissance.amsterdam@renaissancehotels.com
– Fax (0 20) 627 52 45 – www.renaissancehotels.com/amsrd   **G1**
399 rm – †169/340 € ††169/340 €, ⌧ 22 € – 6 suites
Rest 30 € and a la carte 29/43 €
◆ Chain hotel ◆ Business ◆ Classic ◆
A hotel offering superb conference facilities under the dome of a former Lutheran church. Modern comfort in the bedrooms, junior suites and suites. A wide range of guest services, plus a brasserie-restaurant serving international cuisine.

Crowne Plaza City Centre   🔥 ⌂ 🖵 🅰🅲 ↯ 🍴 ᔕ 25/270 ⌂
N.Z. Voorburgwal 5 ✉ *1012 RC – ℰ (0 20) 620 05 00*
– Fax (0 20) 620 11 73 – www.amsterdam-citycentre.crowneplaza.com
268 rm – †150/340 € ††150/340 €, ⌧ 22 € – 2 suites   **G1**
Rest *Dorrius (closed Sunday and Monday)* (dinner only) a la carte 26/46 €
◆ Chain hotel ◆ Business ◆ Modern ◆
Near the station, the Crowne Plaza offers the quality and creature comforts expected of this chain. View of Amsterdam's rooftops from the lounge club on the top floor. Attractive panelled restaurant and authentic 19C café. Traditional menu choices plus a range of local dishes.

Pulitzer ⌘   🍴 🔥 🚗 🅰🅲 ↯ 🖭 ℃ ᔕ 25/150 ⌂ 🖃 VISA ⚫ AE ①
Prinsengracht 323 ✉ *1016 GZ – ℰ (0 20) 523 52 35*
– sales.amsterdam@starwoodhotels.com
– Fax (0 20) 627 67 53 – www.luxurycollection.com/pulitzer   **F1**
227 rm – †220/390 € ††220/415 €, ⌧ 25 € – 3 suites
Rest *Pulitzers* a la carte 44/58 €
◆ Chain hotel ◆ Business ◆ Historic ◆
A group of 25 17C-18C canal houses arranged around a central garden. Bedrooms offering welcome personal touches, and public areas embellished with works of art. A modern, original café-restaurant with humorous references to the painter Frans Hals.

American   🍴 🔥 🔥 ⌂ &rm 🅰🅲 rm ↯ 🍴 🖭 ℃ ᔕ 25/150 VISA ⚫ AE ①
Leidsekade 97 ✉ *1017 PN – ℰ (0 20) 556 30 00 – info@amsterdamamerican.com*
– Fax (0 20) 556 30 01 – www.amsterdamamerican.com   **E3**
172 rm – †345 € ††395 €, ⌧ 21 € – 2 suites
Rest 28 € (weekday lunch), 33/38 €
◆ Chain hotel ◆ Business ◆ Art Deco ◆
This pleasant hotel with an imposing historic façade has identically furnished rooms of varying sizes. Popular with international clientele. The hotel's sophisticated tavern-restaurant has Art Deco touches.

Victoria 🔊 🗗 🛕 rm ⁴⁄⁷ 🍽 🕻 🏊30/150 *VISA* 🌑 🔿 ⓘ

Damrak 1 ⊠ 1012 LG – ℰ (0 20) 623 42 55 – vicres@parkplazahotels.nl
– Fax (0 20) 625 29 97 – www.parkplaza.com   **G1**
295 rm – ♦125/315 € ♦♦125/315 €, ⌧ 20 € – 10 suites
Rest 13 € (weekday lunch)/27 € and a la carte 31/78 €
♦ **Traditional** ♦ **Business** ♦ **Classic** ♦
This classical palace, embellished by a new wing, is in an ideal location for those
arriving in the city by train. Four room categories. The entrance hall is crowned
by an attractive glass roof. Modern cuisine.

The Dylan ⬙ 🍴 🛕 rm ⁴⁄⁷ 🖼 🕻 🏊30 *VISA* 🌑 🔿 ⓘ

Keizersgracht 384 ⊠ 1016 GB – ℰ (0 20) 530 20 10
– hotel@dylanamsterdam.com – Fax (0 20) 530 20 30
– www.dylanamsterdam.com   **F2**
38 rm – ♦260/310 € ♦♦420/920 €, ⌧ 24 € – 3 suites
Rest *(closed Saturday lunch and Sunday dinner)* a la carte 56/103 €
♦ **Luxury** ♦ **Design** ♦
Luxury and peace and quiet best describe this residence with its surprising
Oriental-inspired decor. Highly individual rooms, and a restaurant with a
minimalist feel where the emphasis is on the flavours of the East.

Jolly Carlton 🛕 rm 🛕 ⁴⁄⁷ 🍽 🖼 🕻 🏊25/150 🌫 🔿 *VISA* 🔿 ⓘ

Vijzelstraat 4 ⊠ 1017 HK – ℰ (0 20) 622 22 66 – sales.nl@jollyhotels.com
– Fax (0 20) 626 61 83   **G2**
218 rm – ♦125/430 € ♦♦125/470 €, ⌧ 19 €
Rest *Caruso*, ℰ (0 20) 623 83 20 (dinner only, open until 11p.m.) a la carte
50/64 €
♦ **Chain hotel** ♦ **Business** ♦ **Functional** ♦
This chain hotel, housed in a building from around 1900, is close to the flower
market and Rembrandtplein. Standard rooms with soundproofing and Italian
furnishings. Elegant restaurant serving Italian cuisine, including well-executed
dishes and fixed menus.

Swissôtel 🛕 rm 🛕 ⁴⁄⁷ 🍽 🕻 🏊25/45 🔿 *VISA* 🌑 🔿 ⓘ

Damrak 96 ⊠ 1012 LP – ℰ (0 20) 522 30 00
– ask-us.amsterdam@swissotel.com – Fax (0 20) 522 32 23
– www.swissotel-amsterdam.com   **G1**
104 rm – ♦299/360 € ♦♦299/360 €, ⌧ 20 € – 5 suites
Rest a la carte 20/44 €
♦ **Chain hotel** ♦ **Business** ♦ **Functional** ♦
Various categories of guestrooms, including several junior suites, are on offer at
this hotel near the Dam. Modern facilities, a business centre plus a trendy
brasserie-style restaurant with Mediterranean-inspired cuisine and a distinctly
Italian slant.

Sofitel 🔊 🛕 rm 🛕 ⁴⁄⁷ 🍽 🖼 🏊25/55 🔿 *VISA* 🌑 🔿 ⓘ

N.Z. Voorburgwal 67 ⊠ 1012 RE – ℰ (0 20) 627 59 00 – h1159@accor.com
– Fax (0 20) 623 89 32 – www.sofitel.com   **F1**
148 rm – ♦255/305 € ♦♦255/650 €, ⌧ 20 €
Rest a la carte 31/43 €
♦ **Chain hotel** ♦ **Business** ♦ **Functional** ♦
This chain hotel occupies an old mansion alongside a main road linking the
area surrounding the railway station to the Dam. Classic rooms, each arranged
differently. "Orient Express" atmosphere in the restaurant. Brasserie-style
menu.

Toren without rest ⬙ � 🛕 🖼 🕻 *VISA* 🌑 🔿 ⓘ

Keizersgracht 164 ⊠ 1015 CZ – ℰ (0 20) 622 63 52 – info@hoteltoren.nl
– Fax (0 20) 626 97 05 – www.hoteltoren.nl   **F1**
39 rm – ♦135/240 € ♦♦150/250 €, ⌧ 12 € – 1 suite
♦ **Family** ♦ **Classic** ♦
Anne Frank's House is just 200m/220yd from this family-run hotel with its
tasteful, classic-style bedrooms. Elegant breakfast room next to the hotel's
cosy bar.

NH Amsterdam Centre
&rm AC ⇄ ℅rest 🖂 ☏ ☂ 25/200

Stadhouderskade 7 ✉ 1054 ES
– ℰ (0 20) 685 13 51 – nhamsterdamcentre@nh-hotels.nl – Fax (0 20) 685 16 11
– www.nh-hotels.com   **E3**
228 rm – ♦139/390 € ♦♦139/390 €, ⊑ 22 € – 2 suites – **Rest** a la carte 25/42 €
Rest *Bice* (closed Sunday) (dinner only) a la carte 38/52 €
♦ Chain hotel ♦ Business ♦ Design ♦
This easily accessible chain hotel located along the Singelgracht was given a facelift in 2003. Spacious, highly comfortable rooms with period furniture. Impressive restaurant serving contemporary Italian cuisine and a brasserie that stays open late.

Jan Luyken without rest
AC ⇄ 🖂 ☏ VISA ⑩ AE ⓞ

Jan Luykenstraat 58 ✉ 1071 CS – ℰ (0 20) 573 07 30 – jan-luyken@
bidderberg.nl – Fax (0 20) 676 38 41 – www.janluyken.nl   **E3**
62 rm – ♦99/199 € ♦♦139/279 €, ⊑ 18 €
♦ Family ♦ Business ♦ Classic ♦
An elegant hotel made up of three buildings dating from 1900 with modern interior decor. Large, well-appointed rooms and a good location at the heart of the museum district.

Seven One Seven without rest ⌂
℅ 🖂 ☏ 🛏 VISA ⑩ AE ⓞ

Prinsengracht 717 ✉ 1017 JW – ℰ (0 20) 427 07 17 – info@717hotel.nl
– Fax (0 20) 423 07 17 – www.717hotel.nl   **F3**
8 rm ⊑ – ♦398 € ♦♦450/650 €
♦ Luxury ♦ Family ♦ Personalised ♦
If you're looking for a quiet, intimate hotel, this elegant 18C residence could be just for you, with its exquisite, individually furnished and spacious bedrooms.

Ambassade without rest
≤ 🖂 VISA ⑩ AE ⓞ

Herengracht 341 ✉ 1016 AZ – ℰ (0 20) 555 02 22 – info@ambassade-hotel.nl
– Fax (0 20) 555 02 77 – www.ambassade-hotel.nl   **F2**
51 rm – ♦165/185 € ♦♦185/225 €, ⊑ 16 € – 8 suites
♦ Family ♦ Luxury ♦ Stylish ♦
A group of typical 17C houses is the setting for this charming hotel bordered by two canals. Each bedroom is endowed with its own personal touch. Interesting library.

Estheréa without rest
⇄ ℅ 🖂 ☏ VISA ⑩ AE ⓞ

Singel 305 ✉ 1012 WJ – ℰ (0 20) 624 51 46 – info@estherea.nl
– Fax (0 20) 623 90 01 – www.estherea.nl   **F2**
71 rm – ♦99/231 € ♦♦160/294 €, ⊑ 14 €
♦ Family ♦ Classic ♦
Set back from the hubbub of Amsterdam's central district, between the history museum and the Singel, this hotel is a complex of several adjoining houses with pleasant rooms.

Eden
AC rm ⇄ ℅ VISA ⑩ AE ⓞ

Amstel 144 ✉ 1017 AE – ℰ (0 20) 530 78 78 – res.eden@edenhotelgroup.com
– Fax (0 20) 623 32 67 – www.edenhotelgroup.com   **G2**
225 rm – ♦155/175 € ♦♦175/195 €, ⊑ 15 €
Rest 24 €/35 € and a la carte 26/40 €
♦ Business ♦ Functional ♦
It's hard to believe that hidden behind the façade of these two narrow buildings on the banks of the Amstel is a hotel with over 300 rooms. Tavern-restaurant with views of the river. Popular with both individual visitors and tour groups.

Amsterdam
AC ⇄ ℅rest VISA ⑩ AE ⓞ

Damrak 93 ✉ 1012 LP – ℰ (0 20) 555 06 66 – info@hotelamsterdam.nl
– Fax (0 20) 620 47 16 – www.hotelamsterdam.nl   **G1**
79 rm – ♦225/240 € ♦♦285/340 €, ⊑ 12 €
Rest *De Roode Leeuw* 30 € (weekday lunch), 20/30 €
♦ Business ♦ Functional ♦
This veteran Amsterdam hotel enjoys an unbeatable central location on the busy Damstraat. Rooms beyond reproach, with public parking nearby. The hotel brasserie serves a range of typically Dutch specialities.

NETHERLANDS

NH Schiller 🏠 ⅍ ⅍ 🖵 ☎ 💿 VISA ⓩ AE ①
Rembrandtplein 26 ⊠ 1017 CV – ℰ (0 20) 554 07 00 – nhschiller@
nh-hotels.com – Fax (0 20) 624 00 98 – www.nh-hotels.com G2
91 rm – †89/219 € ††99/229 €, ⊑ 16 € – 1 suite
Rest 18 € (weekday lunch)/35 € and a la carte 22/45 €
◆ Chain hotel ◆ Business ◆ Classic ◆
A 1900s-style building fronting a lively square adorned with a statue of
Rembrandt. Adequately equipped rooms with quality furnishings. Pleasant
lobby. In the Art Deco brasserie, make sure you try the Frisse Frits, the bar's
home-brewed beer.

Albus Gd H. without rest ⅍ ⅍ 🖵 ☎ 🖵 VISA ⓩ AE ①
Vijzelstraat 49 ⊠ 1017 HE – ℰ (0 20) 530 62 00 – info@albusgrandhotel.com
– Fax (0 20) 530 62 99 – www.albusgrandhotel.com G2
74 rm – †180/200 € ††180/270 €, ⊑ 14 €
◆ Business ◆ Stylish ◆
This hotel halfway between the flower market and Rembrandtplein provides
good value for money and high levels of comfort. Ideal for guests in the city for
business or leisure.

NH Caransa without rest ⅍ ⅍ 🖵 ☎ 🔊 25/100 VISA ⓩ AE ①
Rembrandtplein 19 ⊠ 1017 CT – ℰ (0 20) 554 08 00 – nhcaransa@
nh-hotels.com – Fax (0 20) 622 37 73 – www.nh-hotels.com G2
66 rm – †99/229 € ††99/229 €, ⊑ 16 €
◆ Chain hotel ◆ Business ◆ Modern ◆
The Caransa's rooms are functional, well-maintained and reasonably sized. The
warm furnishings add a cosy "British" feel. Four seminar rooms available for
business meetings.

Vondel without rest 🚗 ⅍ 🖵 ☎ VISA ⓩ AE ①
Vondelstraat 28 ⊠ 1054 GE – ℰ (0 20) 612 01 20 – reservation@hotelvondel.nl
– Fax (0 20) 685 43 21 – www.hotelvondel.com E3
78 rm – †99/249 € ††189/429 €, ⊑ 17 €
◆ Family ◆ Functional ◆
The Vondel occupies five houses dating from the late 19C. The building housing
the reception has the best rooms, decorated in "boutique" style. Elegant lounges.

Die Port Van Cleve 🖵 rm ⅍ ☎ 🔊 40 VISA ⓩ AE ①
N.Z. Voorburgwal 178 ⊠ 1012 SJ – ℰ (0 20) 624 48 60 – reservations@
dieportvancleve.com – Fax (0 20) 622 02 40 – www.dieportvancleve.com
119 rm – †150/285 € ††150/295 €, ⊑ 18 € – 1 suite F1
Rest a la carte 32/57 €
◆ Chain hotel ◆ Traditional ◆ Classic ◆
The very first Dutch brewery group was established behind this imposing façade
near the royal palace in the 19C. Noteworthy features today include the six junior
suites and a charming Dutch-style bar. Grill-restaurant where steak holds pride
of place.

Dikker en Thijs Fenice without rest ⅍ 🖵 ☎ VISA ⓩ AE ①
Prinsengracht 444 ⊠ 1017 KE – ℰ (0 20) 620 12 12 – info@dtfh.nl
– Fax (0 20) 625 89 86 – www.dtfh.nl F2
42 rm ⊑ – †125/245 € ††150/345 €
◆ Traditional ◆ Business ◆ Classic ◆
This classical building is located 100m/110yd from the Leidseplein, opposite a
small bridge spanning the Prinsengracht, which is visible from a few of the rooms.

NH City Centre ≤ ⅍ rm ⅍ ⅍ 🖵 ☎ 🚗 🖵 VISA ⓩ AE ①
Spuistraat 288 ⊠ 1012 VX – ℰ (0 20) 420 45 45 – Fax (0 20) 420 43 00
– www.nh-hotels.com F2
209 rm – †100/185 € ††100/215 €, ⊑ 16 €
Rest 20 € (weekday lunch) and a la carte 19/35 €
◆ Chain hotel ◆ Business ◆ Modern ◆
Nestled between the Singel and the Begijnhof, this chain hotel offers rooms
which have been newly refurbished in typical NH style. Spacious, comfortable
lounge plus an informal restaurant serving Italian cuisine.

Mercure Arthur Frommer without rest 🏧 🕭 🕮 🅿
Noorderstraat 46 ⊠ 1017 TV – ℰ (0 20) 622 03 28   VISA 🐵 ㏂ ⓞ
– h1032@accor.com – Fax (0 20) 620 32 08 – www.accorhotels.com   **G3**
90 rm – †105/155 € ††125/175 €, � 14 €
♦ Family ♦ Chain hotel ♦ Classic ♦
A series of houses lining a quiet street close to both the Rijksmuseum and the Museum Van Loon. Fairly standard rooms, basic levels of service, but a useful car park.

Canal House without rest 🕭 VISA 🐵 ㏂ ⓞ
Keizersgracht 148 ⊠ 1015 CX – ℰ (0 20) 622 51 82 – info@canalhouse.nl
– Fax (0 20) 624 13 17 – www.canalhouse.nl   **F1**
26 rm – � – †120/190 € ††140/190 €
♦ Traditional ♦ Historic ♦
This 17C canal-front residence has preserved all its old charm. Individually styled rooms, with good views at the front and less noise at the rear. Eclectic mix of furniture.

Golden Tulip-Centre without rest 🕭 🏧 🕭 🕭 VISA 🐵 ㏂ ⓞ
Nieuwezijdskolk 19 ⊠ 1012 PV – ℰ (020) 530 18 18 – informationams@
goldentuliphotelinntel.com – Fax (020) 422 19 19
– www.goldentulipamsterdamcentre.com   **G1**
239 rm – †290 € ††290/350 €, � 18 €
♦ Chain hotel ♦ Business ♦ Modern ♦
A modern hotel at the heart of the vibrant Nieuwe Zijde shopping district near the station. Soundproofed rooms with double-glazing.

Wiechmann without rest 🕭 🕭 🕭 VISA 🐵
Prinsengracht 328 ⊠ 1016 HX – ℰ (0 20) 626 33 21 – info@hotelwiechmann.nl
– Fax (0 20) 626 89 62 – www.hotelwiechmann.nl   **E-F2**
37 rm ⊑ – †55/95 € ††125/145 €
♦ Family ♦ Traditional ♦ Classic ♦
The Wiechmann occupies three maisonettes overlooking the Prinsengracht. The best rooms, albeit slightly more rustic, are to be found on the corners of the building.

Fita without rest 🕭 🕭 VISA 🐵 ㏂ ⓞ
Jan Luykenstraat 37 ⊠ 1071 CL – ℰ (0 20) 679 09 76 – info@fita.nl
– Fax (0 20) 664 39 69   **E3**
16 rm ⊑ – †90/135 € ††120/145 €
♦ Family ♦ Functional ♦
A small hotel offering a perfect base for individual travellers with its three categories of functional bedrooms and great location close to Amsterdam's major museums.

La Rive – Hotel Amstel 🕭 🏧 🕭 🅿 🕭 VISA 🐵 ㏂ ⓞ
Prof. Tulpplein 1 ⊠ 1018 GX – ℰ (0 20) 520 32 64 – evert.groot@
ichotelsgroup.com – Fax (0 20) 520 32 66 – www.restaurantlarive.com
closed 1 to 11 January, 23 July-7 August, Saturday lunch and Sunday   **H3**
Rest 43 € (weekday lunch), 85/110 € and a la carte 78/109 € 🕭
Spec. Turbot et truffe enrobés de spaghetti de pomme de terre, côtes de blette et jus de veau. Pigeonneau grillé et poivron rouge, sauce au maïs. Feuilleté aux pommes, cannelle, glace vanille et caramel au beurre salé.
♦ Contemporary ♦ Formal ♦
Hushed tones, refined decor, a prestigious wine cellar and incomparable comfort are the main features of the Amstel's gourmet restaurant, from where guests can enjoy superb riverside views.

Excelsior – Hotel de l'Europe 🕭 🕭 🏧 🅿 🕭 VISA 🐵 ㏂ ⓞ
Nieuwe Doelenstraat 2 ⊠ 1012 CP – ℰ (0 20) 531 17 05 – hotel@leurope.nl
– Fax (0 20) 531 17 78
closed 1 to 14 January, Saturday lunch and Sunday lunch   **G2**
Rest (open until 11 p.m.) 45 € (weekday lunch), 65/90 € and a la carte 47/70 €
♦ Contemporary ♦ Formal ♦
This century-old palace provides a delightful backdrop to its elegant, classic restaurant. Views of the Munttoren and the ever-busy Amstel River from the lovely terrace. Exclusive ambience.

XXXX **Vermeer** – Hotel NH Barbizon Palace   🏶 ⚙ **P** 🚕 **VISA** ◐◑ **AE** ①
🕸 *Prins Hendrikkade 59* ✉ *1012 AD – €* *(0 20) 556 48 85*
– vermeer@nh-hotels.nl – Fax (0 20) 624 33 53
– www.restaurantvermeer.nl
closed 1 to 8 January, 24 July-27 August, Saturday lunch and Sunday   **G1**
Rest 40 € (weekday lunch), 65/88 € and a la carte approx. 75 €
Spec. Ravioli de ris de veau aux écrevisses. Faisan, sauce de noix et Oloroso sherry
(nov.-dec.). Millefeuille.
♦ **Innovative** ♦ **Minimalist** ♦
This great restaurant adjoining a luxury hotel is appreciated for its friendly
welcome, attentive service, elaborate classic cuisine and opulent-looking
bourgeois-style decor.

XXX **Christophe** (Royer)   🏶 **VISA** ◐◑ **AE** ①
🕸 *Leliegracht 46* ✉ *1015 DH – €* *(0 20) 625 08 07 – info@christophe.nl*
– Fax (0 20) 623 84 20 – www.christophe.nl
closed Sunday and Monday   **F1**
Rest (dinner only) 45 €/65 € and a la carte 58/69 €
Spec. Galette d'aubergines confites aux anchois frais. Pigeonneau rôti en croûte
d'épices, couscous et croustillant de fruits au curry. Ravioli de mangue et
fromage frais aux fruits de la passion.
♦ **French traditional** ♦ **Trendy** ♦
Restaurant in the simple but impeccable setting of a traditional house alongside
the Lys canal. Good, classic cuisine peppered with modern touches. Avoid the
back room in summer.

XXX **Dynasty**   🏶 🏶 ⚙ **VISA** ◐◑ **AE** ①
Reguliersdwarsstraat 30 ✉ *1017 BM – €* *(0 20) 626 84 00*
– Fax (0 20) 622 30 38
closed 27 December-January and Tuesday   **F2**
Rest (dinner only) 36 €/58 € and a la carte 32/61 €
♦ **Chinese** ♦ **Exotic** ♦
Enjoy a wander through the flower market before sitting down to eat at this
Oriental restaurant with its refreshing, multi-coloured decor. Specialities from
Southeast Asia.

XXX **Radèn Mas**   🏶 ⚙ **VISA** ◐◑ **AE** ①
Stadhooderskade 6 ✉ *1054 ES – €* *(0 20) 685 40 41*
– Fax (0 20) 685 39 81
closed 30 April and 31 December   **E3**
Rest (open until 11 p.m.) 30 € and a la carte 35/68 €
♦ **Indonesian** ♦ **Exotic** ♦
This Indonesian restaurant enjoys a flattering reputation for its embodiment of
the culinary heritage of this former Dutch colony. Live piano music every evening
except Tuesday.

XX **d'Vijff Vlieghen**   🏶 🏶 ⚙ **VISA** ◐◑ **AE** ①
Spuistraat 294 (by Vlieghendesteeg 1) ✉ *1012 VX – €* *(0 20) 530 40 60*
– restaurant@vijffvlieghen.nl – Fax (0 20) 623 64 04
– www.thefiveflies.com   **E3**
Rest (dinner only) 24 €/28 € and a la carte 39/55 €
♦ **Dutch regional cuisine** ♦ **Rustic** ♦
The "Five Flies" (Vijff Vlieghen) is a group of small 17C houses concealing a
maze of charming, rustic-style rooms. Traditional à la carte choices and fixed
menus.

XX **Café Roux** – Hotel The Grand Sofitel Demeure   🏶 🏶 ⚙ **P** 🚕
O.Z. Voorburgwal 197 ✉ *1012 EX – €* *(0 20) 555 35 60*   **VISA** ◐◑ **AE** ①
– h2783-fb@accor.com – Fax (0 20) 555 32 22 – www.thegrand.nl   **G2**
Rest 30 € (weekday lunch)/35 € and a la carte 30/70 €
♦ **Brasserie** ♦ **Retro** ♦
The Sofitel Demeure's Art Deco brasserie is known for its inventive modern
cuisine. A mural by K. Appel, a member of the Cobra artistic group, is visible near
the entrance.

NETHERLANDS

XX **Het Tuynhuys**   🖼 🅰🅲 **VISA** 🆖🆗 🅰🅴 ①
Reguliersdwarsstraat 28 ⊠ 1017 BM – ℰ (0 20) 627 66 03 – info@tuynhuys.nl
– Fax (0 20) 423 59 97 – www.tuynhuys.nl
closed Saturday lunch and Sunday lunch   **F2**
Rest 30 € (weekday lunch), 35/45 € and a la carte 40/65 €
♦ French traditional ♦ Fashionable ♦
The menu is distinctly modern in this stylish split-level restaurant with an attractive garden terrace and contemporary dining room adorned with glazed ceramics.

XX **Indrapura**   🅰🅲 **VISA** 🆖🆗 🅰🅴 ①
Rembrandtplein 42 ⊠ 1017 CV – ℰ (0 20) 62373 29 – info@indrapura.nl
– Fax (0 20) 624 90 78 – www.indrapura.nl – closed 31 December   **G2**
Rest (dinner only) a la carte approx. 58 €
♦ Indonesian ♦ Exotic ♦
A good choice of Indonesian dishes, including the classic "rijsttafel" (rice table). Located on a busy square, this restaurant attracts a mix of customers, including tourists, locals and groups.

XX **Sichuan Food**   🅰🅲 **VISA** 🆖🆗 🅰🅴 ①
Reguliersdwarsstraat 35 ⊠ 1017 BK – ℰ (0 20) 626 93 27 – Fax (0 20) 627 72 81
closed 31 December   **F2**
Rest (dinner only) (booking essential) 31 €/43 € and a la carte 35/65 €
♦ Chinese ♦ Exotic ♦
Hidden behind the unremarkable façade is a Chinese restaurant with a good reputation locally, where the flavours of Szechwan take pride of place. The decor is typical of any local Chinese restaurant.

XX **Hosokawa**   🖼 🛋 **VISA** 🆖🆗 🅰🅴 ①
Max Euweplein 22 ⊠ 1017 MB – ℰ (0 20) 638 80 86 – info@hosokawa.nl
– Fax (0 20) 638 22 19 – www.hosokawa.nl
closed Sunday lunch   **F3**
Rest 14 € (weekday lunch), 59/78 € and a la carte 52/74 €
♦ Japanese ♦ Minimalist ♦
A sober, modern Japanese restaurant with eight teppanyaki (hotplates). Worth the trip just to admire the constant circulation of dishes in front of your eyes. Sushi bar.

XX **Van Vlaanderen**   🖼 🅰🅲 **VISA** 🆖🆗 🅰🅴
Weteringschans 175 ⊠ 1017 XD – ℰ (0 20) 622 82 92
closed last week July- mid August, Christmas-New Year, Sunday and Monday
Rest (dinner only) (booking essential) 43 €/50 € and a la carte 57/69 €   **F3**
♦ Contemporary ♦ Trendy ♦
A relaxed atmosphere awaits customers at this restaurant just outside of the centre near the Museum Van Loon and Rijksmuseum. The plain, patinated decor of the large dining area has a contemporary feel.

XX **Breitner**   🛋 **VISA** 🆖🆗 🅰🅴 ①
Amstel 212 ⊠ 1017 AH – ℰ (0 20) 627 78 79 – info@restaurant-breitner.nl
– Fax (0 20) 330 29 98 – www.restaurant-breitner.nl
closed last week July-first week August, 25 December-2 January and Sunday
Rest (dinner only) 34 €/57 € and a la carte 45/69 €   **G2**
♦ Contemporary ♦ Cosy ♦
This restaurant is named after the Dutch Impressionist artist. Modern cuisine, with Mediterranean and international overtones. Wines from around the world. Views of the Amstel.

XX **Segugio**   🅰🅲 🛋 **VISA** 🆖🆗 🅰🅴 ①
Utrechtsestraat 96 ⊠ 1017 VS – ℰ (0 20) 330 15 03 – adriano@segugio.nl
– Fax (0 20) 330 15 16 – www.segugio.nl
closed 24 December-1 January and Sunday   **G3**
Rest (dinner only) 53 € and a la carte 48/61 €
♦ Italian ♦ Trendy ♦
A good sense of smell is all you need to locate this "ristorante" which takes its name from a breed of hunting dog also used as a truffle hound. Good choice of Italian wines.

XX **Le Pêcheur**   🖼 ℅ 𝑉𝐼𝑆𝐴 ⓒⓢ ⒶⒺ ⓞ

Reguliersdwarsstraat 32 ⊠ 1017 BM – ℰ (0 20) 624 31 21 – rien.vansanten @
chello.nl – Fax (0 20) 624 31 21
closed Sunday   F2
Rest 33 € (weekday lunch) and a la carte approx. 36 €
♦ Seafood ♦ Friendly ♦
As its name (The Fisherman) would suggest, fish and seafood take pride of place
in this restaurant alongside the flower market. Terrace to the rear and parking
nearby.

XX **d'theeboom**   🖼 𝑉𝐼𝑆𝐴 ⓒⓢ ⒶⒺ ⓞ

Singel 210 ⊠ 1016 AB – ℰ (0 20) 623 84 20 – info @ theeboom.com
– Fax (0 20) 421 25 12 – www.theeboom.com
closed 24 December-5 January and Sunday   F1
Rest (dinner only) 33 €/40 € and a la carte approx. 45 €
♦ Traditional ♦ Retro ♦
Firmly established along the Singel, 200m/220yd from the Dam, "The Tea Tree"
is a far cry from the tea room its name might suggest! It is in fact a restaurant with
an interesting menu of inventive dishes.

XX **Le Relais** – Hotel de l'Europe   🔤 ⇥ 𝑉𝐼𝑆𝐴 ⓒⓢ ⒶⒺ ⓞ

(😊) *Nieuwe Doelenstraat 2 ⊠ 1012 CP – ℰ (0 20) 531 17 04 – hotel @ leurope.nl*
– Fax (0 20) 531 17 78   G2
Rest (open until 11 p.m.) 23 € (weekday lunch)/30 € and a la carte 30/45 €
♦ Brasserie ♦ Wine bar ♦
A small, elegant restaurant within a large hotel where you immediately feel in
good hands. Traditional choices on a menu without any particular culinary theme.

XX **Beddington's**   🖼 ℅ 𝑉𝐼𝑆𝐴 ⓒⓢ ⒶⒺ ⓞ

Utrechtsedwarsstraat 141 ⊠ 1017 WE – ℰ (0 20) 620 73 93 – Fax (0 20) 620 01 90
closed 1 to 9 January, 24 July-14 August, 24 December-10 January, Sunday and
Monday   G3
Rest (dinner only) 42 €/48 €
♦ Contemporary ♦ Fashionable ♦
An English chef who has made Amsterdam his home runs the open kitchen of
this modern restaurant serving up dishes in a black and white interior decor.

X **Borderwijk**   🔤 ℅ 𝑉𝐼𝑆𝐴 ⓒⓢ ⒶⒺ ⓞ

Noordermarkt 7 ⊠ 1015 MV – ℰ (0 20) 624 38 99 – Fax (0 20) 420 66 03
closed mid July-mid August and Monday   F1
Rest (dinner only) 37 €/53 € and a la carte 47/61 €
♦ Contemporary ♦ Trendy ♦
One of the trendiest restaurants in the Jordaan district with a lively dining room
furnished in a sober, yet modern style. Appetising classic menu with modern
touches and a good wine list.

X **Haesje Claes**   🖼 🔤 ℅ 𝑉𝐼𝑆𝐴 ⓒⓢ ⒶⒺ ⓞ

Spuistraat 275 ⊠ 1012 VR – ℰ (0 20) 624 99 98 – info @ haesjeclaes.nl
– Fax (0 20) 627 48 17 – www.haesjeclaes.nl
closed 30 April and 25, 26 and 31 December   F2
Rest 19 €/29 € and a la carte 24/34 €
♦ Dutch regional cuisine ♦ Rustic ♦
With its local atmosphere and loyal customers, this welcoming restaurant serves
true Flemish fare: unfussy, generous and satisfying. 100m/110yd from the
History Museum.

X **Entresol**   🔤 ⇥(dinner) 𝑉𝐼𝑆𝐴 ⓒⓢ ⒶⒺ

Geldersekade 29 ⊠ 1011 EJ – ℰ (0 20) 623 79 12 – entresol @ chello.nl
– www.entresol.nu
closed last 2 weeks July-first week August, Monday and Tuesday   G1
Rest (dinner only) 33 €/43 € and a la carte 33/45 €
♦ Contemporary ♦ Rustic ♦
This charming, small family restaurant near Amsterdam's Chinatown is
housed in a 17C building. Dutch-style decor in the dining rooms spread over two
floors.

NETHERLANDS

X **Blue Pepper** VISA ●● AE ●
Nassaukade 366h ⊠ *1054 AB* – ℰ *(0 20) 489 70 39*
– info@restaurantbluepepper.com – www.restaurantbluepepper.com
closed 23 December-2 January **E2**
Rest (dinner only) 45 €/55 € and a la carte approx. 43 €
♦ Indonesian ♦ Exotic ♦
Filtered light, monochrome blues and delicate floral touches provide the basis of Blue Pepper's tranquil decor. Refined Javanese cuisine served on attractive tableware.

X **L'Indochine** AC ⊏✦(dinner) VISA ●● AE ●
Beulingstraat 9 ⊠ *1017 BA* – ℰ *(0 20) 627 57 55*
– indochineamsterdam@hotmail.com – Fax (0 20) 330 09 34
– www.indochine.nl
closed Monday **F2**
Rest (dinner only) 35 € and a la carte 37/62 €
♦ Vietnamese ♦ Exotic ♦
Embark upon a gastronomic journey between the gulfs of Siam and Tonkin in this small, simply furnished restaurant with a "colonial" name. Choice of French wines.

SOUTH and WEST QUARTERS *Plan I*

Okura ⓢ ●● Ĺέ Ŋ ▢ ὸrm AC ↳ ♉ ▣ ℰ⌾ ⅊25/1200 ⌂ ℗
Ferdinand Bolstraat 333 ⊠ *1072 LH* ⊏✦ VISA ●● AE ●
– ℰ (0 20) 678 71 11 – sales@okura.nl – Fax (0 20) 671 23 44
– www.okura.nl **C2**
323 rm � – †260/430 € ††295/465 € – 12 suites
Rest see *Ciel Bleu* and *Yamazato* below
Rest *Sazanka* (dinner only) 53 €/83 € and a la carte 43/107 €
Rest *Brasserie le Camelia* (open until 11p.m.) 25 €/33 € and a la carte approx. 42 €
♦ Grand Luxury ♦ Traditional ♦ Classic ♦
This luxury Japanese-style international hotel overlooks the Noorder Amstel canal. Superb health centre and extensive conference facilities. Japanese restaurant with dishes cooked on typical hobs. The Camelia brasserie serves a variety of French cuisine.

Hilton ← ♉ Ĺέ Ŋ ∰ ὸrm AC ↳ ♉rest ℰ⌾ ⅊25/550 ℗
Apollolaan 138 ⊠ *1077 BG* – ℰ *(0 20) 710 60 00* VISA ●● AE ●
– info.amsterdam@hilton.com – Fax (0 20) 710 60 80
– www.amsterdamhilton.com **B2**
267 rm – †260/395 € ††260/395 €, � 25 € – 4 suites
Rest *Roberto's* a la carte 45/54 €
♦ Chain hotel ♦ Business ♦ Stylish ♦
Spacious modern chain hotel with a canal-side garden and terraces. Rooms and suites offering panoramic views, including one evoking "John and Yoko" in 1969. Roberto's restaurant specialises in Italian cuisine with a choice of menus and antipasti buffets; al fresco dining in summer.

Bilderberg Garden AC ↳ ▣ ℰ⌾ ⅊25/150 ℗ ⊏✦ VISA ●● AE ●
Dijsselhofplantsoen 7 ⊠ *1077 BJ* – ℰ *(0 20) 570 56 00*
– garden@bilderberg.nl – Fax (0 20) 570 56 54
– www.gardenhotel.nl **B2**
120 rm – †140/350 € ††140/350 €, � 21 € – 2 suites
Rest see *Mangerie De Kersentuin* below
♦ Business ♦ Personalised ♦
This small-sized "grand hotel" combines discreet luxury and charm. Rooms with everything you could possibly need, decorated with taste and a fine sense of detail.

NETHERLANDS

Le Meridien Apollo
≤ 🕸 🕎 🎧 🌵 ⅍ 📺 ⚙️ 25/200 🅿️

Apollolaan 2 ⊠ 1077 BA – ℰ (0 20) 673 59 22 — 🖙 VISA ⓶ 🖭 ①
– info.apollo@lemeridien.com – Fax (0 20) 570 57 44
– www.lemeridien.com

B2

217 rm – †305 € ††305 €, � 21 € – 2 suites
Rest *La Sirène* 33 € (weekday lunch) and a la carte 45/53 €

♦ Chain hotel ♦ Business ♦ Classic ♦

Located away from the frenetic pace of the centre at the junction of five canals, this upmarket chain hotel offers guests comfortable rooms and a full range of services. Spacious modern restaurant with a waterfront terrace and an emphasis on fish and seafood.

Holiday Inn
🕎 🎧 &rm 🎧 ⅍ ⅍rest ⚙️ 25/350 🅿️ VISA ⓶ 🖭 ①

De Boelelaan 2 ⊠ 1083 HJ – ℰ (0 20) 646 23 00 – info@vermont.nl
– Fax (0 20) 517 27 64 – www.vermont.nl

C2

254 rm – †135/295 € ††150/340 €, ⊆ 20 € – 2 suites
Rest 24 € (weekday lunch), 33/55 € and a la carte 34/45 €

♦ Chain hotel ♦ Business ♦ Classic ♦

Located close to the RAI exhibition centre, this chain hotel offers guests spacious and discreetly luxurious bedrooms and public areas. American-style dining, encompassing a highly varied menu and salad bar.

The Gresham Memphis without rest
🎧 ⅍ ⅍ ℰ

De Lairessestraat 87 ⊠ 1071 NX — ⚙️40 VISA ⓶ 🖭 ①
– ℰ (0 20) 673 31 49 – info@gresham-memphishotel.nl
– Fax (0 20) 664 70 04 – www.memphishotel.nl

B2

74 rm – †205 € ††250/295 €, ⊆ 18 €

♦ Traditional ♦ Business ♦ Stylish ♦

This hotel has a façade covered with greenery and, on its doorstep, a tramway which runs to the city centre. Modern, elegant and intimate salon-bar, fresh-feeling rooms and a pleasant breakfast area.

Tulip Inn City West
&rm 🎧 ⅍ ⅍rest ⚙️ 25/70 VISA ⓶ 🖭 ①

Reimerswaalstraat 5 ⊠ 1069 AE – ℰ (0 20) 410 80 00
– info@tiamsterdamcw.nl – Fax (0 20) 410 80 30
– www.tiamsterdamcw.nl

A2

162 rm – †135 € ††150/205 €, ⊆ 14 €
Rest (dinner only) a la carte 22/40 €

♦ Chain hotel ♦ Business ♦ Functional ♦

This recently opened chain hotel is situated in a relatively quiet area of the city. Its main selling points are its spacious rooms and lounges, and the good parking facilities nearby. Although traditional, the restaurant menu shows contemporary influence.

Museum Square without rest
⅍ ⅍ 📺 ℰ VISA ⓶ 🖭 ①

De Lairessestraat 7 ⊠ 1071 NR – ℰ (0 20) 671 95 96 – museumsquare@
amsterdamcityhotels.nl – Fax (0 20) 671 17 56
– www.amsterdamcityhotels.nl

B2

34 rm ⊆ – †89/145 € ††109/175 €

♦ Chain hotel ♦ Business ♦ Functional ♦

Despite its unremarkable façade, this hotel is well-maintained and enjoys a superb location close to three of the city's most important museums. Spacious rooms with modern furniture.

Tulip Inn Art
🎧 🎧 ⅍ ⅍ ℰ ⚙️25 ⌂ VISA ⓶ 🖭 ①

Spaarndammerdijk 302 (westerpark) ⊠ 1013 ZX – ℰ (0 20) 410 96 70
– art@westlordhotels.nl – Fax (0 20) 681 08 02
– www.westlordhotels.nl

B1

130 rm – †79/210 € ††79/250 €, ⊆ 10 €
Rest 40 € and a la carte approx. 36 €

♦ Chain hotel ♦ Business ♦ Modern ♦

A thoroughly modern hotel close to the ring-road with rooms designed with the modern business traveller in mind. Exhibition of paintings by contemporary artists. Trendy brasserie-style tavern-restaurant.

NETHERLANDS

Novotel &rm 🏧 🌡 📺 📠 25/225 **P** *VISA* ◑◐ 🜨 ①
*Europaboulevard 10 ⊠ 1083 AD – ℰ (0 20) 541 11 23 – ho515@accor.com
– Fax (0 20) 646 28 23*   **C3**
611 rm – †199 € ††219/285 €, � 18 €
Rest (open until midnight) a la carte 27/40 €
♦ Chain hotel ♦ Business ♦ Functional ♦
This vast hotel is frequented by tour groups and business travellers alike, with
rooms of the standard you would expect from the Novotel name.

NH Museum Quarter without rest 🛗 🏧 🎇 🕏 *VISA* ◑◐ 🜨
*Hobbemakade 50 ⊠ 1071 XL – ℰ (0 20) 537 82 00 – nhmuseumquarter@
nh-hotels.com – Fax (0 20) 573 82 99 – www.nh-hotels.com*   **B-C2**
163 rm – †135/190 € ††135/190 €, ⊷ 16 €
♦ Chain hotel ♦ Business ♦ Design ♦
International hotel chain with uniform, modern rooms. Those at the rear are the
best. Simple food served around the clock in the lounge bar.

De Filosoof without rest 🛝 🎇 📺 🕏 📠 25 *VISA* ◑◐ 🜨
*Anna van den Vondelstraat 6 ⊠ 1054 GZ – ℰ (0 20) 683 30 13 – reservations@
hotelfilosoof.nl – Fax (0 20) 685 37 50 – www.hotelfilosoof.nl*   **B2**
38 rm ⊷ – †115 € ††125/150 €
♦ Family ♦ Personalised ♦
An original hotel on a one-way street skirting the Vondelpark. The decor here is
inspired by cultural and philosophical themes, which can be mused on further in
the garden.

Villa Borgmann without rest 🛝 🎇 📺 *VISA* ◑◐ 🜨 ①
*Koningslaan 48 ⊠ 1075 AE – ℰ (0 20) 673 52 52 – info@hotel-borgmann.nl
– Fax (0 20) 676 25 80 – www.hotel-borgmann.nl*   **B2**
15 rm ⊷ – †85/99 € ††120/189 €
♦ Family ♦ Classic ♦
This attractive, 1900s red-brick villa near the refreshing Vondelpark is family-run
and offers large, modern rooms.

XXXX   **Ciel Bleu** – Hotel Okura (23rd floor)   ≤ ville, 🏧 🎇 **P** ⊒
✿   *Ferdinand Bolstraat 333 ⊠ 1072 LH – ℰ (0 20) 678 83 40*   *VISA* ◑◐ 🜨 ①
      – restaurants@okura.nl – Fax (0 20) 678 77 88 – www.okura.nl
      closed mid July-mid August and end December   **C2**
      Rest (dinner only) 55 €/93 € and a la carte 58/103 €
      Spec. Saint-Jacques grillées aux truffes. Suprême de pigeon d'Anjou. Parade de
      chocolat.
      ♦ Traditional ♦ Formal ♦
      This contemporary-style restaurant at the top of a Japanese palace enjoys a
      superb view of the city's rooftops. You can watch the delicious food being
      prepared via a live video link.

XXX   **Rosarium**   ≤ 🏡 🕭 🎇 **P** *VISA* ◑◐ 🜨 ①
      *Amstelpark 1 ⊠ 1083 HZ – ℰ (0 20) 644 40 85 – info@rosarium.net
      – Fax (0 20) 646 60 04*
      closed Saturday and Sunday   **C3**
      Rest a la carte 38/51 €
      ♦ Contemporary ♦ Friendly ♦
      This modern structure in the Amstelpark is home to a spacious modern
      restaurant, a wine-bar and eight meeting rooms. Polished designer decor.

XX   **Yamazato** – Hotel Okura   🏧 🎇 **P** ⊒ *VISA* ◑◐ 🜨 ①
✿   *Ferdinand Bolstraat 333 ⊠ 1072 LH – ℰ (0 20) 678 83 51 – restaurants@okura.nl
      – Fax (0 20) 678 77 88 – www.okura.nl*   **C2**
      Rest (open until 11p.m.) 49 € (weekday lunch), 55/90 € and a la carte 33/69 €
      Spec. Tokusen Sushi. Tempura de homard. Shabu Shabu (beef)
      ♦ Japanese ♦ Minimalist ♦
      A minimalist ambience pervades this restaurant serving delicious traditional
      Japanese dishes under the watchful gaze of geisha girls. Lunch box menu also
      available.

NETHERLANDS

XX **Visaandeschelde** 🏠 AC 🅿 ⊐🍴(dinner) VISA ⊙⊙ AE ⓪
Scheldeplein 4 ⊠ 1078 GR – ℰ (0 20) 675 15 83 – info @ visaandeschelde.nl
– Fax (0 20) 471 46 53 – www.visaandeschelde.nl
closed 24 December-5 January, Saturday lunch and Sunday lunch **C2**
Rest (open until 11 p.m.) 29 € (weekday lunch) and a la carte 41/134 €
♦ Seafood ♦ Fashionable ♦
The model of the boat in the window leaves little doubt about this restaurant's culinary intentions. A bright, somewhat spartan dining room decorated in maritime blue and white.

XX **Mangerie De Kersentuin** – Hotel Bilderberg Garden 🏠 AC 🅿
Dijsselhofplantsoen 7 ⊠ 1077 BJ – ℰ (0 20) ⊐🍴 VISA ⊙⊙ AE ⓪
570 56 00 – garden @ bilderberg.nl – Fax (0 20) 570 56 54
– www.mangeriedekersentuin.nl
closed 21 December-1 January, Saturday lunch and Sunday **B2**
Rest 25 € (weekday lunch)/30 € and a la carte 36/54 €
♦ Contemporary ♦ Fashionable ♦
A brasserie-style atmosphere pervades this eatery, with its gleaming copper fittings and comfortable red benches. Inviting contemporary menu and welcoming summer terrace.

XX **Le Garage** AC ⊐🍴(dinner) VISA ⊙⊙ AE ⓪
😊 *Ruysdaelstraat 54 ⊠ 1071 XE – ℰ (0 20) 679 71 76 – info @ restaurantlegarage.nl*
– Fax (0 20) 662 22 49
closed Easter, Whitsun, first 2 weeks August, Christmas, New Year, Saturday lunch and Sunday lunch **B-C2**
Rest (open until 11p.m.) 30 € (weekday lunch), 33/50 € and a la carte 44/83 €
♦ Contemporary ♦ Brasserie ♦
A theatrical atmosphere and cosmopolitan exuberance pervade this modern brasserie whose menu is both varied and imaginative. Lively tapas bar-restaurant next door.

X **Blender** 🏠 ⊐🍴 VISA ⊙⊙ AE
Van der Palmkade 16 ⊠ 1051 RE – ℰ (0 20) 486 98 60 – info @ blender.to
– Fax (0 20) 486 98 51 – www.blender.to
closed Sunday in summer and Monday *Plan II* **E1**
Rest (dinner only) 33 €/45 € and a la carte 36/44 €
♦ Contemporary ♦ Trendy ♦
Blender occupies the ground floor of a circular building where the atmosphere is distinctly young and trendy. A semi-circular counter and charming, attentive service.

X **Le Hollandais** AC VISA ⊙⊙ AE ⓪
Amsteldijk 41 ⊠ 1074 HV – ℰ (0 20) 679 12 48 – info @ lehollandais.nl
– www.lehollandais.nl
closed August and Sunday **C2**
Rest (dinner only) 31 €/41 € and a la carte 34/49 €
♦ Traditional ♦ Trendy ♦
An endearing local bistro-cum-restaurant attracting a professional/bohemian clientele. Modern cuisine in a simple, minimalist setting.

X **Pakistan** VISA ⊙⊙ AE ⓪
Scheldestraat 100 ⊠ 1078 GP – ℰ (0 20) 675 39 76 – Fax (0 20) 675 39 76
Rest (dinner only) (open until 11 p.m.) 25 €/45 € and a la carte 30/50 € **C2**
♦ Indian ♦ Family ♦
This authentic Pakistani restaurant near the RAI remains popular thanks to its range of copious set menus. No pork on the menu, but plenty of beef.

X **Spring** 🏠 AC 🍴 VISA ⊙⊙ AE ⓪
Willemsparkweg 177 ⊠ 1071 GZ – ℰ (0 20) 675 44 21 – info @ restaurantspring.nl
– Fax (0 20) 676 94 14 – www.restaurantspring.nl
closed Saturday lunch and Sunday **B2**
Rest 30 € (weekday lunch), 35/44 € and a la carte 44/61 €
♦ Contemporary ♦ Design ♦
This trendy eatery with a long and narrow designer dining room is cut in two by an unusual bench. Highly contemporary cuisine and a collection of canvases by Jasper Krabbé.

X **Brasserie van Baerle** ⌂ VISA ⓪ⓒ AE ⓞ

Van Baerlestraat 158 ⊠ 1071 BG – ✆ (0 20) 679 15 32 – brasserievanbaerle@
xshall.nl – Fax (0 20) 671 71 96 – www.brasserievanbaerle.nl
closed 25 and 26 December and 1 January   **B2**
Rest (open until 11 p.m.) 33 € (weekday lunch) and a la carte 42/64 €
 ♦ **Traditional** ♦ **Brasserie** ♦
A pleasant restaurant popular with a loyal local clientele tempted by an attractive
menu enhanced by a carefully selected wine list. Sunday brunch.

AT SCHIPHOL AIRPORT   *Plan I*

🏨 **Sheraton Airport** ℔ 🕉 ♿rm 🅰 🛗 ▥ 🛗25/500

Schiphol bd 101 ⊠ 1118 BG   ⌂ VISA ⓪ⓒ AE ⓞ
– ✆ (0 20) 316 43 00 – sales.amsterdam@starwoodhotels.com
– Fax (0 20) 316 43 99 – www.sheraton.com/amsterdamair
398 rm – ♦138/345 € ♦♦138/370 €, ⌷ 25 € – 8 suites
Rest *Voyager* 40 € (weekday lunch) and a la carte 54/71 €
 ♦ **Chain hotel** ♦ **Business** ♦ **Modern** ♦
The Schiphol Sheraton is designed predominantly for business clients, with
rooms offering the latest in facilities. An attractive atrium, a comprehensive
range of services, and a modern brasserie crowned by a blue cupola. Evening
buffets.

🏨 **Hilton Schiphol** ℔ 🕉 ♿rm 🅰 🛗 ⅍rest ▥ 🛗25/60

Schiphol bd 701 ⊠ 1118 ZK   P VISA ⓪ⓒ AE ⓞ
– ✆ (0 20) 710 40 00 – hilton.schiphol@hilton.nl – Fax (0 20) 710 40 80
278 rm – ♦199/314 € ♦♦239/349 €, ⌷ 25 € – 2 suites
Rest *East West* (closed 10 July-3 September and Friday-Sunday) (dinner only)
50 €/55 € and a la carte 47/60 €
Rest *Greenhouse* (open until 11p.m.) 39 € and a la carte 33/63 €
 ♦ **Chain hotel** ♦ **Business** ♦ **Classic** ♦
Facilities at the airport Hilton include rooms with high levels of comfort, a
business centre and seminar rooms, not to mention direct access to the airport.
The East West restaurant is known for its fusion of Western and Asian flavours.
The Greenhouse serves international cuisine.

🏨 **Dorint Sofitel Airport** ⌂ ℔ 🕉 ▦ ♿ 🅰 🛗 ⅍ ▥ ☏ 🛗25/640

Stationsplein Zuid-West 951 (Schiphol-Oost)   ⌂ VISA ⓪ⓒ AE ⓞ
⊠ 1117 CE – ✆ (0 20) 540 07 77 – H5332.FB1@accor.com
– Fax (0 20) 540 07 00 – www.accor.com   **A3**
438 rm – ♦320 € ♦♦320 €, ⌷ 20 € – 4 suites
Rest *Nadar* (closed Saturday lunch and Sunday lunch) 25 € (weekday
lunch)/33 € and a la carte 31/49 €
 ♦ **Chain hotel** ♦ **Business** ♦ **Modern** ♦
This modern hotel and conference centre between the airport and Amsterdamse
Bos is arranged around a large patio. Numerous "executive" rooms, plus a
24-hour English-style pub. The Nadar restaurant is named after a famous 19C
French balloonist.

🏨 **Radisson SAS Airport** ⌕ ⌂ ℔ 🕉 ♿rm 🅰 🛗 ⅍rest ▥ ☏

Boeing Avenue 2 (South : 4 km by   🛗25/600 P VISA ⓪ⓒ AE ⓞ
N 201 at Rijk) ⊠ 1119 PB – ✆ (0 20)
655 31 31 – reservations.amsterdam.airport@radissonsas.com
– Fax (0 20) 655 31 00 – www.radissonsas.com
277 rm – ♦219/239 € ♦♦219/239 €, ⌷ 19 € – 2 suites
Rest 34 €/39 € and a la carte 38/59 €
 ♦ **Chain hotel** ♦ **Business** ♦ **Modern** ♦
With its proximity to the airport and motorway, large, friendly feel and
well-equipped, discreetly luxurious rooms, the Radisson is the perfect base for a
business trip. The menu in the Mediterranean restaurant shows a distinct
fondness for all things Italian!

NETHERLANDS

Courtyard by Marriott-Amsterdam Airport　🏠 £å ⑰ ⑤rm
Kruisweg 1401　🖂 ⑭ ↙ ⑰ 🔤 📞 ⑤♨25/160 *VISA* ⑩ AE ①
🖂 *2131 MD (Hoofddorp) –* ⑥ *(0 23) 556 90 00 – jo-habets@courtyard.com*
– Fax (0 23) 556 90 09
148 rm – †85/215 €　††115/395 €, ⊑ 16 €
Rest 20 € (weekday lunch)/30 € and a la carte 19/35 €
♦ Chain hotel ♦ Business ♦ Modern ♦
This modern hotel on the edge of a large park between Haarlem and the airport
is geared towards business clientele. Spacious, modern rooms, plus a sauna and
fitness room.

Schiphol A 4　🏠 ▥ ⑤rm ↙ 🔤 📞 ⑤♨25/1500 **P** *VISA* ⑩ AE ①
Rijksweg A 4 n° 3 (South : 4 km, Den Ruygen Hoek) 🖂 *2132 MA –* ⑥ *(0 252) 67*
53 35 – info@schiphol.valk.nl – Fax (0 252) 62 92 45 – www.hotelschiphol.nl
431 rm – †75/125 €　††90/145 €, ⊑ 15 € – 2 suites
Rest 15 € (weekday lunch) and a la carte 18/80 €
♦ Chain hotel ♦ Business ♦ Functional ♦
A practical option for those with a plane to catch. Numerous room categories and
a huge conference capacity. Part of the Van der Valk group, with its colourful
Toucan logo.

Artemis　🏠 £å ⑰ ⑤ ⑭ ↙ ⑭rm 🔤 📞 ⑤♨25/225 ⊝ *VISA* ⑩ AE ①
John M. Keynesplein 2 (sortie ① Sloten) 🖂 *1066 EP –* ⑥ *(0 20) 718 90 00*
– sales-marketing@aconplazahotels.com – Fax (0 20) 617 04 52
– www.artemisamsterdam.com　**A2**
256 rm – †130/270 €　††130/335 €, ⊑ 18 €
Rest a la carte approx. 35 €
♦ Business ♦ Modern ♦
This modern hotel is nestled in an expanding business district. It offers good
rooms in a contemporary style to match that of the public areas. Huge designer
restaurant and large terrace on the edge of the water.

Mercure Airport　⑤rm ⑭ ↙ 🔤 ⑤♨25/300 **P** *VISA* ⑩ AE ①
Oude Haagseweg 20 (exit ① Sloten) 🖂 *1066 BW –* ⑥ *(0 20) 617 90 05*
– h1315@accor.com – Fax (0 20) 615 90 27 – www.accorhotels.com　**A2**
152 rm – †139/189 €　††159/269 €, ⊑ 18 €
Rest 20 € (weekday lunch)/30 € and a la carte 28/46 €
♦ Chain hotel ♦ Business ♦ Functional ♦
A shuttle service covers the 3km/2mi between this chain hotel and Schiphol
airport. Despite being on the motorway, the Mercure's large, comfortable rooms
offer both peace and quiet.

XX　**De Herbergh** with rm　🏠 ⑭ rest ⑭rm 🔤 ⑤♨35 **P** *VISA* ⑩ AE ①
Sloterweg 259 🖂 *1171 CP Badhoevedorp –* ⑥ *(0 20) 659 26 00*
– info@herbergh.nl – Fax (0 20) 659 83 90 – www.herbergh.nl
24 rm – †75/100 €　††80/110 €, ⊑ 11 €
Rest *(closed Saturday lunch)* 27 € (weekday lunch)/35 € and a la carte 36/45 €
♦ Traditional ♦ Bistro ♦
A hundred-year-old inn serving contemporary cuisine with good facilities for
small business seminars. Functional bedrooms with a full array of creature
comforts.

XX　**Marktzicht**　🏠 *VISA* ⑩ AE ①
Marktplein 31 🖂 *2132 DA Hoofddorp –* ⑥ *(0 23) 561 24 11*
– keesplasmeijer@planet.nl – Fax (0 23) 563 72 91 – restaurant-marktzicht.nl
closed Sunday
Rest 30 € (weekday lunch) and a la carte 38/57 €
♦ Traditional ♦ Family ♦
This traditional "auberge" on the Markt dates from 1860 and was built during
construction of the polder now home to Schiphol airport. Dutch dishes feature
heavily on the menu.

ROTTERDAM

Population (est. 2005): 601 000 (conurbation 3 340 000) – Altitude: sea level

M. Gotin/SCOPE

Rotterdam, the Netherlands' second most populated city, is one of the world's largest ports, located on the Nieuwe Maas which flows into the North Sea, and near the mouth of two important rivers – the Rhine and the Maas – leading to the industrial areas inland. The city of Rotterdam sprawls over both banks of the river and is linked by tunnels, bridges and the metro.

Rotterdam has been improving its port since it was first developed in the late 16C. From 1866 to 1872 the Nieuwe Waterweg (New Waterway) leading to the sea was excavated; several man-made harbours were built in the late 19C. Rotterdam was largely destroyed during the Second World War but has been entirely rebuilt and has a great deal of important modern architecture. Many new buildings erected during the 1980s and 90s have made radical changes to the city's skyline and earned Rotterdam the nickname of Manhattan on the Maas. The latest project is the development of the Kop van Zuid on the south side of the Nieuwe Maas – the creation of a second centre for Rotterdam by around 2010. In 1996 the two halves were linked by Erasmusbrug (Erasmus Bridge).

Rotterdam is the birth place (1469) of the great humanist Erasmus, Geert Geertsz. He travelled widely in Europe and died in Basle in 1536 but he is honoured in the name of the university in his native city.

WHICH DISTRICT TO CHOOSE

The greatest concentration of **hotels** is in the city centre between the railway station *Plan II* **E1** and the Nieuwe Maas *Plan II* **F2**; as the city was rebuilt after the war, the hotels are modern buildings. There are also a few more traditional hotels on the outskirts.

Most **restaurants** are in the city centre, although a few are attached to the hotels in the suburbs.

ARRIVAL – DEPARTURE

ROTTERDAM

♦ **Airport** – About 6km (4 miles) northwest of city centre. ℰ 010 446 34 44; www.rotterdam-airport.nl

From the airport to the city centre – By **taxi** (15min), €20-€23, ℰ 0102 62 04 06 (Rotterdam Airport Taxi). By **shuttle bus** No 33 and No 43 (20min) to Central Railway Station every 10min, single €2.70; ℰ 0900 92 92; www.9292ov.nl; www.ret.nl

Railway Station – Regular train services to the **Centraal Station** *Plan II* **E1** from the major towns in the Netherlands, Belgium, France and Germany; www.ns.nl

Ferry Terminal – Regular ferry services from England: Harwich (www.stenaline.co.uk) and Hull (www.poferries.com).

TRANSPORT

♦ BUSES

The extensive network (RET) consists of metro, bus and train services. ℰ 0900 92 92. Tickets on sale at the service point in front of the railway station or at Coolsingel 141; 1-hour ticket €2.70; 2-strip, 3-strip, 8-strip, 15-strip and 45-strip tickets at €1.60, €2.40, €6.40, €6.70 and €19.80; 1-day, 2-day and 3-day tickets, €6.40, €9.60 and €12.80. In summer the tourist tram, No 10, serves the main sights. ℰ 0800 60 61; www.ret.rotterdam.nl

◆ TAXIS

Taxis bear blue number plates and an illuminated sign on the roof. They may be called by telephone or hired at taxi ranks – airport, railway stations; although they are not supposed to stop, they can also be hailed in the street. Pick-up charge €5.12; price per km €1.94; taxi fares are usually rounded up (5-10%). ✆ 462 60 60 (Rotterdam Taxi Centre).

◆ BICYCLES

Bicycles can be hired at the cycle shop at the station; €6 per day, €25 per week. ✆ 010 412 62 20.

◆ ROTTERDAM CARD

Rotterdam card provides unlimited use of the transport network and free admission to most attractions; 24hr-card €25 and 72hr-card €49.50.

USEFUL ADDRESSES

◆ TOURIST OFFICES

VVV Rotterdam – Coolsingel 67 *Plan II* **E1**; Open Mon-Sat 9.30am-6pm (9pm Fri, 5pm Sat), ✆ 010 403 40 65, 010 414 0000. Coolsingel 197, ✆ 010 489 77 77. Rotterdam Airport Info Desk, Airportplein 60, ✆ 010 446 34 44; www.vvv.rotterdam.nl; www.rotterdam.info; www.gorotterdam.com; www.rotterdam-Airport.nl

◆ POST OFFICES

Post Offices are open Mon-Fri 8.30am-5pm. Longer opening hours (also Saturday 8.30-noon) are available at some large city branches.

◆ BANKS/CURRENCY EXCHANGE

Opening times are Mon-Fri 9am-4pm. Longer opening hours (Thurs 9am-9pm and Sat morning) are available at some large city banks. All close on public holidays. Bank cash machines (ATMs) are open 24hrs (pin number required).

◆ EMERGENCY

Phone ✆ **112** for the emergency services; Police ✆ **0900 88 44**.

BUSY PERIODS

It may be difficult to find a room at a reasonable price (except at weekends) during special events:

International Film Festival: January – 12-day film festival.

Dunya Festival: early June – Multicultural event.

Carnival Street Parade: July – Tropical-style summer event.

FFWD Dance Parade: August – huge techno, hip-hop and big-beat event.

Wereldhavenfestival: early September – Discover the port of Rotterdam.

September in Rotterdam: September – Arts and cultural event.

EXPLORING ROTTERDAM

In two days there is time to visit the main sights and museums.

Rotterdam Welcome Card offers €100 worth of benefits.

Opening times are usually from 10/11am-4/5pm but closed on Mondays and public holidays.

VISITING

Museum Boijmans Van Beuningen *Plan II* **E2** – Fine Arts Museum: rich collection of antiques, modern and contemporary works of art, engravings, decorative arts section (17C glassware and earthenware).

Maritiem Museum Rotterdam *Plan II* **F2** – History of the port of Rotterdam.

Nederlands Architectuurinstituut *Plan II* **E2** – Complex, consisting of four buildings, each in its own style serving a different function: offices and library on Dutch and foreign architecture; auditorium, exhibition wing; collection wing.

Oude Haven *Plan II* **F2** – Rotterdam's first harbour (1325), now a pleasant place for a stroll or for admiring the **Witte Huis**, a 19C office block and the only remnant of the pre-war period; the old Dutch commercial sailing ships of the Inland Waterways Museum *(Openlucht Binnenvaart Museuum)*, and the impressive cable-stayed **Willemsbrug** spanning the Nieuwe Maas. A few steps north is **Overblaak**, cube-shaped apartments spanning the road near the **Blaak Station**, both impressive examples of modern architecture. A few steps south west is **Boompjes**, "little trees", a 17C double row of lime trees, now a modern boulevard with three tower blocks, **Boompjestorens**.

Euromast *Plan II* **E3** – Tower built in 1960 with a viewing platform: remarkable view of the port and city.

Port *Plan II* **E2** – Boat trip along the Nieuwe Maas (River Meuse) to Eemhaven and Botlek: harbours, docks, quay, **Europoort** and **Maasvlakte** facilities.

Molens van Kinderdijk *(30 km – 19 mi – east of Rotterdam)* – Series of 19 windmills used until 1950 to drain the Alblasserwaard, on the banks of the canal amid meadows and reeds (windmill festivals July and August, Saturday afternoons).

SHOPPING

Shops are usually open from Mon-Sat (in town centre also Sun 12-5pm).

The Tourist Information Centre (VVV) sells a guide to some of the more interesting shopping areas.

There are many shopping centres: the *Lijnbaan Plan II* **E2**, Europe's first pedestrian area; the *Beurstraverse Plan II* **E2**, one of the city's architectural highlights; the *Plaza Plan II* **E1**, opposite the railway station (Centraal Station); and the *Zuiderboulevard Plan I* **C3**. The *Vrij Entrepot* is a new shopping area in the **Kop van Zuid district** *Plan I* **C2**. The area in and around the former warehouse **De Vijf Werelddelen** *Plan I* **C2** (late-night shopping on Fridays until 9pm) has all kinds of shops and numerous restaurants and bars. The many commercial art galleries are centred around **Witte de Withstraat** *Plan II* **E2**, the cultural hub of Rotterdam.

MARKETS – **Centrummarkt** (Tues and Sat) in the Binnenrotteterrein; **antiques market** (Sun) on Schiedamsdijk *Plan II* **F2**; **Markt Zuid** (Wed and Sat) in the Afrikaanderplein *Plan I* **C2**; **Markt West** (Thurs and Sat) in Grote Visserijplein *Plan I* **B2** for wide variety of exotic foreign products.

WHAT TO BUY – The local **specialities** are Delft porcelain, Dutch cheese, cigars, Dutch gin and spirits, clogs.

ENTERTAINMENT

R'Uit Magazine gives a full summary of all exhibitions, dance and theatre performances, concerts and other events; published monthly and available free of charge from the tourist information offices or other outlets.

Schouwburg *Plan II* **E2** (Schouwburgplein 25) – Dance, theatre, drama.

Luxor Theatre *Plan I* **C2** (Posthumalaan 125) – Great variety of events.

NIGHTLIFE

Rotterdam's reputation for clubbing attracts fans from all over the Netherlands and abroad: *Off Corso* (Kruiskade 22); *Now-Wow* (Maashaven); *Las Palmas* (Wilhelminakade 66).

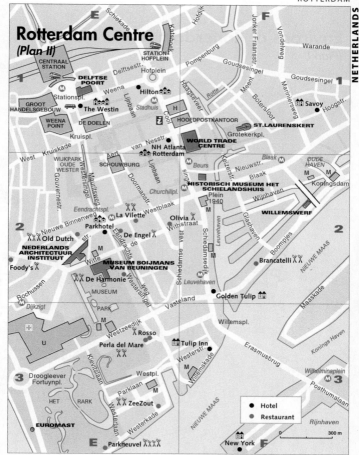

Rotterdam Centre
(Plan II)

Hotel ●
Restaurant ●

0 — 300 m

Environs of Rotterdam
(Plan I)

De Zwethheul

A 13-E 19

Doenkade

ROTTERDAM
ZESTIENHOVEN

SCHIEBROEKSE

G. K. van Hogendorpweg

Delftweg

Schie

Delftweg

Poldervaart

Matlingeweg

Airport

OVERSCHIE

Gordelweg

CENTRAAL
STATION

BEATRIXPARK

A20-E 25

Novotel

Burg. Van Haarenlaan

Parkweg

Troelstralaan

SCHIEDAM

Schiedam
Centrum

Horváthweg

Bistrot Hosman Frères

Schiedamseweg

Vreelust

Verhavenstr.

Beukels dijk

Weena

Van Walsum

Aelbrechtskade

DELFSHAVEN

A 4

Wiltonhaven

Vijfsluizen

Meeuwshaven

MAAS

Westzeedijk

Maastunnel

EUROMAST

Beneluxtunnel

NIEUWE

Petroleumhaven

PERNIS

Pernis

Eemhaven

Waalhaven

Waalhaven O. Z.

Groene Kruisweg

Vondelingenweg

Vondelingenweg

Reeweg

Waalhaven Z. Z.

HOOGVLIET

Tussenwater

Portugaal

Rhoon

Hoogvliet

Zalmplaat

556

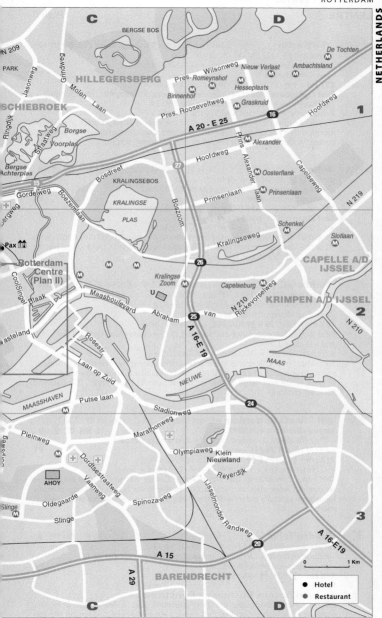

The Westin ≤ ₤ & rm 🅺 🍽 rest 📺 🏋25/100 ➹ 𝘝𝘐𝘚𝘈 ⓜⓞ 🄰🄴 ⓞ
Weena 686 ⊠ 3012 CN – ℰ (0 10) 430 20 00
– rotterdam.westin@westin.com – Fax (0 10) 430 20 01
– www.westin.com E1
227 rm – ♦99/310 € ♦♦99/360 €, � 22 € – 4 suites
Rest *Lighthouse* *(closed 24 December-1 January, Saturday lunch and Sunday)*
19 € *(weekday lunch)*/29 € and a la carte 38/53 €
♦ Luxury ♦ Business ♦ Stylish ♦
This new, futuristic skyscraper in front of the station offers a choice of spacious rooms with a full range of creature comforts. Conference rooms and business centre. Modern cuisine in a resolutely contemporary setting.

Hilton ₤ & 🅺 📺 📞 🏋25/325 🚗 ➹ 𝘝𝘐𝘚𝘈 ⓜⓞ 🄰🄴 ⓞ
Weena 10 ⊠ 3012 CN – ℰ (0 10) 710 80 00
– sales-rotterdam@hilton.com – Fax (0 10) 710 80 80
– www.rotterdam.hilton.com E1
246 rm – ♦75/280 € ♦♦75/280 €, ⊆ 23 € – 8 suites
Rest *(open until 11p.m.)* a la carte 30/47 €
♦ Chain hotel ♦ Business ♦ Classic ♦
A top chain hotel occupying a modern building near the World Trade Center with attractive, well-appointed rooms. The small restaurant in the lounge has an original, "artist's palette" wine list.

Parkhotel ≤ 🚗 ₤ 🐾 🅺 🍽 📺 📞 🏋25/60 🅿 𝘝𝘐𝘚𝘈 ⓜⓞ 🄰🄴 ⓞ
Westersingel 70 ⊠ 3015 LB – ℰ (0 10) 436 36 11
– parkhotel@bilderberg.nl – Fax (0 10) 436 42 12
– www.parkhotelrotterdam.nl E2
187 rm – ♦65/229 € ♦♦90/254 €, ⊆ 21 € – 2 suites
Rest *(closed Saturday lunch and Sunday)* 30 € *(weekday lunch)*, 33/40 €
and a la carte 31/44 €
♦ Traditional ♦ Business ♦ Classic ♦
Six categories of chic rooms are on offer in this silver-grey tower dominating the museum quarter, just a stone's throw from the Lijnbaan shopping area. A fusion of blue, white and beige in the restaurant, with its "New Style", "Global" and "Classic" choices.

NH Atlanta Rotterdam without rest & ↳ 📺 📞 🏋25/325
Aert van Nesstraat 4 ⊠ 3012 CA 🚗 𝘝𝘐𝘚𝘈 ⓜⓞ 🄰🄴 ⓞ
– ℰ (0 10) 206 78 00 – nhatlantarotterdam@nh.hotels.com
– Fax (0 10) 411 74 23 – www.nh.hotels.com E1
213 rm – ♦75/175 € ♦♦75/175 €, ⊆ 16 € – 2 suites
♦ Chain hotel ♦ Business ♦ Art Deco ♦
This hotel overlooking the World Trade Center has undergone large-scale renovation work since its construction in the 1930s but its Art Deco features have been carefully preserved in the lobby, staircase, lounge, bar and breakfast room.

Golden Tulip ≤ ₤ 🐾 🅺 🍽 📺 📞 🏋25/250 𝘝𝘐𝘚𝘈 ⓜⓞ 🄰🄴 ⓞ
Leuvenhaven 80 ⊠ 3011 EA – ℰ (0 10) 413 41 39
– inforotterdam@goldentuliphotelinntel.com – Fax (0 10) 413 32 22
– www.goldentuliphotelinntel.com F2
148 rm – ♦190 € ♦♦190/350 €, ⊆ 19 €
Rest 24 €
♦ Chain hotel ♦ Business ♦ Functional ♦
A chain hotel alongside the port museum, just a few steps from the majestic Erasmusbrug bridge. Panoramic swimming-pool and bar on the top floor.

NETHERLANDS

Savoy without rest   🔥 🅰️ ⚡ 🖥 🛁 25/60 VISA ⓶ ⒶⒺ ⓪
Hoogstraat 81 ⊠ 3011 PJ – ℰ (0 10) 413 92 80
– info.savoy@edenhotelgroup.com – Fax (0 10) 404 57 12
– www.edenhotelgroup.com   **F1**
94 rm – †165/205 € **††**155/190 €, � 17 €
♦ Traditional ♦ Business ♦ Classic ♦
The modern rooms in this pleasant hotel a short distance from Blom's famous "cubic houses" are spread across seven floors. Free internet access on the ground floor.

New York   ⬐ 😶 ⚡rm 🖥 ⓣ 🛁 25/100 ⌂ VISA ⓶ ⒶⒺ ⓪
⊠ 3072 AD – ℰ (0 10) 439 05 00 – info@hotelnewyork.nl – Fax (0 10) 484 27 01
– www.hotelnewyork.nl   **F3**
72 rm – †93/160 € **††**95/173 €, ⊇ 11 €
Rest (open until midnight) a la carte 21/49 €
♦ Traditional ♦ Business ♦ Personalised ♦
This building was once the headquarters of the Holland-America shipping line. Full of character with individually and originally decorated rooms affording views of the port, city or river. Large dining room furnished in bistro style.

Pax without rest   ⬥ 🅰️ ⚡ 🛁 25/80 ⌂ VISA ⓶ ⒶⒺ
Scheikade 658 ⊠ 3032 AK – ℰ (0 10) 466 33 44 – pax@bestwestern.nl
– Fax (0 10) 467 52 78 – www.paxhotel.nl   *Plan I* **C2**
124 rm ⊇ – **†**75/145 € **††**85/185 €
♦ Business ♦ Functional ♦
With its location on a major highway, the Pax is a practical option for both road and rail travellers. Reasonably spacious accommodation with standard furnishings.

Tulip Inn   ⬐ 🅰️ rest 🖥 ⓣ 🛁 25/60 VISA ⓶ ⒶⒺ ⓪
Willemsplein 1 ⊠ 3016 DN – ℰ (0 10) 413 47 90
– reservations@tulipinnrotterdam.nl – Fax (0 10) 412 78 90
– www.tulipinnrotterdam.nl   **F3**
92 rm – †99/165 € **††**139/180 €, ⊇ 13 €
Rest a la carte 19/34 €
♦ Chain hotel ♦ Business ♦ Functional ♦
Small, functional yet comfortable rooms in this hotel built alongside the Nieuwe Maas dock, in the shadow of the Erasmusbrug bridge.

Van Walsum   ⚡ rest ⓣ P. VISA ⓶ ⒶⒺ ⓪
Mathenesserlaan 199 ⊠ 3014 HC – ℰ (0 10) 436 32 75 – info@
hotelvanwalsum.nl – Fax (0 10) 436 44 10 – www.hotelvanwalsum.nl
closed 24 December-2 January   *Plan I* **B2**
29 rm ⊇ – **†**78/95 € **††**98/150 €
Rest (residents only)
♦ Family ♦ Business ♦ Functional ♦
An imposing bourgeois residence with rooms of varying sizes, identical furnishings and double-glazing. The breakfast room opens onto the hotel terrace.

XXXX   **Parkheuvel** (Helder)   ⬐ 😶 P. VISA ⓶ ⒶⒺ ⓪
❀❀❀ *Heuvellaan 21 ⊠ 3016 GL – ℰ (0 10) 436 07 66 – info@parkheuvel.com*
– Fax (0 10) 436 71 40 – www.parkheuvel.com
closed 17 July-5 August, 27 December-4 January,
Saturday lunch and Sunday   **E3**
Rest 50 € (weekday lunch), 78/115 € and a la carte 69/120 € ⅋
Spec. Turbot grillé, crème d'anchois et champignons au basilic. Bar au beurre de maquereau, tomate et basilic (May-June). Côtelettes et selle de chevreuil au poivre noir et aux poires (20 Oct.-26 Dec.)
♦ Innovative ♦ Formal ♦
Delicious, creative cuisine and a wonderful choice of wines are on the menu in this modern, semi-circular building. The tables by the terrace offer the best views of maritime life.

NETHERLANDS

XXX **Old Dutch** 🛱 **P** ⌂ **VISA** **◯◯** **AE** **◯**
Rochussenstraat 20 ⊠ *3015 EK –* ℰ *(0 10) 436 03 44 – info@olddutch.net*
– Fax (0 10) 436 78 26 – www.olddutch.net
closed Saturday in July and August, Sunday and Bank Holidays **E2**
Rest 33 € (weekday lunch), 40/58 € and a la carte 49/71 €
♦ Traditional ♦ Formal ♦
A pleasant restaurant adorned with fine furniture occupying an inn dating from
1932. Traditional cuisine with several fixed menu options. Wines from around the
world.

XX **La Vilette** (Mustert) **AC** ⅍ **VISA** **◯◯** **AE** **◯**
😳 *Westblaak 160* ⊠ *3012 KM –* ℰ *(0 10) 414 86 92 – Fax (0 10) 414 33 91*
closed 17 July-6 August, 24 December-1 January,
Saturday lunch and Sunday **E2**
Rest 33 € (weekday lunch)/45 € and a la carte 45/61 €
Spec. Saint-Jacques et foie de canard aux pommes. Barbue et anguille, risotto et
vinaigrette à l'oseille. Eventail de chocolat et nougat.
♦ Contemporary ♦ Formal ♦
A refined brasserie ambience permeates this pleasant restaurant with an
appetising modern menu and top-notch service. Public car park nearby.

XX **De Harmonie** 🛱 **VISA** **◯◯** **AE** **◯**
Westersingel 95 ⊠ *3015 LC –* ℰ *(0 10) 436 36 10*
– deharmonie@deharmonie.demon.nl – Fax (0 10) 436 36 08
– www.restaurantdeharmonie.nl
closed 26 December-2 January, Saturday lunch and Sunday **E2**
Rest 35 € (weekday lunch), 43/53 € and a la carte 43/58 €
♦ Contemporary ♦ Fashionable ♦
A pleasant restaurant offering cuisine geared to modern tastes, located by the
Museumpark, in a chic avenue with rows of elegant residences. Cosy modern
dining room looking onto a charming terrace and garden.

XX **ZeeZout** 🛱 **AC** **VISA** **◯◯** **AE** **◯**
Westerkade 11b ⊠ *3016 CL –* ℰ *(0 10) 436 50 49 – Fax (0 10) 225 18 47*
closed 25, 26 and 31 December, 1 January, Saturday lunch,
Sunday and Monday **E3**
Rest (booking essential) 30 € (weekday lunch), 37/55 € and a la carte
41/62 €
♦ Seafood ♦ Bistro ♦
A chic and trendy atmosphere, fish and seafood specialities, and a terrace facing
the Nieuwe Maas river are the main attractions of this aptly-named modern
brasserie (meaning "sea salt").

XX **Brancatelli** **AC** **VISA** **◯◯** **AE** **◯**
Boompjes 264 ⊠ *3011 XZ –* ℰ *(0 10) 411 41 51 – pino@brancatelli.nl*
– Fax (0 10) 404 57 34
closed Saturday lunch and Sunday lunch **F2**
Rest (open until 11p.m.) 32 € (weekday lunch), 39/42 € and a la carte
34/46 €
♦ Italian ♦ Friendly ♦
This contemporary-style Italian restaurant on a lively quay offers an authentic
choice of dishes accompanied by a good selection of wines imported directly
from Italy.

XX **Perla del Mare** **AC** ⅍ **VISA** **◯◯** **AE** **◯**
Van Vollenhovenstraat 15 (access by Westerlijk Handelsterrein) ⊠ *3016 BE*
– ℰ *(0 10) 241 04 00 – info@perladelmare.nl – Fax (0 10) 241 03 67*
– www.perladelmare.nl
closed Saturday lunch and Sunday **E3**
Rest 38 € (weekday lunch), 50/70 € and a la carte 49/70 €
♦ Italian ♦ Rustic ♦
As its name suggests, this nautically themed restaurant housed in an old
warehouse specialises in Italian cuisine, with particular emphasis on fish and
seafood.

NETHERLANDS

✕ **Foody's** 🏠 AC ☆ VISA ⬤ AE ⓪

Nieuwe Binnenweg 151 ✉ *3014 GK –* ℰ *(0 10) 436 51 63 – Fax (0 10) 436 54 42*
– www.engelgroep.com
closed Saturday lunch, Sunday lunch and Monday **E2**
Rest (open until midnight) 30 €, 35/47 € and a la carte 40/52 € ☒
♦ **Contemporary ♦ Trendy ♦**
A modern-style brasserie with kitchens in full view. The focus here is on
"natural" modern cuisine using seasonal products. Good choice of wines by the
glass.

✕ **De Engel** AC ☆ VISA ⬤ AE ⓪

Eendrachtsweg 19 ✉ *3012 LB –* ℰ *(0 10) 413 82 56*
– restaurant@engel.com – Fax (0 10) 414 63 86
– www.engelgroep.nl
closed 25 and 26 December and Sunday **E2**
Rest (dinner only) 40 € and a la carte 42/52 €
♦ **Traditional ♦ Trendy ♦**
Currently one of Rotterdam's "in" places. A relaxed atmosphere, contemporary dining room adorned with eclectic furniture, and meticulous, seasonal
cuisine.

✕ **Olivia** 🏠 ☆ VISA ⬤

Witte de Withstraat 15a ✉ *3012 BK –* ℰ *(0 10) 412 14 13*
– info@restaurantolivia.nl – Fax (0 10) 412 70 69
closed Saturday lunch, Sunday lunch and Monday **E2**
Rest 30 €/41 € and a la carte approx. 34 €
♦ **Italian ♦ Trendy ♦**
Trendy Italian restaurant housed in what was formerly an industrial building.
Loft-style decor, lively atmosphere, straightforward menu and daily specials
featured on the board.

✕ **Rosso** AC VISA ⬤ AE ⓪

Van Vollenhovenstraat 15 (access by Westerlijk Handelsterrein) ✉ *3016 BE*
– ℰ *(0 10) 225 07 05 – Fax (0 10) 436 95 04*
closed last week July, 25 and 26 December and Sunday **E3**
Rest (dinner only until 11p.m.) a la carte 49/58 €
♦ **Contemporary ♦ Wine bar ♦**
A bar-restaurant in a trendily modernised 19C former warehouse. With its
fashionable clientele and atmosphere, this is THE place to be seen.

AT THE AIRPORT North: 2,5 km: *Plan I*

 Airport 🏠 ♿rm AC ☆ 🖥 ♨25/425 P VISA ⬤ AE ⓪

Vliegveldweg 59 ✉ *3043 NT –* ℰ *(0 10) 462 55 66 – info@airporthotel.nl*
– Fax (0 10) 462 22 66 – www.airporthotel.nl **B1**
96 rm – †165/195 € ††165/195 €, ☲ 16 € – 2 suites
Rest 32 € and a la carte 35/65 €
♦ **Business ♦ Functional ♦**
A modern airport hotel with functional, well-soundproofed bedrooms and a
lounge and bar popular with a predominantly business clientele. Comfortable,
contemporary dining room offering a range of traditional dishes. Shuttle service
to the airport.

 Novotel 🏠 ♨ 🚗 ♿rm AC 🖥 ✆ ♨25/200 P VISA ⬤ AE ⓪

Hargalaan 2 (near A 20) ✉ *3118 JA Schiedam –* ℰ *(0 10) 471 33 22*
– h0517@accor.com – Fax (0 10) 470 06 56
– www.accorhotels.com **A2**
134 rm – †79/135 € ††79/135 €, ☲ 15 €
Rest a la carte 25/38 €
♦ **Chain hotel ♦ Business ♦ Functional ♦**
A chain hotel in verdant surroundings at a crossroads close to the ring road.
Functional rooms, summer terrace and garden with children's activities by the
pool. Contemporary, brasserie-style restaurant.

NETHERLANDS

XXX **De Zwethheul**

ξ3ξ3 *Rotterdamseweg 480 (at Zweth, canalside) ⊠ 2636 KB Schipluiden – ℰ (0 10)*
470 41 66 – zwethheul@alliance.nl – Fax (0 10) 470 65 22 – www.zwethheul.nl
closed 25 December-7 January, Saturday lunch, Sunday lunch and Monday
Rest 45 € (weekday lunch), 65/132 € b.i. and a la carte 56/147 € ❀   **A1**
Spec. Composition de foie d'oie mariné aux bâtonnets de betterave en
aigre-doux. Ravioli de poulet noir de Bresse aux langoustines sautées. Trois
préparations de veau.
♦ **Innovative** ♦ **Formal** ♦
The culinary delights of this restored former auberge are enhanced by the
magnificent wine list and riverfront views. Open air restaurant.

X **Bistrot Hosman Frères**

☺ *Korte Dam 10 ⊠ 3111 BG Schiedam – ℰ (0 10) 426 40 96 – Fax (0 10) 426 90 41*
– www.hosman-freres.nl
closed 31 December, 1 January, Saturday lunch and Sunday lunch   **A2**
Rest 26 €/40 € and a la carte 34/49 €
♦ **Traditional** ♦ **Bistro** ♦
This charming inn, in a picturesque location near four old windmills in the old
town, will delight customers with its bistro-style fare.

THE HAGUE
DEN HAAG - 'SGRAVENHAGE

Population (est. 2005): 468 500 – Altitude: 3m

E. Valenne / GEOSTORY PICTURES

Although the capital of the country is Amsterdam, The Hague is its seat of government and Parliament. This coastal town is a pleasant and quiet residential community, with many squares, parks and several canals. It sprawls over a large area with a relatively small population, so earning the title of 'biggest village in Europe'. It is marked by an aristocratic charm and is considered the most worldly and elegant town in the Netherlands. It also boasts some important modern architecture – Lucent Danstheater by R. Koolhaas and the Transport and Planning ministry by H. Hertzberger. The development between the Binnenhof and the station has involved famous international architects such as R. Meier.

Until the 13C The Hague was a hunting lodge for Count Floris IV of Holland. In the 17C it became the seat of the States General of the United Provinces, then of the government. In 1806 Amsterdam became the capital of the country but The Hague has kept its diplomatic status, with many foreign embassies. In 1899 and 1907 it was the location for peace conferences and it is now the seat of the International Court of Justice, the Permanent Court of Arbitration and the Academy of International Law.

The philosopher Spinoza (1632-77) lived in The Hague. Between 1870 and 1890 a group of painters in The Hague tried to renew painting, notably the art of landscapes.

WHICH DISTRICT TO CHOOSE

Most of the **hotels** cluster round the Binnenhof *Plan II* **F2.**. Others are by the sea at Scheveningen *Plan I* **B1** or a few miles from the centre at Leidschendam (6 km east), Rijswijk (5 km south), Voorburg (5 km east) and Wassenaar (11 km northeast). As The Hague is not only a diplomatic but also an administrative and commercial centre, the hotels are mostly modern and business-oriented but there are one or two good 19C hotels.

The pattern of **restaurants** is similar, some in the city centre and others in the suburbs.

For a **drink only**, try one of the places near the Binnenhof, in the Dag Groenmarkt or in Hoogstraat.

ARRIVAL – DEPARTURE

♦ ROTTERDAM

Airport – About 16 km (10 mi) southeast of The Hague. ℰ 010 446 34 44; www.rotterdam-airport.nl

From the airport to the city centre – By **taxi** (15min), about €45; ℰ 010 262 04 06. By **Rotterdam Airport Shuttle** (45min) to Central Station. By **train** (30min) to Central Station and Hollands Spoor Station.

Railway Station – Regular train services to **The Hague Central Station** *Plan I* **C2** from Utrecht and to **Hollands Spoor Station** from Amsterdam and Rotterdam; also from Belgium, France and Germany; www.ns.nl

TRANSPORT

♦ BUS AND TRAM

Single tickets can be purchased from the bus driver but saver tickets must be bought in advance from the tourist information office, post offices, most tobacconists, newsagents and hotels. 15-stripcard *(strippenkaart)*, €6.70 or 45-stripcard, €19.80, valid throughout the country on buses, trams and metro; 1-day pass €5.90-€7.90 according to the zone; ℰ 070 384 86 66; www.htm.net

TAXIS

Taxis bear blue number plates and an illuminated sign on the roof. They may be called by telephone or hired at taxi ranks at the railway stations and throughout the city; although they are not supposed to stop, they can also be hailed in the street. Pick-up charge €5.12; price per km €1.94; taxi fares are usually rounded up (5-10%). ℰ 070 390 77 22; 070 317 88 77 (ATC Taxi); www.atc-taxi.nl

♦ BICYCLES

Bicycles can be hired at the railway stations and from Du Nord Rijwielen (Keizerstraat 27-29).

USEFUL ADDRESSES

♦ TOURIST OFFICES

Tourist Office (VVV), Hofweg 1 *Plan I* **C2**; Mon-Fri 10am-6pm, Sat 10am-5pm, Sun 12-5pm; ℰ 0900 340 35 05. City Mondial, Wagenstraat 193, The Hague; Tues-Sat 10am-5pm; ℰ 070 402 33 36; info@vvvdenhaag.nl; www.citylnndial.nl; www.denhaag.com. **Tourist Office (VVV)**, Gevers Deynootweg 1134, Palace Promenade shopping centre, Scheveningen; Apr-Sep Mon-Fri 10am-5pm, Sat 9-5pm, Sun 11-4pm; ℰ 0900 340 35 05; vvvscheveningen@spdh.net

♦ POST OFFICES

Post Offices are open Mon-Fri 9am-5pm (8pm Thurs; 4pm Sat). Longer opening hours are available at some large city branches (also Sat 8.30-noon).

♦ BANKS/CURRENCY EXCHANGE

Opening times are Mon-Fri 9am-4pm. Longer opening hours are available at some large city banks (Thurs 9am-9pm and Sat Morning); all close on public holidays. Bank cash machines (ATMs) are open 24hrs (pin number required).

♦ EMERGENCY

Phone ℰ **112** for the Emergency services. Tourist Assistance Service (TAS) ℰ **070 310 32 74** (daily 9am-9pm).

BUSY PERIODS

It may be difficult to find a room at a reasonable price (except at weekends) during special events:

Herring Festival: May-June – Auction of the first batch of new Dutch herring.

Vliegerfeest: early June – Kite Flying Festival on the beach.

Pasar Malam Besar: June – Indonesian market with stalls, theatre performances, lectures and music in the Malieveld.

North Sea Jazz Festival: July (2nd weekend) – Jazz and blues.

Holland Dance Festival: Oct-Nov (17 days) – In alternate years – 60 performances in 7 locations; also dance parade through the Hague.

CaDance Festival: Oct-Nov (17 days) – In alternate years at the Theater aan het Spui.

Prinsjesdag: September (3rd Tuesday) – State Opening of Parliament by the Queen who arrives in a golden coach.

EXPLORING THE HAGUE

In two days there is time to visit the main sights and museums.

Opening times are usually from 10/11am-4/5pm but closed on Mondays and public holidays.

VISITING

Mauritshuis *Plan II* **F2** – Royal Picture Gallery: Holbein the Younger (16C), Rubens, David Teniers, Rembrandt, Vermeer.

Haags Gemeentemuseum *Plan III* **G3** – Municipal Museum (1935): decorative arts and 19C and 20C sculpture and painting; works by Mondrian and artists from the De Stijl movement.

Scheveningen *Plan I* **B1** – Lively fishing port *(full-day fishing trips)* and elegant seaside resort with a popular long, wide stretch of fine sand, backed by the Strandweg, the main thoroughfare.

SHOPPING

The Hague is best known for its many antique shops and commercial art galleries; the Tourist Information Centre (VVV) publishes brochures full of useful shopping suggestions. In The Hague late-night shopping until 9pm is on Thursdays. In addition to the big city centre department stores and chain stores – *Maison de Bonneterie* (Gravenstraat 2), *De Bijenkorf* (Wagenstraat 32), *V&D* (Grote Marktstraat 50), *Hema* (Grote Marktstraat 57) – there are lots of excellent small shops in the streets and squares around the palaces. Indoor shopping is available at the stylish **Passage** (Hofweg 5-7/Buitenhof 4-5) and at the **Babylon shopping centre** next to the Central Station *Plan I* **C2**.

MARKETS – The Hague has excellent markets: **general goods markets** in Herman Costerstraat (Mon, Wed, Fri and Sat) *Plan I* **B2** and in Markthof (daily except Sun) *Plan I* **B3**; **farmers' market** by the Grote Kerk (Wed); **art and antiques market** in Lange Voorhout *Plan II* **F2** (May-Sept Thurs and Sun) also in the Plein *Plan II* **F2** (Oct-Apr Thurs).

In **Scheveningen** late-night shopping is on Friday. The best places to shop are **Palace Promenade** (open daily 10am-10pm) *Plan III* **G1**, **Gevers Deynootplein** *Plan III* **G1** and the **Boulevard (Strandweg)** *Plan III* **G1**.

WHAT TO BUY – The local **specialities** are Delft porcelain, Hollandsche Waaren, art and antiques, cigars, clogs, fashion, design, books.

ENTERTAINMENT

Dr Anton Philipszaal (Spuiplein 150) for classical music.

Circustheater (Circusstraat 4) for classical music and musicals.

't Paard (Prinsegracht 12) for pop, rock and blues.

Koninklijke Schouwburg (Korte Voorhout 3).

Lucent Danstheater (Spuiplein 152), home of the world-famous **Nederlands Dans Theater.**

Nederlands Congres Centrum (Churchillplein 10).

Theater aan het Spui (Spui 187).

Diligentia (Lange Voorhout 5).

NIGHTLIFE

The place to be is **Schevening's Boulevard** *Plan III* **G1**, crowded and boisterous with street cafés, restaurants, bars and discos; also the *Holland Casino.*

CENTRE

Plan II

Le Méridien Hotel des Indes

AC rm SAT 25/100 P

Lange Voorhoot 54 ✉ 2514 EG – ✆ (0 70) 361 23 45
– info.haghe@lemeridien.com – Fax (0 70) 361 23 50
– www.lemeridien.com

F1

92 rm – †325 € ††375/425 €, ☕ 23 €
Rest 43 € (weekday lunch) and a la carte 38/69 €
◆ Palace ◆ Business ◆ Historic ◆

This 1858 mansion in the European institutions district has finally been restored to its former glory thanks to major renovation works by Jacques Garcia. High degree of comfort, refinement and modernity. Gourmet restaurant and handsome lounge very popular for its High Tea and Afternoon Tea services.

Crowne Plaza Promenade

rm AC SAT 25/425 P VISA MC AE

van Stolkweg 1 ✉ 2585 JL
– ✆ (0 70) 352 51 61 – info@crowneplazadenhaag.nl – Fax (0 70) 354 10 46
– www.crowneplazadenhaag.nl

Plan III **H2**

93 rm – †165/295 € ††165/310 €, ☕ 23 € – 1 suite
Rest ***Brasserie Promenade*** 30 € (weekday lunch)/35 € and a la carte 40/53 €
◆ Chain hotel ◆ Luxury ◆ Modern ◆

This large chain hotel alongside the inner ring road stands opposite a vast park. High levels of comfort in the rooms, a collection of modern paintings and efficient service. A relaxed brasserie serving simple meals.

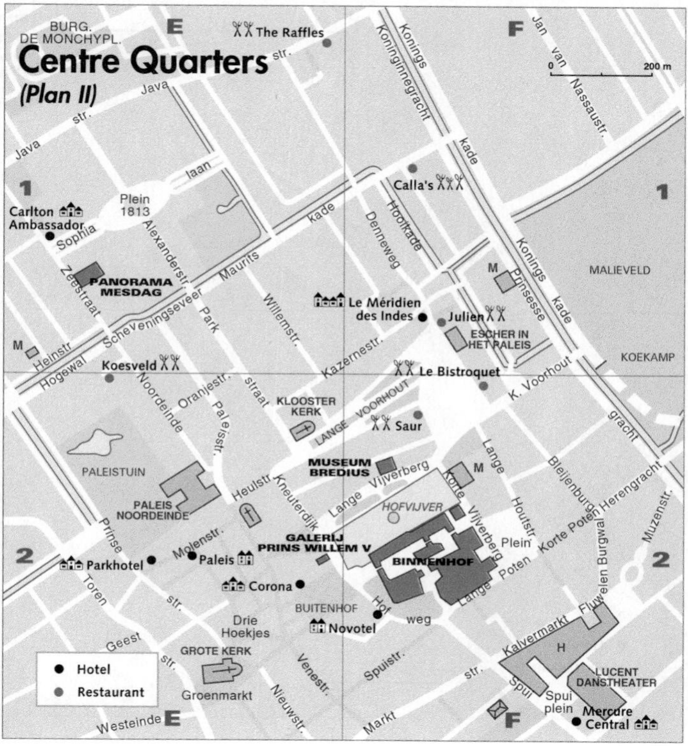

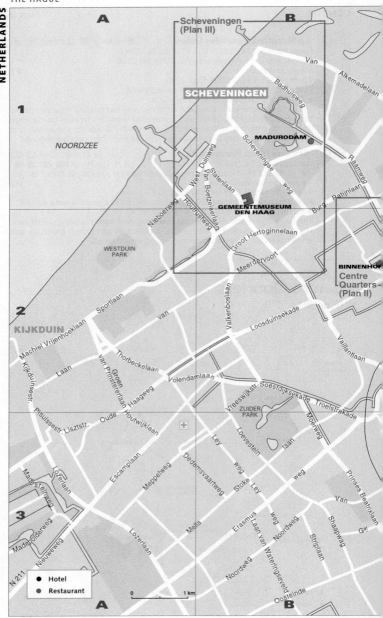

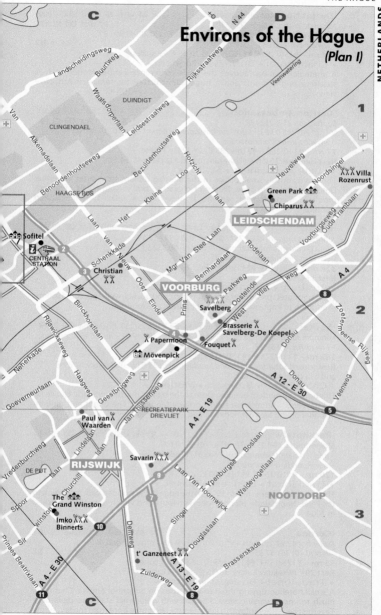

Environs of the Hague
(Plan I)

N 44

N 44

Landscheidingsweg

Buurtweg

Waalsdorperlaan

Rijksstraatweg

Veenwatering

DUINDIGT

Leidsestraatweg

Van Alkemadelaan

CLINGENDAEL

Benoordenhoutseweg

Bezuidenhoutseweg

Hofzicht

Log

Heuvelweg

Noordsingel

Villa Rozenrust

Green Park

Chiparus

HAAGSE BOS

Kleine

Het

Laan van N.

LEIDSCHENDAM

Laan van

Sofitel

CENTRAAL STATION

Christian

Schenkkade

Mgr. Van Stee Laan

Bernhardlaan

Parkweg

Rodelaan

Voorburgseweg

Oude Trambaan

A 4

Oost - Einde

Prins

VOORBURG

Savelberg

West - Vliet - weg

Oosteinde

Donau

Blinckhorstlaan

Papermoon

Brasserie Savelberg-De Koepel

Fouquet

Mövenpick

Rijswijkseweg

Neherkade

Haagweg

Geestbrugweg

Jan Thijssenweg

RECREATIEPARK DRIEVLIET

A 12 - E 30

Donau

Veenweg

Goeverneurlaan

Paul van Waarden

Lindelaan

RIJSWIJK

Savarin

Laan Van Hoornwijck

Boslaan

Ypenburgse laan

Weidevogellaan

NOOTDORP

Vredenburchweg

DE PUT

Churchill

Spoor

Winston

Sir

Prinses Beatrixlaan

The Grand Winston

Imko Binnerts

Delftweg

Singel

Douglaslaan

A 4 - E 30

t' Ganzenest

A 13 - E 19

Zuiderweg

Brasserskade

569

NETHERLANDS

Dorint Novotel without rest ≤ ƒʒ 🖾 ఈ 🖩 4ᵧ ✆ 🏊25/2000
Johan de Wittlaan 42 ⊠ *2517 JR* 🚗 *VISA* 🆎 🆎 ⓪
– ✆ *(0 70) 416 91 00 – h5389@accor.com – Fax (0 70) 416 91 33*
– *www.novotel.com* Plan III **H2**
214 rm – ♦150/310 € ♦♦165/330 €, ⊆ 19 € – 2 suites
◆ Chain hotel ◆ Business ◆ Modern ◆
A strategic location "above" the city's conference centre. Modernist feel,
spacious, bright rooms and a huge infrastructure for seminars. Attractive
views.

Carlton Ambassador 🕭 🕭 🖾 4ᵧ ✕ 🖾 ✆
Sophialaan 2 ⊠ *2514 JP* 🏊25/160 *VISA* 🆎 🆎 ⓪
– ✆ *(0 70) 363 03 63 – info@ambassador.carlton.nl – Fax (0 70) 360 05 35*
– *www.carlton.nl/ambassador* **E1**
77 rm – ♦140/260 € ♦♦160/285 €, ⊆ 22 € – 1 suite
Rest *Henricus* 30 € (weekday lunch) and a la carte 45/54 €
◆ Luxury ◆ Business ◆ Stylish ◆
The rooms in this small palace in the Mesdag diplomatic quarter are either
Dutch or English in style. Plenty of character, but varying levels of soundproofing. Mediterranean cuisine is served in a relaxed, floral-inspired
restaurant.

Bel Air ≤ 🖾 🖙 🖩 4ᵧ ✕rest 🖾 ✆ 🏊25/250 🅿 ⇲ *VISA* 🆎 🆎 ⓪
Johan de Wittlaan 30 ⊠ *2517 JR* – ✆ *(0 70) 352 53 54*
– *info@goldentulipbelairhotel.nl – Fax (0 70) 352 53 53*
– *www.goldentulipbelairhotel.nl* Plan III **H3**
324 rm – ♦99/170 € ♦♦119/195 €, ⊆ 18 €
Rest 35 €/40 €
◆ Business ◆ Functional ◆
This huge hotel spread over nine floors has good quality, well-appointed rooms,
in addition to impressively large public areas and lounges.

Sofitel ㅕrm 🖩 4ᵧ 🖾 ✆ 🏊25/150 🅿 ⇲ *VISA* 🆎 🆎 ⓪
Koningin Julianaplein 35 ⊠ *2595 AA* – ✆ *(0 70) 381 49 01 – h0755@accor.com*
– *Fax (0 70) 382 59 27* Plan I **C2**
142 rm – ♦135/275 € ♦♦150/315 €, ⊆ 21 € – 1 suite
Rest *(closed Saturday lunch and Sunday lunch)* 33 € (weekday lunch)/39 €
and a la carte approx. 40 €
◆ Chain hotel ◆ Business ◆ Modern ◆
This hotel in a modern building close to the train station is a practical choice for
rail travellers. The modern rooms occupy ten floors. The bright and modern
designer dining area overlooks a park.

Parkhotel without rest 🖙 4ᵧ ✆ 🏊25/200 🚗 *VISA* 🆎 🆎 ⓪
Molenstraat 53 ⊠ *2513 BJ* – ✆ *(0 70) 362 43 71*
– *info@parkhoteldenhaag.nl – Fax (0 70) 361 45 25*
– *www.parkhoteldenhaag.nl* **E2**
120 rm – ♦110/150 € ♦♦145/390 €, ⊆ 15 €
◆ Traditional ◆ Business ◆ Classic ◆
This hotel was established in 1912 on the edge of the wooded park belonging to
the Paleis Noordeinde. Modern rooms on four floors which were all refurbished
in 2004.

Corona ✆ 🏊25/100 🚗 *VISA* 🆎 🆎 ⓪
Buitenhof 42 ⊠ *2513 AH* – ✆ *(0 70) 363 79 30 – info@corona.nl*
– *Fax (0 70) 361 57 85* **E2**
35 rm – ♦125/159 € ♦♦125/175 €, ⊆ 16 € – 1 suite
Rest 29 € (weekday lunch), 38/55 € and a la carte 37/55 €
◆ Traditional ◆ Business ◆ Classic ◆
A small hotel occupying three town houses on Buitenhof Square. Charming,
plush rooms of varying sizes. Popular with ministerial staff and diplomats.
Tavern-style restaurant with a lively terrace laid out in front from the first sunny
days.

NETHERLANDS

Mercure Central & AC ⚡ 🍴 📺 📞 ♿ 25/135 VISA ⓾ AE ①

Spui 180 ✉ 2511 BW – 𝒞 (0 70) 363 67 00
– h1317@accor.com – Fax (0 70) 363 93 98
– www.mercure.nl   F2
156 rm – ♦79/185 € ♦♦79/190 €, ☕ 17 € – 3 suites
Rest (dinner only) a la carte 26/52 €
♦ Chain hotel ♦ Business ♦ Functional ♦
Built in the 1980s, this centrally located hotel offers functional, well-maintained rooms with double-glazing. Mainly business clientele. "Minimalist" service.

Paleis without rest AC ⚡ 🍴 📺 📞 🚗 VISA ⓾ AE ①

Molenstraat 26 ✉ 2513 BL – 𝒞 (0 70) 362 46 21
– info@paleishotel.nl – Fax (0 70) 361 45 33
– www.paleishotel.nl   E2
20 rm – ♦160/205 € ♦♦175/275 €, ☕ 15 €
♦ Traditional ♦ Business ♦ Classic ♦
A small luxury hotel with rooms decorated in Louis XVI style and with sumptuous French fabrics by Pierre Frey. Very smart breakfast room.

Novotel ⚡ 📺 📞 ♿ 25/100 🚗 VISA ⓾ AE ①

Hofweg 5 ✉ 2511 AA – 𝒞 (0 70) 364 88 46
– h1180@accor.com – Fax (0 70) 356 28 89
– www.accorhotels.com   F2
106 rm – ♦79/170 € ♦♦79/235 €, ☕ 16 €
Rest (open until 11p.m.) 26 € and a la carte 21/40 €
♦ Chain hotel ♦ Business ♦ Functional ♦
The Novotel is located just opposite the Binnenhof in a former cinema, and still retains a shopping arcade. Modern rooms, which received a facelift in 2004. The spacious restaurant is housed in the old projection room.

Calla's (van der Kleijn) 🍴 VISA ⓾ AE ①
❀
Laan van Roos en Doorn 51a ✉ 2514 BC – 𝒞 (0 70) 345 58 66
– Fax (0 70) 345 57 10 – www.restaurantcallas.nl
closed last week July-mid August, 25 December-6 January, Sunday and
Monday   F1
Rest 38 € (weekday lunch)/70 € and a la carte 62/85 €
Spec. Brochette de Saint-Jacques à la réglisse et witlof (Oct.-April). Turbot en soufflé de pommes de terres aillées (April-Dec.) Crêpes farcies glacées et glace vanille.
♦ Innovative ♦ Fashionable ♦
The design of this modern restaurant, originally a warehouse, is a minimalist one of dazzling white walls. Open views of the kitchens and lounge from the ground floor. Classic cuisine with a modern bent.

Le Bistroquet 🍴 AC VISA ⓾ AE ①

Lange Voorhout 98 ✉ 2514 EJ – 𝒞 (0 70) 360 11 70 – info@bistroquet.nl
– Fax (0 70) 360 55 30 – www.bistroquet.nl
closed 24 December-1 January and Sunday   F1-2
Rest 30 € (weekday lunch), 36/46 € and a la carte 44/67 €
♦ Contemporary ♦ Retro ♦
An intimate atmosphere and distinct nostalgia for the Roaring Twenties pervade this warm restaurant which attracts a clientele of diplomats and staff from the nearby political institutions. Contemporary menu.

Saur 🍴 AC VISA ⓾ AE ①

Lange Voorhout 47 ✉ 2514 EC – 𝒞 (0 70) 346 25 65 – Fax (0 70) 362 13 13
– www.restaurantsaur.nl
closed Sunday and Bank Holidays   F2
Rest 30 € (weekday lunch), 36/50 € and a la carte 47/55 €
♦ Seafood ♦ Brasserie ♦
A long-established culinary address in the city with a chic, contemporary brasserie-style atmosphere and oyster bar. Fish and seafood, particularly lobster, a speciality.

571

NETHERLANDS

XX **Julien** $\overline{VISA}$ **OO** **AE** **O**
Vos in Tuinstraat 2a ⊠ 2514 BX – $\mathscr{C}$ (0 70) 365 86 02 – info@julien.nl
– Fax (0 70) 365 31 47 – www.julien.nl
closed 31 December- 1 January and Sunday   **F1**
Rest 33 € (weekday lunch), 38/40 € and a la carte 48/67 €
♦ Traditional ♦ Retro ♦
The Julien's decor, including a sparkling 1900s-style mezzanine and bar, will thrill
fans of Art Nouveau. A hushed ambience and traditional cuisine with seasonal
influences.

XX **Rousseau** $\widehat{\mathbb{m}}$ $\overline{VISA}$ **OO**
Van Boetzelaerlaan 134 ⊠ 2581 AX – $\mathscr{C}$ (0 70) 355 47 43
– www.restaurantrousseau.com
closed 26 February-6 March, 30 July-21 August, 24 December-2 January, Saturday
lunch, Sunday and Monday   Plan III **G3**
Rest 25 € (weekday lunch), 30/55 € and a la carte 43/62 €
♦ Contemporary ♦ Family ♦
The spirit of the 19C artist Jean Rousseau - the owner's namesake - lives on in this
restaurant adorned with a pleasant Rousseau-style fresco. Imaginative seasonal
menu.

XX **The Raffles**   **AK** **%** $\overline{VISA}$ **OO** **AE** **O**
Javastraat 63 ⊠ 2585 AG – $\mathscr{C}$ (0 70) 345 85 87 – Fax (0 70) 356 00 84
– www.restaurantraffles.com
closed late July-early August, Sunday and Monday   **E1**
Rest (dinner only) 37 €/44 € and a la carte 31/49 €
♦ Indonesian ♦ Friendly ♦
Delicious and authentic Indonesian cuisine is served in this typically decorated
restaurant in the appropriately named Javastraat.

XX **Christian** $\widehat{\mathbb{m}}$ $\overline{VISA}$ **OO** **AE** **O**
Laan van Nieuw Oost Indië 1f ⊠ 2593 BH – $\mathscr{C}$ (0 70) 383 88 56 – info@
restaurantchristian.nl – Fax (0 70) 383 88 56 – www.restaurantchristian.nl
closed Tuesday and Wednesday   Plan I **C2**
Rest 29 € (weekday lunch), 35/58 € and a la carte 45/53 €
♦ Contemporary ♦ Modern ♦
Modern culinary "performance" with equally contemporary interior decor where
orange dominates. Chef's table for 8 to 10 dining companions; courtyard terrace.

XX **Koesveld** $\widehat{\mathbb{m}}$ $\overline{VISA}$ **OO** **AE** **O**
Maziestraat 10 ⊠ 2514 GT – $\mathscr{C}$ (0 70) 360 27 23
closed Sunday   **E1**
Rest 20 € (weekday lunch)/43 € and a la carte 33/46 €
♦ Contemporary ♦ Friendly ♦
This small restaurant between the Panorama Mesdag and Paleis Noordeinde is
known for its modern, well-presented cuisine. Generous portions with a
Mediterranean influence.

SCHEVENINGEN   Plan III

🏛 **Kurhaus**   ≤ ∰ **£6** 🖙 ⟲ rm **AK** **⅙** **%** rest **ṡ4** 35/600 **P.** $\overline{VISA}$ **OO** **AE** **O**
Gevers Deynootplein 30 ⊠ 2586 CK – $\mathscr{C}$ (0 70) 416 26 36
– info@kurhaus.nl – Fax (0 70) 416 26 46
– www.kurhaus.nl   **G1**
245 rm – †215/271 € ††235/291 €, ☞ 22 € – 10 suites
Rest see **Kandinsky** below
Rest **Kurzaal** 26 € (weekday lunch), 29/36 € and a la carte 32/50 €
♦ Palace ♦ Business ♦ Modern ♦
A sumptuous palace by the beach with a remarkable late-19C concert room now
converted into a restaurant. Elegant rooms with modern comforts.
Contemporary cuisine and oyster bar available under the Kurzaal's splendid
cupola.

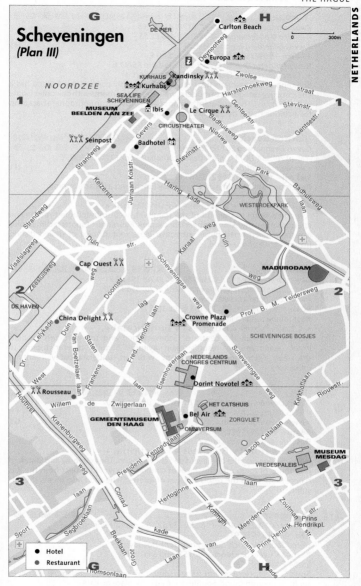

Scheveningen
(Plan III)

NETHERLANDS

NOORDZEE

DE PIER

Carlton Beach

Deynootweg

Europa

Zwolse

KURHAUS Kandinsky

Kurhaus

Harstenhoekweg

Gentsestr.

SEA LIFE
SCHEVENINGEN

Stevinstr.

MUSEUM
BEELDEN AAN ZEE

Ibis   Le Cirque

Badhuisweg

Gentsestr.

CIRCUSTHEATER

Nieuwe

Seinpost

Gevers   Badhotel

Stevinstr.

Park

Badhuisweg

Strandweg

Keizerstr.

Juriaan Kokstr.

Haring   kade

WESTBROEKPARK

laan

Strandweg

Visafslagweg

Zeesluisweg

Duin   str.

Scheveningse

weg

Kanaal   weg

Duin

weg

Cap Ouest

MADURODAM

DE HAVEN

Lelykade

Duin   van Boetzelaer laan

Doornstr.

Iaag

Fred. Hendrik laan

Prof. B. M. Teldersweg

China Delight

Crowne Plaza
Promenade

SCHEVENINGSE BOSJES

Staten

Frankens   laan

Eisenhowerlaan

NEDERLANDS
CONGRES CENTRUM

Scheveningse   weg

West

Dr.

Rousseau

Willem   de   Zwijgerlaan

Dorint Novotel

HET CATSHUIS

Kerkhoflaan

Riouwstr.

Houtrust

Kranenburgweg

weg

Bel Air   ZORGVLIET

GEMEENTEMUSEUM
DEN HAAG

OMNIVERSUM

Jacob Catslaan

VREDESPALEIS

MUSEUM
MESDAG

President Kennedylaan

Hertoginne   laan

Conrad

Zoutman   str.   Prins
Hendrikpl.

Sport   laan

Segbroeklaan

Beeklaan

Groot   kade

Komingh

Laan   van

Meerdervoort

Emma   Prins Hendrik str.   kade

Thomsonlaan

● Hotel
● Restaurant

Europa 🗻 🕙 🖵 🖭 rest 👉 ❄rest ⚓25/460 🚗 🖘 ＶＩＳＡ ⓪❾ ⒶⒺ ①

Zwolsestraat 2 ⊠ *2587 VJ* – *℘ (0 70) 416 95 95*
– *europa@bilderberg.nl* – *Fax (0 70) 416 95 55*
– *www.bilderberg-europa-hotel.nl*   **H1**
174 rm – ♦99/210 € ♦♦119/230 €, ☞ 19 €
Rest *Mangerie Oxo* 38 €/40 € and a la carte 35/47 €

◆ Traditional ◆ Business ◆ Modern ◆

Standing at a crossroads near the dam, the highly comfortable Europa has a choice of five categories of modern, well-appointed rooms with balconies (some with sea views). The restaurant's trendy decor provides an appropriate backdrop for a cuisine that is decidedly cutting-edge.

 Carlton Beach ⇐ 🗻 ℔ 🕙 🖵 👉 ❄rest ⚓25/250

Gevers Deynootweg 201 ⊠ *2586 HZ*   **🅿 ＶＩＳＡ ⓪❾ ⒶⒺ ①**
– *℘ (0 70) 354 14 14* – *info@beach.carlton.nl* – *Fax (0 70) 352 00 20*
– *www.carlton.nl/beach*   **H1**
183 rm – ♦195/240 € ♦♦215/365 €, ☞ 21 €
Rest (open until 11 p.m.) 28 € (weekday lunch) and a la carte approx. 36 €

◆ Chain hotel ◆ Business ◆ Functional ◆

A modern hotel at the end of the dam with well-soundproofed rooms and apartments overlooking the beach or car park. Full range of sports facilities, plus a restaurant crowned by an attractive glass roof. Choice of grilled dishes, including fish and seafood.

 Badhotel 🖭 👉 🖾 🕻 ⚓25/100 🅿 ＶＩＳＡ ⓪❾ ⒶⒺ ①

Gevers Deynootweg 15 ⊠ *2586 BB* – *℘ (0 70) 351 22 21*
– *info@badhotelscheveningen.nl* – *Fax (0 70) 355 58 70*
– *www.badhotelscheveningen.nl*   **G1**
90 rm – ♦105/158 € ♦♦115/158 €, ☞ 15 €
Rest (dinner only) a la carte 26/35 €

◆ Chain hotel ◆ Business ◆ Functional ◆

Halfway between the centre of Scheveningen and the port, this modern hotel overlooks the resort's main avenue. Slightly quieter rooms to the rear. Contemporary restaurant with an understandably maritime influence.

 Ibis ⅙ 👉 ❄rest 🖾 🕻 ⚓25/40 🅿 ＶＩＳＡ ⓪❾ ⒶⒺ ①

Gevers Deynootweg 63 ⊠ *2586 BJ* – *℘ (0 70) 354 33 00*
– *h1153@accor.com* – *Fax (0 70) 352 39 16*
– *www.accorhotels.com*   **G1**
88 rm – ♦82/95 € ♦♦85/105 €, ☞ 12 €
Rest (dinner only) a la carte 23/34 €

◆ Chain hotel ◆ Business ◆ Functional ◆

Hotel overlooking the boulevard de Scheveningen. The economy and standard categories of room offer the level of comfort you would expect from the Ibis name. Close to all the resort's places of interest. The food also meets the Ibis standard.

 XXX **Seinpost** ⇐ 🖭 ＶＩＳＡ ⓪❾ ⒶⒺ ①
❀

Zeekant 60 ⊠ *2586 AD* – *℘ (0 70) 355 52 50* – *mail@seinpost.nl*
– *Fax (0 70) 355 50 93*
closed Saturday lunch, Sunday and Bank Holidays   **G1**
Rest 43 € (weekday lunch), 48/75 € and a la carte 55/84 € 🕸

Spec. Crabe du Nord et King crabe en deux préparations. Lotte laquée aux olives sur lit de poivron rouge. Soufflé glacé au café, glace au café.

◆ Seafood ◆ Fashionable ◆

The god Neptune dominates this round building, where the menu is awash with fish and seafood. Comfortable dining room refurbished in contemporary style. Lovely sea views. Good wines.

XXX **Kandinsky** – Hotel Kurhaus ⟨ 🕭 AK ❄ P ⌂ VISA ⓜ AE ⓞ

Gevers Deynootplein 30 ⊠ 2586 CK – ℰ (0 70) 416 26 36
– info@kurhaus.nl – Fax (0 70) 416 26 46 – www.kurhaus.nl.
closed Saturday lunch and Sunday   **G1**
Rest (dinner only in July and August) 33 € (weekday lunch), 48/63 €
and a la carte 55/80 €
♦ French traditional ♦ Formal ♦
An elegant modern restaurant which is part of the resort's flagship hotel.
Comfortable dining room in beige shades offering a classic menu with modern
undertones.

XX **Le Cirque** (Kranenborg) AK ❄ ⌂(dinner) VISA ⓜ AE ⓞ
😣
Circusplein 50 ⊠ 2586 CZ – ℰ (0 70) 416 76 76
– info@restaurantlecirque.com – Fax (0 70) 416 75 37
– www.restaurantlecirque.com
closed 1 January, 17 July-15 August, 31 December,
Monday and Tuesday   **H1**
Rest (dinner only except Saturday and Sunday) 50 €/98 € and a la carte
55/88 € ⅗
Spec. Saint-Jacques aux witlof et fruits de moutarde (15 Oct.-15 April). Epaule de
cochon de lait laquée, pieds en tempura et parmentier au citron et gingembre.
Noix de ris de veau à la plancha (April-Nov.).
♦ Innovative ♦ Design ♦
A designer restaurant at the resort's Circustheater. Veranda and dining room
decorated in contrasting yet harmonious red and black tones. Both classic and
more creative cuisine.

XX **Cap Ouest** ⟨ 🕭 AK ❄ VISA ⓜ AE ⓞ
Schokkerweg 37 ⊠ 2583 BH – ℰ (0 70) 306 09 35 – info@capouest.nl
– Fax (0 70) 350 84 54   **G2**
Rest 22 € (weekday lunch)/40 € and a la carte 35/113 €
♦ Seafood ♦ Formal ♦
Fish and seafood are the mainstays of this restaurant overlooking the port. The
views from the modern dining room encompass the pleasure marina and fishing
harbour.

XX **China Delight** VISA ⓜ ⓞ
Dr Lelykade 116 ⊠ 2583 CN – ℰ (0 70) 355 54 50
– info@chinadelight.nl – Fax (0 70) 354 66 52
– www.chinadelight.nl   **G2**
Rest (dinner only) a la carte 25/33 €
♦ Chinese ♦ Exotic ♦
This spacious Chinese restaurant is housed in an old warehouse alongside one of
the town's docks. A respectable menu geared towards the cuisine of Beijing and
Szechwan.

ENVIRONS *(Rijswijk, Voorburg, Leidschendam)*   *Plan I*

 The Grand Winston Fa & AK 4⁄ 📼 🛠25/200 P VISA ⓜ AE ⓞ
Generaal Eisenhowerplein 1 ⊠ 2288 AE Rijswijk – ℰ (0 70) 414 15 00
– info@grandwinston.nl – Fax (0 70) 414 15 10
– www.grandwinston.nl   **C3**
245 rm – ♥109/174 € ♥♥109/190 €, � 18 € – 7 suites
Rest see *Imko Binnerts* below
Rest *The Grand Canteen* (open until 11p.m.) 30 € (weekday lunch)
and a la carte 29/51 €
♦ Business ♦ Design ♦
The reception of this new designer-style hotel by the Rijswijk station stands
beneath the watchful gaze of Sir Winston Churchill. The guestrooms here are
split between two modern towers. Lounge bar and trendy brasserie with a varied
menu choice.

NETHERLANDS

Green Park ⟨ 🖶 📺 ⟨ᵗ⟩ 🏖25/250 VISA ⑩ AE ①
Weigelia 22 ⊠ 2262 AB Leidschendam – ℰ (0 70) 320 92 80 – info@greenpark.nl
– Fax (0 70) 327 49 07 – www.greenpark.nl **D1**
92 rm ⊑ – †99/159 € ††99/169 € – 4 suites
Rest see **Chiparus** below
♦ Chain hotel ♦ Business ♦ Modern ♦
This large chain hotel is built on piles on the edge of a lagoon. The bedrooms, laid
out around a bright atrium, offer guests modern comfort. Pleasant service.

Mövenpick 🖭 ⅊rm 🗚 ⅊ ⟨ᵗ⟩ 🏖25/180 🚗 VISA ⑩ AE ①
Stationplein 8 ⊠ 2275 AZ Voorburg – ℰ (0 70) 337 37 37 – hotel.vooburg@
moevenpick.com – Fax (0 70) 337 37 00 – www.movenpick-voorburg.com **C2**
125 rm – †70/138 € ††90/158 €, ⊑ 14 €
Rest 16 € (weekday lunch) and a la carte 15/40 €
♦ Chain hotel ♦ Business ♦ Modern ♦
A chain hotel built along modern lines with good-sized, well-kept, functional
rooms with effective soundproofing. Service with a smile. Excellent choice at lunch
and dinner, with buffets, grilled meats and fish, pasta and various wok dishes.

XXX **Savelberg** with rm ⅗ ⟨ 🖭 ⅄ ⅊ 🏖35 🅿 VISA ⑩ AE ①
🕄 *Oosteinde 14 ⊠ 2271 EH – ℰ (0 70) 387 20 81*
– info@restauranthotelsavelberg.nl – Fax (0 70) 387 77 15
– www.restauranthotelsavelberg.nl
closed 27 to 31 December **D2**
14 rm – †138/195 € ††138/320 €, ⊑ 16 €
Rest *(closed Saturday lunch, Sunday and Monday)* 43 € (weekday lunch),
60/85 € and a la carte 64/105 € 🕸
Spec. Salade de homard. Homard tiède aux pamplemousse et orange (spring).
Pigeon de Bresse rôti au four, artichaut violette, tomates sechées et jus d'olives
vertes.
♦ Traditional ♦ Formal ♦
This magnificent 17C residence offers a treat for the senses with its traditional menu,
vast wine list, terrace overlooking a park and individually furnished bedrooms.

XXX **Imko Binnerts** – Hotel The Grand Winston 🖭 ⅗ VISA ⑩ AE ①
🕄 *Generaal Eisenhowerplein 1 (2nd floor) ⊠ 2288 AE – ℰ (0 70) 414 15 14*
– info@imkobinnerts.nl – Fax (0 70) 414 15 10 – www.imkobinnerts.nl
closed 24 July-15 August, 24 December-10 January, Saturday lunch, Sunday and
Monday **C3**
Rest 33 € (weekday lunch), 38/73 € and a la carte 52/99 € 🕸
Spec. Rouget-barbet au consommé de poivron rouge (April-Oct.). Salade niçoise
maison. Turbot grillé et sa béarnaise.
♦ Seafood ♦ Design ♦
Suspended designer dining room with high-tech lighting via a glass wall which
forms a virtual mosaic to filter external light. Fine cuisine mainly based on fish
and seafood, personalised with finesse and simplicity. Good wine list.

XXX **Villa Rozenrust** 🖭 🅿 VISA ⑩ AE ①
Veursestraatweg 104 ⊠ 2265 CG – ℰ (0 70) 327 74 60 – villarozenrust@
planet.nl – Fax (0 70) 327 50 62 – closed Tuesday and Wednesday **D1**
Rest (dinner only) 45 €/74 € and a la carte 47/72 €
♦ Traditional ♦ Formal ♦
An attractive old villa with a romantic atmosphere is the backdrop for this
restaurant offering contemporary cuisine. Summer dining in the garden.
Home-grown vegetables.

XXX **Savarin** 🖭 🅿 VISA ⑩ AE ①
Laan van Hoornwijck 29 ⊠ 2289 DG – ℰ (0 70) 307 20 50 – info@savarin.nl
– Fax (0 70) 307 20 55 – www.savarin.nl
closed 27 December-1 January, Saturday lunch and Sunday lunch **C3**
Rest 32 € (weekday lunch), 35/45 € and a la carte approx. 44 €
♦ Innovative ♦ Formal ♦
This farm dating from 1916 is known for its inventive cuisine served in a dining
room with rustic and designer decorative features. Summer restaurant and
modern meeting rooms.

XX **Chiparus** – Hotel Green Park ⟨ 🕿 AC 🍴 VISA ⓜⓄ AE Ⓞ

Weigelia 22 ✉ 2262 AB – ℰ (0 70) 320 92 80 – info@greenpark.nl
– Fax (0 70) 327 49 07 – www.greenpark.nl   **D1**
Rest 30 €/38 € and a la carte 40/50 €
♦ Contemporary ♦ Design ♦
The early-20C Romanian sculptor Chiparus lent his name to this restaurant facing
the sea. A fashionable menu, strongly influenced by the Mediterranean. Lakeside
terrace.

XX **t' Ganzenest** ⟨ 🕿 AC 🍴 P VISA ⓜⓄ AE Ⓞ

Deftweg 58 (near A 13-E 19, exit ⑧ Rijswijk-Zuid) ✉ 2289 AL
– ℰ (0 70) 414 06 42 – info@ganzenest.nl – Fax (0 70) 414 07 05
– www.ganzenest.nl
closed late July-early August, 25 December-4 January,
Sunday and Monday   **C3**
Rest (dinner only) 30 €/60 € and a la carte 48/74 €
♦ Contemporary ♦ Friendly ♦
The welcoming "Goose Nest" (Ganzenest) occupies a small farmhouse on the
edge of a golf course. Eye-catching interior décor, an enticing contemporary
menu and a delightful terrace.

X **Paul van Waarden** 🍴 VISA ⓜⓄ AE
🏵
Tollensstraat 10 ✉ 2282 BM – ℰ (0 70) 414 08 12
– info@paulvanwaarden.nl – Fax (0 70) 414 03 91
– www.paulvanwaarden.nl
closed lunch Bank Holidays, Saturday lunch, Sunday and Monday   **C3**
Rest 33 € (weekday lunch), 38/58 € and a la carte 51/63 €
Spec. Quatre préparations de quatre foies différents. Cabillaud croquant au
potage de pois cassés et anguille fumée (Sept.-March). Tatin à la rhubarbe
(March-Aug.)
♦ Contemporary ♦ Friendly ♦
Paul van Waarden serves diners his inventive dishes in one of the several
adjoining rooms that make up this modern, brasserie-style restaurant with its
wall-enclosed terrace.

X **Brasserie Savelberg-De Koepel** 🕿 🎶 VISA ⓜⓄ AE Ⓞ

Oosteinde 1 ✉ 2271 EA – ℰ (0 70) 369 35 72 – Fax (0 70) 360 32 14
– www.brasseriedekoepel.nl   **D2**
Rest (dinner only until 11p.m. except Sunday) 30 €/37 € and a la carte 35/43 €
♦ French traditional ♦ Brasserie ♦
An opulent-looking brasserie in an impressive rotunda-shaped building
crowned by an attractive cupola. Summer terrace, as well as a pleasant park for
a post-prandial stroll.

X **Fouquet** 🕿 AC VISA ⓜⓄ

Kerkstraat 52 ✉ 2271 CT – ℰ (0 70) 386 29 00 – voorburg@fouquet.nl
– Fax (0 70) 386 55 92 – www.fouquet.nl
closed Monday   **D2**
Rest (dinner only) 30 € and a la carte 25/44 €
♦ Contemporary ♦ Bistro ♦
A welcoming, modern brasserie-style eatery occupying two 19C listed houses,
with red seats, yellow walls, tables laid out side-by-side and a number of mirrors.

X **Papermoon** 🕿 AC VISA ⓜⓄ
☺
Herenstraat 175 ✉ 2271 CE – ℰ (0 70) 387 31 61 – info@papermoon.nl
– Fax (0 70) 387 75 20
closed 31 December-1 January and Monday   **C2**
Rest (dinner only) 29 €/53 € b.i. and a la carte approx. 41 €
♦ Contemporary ♦ Bistro ♦
This pleasant restaurant, with its hushed dining room ambience, offers a good
choice of à la carte dishes and fixed menus.

NETHERLANDS

NORWAY
NORGE

PROFILE

- **AREA:**
  323 878 km²
  (125 049 sq mi).

- **POPULATION:**
  4 593 000 inhabitants
  (est. 2005), density =
  14 per km².

- **CAPITAL:**
  Oslo (conurbation
  731 600 inhabitants).

- **CURRENCY:**
  Krone (kr or NOK)
  divided into 100 øre;
  rate of exchange:
  NOK 1 = € 0.13 = US$
  0.15 (Nov 2005).

- **GOVERNMENT:**
  Constitutional
  parliamentary
  monarchy with single-
  chamber Parliament
  (since 1945).

- **LANGUAGES:**
  Norwegian has two
  variants: Bokmål
  (influenced by Danish)

spoken by 80%
of the population
and Nynorsk
(New Norwegian).
Sami is the language
of the Sami people
in the far north.
English is widely
spoken.

- **SPECIFIC PUBLIC
  HOLIDAYS:**
  Maundy Thursday and
  Good Friday (Thursday
  and Friday before
  Easter); Constitution
  Day (17 May); Boxing
  Day (26 December).

- **LOCAL TIME:**
  GMT + 1 hour in winter
  and GMT + 2 hours in
  summer.

- **CLIMATE:**
  Temperate northern
  maritime, with cold
  winters and mild
  summers (Oslo:
  January: -4°C,

July: 16°C). Colder
interior, fairly high
precipitation in the
coastal regions.

- **INTERNATIONAL
  DIALLING CODE:**
  00 47 followed by full
  local number.

- **EMERGENCY:**
  Police: ☎ 112;
  Ambulance service:
  ☎ 113; Fire Brigade:
  ☎ 110.

- **ELECTRICITY:**
  220 volts AC, 50Hz;
  2-pin round-shaped
  continental plugs.

FORMALITIES

Travellers from the European Union (EU), Switzerland, Iceland and the main
countries of North and South America need a national identity card or passport
(America: passport required) to visit Norway for less than three months (tourism
or business purpose). For visitors from other countries a visa may be required, in
addition to a passport, especially for those wishing to stay for longer than three
months. We advise you to check with your embassy before travelling.

Drivers must have a valid national driving licence, together with the vehicle's current registration document or a vehicle on hire certificate. Third party insurance
is compulsory but Green Cards are highly recommended. The minimum age for
drivers in Norway is 18 or 20 depending on the type of vehicle.

MAJOR NEWSPAPERS

The main national newspapers are: *Aftenposten, Verdens Gang, Värt Land,
Dagbladet, Dagvisen*. There are numerous regional papers with wide circulations.
Norway Post, Nettavisen and *Bellona* are English-language dailies.

SMOKING-NO SMOKING

The laws in Norway prohibit smoking in all restaurants, bars and in the public areas of hotels. Some hotel bedrooms are still available for smokers.

USEFUL PHRASES

ENGLISH	NORWEGIAN
Yes	**Ja**
No	**Nei**
Good morning	**God morgen**
Goodbye	**Ha det bra**
Thank you	**Takk**
Please	**Vaer så god**
Excuse me	**Unnskyld**
I don't understand	**Jef forstår ikke**

HOTELS

◆ CATEGORIES

The standard of accommodation is very high and ranges from luxury international hotels and comfortable chain hotels to mountain hotels, chalets, cabins and guesthouses. Bed and breakfast accommodation is developing in Norway.

◆ PRICE RANGE

The price is per room. There is little difference between the price of a single and a double room. In the high season, between mid-June and mid-August, it is advisable to book in advance in tourist areas. There are several hotel passes, discount schemes and cheque systems in operation which offer reduced hotel rates. Hotels in Oslo and the main towns offer substantial discounted rates at weekends and in summer, which are quieter periods for business travel.

◆ TAX

Included in the room price. A service charge (10-12%) is included in hotel bills.

◆ CHECK OUT TIME

Usually between 11am and noon.

◆ RESERVATIONS

By telephone or by the Internet. A credit card is usually required. Tourist Information Offices in Norway often have a reservation service.

◆ TIPS FOR LUGGAGE HANDLING

At the discretion of the client. A small tip (15-20Nkr) is usually appreciated.

◆ BREAKFAST

Breakfast is usually included in the room price. Most hotels offer a substantial self-service buffet of cold meats, pickled herring, eggs, cheese, cereals, fruit, jam and a variety of breads and rolls between 7-8am and 11am.

Reception	**Resepsjon**
Single room	**Enkeltrom**
Double room	**Dobbeltrom**
Bed	**En seng**

Bathroom	**Bad**
Shower	**Dusj**

RESTAURANTS

There are various types of places to eat in Norway besides the traditional restaurants: brasseries, cafés, cafeterias, self-service eateries, pizzerias, bistros, snack bars and sandwich shops. Those who want variety will also find places serving food from all over the world. Norwegians often have a snack at any time of the day.

◆ MEALS

Breakfast	**Frokost**	7/8am-10am
Lunch	**Lunsj**	11am-3pm
Dinner	**Middag**	6pm-10pm

NB: Breakfast tends to be a copious meal while lunch is usually a snack (open sandwiches). Dinner is a hot meal which is eaten fairly early. A smørbrod supper (afens) is taken in the late evening.

Restaurants serving modern international cuisine and fusion food are to be found throughout Norway, particularly in the cities. They offer a comprehensive à la carte menu as well as a fixed price menu. At lunch you may choose to have a light snack or open sandwich or the dish of the day *(dangens rett)*.

◆ RESERVATIONS

Reservations can be made by telephone, Internet or fax. It is not always necessary to book a table except if you want to visit a gourmet restaurant or a popular establishment.

◆ THE BILL

The bill (check) includes service charge, VAT and tip. No additional gratuity is expected but you may wish to reward exceptional service (5-10%).

Appetizer	**Appetittvekker**
Meal	**Måltid**
Starter	**Foretter**
Main dish	**Hovedrett**
Main dish of the day	**Dagens rett**
Dessert	**Dessert**
Water/ mineral water (still, sparkling)	**Vann/ mineralvann (uten kullsyre, med kullsyre)**
Wine (red, white, rosé)	**Vin (rødvin, hvitvin, rosévin)**
Beer	**Øl**
Bread	**Brod**
Meat	**Kjøtt**
Fish	**Fisk**
Salt/pepper	**Salt/pepper**
Cheese	**Ost**
Vegetables	**Grønnsaker**
Hot/cold	**Varm/kald**
The bill (check) please	**Regningen, takk**

LOCAL CUISINE

Norway has an abundance of fresh products: fish and seafood from its long coastline, freshwater fish from its lakes and waterways, lamb and mutton from its verdant pastures and venison from its forests and mountains. The Norwegians have perfected the ways of preserving fish and meat by smoking, drying, pickling and salting. The forest and mountain plateaux provide a profusion of berries, and chanterelles and other wild mushrooms are picked in the forests in the autumn.

Fresh prawns direct from the boat are delicious. Fish – cod, catfish, halibut, haddock, mackerel, ling, ocean perch, coalfish, blenny, Arctic char, grayling, bream, tench – is always well cooked. Poached cod served with boiled potatoes is a delicacy as is poached salmon **(kokt laks)**. Crayfish **(kreps)**, mountain trout **(øret)** preferably broiled and served with fresh lemon are great treats, not to mention smoked salmon, trout and **gravlax**. Fish soufflé **(fiske-gratin)** and a creamy fish soup with shrimps are recommended. The national speciality is **lutefisk**, dried cod treated with lye and salted, which is either boiled or baked; it is very much an acquired taste.

Meat lovers will want to try reindeer, elk, venison or grouse either roasted **(reinsdyrstex, dyrestex)** or served with a creamy game sauce. Reindeer steak with gravy and tart lingonberries, roast lamb, cured leg of mutton **(fenalår)**, salted lamb ribs **(pinnekjøtt)** are specialities. The national dish is a lamb and cabbage stew **(Fårikål)**. Other typical dishes include beef in gravy **(bankebiff)**, beef marinated in beer served with pitta bread **(øllebrod)**, meat patties with onions and gravy **(kjøttkake)** and meatballs with a tomato sauce. **Postei** is a meat pie and **lapskus**, a kind of hash made with leftovers. **Spekemat**, cured meat, is served with flat bread **(flatbrød)**, soured cream and scrambled eggs. **Kjøttpålegg** is cold meat cuts and **spekepølse** air-dried sausage. Boiled, roasted or fried potatoes accompany nearly all dishes.

The secret of the open sandwich **(smørbrod)** is choosing the right mixture of ingredients: a thin slice of rye bread topped with almost anything savoury, cold meats, smoked salmon, smoked eel, pickled herrings, eggs, sausages, cheese and garnished with various salads. You can also have a hot dog **(pølser)** or a waffle as a snack. The evening meal is the main meal of the day and consists of the traditional mixed hors d'œuvre – the **koldtbord** with an extensive choice of cold meats, seafood, salads – and one or two hot dishes. For dessert try the pale-coloured cloudberries **(muiter)**, raspberries and strawberries which are full of flavour, or a pancake with lingonberries. The soft **Jarlsberg** is the best known Norwegian cheese. A great favourite is **giestost**, a sweet, brown goat's cheese. Other varieties are **mysost**, a brown whey cheese, and **pultost**, a soft fermented cheese with caraway seeds.

◆ DRINK

Beer is the national drink. Norway produces the famous Pils lager: Ringses (south) and Mack (north). **Aquavit** is a very strong drink made from potatoes and caraway seeds. The locals usually drink it with a beer chaser. **Linie Akvavit** is reputedly one of the best. It is shipped in casks all the way to Australia because crossing the Equator is deemed to improve the flavour considerably! The fruit juices are particularly delicious. Vinmonopolet stores have the monopoly for selling wines and spirits and are usually to be found in the larger towns.

OSLO

Population (est. 2005): 529 846 (Conurbation 731 600) – Altitude: 96m

Oslo is a pleasant, modern city situated at the head of Oslofjord, on low land surrounded by steep forested hills. Its green open spaces highlight the compact and busy town centre. Its temperate climate with good skiing in winter and long sunny periods during the warm spring and summer allows both locals and tourists to enjoy outdoor activities.

The carefree relaxed attitude of the people is evident as they stroll in the streets and along the harbour, enjoy a drink at pavement cafés and eat outside late into the night. Oslo is a university city with a strong cultural tradition. It boasts a wide choice of museums, a busy theatrical season and an International Jazz Festival in August.

The original Viking settlement was a thriving port by the time the city was founded in 1048 by Harald Handråde. Oslo became the capital of Norway in the late 13C but subsequently suffered various setbacks as the Hanseatic League gained control of the Baltic trade, the population was decimated by the plague and the country was annexed by Denmark. In 1624 after fire destroyed the town, Christian IV built a new Renaissance town and named it Christiana. After Norway's union with Sweden in 1814, the town grew rapidly. The country gained independence in 1905 and in 1925 the capital reverted to the original name of Oslo.

WHICH DISTRICT TO CHOOSE

Prestigious **hotels** with luxury amenities are mostly located along the main street, Karl Johans gate *Plan I* **C2** and near Oslo Central Station *Plan I* **D2** in the city centre. However, there are also less expensive hotels in Karl Johans gate and the neighbouring streets which are reasonably priced for their location. You will find moderately priced chain hotels in the fashionable suburbs of Frogner *Plan I* **A1** and Majorstuen *Plan I* **B1**.

Oslo **restaurants** have won many awards and there are establishments to suit every taste and price range. Karl Johans gate in the city centre has a good variety of places to eat and drink. Some of the more exclusive res-

taurants are to be found in Majorstuen and Frogner which also attract a young, trendy crowd. Grunerløkka *Plan I* **B1** is the area to visit for the more popular bars and restaurants with an informal and relaxed atmosphere and moderate prices. There are lively open-air bars and restaurants along the quaysides near Aker Brygge *Plan I* **B3**.

PRACTICAL INFORMATION

ARRIVAL – DEPARTURE

Oslo International Airport, Gardermoen – 47 km (30 mi) north of the city. ✆ 64 81 20 00; www.osl.no

Sandefjord Airport, Torp – 110 km (68 mi) southwest of the city. ✆ 33 42 70 00; www.torp.no

From Oslo International Airport to the city centre – By **taxi**: time 35min; taxis with Airport taxi logo on the side have special rates NOK500 (4 persons). ✆ 02 323; www.oslotaxi. no; by regular taxi about NOK600. By **express train** to Oslo S station, every 10min; time 19min; fare NOK150; tickets purchased at ticket counters and ticket machines (cash or credit cards). ✆ 47 815 00 77; www.flytoget. no. By **express bus** to Galleri bus terminal, every 20min; time 45min; fare NOK110 one way, NOK160 round trip. ✆ 22 80 49 71; www.flybussen. no/oslo

From Sandefjord Airport to the city centre – By **express bus** to Galleri Terminal: frequent service, time 2hr. *Trafikanten* ✆ 177 or 815 00 176. By **express train**: hourly service (bus or taxi to station 8km-5mi). ✆ 815 00 888; www.nsb.no

Railway Station – Oslo Central Station (Oslo S), Jembanetorget *Plan I* **D2**. ✆ 177 or 815 00 176; www.trafikanten.no

TRANSPORT

◆ BUS, TRAM, METRO

Oslo has an efficient integrated transport system. Single ticket NOK30; Day ticket NOK60. Oslo Pass (24, 48, 72hr) NOK195-395; family pass (2A+2C, 24hr) NOK395, gives unlimited transport, free entry to museums and various discounts. Oslo Pass must be validated by date and time from the start of travel. *Trafikanten*, Jembanetorget 1 *Plan I* **D2**. Open Mon-Fri, 7am-8pm, Sat –Sun, 8am-6pm. ✆ 81 50 01 76; www.trafikanten.no

◆ TAXIS

Taxis, which have a white Taxi sign on the roof, can be hailed in the streets at taxi stands near shopping centres, city squares or can be ordered by phone. *Oslo Taxi* ✆ 023 23; www.oslotaxi.no. *Norgestaxi* ✆ 08000; www.norgestaxi.no. *Taxi 2* ✆ 022 02.

USEFUL ADDRESSES

◆ TOURIST INFORMATION

Norges Informasjonssenter – Fridtjof Nansens plass 5, N-0160 Oslo *Plan I* **C2**.

Open Mon-Sun 9am-7pm; closed public holidays. ✆ 24 14 77 00; info@visitoslo.com; www.visitoslo.com

Tourist Information Centres also at Oslo Central Station (Oslo S) and at the airport.

◆ POST OFFICES

Opening times Mon-Fri 8am-5pm; Sat 9am-3pm. Post boxes are pillar-box red. Main Post Offfice, Dronningensgate 15 *Plan I* **C2** has longer opening hours.

◆ BANKS/CURRENCY EXCHANGE

Banks open mid-May to mid-September, Mon-Fri 9am-3pm; the rest of the year, Mon-Fri 9am-3.30pm (5pm Thu). Banks at Oslo Central Station Airport Express Train and at Oslo Airport Gardermoen open extended hours and have 24hr ATMs. ATMs are available all over the city. Credit cards are widely accepted. It is possible to exchange money and travellers' cheques at post offices.

◆ PHARMACIES

Opening times 10am-5pm. *Jembanetorget Apotek*, Jembanetorget 4b *Plan I* **D2** is open 24hr. *Apoteket Sfinxen*, Bogstraatveien 51and *Sagene Apotek*, Grimstadgata 21are open Mon-Fri 8.30am-9pm, Sat 9am-8pm, Sun 5-8pm.

EXPLORING OSLO

VISITING

It is possible to visit the main sights and museums in Oslo in two days.

Museums and other sights are usually open 9-10am to 5-6pm; some close on Mondays.

Nasjonalgalleriet and **Munch Museum** *Plan I* **C2** – Important collection of Norwegian and international art (19C-20C French painting, Danish and Swedish art). 58 paintings by Edvard Munch including *Moonlight, The Dance of Life*.

Akershus Festning *Plan I* **C3** – Renaissance castle (17C) built on the site of a medieval fortress: large halls and dungeons. **Norges Hjemmefrontmuseum** (Resistance Museum): story of occupied Norway.

Bygdøy – *By car or by ferry from Rådhusbrygga 3*. The pleasant residential quarter is home to five important museums. **Norsk Folkemuseum**: open-air folk art museum displaying rural and urban architecture in wood. Viking Ship Museum **(Vikingskiphuset)**: outstanding display of three boats and their contents used for a funeral ceremony. **Fram Museum**: devoted to the polar vessel *Fram*, used by the Norwegian explorers Fridtjof Nansen and Roald Amundsen. The **Kon-Tiki Museum** illustrates the voyages of Thor Heyerdahl researching the routes followed by ancient civilisations. **Norsk Sjøfartsmuseum**: themed naval collections.

Ibsenmuseet *Plan I* **B2** – Museum dedicated to Norway's most famous dramatist housed in Ibsen's own apartment.

Vigelandsparken *Plan I* **A1** – The Vigeland Park displays monumental sculptures by Norway's most famous 20C sculptor, Gustav Vigeland.

Munchmuseet – Rotating exhibition of Edvard Munch's work.

Views – From the steeple of Domkirken *Plan I* **C2**.

Boat trips – Excursions to Drøbak, the islands and the fjord.

SHOPPING

Shops usually open Mon-Fri 10am-5pm (Thu 9am-6/8pm), Sat 10am-1/3pm. Shopping centres have extended opening hours.

The main shopping streets are **Karl Johans gate** *Plan I* **B2** and **Vikaterrassen** *Plan I* **B2**. There are many shopping centres: *Aker Brygge Plan I* **B3**; *Paleet*, Karl Johans gate 37-43; *Oslo City*, Stenersgate/Fred Olsens gate; *GlasMagasinet*, Stortorvet 9; *Steen & Strøm*, Nedre Slottsgate.

Explore *Basarhallene*, tiny boutiques around and near the main square, Stortorvet *Plan I* **C2** and *Kaare Berntsen*

Art and Antiques, Universitetsgata 12 for handicrafts and antiques. For a wide choice of gifts, Norwegian arts and crafts, woollen garments, visit the *Tourist Office shop*; *Husfliden*, Møllergata 4; *Design Forum*, Øvre Slottsgate 29; *Unique design*, Rosenkrantz gate 13. *Sprell*, Thorvald Meyersgate 27 specialises in wooden toys and Scandinavian designs and *Juhls'*, Roald Amundsensgate 6; *Norway Designs*, Stortingsgaten 28 in designer silver jewellery.

WHAT TO BUY – Jewellery, pewter and enamelware, knitwear, trolls, reindeer leather goods, wooden toys and objects in painted wood (rosemailing); smoked meats and other specialities.

ENTERTAINMENT

Consult the monthly publication *What's On* for an updated calendar of events in Oslo available free from hotels and Tourist Information Offices.

Den Norske Opera *Plan I* **D2** – Opera, ballet.

National Theatret *Plan I* **C2** – Plays by Ibsen and other Norwegian playwrights in the original language.

Oslo Konserthuset *Plan I* **B2** – Home of the Norway Philarmonic Orchestra. Classical music; also pop and rock concerts.

Bryggeteater *Plan I* **B3** – Musical and dance performances.

Black Box Teater *Plan I* **B3**, **Oslo Nye Teater** *Plan I* **C2**, **Nordic Black Theatre**: Plays in English.

Valle Hovin Arena – Outdoor concerts.

Oslo Spektrum *Plan I* **D2** – Pop concerts and sporting events.

NIGHTLIFE

The most popular bars and clubs are to be found along **Karl Johans**

gate. **Grønland** is a multicultural area with lively venues: *Dattera til Hagen*, Grønland 10 and *Gloria Flames* no 18. You should also visit *Frognerveien 6*, Frognerveien and check out the streets around **Møllergata** *Plan I* **C2** and **Torgatta** *Plan I* **D2** lined with a wide range of bars and clubs. For trendy bars and pubs go to **Bogstadveien** *Plan I* **B1** and **Hegdehaugsveien** *Plan I* **B1**. The elegant *Kristiania Bar and Café* is situated in **Jernbanetorget**.

For live music visit *Stortorvets Gjæstgiveri*, Grensen 1; *Blå*, Brenneriveien 9c; *The Place*, Holmens gate 3; *Sør*, Torggata 11; *Mir*, Toftes gate 69; *Liv*, Olav gate 2; *Sam's Bar*, Markveien 32; *Barock*, Universitetsgate 26; *Galleria*, Kristian IV gate 12; *Bar Boca* and *Café Kaos*, Thorvald Meyers gate 30/56. The places for dancing are *Vice*, Pilestredet 9; *Macondo*, Badstugata 1. If you are a jazz fan you will enjoy *Oslo Jazzhus*, Toftesgate 69; *Smuget*, Rosencrantz gate 22. The popular Oslo Jazz Festival is held every summer.

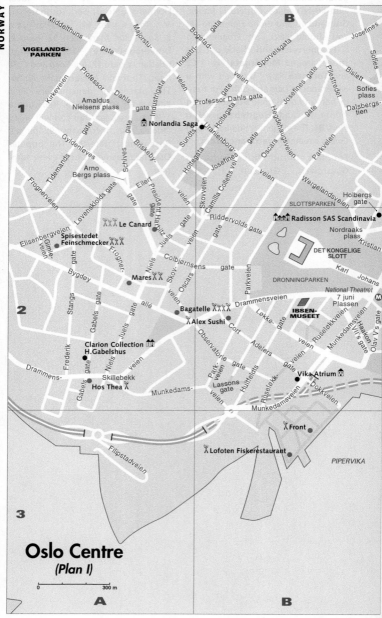

NORWAY

VIGELANDS-
PARKEN

Middelthuns gate

Majorstu...

Bogstad- gata

Josefines

Josefines gate

Sporveisgata

Bislett

Professor Dahls gate

Pilestredet

Sofies plass

Industri- gata

Professor Dahls gate

Sofies tien

Dalsbergs-

Industrigata

gate

Josefines- gate

Oscars

Hegdehaugsveien

Parkveien

🏛 Norlandia Saga

Uranienborg-

gate

Wergelandsveien

Holbergs gate

SLOTTSPARKEN

🏨 Radisson SAS Scandinavia

Nordraaks plass

Kristian

DET KONGELIGE SLOTT

DRONNINGPARKEN

National Theatret
7 juni
Plassen

IBSEN-MUSEET

Vika Atrium 🏛

Front

Lofoten Fiskerestaurant

PIPERVIKA

Le Canard

Spisestedet Feinschmecker

Mares

Bagatelle

Alex Sushi

Clarion Collection H.Gabelshus

Hos Thea

Oslo Centre
(Plan I)

0   300 m

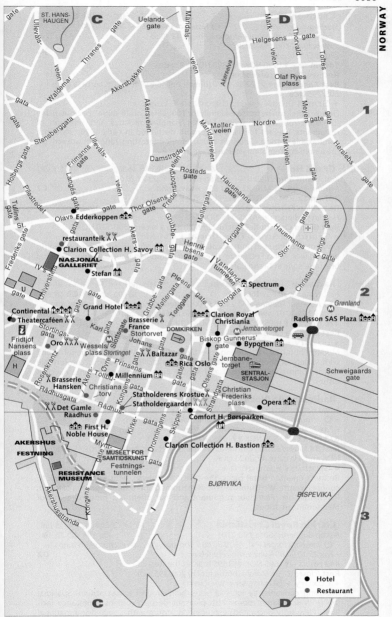

NORWAY

Continental
🏨 ✦✦✦✦   AC ⇔ ⅏ 📺 ♨ ♨300 🚗 **VISA** ⑩⊙ AE ①

Stortingsgaten 24-26 ⊠ 0117 – **Ⓜ** National Theatret – ℰ 22 82 40 00
– booking@hotel-continental.no – Fax 22 42 40 65
– www.hotel-continental.no
closed Christmas   **C2**
146 rm � – ♦1990 NOK ♦♦2390 NOK – 8 suites
Rest see **Theatercaféen** below
Rest Annen Etage ℰ 22 82 40 70 (dinner only)640/1400 NOK and a la carte
605/795 NOK

♦ Grand Luxury ♦ Traditional ♦ Classic ♦

De luxe hotel, run by the same family for 100 years. Comfortable, spacious, richly furnished rooms and suites. Elegant banquet facilities and selection of restaurants. Elegant formal dining room decorated in early 1920s style in a comfortable setting. Gourmet menu offers interesting range of attractively presented contemporary cuisine.

Grand Hotel
🏨 ✦✦✦✦   ♨ ⅏ 📺 AC ⇔ 📺 ⓒ ♨300 🚗 **VISA** ⑩⊙ AE ①

Karl Johans Gate 31 ⊠ 0101 – **Ⓜ** Stortinget – ℰ 23 21 20 00
– grand@rica.no – Fax 23 21 21 00 – www.grand.no   **C2**
281 rm ⊆ – ♦1845 NOK ♦♦2990 NOK – 9 suites
Rest Julius Fritzner (closed Easter, June-July, Christmas, Sunday and Bank Holidays) (dinner only)525/715 NOK
Rest Grand Café (buffet lunch) 235 NOK and a la carte 390/510 NOK

♦ Grand Luxury ♦ Traditional ♦ Classic ♦

Opulent 1874 hotel, in prime location. De luxe well furnished rooms. Swimming pool on roof. Julius Fritzner for fine dining in traditional surroundings. Informal brasserie-style in Grand Café.

Radisson SAS Scandinavia
🏨 ✦✦✦✦   ≤ Oslo and Fjord, ♨ ⅏ 📺 ⓒ AC ⇔

Holbergsgate 30 ⊠ 0166   📺 ⓒ ♨800 🚗 **VISA** ⑩⊙ AE ①
– **Ⓜ** National Theatret – ℰ 23 29 30 00 – reservations.oslo@radissonsas.com
– Fax 23 29 30 01 – www.scandinavia.oslo.radissonsas.com   **B2**
476 rm ⊆ – ♦1695 NOK ♦♦1895 NOK – 12 suites
Rest Enzo a la carte 444/513 NOK

♦ Luxury ♦ Modern ♦

Modern hotel block offering spectacular views. Vast international lobby with variety of shops, and good conference facilities. Spacious comfortable rooms. Panoramic bar. Small and simple Enzo offers popular international dishes.

Radisson SAS Plaza
🏨 ✦✦✦✦   ≤ Oslo and Fjord, ⅏ 📺 ⓒ AC ⇔ 📺 ⓒ ♨950

Sonja Henies Plass 3 ⊠ 0134   🚗 **VISA** ⑩⊙ AE ①
– **Ⓜ** Jernbanetorget – ℰ 22 05 80 00 – sales.plaza@radissonsas.com
– Fax 22 05 80 30 – www.radissonsas.com   **D2**
673 rm ⊆ – ♦1395 NOK ♦♦1595 NOK
Rest 34 (closed Easter, Christmas and Sunday) (tapas buffet lunch) 245/425 NOK and a la carte 475/625 NOK

♦ Business ♦ Modern ♦

Business-oriented hotel block, the tallest in Norway, with footbridge link to congress centre. Well furnished modern rooms. Superb views from top of tower. Panoramic bar. First-floor restaurant and bar offering a modern menu of Mediterranean dishes.

Clarion Royal Christiania
🏨 ✦✦✦✦   ♨ ⅏ 📺 ⓒ AC ⇔ ⅏ ♨450

Biskop Gunnerus' Gate 3 ⊠ 0106   🚗 **VISA** ⑩⊙ AE ①
– **Ⓜ** Jernbanetorget – ℰ 23 10 80 00 – christiania@clarion.choicehotels.no
– Fax 23 10 80 80 – www.choicehotels.no   **D2**
443 rm ⊆ – ♦1695 NOK ♦♦1895 NOK – 60 suites
Rest (closed 27-28 March) (buffet lunch) 200/395 NOK

♦ Luxury ♦ Business ♦ Modern ♦

Imposing conveniently located hotel built around a vast atrium. Spacious lobby. Well lit large rooms with pleasant décor. Excellent conference facilities. Pleasantly decorated restaurant in atrium with a varied international menu.

NORWAY

Opera ⪅ 🛗 🕸 ৬ 🅰🄲 ↤ ※ 📺 🕾 🕿 240 VISA 🕧 AE ①
Christian Frederiks plass 5 ✉ 0103 – **Ⓜ** *Jernbanetorget – 𝒞 24 10 30 00*
– opera @ thonhotels.no – Fax 24 10 30 10 – www.thonhotels.no/opera
closed 23 December-1 January **D2**
432 rm ⌂ – **♥**990 NOK **♥♥**1795 NOK – 2 suites
Rest *(closed lunch Saturday and Sunday)* (buffet lunch) 245/425 NOK
and a la carte 445/475 NOK
♦ Business ♦ Modern ♦
A recent arrival in town, located next to the railway station and overlooking the
harbour. Large modern building with functional yet contemporary furnishings
and décor. Restaurant with huge windows affording panoramic views. Elaborate
traditional cooking.

Clarion Collection H. Bastion *without rest* 🛗 🕸 ↤ 🕿50
Skippergaten 7 ✉ 0152 – 𝒞 22 47 77 00 🅿 VISA 🕧 AE ①
– cc.bastion @ choice.no – Fax 22 33 11 80 – www.hotelbastion.no
closed 7-18 April and 20 December-2 January **C3**
93 rm ⌂ – **♥**1295 NOK **♥♥**1595 NOK – 6 suites
♦ Business ♦ Modern ♦
Comfortable modern hotel handily placed for motorway. Welcoming rooms
with good comforts and facilities. Furniture and paintings in part reminiscent of
English style.

Rica Oslo 🛗 🕸 ৬ 🅰🄲 ↤ ※ 📺 🕿 🕿80 VISA 🕧 AE ①
Europarådets Plass 1 ✉ 0154 – **Ⓜ** *Jernbanetorget – 𝒞 23 10 42 00*
– rica.oslo.hotel @ rica.no – Fax 23 10 42 10 – www.rica.no **D2**
173 rm ⌂ – **♥**1295 NOK **♥♥**1495 NOK – 2 suites
Rest *(closed Sunday)* (buffet lunch)225/350 NOK and a la carte 331/440 NOK
♦ Business ♦ Modern ♦
Modern hotel in three connected buildings close to station. Soundproofed
bedrooms have charming décor and paintings by local artists on walls. Cosy
English style bar. Wood furnished restaurant offering a concise selection of
traditional Norwegian dishes.

Edderkoppen 🛗 🕸 ↤ 📺 🕿 🕿100 🖨 VISA 🕧 AE ①
St Olavs Plass 1 ✉ 0165 – **Ⓜ** *National Theatret – 𝒞 23 15 56 00*
– edderkoppen @ scandic-hotels.com – Fax 23 15 56 11
– www.scandic-hotels.com
closed 23 December-2 January **C2**
235 rm ⌂ – **♥**1595 NOK **♥♥**1795 NOK – 6 suites
Rest *(closed Sunday)* (buffet lunch) 195/590 NOK and a la carte 367/484 NOK
♦ Business ♦ Modern ♦
550 photographs of Norway's famous actors adorn the walls of this renovated
building, incorporating a theatre. Modern functional well-equipped bedrooms.
Modern and traditional fresh Norwegian and international dishes in Jesters and
in the open plan bar.

First H. Noble House *without rest* 🛗 🕸 ↤ ※ 📺 🕾
Kongens Gate 5 ✉ 0153 – 𝒞 23 10 72 00 🖨 VISA 🕧 AE ①
– noble.house @ firsthotels.no – Fax 23 10 72 10 – www.firsthotels.no **C3**
53 rm ⌂ – **♥**1395 NOK **♥♥**1595 NOK – 16 suites
♦ Business ♦ Classic ♦
Charming hotel in good location. Spacious rooms with parquet floors, top
quality furniture and modern facilities. All rooms equipped with kitchenette.
Pleasant roof terrace.

Clarion Collection H. Gabelshus *without rest* 🕸 🕸 ↤ ※ 📺
Gabelsgate 16 ✉ 0272 🕾 🕿50 🅿 VISA 🕧 AE ①
– 𝒞 23 27 65 00 – booking @ gabelshus.no – Fax 23 27 65 60 – www.choice.no
closed Easter and Christmas-New Year **A2**
113 rm ⌂ – **♥**1395 NOK **♥♥**1595 NOK – 1 suite
♦ Traditional ♦ Classic ♦
Attractive early 20C vine-clad hotel with extension in quiet district. Modern
public rooms. Large well-fitted bedrooms; some on front with balconies, quieter
at the rear.

NORWAY

Millennium
                  🖐 ♿ ⚗ 🐕 🚗 ⌣ 🅥🅘🅢🅐 🅞🅞 🅐🅔 ⓪

Tollbugaten 25 ⊠ 0157 – ℰ 21 02 28 00 – millennium @ firsthotels.no
– Fax 21 02 28 30 – www.firsthotels.com   **C2**
102 rm � – †1349 NOK ††1549 NOK – 10 suites
Rest *(closed Sunday)* (dinner only) a la carte 350/550 NOK
♦ Business ♦ Functional ♦
Functional modern hotel near harbour and restaurants. Internet access. Spacious well equipped rooms; top floor with balconies; quietest on inside although overlooked. Simple restaurant on different levels serving global cuisine.

Stefan
                ♿ 🅐🅒 🖐 ⚗ 🔲 🐕 🅥🅘🅢🅐 🅞🅞 🅐🅔 ⓪

Rosenkrantzgate 1 ⊠ 0159 – ℰ 23 31 55 00 – stefan @ thonhotels.no
– Fax 23 31 55 55 – www.thonhotels.no/stefan
closed 12-18 April and 22 December-2 January   **C2**
150 rm ⊻ – †1145 NOK ††1345 NOK
Rest *(closed Sunday)* a la carte 227/274 NOK
♦ Business ♦ Functional ♦
Modern hotel on convenient corner site. Rooms are well equipped with functional furniture and good facilties. Good variety of room types. Families and groups catered for. Eighth floor restaurant with small terrace. Popular buffets.

Clarion Collection H. Savoy
          🖐 ⚗ 🔲 🐕 🅥🅘🅢🅐 🅞🅞 🅐🅔 ⓪

Universitetsgata 11 ⊠ 0164 – Ⓜ National Theatret – ℰ 23 35 42 00
– savoy @ quality.choicehotels.no – Fax 23 35 42 01
– www.choice.no
closed 22 December-2 January   **C2**
93 rm ⊻ – †1395 NOK ††1595 NOK
Rest see *restauranteik* below
♦ Business ♦ Classic ♦
Classic early 20C hotel in the city centre behind the museum. Stylish public areas. Spacious well-kept bedrooms with good facilities.

Byporten without rest
             ♿ 🖐 ⚗ 🔲 🚗 🅥🅘🅢🅐 🅞🅞 🅐🅔 ⓪

Jernbanetorget 6 ⊠ 0154 – Ⓜ Jernbanetorget – ℰ 23 15 55 00
– byporten @ scandic-hotels.com – Fax 23 15 55 11
– www.scandic-hotels.no/byporten   **D2**
236 rm ⊻ – †1695 NOK ††1895 NOK – 4 suites
♦ Business ♦ Modern ♦
Modern hotel in vast office/commercial centre block by station. Functional soundproofed rooms with environmentally friendly decor. Breakfast in nearby public restaurant.

Comfort H. Børsparken without rest
           ♿ 🖐 ⚗ 🔲 🐕
                             🛗75 🅥🅘🅢🅐 🅞🅞 🅐🅔 ⓪

Tollbugaten 4 ⊠ 0152
– Ⓜ Jernbanetorget – ℰ 22 47 17 17
– booking.boersparken @ comfort.choicehotels.no – Fax 22 47 17 18
– www.choicehotels.no   **C-D2**
198 rm ⊻ – †1230 NOK ††1430 NOK
♦ Business ♦ Functional ♦
Modern functional chain hotel on corner site in city centre. Pleasant lobby opening onto tree-lined square. Compact practical rooms, well equipped for business clientele.

Norlandia Saga without rest
         🖐 🔲 🐕 🛗25 🅿 🅥🅘🅢🅐 🅞🅞 🅐🅔 ⓪

Eilert Sundtsgt. 39 ⊠ 0259 – ℰ 22 43 04 85 – service @ saga.norlandia.no
– Fax 22 44 08 63 – www.norlandia.no/saga
closed 7-18 April and 22 December-1 January   **A-B1**
37 rm ⊻ – †1015 NOK ††1225 NOK
♦ Family ♦ Classic ♦
Family-run hotel in quiet area. Cosy winter lounge with fire. Well lit rooms with classic furnishings and facilities; rear rooms are quietest. Complimentary mid-week supper.

NORWAY

Vika Atrium
ᵏᵇ 🛪 ↳ 🍴rest 🖭 📞 ≰240 *VISA* 🐵 🖭 ⓪

Munkedamsveien 45 ⊠ *0121* – Ⓜ *National Theatret* – 𝒞 *22 83 33 00*
– vika.atrium @ thonhotels.no – Fax 22 83 09 57
– www.thonhotels.no/vikaatrium   **B2**
91 rm ☕ – ♥1345 NOK ♥♥1745 NOK
Rest *(closed July, Saturday, Sunday, Friday dinner and Bank Holidays)* (buffet lunch) 175 NOK
◆ Business ◆ Functional ◆
Located in large office block built around an atrium. Comfortable lobby lounge. Well serviced rooms with functional modern fittings. Good conference facilities. Simple menu offers range of international dishes to suit all tastes.

Spectrum without rest
& ↳ 🖭 📞 ≰30 *VISA* 🐵 🖭 ⓪

Brugata 7 ⊠ *0133* – Ⓜ *Grønland* – 𝒞 *23 36 27 00* – *spectrum @ thonhotels.no*
– Fax 23 36 27 50 – www.thonhotel.no/spectrum
closed 22 December-2 January   **D2**
151 rm ☕ – ♥595 NOK ♥♥795 NOK
◆ Business ◆ Functional ◆
Conveniently located hotel in pedestrian street not far from station. Two styles of room: "old" are fairly functional; "new" have more interesting décor and furniture.

Bagatelle (Hellström)
🗚🗚 ↳ 🍴 *VISA* 🐵 🖭 ⓪
🐵🐵
Bygdøy Allé 3 ⊠ *0257* – Ⓜ *National Theatret* – 𝒞 *22 12 14 40*
– bagatelle @ bagatelle.no – Fax 22 43 64 20 – www.bagatelle.no
closed 1 week Easter, 4 weeks July-August, 1 week Christmas-New Year and Sunday   **A2**
Rest (booking essential) (dinner only) 750/1350 NOK and a la carte 800/990 NOK
Spec. Norwegian King crab Royal. Seafood pot-au-feu with lobster butter. Game in season.
◆ Contemporary ◆ Design ◆
Highly reputed classic restaurant with colourful contemporary décor and numerous paintings on walls. Excellent innovative cuisine. Wine cellar may be viewed by diners.

Statholdergaarden (Stiansen)
↳ 🍴 *VISA* 🐵 🖭 ⓪
🐵
Rådhusgate 11, (entrance by Kirkegate) 1st floor ⊠ *0151* – Ⓜ *Stortinget*
– 𝒞 22 41 88 00 – post @ statholdergaarden.no – Fax 22 41 22 24
– www.statholdergaarden.no
closed 9-17 April, 1, 17 and 25 May, 3-5 June, 17 July-8 August, 23 December-2 January and Sunday   **C2**
Rest see also **Statholderens Krostue** below
Rest (booking essential) (dinner only) 695/725 NOK and a la carte 725/740 NOK
Spec. Scallops and crab salad with artichoke, dried tomato and fennel. Peppered fillet of deer with smoked root vegetables, spinach and shallot cream. Chocolate terrine with cloudberry sorbet.
◆ Contemporary ◆ Formal ◆
Fine 17C house offers elegant 1st floor dining room with original décor beneath beautiful period stucco ceilings, whose motifs reappear on the china. High quality cuisine.

Le Canard
🍴 🗚 ↳ 🍴 **P** *VISA* 🐵 🖭 ⓪
🐵
⊠ *0259* – 𝒞 *22 54 34 00* – *lecanard @ lecanard.no – Fax 22 54 34 10*
– www.lecanard.no
closed Easter, 1 July-1 September, Christmas-New Year, Sunday and Monday   **A2**
Rest (dinner only) 670 NOK
Spec. Grilled scallops with foie gras, red onion confit, orange syrup and Port glaze. Duckling with honey, quince purée, leek and lavender. Game and fowl in season.
◆ Contemporary ◆ Formal ◆
Tastefully decorated 1900 villa in residential district. Elegant dining room has beautiful antiques, a wall fresco and Baroque décor. Cuisine for the discerning gourmet.

NORWAY

Spisestedet Feinschmecker
AC ⅍ ⅍ VISA ◍ AE ①

⟨⟩

Balchensgate 5 ⊠ 0265 – ℰ 22 12 93 80
– kontakt@feinschmecker.no – Fax 22 12 93 88
– www.feinschmecker.no
closed Easter, 3 weeks in summer and Sunday　　　　　**A2**
Rest (booking essential) (dinner only) 625/695 NOK and a la carte
640/750 NOK
Spec. Poached turbot with saffron risotto, shrimp and clams. Grilled halibut with
spinach, raisins and truffle vinaigrette. Parsley crusted rack of lamb with
cassoulet of beans and celeriac.
♦ Contemporary ♦ Formal ♦
Busy restaurant in residential building with inviting façade and tasteful colourful
décor. Spacious dining room has warm, cosy atmosphere. Expertly cooked
contemporary fare.

Oro
AC ⅍ ⅍ VISA ◍ AE ①

Tordenskioldsgate 6A ⊠ 0160 – ◍ Stortinget – ℰ 23 01 02 40
– kontakt@ororestaurant.no – Fax 23 01 02 48
– www.ororestaurant.no
closed 10 days Easter, July, 23 December-4 January
and Sunday　　　　　**C2**
Rest (booking essential) (dinner only) 450/575 NOK and a la carte
470/705 NOK
Rest *Del i Oro* 200/300 NOK and a la carte 100/150 NOK
♦ Mediterranean ♦ Trendy ♦
Elegant, modern designer décor in muted tones with an informal atmosphere.
Open-plan kitchen offers inventive cuisine with a Mediterranean influence.
Booking a must. Del i Oro, the adjoining tapas bar with a large counter displaying
cold and some warm dishes.

Det Gamle Raadhus
⍋ ⅍ ⅍ VISA ◍ AE ①

Nedre Slottsgate 1 ⊠ 0157 – ◍ Stortinget – ℰ 22 42 01 07
– gamle.raadhus@gamle-raadhus.no – Fax 22 42 04 90
– www.gamle-raadhus.no
closed 1 week Easter, 3 weeks July, 1 week Christmas
and Sunday　　　　　**C3**
Rest (dinner only) 425 NOK and a la carte 431/594 NOK
♦ Traditional ♦ Rustic ♦
Well run restaurant operating for over a century located in Oslo's original City
Hall, dating from 1641. Elegant rustic interior décor and English style atmosphere
in bar.

Theatercaféen – at Continental H.
⅍ ⅍ VISA ◍ AE ①

Stortingsgaten 24-26 ⊠ 0117 – ◍ National Theatret – ℰ 22 82 40 50
– theatercafeen@hotel-continental.no – Fax 22 41 20 94
– www.hotel-continental.no
closed Sunday lunch　　　　　**C2**
Rest (light lunch) 235/398 NOK and a la carte 518/712 NOK
♦ Traditional ♦ Brasserie ♦
An institution in the city and the place to see and be seen. Elaborate lunchtime
sandwiches make way for afternoon/evening brasserie specials.

restauranteik
AC ⅍ ⅍ VISA ◍ AE ①

☺

Universitetsgata 11 ⊠ 0164 – ◍ Stortinget – ℰ 22 36 07 10
– eikefjord@restauranteik.no – Fax 22 36 07 11
– www.restauranteik.no
closed Sunday-Monday　　　　　**C2**
Rest (dinner only) (set menu only) 335 NOK
♦ Contemporary ♦ Fashionable ♦
Restaurant in striking minimalist style; open-plan kitchen with chef's table. Good
value set menu of 3 or 5 courses of interesting dishes.

XX **Mares** ⚤ ✂ *VISA* ⓪ 匨 ⓪

Frognesveien 12B ✉ *0263 –* ℰ *22 54 89 90 – mares@mares.no – Fax 22 54 89 85*
closed 1 week Easter, 10 July-10 August, 23 December-4 January
and Sunday **A2**
Rest (booking essential) (dinner only) 395/695 NOK and a la carte
365/510 NOK
♦ Seafood ♦ Neighbourhood ♦
Fish restaurant in traditional house in residential area. Well lit pleasant interior
with modern designer décor, black and white photos on walls and local
atmosphere.

XX **Baltazar** 🍴 匨 ⚤ ✂ *VISA* ⓪ 匨 ⓪

Dronningensgt 2-7 ✉ *0154 –* Ⓜ *Jernbanetorget –* ℰ *23 35 70 60*
– baltazar@baltazar.no – Fax 23 35 70 61 – www.baltazar.no
closed 9-19 April, 1 and 17 May, July, 21 December-4 January
and Sunday **C2**
Rest (dinner only) 350/510 NOK and a la carte 300/555 NOK 🏵
Rest *Enoteca* a la carte 280/350 NOK
♦ Italian ♦ Friendly ♦
In courtyard off Karl Johans gate beside cathedral. Serious Italian wine list; small
a la carte or concise chef's menu: home-made pasta, fine Italian produce and
local fish. The rustic décor of the wine bar is just right for an informal lunch.

X **Brasserie Hansken** 🍴 匨 ⚤ ✂ *VISA* ⓪ 匨 ⓪

Akersgata 2 ✉ *0158 –* Ⓜ *Stortinget –* ℰ *22 42 60 88 – Fax 22 42 24 03*
– www.brasseriehansken.no
closed 1 week Easter, 1 week Christmas and Sunday **C2**
Rest (booking essential) 325/615 NOK and a la carte 430/640 NOK
♦ Modern ♦ Brasserie ♦
Busy restaurant in lively district with strictly contemporary bistro-style décor and
dark wood fittings. Good quality brasserie fare. Terrace bar on the square in
summer.

X **Brasserie France** 🍴 匨 ⚤ ✂ *VISA* ⓪ 匨 ⓪

Øvre Slottsgate 16 ✉ *0157 –* Ⓜ *Stortinget –* ℰ *23 10 01 65*
– bord@brasseriefrance.no – Fax 23 10 01 61
– www.brasserie france.no
closed Easter, 22 December-1 January and Sunday **C2**
Rest (dinner only except Saturday) 325/475 NOK and a la carte 340/485 NOK
♦ French ♦ Brasserie ♦
French brasserie-style dining room at D'Artagnan; entrance from pedestrian
street. Wall benches, bistro chairs and open kitchen at end of room. Interesting
French dishes.

X **Hos Thea** ⚤ ✂ *VISA* ⓪ 匨 ⓪

Gabelsgate 11 ✉ *0272 –* ℰ *22 44 68 74 – sergio@hosthea.no – Fax 22 44 68 74*
– www.hosthea.no
closed 10-30 July **A2**
Rest (dinner only) 435 NOK and a la carte 358/564 NOK
♦ Traditional ♦ Family ♦
Discreet black façade in residential area conceals this typical little restaurant
fitted out with simple Scandinavian-style décor. Family atmosphere. Appealing
menu.

X **Statholderens Krostue** – at Statholdergaarden ⚤

Rådhusgate 11, (entrance by Kirkegate) 1st floor ✂ *VISA* ⓪ 匨 ⓪
✉ *0151 –* Ⓜ *Stortinget –* ℰ *22 41 88 00 – post@statholdergaarden.no*
– Fax 22 41 22 24 – www.statholdergaarden.no
closed 9-17 April, 1, 17 and 25 May, 3-5 June, 10 July-9 August, 23 December-
3 January, Sunday and Monday **C2**
Rest a la carte 475/535 NOK
♦ Traditional ♦ Rustic ♦
Three vaulted basement rooms with bistro-style décor and warm candle-lit
ambience. Changing themed menus for dinner and a la carte for light lunch;
friendly service.

NORWAY

Lofoten Fiskerestaurant ⟨ 🛱 ⅍ ⅍ **VISA** **⑯** **AE** **①**
Stranden 75 ⊠ 0250 – ℰ 22 83 08 08 – lofoten @ fiskerestaurant.no
– Fax 22 83 68 66 – www.lofoten-fiskerestaurant.no
closed 22 December-3 January   **B3**
Rest 280/480 NOK and a la carte 398/445 NOK
♦ Seafood ♦ Brasserie ♦
A firm favourite with locals; attractive, modern fjord-side restaurant at Aker Brygge. Chef patron offers a tempting array of seafood and shellfish.

Alex Sushi ⅍ **VISA** **⑯** **AE** **①**
*Cort Adelers Gate 2 ⊠ 0254 – **Ⓜ** National Theatret*
– ℰ 22 43 99 99 – alex @ alexsushi.no – Fax 22 43 99 98
– www.alexsushi.no
closed 1 week Easter, July and 1 week New Year   **B2**
Rest (dinner only) 375/975 NOK
♦ Japanese ♦ Design ♦
Swish Japanese restaurant features central oval sushi bar shaped like small boat with metallic roof. Dining room enlivened by modern art. Appealing tempura and miso dishes.

Front 🛱 ⅍ **VISA** **⑯** **AE** **①**
Stranden 7 ⊠ 0250 – ℰ 22 83 64 00 – post @ restaurant-front.no
– www.restaurant-front.no   **B3**
Rest 395 NOK and a la carte 469/589 NOK
♦ Contemporary ♦ Brasserie ♦
A very popular newcomer on Aker Brygge quay, this contemporary brasserie/restaurant is flooded with light from big windows and has a smart front terrace. Tasty local dishes.

ENVIRONS OF OSLO

at Lillestrøm Northeast: 18 km by E 6:

Arena 🌐 𝄢 ⋒ 🖳 ⅍ 🖾 ⅍ 🖂 ⓦ 🖧1000 🍲 **P** **VISA** **⑯** **AE** **①**
Nesgata 1 ⊠ 2004 – ℰ 66 93 60 00 – arena @ thonhotels.no – Fax 66 93 63 00
– www.thonhotels.no/arena
closed Christmas and Easter
262 rm ⌘ – †1495 NOK ††1695 NOK – 16 suites
Rest *Madame Thrane* (dinner only) a la carte 284/400 NOK
Rest *Amfi* (buffet lunch) 285 NOK
♦ Business ♦ Functional ♦
Large modern hotel in trade fair centre with direct train access to airport and city centre. Spacious, contemporary rooms with every possible facility; a few singles. Madame Thrane for interesting contemporary dishes. Buffet style service at the informal Amfi.

at Holmenkollen Northwest: 10 km by Bogstadveien, Sørkedalsveien
and Holmenkollveien:

Holmenkollen Park 🦫 ⟨ Oslo and Fjord, 🌐 𝄢 ⋒ 🖳 ⅍ 🖾 ⅍ 🖂
Kongeveien 26 ⊠ 0787 ⓦ 🖧500 🍲 **P** **VISA** **⑯** **AE** **①**
– ℰ 22 92 20 00 – holmenkollen.park.hotel.rica @ rica.no – Fax 22 14 61 92
– www.holmenkollenparkhotel.no
closed 22 December-3 January
210 rm ⌘ – †1295 NOK ††1695 NOK – 11 suites
Rest *De Fem Stuer* (buffet lunch) 305/585 NOK and dinner a la carte
540/680 NOK
Rest *Galleriet* (closed Sunday) (buffet lunch) 275/540 NOK and dinner
a la carte 320/410 NOK
♦ Traditional ♦ Personalised ♦
Smart hotel near Olympic ski jump; superb views. Part built (1894) in old Norwegian "dragon style" decorated wood. Chalet style rooms, some with balconies or views or saunas. International cuisine in De Fem Stuer. Informal Galleriet for a more popular menu.

at Oslo Airport Northeast: 45 km by E 6 at Gardermoen:

Radisson SAS Airport

✉ 2061 – ℰ 63 93 30 00
– sales.airport.oslo@radissonsas.com – Fax 63 93 30 30
– www.gardermoen.radissonsas.com
346 rm ⌷ – ♦1850 NOK ♦♦2050 NOK – 4 suites
Rest 285 NOK and a la carte approx. 450 NOK
♦ Business ♦ Modern ♦

Ultra-contemporary business hotel on a semi-circular plan overlooking runway, but well soundproofed. Rooms are a good size, well equipped and have varied décor. Modern restaurant offering a variety of international dishes to appeal to all comers.

Clarion Oslo Airport

(West : 6 km) ✉ 2060 – ℰ 63 94 94 94 – oslo.airport@clarion.choicehotels.no
– Fax 63 94 94 95 – www.choicehotels.no/hotels/no070
357 rm ⌷ – ♦1395 NOK ♦♦1495 NOK – 1 suite
Rest (buffet lunch) 250/295 NOK
♦ Business ♦ Functional ♦

Modern Norwegian design hotel in wood and red tiles on star plan. Compact functional rooms with good modern facilities. Well equipped for conferences. Families at weekend. Vast restaurant offers a standard range of international dishes to cater for all tastes.

Trugstad Gård

Trugstadveien 10 (Southwest : 10 km by Road 120) ✉ 2034 Holter
– ℰ 63 99 58 90 – restaurant@trugstad.no – Fax 63 99 50 87 – www.trugstad.no
closed July and Christmas
Rest (booking essential) 290/545 NOK and a la carte 292/650 NOK
♦ Modern ♦ Family ♦

Attractive and lovingly restored farmhouse yet only a short distance from the airport. Attentive and friendly service of modern set menu using the finest local ingredients.

POLAND
POLSKA

FORMALITIES

Travellers from the European Union (EU), Switzerland, Iceland and the main countries of North and South America need a national identity card or passport (America: passport required) to visit Poland for less than three months (tourism or business purpose). For visitors from other countries a visa may be required, in addition to a passport, especially for those wishing to stay for longer than three months. We advise you to check with your embassy before travelling.

The international car hire companies have branches in Warsaw. Nationals of EU countries require a valid national driving licence; nationals of non-EU countries require an International Driving Licence. Seat belts are compulsory for drivers and all passengers.

MAJOR NEWSPAPERS

The main daily newspapers are *Gazeta Wyborcza*, *Super Express*, *Rzeczpospolita* and *Nasz Dziennik* (Catholic newspaper). The major weeklies are *Przekroj*, *Polityka* and *Wprost*. Poland also has many regional papers, as *Dziennik Gieldowy* (Cracow) or *Gazeta Poznanska* (Poznan).

USEFUL PHRASES

ENGLISH	POLISH
Yes	**Tak**
No	**Nie**
Good morning	**Dzjen dobry**
Goodbye	**Czesc**
Thank you	**Pzie kuje**
Please	**Prosze**
Excuse me	**Przepraszam**
I don't understand	**Nie rozumiem**

HOTELS

◆ CATEGORIES

Accommodation ranges from luxurious international hotels to smaller less expensive hotels; all are classified (1-5 stars). Economy inns and motels are located beside major roads. There are rooms to let *(wolne pokoje)* in tourist resorts. There is also rural and B&B accommodation ☏ 52 398 1434 (www.agritourism.pl). Many old and historic buildings have been converted into tourist accommodation – ☏ 22 433 60 30 (www.leisure-heritage.com).

◆ PRICE RANGE

The price (quoted in Zloty and sometimes in euros also) is per room. Between April and October it is advisable to book in advance, particularly in Cracow. From November to March prices may be lower, some hotels offer special cheap rates.

◆ TAX

7% but not included in the room price.

◆ CHECK OUT TIME

Usually noon.

◆ RESERVATIONS

By telephone or by Internet. A credit card number may be required.

◆ TIP FOR LUGGAGE HANDLING

At the discretion of the customer.

◆ BREAKFAST

It is not usually included in the price of the room and is generally served between 7am and 9.30/10am. Most hotels offer a hot and cold buffet but usually it is also possible to have breakfast served in the room.

Reception	**Recepcja**
Single room	**Pokój 1-Osobowy**
Double room	**Pokój 2-Osobowy**
Bed	**Łozko**
Bathroom	**Łazienka**
Shower	**Prysznic**

RESTAURANTS

Traditional Polish cuisine, hearty and rustic, is served in the many **regional restaurants** and in most hotels but there is also modern Polish cooking by inventive chefs who re-interpret old recipes and create unique dishes using unusual combinations of ingredients. There is also the full range of international cuisine from Mediterranean to Asian. **Cafeteria (bar mlecsny)** offer cheap, basic dishes; there are other fast food outlets.

♦ **MEALS**

Breakfast	**Śniadanie**	7am – 9.30am
Lunch	**Obiad**	12 noon – 2pm
Dinner	**Kolacja**	8pm – midnight

Most restaurants in Poland offer à la carte menus. Menus are usually printed in Polish; they may also be printed in English or explained in English.

♦ **RESERVATIONS**

Reservations are usually made by phone. For famous restaurants, it is advisable to book in advance.

♦ **THE BILL**

The bill (check) does include VAT but not a service charge; in these circumstances tipping (10%) is at the discretion of the diners.

Drink or aperitif	**Drink**
Appetizer	**Snacks**
Meal	**Posłek**
Starter	**Przystawka**
Main dish	**Danie główne**
Main dish of the day	**Speciał**
Dessert	**Deser**
Water	**Woda**
Wine (red, white, rosé)	**Wino (czerwone, białe, rózowe)**
Beer	**Piwo**
Bread	**Chleb**
Meat	**Mięso**
Fish	**Ryba**
Salt/pepper	**Sol/pieprz**
Cheese	**Ser**
Vegetables	**Warzywa**
Hot/cold	**Gorace/zimne**
The bill (check) please	**Rachunek**

LOCAL CUISINE

The cuisine of Poland has been influenced by the Jewish population and by its eastern neighbours, and also by French and Italian royalty. Each region has developed its own particular dishes and culinary customs. Old recipes are passed on from generation to generation, because they preserve the unique flavour of Polish cooking.

On the Baltic coast herring is the most popular fish; in Pomerania and the lake districts there are fish and crayfish dishes; Podlasie offers a variety of cold meats and potato dishes; from the Polish highlands comes a unique **smoked sheep's milk cheese (oscypek)**, served in slices with a glass of spirits. There are dishes typical of just one region: Mazuria's **dzyndzałki** (small meat dumplings served with melted butter and cream), **małdrzyki** from Crakow, or **pork with prunes** in Wielkopolska. General Polish specialities include **sour soup (żurek)**, **cold soups**, **fruit soups**, **potato pancakes** and **black pudding**. **Pork** is ubiquitous and served in many different ways: as sausages with pickled cabbage, mushrooms and **prunes (bigos)**. **Goose** is popular, roasted, in the Jewish style **(gęsie pipki)**, or as pickled and smoked goose breast **(półgęsek)**. **Game** may be served marinated, as pâté or in sausages **(kiełbasa)**. There are numerous varieties of **dumplings** and **pancakes** unknown in other countries; every region produces **pierogi**, turnovers with various fillings: buckwheat and mushroom, cabbage and mushroom, buckwheat and cheese, minced offal and pickled cabbage, cottage cheese, potato and onion, berries of all kinds.

For dessert there is a variety of cream cakes and cheesecake **(sernik)**: two squares of puff pastry filled with a thick layer of cream and custard **(kremówka)**, cottage-cheese cakes **(małdrzyke)**, **Toruń gingerbread**.

◆ DRINK

There is a broad range of Polish beers which are of the lager type. Poland also produces many fruit juices and several mineral waters. **Juniper Beer** is the pride of Kurpie, in northeast of the country. **Pepper water** is made from onion juice, salt, pepper and vinegar. Imported wines and spirits tend to be expensive.

Polish **vodka** comes in many varieties. **White vodka** made from distilled spirit and water. **Flavoured vodka** is produced by adding various ingredients to give flavour, colour and aroma: fresh and dried fruit, spices, grass, flowers, seeds, aromatic oils, honey and sugar. It is worth mentioning by name **Żubrówka**, a light-yellow herbal vodka named bison vodka after the vanilla grass (called bison grass in Polish) which grows in the Bialowieska Forest, a refuge of European bison and the oldest primeval forest in Europe; **Jarzębiak**, made from rowanberries; **Żołądkowa Gorzka**, a spicy vodka made with unripe oranges and cloves; the famous **sliwowica from Łąck**, made from ripe plums and very potent (70-140%) owing to double distillation.

Poland is famous for its **mead (trójniak)**, an alcoholic drink (9-18%) made by fermenting diluted natural honey; the flavour may be enhanced by the addition of spices or herbs, as well as hops, also cinnamon, cloves, ginger, juniper berries, vanilla, mint, rose petals. Fruit mead is made by adding fruit juice instead of water. Mead may be drunk like wine, cold or hot; mulled mead is good for cold winter weather, served in ceramic cups rather than glasses. Other liqueurs sweetened with local honey are also famous: **krupnik kurpiowski** and **mioduszka**.

WARSAW
WARZSAWA

Population (est. 2005): 1 593 000 (conurbation 2 135 000) – Altitude: 106m

B. Morandi / MICHELIN

The capital of Poland lies on the banks of the Vistula at the heart of the Mazovian lowlands. According to legend, a mermaid asked two young lovers, Wars and Zawa, to found a city and call it Warszawa, hence the city emblem of a mermaid in the Old Town Square. In fact the town was founded in the 10C and 11C when large villages spread along each side of the Vistula. It became the capital during the reign of Sigismund III in 1596, when the royal castle in Cracow was destroyed in a terrible fire. Over the centuries the city has expanded from its medieval core, which was laid waste during the Second World War and afterwards rebuilt as an almost exact copy of its former self from old documents and plans; it is now on the UNESCO World Heritage List.

Today Warsaw is a lively, bustling and modern metropolis, the most cosmopolitan, dynamic and progressive of Poland's cities, with good shops and restaurants. It is not only the seat of the government and administration but also a scientific, cultural and arts centre, with many theatres and concert halls, art galleries and museums, a university and institutes of higher education.

From 1826 to 1829 the Central Academy of Music numbered among its pupils F. Chopin who was born in 1810 in Zelazowa Wola (53 km west). Although he left Poland at 20, his work has a strong Polish accent.

WHICH DISTRICT TO CHOOSE

Most of the **hotels** are in the commercial district west of the Royal Way. There are **restaurants** in the commercial dis-trict and also in the Old Town *Plan I* **A2**. Both districts offer places where you can have a drink in the evening.

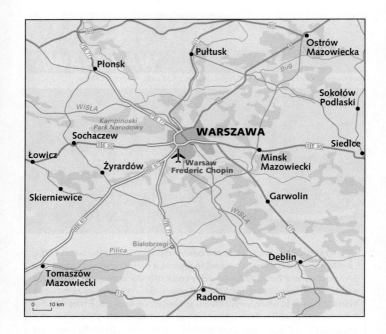

PRACTICAL INFORMATION

ARRIVAL – DEPARTURE

Warsaw F. Chopin (Okęcie) International Airport – About 10 km (6 mi) south of the city centre. ✆ 226 50 11 11 (info desk), 650 39 43 (flight information).

From the airport to the city centre – By **bus** 175 (611 at night) to the city centre. By **taxi**: it is advisable to order a taxi from one of the licensed firms: *Merc, MPT, Sawa-Taxi*; taxis touting for custom at the airport tend to be expensive. Initial charge 5-6zł.

Sea Ferries – *Polska Żegluga Bałtycka (Polish Baltic Shipping)*, Portowa 3, Gdynia; ✆ 35 52 102; www.polferries. com.pl; *Polskie Linie Oceaniczne (Polish Ocean Lines)*, 10 Lutego 24, Gdynia, ✆ 690 06 70; www.pol.com.pl; *Stena Line*, Kwiatkowskiego 60, Gdynia; ✆ 660 92 00; www.stenaline.pl

Railway Stations – Dworzec Warszawa Centralna (Central), 54 Jerozolimskie Ave; **Dworzec Wschodni (West)**, 1 Lubelska St; for trains to the west; **Dworzec Zachodni (East)**, 144 Jerozolimskie Ave; for trains to the north and east.

TRANSPORT

◆ TRAM, BUS AND METRO

Operate 5am-11pm. Single zł2.40; 1 day travelcard zł7.20; 3-day travelcard zł12; 30-day travelcard zł66; 90-day travelcard zł166; double fare for journeys outside the city limits; discounted fares for foreigners under 26 with valid ISIC card. All tickets can be bought at RUCH kiosks, from automatic ticket machines at stops, at newsagents and (for trams and buses) from the driver (additional fee) as rechargeable magnetic cards which must be validated (www.ztm.waw.pl).

◆ TAXIS

Taxis are distinguished by a horizontal red and yellow line. It is advisable to take a taxi from a taxi rank, indicated by a blue sign, or book with one of the licensed firms: *MPT* ℰ 919, *Euro Taxi* ℰ 9662, *Halo Taxi* ℰ 9623, *Super-Taxi* ℰ 9622, *Volfra-Taxi* ℰ 9625. Initial charge 5-6zł; minimal day rate zł2 pkm (check the sticker on the window); official night (10pm-6am) and weekend rate zł4 pkm.

◆ WARSAW TOURIST CARD

For free travel on public transport in Warsaw, free admission to 21 museums, discounts in some shops, restaurants and leisure centres.

USEFUL ADDRESSES

◆ TOURIST INFORMATION

Tourist Help Line ℰ 48 22 94 31, May-Sep daily 8am-8pm, Oct-Apr daily 8am-6pm. **Tourist Information Centre**, 39 Krakowskie Przedmieście *Plan II* **D1**, May-Sep daily 9am-9pm, Oct-Apr daily 9am-6pm. **Dworzec Centralny (Central Railway Station)**, Jerozolimskie 54; May-Sep daily 8am-8pm, Oct-Apr daily 8am-6pm. **Dworzec Zachodni (Zachodni Coach Station)**, Jerozolimskie 144, May-Sep daily 10am-6pm, Oct-Apr daily 9am-5pm. **F. Chopin International Airport**, Arrival Hall, May-Sep daily 8am-8pm, Oct-Apr daily 8am-6pm. **Warsaw Tourist and Cultural Information**, Palace of Culture and Science (entrance Marszałkowska), daily 9am-6pm, ℰ 656 68 54, 656 71 36. **MUFA Warsaw Tourist Information Centre**, Zamkowy Square 1/13 *Plan II* **C1**; Mon-Fri 9am-6pm, Sat 10am-6pm, Sun 11am-6pm, ℰ 635 18 81; info@warsawtour.pl; www.warsawtour.pl

◆ POST OFFICES

Mon-Fri 8am-8pm, Sat 8am-1pm. Main Post Office, Żwiętokrzyska 31/33 *Plan II* **C2**; open daily, 24-hr.

◆ BANKS/CURRENCY EXCHANGE

Mon-Fri, 8am-6pm, Sat 8am-2pm. There are cash machines (24hr); most credit cards can be used in those connected to the Euronet system.

◆ EMERGENCY

Ambulance: ℰ **999**; Fire Brigade: ℰ **998**; Police: ℰ **997**; Police from mobile: ℰ **112**.

BUSY PERIODS

It may be difficult to find a room at a reasonable price when special events are held in the city:

International Poster Biennial: March (even years) – Welcomes many artists of international reputation from all fields of culture and art; organised by the Poster Museum in Wilanów.

Mozart Festival: June-July – Mozart operas, symphonic and chamber music and masses performed in Warsaw Chamber Opera and churches.

International Festival of Organ Music: summer – in the cathedral.

Warsaw Autumn: September – International Festival of Contemporary Music.

Chopin Piano Competition: October, every fifth year (next in 2010) – International competition for young pianists playing music by Chopin, which attracts about 150 participants.

Jazz Jamboree: October – International Jazz Festival.

Old Music Festival: October-November – At the Royal Castle.

DIFFERENT FACETS OF THE CITY

It is possible to visit the main sights and museums in two to three days.

Most museums and sights are usually open Tues-Sat 10am-4pm. Some are closed on Mon; most are closed on Sun or vary their hours. To Wilanów Palace (8 km/5 mi south): bus 180 from Powązki Cemetery, daily 4.30am-10pm, every 15min.

VIEW OF WARSAW – Pałac Kultury i Nauki *Plan II* **C2**: panoramic view of the city and multimedia tourist information centre on 30th floor of the Palace of Culture and Science, a skyscraper (234m) in the Stalinist style of architecture, a 'gift' from the former USSR.

OLD TOWN – Plac Zamkowy *Plan II* **C1**: Castle Square marked by the Sigismund Column (1644). **Zamek Królewski** *Plan II* **C1**: the Royal Palace, reconstructed to create the luxury of the 17C and 18C. **Katedra Św Jana** *Plan II* **C1**: St John's Cathedral, a Gothic church with stained-glass windows depicting major figures from Polish history. **Rynek Starego Miasta** *Plan II* **C1**: Old Town Market Square, bordered by narrow-fronted houses and alive with cafés, restaurants, artists, souvenir stalls and horse-drawn carriages for hire.

MUSEUMS AND GALLERIES – Muzeum Historyczne Warszawy *Plan II* **C1**: the Warsaw History Museum; short film in English on the destruction and reconstruction of Warsaw. **Muzeum Narodowe** *Plan II* **D2**: National Museum devoted to medieval Polish art and other European artists; frescoes from Farras in Sudan. **Muzeum Kolekcji im. Jana Pawla II** *Plan II* **C1**: the John Paul II Collection of six centuries of outstanding European art; religious subjects, landscapes, mythology, portraits and works by the Impressionists. **Jewish History Museum**: the history of the Warsaw ghetto.

ROYAL ROAD – Trakt Królewski. The Royal Way (4 km/2.5 mi) linking the castle to the summer residence, is divided into several streets lined with historic buildings reflecting several centuries of history: St Anne's Church (**view** from the tower – *summer only*), Radziwiłł Palace, now the Residence of the President of Poland, Hotel Bristol, Warsaw University, Chopin's residence, Holy Cross Church (urn containing Chopin's heart), Pilsudski Square *(side street west)* with the changing of the guard every 1hr before the Tomb of the Unknown Soldier, Staszic Palace, St Aleksander's Church, Paderewski Monument in Ujazdowski Park.

ROYAL PALACES – Park Łazienkowski *Plan I* **B2**. 18C park (lakes, trees, lawns, flower beds; Botanic Gardens) containing Chopin Memorial; 18C orangery housing the royal theatre; Biały Dom, royal summer residence known as the White House; Pałac na Wodzie, royal residence designed by Merlini, standing on a tiny island: superbly furnished and decorated rooms; Palac Myślewicki, second summer residence by Merlini; Teatr na Wyspie, amphitheatre on the edge of the lake; Belweder, 18C building now the official residence of the President of the Republic. **Wilanów** Residence of King John III Sobieski, a Baroque palace with lavishly furnished rooms, surrounded by a park and gardens: Baroque, English-style and Anglo-Chinese on the edge of the lake.

GOURMET TREATS

Warsaw is good for coffee and cakes (kawiarnia): *Hortex* chain, for a range of patisserie; *Blikle*, Nowy Świat 33, famous for its traditional interior, doughnuts and cream cakes; *Antykwariat*, Żurawia 45; *Cafe Brama*, Krucsz 16/22; *Coffeeheaven*, Nowy Świat 40. For a traditional Polish eating house: *U Fukiera*, Rynek Starego Miasta 27; *Dom Polski*, Francuska 11, with pleasant terrace garden; *Restauracja Polska 'Tradycja'*, Belwederska 18A; *Restauracja Polska*, Nowy Świat 21; *Restauracja Polska*, Chocimska 7.

SHOPPING

Shops are generally open from Mon-Fri 10am-7pm, Sat 9am-3pm. Food shops open earlier and close at 8pm or 10pm. Large shopping centres and tourist shops tend to open on Sundays.

There are some shops in the Old Town but the main shopping streets are: **Chmielna** *Plan II* **D2**, **Marszałkowska** *(Galeria Centrum)*, **Krakowskie Przedmiescie** *Plan II* **D1**, **Nowy Świat** *Plan II* **D2**, **Świętojańska**, **Jerozolimskie** *(Smylg) Plan II* **D2**.

MARKETS – The street markets offer the lowest prices; the most famous **food market** is Polna St *Plan I* **B2**.

WHAT TO BUY – Woodcarvings, pottery, paintings on glass, embroidery, tapestries, striped woollen fabrics known as *pasiak* used to make skirts and aprons (all available in Cepelia shops). Amber, the gold of the north, is found in yellow, russet and brown, and used to make necklaces and earrings; sometimes it is mounted in silver as jewellery. Works of art and antiques (large selection in the *DESA* stores).

ENTERTAINMENT

What When Where, published in English, gives a calendar of current events in Warsaw and other towns. *What's up in Warsaw*, published monthly in English (no charge) also provides current information. Details about cultural events in Warsaw – theatre shows, concerts – can be obtained from the telephone Cultural Information Centre, ✆ 629 84 89 (Mon-Fri 10am-9pm, Sat-Sun 10am-6pm).

Tickets can be obtained at *ZASP Theatre Booking Office*, Jerozolimskie 25 *Plan II* **D2**, ✆ 621 94 54 or 621 93 83; *Empik*, Nowy Świat 15/17, ✆ 625 12 19; Marszałkowska 104/122, ✆ 551 4 37.

Grand Theatre-National Opera *Plan II* **D1** – National opera and ballet.

Warsaw Chamber Opera *Plan II* **C1** – Baroque opera.

National Philharmonic Hall *Plan II* **C2** – Two auditoria for orchestral concerts; venue for the Chopin Piano Competition.

Roma Music Theatre *Plan II* **D2** – Classical operettas and musicals.

National Theatre *Plan II* **D1** – Foremost Polish drama.

NIGHTLIFE

Warsaw has a lively clubbing scene, including *Piekarnia*, Młocińska 11; *Vanilla*, Sienkiewicza 6; *Techno*, Instytut Energetyki, Mory 8; *Lucid*, Jerozolimskie 179; *Organza*, Sienkiewicza 4; *Klubo Kawiarnia*, Czackiego; NoBo, Wilcza 58a.

A

B

Environs of Warsaw
(Plan I)

0   2 km

61

8

Płochocińska

Marywilska

Modlińska

Toruńska

Ludwika

Kondratowicza

Łodygowa

P. Wysockiego

Wybrzeże

WISŁA

Jagiellońska

Radzymińska

TARGÓWEK

1

Krajowej

Armii

Gdyńskie

Stefana
Starzyńskiego

Solidarności

Grochowska

Warsaw Centre
(Plan II)

Jerzego Waszyngtona

Ostrobramska

Okopowa

🏨 Ibis Stare
Miasto

ZAMEK
KRÓLEWSKI

Wał

Al.

Dom Polski ✕✕✕

2

🏨 Ibis Centrum

Solidarności

Towarowa

WARSZAWA
CENTRALNA

Miedzeszyński

WISŁA

Wólska

🏨🏨 Jan III Sobieski

🏨 Rialto

Al. Ludowej

Casa Valdemar ✕✕

PARK
ŁAZIENKOWSKI

Prymasa
Tysiąclecia

✕ Inaba

✕✕ Kurt
Scheller's

Wawelska

Politechnika

Belvedere ✕✕✕

Restauracja Polska "Rozana" ✕✕

Pole Mokotowskie

✕✕ Flik

● Hyatt Regency 🏨🏨🏨

Restauracja
Polska "Tradycja" ✕✕✕

Jerozolimskie

Al.

Żwirki

Pułaskiego

Racławicka

Jana

Powsińska

Grójecka

Niepodległości

Wierzbno

Al. Gen.

W. Sikorskiego

Sobieskiego

🛈

3

Wilanowska

Al. Wilanowska

🏨🏨 Novotel
Warszawa Airport

Łopuszańska

F. Hynka

Wigury

Marynarska

Al. Wilanowska

WŁOCHY

Lord 🏨🏨

🏨🏨 Airport
H. Okecie

Służew

Dolina Służewiecka

8(7) E 77

Al. Krakowska

Courtyard 🏨🏨
by Marriott

WARSAW
FREDERIC CHOPIN
AIRPORT

W.
Rzymowskiego

● Hotel
● Restaurant

A

B

Ursynów

POLAND

⭤ **Le Royal Meridien Bristol** 🍴 ⊕ ₤ 🗅 🛅 ﹠ 🗚 ⅙rm 🖾 ⓦ
Krakowskie Przedmieście 42-44 ⊠ 00 325 🕭180 *VISA* ⓞⓒ 🖭 ⓞ
– ⓜ Świętokrzyska – ℰ (022) 551 10 00 – bristol@lemeridien.com.pl
– Fax (022) 625 25 77 – www.warsaw.lemeridien.com **D1**
174 rm – †1400/1700 PLN ††1400/1700 PLN, ⊆ 85 PLN – 31 suites
Rest see *Malinowa* below
Rest *Marconi* 85 PLN (weekday lunch) and a la carte 124/182 PLN
♦ Grand Luxury ♦ Classic ♦
Imposing late 19C façade, partly decorated in Art Nouveau style fronts classic
hotel, a byword for luxury and meeting place for Warsaw high society. Spacious
elegant rooms. Fairly informal restaurant with terrace offers a varied menu of
Mediterranean fare.

⭤ **Intercontinental** ⊕ ₤ 🛅 🗅 ﹠ 🗚 ⅙rm 🖾 ⓦ 🕭500
Ul. Emilii Plater 49 ⊠ 00 125 – ⓜ Centrum 🚭 *VISA* ⓞⓒ 🖭 ⓞ
– ℰ (022) 328 88 88 – wrs_reservation@interconti.com – Fax (022) 328 88 89
– www.warsaw.intercontinental.com **C2**
305 rm ⊆ – †532/684 PLN ††532/684 PLN – 21 suites
Rest *Frida (closed Sunday and Saturday lunch)* a la carte 66/169 PLN
Rest *Downtown*66/100 PLN and a la carte 66/110 PLN
Rest *Hemisphere* a la carte 69/108 PLN
♦ Grand Luxury ♦ Business ♦ Modern ♦
Architecturally striking high-rise hotel. Richly furnished, contemporary
bedrooms. Stunning 44th floor wellness centre. Frida for Mexican dishes from
open plan kitchen. Cosmopolitan New York style in Downtown. Hemisphere
with Hemingway theme and live music.

⭤ **Hyatt Regency** 🍴 ⊕ ₤ 🛅 🗅 ﹠ 🗚 ⅙rm 🖾 🕭350 🚭
Belwederska Ave 23 ⊠ 00 761 – ℰ (022) 🅿 *VISA* ⓞⓒ 🖭 ⓞ
558 12 34 – info@hyattwarsaw.pl – Fax (022) 558 12 35
– www.warsawregency.hyatt.com *Plan I* **B3**
231 rm – †290/635 PLN ††365/670 PLN – 19 suites
Rest *Venti Tre , ℰ (022) 558 10 94* – 85 PLN/150 PLN and a la carte
110/149 PLN
Rest *Q Club (closed Saturday, Sunday and Bank Holidays)* (dinner only)
a la carte 79/144 PLN
♦ Business ♦ Modern ♦
Striking glass fronted and ultra modern corporate hotel beside Lazienki Park.
Spacious bedrooms with every facility and comfort. Contemporary Italian meal in
relaxed Venti Tre. Open kitchen with wood fired specialities. Q Club for
contemporary Asian menu.

⭤ **The Westin** ₤ 🗅 ﹠ 🗚 ⅙rm 🖾 ⓦ 🕭560 🚭 *VISA* ⓞⓒ 🖭 ⓞ
Al. Jana Pawła II 21 ⊠ 00 854 – ⓜ Świętokrzyska – ℰ (022) 450 80 00
– warsaw@westin.com – Fax (022) 450 81 11 – www.westin.com/warsaw
346 rm ⊆ – †514/790 PLN ††514/790 PLN – 15 suites **C2**
Rest *Fusion* a la carte 65/208 PLN
♦ Luxury ♦ Business ♦ Modern ♦
Impressive modern façade, splendid glass atrium with glass lifts and spacious
public areas. 'Heavenly beds' and modern facilities in comfortable bedrooms.
Contemporary Fusion offers culinary delights as East meets West.

⭤ **Sheraton** ₤ 🗅 ﹠ 🗚 ⅙rm 🖾 ⓦ 🕭700 🚭 *VISA* ⓞⓒ 🖭 ⓞ
Ul. B. Prusa 2 ⊠ 00493 – ⓜ Centrum – ℰ (022) 450 61 00 – warsaw@
sheraton.com – Fax (022) 450 62 00 – www.sheraton.com/warsaw **D2**
331 rm – †514/775 PLN ††514/775 PLN, ⊆ 90 PLN – 19 suites
Rest *The Oriental (closed Saturday lunch and Sunday dinner)* a la carte
120/216 PLN
Rest *Lalka* 90 PLN/160 PLN and a la carte 78/179 PLN
♦ Luxury ♦ Business ♦ Modern ♦
Up-to-date business hotel in well located imposing building. Very comfortable,
spacious modern rooms with latest hi-tech facilities. Authentic Asian fare in
ornately decorated Oriental. All day bistro; Old City mural; Mediterranean/
traditional Polish dishes.

POLAND

Marriott ⪡ City, Ⅰ₅ 🈲 🔲 ⚅ 𝔸𝔼 ⅔rm 📺 🚬 🏊700 🚗 🆅🇮🇸🇦 🆎 🆎 🆔
Al. Jerozolimskie 65-79 ⌖ 00 697 – **Ⓜ** Centrum – 𝒞 (022) 630 63 06 – marriott@
it.com.pl – Fax (022) 830 03 11 – www.marriott.com/wawpl **C2**
491 rm 🛏 – ♥440 PLN ♥♥520 PLN – 31 suites
Rest *Parmizzano's* 115 PLN/384 PLN and a la carte 92/269 PLN
Rest *Lila Weneda* 86 PLN (lunch) and a la carte 69/134 PLN
♦ Business ♦ Modern ♦
Modern high-rise business hotel opposite station. Well equipped up-to-date
bedrooms with city views; good facilities for business travellers. Formal
Parmizzano's offers Italian fare. Classic Polish cooking in Lila Weneda.

Sofitel Victoria 🈲 🔲 ⚅ 𝔸𝔼 ⅔rm 📺 🕻 🏊650 🚗 🆅🇮🇸🇦 🆎 🆎 🆔
Ul. Krølewska 11 ⌖ 00 065 – **Ⓜ** Świętokrzyska – 𝒞 (022) 657 80 11
– sof.victoria@orbis.pl – Fax (022) 657 80 77 – www.sofitel.com **C1-2**
329 rm 🛏 – ♥760 PLN ♥♥840 PLN – 12 suites
Rest *Canaletto* 99 PLN/150 PLN and a la carte 99/200 PLN
♦ Business ♦ Classic ♦
Large hotel overlooking Pilsudski Square and Saxon Gardens. Rooms are well
equipped and comfortable with muted classic modern décor. Good business
facilities available. Formal restaurant with Italian influence.

Radisson SAS Centrum Ⅰ₅ 🈲 🔲 ⚅ 𝔸𝔼 ⅔rm 📺 🕻 🏊400
Grzybowska 24 ⌖ 00 132 – **Ⓜ** Świętokrzyska 🚗 🆅🇮🇸🇦 🆎 🆎 🆔
– 𝒞 (022) 321 88 88 – reservation.warsaw@radissonsas.com
– Fax (022) 321 88 98 – www.radissonsas.com **C2**
292 rm 🛏 – ♥520/650 PLN ♥♥520/650 PLN – 19 suites
Rest *Latino Brasserie at Ferdy's* 80/120 PLN
♦ Business ♦ Modern ♦
Popular corporate hotel in business district with state of the art meeting facilities.
Modern bedrooms in maritime, Scandinavian or Italian style. Informal bar-
restaurant with Latin American influences.

Le Régina 🈷 🈲 ⚅ 𝔸𝔼 ⅔rm 📺 🚬 🏊100 🚗 🆅🇮🇸🇦 🆎 🆎 🆔
U. Kościelna 12 ⌖ 00 218 – **Ⓜ** Ratusz – 𝒞 (022) 531 60 00 – info@leregina.com
– Fax (022) 531 60 01 – www.leregina.com **C1**
59 rm – ♥1000/1200 PLN ♥♥1600 PLN, 🛏 92 PLN – 2 suites
Rest *La Rotisserie* 95 PLN (weekday lunch) and a la carte 150/248 PLN
♦ Luxury ♦ Design ♦
Boutique hotel close to the Old Town; neo-18C exterior but stylish,
contemporary interior. Pleasant courtyard. Individually decorated, spacious
high-tech bedrooms. Small, intimate restaurant offering original modern
cuisine.

Jan III Sobieski Ⅰ₅ 🈲 ⚅ 𝔸𝔼 ⅔rm 🚬 🏊400 🚗 🆅🇮🇸🇦 🆎 🆎 🆔
Plac Artura Zawiszy 1 ⌖ 02 025 – **Ⓜ** Politechnika – 𝒞 (022) 579 10 00 – hotel@
sobieski.com.pl – Fax (022) 659 88 28 – www.sobieski.com.pl *Plan I* **A2**
392 rm – ♥350 PLN ♥♥350 PLN, 🛏 46 PLN – 35 suites
Rest 69 PLN and a la carte approx. 69 PLN
♦ Business ♦ Modern ♦
Up-to-date business hotel on busy thoroughfare. Pleasant first-floor terrace
garden. Comfortable well equipped bedrooms. Good conference facilities.
Restaurant offers classic menu of traditional local fare with international
overtones.

Holiday Inn Ⅰ₅ 🈲 ⚅ 𝔸𝔼 ⅔rm 📺 🕻 🏊220 🚗 🆅🇮🇸🇦 🆎 🆎 🆔
Ul. Złota 48-54 ⌖ 00 120 – **Ⓜ** Centrum – 𝒞 (022) 697 39 99 – holiday@orbis.pl
– Fax (022) 697 38 99 **C2**
326 rm 🛏 – ♥500 PLN ♥♥640 PLN – 10 suites
Rest *Symfonia* a la carte 92/145 PLN
Rest *Brasserie* 89 PLN
♦ Business ♦ Functional ♦
Business hotel in the shadow of the Palace of Culture; ideal for shopping.
Comfortable bedrooms with good level of facilities. International cuisine in
Symfonia accompanied by piano music. Brasserie for buffet lunch.

POLAND

 Mercure Fryderyk Chopin
Al. Jana Pawła II 22 ⊠ *00 133*
– Ⓜ *Świętokrzyska* – ✆ *(022) 528 03 00*
– *h1597@accor.com* – *Fax (022) 528 03 13*
– *www.mercure.com*

😩 🐱 ⅁ 🆎 ↔rm 🏋300 ☕
🅿 VISA ⦿ 🆎 ⓪

C2

242 rm – 📍500 PLN 📍📍500 PLN, ☕ 58 PLN – 7 suites
Rest *Stanislas Brasserie*, ✆ *(022) 620 02 01* – a la carte 46/69 PLN
◆ Business ◆ Functional ◆
Up-to-date hotel located in business district, catering for business clientele.
Practically appointed rooms. Comfortable brasserie-style restaurant for
international dishes.

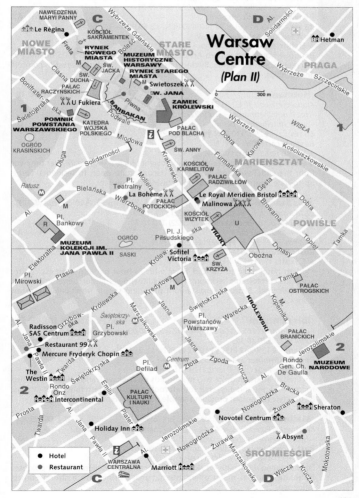

● Hotel
● Restaurant

POLAND

Novotel Centrum　　　& 📺 ↳rm 🖭 📞 🔥450 VISA 🕥 AE ①
Ul. Nowogrodzka 24-26 ⊠ 00 511 – Ⓜ *Centrum*
– ℰ (022) 621 02 71 – nov.warszawa@orbis.pl
– Fax (022) 625 04 76　　　　　　　　　　　　　　　　　**D2**
724 rm ⬚ – ♦520 PLN ♦♦575 PLN – 10 suites
Rest 80 PLN/120 PLN and a la carte 80/120 PLN
♦ Business ♦ Functional ♦
1970s style high-rise hotel in central but noisy location on central shopping
street. Contemporary style, well serviced bedrooms; all with city views.
Traditional-style restaurant for international cuisine.

Rialto　　　　⅃ ⌂ & 📺 ↳rm 🖭 📞 🔥25 P VISA 🕥 AE ①
Ul. Wilcza 73 ⊠ 00 670 – Ⓜ *Politechnika – ℰ (022) 584 87 00*
– info@hotelrialto.com.pl – Fax (022) 584 87 01
– www.hotelrialto.com.pl　　　　　　　　　　　　*Plan I* **A2**
33 rm – ♦460/615 PLN ♦♦540/690 PLN, ⬚ 59 PLN – 11 suites
Rest see *Kurt Scheller's* below
♦ Business ♦ Art Deco ♦
Boutique hotel with superb Art Deco features in converted 1906 building in
discreet location. Individually decorated bedrooms with the latest in comfort
and facilities.

Hetman　　　　　　& 📺 ↳rm 🖭 📞 🔥110 🛳 VISA 🕥 AE
Klopotowskiego 36 ⊠ 03 717 – ℰ (022) 511 98 00
– rez@hotelhetman.pl – Fax (022) 618 51 39
– www.hotelhetman.pl　　　　　　　　　　　　　　　**D1**
68 rm ⬚ – ♦290/330 PLN ♦♦330/380 PLN
Rest a la carte 38/115 PLN
♦ Business ♦ Functional ♦
Modern hotel in a 19C converted apartment block, a short walk over the river
from the Old Town and city centre. Jacuzzi suite open to residents. Large
up-to-date bedrooms. International cuisine in restaurant.

Ibis Stare Miasto　　　& 📺 ↳rm 🖭 🔥40 🛳 VISA 🕥 AE
Ul. Muranowska 2 ⊠ 00 209 – ℰ (022) 310 10 00
– h3714@accor-hotels.com – Fax (022) 310 10 10
– www.ibishotel.com　　　　　　　　　　　　　　*Plan I* **A2**
333 rm – ♦259 PLN ♦♦259 PLN, ⬚ 28 PLN
Rest *L'Estaminet* a la carte 53/138 PLN
♦ Chain hotel ♦ Functional ♦
Modern hotel close to the Old Town with 24-hour bar and business centre.
Spacious, comfortable bedrooms with en suite shower; larger rooms on 6th floor
with balconies. Bistro-style restaurant providing simple traditional European
dishes.

Ibis Centrum　　　　& 📺 ↳rm 🖭 🔥60 🛳 VISA 🕥 AE
Al. Solidarności 165 ⊠ 00 876 – ℰ (022) 520 30 00 – h2894@accor.com
– Fax (022) 520 30 30　　　　　　　　　　　　　*Plan I* **A2**
189 rm – ♦199/249 PLN ♦♦199/249 PLN, ⬚ 28 PLN
Rest *L'Estaminet* a la carte 53/138 PLN
♦ Chain hotel ♦ Functional ♦
Located at intersection of two main roads by Warsaw Trade Tower. Good size
rooms are light and airy, well soundproofed, with modern functional fittings.
Bistro-style restaurant providing simple traditional European dishes.

XXXX **Malinowa** – at Le Royal Meridien Bristol H.　　📺 ↳ VISA 🕥 AE ①
Krakowskie Przedmieście 42-44 – Ⓜ *Świętokrzyska – ℰ 551 18 32*
– bristol@lemeridien.pl – Fax 551 18 27　　　　　　　　　　**D1**
Rest *(closed January)* (dinner only) a la carte 167/265 PLN
♦ International ♦ Formal ♦
Formal dining room with Art Nouveau décor and chandeliers adding opulence.
Elaborate gourmet menu offers international cuisine with a strong French
influence.

POLAND

XXX **Belvedere** ⇐ 斎 ⚘ ℗ *VISA* ⓪ 伍 ①
Ul. Agrykoli 1 (entry from Parkowa St) ⊠ *00 460 –* ✆ *(022) 841 22 50*
– restauracja@belvedere.com.pl – Fax (022) 841 71 35
– www.belvedere.com.pl
closed 23 December- 4 January   *Plan I* **B2**
Rest (booking essential) a la carte 86/207 PLN
♦ International ♦ Formal ♦
Elegant restaurant occupying late 19C orangery in Lazienki park. Dining room
filled with statuesque plants. French-influenced International and Polish cuisine.

XXX **Restauracja Polska "Tradycja"** 斎 圃 ℗ *VISA* ⓪ 伍 ①
Belwederska Ave 18A ⊠ *00 762 –* ✆ *(022) 840 09 01 – Fax (022) 840 09 50*
– www.restauracjapolska.com.pl   *Plan I* **B3**
Rest (booking essential) a la carte 42/77 PLN
♦ Traditional ♦ Family ♦
Several homely dining rooms offer traditional Polish atmosphere; live piano,
candles and lace tableclothes. Professional service. Well prepared traditional
Polish cooking.

XXX **Dom Polski** 斎 圃 ⅓ *VISA* ⓪ 伍 ①
Ul. Francuska 11 ⊠ *03 906 –* ✆ *(022) 616 24 32 – restauracjadompolski@wp.pl*
– Fax (022) 616 24 88 – www.restauracjadompolski.pl   *Plan I* **B2**
Rest a la carte 57/161 PLN
♦ Traditional ♦ Friendly ♦
Elegant house in city suburb with pleasant terrace-garden. Comfortable dining
rooms on two floors with welcoming ambience. Interesting well presented
traditional cuisine.

XX **U Fukiera** 斎 ⅓ *VISA* ⓪ 伍 ①
Rynek Starego Miasta 27 ⊠ *00 272 –* Ⓜ *Ratusz –* ✆ *(022) 831 10 13*
– Fax (022) 831 58 08
closed 24, 25 and 31 December   **C1**
Rest a la carte 68/266 PLN
♦ Traditional ♦ Rustic ♦
On historic central city square, well known restaurant with character; 17C vaulted
cellar and pleasant rear courtyard. Traditional Polish cuisine.

XX **La Bohème** 斎 圃 *VISA* ⓪ 伍 ①
Plac Teatralny 1 ⊠ *00 077 –* Ⓜ *Ratusz –* ✆ *(022) 692 06 81*
– restauracja.laboheme@laboheme.com.pl – Fax (022) 692 06 84
– www.laboheme.com.pl
closed 25 December, 1 January and Easter   **C1**
Rest a la carte 73/124 PLN
♦ International ♦ Rustic ♦
Elegant bar-restaurant with intimate vaulted cellar and attractive terrace located
at Grand Theatre; classic cuisine with international influences; pre and post
theatre menu.

XX **Restauracja Polska "Rozana"** 斎 圃 *VISA* ⓪ 伍 ①
Chocimska 7 – ✆ *(022) 848 12 25 – Fax (022) 848 15 90*
– www.restauracjapolska.com.pl   *Plan I* **B3**
Rest a la carte 42/77 PLN
♦ Traditional ♦ Friendly ♦
Typical of the Restauracja Polska style; traditional homely ambience;
professional service; classic Polish cuisine.

XX **Kurt Scheller's** *– at Rialto H.* 圃 ℗ *VISA* ⓪ 伍 ①
Ul. Wilcza 73 ⊠ *00 670 –* Ⓜ *Politechnika –* ✆ *(022) 584 87 00*
– restaurant@hotelrialto.com.pl – Fax (022) 584 87 01   *Plan I* **A2**
Rest a la carte 45/63 PLN
♦ Modern ♦ Fashionable ♦
Superb Art Deco style with reproduction 1930s furniture and posters. Modern
slant on traditional Polish cooking by Kurt Scheller.

POLAND

XX **Casa Valdemar**   🏠 AC VISA 🅼🅾 AE ⓪
Ul. Piekna 7-9 ⊠ 00 539 – Ⓜ Politechnika – ℰ (022) 628 81 40
– restauracja@casavaldemar.pl – Fax (022) 622 88 96
– www.casavaldemar.pl   Plan I **B2**
Rest 134 PLN (dinner) and a la carte 138/142 PLN
♦ Spanish ♦ Rustic ♦
Elegant Spanish-style installation inside and out with pleasant wooden terrace
to front. Authentic Spanish cooking; try the meat and fish from the clay
oven.

XX **Flik**   🏠 AC VISA 🅼🅾 AE ⓪
😊 Ul. Puławska 43 ⊠ 02 508 – ℰ (022) 849 44 34
– restauracja@flik.com.pl – Fax (022) 849 44 06
– www.flik.com.pl
closed 25 December   Plan I **B3**
Rest a la carte 54/94 PLN
♦ Traditional ♦ Neighbourhood ♦
Welcoming neighbourhood restaurant with Polish art collection, overlooking
park. Good reputation and friendly service. Good quality well prepared
traditional fare.

XX **Swietoszek**   VISA 🅼🅾 AE ⓪
Ul. Jezuicka 6-8 ⊠ 00 281 – Ⓜ Ratusz – ℰ (022) 831 56 34
– info@swietoszek.com.pl – Fax (022) 635 59 47
– www.swietoszek.com.pl   **C1**
Rest 45 PLN/85 PLN and a la carte 66/95 PLN
♦ Traditional ♦ Rustic ♦
Characterful restaurant in charming vaulted cellar in historic district. Rustic
furniture, spotlights and candles add to ambience. Serves tasty traditional
specialities.

XX **Restaurant 99**   🏠 AC VISA 🅼🅾 AE ⓪
Al. Jana Pawła II 23 ⊠ 00 854 – Ⓜ Świętokrzyska
– ℰ (022) 620 19 99 – nn@restaurant99.com
– Fax (022) 620 19 98   **C2**
Rest 59 PLN (lunch) and a la carte 87/183 PLN
♦ Modern ♦ Fashionable ♦
Lively noisy restaurant with informal atmosphere. Eclectic menu with dishes
from wood burning oven and rotisserie. Stylish bar and lounge popular in the
evening.

X **Absynt**   AC ↯ VISA 🅼🅾 AE ⓪
😊 Ul. Wspølna 35 ⊠ 00 519 – Ⓜ Centrum – ℰ (022) 621 18 81
– absynt@siesta.com.pl – Fax (022) 622 11 01
– www.siesta.com.pl   **D2**
Rest a la carte 73/135 PLN
♦ French ♦ Bistro ♦
Informal restaurant with a strong 'French' accent; more intimate basement.
Friendly service. Good value classic French dishes.

X **Inaba**   AC VISA 🅼🅾 AE ⓪
Ul. Nowogrodzka 84-86 ⊠ 02 018 – ℰ (022) 622 59 55
– inaba@inaba.com.pl – Fax (022) 622 59 56
– www.inaba.com.pl
closed 24-26 December   Plan I **A2**
Rest 100 PLN/190 PLN (dinner) and a la carte 42/87 PLN
♦ Japanese ♦ Minimalist ♦
Choose from the lively sushi-bar or the relaxed restaurant in this discreetly
located basement restaurant. Authentic Japanese cuisine prepared with skill
and precision.

at Warsaw Frederick Chopin Airport Southwest : 10 km by Zwirki i Wigury

POLAND

Courtyard by Marriott　　　🖪 ♿ Ⓐ ↔rm 🖾 🛜420

W. Zwirki i Wigury 1 ✉ 00 906 – ℰ (022) 650 01 00　　　**P** **VISA** 🟠 🗛 ⓞ
– wcy@courtyard.com – Fax (022) 650 01 01
– www.courtyard.com/wawcy　　　　　　　　　　　　**A3**
219 rm – †326/480 PLN ††326/480 PLN, � 32 PLN – 7 suites
Rest *Brasserie* a la carte 50/122 PLN
♦ Business ♦ Modern ♦
Modern hotel opposite the airport entrance. Bar and cyber café with internet access; conference facilities. Well-equipped modern bedrooms with effective soundproofing. Mezzanine brasserie offering an eclectic range of international dishes.

Airport H. Okęcie　　　🖪 🛜 ✕ ♿ Ⓐ ↔rm 🖾 ☏ 🛜200 🗑

Ul. 17 Stycznia 24 ✉ 02 146 – ℰ (022) 456 80 00　　　**P** **VISA** 🟠 🗛 ⓞ
– reservation@airporthotel.pl – Fax (022) 456 80 29
– www.airporthotel.pl　　　　　　　　　　　　**A3**
173 rm ⊃ – †376/410 PLN ††460/500 PLN – 7 suites
Rest *Mirage* a la carte approx. 75 PLN
♦ Business ♦ Modern ♦
Bright and modern corporate hotel 800 metres from the airport. Spacious meeting and bedrooms have both the international traveller and conference delegate in mind. Lively and popular 'Mirage' with open plan kitchen and buffet.

Lord　　　🗺 🖪 🛜 ♿ Ⓐ 🖾 ☏ 🛜220 **P** **VISA** 🟠 🗛 ⓞ

Al. Krakowska 218 ✉ 02 219 – ℰ (022) 574 20 20 – okecie@hotellord.com.pl
– Fax (022) 574 20 01　　　　　　　　　　　　**A3**
87 rm ⊃ – †225/310 PLN ††246/353 PLN – 5 suites
Rest a la carte 75/105 PLN
♦ Business ♦ Modern ♦
Bright and modern corporate hotel convenient for Warsaw Frederick Chopin Airport. Well kept and functional bedrooms. 6th floor café bar with terrace and city views. Elegant dining room offers classic Polish cooking.

Novotel Warszawa Airport　　　🗺 🖪 🛜 ⊃ ♿ Ⓐ ↔rm 🛜300

Ul. 1 Sierpnia 1 ✉ 02 134 – ℰ (022) 575 60 00　　　**P** **VISA** 🟠 🗛 ⓞ
– nov.airport@orbis.pl – Fax (022) 575 69 99
– www.orbis.pl/novotelwarszawaairport　　　　　　　　**A3**
269 rm – †450 PLN ††450 PLN, ⊃ 38 PLN – 1 suite
Rest a la carte 73/111 PLN
♦ Business ♦ Functional ♦
Modern functional hotel not far from airport, which caters well for families and business people. Rooms are of adequate size, practical and well maintained. Private garden. Bright and modern restaurant specialises in international cuisine to suit all tastes.

- *Discover the best restaurant ?*
- *Find the nearest hotel ?*
- *Find your bearings using our maps and guides ?*
- *Understand the symbols used in the guide...*

Follow the red Bibs !

Advice on restaurants from Chef Bib.

Advice on hotels from Bellboy Bib.

Tips and advice from Clever Bib on finding your way around the guide and on the road.

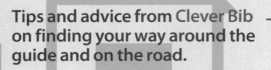

PORTUGAL

PORTUGAL

PROFILE

- **AREA:**
  88 944 km² (34 341 sq mi).

- **POPULATION:**
  10 566 000 (est. 2005), density = 119 per km².

- **CAPITAL:**
  Lisbon (conurbation 2 398 000 inhabitants).

- **CURRENCY:**
  Euro (€); rate of exchange: € 1 = US$1.17 (Nov 2005).

- **GOVERNMENT:**
  Parliamentary republic (since 1976). Member of European Union since 1986.

- **LANGUAGE:**
  Portuguese.

- **SPECIFIC PUBLIC HOLIDAYS:**
  Shrove Tuesday (February); Good Friday (Friday before Easter); Freedom Day (25 April), Corpus Christi (May or June); Portugal Day (10 June); Republic Day (5 October); Restoration of Independence Day (1 December); Immaculate Conception (8 December).

- **LOCAL TIME:**
  GMT in winter and GMT + 1 hour in summer.

- **CLIMATE:**
  Temperate Mediterranean with warm winters and hot summers (Lisbon: January 15°C, July 26°C).

- **INTERNATIONAL DIALLING CODE:**
  00 351 followed by a nine-digit number. International directory enquiries : ☎ 098.

- **EMERGENCY:**
  Dial ☎ 112.

- **ELECTRICITY:**
  230-240 volts AC, 50 Hz; 2-pin round-shaped continental plugs.

FORMALITIES

Travellers from the European Union (EU), Switzerland, Iceland and the main countries of North and South America need a national identity card or passport (America: passport required) to visit Portugal for less than three months (tourism or business purpose). For visitors from other countries a visa may be required, in addition to a passport, especially for those wishing to stay for longer than three months. We advise you to check with your embassy before travelling.

A valid national driving licence is required by nationals of EU countries; an international driving licence is required by nationals of non-EU countries. Valid insurance cover is compulsory. Drivers must be at least 21 or 25 to hire a car and to have held a driving licence for more than 1 year.

MAJOR NEWSPAPERS

The main dailies are : *O Diário de Notícias*, *O Correio da Manhã* and *O Público* (from Lisbon) and *O Jornal de Notícias* (from Porto).

ENGLISH	PORTUGUESE
Yes	**Sim**
No	**Não**
Good morning	**Bom dia**
Goodbye	**Adeus**
Thank you	**Obrigado (a)**
Please	**(se) faz favor**
Excuse me	**Desculpe**
I don't understand	**Não percebo**

HOTELS

◆ CATEGORIES

Accommodation is classified in several different categories: **hotels** (1-5 stars); **inns** (estalagens); smaller, **family-run guesthouses** (residenciais which do not serve meals); **more modest guesthouses** (pensões); **bed and breakfast in manor houses** (turismo de habitação); **country houses** (casas de campo); **farmhouses** (agro-turismo). The **pousadas**, hotels in restored historic buildings (castles, palaces and convents) in beautiful sites or excursion centres, are state-owned; there are similar privately-owned hotels. As **pousadas** are very popular, it is wise to book in advance – www.pousadas.pt

◆ PRICE RANGE

The price is per room. There is little difference between the price of a single and a double room.

Between April and October it is advisable to book in advance. From November to March prices may be slightly lower, some hotels offer special cheap rates and some may be closed.

◆ TAX

Included in the room price (5% or 16%).

◆ CHECK OUT TIME

Usually between 11am and noon.

◆ RESERVATIONS

By telephone or by Internet; a credit card number may be required.

◆ TIP FOR LUGGAGE HANDLING

At the discretion of the customer (about €1 per bag).

◆ BREAKFAST

Breakfast is usually included in the price of the room and is generally served between 7am and 10am. Most hotels offer a buffet but usually it is possible to have continental breakfast served in the room.

Reception	**Recepção**
Single room	**Quarto indivudual**
Double room	**Quarto duplo**
Bed	**Cama**
Bathroom	**Casa de banho**
Shower	**Duche**

RESTAURANTS

Restaurants serve lunch from noon to 3pm and dinner from 7pm to 10pm, although some restaurants continue to serve after 10pm. Besides the traditional restaurants there are cafés and bars, which serve simpler fare.

Breakfast	**Pequeno-almoço**	7am – 10am
Lunch	**Almoço**	12.30pm – 2-3pm
Dinner	**Jantar**	6.30pm – 10-11pm
		sometimes later

Restaurants offer fixed price menus (starter, main course and dessert) or à la carte. Menus are usually printed in Portuguese and often in English. A fixed price menu is usually less expensive than the same dishes chosen from the à la carte. Hors-d'œuvre are often served prior to the meal and the cost is added to the bill if they are eaten.

In some of the more popular restaurants, particularly in the north, there are two prices against an item on the menu; the first is for a full portion *(dose)* and the second for a half-portion *(meia dose)*.

Reservations are usually made by phone, fax or Internet. For famous restaurants (including Michelin starred restaurants), it is advisable to book several days – in some instances weeks – in advance. A credit card number or a phone number may be required to guarantee the booking.

The bill (check) includes service charge and VAT. It is customary to leave a tip of about 10% of the total bill.

Drink		Wine (red,	**Vinho (tinto,**
or aperitif	**Bebida**	white, rosé)	**branco, rosé)**
Aperitif	**Aperitivo**	Beer	**Cerveja**
Meal	**Comida, refeição**	Bread	**Pão**
Starter	**Entrada**	Meat	**Carne**
Main dish	**Prato principal**	Fish	**Peixe**
Main dish		Salt/pepper	**Sal/pimenta**
of the day	**Prato do dia**	Cheese	**Queijo**
Dessert	**Sobremesa**	Vegetables	**Hortaliças, vegetais**
Water,		Hot/cold	**Quente/frio**
still, sparkling	**Água, sem gás,**	The bill (check)	
	com gás	please	**A conta por favor**

LOCAL CUISINE

Portuguese meals are usually copious and prepared with olive oil and aromatic herbs.

Soup is served at most meals. **Caldo verde**, the most famous, consists of mashed potato mixed with finely shredded green cabbage, olive oil and slices of black pudding *(tora)*. Bread soup *(açorda)* is common to all regions but **gaspacho** – made of tomatoes, onions, cucumbers and chillies seasoned with garlic and vinegar, which is served cold with croutons – is mostly found in the south.

Fish is a basic element in Portuguese cooking. The commonest is **cod** *(bacalhau)* for which there are 365 different recipes; **caldeirada** is a stew of many types of fish. Seafood *(mariscos)* including octopus is plentiful. Shellfish are delicious and very varied, especially in the Algarve where **cataplana**, a special copper vessel, gives its name to a dish of clams and sausages spiced with herbs.

Pork is cooked and served in a variety of ways: **carne de porco à Alentejana**, pork marinated in wine and garnished with clams, **leitão assado**, roast suckling-pig and **presunto**, smoked ham. Other meat is usually minced and served as meatballs, although lamb and kid are sometimes roasted or served on skewers.

There are various types of cheese (queijo) made from ewe's milk (October to May) and goat's milk.

Nearly all cake and pastry recipes include eggs and come from old specialities prepared in convents: **Queijadas de Sintra**, with almonds and fresh ewe's milk, **Toucinho-do-Céu** and **Barriga-de-Freira**. The commonest dessert is the **pudim flan**, a sort of crème caramel; **leite-creme** is a creamier version. Particularly delicious is **pasteis de nata**, a small custard tart sprinkled with cinnamon. On festive occasions **Arroz doce** (rice pudding) sprinkled with cinnamon is served. In the Algarve the local figs (figos) and almonds (amêndoas) are made into appetising sweetmeats.

DRINK

Portugal has a rich variety of wines. **Vinho Verde** can be white or deep red; it is best enjoyed young and chilled; as an aperitif or with fish and seafood; its name which means green wine, comes from its early harvest and short fermentation period, which make it light and sparkling with a distinctive bouquet and a low alcohol content. **Bucelas** is a dry, somewhat acidic white wine. **Dão** wine may be a fresh white wine or a sweet red wine with a velvety texture and a heady bouquet. **Bairrada** is a robust, fragrant red with a natural sparkle. **Colares** is a velvety, dark red wine, famous since the 13C.

Portugal is best known for the world famous **Port**, named after Oporto. After fermentation brandy is added and the wine is matured in huge vats and then aged in wooden barrels (pipes). Port is red or white according to the colour of the grapes, and can be dry, medium or sweet. Port aged in casks matures through oxidation and turns an amber colour; port aged in the bottle matures by reduction and is a dark red colour. Red ports are blended: **Tinto** is young, distinctly coloured and fruity; **Tinto-alourado** or **Ruby** is older, rich in colour, fruity and sweet; **Alourado** or **Tawny** turns to a brownish gold as it ages; **Alourado-Claro** or **Light Tawny** is the culmination of the former.

Maderia wine, famous in England as Malmsey, comes in four principal types – **Sercial**, a dry wine with a good bouquet, amber in colour and served chilled as an aperitif; **Verdelho**, slightly sweeter but also drinkable ar an aperitif; **Bual**, with a rich, full bodied flavour, primarily a dessert wine; **Malmsey**, now rare, is also a dessert wine with a honeyed flavour and a deep-red colour.

Dessert wines include **Setúbal** moscatel, a generous fruity wine, and fruity amber-coloured **Carcavelos**, which is also drunk as an aperitif.

The wide variety of Portuguese brandies includes cherry brandy from Alcobaça (ginginha), arbutus berry brandy (medronho) and honey brandy (brandimel) from the Algarve. The most popular spirit is a grape marc (bagaço or bagaceira) which is served chilled.

The commonest beer is light and similar to lager. Fruit juices, still or sparkling, are also excellent and refreshing.

LISBON
LISBOA

Population (est. 2005): 518 000 (conurbation 2 398 000) – Altitude: at sea level

B. Morandi/MICHELIN

The capital of Portugal stands midway on the Atlantic coast on the Tagus estuary. At the time of the Great Discoveries (15C-16C), Lisbon became the cosmopolitan centre of a huge overseas empire.

The old town was built on 7 hills on the northern shore of the 'Straw Sea', as the bulge in the Tagus is called because of the golden reflections of the sun on the water. The attraction of the city lies in its light, its pastel ochres, pinks, blues and greens, its streets and squares with mosaic paving (small black and white stones named *empedrados*). With its narrow old streets, its magnificent vistas along wide avenues, its lively harbour, old trams, exotic gardens and *Fado* lyrical chants which celebrate nostalgia *(saudade)*, Lisbon is a delightful patchwork.

While Lisbon bears the stamp of its past, it has set its sights firmly on the future ever since Portugal became a member of the EEC (1986). New Business districts are growing, particularly around Campo Pequeno and Campo Grande, while the Centro Cultural de Belém (1992) was built to enhance the historical and cultural importance of this part of the city. The famous post-modern towers of Amoreiras, by the architect T. Taveira, caused a sensation when they first went up, while other towers have sprung up around Campo Grande to become landmarks within the city.

WHICH DISTRICT TO CHOOSE

For **hotels** there is a choice between the borders of the Parque Eduardo VII *Plan III* **G3** where most of the luxury hotels are to be found, and the residential districts such as Lapa *Plan I* **B3** near the embassies, which offers a number of charming hotels in old private houses, or Belém, which is further from the centre.

For **restaurants** it is best to go to the more central and lively districts such as Rossio *Plan I* **H1** and Baixa *Plan II* **F2** or climb up to Bairro Alto *Plan II* **E2** which has become the in-district in Lisbon.

621

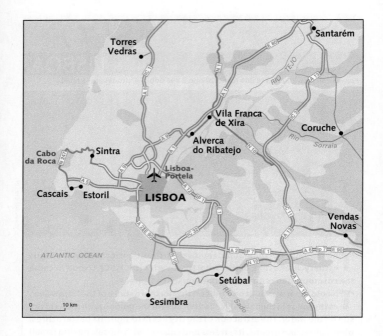

If you are going out for a **drink**, take a stroll along the banks of the Tagus in Alcantara *Plan I* **B3** where the old docks *(Docas)* are now lined with bars and nightclubs.

PRACTICAL INFORMATION

ARRIVAL – DEPARTURE

Portela Airport – About 8 km (5 mi) north of the city centre. ✆ 218 450 660, 218 413 500; Lisbon.airport@ana-aeroportos.pt; www.ana-aeroportos.pt

From the airport to the city centre – By **taxi**: 10 mins, €12.15 (+ €1.50 for luggage). By **shuttle bus** to Praça do Comércio *Plan II* **E2** and Cais do Sodré *Plan II* **E2** 15mins (7.45am-8.45pm, every 20min). Fare €2.95.

Railway Stations – Estação de Santa Apolónia *Plan I* **C3** for international routes and trains to the north of the country. ✆ 218 821 604; www.

cp.pt – **Estação do Cais do Socré** for trains to Estoril and Cascais; departures approximately every 20min until 2.30am; journey time about 30min – **Estação do Rossio** for trains to the NW suburbs including Sintra and Leiria; departures to Sintra approximately every 20min until 2.30am; journey time about 30min – **Estação Sul e Sueste** for trains to Alentejo and Algarve via the ferry which crosses the river to Barreiro railway station – **Estação do Oriente** intermodal transport terminal (bus, metro and train) serving the north: the station is linked to Santa Apolónia and Sintra railway stations.

TRANSPORT

◆ METRO

4 lines (Gaivota, Girassol, Caravela and Oriente) operate from 6.30am to 1am; the stations are works of art. Single ticket €0.70; 10 tickets €6.35; 1-day ticket €2.90 – www.metrolisboa.pt

◆ BUSES, TRAMS AND FUNICULAR

There are 6 main bus routes and 3 funiculars. The buses and trams *(eléctricos)* operate from 7am to 1am, every 11-15min until 9.30pm; the last no 45 bus (Cais do Sodré, Baixa, Av. da Liberdade) is at 1.55am. Tram routes no 15 and 28 serve the main sights. Funiculars operate from 7am to 11pm. Tickets can be bought individually on both buses and trams; single fare €1, 1-day ticket €2.35, 3-day ticket €5.65 on sale in metro stations and in kiosks *(Venda de Passe)*. For bus, trams and funiculars: 4-day pass *(passe turístico)* €9.95; 7-day pass €14.10. Bus and tram route maps (€5) available at the kiosks. ☏ 213 632 021, 213 613 000, www.carris.pt

◆ LISBOA CARD

Valid for unlimited travel on public transport (metro, buses, trams except trams no 15 and 28) and for free or reduced admission to most museums and cultural sites; on sale at certain venues and museums; €11 (24hr); €18 (48hr); €28 (72hr); ☏ 213 610 250 or 210 312 810.

◆ TAXIS

Taxis are usually beige or cream but older ones are still black with green roofs; they are occupied if the illuminated sign on the roof is lit. They are numerous and relatively cheap. Initial charge €2 (daytime rate), €2.35 (night rate); €1.50 fixed rate for luggage; €0.75 surcharge if called by phone; 20% surcharge between 10pm and 6am. Journeys within the city are metered; outside the tariff is per km, including the return trip to the pick-up point and any road tolls, price to be agreed in advance. Tipping at 10% or by rounding up. ☏ 218 119 000 *(Rádio Táxis de Lisboa)*, ☏ 214 186 206 or 217 996 460 *(Autocoop)*, ☏ 2183 649 538 *(Auto Táxis Progresso do Príncipe Real)*, ☏ 218 155 061 or 218 111 100 *(Teletáxis)*.

◆ RIVER BOAT AND FERRY STATIONS

Five ferries *(cacilheiros)* link Lisbon with the opposite bank of the Tagus; departures every 15min; tickets available at the ferry stations; also boat rides on the Tagus (2hr) 11am-5pm daily; €15 (€7.50 child 6-12 yrs).

USEFUL ADDRESSES

◆ TOURIST INFORMATION

Tourist Office, Palácio Foz, Praça dos Restauradores *Plan II* **H1**; open 9am-8pm, ☏ 213 463 314/213 463 658. **Airport Tourist Office**; open 7am-midnight, ☏ 218 494 323/218 493 689. **Lisboa Welcome Center Plan**, Rua do Arsenal; open 9am-9pm; café, restaurant, food shop, designer and fashion shop, art gallery. **Tourist Help Line** ☏ 800 296 296; www.atl-turismolisboa.pt/welcomecenter

◆ POST OFFICES

Opening times Mon-Fri 9am-8pm, Sat 9am-6pm, Sun and public holidays 9am-1pm and 2-5pm; Airport 24 hrs.

◆ BANKS/CURRENCY EXCHANGE

Opening times Mon-Fri, 8.30am-3pm. National network (24hrs) of ATMs (MB-*multibanco*) for withdrawing money using all major bank cards.

◆ EMERGENCY

☏ **112**; Police: ☏ **213 466 141/213 474 730**.

It may be difficult to find a room at a reasonable price (except at weekends) during special events:

Meia Martona Internacional de Lisboa: March – Lisbon International Half Marathon.

Holy Week: Easter.

Summer Festivals: 12-29 June – Popular saints' festivals with processions of young people in traditional costume *(marchas populares)*.

Meia Martona de Portugal: September – Portugal Half Marathon.

EXPLORING LISBON

DIFFERENT FACETS OF THE CITY

It is possible to visit the main sights and museums in three days.

Museums and sights are usually open from 10am to 5pm. Most are closed on Mondays and on Tuesday mornings and public holidays (national palaces are closed on Wednesdays).

HISTORIC CITY – Mosteiro dos Jerónimos *Plan I* **A3** – 16C Manueline Gothic monastery: church and cloisters. **Torre de Belém** *Plan I* **A3** – 16C Manueline defensive tower. **Baixa** *Plan II* **F2** – District re-built to the plans of the Marquis of Pombal in 1755 after the earthquake. **Alfama** *Plan II* **F2** – Cobbled maze of narrow twisting streets and steps. **Cathedral** *Plan II* **F2** – Romanesque cathedral, built as a 12C fortress but remodelled in 17C and 18C; Treasury. **Castelo de São Jorge** *Plan II* **F2** – 5C Visigoth castle, with 9C Moorish extensions and 12C modifications, converted into a shaded flower garden with magnificent **views**. **Palácio dos Marqueses de Fronteira** *Plan I* **B2** – 17C hunting lodge set in formal gardens: outstanding decorative tiles.

ARTISTIC LISBON – Museu Nacional de Arte Antiga *Plan I* **B3** – 17C palace: 12C to early 19C paintings, sculptures and decorative art. **Museu de Artes Decorativas** *Plan II* **F2** – 17C and 18C interiors with silver, porcelain, tapestries and furniture. **Museu Nacional do Azulejo** *Plan I* **D3** – Former convent displaying decorative tiles: 15C Hispano-Moorish to the present day. **Museu da**

Marinha *Plan I* **A3** – Portuguese ships and maritime history. **Museu Calouste Gulbenkian** *Plan III* **G2** – Oriental and European art beautifully presented. **Casa do Fado e da Guitarra Portuguesa** *Plan II* **F2** – History of **Fado**.

OUTDOOR LISBON – Parque das Naçoes *Plan I* **D1** – Site of Expo'98: contemporary works of art, gardens and pedestrianised areas, bars, restaurants, entertainment venues and shopping centre; **Torre Vasco da Gama**, belvedere with **views** of the Tagus. **Parque Eduardo VII** *Plan III* **G3** – Elegant landscaped park with a magnificent **view** over the Baixa and the Tagus. **Jardim Zoológico** *Plan I* **B2** – Magnificent palm trees in one of the finest gardens for subtropical plants in Europe.

GOURMET TREATS

A favourite pastime in Lisbon is to go to a bar or café for an after-lunch or after-dinner coffee *(bica)*; excellent cafés and pastry shops can be found all over the city. *Confeitaria Nacional*, Pç Figueira 18B – one of the best old cafés in Lisbon, has a huge choice of pastries and traditional sweets; *Pastelaria Suiça*, Praça. D. Pedro IV/Rossio – for an outdoor terrace where you can consume snacks, excellent cakes and fruit juices with views of the Castelo de São Jorge; *Pastéis de Belém Café*, Rua Belém 84/8 – serving the famous cakes of this name; *Pastelaria Benard*, Rua Garrett 104 – for delicious pastries or a meal served in its quiet, dignified atmosphere.

For traditional family cuisine at reasonable prices it is worth trying one of the museum cafeterias or restaurants, which are often set in attractive surroundings: patios, gardens, modern décor.

SHOPPING

Shops are usually open from 9am to 1pm and 3-7pm. On Saturdays they close at 1pm. Shopping centres are usually open 10am-11pm.

The traditional shopping district is **Baixa** *Plan II* **F2**. **Chiado** *Plan II* **E2**, in particular Rua do Carmo and Rua do Garret, has shops selling international brand names, also bookshops and some old boutiques. For fashion try Av. Da Liberdade, Pç. D. Pedro IV, Rua do Carmo and the Bairro Alto district.

Shopping centres outside the city centre but worth visiting: **Amoreiras Shopping Centre**, Av. Eng. Duarte Pacheco *Plan I* **B2**; **Colombo**, Avenida do Colégio Militar *Plan I* **B1**; **Vasco da Gama**, Parque das Naçoes *Plan I* **B1**.

MARKETS – **Feira da Ladra**, Campo Sta Clara *Plan I* **C3** is a good flea market for second-hand silverware, furniture, old books, clothes, etc. (Tues, 7am-1pm and Sat, 7am-6pm).

WHAT TO BUY – Wines, port, cheeses, footwear, handbags, embroidery, lace, household textiles, clothing, Vista Alegre porcelain, crystal from the Alcobaça and Marinha Grande regions, decorative tiles *(azulejos)*, regional pottery, copper utensils, wicker baskets.

ENTERTAINMENT

Agenda Cultural, a monthly publication, provides information on cultural events, available free of charge at the main tourist offices, hotels and kiosks (www.agendacultural.pt). *Lisboa em*, another monthly publication (in Portuguese and English) publishes details of cultural events as well as practical information, available free of charge at tourist sights and in some bars. *What's on in Lisbon* (in English) lists concerts and other

events (publituris@mail.telepac.pt)

Tickets can be obtained at the following kiosks: *ABEP*, Praça dos Restauradores, ℘ 213 425 360; *Quiosque Cultural de São Mamede*, R. de São Mamede.

Coliseu dos Recreios *Plan II* **E2** – Opera, concerts and a wide range of other events.

Teatro Nacional de São Carlos *Plan II* **E2** – Opera, ballet and concerts of classical music.

Grande Auditório Gulbenkian *Plan III* **G2** – Musical concerts.

Centro Cultural de Belém *Plan I* **A3** – Concerts and temporary exhibitions.

Comuna *Plan III* **G2** – Traditional programme of theatre with a bistro-style café-theatre for contemporary music concerts (rock, jazz) (Sat at 10pm).

Culturgest – **Caixa Geral de Depósitos** *Plan II* **E2** – Cultural centre with two auditoria and two exhibition galleries and a programme of musical events of high quality.

Escola Portuguesa de Arte Equestre (Palácio Nacional de Queluz, 2475 Queluz) – School maintaining Portuguese equestrian art, particularly with Lusitanian thoroughbreds.

Praça de Touros do Campo Pequeno *Plan III* **H1** – Neo-Moorish red-brick arena for bullfights *(touradas)* (May-Sep, Thur at 10pm – the bulls are not killed).

NIGHTLIFE

Nightclubs rarely get going until after midnight. The best-known districts are **Chiado** and **Bairro Alto** *Plan II* **E2** ; there is also a string of restaurants, bars and nightclubs along the docks in **Alcântara** and **Santo Amaro** *Plan I* **B3**. Another address is **Avenida 24 de Julho**. **Principe Real**, a small elegant district, is the centre of gay nightlife.

For **fado** restaurants go to the historic **Alfama district** *Plan II* **F2** or **Chiado** and **Bairro Alto**: *Sr. Vinho*, Rua do Meio-à-Lapa 18; *A Severa*, Rua das Gàveas 51; *Adega Machado*, Rua do Norte 91.

Environs of Lisbon and Belem

(Plan I)

A

IC 17

CRIL

B

MUSEU NACIONAL DO TEATRO

PAÇO DO LUMIAR

1

N 249

Falagueiros

Estr.

de

Benfica

Affornelos

Pontinha ⓜ

CARNIDE

AMADORA

BENFICA

Carnide ⓜ

Av. Lusíada

Colégio Militar Luz

CALHARIZ

Alto des Moinhes ⓜ

Av. Lusíada

IC 19

Laranjeiras ⓜ

JARDIM ZOOLÓGICO

J. Zoológico ⓜ

PALÁCIO DE FRONTEIRA

dos

N 117

FORTE DE MONSANTO

Estr. das Laranjeiras

2

PARQUE FORESTAL

Av. Gulbenkian

OEIRAS

A 5

5

4

3

2

Calouste

1

CAMPOLIDE

A 5

DE MONSANTO

Ceuia

Av. Engenheiro Duarte Pacheco

R. Ferreira Borges

CAMPO DE OURIQUE

BASÍLICA DA ESTRELA

IC 17

Av. das Descobertas

U

AJUDA

JARDIM BOTÂNICO

Calç. da Ajuda

PALÁCIO DA AJUDA

de

Av. da Ponte

Santo

LAPA

MUSEU NACIONAL DE ARTE ANTIGA

ALGÉS

FORTE DO ALTO DUQUE

✕✕ Estufa Real

SANTO AMARO

ALCÂNTARA

Av. Infante

24

Av. Dom Vasco da Gama

RESTELO

MOSTEIRO DOS JERÓNIMOS

MUSEU DA MARINHA

BELÉM

CENTRO CULTURAL

Caseiro ✕

Índia

Av. da

PONTE 26 DE ABRIL

E 1-90

TORRE DE BELÉM

MUSEU DE ARTE POPULAR

PADRÃO DOS DESCOBERTAS

3

● Hotel

● Restaurant

A

B

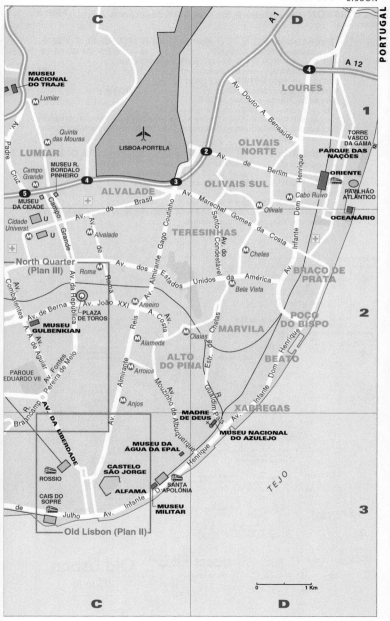

PORTUGAL

OLD LISBON (Alfama, Castelo de São Jorge, Rossio, Baixa, Chiado, Bairro Alto)   *Plan II*

🏨🏨🏨🏨 **Tivoli Lisboa** ⬉ city from the terrace, 🛎 🕭 ⌸ (heated) 🏧 ⅋ 🖨 📞
av. da Liberdade 185 ✉ 1269-050   🛗40/200 🅿 *VISA* 🆗 🅰🅴 ⓘ
– Ⓜ Avenida – ✆ 21 319 89 00 – htlisboa@tivolihotels.com
– Fax 21 319 89 50 – www.tivolihotels.com   **E1**
300 rm ⬒ – †400 € ††420 € – 29 suites
Rest *Terraço* a la carte 46/60 €
Rest *Beatriz Costa* a la carte 26/36 €
♦ Business ♦ Traditional ♦ Classic ♦
Elegant, comfortable and with fine views from the top floor. Pleasant, tastefully decorated and well-equipped bedrooms. The Terraço restaurant is both smart and traditional.

🏨🏨🏨 **Sofitel Lisboa** ⅃ 🏧 ⅋ 🖨 📞 🛗25/250 🅿 *VISA* 🆗 🅰🅴 ⓘ
av. da Liberdade 127 ✉ 1269-038 – Ⓜ Avenida – ✆ 21 322 83 00
– h1319@accor.com – Fax 21 322 83 60 – www.sofitel.com   **E1**
166 rm – †201/245 € ††258/335 €, ⬒ 17 € – 5 suites
Rest *Ad Lib* 29 €
♦ Business ♦ Design ♦
A friendly welcome, comfortable and with a contemporary classic feel. Enjoy a pleasant stay in agreeable surroundings.

PORTUGAL

Lisboa Plaza   ⓐⓒ ✇ 📧 📞 ♨25/140 🅿 𝘝𝘐𝘚𝘈 ⓜⓢ ⒶⒺ ⓪
Travessa do Salitre 7 ✉ 1269-066 – Ⓜ Avenida – ☎ 21 321 82 18
– plaza.hotels@heritage.pt – Fax 21 347 16 30
– www.heritage.pt   **E1**
94 rm – ♦146/215 € ♦♦156/235 €, ☲ 14 € – 12 suites
Rest 30 €
♦ Business ♦ Traditional ♦ Classic ♦
Near the famous Avenida da Liberdade. Very traditional with distinguished
and tasteful atmosphere and classic décor. A large buffet is available in the
dining room.

Tivoli Jardim   ⛱ (heated) & ⓐⓒ ✇ 📧 📞 ♨25 ⌂ 🅿 𝘝𝘐𝘚𝘈 ⓜⓢ ⒶⒺ ⓪
Rua Julio Cesar Machado 7 ✉ 1250-135 – Ⓜ Marquês de Pombal
– ☎ 21 359 10 00 – htjardim@mail.telepac.pt – Fax 21 359 12 45
– www.tivolihotels.com   **E1**
119 rm ☲ – ♦310 € ♦♦320 €
Rest 26 €
♦ Business ♦ Functional ♦
Modern efficiency for the business traveller. A large foyer, conference rooms and
pleasantly decorated bedrooms. The brightly-lit dining room offers traditional
dishes.

Britania without rest   ⓐⓒ ✇ 📧 📞 𝘝𝘐𝘚𝘈 ⓜⓢ ⒶⒺ ⓪
Rua Rodrigues Sampaio 17 ✉ 1150-278 – Ⓜ Avenida – ☎ 21 315 50 16
– britania.hotel@heritage.pt – Fax 21 315 50 21
– www.heritage.pt   **E1**
30 rm – ♦154/225 € ♦♦164/245 €, ☲ 14 €
♦ Business ♦ Traditional ♦ Art Deco ♦
The lounge area consists of a bar which boasts a beautiful wooden floor
and paintings of Portugal's former colonies. Spacious Art Deco-style
rooms.

Lisboa Regency Chiado without rest   & ⓐⓒ ⇜ ✇ 📧
Rua Nova do Almada 114 ✉ 1200-290   ⌂ 𝘝𝘐𝘚𝘈 ⓜⓢ ⒶⒺ ⓪
– Ⓜ Baixa-Chiado – ☎ 21 325 61 00
– reservations.chiado@madeiraregency.pt – Fax 21 325 61 61
– www.regency-hotels-resorts.com   **E2**
40 rm ☲ – ♦152/304 € ♦♦164/354 €
♦ Business ♦ Personalised ♦
Pleasantly situated in a building in the old part of the city. Friendly, professional
service, with bedrooms decorated in oriental style.

NH Liberdade   ⛱ & ⓐⓒ ✇ 📧 📞 ♨25/50 ⌂ 𝘝𝘐𝘚𝘈 ⓜⓢ ⒶⒺ ⓪
av. da Liberdade 180-B ✉ 1250-146 – Ⓜ Avenida
– ☎ 21 351 40 60 – nhliberdade@nh-hotels.es
– Fax 21 314 36 74 – www.nh-hotels.com   **E1**
58 rm ☲ – ♦100/219 € ♦♦110/232 € – 25 suites
Rest 28 €
♦ Business ♦ Chain hotel ♦ Modern ♦
Situated in Lisbon's most important business district. A comfortable and
functional hotel with all the quality and characteristic style of this hotel
chain.

Veneza without rest   ⓐⓒ ✇ 📧 🅿 𝘝𝘐𝘚𝘈 ⓜⓢ ⒶⒺ ⓪
av. da Liberdade 189 ✉ 1250-141 – Ⓜ Avenida – ☎ 21 352 26 18
– veneza@3khoteis.com.pt – Fax 21 352 66 78
– www.3khoteis.com.pt   **E1**
37 rm – ♦100 € ♦♦125 €
♦ Traditional ♦ Business ♦ Cosy ♦
In a small former palace with a lovely façade. A perfect balance of old grandeur
and modern day functionality.

Solar do Castelo without rest   AK ⚇ 🚹 (t) VISA ◐◑ AE ①
Rua das Cozinhas 2 ⊠ 1100-181 – 𝒞 21 880 60 50 – solar.castelo @ heritage.pt
– Fax 21 887 09 07 – www.heritage.pt   **F2**
14 rm – 🛉183/275 € 🛉🛉196/305 €, � 14 €
♦ Family ♦ Cosy ♦
A small 18C palace in an area with lots of historic monuments. A comfortable
and completely renovated interior. Modern bedrooms with attractive design
details.

Solar dos Mouros without rest 🅱   ≤ AK ⚇ 🚹 (t) VISA ◐◑ AE ①
Rua do Milagre de Santo António 6 ⊠ 1100-351 – ⓜ Baixa-Chiado
– 𝒞 218 85 49 40 – reservation @ solardosmouros.pt – Fax 218 85 49 45
– www.solardosmouros.com   **F2**
11 rm ⊑ – 🛉88/156 € 🛉🛉106/216 €
♦ Family ♦ Personalised ♦
A typical house which has been modernised and furnished with personal
touches, including four paintings by the owner himself. Colourful bedrooms,
some with excellent views.

Lisboa Tejo without rest   & AK ⚇ 🚹 VISA ◐◑ AE ①
Rua dos Condes de Monsanto 2 ⊠ 1100-159 – ⓜ Rossio – 𝒞 21 886 61 82
– hotellisboatejo.reservas @ evidenciagrupo.com – Fax 21 886 51 63
– www.evidenciahoteis.com   **F2**
51 rm ⊑ – 🛉80/105 € 🛉🛉85/120 € – 7 suites
♦ Business ♦ Traditional ♦ Personalised ♦
Moderate prices and pleasant, well-appointed bedrooms in the Baixa Pombalina
district. A modern, refurbished and central hotel with a traditional atmosphere
and elegant décor.

XXXX **Tavares**   AK ⚇ VISA ◐◑ AE ①
Rua da Misericórdia 37 ⊠ 1200-270 – ⓜ Baixa-Chiado – 𝒞 213 42 11 12
– reservas @ tavaresrico.pt – Fax 213 47 81 25 – www.tavaresrico.pt
closed Christmas, 1 to 15 August, Saturday lunch, Sunday and Bank
Holidays   **E2**
Rest a la carte 65/85 €
♦ Inventive ♦ Formal ♦
Founded in 1784, Lisbon's oldest restaurant has retained all its aristocratic
elegance and ambience. A sumptuous decor of gilded work, mirrors and
chandeliers.

XXX **Gambrinus**   AK ⚇ ⇄18/30 P VISA ◐◑ AE
Rua das Portas de Santo Antão 25 ⊠ 1150-264 – ⓜ Restauradores
– 𝒞 21 342 14 66 – Fax 21 346 50 32   **E1**
Rest a la carte 65/85 €
♦ Traditional ♦ Formal ♦
In the historic centre of the city near the Rossio district. A restaurant with a
well-established reputation backed up by fine cuisine and an excellent wine
list.

XXX **Casa do Leão**   ≤ 🌇 AK ⚇ VISA ◐◑ AE ①
Castelo de São Jorge ⊠ 1100-129 – ⓜ Rossio – 𝒞 21 887 59 62
– guest @ pousadas.pt – Fax 21 887 63 29 – www.pousadas.pt   **F2**
Rest a la carte 37/41 €
♦ Traditional ♦ Formal ♦
Situated in the walls of the castle of São Jorge. An elegant restaurant in traditional
Portuguese-style with an exclusive ambience.

XX **Solar dos Presuntos**   AK ⚇ VISA ◐◑ AE ①
Rua das Portas de Santo Antão 150 ⊠ 1150-269 – ⓜ Restauradores
– 𝒞 21 342 42 53 – restaurante @ solardospresuntos.com – Fax 21 346 84 68
closed Sunday   **E1**
Rest a la carte approx. 35 €
♦ Minho cuisine ♦ Family ♦
A locally-run, comfortable restaurant with a wide selection of well-prepared
traditional dishes and some specialities from Minho.

FADO RESTAURANTS *You can hear the typical Portuguese fado songs while dining in these restaurants.* *Plan II*

PORTUGAL

XX **Clube de Fado** 　　　　　　　AC ✗ VISA ◉◉ AE ①
São João da Praça 94 ✉ 1100-521 – 𝒞 21 885 27 04 – info @ clube-de-fado.com
– Fax 21 888 26 94 – www.clube-de-fado.com 　　　　　　　**F2**
Rest (dinner only) a la carte 31/47 €
♦ Traditional ♦ Musical ♦
A restaurant with a well-cared for appearance, a pleasant ambience and a bar with a friendly atmosphere. Simple décor.

XX **A Severa** 　　　　　　　　　　AC ✗ VISA ◉◉ AE ①
Rua Das Gáveas 51 ✉ 1200-206 – Ⓜ Baixa-Chiado – 𝒞 21 342 83 14
– Fax 21 346 40 06 – www.asevera.com – closed Thursday 　　　**E2**
Rest a la carte 30/56 €
♦ Traditional ♦ Musical ♦
A traditional fado restaurant run by a large family who base their success on good cuisine. Comfortable and with classic Portuguese décor.

NORTH QUARTER *(Av. da Liberdade, Parque Eduardo VII,* *Plan III*
Museu Gulbenkian)

🏠🏠🏠🏠 **Four Seasons H. Ritz Lisbon** 　　≤ 🕾 Fб 🔲 ፚ AC ▣ ⅀å25/500 🕾
Rua Rodrigo da Fonseca 88 ✉ 1099-039 　　　　　Ⓟ VISA ◉◉ AE ①
– Ⓜ Marquês de Pombal – 𝒞 21 381 14 00 – fsh.lisbon @ fourseasons.com
– Fax 21 383 17 83 – www.fourseasons.com 　　　　　　　**G3**
262 rm – ♦310/505 € ♦♦335/530 €, � 26 € – 20 suites
Rest *Varanda* a la carte 59/73 €
♦ Luxury ♦ Business ♦ Classic ♦
Luxury is the keynote in these exquisite bedrooms, more than matched by the superb public rooms. The exclusive restaurant in classic style serves sophisticated, immaculately presented cuisine.

🏠🏠🏠🏠 **Sheraton Lisboa H. & Towers** 　　≤ Fб 🔲 (heated) ፚ AC å25/550
Rua Latino Coelho 1 ✉ 1069-025 – Ⓜ Picoas 　　　🕾 VISA ◉◉ AE ①
– 𝒞 21 312 00 00 – sheraton.lisboa @ sheraton.com – Fax 21 354 71 64
– www.sheraton.com/lisboa 　　　　　　　　　　　**H2**
376 rm – ♦217 € ♦♦237 €, ⅀ 17 € – 8 suites
Rest *Panorama* (dinner only) a la carte 47/62 €
Rest *Caravela* (lunch only) a la carte 32/47 €
♦ Business ♦ Modern ♦
Business travellers should ask for the wonderful, fully equipped executive bedrooms. Conferences, receptions and dinners catered for. The Alfama restaurant is a very pleasant setting in which to sample finely prepared dishes.

🏠🏠🏠🏠 **Le Meridien Park Atlantic Lisboa** 　　≤ ፚ AC å25/550 🕾
Rua Castilho 149 ✉ 1099-034 – Ⓜ Marquês de Pombal – 𝒞 21 381 87 00
– reservas.lisboa @ lemeridien.pt – Fax 21 389 05 05 　　　**G3**
314 rm – 17 suites – **Rest** *L'Appart*
♦ Business ♦ Chain hotel ♦ Modern ♦
A full range of facilities and professional service in the comfort of modern bedrooms and suites. Bathrooms fitted with marble and high quality furnishings. A pleasantly decorated restaurant offering à la carte, buffet or dish of the day.

🏠🏠🏠 **Holiday Inn Lisbon Continental** 　　ፚ AC ✗ ▣ 🕿 å25/180
Rua Laura Alves 9 ✉ 1069-169 – Ⓜ Campo 　　　🕾 VISA ◉◉ AE ①
Pequeno – 𝒞 21 004 60 00 – hic @ grupo-continental.com – Fax 21 797 36 69
– www.holiday-inn.com 　　　　　　　　　　　　**H1**
210 rm – ♦95/180 € ♦♦105/205 €, ⅀ 11 € – 10 suites
Rest 18 €
♦ Business ♦ Chain hotel ♦ Functional ♦
A hotel with a modern exterior that is very popular for business meetings. Pleasant, well-appointed bedrooms and adequate public areas. The dining room is not up to the standards of the rest of the hotel.

Real Parque

⚫ 🏅 🅰 🛜 📺 🔊 𝔐25/100 ⌂ **VISA** **MC** 🅰 ⓘ

av. Luís Bívar 67 ✉ *1069-146 –* 🚇 *Saldanha –* 𝒞 *21 319 90 00 – realparque@
hoteisreal.com – Fax 21 357 07 50 – www.hoteisreal.com*   G2
147 rm 🖳 – 🛉155 € 🛉🛉175 € – 6 suites
Rest *Cozinha do Real* a la carte 25/32 €
♦ Business ♦ Classic ♦
Ideal for meetings, business and leisure travel. Elegant furnishings, quality and
good taste everywhere. A modern exterior, classic contemporary décor and a
charming lounge area. Good food served in a pleasant dining room.

Suites do Marquês

🛏 🏅 🅰 🛜 📺 𝔐25/50 ⌂ **VISA** **MC** 🅰 ⓘ

av. Duque de Loulé 45 ✉ *1050-086 –* 🚇 *Picoas –* 𝒞 *21 351 04 80
– suitesdomarques@viphotels.com – Fax 21 353 18 65
– www.viphotels.com*   H3
80 rm 🖳 – 🛉97/107 € 🛉🛉105/115 € – 4 suites
Rest a la carte approx. 30 €
♦ Business ♦ Functional ♦
Central location near the famous Praça Marquês de Pombal square. All the
comfort and characteristic style of the Meliá chain in large, quiet and functional
bedrooms.

Holiday Inn Lisbon

 🏅 🅰 🛜 📺 🔊 𝔐25/300

av. António José de Almeida 28-A ✉ *1000-044*   ⌂ **VISA** **MC** 🅰 ⓘ
– 🚇 *Alameda –* 𝒞 *21 004 40 00 – hil@grupo-continental.com
– Fax 21 793 66 72*   H2
161 rm – 🛉120/180 € 🛉🛉140/200 €, 🖳 11 € – 8 suites
Rest 22 €
♦ Business ♦ Chain hotel ♦ Modern ♦
Centrally located: ideal for the business or leisure traveller. Few public rooms but
comfortable bedrooms. A pleasant dining room with wickerwork furniture and
a buffet.

AC Lisboa

 🏅 🅰 🛜 📺 🔊 𝔐25/60 **VISA** **MC** 🅰 ⓘ

Rua Largo Andaluz 13 ✉ *1050-121 –* 🚇 *Marquês de Pombal
–* 𝒞 *210 05 09 30 – aclisboa@ac-hotels.com – Fax 210 05 09 31
– www.ac-hotels.com*   H3
81 rm 🖳 – 🛉115/130 € 🛉🛉128/143 € – 2 suites
Rest 16 €
♦ Business ♦ Chain hotel ♦ Modern ♦
Located in the rear part of the palace, this hotel has a modern façade and a
reception area that is typical of the AC chain. Pleasant lounge and meeting areas,
plus modern, well-appointed bedrooms. An attractive, albeit soberly decorated
restaurant.

Real Palacio

 🏅 🅰 🛜 📺 𝔐25/230 ⌂ **VISA** **MC** 🅰 ⓘ

Rua Tomás Ribeiro 115 ✉ *1050-228 –* 🚇 *São Sebastião –* 𝒞 *213 19 95 00
– realpalacio@hoteisreal.com – Fax 213 19 95 01
– www.hoteisreal.com*   G2
143 rm 🖳 – 🛉225 € 🛉🛉250 € – 4 suites
Rest *Guarda Real* a la carte 25/33 €
♦ Business ♦ Classic ♦
The Real Palacio is a mix of the modern and traditional with its stylish marble and
elegant woodwork. Panelled meeting rooms and fully-equipped bedrooms.
Options in the restaurant include the à la carte menu and an extensive buffet.

Marquês de Pombal

 🏅 🅰 🛜 📺 𝔐25/120 ⌂ **VISA** **MC** 🅰 ⓘ

av. da Liberdade 243 ✉ *1250-143 –* 🚇 *Marquês de Pombal –* 𝒞 *21 319 79 00
– info@hotel-marquesdepombal.pt – Fax 21 319 79 90
– www.hotel-marquesdepombal.pt*   G3
120 rm 🖳 – 🛉118/170 € 🛉🛉130/182 € – 3 suites
Rest a la carte 23/34 €
♦ Business ♦ Modern ♦
A recently built hotel. Conferences and business meetings in an atmosphere of
modern efficiency. Elegantly furnished with up-to-date technology and
conference hall.

Barcelona without rest ⅙ 𝔸𝕔 ⌘ 𝗦𝗔 25/230 ⌨ **VISA** **𝗠𝗖** 𝔸𝔼 ⓞ

Rua Laura Alves 10 ⊠ *1050-138 –* Ⓜ *Campo Pequeno –* 𝒞 *21 795 42 73*

– barcelona@3khoteis.com.pt – Fax 21 795 42 81 – www.3khoteis.com

H1

120 rm ⌑ – ♟100/125 € – ♟♟125/150 € – 5 suites

♦ Business ♦ Modern ♦

An up-to-date hotel in the financial district of the city. Modern surroundings with avant-garde touches. Cheery, colourful décor and good level of comfort.

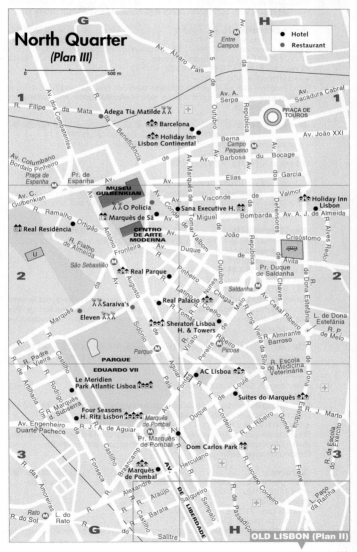

PORTUGAL

Dom Carlos Park   🕅 🕸 🖾 🖄 25/40 VISA ⓪ⓔ AE ⑩
av. Duque de Loulé 121 ⊠ *1050-089 –* ⑩ *Marquês de Pombal –* ℰ *21 351 25 90*
– comercial@domcarloshoteis.com – Fax 21 352 07 28
– www.domcarloshoteis.com   **G-H3**
76 rm ⊇ – †77/117 € ††91/152 €
Rest (Coffee shop only)
♦ Traditional ♦ Business ♦ Classic ♦
Traditional and elegant hotel in a very good location with restful ambience.
Pleasant rooms with bathrooms decorated in marble and a small sitting area.

Sana Executive H. without rest   ⚿ 🕅 🕸 🖾 🖄 25/55
av. Conde Valbom 56 ⊠ *1050-069*   🚗 VISA ⓪ⓔ AE ⑩
– ⑩ *São Sebastião –* ℰ *21 795 11 57 – sanaexecutive@sanahotels.com*
– Fax 21 795 11 66 – www.sanahotels.com   **G-H2**
72 rm ⊇ – †110/155 € ††120/165 €
♦ Business ♦ Modern ♦
Good location and ideal for the business traveller. Practical and functional. A
modern foyer-reception, comfortable, well-equipped rooms and bathrooms
with marble fittings.

Marquês de Sá   ⚿ 🕅 🕸 🖾 🖄 25/300 🚗 VISA ⓪ⓔ AE ⑩
av. Miguel Bombarda 130 ⊠ *1050-167 –* ⑩ *Saldanha –* ℰ *21 791 10 14*
– reservas.oms@olissippohotels.com – Fax 21 793 69 83
– www.olissippohotels.com   **G2**
163 rm ⊇ – †96/135 € ††106/165 € – 1 suite
Rest 20 €
♦ Business ♦ Functional ♦
Beside the Gulbenkian Foundation. Business and pleasure in a pleasant
atmosphere of quality. Friendly service and well-appointed rooms. Well-lit
dining room with décor in blue tones and a large foyer.

Real Residência   🕅 🕸 🖾 🖄 25/70 P. VISA ⓪ⓔ AE ⑩
Rua Ramalho Ortigão 41 ⊠ *1070-228 –* ⑩ *Praça de Espanha –* ℰ *21 382 29 00*
– realresidencia@hoteisreal.com – Fax 21 382 29 30
– www.hoteisreal.com   **G2**
24 suites – †155 € ††185 €
Rest a la carte approx. 25 €
♦ Traditional ♦ Classic ♦
Quality, comfort and elegance. Large, well-equipped apartments: bathrooms
fitted with marble, traditional décor of good quality furnishings and fittings. The
smallish dining room is pleasant and combines modern elements with attractive
rustic details.

XXX   **Eleven**   ≼ park, city and river Tejo, 🕅 🕸 ⬦ 20/40 P. VISA ⓪ⓔ AE ⑩
⁕   *Rua Marquês de Fronteira* ⊠ *1070 –* ⑩ *São Sebastião –* ℰ *21 386 22 11 – 11@*
restauranteleven.com – Fax 21 386 22 14
– www.restauranteleven.com
closed August, Sunday and Monday   **G2**
Rest 85 € and a la carte 53/70 €
Spec. Salada de pombo com fígado de pato e vinagrete de lentilhas. Robalo em
crosta mediterrânica e arroz de laranja. Soufflé de maracujá.
♦ Inventive ♦ Design ♦
This establishment has already gained wide acceptance in a short time. Excellent,
modern facilities, a private lobby bar and a dining room with magnificent views.
Enticing creative cooking.

XX   **Saraiva's**   🕅 🕸 ⬦ 12/22 VISA ⓪ⓔ AE ⑩
Rua Engenheiro Canto Resende 3 ⊠ *1050-104 –* ⑩ *Parque –* ℰ *21 354 06 09*
– Fax 21 353 19 87
closed Saturday   **G2**
Rest a la carte 21/33 €
♦ Traditional ♦ Design ♦
Carpeted floors and elegant modern-style furnishings. Very professional service,
a well-heeled clientele and a lively ambience.

PORTUGAL

XX **Adega Tia Matilde** 🔲 ⚘ ⇧40 🅿 𝗩𝗜𝗦𝗔 ⓌⓈ ⅍ ⓞ
Rua da Beneficéncia 77 ⊠ 1600-017 – Ⓜ Praça de Espanha
– 𝒞 21 797 21 72 – adegatiamatilde@netcabo.pt
– Fax 21 797 21 72
closed Saturday dinner and Sunday   **G1**
Rest a la carte 25/30 €
♦ Traditional ♦ Family ♦
A popular establishment, friendly and professional. Portuguese specialities.
Classic-modern style with plants and fresh flowers on the tables.

XX **Varanda da União** ⇐ 🔲 ⚘ ⇧10/25 𝗩𝗜𝗦𝗔 ⓌⓈ ⅍ ⓞ
Rua Castilho 14 C-7° ⊠ 1250-069 – Ⓜ Marquês de Pombal – 𝒞 21 314 10 45
– Fax 21 314 10 46 – www.varandadauniao.restaunet.pt
closed Saturday lunch and Sunday   *Plan II* **E1**
Rest a la carte approx. 38 €
♦ Traditional ♦ Formal ♦
A fine panorama of Lisbon rooftops from the 7th floor of a residential building.
A large number of waiting staff and success based on the quality of the cuisine.

XX **O Polícia** 🔲 ⚘ ⇧15/40 𝗩𝗜𝗦𝗔 ⓌⓈ ⅍ ⓞ
Rua Marquês Sá da Bandeira 112 ⊠ 1050-150 – Ⓜ São Sebastião
– 𝒞 21 796 35 05 – Fax 21 796 97 91 – www.opolicia.restaunet.pt
closed Saturday dinner, Sunday and Bank Holidays   **G2**
Rest a la carte 20/35 €
♦ Traditional ♦ Brasserie ♦
Renowned for fish. Well-decorated establishment, with large dining room,
friendly service and a busy atmosphere. Reservation recommended.

BELÉM   *Plan I*

XX **Estufa Real** 🔲 ⚘ ⇧19 🅿 𝗩𝗜𝗦𝗔 ⓌⓈ ⅍ ⓞ
Jardim Botânico da Ajuda-Calçada do Gâlvao ⊠ 1400 – 𝒞 21 361 94 00
– estufa.real@mail.telepac.pt – Fax 21 361 90 18
closed Saturday   **A3**
Rest (lunch only) a la carte 25/39 €
♦ Traditional ♦ Fashionable ♦
A relaxing location in the Jardim Botânico da Ajuda. A lovely glassed-in
conservatory with attractive modern design details.

X **Caseiro** 🔲 ⚘ 𝗩𝗜𝗦𝗔 ⓌⓈ ⅍ ⓞ
Rua de Belém 35 ⊠ 1300-354 – Ⓜ Cais do Sodré – 𝒞 21 363 88 03
– Fax 21 364 23 39
closed August and Sunday   **A3**
Rest a la carte 21/31 €
♦ Traditional ♦ Rustic ♦
Traditional establishment serving delicious, simply prepared dishes which have
made this restaurant well known in the locality.

SPAIN
ESPAÑA

PROFILE

+ **AREA:**
504 782 km² (194 897 sq mi).

+ **POPULATION:**
40 350 000 inhabitants (est. 2005), density = 80 per km².

+ **CAPITAL:**
Madrid (conurbation 4 858 000 inhabitants).

+ **CURRENCY:**
Euro (€); rate of exchange: € 1 = US$ 1.17 (Nov 2005).

+ **GOVERNMENT:**
Constitutional parliamentary monarchy (since 1978). Member of European Union since 1986.

+ **LANGUAGES:**
Spanish (Castilian) but also Catalan in Catalonia, Gallego in Galicia, Euskera in the Basque Country, Valencian in the Valencian Region and Mallorquin in the Balearic Isles.

+ **SPECIFIC PUBLIC HOLIDAYS:**
Epiphany (6 January); San Jose (19 March); Maundy Thursday (the day before Good Friday); Good Friday (Friday before Easter); National Day (12 October); Constitution Day (6 December); Immaculate Conception (8 December). Some public holidays may be replaced by the autonomous communities with another date.

+ **LOCAL TIME:**
GMT + 1 hour in winter and GMT + 2 hours in summer.

+ **CLIMATE:**
Temperate Mediterranean with mild winters (colder in interior) and sunny, hot summers (Madrid: January: 6°C, July: 25°C).

Barcelona
Madrid

+ **IINTERNATIONAL DIALLING CODE:**
00 34 followed by full 9-digit number. Directory enquiries: ℰ **1003**. International directory enquiries: ℰ **025**. On-line telephone directory: www.paginas-blancas.es

+ **EMERGENCY:**
Dial ℰ **112**; Medical Assistance: ℰ **061**; National Police: ℰ **091**.

+ **ELECTRICITY:**
220 or 225 volts AC (previously 110 V), 50 Hz; 2-pin round-shaped continental plugs.

FORMALITIES

Travellers from the European Union (EU), Switzerland, Iceland and the main countries of North and South America need a national identity card or passport (America: passport required) to visit Spain for less than three months (tourism or business purpose). For visitors from other countries a visa may be required, in addition to a passport, especially for those wishing to stay for longer than three months. We advise you to check with your embassy before travelling.

An International Driving Licence or an EU driving licence is required. Third party insurance is compulsory in Spain. For traffic offences on-the-spot payment of fines (reduced by 30%) is compulsory for non-residents. The minimum age for driving is 18 and for car hire is 21. For information in English on regulations and road conditions contact the National Traffic Agency ℰ 900 12 35 05; www.dgt.es

MAJOR NEWSPAPERS

The main dailies distributed nationally are *El País*, *ABC* and *El Mundo* (from Madrid), *La Vangardia* and *El Periódico* (from Barcelona). Major regional newspapers: *El Correo* (Bilbao), *La Voz de Galicia* (A Coruña), *Levante* (Valencia) and *El Correo de Andalucia* (Sevilla).

USEFUL PHRASES

ENGLISH	**SPANISH**		
Yes	**Si**	Goodbye	**Hasta luego, adios**
No	**No**	Thank you	**Gracias**
Good		Please	**Por favor**
morning	**Buenos dias!**	Excuse me	**Perdone**
		I don't understand	**No entiendo**

HOTELS

◆ CATEGORIES

Accommodation ranges from luxurious international hotels, classified from 1-5 stars, via smaller hotels *(hostales)* and family-run guesthouses *(pensiones)*, classified from 1-3 stars to rural accommodation, sometimes in private houses. Most hotels have a restaurant except *hoteles-residencias*, which usually serve only breakfast. Ratings are granted by the regional governments and standards may vary from region to region. The state-run network of luxury hotels *(paradores)*, classified from 3-5 stars and located in restored historic buildings (castles, palaces, monasteries etc), often has special weekend offers in addition to a 5-night 'go as you please' accommodation card – www.parador.es

◆ PRICE RANGE

The price is per room. There is little difference between the price of a single and a double room.

Between April and October it is advisable to book in advance, particularly on the coast. From November to March prices may be slightly lower, some hotels offer special cheap rates and some may be closed. At the weekend out of season chain hotels in the capital usually offer lower rates.

◆ TAX

On the mainland 7%, which is not always included in the room price.

◆ CHECK OUT TIME

Usually at noon.

◆ RESERVATIONS

By telephone or by Internet. A credit card number may be required.

◆ TIP FOR LUGGAGE HANDLING

At the discretion of the customer (about €1).

◆ BREAKFAST

It is not always included in the price of the room and is generally served from 8am to 11am. Most hotels offer a buffet but usually it is possible to have continental breakfast served in the room.

Reception	**Recepción**	Bed	**Cama**
Single room	**Habitación individual**	Bathroom	**Baño**
		Shower	**Ducha**
Double room	**Habitación doble**		

RESTAURANTS

Spaniards usually eat lunch between 1pm and 3.30pm and dinner from 8.30 to 11pm. Besides the traditional **restaurants** there are the ubiquitous **tapas bars**, serving the traditional appetizers, which come in two different sizes: small saucer-size portions *(tapas)* or more substantial portions *(raciones)*; two or three *tapas* or one or two *raciones*, together with a draught beer *(una caña)* or a glass of sherry *(una copa de fino)*, make a good light lunch. In the smallest village as in the large towns, the many **bars** are a local focal point where people look in for refreshment at any time of day. In summer **terraces** spring up on the pavements and in shady alleys where you can sit down for a drink or a whole meal. The **beach bars** *(chiringuitos)* are particularly popular as you can enjoy a drink or a meal without changing out of swimming garb.

Breakfast	**Desayuno**	7am – 10am
Lunch	**Almuerzo**	1.30pm – 3.30pm
Dinner	**Cena**	9pm – 11pm

Spanish restaurants offer fixed price menus *(menú del día)*, comprising starter, main course, dessert and drink, or à la carte. Menus are usually printed in Spanish and English, and sometimes also in French and German, depending on the location. A fixed-price menu is usually less expensive than the same number of dishes chosen à la carte.

Reservations are usually made by phone, fax or Internet. For famous restaurants (including Michelin starred restaurants), it is advisable to book several days – or weeks in some instances – in advance. A credit card number or a phone number may be required to guarantee the booking.

The **bill** (check) includes service charge and VAT. Tipping is optional but, if you are particularly pleased with the service, it is customary to add between 5% and 10% of the total bill.

Drink or aperitif	**Bebida**	Meat (medium, rare, blue)	
Appetizers	**Tapas/Aperitivo**		**Carne**
Meal	**Comida**		**(muy hecha,**
Starter	**Entrante**		**medio hecha,**
Main dish	**Plato principal**		**poco hecha)**
Main dish of the day	**Plato de día**	Fish	**Pescados**
		Salt/pepper	**Sal/pimienta**
Dessert	**Postre**	Cheese	**Queso**
Water	**Agua**	Vegetables	**Legumbres**
Wine (red, white, rosé)	**Vino (tinto, blanco, rosado)**	Hot/cold	**Caliente/frío**
		The bill (check) please	**La nota, por favor**
Beer	**Cerveza**		
Bread	**Pan**		

LOCAL CUISINE

Spanish food is distinctively Mediterranean – cooked with olive oil, seasoned with aromatic herbs and spiced with garlic and peppers – but it also varies enormously from region to region.

The commonest dish is stew (*cocido*; also known as *olla, pote, escudella…*) made with pulses (beans or chick-peas), vegetables and meat, cooked together slowly but served as two or three separate courses. Other dishes served throughout the country include garlic soup (made of bread, garlic, oil and paprika with additional regional ingredients), spicy pork sausages (**chorizo**), delicious lean Serrano hams and omelette (**tortilla**) such as the famous **Spanish omelette** which contains potatoes. Fish and seafood are also used in a great many dishes, particularly along the coasts. There are also many savoury rice dishes, particularly in the eastern region, including the well-known **paella** which was first produced in the mid-19C in Valencia and consist of saffron rice with a variety of fish, meat and vegetables. Meat plays a leading role in Spanish cooking; beef and veal, pork, both cooked and cured, lamb and goat, and game of all kinds. Some of the more unusual specialities include **perdices con chocolate** (partridge with chocolate) from Aragon, **mar y muntanya** in Girona (fish and meat in the same dish, usually lobster and chicken); **gazpacho**, a cold soup made of cucumber, tomato, oil, garlic and bread; **habas a la granadina** (broad beans Granada style); **roast sucking pig** in Segovia; **bacalao al ajoarriero** (salt cod) from Castile, and **migas**, a dish of breadcrumbs softened in water and then gently fried, which must be ordered in advance.

The ubiquitous **tapas**, invented in Seville but now found throughout Spain, appear on the counters of most bars and cafés just before lunch and dinner. This often vast array of colourful appetisers may include cheese, ham, sausage or a selection of vegetarian, fish, seafood or meat dishes.

Every region of Spain has its own cheeses; hard cheeses such as Roncal from Navarra and Manchego from La Mancha; soft creamy curd cheeses from Burgos and Valladolid.

Spain has a wide range of sweets, many of Arab origin: **quesada**, a mixture of cream cheese, honey and milk, from Santander; nougat (**turrón**) in Valencia; **pan de Alá**, **tocino de cielo** and **roscos de vino** in Murcia; **tortas de aceite** (olive oil cakes), once an essential part of breakfast in Seville but now found throughout Spain; **yemas de Santa Teresa**, a sweet made of sugar and egg yolk in Avila; **mazapán** (marzipan made with sugar and almonds) from Toledo.

◆ DRINK

Wine is produced in most of the regions of Spain, which has 50 wine producing areas recognised by the Instituto Nacional de Denominaciones de Origen (INDO). The red table wines of **La Rioja** have an international reputation. Castile produces some reds and rosés of international renown – Cigales, Rueda, Ribera de Duero, Toro, Bierzo. The art of viniculture goes back centuries in Catalonia, which produces excellent light wines: reds in Priorato, fruity white in Penedès and Tarragona as an appetiser or with fish. The main source of Spanish wine is La Mancha; the best known are the light reds and white from Valdepeñas. The full-flavoured reds of Aragon are ideal with meat dishes. From Levante come crisp, dry white Valencias and red Jumillas. The light whites of Galicia go well with the local cuisine.

Andalusia is famous for its **dessert wines** and sherries (Jerez), Manzanilla, Montilla-Moriles and Málaga. The sparkling wines known as **cavas** are produced in the region of Barcelona. In the northern provinces of Asturias and Cantabria **cider** (*sidra*), made from locally-grown apples, is often drunk at meals. Orgeat (**horchata**), a sweet, light, refreshing drink made from chufa (tiger nut), is enjoyed in summer all over Spain.

MADRID

MADRID

Population (est. 2005): 2 890 000 (conurbation 4 858 000) – Altitude: 646m

J. Malburet / MICHELIN

Madrid is one of Europe's most hospitable, cosmopolitan and lively cities, with wide avenues, attractive parks and a great sense of joie de vivre. In 1561 Charles V moved his capital from Toledo to Madrid; at this time Spain ruled over a vast empire. Madrid was chosen because it was more or less in the geographic centre of Spain and has attracted people from every corner of the country.

As the capital of Spain, Madrid is the leading city for banks and insurance, administrative and political institutions. It is an important industrial and technological centre with most of these activities developing on the outskirts of the city.

When Charles V made it the capital of Spain in 1561 it began to grow and it was further transformed in the 18C under the Bourbons. The City's main monuments, Classical and Baroque in style, were built during the 17C, 18C and 19C. As a result of the artistic legacies of the Habsburgs and Bourbons, Madrid is home to an exceptional wealth of paintings, enhanced considerably in recent years by the superb collections on display in the Museo Thyssen-Bornemisza and the Centro de Arte Reina Sofía.

WHICH DISTRICT TO CHOOSE

The central districts of Madrid are well provided with **places to stay**, **restaurants**, sights and attractions. The Centro district, especially round Sol, Callao *Plan I* **B2** is good for dinner or a drink in one of the many local cafés and restaurants. Barrio de los Austrias *Plan II* **E3** is also excellent for **tapas**, dinner or a drink. Home of the 17C literary community, Huertas *Plan II* **G3** is now packed with bars and restaurants and attracts an interesting mixture of late-night revellers. Malasaña *Plan II* **F1** is transformed at night by the crowds of young people heading for the many bars, although there are some quieter cafés. The rich and famous congregate in the upmarket bars and restaurants in Alonso Martínez *Plan II* **G2**. Chueca *Plan II* **G2** is now Madrid's gay area with a multitude of small and sophisticated boutiques.

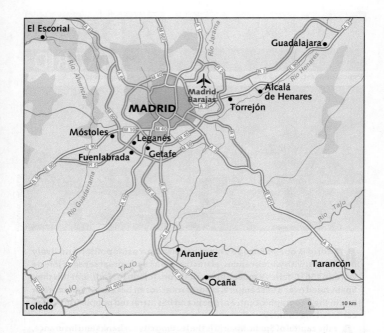

0   10 km

PRACTICAL INFORMATION

ARRIVAL – DEPARTURE

Madrid-Barajas Airport – About 13 km (8 mi) east of the city centre. ℰ 917 477 570 (Terminals 1 & 2), 913 058 343/4/5/6 or 913 058 656. Airport Information ℰ 902 353 570, 913 058 346; www.aena.es

From the airport to the city centre – By **taxi**: Fare €18-€20 + charge for luggage; journey time 25 min. By **Metro Line 8** €1.15; 6am-2.00am, every 4-7min; journey time 50min; terminus Nuevos Ministerios (check-in facilities 6.30am-10.30pm). By **bus** (red buses): lines **101** (approx. every 20 min) and **200** (approx. every 10 min); journey time 30min; €3; terminus Plaza de Colón.

Railway Stations – **Chamartín Station** *Plan V* **M1** for services to the

642

north of Spain and to France. **Atocha Station** *Plan II* **H3** for services to the south of Spain. ℰ 902 240 202 (24hr information line; bookings 5.30am-11.50pm); www.renfe.es

TRANSPORT

♦ METRO AND BUS

Single journey €1; **Metrobus** 10-trip ticket *(un bono de 10 viajes)* €5.80; these tickets are valid on both bus and metro networks and are available from underground stations, bus ticket offices, news-stands and tobacconists *(estancos)*. The **Tourist Travel Card** *(abono turístico de transportes)*, valid for from 1 to 7 days for unlimited travel on all public transport in Zone A or Zone T in the Madrid region and available at Metro ticket offices, at Chamartín and Atocha Stations, and at the Travel Information Point at the Airport station. Metro trains operate on 12 lines from 6am-1.30am. ℰ 902 444 403; www.metromadrid.es. Bus services operate on 189 routes generally from 6am-11.30pm. ℰ 902 507 850; www.emtmadrid.es

◆ TAXIS

Taxis are distinguished by their white paintwork with a red diagonal stripe on the rear doors; they show a green light *(Libre)* on the windscreen when not engaged and can be hailed in the street. Minimum pick up charge is €1.65; supplementary charge between 10pm and 6am. It is customary to round up taxi fares. *Radio-Taxi* ℰ 914 475 180; *Tele-Taxi* ℰ 914 459 008; *Radio-Teléfono Taxi* ℰ 902 (or 915) 478 200.

◆ MADRID CARD

1-day ticket €25; 2-day ticket €35, 3-day ticket €45; available from Madrid Tourist Office, Madrid Municipal Tourism, tobacco shops *(estancos)*, Barajas Airport, Atocha Station, at news-stands (64 Gran Vía, 11 Puerta del Sol, Madrid Visión, beside the Prado Museum); valid for travel by all public transport plus admission to more than 40 museums; also valid for discounts in some night clubs, shops and restaurants. To buy the card by phone: 902 877 996; information: ℰ 917 130 444 or 915 882 900 (Mon-Fri, 9.30am-1.30pm); www.madrid card.com

◆ MADRID VISION SIGHTSEEING TOURS

1-day ticket €13, no charge for holders of Madrid Card. Service operates all year, 9.30/10am-7pm/midnight – Route 1 (thema: Historical Madrid) from the Palacio Real; Route 2 (thema: Modern Madrid) from the Prado Museum, Route 3 (thema: Monumental Madrid) from Atocha. ℰ 917 791 888; www. madridvision.es

USEFUL ADDRESSES

◆ TOURIST INFORMATION

Municipal Tourist Office *Plan II* **F2** 3 Plaza Mayor, ℰ 914 881 636; Mercado Puerta de Toledo; 2 Duque de Medinaceli; **Barajas Airport Tourist Office**, (Terminal 1 – arrivals); **Chamartín Railway Station** *Plan V* **M1**, Gate 15; **Atocha Station** *Plan II* **H3**; ℰ 902 100 007; info@turmadrid. com; turismo@madrid.org; turismo@ comadrid.es; www.madrid.org; www.comadrid.es

◆ POST OFFICES

Opening times Mon-Sat, 8.30am-2.30pm (1pm Sat). Main Office, Plaza de Cibeles (8am-midnight). ℰ 902 197 197. Stamps can be bought in tobacconists *(estancos)*.

◆ BANKS / CURRENCY EXCHANGE

Opening times Mon-Fri, 8.30am-2pm, Sat 9am-1pm but closed Saturdays in summer.

◆ EMERGENCY

Dial ℰ **112**; for National Police ℰ **091**; for Medical assistance and Ambulance ℰ **061**.

BUSY PERIODS

It may be difficult to find a room at a reasonable price when special events are held in the city:

Madrid Regional Festival: 1-4 May.

Feria de San Isidro: from 15 May for a month – Concerts, open-air dancing, outdoor picnics and a famous bullfighting festival, lasting six weeks.

Veranos de la Villa: Summer – Variety of cultural performances.

Autumn Festival: mid-October to mid-November – Theatre, dance, music.

Festival Internacional de Jazz: November.

DIFFERENT FACETS OF THE CITY

It is possible to visit the main sights and museums in two to three days.

Museums and sights are usually open from 9/10am to 5pm. Some close on Mondays.

Museum Card (Paseo del Arte): €7.66; special ticket valid for and available at the 3 main museums; www.munimadrid.es

ARTISTIC CITY – **Museo del Prado** *Plan III* **I3**: one of the greatest galleries of Classical paintings in the world, housing the collections of Spanish painting made by the Habsburg and Bourbon kings; also works by Flemish painters and many paintings from the Italian School favoured by Emperor Charles V and Philip II. **Museo Thyssen-Bornemisza** *Plan II* **G2**: the museum contains approximately 800 works (mainly paintings) from the late 13C to the present day – one of the largest private collections, assembled by Baron Heinrich Thyssen-Bornemisza. **Museo Nacional Centro de Arte Reina Sofía** *Plan II* **G3**: an outstanding collection of contemporary art housed in a former hospital. **Monasterio de la Descalzas Reales** *Plan II* **F2**: the convent of the Poor Clares, founded by Joanna of Austria in the palace where she was born, served for two centuries as a retreat for nobles, who heaped gifts upon the order. **Museo Arqueológico Nacional** *Plan III* **I2**: this museum, founded in 1867 by Queen Isabel II, traces the development of artistic creativity; Prehistoric Art and Archaeology, Iberian and Classical Antiquities, Medieval and Renaissance Decorative Art, 16-19C Art.

HABSBURG AND BOURBON MADRID – **Plaza Mayor** *Plan II* **F2**: the architectural centre of Habsburg Madrid, built in the 17C, and surrounded by historic houses. **Palacio Real** *Plan II* **E2**: the official residence of the royal family until 1931 was built by the Bourbons to replace the old Habsburg Alcázar which was destroyed in a fire. The north front faces the **Jardines de Sabatini**; the west is flanked by the **Campo del Moro** *Plan II* **E2** and the Manzanares River. On the east side is the Plaza de Oriente, where you can stroll up to the magnificent equestrian statue of Philip IV by Pietro Tacca (17C), and the **Teatro Real** *Plan II* **E2**, a hexagonal neo-Classical building by López de Aguacio, inaugurated as an opera house in 1850 for Isabel II.

OUTDOOR MADRID – **Parque del Buen Retiro** *Plan III* **I2**: 32 acres in the middle of the city, created in the 17C, with dense clumps of trees, formal flower-beds, fountains, temples, colonnades and statues, lake with boats for hire, music, puppets, exhibitions in the **Palacio de Cristal** *Plan III* **I3**. Flanking the park is **Calle de Alfonxo XII** *Plan III* **I2** running north to **Puerta de Alcalá**, built (1769-78) by Sabatini to celebrate the triumphant entrance of Charles III into Madrid: impressive perspective at night. **Casa de Campo** *Plan I* **A2**: 4,000 acres on the right bank of the Manzanares River, once part of the royal estate, with the Zoo, an amusement park, rowing boats on the lake, swimming and tennis.

GOURMET TREATS

In Madrid going out for **tapas** (*ir de tapeo*) is a tradition; the most popular district is in and around Plaza Mayor but there are hundreds of bars throughout the city which serve tapas – small portions of a variety of savoury dishes served as appetizers – accompanied by a draught beer (*una caña*) or a small glass of wine or sherry (*una copa de fino*). Wine from La Mancha is usually served in Madrid during the *chateo*, when people go from bar to bar having a glass of wine in each.

Gourmets may argue whether Madrid has its own cuisine but several dishes can be considered typical. **Cocido madrileño** is a huge succulent stew combining chickpeas with vegetables (cabbage, celery, carrots, turnips and potatoes) and chicken, beef and pork. **Callos** (tripe) is found in some of the well-known restaurants. Other typical dishes include **sopa de ajo** (garlic soup), **caracoles** (snails), **tortilla de patatas** (potato omelette), **besugo al horno** (baked bream) and **bacalao** (cod).

The year is marked by seasonal sweets – **torrijas** in the spring and Holy Week, **barquillos** (rolled wafers), **bartolillos con crema** (a type of small pie with custard), **buñuelos** (a type of fritter filled with custard and whipped cream); **mazapán** (marzipan) in November, **turrón** (nougat) at Christmas and **rosquillas de anis** (aniseed-flavoured doughnuts) during the festival of San Isidro.

SHOPPING

Department stores are usually open 10am-8.30pm. Smaller shops and boutiques open 10am-2pm and 5-8pm. The majority of shops close on Sundays.

The shopping district par excellence is **Sol-Callao** *Plan II* **F2** including **Preciados**, the pedestrianised precinct north of Puerta de Sol. Other streets with large department stores are **Princesa** *Plan IV* **K3**, **Goya** and **Castellana** *Plan I* **C2**. For designer boutiques and an impressive collection of stores selling luxury goods visit **Almirante** *Plan II* **G2**, **Conde Xiquena** *Plan II* **G2** and **Salamanca** *Plan IV* **L2**: Serrano and Ortega y Gasset. The shops in and around Plaza Mayor sell traditional articles such as espadrilles, fabrics, ropes, hats and religious articles.

MARKETS – The best known flea market is **El Rastro** *Plan I* **C2**; there are other markets in **Las Cortes** *Plan II* **G2** and **Serrano** *Plan III* **J1**.

WHAT TO BUY – Leather goods, shoes, jewellery, pottery and wrought-iron.

ENTERTAINMENT

The *Guia del Ocio*, a weekly publication, contains information on shows, entertainment, night life and restaurants – www.guiadelocio.es; www.cajamadrid.es (for theatre tickets)

Teatro Real *Plan II* **E2** – Offers a season of opera.

Auditorio Nacional *Plan V* **M3** – Varied programme of classical music

Zarzuela Theatre *Plan II* **G2** – Wide range of shows including ballets and Spanish operettas (*zarzuelas*).

Plaza de la Ventas *Plan I* **C2** – Bull fights on Sunday afternoons; ℰ 914 220 780; reservations ℰ 902 332 211; www.las-ventas.com; reservations www.mundotoro.com; www.ticketstoro.com; www.tauroentrada.com

Warner Brothers Movie World Park – Entertainment for young and old with Hollywood characters, thrilling rides and live performances; www.warnerbrospark.com

NIGHTLIFE

Madrid is a great city for a night out any evening of the week; as people tend to eat late some places stay open until the early hours. **Malasaña** *Plan II* **E1** has many cafés and bars with live music, as well as moderately-price restaurants. Young people generally frequent **Argüelles** *Plan I* **B1** and **Moncloa** *Plan I* **A2**. Other districts with a lively nightlife – popular bars, pubs, fast-food outlets and ice cream parlours – are **Huertas** *Plan II* **G3** and **Alonso Martínez** *Plan II* **G2**. **Paseo de la Castellana**, **Paseo de Recoletos** and **Paseo del Prado** *Plan II* **H3** cater to more expensive tastes. For open-air terraces in the summer months and especially at night, try the district of **Paseo de la Castellana** and **Parque del Oeste** *Plan I* **A2**.

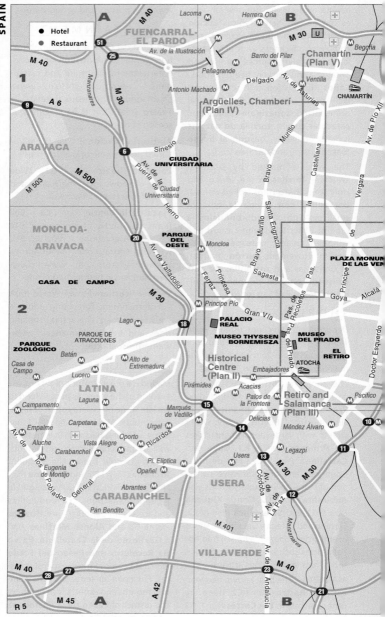

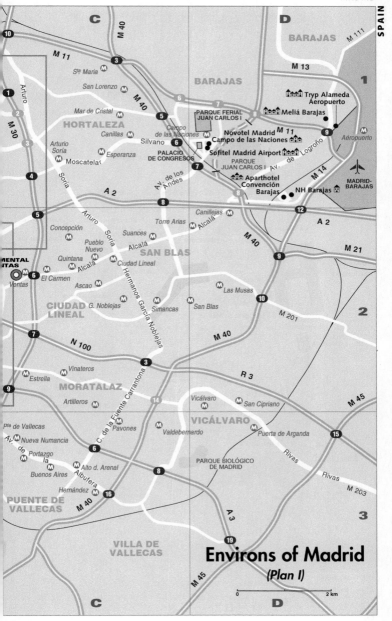

Environs of Madrid
(Plan I)

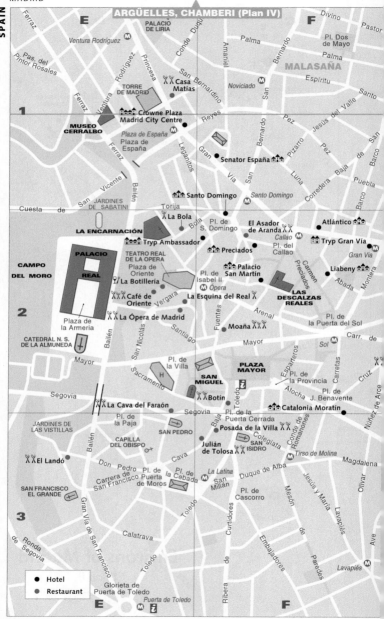

ARGÜELLES, CHAMBERI (Plan IV)

MALASAÑA

Ventura Rodríguez

PALACIO
DE LIRIA

Casa Matías

TORRE
DE MADRID

Crowne Plaza
Madrid City Centre

MUSEO
CERRALBO

Plaza de España

Senator España

Santo Domingo

Atlántico

JARDINES
DE SABATINI

La Bola

El Asador
de Aranda

Tryp Gran Via

LA ENCARNACIÓN

Tryp Ambassador

Preciados

Liabeny

CAMPO
DEL MORO

PALACIO
REAL

TEATRO REAL
DE LA ÓPERA
Plaza de
Oriente

Palacio
San Martín

LAS
DESCALZAS
REALES

La Botillería

Pl. de
Isabel II

Café de
Oriente

La Esquina del Real

La Ópera de Madrid

Plaza de
la Armería

CATEDRAL N. S.
DE LA ALMUNEDA

Moaña

Pl. de
la Puerta del Sol

SAN
MIGUEL

PLAZA
MAYOR

La Cava del Faraón

Botín

Catalonia Moratín

JARDINES
DE LAS VISTILLAS

SAN PEDRO

Posada de la Villa

CAPILLA
DEL OBISPO

Julián
de Tolosa

SAN
ISIDRO

El Landó

SAN FRANCISCO
EL GRANDE

Puerta
de Moros

La Latina
San
Millán

Pl. de
Cascorro

Lavapiés

● Hotel
● Restaurant

Glorieta de
Puerta de Toledo

Puerta de Toledo

648

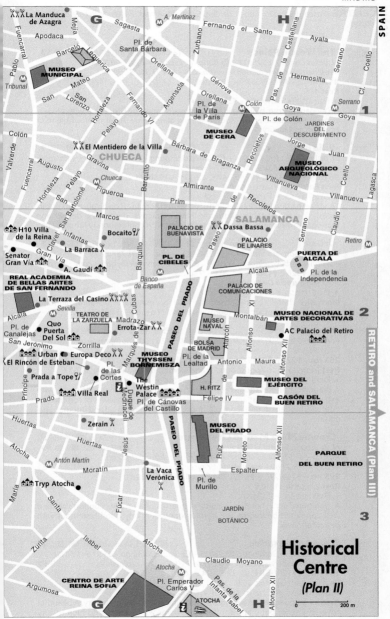

Historical
Centre
(Plan II)

0   200 m

649

SPAIN

CENTRE *(Paseo del Prado, Puerta del Sol, Gran Vía, Alcalá, Paseo de Recoletos, Plaza Mayor)* *Plan II*

The Westin Palace 🛗 ♿ 🕮 ♨25/500 🚫 *VISA* ⦾ ⲀⒺ ①
pl. de las Cortes 7 ⊠ 28014 – Ⓜ Banco de España – ℰ 91 360 80 00
– reservation.palacemadrid@westin.com – Fax 91 360 81 00 **G2**
417 rm ⌖ – ♦♦449/567 € – 48 suites
Rest 48 €
♦ Palace ♦ Luxury ♦ Classic ♦
An elegant historic building in front of the Congreso de Diputados with a lovely patio in the middle and a Modernist-style glass dome. A harmonious blend of tradition and luxury.

Villa Real 🛗 🅰🅲 🕮 ♨35/220 🚫 *VISA* ⦾ ⲀⒺ ①
pl. de las Cortes 10 ⊠ 28014 – Ⓜ Banco de España – ℰ 91 420 37 67 – villareal@derbyhotels.es – Fax 91 420 25 47 – www.derbyhotels.es **G2**
96 rm – ♦219/310 € ♦♦246/347 €, ⌖ 19 € – 19 suites
Rest *Europa* a la carte 41/50 €
♦ Business ♦ Personalised ♦
This hotel has a valuable collection of Greek and Roman art on display in its public areas. The comfortable bedrooms have attractive decorative details and mahogany furnishings. A pleasant restaurant with contemporary lithographs.

Urban Egyptian Museum 🛗 ⌾ ♿ 🅰🅲 ♨25/120 🚫 *VISA* ⦾ ⲀⒺ ①
Carrera de San Jerónimo 34 ⊠ 28014 – Ⓜ Sevilla – ℰ 91 787 77 70
– urban@derbyhotels.com – Fax 91 787 77 79 – www.derbyhotels.com
87 rm – ♦326 € ♦♦364 €, ⌖ 20 € – 9 suites **G2**
Rest see *Europa Deco* below
♦ Business ♦ Design ♦
Innovative hotel, characterized by quality materials, beautiful lighting, numerous works of art, and rooms which boast a range of details.

Husa Princesa 🛗 ⌾ ♿ 🅰🅲 🕮 ♨ ♨25/500 🚫 *VISA* ⦾ ⲀⒺ ①
Princesa 40 ⊠ 28008 – Ⓜ Argüelles – ℰ 91 542 21 00 – husaprincesa@husa.es
– Fax 91 542 73 28 – www.hotelhusaprincesa.com *Plan IV* **K3**
263 rm – ♦275 € ♦♦345 €, ⌖ 23 € – 12 suites
Rest *(closed 1 to 15 August, Sunday and Monday dinner)* a la carte 39/53 €
♦ Business ♦ Chain hotel ♦ Classic ♦
A magnificent hotel situated on one of the principal arteries of the city, with expansive lounge areas and spacious rooms offering high levels of comfort. An intimate, modern dining room offering a choice of traditional and international cuisine.

Crowne Plaza Madrid City Centre ⟨ 🛗 ♿ 🅰🅲 ✄ 🕮 ♨
pl. de España ⊠ 28013 – Ⓜ Plaza de ♨25/220 *VISA* ⦾ ⲀⒺ ①
España – ℰ 91 454 85 00 – reservas@crowneplazamadrid.com
– Fax 91 548 23 89 – www.madrid-citycentre.crowneplaza.com **E1**
295 rm – ♦140/270 € ♦♦160/294 €, ⌖ 17 € – 11 suites
Rest a la carte 31/40 €
♦ Business ♦ Classic ♦
A traditional-style hotel in a cultural quarter of the city. Comfortable and well-appointed bedrooms and several lounges. A very good restaurant with beautiful views.

Tryp Ambassador 🅰🅲 ✄ 🕮 ♨25/300 *VISA* ⦾ ⲀⒺ ①
Cuesta de Santo Domingo 5 ⊠ 28013 – Ⓜ Santo Domingo – ℰ 91 541 67 00
– ambasador@trypnet.com – Fax 91 559 10 40 – www.somelia.es **E-F2**
159 rm – ♦♦120/158 €, ⌖ 17 € – 24 suites
Rest a la carte approx. 36 €
♦ Business ♦ Chain hotel ♦ Classic ♦
A rather grand hotel in keeping with the tone of this area of the city. A beautiful covered interior patio and comfortable rooms with elegant and high-quality furnishings. With its glass roof, the restaurant has the feel of a winter garden.

SPAIN

Quo Puerta Del Sol without rest   🔳 🍴 📺 *VISA* 🇺🇸 🇦🇪
*Sevilla 4 ⊠ 28014 – Ⓜ Sevilla – 𝒞 91 532 90 49 – puertadelsol@hotelesquo.com
– Fax 91 531 28 34 – www.hotelesquo.com*   **G2**
61 rm – ♦125/180 € ♦♦140/225 €, ☲ 15 € – 1 suite
♦ Business ♦ Design ♦
What the hotel lacks in lounge and public areas is compensated by the magnificent bedrooms with their avant-garde design and high technical specification.

Liabeny   ♿ 🔳 🍴 📺 📞 🆑 25/125 🌳 *VISA* 🇺🇸 🇦🇪 ①
*Salud 3 ⊠ 28013 – Ⓜ Sol – 𝒞 91 531 90 00 – info@hotelliabeny.com
– Fax 91 532 74 21 – www.liabeny.es*   **F2**
220 rm – ♦88/118 € ♦♦120/168 €, ☲ 14 € – **Rest** 23 €
♦ Business ♦ Traditional ♦ Classic ♦
A hotel in a busy commercial area. The old-fashioned English-style bar lends a touch of class to the public areas. Comfortable rooms with classic functional décor and furnishings. The restaurant has an intimate ambience.

Senator España   🛗 📺 ♿ 🔳 🍴 📺 🆑 25/200 *VISA* 🇺🇸 🇦🇪 ①
*Gran Vía 70 ⊠ 28013 – Ⓜ Plaza de España – 𝒞 91 522 82 65 – senator.espana@
playasenator.com – Fax 91 522 82 64 – www.playasenator.com*   **F1**
171 rm – ♦143/147 € ♦♦165/220 €, ☲ 12 € – **Rest** 16 €
♦ Business ♦ Chain hotel ♦ Functional ♦
Excellent leisure facilities, which include a beauty salon and hydromassage pool. The hotel's guestrooms are well-appointed, and offer full soundproofing.

Santo Domingo   🔳 🍴 📺 🆑 25/200 *VISA* 🇺🇸 🇦🇪 ①
*pl. de Santo Domingo 13 ⊠ 28013 – Ⓜ Santo Domingo – 𝒞 91 547 98 00 – reserva
@hotelsantodomingo.com – Fax 91 547 59 95 – www.hotelsantodomingo.net*
120 rm – ♦100/138 € ♦♦140/175 €, ☲ 11,50 € – **Rest** 32 €   **F2**
♦ Business ♦ Traditional ♦ Personalised ♦
Numerous works of art decorate the walls of this hotel. Comfortable rooms with modern bathrooms, some with hydro-massage baths.

Palacio San Martín   🛗 ♿ 🔳 🍴 📺 📞 🆑 25 *VISA* 🇺🇸 🇦🇪 ①
*pl. San Martín 5 ⊠ 28013 – Ⓜ Sol – 𝒞 91 701 50 00 – sanmartin@intur.com
– Fax 91 701 50 10 – www.intur.com*   **F2**
93 rm – ♦109/170 € ♦♦109/210 €, ☲ 17 € – 1 suite
Rest *(closed August, Sunday and Bank Holidays)* a la carte 28/38 €
♦ Business ♦ Stylish ♦
A historic building which in the 1950s was the United States Embassy. A patio with a glass roof serves as a lounge area. Traditional-style bedrooms, plus a panoramic restaurant on the top floor.

H10 Villa de la Reina   🔳 🍴 📺 🆑 25/40 *VISA* 🇺🇸 🇦🇪 ①
*Gran Vía 22 ⊠ 28013 – Ⓜ Gran Vía – 𝒞 91 523 91 01 – h10.villa.delareina@
h10.es – Fax 91 521 75 22 – www.h10.es*   **G2**
73 rm – ♦85/180 € ♦♦115/195 €, ☲ 14,50 € – 1 suite – **Rest** a la carte 21/34 €
♦ Business ♦ Chain hotel ♦ Stylish ♦
An attractive building dating from the early 20C with an elegant foyer-reception decked in marble and fine wood. All the charm of former times and comfortable rooms.

Preciados   🔳 🍴 📺 📞 🆑 25/100 🌳 *VISA* 🇺🇸 🇦🇪 ①
*Preciados 37 ⊠ 28013 – Ⓜ Santo Domingo – 𝒞 91 454 44 00
– preciadoshotel@preciadoshotel.com – Fax 91 454 44 01*   **F2**
68 rm – ♦105/120 € ♦♦110/140 €, ☲ 13 € – 5 suites – **Rest** 18 €
♦ Business ♦ Modern ♦
The severe 19C Classicism of this hotel's architecture is in complete contrast to its modern and well-appointed facilities. A small but pleasant lounge.

A. Gaudí   🛗 ♿ 🔳 🍴 📺 📞 🆑 25/120 *VISA* 🇺🇸 🇦🇪 ①
*Gran Vía 9 ⊠ 28013 – Ⓜ Gran Vía – 𝒞 91 531 22 22 – gaudi@
hoteles-catalonia.es – Fax 91 531 54 69 – www.hoteles-catalonia.es*   **G2**
185 rm – ♦122/165 € ♦♦161/198 €, ☲ 13 € – **Rest** 15 €
♦ Business ♦ Chain hotel ♦ Functional ♦
Right in the centre of Madrid with an attractive early 20C façade behind which is a lively and modern interior. Well-lit, comfortable and modern rooms.

Senator Gran Vía
🔧 (heated) & 🅰️ ⚗️ ♨25 VISA 🔵 🅰️🅴 ①
Gran Vía 21 ⊠ 28013 – Ⓜ Gran Vía – ℰ 91 531 41 51
– senator.granvia@playasenator.com – Fax 91 524 07 99   **G2**
136 rm – ♦100/170 € ♦♦120/200 €, ⊇ 12 €
Rest 16 €
♦ Business ♦ Chain hotel ♦ Functional ♦
Behind the Senator's distinctive classical façade is an interior with the latest in modern comforts, including avant-garde bedrooms. Dining options include a simply styled restaurant offering à la carte and buffet dining, and a spacious cafeteria.

Catalonia Moratín
& 🅰️ ⚗️ 📺 ♨️ ♨25/30 VISA 🔵 🅰️🅴 ①
Atocha 23 ⊠ 28012 – Ⓜ Sol – ℰ 91 369 71 71
– moratin@hoteles-catalonia.es – Fax 91 360 12 31
– www.hoteles-catalonia.es   **F2-3**
59 rm – ♦122/165 € ♦♦161/198 €, ⊇ 13 € – 4 suites
Rest a la carte approx. 25 €
♦ Business ♦ Chain hotel ♦ Functional ♦
This 18C building combines original features, such as the staircase, with others of a more modern, practical design, including the stylish bedrooms. Attractive inner patio, as well as a pleasant restaurant in the basement serving refined cuisine.

Tryp Atocha without rest
🅰️ ⚗️ 📺 ♨25/210 VISA 🔵 🅰️🅴 ①
Atocha 83 ⊠ 28012 – Ⓜ Antón Martín – ℰ 91 330 05 00
– tryp.atocha@solmelia.com – Fax 91 420 15 60
– www.trypatocha.solmelia.com   **G3**
150 rm – ♦♦90/150 €, ⊇ 15 €
♦ Business ♦ Chain hotel ♦ Functional ♦
This small palace dating from 1913 offers guests modern, functional facilities. The spacious lounge areas include the glass-adorned "salón de actos" and a superb staircase.

Atlántico without rest
🅰️ ↯ ⚗️ 📺 VISA 🔵 🅰️🅴 ①
Gran Vía 38 ⊠ 28013 – Ⓜ Callao – ℰ 91 522 64 80 – informacion@
hotelatlantico.es – Fax 91 531 02 10 – www.hotelatlantico.es   **F2**
116 rm – ♦100/110 € ♦♦125/140 €, ⊇ 8,50 €
♦ Business ♦ Family ♦ Classic ♦
The comfort in this centrally located mansion has increased following a recent expansion. Harmonious decor in the bedrooms with matching wallpaper and curtains.

Tryp Gran Vía without rest
& 🅰️ ⚗️ 📺 ♨25/50 VISA 🔵 🅰️🅴 ①
Gran Vía 25 ⊠ 28013 – Ⓜ Gran Vía – ℰ 91 522 11 21
– tryp.gran.via@solmelia.com – Fax 91 521 24 24
– www.solmelia.es   **F2**
175 rm – ♦87/118 € ♦♦96/132 €, ⊇ 10 €
♦ Business ♦ Chain hotel ♦ Functional ♦
A landmark hotel frequented by Ernest Hemingway. Facilities here include a small foyer, a good breakfast room and pleasant bedrooms with marble bathrooms.

La Terraza del Casino
🍴 🅰️ ⚗️ VISA 🔵 🅰️🅴 ①
Alcalá 15-3° ⊠ 28014 – Ⓜ Sevilla – ℰ 91 521 87 00
– laterraza@casinodemadrid.es – Fax 91 523 44 36
– www.casinodemadrid.es
closed August, Saturday lunch, Sunday and Bank Holidays   **G2**
Rest 100 € and a la carte 64/98 €
Spec. Tortilla de piel de leche con sémola nitro de aceite de oliva virgen (spring-summer). Tuétano con caviar Beluga y puré de coliflor. Espaldita de cordero confitada a baja temperatura con puré de limón.
♦ Inventive ♦ Formal ♦
In the 19C Madrid Casino building. The lounges have a classy feel and the very attractive terrace is a delightful setting in which to eat.

SPAIN

XXX   Café de Oriente   🔣 ⌖ ⟷4/40 VISA ⓪ AE ⓪

pl. de Oriente 2 ✉ 28013 – Ⓜ Ópera – ℰ 91 541 39 74 – cafeoriente @
grupolezama.com – Fax 91 547 77 07 – www.grupolezama.com   **E2**
Rest a la carte 49/54 €
♦ International ♦ Formal ♦
In front of the Palacio Real with a luxury café and an attractive wine cellar-style
dining room. International menu with a modern twist.

XXX   La Manduca de Azagra   🔣 ⌖ ⟷4/12 VISA ⓪ AE ⓪

Sagasta 14 ✉ 28004 – Ⓜ Alonso Martínez – ℰ 91 591 01 12
– Fax 91 591 01 13
closed August, Sunday and Bank Holidays   **G1**
Rest a la carte 36/45 €
♦ Navarrese specialities ♦ Minimalist ♦
A privileged central location for this spacious restaurant with a minimalist
feel in both its design and lighting. The cuisine here is based on quality
products.

XXX   Moaña   🔣 ⌖ ⟷4/40 ⓟ VISA ⓪ AE ⓪

Hileras 4 ✉ 28013 – Ⓜ Ópera – ℰ 91 548 29 14 – Fax 91 541 65 98
closed Sunday dinner   **F2**
Rest a la carte 39/53 €
♦ Galician specialities ♦ Formal ♦
A comfortable, elegant restaurant in a central and historic area. A busy, popular
bar, various private rooms and a large fish-tank containing a tempting selection
of seafood.

XX   Errota-Zar   🔣 ⌖ ⟷4/20 VISA ⓪ AE ⓪

Jovellanos 3-1° ✉ 28014 – Ⓜ Banco de España – ℰ 91 531 25 64
– errota @ errota-zar.com – Fax 91 531 25 64 – www.errota-zar.com
closed Holy Week, August and Sunday   **G2**
Rest a la carte 34/39 €
♦ Basque ♦ Family ♦
In front of the Zarzuela theatre. The sober but elegant dining room serves Basque
cuisine accompanied by an extensive wine and cigar list. One private room is also
available.

XX   El Asador de Aranda   🔣 ⌖ VISA ⓪ AE ⓪

Preciados 44 ✉ 28013 – Ⓜ Cuzco – ℰ 91 547 21 56 – Fax 91 556 62 02
– www.asadordearanda.com
closed 18 July-8 August and Monday dinner   **F2**
Rest a la carte approx. 28 €
♦ Roast lamb ♦ Rustic ♦
An attractive Castilian restaurant with beautiful wood ceilings. Traditional dishes
and roast meats cooked in a wood fired oven a speciality.

XX   Casa Matías   🔣 ⌖ VISA ⓪ AE ⓪

San Leonardo 12 ✉ 28015 – Ⓜ Plaza de España – ℰ 91 541 76 83
– Fax 91 541 93 70
closed Sunday dinner   **E1**
Rest a la carte 35/45 €
♦ Grills ♦ Rustic ♦
This Basque-style cider-house, adorned with large casks of its trademark brew for
customers to taste, has two spacious rustic-modern rooms, one with an open
grill.

XX   Julián de Tolosa   🔣 ⌖ VISA ⓪ AE ⓪

Cava Baja 18 ✉ 28005 – Ⓜ La Latina – ℰ 91 365 82 10 – Fax 91 366 33 08
closed Sunday dinner   **F3**
Rest a la carte approx. 54 €
♦ Grills ♦ Rustic ♦
A pleasant restaurant in neo-rustic style offering the best T-bone steaks in
the city. The limited menu is more than compensated for by the quality of the
food.

SPAIN

XX **La Ópera de Madrid**　　　　　　　　🔲 📶 _VISA_ 🅾 🅰🅴 ⓪
Amnistía 5 ⊠ 28013 – ⓜ Ópera – ℰ 91 559 50 92 – Fax 91 559 50 92
closed August, Sunday and Monday dinner　　　　　　　　E2
Rest a la carte approx. 35 €
♦ International ♦ Cosy ♦
A good place to start an evening out or to discuss a play seen in the nearby
theatre while enjoying something delicious. Elegant décor and a well-balanced
menu.

XX **Europa Deco** – Hotel Urban　　　　　🔲 🄿 _VISA_ 🅾 🅰🅴 ⓪
Carrera de San Jerónimo 34 ⊠ 28014 – ⓜ Sevilla – ℰ 91 787 77 80
– europadeco@derbyhotels.com – Fax 91 787 77 70
– www.derbyhotels.com　　　　　　　　G2
Rest a la carte approx. 65 €
♦ Inventive ♦ Trendy ♦
The name on everyone's lips, with its innovative design and excellent restaurant,
serving Mediterranean and international fusion cuisine, produced using both
fresh local produce and more exotic ingredients.

XX **El Mentidero de la Villa**　　　　🔲 📶 ⇔8/40 _VISA_ 🅾 🅰🅴 ⓪
Santo Tomé 6 ⊠ 28004 – ⓜ Colón – ℰ 91 308 12 85 – info@
mentiderodelavilla.com – Fax 91 651 34 88 – www.elmentiderodelavilla.com
closed August, Saturday lunch, Sunday and Bank Holidays　　　　G1
Rest a la carte 45/60 €
♦ International ♦ Cosy ♦
A friendly, intimate restaurant with original and tasteful decor. Very carefully
prepared and bold international cuisine.

XX **Posada de la Villa**　　　　　　　🔲 📶 _VISA_ 🅾 🅰🅴 ⓪
Cava Baja 9 ⊠ 28005 – ⓜ La Latina – ℰ 91 366 18 60 – povisa@
posadadelavilla.com – Fax 91 366 18 80 – www.posadadelavilla.com
closed August and Sunday dinner except May　　　　　　　　F3
Rest a la carte 24/38 €
♦ Spanish ♦ Rustic ♦
An old inn with a friendly ambience and Castilian décor. Regional menu and
traditional roasts cooked in a wood fired oven. Madrid-style chickpea stew a
speciality.

XX **Botín**　　　　　　　　　　　　🔲 📶 _VISA_ 🅾 🅰🅴 ⓪
Cuchilleros 17 ⊠ 28005 – ⓜ Puerta del Sol – ℰ 91 366 42 17
– Fax 91 366 84 94 – www.botin.es　　　　　　　　F2
Rest a la carte 30/41 €
♦ Spanish ♦ Rustic ♦
Founded in 1725 and said to be the oldest restaurant in the world. The old-style
décor, traditional wine-cellar and wood fired oven all convey a strong feeling of
the past.

XX **El Landó**　　　　　　　　　　🔲 📶 _VISA_ 🅾 🅰🅴 ⓪
pl. Gabriel Miró 8 ⊠ 28005 – ⓜ La Latina – ℰ 91 366 76 81
– ellandomadrid@hotmail.com – Fax 91 366 25 56
closed Holy Week, August and Sunday　　　　　　　　E3
Rest a la carte approx. 47 €
♦ Spanish ♦ Formal ♦
Near to the Basílica de San Francisco el Grande, this restaurant has a bar, dining
room in the basement, and private room, all classically furnished with a profusion
of wood.

XX **El Rincón de Esteban**　　　　　　🔲 📶 _VISA_ 🅾 🅰🅴 ⓪
Santa Catalina 3 ⊠ 28014 – ⓜ Sevilla – ℰ 91 429 92 89 – Fax 91 365 87 70
closed August and Sunday　　　　　　　　G2
Rest a la carte 40/58 €
♦ Spanish ♦ Family ♦
Frequented by politicians because of its proximity to the Palacio de Congresos.
Intimate and elegant and offering traditional-style dishes.

SPAIN

XX **La Cava del Faraón**   🔳 🎖️ _VISA_ 🅰️🅴 ①
Segovia 8 ⊠ 28005 – Ⓜ Tirso de Molina – 𝒞 91 542 52 54
– Fax 91 457 45 30
closed Monday   E2
Rest (dinner only) a la carte 25/30 €
♦ Egyptian ♦ Exotic ♦
A typical Egyptian setting, with a tea-room, domed ceilings and a dining room
where you can sample the cuisine of the country and enjoy a belly-dancing
performance.

X **La Barraca**   🔳 🎖️ 🔁6/30 _VISA_ 🅰️🅴 ①
Reina 29 ⊠ 28004 – Ⓜ Banco de España – 𝒞 91 532 71 54
– info@labarraca.es – Fax 91 523 82 74 – www.labarraca.es   G2
Rest a la carte 23/40 €
♦ Rice specialities ♦ Rustic ♦
Popular with tourists because of its renown and its location. Traditional
Valencian décor with lots of ceramic tiles. Rice dishes a speciality.

X **Zerain**   🔳 🎖️ 🔁8/24 _VISA_ 🅰️🅴 ①
😊 *Quevedo 3 ⊠ 28014 – Ⓜ Antón Martín – 𝒞 91 429 79 09*
– Fax 91 429 17 20
closed Holy Week, August and Sunday   G3
Rest a la carte approx. 30 €
♦ Basque ♦ Rustic ♦
A Basque cider house with huge barrels. Friendly atmosphere and attractive
décor with pictures of the Basque Country. Traditional cider house menu at
reasonable prices.

X **La Vaca Verónica**   🔳 _VISA_ 🅰️🅴 ①
Moratín 38 ⊠ 28014 – Ⓜ Antón Martín – 𝒞 91 429 78 27
closed Saturday lunch   G3
Rest a la carte 24/32 €
♦ International ♦ Friendly ♦
This delightfully intimate and friendly restaurant is decorated in original style
with colourful paintings, mirrored ceilings and candles on every table.

X **La Bola**   🔳 🎖️
😊 *Bola 5 ⊠ 28013 – Ⓜ Santo Domingo – 𝒞 91 547 69 30*
– labola1870@hotmail.com – Fax 91 541 71 64
– www.labola.es
*closed Saturday dinner and Sunday in Summer, Sunday dinner the rest
of the year*   E2
Rest a la carte approx. 30 €
♦ Spanish ♦ Friendly ♦
A long-established Madrid tavern with the flavour of old Madrid. Traditional
stewed dishes a speciality. Try the meat and chickpea stew.

X **La Esquina del Real**   🔳 🎖️ _VISA_ 🅰️🅴
Amnistía 2 ⊠ 28013 – Ⓜ Ópera – 𝒞 91 559 43 09
closed 15 August-15 September, Saturday lunch and Sunday   E-F2
Rest a la carte 38/42 €
♦ International ♦ Friendly ♦
An intimate and pleasant rustic-style restaurant with stone and brick walls.
Friendly service and French dishes.

Ⓨ **La Botillería**   🏠 🔳 🎖️ _VISA_ 🅰️🅴 ①
pl. de Oriente 4 ⊠ 28013 – Ⓜ Ópera – 𝒞 91 548 46 20
– cafeoriente@grupolezama.com – Fax 91 547 77 07
– www.grupolezama.es   E2
Tapa 3,40 € **Ración** approx. 12 €
♦ Spanish ♦ Tapas bar ♦
In an area that is very lively at night. Traditional Viennese café-style décor
and a wide variety of canapes accompanied by good wines served by the
glass.

655

SPAIN

℉ **Prada a Tope**   AC ॐ VISA ⊙⊙

Príncipe 11 ⊠ 28012 – Ⓜ Sevilla – ℰ 91 429 59 21
closed August, Sunday dinner and Monday   **G2**
Tapa 6 € **Ración** approx. 12 €
♦ Spanish ♦ Tapas bar ♦
A traditional establishment with a bar and rustic-style tables. Wood décor,
photos on the walls and the opportunity to buy various products.

℉ **Taberna de San Bernardo**   AC ॐ VISA ⊙⊙ AE ⊙

San Bernardo 85 ⊠ 28015 – Ⓜ San Bernardo
– ℰ 91 445 41 70   *Plan IV* **K3**
Tapa 2 € **Ración** approx. 7 €
♦ Spanish ♦ Tapas bar ♦
An informal, rustic tavern with three separate sections. Popular house spe-
cialities include two vegetarian dishes - papas con huevo and fritura de
verduras.

℉ **Bocaito**   AC ॐ VISA ⊙⊙ ⊙

Libertad 6 ⊠ 28004 – Ⓜ Chueca – ℰ 91 532 12 19
– bocaito@bocaito.com – Fax 91 522 56 29
– www.bocaito.com
closed August, Saturday lunch and Sunday   **G2**
Tapa 2,40 € **Ración** approx. 9 €
♦ Spanish ♦ Tapas bar ♦
A taurine atmosphere and décor. Ideal for sampling tapas either at the splendid
bar or at a table. Deep fried and egg-based tapas are specialities.

RETIRO and SALAMANCA *(Paseo de la Castellana, Velázquez, Serrano, Goya,*
Príncipe de Vergara, Narváez, Don Ramón de la Cruz)   *Plan III*

🏨🏨🏨🏨 **Ritz**   ⌨ ₤₰ ₺ AC ॐ ₰25/250 VISA ⊙⊙ AE ⊙

pl. de la Lealtad 5 ⊠ 28014 – Ⓜ Banco de España – ℰ 91 701 67 67
– reservations@ritz.es – Fax 91 701 67 76   **I2**
137 rm – †250 € ††480 €, ☲ 30 € – 30 suites
Rest a la carte approx. 100 €
♦ Grand Luxury ♦ Traditional ♦ Classic ♦
A hotel of international renown in a 19C former palace which had diplomatic
connections. Sumptuous décor in the bedrooms and beautiful public areas. The
well-known restaurant has attractive lounges and a pleasant terrace.

🏨🏨🏨🏨 **Villa Magna**   ⌨ ₤₰ AC ▦ ☎ ₰25/400 ⇔ VISA ⊙⊙ AE ⊙

Paseo de la Castellana 22 ⊠ 28046 – Ⓜ Rubén Darío – ℰ 91 587 12 34
– hotel@villamagna.es – Fax 91 431 22 86
– www.madrid.park.hyatt.com   **I1**
164 rm – †275/400 € ††295/455 €, ☲ 26 € – 18 suites
Rest 39 €
Rest *Tsé Yang* a la carte approx. 50 €
♦ Luxury ♦ Classic ♦
Luxury, elegance and décor in the style of Charles IV. Spacious rooms. Le Divellec
restaurant is tasteful and has fine wood furnishings.

🏨🏨🏨🏨 **Wellington**   ☒ AC ॐ ₰25/200 ⇔ VISA ⊙⊙ AE ⊙

Velázquez 8 ⊠ 28001 – Ⓜ Retiro – ℰ 91 575 44 00
– wellington@hotel-wellington.com – Fax 91 576 41 64
– www.hotel-wellington.com   **I2**
259 rm – †250/260 € ††325/335 €, ☲ 20 € – 25 suites
Rest see *Goizeko Wellington* below
♦ Luxury ♦ Classic ♦
In an elegant area of Madrid close to the Retiro. Classic style which has been
updated in public rooms and bedrooms. Bullfighting aficionados meet here
regularly.

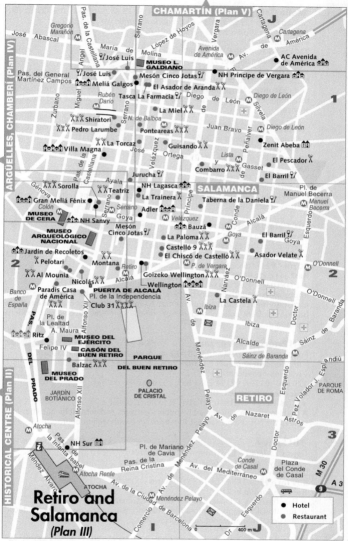

Retiro and Salamanca
(Plan III)

● Hotel
● Restaurant

0 ⸺ 400 m

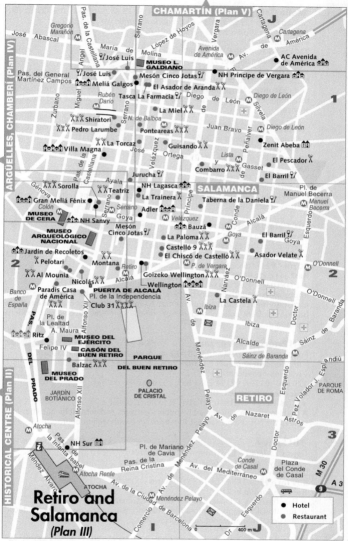

Gran Meliá Fénix   & 🅰️ 🌀 🔟 🛁 25/100 🚗 **VISA** 🅜🅞 AE ①

Hermosilla 2 ✉ *28001* – Ⓜ *Colón* – ☏ *91 431 67 00* – *gran.melia.fenix@*
solmelia.com – *Fax 91 576 06 61* – *www.solmelia.com*   **12**
199 rm – 🛏️*185/365 €,* ⌑ *25 €* – **16 suites** – **Rest** a la carte 49/55 €
◆ Luxury ◆ Chain hotel ◆ Classic ◆
A distinguished hotel. Large public areas such as the elegant foyer with its
cupola. Rooms comfortably furnished.

SPAIN

Meliá Galgos 🔥 🎧 ※ 🖼 🛗 25/300 🅿️ **VISA** 🅜 🅐 ①
Claudio Coello 139 ✉ *28006 –* Ⓜ *Gregorio Marañón –* ☎ *91 562 66 00*
– melia.galgos@solmelia.es – Fax 91 561 76 62
– www.meliagalgos.solmelia.es **I1**
350 rm – ♦100/300 € ♦♦100/380 €, ☲ 17 € – 6 suites
Rest *Diábolo* a la carte 31/50 €
♦ Business ♦ Chain hotel ♦ Functional ♦
Modern but traditional in style and frequented by business travellers
and executives. Large and attractive public areas and bedrooms refurbished
to a high level of comfort. Pleasant décor in the restaurant and excellent
service.

Adler 🎧 ※ 🖼 🕻 🅿️ **VISA** 🅜 🅐 ①
Velázquez 33 ✉ *28001 –* Ⓜ *Velázquez –* ☎ *91 426 32 20*
– hoteladler@iova-sa.com – Fax 91 426 32 21 **I2**
45 rm – ♦352 € ♦♦435 €, ☲ 22 €
Rest a la carte 47/54 €
♦ Luxury ♦ Personalised ♦
An exclusive hotel with an elegant décor. High-quality furnishings and
comfortable and very well-appointed rooms. A pleasant restaurant with a
friendly atmosphere.

AC Palacio del Retiro 🔥 ♿ 🎧 🖼 🕻 🛗 25/40 🅿️ **VISA** 🅜 🅐 ①
Alfonso XII - 14 ✉ *28014 –* Ⓜ *Retiro –* ☎ *91 523 74 60*
– pretiro@ac-hotels.com – Fax 91 523 74 61
– www.ac-hotels.com *Plan II* **H2**
50 rm – ♦217/255 € ♦♦261/307 €, ☲ 26 € – 1 suite
Rest a la carte 41/48 €
♦ Luxury ♦ Personalised ♦
Imposing, early 20th century building. The reception area occupies the former
carriage entrance, and is complemented by an elegant lounge area and excellent
bedrooms. Dark colours and design details combine to create a modern
restaurant.

NH Príncipe de Vergara 🔥 ♿ 🎧 ※ 🛗 25/300 🅿️ **VISA** 🅜 🅐 ①
Príncipe de Vergara 92 ✉ *28006 –* Ⓜ *Av. de América –* ☎ *91 563 26 95*
– nhprincipedevergara@nh-hotels.com – Fax 91 563 72 53
– www.nh-hotels.com **J1**
170 rm – ♦172 € ♦♦194 €, ☲ 18 € – 3 suites
Rest a la carte approx. 40 €
♦ Business ♦ Chain hotel ♦ Functional ♦
A hotel in an area well-served by public transport and with all the facilities and
style of the NH chain. Practical, functional and with well-lit bedrooms.

NH Sanvy 🎧 ※ 🖼 🕻 🛗 25/160 🅿️ **VISA** 🅜 🅐 ①
Goya 3 ✉ *28001 –* Ⓜ *Serrano –* ☎ *91 576 08 00*
– nhsanvy@nh-hotels.com – Fax 91 575 24 43
– www.nh-hotels.com **I2**
139 rm – ♦♦90/183 €, ☲ 18 € – 10 suites
Rest see *Sorolla* below
♦ Business ♦ Chain hotel ♦ Functional ♦
A functional though comfortable building with attractive modern décor.
Professional management and good service.

Bauzá 🔥 ♿ 🎧 ※ 🖼 🛗 25/425 🅿️ **VISA** 🅜 🅐 ①
Goya 79 ✉ *28001 –* Ⓜ *Goya –* ☎ *91 435 75 45 – info@hotelbauza.com*
– Fax 91 431 09 43 – www.hotelbauza.com **J2**
169 rm – ♦97/174 € ♦♦130/240 €, ☲ 13 € – 8 suites
Rest a la carte approx. 38 €
♦ Business ♦ Design ♦
This is the refurbished former Hotel Pintor Goya. Modern facilities and elegant
comfort. A beautiful lounge/library with a fireplace and a light and airy modern
dining room.

SPAIN

AC Avenida de América
AC % M 📞 👬 25/50 ⬅ VISA ⬤ AE ⓘ

Cartagena 83 ⊠ *28028 –* Ⓜ *Av. de América – ℰ 91 724 42 40 – acamerica@
ac-hoteles.com – Fax 91 724 42 41 – www.ac-hotels.com* **J1**
145 rm – 👤70/149 €, � 11 €
Rest (coffee shop) (dinner only)
♦ Business ♦ Chain hotel ♦ Functional ♦
Ideal for business executives and with good communications. Modern and functional and with a coffee shop that is also a bar depending on the time of day.

Jardín de Recoletos
🏠 AC % M 📞 ⬅ VISA ⬤ AE ⓘ

Gil de Santiváñes 4 ⊠ *28001 –* Ⓜ *Serrano – ℰ 91 784 16 40 – Fax 91 781 16 41
– www.vphoteles.com* **I2**
43 rm ⊠ **–** 👤132/199 € 👬140/207 €
Rest 23 €
♦ Business ♦ Classic ♦
A hotel with an attractive façade embellished with balustraded balconies. An
elegant glass-crowned foyer-reception area, large studio-type bedrooms and an
attractive patio-terrace. The walls of the pleasant dining room are adorned with
landscape murals.

NH Lagasca
AC % M 📞 👬25/60 VISA ⬤ AE ⓘ

Lagasca 64 ⊠ *28001 –* Ⓜ *Serrano – ℰ 91 575 46 06 – nhlagasca@
nh-hotels.com – Fax 91 575 16 94 – www.nh-hotels.com* **I2**
100 rm – 👤112/190 € 👬112/195 €, ⊠ 14,50 €
Rest *(closed August, Saturday and Sunday)* 30 €
♦ Business ♦ Chain hotel ♦ Functional ♦
Good and comfortable rooms in a functional hotel where great thought is given
to the needs and comfort of guests. Professional management.

Zenit Abeba
AC % ⬅ VISA ⬤ AE ⓘ

Alcántara 63 ⊠ *28006 –* Ⓜ *Diego de León – ℰ 91 401 16 50 – abeba@
zenithoteles.com – Fax 91 402 75 91 – www.zenithoteles.com* **J1**
90 rm – 👤70/150 € 👬85/200 €, ⊠ 12 €
Rest a la carte 30/37 €
♦ Business ♦ Functional ♦
In the Salamanca district of Madrid. A functional and modern hotel with
refurbished rooms, contemporary furniture and up-to-date bathrooms.

NH Sur without rest
AC % 👬25/30 VISA ⬤ AE ⓘ

Paseo Infanta Isabel 9 ⊠ *28014 –* Ⓜ *Atocha – ℰ 91 539 94 00
– nhsur@nh-hotels.com – Fax 91 467 09 96* **I3**
68 rm – 👤50/138 € 👬50/173 €, ⊠ 13 €
♦ Business ♦ Chain hotel ♦ Functional ♦
A hotel with décor in keeping with modern standards and the small lounge is
complemented by a breakfast room. Comfortable bedrooms.

XXXX ### Club 31
AC % ⇔6/24 VISA ⬤ AE ⓘ

Alcalá 58 ⊠ *28014 –* Ⓜ *Retiro – ℰ 91 531 00 92 – club31@club31.net
– Fax 91 531 00 92 – www.club31.net*
closed August **I2**
Rest a la carte approx. 60 €
♦ International ♦ Formal ♦
A long-established and well-respected restaurant which successfully combines
classical style and modern decor. International cuisine and an excellent wine-list.

XXX ### Combarro
AC % VISA ⬤ AE ⓘ

José Ortega y Gasset 40 ⊠ *28006 –* Ⓜ *Núñez de Balboa – ℰ 91 577 82 72
– combarro@combarro.com – Fax 91 435 95 12*
closed Holy Week, August and Sunday dinner **J1**
Rest a la carte approx. 60 €
♦ Galician specialities ♦ Formal ♦
Large and rather magnificent restaurant with a fish-tank and granite and wood
décor.

SPAIN

XXX **Pedro Larumbe** 🏧 ⌘ VISA 🌑 AE ①

Serrano 61 (2nd floor) ✉ *28006 –* Ⓜ *Rubén Darío – ℰ 91 575 11 12*
– info@larumbe.com – Fax 91 576 60 19
closed Holy Week, 15 days in August, Saturday lunch, Sunday and Bank
Holidays   I1
Rest a la carte 45/60 €
♦ International ♦ Retro ♦
In an elegant palace with three grand dining rooms, each individually decorated with great taste. Interesting menu of dishes elaborated with a creative touch.

XXX **Goizeko Wellington** – Hotel Wellington 🏧 ⌘ VISA 🌑 AE ①

Villanueva 34 ✉ *28001 –* Ⓜ *Retiro – ℰ 91 577 01 38*
– goizeko@goizekowellington.com – Fax 91 555 16 66
– www.hotel-wellington.com
closed 10 to 17 August, Sunday and Saturday in summer   I2
Rest a la carte 64/90 €
♦ Spanish ♦ Minimalist ♦
An exquisite atmosphere characterised by a fusion of the contemporary and traditional. Refined cuisine which mirrors the ambience.

XXX **Sorolla** – Hotel NH Sanvy 🏧 ⌘ VISA 🌑 AE ①

Hermosilla 4 ✉ *28001 –* Ⓜ *Serrano – ℰ 91 576 08 00 – Fax 91 431 83 75*
closed August and Sunday   I2
Rest a la carte 27/46 €
♦ Spanish ♦ Formal ♦
Excellent, traditional-style restaurant with four private rooms. International cuisine plus dishes prepared on a charcoal grill. A fine selection of coffees, teas and cigars.

XXX **Shiratori** 🏧 ⌘ P VISA 🌑 AE ①

Paseo de la Castellana 36 ✉ *28046 –* Ⓜ *Rubén Darío – ℰ 91 577 37 34*
– jarmas@todocep.es – Fax 91 577 44 55
closed Sunday and Bank Holidays   I1
Rest a la carte 44/55 €
♦ Japanese ♦ Exotic ♦
Japanese specialities and elegant traditional atmosphere in a large restaurant. Dishes prepared in front of the diner.

XXX **Balzac** 🏧 ⌘ ⇔6/40 VISA 🌑 AE ①

Moreto 7 ✉ *28014 –* Ⓜ *Banco de España – ℰ 91 420 01 77*
– restaurantebalzac@yahoo.es – Fax 91 429 83 70
closed 1 to 15 August, Saturday lunch and Sunday   I2-3
Rest a la carte 50/64 €
♦ Inventive ♦ Design ♦
An ideal place to rest after visiting the nearby museums. Classic comfortable style with modern and innovative cuisine.

XXX **Ponteareas** 🏧 ⌘ ⇔6/20 P VISA 🌑 AE ①

Claudio Coello 96 ✉ *28006 –* Ⓜ *Núñez de Balboa – ℰ 91 575 58 73*
– Fax 91 431 99 57
closed 20 days in August, Sunday and Bank Holidays   I1
Rest a la carte 39/53 €
♦ Galician specialities ♦ Formal ♦
Traditional Galician dishes in large traditional dining rooms with wood décor and chandeliers. Private bar at the front of the restaurant. Many regular customers.

XXX **Paradis Casa de América** 🍴 🏧 ⌘ ⇔8/17 VISA 🌑 AE ①

Paseo de Recoletos 2 ✉ *28001 –* Ⓜ *Banco de España – ℰ 91 575 45 40*
– casa-america@paradis.es – Fax 91 576 02 15 – www.paradis.es
closed Saturday lunch, Sunday and Bank Holidays   I2
Rest a la carte 36/42 €
♦ Inventive ♦ Trendy ♦
An attractive restaurant with elegant decor inside the Palacio de Linares. A minimalist feel pervades the restaurant, where the emphasis is on innovative cuisine.

XXX **Castelló 9**   AC   ⌘ ⟷10/20 VISA ⓶ AE ①
Castelló 9 ⊠ 28001 – Ⓜ Príncipe de Vergara – ℰ 91 435 00 67
– castello9@castello9.com – Fax 91 435 91 34
closed Holy Week, August, Sunday and Bank Holidays   I2
Rest a la carte approx. 43 €
♦ International ♦ Formal ♦
Classic elegance in the Salamanca district. Intimate dining rooms offering an international à la carte choice plus a tasting menu featuring a variety of shared dishes.

XX **La Paloma**   AC   ⌘ VISA ⓶ AE ①
Jorge Juan 39 ⊠ 28001 – Ⓜ Príncipe de Vergara – ℰ 91 576 86 92
– Fax 91 575 51 41
closed 23 December-2 January, Holy Week, August, Sunday and Bank Holidays   I2
Rest a la carte 39/49 €
♦ International ♦ Trendy ♦
A well-established and successful restaurant with a dining room on two levels and excellent service. An interesting menu and good wine-list.

XX **La Torcaz**   AC   ⌘ VISA ⓶ AE ①
Lagasca 81 ⊠ 28006 – Ⓜ Núñez de Balboa – ℰ 91 575 41 30 – Fax 91 431 83 88
closed Holy Week, August and Sunday   I1
Rest a la carte 34/48 €
♦ International ♦ Formal ♦
A friendly restaurant with a display of different wines near the entrance, a dining room divided into two areas and mirrors on the walls. Excellent service.

XX **Dassa Bassa**   AC   ⌘ VISA AE ①
Villalar 7 ⊠ 28001 – Ⓜ Retiro – ℰ 91 576 73 97 – dassabassa@dassabassa.com
– www.dassabassa.com
closed Holy Week, 21 days in August, Sunday and Monday   Plan II **H2**
Rest a la carte 41/51 €
♦ Inventive ♦ Design ♦
Occupying the former headquarters of a coal merchant, this establishment is expertly managed by its owners. It has a fine lobby and four modern lounges with design details. Creative cooking.

XX **Montana**   AC   ⌘ VISA ⓶ AE ①
Lagasca 5 ⊠ 28001 – Ⓜ Retiro – ℰ 91 435 99 01 – restaurantemontana@
hotmail.com – Fax 91 297 47 40
closed 14 to 25 August and Sunday   I2
Rest a la carte 24/35 €
♦ Spanish ♦ Minimalist ♦
The Retiro's atmosphere is best defined by its wood flooring and minimalist décor. A modern take on traditional cuisine, with an emphasis on presentation and natural products.

XX **Al Mounia**   AC   ⌘ VISA ⓶ AE ①
Recoletos 5 ⊠ 28001 – Ⓜ Banco de España – ℰ 91 435 08 28 – Fax 91 575 01 73
closed Holy Week, Sunday and Monday   I2
Rest a la carte 23/34 €
♦ North African ♦ Exotic ♦
An exotic restaurant near the National Archaeological Museum. Moroccan décor with carved wood, plasterwork and low tables. Traditional Arab dishes.

XX **Teatriz**   AC   ⌘ ⟷10/40 VISA ⓶ AE ①
Hermosilla 15 ⊠ 28001 – Ⓜ Serrano – ℰ 91 577 53 79
– Fax 91 431 69 10   I2
Rest a la carte 30/40 €
♦ International ♦ Design ♦
In the stalls of the former Teatro Beatriz. A tapas bar near the entrance and a dining area and a bar on the stage, all with attractive Modernist décor.

SPAIN

XX **La Miel** 🔠 ½ ⚹ 𝘝𝘐𝘚𝘈 🟠 AE ①
Maldonado 14 ⊠ 28006 – ⓜ Núñez de Balboa – ℰ 91 435 50 45
– manuelcoto@restaurantelamiel.com – www.restaurantelamiel.com
closed August and Sunday **I1**
Rest a la carte 34/42 €
♦ International ♦ Family ♦
A traditional, comfortable restaurant run by the proprietors. Attentive service, a
good menu of international dishes and an impressive wine cellar.

XX **El Chiscón de Castelló** 🔠 ↔6/20 𝘝𝘐𝘚𝘈 🟠 AE
Castelló 3 ⊠ 28001 – ⓜ Príncipe de Vergara – ℰ 91 575 56 62 – Fax 91 575 56 05
closed August, Sunday and Bank Holidays **I2**
Rest a la carte 33/46 €
♦ Spanish ♦ Friendly ♦
Hidden behind the typical façade is a warmly decorated interior that gives it the
feel of a private house, particularly on the first floor. Well-priced traditional
cuisine.

XX **El Asador de Aranda** 🔠 ⚹ 𝘝𝘐𝘚𝘈 🟠 AE ①
Diego de León 9 ⊠ 28006 – ⓜ Núñez de Balboa – ℰ 91 563 02 46
– Fax 91 556 62 02 – www.asadordearanda.com
closed 1 to 28 August and Sunday dinner **I1**
Rest a la carte 28/35 €
♦ Roast lamb ♦ Rustic ♦
Classic Castilian décor and a wood fired oven for roasting meat. The main dining
room, with stained-glass windows, is on the 1st floor.

XX **Nicolás** 🔠 ⚹ ↔4/14 𝘝𝘐𝘚𝘈 🟠 AE ①
Villalar 4 ⊠ 28001 – ⓜ Retiro – ℰ 91 431 77 37 – jam@mail.ddnet.es
– Fax 91 577 86 65
closed Holy Week, August, Sunday and Monday **I2**
Rest a la carte 28/38 €
♦ Spanish ♦ Minimalist ♦
A restaurant with minimalist décor. The traditional menu does not have many
dishes but the quality of the food more than compensates for this.

XX **Guisando** 🔠 ⚹ 𝘝𝘐𝘚𝘈 🟠 AE ①
Núñez de Balboa 75 ⊠ 28006 – ⓜ Núñez de Balboa – ℰ 91 575 10 10
– Fax 91 575 09 00
closed Holy Week, August and Sunday dinner **I1**
Rest a la carte approx. 35 €
♦ Syrian ♦ Formal ♦
Very popular with a younger clientele and very good prices. Bar near the
entrance and also a spacious and light dining room. Different dishes available on
a daily basis.

X **Asador Velate** 🔠 ⚹ 𝘝𝘐𝘚𝘈 🟠 AE ①
Jorge Juan 91 ⊠ 28009 – ⓜ Goya – ℰ 91 435 10 24
– catering@velatecatering.com – Fax 91 435 10 24
closed August and Sunday **J2**
Rest a la carte 33/48 €
♦ Basque ♦ Rustic ♦
A traditional Basque-Navarrese grill-restaurant specialising in grilled hake and
T-bone steaks. Dining areas with décor resembling a farmhouse of the region.
Traditional menu.

X **Pelotari** 🔠 ⚹ ↔15/20 𝘝𝘐𝘚𝘈 🟠 AE ①
Recoletos 3 ⊠ 28001 – ⓜ Colón – ℰ 91 578 24 97 – informacion@
asador-pelotari.com – Fax 91 431 60 04 – www.asador-pelotari.com
closed 15 to 21 August and Sunday **I2**
Rest a la carte 33/43 €
♦ Basque ♦ Rustic ♦
A traditional Basque grill-restaurant which has improved both its service and its
décor which is in the classic style of the Basque region.

SPAIN

La Trainera 🞩 🎴 🖷 VISA ◍◐ AE ◉

Lagasca 60 ⊠ 28001 – Ⓜ Serrano – ℰ 91 576 05 75 – resta @ latrainera.es
– Fax 91 575 06 31 – www.latrainera.es – closed August and Sunday
I2
Rest a la carte 45/70 €
♦ Seafood ♦ Rustic ♦
A fish restaurant which is just about comfortable enough. Simple dining rooms with maritime décor which offer very high quality food. No tablecloths.

El Pescador 🎴 🖷 VISA ◍◐

José Ortega y Gasset 75 ⊠ 28006 – Ⓜ Lista – ℰ 91 402 12 90 – Fax 91 401 30 26
closed Holy Week, August and Sunday
J1
Rest a la carte 50/80 €
♦ Seafood ♦ Rustic ♦
A modest restaurant with simple maritime décor which looks a little outdated. Excellent fish and seafood.

La Castela 🎴 🖷 ⇦12 VISA ◍◐ AE ◉

Doctor Castelo 22 ⊠ 28009 – Ⓜ Ibiza – ℰ 91 574 00 15
closed Holy Week, August and Sunday
J2
Rest a la carte approx. 35 €
♦ Spanish ♦ Formal ♦
An establishment in the tradition of Madrid taverns with a tapas bar and a simple traditional dining room offering traditional dishes.

José Luis 🕱 🎴 🖷 VISA ◍◐ AE ◉

General Oráa 5 ⊠ 28006 – Ⓜ Gregorio Marañón – ℰ 91 561 64 13
– joseluis @ nexo.es
I1
Tapa 1,50 € **Ración** approx. 10 €
♦ Spanish ♦ Tapas bar ♦
A well-known establishment with a wide range of canapés, Basque-style tapas and servings of different dishes in elegant surroundings with traditional décor.

Mesón Cinco Jotas 🕱 🎴 🖷 VISA ◍◐ AE ◉

Puigcerdá ⊠ 28001 – Ⓜ Serrano – ℰ 91 575 41 25 – m5jjorgejuan @ osborne.es
– Fax 91 575 56 35 – www.mesoncincojotas.com
I2
Tapa 2,50 € **Ración** approx. 11 €
♦ Spanish ♦ Tapas bar ♦
Well-known for the high quality of its hams and other fine pork products. A wonderful terrace where you can enjoy well-made and appetising tapas.

Tasca La Farmacia 🎴 🖷 VISA ◍◐ AE

Diego de León 9 ⊠ 28006 – Ⓜ Núñez de Balboa – ℰ 91 564 86 52
– Fax 91 556 62 02 – closed 18 July-14 August and Sunday
I1
Tapa 3 € **Ración** approx. 5 €
♦ Codfish specialities ♦ Tapas bar ♦
A traditional establishment with a beautiful tiled bar. Don't miss the opportunity to try the tapas or larger servings of salt-cod dishes.

Mesón Cinco Jotas 🕱 🎴 🖷 VISA ◍◐ AE ◉

Serrano 118 ⊠ 28006 – Ⓜ Núñez de Balboa – ℰ 91 563 27 10 – m5jserrano @
osborne.es – Fax 91 561 32 84 – www.mesoncincojotas.com
I1
Tapa 2,20 € **Ración** approx. 10,50 €
♦ Spanish ♦ Tapas bar ♦
Good service in a modern establishment with a variety of tapas and larger portions of different dishes. The hams and fine pork products are very good.

El Barril 🎴 VISA ◍◐ AE ◉

Goya 86 ⊠ 28009 – Ⓜ Goya – ℰ 91 578 39 98
closed Sunday dinner
J2
Ración approx. 21 €
♦ Seafood ♦ Tapas bar ♦
A good fish restaurant with a bar and a wide display of fish and seafood. Eat at the bar or enjoy the food in greater comfort in the dining room.

SPAIN

ॷ/ **José Luis** 🕤 AK ℁ *VISA* ⓶ AE ⓵
Serrano 89 ⊠ 28006 – Ⓜ *Gregorio Marañón –* ℰ *91 563 09 58*
– joseluis@nexo.es – Fax 91 563 31 02 I1
Tapa 1,50 € **Ración** approx. 10 €
♦ Spanish ♦ Tapas bar ♦
This was the first bar opened in Madrid by this chain and it is in a very good
location. A wide variety of Basque and traditional-style tapas.

ॷ/ **Taberna de la Daniela** AK ℁ *VISA* ⓶ AE
General Pardiñas 21 ⊠ 28001 – Ⓜ *Goya –* ℰ *91 575 23 29*
– Fax 91 409 07 11 J2
Tapa 3 € **Ración** approx. 6 €
♦ Spanish ♦ Tapas bar ♦
Behind the tiled façade of this typical Madrid tavern are a number of dining
rooms where you can enjoy a range of creative tapas, raciones, stews and fish
dishes.

ॷ/ **El Barril** AK ℁ *VISA* ⓶ AE ⓵
Don Ramón de la Cruz 91 ⊠ 28006 – Ⓜ *Manuel Becerra –* ℰ *91 401 33 05*
– www.elbarrilalcantara.com J1
Ración approx. 21 €
♦ Seafood ♦ Tapas bar ♦
A fish restaurant which is both well-known and popular as much for the service as
for the quality of the food. A bar specialising in different beers near the entrance.

ॷ/ **Jurucha** AK ℁
Ayala 19 ⊠ 28001 – Ⓜ *Serrano –* ℰ *91 575 00 98 – jurucha@telefonica.net*
closed August, Sunday and Bank Holidays I1
Tapa 1,40 € **Ración** approx. 4 €
♦ Spanish ♦ Tapas bar ♦
Delicious Basque-style tapas along with the Spanish omelette and croquettes
have made this bar very popular with anybody enjoying an evening of tapas in
Madrid.

ARGÜELLES *(Princesa, Paseo del Pintor Rosales, Paseo de la Florida,*
Casa de Campo) *Plan IV*

🏨🏨🏨 **Meliá Madrid Princesa** Ⅰ₆ ᵹ AK ぬ25/350
Princesa 27 ⊠ 28008 – Ⓜ *Ventura Rodríguez –* ℰ *91 541 82 00*
– melia.madrid.princesa@solmelia.com – Fax 91 541 19 88 K3
253 rm – 23 suites
Rest
♦ Business ♦ Chain hotel ♦ Modern ♦
This hotel's location and facilities make it ideal for conferences and other group
functions. Politicians, business executives and artists frequent this modern and refurbished hotel. There is a very good restaurant where you can enjoy fine cuisine.

🏨🏨 **Sofitel Madrid Plaza de España** without rest ᵹ AK ▥
Tutor 1 ⊠ 28008 – Ⓜ *Ventura Rodríguez* �📶 *VISA* ⓶ AE ⓵
– ℰ 91 541 98 80 – h1320@accor.com – Fax 91 542 57 36 – www.sofitel.com
97 rm – ☗90/276 € ☗☗90/296 €, � 19 € K3
♦ Business ♦ Chain hotel ♦ Cosy ♦
Well refurbished with high-quality furnishings in the bedrooms and marble
fittings in the bathrooms. A perfect balance of elegance and comfort.

XX **Neo** AK ℁ *VISA* ⓶ AE ⓵
Quintana 30 ⊠ 28008 – Ⓜ *Argüelles –* ℰ *91 540 04 98*
closed August, Saturday lunch, Sunday and Bank Holidays K3
Rest a la carte 35/46 €
♦ Inventive ♦ Minimalist ♦
An attractive minimalist-style restaurant popular with a younger crowd. One
room on two levels with wood floors and numerous design features. Excellent
at-table service.

XX **El Molino de los Porches** 佡 AC 氷 **VISA** ❻ AE ①

Paseo Pintor Rosales 1 ✉ *28008 –* Ⓜ *Ventura Rodríguez – 𝒞 91 548 13 36*
– Fax 91 547 97 61 – **Rest** *a la carte 32/41 € –*

K3

◆ Grills ◆ Rustic ◆

A hotel located in the Parque del Oeste with several lounges and a pleasant glazed-in terrace. The meat produced from the wood fired oven and charcoal grill is delicious.

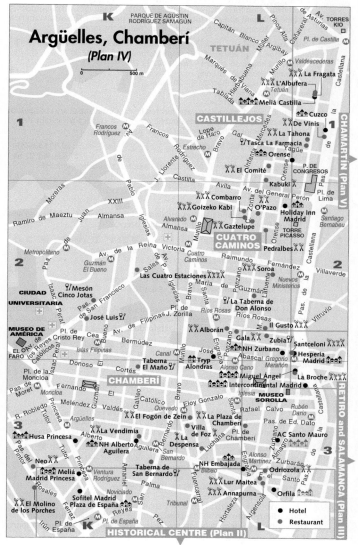

CHAMBERÍ *(San Bernardo, Fuencarral, Alberto Aguilera, Santa Engracia)*   *Plan IV*

AC Santo Mauro   🔊 Ⅰ⚄ 🔲 ⚟ 🅰🅲 ⚟ 📺 ♨ ♨25/50
Zurbano 36 ⊠ 28010 – Ⓜ Alonso Martínez   ⚟ **VISA** ⓜ AE ①
– ✆ 91 319 69 00 – santo-mauro@ac-hotels.com – Fax 91 308 54 77   **L3**
43 rm – ♥♥307 €, � 20 € – 8 suites
Rest *Santo Mauro* a la carte 62/73 €
♦ Palace ♦ Grand Luxury ♦ Classic ♦
A hotel in a beautiful French-style palace with garden situated in a classy district of Madrid. Elegant and with touches of luxury in the rooms. The restaurant is in a beautiful library-room which lends distinction to the food.

Miguel Ángel   🔊 Ⅰ⚄ 🔲 ⚄ 🅰🅲 ⚟ 📺 ♨25/200 ⚟ **VISA** ⓜ AE ①
Miguel Ángel 31 ⊠ 28010 – Ⓜ Gregorio Marañón – ✆ 91 442 00 22
– comercial.hma@oh-es.com – Fax 91 442 53 20
– www.miguelangelhotel.com   **L3**
243 rm – ♥♥160/350 €, ⊑ 24 € – 20 suites
Rest *Arco* a la carte 33/49 €
♦ Luxury ♦ Classic ♦
A prestigious and up-to-date hotel located in the Castellana district of Madrid. Well-appointed rooms and large public areas with classically elegant decor. Superb restaurant with a terrace for the summer months.

Intercontinental Madrid   🔊 Ⅰ⚄ 🅰🅲 📺 ♨ ♨25/450
Paseo de la Castellana 49 ⊠ 28046   ⚟ **VISA** ⓜ AE ①
– Ⓜ Gregorio Marañón – ✆ 91 700 73 00 – madrid@ichotelsgroup.com
– Fax 91 308 54 23 – www.intercontinental.com   **L3**
270 rm – ♥♥199/259 €, ⊑ 28 € – 28 suites
Rest a la carte 50/74 €
♦ Luxury ♦ Classic ♦
Right in the heart of the banking and financial district. Totally refurbished and offering a high level of comfort and elegant décor.

Hesperia Madrid   ⚄ 🅰🅲 📺 ♨ ♨25/300 **VISA** ⓜ AE ①
Paseo de la Castellana 57 ⊠ 28046 – Ⓜ Gregorio Marañón – ✆ 91 210 88 00
– hotel@hesperia-madrid.com – Fax 91 210 88 99
– www.hesperia-madrid.com   **L2**
139 rm – ♥150/325 € ♥♥150/375 €, ⊑ 27 € – 32 suites
Rest see also rest. *Santceloni* below – **Rest** 30 €
♦ Business ♦ Modern ♦
A hotel with modern décor and attractive design. A large lounge and light and airy foyer and reception area and a patio in the middle. Traditional bedrooms. A good dining room with many very tasteful details of décor.

Orfila   🔊 🅰🅲 ⚟ 📺 ♨ ♨25/80 ⚟ **VISA** ⓜ AE ①
Orfila 6 ⊠ 28010 – Ⓜ Alonso Martínez – ✆ 91 702 77 70 – inforeservas@
hotelorfila.com – Fax 91 702 77 72
– www.hotelorfila.com   **L3**
28 rm – ♥310 € ♥♥380 €, ⊑ 25 € – 4 suites
Rest *(closed August)* 80 €
♦ Palace ♦ Luxury ♦ Classic ♦
A hotel in a late 19C palace situated in an exclusive residential zone. A grand atmosphere and rooms with traditional and elegant furnishings. A welcoming dining room and interior garden where you can enjoy the à la carte menu.

NH Zurbano   ⚄ 🅰🅲 📺 ♨ ♨25/180 ⚟ **VISA** ⓜ AE ①
Zurbano 79-81 ⊠ 28003 – Ⓜ Gregorio Marañón – ✆ 91 441 45 00
– nhzurbano@nh-hotels.com – Fax 91 441 32 24
– www.nh-hotels.com   **L2**
255 rm – ♥63/156 € ♥♥63/175 €, ⊑ 19 € – 11 suites
Rest a la carte approx. 38 €
♦ Business ♦ Chain hotel ♦ Functional ♦
A hotel divided into two buildings each with its own facilities. Tasteful décor in a functional style. Regular guests are business travellers and well-known sports teams.

SPAIN

NH Embajada

ĀĶ ⁇ 👪 25/60 *VISA* ⓪ ₳ℰ ⓪

Santa Engracia 5 ✉ 28010 – Ⓜ Alonso Martínez – ℰ 91 594 02 13
– nhembajada@nh-hotels.com – Fax 91 447 33 12

L3

101 rm – 👫 50/168 €, ⊑ 13 €
Rest *(closed August, Saturday and Sunday)* 25 €
♦ Business ♦ Chain hotel ♦ Functional ♦
A hotel with a refurbished interior that leans towards the avant-garde in contrast to the very traditional façade. Contemporary and practical feel.

NH Alberto Aguilera

ᗭ ĀĶ ⁇ 👪 25/100 ⌲ *VISA* ⓪ ₳ℰ ⓪

Alberto Aguilera 18 ✉ 28015 – Ⓜ San Bernardo – ℰ 91 446 09 00
– nhalbertoaguilera@nh-hotels.com – Fax 91 446 09 04

K3

148 rm – 👫 101/166 €, ⊑ 14 € – 5 suites
Rest *(closed August)* 24 €
♦ Business ♦ Chain hotel ♦ Functional ♦
Modern and welcoming although the public areas are limited to a lounge-coffee shop and the dining room. Comfort and well-equipped rooms are the hallmarks of this chain.

Tryp Alondras

ĀĶ ⁇ 🖂 *VISA* ⓪ ₳ℰ ⓪

José Abascal 8 ✉ 28003 – Ⓜ Alonso Cano – ℰ 91 447 40 00 – tryp.alondras@
solmelia.com – Fax 91 593 88 00 – www.solmelia.com

L2

72 rm – 👫 55/146 €, ⊑ 10 €
Rest (coffee shop) (dinner only)
♦ Business ♦ Chain hotel ♦ Classic ♦
A traditional-style hotel with spacious, bright rooms which have all been refurbished. A good foyer-reception with a coffee shop on one side offering a limited menu.

Santceloni – Hotel Hesperia Madrid

ĀĶ ⁇ ⇄ 7/20 *VISA* ⓪ ₳ℰ ⓪

🕸🕸

Paseo de la Castellana 57 ✉ 28046 – Ⓜ Gregorio Marañón – ℰ 91 210 88 40
– santceloni@hesperia-madrid.com – Fax 91 210 88 92
– www.restaurantesantceloni.com
closed Holy Week, August, Saturday lunch,
Sunday and Bank Holidays

L2

Rest a la carte 90/129 €
Spec. Caviar con blinis y crema de cebolla. Jarrete de ternera lechal con puré de patatas. Sorpresas de fruta de la pasión.
♦ Inventive ♦ Minimalist ♦
A restaurant with a modern façade and neo-rustic beams in the entrance. A spacious room with décor in minimalist style and designer tableware. Quite a culinary experience.

La Broche

ĀĶ ⁇ *VISA* ⓪ ₳ℰ ⓪

🕸🕸

Miguel Ángel 29 ✉ 28010 – Ⓜ Gregorio Marañón – ℰ 91 399 34 37
– info@labroche.com – Fax 91 399 37 78 – www.labroche.com
closed Holy Week, August, Saturday and Sunday

L3

Rest 75 € and a la carte 66/84 €
Spec. Fondos de patata confitados con tomate y 'all i oli'. Coca de higado de pato con verduras asadas al horno, al aceite de oliva (spring-summer). Geometria de chocolate y fruta.
♦ Inventive ♦ Minimalist ♦
A spacious restaurant with bare white walls which allow all attention to be focused on the very innovative cuisine.

Las Cuatro Estaciones

ĀĶ ⁇ *VISA* ⓪ ₳ℰ ⓪

General Ibáñez de Íbero 5 ✉ 28003 – Ⓜ Guzmán El Bueno – ℰ 91 553 63 05
– Fax 91 535 05 23
closed August, Saturday lunch and Sunday

K2

Rest a la carte 51/68 €
♦ International ♦ Formal ♦
A classic-style restaurant with a carpeted floor and fibre-optic lighting. The exclusive bar and waiting area lead into a pleasant and intimate dining room.

SPAIN

Il Gusto
XXX   🅐🅒 ✾ ↔4/20 *VISA* 🅜🅒 🅐🅔 ⓞ

Espronceda 27 ⊠ 28003 – Ⓜ *Alonso Cano – ℰ 91 535 39 02 – Fax 91 535 08 61*
– www.grupo-oter.com
closed 6 to 20 August   **L2**
Rest a la carte 38/46 €
♦ Italian ♦ Design ♦
Discover the delicious nuances of Italian cuisine in this modern restaurant with an entrance hall and elegant restaurant, where the decor is a combination of wood and marble.

Annapurna
XXX   🅐🅒 ✾ *VISA* 🅜🅒 🅐🅔 ⓞ

Zurbano 5 ⊠ 28010 – Ⓜ *Alonso Martínez – ℰ 91 319 87 16*
– rteannapurna@yahoo.com – Fax 91 308 32 49
closed Saturday lunch, Sunday and Bank Holidays   **L3**
Rest a la carte approx. 32 €
♦ Indian ♦ Exotic ♦
A spacious restaurant with a private garden. Traditional Hindu decorative motifs and some colourful dishes with all the aromas and sensuousness of India.

Lur Maitea
XXX   🅐🅒 ✾ *VISA* 🅜🅒 🅐🅔 ⓞ

Fernando el Santo 4 ⊠ 28010 – Ⓜ *Alonso Martínez – ℰ 91 308 03 05*
– restaurante@lurmaitea.com – Fax 91 308 62 25
closed August, Sunday and Bank Holidays   **L3**
Rest a la carte approx. 46 €
♦ Basque ♦ Formal ♦
A carriage entrance is the way in to one of the best known places to try Basque cuisine. Traditional, with a large menu and a delicatessen.

Soroa
XXX   🅐🅒 ✾ ↔8/22 *VISA* 🅜🅒 🅐🅔 ⓞ

Modesto Lafuente 88 ⊠ 28003 – Ⓜ *Nuevos Ministerios – ℰ 91 553 17 95*
– soroa@restaurantesoroa.com – Fax 91 553 17 98
– www.restaurantesoroa.com
closed August and Sunday   **L2**
Rest a la carte 39/44 €
♦ Inventive ♦ Trendy ♦
An interesting menu of innovative dishes. Modern décor with a spacious dining room in light shades and a private dining area with wine-cellar décor in the basement.

La Vendimia
XX   🅐🅒 ✾ *VISA* 🅜🅒 🅐🅔 ⓞ

pl. del Conde del Valle de Suchil 7 ⊠ 28015 – Ⓜ *San Bernardo – ℰ 91 445 73 77*
– Fax 91 448 86 72   **K3**
Rest a la carte 32/42 €
♦ Spanish ♦ Formal ♦
A menu offering traditional and Basque dishes in a classic contemporary restaurant. Good service. Regular customers from nearby offices.

El Fogón de Zein
XX   🅐🅒 ✾ *VISA* 🅜🅒 🅐🅔 ⓞ

Cardenal Cisneros 49 ⊠ 28010 – Ⓜ *Bilbao – ℰ 91 593 33 20*
– info@restaurantesoroa.com – Fax 91 591 00 34
– www.elfogondezein.com
closed Sunday   **L3**
Rest a la carte 28/37 €
♦ Inventive ♦ Formal ♦
A highly professional restaurant with a bar near the entrance leading to a small private room and the redecorated dining room, hung with contemporary paintings.

Odriozola
XX   🅐🅒 ✾ ↔4/16 *VISA* 🅜🅒 🅐🅔 ⓞ

Zurbano 13 ⊠ 28010 – Ⓜ *Alonso Martínez – ℰ 91 319 31 50*
– Fax 91 319 12 93
closed Holy Week, 10 to 31 August, Saturday lunch and Sunday   **L3**
Rest a la carte 41/56 €
♦ Basque ♦ Formal ♦
A restaurant with a bar and a pleasant but small dining area. Traditional furnishings, slate floor and a private dining area on the mezzanine.

SPAIN

XX **Gala**   AC ✗ VISA ⬤ AE
Espronceda 14 ✉ 28003 – Ⓜ Ríos Rosas – 𝒸 91 442 22 44
– www.restaurantegala.com
closed 10 to 20 August and Sunday   **L2**
Rest a la carte 33/40 €
♦ International ♦ Design ♦
A pleasant modern restaurant with avant-garde decor which is in contrast
to the wine-cellar-style private dining area. Very popular with a younger
clientele.

XX **Alborán**   AC ✗ ⟨⟩12/32 VISA ⬤ AE ⬤
Ponzano 39-41 ✉ 28003 – Ⓜ Alonso Cano – 𝒸 91 399 21 50
– alboran@alboran-rest.com – Fax 91 399 21 50
– www.alboran-rest.com
closed Sunday dinner   **L2**
Rest a la carte 38/45 €
♦ Spanish ♦ Rustic ♦
A coffee shop with tapas near the entrance and two dining areas with
high-quality furnishings. Decor on a maritime theme with wooden floors and
walls.

XX **La Plaza de Chamberí**   AC ✗ VISA ⬤ AE ⬤
pl. de Chamberí 10 ✉ 28010 – Ⓜ Iglesias – 𝒸 91 446 06 97 – Fax 91 594 21 20
– www.laplazadechamberi.com
closed Sunday   **L3**
Rest a la carte 29/34 €
♦ Spanish ♦ Formal ♦
A restaurant which deserves the success it now has. A private bar and a pleasant
dining room on two levels. A select menu of traditional dishes.

X **Villa de Foz**   AC ✗ VISA ⬤ AE
Gonzalo de Córdoba 10 ✉ 28010 – Ⓜ Bilbao – 𝒸 91 446 89 93
– www.villadefoz.es
closed August and Sunday   **L3**
Rest a la carte 26/35 €
♦ Galician specialities ♦ Trendy ♦
Good traditional Galician cuisine in a modern dining room. The menu is limited
but the food is of very high quality.

X **La Despensa**   AC ✗ VISA ⬤ AE ⬤
😊 *Cardenal Cisneros 6 ✉ 28010 – Ⓜ Bilbao – 𝒸 91 446 17 94*
closed August, Sunday dinner and Monday   **L3**
Rest a la carte 24/30 €
♦ Spanish ♦ Family ♦
A pleasant and friendly restaurant offering simple home cooking at reasonable
prices. An intimate setting, functionally refurbished in classical style.

Y/ **Mesón Cinco Jotas**   🏛 AC ✗ VISA ⬤ AE ⬤
Paseo de San Francisco de Sales 27 ✉ 28003 – Ⓜ Guzmán El Bueno
– 𝒸 91 544 01 89 – m5jsfsales@osborne.es – Fax 91 549 06 51
– www.mesoncincojotas.com   **K2**
Tapa 2,50 € **Ración** approx. 11 €
♦ Spanish ♦ Tapas bar ♦
In the style of this chain with two areas where you can have a single dish or eat
à la carte. Also a variety of tapas, fine hams and pork products.

Y/ **José Luis**   🏛 AC ✗ VISA ⬤ AE ⬤
Paseo de San Francisco de Sales 14 ✉ 28003 – Ⓜ Islas Filipinas
– 𝒸 91 441 20 43 – joseluis@nexo.es   **K2**
Tapa 1,50 € **Ración** approx. 10 €
♦ Spanish ♦ Tapas bar ♦
One of the more simple establishments in this well-known chain. A variety of
Basque-style tapas and larger portions of dishes. Also a terrace.

SPAIN

⏱ Zubia ⏍ 🛂 *VISA* 🐵 🖭 ①
Espronceda 28 ⊠ 28003 – ⓜ Ríos Rosas – ℰ 91 441 04 32 – info@
restaurantezubia.com – Fax 91 441 10 43 – www.restaurantezubia.com
closed Holy Week, 15 August-15 September,
Saturday lunch and Sunday **L2**
Tapa 1,80 € **Ración** approx. 8 €
♦ Spanish ♦ Tapas bar ♦
This professionally run bar is known for its high-quality Basque-style tapas
and raciones. The reasonable menu on offer here is served in two small dining
rooms.

⏱ La Taberna de Don Alonso 🛅 🛂
Alonso Cano 64 ⊠ 28003 – ⓜ Ríos Rosas – ℰ 91 533 52 49
closed Holy Week, August and Sunday dinner **L2**
Tapa 1,90 € **Ración** approx. 10 €
♦ Spanish ♦ Tapas bar ♦
A tavern with a selection of Basque-style tapas and a blackboard listing
tapas prepared to order and larger servings of dishes available. Wine by
the glass.

⏱ Taberna El Maño 🛋 *VISA* 🐵
Vallehermoso 59 ⊠ 28015 – ⓜ Canal – ℰ 91 448 40 35
closed 1 to 8 January, Holy Week, 8 August-8 September,
Sunday dinner and Monday **K3**
Tapa 3 € **Ración** approx. 12 €
♦ Spanish ♦ Tapas bar ♦
A popular bar with a taurine atmosphere with lots of tapas and larger servings of
dishes. Good seafood and ham. Relaxed atmosphere.

CASTILLEJOS and CUATRO CAMINOS *(Paseo de la Castellana, Capitán*
Haya, Orense, Alberto Alcocer, Paseo de la Habana) **Plan IV**

🏨🏨🏨🏨 Meliá Castilla 🍽 ♿ 🛅 🛂 🖭 🏊25/800 🕳 *VISA* 🐵 🖭 ①
Capitán Haya 42 ⊠ 28020 – ⓜ Cuzco – ℰ 91 567 50 00
– melia.castilla@solmelia.com – Fax 91 567 50 51
– www.meliacastilla.solmelia.com **L1**
904 rm – ♥♥120/299 €, � 20 € – 12 suites
Rest see **L'Albufera** and **La Fragata** below
♦ Business ♦ Chain hotel ♦ Modern ♦
An entrance with lots of plants and large and attractive rooms. A large hotel
popular for social functions and conventions.

🏨🏨🏨 Holiday Inn Madrid 🏋 🍽 ♿ 🛅 🛂 🖭 📞 🏊25/400 *VISA* 🐵 🖭 ①
pl. Carlos Trías Beltrán 4 (entrance by Orense 22-24) ⊠ 28020
– ⓜ Santiago Bernabeu – ℰ 91 456 80 00 – Fax 91 456 80 01
– www.holiday-inn.es **L2**
282 rm – ♥♥110/250 €, ⊆ 20 € – 31 suites
Rest *Big Blue* a la carte 30/42 €
♦ Business ♦ Chain hotel ♦ Functional ♦
A good location near the Azca Complex with its many offices and leisure facilities.
A classic foyer, shops and Internet facilities. The Big Blue restaurant has unusual
modern décor and a good menu.

🏨🏨🏨 Orense 🛅 🛂 🖭 📞 🏊25/50 🕳 *VISA* 🐵 🖭 ①
Pedro Teixeira 5 ⊠ 28020 – ⓜ Santiago Bernabeu – ℰ 91 597 15 68
– reservas@hotelorense.com – Fax 91 597 12 95 – www.hotelorense.com
140 rm – ♥180 € ♥♥214 €, ⊆ 12,50 € **L1**
Rest 16 €
♦ Traditional ♦ Cosy ♦
A modern hotel featuring comfortable well-appointed rooms with attractive
décor. Small lounge area but a good range of meeting rooms.

SPAIN

Cuzco 🗗 🕭 🗚 🕸 🖭 📞 🖧 25/450 🕭 **P** 🗷 🐠 🗚 ⓘ
Paseo de la Castellana 133 ⊠ 28046 – **Ⓜ** Cuzco – ℰ 91 556 06 00
– hotelcuzco@mundivia.es – Fax 91 556 03 72 – www.hotelcuzco.net
322 rm – 🛉162 € 🛉🛉203 €, ⊑ 12 € – 8 suites   **L1**
Rest (coffee shop only)
♦ Business ♦ Functional ♦
A traditional hotel a few metres from the Palacio de Congresos. Spacious,
well-maintained bedrooms with somewhat old-fashioned decor. Popular with
business travellers.

L'Albufera – Hotel Meliá Castilla   🗚 🕸 **P** 🗷 🐠 🗚 ⓘ
Capitán Haya 45 ⊠ 28020 – **Ⓜ** Cuzco – ℰ 91 567 51 97
– Fax 91 567 50 51   **L1**
Rest a la carte 38/50 €
♦ Rice specialities ♦ Formal ♦
A restaurant with three attractive dining rooms and another in a conservatory in
a central patio with numerous plants.

Combarro 🗚 🕸 ❖8/17 🗷 🐠 🗚 ⓘ
Reina Mercedes 12 ⊠ 28020 – **Ⓜ** Alvarado – ℰ 91 554 77 84
– combarro@combarro.com – Fax 91 534 25 01
closed Holy Week, August and Sunday dinner   **L2**
Rest a la carte approx. 60 €
♦ Galician specialities ♦ Formal ♦
Galician cuisine based on good quality seafood and fish. Public bar, dining room
on the 1st floor and two more rooms in the basement all in distinguished
traditional style.

La Fragata – Hotel Meliá Castilla   🗚 🕸 **P** 🗷 🐠 🗚 ⓘ
Capitán Haya 45 ⊠ 28020 – **Ⓜ** Cuzco – ℰ 91 567 51 96 – Fax 91 567 50 51
closed August and Bank Holidays   **L1**
Rest a la carte 44/58 €
♦ Spanish ♦ Formal ♦
A separate entrance and an elegant private bar. The dining area surrounds a
central patio with lots of plants. A good traditional menu.

Goizeko Kabi 🗚 🕸 🗷 🐠 🗚 ⓘ
Comandante Zorita 37 ⊠ 28020 – **Ⓜ** Alvarado – ℰ 91 533 01 85
– Fax 91 533 02 14 – www.goizekogaztelupe.com
closed Sunday   **L2**
Rest a la carte 49/58 €
♦ Basque ♦ Formal ♦
A Basque restaurant with prestige in the city. Elegant and comfortable although
the tables are a little close together.

De Vinis 🗚 🕸 ❖8/30 🗷 🐠 🗚 ⓘ
Paseo de la Castellana 123 ⊠ 28046 – **Ⓜ** Cuzco – ℰ 91 556 40 33
– vic.vino@teleline.es – Fax 91 556 08 58
closed 15 days in August, Saturday lunch and Sunday   **L1**
Rest a la carte 41/49 €
♦ Inventive ♦ Minimalist ♦
Modern and intimate dining areas and excellent service. An innovative menu
and a wide selection of wines served by the glass.

La Tahona 🗚 🕸 🗷 🐠 🗚 ⓘ
Capitán Haya 21 (side) ⊠ 28020 – **Ⓜ** Cuzco – ℰ 91 555 04 41 – Fax 91 556 62 02
– www.asadordearanda.com
closed 1 to 28 August and Sunday dinner   **L1**
Rest a la carte approx. 30 €
♦ Roast lamb ♦ Rustic ♦
A bar near the entrance with a wood fired oven and wood ceiling from which lead
off several dining areas. Traditional roast meat accompanied by the house rosé
is delicious.

SPAIN

XX **O'Pazo**   AK ⁶⁄⁄ VISA Ⓜ◎

Reina Mercedes 20 ⊠ 28020 – Ⓜ *Santiago Bernabeu – ℰ 91 553 23 33*
– Fax 91 554 90 72 – closed Holy Week, August and Sunday   L2
Rest a la carte 39/70 €
♦ Seafood ♦ Formal ♦
Although the decor is a little out of date, O'Pazo has a large dining room and a
library-lounge for private meetings. A good choice of fish and seafood always on
display here.

XX **Pedralbes**   🛋 AK ⁶⁄⁄ VISA Ⓜ◎ AE ◎

Basílica 15 ⊠ 28020 – Ⓜ *Nuevos Ministerios – ℰ 91 555 30 27*
– Fax 91 570 95 30 – closed August, Sunday dinner and Monday   L2
Rest a la carte 20/46 €
♦ Catalan cuisine ♦ Cosy ♦
Restaurant with Mediterranean feel with lots of plants and pictures, evoking the
palace after which it is named. Dining areas on three levels and traditional
Catalan cuisine.

XX **Gaztelupe**   AK ⁶⁄⁄ VISA Ⓜ◎ AE ◎

Comandante Zorita 32 ⊠ 28020 – Ⓜ *Alvarado – ℰ 91 534 90 28*
– Fax 91 554 65 66
closed Sunday dinner in July and August and Sunday for rest of year   L2
Rest a la carte 36/47 €
♦ Basque ♦ Friendly ♦
A bar at the entrance, refurbished dining areas with decor in regional style, and two
private rooms in the basement. An extensive menu of traditional Basque dishes.

XX **El Comité**   AK ⁶⁄⁄ VISA Ⓜ◎ AE ◎

pl. de San Amaro 8 ⊠ 28020 – Ⓜ *Santiago Bernabeu – ℰ 91 571 87 11*
– Fax 91 435 43 27 – closed Saturday lunch and Sunday   L1
Rest a la carte 21/38 €
♦ French ♦ Bistro ♦
Restaurant in a welcoming bistro-style, with café-type furniture and lots of old
photos on the walls. French cuisine.

X **Kabuki**   🛋 AK ⁶⁄⁄ VISA Ⓜ◎ AE ◎

av. Presidente Carmona 2 ⊠ 28020 – Ⓜ *Santiago Bernabeu – ℰ 91 417 64 15*
– Fax 91 556 02 32
closed Holy Week, 7 to 27 August, Saturday lunch, Sunday and Bank Holidays
Rest a la carte 46/62 €   L1-2
♦ Japanese ♦ Minimalist ♦
An intimate Japanese restaurant with tasteful, minimalist decor. A modern
terrace, in addition to a bar/kitchen serving popular dishes such as sushi.

Ⴘ⁄ **Tasca La Farmacia**   AK ⁶⁄⁄ VISA Ⓜ◎ AE

Capitán Haya 19 ⊠ 28020 – Ⓜ *Cuzco – ℰ 91 555 81 46 – Fax 91 556 62 02*
closed 8 August-4 September and Sunday   L1
Tapa 2,15 € **Ración** approx. 6 €
♦ Codfish specialities ♦ Tapas bar ♦
A beautiful restaurant with décor of exposed brickwork, tiles, wood and
wonderful stained glass. A wide selection of tapas although cod dishes are the
house speciality.

CHAMARTÍN *(Paseo de la Castellana, Capitán Haya, Orense, Alberto Alcocer, Paseo de la
Habana)*   *Plan V*

🏨 **NH Eurobuilding**   ┠ 🗗 ⚐ ⑁ AK ⁶⁄⁄ 🔧 25/900 🛱 VISA Ⓜ◎ AE ◎

Padre Damián 23 ⊠ 28036 – Ⓜ *Cuzco – ℰ 91 353 73 00*
– nheurobuilding@rh-hoteles.es – Fax 91 345 45 76   M2
421 rm – ♥♥98/223 €, � 19 € – 39 suites
Rest *Magerit (closed August and Sunday)* a la carte approx. 40 €
♦ Business ♦ Chain hotel ♦ Functional ♦
Recently refurbished in keeping with this chain's usual standards of comfort.
Spacious, modern and well-appointed bedrooms plus a variety of meeting areas.
An attractive, high-quality restaurant in welcoming surroundings.

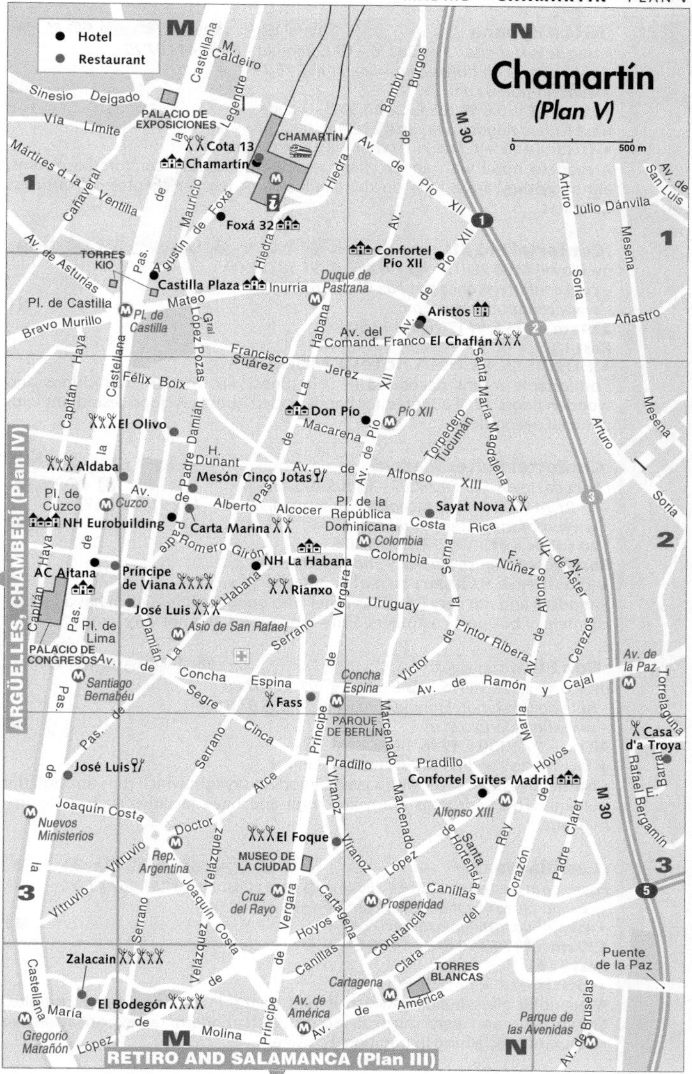
Hotel
Restaurant
M
N
Chamartín
(Plan V)
0
500 m
1
2
3
Sinesio Delgado
Vía Límite
Mártires d. la Ventilla
Cañaveral
PALACIO DE EXPOSICIONES
Castellana
M. Caldeiro
Legendre
Cota 13
Chamartín
CHAMARTÍN
Hiedra
Mauricio
Foxá
Foxá 32
Av. de Pío XII
Bambú
Burgos
M 30
Julio Dánvila
Arturo Soria
Mesena
Av. de San Luis
Añastro
Av. de Asturias
TORRES KIO
Pas. de la Castellana
Agustín de Foxá
Castilla Plaza
Inurria
Duque de Pastrana
Confortel Pío XII
Aristos
El Chaflán
Pl. de Castilla
Bravo Murillo
Pl. de Castilla
Mateo Inurria
Gral López Pozas
Habana
Av. del Comand. Franco
Francisco Suárez
Jerez
Félix Boix
Capitán Haya
Don Pío
Macarena
Pío XII
Torpedero Tucumán
Santa María Magdalena
El Olivo
Padre Damián
H. Dunant
Aldaba
Mesón Cinco Jotas
Av. de Alfonso XIII
Pl. de Cuzco
Cuzco
Av. de Alberto Alcocer
Pl. de la República Dominicana
Sayat Nova
NH Eurobuilding
Carta Marina
Costa Rica
Romero Girón
Colombia
NH La Habana
F. Núñez
Av. de Alfonso XIII
Av. de Aster
AC Aitana
Príncipe de Viana
Rianxo
Uruguay
José Luis
Pas. de La Habana
Vergara
Asio de San Rafael
Serrano
Pintor Ribera
Cerezos
PALACIO DE CONGRESOS
Av. de Concha Espina
Concha Espina
Víctor de la Serna
Av. de Ramón y Cajal
Av. de la Paz
Torrelaguna
Santiago Bernabéu
Segre
Fass
PARQUE DE BERLÍN
Marcenado
María de Molina
Casa d'a Troya
Barral
Rafael Bergamín
Cinca
Príncipe de Vergara
Pradillo
Hoyos
José Luis
Arce
Confortel Suites Madrid
Joaquín Costa
Viranoz
Alfonso XIII
Nuevos Ministerios
Doctor
Vitruvio
Rep. Argentina
Velázquez
El Foque
MUSEO DE LA CIUDAD
López de Hoyos
Santa Hortensia
Corazón de María
Padre Claret
Rey
Cruz del Rayo
Cartagena
Prosperidad
Canillas
Constancia
5
Zalacain
Clara del Rey
TORRES BLANCAS
Puente de la Paz
El Bodegón
Av. de América
Cartagena
Parque de las Avenidas
Av. de Bruselas
Gregorio Marañón
López de Hoyos
Molina
ARGÜELLES, CHAMBERÍ (Plan IV)
RETIRO AND SALAMANCA (Plan III)

AC Aitana

Paseo de la Castellana 152 ✉ 28046 – Ⓜ Cuzco – ☎ 91 458 49 70 – aitana@ac-hotels.com – Fax 91 458 49 71 – **109 rm** – 152/220 €, ☕ 16 € – 2 suites
Rest a la carte approx. 35 € **M2**

◆ Business ◆ Chain hotel ◆ Functional ◆

Completely refurbished and with the latest mod cons. The décor and furnishings are very modern in style and with wood decoration.

SPAIN

NH La Habana   🔠 🕸 📺 📞 🖾 25/250 🚗 *VISA* 🚭 🖭 ⓪
Paseo de la Habana 73 ✉ *28036 –* Ⓜ *Colombia –* 𝒞 *91 443 07 20*
– nhhabana@nh-hotels.com – Fax 91 457 75 79
– www.nh-hotels.com   **M2**
155 rm – 🛏170 € 🛏🛏205 €, ⌦ 14,50 € – 1 suite
Rest *(closed August)* a la carte 23/34 €
♦ Business ♦ Chain hotel ♦ Functional ♦
A modern hotel with an excellent reception and very comfortable rooms,
although they are a little on the small side. A regular clientele of business
travellers.

Confortel Pío XII   🕭 🔠 🕸 📺 📞 🖾 25/350 🚗 *VISA* 🚭 🖭 ⓪
av. Pío XII-77 ✉ *28016 –* Ⓜ *Pio XII –* 𝒞 *91 387 62 00*
– com.confortel@once.es – Fax 91 302 65 22
– www.confortelhoteles.com   **N1**
214 rm – 🛏75 € 🛏🛏170 €, ⌦ 13,50 €
Rest 18 €
♦ Business ♦ Chain hotel ♦ Modern ♦
Comfortable rooms decorated in soft tones with modern furnishings and
wooden floors. Well-adapted for handicapped guests. A good restaurant with
minimal decoration.

Confortel Suites Madrid   🕭 🔠 🕸 📺 📞 🖾 25/350
López de Hoyos 143 ✉ *28002 –* Ⓜ *Alfonso XIII*   🚗 *VISA* 🚭 🖭 ⓪
– 𝒞 *91 744 50 00 – info@confortelsuitesmadrid.com – Fax 91 415 30 73*
– www.confortelsuitesmadrid.com   **N3**
120 suites – 🛏🛏90/155 €, ⌦ 13,50 €
Rest *(closed August, Saturday and Sunday)* 15 €
♦ Business ♦ Chain hotel ♦ Modern ♦
A modern and not very luxurious hotel with good facilities which has a regular
clientele of business customers. Suite-type rooms, but not very large.

Don Pío without rest   🔠 🕸 📺 📞 **P** *VISA* 🚭 🖭
av. Pío XII-25 ✉ *28016 –* Ⓜ *Pio XII –* 𝒞 *91 353 07 80*
– hoteldonpio@hoteldonpio.com – Fax 91 353 07 81
– www.hoteldonpio.com   **N2**
40 rm – 🛏72/130 € 🛏🛏96/144 €, ⌦ 13 €
♦ Business ♦ Traditional ♦ Cosy ♦
An attractive patio foyer with a classic-modern skylight which runs through the
building. The bedrooms are quite large and have facilities such as hydro-
massage.

Castilla Plaza   🔠 🕸 📺 📞 🖾 25/150 🚗 *VISA* 🚭 🖭 ⓪
Paseo de la Castellana 220 ✉ *28046 –* Ⓜ *Plaza Castilla –* 𝒞 *91 567 43 00*
– castilla-plaza@abbahoteles.com – Fax 91 315 54 06
– www.abbacastillaplazahotel.com   **M1**
139 rm – 🛏🛏79/170 €, ⌦ 14,80 €
Rest 22 €
♦ Business ♦ Modern ♦
A beautiful glass building which is part of the Puerta de Europa complex.
Comfortable and very much in accord with modern tastes. An attractive
restaurant specialising in traditional cuisine.

Foxá 32   🔠 🕸 📺 🖾 25/250 🚗 *VISA* 🚭 🖭 ⓪
Agustín de Foxá 32 ✉ *28036 –* Ⓜ *Chamartín –* 𝒞 *91 733 10 60*
– foxa32@foxa.com – Fax 91 314 11 65 – www.foxa.com   **M1**
63 rm – 🛏174 € 🛏🛏195 € – 98 suites, ⌦ 10 €
Rest 15 €
♦ Traditional ♦ Personalised ♦
Although the foyer-reception is on the small side, the hotel's apartment-type
rooms are elegantly decorated and furnished with high-quality antiques. The
restaurant has an attractive covered terrace.

SPAIN

Chamartín   🄰 🕉 📺 🔼 25/500 VISA 🆗 🄰🄴 ①

Agustín de Foxá ✉ 28036 – Ⓜ *Chamartín – ℰ 91 334 49 00*
– chamartin@husa.es – Fax 91 733 02 14
– www.hotelchamartin.com   **M1**
360 rm – ❢84/150 € ❢❢90/180 €, ☲ 11,60 € – 18 suites
Rest see **Cota 13** below
♦ Business ♦ Functional ♦
Situated at Chamartín train station and with a very busy foyer. Functional
bedrooms and some lounges which are used for more than one purpose.

Aristos   🄰 🕉 📺 📞 VISA 🆗 🄰🄴 ①

av. Pío XII-34 ✉ 28016 – Ⓜ *Pio XII – ℰ 91 345 04 50*
– hotelaristos@elchaflan.com – Fax 91 345 10 23
– www.hotelaristos.com   **N1**
22 rm – ❢102 € ❢❢139 €, ☲ 8,75 € – 1 suite
Rest see *El Chaflán* below
♦ Traditional ♦ Functional ♦
A functional hotel with very well-equipped rooms and décor reminiscent of the
1980s. Good management and service.

XXXXX   Zalacain   🄰 🕉 ⇔8/40 VISA 🆗 🄰🄴 ①
💠
Álvarez de Baena 4 ✉ 28006 – Ⓜ *Gregorio Marañón – ℰ 91 561 48 40*
– Fax 91 561 47 32 – www.restaurantezalacain.com
closed Holy Week, August, Saturday lunch, Sunday and Bank Holidays
Rest 86 € and a la carte 51/75 €   **M3**
Spec. Consomé gelée con foie de oca, pichón ahumado y fina crema de boletus
edulis. Rodaballo a la plancha con tomate macerado en finas hierbas y reducción
de vinagre balsámico. Manita de cerdo rellena de cordero a la mostaza en grano
con trio de pimientos asados.
♦ International ♦ Formal ♦
A refined restaurant with traditional and intimate dining rooms and
highly-trained staff. An elegant atmosphere enhanced by decor showing fine
attention to detail.

XXXX   Príncipe de Viana   🄰 🕉 VISA 🆗 🄰🄴 ①

Manuel de Falla 5 ✉ 28036 – Ⓜ *Cuzco – ℰ 91 457 15 49 – principeviana@*
ya.com – Fax 91 457 52 83
closed Holy Week, August, Saturday lunch, Sunday and Bank Holidays
Rest a la carte approx. 63 €   **M2**
♦ Basque ♦ Formal ♦
Well-known restaurant serving Basque-Navarrese inspired cooking. Traditional
dining areas and excellent service.

XXXX   El Bodegón   🄰 🕉 ⇔8/30 VISA 🆗 🄰🄴 ①

Pinar 15 ✉ 28006 – Ⓜ *Gregorio Marañón – ℰ 91 562 88 44 – Fax 91 562 97 25*
closed August, Saturday lunch, Sunday and Bank Holidays   **M3**
Rest a la carte 55/68 €
♦ Spanish ♦ Formal ♦
A rather grand and elegant restaurant with a private bar and a dining room on
various levels with windows overlooking a pleasant garden.

XXX   El Chaflán – Hotel Aristos   🕅 🄰 🕉 VISA 🆗 🄰🄴 ①
💠
av. Pío XII-34 ✉ 28016 – Ⓜ *Pio XII – ℰ 91 350 61 93 – restaurante@*
elchaflan.com – Fax 91 345 10 23 – www.elchaflan.com
closed 15 days in August, Saturday lunch and Sunday   **N1**
Rest 60 € and a la carte 54/71 €
Spec. Alcachofas con vieiras y tuétano con toffe de naranja. Solomillo de atún
rojo, royal de avellanas y tomate provenzal. Buey 'Casin', el lomo a la brasa, migas
trufadas, royal de foie y alcachofas.
♦ Inventive ♦ Minimalist ♦
A restaurant in minimalist style which prides itself on its service. An olive tree has
pride of place in the centre of the room. Interesting and innovative cuisine.

SPAIN

XXX Aldaba
`AC` `⌇` `VISA` `MO` `AE` `O`

av. de Alberto Alcocer 5 ✉ 28036 – Ⓜ Cuzco – ℰ 91 345 21 93
– Fax 91 345 21 93
closed Holy Week, August, Saturday lunch, Sunday and Bank Holidays
Rest a la carte 42/68 € **M2**

♦ Spanish ♦ Friendly ♦

A bar near the entrance from which follows a pleasant dining room in classic-modern style. There are also private rooms. Excellent wine-list.

XXX José Luis
`AC` `⌇` `VISA` `MO` `AE` `O`

Rafael Salgado 11 ✉ 28036 – Ⓜ Santiago Bernabeu – ℰ 91 457 50 36
– joseluis@nexo.es – Fax 91 344 10 46
closed August **M2**
Rest a la carte approx. 50 €

♦ International ♦ Formal ♦

A well-known restaurant in front of the Santiago Bernabeu Stadium. A pleasant dining room with a tapas bar and two glass covered terraces. International and Basque dishes.

XXX El Olivo
`AC` `⌇` `VISA` `MO` `AE` `O`

General Gallegos 1 ✉ 28036 – Ⓜ Cuzco – ℰ 91 359 15 35
– bistrotelolivosl@retemail.es – Fax 91 345 91 83
– www.elolivorestaurante.com
closed 15 to 31 August, Sunday and Monday **M2**
Rest a la carte 40/63 €

♦ International ♦ Friendly ♦

Modern décor in shades of green and attractive decorative details alluding to olive oil. Carefully prepared cosmopolitan and Mediterranean dishes.

XXX El Foque
`AC` `⌇` `VISA` `MO` `O`

Suero de Quiñones 22 ✉ 28002 – Ⓜ Cruz del Rayo – ℰ 91 519 25 72
– restaurante@elfoque.com – Fax 91 561 07 99 – www.elfoque.com
closed Sunday **M3**
Rest a la carte 34/42 €

♦ Codfish specialities ♦ Friendly ♦

An intimate restaurant near the Auditorio Nacional de Música. A dining room on two levels decorated in maritime style. An interesting menu which specialises in cod dishes.

XX Rianxo
`AC` `⌇` `VISA` `MO` `AE` `O`

Oruro 11 ✉ 28016 – Ⓜ Colombia – ℰ 91 457 10 06 – Fax 91 457 22 04
closed 15 August-15 September and Sunday **M2**
Rest a la carte 38/68 €

♦ Galician specialities ♦ Formal ♦

Galician cuisine prepared in the classic way and based more on the quality of ingredients than elaborate preparation. A bar and attractive traditional dining room.

XX Carta Marina
`AC` `⌇` `↔12/40` `VISA` `MO` `AE` `O`

Padre Damián 40 ✉ 28036 – Ⓜ República Dominicana – ℰ 91 458 68 26
– Fax 91 458 68 26
closed August and Sunday **M2**
Rest a la carte 43/57 €

♦ Galician specialities ♦ Formal ♦

A restaurant with wood decor and an attractive private bar. Pleasant dining rooms with terrace. Traditional Galician cooking.

XX Cota 13 – Hotel Chamartín
`AC` `⌇` `VISA` `MO` `AE` `O`

Chamartín railway station ✉ 28036 – Ⓜ Chamartín – ℰ 91 334 49 00
– chamartin@husa.es – Fax 91 733 02 14 – www.hotelchamartin.com
closed August **M1**
Rest a la carte approx. 36 €

♦ International ♦ Retro ♦

A dining room with a ceiling like the roof of an old railway station. Décor in the style of a restaurant-car, circa 1900. Simple international cuisine.

SPAIN

XX **Sayat Nova** 　　　　　　　　　 AC � VISA ⚫⚫ AE ①
Costa Rica 13 ✉ *28016 –* Ⓜ *Colombia –* ℰ *91 350 87 55*
closed Sunday dinner　　　　　　　　　　　　　　　　N2
Rest a la carte 28/36 €
♦ Armenian ♦ Cosy ♦
A good address to discover the gastronomics merits of Armenian cuisine. Two rooms with parquet flooring and decor alluding to the minstrel who gives the restaurant its name.

X **Casa d'a Troya** 　　　　　　　 AC ⚫ ↔16/24 VISA ⚫⚫ AE ①
❀ *Emiliano Barral 14* ✉ *28043 –* Ⓜ *Avenida de la Paz –* ℰ *91 416 44 55*
– Fax 91 416 42 80
closed 24 December-3 January, Holy Week, 15 July-1 September, Sunday and Bank Holidays　　　　　　　　　　　　　　　　N3
Rest a la carte 34/45 €
Spec. Pulpo a la gallega. Merluza a la gallega. Tarta de Santiago.
♦ Galician specialities ♦ Family ♦
A family-run restaurant offering excellent Galician food prepared in a traditionally simple way. A bar-entrance area and traditional furnishings in the dining room.

X **Fass** 　　　　　　　　　　　　 AC ⚫ VISA ⚫⚫ AE ①
Rodríguez Marín 84 ✉ *28002 –* Ⓜ *Concha Espina –* ℰ *91 563 74 47*
– info@fassgrill.com – Fax 91 563 74 53 – www.fassgrill.com　　　M2
Rest a la carte approx. 32 €
♦ German ♦ Rustic ♦
A bar at the front but a separate entrance for the restaurant. Rustic décor with lots of wood in pure Bavarian style. German cuisine.

Ϋ/ **Mesón Cinco Jotas** 　　　　　　　 ⚫ AC ⚫ VISA ⚫⚫ AE ①
Padre Damián 42 ✉ *28036 –* Ⓜ *Cuzco –* ℰ *91 350 31 73*
– m5jpdamian@osborne.es – Fax 91 345 79 51
– www.mesoncincojotas.com　　　　　　　　　　　　M2
Tapa 2,50 € **Ración** approx. 11 €
♦ Spanish ♦ Tapas bar ♦
This establishment belongs to a chain specialising in ham and other pork products. Two attractive eating areas plus a limited choice of set menus.

Ϋ/ **José Luis** 　　　　　　　　　　 AC ⚫ VISA ⚫⚫ AE ①
Paseo de la Habana 4 ✉ *28036 –* Ⓜ *Nuevos Ministerios*
– ℰ 91 562 75 96 – joseluis@nexo.es – Fax 91 562 31 18
– www.joseluis.es　　　　　　　　　　　　　　　　M3
Tapa 1,40 € **Ración** approx. 10 €
♦ Spanish ♦ Tapas bar ♦
Well-known to lovers of tapas. A relaxed and youthful ambience and a good selection of various dishes served in an adjoining room.

PARQUE FERIAL　　　　　　　　　　　　　　　　　*Plan I*

🏨 **Sofitel Madrid Airport** 　　　　 ⚫ & AC ⚫ ☎ ⚫50/120
av. de la Capital de España Madrid 10　　　　　　 ⚫ VISA ⚫⚫ AE ①
✉ *28042 –* Ⓜ *Campo de las Naciones –* ℰ *91 721 00 70*
– h1606@accor-hotels.com – Fax 91 721 05 15
– www.sofitel.com　　　　　　　　　　　　　　　　D1
176 rm – ♦130/280 € ♦♦130/300 €, ⊊ 24 € – 3 suites
Rest *Mare Nostrum (closed 20 December-9 January, 15 July-August, Saturday and Sunday)* a la carte approx. 50 €
♦ Business ♦ Chain hotel ♦ Classic ♦
Near the Recinto Ferial. Fine hall, well-fitted rooms and an attractive dining room styled like a southern patio. Inventive à la carte in the stylish Mare Nostrum restaurant.

SPAIN

Novotel Madrid Campo de las Naciones
Amsterdam 3 ✉ 28042 – Ⓜ Campo de las Naciones – ☎ 91 721 18 18 – h1636@accor-hotels.com – Fax 91 721 11 22 – www.accorhotels.com 25/200 VISA AE **D1**
240 rm – †50/159 € ††50/189 €, ☕ 14 € – 6 suites
Rest *Claravía* a la carte 22/40 €
◆ Business ◆ Chain hotel ◆ Functional ◆
A classic-modern hotel near the Parque Ferial. Sufficiently large public rooms and comfortable bedrooms with functional furniture. A bright dining room with a summer terrace.

AT BARAJAS AIRPORT *Plan I*

Meliá Barajas 25/675 VISA AE
av. de Logroño 305 (A2 and detour to Barajas city: 15km) ✉ 28042 – Ⓜ Barajas – ☎ 91 747 77 00 – reservas.tryp.barajas@solmelia.com – Fax 91 747 87 17 – www.meliabarajas.solmelia.com **D1**
220 rm – †85/199 € ††110/199 €, ☕ 18 € – 9 suites
Rest 28 €
◆ Business ◆ Chain hotel ◆ Classic ◆
Comfortable and traditional with extremely well-equipped rooms and refurbished bathrooms. A number of conference/meeting rooms around the swimming pool and garden. One dining room serves à la carte cuisine, the other food prepared on a charcoal grill.

Tryp Alameda Aeropuerto 25/280 VISA AE
av. de Logroño 100 (A2 and detour to Barajas city: 15km) ✉ 28042 – Ⓜ Barajas – ☎ 91 747 48 00 – tryp.alameda.aeropuerto@solmelia.com – Fax 91 747 89 28 – www.trypalamedaaeropuerto.solmelia.com **D1**
145 rm – †90 € ††180 €, ☕ 15 € – 3 suites
Rest 24 €
◆ Business ◆ Chain hotel ◆ Modern ◆
Bright and comfortable guest rooms furnished in modern style with cherry tones and well-equipped bathrooms. The hotel's lounges and meeting areas are in the process of being refurbished.

Aparthotel Convención Barajas without rest
Noray 10 (A2 detour to Barajas city and industrial zone :10km) ✉ 28042 – Ⓜ Canillejas – ☎ 91 371 74 10 – aparthotel@hotel-convencion.com – Fax 91 371 79 01 – www.hotel-convencion.com 25 VISA AE **D1**
95 suites – †79/144 € ††79/180 €
◆ Business ◆ Functional ◆
Two towers with few areas in common although they have spacious apartment-type bedrooms with a small sitting room and kitchen.

NH Barajas without rest
Catamarán 1 (A2 detour to Barajas city and industrial zone: 10km) ✉ 28042 – ☎ 91 742 02 00 – exbarajas@nh-hoteles.es – Fax 91 741 11 00 **D1**
173 rm
◆ Business ◆ Chain hotel ◆ Functional ◆
This budget hotel, part of the NH chain, offers reasonable comfort and value for money, although its lounges and public areas are somewhat on the small side.

BARCELONA

BARCELONA

Population (est. 2005): 1 449 000 (conurbation 4 062 000) – Altitude: at sea level

R. Mattes/MICHELIN

Barcelona is perhaps the most cosmopolitan of all Spanish cities, combining the traditional and the avant-garde to create an identity which is open and welcoming. Barcelona is not only the capital of an autonomous community but a major Mediterranean port and industrial centre. It is also a Catalan town where Catalan is considered the official language along with Castilian Spanish. Barcelona is a university town and an important cultural centre with an opera house and many museums, theatres and concert halls. It has been the place of residence for many artists – Picasso, Miró, Dalí, Tàpies, the sculptor Subirachs and the architects Gaudí, Josep Lluís Sert, Bofill and Bohigas – and is now a centre for modern art, with cultural and nocturnal attractions which regularly attract millions of visitors.

The city was founded by the Phocaeans, prospered under the Romans and in the 12C became the capital of Catalonia. In the mid 19C, when the ban on building outside its fortifications was lifted, the ramparts were demolished and city spread in an elegant town-planning grid divided by great diagonal avenues. There was a flurry of building on Montjuïc for the International Exhibition in 1929 and another surge of development took place when the Olympic Games were held in Barcelona in 1992.

WHICH DISTRICT TO CHOOSE

For **hotels** the selection is wide and varied. The most charming buildings are situated in the narrow streets of the Old Town, formerly enclosed within the city walls, an attractive location close to the harbour and the lively Barceloneta *Plan II* **H2** and Ribera *Plan II* **G1** districts. The most modern buildings are to be found in the Vila Olimpica *Plan I* **C2**. Many more hotels are located in the streets near the Passeig de Gràcia *Plan II* **E1** and the large avenues of Eixample *Plan II* **E1**, the districts with a formal grid plan of wide streets south and north of the Diagonal in the extended city.

As for **restaurants**, the cuisine of Catalonia in general and of Barcelona in particular is improving constantly;

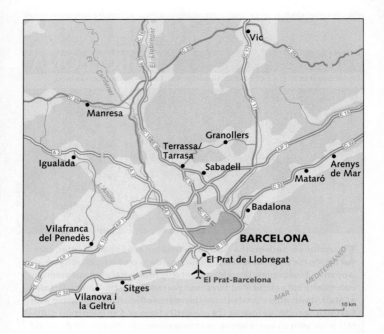

magnificent inventive dishes are often created in restaurants of rare beauty:

early 20C modernist houses and more futuristic architecture.

PRACTICAL INFORMATION

ARRIVAL – DEPARTURE

Barcelona Airport – In El Prat de Llobregat, about 13 km (8 mi) southwest of the city centre. ℘ 932 983 838, www.aena.es

From the airport to the city centre – By **taxi**: €15-€20 + charge for luggage. By **train**: Rodalíes/Cercanías (marked C beside Terminal A) €3 (Mon-Fri), €2.50 (Sat-Sun) every 30min from 5.43am to 10.16pm. Journey time: 30min. By **shuttle bus**: €3; every 15mins from 5.30am to 11pm, via Sants Station, Avenida Roma/Comte d'Urgell, Passeig de Gràcia/Conseil de Cent, Plaça Catalunya. Last stop: Plaça d'Espanya (opposite the Fira de Barcelona).

Railway Station – Estació de França *Plan II* **H1** regional and long-distance services to Paris, Geneva, Zurich and Milan; trains to El Prat Airport. Estació de Sants *Plan III* **I3** Domestic and international services; trains to El Prat Airport. ℘ 902 24 02 02 (information and booking for domestic services) and ℘ 902 24 34 02 (international services); www.renfe.es

TRANSPORT

♦ BUSES AND METRO

The majority of bus services operate 4.30am-11pm. The 6 metro lines operate Mon-Thu and Sun 5am-midnight (2am Fri, Sat and preceding public holidays). Single ticket €1.15; T-1 (1 day) ticket €4.80 to €13.55 (according to the zone), T-10

(10 trips) €6.30 to €27.40 (according to the zone), T-5/30 (50 trips in 30 days) €26.25 to €101 (according to the zone), valid for underground, bus and local trains and available from underground ticket offices, tobacco shops (*estancos*), regional train offices (FGC), Barcelona Metropolitan Transport (TMB) office and in Savings Banks (Caixas). 2-day ticket €8,80; 3-day ticket €12.40, 4-day ticket €16, 5-day ticket €19, monthly ticket €40.75 to €115.40 (according to the zone), valid for underground, bus and regional trains, available from underground ticket offices and Tourist Offices. Information ℰ 93 318 70 74; www.tmb.net

◆ BARCELONA CARD

1-day €17, 2-day €20, 3-day €24, 4-day €27, 5-day €30, valid for travelling on all Barcelona public transport plus discounts (30%-50%) on some museums, art galleries, shops, nightclubs and restaurants, available from Tourist Offices, Savings Banks (*Caixa Catalunya*). ℰ 932 853 832.

◆ TAXIS

The city's black and yellow taxis are not expensive and can be hailed in the street. Minimum pick up charge is €1.65; supplementary charge between 10pm and 6am. It is customary to round up taxi fares. *Radio-Taxi* ℰ 932 250 000; *Servi-Taxi* ℰ 933 300 300; *Taxi-Radio-Móvil* ℰ 933 581 111.

◆ TOURIST BUS

€17 official sightseeing tour (2hrs) with 3 routes (north and south of the city and Forum route) and 42 stops from 9am or 9.30am every 6 to 20min, until 7pm or 8pm according to season Ticket available from the bus and Tourist Offices.

USEFUL ADDRESSES

◆ TOURIST INFORMATION

Barcelona Tourist Information, 17-S Plaza Catalunya *Plan II* **E1** ℰ 906 301 282;

Catalonia Tourist Information, Palau Robert 107 Passeig de Gràcia *Plan III* **K2** ℰ 932 384 000; **Barcelona Airport Tourist Office** ℰ 934 785 000; **Tourist Information** ℰ 901 300 600; **Sants Station** (Hall) ℰ 93 491 44 31; turisme.bcn@bcn.servicom.es, www.gencat.es, www.barcelonaturisme.com, www.catalunyaturisme.com, www.tourspain.es

◆ POST OFFICES

G.P.O., Plaça de Antoni López (at the end of Via Laietana) *Plan II* **G2** Mon-Fri, 8.30am-9pm, Sat 8am-2pm; branch post offices at 282 C. Aragó *Plan III* **K1** and 54 Via Laietana *Plan II* **F2** close at 8.30pm. Opening times 9am to 4-5pm. Stamps can be bought in tobacconists (*estancos*).

◆ BANKS / CURRENCY EXCHANGE

Opening times Mon-Fri 8.30am to 2pm; Sat (Oct to May) 8.30am-12.30pm.

◆ EMERGENCY

Dial ℰ **112**; for National Police: ℰ **091**; for Medical assistance and Ambulance: ℰ **061**.

BUSY PERIODS

It may be difficult to find a room at a reasonable price when special events are held in the city:

Carnival: February – Parades and fireworks.

Sant Medir: 3 March – Festival and procession in Gràcia district.

Sant Jordi: 23 April – St George's Day with bookstalls throughout the city.

Corpus Christi: June – Parades of giants and carnival figures.

Sant Joan: 23 June – St John's Day with bonfires and fireworks at night.

Assumption: 15 August – Gràcia district.

Cardona: 9-13 September – Celebration with bull-centred events.

La Mercè: 24 September – 4-day Patronal festival of Barcelona.

DIFFERENT FACETS OF THE CITY

It is possible to visit the main sights and museums in two to three days.

Barcelona Art ticket: €15. Voucher for 6 museums and art galleries, available from museums, Tourist Offices, Savings Banks (Caixa Catalunya). ℰ 902 101 313 (in Spain), ℰ 93 479 99 20 (from abroad).

Museums and sights are usually open from 10am to 6pm or later according to season. Some close on Mondays; others on Tuesdays.

ARTISTIC CITY – Museu Nacional d'Art de Catalunya *Plan I* **B3**: remarkable Romanesque and Gothic collections from many churches in Catalunya and Aragón. **Fundació Joan Miró** *Plan I* **B3**: over 10 000 exhibits (paintings, sculptures, drawings, collages and other graphic works) housed in a modern building in the artist's native city. **Fundació Antoni Tàpies** *Plan II* **E1**: 300 paintings and sculptures tracing the development of this local artist since 1948, housed in a Modernist building. **Museu d'Art Contemporàni de Barcelona** (MACBA) *Plan II* **E1**: works influenced by Constructivism and Abstract art, creations by experimental artists and names associated with the 1980s. **Drossanes and Museu Maritim** *Plan II* **F3**: Catalan naval history presented in an historic former shipyard building. **Museu Picasso** *Plan II* **G1**: works by Picasso presented in two Gothic palaces.

MODERNIST ARCHITECTURE – La **Sagrada Familia** *Plan III* **L1**: the unfinished church planned by Gaudí in 1883 and continued (1940-81) after his death. **Palau Güell** *Plan II* **F3**: family residence designed by Gaudí in 1889 for his patron and admirer the banker, Eusebi Güell. **Palau de la Música Catalana** *Plan II* **F1**: Barcelona's most important concert hall and the most famous work by Domenech I Montaner with lavish external mosaic decoration and an inverted internal cupola. **Passeig de Gràcia** *Plan II* **E1**: elegant street adorned with wrought-iron street lamps by Pere Falqués (1900) and the finest examples of Modernist architecture in Barcelona. **Park Güell** *Plan I* **B1**: the most famous of Gaudí's undertakings commissioned by Güell. www.rutadelmodernisme.com

OLD TOWN – Gothic City *Plan II* **F2**: a network of streets, square and hidden corners, incorporating the **Cathedral**, many **medieval monuments** and **Roman walls**, on the site of an ancient fortified Roman village. **Santa Maria del Mar** *Plan II* **G2**: fine example of Catalan Gothic, build in the 14C by local sailors.

LOCAL COLOUR – La Rambla *Plan II* **F2**: the most famous street in Barcelona, in five different sections, where a colourful crowd of locals, tourists and down-and-outs strolls along beneath the plane trees at all hours of the day, passing the bird- and flower-sellers and the news-stands which sell papers and magazines in every language. **Plaça Reial** *Plan II* **F2**: vast pedestrian-only square shaded by palm trees and lined with cafés and neo-Classical buildings (19C); central fountain flanked by lamp-posts designed by Gaudí.

GOURMET TREATS

In Barcelona going out for **tapas** (*ir de tapeo*) is as popular as elsewhere in Spain; hundreds of bars throughout the city serve a **tapa** – small portions of a variety of savoury dishes served as appetizers – accompanied by a draught beer (*una caña*) or a small glass of wine or sherry (*una copa de fino*). Barcelona has a long gastronomic tradition, more influenced by France and Italy than other regions. The typical dish is **escudella i carn d'olla**, once eaten on a daily basis but now not so frequent; it consists of two courses *(vuelcos)*: a thin noodle and rice soup and then the vegetables and meat, inlcuding the famous *pilota*, a ball made from minced meat, parsley, breadcrumbs and egg. Other specialities of Barcelona are **fideos a la cazuela** (noodles cooked in an earthenware dish), **habas a la catalana** (broad beans Catalonia style) in which the beans are prepared with herbs and spices and **butifarra** (sausages).

For dessert there is **crema catalana**, similar to **natillas** (a custard covered with a layer of caramel). The most traditional sweets are cakes prepared for various feast days: **pa de pessic** and **coques** for St John's Eve, **panellets**, made from almonds and pine nuts in November and **mel i mató** with cottage cheese.

SHOPPING

Department stores are usually open 10am-8.30pm. Smaller shops and boutiques open 10am-2pm and 5-8pm. The majority of shops close on Sundays.

Between **Plaça Catalunya** *Plan II* **E1** and **C. Portaferrisso** *Plan II* **F2** and along **Av. Portal de l'Angel** *Plan II* **F3**: two department stores and many shops selling fashion, accessories and other articles. **Eixample** *Plan III* **K1**: select fashion and jewellery shops. **Passeig de Gràcia** *Plan II* **E1**: shopping arcades. **Diagonal** *Plan II* **K1**: two department stores and the most famous **designer boutiques** in the city.

MARKETS – **Boquería Market** *Plan II* **F2**: a succession of stalls selling fresh vegetables, meat and fish, as well as bars for a bite to eat or a drink. **Mercat de les Encants** *Plan I* **C2**: a flea market selling all kinds of new, old and even antique articles (Mon, Wed, Fri-Sat, 8am-7pm). **Mercat de Sant Antoni** *Plan III* **J2**: another flea market (Mon, Wed, Fri-Sat, 8am-7pm); on Sunday mornings: old books, collector cards, movie posters and records.

ENTERTAINMENT

The *Guía del Ocio*, a weekly publication containing a list of every cultural event in the city, is on sale at newspaper stands. The city airport and tourist offices supply a full range of booklets and leaflets produced by the Generalitat de Catalunya's Department of Industry, Commerce and Tourism.

Gran Teatre de Liceu *Plan II* **F2** – The opera house, rebuilt in 1994 following a fire.

Palau de la Música Catalana *Plan II* **F1**; **Auditorio** *Plan I* **C2** – Barcelona's biggest concert halls.

Palau Sant Jordi *Plan I* **B3**; **Velódromo de Horta** *Plan I* **C2**; **Plaza de Toros Monumental** *Plan III* **L1**; **Sot del Migdia** *Plan I* **B3** – Venues for major pop and rock concerts.

Plaza de Toros Monumental *Plan III* **L1** – Bullfights on Sunday afternoons; reservations T 934 533 821; Fax 934 516 998 (11am-2pm and 4-8pm); www.torosbarcelona.com; www.mundotoro.com; www.ticketstoro.com; www.tauroentrada.com

NIGHTLIFE

The district south of **Av. Diagonal** between **C. Pau Claris** and **C. Aribau** *Plan III* **K2** abounds in bars, cafés, club and discotheques, which cater to all tastes with a variety of styles of music. There are more nightspots north of **Av. Diagoal**, in **C. Santaló** and around **Plaça Francesc Macià** *Plan III* **J2**. The streets of **C. Aribau** and **C. Muntaner** *Plan III* **J1** are also very lively at night. The district of **Av. de Tibidabo** *Plan I* **B1** *(terminus of the Tramvia blau)* provides a more relaxed environment which is popular in summer. There are several small nightclubs and outdoor cafés in the squares in the **Gràcia** district *Plan III* **K1**. The **Spanish Village** *(Poble Espanyol)* on Montjuïc is a striking and unique location and there is a good selection of bars with music and discotheques in the Olympic Village in **Poble Nou** *Plan I* **D2**.

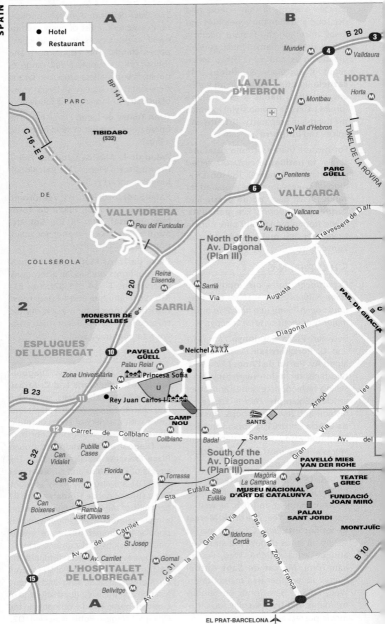

SPAIN

A   **B**

● Hotel
● Restaurant

B 20

B 20   3

Mundet   4   *Valldaura*

**LA VALL
D'HEBRON**   **HORTA**

Horta

Montbau

1

PARC

BP 1417

C 16 - E 9

Vall d'Hebron

TÚNEL DE LA ROVIRA

TIBIDABO
(532)

Penitents   **PARC
GÜELL**

DE

6   **VALLCARCA**

VALLVIDRERA   *Vallcarca*

Peu del Funicular   *Av. Tibidabo*   Travessera de Dalt

North of the
Av. Diagonal
(Plan III)

COLLSEROLA

*Reina
Elisenda*   *Sarrià*   Augusta

B 20   **SARRIÀ**   Via

2   Diagonal   **PAS. DE GRÀCIA**

**MONESTIR DE
PEDRALBES**

**ESPLUGUES
DE LLOBREGAT**   10   **PAVELLÓ
GÜELL**   ● *Neichel*

Palau Reial

Zona Universitària   ▲▲ *Princesa Sofia*

B 23   Av.   U   Aragó   de   les

11   ● *Rey Juan Carlos Hotel* ●

**CAMP
NOU**   SANTS

12   Carret.   de   Collblanc   Via

Collblanc   *Badal*   Sants   Av.   del

C 32   *Pubilla
Cases*   South of the
Av. Diagonal
(Plan III)

*Can
Vidalet*   Gran   **PAVELLÓ MIES
VAN DER ROHE**

3   *Florida*   *Magòria
La Campana*   **TEATRE
GREC**

Can Serra   *Torrassa*   **MUSEU NACIONAL
D'ART DE CATALUNYA**   **FUNDACIÓ
JOAN MIRÓ**

*Can
Boixeres*   *Sta
Eulàlia*   *Sta
Eulàlia*

*Rambla
Just Oliveras*   Sta   Eulàlia   **PALAU
SANT JORDI**   **MONTJUÏC**

Carrilet   Via

del   *St Josep*   Gran

*Ildefons
Cerdà*   Pas. de la Zona Franca

Av.   *Av. Carrilet*   *Gornal*   B 10

15   **L'HOSPITALET
DE LLOBREGAT**   C 31   la

Bellvitge

A   **B**

EL PRAT-BARCELONA ✈

SPAIN

Environs of Barcelona

(Plan I)

0   1 km

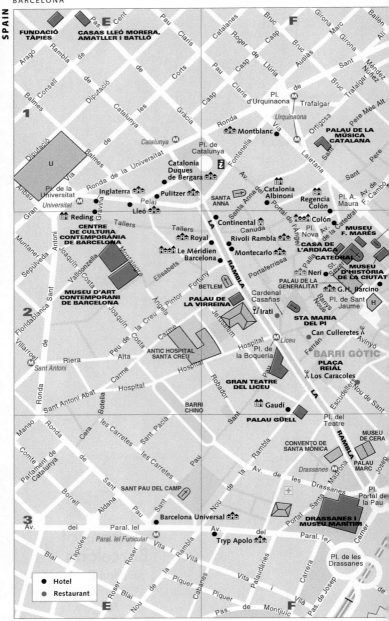

FUNDACIÓ TÀPIES

CASAS LLEÓ MORERA, AMATLLER I BATLLÓ.

E

F

Pl. d'Urquinaona

Urquinaona

Trafalgar

1

Montblanc

PALAU DE LA MÚSICA CATALANA

Pl. de Catalunya

Catalonia Duques de Bergara

Inglaterra

Pulitzer

SANTA ANNA

Catalonia Albinoni

Regencia Colón

Lleó

Reding

Continental

Colón

MUSEU F. MARÉS

CENTRE DE CULTURA CONTEMPORÀNIA DE BARCELONA

Royal

Rivoli Rambla

CASA DE L'ARDIACA

Le Méridien Barcelona

Montecarlo

CATEDRAL

MUSEU D'HISTÒRIA DE LA CIUTAT

PALAU DE LA GENERALITAT

Neri

G.H. Barcino

MUSEU D'ART CONTEMPORANI DE BARCELONA

PALAU DE LA VIRREINA

BETLEM

Cardenal Casañas

Irati

STA MARIA DEL PI

Pl. de Sant Jaume

H

2

Can Culleretes

ANTIC HOSPITAL SANTA CREU

Liceu

Pl. de la Boqueria

BARRI GÒTIC

PLAÇA REIAL

Los Caracoles

GRAN TEATRE DEL LICEU

BARRI CHINO

Gaudí

PALAU GÜELL

Pl. del Teatre

MUSEU DE CERA

CONVENTO DE SANTA MÓNICA

Drassanes

PALAU MARC

SANT PAU DEL CAMP

Pl. Portal de la Pau

3

Barcelona Universal

DRASSANES I MUSEU MARÍTIM

Paral. lel Funicular

Tryp Apolo

Pl. de les Drassanes

E

F

● Hotel
● Restaurant

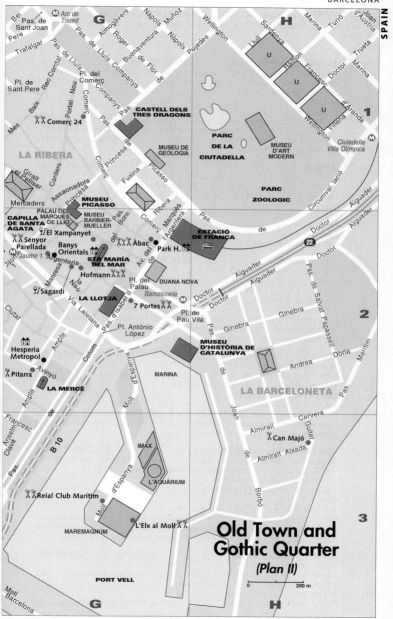

Old Town and Gothic Quarter

(Plan II)

SPAIN

0   200 m

OLD TOWN and the GOTHIC QUARTER *(Ramblas, Pl. de Catalunya, Via Laietana, Pl. St-Jaume, Passeig de Colom, passeig de Joan Borbó Comte de Barcelona)*
Plan II

Le Méridien Barcelona   🚿 AC GB 🛗25/150 ⌚ VISA MO AE ①
La Rambla 111 ⊠ 08002 – Ⓜ Catalunya – ℰ 93 318 62 00 – info.barcelona@
lemeridien.com – Fax 93 301 77 76 – www.lemeridien.com   **F2**
202 rm – ♥♥390 €, ⌚ 24 € – 10 suites
Rest 30 €
♦ Business ♦ Chain hotel ♦ Classic ♦

This elegant, traditional hotel combines local flavour and a cosmopolitan contemporary look in a superb location right on the Ramblas. The patio-style restaurant, partly illuminated by natural light, offers a lunchtime buffet as well as à la carte choices.

Colón   AC GB 🛗25/150 VISA MO AE ①
av. de la Catedral 7 ⊠ 08002 – Ⓜ Jaume I – ℰ 93 301 14 04
– info@hotelcolon.es – Fax 93 317 29 15 – www.hotelcolon.es   **F2**
140 rm – ♥100/160 € ♥♥120/230 €, ⌚ 15 € – 5 suites
Rest 20 €
♦ Traditional ♦ Functional ♦

The Colón enjoys an enviable position opposite the cathedral, enhanced by the pleasant terrace at its entrance. Traditional in style with comfortable, well-appointed rooms. The dining room has a welcoming and intimate feel.

Rivoli Rambla   🍴 ⅃δ 🚿 AC 🍽 GB 🛗25/100 VISA MO AE ①
La Rambla 128 ⊠ 08002 – Ⓜ Catalunya – ℰ 93 481 76 76 – reservas@
rivolihotels.com – Fax 93 317 50 53 – www.rivolihotels.com   **F2**
114 rm – ♥127/222 € ♥♥127/265 €, ⌚ 19 € – 15 suites
Rest a la carte 16/34 €
♦ Business ♦ Design ♦

This historic building has an avant-garde interior embellished with Art Deco touches, elegant bedrooms, plus a terrace offering panoramic views of the city. The restaurant menu offers a range of international dishes.

Royal   🚿 AC 🍽 GB 📞 ⌚ VISA MO AE ①
La Rambla 117 ⊠ 08002 – Ⓜ Catalunya – ℰ 93 301 94 00
– hotelroyal@hroyal.com – Fax 93 317 31 79 – www.hroyal.com   **F2**
108 rm – ♥110/172 € ♥♥120/215 €, ⌚ 13 €
Rest La Poma a la carte 20/47 €
♦ Business ♦ Classic ♦

Located in the liveliest part of the city, the Royal is a pleasant hotel with classic style, attentive service and high levels of comfort. The restaurant, specialising in grilled meats, has a separate entrance.

Catalonia Duques de Bergara   ⅃ AC 🍽 GB 📞
Bergara 11 ⊠ 08002 – Ⓜ Catalunya   🛗25/400 VISA MO AE ①
– ℰ 93 301 51 51 – duques@hoteles-catalonia.es – Fax 93 317 34 42
– www.hoteles-catalonia.com   **E1**
146 rm – ♥143/210 € ♥♥171/242 €, ⌚ 13 € – 2 suites
Rest 20 €
♦ Business ♦ Chain hotel ♦ Functional ♦

Partly occupying an attractive late-19C Modernist building, with an interior that combines a sense of the past with contemporary comfort. The hotel restaurant offers a wide range of fine international cuisine. Swimming pool-solarium.

Montecarlo without rest   AC 🍽 GB 📞 ⌚ VISA MO AE ①
La Rambla 124 ⊠ 08002 – Ⓜ Liceu – ℰ 93 412 04 04 – hotel@
montecarlobcn.com – Fax 93 318 73 23 – www.montecarlobcn.com   **F2**
54 rm – ♥129 € ♥♥192 €, ⌚ 15 € – 1 suite
♦ Traditional ♦ Design ♦

This magnificent hotel, housed in a 19C palace, harmoniously combines the classicism of the past with the modern design features of its exquisitely furnished guestrooms.

SPAIN

Neri 🔲 ⬛ 🔲 📞 VISA 🔲 AE 🔘

Sant Sever 5 ✉ 08002 – Ⓜ Liceu – ☎ 93 304 06 55 – info@hotelneri.com
– Fax 93 304 03 37 – www.hotelneri.com   **F2**
21 rm – 🛏215/270 € 🛏🛏215/359 €, ☲ 18 € – 1 suite
Rest 60 €
♦ Business ♦ Design ♦
A large 18C mansion with a unique and bold avant-garde look just a few yards
from the cathedral. Small library-lounge, superb bedrooms and an intimate
restaurant dominated by two stone arches in which the cuisine is equally
innovative.

Montblanc 🔲 ⬛ ↲ 🔲 🔲 25/450 🚗 VISA 🔲 AE 🔘

Via Laietana 61 ✉ 08003 – Ⓜ Urquinaona – ☎ 93 343 55 55
– montblanc@hcchotels.es – Fax 93 343 55 58 – www.hcchotels.es   **F1**
157 rm – 🛏103 € 🛏🛏119/206 €, ☲ 15 €
Rest 19 €
♦ Traditional ♦ Functional ♦
A hotel in classic yet contemporary style with spacious lounges and an elegant
piano bar. The comfortable bedrooms are modern in style with carpeted floors
and marble bathrooms. The circular dining room offers a choice of Catalan and
international dishes.

Tryp Apolo 🔲 ⬛ 🔲 🔲 25/500 🚗 VISA 🔲 AE 🔘

av. del Paral.lel 57-59 ✉ 08004 – Ⓜ Paral.lel – ☎ 93 343 30 00 – tryp.apolo@
solmelia.com – Fax 93 443 00 59 – www.solmelia.com   **F3**
290 rm ☲ – 🛏🛏193 € – 24 suites
Rest 9 €
♦ Business ♦ Chain hotel ♦ Functional ♦
Friendly and functional and ideal for the business traveller. Lounges fitted with
marble and bedrooms that have recently been refurbished. The bright
restaurant overlooks a garden terrace.

Barcelona Universal ⎰ 🔲 🔲 🔲 🔲 📞

av. del Paral.lel 80 ✉ 08001 – Ⓜ   🔲 25/100 VISA 🔲 AE 🔘
Paral.lel – ☎ 93 567 74 47 – bcnuniversal@nnhotels.es – Fax 93 567 74 40
– www.nnhotels.es   **E3**
164 rm – 🛏100/180 € 🛏🛏100/200 €, ☲ 13,50 € – 3 suites
Rest (dinner only) a la carte 21/30 €
♦ Business ♦ Functional ♦
A new hotel built in modern style with large, well-appointed bedrooms
embellished with wooden floors and well-equipped bathrooms. The panoramic
swimming pool on the roof is an added bonus. Contemporary-style restaurant
adorned with a profusion of wood.

G.H. Barcino without rest 🔲 🔲 VISA 🔲 AE 🔘

Jaume I-6 ✉ 08002 – Ⓜ Jaume I – ☎ 93 302 20 12
– reserve@gargallo-hotels.com – Fax 93 301 42 42
– www.gargallohotels.es   **F2**
53 rm – 🛏118/184 € 🛏🛏138/223 €, ☲ 15 €
♦ Traditional ♦ Classic ♦
Right in the heart of the Gothic Quarter. The hotel's main selling points are the
elegant entrance hall and attractively designed bedrooms, all equipped with
modern bathrooms. Some rooms on the top floor enjoy views of the cathedral
from their terrace.

Inglaterra 🔲 ⬛ 🔲 🔲 📞 🔲 25 VISA 🔲 AE 🔘

Pelai 14 ✉ 08001 – Ⓜ Universitat – ☎ 93 505 11 00 – recepcion@
hotel-inglaterra.com – Fax 93 505 11 09 – www.hotel-inglaterra.com   **E1**
55 rm – 🛏90/180 € 🛏🛏99/200 €, ☲ 12 €
Rest (coffee shop only)
♦ Traditional ♦ Functional ♦
A smart, modern hotel with a classical façade and welcoming feel. Multi-purpose
function areas, plus bedrooms with large wooden headboards. Pleasant
terrace-solarium.

Pulitzer   & 🅰🅲 ⅋ 𝑽𝑰𝑺𝑨 ⑩ 🅰🅴 ⓪

Bergara 8 ⊠ 08002 – Ⓜ *Catalunya –* ℰ *93 481 67 67 – info@hotelpulitzer.es*
– Fax 93 481 64 64 – www.hotelpulitzer.es   **E1**
91 rm – ▪100/255 € ▪▪120/275 €, � 15 €
Rest *(closed Sunday)* (lunch only except Thursday, Friday and Saturday) 20 €
♦ Business ♦ Functional ♦
Modern facilities with a spacious lounge area and café. Functional, comfortable
rooms with wood floors. The restaurant has a contemporary design and looks
out onto a terrace.

Lleó   & 🅰🅲 ⅋ 🄲 ℂ⁾ 🄰25/150 𝑽𝑰𝑺𝑨 ⑩ 🅰🅴

Pelai 22 ⊠ 08001 – Ⓜ *Universitat –* ℰ *93 318 13 12 – reservas@hotel-lleo.es*
– Fax 93 412 26 57 – www.hotel-lleo.es   **E1**
89 rm – ▪115/125 € ▪▪135/160 €, ⊶ 10 €
Rest (coffee shop only)
♦ Family ♦ Personalised ♦
A well-run family hotel with an elegant façade, bedrooms offering adequate
levels of comfort, and a large lounge area.

Catalonia Albinoni without rest   & 🅰🅲 ⅋ 🄲 ℂ⁾ 𝑽𝑰𝑺𝑨 ⑩ 🅰🅴 ⓪

av. Portal de l'Ángel 17 ⊠ 08002 – Ⓜ *Catalunya –* ℰ *93 318 41 41*
– albinoni@hoteles-catalonia.es – Fax 93 301 26 31   **F1**
74 rm – ▪90/185 € ▪▪99/198 €, ⊶ 13 €
♦ Business ♦ Chain hotel ♦ Functional ♦
In the former Rocamora Palace and near the Gothic Quarter. The foyer area has
original decorative details and bedrooms in the style of the period.

Reding   & 🅰🅲 ⅋ 🄲 ℂ⁾ 𝑽𝑰𝑺𝑨 ⑩ 🅰🅴 ⓪

Gravina 5-7 ⊠ 08001 – Ⓜ *Universitat –* ℰ *93 412 10 97 – reding@*
occidental-hoteles.com – Fax 93 268 34 82 – www.hotelreding.com
44 rm – ▪120/200 € ▪▪138/200 €, ⊶ 11,50 €   **E1-2**
Rest *(closed Sunday and Bank Holidays)* 10 €
♦ Traditional ♦ Functional ♦
Located close to Plaça de Catalunya. Despite being on the small side, the lounge
areas and bedrooms are comfortable and well-equipped. The hotel's dining
room offers a menu featuring traditional and Catalan dishes.

Banys Orientals   & 🅰🅲 ⅋ 🄲 𝑽𝑰𝑺𝑨 ⑩ 🅰🅴 ⓪

L'Argenteria 37 ⊠ 08003 – Ⓜ *Jaume I –* ℰ *93 268 84 60 – reservas@*
hotelbanysorientals.com – Fax 93 268 84 61 – www.hotelbanysorientals.com
43 rm – ▪80 € ▪▪95 €, ⊶ 10 €   **G2**
Rest see *Senyor Parellada* below
♦ Business ♦ Design ♦
Comfortable minimalist rooms with design features galore, wooden floors and
four-poster-style beds. No lounge area.

Park H. without rest   & 🅰🅲 ⅋ 🄲 ℂ⁾ 𝑽𝑰𝑺𝑨 ⑩ 🅰🅴 ⓪

av. Marquès de l'Argentera 11 ⊠ 08003 – Ⓜ *Barceloneta –* ℰ *93 319 60 00*
– parkhotel@parkhotelbarcelona.com – Fax 93 319 45 19
– www.parkhotelbarcelona.com   **G2**
91 rm ⊶ – ▪97/117 € ▪▪120/155 €
♦ Traditional ♦ Modern ♦
A modern, avant-garde feel permeates this well-maintained hotel with a friendly
atmosphere and large breakfast room. Pleasant entrance-cum-reception area
with adjoining bar.

Gaudí   🄵& 🅰🅲 ⅋ 🄲 🄰25 ⌂ 𝑽𝑰𝑺𝑨 ⑩ 🅰🅴 ⓪

Nou de la Rambla 12 ⊠ 08001 – Ⓜ *Liceu –* ℰ *93 317 90 32*
– gaudi@hotelgaudi.es – Fax 93 412 26 36 – www.hotelgaudi.es   **F2**
73 rm – ▪80/120 € ▪▪100/160 €, ⊶ 10 €
Rest (coffee shop only)
♦ Family ♦ Functional ♦
The Gaudí's main features are its Modernist fountain in the foyer and an
attractive cafeteria. The hotel's bedrooms, some with balcony, are gradually
being refurbished.

SPAIN

🏨 **Regencia Colón** without rest　　　　ⓐ 🖼 𝐕𝐈𝐒𝐀 ⑩ 🆎 ①
Sagristans 13 ⊠ *08002 –* Ⓜ *Jaume I –* ℰ *93 318 98 58 – info@
hotelregenciacolon.com – Fax 93 317 28 22 – www.hotelregenciacolon.com*
50 rm – †50/130 € ††60/160 €, ⊑ 10 €　　　　　　　　　F1-2
♦ Traditional ♦ Functional ♦
A great base from which to explore one of the city's most distinctive districts.
Functional bedrooms with modern bathrooms and wood flooring.

🏨 **Hesperia Metropol** without rest　　　　&. ⓐ ⅗ 𝐕𝐈𝐒𝐀 ⑩ 🆎 ①
Ample 31 ⊠ *08002 –* Ⓜ *Jaume I –* ℰ *93 310 51 00
– hotel@hesperia-metropol.com – Fax 93 319 12 76*　　　　G2
68 rm – †105/150 € ††120/165 €, ⊑ 10 €
♦ Business ♦ Chain hotel ♦ Functional ♦
Situated in the old town with comfortable and well-decorated rooms. Friendly
atmosphere and pleasant staff.

🏠 **Continental** without rest　　　　ⓐ 🖼 𝐕𝐈𝐒𝐀 ⑩ 🆎 ①
Rambles 138-2° ⊠ *08002 –* Ⓜ *Catalunya –* ℰ *93 301 25 70 – barcelona@
hotelcontinental.com – Fax 93 302 73 60 – www.hotelcontinental.com*
35 rm ⊑ *–* †75 € ††100 €　　　　　　　　　　　　F2
♦ Family ♦ Personalised ♦
Friendly hotel located close to the Plaza Catalunya square which gets much of its
character from the bedrooms which are furnished in an English style.

✗✗✗ **Àbac**　　　　ⓐ ⅗ ⟲10/14 🅿 𝐕𝐈𝐒𝐀 ⑩ 🆎 ①
⚘ *(possible transfer to av. del Tibidabo 7), Rec 79-89* ⊠ *08003 –* Ⓜ *Barceloneta
– ℰ 93 319 66 00 – abac12@telefonica.net – Fax 93 319 45 19
closed 6 to 13 January, 3 weeks in August, Sunday and Monday lunch*
Rest 84 € and a la carte 63/85 €　　　　　　　　　　G2
Spec. Vieiras con caviar, hierbas y lima. Esturión del Valle de Arán caramelizado,
emulsión de setas. Cabrito confitado a 72° y lacado.
♦ Inventive ♦ Minimalist ♦
Modern restaurant with minimalist design details. Excellent service and creative
Mediterranean cuisine. Popular with a young clientele.

✗✗✗ **Hofmann**　　　　ⓐ ⅗ ⟲6/20 𝐕𝐈𝐒𝐀 ⑩ 🆎 ①
⚘ *L'Argenteria 74-78 (1°)* ⊠ *08003 –* Ⓜ *Jaume I –* ℰ *93 319 58 89 – hofmann@
ysi.es – Fax 93 319 58 82 – www.hofmann-bcn.com
closed Christmas, Holy Week, August, Saturday and Sunday*　　　G2
Rest a la carte 47/64 €
Spec. Nuestra tradicional tarta de sardinas con tomate y cebollitas nuevas en
caliente. Farcellets de acelgas rellenos de mascarpone, piñones y pasas con
crujiente de panceta. Tarta cremosa caramelizada, helado y chupito de Chivas
12 años, crujiente de café.
♦ Inventive ♦ Design ♦
Housed in an old building which doubles as a catering school, the Hofmann is
known for its classical design and innovative, imaginatively presented cuisine.

✗✗ **Reial Club Marítim**　　　　≤ �おります ⓐ ⅗ 𝐕𝐈𝐒𝐀 ⑩ 🆎 ①
Moll d'Espanya ⊠ *08039 –* Ⓜ *Drassanes –* ℰ *93 221 71 43 – Fax 93 221 44 12
closed August, Sunday dinner and Monday*　　　　　　　G3
Rest a la carte 28/42 €
♦ International ♦ Formal ♦
A large, attractively laid out dining room with wonderful views of the marina
through the extensive windows. The culinary emphasis here is on the traditional.

✗✗ **Senyor Parellada** – Hotel Banys Orientals　　ⓐ ⅗ 𝐕𝐈𝐒𝐀 ⑩ 🆎
L'Argenteria 37 ⊠ *08003 –* Ⓜ *Jaume I –* ℰ *93 310 50 94
– fondaparellada@hotmail.com – Fax 93 268 31 57*　　　　G2
Rest a la carte 12/25 €
♦ Catalan cuisine ♦ Cosy ♦
A pleasant restaurant with classic-contemporary decor, bar and several
attractive dining rooms. The small central patio, crowned by a glass roof, is
worthy of particular note.

XX **7 Portes**   AK ✗ *VISA* ✱ AE ①
Passeig d'Isabel II-14 ✉ *08003 –* ⓜ *Barceloneta –* ✆ *93 319 30 33*
– reservas@7portes.com – Fax 93 319 30 46   **G2**
Rest a la carte 24/41 €
♦ Catalan cuisine ♦ Retro ♦
A venerable Barcelona institution dating back to 1836, whose dining areas retain their old-fashioned feel. The traditional menu is strong on fish, seafood and rice dishes.

XX **Comerç 24**   ✗ *VISA* AE
Comerç 24 ✉ *08003 –* ⓜ *Arc de Triomf –* ✆ *93 319 21 02*
– info@comerc24.com – Fax 93 319 10 74
– www.comerc24.com
closed 15 days at Christmas, 15 Days in August, Sunday and Monday   **G1**
Rest a la carte 25/30 €
♦ Inventive ♦ Design ♦
A modern restaurant with avant-garde décor offering different menus of creative cuisine. Popular with a younger clientele.

XX **L'Elx al Moll**   ← 🍽 AK *VISA* ✱ AE ①
Moll d'Espanya-Maremagnum (Local 9) ✉ *08039*
– ⓜ *Drassanes –* ✆ *93 225 81 17 – Fax 93 225 81 20*
– www.restauratelx.com   **G3**
Rest a la carte 17/30 €
♦ Rice specialities ♦ Formal ♦
A restaurant with impressive views of the marina, a modern-rustic dining room and pleasant covered terrace. Popular for its fish, seafood and good choice of rice-based dishes.

X **Pitarra**   AK ✧12/30 *VISA* ✱ AE ①
Avinyó 56 ✉ *08002 –* ⓜ *Liceu –* ✆ *93 301 16 47 – Fax 93 301 85 62*
– www.pitarra.com
closed August, Sunday and dinner Bank Holidays   **G2**
Rest a la carte 20/41 €
♦ Catalan cuisine ♦ Cosy ♦
A pleasant and welcoming interior adorned with old clocks and mementoes of the poet Pitarra. The comprehensive, moderately priced menu is strong on traditional cuisine.

X **Can Culleretes**   AK *VISA* ✱
Quintana 5 ✉ *08002 –* ⓜ *Liceu –* ✆ *93 317 64 85 – info@culleretes.com*
– Fax 93 412 59 92 – www.culleretes.com
closed July, Sunday dinner and Monday   **F2**
Rest a la carte 16/28 €
♦ Catalan cuisine ♦ Friendly ♦
A family-run restaurant dating back to 1786. Traditional décor with beams and lots of paintings, creating a welcoming atmosphere.

X **Los Caracoles**   AK ✗ ✧10/20 *VISA* ✱ AE ①
Escudellers 14 ✉ *08002 –* ⓜ *Liceu –* ✆ *93 302 31 85 – caracoles@versin.com*
– Fax 93 302 07 43   **F2**
Rest a la carte 29/40 €
♦ Catalan cuisine ♦ Retro ♦
Established in 1835, this typically rustic restaurant in the city's old quarter has retained all its old charm. Interesting menu and as popular as ever.

X **Can Majó**   🍽 AK ✗ *VISA* ✱ AE ①
Almirall Aixada 23 ✉ *08003 –* ⓜ *Barceloneta –* ✆ *93 221 54 55*
– majocan@terra.es – Fax 93 221 54 55
closed Sunday dinner and Monday   **H3**
Rest a la carte 32/40 €
♦ Seafood ♦ Family ♦
This popular, family-run restaurant is renowned for its impressive fish and seafood menu. Attractive seafood counter plus a panoramic terrace.

¶/ **Sagardi** 🏠 AK ⚑ **VISA** 🅮🅒 AE ①
L'Argenteria 62 ✉ 08003 – ⓜ Jaume I – ℰ 93 319 99 93 – sagardi@sagardi.es
– Fax 93 268 48 86 – www.sagardi.com **G2**
Tapa 1,30 € **Ración** approx. 10 €
♦ Basque ♦ Tapas bar ♦
A Basque cider house situated near the historic church of Santa María del Mar. A
very wide range of Basque-style tapas and dining room with cider barrels and
charcoal grill.

¶/ **Irati** AK ⚑ **VISA** 🅮🅒 AE ①
Cardenal Casanyes 17 ✉ 08002 – ⓜ Liceu – ℰ 93 302 30 84
– sagardi@sagardi.es – Fax 93 412 73 76 **F2**
Tapa 1,50 €
♦ Basque ♦ Tapas bar ♦
This traditional-style Basque tavern close to the Liceo theatre offers a good
choice of typical Basque dishes with an innovative touch.

¶/ **El Xampanyet** **VISA** 🅮🅒
Montcada 22 ✉ 08003 – ⓜ Jaume I – ℰ 93 319 70 03
closed Holy Week, August, Sunday dinner and Monday **G2**
Tapa 3 € **Ración** approx. 7 €
♦ Spanish ♦ Tapas bar ♦
This well-established family-run tavern is attractively adorned with typical azu-
lejo panelling. A varied selection of tapas, with the emphasis on fish and meat.

SOUTH of AV. DIAGONAL (Gran Via de les Corts Catalanes, Passeig de Gràcia,
Balmes, Muntaner, Aragó) **Plan III**

🏨🏨🏨🏨 **Rey Juan Carlos I** ⑤ ⟨ 🏠 ⅙ ⌁ (heated) ⊠ ⏛ ⅙ AK ⚑ 🖂 ☏
av. Diagonal 661 ✉ 08028 – ⓜ ⑭ 25/1000 ⟨ P **VISA** 🅮🅒 AE ①
Zona Universitaria – ℰ 93 364 40 40 – hotel@hrjuancarlos.com
– Fax 93 364 42 32 – www.hrjuancarlos.com Plan I **A2**
375 rm – ♦280/315 € ♦♦350/420 €, ☑ 19 € – 37 suites
Rest The Garden (closed August, Sunday and Monday) a la carte approx. 70 €
Rest Café Polo (buffet) a la carte approx. 31 €
Rest Tati (closed August, Sunday and Monday) a la carte approx. 60 €
♦ Luxury ♦ Business ♦ Modern ♦
A hotel with impressive modern facilities surrounded by an area of parkland with
a small lake and swimming pool. An exclusive atmosphere pervades this hotel,
which is tastefully decorated throughout. The Garden restaurant has a pleasant
terrace.

🏨🏨🏨 **Claris** ⑤ 🏠 ⅙ ⌁ AK 🖂 ☏ ⑭ 25/120 ⟨ **VISA** 🅮🅒 AE ①
Pau Claris 150 ✉ 08009 – ⓜ Passeig de Gràcia – ℰ 93 487 62 62
– claris@derbyhotels.es – Fax 93 215 79 70 – www.derbyhotels.com **K2**
80 rm – ♦160/345 € ♦♦160/383 €, ☑ 20 € – 40 suites
Rest East 47 a la carte 39/50 €
♦ Traditional ♦ Modern ♦
An elegant hotel with an aristocratic feel in the former Palacio Vedruna, where
tradition and modernity combine in perfect harmony. The decor in the refined
restaurant is inspired by Andy Warhol. The hotel also houses an important
archaeological collection.

🏨🏨🏨 **Majestic** ⅙ ⌁ ⅙ AK ⚑ ⑭ 25/400 ⟨ **VISA** 🅮🅒 AE ①
Passeig de Gràcia 68 ✉ 08007 – ⓜ Passeig de Gràcia – ℰ 93 488 17 17
– recepcion@hotelmajestic.es – Fax 93 448 18 80 **K2**
273 rm – ♦♦199/390 €, ☑ 20 € – 31 suites
Rest see **Drolma** below
Rest 30 €
♦ Traditional ♦ Classic ♦
A well-established and modern hotel on the Paseo de Gràcia. Good facilities for
business meetings and conferences. Attractive, spacious and well-equipped
rooms. Functional dining room with both an à la carte menu and a buffet.

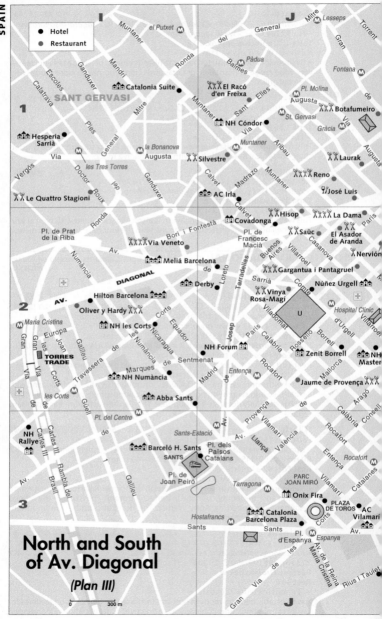

North and South of Av. Diagonal

(Plan III)

0   300 m

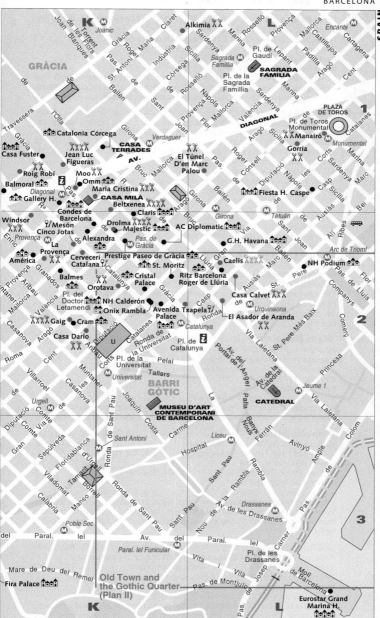

K

Joanic

GRÀCIA

Alkimia ✗✗

L

Encants

Pl. de Gaudí

Sagrada Familia

SAGRADA FAMILIA

Pl. de la Sagrada Familia

PLAZA DE TOROS

1

Pl. de Toros Monumental

DIAGONAL

Manairó ✗✗

Catalonia Córcega

CASA TERRADES

✗✗ El Túnel D'en Marc Palou

Gorría ✗✗

Casa Fuster

Jean Luc Figueras ✗✗✗✗

AV.

Roig Robí ✗✗

Moo ✗✗

Omm

Fiesta H. Caspe

Balmoral

Gallery H.

Diagonal

Maria Cristina ✗✗✗

CASA MILÀ

Beltxenea ✗✗✗

Condes de Barcelona

Claris

Tetuán

Windsor ✗✗✗

Mesón Cinco Jotas

Drolma ✗✗✗✗

Majestic

AC Diplomatic

Arc de Triomf

Alexandra

Pas. de Gràcia

G.H. Havana

La Provença

Amèrica

Cerverceri Catalana

Prestige Paseo de Gràcia

St. Moritz

Caelis ✗✗✗

NH Podium

Balmes

Orotava ✗✗

Cristal Palace

Ritz Barcelona Roger de Llúria

Casa Calvet ✗✗✗

Pl. del Doctor Letamendi

NH Calderón

Onix Rambla

Avenida Txapela ✗/ Palace

Urquinaona

El Asador de Aranda ✗✗

Gaig ✗✗✗✗ Cram

Diputació

Catalanes

Ronda de Catalunya

Casa Darío ✗✗

Ronda de la Universitat

Pl. de Catalunya

Casa Darío

Pl. de la Universitat

Pelaí

Universitat

Tallers

BARRI GÒTIC

Av. del Portal de l'Angel

CATEDRAL

Jaume 1

MUSEU D'ART CONTEMPORANI DE BARCELONA

Liceu

Hospital

Drassanes

Av. de les Drassanes

Poble Sec

Paral. lel

Paral. lel Funicular

Pl. de les Drassanes

Old Town and the Gothic Quarter (Plan II)

Mare de Deu del Remei

Fira Palace

K

Eurostar Grand Marina H.

L

695

Fira Palace　　🔽 🔲 ⬆ 🗚 ❄ 🔲 📞 🏊25/1300 ☕ **VISA** 🅜 🅐 ①
av. Rius i Taulet 1 ⊠ 08004 – ⓜ Espanya – ☎ 93 426 22 23 – sales @
fira-palace.com – Fax 93 425 50 47 – www.fira-palace.com　　　　**J-K3**
258 rm – ♦115/242 € ♦♦129/282 €, ⌣ 15 € – 18 suites
Rest 25 € – **Rest El Mall** a la carte 32/43 €
♦ Business ♦ Classic ♦
Close to the exhibition and trade fair sector. Modern-style hotel with very
well-equipped rooms. Ideal for conventions, conferences and social functions.
Restaurant with a rustic feel, exposed brickwork and pleasant furnishings.

Hilton Barcelona　　　🔲 🔲 ⬆ 🗚 ❄ 🔲 📞 🏊25/600
av. Diagonal 589 ⊠ 08014 – ⓜ Maria Cristina　　　☕ **VISA** 🅜 🅐 ①
– ☎ 93 495 77 77 – barcelona @ hilton.com – Fax 93 495 77 00
– www.barcelonahilton.com　　　　　**I2**
275 rm – ♦195/330 € ♦♦225/360 €, ⌣ 20 € – 11 suites
Rest Mosaic a la carte 36/45 €
♦ Traditional ♦ Business ♦ Modern ♦
Situated on one of the main arteries of the city, the Hilton has a spacious lobby,
well-equipped meeting rooms and comfortable bedrooms in contemporary style. Its
bright restaurant is enhanced by a pleasant terrace during the summer months.

G.H. Havana　　🔲 🔽 ⬆ 🗚 🔲 📞 🏊25/150 ☕ **VISA** 🅜 🅐 ①
Gran Via de les Corts Catalanes 647 ⊠ 08010 – ⓜ Girona – ☎ 93 412 11 15
– granhotelhavana @ hoteles-silken.com – Fax 93 412 26 11
– www.granhotelhavana.com　　　　**L2**
141 rm – ♦160 € ♦♦175 €, ⌣ 17 € – 4 suites
Rest 24 €
Rest Grand Place a la carte 28/40 €
♦ Traditional ♦ Retro ♦
This centrally located hotel has retained the building's original façade, dating
from 1882. The refurbished interior includes a modern entrance hall, guestrooms
which are contemporary in style, and an elegant restaurant serving international
cuisine.

Meliá Barcelona　　≤ 🔲 ⬆ 🗚 ❄ 🔲 🏊25/500 ☕ **VISA** 🅜 🅐 ①
av. de Sarrià 50 ⊠ 08029 – ⓜ Hospital Clinic – ☎ 93 410 60 60
– melia.barcelona @ solmelia.com – Fax 93 410 77 44
– www.meliabarcelona.solmelia.com　　　　**J2**
299 rm – ♦♦135/225 €, ⌣ 20 € – 15 suites
Rest a la carte approx. 45 €
♦ Business ♦ Chain hotel ♦ Functional ♦
A traditional-style hotel in the city's most modern district. Large, well-equipped
rooms, excellent services and facilities, plus a spacious and welcoming restaurant.

Princesa Sofía　　≤ 🔲 🔽 ⬆ 🗚 ❄ 🔲 📞 🏊25/1000
pl. Pius XII-4 ⊠ 08028 – ⓜ Maria Cristina　　　☕ **VISA** 🅜 🅐 ①
– ☎ 93 508 10 00 – psofia @ expogrupo.com – Fax 93 508 10 01
– www.princesasofia.com　　　　Plan I **A2**
475 rm – ♦290/370 € ♦♦300/380 €, ⌣ 20 € – 25 suites
Rest a la carte 27/49 €
♦ Business ♦ Classic ♦
In the city's main business and commercial district. The hotel's excellent facilities,
luxurious lounges and comfortable rooms make it an ideal location for business
trips and conventions. The modern-style restaurant offers à la carte and buffet
options.

AC Diplomatic　　🔲 ⬆ 🗚 ❄ 🔲 📞 🏊25/70 ☕ **VISA** 🅜 🅐 ①
Pau Claris 122 ⊠ 08009 – ⓜ Diagonal – ☎ 93 272 38 10 – diplomatic @
ac-hotels.com – Fax 93 272 38 11 – www.ac-hotels.com　　　**K2**
209 rm – ♦190 € ♦♦245 €, ⌣ 16 € – 2 suites
Rest a la carte approx. 33 €
♦ Business ♦ Chain hotel ♦ Functional ♦
Located at the heart of the Ensanche district, this functional hotel offers guests
comfortable, contemporary bedrooms with modern bathrooms and good
sound-proofing.

NH Calderón
🗻 & 🖭 ⚒ 🖵 ☏ ⚙ 25/200 🚗 VISA ⚫ AE ⑩

Rambla de Catalunya 26 ⊠ *08007 –* Ⓜ *Passeig de Gràcia –* ℰ *93 301 00 00*
– nhcalderon@nh-hoteles.com – Fax 93 412 41 93
– www.nh-hotels.com   **K2**
224 rm – ♛♛115/227 €, ⌴ 18 € – 29 suites
Rest a la carte 24/32 €
◆ Business ◆ Chain hotel ◆ Functional ◆
This hotel's location in the city's main financial district makes it an ideal base for
business travellers. Excellent facilities and high levels of comfort.

Fiesta H. Caspe
🖪 🖭 ⚒ 🖵 ☏ ⚙ 25/200 🚗 VISA ⚫ AE ⑩

Casp 103 ⊠ *08013 –* Ⓜ *Arc de Triomf –* ℰ *93 246 70 00 – caspe@*
fiesta-hotels.com – Fax 93 246 70 01 – www.fiestahotelgroup.com   **L1**
141 rm – ♛150 € ♛♛164 €, ⌴ 14 €
Rest 3 Plats a la carte approx. 20 €
◆ Business ◆ Chain hotel ◆ Functional ◆
The hotel's lounge area and modern foyer are both embellished with design
furniture. Wide choice of meeting rooms and guest bedrooms, with a shower
and bathtub as standard. A combination of Mediterranean and international
cuisine is on offer in the restaurant.

Catalonia Barcelona Plaza
🖪 🗻 (heated) & 🖭 ⚒ 🖵 ☏

pl. d'Espanya 6 ⊠ *08014 –* Ⓜ   ⚙ 25/600 🚗 VISA ⚫ AE ⑩
Espanya – ℰ *93 426 26 00 – plaza@hoteles-catalonia.es – Fax 93 426 04 00*
– www.hoteles-catalonia.es   **J3**
338 rm – ♛136/242 € ♛♛171/242 €, ⌴ 12 € – 9 suites
Rest Gourmet Plaza a la carte approx. 40 €
◆ Business ◆ Chain hotel ◆ Functional ◆
A modern hotel facing Barcelona's main exhibition centre, with excellent
facilities aimed mainly at business clientele, as well as a functional restaurant
decorated in minimalist style.

Barceló H. Sants
≪ 🖪 & 🖭 ⚒ 🖵 ☏ ⚙ 25/1500 P VISA ⚫ AE ⑩

pl. dels Països Catalans ⊠ *08014 –* Ⓜ *Sants-Estació –* ℰ *93 503 53 00*
– sants@bchoteles.com – Fax 93 490 60 45 – www.bchoteles.com   **J3**
364 rm – ♛150/185 € ♛♛175/200 €, ⌴ 12 € – 13 suites
Rest *(closed August and Sunday)* a la carte 32/45 €
◆ Business ◆ Chain hotel ◆ Functional ◆
Located within the confines of the Sants railway station with views of the city.
Functional in style with good facilities and a spacious lobby. The well-lit dining
room offers two contrasting sections, one for à la carte, the other a more relaxed
buffet.

Condes de Barcelona
& 🖭 ⚙ 25/200 🚗 VISA ⚫ AE ⑩

passeig de Gràcia 75 ⊠ *08008 –* Ⓜ *Passeig de Gràcia –* ℰ *93 445 00 00*
– reservas@condesdebarcelona.com – Fax 93 445 32 32   **K2**
181 rm – ♛♛165/425 €, ⌴ 16 € – 2 suites
Rest *(closed Holy Week, 21 days in August, Sunday and Monday)* 120 €
◆ Traditional ◆ Modern ◆
A hotel set in two well-known and emblematic Barcelona buildings, the Casa
Batlló and the Casa Durella. The rooms are comfortable and the décor has many
period details. A charming restaurant with a wide variety of dishes.

Avenida Palace
🖭 ⚒ 🖵 ☏ ⚙ 25/300 VISA ⚫ AE ⑩

Gran Via de les Corts Catalanes 605 ⊠ *08007 –* Ⓜ *Passeig de Gràcia*
– ℰ *93 301 96 00 – avpalace@husa.es – Fax 93 318 12 34*
– www.avenidapalace.com   **K2**
136 rm – ♛125/235 € ♛♛140/265 €, ⌴ 20 € – 14 suites
Rest 23 €
◆ Traditional ◆ Classic ◆
An elegant, traditional-style hotel in which the attention to detail is evident
throughout and the recently refurbished rooms offer high levels of comfort. The
restaurant has a distinguished atmosphere, pleasant furnishings and
impeccable service.

Ritz Barcelona Roger de Llúria ♿ 🅰🅒 ℅ 📺 ℡

Roger de Llúria 28 ⊠ 08010 – Ⓜ Urquina- 🛗25/60 *VISA* 🆗 🅰🅔 ⓪
ona – ℰ 93 343 60 80 – ritzbcn@rogerdelluria.com – Fax 93 343 60 81
– www.rogerdelluria.com **L2**
46 rm – ♦99/199 € ♦♦168/299 €, � 17 € – 2 suites
Rest *(closed Sunday)* a la carte approx. 43 €

♦ Traditional ♦ Classic ♦

A hotel with a welcoming and intimate feel, a small foyer, and large, extremely comfortable and well-appointed bedrooms. The spacious restaurant is traditionally furnished in elegant style.

Omm 🍴 🅰🅒 ℅ 📺 ℡ 🛗25/30 🚗 *VISA* 🆗 🅰🅔 ⓪

Rosselló 265 ⊠ 08008 – Ⓜ Diagonal – ℰ 93 445 40 00
– reservas@hotelomm.es – Fax 93 445 40 04 – www.hotelomm.es **K1**
59 rm – ♦♦195/350 €, ⊒ 18 €
Rest see *Moo* below

♦ Business ♦ Design ♦

Hiding behind the original façade is a boutique hotel with a bright and spacious lounge area with a designer feel laid out in three parts. Contemporary rooms with restrained decor, plus a restaurant serving varied and inventive cuisine.

Abba Sants ♿ 🅰🅒 ℅ 🛗25/200 🚗 *VISA* 🆗 🅰🅔 ⓪

Numància 32 ⊠ 08029 – Ⓜ Sants-Estació – ℰ 93 600 31 00
– abba-sants@abbahoteles.com – Fax 93 600 31 01 **I2**
140 rm – ♦108/250 € ♦♦118/250 €, ⊒ 15 €
Rest *Amalur* a la carte approx. 35 €

♦ Business ♦ Chain hotel ♦ Modern ♦

A newly constructed hotel of modern design. Adequate public areas and bedrooms, which are smallish but comfortable. Functional dining room where the menu is a mix of traditional and Basque cuisine.

Gallery H. 🍴 🛗 ♿ 🅰🅒 ℅ 📺 🛗25/200 🚗 *VISA* 🆗 🅰🅔 ⓪

Rosselló 249 ⊠ 08008 – Ⓜ Diagonal – ℰ 93 415 99 11
– email@galleryhotel.com – Fax 93 415 91 84
– www.galleryhotel.com **K1**
108 rm – ♦116/245 € ♦♦134/280 €, ⊒ 16 € – 5 suites
Rest 20 €

♦ Business ♦ Modern ♦

This spacious, modern hotel has a roomy foyer, a number of meeting rooms and comfortable bedrooms with attractive, fully equipped bathrooms. The pleasant atmosphere in the restaurant is enhanced by the large windows, interior patio and welcoming terrace.

St. Moritz 🍴 ♿ 🅰🅒 ℅ 📺 ℡ 🛗25/200 🚗 *VISA* 🆗 🅰🅔 ⓪

Diputació 264 ⊠ 08007 – Ⓜ Passeig de Gràcia – ℰ 93 412 15 00
– stmoritz@hchotels.es – Fax 93 412 12 36
– www.hchotels.es **K2**
91 rm – ♦133/210 € ♦♦151/255 €, ⊒ 18 €
Rest 26 €

♦ Business ♦ Functional ♦

A well-run hotel with a traditional façade, well-appointed rooms and a number of private rooms suitable for any social function.

Prestige Paseo de Gràcia without rest ♿ 🅰🅒 ℅ *VISA* 🆗 🅰🅔 ⓪

Passeig de Gràcia 62 ⊠ 08007 – Ⓜ Passeig de Gràcia
– ℰ 93 272 41 80 – reservas@prestigehotels.com
– Fax 93 272 41 81 **K2**
45 rm – ♦♦142/620 €, ⊒ 18 €

♦ Traditional ♦ Minimalist ♦

The design concept figures strongly here, with aesthetically pleasing pure lines and minimalist decor which is most evident in the hotel's bedrooms.

SPAIN

SPAIN

Cram   🔥 AC ⚘ 🖂 ☏ 🍸 VISA ⓜ AE ①

Aribau 54 ⊠ 08011 – Ⓜ Universitat – 𝒞 93 216 77 00 – info@hotelcram.com
– Fax 93 216 77 07 – www.hotelcram.com   **K2**
67 rm ⌂ – †160/250 € ††180/270 €
Rest see *Gaig* below
♦ Business ♦ Design ♦
Bedrooms on the small side are more than compensated for by the use of
innovative technology and cutting-edge work by leading interior designers.

NH Podium   🔥 🏊 🔥 AC ⚘ 🔥 25/240 ☏ VISA ⓜ AE ①

Bailén 4 ⊠ 08010 – Ⓜ Arc de Triomf – 𝒞 93 265 02 02 – nhpodium@
nh-hotels.com – Fax 93 265 05 06   **L2**
140 rm – †95/160 € ††115/210 €, ⌂ 17 € – 5 suites
Rest *Corella* a la carte 28/40 €
♦ Business ♦ Chain hotel ♦ Functional ♦
In the Modernist part of the Ensanche area. A traditional façade with a modern
interior with avant-garde design details. Welcoming and well-lit rooms. Intimate
restaurant with pleasant décor and contemporary paintings.

Balmes   🏊 AC ⚘ 🔥 25/30 ☏ VISA ⓜ AE ①

Mallorca 216 ⊠ 08008 – Ⓜ Provença – 𝒞 93 451 19 14 – balmes@
derbyhotels.es – Fax 93 451 00 49   **K2**
93 rm – †70/189 € ††90/210 €, ⌂ 14 € – 8 suites
Rest *(closed Saturday and Sunday)* (lunch only) 12 €
♦ Traditional ♦ Functional ♦
A modern-style hotel with pleasantly furnished rooms with wooden floors and
exposed brick walls. One of the hotel's main features is its pleasant pool and terrace.

Derby   AC 🖂 🍸 🔥 25/60 ☏ VISA ⓜ AE ①

Loreto 21 ⊠ 08029 – Ⓜ Entença – 𝒞 93 322 32 15 – derby@derbyhotels.com
– Fax 93 410 08 62 – www.derbyhotels.com   **J2**
111 rm – †75/209 € ††90/209 €, ⌂ 14 € – 4 suites
Rest (coffee shop only)
♦ Traditional ♦ Functional ♦
A classic hotel in the business district of the city. Spacious public areas and a coffee
shop with a separate entrance, an English-style bar and comfortable rooms.

AC Vilamarí   🔥 🔥 AC ⚘ 🖂 🍸 🔥 25/35 ☏ VISA ⓜ AE ①

Vilamarí 34-36 ⊠ 08015 – Ⓜ Espanya – 𝒞 93 289 09 09 – acvilamari@
ac-hotels.com – Fax 93 289 05 01 – www.ac-hotels.com   **J3**
90 rm – ††130 €, ⌂ 12 €
Rest 22 €
♦ Business ♦ Chain hotel ♦ Functional ♦
Meticulous in style, this hotel successfully combines functionality with the world
of design. Comfortable bedrooms, half of which have bathtubs, the remainder
showers. The subtly lit restaurant is modern yet intimate.

Alexandra   🔥 AC ⚘ 🖂 🍸 🔥 25/100 ☏ VISA ⓜ AE ①

Mallorca 251 ⊠ 08008 – Ⓜ Passeig de Gràcia – 𝒞 93 467 71 66 – informacion@
hotel-alexandra.com – Fax 93 488 02 58 – www.hotel-alexandra.com
106 rm – †120/270 € ††120/320 €, ⌂ 17 € – 3 suites   **K2**
Rest (set menu only) 22 €
♦ Business ♦ Functional ♦
A modern and welcoming hotel with spacious, well-equipped rooms, pleasant
furnishings, carpeted floors and bathrooms with marble fittings. Pleasant public
areas.

NH Master   AC 🔥 25/100 ☏ VISA ⓜ AE ①

València 105 ⊠ 08011 – Ⓜ Hospital Clinic – 𝒞 93 323 62 15
– nhmaster@nh-hotels.com – Fax 93 323 43 89   **J2**
80 rm – †60/126 € ††70/169 €, ⌂ 12 € – 1 suite
Rest 12,50 €
♦ Business ♦ Chain hotel ♦ Functional ♦
Both central and modern, with the characteristic style of this hotel chain. Pleasantly decorated and functional bedrooms which are ideal for business travellers.

SPAIN

Cristal Palace
ᴀᴄ ⁂ 🖼 ❄ ᵴᴀ 25/100 🚗 VISA ⓂⓄ ᴀᴇ ⓪

Diputació 257 ⊠ 08007 – Ⓜ *Passeig de Gràcia* – ℰ 93 487 87 78
– *reservas@hotelcristalpalace.com* – Fax 93 487 90 30
– *www.eurostarscristalpalace.com* **K2**
147 rm – ♥98/225 € ♥♥115/250 €, ⌑ 12,50 € – 1 suite
Rest 18 €
♦ Business ♦ Modern ♦
Modern in design with a glass façade and well-equipped rooms offering a high
levels of comfort. Efficiently managed by friendly staff.

NH Numància
ᴀᴄ ⁂ 🖼 ❄ ᵴᴀ 25/65 🚗 VISA ⓂⓄ ᴀᴇ ⓪

Numància 74 ⊠ 08029 – Ⓜ *Sants-Estació* – ℰ 93 322 44 51 – *nhnumancia@
nh-hotels.com* – Fax 93 410 76 42 – *www.nh-hotels.com* **I2**
140 rm – ♥85/123 € ♥♥98/215 €, ⌑ 12,50 €
Rest 22 €
♦ Business ♦ Chain hotel ♦ Functional ♦
Close to Sants train station. Pleasant public areas and comfortable bedrooms
with modern décor and furnishings.

América without rest
🛁 ⊼ ⴕ ᴀᴄ ⁂ 🖼 ᵴᴀ 25/50 VISA ⓂⓄ ᴀᴇ ⓪

Provença 195 ⊠ 08008 – Ⓜ *Provença* – ℰ 93 487 62 92
– *america@hotel-america-barcelona.com* – Fax 93 487 25 18
– *www.hotelamericabarcelona.com* **K2**
60 rm – ♥143/196 € ♥♥164/230 €, ⌑ 15 €
♦ Traditional ♦ Cosy ♦
A modern and spacious hotel with a combined reception and public areas.
Comfortable bedrooms with minimalist décor and personalised service.

Núñez Urgell without rest
ᴀᴄ ᵴᴀ 25/150 🚗 VISA ⓂⓄ ᴀᴇ ⓪

Comte d'Urgell 232 ⊠ 08036 – Ⓜ *Hospital Clinic* – ℰ 93 322 41 53
– *nunezurgell@nnhotels.es* – Fax 93 419 01 06 **J2**
106 rm – ♥105/170 € ♥♥115/190 €, ⌑ 12,50 € – 2 suites
♦ Business ♦ Functional ♦
A hotel with a welcoming foyer, coffee shop and comfortable bedrooms, most of
which are pleasantly furnished and have a terrace-balcony.

Onix Rambla
🛁 ⊼ ⴕ ᴀᴄ ⁂ 🖼 ᵴᴀ 25/80 🚗 VISA ⓂⓄ ᴀᴇ ⓪

Rambla de Catalunya 24 ⊠ 08007 – Ⓜ *Catalunya* – ℰ 93 342 79 80
– *reservas.hotelsonix@icyesa.es* – Fax 93 342 51 52
– *www.horelsonix.com* **K2**
40 rm – ♥106/144 € ♥♥116/158 €, ⌑ 10 €
Rest (coffee shop only)
♦ Business ♦ Functional ♦
The Onix Rambla's seigneurial exterior contrasts with its welcoming,
contemporary interior, with reasonably spacious and functionally furnished
rooms with wood flooring.

Zenit Borrell
ⴕ ᴀᴄ ⁂ 🖼 ❄ ᵴᴀ 25/60 🚗 VISA ⓂⓄ ᴀᴇ ⓪

Comte Borrell 208 ⊠ 08029 – Ⓜ *Hospital Clinic* – ℰ 93 452 55 66
– *borrell@zenithoteles.com* – Fax 93 452 55 60 **J2**
73 rm – ♥85/250 € ♥♥90/275 €, ⌑ 11 € – 1 suite
Rest 13 €
♦ Traditional ♦ Modern ♦
The emphasis here is on impeccable taste, with bedrooms that have
contemporary furnishings, wood floors and top-notch bathrooms. Small,
Modernist-style lounge area.

NH Forum
ᴀᴄ ⁂ 🖼 ❄ ᵴᴀ 25/50 🚗 VISA ⓂⓄ ᴀᴇ ⓪

Ecuador 20 ⊠ 08029 – Ⓜ *Sants-Estació* – ℰ 93 419 36 36 – *nhforum@
nh-hotels.com* – Fax 93 419 89 10 – *www.nh-hotels.com* **J2**
47 rm – ♥♥78/182 €, ⌑ 13 € – 1 suite
Rest (closed Christmas, August, Saturday, Sunday and Bank Holidays) 24 €
♦ Business ♦ Chain hotel ♦ Functional ♦
A modern hotel with the characteristic style of the NH chain. Pleasant and
well-equipped rooms.

SPAIN

NH Rallye

25/250 VISA

Travessera de les Corts 150 ✉ 08028 – Ⓜ Les Corts – ✆ 93 339 90 50 – nhrallye@nh-hotels.com – Fax 93 411 07 90 – www.nh-hotels.com I3

105 rm – 60/119 € 70/169 €, 12,50 € – 1 suite

Rest a la carte 21/31 €

♦ Business ♦ Chain hotel ♦ Functional ♦

A modern, functional hotel with the characteristic style of the NH chain. Comfortable, well-equipped rooms, plus an attractive terrace-bar on the top floor.

NH les Corts

25/80 VISA

Travessera de les Corts 292 ✉ 08029 – Ⓜ Les Corts – ✆ 93 322 08 11 – nhlescorts@nh-hotels.com – Fax 93 322 09 08 – www.nh-hotels.com I2

80 rm – 78/130 € 78/175 €, 13 € – 1 suite

Rest (coffee shop) (dinner only)

♦ Business ♦ Chain hotel ♦ Functional ♦

Pleasant rooms, each with a terrace, furnished in brightly coloured modern decor. Multi-functional meeting rooms are also available. Efficiently managed by friendly staff.

Onix Fira without rest

25/80 VISA

Llançà 30 ✉ 08015 – Ⓜ Espanya – ✆ 93 426 00 87 – reservas.hotelsonix@icyesa.es – Fax 93 426 19 81 – www.hotelsonix.com J3

80 rm – 84/107 € 95/133 €, 9 €

♦ Business ♦ Functional ♦

Close to the old bullring. An intimate and comfortable hotel with a large coffee shop and functional rooms. Décor with an attractive use of marble.

Caelis

VISA

Gran Via de les Corts Catalanes 668 ✉ 08010 – Ⓜ Urquinaona – ✆ 93 510 12 05 – restaurante@caelis.com – Fax 93 510 12 05 – www.caelis.com L2

Rest *(closed August, Saturday lunch, Sunday, Monday and Bank Holidays)* a la carte 60/78 €

Spec. Foie-gras de pato parrilla y enfriado. Merluza sobre carpaccio de manitas de cerdo y jugo de asado. Manzana Golden en tatin.

♦ Inventive ♦ Design ♦

Modern restaurant with minimalist design within a classical setting. Excellent service and creative cuisine.

La Dama

VISA

av. Diagonal 423 ✉ 08036 – Ⓜ Diagonal – ✆ 93 202 06 86 – reservas@ladama-restaurant.com – Fax 93 200 72 99 – www.ladama-restaurant.com

closed 3 weeks in August J2

Rest a la carte 48/64 €

♦ International ♦ Retro ♦

An elegant restaurant with Modernist decorative details both inside and on the façade. Professional staff.

Drolma – Hotel Majestic

12/18 P VISA

Passeig de Gràcia 68 ✉ 08007 – Ⓜ Passeig de Gràcia – ✆ 93 496 77 10 – drolma@hotelmajestic.es – Fax 93 445 38 93

closed Sunday K2

Rest (dinner only in August) a la carte 95/126 €

Spec. Espardenyes con espárragos. Sopa de pan con trufas negras (20 December-15 March). Cabrito embarrado a la cuchara.

♦ International ♦ Formal ♦

Traditional style, predominantly wood, décor creating an elegant and refined atmosphere. Professional staff.

SPAIN

XXXX ✿ **Gaig** – Hotel Cram   🔳 ❄ ⇔4/40 **P** 𝚅𝙸𝚂𝙰 ⓒⓞ 🄰🄴 ⓞ
Aragó 214 ⊠ 08011 – Ⓜ Passeig de Gràcia – ℰ 93 429 10 17 – info @
restaurantgaig.com – Fax 93 429 70 02 – www.restaurantgaig.com
closed Holy Week, August and Sunday   **K2**
Rest 74 € and a la carte 55/77 €
Spec. Canelones tradicionales a la crema de trufa negra. Escórpora asada,
rebozuelos, espinacas y cítricos. Foie gras con almendras texturizadas.
♦ Inventive ♦ Design ♦
A refined setting with professional service of the highest order. Creative cuisine
which takes its inspiration from the Mediterranean and Catalunya.

XXXX **Beltxenea**   🛋 🔳 ❄ 𝚅𝙸𝚂𝙰 ⓒⓞ 🄰🄴 ⓞ
Mallorca 275 entlo ⊠ 08008 – Ⓜ Diagonal – ℰ 93 215 30 24 – Fax 93 487 00 81
closed Christmas, Holy Week, August, Saturday lunch and Sunday   **K1**
Rest a la carte 41/55 €
♦ Basque ♦ Formal ♦
An elegant restaurant in a historic building with an atmosphere of the past. A
dining room with views of the garden and an attractive, carved wooden fireplace.

XXX **Casa Calvet**   🔳 ❄ ⇔5/12 𝚅𝙸𝚂𝙰 ⓒⓞ 🄰🄴 ⓞ
Casp 48 ⊠ 08010 – Ⓜ Urquinaona – ℰ 93 412 40 12 – restaurant @ casacalvet.es
– Fax 93 412 43 36 – www.casacalvet.es
closed Holy Week, 15 days in August, Sunday and Bank Holidays   **L2**
Rest a la carte 49/62 €
♦ Inventive ♦ Formal ♦
A restaurant in an attractive building designed by Gaudí. The dining room is
welcoming and there is an excellent à la carte menu.

XXX **Jaume de Provença**   🔳 ❄ 𝚅𝙸𝚂𝙰 ⓒⓞ 🄰🄴 ⓞ
Provença 88 ⊠ 08029 – Ⓜ Entença – ℰ 93 430 00 29 – Fax 93 439 29 50
– www.jaumeprovenza.com
closed Holy Week, August, Sunday dinner and Monday   **J2**
Rest a la carte 33/52 €
♦ International ♦ Formal ♦
A traditional-style restaurant with a small bar, which leads to a spacious dining
room with an intimate atmosphere and attentive service.

XXX **Windsor**   🔳 ❄ 𝚅𝙸𝚂𝙰 ⓒⓞ 🄰🄴 ⓞ
Còrsega 286 ⊠ 08008 – Ⓜ Diagonal – ℰ 93 415 84 83 – info @
restaurantwindsor.com – Fax 93 238 66 08 – www.restaurantwindsor.com
closed 1 to 7 January, Holy Week, August, Saturday lunch and Sunday
Rest a la carte 34/50 €   **K2**
♦ Catalan cuisine ♦ Formal ♦
An elegant restaurant with a beautiful interior patio, several dining areas and a
private bar. An interesting menu and a good wine-list.

XXX **Gargantua i Pantagruel**   🔳 ❄ ⇔6/28 𝚅𝙸𝚂𝙰 ⓒⓞ 🄰🄴 ⓞ
Còrsega 200 ⊠ 08036 – Ⓜ Hospital Clinic – ℰ 93 453 20 20
– gip @ gargantuaipantagruel.com – Fax 93 419 29 22
– www.gargantuaipantagruel.com
closed August and Sunday dinner   **J2**
Rest a la carte 33/44 €
♦ Catalan cuisine ♦ Trendy ♦
The main restaurant and private rooms are classic in style, enhanced by
contemporary design features. Traditional cuisine with a modern twist,
including dishes from Lérida.

XXX **Oliver y Hardy**   🛋 🔳 ❄ 𝚅𝙸𝚂𝙰 ⓒⓞ 🄰🄴 ⓞ
av. Diagonal 593 ⊠ 08014 – Ⓜ Maria Cristina – ℰ 93 419 31 81 – oliveryhardy @
husa.es – Fax 93 419 18 99 – www.husarestauracion.com
closed Holy Week, Saturday lunch and Sunday   **I2**
Rest a la carte 32/42 €
♦ International ♦ Formal ♦
A renowned dinner venue divided between a night-club and restaurant. Refined
dining room with a terrace used for private functions.

XxX **Maria Cristina**   AC ⌁ VISA ⓪ AE ⓪

Provença 271 ⊠ 08008 – Ⓜ Provença – 𝒞 93 215 32 37 – Fax 93 215 83 23
closed 16 to 31 August and Sunday   **K1**
Rest a la carte approx. 52 €
♦ Catalan cuisine ♦ Formal ♦
The attractive opaque glass frontage leads to a small foyer and several dining rooms with a mixed classic-modern ambience. Traditional cuisine based on high-quality products.

XX **Moo** – Hotel Omm   AC ⌁ VISA ⓪ AE ⓪

✿ *Rosselló 265 ⊠ 08008 – Ⓜ Diagonal – 𝒞 93 445 40 00*
– reservas@hotelomm.es – Fax 93 445 40 04 – closed Sunday   **K 1**
Rest a la carte 46/57 €
Spec. Cigala con curry, rosa y regaliz. Lubina ligeramente ahumada con judia verde. Viaje a La Habana.
♦ Inventive ♦ Design ♦
Modern restaurant with coffee area and cosmopolitan atmosphere. Creative cuisine and original wine list.

XX **Orotava**   AC VISA ⓪ AE ⓪

Consell de Cent 335 ⊠ 08007 – Ⓜ Passeig de Gràcia – 𝒞 93 487 73 74
– nuriaposo@terra.es – Fax 93 488 26 50   **K2**
Rest a la carte approx. 49 €
♦ International ♦ Formal ♦
A classic-style restaurant close to the Fundació Tàpies with contemporary paintings hanging on the walls and a cosmopolitan menu.

XX **El Asador de Aranda**   AC ⌁ VISA ⓪ AE ⓪

Londres 94 ⊠ 08036 – Ⓜ Tibidabo – 𝒞 93 414 67 90 – Fax 93 414 67 90
– www.asadoraranda.com
closed Holy Week, and Sunday dinner   **L2**
Rest a la carte 25/34 €
♦ Roast lamb ♦ Rustic ♦
In a street off the Avenida Diagonal. A spacious restaurant with traditional Castilian-style décor, bar and a wood fired oven for roasting suckling pig and lamb.

XX **La Provença**   AC VISA ⓪ AE ⓪

☺ *Provença 242 ⊠ 08008 – Ⓜ Diagonal – 𝒞 93 323 23 67*
– restofi@laprovenza.com – Fax 93 451 23 89 – www.laprovenza.com
Rest a la carte 21/29 €   **K2**
♦ Catalan cuisine ♦ Trendy ♦
A fusion of the traditional and modern restaurant close to the Paseo de Gràcia in a comfortable, cheerful setting. The well-priced menu is based on fresh market produce.

XX **El Asador de Aranda**   AC ⌁ VISA ⓪ AE ⓪

Pau Clarís 70 ⊠ 08010 – Ⓜ Urquinaona – 𝒞 93 342 55 77
– asador@asadoraranda.com – Fax 93 342 55 78 – www.asadoraranda.com
closed Holy Week, Sunday in August and Sunday dinner the rest of the year
Rest a la carte 25/34 €   **J2**
♦ Roast lamb ♦ Rustic ♦
The standard features of this chain are evident here, with a bar at the entrance, a roasting oven in open view, and two inviting dining rooms with elegant Castilian decor.

XX **El Túnel D'en Marc Palou**   AC ⌁ VISA ⓪ AE ⓪

Bailén 91 ⊠ 08009 – Ⓜ Girona – 𝒞 93 265 86 58 – Fax 93 246 01 14
closed August and Sunday   **L1**
Rest a la carte 31/37 €
♦ Inventive ♦ Trendy ♦
In a glass-fronted corner building with three small and contemporary dining rooms on various levels. A refined setting for cuisine that is interestingly inventive.

SPAIN

XX **Vinya Rosa-Magí**   AC ⟷6/20 VISA ⓜⓢ AE ⓞ
av. de Sarrià 17 ⊠ 08029 – Ⓜ Hospital Clínic – ℰ 93 430 00 03
– info@vinyarosamagi.com – Fax 93 430 00 41 – www.vinyarosamagi.com
closed Saturday lunch and Sunday   **J2**
Rest a la carte 36/54 €
♦ International ♦ Friendly ♦
This small restaurant has an intimate and welcoming atmosphere and attractive décor details. Cosmopolitan cuisine.

XX **Gorría**   AC ℅ VISA ⓜⓢ AE ⓞ
Diputació 421 ⊠ 08013 – Ⓜ Sagrada Familia – ℰ 93 245 11 64
– info@restaurantegorria.com – Fax 93 232 78 57 – www.restaurantegorria.com
closed Holy Week, August, Sunday and dinner Bank Holidays   **L1**
Rest a la carte 35/46 €
♦ Basque ♦ Rustic ♦
A well-established and pleasant restaurant with good service. Very good menu and cuisine.

XX **Casa Darío**   AC ℅ ⟷4/40 VISA ⓜⓢ AE ⓞ
Consell de Cent 256 ⊠ 08011 – Ⓜ Universitat – ℰ 93 453 31 35
– casadario@casadario.com – Fax 93 451 33 95 – www.casadario.com
closed August and Sunday   **K2**
Rest a la carte 32/47 €
♦ Seafood ♦ Formal ♦
A classic-style restaurant with a bar near the entrance leading to three pleasantly furnished dining areas and a private room upstairs. Cuisine based on quality ingredients.

XX **Saüc**   AC ℅ VISA ⓜⓢ AE
Passatge Lluís Pellicer 12 ⊠ 08036 – Ⓜ Hospital Clínic – ℰ 93 321 01 89
– sauc@saucrestaurant.com – www.saucrestaurant.com
closed 1 to 9 January, 7 to 29 August, Sunday, Monday and
Bank Holidays   **J2**
Rest a la carte 33/44 €
♦ Inventive ♦ Family ♦
The couple who run this restaurant, functional in style but with the occasional avant-garde touch, offer a personal slant on regional cuisine based on high-quality products.

XX **Manairó**   AC ℅ VISA ⓜⓢ AE ⓞ
Diputació 424 ⊠ 08013 – Ⓜ Monumental – ℰ 93 231 00 57
– info@manairo.com – www.manairo.com
closed 1 to 7 January, 10 to 31 August, Sunday and Monday   **L1**
Rest a la carte 34/53 €
♦ Inventive ♦ Cosy ♦
This establishment has already built up a strong reputation locally. The small lounge is decorated with works by a range of artists, and the restaurant serves food produced by the marriage of innovative techniques with culinary tradition.

X **Nervión**   AC ℅ VISA ⓜⓢ AE ⓞ
Còrsega 232 ⊠ 08036 – Ⓜ Diagonal – ℰ 93 218 06 27
closed August, Sunday and Bank Holidays   **J2**
Rest a la carte approx. 40 €
♦ Basque ♦ Cosy ♦
A small and well-managed restaurant. Delicious traditional Basque dishes and friendly service.

Ⴘ/ **Mesón Cinco Jotas**   ⌂ ℅ VISA ⓜⓢ AE ⓞ
Rambla de Catalunya 91-93 ⊠ 08008 – Ⓜ Diagonal – ℰ 93 487 89 42
– m5jrambla@osborne.es – Fax 93 487 91 21 – www.mesoncincojotas.com
Tapa 2,50 € **Ración** approx. 15 €   **K2**
♦ Spanish ♦ Tapas bar ♦
A spacious bar with traditional wood décor where customers can sample a good selection of fine hams and other pork products. Beyond the bar there is a dining room.

SPAIN

⅋/ **Txapela** 🛱 AC ⅋ **VISA** **MO** AE **O**
*Passeig de Gràcia 8-10 ⊠ 08007 – **Ⓜ** Passeig de Gràcia – 𝒞 93 412 02 89*
– txapela@angrup.com – Fax 93 412 24 78 – www.angrup.com **K2**
Tapa 1,45 €
♦ Basque ♦ Tapas bar ♦
A Basque-style bar and restaurant situated on the Paseo de Gràcia. Spacious and
with a pleasant terrace.

⅋/ **Cervecería Catalana** 🛱 AC ⅋ **VISA** **MO** AE **O**
*Mallorca 236 ⊠ 08008 – **Ⓜ** Diagonal – 𝒞 93 216 03 68*
– jahumada@62online.com – Fax 93 488 17 97 **K2**
Tapa 4,50 € **Ración** approx. 6 €
♦ Spanish ♦ Brasserie ♦
A bar specialising in different beers with wood décor and a wide range of
well-presented tapas made from carefully selected ingredients.

SANT MARTÍ
Plan I

🏨🏨🏨 **Arts** 📇 ⊰ 🛱 *ʄ₆* ⊼ & AC ♨25/900 ⌖ **VISA** **MO** AE **O**
*Marina 19 ⊠ 08005 – **Ⓜ** Ciutadella-Vila Olímpica – 𝒞 93 221 10 00*
– rc.barcelonareservations@ritzcarlton.com – Fax 93 221 10 70 **C2**
397 rm – ♥♥345/550 €, � 25 € – 86 suites
Rest *Arola (closed January, Monday and Tuesday)* a la carte approx. 60 €
♦ Grand Luxury ♦ Design ♦
Housed in one of the two towers overlooking the Olympic port, this superb hotel
is justifiably renowned for the luxurious design of its guestrooms and lounges.
The Arts has several restaurants, most notably the Arola, renowned for its
creative cuisine.

🏨🏨🏨 **Eurostar Grand Marina H.** 🛱 *ʄ₆* ⊼ & AC ⅋ ♨25/500
Moll de Barcelona (World Trade Center) ⌖ **VISA** **MO** AE **O**
⊠ 08039 – 𝒞 93 603 90 00 – info@grandmarinahotel.com
– Fax 93 603 90 90 *Plan III* **L3**
258 rm – ♥190/475 € ♥♥190/500 €, �⵿ 21 € – 15 suites
Rest a la carte approx. 65 €
♦ Grand Luxury ♦ Modern ♦
A circular building in a very modern style with a patio in the middle. Rooms with
a high level of comfort, attractive design details and original works of art. A
well-lit restaurant with good service.

🏨🏨🏨 **Diagonal Barcelona** 🛱 ⊼ & AC ⅋ ▥ ♨25/250
*av. Diagonal 205 ⊠ 08018 – **Ⓜ** Glòries* ⌖ **VISA** **MO** AE **O**
– 𝒞 93 489 53 00 – reservas.diagonal@hoteles-silken.com – Fax 93 489 53 09
– www.hoteldiagonalbarcelona.com **C2**
228 rm – ♥100/145 € ♥♥115/165 €, � 16 € – 12 suites
Rest a la carte 38/51 €
♦ Business ♦ Design ♦
Pure design is what you get when you ask several well-known artists to give free
rein to their creativity. Ultra-modern bedrooms with baths on view and a sun
terrace on the roof.

🏨🏨 **Barceló H. Atenea Mar** ⊰ *ʄ₆* & AC ▥ ℣ ♨25/400
*Passeig Garcia Faria 47 ⊠ 08019 – **Ⓜ** Selva de* ⌖ **VISA** **MO** AE **O**
Mar – 𝒞 93 531 60 40 – ateneamar@bchoteles.com – Fax 93 531 60 90
– www.bchoteles.com **D2**
191 rm – ♥75 € ♥♥200 €, � 12 €
Rest *El Comedor* a la carte 29/37 €
♦ Business ♦ Chain hotel ♦ Functional ♦
On an avenue facing out to sea, the Atenea Mar offers a number of modular
meeting rooms, reasonable fitness area and functional bedrooms, the majority
with Mediterranean views. Restaurant with a separate entrance and menu based
on traditional seasonal cuisine.

SPAIN

Rafael H. Diagonal Port 🐚 🗛 ⚄ ⌨ 🕸25/175 🚗 **VISA** **⚄** 🗛 ⓪
Lope de Vega 4 ✉ 08005 – **Ⓜ** *Poblenou* – 𝒞 93 230 20 00
– diagonalport@rafaelhoteles.com – Fax 93 230 20 10
– www.rafaelhoteles.com   **D2**
115 rm – 🛏80/200 € 🛏🛏80/220 €, � 14 €
Rest 16 €
♦ Business ♦ Functional ♦
A modern, functional hotel with spacious public areas, comfortable, carpeted
bedrooms, bathrooms fitted with marble, and good sound-proofing.

Hesperia del Mar 🏡 🐚 🗛 ⚄ ⌨ 🕸25/175 🚗 **VISA** **⚄** 🗛 ⓪
Espronceda 6 ✉ 08005 – **Ⓜ** *Poblenou* – 𝒞 93 502 97 00
– hotel@hesperia-delmar.com – Fax 93 502 97 01
– www.hesperia-delmar.com   **D2**
78 rm – 🛏90/180 € 🛏🛏100/190 €, ⊻ 14,50 € – 6 suites
Rest a la carte approx. 32 €
♦ Business ♦ Chain hotel ♦ Functional ♦
This hotel is located close to the sea in an area in the process of redevelopment.
Facilities here include spacious lounge areas, well-equipped guest rooms with
modern, practical furnishings, and a bright, airy restaurant.

Vincci Marítimo 🏡 🐚 🗛 ⚄ ⌨ 🕸25/250 🚗 **VISA** **⚄** 🗛 ⓪
Llull 340 ✉ 08019 – **Ⓜ** *Selva de Mar* – 𝒞 93 356 26 00
– maritimo@vinccihoteles.com – Fax 93 356 06 69
– www.vinccihoteles.com   **D2**
144 rm – 🛏130/175 € 🛏🛏138/203 €, ⊻ 13 €
Rest 27 €
♦ Business ♦ Chain hotel ♦ Design ♦
A good level of general comfort, although the hotel's outstanding feature is its
designer decor, with original avant-garde features in the bathrooms and on the
bed headboards. The restaurant is bright and simply designed.

Els Pescadors 🏡 🗛 ⟷5/30 **VISA** **⚄** 🗛 ⓪
pl. Prim 1 ✉ 08005 – **Ⓜ** *Poblenou* – 𝒞 93 225 20 18
– contacte@elspescadors.com – Fax 93 224 00 04
– www.elspescadors.com
closed Holy Week   **D2**
Rest a la carte 34/48 €
♦ Rice specialities ♦ Formal ♦
This restaurant has one dining room in the style of an early-20C café-bar and two
with more modern decor. A varied menu of fish and seafood, including cod and
rice dishes.

Anfiteatro 🏡 🗛 ⚄ **VISA** **⚄** 🗛
av. Litoral (Parc del Port Olímpic) ✉ 08005 – **Ⓜ** *Ciutadella-Vila Olímpica*
– 𝒞 659 69 53 45 – anfiteatrobcn@telefonica.net
– Fax 93 457 14 19
closed Sunday dinner and Monday   **C2**
Rest a la carte 40/52 €
♦ Inventive ♦ Trendy ♦
This modern restaurant has a friendly atmosphere, an abundance of natural
light and careful attention to detail. A large fountain adds to the overall
charm.

El Túnel del Port ⟷ 🏡 🗛 ⟷20/40 **VISA** **⚄** 🗛 ⓪
Moll de Gregal 12 (Port Olímpic) ✉ 08005 – **Ⓜ** *Ciutadella-Vila Olímpica*
– 𝒞 93 221 03 21 – info@eltuneldelport.com – Fax 93 221 35 86
– www.eltuneldelport.com
closed Sunday dinner and Monday   **C2**
Rest a la carte 35/57 €
♦ Catalan cuisine ♦ Formal ♦
A traditional restaurant in an elegant setting with service in keeping with its
reputation. Two dining rooms, one private section and two large-capacity
terraces.

NORTH of AV. DIAGONAL *(Via Augusta, Capità Arenas, Ronda General Mitre, Passeig de la Bonanova, Av. de Pedralbes)* **Plan III**

SPAIN

Casa Fuster 🔥 ⚄ 🅰🅲 ❄ 🖼 🕰25/110 𝗩𝗜𝗦𝗔 🆎 🅰🅴 ⓪
passeig de Gràcia 132 ✉ *08008 –* Ⓜ *Diagonal –* ☎ *93 255 30 00 – casafuster@*
hotelescenter.es – Fax 93 255 30 02 – www.hotelescenter.es **K1**
76 rm – ♦305 € ♦♦381 €, ⌑ 25 € – 20 suites
Rest *Galaxó* a la carte 40/66 €
♦ Luxury ♦ Modern ♦
Magnificent hotel housed in a beautiful modernist building dating back to 1908. It has an attractive café-lounge, and the bedrooms are equipped to the highest level, with well-appointed bathrooms. You can enjoy sophisticated, innovative cooking in the hotel's elegant restaurant.

Hesperia Sarrià 🅰🅲 ❄ 🖼25/300 🍽 𝗩𝗜𝗦𝗔 🆎 🅰🅴 ⓪
Vergós 20 ✉ *08017 –* Ⓜ *Les Tres Torres –* ☎ *93 204 55 51*
– hotel@hesperia-sarria.com – Fax 93 204 43 92 **I1**
134 rm – ♦100/250 € ♦♦100/350 €, ⌑ 13,50 €
Rest 28 €
♦ Business ♦ Chain hotel ♦ Functional ♦
A modern hotel with a spacious foyer and reception area and comfortable and very well-appointed bedrooms. Large meeting rooms.

Balmoral 🅰🅲 ❄ 🖼 🕰25/150 🍽 𝗩𝗜𝗦𝗔 🆎 🅰🅴 ⓪
Via Augusta 5 ✉ *08006 –* Ⓜ *Diagonal –* ☎ *93 217 87 00 – info@*
hotelbalmoral.com – Fax 93 415 14 21 – www.hotelbalmoral.com **K1**
106 rm – ♦100/155 € ♦♦100/218 €, ⌑ 12 €
Rest (coffee shop only)
♦ Traditional ♦ Classic ♦
A comfortable, traditional-style hotel offering professional service. Bright, well-appointed bedrooms and a choice of panelled-off function rooms.

AC Irla 🔥 🅰🅲 ❄ 🖼25/30 𝗩𝗜𝗦𝗔 🆎 🅰🅴 ⓪
Calvet 40-42 ✉ *08021 –* Ⓜ *Muntaner –* ☎ *93 241 62 10*
– acirla@ac-hotels.com – Fax 93 241 62 11 **J1**
36 rm – ♦♦135/165 €, ⌑ 14 €
Rest a la carte approx. 30 €
♦ Business ♦ Chain hotel ♦ Functional ♦
Quality materials, design features and a sense of the functional add to the overall charm of this welcoming hotel. Spacious bathrooms with showers rather than baths.

Catalonia Suite ⚄ 🅰🅲 ❄ 🖼 📞 🕰25/90 🍽 𝗩𝗜𝗦𝗔 🆎 🅰🅴 ⓪
Muntaner 505 ✉ *08022 –* Ⓜ *El Putxet –* ☎ *93 212 80 12*
– suite@hoteles-catalonia.es – Fax 93 211 23 17
– www.hoteles-catalonia.com **I1**
117 rm – ♦105/160 € ♦♦136/172 €, ⌑ 13 €
Rest 16 €
♦ Business ♦ Chain hotel ♦ Functional ♦
Located in an exclusive residential and business district, the Catalonia Suite offers guests functional, elegantly decorated rooms in a welcoming, restful atmosphere.

Catalonia Córcega ⚄ 🅰🅲 ❄ 🖼 📞 𝗩𝗜𝗦𝗔 🆎 🅰🅴 ⓪
Còrsega 368 ✉ *08037 –* Ⓜ *Verdaguer –* ☎ *93 208 19 19*
– corcega@hoteles-catalonia.es – Fax 93 208 08 57
– www.hoteles-catalonia.com **K1**
77 rm – ♦118/160 € ♦♦149/172 €, ⌑ 13 € – 2 suites
Rest 15 €
♦ Business ♦ Chain hotel ♦ Functional ♦
A modern hotel with attractive, spacious rooms, a mix of contemporary and traditional furniture and facilities in keeping with its rating, although the hotel lounge is on the small side. Fixed menu in the restaurant, with a small à la carte choice.

SPAIN

NH Cóndor 🔲 📺 📞 📶 25/50 *VISA* 🔴 🔵 ①
Via Augusta 127 ⊠ 08006 – Ⓜ *Muntaner – ℰ 93 209 45 11*
– nhcondor@nh-hotels.es – Fax 93 202 27 13 – www.nh-hotels.com **J1**
66 rm – ♥75/119 € ♥♥75/158 €, ⊑ 12,50 € – 12 suites
Rest *(closed August, Saturday and Sunday)* 20 €
♦ Business ♦ Chain hotel ♦ Functional ♦
A functional and comfortable hotel with all the characteristic style of this hotel
chain. Modern furnishings and wood décor creating an intimate atmosphere.

Covadonga without rest 🔲 🕏 📺 📶 25/50 *VISA* 🔴 🔵 ①
av. Diagonal 596 ⊠ 08021 – Ⓜ *Hospital Clinic – ℰ 93 209 55 11*
– covadonga@hcchotels.com – Fax 93 209 58 33
– www.hcchotels.es **J2**
101 rm – ♥103/165 € ♥♥119/206 €, ⊑ 15 €
♦ Traditional ♦ Functional ♦
A good location in a lively shopping area. A classical façade, intimate ambience,
and bright rooms with all creature comforts. Popular with groups.

XXXX **Neichel** 🔲 🕏 *VISA* 🔴 🔵 ①
❄️ *Beltran í Rózpide 1 ⊠ 08034 –* Ⓜ *Maria Cristina – ℰ 93 203 84 08*
– neichel@relaischateaux.com – Fax 93 205 63 69 – www.neichel.es
closed 1 to 9 January, 1 to 20 August, Sunday and Monday *Plan I* **A2**
Rest 76 € and a la carte 58/76 €
Spec. Ravioli de foie y centollo, jugo de trufas con puerros, chips de alcachofas.
Cordero lechal 'churra' con especias, cuscus de frutas, emulsión de leche de oveja
al cardamomo. Torrija de leche de coco caramelizada, helado de tomate/ vainilla,
chips de plátano, gelée de agua de rosas.
♦ Inventive ♦ Design ♦
Creative and innovative cuisine to satisfy even the most demanding palate. An
elegant and pleasant restaurant with a garden.

XXXX **Via Veneto** 🔲 🕏 *VISA* 🔴 🔵 ①
❄️ *Ganduxer 10 ⊠ 08021 –* Ⓜ *Hospital Clinic – ℰ 93 200 72 44 – pmonje@adam.es*
– Fax 93 201 60 95 – www.viavenetorestaurant.com
closed 1 to 20 August, Saturday lunch and Sunday **I2**
Rest 68 € and a la carte 46/68 €
Spec. Yema de huevo de Calaf con salmón, salsa smitana y caviar de arenque.
Rodaballo asado con salsifis crujientes y caldo de bullabesa. Crema de limón con
helado de albahaca y dados de manzana asada
♦ International ♦ Retro ♦
A restaurant with elegant Belle Epoque décor and impeccable service with an
interesting menu. A highly professional staff.

XXXX **Jean Luc Figueras** 🔲 🕏 *VISA* 🔴 🔵 ①
❄️ *Santa Teresa 10 ⊠ 08012 –* Ⓜ *Passeig de Gràcia – ℰ 93 415 28 77*
– jlf@jeanlucfigueras.com – Fax 93 218 92 62
– www.jeanlucfigueras.com
closed Sunday **K1**
Rest a la carte 65/87 €
Spec. Farcellet de col y butifarra de perol con caviar osietra. Lubina al vapor con
espinacas. Canelón helado de piña y eucalipto.
♦ Inventive ♦ Cosy ♦
A very pleasant setting in which to enjoy creative and innovative dishes. Several
elegant dining areas and décor with exquisitely tasteful design details.

XXXX **Reno** 🔲 🕏 *VISA* 🔴 🔵 ①
Tuset 27 ⊠ 08006 – Ⓜ *Gràcia – ℰ 93 200 91 29 – reno@restaurantreno.com*
– Fax 93 414 41 14
closed August, Saturday lunch and Sunday **J1**
Rest a la carte approx. 65 €
♦ Catalan cuisine ♦ Formal ♦
A traditional-style restaurant with a welcoming atmosphere and a menu firmly
rooted in the gastronomic culture of the region but with a modern twist. A very
good wine-list.

XxX **El Racó d'en Freixa** Ⓐ Ⓒ ⟨◇⟩4/16 ⟨VISA⟩ ⟨MC⟩ ⟨AE⟩ ⟨①⟩

✿ *Sant Elies 22* ⊠ *08006 –* Ⓜ *Plaça Molina –* ☏ *93 209 75 59*
– info@elracodenfreixa.com – Fax 93 209 79 18
– www.elracodenfreixa.com
closed Holy Week, 21 days in August, Sunday and Monday   **J1**
Rest a la carte 57/69 €
Spec. Transparente, crudo, confitado y helado de tomate con gambas de
Palamós. Liebre a la royal. Frutas y verduras vaporosas con helado de flor de
sauco.
◆ Inventive ◆ Family ◆
Recently redecorated in a more contemporary style with pure, minimalist lines
and designer touches to mirror the excellent service and interestingly creative
cuisine.

XxX **Botafumeiro** Ⓐ Ⓒ ⟨VISA⟩ ⟨MC⟩ ⟨AE⟩ ⟨①⟩

Gran de Gràcia 81 ⊠ *08012 –* Ⓜ *Fontana –* ☏ *93 218 42 30*
– info@botafumeiro.es – Fax 93 217 13 05
– www.botafumeiro.es   **J1**
Rest a la carte 40/60 €
◆ Seafood ◆ Formal ◆
A well-known restaurant in the Gràcia district of the city with a maritime feel to
it and a menu to match.

XX **Roig Robí** ⟨⌂⟩ Ⓐ Ⓒ 🅿 ⟨VISA⟩ ⟨MC⟩ ⟨AE⟩ ⟨①⟩

Sèneca 20 ⊠ *08006 –* Ⓜ *Diagonal –* ☏ *93 218 92 22*
– roigrobi@roigrobi.com – Fax 93 415 78 42
– www.roigrobi.com
closed 3 weeks in August, Saturday lunch and Sunday   **K1**
Rest a la carte 46/67 €
◆ Catalan cuisine ◆ Family ◆
A modern restaurant in a splendid setting with a pleasant garden-terrace. A very
varied and original menu.

XX **Alkimia** Ⓐ ⟨⤢⟩ Ⓒ ⟨VISA⟩ ⟨MC⟩ ⟨①⟩

✿ *Indústria 79* ⊠ *08025 –* Ⓜ *Sagrada Familia –* ☏ *93 207 61 15*
– alkimia@telefonica.net
closed Holy Week, 3 weeks in August, Saturday and Sunday   **K1**
Rest 58 € and a la carte 44/56 €
Spec. Atadillo de brandada de bacalao con col, canaillas, salsa de ajo y perejil.
Arroz de ñoras y azafrán con cigalas. Lechazo churro con fondue de queso de
cabra.
◆ Inventive ◆ Minimalist ◆
Dining room with soothing, minimalist decor, very good service and individual
lighting. Modern cuisine based on Catalonian traditions and a "sampler" menu
for tasting a variety of dishes.

XX **Laurak** Ⓐ Ⓒ ⟨◇⟩6/16 ⟨VISA⟩ ⟨MC⟩ ⟨AE⟩ ⟨①⟩

La Granada del Penedès 14-16 ⊠ *08006 –* Ⓜ *Passeig de Gràcia –* ☏ *93 218 71 65*
– Fax 93 218 98 67 – www.laurak.net
closed 22 December-3 January and Sunday   **J1**
Rest a la carte approx. 61 €
◆ Basque ◆ Design ◆
A modern restaurant which is efficiently run by the owner-chef. Airy dining room
with a wooden floor, design features and two private sections.

XX **Hisop** Ⓐ Ⓒ ⟨VISA⟩ ⟨MC⟩ ⟨AE⟩ ⟨①⟩

Passatge de Marimon 9 ⊠ *08021 –* Ⓜ *Hospital Clinic –* ☏ *93 241 32 33*
– hisop@hisop.com – www.hisop.com
closed 15 days in August, Saturday lunch and Sunday   **J2**
Rest a la carte 49/56 €
◆ Inventive ◆ Minimalist ◆
Hisop enjoys an excellent local reputation based upon its highly creative
cuisine and good service. A minimalist look with floral decoration on the
walls.

SPAIN

SPAIN

XX **Le Quattro Stagioni**   🕎 AC ⅍ ⇆8/16 VISA ⓜⓞ AE ⓞ

Dr. Roux 37 ⊠ 08017 – Ⓜ Les Tres Torres – ℰ 93 205 22 79 – restaurante @
4stagioni.com – Fax 93 205 78 65 – www.4stagioni.com
closed Holy Week, Sunday and Monday lunch (July-15 September),
Sunday dinner and Monday for rest of the year   **I1**
Rest a la carte 24/32 €
♦ Italian ♦ Cosy ♦
A well-run restaurant with comfortable dining areas with modern décor and a
pleasant patio-terrace. Cuisine in the Italian tradition.

XX **Silvestre**   AC ⅍ VISA ⓜⓞ AE ⓞ

😊 *Santaló 101 ⊠ 08021 – Ⓜ Muntaner – ℰ 93 241 40 31 – Fax 93 241 40 31*
closed Holy Week, 2 weeks in August, Saturday lunch, Sunday and Bank
Holidays   **J1**
Rest a la carte 27/30 €
♦ Catalan cuisine ♦ Cosy ♦
The couple who own this restaurant have created a popular eatery with several
sections which add intimacy to this classic setting. Good value-for money and
seasonal produce.

𝒴/ **José Luis**   🕎 AC ⅍ VISA ⓜⓞ AE ⓞ

av. Diagonal 520 ⊠ 08006 – Ⓜ Diagonal – ℰ 93 200 83 12
– joseluis@nexo.es – Fax 93 200 83 12 – www.joseluis.es   **J2**
Tapa 2 € **Ración** approx. 10 €
♦ Spanish ♦ Tapas bar ♦
On the city's main artery. A tapas bar with tables and on the first floor two
pleasant dining areas.

AT EL PRAT AIRPORT

🏠 **Ciutat del Prat**   🗲 🖃 🕭 AC ⅍ 🔥25/100 🛏 VISA ⓜⓞ AE ⓞ

av. Remolar 46 ⊠ 08820 – ℰ 93 378 83 33 – ciutatdelprat @ euro-mar.com
– Fax 93 478 60 63 – www.euro-mar.com
130 rm – ♦64/120 € ♦♦64/150 €, ⊑ 10 €
Rest 20 €
♦ Business ♦ Cosy ♦
Modern building with brightly coloured fully furnished rooms, and marble
bathrooms. The lounge areas are cheerful and comfortable, and the restaurant
is elegantly furnished and decorated.

🏠 **Tryp Barcelona Aeropuerto**   🗲 🕭 AC ⅍ 🔥25/300

pl. del Pla de L'Estany 1-2 ⊠ 08820 – ℰ 93   🛏 VISA ⓜⓞ AE ⓞ
378 10 00 – tryp.barcelona.aeropuerto @ solmelia.com – Fax 93 378 10 01
205 rm – ♦50/132 € ♦♦50/167 €, ⊑ 15 €
Rest 23 €
♦ Business ♦ Chain hotel ♦ Functional ♦
Functional establishment located in a business park close to the airport. The
interesting lobby layout means that it opens directly onto all the corridors
leading to the hotel's comfortable, practical bedrooms.

SWEDEN
SVERIGE

PROFILE

- **AREA:**
  449 964 km² (173 731 sq mi).

- **POPULATION:**
  9 002 000 inhabitants (est. 2005), density = 20 per km².

- **CAPITAL:**
  Stockholm (conurbation 1 417 000 inhabitants).

- **CURRENCY:**
  Swedish Kronor (Skr or SEK); rate of exchange: SEK 1 = € 0.10 = US$ 0.12 (Nov 2005).

- **GOVERNMENT:**
  Constitutional parliamentary monarchy (since 1950). Member of European Union since 1995.

- **LANGUAGE:**
  Swedish; many Swedes also speak good English.

- **SPECIFIC PUBLIC HOLIDAYS:**
  Epiphany (6 January), Good Friday (Friday before Easter), Midsummer's Day (Saturday between June 20-26), Halloween (Saturday between Oct 31-Nov 6), Boxing Day (26 December). National Day, 6 June, is not a public holiday.

- **LOCAL TIME:**
  GMT + 1 hour in winter and GMT + 2 hours in summer.

- **CLIMATE:**
  Temperate continental with cold winters and mild summers (Stockholm: January: -3°C, July: 16°C).

- **INTERNATIONAL DIALLING CODE:**
  00 46 followed by area code without the initial **0** and then the local number. International Directory Enquiries: ✆ **079 77**.

- **EMERGENCY:**
  Dial ✆ **112** for Police, Fire Brigade, Ambulance, Poison hot-line, on-call doctors and 24hr Roadside breakdown service.

- **ELECTRICITY:**
  220 volts AC, 50 Hz; 2-pin round-shaped continental plugs.

FORMALITIES

Travellers from the European Union (EU), Switzerland, Iceland and the main countries of North and South America need a national identity card or passport (America: passport required) to visit Sweden for less than three months (tourism or business purpose). For visitors from other countries a visa may be required, in addition to a passport, especially for those wishing to stay for longer than three months. We advise you to check with your embassy before travelling.

The major international car hire companies have offices in Stockholm and Gothenburg and at Arlanda and Landvetter airports. Drivers must not drink any alcoholic beverages.

MAJOR NEWSPAPERS

The main daily newspapers are *Dagens Nyheter* (Stockholm), *Göteborgs-Posten* (Göteborg) and *Sydsvenska Dagbladet* (Malmö); also *Expressen* and *Aftonbladet*. Most of the dailies are sold by subscription, with early morning home delivery.

USEFUL PHRASES

ENGLISH	SWEDISH
Yes	**Ja**
No	**Nej**
Good morning	**God dag, Hej**
Goodbye	**Adjö, Hej då**
Please	**Varsågod**
Thank you	**Tack**
Excuse me	**Förlåt**
I don't understand	**Jag förstår inte**

HOTELS

◆ CATEGORIES

Accommodation ranges from luxurious 5-star international hotels, to smaller, family-run guesthouses and bed and breakfast establishments *(rum & frukost)*, where guests are usually expected to stay 2 nights.

◆ PRICE RANGE

The price is per room. There is little difference between the price of a single and a double room. Between April and October it is advisable to book in advance. From November to March prices may be slightly lower, some hotels offer discounts throughout the year and during the summer. In Stockholm hotel chains frequently offer special discounts or hotel cheques.

◆ TAX

Included in the room price, together with service charge and breakfast.

◆ CHECK OUT TIME

Usually between 10am and noon.

◆ RESERVATIONS

By telephone or by Internet. A credit card number or a deposit may be required.

◆ TIP FOR LUGGAGE HANDLING

At the discretion of the customer (about Skr 3 per bag).

◆ BREAKFAST

It is usually included in the price of the room and is generally served between 7am and 10am. Most hotels offer a generous self-service buffet but usually it is possible to have continental breakfast served in the room.

Reception	**Reception**
Single room	**Enkelrum**
Double room	**Dubbelrum**
Bed	**Säng**
Bathroom	**Badrum**
Shower	**Dusch**

RESTAURANTS

Besides the traditional **restaurants** there are **brasseries** which serve simpler meals.

712

Breakfast	**Frukost**	7am – 10am
Lunch	**Lunch**	11am – 2pm
Dinner	**Middag**	6pm – 10pm

All restaurants display a menu in the window; the prices include VAT (Moms) and a service charge. Menus are usually printed in Swedish, Finnish, English and German. In the evening at dinner it is a good idea to opt for the speciality of the house or try the great Swedish buffet *(smörgåsbord)*. Many formal restaurants are closed at lunchtime but the dish of the day *(dagens rätt)* is usually good value as it includes unlimited salad, a soft drink bread and coffee. An alternative is to try a café for one of the tempting open sandwiches which make a refreshing and sustaining snack. At any time of year, as soon as the sun shines, the locals sit out on the terraces and at pavement tables.

◆ RESERVATIONS

Reservations are usually made by phone, fax or Internet. For famous restaurants (including Michelin starred restaurants), it is advisable to book several days – or weeks in some instances – in advance. A credit card number or a phone number may be required as guarantee.

◆ THE BILL

The bill (check) includes service charge (13-15%) and VAT. Tipping is optional but, if you are particularly pleased with the service, it is customary to round up the total – 10% in larger restaurants and the value of the small change elsewhere. In winter there is often a compulsory cloakroom charge of Skr 2.

Drink or aperitif	**Drycker**
Meal	**Måltid**
First course, starter	**Förrätter**
Main dish	**Huvudrätter / Varmrätter**
Main dish of the day	**Dagens rätt**
Dessert	**Efterrätter**
Water	**Vatten**
Wine (red, white, rosé)	**Vin (röd, vitt, rosé)**
Beer	**Öl**
Bread	**Bröd**
Meat	
(rare, medium, well done)	**Kött (blodig, medium, välstekt)**
Fish	**Fisk**
Salt/pepper	**Salt / peppar**
Cheese	**Ost**
Vegetables	**Grönsaker**
Hot/cold	**Varm / kall**
The bill (check) please	**Får jag be om notan**

LOCAL CUISINE

Breakfast is a mouth-watering display of bread, rolls, pastries, crispbread, sliced sausage, cheese, boiled and scrambled eggs, meatballs, pickles, cereals, yoghurt and fruit, accompanied with thin yoghurt *(filmjlk)*, milk, fruit juices, tea and coffee.

The great Swedish buffet *(smörgåsbord)* is served as a celebratory meal and should be approached in a leisurely way. Start with herring in many delectable forms in a mustard or horseradish sauce accompanied by boiled potatoes, garnished with fresh herbs and juniper berries; this stage is usually accompanied with beer and acquavit. Next try the thin slices of salmon cured in dill and then cleanse the palate with a course of cheese or eggs stuffed with caviar and shrimps. After that comes the main course of cold meat or fish or a hot dish of meatballs.

Seafood is always popular: cod, haddock, Baltic herring and fermented herring *(surströmming)*, whitefish and whitefish caviar, prawns *(räkor)*, mussels *(blåmusslor)*, crab and lobster *(hummer)*, salmon *(lax)* and trout *(forell)*. **Eel** *(ål)* is a delicacy served in a wide variety of ways. August is the time for **crayfish** *(kräftor)* parties when these delicious freshwater shellfish, boiled with dill, salt and sugar, are served cold with hot buttered toast and caraway cheese accompanied by the odd schnapps and beer. **Lutfisk**, dried and boiled ling, is served on Christmas Eve. **Janssons frestelse** (Jansson's Temptation) is a gratin of anchovies, potatoes, onions and cream baked in the oven.

Menus feature pork *(fläsk)*, beef *(biff)*, veal *(kalvkött)*, lamb *(lammkött)*, chicken *(kyckling)* and sausage *(korv)*. A very popular meat dish is succulent **meatballs** *(köttbullar)*, mixed with herbs and served in a cream sauce with mashed potatoes. Goose makes a festive dinner on St Martin's Eve. Venison, reindeer *(ren)* and elk *(älg)* may appear on the menu: **smoked reindeer** with a pesto of beetroot and horseradish, **roast elk** with boiled potatoes, cream sauce and blackcurrant or redcurrant jelly. Wild berries figure largely in many dishes: blueberries for soup and fruit pies, loganberries for juice and jam, lingonberries to accompany meatballs, elk and pancakes. Dinner on Thursday is often pea soup *(ärtsoppa)* and pancake with a sweet alcoholic drink called punsch.

Sweet cakes and pastries are popular: waffles *(våfflor)*, mini pancakes served with cream and jam *(plättar)*, cinnamon buns *(kanelbullar)*, gingerbread biscuits *(pepparkaka)*, saffron cakes *(lussekatt)*, a cake made of eggs and sugar *(spettekaka)*, a regional speciality from Skåne.

◆ DRINK

Most Swedes prefer to drink **beer**, which is produced in 3 grades – light, ordinary and export. Wine is widely available in nearly all restaurants, most of which offer an interesting range from France and other countries, often by the glass. As alcohol is expensive and sold only in government-owned shops *(Systembolaget)* (Mon-Fri 9.30am-6pm), soft drinks, mineral water, alcohol-free beer and coffee are usually drunk at meal times. The coffee is fairly strong and tea is usually made with warm water. In December you can warm up with a glass of spicy mulled wine *(glögg)*. The most popular Swedish spirit is aquavit *(akvavit)* and the most popular brand is Skåne. Aquavit is distilled from barley or potatoes but each brand is flavoured with juniper or coriander or myrtle or some other herb. It is served in tiny glasses and quaffed ice cold usually at the beginning of a meal with the fish course.

STOCKHOLM
STOCKHOLM

Population (est. 2005): 782 000 (conurbation 1 417 000) – Altitude: sea level

R.Mattes/MICHELIN

Enthusiastic admirers say that Stockholm is the most beautiful city in the world. The Swedish capital is set in an archipelago so that the city, which is built on 14 islands linked by bridges, is surrounded on all sides by water. It is located where freshwater Lake Mälaren joins the Baltic Sea, amid a seascape of countless islands, each seemingly more beautiful than the last. Parks and gardens add to Stockholm's undeniable beauty and contrast with the high-rise buildings of the commercial centre. The residence of the royal household is not far from Stockholm at Drottningholm.

Stockholm is modern and efficient, with a rich historical and cultural heritage. During the summer Stockholmers live outdoors, like the citizens of Oslo and Copenhagen, making for the city's animated streets and parks, where there are staged entertainments. Stockholm, cultural capital of Europe in 1998, is rich in cultural activities with a wide selection of museums, theatres, art galleries and music performances. Early in December brightly decorated stalls are set up in the Old Town square for the Christmas Fair.

WHICH DISTRICT TO CHOOSE

Many of the **hotels** are located in the Old Town (Gamla Stan) *Plan I* **C2** and in Norrmalm *Plan I* **B2** but there are a good number in the suburbs and at the airport.

Stockhom has a great diversity of **restaurants** and the highest concentrations are to be found in Norrmalm, Östermalm *Plan I* **C1**, Södermalm *Plan I* **C3** and Gamla Stan; the latter boasts many restaurants, some of them established in picturesque old houses; the triangle formed by Birger Jarlsgatan and Nybrogatan up to Östermalmstorg has a good selection of restaurants, brasseries, cafés and snack bars. There are also restaurants in the suburbs where there are hotels and at the airport.

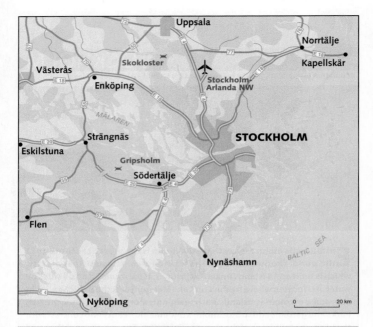

0   20 km

PRACTICAL INFORMATION

ARRIVAL – DEPARTURE

Stockholm Arlanda Airport – About 40 km (25 mi) northwest of city centre, ℰ 797 60 00.

From the airport to the city centre – By **train**: Arlanda Express (20min) to Centralstation (5am-12.35am, every 15min), Skr 140. By **airport bus** *(Flygbus)* (40min) to Cityterminalen, the central bus station (6.30am-11.45pm every 5-10min), Skr 80. By **taxi**: 35min, Skr 375.

Railway Station – **Centralstation** *Plan I* **B2** for services from the main towns of Sweden.

Ferry Terminal – Ferry services from Helsinki (Finland) – *Silja Line*, ℰ 22 21 40; www.silja.com; *Viking Line*, ℰ 452 20 00; www.vikingline.se. From Tallinn (Estonia) – *Tallink*, www.tallink.se

TRANSPORT

◆ BUS, TRAM AND METRO

Buses (450 routes), trams, the underground railway *(Tunnelbanan)* and suburban trains. Timetables and maps from the buses or at Stockholm's Local Traffic Information Centre in Central Station. The metro is often quicker as it offers a more direct route. The tram No 7 (June-August daily 11am-6/7pm) takes in quite a few of the main attractions. **Travel passes** for unlimited travel by bus, metro and regional train and ferries to Djurgården: 1-day card Skr 95; 3-day card Skr 180, available from travel centres and newsagents *(pressburå)*. **Ticket coupons** *(rabattkuponger)* valid on buses and underground Skr 110, available from bus drivers or at any underground station. **Monthly card** *(månadskort)* for unlimited travel on public transport for 31 days Skr 600.

◆ TAXIS

Taxis can be hailed in the street or picked up at a taxi rank. A lit sign *Ledig* means a taxi is free. A 10% tip is included in the amount shown on the meter. The basic charge is Skr 35 within the city area (some taxis charge Skr 75) plus Skr 10 per km. Special fares operate after midnight, at weekends and on public holidays. *Taxi Stockholm* ℰ 15 00 00, *Taxi Kurir* ℰ 30 00 00, *Top Cab* ℰ 33 33 33.

◆ BOATS

Ferry between **Skeppsbron** and **Djurgården**, daily (extra service in summer from Nybroplan stopping at Skeppsholmen and Vasamuseet).

Boat tours under the Bridges of Stockholm or on the Royal Canal, discovering the network of waterways of this island city; daily from **Strömkajen** or **Nybroplan**. Combined sightseeing boat and bus tour. Information and bookings from Stockholm Sightseeing, Skeppsbron 22. ℰ 587 140 20; www.stockholmsightseeing.com

Boat tours to different parts of the **National City Park**: round Djurgården April to mid-Dec daily; round Brunnsviken (north of city centre) late June to early August daily (last tour in English); Fjäderholmarna Islands (east of Djurgården) from May to mid-Sep daily. ℰ 587 140 40.

◆ STOCKHOLM CARD

Valid for free public transport (city centre and suburbs but not airport buses), parking, a sightseeing tour by boat and free admission to 70 museums and other attractions. 24hr-card Skr 220 ; 48hr-card Skr 380; 72hr-card Skr 540.

USEFUL ADDRESSES

◆ TOURIST OFFICES

Tourist Centre, Sweden House, Hamngatan 27 (entrance in Kungsträdgården) *Plan I* **C2**; open Mon-Fri 9am-6pm, Sat-Sun 9am-3pm; ℰ 508 28 508, 789 24 00 (Mon-Fri), 789 24 90 (weekends; Excursion Shop and Tourist Centre only). **Kaknastornet,**

Ladugardsgardet, ℰ 789 24 35 (9am-10pm); kaknas@stoinfo.se. **Stadshuset** (Town Hall), Hantverkargatan 1, ℰ 651 21 12; www.stockholm.com.

Accommodation Booking Office – Hotel Centralen *Plan I* **B2**, ℰ 789 24 90.

◆ POST OFFICES

Opening times Mon-Sat 10am-6pm (Sat 1pm); longer hours at the main post office in Drottninggatan 53.

◆ BANKS/CURRENCY EXCHANGE

Opening times Mon-Fri 9.30am-3pm; most banks in the city centre close at 3.30pm. Banking facilities at the Arlanda Airport daily 7am-10pm. Exchange facilities at the Tourist Centre and in most large hotels.

◆ EMERGENCY

Dial ℰ **112** for Police, Fire Brigade, Ambulance, Poison hot-line, on-call doctors and 24hr Roadside breakdown service.

BUSY PERIODS

It may be difficult to find a room at a reasonable price (except at weekends) during special events:

Restaurant Festival: early June – Kungsträdgården becomes a large outdoor restaurant.

Midsummer Eve: June (next to last Saturday) – Major Swedish festival celebrated at Skansen over three days; maypole and ring dancing.

Music at the Palace: June-August – Summer concert season starts in the Royal Palace.

Drottningholms Slottsteater: June-August – Summer season of concerts, opera and dance in the 18C court theatre.

Stockholm International Jazz and Blues Festival: July.

Stockholm Water Festival: August – Water sports, fireworks and other events.

Christmas Markets: early December – Christmas goods on sale at traditional markets at Skansen, Rosendals Slott, Stortorget in Gamla Stan and Drottningholms Slott.

DIFFERENT FACETS OF THE CITY

It is possible to visit the main sights and museums in two to three days.

Museums and sights are usually open from 10/11am to 4-6pm; some close on Mondays.

GAMLA STAN – Historic heart of the city, an architecturally harmonious maze of narrow 17C streets and several prestigious buildings erected on three islands – Stadsholmen, Riddarholmen and Helgeandsholmen. **Kungliga Slottet** *Plan II* **F**: Royal castle rebuilt in the baroque style after a fire; now houses several museums and is occasionally used for official receptions; Royal Armoury in the vaults; Royal Treasury; changing of the guard weekdays at noon and Sundays and holidays at 1.10pm. **Storkyrkan** *Plan II* **F**: Cathedral, consecrated in 1306 and later remodelled, with a magnificent wooden 15C sculpture depicting St George and the Dragon by Bernt Notke from Lübeck. **Stortorget** *Plan II* **F**: Old Town main square, fronted by a late 18C rococo-style building, the former **Börsen** (Stock Exchange), now the Royal Academy, where the winner of the Nobel Prize for literature is announced. **Riddarholmskyrkan** *Plan II* **E**: set on a small island, one of the oldest churches in Stockholm, containing the tombs of the Swedish monarchs, now houses a museum. **Medeltidsmuseet** *Plan II* **E**: situated on Helgeandsholmen, beneath the Parliament House, contains medieval ruins.

NORRMALM – Modern, functional district north of the old town consisting of wide straight streets with offices and shops clustered round Sergels Torg. **Kungsträdgården** *Plan I* **C2**: a popular meeting place

offering a range of activities – large chessboards and boules alleys – on the site of the royal vegetable plot. **Nationalmuseum** *Plan I* **C2**: national museum of fine arts.

DJURGÅRDEN – Vast park containing three museums in former hunting ground: picnicking, rambling, horse-riding and other outdoor pursuits. **Skansen** *Plan I* **D2**: the world's first open-air museum, founded in 1891, containing 150 houses from different regions of Sweden; the interiors have all been reconstructed. **Vasamuseet** *Plan I* **D2**: *Vasa* warship which sank in 1628 in Stockholm harbour and was raised and restored in 1961. **Nordiska Museet** *Plan I* **D2**: cultural history of Sweden with a particularly interesting section on the Lapps.

OUTSKIRTS – **Drottningholm Slott** *(1hr by boat from Stadshusbron on Kungsholmen)*: late 17C royal castle in the Baroque style, the official residence of the monarch; monumental staircase, Court Theatre, formal gardens, French gardens, English park. **Millesgården**: Museum dedicated to the sculptor Carl Milles (1875-1955) in his former residence magnificently set on the island of Lidingö. **Archipelago**: take a mini-cruise to visit some of the 24 000 islands and reefs in the area around Stockholm, where many locals have island summer houses; swimming possible.

GOURMET TREATS

For a light lunch go into **Östermalms Saluhall** (covered market) *Plan I* **C1** where individual stalls sell an array of fish, meat, cheese and vegetables and offer a choice of Scandinavian sandwiches *(Smörgasbord)*, salads and snacks, served directly at the counter or on tables set inside the market hall.

Many of Stockholm's cafés are distinctive places in pleasantly rural or lakeside settings with excellent views. They also provide a mouth-watering selection of open sandwiches and home-made delicacies: pastries, apple, walnut and fudge, raspberry and blueberry pies, cheesecakes or waffles with cloudberry jam. Quite a number offer light lunches. Coffee may be expensive but you are entitled to a second cup. Museum cafés often offer good value for money and department stores are good for coffee, snacks and light meals.

SHOPPING

Stores are usually open on weekdays from 9/10am to 6/7pm. On Friday some department stores close at 8-9pm. In many districts, some shops also open on Sunday and/or in the evening.

Stockholm has a great variety of shops from small boutiques to large stores. The largest department store is *Åhlens* (Klarabergsgatan 50) and the most exclusive is *NK* (Hamngatan 18-20). The main shopping streets in the centre of Stockholm are **Hamngatan** *Plan I* **C2**, **Biblioteksgatan** *Plan I* **C2**, **Drottninggatan** *Plan I* **B2**, **Sturegallerian**; also in the Old Town mainly **Västerlånggatan** *Plan I* **C2**, which has many speciality shops. Certain streets or districts in the city centre tend to specialise in one kind of shop: department stores in **Hamngatan**; expensive boutiques in the narrow streets of **Gamla Stan** *Plan I* **C2**; design shops in **Strandvågen**; individual shops selling trendy clothes in pedestrianised **Drottninggatan**, the rendezvous for the young. When looking for bargains *Rea* means sale, *Extrapris* means discount and *Fynd* indicates a special offer.

WHAT TO BUY – Glassware (Orrefors, Kosta, Boda), ceramics, textiles, knitwear, needlework, craft work, wood carvings; the museum shops are good for gifts.

ENTERTAINMENT

For information about times and venues consult *Stockholm This* Week, published monthly by the Stockholm Information Service, *What's On*, a monthly publication from the Tourist Office, and the *På Stan* (On the Town) section of the Friday edition of the daily newspapers *Svenska Dagbladet* and *Dagens Nyheter*.

MUSIC – **Opera** *Plan I* **C2**. **Berwalk Hallen** *Plan I* **D1**. **Konserthuset** *Plan I* **B2**. Many city churches. **Skeppsholmen** *Plan I* **D2**: the Stockholm Jazz and Blues Festival in July. **Circus** (Djurgården) for rock and pop concerts. **Skansen** *Plan I* **D1** and **Grona Lund**: for concerts in summer. **Stampen** (Stora Nygatan 5) *Plan II* **E**: for jazz and swing.

THEATRE – **Kungliga Dramatiska Teatern** *Plan I* **C2**: the stamping ground of Strindberg and Bergman. **Stadsteatern** *Plan I* **C2** and **Fasching Jazzclub** (Kungsgatan) *Plan I* **B2**: modern and classical plays in Swedish.

NIGHTLIFE

For information on nightclubs consult *What's On*, a monthly publication from the Tourist Office, and the *På Stan* (On the Town) section of the Friday edition of the daily newspapers *Svenska Dagbladet* and *Dagens Nyheter*. The area around **Kungstradgarden** *Plan I* **C2** and **Stureplan** *Plan I* **C1** has a thriving nightlife: *Café Opera* (Operahuset, Kungsträdgården), known for its celebrity clientele and long queues, has dancing every night; *Kolingen* (Kornhamnstorg 59B) a basement night club; *Sturecom-pagniet* (Stureplan) a multi-storey complex of eating, drinking and dancing spots.

SWEDEN

A
B

Tekniska
Högskolan

Sankt Eriksgatan
Norrtullsgatan
Sveavägen
Freigatan
Vanadis-
vägen
Surbrunns-
Odengatan
Karlavägen
Östermalmsgatan

Clas På
Hörnet

Dalagatan
Vanadis-
plan
VASASTADEN

Tulegatan
Döbelnsgatan
Birger
Kungstens-
Karlavägen
Jarlsgatan
Birger Jarl

Freigatan
Odenplan
Karlbergsvägen
Nortullsgatan

Sankt Eriksgatan
Torsgatan
Odengatan
Upplands-
Kungstens-
gatan
Västmanna-
Rådmansgatan
Sveavägen
Tegnérgatan
Regerings-
Birger

VASAPARKEN
U
U
U
Grill
RolfsKok
Drottninggatan
Hollandargatan
Gata
Vassa Eggen
Elite H.
Stockholm Plaza

Sankt
Eriksplan
STRINDBERGSMUSEET
Tegnér-
lunden

Hötorget
Kungs-

Klarastrands-
Torsgatan
Tegnér-
gatan
Dalagatan
Olof Palmes
Drottning
gatan
Restaurangen
KONSERTHUSET
Oxtorgs-
gatan
Sveav.
Regerings-

Barnhusbron
leden
Norra
Bantorget
Vasa-
gatan
Kungs-
gatan
Rica H.
Stockholm
Freys
Slöjdgatan
Hötorget
NORRMALM

Flemming-
Kungsbron-
gatan
Nordic Light
Bryggar
T-Centralen
Nordic Sea
Karlabergs-
Hamn
Vasagatan
KULTUR-
HUSET

Kungsbron
Radisson SAS
Royal Viking
Klarabergsviadukten
Sheraton
Stockholm
H. and Towers
Herkules-
gatan
Jakobs-
gatan

Kungsholms-
gatan
First H.
Amaranten
Scheelegatan
CENTRAL-
STATIONEN
Vasa-
gatan
Fredsgata
12

Rådhuset
Bergs-
gatan
Hantverkargatan
Kungsholms-
torg
Hantverkargatan
STADHUSET
RIDDARHOLME

KUNGSHOLMEN
Norr
Mälarstrand

RIDDARFJÄRDEN

Mälarstrand

Söder
Brännkyrka-
Horns-

| ● | Hotel |
| ● | Restaurant |

A
B
Mariatorget

720

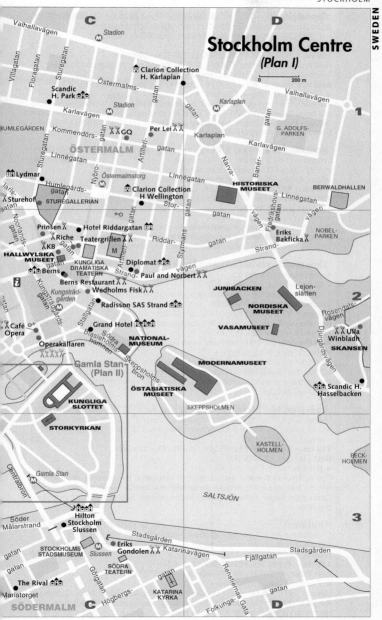

Stockholm Centre
(Plan I)

0   200 m

C

Valhallavägen

Stadion

Clarion Collection
H. Karlaplan

Scandic
H. Park

Östermalms-gatan

Karlavägen

Karlaplan

Valhallavägen

D

Karlaplan

G. ADOLFS-PARKEN

HUMLEGÅRDEN

Kommendörs-gatan

Per Lei

Karlaplan

Karlavägen

ÖSTERMALM

Artilleri-gatan

GQ

Stadion

Linnégatan

Östermalmstorg

Lydmar

Humlegårds-gatan

STUREGALLERIAN

Clarion Collection
H Wellington

Linnégatan

Narva-vägen

Banér-gatan

HISTORISKA
MUSEET

BERWALDHALLEN

Sturehof

Stor-gatan

Linnégatan

Fredrikshovs-gatan

Prinsen

Riche

KB

HALLWYLSKA
MUSEET

Nybro-gatan

Hotel Riddargatan

Teatergrillen

Riddar-gatan

Styrmans-gatan

gatan

Eriks
Bakficka

NOBEL-PARKEN

Diplomat

Strand-vägen

Paul and Norbert

Berns Restaurant

KUNGLIGA
DRAMATISKA
TEATERN

Wedholms Fisk

Strand-

JUNIBACKEN

Lejon-slätten

Berns

Kungsträd-gården

Radisson SAS Strand

NORDISKA
MUSEET

Rosendals-vägen

Café
Opera

Grand Hotel

VASAMUSEET

Ulla
Winblad

Djurgårdsvägen

SKANSEN

Operakällaren

Stallgatan

Blasieholms-hamnen

Södra

NATIONAL-
MUSEUM

Skeppsholms-bron

MODERNAMUSEET

Gamla Stan
(Plan II)

KUNGLIGA
SLOTTET

ÖSTASIATISKA
MUSEET

Scandic H.
Hasselbacken

SKEPPSHOLMEN

STORKYRKAN

KASTELL-HOLMEN

BECK-HOLMEN

Centralbron

Gamla Stan

SALTSJÖN

Söder
Mälarstrand

Hilton
Stockholm
Slussen

STOCKHOLMS
STADSMUSEUM

Slussen

Eriks
Gondolen

Stadsgården

Katarinavägen

Fjällgatan

Stadsgården

Renstiernas Gata

The Rival

Mariatorget

Götgatan

SÖDRA
TEATERN

KATARINA
KYRKA

Högbergs-gatan

Folkunga-Gata

SÖDERMALM   **C**   **D**

Grand Hôtel

rest 350 VISA MC AE

Södra Blasieholmshamnen 8 ✉ S-111 47 – Ⓜ Kungsträdgarden – ✆ (08) 679 35 00 – info@grandhotel.se – Fax (08) 611 86 86 – www.grandhotel.se **C2**

290 rm – 2500 SEK 4600 SEK, 220 SEK – 10 suites

Rest *Franska Matsalen*, *✆ (08) 679 35 84 (closed July, Sunday and Saturday lunch)*685/1400 SEK and a la carte 625/1105 SEK

Rest *Verandan*, *✆ (08) 679 35 86* – 365/495 SEK and a la carte 355/635 SEK

◆ Grand Luxury ◆ Classic ◆

Sweden's top hotel occupies a late 19C mansion on the waterfront overlooking the Royal Palace and Old Town. Combines traditional elegance with the latest modern facilities. Classic mahogany and crystal Franska Matsalen. Verandan boasts famous smörgåsbord.

Radisson SAS Royal Viking

130 VISA MC AE

Vasagatan 1 ✉ S-101 24 – Ⓜ T-Centralen – ✆ (08) 506 540 00 – sales.royal.stockholm@radissonsas.com – Fax (08) 506 540 01 – www.radissonsas.com **B2**

456 rm – 1795 SEK 2595 SEK, 125 SEK – 3 suites

Rest *Stockholm Fisk*, *✆ (08) 506 541 02 (closed Sunday lunch)* a la carte approx. 550 SEK

◆ Business ◆ Modern ◆

Panoramic Sky Bar with impressive views over Stockholm, at the top of 9 floors of comfortable bedrooms. In busy part of the city but completely soundproofed. Stylish contemporary restaurant offers an array of seafood dishes.

Sheraton Stockholm H. and Towers

rest 380 VISA MC AE

Tegelbacken 6 ✉ S-101 23 – Ⓜ T-Centralen – ✆ (08) 412 34 00 – stockholm.sheraton@sheraton.com – Fax (08) 412 34 09 – www.sheraton.com/stockholm **B2**

445 rm – 3100 SEK 3300 SEK, 195 SEK – 17 suites

Rest *Dining Room* *(closed lunch Saturday and Sunday)* (buffet lunch) 195/255 SEK and a la carte 385/445 SEK

Rest *Die Ecke* *(closed Sunday and lunch Saturday)* a la carte approx. 400 SEK

◆ Business ◆ Modern ◆

International hotel popular with business people, overlooking Gamla Stan and offering the largest rooms in town. Comprehensive guest facilities. Open-plan all day restaurant with Swedish dishes. Authentic German dishes in classic wood panelled Die Ecke.

Radisson SAS Strand

50 VISA MC AE

Nybrokajen 9 ✉ S-103 27 – Ⓜ Kungsträdgarden – ✆ (08) 506 640 00 – sales.strand.stockholm@radissonsas.com – Fax (08) 506 640 01 – www.radissonsas.com **C2**

132 rm – 2150 SEK 2595 SEK, 180 SEK – 20 suites

Rest a la carte 295/425 SEK

◆ Business ◆ Classic ◆

Characterful old world architecture in red brick overlooking the harbour. Rooms feature classic elegant décor with traditional Swedish style furniture. Open plan lobby restaurant with accomplished Swedish and international cooking.

Diplomat

VISA MC AE

Strandvägen 7c ✉ S-104 40 – Ⓜ Kungsträdgarden – ✆ (08) 459 68 00 – info@diplomathotel.com – Fax (08) 459 68 20 – www.diplomathotel.com closed Christmas **C2**

128 rm – 1995 SEK 2495 SEK, 170 SEK

Rest *T Bar*, *✆ (08) 459 68 02* – a la carte 370/570 SEK

◆ Traditional ◆ Classic ◆

Elegant 1911 Art Nouveau building converted into hotel from diplomatic lodgings pleasantly located overlooking the harbour. Traditional and contemporary bedrooms. A popular terrace adjoins contemporary style hotel restaurant offering traditional Swedish cooking.

Berns 🕏 ↳ ⅌rest 🖭 ⚿180 **VISA** 🐠 ⚞ ①
Näckströmsgatan 8, Berzelii Park ⊠ *S-111 47 –* ⑩ *Kungsträdgarden*
– ℰ *(08) 566 322 00 – frontoffice@berns.se – Fax (08) 566 322 01*
– www.berns.se   **C2**
61 rm � – ♥2400 SEK ♥♥3100 SEK – 4 suites
Rest see **Berns Restaurant** below
Rest *The Summer Terrace* *(closed October-April)* a la carte 175/550 SEK
♦ Business ♦ Stylish ♦
Boutique hotel with a modern minimalist interior décor verging on trendy;
details in cherry wood and marble. Modern facilities in bedrooms, some have
balconies. The Summer Terrace for dinner, drinking, nightclubbing and breakfast.

 Nordic Light 🖪 🕏 ↻ ⚿ ↳ 🖭 ⚿40 ⌬ **VISA** 🐠 ⚞ ①
Vasaplan ⊠ *S-101 37 –* ⑩ *T-Centralen –* ℰ *(08) 505 630 00*
– info@nordichotels.se – Fax (08) 505 630 30
– www.nordiclighthotel.com   **B2**
175 rm � – ♥2560 SEK ♥♥2990 SEK
Rest a la carte 360/465 SEK 🏵
♦ Business ♦ Design ♦
Sister hotel to Nordic Sea boasting most facilities. Modern harmonious black and
white designer décor features symphony of lights on the Nordic Lights theme.
Also, an ice bar! Modern restaurant in the main hall: modish cooking.

 Nordic Sea without rest ↻ ⚿ ↳ 🖭 ⚿100 ⌬ **VISA** 🐠 ⚞ ①
Vasaplan ⊠ *S-101 37 –* ⑩ *T-Centralen –* ℰ *(08) 505 630 00*
– info@nordichotels.se – Fax (08) 505 630 90
– www.nordicseahotel.com   **B2**
367 rm � – ♥2140 SEK ♥♥2570 SEK
♦ Business ♦ Design ♦
Stylish modern hotel with an appropriately nautical theme. Accordingly, the
modish bedrooms all have a cool blue backdrop.

 First H. Amaranten 🖪 🕏 ↻ ⚿ rest ↳ ⅌rest 🖭 ℰ **VISA** 🐠 ⚞ ①
Kungsholmsgatan 31 ⊠ *S-104 20 –* ⑩ *Rådhuset –* ℰ *(08) 692 52 00*
– amaranten@firsthotels.se – Fax (08) 652 62 48
– www.firsthotels.com/amaranten   **A2**
422 rm � – ♥1798 SEK ♥♥2198 SEK – 1 suite
Rest *Amaranten* 265 SEK (lunch) and a la carte 264/514 SEK
♦ Business ♦ Modern ♦
Modernised, commercial hotel conveniently located with easy access to subway.
Stylish, quiet public areas with American Bar; compact but up-to-date bedrooms.
Stylish modern eating area with a large menu of modern Swedish cooking.

 Scandic H. Park 🕏 🕏 ↻ ↳ 🖭 ℰ ⚿50 ⌬ **VISA** 🐠 ⚞ ①
Karlavägen 43 ⊠ *S-102 46 –* ⑩ *Stadion –* ℰ *(08) 517 348 00*
– park@scandic-hotels.com – Fax (08) 517 348 11
– www.scandic-hotels.com/park   **C1**
190 rm � – ♥2140 SEK ♥♥2240 SEK – 8 suites
Rest *Park Village* a la carte 310/440 SEK
♦ Business ♦ Modern ♦
Convenient location by one of the city's prettiest parks (view from suites). All
rooms are a good size, modern and comfortable with good range of facilities and
comforts. Modern restaurant with small summer terrace; traditional Swedish
and international fare.

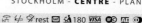 **Birger Jarl** 🖪 🕏 ↻ ↳ ⅌ 🖭 ⚿150 ⌬ **VISA** 🐠 ⚞ ①
Tulegatan 8 ⊠ *S-104 32 –* ⑩ *Rådmansgatan –* ℰ *(08) 674 18 00*
– info@birgerjarl.se – Fax (08) 673 73 66 – www.birgerjarl.se   **B1**
230 rm � – ♥1745 SEK ♥♥2400 SEK – 5 suites
Rest *(closed lunch Saturday and Sunday)* a la carte 210/444 SEK
♦ Business ♦ Modern ♦
Modern hotel building in quieter part of city. Lobby features many art and
sculpture displays. Some rooms decorated by local artists of international
reputation. Simple and stylish restaurant with unfussy Swedish cooking.

SWEDEN

🔒 **Elite H. Stockholm Plaza** ⚉ ⮂ ⇄ 🖵 🕻 ⚙50 *VISA* 🌎 🆎 ⓿
Birger Jarlsgatan 29 ⌧ *S-103 95* – **Ⓜ** *Östermalmstorg* – ✆ *(08) 566 220 00*
– info.stoplaza@elite.se – Fax (08) 566 220 20 – www.elite.se
closed 23-27 December   **B1**
147 rm ⌚ – **†**1945 SEK **††**2445 SEK – 4 suites
Rest see *Vassa Eggen* below
◆ Business ◆ Functional ◆
Well preserved 1884 building with up-to-date comforts. Compact well run
commercial hotel with conference rooms, basement sauna and high percentage
of single rooms.

🔒 **Freys** ⇗ ⚉ ⮂ ⇄ 🖵 ⚙30 *VISA* 🌎 🆎 ⓿
Bryggargatan 12 ⌧ *S-101 31* – **Ⓜ** *T-Centralen* – ✆ *(08) 506 213 00*
– freys@freyshotels.com – Fax (08) 506 213 13 – www.freyshotels.com
closed 22-28 December   **B2**
123 rm ⌚ – **†**1650 SEK **††**2250 SEK – 1 suite
Rest *belgobaren* 295 SEK (dinner) and a la carte 196/342 SEK
◆ Business ◆ Functional ◆
Completely renovated hotel near Central station. Local paintings for sale.
First-floor terrace. Fairly compact rooms with informal furnishings; superior
rooms with balconies. Belgian specialities, including more than 100 different
beers, on exclusive menu.

🔒 **Hotel Riddargatan** without rest ⮂ ⇄ 🖵 🕻 *VISA* 🌎 🆎 ⓿
Riddargatan 14 ⌧ *S-114 35* – **Ⓜ** *Östermalmstorg* – ✆ *(08) 555 730 00*
– hotelriddargatan@profilhotels.se – Fax (08) 555 730 11
– www.profilhotels.se   **C2**
56 rm ⌚ – **†**1945 SEK **††**2295 SEK – 2 suites
◆ Business ◆ Design ◆
Modern style hotel in quiet location behind the Royal Dramatik Theatre, near
shops and restaurants. Swedish design bedrooms with good internet facilities.

🔒 **Lydmar** ⮂ ⇄ 🖵 🕻 *VISA* 🌎 🆎 ⓿
Sturegatan 10 ⌧ *S-114 36* – **Ⓜ** *Östermalmstorg* – ✆ *(08) 566 113 00*
– info@lydmar.se – Fax (08) 566 113 01 – www.lydmar.se   **C1**
61 rm ⌚ – **†**1550 SEK **††**2800 SEK – 1 suite
Rest *The Dining Room* *(closed Sunday in low season)* (light lunch)
a la carte approx. 525 SEK
◆ Business ◆ Stylish ◆
Well located in the shopping and nightlife area, this boutique hotel overlooking
the park offers style: bar with regular light music; individually furnished
bedrooms. Stylish, informal dining and original, modern cooking with eclectic
influences.

🔒 **Rica H. Stockholm** ⚉ ⮂ 🖨 ⇄ ⚗ 🖵 ⚙60 *VISA* 🌎 🆎 ⓿
Slöjdgatan 7 ⌧ *S-111 57* – **Ⓜ** *T-Centralen* – ✆ *(08) 723 72 00*
– info.stockholm@rica.se – Fax (08) 723 72 09 – www.rica.se
closed 22 December-2 January   **B2**
292 rm ⌚ – **†**1740 SEK **††**2175 SEK
Rest *Oasen* *(closed Saturday and Sunday)* (lunch only) (snacks only) a la carte
82/88 SEK
◆ Business ◆ Functional ◆
Conveniently located at heart of shopping district so popular with tourists.
Rooms distributed around atrium, beneath which is a winter garden. Functional
modern bedrooms. Street-side restaurant offering narrow range of daily
changing platters.

🔒 **Clarion Collection H. Wellington** without rest ⚉ ⮂ ⇄ 🖵 🕻
Storgatan 6 ⌧ *S-114 51* – **Ⓜ** *Östermalmstorg* ⇨ *VISA* 🌎 🆎 ⓿
– ✆ (08) 667 09 10 – cc.wellington@choice.se – Fax (08) 667 12 54
– www.wellington.se – closed Christmas   **C1**
58 rm ⌚ – **†**1945 SEK **††**2245 SEK – 2 suites
◆ Business ◆ Functional ◆
Apartment block converted to hotel in 1960s, well placed for shopping and
clubs. Compact, refurbished and well-equipped rooms; good city views from
upper floor balconies.

Clarion Collection H. Karlaplan without rest
Skeppargatan 82 ⊠ *S-114 59 Stockholm –*
ℰ (08) 31 32 20 – info.karlaplan@choicehotels.se – Fax (08) 31 32 21
– www.hotelkarlaplan.se
85 rm ☷ – ♥1599 SEK ♥♥2399 SEK
♦ Business ♦ Modern ♦
18C building on edge of city centre. Functionality is the key here, with both breakfast room and bedrooms being simple and unfussily adorned. Buffet included in room rate.

Plan I **C-D1**

Operakällaren (Catenacci)
Operahuset, Karl XII's Torg ⊠ *S-111 86 –* Ⓜ *Kungsträdgarden*
– ℰ (08) 676 58 00 – matsal@operakallaren.se – Fax (08) 676 58 72
– www.operakallaren.se
closed mid July-mid August, 25 December-8 January,
Sunday and Monday
Rest (dinner only) 890 SEK/1050 SEK and a la carte 515/780 SEK 🕮
Spec. Swedish salmon in three ways. Fillet of reindeer with horn of plenty mushroom powder, baked fig and potato with Gorgonzola. Cloudberry soufflé with vanilla ice cream.
♦ Traditional ♦ Formal ♦
Magnificent dining room with original 19C carved wood décor and fresco paintings situated in the historic Opera House. Extensive menu of well prepared gourmet dishes.

C2

Vassa Eggen – at Elite H. Stockholm Plaza
Birger Jarlsgatan 29 ⊠ *S-114 25 –* Ⓜ *Östermalmstorg – ℰ (08) 21 61 69*
– info.vassaeggen.com – Fax (08) 20 34 46
– www.vassaeggen.com
closed 23-27 December
Rest *(closed lunch Saturday and Sunday)* (light lunch) 315 SEK/700 SEK and a la carte 650/700 SEK
♦ Innovative ♦ Fashionable ♦
Refined restaurant popular with those in the know. Modern style reflected in both the décor and the cuisine, which is original and innovative.

B1

Paul and Norbert
Strandvägen 9 ⊠ *S-114 56 –* Ⓜ *Kungsträdgarden – ℰ (08) 663 81 83*
– restaurang.paul.norbert@telia.se – Fax (08) 661 72 36
– www.paulochnorbert.se
closed 21 December-7 January, Sunday and lunch June-August, Saturday
and Monday
Rest (booking essential) 350 SEK/1100 SEK and a la carte 495/715 SEK
♦ Traditional ♦ Formal ♦
Small sophisticated well run restaurant on harbour with stylish modern décor and artwork. Some tables in booths. Numerous menus featuring seasonal produce.

C2

Fredsgatan 12 (Couet)
Fredsgatan 12 ⊠ *S-111 52 –* Ⓜ *T-Centralen – ℰ (08) 24 80 52*
– info@fredsgatan12.com – Fax (08) 23 76 05
– www.fredsgatan12.com
closed 11 July-15 August, 22 December-3 January,
Sunday and lunch Saturday
Rest (booking essential) 315 SEK (lunch) and a la carte 450/650 SEK
Spec. Beetroot "glacé" eel, wasabi and caviar. Peach en gelée foie gras, beef ribs and brioche. Cassoulet of suckling pig, tonka bean and baby greens.
♦ Innovative ♦ Fashionable ♦
Stylish retro interior design with predominant 1970s theme in a wing of the Academy of Arts. Good value business lunch offered. Creative and original modern cuisine.

B2

✗✗ GQ
    4/ 𝗩𝗜𝗦𝗔 ⓌⓄ ᴀᴇ ①

Kommendörsgatan 23 ✉ *S-114 48 Stockholm –* Ⓜ *Stadion –* ✆ *(08) 545 674 30*
– upplev@gqrestaurang.se – Fax (08) 663 35 10
– www.gqrestaurang.se
closed 2 July-14 August, 24 December-9 January and Sunday   Plan I   **C1**
Rest (set menu only) 295 SEK/795 SEK 🍷
♦ Innovative ♦ Trendy ♦
"Gastronomic intelligence" in a trendy, eye-catching restaurant with its own
cookery school. Specially chosen wines complement seriously considered and
ambitious dishes.

✗✗ Berns Restaurant – at Berns H.
    4/ 𝗩𝗜𝗦𝗔 ⓌⓄ ᴀᴇ ①

Berzelii Park – Ⓜ *Kungsträdgarden –* ✆ *(08) 566 322 22*
– info@berns.se – Fax (08) 566 323 23 – www.berns.se   **C2**
Rest a la carte 175/550 SEK
♦ Modern ♦ Fashionable ♦
A stunningly restored 19C rococo ballroom with galleries overlooking the dining
room. Modern international cuisine. Live music. The place to be seen in.

✗✗ Wedholms Fisk
    🍴 🅺 4/ 🍷 𝗩𝗜𝗦𝗔 ⓌⓄ ᴀᴇ ①

Nybrokajen 17 ✉ *S-111 48 –* Ⓜ *Kungsträdgarden –* ✆ *(08) 611 78 74*
– info@wedholmsfisk.se – Fax (08) 678 60 11
– www.melanders.se
closed Sunday and Saturday lunch   **C2**
Rest a la carte 425/915 SEK
♦ Seafood ♦ Formal ♦
Classic 19-20C building near harbour. Elegant restaurant serving a good
choice of fish and shellfish, simply but accurately prepared; similar dishes in the
bar.

✗✗ Per Lei
    4/ 🍷 𝗩𝗜𝗦𝗔 ⓌⓄ ᴀᴇ ①

Artillerigatan 56 ✉ *S-114 45 –* Ⓜ *Karlaplan –* ✆ *(08) 411 38 11*
– info@perlei.se – Fax (08) 662 64 45 – www.perlei.se
closed 10 July-10 August, 3 days Christmas,
Sunday and Saturday lunch   **C1**
Rest (booking essential) (light lunch) 395 SEK/595 SEK
♦ Italian influences ♦ Cosy ♦
Popular neighbourhood restaurant in converted boutique; elegant décor with
Murano chandelier. Modern Italian menu: two dinner menus of three or five
courses. Refined cooking.

✗✗ Teatergrillen
    4/ 🍷 𝗩𝗜𝗦𝗔 ⓌⓄ ᴀᴇ ①

Nybrogatan 3 ✉ *S-111 48 –* Ⓜ *Östermalmstorg –* ✆ *(08) 545 035 65*
– riche@riche.se – Fax (08) 545 035 69 – www.teatergrillen.se
closed 24-25 December, 1 and 5-6 January, 9 April, 20 May, 20-21 and 31 June,
Sunday and Monday dinner   **C2**
Rest a la carte 300/600 SEK
♦ Traditional ♦ Brasserie ♦
Intimate, traditional city institution, most pleasant in the evening. Menus are
more expensive than its sister Riche. Expect traditional cooking of Scandinavian
classics.

✗✗ Café Opera
    🍴 🅺 4/ 🍷 𝗩𝗜𝗦𝗔 ⓌⓄ ᴀᴇ ①

Operahuset, Karl XII's Torg ✉ *S-111 86 –* Ⓜ *Kungsträdgarden*
– ✆ *(08) 676 58 09 – info@cafeopera.se – Fax (08) 676 58 71*
– www.cafeopera.se
closed midsummer eve, 24 December and Monday except summer
and December   **C2**
Rest (booking essential) (dinner only - music and dancing after 12pm)
a la carte 340/539 SEK
♦ International ♦ Brasserie ♦
Characterful rotunda-style historic restaurant with ceiling painted in 1895,
Corinthian pillars, fine mouldings and covered terrace. Swedish-influenced,
international menu.

SWEDEN

XX Clas På Hörnet with rm 🛋 🅰️ ⇹ ℁ 🖼 VISA ⓂⓈ AE ①

Surbrunnsgatan 20 ✉ *S-113 48 –* Ⓜ *Tekniska Högskolan –* ℰ *(08) 16 51 30*
– boka@claspahornet.se – Fax (08) 612 53 15
– www.claspahornet.se   **B1**
10 rm 🛏 – 🛉1295 SEK 🛉🛉2395 SEK
Rest *(closed Sunday and Saturday lunch)* 450 SEK/595 SEK
♦ Traditional ♦ Rustic ♦
Well established and busy restaurant in part 18C inn with character. Simple
traditional rustic cooking using good quality local produce. Cosy, well-equipped
bedrooms.

X Restaurangen 🛋 ⇹ ℁ VISA ⓂⓈ AE ①
(☺)
Oxtorgsgatan 14 ✉ *S-111 57 –* Ⓜ *Hötorget –* ℰ *(08) 22 09 52 – reservation@*
restaurangentm.com – Fax (08) 22 09 54 – www.restaurangentm.com
closed 1 month in summer, 1 week Christmas and Sunday   **B2**
Rest (booking essential) (light lunch) 275 SEK/475 SEK
♦ Inventive ♦ Trendy ♦
Contemporary interior with clean-cut minimalist décor and modern furnishings.
Unusual menu concept based on a tasting of several small dishes.

X Grill 🅰️ ⇹ VISA ⓂⓈ AE ①

Drottninggatan 89 ✉ *S-113 60 –* Ⓜ *Rådmansgatan –* ℰ *(08) 31 45 30*
– info@grill.se – Fax (08) 31 45 80 – www.grill.se
closed mid July-early August and lunch Saturday and Sunday   **B1**
Rest (light buffet lunch) a la carte 335/610 SEK
♦ Grills ♦ Minimalist ♦
Stylish city centre restaurant with spacious lounge area; modern minimalist
décor. Open plan kitchen. Menu based on different cooking methods - grilling,
rotisserie, BBQ etc.

X Rolfskök 🛋 ⇹ VISA ⓂⓈ AE ①
(☺)
Tegnérgatan 11 ✉ *S-111 61 –* Ⓜ *Rådmansgatan –* ℰ *(08) 10 16 96*
– info@rolfskok.se – Fax (08) 789 88 80 – www.rolfskok.se
closed July, 24-26 December, 31 December-1 January and lunch Saturday and
Sunday   *Plan I* **B1**
Rest (booking essential) (light lunch) a la carte 390/560 SEK 🕏
♦ International ♦ Bistro ♦
Compact, trendy bar-restaurant: buzzy atmosphere guaranteed. Home-made
fresh bread and ice cream. Modern international cooking. Up to 750 wines can be
ordered by the glass!

BRASSERIES AND BISTRO   *Plan I*

X KB ⇹ ℁ VISA ⓂⓈ AE ①
(☺)
Smålandsgatan 7 ✉ *S-111 46 –* Ⓜ *Östermalmstorg –* ℰ *(08) 679 60 32*
– info@konstnarsbaren.se – Fax (08) 611 39 32
– www.konstnarsbaren.se   **C2**
Rest 295 SEK (dinner) and a la carte 255/610 SEK
♦ Traditional ♦ Brasserie ♦
19C building with impressive façade and original wall frescoes in bar - a home of
Swedish artists with interesting modern art on the walls. Traditional Swedish
cooking.

X Prinsen 🛋 ⇹ ℁ VISA ⓂⓈ AE ①

Mäster Samuelsgatan 4 ✉ *S-111 44 –* Ⓜ *Östermalmstorg –* ℰ *(08) 611 13 31*
– kontoret@restaurangprinsen.se – Fax (08) 611 70 79
– www.restaurangprinsen.se
closed 24-25 and 31 December, 23 June and Sunday lunch   **C2**
Rest (booking essential) a la carte 335/569 SEK
♦ Traditional ♦ Brasserie ♦
Long-standing and classic, busy but well run brasserie with literary associations.
Exhibition of graphic art renewed monthly in basement room. Classic Swedish
cooking.

SWEDEN

✗ **Eriks Bakficka** ☐ ⪚ ✵ VISA ⓶ AE ①
Fredrikshovsgatan 4 ⊠ S-115 23 – ℰ (08) 660 15 99 – info.bakfickan @ eriks.se
– Fax (08) 663 25 67 – www.eriks.se
closed July, 23-26 December, 1 January and lunch Saturday
and Sunday **D2**
Rest a la carte 95/295 SEK
♦ Modern ♦ Bistro ♦
Quiet residential setting and well-run, with small terrace, bistro and bar-counter.
Cosy dining rooms in the basement. Traditional Swedish dishes with modern
global twists.

✗ **Sturehof** ☐ ⪚ VISA ⓶ AE ①
Stureplan 2-4 ⊠ S-114 46 – Ⓜ Östermalmstorg – ℰ (08) 440 57 30
– info @ sturehof.com – Fax (08) 678 11 01 – www.sturehof.com **C1**
Rest a la carte 320/575 SEK
♦ Traditional ♦ Brasserie ♦
Very popular classic café-brasserie with closely packed tables and a busy
atmosphere due to the steady stream of local business clientele. Good choice of
seafood dishes.

✗ **Riche** ⪚ ✵ VISA ⓶ AE ①
Birger Jarlsgatan 4 ⊠ S-114 53 – Ⓜ Östermalmstorg – ℰ (08) 545 035 60
– riche @ riche.se – Fax (08) 545 035 69 – www.riche.se
closed 1 and 6 January, 9 and 12 April, 20-21 June, 24-25 December and
Sunday **C2**
Rest a la carte 225/494 SEK
♦ Traditional ♦ Brasserie ♦
Lively bar and bustling restaurant, very different from, but with same menu as,
its sister Teatergrillen. Serves classic Scandinavian as well as international dishes.

---

at Gamla Stan (Old Stockholm) : *Plan II*

 First H. Reisen ≤ 🕅 ⪚ ✵ 📺 ℃ ♨20 VISA ⓶ AE ①
Skeppsbron 12 ⊠ S-111 30 – Ⓜ Gamla Stan – ℰ (08) 22 32 60
– reisen @ firsthotels.se – Fax (08) 20 15 59 – www.firsthotels.com **F1**
137 rm – ♥2398 SEK ♥♥2598 SEK, ☲ 160 SEK – 7 suites
Rest *Reisen Bar and Dining Room* (light lunch) 95 SEK/265 SEK and a la carte
280/400 SEK
♦ Business ♦ Modern ♦
19C hotel on waterfront with original maritime décor. Popular piano bar. Sauna
in 17C vault. De luxe and superior rooms offer quayside view and small balconies.
Maritime interior and a warm and welcoming atmosphere. Traditional Swedish
and international menu.

 Victory 🕅 ⪚ ✵ 📺 ℃ ♨55 VISA ⓶ AE ①
Lilla Nygatan 5 ⊠ S-111 28 – Ⓜ Gamla Stan – ℰ (08) 506 400 00
– info @ victoryhotel.se – Fax (08) 506 400 10 – www.victoryhotel.se
closed Christmas and New Year **E1**
45 rm – ♥2050 SEK ♥♥2550 SEK, ☲ 170 SEK – 4 suites
Rest see *Leijontornet* below
♦ Historic ♦ Classic ♦
Pleasant 17C hotel with Swedish rural furnishings and maritime antiques. Rooms
named after sea captains with individually styled fittings, mixing modern and
antique.

 Rica H. Gamla Stan without rest ⪚ 📺 ℃ ♨20 VISA ⓶ AE ①
Lilla Nygatan 25 ⊠ S-111 28 – Ⓜ Gamla Stan – ℰ (08) 723 72 50
– info.gamlastan @ rica.se – Fax (08) 723 72 59 – www.rica.se **F1**
50 rm ☲ – ♥1705 SEK ♥♥1905 SEK – 1 suite
♦ Business ♦ Classic ♦
Conveniently located 17C house with welcoming style. Well-furnished rooms
with traditional décor and antique style furniture. Pleasant top-floor terrace with
rooftop outlook.

SWEDEN

Lady Hamilton without rest

☆ ⇄ ⅍ 🄶🅐🅣 VISA ⓜⓢ 🄰🄴 ⓞ

Storkyrkobrinken 5 ⊠ *S-111 28* – ⓜ *Gamla Stan* – ℰ *(08) 506 401 00*
– info@ladyhamiltonhotel.se – Fax (08) 506 401 10
– www.ladyhamiltonhotel.se   **E-F1**
34 rm – ♥1850 SEK ♥♥2350 SEK, � 140 SEK

◆ Historic ◆ Classic ◆

15C houses of character full of fine Swedish rural furnishings. Rooms boast antique pieces and modern facilities. Sauna and 14C well plunge pool in basement.

Lord Nelson without rest

☆ ⇄ ⅍ 🄶🅐🅣 VISA ⓜⓢ 🄰🄴 ⓞ

Västerlånggatan 22 ⊠ *S-111 29* – ⓜ *Gamla Stan* – ℰ *(08) 506 401 20*
– info@lordnelsonhotel.se – Fax (08) 506 401 30
– www.lordnelsonhotel.se
closed Christmas and New Year   **E1**
29 rm – ♥1750 SEK ♥♥2050 SEK, ⊡ 90 SEK

◆ Historic ◆ Classic ◆

Charming late 17C house located in lively Old Town, with ship-style interior and maritime antiques. Small cabin-style rooms with good level of comfort and compact bathrooms.

Pontus in the Green House

⇄ VISA ⓜⓢ 🄰🄴 ⓞ

Österlånggatan 17 ⊠ *S-111 31* – ⓜ *Gamla Stan* – ℰ *(08) 23 85 00*
– pontusfrithiof@pontusfrithiof.com – Fax (08) 796 60 69
– www.pontusfrithiof.com
closed Sunday   **F1**
Rest (booking essential) 375 SEK/1200 SEK and a la carte
560/1110 SEK

◆ Innovative ◆ Formal ◆

Restaurant with charm and style in 15C house. Classic décor and some booths in more formal upstairs room. Modern innovative or 'classic rustique' menu; accomplished cuisine.

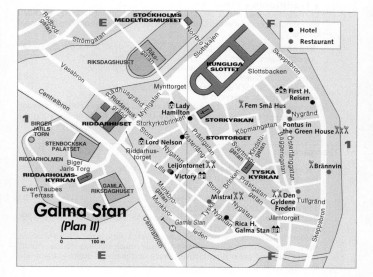

SWEDEN

XX **Leijontornet** – at Victory H.   AK 4/ 🏶 VISA ◐◐ AE ⓞ
Lilla Nygatan 5 ⊠ S- 111 28 – ⓜ Gamla Stan – 𝒞 (08) 506 400 80
– info@leijontornet.se – Fax (08) 506 400 85 – www.leijontornet.se
closed 23 December-7 January and Sunday   **E1**
Rest (booking essential) (light lunch) 290 SEK/650 SEK 🍴
♦ Traditional ♦ Formal ♦
Characterful restaurant with remains of a 14C fortified tower and a glass fronted wine cellar sunk into floor. Light lunch in bistro; dinner in main basement dining room.

XX **Mistral** (Andersson)   4/ 🏶 VISA ◐◐ AE ⓞ
🏵 Lilla Nygatan 21 ⊠ S-111 28 – ⓜ Gamla Stan – 𝒞 (08) 10 12 24
– rest.mistral@telia.com – Fax 10 12 17
closed 14-18 April, 1 July-7 August, 23 December-3 January
and Saturday-Monday   **F1**
Rest (booking essential) (dinner only) (set menu only) 975 SEK
Spec. Scallop with dried celeriac and crushed juniper berries. Creamy potato with vanilla, olive oil, thyme and lemon emulsion. Parsnip with flavours of salted butter and the ocean.
♦ Innovative ♦ Minimalist ♦
Small personally-run restaurant with modern décor. Open-plan kitchen preparing original and creative dishes; degustation menu of 10 courses.

XX **Den Gyldene Freden**   4/ 🏶 VISA ◐◐ AE ⓞ
🐌 Österlånggatan 51 ⊠ S-103 17 – ⓜ Gamla Stan – 𝒞 (08) 24 97 60
– info@gyldenefreden.se – Fax (08) 21 38 70 – www.gyldenefreden.se
closed Sunday and Saturday lunch   **F1**
Rest 545 SEK/695 SEK and a la carte 525/680 SEK
♦ Traditional ♦ Rustic ♦
Restaurant in early 18C inn with fine vaulted cellars owned by Swedish Academy. Traditional, Swedish, robust cooking incorporating plenty of flavours and good local produce.

X **Fem Små Hus**   4/ VISA ◐◐ AE ⓞ
Nygränd 10 ⊠ S-111 30 – ⓜ Gamla Stan – 𝒞 (08) 10 87 75
– info@femsmahus.se – Fax (08) 14 96 95 – www.femsmahus.se
closed 14 April, 24-26 December and 1 January   **F1**
Rest (dinner only) 375 SEK/545 SEK 🍴
♦ Traditional ♦ Rustic ♦
Characterful restaurant located in 17C cellars of five adjacent houses and filled with antiques. Popular with tourists. Several menus available offering traditional cuisine.

X **Brännvin**   ≤ 🏠 4/ VISA ◐◐ AE ⓞ
Skeppsbrokajen, Tullhus 2 ⊠ S-111 30 – ⓜ Gamla Stan – 𝒞 (08) 22 57 55
– info@brannvin-stockholm.se – www.brannvin-stockholm.se
closed Sunday dinner   **F1**
Rest 340 SEK/500 SEK and a la carte 340/500 SEK
♦ Traditional ♦ Bistro ♦
Modern quayside bistro; its neat terrace runs to the water's edge. Interesting food concept: small portions of traditional Swedish dishes emphasising the different flavours.

---

at Djurgården: *Plan I*

 Scandic H. Hasselbacken   🏠 🏠 🛋 ⅙ AK 4/ 🖂 📞 🔧 250
Hazeliusbacken 20 ⊠ S-100 55   🏠 VISA ◐◐ AE ⓞ
– 𝒞 (08) 517 343 00 – hasselbacken@scandic-hotels.com – Fax (08) 517 343 11
– www.scandic-hotels.se/hasselbacken   **D2**
111 rm ⊡ – ♦2090 SEK ♦♦2190 SEK – 1 suite
Rest *Restaurang Hasselbacken* (buffet lunch) 155 SEK and a la carte 394/690 SEK
♦ Business ♦ Modern ♦
Modern hotel situated on island in former Royal park, close to the Vasa Museum. Up-to-date bedrooms, some with views. Regular musical events. Restaurant with ornate mirrored ceilings, attractive terrace and pleasant outlook; traditional Swedish cooking.

XX **Ulla Winbladh** ⌂ ⇔ ⅏ 𝗩𝗜𝗦𝗔 ⓪ ᴬᴱ ⓪

SWEDEN

Rosendalsvägen 8 ✉ S-115 21 – ℰ (08) 663 05 71 – info @ ullawinbladh.se
– Fax (08) 663 05 73 – www.ullawinbladh.se
closed 25 December   **D2**
Rest (booking essential) a la carte 170/550 SEK
 ◆ Traditional ◆ Formal ◆
Pleasant late 19C pavilion in former Royal hunting ground houses several
welcoming dining rooms and extensive terraces in summer. Traditional Swedish
cuisine.

at Södermalm   *Plan I*

🏨 **Hilton Stockholm Slussen** ≤ ⌂ 𝐈𝐬 𝕟 ⅗ 𝐀𝐂 ⇔ 🖭 ℭ 𝒔𝒂 300

Guldgränd 8 ✉ S-104 65 – ⓜ Slussen –   ⌂ 𝗩𝗜𝗦𝗔 ⓪ ᴬᴱ ⓪
ℰ (08) 517 353 00 – stockholm-slussen @ hilton.com – Fax (08) 517 353 11
– www.hilton.com   **C3**
276 rm – 👤2490 SEK 👤👤2490 SEK, ⌑ 150 SEK – 13 suites
Rest *Eken* (buffet lunch) 235 SEK/395 SEK and a la carte 350/515 SEK
 ◆ Business ◆ Modern ◆
Busy commercial hotel, overlooking Old Town and surrounding water, housed
in three buildings with central lobby. Stylish rooms with elegant, coloured
Scandinavian wood panels. Traditional and modern Swedish cuisine.

🏨 **The Rival** ⌂ 𝒌 ⇔ ⅏ 🖭 ℭ 𝒔𝒂 50 𝗩𝗜𝗦𝗔 ⓪ ᴬᴱ ⓪

Mariatorget 3 ✉ S-118 91 – ⓜ Mariatorget – ℰ (08) 545 789 00
– reservations @ rival.se – Fax (08) 545 789 24
– www.rival.se   **C3**
97 rm – 👤2290 SEK 👤👤2490 SEK, ⌑ 145 SEK – 2 suites
Rest *The Bistro* (dinner only) 325 SEK/395 SEK and a la carte 285/485 SEK
 ◆ Business ◆ Stylish ◆
Modern boutique hotel and Art Deco cinema in 1930s building. Stylish
bedroooms with cinema theme décor and high-tech facilities. First floor
open-plan bar and bistro/restaurant. Classic Swedish cooking in the bistro; more
modern dishes in the restaurant.

XX **Eriks Gondolen** ≤ Stockholm and water, ⌂ ⇔ ⅏ 𝗩𝗜𝗦𝗔 ⓪ ᴬᴱ ⓪

Stadsgården 6 (11th floor) ✉ S-104 56 – ⓜ Slussen – ℰ (08) 641 70 90
– info @ eriks.se – Fax (08) 641 11 40 – www.eriks.se
closed 17 April, 10 July-13 August, 24-26 December,
Saturday and Sunday   **C3**
Rest 295 SEK/535 SEK and a la carte 370/615 SEK
 ◆ Traditional ◆ Brasserie ◆
Glass enclosed suspended passageway, renowned for stunning panoramic view
of city and water. Open-air dining and barbecue terraces on 12th floor.
Traditional Swedish fare.

at Arlanda Airport *Northwest: 40 km by Sveavägen and E 4:*

🏨 **Radisson SAS Sky City** 𝐈𝐬 𝕟 𝒌 𝐀𝐂 ⇔ ⅏ 🖭 ℭ 𝗩𝗜𝗦𝗔 ⓪ ᴬᴱ ⓪

at Terminals 4-5, 2nd floor above Street level (Stockholm-Arlanda, Sky City)
✉ 190 45 – ℰ (08) 506 740 00
– reservations.skycity.stockholm @ radissonsas.com – Fax (08) 506 740 01
– www.radissonsas.com
229 rm – 👤1995 SEK 👤👤 1995 SEK, ⌑ 135 SEK – 1 suite
Rest *Stockholm Fish* a la carte approx. 350 SEK
 ◆ Business ◆ Modern ◆
The perfect place not to miss your plane: modern, corporate airport hotel. Varied
décor to rooms: older Scandinavian or a choice of three modern styles. Balcony
restaurant overlooking airport terminal offering fish-based menu.

SWEDEN

Radisson SAS Arlandia 🛋 🕸 🗑 ⅙ 🎬 ⅙ 📟 💰100 **P**
P **VISA** **◑** **AE** **①**
Benstocksvägen (Stockholm-Arlanda,
Southeast : 1 km) ✉ *190 45*
– ℰ *(08) 506 840 00 – reservations.arlandia.stockholm@radissonsas.com*
– *Fax (08) 506 840 01 – www.radissonsas.com*
closed 23 December-3 January
327 rm ⌧ – 🛉1400 SEK 🛉🛉1800 SEK – 8 suites
Rest *Cayenne* (buffet lunch) 197 SEK and a la carte approx.
250 SEK
♦ Business ♦ Functional ♦
A short shuttle ride from the terminal. Bright and modern corporate hotel and
congress hall. Ecological, maritime and Scandinavian themed bedrooms.
Contemporary-styled restaurant and adjacent bar for light snacks, pastas and
traditional Scandinavian fare.

ENVIRONS OF STOCKHOLM

to the North: 2 km by Sveavägen (at beginning of E 4):

Stallmästaregården 🚗 ⅙ 𝒴 📟 💰200 **P** **VISA** **◑** **AE** **①**
Nortull (North : 2 km by Sveavägen (at beginning of E 4)) ✉ *S-113 47*
– ℰ *(08) 610 13 00 – info@stallmastaregarden.se*
– *Fax (08) 610 13 40 – www.stallmastaregarden.se*
closed 25-30 December
46 rm ⌧ – 🛉2095 SEK 🛉🛉2395 SEK – 3 suites
Rest see below
♦ Inn ♦ Classic ♦
Attractive 17C inn with central courtyard and modern bedroom wing. Quieter
rooms overlook waterside and park. 18C style rustic Swedish décor with modern
comforts.

✗✗ **Stallmästaregården** – at Stallmästaregården H. 🍴 🛋 🚗 𝒴
Nortull (North : 2 km by Sveavägen (at **P** **VISA** **◑** **AE** **①**
beginning of E 4)) ✉ *S-113 47* – ℰ *(08)*
610 13 00 – info@stallmastaregarden.se – Fax (08) 610 13 40
– *www.stallmastaregarden.se*
closed 25-30 December
Rest 425 SEK/495 SEK (dinner) and a la carte 425/525 SEK
♦ Modern ♦ Inn ♦
Part 17C inn with elegant 18C Swedish décor. Beautiful waterside terrace in
summer. Open kitchen. Modern Swedish cuisine.

at Ladugårdsgärdet:

✗✗ **Villa Källhagen** with rm 🍴 🛋 🕸 🚗 ⅙ 𝒴 📞 💰55
Djurgårdsbrunnsvägen 10 (East: 3km by **P** **VISA** **◑** **AE** **①**
Strandvägen) ✉ *S-115 27* – ℰ *(08) 665 03 00*
– *villa@kallhagen.se – Fax (08) 665 03 99*
– *www.kallhagen.se*
closed 1 week Christmas
18 rm ⌧ – 🛉1700 SEK 🛉🛉2400 SEK – 2 suites
Rest *(closed 4 weeks in summer, Sunday dinner and Monday dinner*
September-April) 455 SEK/525 SEK (dinner) and a la carte
370/564 SEK
Rest *Bistro* – a la carte approx. 380 SEK
♦ Modern ♦ Brasserie ♦
Modern building in lovely waterside setting. Contemporary bedrooms, all with
view of water. Extensive open-air terraces amid trees. Traditional modern
Scandinavian cuisine.

at Fjäderholmarna Island:

XX
(☺)
Fjäderholmarnas Krog   ≼ neighbouring islands and sea,
Stora Fjäderholmen ⊠ *S-100 05 – 𝒞 (08)*   ☐ **VISA** **MO** **AE** **①**
718 33 55 – fjaderholmarna@atv.se – Fax (08) 716 39 89
– www.fjaderholmarnaskrog.se
closed January-April, October-November and midsummer eve
Rest (booking essential) 545 SEK/635 SEK and a la carte
430/620 SEK
♦ Seafood ♦ Friendly ♦
Delightful waterside setting on archipelago island with fine view. Fresh produce, mainly fish, delivered daily by boat. Wide selection of traditional Swedish dishes.

at Nacka Strand: Southeast: 10 km by Stadsgarden or 20 mins by boat from Nybrokajen:

🏨
Hotel J ⌂   ≼ Sea, 🚗 ♿ 🅐🅚 ⇿ ⊠ 🕸30 🅿 **VISA** **MO** **AE** **①**
Ellensviksvägen 1 ⊠ *S-131 28 – 𝒞 (08) 601 30 00*
– nackastrand@hotelj.com – Fax (08) 601 30 09
– www.hotelj.com
41 rm ⊑ – ♦1795 SEK ♦♦ 2995 SEK – 4 suites
Rest see **Restaurant J** below
♦ Luxury ♦ Design ♦
Former politician's early 20C summer residence in quiet waterside setting. 'Boutique'-style hotel with maritime theme. Stylish spacious rooms, some with sea view.

X
Restaurant J   ≼ Sea, ☐ ⇿ ℅ **VISA** **MO** **AE** **①**
Augustendalsvägen 52 ⊠ *S- 131 28 – 𝒞 (08) 601 30 25*
– info@restaurantj.com – Fax (08) 601 30 09
– www.restaurantj.com
Rest 295 SEK (lunch) and a la carte 390/525 SEK
♦ Traditional ♦ Brasserie ♦
Bright, informal restaurant with sleek maritime décor and attractive terrace beside marina. Selective menu of Swedish and international dishes.

at Lilla Essingen: West: 5.5 km by Norr Mälarstrand:

XX
❀
Lux Stockholm (Norström)   ≼ ☐ 🅐🅚 ⇿ ℅ **VISA** **MO** **AE** **①**
Primusgatan 116 ⊠ *S-112 62 – 𝒞 (08) 619 01 90*
– info@luxstockholm.com – Fax (08) 619 04 47
– www.luxstockholm.com
closed 22 December-5 January, Monday and lunch Saturday and Sunday
Rest (booking essential) (light lunch) a la carte 525/615 SEK
Spec. Lobster with salted veal, dill and melon. Lightly smoked truffle pork sausage, horseradish, cauliflower and artichoke. Caramelised apple with vanilla cream, Calvados and hazelnuts.
♦ Innovative ♦ Fashionable ♦
Converted brick warehouse overlooking waterways. Light and airy with green and white décor. Large window into kitchen; innovative Swedish cooking with distinctive twists.

at Bromma: West: 5.5 km by Norr Mälarstrand and Drottningholmsvägen:

XX
(☺)
Sjöpaviljongen   ≼ ☐ ⇿ **VISA** **MO** **AE** **①**
Tranebergs Strand 4, Alvik (East : 1 ½ km) ⊠ *167 40 – 𝒞 (08) 704 04 24*
– info@sjopaviljongen.se – Fax (08) 704 82 40 – www.sjopaviljongen.se
closed 23 December-6 January
Rest (booking essential) (light lunch) 275 SEK/595 SEK and a la carte 355/475 SEK
♦ Traditional ♦ Friendly ♦
Modern pavilion in attractive lakeside setting. Swedish style décor. Good value classic Swedish cuisine at lunch; more modern dishes at dinner.

to the Northwest : 8 km by Sveavägen and E 18 towards Norrtälje:

XXX **Ulriksdals Wärdshus** ⟨ 🛁 🍽 ⅍ ⅍ **P** ᴠɪsᴀ ⓒⓞ ᴀᴇ ⓞ
(take first junction for Ulriksdals Slott) ⊠ *170 79 Solna –* ℰ *(08) 85 08 15*
– info@ulriksdalswardshus.se – Fax (08) 85 08 58 – www.ulriksdalswardshus.se
closed 14-28 July, 24-26 December, Monday September-April and dinner Tuesday
except December
Rest (booking essential) 300 SEK/350 SEK and a la carte 350/610 SEK 🍴
  ♦ Traditional ♦ Inn ♦
19C former inn in Royal Park with classic winter garden-style décor. Wine cellar
features in Guinness Book of Records. Extensive smorgasbord at weekends.

at Sollentuna: Northwest: 15 km by Sveavägen and E 4, (exit Sollentuna c):

XXXX **Edsbacka Krog** (Lingström) 🍽 ⅍ ⅍ **P** ᴠɪsᴀ ⓒⓞ ᴀᴇ ⓞ
£3£3 *Sollentunavägen 220* ⊠ *191 35 –* ℰ *(08) 96 33 00 – info@edsbackakrog.se*
– Fax (08) 96 40 19 – www.edsbackakrog.se
closed midsummer weekend, 9 July-3 August, 23 December-5 January, Sunday,
Monday and Bank Holidays
Rest (dinner only) 735 SEK and a la carte 625/895 SEK
Spec. Salmon with whitebait roe, shrimps and vanilla. Saddle of roe deer with
blackcurrant sauce and potato dumpling. Artic raspberry soufflé.
  ♦ Innovative ♦ Inn ♦
Charming part 17C inn in small park with elegant rustic Swedish décor. Superb
range of menus offering highly accomplished and original modern dishes.

X **Bistro Edsbacka** 🍽 ⅍ ⅍ **P** ᴠɪsᴀ ⓒⓞ ᴀᴇ ⓞ
🙂 *Sollentunavägen 223* ⊠ *191 35 –* ℰ *(08) 631 00 34 – info@svenskasmaker.se*
– Fax (08) 96 40 14 – www.svenskasmaker.se
closed 23-25 June, 17-23 July, 23-26 December and 1 January
Rest (booking essential) 395 SEK/425 SEK and a la carte 293/473 SEK
  ♦ Traditional ♦ Bistro ♦
Simple modern bistro, contrasting the restaurant opposite, with black and white
décor. Smart rear terrace shielded from traffic. Good value menu of classic
Swedish dishes.

GOTHENBURG
GÖTEBORG

Population (est. 2005): 481 500 (conurbation 872 200) – Altitude: sea level

Assner GÖRAN/VISITSWEDEN

Not without reason Gothenburg has been designated by Swedes themselves as Sweden's most friendly town. Sweden's second city and gateway to the west is favourably located on the west coast, equidistant from three Scandinavian capitals – Stockholm, Copenhagen and Oslo. With strong maritime traditions Gothenburg, at the mouth of the River Göta, is Scandinavia's number one seaport and a bustling commercial centre, including the head offices of some of Sweden's best known industrial companies – Volvo, SKF, ESAB and Hasselblad. It is set among hills, bridges, water and islands and is known for its seafood restaurants. The coast to the south boasts miles of sandy beaches backed by dunes – the Swedish Riviera. The archipelago provides many places for cycling, fishing, surfing and bathing.

The city boasts excellent facilities for conferences, trade fairs, sporting events and rock concerts but its popularity is mostly due to its cosmopolitan, lively and friendly welcome. Shoppers may enjoy Nordstan, Northern Europe's largest indoor shopping centre. Ullevi, Scandinavia's largest stadium with 47 000 seats, and Scandinavium (12 500 seats) are stages for events ranging from rock concerts to sports events. The annual Gothia Cup is the world's greatest junior football tournament, with about 25 000 participants.

WHICH DISTRICT TO CHOOSE

Most **hotels** are to be found in and around the city centre *Plan I* **B1** and Götaplatsen *Plan I* **C3**. **Restaurants** follow much the same pattern; some are in the parks and some on the waterfront or accessible by boat. For lunch the best places are cafés, which offer good food at reasonable prices, or the traditional *konditori* (bakery with tearoom attached) in Haga and Linné. For a **drink only**, choose one of the places in Avenyn *Plan I* **B2** or Haga *Plan I* **A3**.

735

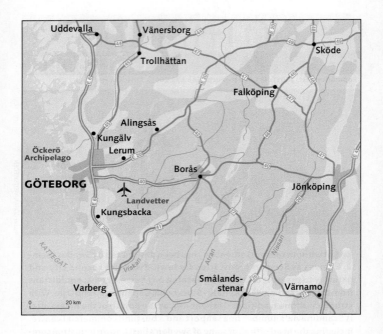

PRACTICAL INFORMATION

ARRIVAL – DEPARTURE

Landvetter Airport – About 25 km (16 mi) east of the city centre, ☎ 94 10 00.

From the airport to the city centre – By **taxi** (30min) Skr 310. By **airport bus** *(Flygbus)* (30min) every 15min, Skr 50; ☎ 80 12 35, 94 10 00; www.landvetter.lfv.se

Railway Stations – There are regular train services to **Gothenburg Centralstationen** *Plan I* **B2** from the major towns in Sweden.

Ferry Terminal – There are regular ferry services from Kiel (Germany), Frederikshavn (Denmark) ☎ 705 70 70 70; www.stenaline.co.uk; Harwich and Newcastle (England), Kristiansand (Norway) ☎ 650 650; www.dfdsseaways.co.uk

TRANSPORT

◆ BUS AND TRAM

The blue and white tram cars are named after personalities with Gothenburg connections. Tickets, timetables, routes and fares for buses and trams are available at Travel Information Centres *(tidpunkten)* at Brunnsparken, Drottningtorget, Nils Ericssons-platsen or Folkungabron. Tickets also sold by bus/tram drivers: Single ticket Skr 16; 10-trip carnet Skr 100. ☎ 80 12 35 (enquiries).

Vintage trams (Lisebergslinjen) operate in summer (12 noon to 6pm) between Central Station and Liseberg.

Punts *(paddan)* are a fascinating way to explore this maritime city, gliding along the canals past stately canalside buildings and under 20 bridges *(depart from the bridge at Kungsportsplatsen)*, Skr 80.

◆ TAXIS

Taxis can be hired at a taxi stand – Central Station, Kungsportplatsen, Kungsportsavenyn. When the *Ledig* sign is lit up, the taxi is free. The basic charge is Skr27 plus Skr9 per km within the city area. *Taxi Göteborg*, ℰ 65 00 00.

◆ GOTHENBURG CARD

This card *(Göteborgskortet)* is valid for free boat and trams rides, parking in municipal car parks, a sightseeing tour, admission to the Liseberg amusement park and museums and discounts in certain shops and restaurants. 1-day card Skr210, 2-day card Skr295 on sale at Tourist Information Offices, the amusement park, newspaper kiosks *(pressbyrån)*, hotels and campsites.

USEFUL ADDRESSES

◆ TOURIST OFFICE

Göteborgs Turistbyrå, Kungsportsplatsen 2 *Plan I* **B2**; ℰ 61 25 00; www. goteborg.com. Nordstan Shopping Centre, Nordstadstorget; ℰ 15 07 05; www.goteborg.com; www.scandina

vium.se. For information and tickets to concerts, theatres and sports events: *Scandinavium*, Ullevi, Skånegatan, ℰ 61 56 80.

◆ POST OFFICES

Opening times are Mon-Fri 9am-6pm, Sat 10am-1pm.

◆ BANKS/CURRENCY EXCHANGE

Opening times 9.30am-3pm; some stay open until 5.30pm. At Landvetter Airport, Mon-Fri 8am-6pm, Sat until 5pm, Sun 12.30-8pm. Bank cash machines (ATMs) are open 24hrs (pin number required).

◆ EMERGENCY

ℰ **112** for Police, Fire Brigade, Ambulance, Poison hot-line, on-call doctors and 24hr Roadside breakdown service.

BUSY PERIODS

It may be difficult to find a room at a reasonable price (except at weekends) during special events:

International Travel and Tourism Fair: Spring – In the exhibition centre Svenska Mässan.

Book Fair: Autumn – In the exhibition centre Svenska Mässan.

EXPLORING GÖTHENBURG

In two days there is time to visit the main sights and museums.

Opening times are usually from 10/11am-4/6pm but closed on Mondays and public holidays.

VISITING

Waterfront: Göteborgs-Utkiken *Plan I* **B1** – Distinctive red and white office skyscraper (late 1980s) with **panoramic view** of the town from the café *(lift)*. **Lilla Bommens Hamn** *Plan I* **B1** – Departure point for local excur-

sions by boat; 4-masted barque *Viking* (1906) converted to a restaurant. **Göteborgsoperan** *Plan I* **B1** – Modern opera house resembling a ship. **Göteborgs Maritima Centrum** *Plan I* **A1** – Floating museum of 11 historic vessels and boats. **Masthuggskyrkan** *Plan I* **B2** – Church built in the Swedish National Romantic style with an interesting wooden interior and a good view of the city.

Göteborgs Stadsmuseum *Plan I* **B2** – Historical and industrial museums housed in the Swedish East India House (1750-62), which served as HQ, warehouse and auction room. **Sjöfartsmuseet** – History of the Gothenburg East India trade: merchant ship *Finland*.

Town Centre: Gustaf Adolfs Torg is bordered by the stock exchange, **Börsen** (1849), **Wenngren's House** (1759), **Stadshuset** (1758) and **Rådhuset** (1672). **Avenyn** *Plan / B2* – The main artery of Gothenburg, properly called Kungsportsavenyn, a tree-lined boulevard, lined with cafés and restaurants, running south from Kungsportplatsen over the canal and through the park to the Götaplatsen.

Göteborgs Konstmuseum *Plan / C3* – Collection of 19C and 20C Scandinavian art, 17C Dutch and Flemish art, 16C-18C Italian and Spanish art, 19C and 20C French art as well as contemporary international art: Göteborg Colourists, humerous pictures by Ivar Arosenius.

Röhsska Konstslöjdmuseet *Plan / C* – Arts and crafts museum: latest in Nordic and international design.

Trädgårdsföreningen *Plan / C2* – Laid out by the horticultural society in 1842 with a Butterfly house, Palm House and rose garden beside the canal.

Liseberg *Plan / D3* – Fantastic amusement park with many rides, bandstands, theatres, dancing, cafés and restaurants in a pleasant green setting.

Botanisk Trädgården – Botanical gardens with Rock Garden, Bamboo Grove, Japanese Dale, Rhododendron Valley, wide expanses of lawn, winding paths and woodland.

SHOPPING

The main shopping streets are **Nordstan Mall**, **Avenyn**, **Linnégatan** and **Haga**. NK (Östra Hamngatan 42) and *Åhlens* (Nordstan) are two leading department stores. *Kronhusbodarna* (Kronhusgtan) is good for buying glassware and handicrafts; *Bohusslöjden* (Kungsportsavenyn 25) for local handicrafts.

MARKETS – The **fish and seafood** market (closed Monday) is held in the fish church *(Feskekörke)*, so called because of its architecture.

WHAT TO BUY – Glassware (Orrefors, Kosta, Boda), ceramics, textiles, knitwear, needlework, craft work, wood carvings; the museum shops are good for gifts.

ENTERTAINMENT

Theatre, cinema, bars and restaurants, clubs and other listings are printed in the Friday edition of *Göteborg Posten* and its weekly supplement *Aveny*.

Göteborgsoperan *Plan / B1* – Opera, ballet, light opera, musicals.

Concert Hall *Plan / C3* – Home of the Gothenburg Symphony Orchestra; also Stenhammar Room for chamber music recitals.

City Theatre and Folkteatern *Plan / C3*.

NIGHTLIFE

Gothenburg has a lively nightlife: *Dojan* (Vallgatan) the oldest and biggest music pub in the city with dance floor and rock bar and live performances on Thursdays and Sundays; *Henriksberg* (Stigbergsliden) old premises with nightclub, pub and restaurant. There is also the *Casino Cosmopol* (Packhusplatsen).

SWEDEN

Radisson SAS Scandinavia   ⅃⅙ 🏠 ⊠ ᕦ 🎦 ⅍ ℁ 🖭 ℭ 🕭450

Södra Hamngatan 59-65 ⊠ S-401 24 –   🚗 𝗩𝗜𝗦𝗔 ⓜⓞ 𝖠𝖤 ⓞ
℘ (031) 758 50 00 – reservations.scandinavia.gothenburg@radissonsas.com
– Fax (031) 758 50 01 – www.radissonsas.com   **B2**
332 rm – ♦1920 SEK ♦♦2020 SEK, ⊊ 125 SEK – 17 suites
Rest *Atrium Bar & Restaurant* (buffet lunch)115/460 SEK and a la carte
235/460 SEK
♦ Business ♦ Modern ♦
Grand commercial hotel with impressive atrium courtyard complete with water
and glass elevators. Renovated, airy rooms boast choice of décor and
impressive mod cons. A range of international dishes offered in restaurant
housed within the atrium.

Gothia Towers   ≼ 🏠 ᕦ 🎦 ⅍ 🖭 🕭1500 🚗 𝗩𝗜𝗦𝗔 ⓜⓞ 𝖠𝖤 ⓞ

Mässans Gata 24 ⊠ S-402 26 – ℘ (031) 750 88 00 – infomaster@
gothiatowers.com – Fax (031) 750 88 82 – www.gothiatowers.com   **D3**
695 rm ⊊ – ♦2095 SEK ♦♦2395 SEK – 9 suites
Rest *Heaven 23* (buffet lunch)199/465 SEK and a la carte 385/555 SEK
Rest *Incontro* (closed Sunday dinner) (buffet lunch)115/380 SEK and a la carte
265/425 SEK
♦ Business ♦ Modern ♦
Large twin tower hotel owned by Gothenburg Exhibition Centre, popular with
conference delegates and business people. Elegant modern Scandinavian
décor. Top floor Heaven 23, for spectacular city views and modern cuisine.
Modern Italian dishes in Incontro.

Elite Plaza   ⅃⅙ 🏠 ᕦ 🎦 ⅍ ℁ 🖭 🕭50 𝗩𝗜𝗦𝗔 ⓜⓞ 𝖠𝖤 ⓞ

Västra Hamngatan 3 ⊠ S-402 22 – ℘ (031) 720 40 40 – info.gbgplaza@elite.se
– Fax (031) 720 40 10 – www.elite.se
closed 24-26 December   **B2**
141 rm ⊊ – ♦2025 SEK ♦♦2925 SEK – 2 suites
Rest see *Swea Hof* below
♦ Luxury ♦ Modern ♦
Discreet and stylishly converted late 19C building. Rooms embody understated
luxury with those overlooking the atrium sharing its lively atmosphere. Smart
cocktail bar.

Clarion Collection H. Odin without rest   ⅃⅙ 🏠 ⅍ 🖭 ℭ 🕭30

Odinsgatan 6 ⊠ S-411 03 – ℘ (031) 745 22 00   𝗣 𝗩𝗜𝗦𝗔 ⓜⓞ 𝖠𝖤 ⓞ
– info.cc.odin@choicehotels.se – Fax (031) 711 24 60 – www.hotelodin.se
112 rm ⊊ – ♦1845 SEK ♦♦2055 SEK – 24 suites   **C2**
♦ Business ♦ Modern ♦
Central location near railway station. Smart, Scandic-style, well equipped,
serviced apartments, with mini-kitchen; also spacious and appealing suites.

Scandic H. Rubinen   🏠 ⅍ 🖭 🕭40 𝗩𝗜𝗦𝗔 ⓜⓞ 𝖠𝖤 ⓞ

Kungsportsavenyn 24 ⊠ S-400 14 – ℘ (031) 751 54 00 – rubinen@
scandic-hotels.com – Fax (031) 751 54 11 – www.scandic-hotels.com/rubinen
190 rm ⊊ – ♦1890 SEK ♦♦2190 SEK – 1 suite   **C3**
Rest (closed Sunday lunch) a la carte 336/458 SEK
♦ Business ♦ Modern ♦
Well located central hotel with smart, modern style. Comfy rooms exude a rich
"red" theme, including a painting in that style. Junior suites boast delightful roof
terraces. Modish restaurant with dominant bar: trendy "New Latino" style cuisine.

Riverton   ≼ 🏠 ᕦ 🎦 ⅍ ℁ 🖭 🕭300 𝗣 𝗩𝗜𝗦𝗔 ⓜⓞ 𝖠𝖤 ⓞ

Stora Badhusgatan 26 ⊠ S-411 21 – ℘ (031) 750 10 00 – riverton@riverton.se
– Fax (031) 750 10 01 – www.riverton.se   **A2**
187 rm ⊊ – ♦1495 SEK ♦♦1995 SEK – 4 suites
Rest (closed Sunday) a la carte approx. 450 SEK
♦ Business ♦ Modern ♦
Modern hotel offering fine view of city and docks from upper floors. Sleek
Swedish décor with wood floors and warm bright colours. Good business
facilities. 12th floor restaurant, overlooking Göta Älv river and docks. Local and
international cuisine.

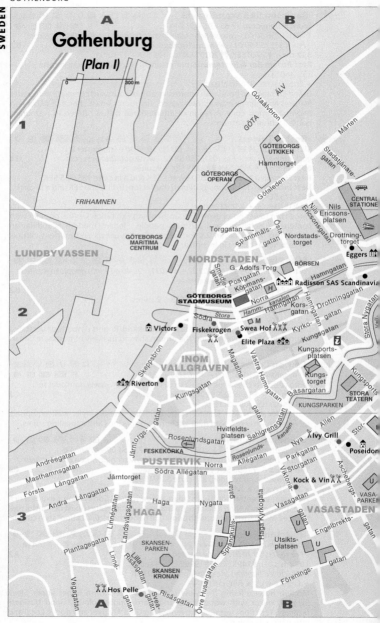

Gothenburg

(Plan I)

0   300 m

GÖTA ÄLV

GÖTA

Götaälvbron

Mårten

Stadstjänare gatan

GÖTEBORGS UTKIKEN

Hamntorget

Nils Ericsonsplatsen

CENTRAL STATIONE

GÖTEBORGS OPERAN

Götaleden

FRIHAMNEN

Nils Ericsonsgatan

Torggatan

Spannmåls- Göta gatan

Nordstadstorget

Drottningtorget

GÖTEBORGS MARITIMA CENTRUM

NORDSTADEN

LUNDBYVASSEN

Smedje- gatan

G. Adolfs Torg

BÖRSEN

Eggers

Postgatan

Köpmans- gatan

Hamngatan

Radisson SAS Scandinavia

GÖTEBORGS STADMUSEUM

Norra Hamm- Hamngatan

H

Stora kanalen

Drottninggatan

Stora Nygata

Victors

Södra Stora

Hamm- Hamngatan

Kors- gatan

Kyrko-

Drottninggatan

Vall-

Fiskekrogen

Swea Hof

M

Kungsports- platsen

Elite Plaza

Skeppsbron

INOM VALLGRAVEN

Magasins-

Västra Hamngatan

Kungs- torget

Kungsports

Riverton

Kungsgatan

Basargatan

KUNGSPARKEN

STORA TEATERN

Hvitfeldts- platsen

Allén

Stor-

Järntorgs- gatan

Rosenlundsgatan

Sahlgrens

kanalen

Nya

Ivy Grill

Poseidon

FESKEKORKA

Rosenlunds- Allégatan

Parkgatan

Ascheberg

Andréegatan

PUSTERVIK

Norra

Storgatan

Masthamnsgatan

Södra Allégatan

Viktoria

Kock & Vin

gatan

Första Långgatan

Järntorget

Nygata

Vasagatan

VASA- PARKEN

Andra Långgatan

Haga

Haga Kyrkogata

VASASTADEN

HAGA

U

U

Engelbrekts-

Plantagegatan

Limnegatan

Landsvägsgatan

Sprängkullsgatan

U

U

Utsikts- platsen

gatan

SKANSEN- PARKEN

U

Veggagatan

Linné-

Lilla Risåsgatan

SKANSEN KRONAN

Övre Husargatan

Förenings-

Hos Pelle

Risåsgatan

Svea- gatan

740

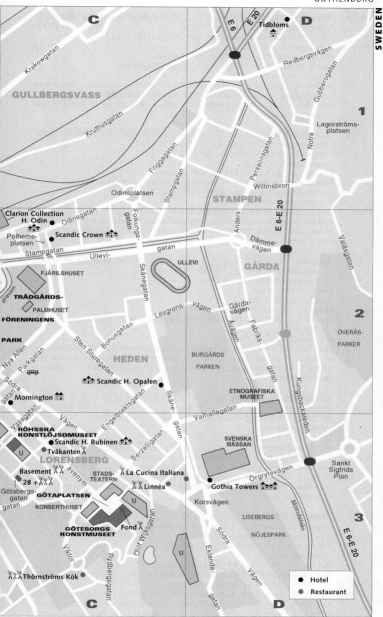

Krakowgatan

C

E 6

E 20

Tidbloms

D

Redbergsvägen

GULLBERGSVASS

Kruthusgatan

Gubberogatan

Lagorströms-
platsen

1

Friggagatan

Notra

Odinsplatsen

Stampgatan

Perssonsgatan

Willinsbron

STAMPEN

E 6-E 20

Clarion Collection
H. Odin

Odinsgatan

Folkunga-
gatan

Anders

Dämme-
vägen

Valasgatan

Polhems-
platsen

Scandic Crown

gatan

Stampgatan

Ullevi-

GÅRDA

FJÄRILSHUSET

Skånegatan

ULLEVI

gravitt

TRÄDGÅRDS-

PALMHUSET

Levgrens-
vägen

Gårda-
vägen

Gårda-
vägen

Fabriks-

FÖRENINGENS

Bohusgatan

2

PARK

Sten Sturegatan

ÖVERÅS-
PARKER

Nya Allén

Parkgatan

Kungsbackaleden

Södra

HEDEN

BURGÅRDS

PARKEN

gata

Scandic H. Opalen

Skåne-

Valhallagatan

ETNOGRAFISKA
MUSEET

Mornington

Engelbrektsgatan

gatan

Vägen

Vasagatan

RÖHSSKA
KONSTLÖJSDMUSEET

Berzeliigatan

SVENSKA
MÄSSAN

Scandic H. Rubinen

Tvåkanten

LORENSBERG

Örgry,tevägen

Sankt
Sigfrids
Plan

Basement

avenym

STADS-
TEATERN

La Cucina Italiana

Linnéa

Gothia Towers

28 +

Mölndalsän

E 6-E 20

Götabergs-
gatan

GÖTAPLATSEN

KONSERTHUSET

Korsvägen

LISEBERGS

3

gatan

GÖTEBORGS
KONSTMUSEET

Fond

Olof Wijksgatan

U

NÖJESPARK

Viktor

Rydbergsgatan

Södra

Thörnströms Kök

Eklanda-

Vägen

gatan

U

Hotel

Restaurant

C

D

SWEDEN

Scandic Crown
🖼 🏠 ♿ Ⓜ 🤸 ⑁rest 📺 🕻 ♨300 🛏

Polhemsplatsen 3 ⊠ S-411 11 – ℰ (031)   **P** **VISA** **MC** **AE** **①**
751 51 00 – crown@scandic-hotels.com – Fax (031) 751 51 11
– www.scandic-hotels.se   **C2**
336 rm � – ♦1490 SEK ♦♦1950 SEK – 2 suites
Rest (buffet lunch)98/245 SEK and a la carte 289/364 SEK
♦ Business ♦ Modern ♦
Modern group hotel in good location for transport connections. Fresh bright
functional rooms with wood floors and colourful fabrics. Executive rooms with
balconies. Pleasant atrium restaurant with a wide range of Swedish and
international cuisine.

Scandic H. Opalen
🏠 ♿ Ⓜ rest 🤸 📺 🕻 ♨180 🛏 **VISA** **MC** **AE** **①**

Engelbrektsgatan 73 ⊠ S-402 23 – ℰ (031) 751 53 00
– opalen@scandic-hotels.com – Fax (031) 751 53 11
– www.scandic-hotels.se   **C2**
238 rm ⊻ – ♦1700 SEK ♦♦2000 SEK – 4 suites
Rest (closed Sunday) (dancing Thursday-Saturday evenings except mid
June-mid August) a la carte approx. 350 SEK
♦ Business ♦ Modern ♦
Corporate hotel near the business centre and stadium. Rooms vary in size but all
with same good level of facilities. Large restaurant, varied choice of Swedish and
international dishes. Popular weekend entertainment, with dancing several
nights a week.

Eggers
🏠 🤸 ⑁ 📺 ♨50 **VISA** **MC** **AE** **①**

Drottningtorget ⊠ S-401 25 – ℰ (031) 333 44 40
– hotel.eggers@telia.com – Fax (031) 333 44 49
– www.hoteleggers.se
closed 23-26 December   **B2**
69 rm ⊻ – ♦1455 SEK ♦♦1990 SEK
Rest (closed July and 20 December-8 January)179/250 SEK and a la carte
312/405 SEK
♦ Traditional ♦ Classic ♦
Charming 1850s hotel, one of Sweden's oldest: wrought iron and stained glass
on staircase, Gothenburg's oldest lift. Rooms feature period furniture and
fittings. Ornate restaurant busy during day, more elegant in evening. Traditional
Swedish cuisine.

Quality H. Panorama
≤ 🖼 🏠 ♿ Ⓜ 🤸 📺 ♨90

Eklandagatan 51-53 ⊠ S-400 22 – ℰ (031)   🛏 **VISA** **MC** **AE** **①**
767 70 00 – info.panorama@quality.choicehotels.se – Fax (031) 767 70 75
– www.panorama.se
339 rm – ♦1495 SEK ♦♦1995 SEK
Rest (closed lunch Saturday and Sunday) a la carte approx. 450 SEK
♦ Chain hotel ♦ Business ♦ Functional ♦
Commercial hotel popular with business people; good conference facilities.
Compact, refurbished rooms, larger on top floors. Small spa area for
relaxation. First floor hotel restaurant in Scandinavian brasserie style.
International menu.

Novotel Göteborg
≤ 🏠 ♿ Ⓜ 🤸 📺 ♨70 **P** **VISA** **MC** **AE** **①**

Klippan 1 (Southwest : 3 ½ km by Andréeg taking Kiel-Klippan Ö exit,
or boat from Rosenlund) ⊠ S-414 51 – ℰ (031) 720 22 00
– info@novotel.se – Fax (031) 720 22 99
– www.novotel.se
143 rm ⊻ – ♦1560 SEK ♦♦1690 SEK – 5 suites
Rest Carnegie Kaj (buffet lunch)159 SEK and a la carte 282/425 SEK
♦ Chain hotel ♦ Business ♦ Functional ♦
Converted brewery on waterfront with view of Göta Älv. Central atrium
style lobby. Spacious rooms with international style décor and sofabeds.
Restaurant overlooking the harbour. International cooking to appeal to all
tastes.

SWEDEN

Mornington 🏠 🕭 📖 rest ↔ 🖭 ☎ ⚙45 ⛱ VISA ⚫ AE ⓐ

Kungsportsavenyn 6 ⊠ S-411 36 – ℰ (031) 767 34 00 – goteborg @
mornington.se – Fax (031) 711 34 39 – www.mornington.se   **C2**
91 rm ⬜ – ♦1440 SEK ♦♦1950 SEK
Rest *Brasserie Lipp* a la carte 364/435 SEK
♦ Business ♦ Modern ♦
Modern office block style façade conceals hotel on famous shopping street.
Compact rooms of dark brown, comfortable functional furniture, with slightly
English "feel" to them. Pleasant brasserie-style restaurant, hearty home cooking
and international fare.

Victors ≼ Göta Älv river and harbour, 🕭 ⛯ ↔ 🖭 ⚙50 VISA ⚫ AE ⓐ

Skeppsbroplatsen 1 (4th floor) ⊠ S-411 18 – ℰ (031) 17 41 80 – info @
victors-hotel.com – Fax (031) 13 96 10 – www.victors-hotel.com
closed 23 December-2 January   **A2**
41 rm ⬜ – ♦1400 SEK ♦♦2000 SEK – 10 suites
Rest *(closed Friday-Sunday)* (dinner only) a la carte 260/410 SEK
♦ Traditional ♦ Functional ♦
Hotel occupies floors 4-6 of an office block on busy intersection but overlooking
harbour. Compact reception and all purpose dining/breakfast/coffee area.
Functional rooms. Good view from restaurant. Choice of international cuisine.

Tidbloms 🕭 ⛯ ↔ ⅌rest ☎ ⚙45 P VISA ⚫ AE ⓐ

Olskroksgatan 23 ⊠ S-416 66 – ℰ (031) 707 50 00 – info @ tidbloms.se
– Fax (031) 707 50 99 – www.tidbloms.se   **D1**
42 rm ⬜ – ♦1190 SEK ♦♦1450 SEK
Rest *(closed lunch Saturday and Sunday)*155 SEK
♦ Business ♦ Functional ♦
Old red brick hotel in quiet residential area. Quaint turret and semi-circular
veranda-cum-conservatory. Sunny rooms with standard comforts. Rustic
restaurant in the round, serving modern international cuisine.

Poseidon without rest ↔ ⅌ 🖭 ☎ VISA ⚫ AE ⓐ

Storgatan 33 ⊠ S-411 38 – ℰ (031) 10 05 50 – info @ hotelposeidon.com
– Fax (031) 13 83 91 – www.hotelposeidon.com
closed 23 December-2 January   **B3**
49 rm ⬜ – ♦980 SEK ♦♦1100 SEK
♦ Family ♦ Functional ♦
Informal hotel in residential area not far from main shopping street. Comfortable
neutral décor and functional furnishings in rooms. Accommodation for families
available.

XXX Sjömagasinet (Mannerström) ≼ 🏠 ↔ ⅌ P VISA ⚫ AE ⓐ
✿

Klippans Kulturreservat 5 (Southwest : 3 ½ km by Andréeg taking
Kiel-Klippan Ó exit, or boat from Rosenlund. Also evenings and weekends in
summer from Lilla Bommens Hamn) ⊠ S-414 51 – ℰ (031) 775 59 20
– info @ sjomagasinet.se – Fax (031) 24 55 39 – www.sjomagasinet.se
closed 17 April, 23 June, 24-26 and 31 December and Sunday January-March
Rest (booking essential) (buffet lunch in summer)275/375 SEK (lunch)
and a la carte 550/665 SEK 🍷
Spec. Mannerström's herring platter. Poached fillet of sole with lobster sauce.
Cloudberry tart, red fruit coulis.
♦ Seafood ♦ Rustic ♦
Delightful 18C former East India Company waterfront warehouse. Forever busy
restaurant on two floors with ship's mast and charming terrace. Accomplished
seafood cooking.

XXX Thörnströms Kök 📖 ↔ ⅌ VISA ⚫ AE ⓐ

Teknologgatan 3 ⊠ S-411 32 – ℰ (031) 16 20 66 – info @ thornstromskok.com
– Fax (031) 16 40 17 – www.thornstromskok.com   **C3**
closed 22 June-8 August, 25 December-1 January, Sunday and Monday
Rest (booking essential) (dinner only)410/535 SEK and a la carte 410/535 SEK
♦ Modern ♦ Neighbourhood ♦
Eternally popular and stylishly elegant restaurant, set in a quiet area near
university. Accomplished, well-priced international gourmet dishes; very good
service can be expected.

XXX **Swea Hof** – at Elite Plaza H.　　　　　　AK ℀ VISA ⓪ AE ⓪
Västra Hamngatan 3 – ℰ (031) 720 40 40 – Fax (031) 720 40 10
closed 24-26 December　　　　　　　　　　　　　　　**B2**
Rest *(closed Sunday)* 295/795 SEK and a la carte 465/635 SEK
♦ Modern ♦ Formal ♦
Striking atrium-style restaurant in heart of hotel with glass roof on metal
framework and open-plan kitchen. Dinner menu offers elaborate and
accomplished modern cuisine.

XXX **28 +** (Lyxell)　　　　　　　　　　　⇄ ℀ VISA ⓪ AE ⓪
⚘ *Götabergsgatan 28 ⊠ S-411 34 – ℰ (031) 20 21 61 – 28plus@telia.com*
– Fax (031) 81 97 57 – www.28plus.se
closed 14-17 April, 3 July-2 August, 23-26 December, 31 December-2 January and
Sunday　　　　　　　　　　　　　　　　　　　**C3**
Rest (dinner only) a la carte 400/775 SEK ⚘
Spec. Scallops with roast carrot purée, pine nuts and tarragon. Baked halibut with
ginger, eggplant and red curry. Valrhona chocolate pastry with pistachio ice cream.
♦ Innovative ♦ Cosy ♦
Go down a steep flight of steps to beautiful, fine wine cellar accessible to diners.
Special chef to describe cheeses. Seafood emphasis underpins modern Swedish
cuisine.

XX **Linnéa**　　　　　　　　　　　　⇄ ℀ VISA ⓪ AE ⓪
Södra Vägen 32 ⊠ S-412 54 – ℰ (031) 16 11 83 – info@restauranglinnea.com
– Fax (031) 18 12 92 – www.restauranglinnea.com
closed Easter, July, 24 December-9 January, Sunday, Saturday lunch and Bank
Holidays　　　　　　　　　　　　　　　　　**C3**
Rest 395 SEK (dinner) and a la carte 315/647 SEK
♦ Modern ♦ Neighbourhood ♦
Well run restaurant; changing summer and winter décor. Simple lunch venue;
more formal and elaborate for dinner - stylish place settings. Well prepared
modern Swedish cuisine.

XX **Basement** (Wagner)　　　　　　　AK ⇄ ℀ VISA ⓪ AE ⓪
⚘ *Götabergsgatan 28 ⊠ S-411 34 – ℰ (031) 28 27 29 – bokning@*
restbasement.com – Fax (031) 28 27 37 – www.restbasement.com
closed 7 July-15 August, 24 December-6 January and Sunday　　**C3**
Rest (dinner only)560 SEK
Spec. Terrine of seared duck liver with an apple and bayleaf marmalade.
Butter-fried lobster salad.
♦ Modern ♦ Fashionable ♦
Restaurant below street level with white walls enlivened by contemporary
paintings and lithographs. Imaginative modern cuisine using Swedish produce;
speciality tasting menus.

XX **Fiskekrogen**　　　　　　　　　AK ⇄ ℀ VISA ⓪ AE ⓪
Lilla Torget 1 ⊠ S-411 18 – ℰ (031) 10 10 05 – info@fiskekrogen.com
– Fax (031) 10 10 06 – www.fiskekrogen.com
closed 4 weeks summer, 1 week Christmas, Sunday except December and Bank
Holidays　　　　　　　　　　　　　　　　　**B2**
Rest (buffet lunch)195/289 SEK and a la carte 445/690 SEK
♦ Seafood ♦ Brasserie ♦
Busy 1920s restaurant with reputation for its seafood. Striking room with high
ceiling, wood panelling, columns and modern Scandinavian art. Good choice
seafood buffet lunch.

XX **Hos Pelle**　　　　　　　　　　　　⇄ VISA ⓪ AE
Djupedalsgatan 2 ⊠ S-413 07 – ℰ (031) 12 10 31 – info@hospelle.com
– Fax (031) 775 38 32 – www.hospelle.com
closed Sunday and Bank Holidays　　　　　　　　**A3**
Rest (dinner only) a la carte 420/650 SEK
♦ Traditional ♦ Neighbourhood ♦
Popular local restaurant with comfortable atmosphere, displaying Swedish art.
Serves classic and modern Swedish cuisine prepared to high standard. Ground
floor bistro.

SWEDEN

✗✗ Kock & Vin 🔤 ↳ ⅔ VISA ⑩ ㎒ ◎

*Viktoriagatan 12 ⊠ S-411 25 – ℰ (031) 701 79 79 – info @ kockvin.se
– www.kockvin.se*
closed July, 23-26 and 31 December **B3**
Rest (dinner only) a la carte 375/605 SEK ⅜
♦ Modern ♦ Romantic ♦

Attractive candlelit neighbourhood restaurant. Modern paintings but 19C painted ceiling. A la carte or set menu with complementary wines; best of Swedish ingredients.

✗ Fond 🍴 ↳ ⅔ VISA ⑩ ㎒ ◎

※

*Götaplatsen ⊠ S-412 56 – ℰ (031) 81 25 80 – fond @ fondrestaurang.com
– Fax (031) 18 37 90 – www.fondrestaurang.com*
closed 1 month in summer, 1 week Christmas, Sunday, Saturday lunch and Bank Holidays **C3**
Rest a la carte 360/690 SEK
Spec. Halibut with pickled tomatoes and dill, crayfish and fennel. Sugar-fried lamb with sausage, parsley root and thyme flavoured gravy. Baked chocolate terrine with almond pear and rosehip ice cream.
♦ Modern ♦ Trendy ♦

Bright semi-circular glass structure outside Art Museum houses contemporary restaurant. Traditional Swedish lunch as lighter option and modern elaborate dinner menus.

✗ La Cucina Italiana ↳ ⅔ VISA ⑩ ㎒ ◎

☺

*Skånegatan 33 ⊠ S-412 52 – ℰ (031) 16 63 07 – pietro @ swipnet.ie
– Fax (031) 16 63 07 – www.lacucinaitaliana.nu* **C3**
Rest (booking essential) (dinner only)189/299 SEK and a la carte 349/574 SEK
♦ Italian ♦ Bistro ♦

Snugly intimate and authentic Italian restaurant, away from the city centre, with a smart line in modern furnishings. Good value modish menus which change daily.

✗ Tvåkanten 🍴 🔤 ↳ ⅔ VISA ⑩ ㎒ ◎

☺

*Kungsportsavenyn 27 ⊠ S-411 36 – ℰ (031) 18 21 15 – info @ tvakanten.se
– Fax (031) 20 13 98 – www.tvakanten.se*
closed 23-24 June, 23-24 December and Sunday lunch **C3**
Rest 280/745 SEK and a la carte 365/655 SEK
♦ Traditional ♦ Brasserie ♦

Busy character restaurant in city centre setting attracting varied clientele. Dining rooms with brick walls, plus elegant first-floor private dining room. Swedish fare.

✗ Ivy Grill 🍴 🔤 ↳ ⅔ VISA ⑩ ㎒ ◎

*Vasaplatsen 2 ⊠ S-411 28 – ℰ (031) 711 44 04 – info @ ivygrill.com
– Fax (031) 711 29 55 – www.ivygrill.com*
closed 30 June-30 August and Sunday-Monday **B3**
Rest (dinner only)375/495 SEK and a la carte 329/493 SEK
♦ Grills ♦ Brasserie ♦

Step down from the lively bar to this trendy restaurant with its unusual décor. Menu specialises in grills; simple lunch on the terrace in summer only.

at Eriksberg West: 6 km by Götaälvbron and Lundbyleden, or boat from Rosenlund:

🏨 Quality Hotel 11 ≤ 🔤 ↳ 🖾 ⅍ 1500 🅿 VISA ⑩ ㎒ ◎

*Maskingatan 11 ⊠ S-417 64 – ℰ (031) 779 11 11 – info.hotel11 @ choice.se
– Fax (031) 779 11 10 – www.hotel11.se*
closed Christmas-New Year
260 rm ⊇ – ∱1565 SEK ∱∱2020 SEK
Rest *Kök & Bar 67* *(closed Sunday and Saturday lunch)* a la carte approx. 400 SEK
♦ Business ♦ Functional ♦

Striking former shipbuilding warehouse, part see-through there is so much glass! Rooms feature stylish modern Scandinavian interior design with pale wood and bright fabrics. Upper floor restaurant with bar area, waterway views, and international cooking.

SWEDEN

XX **River Café** ≤ Göta Älv river and harbour, 🌫 🗚 ↳ 📧 🐵 🖭 ⓞ
Dockepiren ✉ S-417 64 – ℰ *(031) 51 00 00 – info@rivercafe.se*
– Fax (31) 51 00 01 – www.rivercafe.se
closed Sunday and Saturday lunch
Rest 250/600 SEK
♦ Modern ♦ Friendly ♦
Delightfully set on the pier in Eriksburg, with fine view to harbour. Agreeable bar;
elegant first-floor restaurant with panoramic glass frontage. Modish worldwide
menus.

at Landvetter Airport East: 30 km by Rd 40:

Landvetter Airport H. 🌫 🕉 ⅙ 🗚 ↳ 🍽 📧 🐵 📱 📧 🐵 🖭 ⓞ
✉ S-438 13 – ℰ *(031) 97 75 50 – info@landvetterairporthotel.se*
– Fax (031) 94 64 70 – www.landvetterairporthotel.se
103 rm ☕ – ♦1345 SEK ♦♦1495 SEK – 1 suite
Rest (buffet lunch)149/198 SEK and a la carte 214/454 SEK
♦ Business ♦ Modern ♦
Hotel benefitting from immediate proximity to airport. Rooms are bright and
welcoming and feature typical Swedish décor in bright colours. Full modern and
business facilities. Relaxed restaurant and terrace off the main lobby. Offers
Swedish and global fare.

SWITZERLAND
SUISSE, SCHWEIZ, SVIZZERA

PROFILE

- ◆ **AREA:**
  41 284 km² (15 940 sq mi).

- ◆ **POPULATION:**
  7 489 000 (est. 2005), density = 181 per km².

- ◆ **CAPITAL:**
  Bern (Berne) (conurbation 349 100 inhabitants).

- ◆ **CURRENCY:**
  Swiss Franc (CHF); rate of exchange CHF 1 = € 0.65 = US$ 0.76 (Nov 2005).

- ◆ **GOVERNMENT:**
  Federation of 26 cantons with 2 assemblies (National Council and Council of State) forming the Federal Assembly.

- ◆ **LANGUAGES:**
  German (64% of population), French (20%), Italian (7%) are spoken in all administrative departments, shops, hotels and restaurants. Romansh (1%) in the Grisons canton.

- ◆ **SEPCIFIC PUBLIC HOLIDAYS:**
  Berchtold's Day (2 January); Good Friday (Friday before Easter); Swiss National Holiday (1 August); St. Stephen's Day (26 December). Thanksgiving (Jeûne Fédéral in French; Bettag in German) is observed in all cantons, except Geneva, on the third Sunday in September; the Geneva canton holds Thanksgiving on the second Thursday in September.

- ◆ **LOCAL TIME:**
  GMT + 1 hour in winter, GMT+ 2 hours in summer.

- ◆ **CLIMATE**
  Temperate continental, varies with altitude – most of the country has

cold winters and warm summers (Bern: January: 0°C, July: 19°C).

- ◆ **INTERNATIONAL DIALLING CODE**
  00 41 followed by the area or city code (Geneva: **22**, Bern: **31**, Zurich: **44** or **43**) and then the local number.

- ◆ **EMERGENCY**
  Police: ☎ **117**; Medical emergencies: ☎ **144**; Fire Brigade: ☎ **118**. Anglo-Phone (24 hr information and helpline in English): ☎ **0900 576 444**.

- ◆ **ELECTRICITY:**
  220 volts AC, 50 Hz; 2-pin round-shaped continental plugs.

FORMALITIES

Travellers from the European Union (EU), Iceland and the main countries of North and South America need a national identity card or passport (America: passport required) to visit Switzerland for less than three months (tourism or business purpose). For visitors from other countries a visa may be required, in addition to a passport, especially for those wishing to stay for longer than three months. We advise you to check with your embassy before travelling.

A valid driving licence or international driving permit, car registration papers and a nationality plate of the approved size are required. An international Insurance Certificate (Green Card) is advisable. Roads are toll-free but all vehicles must display a road tax disc (vignette) which is available at border posts. It can be purchased in advance from the Swiss National Tourist Office.

747

MAJOR NEWSPAPERS

Le Matin, La Tribune de Genève, 24 Heures are the main French-language papers; *Neue Zürcher Zeitung, Basler Zeitung, Tages-Anzeiger, Berner Zeitung* are published in German.

USEFUL PHRASES

ENGLISH	FRENCH	GERMAN	ITALIAN
Yes	**Oui**	**Ja**	**Si**
No	**Non**	**Nein**	**No**
Good morning	**Bonjour**	**Guten Morgen**	**Buongiorno**
Goodbye	**Au revoir**	**Auf Wiedersehen**	**Arrivederci**
Thank you	**Merci**	**Danke**	**Grazie**
Please	**S'il vous plaît**	**Bitte**	**Per favore**
Excuse me	**Excusez-moi**	**Verzeihung**	**Mi scusi**
I don't understand	**Je ne comprends pas**	**Ich verstehe nicht**	**Non capisco**

HOTELS

◆ CATEGORIES

Prestigious international hotels offer high standards of accommodation and service. Motels, resorts, moderately priced hotels, garni (hotel with no restaurant) provide a very good standard of comfort. Inns (Gasthaus), B&Bs and guesthouses (pension) have clean, simple accommodation. The Swiss Hotel Association has a star-rating classification but this is on a voluntary basis.

◆ PRICE RANGE

Prices may be quoted per person or per room. Make sure to check when you contact the hotel directly. Hotel prices usually include breakfast in summer but tend to quoted for half-board in winter.

◆ TAX

Prices are inclusive of VAT (7.6%) and service charge but an additional tax may be payable depending on the canton.

◆ CHECK OUT TIME

Between 11am and noon.

◆ RESERVATIONS

Bookings can be made by phone or on the Internet. Discounts apply for booking on line.

◆ TIPS FOR LUGGAGE HANDLING

No gratuities are expected but it is at the discretion of the customer (2CHF per item) whether to tip the porter.

◆ BREAKFAST

Breakfast is usually included in the price of the room and consists of a self-service buffet. You may be able to order continental breakfast to be served in the room.

Reception	**Réception**	**Empfang**	**Ufficio ricevimento**
Single room	**Chambre simple**	**Einzelzimmer**	**Camera singola**
Double room	**Chambre double**	**Doppelzimmer**	**Camera doppia**
Bed	**Lit**	**Bett**	**Letto**
Bathroom	**Salle de bains**	**Bad**	**Bagno**
Shower	**Douche**	**Dusche**	**Doccia**

748

RESTAURANTS

Set menus usually include an entrée, a meat dish with vegetables and dessert. A la carte dishes are very generous. Inns serve simple local cuisine, 'cuisine du terroir'.

Wirtschaft is a modest local inn or pub. **Grotto** means, in the Ticino area, a typical restaurant serving local wines and a selection of dishes of the region. In Switzerland **Café** is a tea-room.

◆ MEALS

Breakfast	**Petit-déjeuner**	**Frühstück**	**La collazione**	6am – 8am
Lunch	**Déjeuner**	**Mittagessen**	**Il pranzo**	noon –2-3pm
Dinner	**Dîner**	**Abendessen**	**La cena**	8pm – 11.30pm

NB: The Swiss often call the midday meal 'dinner'.

◆ RESERVATIONS

Booking should be made by phone or by email. It is advisable to book, especially if you want to visit a popular restaurant or a restaurant which has won special commendation.

◆ THE BILL

The bill (check) includes service charge and VAT. No extra tip required unless you wish to reward exceptional service.

Drink or aperitif	**Apéritif**	**Aperitif**	**Aperitivo**
Appetizer	**Amuse-bouche**	**Appetitanreger**	**Antipasto**
Meal	**Repas**	**Essen**	**Pasto**
First course, starter	**Entrée**	**Vorspeise**	**Primo piatto**
Main dish	**Plat principal**	**Hauptgericht**	**Piatto principale**
Main dish of the day	**Plat du jour**	**Tagesteller**	**Piatto del giorno**
Dessert	**Dessert**	**Nachtisch**	**Dolce**
Water/mineral water (still, sparkling)	**Eau/eau minérale (plate, gazeuse)**	**Wasser/ Mineralwasser (ohne/mit Kohlensäure)**	**Acqua/acqua minerale (naturale, gasata)**
Wine (red, white, rosé)	**Vin (rouge, blanc, rosé)**	**Wein (rot, weiss, rosé)**	**Vino (rosso, bianco, rosatello)**
Beer	**Bière**	**Bier**	**Birra**
Bread	**Pain**	**Brot**	**Pane**
Meat (rare, medium, well done)	**Viande (saignant, à point, bien cuit)**	**Fleisch (blutig, mittel, gut durchgebraten)**	**Carne (al sangue, a puntino, ben cotto)**
Fish	**Poisson**	**Fisch**	**Pesce**
Salt/pepper	**Sel/poivre**	**Salz/Pfeffer**	**Sale/pepe**
Cheese	**Fromage**	**Käse**	**Formaggio**
Vegetables	**Légumes**	**Gemüse**	**Verdure**
Hot/cold	**Chaud/froid**	**Heiss/Kalt**	**Caldo/freddo**
The bill (check) please	**L'addition s'il vous plaît**	**Die Rechnung bitte**	**Il conto per favore**

749

LOCAL CUISINE

Switzerland combines the gastronomic traditions of France, Germany and Italy and is rich in culinary specialities, often simple but wholesome and tasty.

The national dish of German Swiss is the golden **Rösti**, often topped with cheese, ham or fried egg. The **fondue** made from the hard cheeses, Vacherin and Gruyère, melted with spices, kirsch and wine, is a national institution among the French Swiss. The fondue is eaten by dipping little cubes of bread, held on a long fork, into the pot. **Raclette** is a Valais speciality – melted Valais cheese is eaten with gherkins or potatoes. Other tasty cheeses are Emmental, Vacherin Mont d'Or, Tête de moine, L'Etivaz, Formaggio d'alpe ticinese. **Bündnerfleisch**, thin slices of smoked, dried beef is a Grisons delicacy. Varieties of sausages (Wurst, saucisse, salsiccia) are numerous: Cervelat, Schüblig (long beef and pork sausage), Longeole (raw sausage with spices and white wine), boutefas, saucisson neuchâtelois, saucisse d'Ajoie, saucisson vaudois, dried house sausages from the Valais, salami, mortadella ticinese, cicitt (goat sausages), salsiz (small sausages), veal and venison sausages. The monumental **Berner Platte** brings together bacon, sausages, ham, boiled beef, pickled cabbage (Sauerkraut), potatoes or green beans.

Among regional specialities are: air-dried Graubünden meat, **Capuns** (stuffed mangel leaves), **Beinwurst** (pork ragout in wine sauce), Schaffhauser **Bölletüne** (onion pie), **busecca** (entrails and vegetable soup), **Papet vaudois** (cream-leek casserole), **geschnetzeltes Kalbsfleisch** (minced veal or calf's liver with cream), **Leberspiessli** (calf's liver on a spit with bacon), **Pastetli** (puff pastry with creamy diced veal), **cardoons au gratin**. The rivers and lakes provide a wide variety of fish (pike, trout, carp, tench, perch, which are prepared to traditional recipes: baked, in white wine sauce, in pastry, pickled.

Desserts and sweets should not be missed: tarte au vin (wine cake), torta di pane (bread cake), kirsch cake, meringues, Schaffhauserzungen (baked biscuits), Leckerli (spiced honey and almond bread). Swiss chocolate, of time-honoured renown, is used to make delicious cakes and sweets.

DRINK

The wine growing tradition of Switzerland goes back to the Roman era. The diversity of vines, soil and climate accounts for the quality and originality of its wines. The Vaud produces excellent vintages in the regions La Côte, Lavaux and Chablais: Chasselas, Salvagnin and fruity, light Pinot Noir. The best known wines from the Valais, the largest wine canton, include **Fendant**, Johannisberg (white) and the fragrant red **Dôle**. The Geneva canton produces interesting dry whites: Chasselas, Pinot Gris and full-bodied Aligoté as well as the mellow, aromatic **Gewürztraminer**. The fruity red Gamay and dry Pinot Noir and the lively fresh rosé, **Oeil-de-Perdrix**, are also noteworthy. The principal wines from Neuchâtel are Chasselas, Pinot Noir and the delicately fruity **Oeil-de-Perdrix**. The warm climate of the south yields outstanding wines: tannic Merlot del Ticino and Merlot Bianco. The red, white, rosé wines from the eastern area of the country and the Alpine Valley of the Rhine are most appreciated for their light and subtle quality. There are also some excellent dessert wines (Malvoisie, Johannisberg).

Kirsch from Zug, Marc (grape schnapps), Grappa from Ticino, Williams (pear schnapps) from the Valais, Zwetschgenwasser (plum eau-de-vie), Damassine (wild plum schnapps), pleasantly round off a meal. Strong absinthe is a speciality of the Watch Valley (Val-de-Travers). Beer, in particular Feldschlösschen from Basle and Cardinal from Fribourg, and strong alcoholic cider are also popular.

BERN
BERNE

Population (est. 2005): 122 300 (conurbation 349 100) – Altitude: 548m

C. Bowman/SCOPE

The attraction of Bern is enhanced by its situation on a spur overlooking a verdant loop of the Aare, facing the Alps. The old town, a World Heritage Site, is characterised by its long stretch of arcades, home to a wide range of shops, its attractive towers and flower-decked fountains; it is best explored on foot.

The foundation of Bern on a former hunting ground by Duke Berchtold V of Zähringen dates back to the 12C. It was named after the first animal killed by the duke and his followers while hunting during the construction of the city. This was a bear (Bär); it appears on its coat of arms and is the town's mascot. From the 14C to the 16C, the town followed a clever policy of expansion and played a dominant part in the Confederation. When the Constitution was drafted in 1848, Bern was chosen as the seat of the federal authority. It holds a privileged position at the dividing line between the Latin and German cultures. It is the seat of the Swiss federal authorities, 70 embassies and the headquarters of several international organisations. Its famous sons include the artists Ferdinand Hodler and Paul Klee and it was home to the Nobel prize-winning physicist, Albert Einstein, who worked out his theory of relativity while employed as a clerk at the Bern patent office.

WHICH DISTRICT TO CHOOSE

The attractive old town is where you will find luxury **accommodation** in tastefully converted old town houses and with stunning views. It is also relatively easy to find moderately priced hotels in the quiet cobbled streets. There are business hotels near the station and the Bern Expo complex.

There is a great variety of **restaurants** where you can treat yourself in the old town from establishments offering refined international cuisine and brasseries with a congenial ambience to charming inns serving traditional and seasonal dishes.

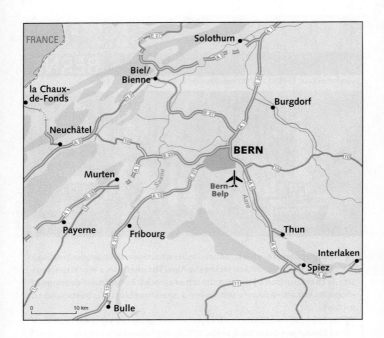

PRACTICAL INFORMATION

ARRIVAL – DEPARTURE

Bern-Belp International Airport – 9 km (5.5 mi) southeast of the city. ℘ 031 960 21 11, www.alpar.ch

From the airport to the city centre – By **taxi**: 45-50CHF, time 20-30min. By **shuttle bus**: 15CHF, every 30min, time: 20min. By **Airliner** Regional bus: 3CHF, 1-2 buses an hour.

Railway Station – Bahnhof, Bahnhofplatz *Plan II* **C2**: inter-city and intercontinental services. Fast trains to Zurich and Geneva airports. ℘ 0900 300 300; www.sbb.ch

TRANSPORT

◆ BUSES AND TRAMS

The bus and tram network is very efficient. A short cable-railway links the Marzili quarter to the Bundeshaus. Single ticket 1.90CHF (1-6 stops, valid 30min), 3.20CHF (7 or more stops, valid 1hr). Buy your ticket from the ticket machine at the bus or tram stop. The BernCard – 17CHF (€11.50, 24hr), 27CHF (€18, 48hr), 33CHF (€22, 72hr) – which gives unlimited travel, free admission to museums and gardens and various reductions, is available from the Tourist Office, museums and hotels. *BernMobil*, ℘ 031 321 88 88; www.bernmobil.ch

◆ TAXIS

There are taxi ranks in **Casinoplatz** *Plan II* **D2** and at the railway station or taxis can also be ordered by phone. An average ride in town costs 12-15CHF. Supplements are charged for evenings and luggage. *Bären Taxi* ℘ 031 371 11 11; *Nova-Taxi* ℘ 031 331 33 13.

Bern Tourismus – In **Bahnhof** *Plan II* **C2**: open Jun-Sep, daily 9am-8.30pm; Oct-May, Mon-Sat 9am-6.30pm, Sun 10am-5pm. **Bärengraben**: open Jun-Sep, daily 9am-6pm; Oct, Mar-May, daily 10am-4pm; Nov-Feb, Fri-Sun 11am-4pm. ℰ 031 328 12 12; www. bernetourism.ch

◆ POST OFFICES

Main Post Office (Schanzenpost), Schanzenstrasse *Plan II* **C2**; open Mon-Fri 7.30am-9pm, Sat 8am-4pm, Sun 4pm-9pm.

◆ BANKS/CURRENCY EXCHANGE

Banks open Mon-Fri 8.30am-4.30pm (6pm Thu). Exchange offices at the railway station open extended hours.

There are cash dispensers all over the city. Credit cards are widely accepted and require a PIN.

◆ PHARMACIES

Pharmacy Hörning, Bahnhof (upper level) *Plan II* **C2** is open daily, 6.30am-10pm.

◆ EMERGENCY

Police ℰ **117**. Fire Brigade ℰ **118**. Medical Emergency service ℰ **144**.

BUSY PERIODS

It may be difficult to find a room at a reasonable price during special events:

International Jazz Festival Gala: one week end in May – In the Kursaal.

Zibelemärit: Fourth Monday in November – Traditional onion market to mark the beginning of winter.

EXPLORING BERN

It is possible to visit the main sights and museums in two days.

Museums and other sights are usually open from 9-10am to 5pm. Some close on Mondays.

VISITING

Old Town – **Marktgasse** *Plan II* **D2**: fine 17-18C houses and arcades, fountains, clock tower **(Zeitglockenturm)** with painted figurines. **Kramgasse** *Plan II* **E1**: old houses with oriel windows and corner turrets, Samson fountain, **Einsteinhaus** (home of Nobel physicist). 15C **Rathaus** with double staircase and covered porch. **Nydeggbrücke** *Plan II* **F1**: view of the town, river and wooded setting. **Bärengraben** *Plan II* **F1**: city mascots, Bern Show (history of the town). **Junkerngasse** lined with old houses (Baroque **Erlacher Hof**). Gothic **Münster Sankt Vincenz** *Plan II* **H2** (panorama from belltower, painted tympanum of main portal,

stained glass in chancel, 16C stalls). **Bundeshaus** *Plan II* **D2**, home of the Federal Council and Swiss Parliament; view from the terrace.

Kunstmuseum *Plan II* **C1** – Splendid collection of 13C-20C paintings: Swiss Primitives, Hodler, French schools and contemporary Swiss art.

Zentrum Paul Klee *Plan I* **B2** – Three spectacular buildings are devoted to the life and works of the artist Paul Klee.

Bernisches Historisches Museum *Plan I* **A2** – Collection of historical, archaeological and ethnographic exhibits.

Schweizerisches Alpines Museum *Plan II* **D2** – A good introduction to the Alps: Alpine life, traditional customs and folklore.

Naturhistorisches Museum *Plan I* **A2** – One of the largest natural history museums in the country: remarkable

Wattenwyl Hall, dioramas and fine collections.

Museum für Kommunikation *Plan I* **A2** – It traces the history of communication from smoke signals to digital systems.

Excursions – The **Gurten** *(2.5 km-1.5 mi S by road and funicular)*: views. **Murten** (Murat, *18km-11mi W*): picturesque fortified town. **Fribourg** *(27 km-18 mi SW)*: in a remarkable site, it marks the boundary between Switzerland's French- and German-speaking areas.

SHOPPING

Shops open Mon 2pm (department stores 9am)-6.30pm; Tue-Fri 9am-6.30pm (9pm Thu); Sat 8am-4pm; closed Sun except shops at the railway station.

The main shopping streets are **Spitalgasse** *Plan II* **C2** (*Globus* No 37, *Loeb* No 47-57), **Marktgasse** *Plan II* **D2**, **Kramgasse** *Plan II* **E1** and **Gerechtigkeitsgasse** *Plan II* **E1**. Smaller specialist boutiques (antiques, wooden toys, arts and crafts) are located in the side streets near the river bank. Visit *Grieder*, Waisenhausplatz 3; *Bürki*, Münzgraben 2; *Gygax* and *Bally*, Spitalgasse 4/9 for leather goods. *Indigo Moda Donna*, Spitalgasse 27; *Jutta van D* and *Stoff-Ciolina*, Kramgasse 8/52; *Bayard Wartmann*, Marktgasse 45 specialise in ladies fashion.

MARKETS – In **Bundesplatz** *Plan II* **D2**, **Bärenplatz** *Plan II* **D2**, **Waisenhausplatz** *Plan II* **D1** on Tue, Sat mornings. **Craft market**: Mar-Dec, every first Sun on the Münster platform *Plan II* **E2**. Traditional **onion market** (*Zwiebelmarkt*) on the fourth Mon in Nov at various locations in the city. **Christmas market** on Münsterplatz *Plan II* **E2**.

WHAT TO BUY – Designer items, watches, jewellery, chocolates (Toblerone), handicrafts, toys.

ENTERTAINMENT

Stadttheater *Plan II* **D1** – Drama, music.

Theater am Käfigturm *Plan II* **C2** and **Schlachthaus Theater** *Plan II* **E1** – Cultural events.

Kursaal *Plan II* **D1** – Nightclub, cabaret; international variety shows, Jazz Festival.

Puppentheater *Plan II* **E1** – Puppet theatre, shadow play, masques.

Narrenpack Theater *Plan II* **E1** – Lively folk theatre.

Zytglogge Theater *Plan II* **D1** – Plays in dialect.

Gaskessel *Plan I* **A2**, **Reitschule Bern** *Plan II* **C1**, **Dampfzentrale** *Plan I* **A2** – Cultural centres.

NIGHTLIFE

There is a multitude of bars, cafés, restaurants in **Spitalgasse** *Plan II* **C2**, **Marktgasse** *Plan II* **D2**. Enjoy the evening at the elegant *Belle Epoque* and *Klötzkeller*, the oldest tavern in town, Gerechtigkeitsgasse 18/62; *Kreissaal*, Brunngasshalde 63; *Kornhaus*, Kornhausplatz 18; *Arcady* piano bar, Bahnhofplatz 11; *Bierhübeli*, Neubrückstrasse 43; *Schwellenmätteli*, Dalmaziquai 11. Listen to music at *Markthalle Bern*, Bubenbergplatz 9; *Nordsüd* and *Propeller*, Aabergergasse 10/30; *Lirum Larum*, Kramgasse 19A. Trendy places to visit are *Lorenzini*, Hotelgasse 10; *Pery Bar*, Zeughausgasse 3. Dance the night away at *Via Felsenau*, Spinnereiweg 17; *Guayas*, Parkterrasse 16; *Le Club*, Kornhausstrasse 3; *Silo*, Mühlenplatz 11. *Marian's Jazzroom* (Hotel Innere Enge), Engestrasse 54 and *Mahogany Hall*, Klösterlistutz 18 are popular with jazz connoisseurs. Lady luck beckons at the *Grand Casino*, Herrengasse 25.

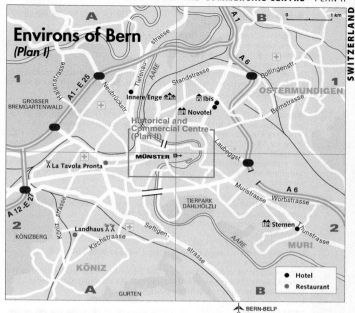

SWITZERLAND

BERN-BELP

HISTORICAL AND COMMERCIAL CENTRE

Plan II

Bellevue Palace   ≤ 斎 & 旭 rm %rest 🖂 ☎ 🛗 15/350
Kochergasse 3 ⊠ 3001 – ℰ 0313 204 545   *VISA* *MO* *AE* *①*
– direktion @ bellevue-palace.ch – Fax 0313 114 743 – www.bellevue-palace.ch
115 rm ☲ – ♟350/430 CHF ♟♟460/540 CHF – 15 suites   **D2**
Rest *Bellevue Grill / Bellevue Terrasse* (Grill: closed lunch and in summer;
Terrasse: closed dinner in winter) 68 CHF (lunch)/125 CHF and a la carte
84/151 CHF
♦ Palace ♦ Classic ♦
This recently renovated luxury hotel breathes an air of aristocratic refinement,
effortlessly combining tradition and modernity. Beautiful views of the river from
the terrace.

Allegro   ≤ 斎 Ⅰ6 ㈱ & 旭 rm ↩rm ☎ 🛗 15/350 🅿 *VISA* *MO* *AE* *①*
Kornhausstr. 3 ⊠ 3013 – ℰ 0313 395 500 – info @ kursaal-bern.ch
– Fax 0313 395 510 – www.kursaal-bern.ch   **D1**
171 rm – ♟220/255 CHF ♟♟300/450 CHF, ☲ 25 CHF
Rest see also *Meridiano* below
Rest *Allegretto* 38 CHF (lunch)/65 CHF and a la carte 57/93 CHF
♦ Business ♦ Modern ♦
Furnished in ultra-modern and functional style, this trendy hotel is designed
especially for the business guest. There is also a casino. The Allegretto has a
friendly atmosphere and contemporary cuisine.

Savoy without rest   旭 ↩ ☎ *VISA* *MO* *AE* *①*
Neuengasse 26 ⊠ 3011 – ℰ 0313 114 405 – info @ zghotels.ch
– Fax 0313 121 978 – www.zghotels.ch   **C1**
56 rm ☲ – ♟205/225 CHF ♟♟270/290 CHF
♦ Business ♦ Classic ♦
This fine old town house is in Bern's pedestrianised centre. Bright, tastefully deco-
rated, and reasonably spacious rooms, with up-to-the-minute technical facilities.

Bristol without rest   ⋒ ⅍ ⅍ ⅏ 🖂 ℭ VISA ⦿ AE ①
Schauplatzgasse 10 🖂 3011 – ℰ 0313 110 101
– reception @ bristolbern.ch – Fax 0313 119 479
– www.bristolbern.ch   **C2**
92 rm ⌖ – ♦195/215 CHF ♦♦255/310 CHF
♦ Business ♦ Modern ♦
This old town house has been completely refurbished and accommodates its
guests in modern rooms with massive wooden furniture. Small sauna shared
with the Hotel Bern.

Bären without rest   ⋒ ⅍ 🖂 ℭ VISA ⦿ AE ①
Schauplatzgasse 4 🖂 3011 – ℰ 0313 113 367 – reception @ baerenbern.ch
– Fax 0313 116 983 – www.baerenbern.ch   **C2**
57 rm ⌖ – ♦195/215 CHF ♦♦255/310 CHF
♦ Business ♦ Modern ♦
Just a stone's throw from the Bundesplatz, a hotel with rooms furnished in
contemporary style with a good range of technical facilities for business
travellers.

Belle Epoque   ⇲ ᶜᵘᵣm ⅍rm 🖂 ℭ VISA ⦿ AE ①
Gerechtigkeitsgasse 18 🖂 3011 – ℰ 0313 114 336
– info @ belle-epoque.ch – Fax 0313 113 936
– www.belle-epoque.ch   **E1**
17 rm – ♦245 CHF ♦♦340 CHF, ⌖ 19 CHF
Rest (only snacks at lunch) 65 CHF (dinner) and a la carte 51/95 CHF
♦ Business ♦ Cosy ♦
A charming hotel in Bern's beautiful Old Town. From the lovely foyer to the
tasteful rooms, there is a wealth of Art Nouveau details and original pieces. Light
lunches and speciality roasts in the evening.

HOTELBERN   ⇲ ᶜ ⅍rm 🖂 ℭ ⅍15/120 VISA ⦿ AE ①
Zeughausgasse 9 🖂 3011 – ℰ 0313 292 222 – hotelbern @ hotelbern.ch
– Fax 0313 292 299 – www.hotelbern.ch   **D1**
100 rm ⌖ – ♦205/240 CHF ♦♦250/310 CHF
Rest *Kurierstube* (closed July and Sunday) 33 CHF (lunch)/68 CHF
and a la carte 52/111 CHF
Rest *7 Stube* a la carte 40/98 CHF
♦ Business ♦ Modern ♦
This establishment in the heart of the Old Town is proud to bear the name
of the city and canton. Rooms with functional furniture and fittings, plus good
facilities for seminars. Classically elegant Kurierstube. Traditional cuisine in the
7 Stube.

CITY without rest   🖂 VISA ⦿ AE ①
Bahnhofplatz 🖂 3011 – ℰ 0313 115 377 – city @ fhotels.ch – Fax 0313 110 636
– www.fhotels.ch   **C2**
58 rm – ♦135/170 CHF ♦♦175/210 CHF, ⌖ 18 CHF
♦ Business ♦ Functional ♦
This hotel is located right by the station. Contemporary rooms with decent,
timeless furnishings and parquet floors throughout.

Kreuz   ⇲ ᶠᵃ ᶜrest ⅍rm 🖂 ℭ ⅍15/120 VISA ⦿ AE ①
Zeughausgasse 41 🖂 3011 – ℰ 0313 299 595
– info @ hotelkreuz-bern.ch – Fax 0313 299 596
– www.hotelkreuz-bern.ch   **D1**
100 rm ⌖ – ♦150/155 CHF ♦♦210 CHF
Rest (closed 1 July - 7 August, Saturday and Sunday) a la carte 31/
63 CHF
♦ Business ♦ Modern ♦
This hotel specialises in meetings and conferences. Rooms are in functional
style with grey, fitted furniture. Seminar rooms of various types are
available.

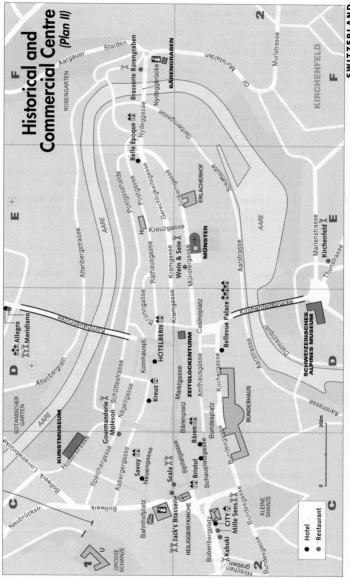

Historical and Commercial Centre *(Plan II)*

- Hotel
- Restaurant

BOTANISCHER GARTEN

KUNSTMUSEUM

GROSSE SCHANZE

Neubrückstr.

Bollwerk Lorrainebrücke

Bollwerk

Altenbergrain

Altenbergstrasse

AARE

Kornhausbrücke

Speichergasse

Hodlerstrasse

Aarbergergasse

Gourmanderie Moléson

Savoy

Neuengasse

Bristol

Scala

Spitalgasse

Schauplatgasse

Bahnhofplatz

Bubenbergplatz

HEILIGGEISTKIRCHE

Jack's Brasserie

Kabuki

CITY

Mille Sens

Bundesgasse

KLEINE SHANZE

Hirschen-graben

Bundesgasse

Bundesgasse

Bundesplatz

BUNDESHAUS

Bären

Bärenplatz

Marktgasse

Nägeligasse

Schüttestrasse

Komhauspl.

Kreuz

HOTELBERN

Brunngasse

Amthausgasse

Kochergasse

ZEITGLOCKENTURM

Casinoplatz

Kramgasse

Münstergasse

Rathausgasse

Kramgasse

Postgasse

Postgasshalde

Kreuzgasse

MÜNSTER

Wein & Sein

Gerechtigkeitsgasse

Junkerngasse

ERLACHERHOF

Bellevue Palace

Aarstrasse

Schifflaube

AARE

Belle Epoque

Nydeggasse

Gerberngasse

Brasserie Bärengraben

BÄRENGRABEN

Nydeggbrücke

ROSENGARTEN

Stalden

Aargauer

Bellevue Palace

Kirchenfeldbrücke

Aarstrasse

Dalmaziquai

Aarstrasse

Marienstrasse

Kirchenfeld

Thunstrasse

SCHWEIZERISCHES ALPINES MUSEUM

KIRCHENFELD

Muristrasse

Muristalden

Gr. Muristalden

Allegro

Meridiano

0 200m

757

SWITZERLAND

XXX **Meridiano** – Hotel Allegro   ≤ Bern and Mountains, ⌂
Kornhausstr. 3 ✉ *3013* – ℰ *0313 395 245*   A/C P. VISA ◐◐ AE ◐
– info @ kursaal-bern.ch – Fax 0313 395 510 – www.allegro-hotel.ch
closed mid July - mid August, Saturday lunch, Sunday and Monday   **D1**
Rest 54 CHF (lunch)/155 CHF and a la carte 88/153 CHF
♦ Contemporary ♦ Fashionable ♦
The highlights of this restaurant on the fifth floor of the Hotel Allegro are the modern Mediterranean cuisine and the striking panorama of Bern and the mountains from the terrace.

XX **Scala**   ⌂ VISA ◐◐ AE ◐
Schweizerhofpassage 7 ✉ *3011* – ℰ *0313 264 545 – info @ ristorante-scala.ch*
– Fax 0313 264 546 – www.ristorante-scala.ch
closed 15 July - 15 August, Saturday (except from November - December) and Sunday   **C1**
Rest (Italian rest.) a la carte 56/95 CHF
♦ Italian ♦ Fashionable ♦
Bright, modern restaurant in elegant Italian style on the first floor of one of Bern's shopping arcades. Parquet floors add to the congenial ambience.

XX **Jack's Brasserie**   A/C VISA ◐◐ AE ◐
Bahnhofplatz 11 ✉ *3011* – ℰ *0313 268 080 – jacks @ schweizerhof-bern.ch*
– Fax 0313 268 090 – www.schweizerhof-bern.ch   **C2**
Rest 52 CHF (lunch)/80 CHF and a la carte 65/111 CHF
♦ Contemporary ♦ Brasserie ♦
This eating place is in refined brasserie style with nicely upholstered benches and offers a contemporary menu.

XX **Mille Sens**   VISA ◐◐ AE ◐
Bubenbergplatz 9, (in the market hall) ✉ *3011* – ℰ *0313 292 929*
– info @ millesens.ch – Fax 0313 292 991 – www.millesens.ch   **C2**
closed Sunday and Bank Holidays and Saturday lunch June-August
Rest *(closed also dinner from June - August)* (only menu at lunch) 59 CHF (lunch)/98 CHF and a la carte 73/111 CHF ❀
Rest *Marktplatz* a la carte 52/95 CHF
♦ Contemporary ♦ Trendy ♦
A modern restaurant in the midst of busy shops: black leather chairs, smart white tablecloths, parquet beneath your feet and air ducts along the ceiling. The no-nonsense 'Marktplatz' bistro serves a concise and well-priced menu.

X **Gourmanderie Moléson**   ⌂ ↳ ⟲30 VISA ◐◐
Aarbergergasse 24 / Speichergasse 21 ✉ *3011* – ℰ *0313 114 463*
– info @ moleson-bern.ch – Fax 0313 120 145 – www.moleson-bern.ch   **C1**
Rest *(closed Saturday lunch, Sunday and Bank Holidays)* 66 CHF/77 CHF and a la carte 48/105 CHF
♦ Traditional ♦ Brasserie ♦
Cooking like in grandmother's time is the motto of this cosy restaurant in the Old Town. Specialities are traditional Bernese dishes and Alsatian Flammkuchen.

X **Brasserie Bärengraben**   ⌂ VISA ◐◐ AE ◐
Grosser Muristalden 1 ✉ *3006* – ℰ *0313 314 218 – edy_juillerat @ hotmail.com*
– Fax 0313 312 560 – www.brasseriebaerengraben.ch   **F1**
Rest (booking essential) 65 CHF and a la carte 35/94 CHF
♦ Traditional ♦ Brasserie ♦
One of the most popular and traditional Brasseries in the city is accommodated in the historic little customs house on the Nydeggbrücke near the Bärengraben.

X **Kabuki**   A/C ↳ ℀ VISA ◐◐ AE
Bubenbergplatz 9, (in the market hall) ✉ *3011* – ℰ *0313 292 919*
– kabuki @ kabuki.ch – Fax 0313 292 917 – www.kabuki.ch
closed 24 July - 6 August, Sunday and Bank Holidays   **C2**
Rest (Japanese rest.) 82 CHF (dinner) and a la carte 41/99 CHF
♦ Japanese ♦ Exotic ♦
An understated, modern style and a long sushi bar define the ambience of this restaurant in the basement of the market hall.

Wein & Sein (Blum) 🎇 VISA ⓪

Münstergasse 50 ⊠ 3011 – ℰ 0313 119 844 – blum@weinundsein.ch
– www.weinundsein.ch
closed 16 July - 14 August, 24 December - 4 January,
Sunday and Monday **E2**
Rest (dinner only) (booking essential) (set menu only) 88 CHF
Spec. Berner Trüffel (autumn). Sommerwild (June - July). Gebackene Desserts
(winter)

♦ Contemporary ♦ Trendy ♦

This is an attractive, typical Bern cellar restaurant, with a wine bar. It presents a
contemporary menu, changed daily – the fare is written on a board.

SWITZERLAND

Kirchenfeld 🍴 ⇔30 VISA ⓪ AE ⓪

Thunstr. 5 ⊠ 3005 – ℰ 0313 510 278 – restaurant@kirchenfeld.ch
– Fax 0313 518 416 – www.kirchenfeld.ch
closed Sunday and Monday **E2**
Rest 55 CHF (lunch)/62 CHF and a la carte 50/92 CHF

♦ International ♦ Brasserie ♦

Stucco decoration and antiques give this establishment a stylish note. A tasty
range of meals are served here, ranging from the traditional to the
contemporary.

ENVIRONS OF BERN *Plan I*

 Innere Enge ⌂ 🍴 ⅙rm 📶20 P VISA ⓪ AE ⓪

Engestr. 54 ⊠ 3012 – ℰ 0313 096 111 – info@zghotels.ch – Fax 0313 096 112
– www.zghotels.ch **A1**
26 rm � – †220/260 CHF ††270/290 CHF
Rest 50 CHF (lunch)/75 CHF and a la carte 50/103 CHF

♦ Business ♦ Classic ♦

Quiet establishment almost in the countryside. The rooms are fitted with elegant
furniture and feature Provençal colour schemes. Breakfast is served in the
historic Pavillon. The Jazz Cellar is a city institution. Welcoming bistro-style café
and restaurant.

 Novotel &rm 🅰 ⅙rm 📺 📶15/120 VISA ⓪ AE ⓪

Guisanplatz 2 ⊠ 3014 – ℰ 0313 390 909 – H5009@accor.com
– Fax 0313 390 910 – www.novotel.com **B1**
112 rm – †175/220 CHF ††195/240 CHF, ⊠ 25 CHF
Rest a la carte 44/84 CHF

♦ Chain hotel ♦ Modern ♦

Modern rooms with good technical mod cons, plus a light, contemporary
restaurant, right next to the Bern Expo complex. The bar pays tribute to
Germany's 1954 World Cup win - "The Miracle of Bern" - at the now rebuilt
Wankdorf Stadium nearby.

 Sternen 🍴 & ⅙ 📺 📶15/120 P VISA ⓪ AE ⓪

Thunstr. 80 ⊠ 3074 Muri – ℰ 0319 507 111 – info@sternenmuri.ch
– Fax 0319 507 100 – www.sternenmuri.ch **B2**
44 rm ⊠ – †160/170 CHF ††220/235 CHF
Rest 37 CHF (lunch) and a la carte 45/90 CHF

♦ Traditional ♦ Functional ♦

Village centre hotel in typical Bernese country style. Bright, functional rooms in
the original house and annex. The "Läubli" serve contemporary dishes.

 Ibis without rest & 🅰 📶 VISA ⓪ AE ⓪

Guisanplatz 4 ⊠ 3014 – ℰ 0313 351 200 – H5007@accor.com
– Fax 0313 351 210 – www.ibishotel.com **B1**
96 rm – †112/129 CHF ††112/129 CHF, ⊠ 14 CHF

♦ Chain hotel ♦ Minimalist ♦

Simple, practical and affordable, the bedrooms here are clean and bright. A snack
menu is available around the clock at the bar.

XX **Landhaus** ⚮ ✿80 **P** *VISA* ◍◍ ⒶⒺ ①
Schwarzenburgstr. 134 ✉ 3097 Liebefeld – ☏ 0319 710 758
– info@landhaus-liebefeld.ch – Fax 0319 720 249
– www.landhaus-liebefeld.ch **A2**
Rest *(closed Sunday)* (booking essential) 56 CHF (lunch)/90 CHF and a la carte
58/94 CHF
♦ Contemporary ♦ Formal ♦
The restaurant in the former governor's residence was destroyed by fire. Now rebuilt, it continues to offer the much-prized contemporary cuisine. Guest rooms available.

X **La Tavola Pronta** ⚮ *VISA* ◍◍ ⒶⒺ ①
Laupenstr. 57 ✉ 3008 – ☏ 0313 826 633 – Fax 0313 815 693
– www.latavolapronta.ch
closed Saturday lunch and Sunday **A2**
Rest (booking essential) 40 CHF (lunch)/74 CHF and a la carte 58/90 CHF
♦ Italian ♦ Friendly ♦
This small cellar restaurant, a comfortable lounge with a fireplace, has a very welcoming atmosphere. The classic Piedmont fare is written on a mirror.

GENEVA
GENÈVE

Population (est. 2005): 198 500 (conurbation 698 000) – Altitude: 375m

AGE Moya/HOA QUI

An exceptional location on the shimmering shores of Lake Geneva, set against a backdrop of lush vegetation and wooded mountains, makes Geneva one of Switzerland's most privileged cities. It enjoys a pristine natural environment and the best possible living conditions. Visitors will be charmed by the opulent mansions, the harbour and its Jet d'Eau, the green spaces, its busy streets and elegant shopping centres.

Geneva is home to the second seat of the United Nations after New York and it houses the headquarters of several UN agencies as well as many international bodies. But Geneva, clustering around its cathedral, also remains the town of Calvin and the stronghold of the Reformation. The city was occupied by French troops in 1798 and for 16 years it was the capital of the French department of Léman. After the collapse of the Napoleonic Empire, it joined the Swiss Confederation on 19 May 1815 when the unification treaty was signed. The metropolis of French-speaking Switzerland, Geneva is an intellectual city which has welcomed many luminaries such as Jean-Jacques Rousseau and Voltaire as well as many eminent writers and men of science. These diverse influences are bound together by a very Helvetian atmosphere of order and discipline.

WHICH DISTRICT TO CHOOSE

The city offers exceptionally high standards of **accommodation** to suit the most demanding visitors. Opulent hotels with splendid views are located along the quays on both sides of the lake and there are charming, quiet hotels at moderate prices near the station, in the little streets by the Rhône. You will find business hotels by the station *Plan II* **E3**, near the airport *Plan I* **A1** and the Palais des Expositions *Plan I* **B1** and modern chain hotels on the outskirts.

The quality and number of **restaurants** in Geneva rank very high with many award-winning establishments. Elegant restaurants overlook the lake or are to be found

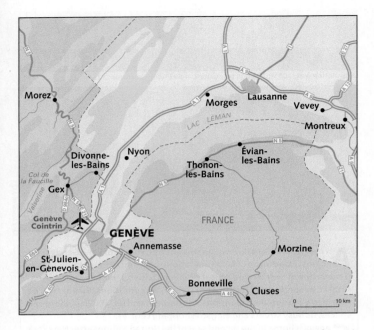

in the surrounding countryside *(see listing)*. Delightful small restaurants and modern brasseries in the town centre and country inns in the environs serve regional and seasonal specialities.

PRACTICAL INFORMATION

ARRIVAL – DEPARTURE

Geneva International Airport – Cointrin *Plan I* **A1**. ✆ 022 717 71 11; www.gva.ch

From the airport to the city centre – By **taxi**: 30-35CHF; time 15min. By **train**: 3CHF; every 10min; time 8min. By **bus**: 3CHF; No 10 to Geneva city (every 10min), No 20 to Meyrin, UN complex and the lake (every 20min), No 18 to UN (every 30min); time 20min.

Railway Stations – Cornavin Station, place Cornavin *Plan II* **E3** and **Geneva Airport Station**: international and inter-city services. ✆ 0900

300 300; www.cff.ch. **Eaux Vives Station**: services to Évian, Annecy and Annemasse over the border in France.

TRANSPORT

✦ BUSES, TRAMS, TRAINS, BOATS

The city is served by an efficient public transport network. A single All Geneva ticket costs 3-5CHF and is valid 1hr. A day card is 10-12CHF and a 9am-midnight card 7-11.60CHF (city), 12-20CHF (Regional). Also Tourist Cards: 20CHF (valid 48hr), 30CHF (72hr). A short hop ticket 2CHF is valid for 3 stops or 1 ferry crossing. ✆ 0900 022 021; www.unireso.com, www.tpg.ch

◆ TAXIS

Metered taxis can be hailed at taxi ranks, near the stations and at the airport or can be ordered by phone. Fares are based on a standard charge of 6.30CHF and 3.20CHF/km. There are supplements for travel at night, Sundays and public holidays (3.80CHF) and luggage (1.50CHF). Tips and VAT are included but it is usual to round up the fare. *Taxiphone* ℰ 022 331 41 33. *Ambassador* ℰ 022 731 41 41. *Europa* ℰ 022 906 79 79, 0800 141 141.

USEFUL ADDRESSES

◆ TOURIST OFFICE

Geneva Tourism – Rue du Mont-Blanc 18 *Plan II* **E3**, P.O.Box 1602, CH – 1211 Geneva 1. Open 9am (10am Mon) to 6pm; closed Sun, Sep to mid-Jun. ℰ 022 909 70 00; www.geneva-tourism.ch; also at Pont de la Machine 1 *Plan II* **E3**, CH-1204 Geneva. ℰ 022 311 98 27.

◆ POST OFFICES

Main Post Office, Rue du Mont-Blanc 18 *Plan II* **E3** is open Mon-Fri 7.30am-6pm; Sat 9am-4pm. The post office Cornavin Station at 16 Rue des Gares

Plan II **E3** is open Mon-Fri, 8am-8pm; Sat 8am-noon, Sun 4-7pm.

◆ BANKS/CURRENCY EXCHANGE

Banks open Mon-Fri 8am-4.30pm (5.30pm). Exchange offices at Cornavin Station and at the airport open longer hours. There are cash dispensers, which require a PIN, all over the city. Credit cards are widely accepted for all transactions.

◆ EMERGENCY

Police ℰ **117**; Fire Brigade: ℰ **118**; Medical Emergency Service: ℰ **144**.

BUSY PERIODS

It may be difficult to find a room at a reasonable price during special events:

International Motor Show: early March.

Geneva Festival: first two weeks in August – Various shows and attractions (floral floats, fireworks).

Feast of the Escalade: December – Commemorates the successful defence of the town against the Savoyards in 1602: torchlight procession, fireworks, chocolate cauldrons.

EXPLORING GENEVA

It is possible to visit the main sights and museums in two days.

Museums and other sights are usually open from 10-11am to 5pm. Some close on Mondays.

VISITING

Boat trips on the lake and on the Rhône from Quai du Mont-Blanc *Plan II* **F3**, Quai des Moulins en l'Île *Plan III* **G1** and Quai Gustave-Ador, Jardin Anglais *Plan III* **H1**.

HARBOUR AND LAKE SHORES – Splendid views of the majestic **Jet d'Eau** *Plan III* **H1** and bustling harbour. **North**

Bank – Parks (**Villa Barton, La Perle du Lac, Mon Repos**) *Plan II* **F1**: the finest landscaped area lined with 19C mansions (Musée d'Histoire des Sciences in Villa Bartholoni, Parc de la Perle du Lac); views of Little Lake. **Conservatoire** and **Jardin Botanique** *Plan II* **E1**: living plant museum and rock garden. **South Bank** – **Jardin Anglais** *Plan III* **H1**: floral clock, panorama of harbour and the Jura mountain range, marina; **Parc de la Grange** (wonderful rose garden) *Plan I* **C2** and **Parc des Eaux Vives** *Plan I* **D2**.

INTERNATIONAL DISTRICT – Place des Nations leads to the imposing

763

Palais des Nations (Armillary Sphere) *Plan II* **E1** in Ariana Park: tour including the Salle des Pas Perdus, the impressive Assembly Room and the Council Chamber. **Musée Ariana** *Plan II* **E1**: Overview of ten centuries of ceramic-making in Europe. **Musée International de la Croix Rouge et du Croissant Rouge** *Plan I* **B2** the museum traces events which have left their mark on history. **Domaine de Penthes – Musée des Suisses à l'Étranger** *Plan I* **B1**: focus on the Papal Guard, Swiss mercenaries and celebrities.

OLD TOWN – Narrow streets and squares lined with old houses and aristocratic residences: **Grand-Rue, Rue des Granges, Place du Bourg-de-Four** *Plan III* **H2** with flower-decked fountain. Impressive **Cathédrale St-Pierre** *Plan III* **H2**: superb view from the tower; archaeological site. **Hôtel de Ville** (16C-17C) *Plan III* **H2**: Tour Baudet, Alabama Room where the Geneva Convention was signed. Elegant **Maison Tavel,** *Plan III* **H2** the oldest house in the city: museum devoted to the history of Geneva.

Musée d'Art et d'Histoire *Plan III* **H2** – An outline of the history of civilisation from prehistoric times to the 21C: archaeology, applied art, coins, paintings.

Petit Palais *Plan III* **H2** – 19C mansion housing the **Musée d'Art Moderne**: French and European avant-garde painting (Impressionism, Surrealism, Abstract art).

Musée d'Histoire Naturelle *Plan I* **C3** – Dioramas of regional fauna; displays devoted to paleontology, mineralogy and the geology of the country.

Patek Philippe Museum *Plan III* **G2** – Housed in a beautifully restored factory, it displays a collection of magnificent timepieces.

Musée de l'Horlogerie et de l'Émaillerie *Plan I* **C3** – An illuminating history of the science of horology from its origins to the present day and the art of enamelling.

Musée International de l'Automobile *Plan I* **B1** – A fabulous array of vintage vehicles, some owned by famous people.

SHOPPING

Shops are usually open Mon-Wed 9am-7pm (9pm Thu, 7.30pm Fri, 6pm Sat).

The main shopping areas are located on the North bank: **Quai des Bergues** *Plan III* **G1**, **Quai du Mont-Blanc** *Plan II* **F3** and **Rue du Mont-Blanc** *Plan II* **E3**. South bank: around the chic **Rue du Rhône** *Plan III* **H2**, in the **Rues du Molard** *Plan III* **H2**, **de la Confédération** *Plan III* **G1**, **du Marché** *Plan III* **G1**, **de la Croix-d'Or** *Plan III* **H2**, **de Rive** *Plan III* **H2**, **de la Corraterie** *Plan III* **H1**, **cours de Rive** *Plan III* **H2** and **galerie Malbuisson**. The more popular **Saint-Gervais** and **Pâquis** *Plan II* **F3** areas are also worth a visit. Department stores: *Globus*, 48 Rue du Rhône and Rue de la Confédération; *Manor*, Rue Cornavin 6. Browse in **Grand-Rue** *Plan III* **G2** for bookstores, art galleries, antique shops. Visit *Aux Arts du Feu*, 18 Quai du Général Guisan (antiques); *Linen Langenthal*, 13 Rue du Rhône (fine linen, lace); *Les Galeries du Lac*, 16 Chemin de la Voie-Creuse and *Molard Souvenirs*, Rue de la Croix-d'Or (gifts); *Buzzano*, 15 Rue de Rive and 1 Rue de la Croix-d'Or and *Bally*, 18 Rue du Marché (leather goods); *Pinocchio*, 10 Rue Étienne-Dumont (wooden toys); *Chocolaterie du Rhône*, 3 Rue de la Confédération; *Arn Chocolatier*, 12 Rue Bourg-de-Four; *La Bonbonnière*, 11 Rue de Rive and *Teuscher Confiserie*, 2 Rue du Rhône (chocolates).

MARKETS – Plaine de Plainpalais *Plan III* **G2**: **produce market** open Tue, Fri 8am-1pm, Sun 8am-6pm; **flea market** (antiques and other goods) Wed, Sat 8am-5pm. Place de la Fusterie *Plan III* **G1**: **produce market** open Wed, Sat 8am-6.45pm; **handicrafts** Thu 8am-7pm; books Fri 8am-6.45pm. **Produce market** in Place de la Navigation *Plan II* **F3**: Tue, Fri 8am-1pm; Place de Grenus *Plan II* **E3**: Sat 8am-1.30pm; Boulevard Helvétique *Plan III* **H2**: Wed 8am-1pm, Sat 8am-1.30pm. **Flower market**: Place du Molard *Plan III* **H2** daily.

WHAT TO BUY – Jewellery, watches, linen, lace, cuckoo clocks, music boxes, toys, chocolates (Pavés de Genève).

ENTERTAINMENT

Consult Genève-Agenda, a monthly publication listing events and entertainment in the city. It is available free from the Tourist Office, hotels, stations and many public places.

Grand Théâtre *Plan III* **G2** – Opera, ballet and music.

Bâtiment des Forces Motrices *Plan I* **B3** – Plays, opera and conferences.

Conservatoire de Musique and **Victoria Hall** *Plan III* **G2** – Classical music concerts.

Comédie de Genève *Plan III* **G2** – Contemporary and classical drama.

Les Salons *Plan III* **G2** – Musical performances and plays by modern authors.

Casino-Théâtre *Plan III* **G3** – Satirical reviews, operetta and variety shows.

Les Marionettes de Genève *Plan III* **G3** and **Am Stram Gram** *Plan I* **C3** – Puppet theatre and shows for children.

Forum Meyrin *Plan I* **A1** – Drama, dance, classical and modern music performances.

NIGHTLIFE

The bustling area between **Cornavin Station** and **Les Pâquis** abounds in cinemas, bars, pubs and restaurants. You may also visit **Carouge** *Plan I* **C3** to the south of the city for its lively cafés and restaurants. Enjoy a drink at the microbrewery *Les Brasseurs*, Place Cornavin ; *Mortimer* and *Clémence* around Place du Bourg-de-Four; *Bohème* piano bar, *Griffin's*, Boulevard Helvétique 56/36. A fashionable crowd flocks to *Demi-Lune* café, 3 Rue Étienne-Dumont; *Brasserie Lipp*, 8 Rue de la Confédération; *La Coupole*, 116 Rue du Rhône; *Club 58*, 15 Rue des Glacis de Rive; the stylish cafés in the **Eaux-Vives quartier** *Plan I* **D2**. For live music and dancing, visit *Au Chat Noir*, 13 Rue Vautier; *L'Usine*, 4 Place des Volontaires; *Le Baroque*, 12 Place de la Fusterie; *CREM*, Boulevard Helvétique 10; *Arthur's Club*, 20 Rue du Pré-Bois and *Macumba*, 403 Route d'Annecy. Go to *Grand Casino du Lac*, 20 Route de Pré-Bois, for a sophisticated evening.

Around Geneva
(Plan I)

D 35

A

B

FRANCE

Colovrex

PREGNY-CHAMBÉSY

1

Route

de

MEYRIN

Av. de Mategnin

MUSÉE INTERNATIONAL
DE L'AUTOMOBILE

Crowne Plaza

Route

PALEXPO

GENÈVE

ep

NH Geneva
Airport Hotel

Sarazin

SACONNEX

Edouard

de

Av.

Appia

Avenue

MUSÉE INTERNATIONAL
DE LA CROIX-ROUGE ET
DU CROISSANT-ROUGE

Ibis

COINTRIN

Ch.

Intercontinental

Ferney

Mövenpick
Genève

Route

de

Meyrin

Pré

Bois

Ramada
Park Hotel

Av.

Louis

Chin des Coudriers

R.

Giuseppe

Motta

Express by Holiday Inn

Rte

de

SuiteHotel

Chin de Av. J. Trembley de Molliebeau

Route

de

Casai

2

Route

du

Nant

d'Avril

VERNIER

Meyrin

Carr.
du Bouchet   Route de Meyrin

Les Nations

R.

du

Grand

Route

de

Vernier

Av. du Pailly

Av. H. Golay Av. E. Vaucher

Av.

Wendt

Nash
Rex Hotel

R. de la Servette

A 1- E 62

Rte du Bois des Frères

Av. de l'Ain

Rue

de

Lyon

d' Aire

Avenue

Pont Butin

Bd des Deux Ponts

Bd de
St- Georges

Pont de
St-Georges

Rte de St-Georges

ARVE

Chin des Sellières

RHÔNE

3

Chancy

Route

du

Hostellerie
de la Vendée

Av. du Bois de la Chapelle

Route

Pont

de

Butin

ÉGLISE
DU CHRIST-ROI

R. des Acacias

A

LANCY

B

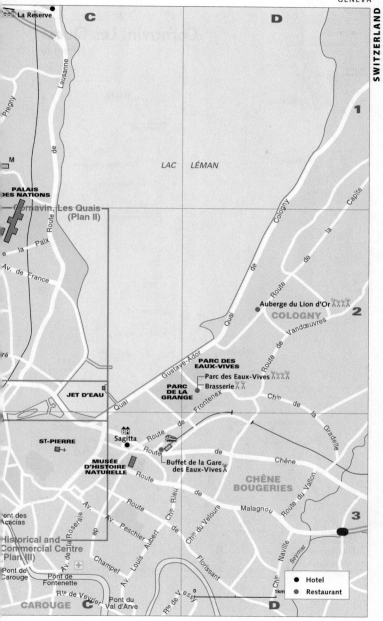

La Reserve

C

D

1

LAC LÉMAN

Lausanne

Pregny

de

M

**PALAIS
DES NATIONS**

Cornavin, Les Quais
(Plan II)

Route

la Paix

Av. de France

ré

Av. de

de Cologny

de la Capite

de

Route

Quai

Gustave-Ador

Auberge du Lion d'Or ✕✕✕✕

COLOGNY

2

Route de Vandœuvres

**PARC DES
EAUX-VIVES**

Parc des Eaux-Vives ✕✕✕✕
Brasserie ✕✕

**PARC
DE LA
GRANGE**

JET D'EAU

Quai

Frontenex

Ch'n de la Gradelle

ST-PIERRE

Sagitta

Route de

Route

de

Chêne

**CHÊNE
BOUGERIES**

Route du Vallon

**MUSÉE
D'HISTOIRE
NATURELLE**

Route

Buffet de la Gare
des Eaux-Vives ✕

Malagnou

Naville

Seymaz

3

ont des
Acacias

Av. de la Roseraie

Route

Av. Peschier

Av. Louis Aubert

Ch'n Rieu

Ch'n du Velours

de

de

Ch'n de V essy

**Historical and
Commercial Centre
(Plan III)**

Pont de
Carouge

Pont de
Fontenette

Champel

Florissant

Rte de Vessy

C

CAROUGE

Rte de Veyrier

Pont du
Val d'Arve

D

0   1km

● Hotel
● Restaurant

SWITZERLAND

E   F

Cornavin, Les Quais
(Plan II)

● Hotel
● Restaurant

MUSÉE
ARIANA

PALAIS
DES
NATIONS

JARDIN
BOTANIQUE

0   200m

PARC
DE L'ARIANA

1   1

Av. de la Paix   R. de la Paix   Eden

PARC VILLA
BARTON

Av. de la Paix   Pl. des Nations

Chemin E. Rigot

Rue de France   Thai Phuket

LA PERLE DU LAC

Av. de France   La Perle du Lac

Sagano

Rue de Vermont   La Voie-Creuse   Rue de Montbrillant   Av. de France   R. de Lausanne

PARC
MON REPOS

LAC

LÉMAN

du Valais

LE PRIEURÉ

2   2

Rue de Montbrillant   R. Butini   R. de Richemont   Epsom

R. des Gares   Jade   Quai Wilson

R. du Prieuré   R. de Bâle   Président Wilson

Boulevard   Rue de Montbrillant   Royal   R. de Lausanne

Auteuil   Kipling   R. du Môle

R. du Grand-Pré   R. du Fort-Barreau   PARC DES CROPETTES

PORT DES PÂQUIS

LES PÂQUIS

Novotel   R. de Berne   R. de Zurich   Edelweiss   Mont-Blanc   Plantamour

R. des Grottes   Le Montbrillant   Warwick   Pl. de Cornavin   Bistrot du Boeuf Rouge   R. de Monthoux   Noga Hilton

CORNAVIN   L'Entrecôte Couronnée   Green   Tsé Yang

R. de la Servette   R. de la Pépinière   Strasbourg-Univers   R. des   D'Angleterre

Rue de Lyon   Cornavin   Beau-Rivage

R. de Malatrex   R. de Chantepoulet   R. du Mont-   Alpes   De la Paix

3   Ibis   Sofitel   R. Kléberg   Bristol   JET D'EAU   3

R. Voltaire   Bd James-Fazy   R. Rousseau   Du Midi

Ambassador   PIERRE DU NITON

R. du Temple   R. du Valin   Pont du Mont-Blanc

Mandarin Oriental du Rhône   Q. des Bergues

Le Neptune   Q. Turrettini   ÎLE J. J. ROUSSEAU

RHÔNE   Pont de la Couloubrenière   E

Historical and Commercial Centre (Plan III)

RIGHT BANK (Cornavin Railway Station-Les Quais-Palais des Nations) *Plan II*

Mandarin Oriental du Rhône ⪡ 😋 ſ₅ 🍸 ᘓrm ⅍ ⅍rm ⅍ 🔤

1 quai Turrettini ✉ *1201* 📞 ⅍15/150 ⇔ **VISA** **MO** **AE** **①**
– 𝒞 *0229 090 000 – mogva-reservation@mohg.com*
– *Fax 0229 090 010*
– *www.mandarinoriental.com* **E3**
180 rm – †530/990 CHF ††750/1050 CHF, � 40 CHF – 12 suites
Rest see also *Le Neptune* below
Rest Café Rafael, 𝒞 *0229 090 0 05* – 61 CHF (lunch) and a la carte
71/113 CHF
♦ Grand Luxury ♦ Art Deco ♦
Central location on the right bank of the Rhone. Sumptuous rooms with Art Deco
furnishings and sparkling marble bathrooms. The Café Rafael offers a choice of
traditional recipes showing occasional local influence.

Président Wilson ⪡ 😋 ſ₅ 🍸 ⅂ 🅐 ⅍rm ⅍ 🔤 ⅍15/600

47 quai Wilson ✉ *1201* – 𝒞 *0229 066 666* ⇔ **VISA** **MO** **AE** **①**
– *sales@hotelpwilson.com – Fax 0229 066 667*
– *www.hotelpwilson.com* **F2**
219 rm – †580/750 CHF ††750/1100 CHF, ⊆ 40 CHF – 11 suites
Rest Spice's *(closed mid July - mid August, Saturday lunch and Sunday)* 55 CHF
(lunch)/128 CHF and a la carte 101/147 CHF
Rest L'Arabesque (Lebanese rest.) 55 CHF (lunch)/95 CHF and a la carte
52/90 CHF
Rest Pool Garden *(May - September)* 47 CHF (lunch)/68 CHF and a la carte
80/130 CHF
♦ Grand Luxury ♦ Stylish ♦
Wood and marble abound in this hotel whose finest rooms look onto the lake.
Spice's Café has "World Cuisine" in a modern setting, while the Arabesque offers
mouthwatering Lebanese delights. Try eating al fresco in the Pool Garden in summer.

Noga Hilton ⪡ 😋 ⊛ ſ₅ ⅂ ᘓrm 🅐 ⅍rm 🔤 📞

19 quai du Mont-Blanc ✉ *1201* ⅍15/800 **VISA** **MO** **AE** **①**
– 𝒞 *0229 089 081 – reservations.geneva@hilton.com – Fax 0229 089 090*
– *www.hiltongeneve.com* **F3**
401 rm – †385/570 CHF ††605/790 CHF, ⊆ 40 CHF – 9 suites
Rest Le Cygne – (1st floor) , 𝒞 *0229 089 0 85 (closed 23 March - 2 April, 14*
August - 4 September, 1 to 8 January, Saturday and Sunday) 88 CHF/115 CHF
and a la carte 90/161 CHF
Rest La Grignotière a la carte 53/108 CHF
♦ Grand Luxury ♦ Classic ♦
An imposing modern hotel on Lake Geneva with spacious bedrooms, a
number of which are somewhat dated in style but awaiting an overhaul.
Modern gourmet cuisine at Le Cygne, which enjoys a backdrop of the harbour
and water jet. La Grignotière serves brasserie-style food and has a panoramic
terrace.

D'Angleterre ⪡ ſ₅ 🍸 🅐 ⅍rm 🔤 📞 ⅍15/35 ⇔ **VISA** **MO** **AE** **①**

17 quai du Mont-Blanc ✉ *1201* – 𝒞 *0229 065 555*
– *angleterre@rchmail.com – Fax 0229 065 556*
– *www.hoteldangleterre.ch* **F3**
45 rm – †530/820 CHF ††720/950 CHF, ⊆ 42 CHF
Rest Windows 38 CHF (lunch)/155 CHF and a la carte
90/126 CHF
♦ Grand Luxury ♦ Stylish ♦
A lakeside hotel with a calm, distinguished air offering spacious, welcoming
guest rooms. Relaxed atmosphere and attentive service in the Leopard
Lounge. Cosy veranda-restaurant with a contemporary menu and views of the
lake.

SWITZERLAND

Beau-Rivage ⪵ 🍴 🛴 🗚 ⅍rm 🖿 ℡ ᠕15/120 🍷 *VISA* ⓬ 🄰🄴 ⓪
13 quai du Mont-Blanc ✉ *1201 – ℰ 0227 166 666 – info @ beau-rivage.ch*
– Fax 0227 166 060 – www.beau-rivage.ch   **F3**
86 rm – †790/1100 CHF ††890/1200 CHF, � 39 CHF – 7 suites
Rest *Le Chat Botté* 60 CHF (lunch)/185 CHF and a la carte
102/172 CHF ॐ
Rest *Le Patara* – ℰ 0227 315 5 66 (closed 14 to 17 april, 3 to 5 June, 24
December - 8 January, Saturday lunch and Sunday lunch) (Thai rest.)
34 CHF (lunch)/85 CHF and a la carte 61/123 CHF
♦ Grand Luxury ♦ Stylish ♦
Facing the lake, this atmospheric establishment has been in the family since
1865. The bedrooms have a refined retro feel. Elegant atrium with fountain and
colonnades. Up-to-date cooking in an elegant setting at "Le Chat Botté".
Experience the flavours of Thailand in the inviting atmosphere of the Patara
restaurant.

Intercontinental ⪵ 🍴 🛴 🍃 🔼 ᠖rm 🗚 ⅍ ✂rest 🖿 ℡
7-9 ch. du Petit-Saconnex ᠕15/450 🍷 🄿 🄿 *VISA* ⓬ 🄰🄴 ⓪
✉ *1209 – ℰ 0229 193 939 – geneva @ interconti.com – Fax 0229 193 838*
– www.intercontinental.com/geneva   *Plan I* **B2**
260 rm – †480/525 CHF ††480/600 CHF, ⊠ 39 CHF – 67 suites
Rest *Woods* 59 CHF (lunch) and a la carte 63/125 CHF
♦ Chain hotel ♦ Classic ♦
Next door to the Palais des Nations and ideal for conferences, this 1960s-built
hotel has given its public areas a facelift, while the rooms await a similar overhaul.
Extensive conference facilities. Spacious and comfortable restaurant serving
contemporary cuisine in a modern setting.

De la Paix ⪵ 🗚 ⅍rm ✂rest 🖿 ℡ ᠕15/50 *VISA* ⓬ 🄰🄴 ⓪
11 quai du Mont-Blanc ✉ *1201 – ℰ 0229 096 000*
– reservation @ hoteldelapaix.ch – Fax 0229 096 001 – www.hoteldelapaix.ch
Reopening after restoration in February   **F3**
80 rm – †360/750 CHF ††550/920 CHF, ⊠ 40 CHF – 4 suites
Rest *Vertig'O* (closed Sunday) 49 CHF (lunch)/95 CHF and a la carte
68/125 CHF
♦ Luxury ♦ Classic ♦
In 2005 a new lease of life was given to this grand hotel built in 1865 next to Lake
Geneva. Today's guests can enjoy elegant public rooms, various categories of
bedrooms in classic-modern style, and a contemporary bar-restaurant with a
menu to match. Traditional meals.

Bristol 🛴 🍃 🗚 ⅍rm ✂ 🖿 ℡ ᠕15/100 *VISA* ⓬ 🄰🄴 ⓪
10 r. du Mont-Blanc ✉ *1201 – ℰ 0227 165 700*
– reservations @ bristol.ch – Fax 0227 389 039 – www.bristol.ch   **F3**
95 rm – †330/590 CHF ††450/625 CHF, ⊠ 33 CHF – 5 suites
Rest *Relais Bristol* 49 CHF (lunch)/86 CHF and a la carte 66/108 CHF
♦ Business ♦ Classic ♦
An opulent entrance hall leads to the reception area of this hotel near the lake.
Spacious, refurbished rooms, fitness centre, sauna, steam room and collection of
old canvasses. Cuisine with a modern twist is served in a spruce, classic dining
room. Piano bar.

Epsom 🛴 🔼rm 🗚 ⅍rm ✂ 🖿 ℡ ᠕15/60 *VISA* ⓬ 🄰🄴 ⓪
18 r. de Richemont ✉ *1202 – ℰ 0225 446 666 – epsom @ manotel.com*
– Fax 0225 446 699 – www.manotel.com   **F2**
153 rm ⊠ – †250/380 CHF ††280/410 CHF
Rest *Portobello* (closed 25 December - 2 January) 39 CHF (lunch) and a la carte
50/105 CHF
♦ Business ♦ Classic ♦
Very contemporary hotel on a quiet city-centre street. Relaxing atmosphere,
homely rooms and high-tech conference facilities. Modern rotisserie with a glass
roof.

Royal 🛜 👪 🕭 🕭 🖭 🛏rm 🛏 📞 ♨15/30 VISA ⚫ 🆎 ⓪

41 r. de Lausanne ✉ 1201 – ℰ 0229 061 414 – royal@manotel.com
– Fax 0229 061 499 – www.manotel.com/royal
closed 6 months for restoration at the beginning of the year   **E2**
166 rm – †275/520 CHF ††320/530 CHF, ☲ 28 CHF – 6 suites
Rest *Rive Droite* 65 CHF and a la carte 42/94 CHF
♦ Business ♦ Classic ♦
Situated between the station and the lake, the Royal's classically furnished rooms are elegant and plush; it also has several luxury suites. Parisian brasserie-style restaurant offers a good value menu chalked up on the slate board.

 Warwick 🛠 🖭 🛏rm 🖭 📞 ♨15/150 VISA ⚫ 🆎 ⓪

14 r. de Lausanne ✉ 1201 – ℰ 0227 168 000
– res.geneva@warwickhotels.com – Fax 0227 168 001
– www.warwickgeneva.com   **E3**
167 rm – †320/440 CHF ††350/520 CHF, ☲ 27 CHF
Rest *La Brasserie* a la carte 55/86 CHF
♦ Business ♦ Functional ♦
Located in front of the station, the Warwick is ideal for tourists and conference guests travelling by train. Contemporary, functional rooms. The restaurant cultivates a Parisian bistro atmosphere.

Sofitel 🛜 🖭 🛏rm 🕽 🖭 📞 VISA ⚫ 🆎 ⓪

18-20 r. du Cendrier ✉ 1201 – ℰ 0229 088 080 – h1322@accor-hotels.com
– Fax 0229 088 081 – www.sofitel.com   **E3**
95 rm – †410/470 CHF ††440/530 CHF, ☲ 35 CHF
Rest 49 CHF and a la carte 65/108 CHF
♦ Chain hotel ♦ Stylish ♦
A city-centre hotel with a choice of rustic- or Louis XVI-style rooms awaiting refurbishment. Lounge with an open fire and pianist in the evening. Classic/traditional fare in the restaurant, which has a terrace for those lazy summer days.

 Novotel 🖭 🛏rm 🖭 ♨25 🚗 VISA ⚫ 🆎 ⓪

19 r. de Zurich ✉ 1201 – ℰ 0229 099 000 – h3133@accor.com
– Fax 0229 099 001 – www.novotel.com   **F3**
194 rm – †145/450 CHF ††145/450 CHF, ☲ 27 CHF – 12 suites
Rest 29 CHF (lunch)/46 CHF and a la carte 47/80 CHF
♦ Chain hotel ♦ Functional ♦
A chain hotel recognisable by its glass façade, ideally located close to both the train station and lake. Good-sized, well-appointed bedrooms, in the process of being renovated. Contemporary-style "spice"-themed decor in the restaurant. Traditional cuisine.

 Nash Rex Hotel without rest 🛏 🖭 📞 VISA ⚫ 🆎 ⓪

42-44 av. Wendt ✉ 1203 – ℰ 0225 447 474 – hotel.rex@nash-holding.com
– Fax 0225 447 499
– www.nashrex.com   *Plan I* **B2**
70 rm – †195/295 CHF ††235/385 CHF, ☲ 25 CHF
♦ Business ♦ Classic ♦
Opened in 2004 in a residential area, this hotel offers opulent-looking reception areas and rooms of various sizes: at its best, the accommodation is bright, spacious and furnished with period pieces.

 Le Montbrillant 🛜 🛏rm 🖭 📞 ♨15/40 🅿 VISA ⚫ 🆎 ⓪

2 r. de Montbrillant ✉ 1201 – ℰ 0227 337 784
– contact@montbrillant.ch – Fax 0227 332 511
– www.montbrillant.ch   **E3**
82 rm ☲ – †150/195 CHF ††220/360 CHF
Rest a la carte 45/80 CHF
♦ Family ♦ Personalised ♦
Invaluable accommodation for those who want to be near the station. Similar to a mountain retreat, with quirkily-shaped public spaces and studios with kitchenette. The restaurant offers traditional fare.

SWITZERLAND

Les Nations without rest   🛬 📺 ✆ 𝘝𝘐𝘚𝘈 ⓪ 🅰🅴 ⓞ

62 r. du Grand-Pré ⊠ 1202 – ℰ 0227 480 808 – info@hotel-les-nations.com
– Fax 0227 343 884 – www.hotel-les-nations.com   *Plan I* **B2**
71 rm � – 🛏220/280 CHF 🛏🛏280/350 CHF
♦ Business ♦ Classic ♦
Popular with business travellers, Les Nations has been totally refurbished. The
rooms, though on the small side, are as charming as they are smart.

Auteuil without rest   🅰🅲 🛬 ✆ 🕭25 🈂 𝘝𝘐𝘚𝘈 ⓪ 🅰🅴 ⓞ

33 r. de Lausanne ⊠ 1201 – ℰ 0225 442 222 – auteuil@manotel.com
– Fax 0225 442 299 – www.manotel.com   **E2**
104 rm ⊆ – 🛏280/310 CHF 🛏🛏355/395 CHF
♦ Business ♦ Classic ♦
A contemporary reception hall with Warhol-style portraits of the stars leads on
to modern rooms in dark wood, designer bathrooms and a very trendy breakfast
room.

Cornavin without rest   🅰🅲 🛬 📺 ✆ 🕭60 ⓪ 🅰🅴 ⓞ

Cornavin Station ⊠ 1201 – ℰ 0227 161 212 – cornavin@fhotels.ch
– Fax 0227 161 200 – www.fhotels.ch   **E3**
162 rm – 🛏251/387 CHF 🛏🛏301/437 CHF, ⊆ 18 CHF
♦ Business ♦ Modern ♦
Patronised by Tintin in "The Calculus Affair", this hotel is home to the world's
biggest clock. Modern guest rooms with Le Corbusier armchairs, and a
panoramic breakfast room.

Kipling without rest   🅰🅲 🛬 🈺 📺 ✆ 🕭10 🅿 𝘝𝘐𝘚𝘈 ⓪ 🅰🅴 ⓞ

27 r. de la Navigation ⊠ 1201 – ℰ 0225 444 040
– kipling@manotel.com – Fax 0225 444 099
– www.manotel.com   **E-F2**
62 rm ⊆ – 🛏235/300 CHF 🛏🛏275/320 CHF
♦ Business ♦ Modern ♦
A delicate waft of incense greets you as you enter this colonial-styled hotel
dedicated to the author of "The Jungle Book".

Jade without rest   🅰🅲 🛬 📺 ✆ 𝘝𝘐𝘚𝘈 ⓪ 🅰🅴 ⓞ

55 r. Rothschild ⊠ 1202 – ℰ 0225 443 838 – jade@manotel.com
– Fax 0225 443 899 – www.manotel.com   **F2**
47 rm ⊆ – 🛏234/258 CHF 🛏🛏276/315 CHF
♦ Business ♦ Modern ♦
The interior of this hotel has been designed according to the principles of the
fashionable Chinese philosophy of Feng Shui. The result is a refined, modern
setting aiming to promote harmony and serenity.

Du Midi   🈺 🅶rm 🅰🅲 📺 ✆ 𝘝𝘐𝘚𝘈 ⓪ 🅰🅴 ⓞ

4 pl. Chevelu ⊠ 1201 – ℰ 0225 441 500 – info@hotel-du-midi.ch
– Fax 0225 441 520 – www.hotel-du-midi.ch   **E-F3**
87 rm – 🛏250/350 CHF 🛏🛏300/400 CHF, ⊆ 25 CHF
Rest *(closed Saturday and Sunday)* 35 CHF (lunch) and a la carte 54/88 CHF
♦ Business ♦ Functional ♦
On a little square by the Rhône, this spacious hotel has great rooms. In the
evenings, a pianist plays relaxing melodies in the lounge. Comfortable modern
restaurant with summer terrace.

Edelweiss   🅰🅲 🛬rm 🈺rest 📺 ✆ 𝘝𝘐𝘚𝘈 ⓪ 🅰🅴 ⓞ

2 pl. de la Navigation ⊠ 1201 – ℰ 0225 445 151 – edelweiss@manotel.com
– Fax 0225 445 199 – www.manotel.com   **F3**
42 rm ⊆ – 🛏235/300 CHF 🛏🛏275/320 CHF
Rest *(closed 1 to 18 January)* (dinner only) a la carte 44/97 CHF
♦ Business ♦ Cosy ♦
The outside of this establishment gives a good idea of the pleasures within. It's
a real Swiss chalet, with cosy bedrooms and a congenial galleried dining room
where you can enjoy traditional fare and typical cheese dishes to the
accompaniment of music.

Ambassador 🚭 AC ⬜ 📞 🛁 30 VISA ⊕ AE ①
21 quai des Bergues ⊠ *1201* – ℰ *0229 080 530*
– info@hotel-ambassador.ch – Fax 0227 389 080
– www.hotel-ambassador.ch **E3**
81 rm – ♦250/350 CHF ♦♦300/450 CHF, � 24 CHF
Rest *(closed Sunday lunch and Saturday)* 40 CHF (lunch)/60 CHF and a la carte
53/98 CHF
♦ Business ♦ Classic ♦
Traffic hurries by outside, following the river Rhône, but excellent
soundproofing in the bedrooms keeps out all but a murmur. Traditional meals
served in wood-fitted dining room or on the terrace in summer.

Eden AC ⬜ 📞 🛁 20 VISA ⊕ AE ①
135 r. de Lausanne ⊠ *1202* – ℰ *0227 163 700* – *eden@eden.ch*
– Fax 0227 315 260 – www.eden.ch **F1**
54 rm ⊆ – ♦175/260 CHF ♦♦235/310 CHF
Rest *(closed 22 July - 13 August, 23 December - 8 January, Saturday and Sunday)*
32 CHF/44 CHF and a la carte 40/63 CHF
♦ Business ♦ Classic ♦
This establishment facing the Palais des Nations is regularly refurbished. Bright
and functional classically furnished rooms. Traditional restaurant where local
people rub shoulders with guests and passers-by.

Strasbourg-Univers without rest ⇔ 🖎 ⬜ 📞 VISA ⊕ AE ①
10 r. Pradier ⊠ *1201* – ℰ *0229 065 800* – *info@hotel-strasbourg-geneva.ch*
– Fax 0227 384 208 – www.strasbourg-geneva.ch **E3**
51 rm ⊆ – ♦170/210 CHF ♦♦220/290 CHF
♦ Business ♦ Functional ♦
Close to the station and the Cornavin car park, this refurbished establishment has
small, functional rooms with cosy public areas.

Ibis without rest 🕭 AC ⇔ ⬜ 📞 VISA ⊕ AE ①
10 r. Voltaire ⊠ *1201* – ℰ *0223 382 020*
– h2154@accor.com – Fax 0223 382 030
– www.ibishotel.com **E3**
65 rm – ♦131 CHF ♦♦131 CHF, ⊆ 14 CHF
♦ Chain hotel ♦ Minimalist ♦
This completely refurbished establishment is typical of the new generation of
Ibis hotels. Contemporary comfort in rooms with modern, no-nonsense
furnishings.

Le Neptune – Hotel Mandarin Oriental du Rhône 🚭 AC
1 quai Turrettini ⊠ *1201* – ℰ *0229 090 006* 🖎 🚭 VISA ⊕ AE ①
– mogva-reservation@mohg.com – Fax 0229 090 010
– www.mandarinoriental.com
closed 29 July - 27 August, 24 to 30 December, Saturday, Sunday and Bank
Holidays **E3**
Rest 98 CHF (lunch)/180 CHF and a la carte 137/214 CHF
Spec. La langoustine de Guilvinec, les girolles Crête-de-coq et les fevettes. Le
turbot de ligne, l'encornet du bassin méditerranéen et les légumes de Provence.
Tarte tout chocolat Guanaja.
♦ Contemporary ♦ Formal ♦
Culinary artistry and modern cuisine from the Mandarin Oriental du Rhône's Le
Neptune restaurant – the god himself appears in the wall-paintings.

Tsé Yang ≤ AC ⇔ 20 VISA ⊕ AE ①
19 quai du Mont-Blanc (1st floor) ⊠ *1201* – ℰ *0227 325 081*
– Fax 0227 310 582 **F3**
Rest 45 CHF (lunch)/139 CHF and a la carte 67/165 CHF
♦ Chinese ♦ Exotic ♦
Elegant restaurant with oriental décor and carved wooden partitions. Savour
Chinese specialities while admiring the view over Lake Léman.

SWITZERLAND

XxX   La Perle du Lac   ≤ Lake, ☆ ⚙ 〽 〽 ↔8/60 🅿 _VISA_ ⦿⦿ 쬬 ⦾

128 r. de Lausanne ⊠ 1202 – ℰ 0229 091 020
– info@perledulac.ch – Fax 0229 091 030
– www.laperledulac.ch
closed 24 December - 25 January and Monday   **F1**
Rest 58 CHF (lunch)/115 CHF and a la carte 88/131 CHF
♦ Contemporary ♦ Formal ♦
Established over a century ago, this chalet with a spacious panoramic terrace is
located in a park facing the lake. Bold colours enliven the more modern of the two
dining rooms.

XX   Green   〽 _VISA_ ⦿⦿ 쬬 ⦾

5 r. Alfred Vincent ⊠ 1201 – ℰ 0227 311 313 – Fax 0227 381 345
– www.green-gr.com
closed 14 to 23 April, 30 July - 26 August, 24 December - 1 January, Saturday
lunch, Monday lunch and Sunday   **F3**
Rest 58 CHF (lunch) and a la carte 121/157 CHF
♦ Contemporary ♦ Friendly ♦
Behind a dark grey façade, an elegant and modern dining room in strades of
mauve. Contemporary cooking; intinate lighting in the evening.

X   Thai Phuket   🅰🅲 〽 _VISA_ ⦿⦿ 쬬

33 av. de France ⊠ 1202 – ℰ 0227 344 100
– Fax 0227 344 240   **E1**
Rest (closed Saturday lunch) 35 CHF (lunch)/90 CHF and a la carte 41/111 CHF 🕸
♦ Thai ♦ Exotic ♦
A respected address with attentive service from waitresses dressed in traditional
costume. Vintage wines, including top clarets, and a superb aquarium of exotic
fish.

X   Bistrot du Boeuf Rouge   _VISA_ ⦿⦿ 쬬 ⦾
😊
17 r. Alfred Vincent ⊠ 1201 – ℰ 0227 327 537 – Fax 0227 314 684
– www.boeufrouge.ch
closed 3 weeks in July - August, 24 December - 2 January, Saturday and
Sunday   **F3**
Rest (Specialities of Lyons) 37 CHF (lunch)/54 CHF and a la carte
54/92 CHF
♦ Brasserie ♦ Bistro ♦
A typically French brasserie ornamented with mirrors, a bar and comfortable
benches. The menu features specialities from the city of Lyon, local dishes and
daily specials.

X   Sagano   ☆ 🅰🅲 ↔80 _VISA_ ⦿⦿ 쬬

86 r. de Montbrillant ⊠ 1202 – ℰ 0227 331 150
– Fax 0227 332 755   **E1**
Rest (closed Saturday lunch and Sunday) 23 CHF (lunch)/90 CHF and a la carte
46/113 CHF 🕸
♦ Japanese ♦ Exotic ♦
Hungry for a taste of the exotic with a little zen? Head for this Japanese restaurant
with its tatami mats and low tables. A culinary voyage from the Land of the Rising
Sun.

X   L'Entrecôte Couronnée   _VISA_ ⦿⦿ 쬬 ⦾

5 r. des Pâquis ⊠ 1201 – ℰ 0227 328 445
– Fax 0227 328 446
closed 23 December - 3 January, Saturday lunch and Sunday   **F3**
Rest 58 CHF and a la carte 56/82 CHF
♦ Contemporary ♦ Bistro ♦
This is the place to experience the real Geneva. Bistro-style ambience
with contemporary food. Plenty of prints and paintings evoke the spirit of this old
city.

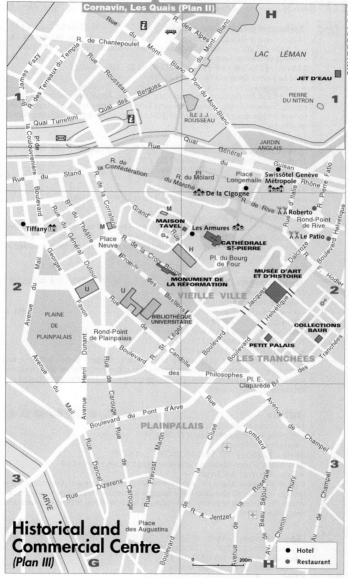

Historical and Commercial Centre
(Plan III)

● Hotel
● Restaurant

0   200m

SWITZERLAND

LEFT BANK *(Commercial Centre)* — *Plan III*

Swissôtel Genève Métropole

34 quai Général-Guisan ⊠ *1204*
– ℰ 0223 183 200 – reservations.geneva @ swissotel.com – Fax 0223 183 300
– www.swissotel-geneva.com — **H1**
118 rm – ✦355/580 CHF ✦✦470/950 CHF, ⊃ 37 CHF – 9 suites
Rest *Le Grand Quai* a la carte 58/124 CHF
♦ Luxury ♦ Classic ♦

Built in 1854 overlooking the landmark Jet d'Eau. Attractive, traditional guest rooms, many with lake views, plus new king-size suites and a panoramic roof terrace and fitness centre. Le Grand Quai, with its trompe l'oeil frescoes, serves traditional French fare.

Les Armures ♨

1 r. du Puits-Saint-Pierre ⊠ *1204 – ℰ 0223 109 172*
– armures @ span.ch – Fax 0223 109 846
– www.hotel-les-armures.ch — **H2**
32 rm ⊃ – ✦360/445 CHF ✦✦520/545 CHF
Rest *(closed Easter, Christmas and New Year)* 55 CHF and a la carte 49/91 CHF
♦ Traditional ♦ Historic ♦

An elegant 17C town house tucked away in the heart of the old town. Attractive bedroom decor with antique furniture and exposed beams. A choice of traditional dishes in the newly renovated restaurant, including fondue served in the "carnotset" (drinking den).

De la Cigogne

17 pl. Longemalle ⊠ *1204 – ℰ 0228 184 040*
– cigogne @ relaischateaux.com – Fax 0228 184 050
– www.relaischateaux.com/cigogne — **H1-2**
46 rm ⊃ – ✦370 CHF ✦✦465 CHF – 6 suites
Rest *(closed Sunday lunch and Saturday from July - August)* 59 CHF (lunch)/ 105 CHF and a la carte 72/121 CHF
♦ Traditional ♦ Historic ♦

The early-20C façade overlooks a busy square. Elegant decor, public areas adorned with objets d'art, and bedrooms and suites embellished with personal touches and antique furniture. Traditional cuisine beneath the glass roof of the Art Deco-style restaurant.

Tiffany

1 r. des Marbriers ⊠ *1204 – ℰ 0227 081 616*
– info @ hotel-tiffany.ch – Fax 0227 081 617
– www.hotel-tiffany.ch — **G2**
46 rm – ✦240/290 CHF ✦✦350/420 CHF, ⊃ 18 CHF
Rest *(closed Easter, Christmas and New Year)* a la carte 51/91 CHF
♦ Traditional ♦ Classic ♦

Built on the site of a late-19C monument. Modern facilities with bedrooms, cosy lounge and bar all showing Belle Époque influence. Retro-style dining room which fits perfectly with the house style. A la carte menu featuring salads and low-calorie dishes.

Sagitta *without rest* ♨

6 r. de la Flèche ⊠ *1207 – ℰ 0227 863 361*
– sagitta @ span.ch – Fax 0228 498 110
– www.hotels.suisse.ch/hotel-sagitta — *Plan I* **C3**
42 rm ⊃ – ✦169/279 CHF ✦✦209/279 CHF
♦ Business ♦ Modern ♦

In the commercial district but secluded, this establishment has rooms, studios, apartments and numerous kitchenettes. The uninspiring façade belies renovated facilities.

SWITZERLAND

XXXX **Parc des Eaux-Vives** with rm
£3 £3 *82 quai Gustave-Ador* ⊠ *1207*
– ℰ *0228 497 575 – info@parcdeseauxvives.ch – Fax 0228 497 570*
– *www.parcdeseauxvives.ch* Plan I **D2**
7 rm – †550/750 CHF ††650/850 CHF, ⊡ 29 CHF – **Rest** see *Brasserie* below
Rest *(closed 1 to 16 January, Sunday and Monday)* (1st floor) 79 CHF
(lunch)/275 CHF and a la carte 161/219 CHF
Spec. L'omble chevalier du Lac Léman (May-August). Le lièvre à la royale (Sept.-
Déc.). Menu Caviar.
♦ Innovative ♦ Design ♦
Housed in a lavish 18C building in a public park. Fine Art Deco-style dining room,
mouth-watering, creative cuisine, summer restaurant and high-tech guest rooms.

XX **Brasserie** – Parc des Eaux-Vives
82 quai Gustave-Ador ⊠ *1207* – ℰ *0228 497 575 – info@parcdeseauxvives.ch*
– *Fax 0228 497 570 – www.parcdeseauxvives.ch* Plan I **D2**
Rest 49 CHF (lunch) and a la carte 62/114 CHF
♦ Contemporary ♦ Trendy ♦
Elegant modern brasserie on the ground floor of the pavilion of the Parc des
Eaux-Vives. Contemporary cuisine, a beautiful view of the lake and an inviting
teak-decked terrace.

XX **Roberto**
10 r. Pierre Fatio ⊠ *1204* – ℰ *0223 118 033 – Fax 0223 118 466*
closed 25 December - 1 January, Saturday dinner, Sunday and Bank Holidays
Rest a la carte 68/123 CHF **H2**
♦ Italian ♦ Formal ♦
Vast restaurant made to look even more spacious by the mirrors on the walls.
Intimate ambience for Italian cuisine showing Milanese influence.

XX **Le Patio**
19 bd Helvétique ⊠ *1207* – ℰ *0227 366 675 – lepatio.ch@freesurf.ch*
– *Fax 0227 864 074*
closed 23 December - 3 January, Saturday and Sunday **H2**
Rest a la carte 65/106 CHF
♦ Contemporary ♦ Fashionable ♦
This establishment has two modern dining rooms, one of them designed as a
winter garden. A selection of seasonal recipes and Provençal specialities make
easy bedfellows.

X **Buffet de la Gare des Eaux-Vives** (Labrosse)
£3 *7 av. de la Gare des Eaux-Vives* ⊠ *1207* – ℰ *0228 404 430 – Fax 0228 404 431*
closed 23 December - 9 January, Saturday and Sunday Plan I **C-D3**
Rest 52 CHF (lunch)/135 CHF and a la carte 86/129 CHF
Spec. Fraîcheur de homard à l'avocat et fine gelée d'herbes (spring). Pavé de
turbot rôti, sauté de fèves et patta negra (spring). Côte de veau rôtie aux morilles,
jus au vin jaune, ravioles de pommes (spring).
♦ Innovative ♦ Formal ♦
Not your ordinary station buffet, here is a boldly contemporary yet sober interior
with a railway fresco, a waterside summer terrace and an inventive
up-to-the-minute menu.

ENVIRONS AND COINTRIN AIRPORT *Plan I*

La Réserve
301 rte de Lausanne ⊠ *1293 Bellevue*
– ℰ *0229 595 959 – info@lareserve.ch – Fax 0229 595 960*
– *www.lareserve.ch* **C1**
85 rm – †400/730 CHF ††540/990 CHF, ⊡ 45 CHF – 17 suites
Rest *Tsé-Fung* (Chinese rest.) 70 CHF/150 CHF and a la carte 68/148 CHF
Rest *Le Loti* a la carte 64/139 CHF
♦ Grand Luxury ♦ Stylish ♦
Most of the modern rooms of this luxury hotel have a terrace overlooking the
park with its swimming pool. Splendid Garcia décor. Sample fine Chinese cuisine
at the Tsé-Fung or contemporary food at the Loti.

Crowne Plaza   🛜 📶 🛗 🌀 🔲 ⚕ 🅰 ⁴⁄rm 🔲 🕍 15/180 🚗
34 r. François-Peyrot ✉ *1218 Grand-Saconnex*   🅿 🆅🅸🆂🅰 ⓶ 🅰🅴 ⓪
– ℰ 0227 470 202 – sales@cpgeneva.ch
– Fax 0227 470 303 – www.geneva.crowneplaza.com   **B1**
496 rm ⥮ – ♦274/594 CHF ♦♦348/638 CHF
Rest L'Olivo – 26 voie de Moëns *(closed Saturday and Sunday)* a la carte
57/113 CHF
♦ Business ♦ Classic ♦
The facilities at this American-style hotel close to the airport include modern
bedrooms, conference halls and a fitness centre. Contemporary cuisine in the
restaurant whose decor is inspired by the south of France.

Mövenpick Genève   🛗 🛜 🌀 🅰 ⁴⁄rm 🔲 📞 🕍 15/400
20 rte de Pré-Bois ✉ *1216 Cointrin*   🚗 🆅🅸🆂🅰 ⓶ 🅰🅴 ⓪
– ℰ 0227 171 111 – hotel.geneva.airport@moevenpick.com
– Fax 0227 171 122
– www.moevenpick-geneva.com   **A2**
344 rm – ♦350/460 CHF ♦♦420/560 CHF, ⥮ 34 CHF – 6 suites
Rest a la carte 48/104 CHF
Rest Kamome *(closed Saturday lunch, Monday lunch and Sunday)* (Japanese
rest.) 38 CHF (lunch)/110 CHF and a la carte
59/117 CHF
♦ Chain hotel ♦ Functional ♦
A chain hotel close to the airport. Facilities include lounges, bars, casino,
conference rooms, business centre and various categories of bedrooms. Classic
cuisine in the Brasserie, plus Japanese specialities at the Kamome, including
teppanyaki and sushi bar.

Ramada Park Hotel   🛗 🛜 🌀 🅰 ⁴⁄rm 🍽rest 🔲 🕍 15/550
75 av. Louis Casaï ✉ *1216 Cointrin*   🚗 🆅🅸🆂🅰 ⓶ 🅰🅴 ⓪
– ℰ 0227 103 000 – resa@ramadaparkhotel.ch – Fax 0227 103 100
– www.ramadaparkhotel.ch   **A2**
302 rm – ♦195/440 CHF ♦♦270/440 CHF, ⥮ 33 CHF – 6 suites
Rest La Récolte – 34 CHF and a la carte 51/94 CHF
♦ Chain hotel ♦ Modern ♦
Next door to the airport, a hotel with a wide range of amenities including a
newspaper kiosk, a hairdresser's, a sauna and fitness centre, and meeting rooms.
The bedrooms are modern. Some weeks the contemporary restaurant stages a
themed menu.

Hostellerie de la Vendée   🛜 🅰 🔲 📞 🕍 15/60
28 ch. de la Vendée ✉ *1213 Petit-Lancy*   🚗 🆅🅸🆂🅰 ⓶ 🅰🅴 ⓪
– ℰ 0227 920 411 – info@vendee.ch – Fax 0227 920 546
– www.vendee.ch
closed 14 to 17 April and 24 December - 8 January   **B3**
34 rm ⥮ – ♦195/350 CHF ♦♦300/350 CHF
Rest *(closed Saturday lunch, Sunday and Bank Holidays)* 57 CHF (lunch)/
157 CHF and a la carte 77/152 CHF
Rest Bistro *(closed Saturday lunch, Sunday and Bank Holidays)* 44 CHF/59 CHF
and a la carte 58/102 CHF
Spec. Terrine de foie gras de canard, réduction de Porto rouge et cake à la truffe
noire (winter). Filet de chevreuil rôti, sauce poivrade. Bolets au jus et aux gousses
d'ail en chemise (autumn). Superposé d'ananas au chocolat blanc et noix de
coco, caramel aux griottes (winter).
♦ Business ♦ Classic ♦
In a quiet residential area, this hotel is just the place for a good night's sleep.
The elegant dining room of the gourmet restaurant is extended by a veranda.
Classic French meals much loved by foodies. Bistro serving a contemporary
selection.

SWITZERLAND

NH Geneva Airport Hotel
AC 4→rm 🖂 ☎ 🔊 15/60

21 av. de Mategnin ✉ *1217 Meyrin*
🅿 VISA ⑳ AE ①
– ✆ *0229 899 000* – *nhgenevaairport@nh-hotels.ch* – *Fax 0229 899 999*
– *www.nh-hotels.com*
A1
190 rm – ♦155/360 CHF ♦♦155/390 CHF, ☲ 27 CHF
Rest *Le Pavillon* a la carte 46/94 CHF
♦ Chain hotel ♦ Functional ♦
A circular red-brick construction whose outer appearance provides a foretaste of
the contemporary interior. Designer hall and lobby, friendly bar and well-kept
rooms. Modern cuisine is served in the contemporary setting beneath the
Pavillon's cupola.

Express by Holiday Inn without rest
& AC 4→ 🖂 15/25

16 rte de Pré-Bois ✉ *1216 Cointrin*
🅿 VISA ⑳ AE ①
– ✆ *0229 393 939* – *info@expressgeneva.com* – *Fax 0229 393 930*
– *www.expressgeneva.com*
A2
154 rm ☲ – ♦150/230 CHF ♦♦150/230 CHF
♦ Chain hotel ♦ Functional ♦
Intended to be modern and practical, this new addition to the Holiday Inn chain
is tailor-made for business travel. Good triple-glazed rooms.

Suitehotel
🛱 & rm AC 4→ ☎ 🅿 VISA ⑳ AE ①

28 av. Louis Casaï ✉ *1216 Cointrin* – ✆ *0227 104 626* – *H5654@accor.com*
– *Fax 0227 104 600* – *www.suite-hotel.com*
B2
86 rm – ♦159 CHF ♦♦159 CHF, ☲ 15 CHF
Rest *Swiss Bistro* a la carte 33/77 CHF
♦ Business ♦ Modern ♦
This hotel located between the airport and the town centre offers
up-to-the-minute rooms, each with an office which can be separated off by a
sliding door. The public areas are bright and modern. Contemporary-style
brasserie serving bistro-type meals with a Swiss twist.

Ibis
🛱 & AC 4→rm ☎ 🅿 VISA ⑳ AE ①

10 ch. de la Violette ✉ *1216 Cointrin* – ✆ *0227 109 500* – *H3535@accor.com*
– *Fax 0227 109 595* – *www.ibishotel.com*
A2
109 rm – ♦131 CHF ♦♦131 CHF, ☲ 14 CHF
Rest (dinner only) a la carte approx. 45 CHF
♦ Chain hotel ♦ Minimalist ♦
Near the motorway and Geneva airport, you can find the whole range of the Ibis
chain's hotel services. Standard rooms with bathroom units. The restaurant has
a slightly globe-trotting menu and a comfortable terrace.

XXXX Auberge du Lion d'Or (Byrne/Dupont)
< 🛱 & AC

❀ *5 pl. Pierre-Gautier* ✉ *1223 Cologny*
🅿 VISA ⑳ AE ①
– ✆ *0227 364 432* – *Fax 0227 867 462* – *www.liondor.ch*
closed 23 December - 9 January
D2
Rest *(closed Saturday lunch, Sunday and Monday)* 70 CHF (lunch)/170 CHF
and a la carte 118/172 CHF ❀
Rest *Le Bistro de Cologny (closed Saturday and Sunday)* 42 CHF (lunch)
and a la carte 65/118 CHF
Spec. Croustillant de thon rouge de la Méditerranée, vinaigrette de légumes
crus, huile aux saveurs de fruits et fleurs (summer). Dos de cabillaud, minestrone
de légumes, compotée de tomate, origan et peau d'orange (spring). Noisette de
selle d'agneau de Sisteron marinées au safran, bois de cannelle, fruits secs
et épices douces.
♦ Contemporary ♦ Formal ♦
The superb backdrop to this elegant, contemporary-style restaurant
encompasses both the lake and surrounding mountains. Attractive terrace and
modern bar, also with panoramic views. Bistro serving contemporary fare and in
summer a sumptuously flower-decked restaurant.

ZURICH

ZÜRICH

Population (est. 2005): 345 300 (conurbation 1 081 700) – Altitude: 409m

The site of Zurich, framed by the wooded slopes of the Üetliberg and the Zürichberg at the point where the Limmat, flowing out of Lake Zürich, meets the Sihl river, is particularly charming. It is Switzerland's largest city and an important financial, industrial and commercial centre. It has a reputation for good living with a rich cultural life, outdoor cafés and gourmet restaurants; it is also a busy university city.

Zurich became a stronghold of the Reformation movement in the 16C. The pastor Ulrich Zwingli denounced social institutions and corruption and instituted controversial religious reforms. Several cantons formed an alliance against Zurich; the city was excluded from the direction of federal affairs and war broke out in 1531. However, his religious theories spread throughout German Switzerland. In the early 20C, the city was the cradle of the avant-garde Dada Movement as a reaction to established art. Its members included friends and artists from a variety of backgrounds, among them Tristan Tzara, Maurice Janco, Jean Arp and Sophie Taeuber.

WHICH DISTRICT TO CHOOSE

For the finest **accommodation** and boutique hotels look in the old city, around Niederdorfstrasse *Plan II D2* and Bahnhofstrasse *Plan II C2*. Business travellers will find first-class hotels with all facilities near the airport, in the city centre and in the downtown area. Hotels in the lake-side area and on the outskirts will suit visitors who appreciate peace and tranquillity. There are also delightful smaller hotels with an intimate atmosphere in the city.

The city boasts a variety of **eating places** in the old town, in a pleasant location along the quays and in the up and coming area to the west near the Schiffbau complex *Plan I A3*. For a gourmet experience, visit also the starred restaurants at Küsnacht, Uetikon am See (SE) and Gattikon (S) on the outskirts of the city.

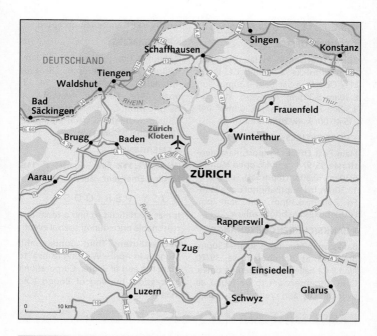

PRACTICAL INFORMATION

ARRIVAL – DEPARTURE

Zurich International Airport (Kloten) – 10 km (6 mi) north of the city. ℰ 0438 162 211; www.zurichairport.com

From the airport to the city centre – By **taxi**: about 50CHF, time 20-40min. By **train**: 5.80CHF, every 10-15min, time 10min. By **shuttle minibus** to hotels: about 20CHF, every 45min. By **bus**: several buses go to the city centre, 3.80CHF, time 20-30min.

Railway Station – Zürich Hauptbahnhof *Plan II C1*; main station for international and intercity trains. ℰ 0900 300 300; www.sbb.ch

TRANSPORT

◆ BUS, METRO, TRAM, TRAIN, BOAT

The city operates an efficient public transport network in the city centre and suburbs. Single ticket 3.80CHF; day ticket 7.60CHF (€5.15); 9 o'clock Pass 22-37CHF (€14.85-25). Tickets are available from ticket machines and offices. Make sure you validate the ticket before boarding at the ticket machine or the special orange-coloured machine. Zurich Card gives unlimited travel, free entry to several museums and various discounts: 15CHF (€10.15, 24hr); 30CHF (€20.25, 72hr). It is available from the Tourist Office, hotels, museums and stations.

◆ TAXIS

Metered taxis can be hailed at taxi stands, near the stations, at the airport or ordered by phone. Tips are included in the fare. Average ride in town: 25CHF. *Alpha Taxi AG* ℰ 044 777 77 77; www.alphataxi.ch; *Taxi 444 AG* ℰ 044 444 44 44; www.taxi444.ch

◆ TOURIST OFFICE

Zürich Tourismus – In Hauptbahnhof, Bahnhofbrücke 1 *Plan II C1*. Open May-Oct, Mon-Sat 8am-8.30pm; Sun 8.30am-6.30pm; Nov-Apr, Mon-Sat 8.30am-7pm; Sun 9am-6.30pm.℘ 041 215 40 00; www.zurichtourism.ch

◆ POST OFFICES

Main Post Office: Sihlpost, Kasernenstrasse 95-97 *Plan I A3*: open Mon-Fri 6.30am-10.30pm (8pm Sat), Sun 10am-10.30pm. In Hauptbahnhof open Mon-Fri 7.30am-6.30pm, Sat 8am-7pm. Letter boxes are bright yellow.

◆ BANKS/CURRENCY EXCHANGE

Banks open Mon-Fri, 8.30am-4.30pm. Branches at Bahnhofstrasse 39/70 *Plan II C2* have longer opening times. Cash dispensers are to be found all over the city and credit cards, which require a PIN, are widely accepted.

◆ PHARMACIES

Opening times Mon-Fri 7.30am-6.30pm, Sat 8am-4pm. *Bellevue Apotheke*, Theaterstrasse 14, is open 24hr. *Bahnhof Apotheke*, in Hauptbahnhof, Bahnhofplatz 15, 7.30am-midnight. *Odeon Apotheke*, Limmatquai 2, 7am-11pm.

◆ EMERGENCY

Police: ℘ **117**. Fire Brigade: ℘ **118**. Medical Emergency Service: ℘ **144**.

BUSY PERIODS

It may be difficult to find a room at a reasonable price during special event:

Sechseläuten: Third Sunday and Monday in April – A spring festival to mark the end of winter. Corporation's procession; burning of Böögg (Old Man Winter).

EXPLORING ZURICH

It is possible to visit the main sights and museums in two days.

Museums and other sights are usually open from 9-10am to 5-6pm. Some close on Mondays.

VISITING

Grossmünster *Plan II D2* – Imposing 11C-13C cathedral with domed towers (statue of Charlemagne) and Romanesque cloisters.

Old Town – Follow the tree-lined **Bahnhofstrasse** *Plan II C2* to Paradeplatz *Plan II C2* – take Bleicherweg *Plan II C3* to view the old moat, **Schanzengraben**; Poststrasse leads to **Münsterhof** *Plan II C2* and 13C **Fraumünster** *Plan II C2* – Romanesque chancel, stained-glass windows, cloisters. Proceed to **St Peterkirche** (7C) *Plan II C2*: 16C clock; and pretty **Weinplatz** *Plan II C2* (view of the east bank). **Schipfe** *Plan II C2*, the heart of the old town, boasts narrow, medieval streets lined with old houses (Augustinerstrasser). The shady **Lindenhof** *Plan II C2* (views of old quarter on opposite bank) marks the site of Celtic and Roman encampments.

Schweizerisches Landesmuseum *Plan II C1* – Magnificent collections of the Swiss National Museum tracing Switzerland's artistic and cultural heritage.

Kunsthaus *Plan II D2* – The Fine Arts Museum displays medieval sculpture, Swiss and German 15C Primitives and paintings by major European artists (Hodler, Cézanne, Renoir, Matisse, Braque, Picasso); also works by E. Munch, Man Ray, Arp and Giacometti.

Museum Rietberg *Plan I A3* – The eclectic collection of a private art patron: art from Asia, Africa, the South Sea Islands, South America and the Near East.

Sammlung Bührle – Splendid collection of paintings and sculpture assembled by a private collector: the exhibits illustrate all major European trends from the Dutch schools, the Impressionist movement to Cubism and Fauvism.

Boat trips – Cruises on Lake Zurich and the River Limmat from Bürkliplatz landing-stage *Plan II C3*.

Views – From Jules Verne Bar Panorama *Plan II C2*. Top of Üetliberg Tower. Bürkliplatz *Plan II C3*.

Excursions – **Üetliberg** and **Felsenegg** *(2hr round trip by train)*. **Albis Pass Road**, former Abbey of Kappel and plunging views of the lake beyond Hütten *(53 km-33 mi SW)*. **Eglisau** *(27 km-17 mi N)*.

SHOPPING

Department stores are usually open Mon-Fri 9am-8pm, Sat 8am-4pm. Smaller shops open later and close on Mon.

Bahnhofstrasse *Plan II C2*, the most famous shopping boulevard, is lined by smart boutiques and department stores *(Globus, Vilan, Jelmoli)*. You will also find boutiques, antique stores, trendy shops *(Trois Pommes No 18)* in the narrow streets around **Weinplatz** *Plan II C2*, **Münsterhof** *Plan II C2* and in the district around **Niederdorfstrasse** *Plan II D2* in the picturesque Old Town. There are also some fine shops in **Rennweg** *Plan II C2*, **Limmatquai** and **Langstrasse** *Plan I A3*. Visit *Fabric Frontline*, Ankerstrasse 118 (fine silks). For designer collectibles browse in *Time Tunnel*, Stüssihofstatt 7. For mouthwatering chocolates and specialities, do not miss *Sprüngli* and *Merkur*, Bannhofstrasse 21/106; *Teuscher*, Storchengasse 9 and *Globus* Delikatessen. *Pastorini*, Weinplatz 3, specialises in wooden toys, and *Schweizer Heimatwerk*, Rudolf Brun-Brücke, in gifts and handicrafts. *Christie's*, Steinwiesstrasse 26, and *Sotheby's*, Gessnerallee 1, hold international auctions of art and antiques.

MARKETS – **Flea market** on Bürkliplatz *Plan II C3* (May-Oct, Sat 6am-3.30pm).

WHAT TO BUY – Designer items, jewellery, watches, toys, children's clothes, lace, linen, dolls, wall hangings, confectionery (truffles, chocolates, Luxemburgerli), cheese and other delicacies.

ENTERTAINMENT

Consult ZüriTipp (in German), the Friday supplement of Tages-Anzeiger, for listings of cultural events. English language web site www.zürtipp.ch/essentials

Opernhaus *Plan II D3* – Opera.

Tonhalle *Plan II C3* – Large hall inaugurated by Johannes Brahms in 1895.

Schauspielhaus *Plan II D2* – Plays.

Theatre Neumarkt *Plan II D2* and **Theater Stock** *Plan II D2* – Contemporary theatre.

Bernhard-Theater *Plan II D3* – Comedy, cabaret.

Theatersaal Rigiblick *Plan I B2* – Plays, dance, music.

Theatre Stadelhofen *Plan II D3* – Puppet plays, object and figure theatre.

Herzbaracke (Bellevuesteg) *Plan II D3* – Floating theatre for variety entertainment.

NIGHTLIFE

The Old Town (**Bahnhofstrasse**, **Niederdorfstrasse** and **the quays**) boasts a multitude of eating, drinking and entertainment venues. To the west, the area around **Escher-Wyss Platz/Pfingstweidstrasse** is lively with cafés, restaurants, nightclubs. Trendy venues include *4.Akt*, Heinrichstrasse 262; *Toni Molkerei*, Förrlibuckstrasse 109; *Rohstofflager*, Duttweilerstrasse; *Labor Bar*, Schiffbaustrasse 3; *Supermarket*, Geroldstrasse 17; *X-Tra* and *Indochine*, Limmatstrasse 118/275; *Kunsthaus*, Heimplatz 1. Relax at the famous *Café Odéon* and *Café Select*, Limmatquai 2/16; at the *Splendid* piano bar, Rosengasse 5 and the sophisticated *Kronenhalle*, Rämistrasse 4. Listen to cool jazz at *Blue Note*, Stockerstrasse 45; *Casa Bar*, Münstergasse 30; *Moods*, Schiffbaustrasse 6. Visit *Grand Casino Baden*, Haselstrasse 2, Baden, for an elegant evening out.

Environs of Zurich
(Plan I)

0   1 Km

ZÜRICH-KLOTTEN

Glattalstrasse

A

B

Rias

NH Zürich Airport

Fly Away

Allegra

Hilton

KLOTTEN

Flughofstrasse

Glattalstrasse

Kalzenrüti-strasse

1

Mövenpick

Vivendi

GLATTBRUGG

Schaffhauserstr.

Kloten-erstr.

A 50

Wallisellerstr.

1

A1 - E - 60

Kasnadelstrasse

Novotel Zürich Airport Messe

Schaffhauserstr.

Renaissance Zürich Hotel

Thurgauerstr.

Hagenholzstr.

WALLISELLEN

Weststrasse

Wallisellerstr.

A1- E 60- E 41

Wehntalerstrasse

Glaubtenstr.

Binzmühlestr.

Regensbergstrasse

Wehntalerstrasse

Wallisellenstrasse

Ueberland

strasse

KÄFERBERG

Bucheggstrasse

Winterthurerstrasse

Dübendorfstrasse

2

Elli

Klöti

Strasse

Rottluchstr.

Schaffhauserstr.

Winterthurerstr.

U

ZÜRICHBERG

2

Peterstrasse

Nordstr.

Limmattalstrasse

Hardturm.

Limmat

ZOO ZÜRICH

Pfingstweidstr.

A3

Ibis

Hardstr.

Krone Unterstrass

Rigiblick

Novotel Zürich City-West

Josef

Sihlquai

Rigihof

Stapferstube

Inter-Continental Zurich

SCHWEIZERISCHES LANDESMUSEUM

Badenerstr.

Caduff's Wine Loft

Greulich

Historical and Commercial Centre (Plan II)

ADLISBERG

Dolder Waldhaus

Mercure Hotel Stoller

Ciro

Kasernenstr.

Weststr.

Casa Piccoli "Il Gattopardo"

Gustrasse

Zentraleck

KUNSTHAUS

Ramistr.

Talstr.

Asylstrasse

Bergstr.

Sonnenberg

Birmensdorferstr.

3

Alden Hotel Splügenschloss

Ascot

Eden au Lac

Steigenberger Bellerive au Lac

Forchstr.

Wittikonerstr.

3

Engimatt

RIETBERGMUSEUM

Seestrasse

Bellevuestr.

Riesbächli

Blaue Ente

FRIESENBERG

Schweighofstr.

Sihl

Muschellaustr.

Mythenquai

Lake Side

ZÜRICHSEE

Wirtschaft Flühgass

Zollikerstr.

Forchstr.

ZOLLIKON

A 3

A 3

B

- ● Hotel
- ● Restaurant

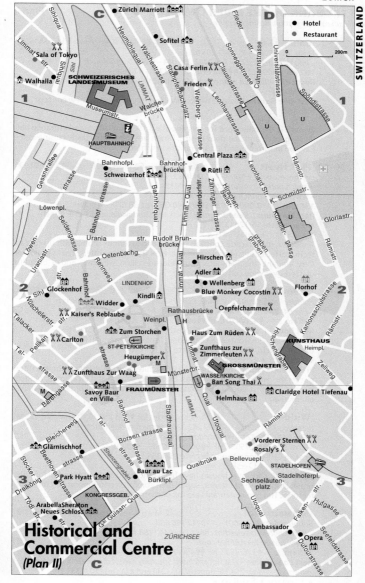

SWITZERLAND

C — Zürich Marriott 🏨

● Hotel
● Restaurant

0   200m

Sofitel 🏨

XX Sala of Tokyo
🏛 Walhalla

Casa Ferlin XX
Frieden X

SCHWEIZERISCHES LANDESMUSEUM

HAUPTBAHNHOF

Bahnhofpl.

Central Plaza 🏨

Schweizerhof 🏨

Bahnhof-brücke

● Rütli 🏛

Löwenpl.

Urania   str.   Rudolf Brun-brücke

Oetenbachg.

● Hirschen 🏛

Glockenhof ●

● Adler 🏨

LINDENHOF

● Wellenberg 🏨

Florhof

Widder 🏨   ● Kindli ●

● Blue Monkey Cocostin XX

XX Kaiser's Reblaube

Weinpl.

Oepfelchammer X

Rathausbrücke

XX Carlton

H

Zum Storchen 🏨

Haus Zum Rüden XX

ST-PETERKIRCHE

Heugümper X

Zunfthaus zur Zimmerleuten XX

M

XX Zunfthaus Zur Waag

GROSSMÜNSTER

KUNSTHAUS
Heimpl.

Münsterbr.

WASSERKIRCHE

Ban Song Thai X

M

Savoy Baur en Ville 🏨

FRAUMÜNSTER

● Helmhaus 🏨

Claridge Hotel Tiefenau 🏨

Glärnischhof 🏨

Vorderer Sternen XX
Rosaly's X

STADELHOFEN

Park Hyatt 🏨

Baur au Lac 🏨

Bürklipl.

Quaibrüke

Bellevuepl.

Stadelhoferpl.

ArabellaSheraton
Neues Schloss 🏨

KONGRESSGEB.

Sechseläuten-platz

🏨 Ambassador

ZÜRICHSEE

Opera 🏨

Historical and Commercial Centre
(Plan II)

C   D

SWITZERLAND

LEFT BANK OF THE RIVER LIMMAT
Plan II
(Main railway station, Business centre)

Baur au Lac 🗘 🖪 🚗 ⅙rm 📶rm ⅔rest 🎬 📞 🚗15/60
Talstr. 1 ⊠ 8001 – 𝒞 0442 205 020 🚗 VISA ⑳ 🖭 ⓪
– info@bauraulac.ch – Fax 0442 205 044 – www.bauraulac.ch **C3**
107 rm – ♥490 CHF ♥♥740 CHF, 😅 38 CHF – 17 suites
Rest *Le Pavillon/Le Français* 90 CHF (lunch)/140 CHF and a la carte
80/173 CHF
Rest *Rive Gauche* *(closed 3 weeks July - August and Sunday)* (new concept
planned)
♦ Grand Luxury ♦ Stylish ♦
Elegant is the only word for this imposing 19C hotel, its grand entrance hall,
lovely garden and luxurious rooms. Diners are treated to classic cuisine in the
Pavillon in summer and in the Français in winter.

Park Hyatt 🗘 🖪 🕉 ⅙ 📶 ⅙rm 🎬 📞 🚗15/280 🚗 VISA ⑳ 🖭 ⓪
Beethovenstr. 21 ⊠ 8002 – 𝒞 0438 831 234
– zurich.park@hyattintl.com – Fax 0438 831 235
– www.zurich.park.hyatt.ch **C3**
138 rm – ♥410/990 CHF ♥♥560/1140 CHF, 😅 38 CHF – 4 suites
Rest *Parkhuus* *(closed Saturday lunch and Sunday dinner)* 57 CHF (lunch)
and a la carte 56/128 CHF
♦ Luxury ♦ Modern ♦
A modern glass façade conceals tasteful and luxurious rooms with up-to-date
technical facilities and professional service. The Lounge offers snacks. Onyx Bar.
Very elegant: the Parkhuus with floor-to-ceiling windows and a beautiful
glassed-over wine cellar on 2 floors.

Savoy Baur en Ville ⅙ 📶 ⅔ 📞 🚗15/70 VISA ⑳ 🖭 ⓪
Paradeplatz ⊠ 8001 – 𝒞 0442 152 525 – welcome@savoy-zuerich.ch
– Fax 0442 152 500 – www.savoy-zuerich.ch **C3**
104 rm 😅 – ♥420/470 CHF ♥♥650/720 CHF – 8 suites
Rest *Baur* – (1st floor) – 64 CHF (lunch) and a la carte 70/150 CHF
Rest *Orsini* – (in front of the cathedral) (booking essential) (Italian rest.)
62 CHF (lunch)/98 CHF and a la carte 76/153 CHF
♦ Luxury ♦ Stylish ♦
In the heart of town, the grandiose 19 C architecture of this establishment offers
guests the most stylish of settings. Exemplary service and an elegant, modern
interior. The first-floor Baur is classically elegant; the Orsini provides an Italian
alternative.

Widder 🗘 🖪 📶 ⅙rest ⅔rest 🎬 📞 🚗15/120 🚗 VISA ⑳ 🖭 ⓪
Rennweg 7 ⊠ 8001 – 𝒞 0442 242 526 – home@widderhotel.ch
– Fax 0442 242 424 – www.widderhotel.ch **C2**
42 rm 😅 – ♥430/505 CHF ♥♥665/810 CHF – 7 suites
Rest 88 CHF (dinner) and a la carte 75/135 CHF
♦ Luxury ♦ Design ♦
Ten historic Old Town houses have been renovated and combined to form this
hotel. Distinguished interior, superlative comfort, contemporary architectural
features. The two restaurants are full of charm and character.

Schweizerhof 📶 ⅙rm ⅔rest 📞 🚗15/40 VISA ⑳ 🖭 ⓪
Bahnhofplatz 7 ⊠ 8001 – 𝒞 0442 188 888
– info@hotelschweizerhof.com – Fax 0442 188 181
– www.hotelschweizerhof.com **C1**
115 rm 😅 – ♥315/495 CHF ♥♥490/700 CHF
Rest *La Soupière* – (1st floor) *(closed Saturday except dinner from October -
June and Sunday)* 75 CHF (lunch)/104 CHF and a la carte 87/133 CHF
♦ Luxury ♦ Stylish ♦
This historic establishment stands in the very heart of town directly opposite the
main station. Beyond the imposing façade is an interior of contemporary
elegance and great comfort. La Soupière restaurant has a classically tasteful
ambience.

SWITZERLAND

Zum Storchen
← 📷 🌐 rm ↔rm 🍴 rest 🏛15/20 VISA ⚫ ⍺ ⑩

Weinplatz 2 ⊠ 8001 – 𝒞 0442 272 727 – info@storchen.ch – Fax 0442 272 700
– www.storchen.ch
C2
73 rm ⊑ – ♦340/460 CHF ♦♦530/730 CHF
Rest *Rôtisserie* – (1st floor) – 68 CHF and a la carte 67/110 CHF
♦ Traditional ♦ Functional ♦
This traditional hotel - one of the city's oldest - stands right on the Limmat. Elegant, comfortable rooms, with tasteful toile de Jouy fabrics, ensure a relaxing stay. The restaurant's lovely riverside terrace offers a fine view of the Old Town.

ArabellaSheraton Neues Schloss
📷 ↔rm 📞 🏛20

Stockerstr. 17 ⊠ 8002 – 𝒞 0442 869 400
– neuesschloss@arabellasheraton.com – Fax 0442 869 445
– www.arabellasheraton.com
C3
60 rm – ♦305/425 CHF ♦♦345/475 CHF, ⊑ 30 CHF
Rest *Le Jardin* (closed Saturday lunch, Sunday lunch and lunch Bank Holidays)
57 CHF (lunch) and a la carte 59/102 CHF
♦ Traditional ♦ Modern ♦
Not far from the lakeside, this establishment makes an excellent base for your stay in Zurich. The recently renovated rooms have elegant wooden furnishings in contemporary style. The ground floor restaurant is lavishly decorated with indoor plants.

Glärnischhof
📷 ↔rm 📷 📞 🏛25 🅿 VISA ⚫ ⍺ ⑩

Claridenstr. 30 ⊠ 8002 – 𝒞 0442 862 222 – info@hotelglaernischhof.com
– Fax 0442 862 286 – www.hotelglaernischhof.ch
C3
62 rm ⊑ – ♦340/370 CHF ♦♦440/490 CHF
Rest *Le Poisson* (closed Saturday and Sunday) (Fish specialities) 59 CHF (lunch)/95 CHF and a la carte 72/115 CHF
Rest *Vivace* (Italian rest.) a la carte 41/95 CHF
♦ Business ♦ Modern ♦
This building on the edge of the city centre has functional rooms with fine wood furnishings and fresh and bright colour schemes. The restaurants' names spell out their wares: fish dishes in Le Poisson, Italian cuisine in Vivace.

Glockenhof
📷 ♿rm 📷 rest ↔rm 📞 🏛15/40 🅿 VISA ⚫ ⍺ ⑩

Sihlstr. 31 ⊠ 8001 – 𝒞 0442 259 191 – info@glockenhof.ch – Fax 0442 259 292
– www.glockenhof.ch
C2
95 rm ⊑ – ♦270/340 CHF ♦♦380/470 CHF
Rest 45 CHF (lunch) and a la carte 45/98 CHF
♦ Business ♦ Modern ♦
Its city centre location is only one of the advantages of this well-run hotel. Choose from traditionally decorated rooms or tasteful modern ones. Enjoy the pleasantly relaxed terrace of the traditional Glogge-Stube restaurant or Bistro Glogge-Egge.

Kindli
📷 🍴rm 📞 VISA ⚫ ⍺ ⑩

Pfalzgasse 1 ⊠ 8001 – 𝒞 0438 887 676 – reservations@kindli.ch
– Fax 0438 887 677 – www.kindli.ch
C2
20 rm – ♦260/340 CHF ♦♦360/420 CHF
Rest *Zum Kindli* (closed Sunday and Bank Holidays) a la carte 51/96 CHF
♦ Traditional ♦ Cosy ♦
This historic town house with a friendly, informal ambience is decorated in English country-house style; Laura Ashley design sets the tone in its individually styled rooms. Family atmosphere. Discreetly elegant restaurant offers contemporary cooking.

Walhalla without rest
↔ 📷 📞 🏛15/20 VISA ⚫ ⍺ ⑩

Limmatstr. 5 ⊠ 8005 – 𝒞 0444 465 400 – walhalla-hotel@bluewin.ch
– Fax 0444 465 454 – www.walhalla-hotel.ch
C1
48 rm – ♦140/170 CHF ♦♦190/220 CHF, ⊑ 15 CHF
♦ Business ♦ Functional ♦
Good public transport access, by a tram stop behind the main station. Rooms with dark wood furniture and paintings of gods disporting themselves.

SWITZERLAND

XX Carlton   🛱 🔼 ⟷30/60 _VISA_ 🐾 🔼 ①
Bahnhofstr. 41 ⊠ *8001 –* ℰ *0442 271 919 – info@carlton.ch*
– Fax 0442 271 927 – www.carlton.ch   **C2**
Rest *(closed Sunday and Bank Holidays)* 43 CHF (lunch)/99 CHF and a la carte
55/108 CHF 🌸
• Contemporary • Trendy •
A spacious restaurant, elegantly decorated in Art Deco style. The kitchen
produces modern dishes, the wine cellar is open to diners and they also serve
afternoon tea.

XX Zunfthaus Zur Waag   🛱 ⟷50/60 _VISA_ 🐾 🔼 ①
Münsterhof 8 ⊠ *8001 –* ℰ *0442 169 966 – zunfthaus-zur-waag@bluewin.ch*
– Fax 0442 169 967 – www.waag.ch   **C2**
Rest (1st floor) 64 CHF (dinner) and a la carte 58/115 CHF
• Traditional • Formal •
The first floor of the hatters' and weavers' guildhall now houses a well-stocked
restaurant with Biedermeier-style décor. Contemporary offerings on the menu.

XX Sala of Tokyo   🛱 _VISA_ 🐾 🔼 ①
Limmatstr. 29 ⊠ *8005 –* ℰ *0442 715 290 – sala@active.ch – Fax 0442 717 807*
– www.sala-of-tokyo.ch
closed 14 to 17 April, 16 July - 7 August, 24 December - 9 January, Saturday lunch,
Sunday and Monday   **C1**
Rest 68 CHF/120 CHF and a la carte 48/122 CHF
• Japanese • Exotic •
Wood-panelled interior with sushi-bar and restaurant, to the rear a section in con-
temporary style with yakitori grills. The kitchen is sure to bring a smile to your lips.

XX Kaiser's Reblaube   🛱 🌸 _VISA_ 🐾 🔼 ①
Glockengasse 7 ⊠ *8001 –* ℰ *0442 212 120 – rest.reblaube@bluewin.ch*
– Fax 0442 212 155 – www.restaurant-reblaube.ch
closed 17 July - 10 August, Monday dinner (except from October - March),
Saturday lunch and Sunday   **C2**
Rest (booking essential) 58 CHF (lunch)/134 CHF and a la carte 74/110 CHF
• Contemporary • Rustic •
Historic townhouse hidden in a maze of streets. Modern cooking in the first floor
Goethe-Stübli; modern cuisine in the lively wine bar, which has a garden.

X Heugümper   🔼 ⟷35 _VISA_ 🐾 🔼 ①
Waaggasse 4 ⊠ *8001 –* ℰ *0442 111 660 – info@restaurantheuguemper.ch*
– Fax 0442 111 661 – www.restaurantheuguemper.ch
closed 15 July - 13 August, 31 December - 8 January, Saturday (except dinner from
October - December), Sunday and Bank Holidays   **C2**
Rest a la carte 74/130 CHF
• Contemporary • Bistro •
In the part of the Old Town around the Fraumünster this restaurant consists of a
smart bistro and an elegant dining room, both serving dishes with a modern
twist.

RIGHT BANK OF THE RIVER LIMMAT *(University, Fine Arts Museum)*
Plan II

🏨 Zürich Marriott   ⇐ 🛁 🛏 🔲 ੬.rm 🔼 ↻rm 🌸rest 📺 📞 🛁15/250
Neumühlequai 42 ⊠ *8001 –* ℰ *0443 607 070*   ⟴ _VISA_ 🐾 🔼 ①
– marriott.zurich@marriotthotels.com – Fax 0443 607 777   **C1**
252 rm – †295/405 CHF ††305/450 CHF, ⟳ 34 CHF – 9 suites
Rest *White Elephant (closed Saturday lunch and Sunday lunch)* (Thai rest.)
38 CHF (lunch)/75 CHF and a la carte 54/105 CHF
Rest *La Brasserie* – a la carte 45/97 CHF
• Chain hotel • Classic •
This tall building with basement parking and riverside location offers
comfortable, modern, recently renovated rooms varying in size and décor. The
White Elephant restaurant is modern, in bold lines, while the Brasserie is
elegantly simple.

Sofitel 🛋 ⚹ 🆔 ⅓rm 🖿 📞 🔖15/40 🚗 **VISA** **⓪** **AE** **①**
Stampfenbachstr. 60 ⊠ 8006 – ℰ 0443 606 060 – h1196@accor.com
– Fax 0443 606 061 – www.sofitel.com **C1**
149 rm – ♦220/450 CHF ♦♦260/450 CHF, ☷ 32 CHF – 4 suites
Rest *Bel Etage* 32 CHF (lunch)/68 CHF and a la carte 54/102 CHF
◆ Chain hotel ◆ Stylish ◆
Attractive décor throughout, based on the use of wood and warm colours, from the foyer in the style of an elegant Swiss chalet to the soundproofed rooms. A wide-ranging menu is served in the Bel Etage restaurant.

Central Plaza 🛋 ⅙ 🆔 rm ⅓rm 🖿 📞 🔖30 🚗 **VISA** **⓪** **AE** **①**
Central 1 ⊠ 8001 – ℰ 0442 565 656 – info@central.ch – Fax 0442 565 657
– www.central.ch **D1**
97 rm – ♦360/385 CHF ♦♦360/385 CHF, ☷ 18 CHF – 5 suites
Rest *King's Cave* (closed Saturday lunch and Sunday lunch) (Grill room)
a la carte 42/92 CHF
◆ Business ◆ Modern ◆
This establishment is right on the River Limmat directly opposite the main station. Rooms are all in the same modern and comfortable style, calculated to meet guests' every need. The vaulted cellars house the King's Cave grill.

Florhof 🛋 ⅓rm 🖿 **VISA** **⓪** **AE** **①**
Florhofgasse 4 ⊠ 8001 – ℰ 0442 502 626 – info@florhof.ch
– Fax 0442 502 627 – www.florhof.ch **D2**
35 rm ☷ – ♦245/290 CHF ♦♦360/380 CHF
Rest (closed 14 to 30 April, 8 to 15 October, 24 December - 8 January, Saturday lunch, Monday -except dinner in summer-, Sunday and Bank Holidays) 44 CHF (lunch)/88 CHF and a la carte 81/118 CHF
◆ Family ◆ Personalised ◆
Tasteful décor characterises the rooms in this lovely old patrician mansion from the 16C. Careful attention to detail and excellent technical facilities throughout. Tempting dishes await diners in the elegant restaurant.

Ambassador 🆔 ⅓rm 🖿 📞 **VISA** **⓪** **AE** **①**
Falkenstr. 6 ⊠ 8008 – ℰ 0442 589 898 – mail@ambassadorhotel.ch
– Fax 0442 589 800 – www.ambassadorhotel.ch **D3**
45 rm – ♦245/335 CHF ♦♦350/470 CHF, ☷ 24 CHF
Rest 59 CHF (dinner) and a la carte 51/116 CHF
◆ Business ◆ Functional ◆
This stately hotel is located right by the opera house on the edge of the city centre. Rooms and suites furnished in contemporary style and provided with excellent technical facilities. Restaurant with fantastical murals depicting scenes from the opera.

Wellenberg without rest ⅓ 📞 **VISA** **⓪** **AE** **①**
Niederdorfstr. 10 ⊠ 8001 – ℰ 0438 884 444
– reservation@hotel-wellenberg.ch – Fax 0438 884 445
– www.hotel-wellenberg.ch **D2**
45 rm ☷ – ♦295/350 CHF ♦♦380/420 CHF
◆ Business ◆ Functional ◆
This establishment is located right in the middle of the Old Town. Modern bedrooms, some in Art Deco style. Elegant breakfast room with a sun terrace and pergola.

Claridge Hotel Tiefenau 🛋 ⅓rm 🖿 📞 **P** **VISA** **⓪** **AE** **①**
Steinwiesstr. 8 ⊠ 8032 – ℰ 0442 678 787 – info@claridge.ch – Fax 0442 512 476
– www.claridge.ch
closed 23 December - 1 January **D3**
31 rm ☷ – ♦205/320 CHF ♦♦320/420 CHF
Rest *Orson's* (closed Sunday) a la carte 52/98 CHF
◆ Traditional ◆ Stylish ◆
This establishment near the city centre dates from 1835. Rooms based on diverse design concepts, some with Louis XV furnishings. Orson's serves contemporary cuisine with an Asian touch.

SWITZERLAND

Opera without rest   AC 🛏 📺 📞 *VISA* 🅌 🆊 ①
Dufourstr. 5 ⊠ 8008 – 𝒞 0442 589 999 – mail@operahotel.ch
– Fax 0442 589 900 – www.operahotel.ch   **D3**
62 rm – ♦225/335 CHF ♦♦320/410 CHF, ⊊ 24 CHF
♦ Business ♦ Functional ♦
Directly opposite the opera house to which this business hotel owes its name.
Well-maintained rooms with contemporary comforts.

Adler   🍴 🛏rm 📺 📞 *VISA* 🅌 🆊 ①
Rosengasse 10, at Hirschenplatz ⊠ 8001 – 𝒞 0442 669 696
– info@hotel-adler.ch – Fax 0442 669 669 – www.hotel-adler.ch   **D2**
52 rm ⊊ – ♦170/270 CHF ♦♦220/270 CHF
Rest *Swiss Chuchi* (closed Christmas) a la carte 42/90 CHF
♦ Business ♦ Functional ♦
Rooms with bright, functional wooden furniture and up-to-the-minute technical
facilities are also hung with pictures of old Zurich by Haus Blum. Country-style
ambience in the rustic Swiss-Chuchi restaurant facing the street.

Helmhaus without rest   AC 🛏 🍽 📺 📞 *VISA* 🅌 🆊 ①
Schifflände 30 ⊠ 8001 – 𝒞 0442 669 595 – hotel@helmhaus.ch
– Fax 0442 669 566 – www.helmhaus.ch   **D3**
24 rm ⊊ – ♦175/280 CHF ♦♦240/342 CHF
♦ Business ♦ Functional ♦
In the very heart of the city, this hotel offers rooms most of which have bright
and functional décor featuring white built-in furniture. Breakfast on the first
floor.

Rütli without rest   ⇐ 🛏 🛏 📞 *VISA* 🅌 🆊 ①
Zähringerstr. 43 ⊠ 8001 – 𝒞 0442 545 800 – info@rutli.ch – Fax 0442 545 801
– www.rutli.ch
closed 22 December - 3 January   **D1**
62 rm ⊊ – ♦170/195 CHF ♦♦260/290 CHF
♦ Business ♦ Functional ♦
Located near the station, this hotel has a prettily furnished lobby, bedrooms with
straightforward modern furnishings, and a generous breakfast buffet.

Hirschen without rest   🛏 📺 *VISA* 🅌
Niederdorfstr. 13 ⊠ 8001 – 𝒞 0432 683 333
– info@hirschen-zuerich.ch – Fax 0432 683 334
– www.hirschen-zuerich.ch   **D2**
27 rm ⊊ – ♦135/150 CHF ♦♦175/200 CHF
♦ Family ♦ Functional ♦
The 300 year-old Hirschen offers practical, modern rooms and a wine bar in the
vaulted cellars, which date back to the 16C.

✗✗ **Stapferstube**   🍴 🛏 ☼15 *VISA* 🅌 🆊
Culmannstr. 45 ⊠ 8006 – 𝒞 0443 613 748 – restaurant@stapferstube.ch
– Fax 0443 640 060 – www.stapferstube.ch
closed 23 July - 14 August, Sunday and Monday   Plan I **B3**
Rest a la carte 63/113 CHF
♦ Traditional ♦ Formal ♦
Under new management this tradition-laden address still offers classic dishes
such as boiled meat and the legendary veal steak – but also contemporary
cuisine with Mediterranean influences.

✗✗ **Haus Zum Rüden**   AC ☼30/150 *VISA* 🅌 🆊 ①
Limmatquai 42 (1st floor) ⊠ 8001 – 𝒞 0442 619 566
– info@hauszumrueden.ch – Fax 0442 611 804
– www.hauszumrueden.ch
closed Christmas, Saturday and Sunday   **D2**
Rest 58 CHF (lunch)/138 CHF and a la carte 71/140 CHF
♦ International ♦ Rustic ♦
This restaurant, with an amazing wooden ceiling, is in a 13C guild house. The
elegant, historical atmosphere is in keeping with a classic menu.

XX **Zunfthaus zur Zimmerleuten** 🕽 🎟 ⇕25/120 *VISA* ⚫⚫ 🎟 ⓪

Limmatquai 40 ⊠ 8001 – ℰ 0442 505 363
– zimmerleuten@kramergastro.ch – Fax 0442 505 364
– www.zunfthaus-zimmerleuten.ch
closed 24 July - 8 August, Christmas and New Year **D2**
Rest (1st floor) 37 CHF (lunch) and a la carte 59/114 CHF
Rest *Küferstube* 58 CHF/76 CHF and a la carte 36/82 CHF
♦ Traditional ♦ Rustic ♦
Built in 1708 as a carpenters' guildhall: carved beams set a welcoming tone in the
first floor restaurant; with old barrels and dark wood fittings in the Küferstube.
Attractive terrace.

XX **Casa Ferlin** 🎟 *VISA* ⚫⚫ 🎟 ⓪

Stampfenbachstr. 38 ⊠ 8006 – ℰ 0443 623 509 – casaferlin@bluewin.ch
– Fax 0443 623 534 – www.casaferlin.ch
closed mid July - mid August, Saturday and Sunday **C-D1**
Rest (booking essential) 52 CHF (lunch)/105 CHF and a la carte 61/127 CHF
♦ Italian ♦ Rustic ♦
This classically styled restaurant, with its open fireplace and rustic furnishings,
has been family run since 1907: it's one of the oldest Italian restaurants in the city.

XX **Vorderer Sternen** 🕽 ⅘ *VISA* ⚫⚫ 🎟 ⓪
😳
Theaterstr. 22 ⊠ 8001 – ℰ 0442 514 949 – info@vorderer-sternen.ch
– Fax 0442 529 063 – www.vorderer-sternen.ch **D3**
Rest (1st floor) a la carte 51/106 CHF 🍴
♦ Traditional ♦ Rustic ♦
Straightforward café on the ground floor, above it a homely restaurant with dark
wood décor. Traditional menu.

XX **Blue Monkey Cocostin** 🕽 ⇕20 *VISA* ⚫⚫ 🎟 ⓪

Stüssihofstatt 3 ⊠ 8001 – ℰ 0442 617 618 – koenigstuhl@bluewin.ch
– Fax 0442 627 123 – www.bluemonkey.ch
closed Saturday lunch and Sunday lunch **D2**
Rest (1st floor) 60 CHF (dinner) and a la carte 53/96 CHF
♦ Thai ♦ Exotic ♦
A Thai restaurant has been established on two floors of the historic guildhall
called the Zunfthaus zur Schneidern. Ground floor bar-bistro, fine dining above.

X **Oepfelchammer** 🕽 ⇕30 *VISA* ⚫⚫ 🎟 ⓪

Rindermarkt 12 ⊠ 8001 – ℰ 0442 512 336 – Fax 0442 627 533
closed 17 July - 12 August, 24 December - 7 January, Monday, Sunday and Bank
Holidays **D2**
Rest (1st floor) a la carte 53/93 CHF
♦ Traditional ♦ Rustic ♦
The famous 19C Swiss writer Gottfried Keller was a regular in the wine bar in this
14C establishment. Good solid fare in the restaurant including local specialities.

X **Rosaly's** 🕽 *VISA* ⚫⚫ 🎟 ⓪
😳
Freieckgasse 7 ⊠ 8001 – ℰ 0442 614 430 – info@rosalys.ch – Fax 0442 614 413
– www.rosalys.ch **D3**
Rest *(closed Saturday lunch and Sunday lunch)* a la carte 44/83 CHF
♦ Contemporary ♦ Trendy ♦
Contemporary, simply furnished restaurant with relaxed atmosphere, offering
interesting international dishes prepared in a refined traditional style.

X **Frieden** 🕽 ⅘ *VISA* ⚫⚫ 🎟 ⓪

Stampfenbachstr. 32 ⊠ 8006 – ℰ 0442 531 810 – Fax 0442 531 812
closed 2 to 18 April, 1 to 15 October, 23 December - 3 January,
Saturday and Sunday **D1**
Rest a la carte 55/104 CHF
♦ Euro-asiatic ♦ Bistro ♦
Housed in a municipal building, this is a bistro-style restaurant with plain
wooden furnishings and parquet flooring. Friendly service.

SWITZERLAND

Ban Song Thai
 VISA ●● AE

Kirchgasse 6 ⊠ 8001 – ℰ 0442 523 331 – bansong @ bluewin.ch
– Fax 0442 523 315 – www.bansongthai.ch
closed 17 July - 7 August, 24 December - 3 January, Saturday lunch and
Sunday   **D2**
Rest (booking essential) 59 CHF and a la carte 47/99 CHF
   ◆ Thai ◆ Exotic ◆
This restaurant is very close to the Kunsthaus and Cathedral. Its name evokes its offerings - you are cordially invited by your hosts to take a gastronomic trip to Thailand.

NEAR THE AIRPORT *(Glattbrugg, Kloten)*   *Plan I*

Renaissance Zürich Hotel
 ㄈ 孙 ☒ ㅎrm ⅘ ⅙rest 📶 📞

Talackerstr. 1 ⊠ 8152 Glattbrugg   ⅍15/300 ☎ VISA ●● AE ①
– ℰ 0448 745 000 – renaissance.zurich @ renaissancehotels.com
– Fax 0448 745 001 – www.renaissancehotels.com/zrhrn   **B2**
196 rm – ♥255/295 CHF ♥♥255/385 CHF, ☲ 30 CHF – 8 suites
Rest *Asian Place (closed 17 July - 20 August, 23 December - 2 January, Saturday lunch and Sunday lunch)* (Asian rest.) a la carte 54/120 CHF
Rest *Brasserie* a la carte 48/97 CHF
   ◆ Business ◆ Classic ◆
In a building complex with an extensive basement-level leisure area, this establishment offers rooms nearly all of which have tasteful, dark furnishings. To the rear of the foyer, the brasserie offers a range of contemporary cuisine.

Hilton
ㄈ 孙 Ⓐⓒ ⅙rm 📶 📞 ⅍15/280 ℗ VISA ●● AE ①

Hohenbühlstr. 10 ⊠ 8152 Glattbrugg – ℰ 0448 285 050 – zurich @ hilton.ch
– Fax 0448 285 151 – www.hilton.de/zurich   **B1**
310 rm – ♥199/404 CHF ♥♥199/404 CHF, ☲ 35 CHF – 13 suites
Rest *Market Place* 59 CHF and a la carte 58/112 CHF
   ◆ Chain hotel ◆ Modern ◆
Close to the airport, this establishment offers freshly refurbished rooms with bright maplewood furnishings. New executive rooms have been provided on two floors. Open kitchen in the Market Place restaurant.

Mövenpick
ㄈ ㅎrm Ⓐⓒ ⅙rm 📶 📞 ⅍15/220 ℗ VISA ●● AE ①

Walter Mittelholzerstr. 8 ⊠ 8152 Glattbrugg – ℰ 0448 088 888
– hotel.zurich.airport @ moevenpick.ch – Fax 0448 088 877
– www.movenpick-zurich.com   **B1**
333 rm – ♥199/485 CHF ♥♥199/485 CHF, ☲ 29 CHF
Rest *Appenzeller Stube (closed Saturday lunch)* 45 CHF (lunch)/85 CHF
and a la carte 54/121 CHF
Rest *Mövenpick Rest.* a la carte 36/107 CHF
Rest *Dim Sum (closed Sunday)* (Chinese rest.) a la carte 42/112 CHF
   ◆ Chain hotel ◆ Modern ◆
This hotel is right by the exit off the motorway. All of the rooms have tasteful, some have exercise equipment. Enjoy the typically Swiss atmosphere in the Appenzeller Stube or try International dishes in the Mövenpick restaurant.

Novotel Zürich Airport Messe
ℛ ㄈ 孙 ㅎrm Ⓐⓒ rm ⅘rest 📶

Talackerstr. 21 ⊠ 8152 Glattbrugg   ⅍15/150 ☎ ℗ VISA ●● AE ①
– ℰ 0448 299 000 – h0884-fb @ accor.com – Fax 0448 299 999
– www.novotel.com   **A-B1**
255 rm – ♥205 CHF ♥♥205 CHF, ☲ 25 CHF
Rest a la carte 42/90 CHF
   ◆ Chain hotel ◆ Modern ◆
On the edge of the town centre and just a few minutes from the new trade fair centre, this hotel offers convenient parking and functional rooms with lightwood furnishings.

NH Zürich Airport
Ƙ 𝕞 ⅙rm 🅐🅚 ⅔rm ⅀rest 🆔 🕻 🕻 🔒15/45

Schaffhauserstr. 101 ⊠ 8152 Glattbrugg – ℰ 0448 085 000 – 🚗 🆅🅸🆂🅰 🄼🄾 🄰🄴 🄾
– nhzurichairport@nh-hotels.com – Fax 0448 085 100
– www.nh-hotels.com **B1**
140 rm – ♥200/340 CHF ♥♥200/340 CHF, � 26 CHF
Rest (closed Saturday lunch and Sunday lunch) 30 CHF (lunch)/60 CHF
and a la carte 57/86 CHF
◆ Chain hotel ◆ Functional ◆
The rooms of this airport hotel with their contemporary, functional décor and furnishings are above all suitable for business travellers. Shuttle service to the airport.

Allegra
🏠 Ƙrm ⅙ ⅀rest 🆔 🕻 🔒15/30 🄿 🆅🅸🆂🅰 🄼🄾 🄰🄴 🄾

Hamelirainstr. 3 ⊠ 8302 Kloten – ℰ 0448 044 444
– reservation@hotel-allegra.ch – Fax 0448 044 141
– www.hotel-allegra.ch **B1**
132 rm ⊟ – ♥185 CHF ♥♥230 CHF
Rest a la carte 36/80 CHF
◆ Business ◆ Modern ◆
New business hotel offers spacious, well-soundproofed rooms with colourful built-in furniture. Free airport bus service. Modern restaurant: Swiss favourites and a salad bar.

Fly Away
🏠 Ƙrm 🅐🅚 rm ⅙rm 🆔 🕻 🚗 🄿 🆅🅸🆂🅰 🄼🄾 🄰🄴 🄾

Marktgasse 19 ⊠ 8302 Kloten – ℰ 0448 044 455 – reservation@hotel-flyaway.ch
– Fax 0448 044 450 – www.hotel-flyaway.ch
closed 23 December - 3 January (Hotel only) **B1**
42 rm – ♥120/155 CHF ♥♥176/202 CHF, ⊟ 15 CHF
Rest Mercato (Italian rest.) a la carte 33/81 CHF
◆ Business ◆ Functional ◆
Close to the station, this hotel has spacious rooms all similar in décor and layout and all with timeless, functional furnishings.The Mercato restaurant is Mediterranean in style with contemporary décor and wooden furnishings.

✗✗ Vivendi
🏠 🅐🅚 ⟷20 🄿 🆅🅸🆂🅰 🄼🄾 🄰🄴 🄾

Europastr. 2 – ℰ 0432 113 242 – info@restaurant-vivendi.ch – Fax 0432 113 241
– www.restaurant-vivendi.ch
closed 24 December - 2 January, Saturday,
Sunday and Bank Holidays **B1**
Rest 49 CHF and a la carte 52/100 CHF
◆ Traditional ◆ Trendy ◆
Clean lines and a pleasantly muted colour scheme set the tone in this modern restaurant, which serves traditionally presented cuisine with modern touches.

✗ Rias
🏠 🆅🅸🆂🅰 🄼🄾 🄰🄴

Gerbegasse 6 ⊠ 8302 Kloten – ℰ 0448 142 652 – info@rias.ch
– Fax 0448 135 504 – www.rias.ch **B1**
Rest (closed Saturday dinner and Sunday) a la carte 44/99 CHF
◆ Traditional ◆ Family ◆
This contemporary style restaurant is tucked away rather unobtrusively down a little street. Separate bar and à la carte dining room offering reliable traditional fare.

ENVIRONS OF ZURICH
Plan I

Eden au Lac
≤ 𝕞 🅐🅚 ⅀rest 🆔 🕻 🔒20 🄿 🆅🅸🆂🅰 🄼🄾 🄰🄴 🄾

Utoquai 45 ⊠ 8008 – ℰ 0442 662 525 – info@edenaulac.ch – Fax 0442 662 500
– www.edenaulac.ch **B3**
45 rm ⊟ – ♥420/490 CHF ♥♥640/710 CHF – 5 suites
Rest 59 CHF (lunch)/120 CHF and a la carte 71/140 CHF
◆ Luxury ◆ Classic ◆
Having set the architectural tone for Zurich's lakeside in 1909, this neo-Baroque hotel is now a listed cultural monument. Inside you will find everything you expect from a luxury hotel. The restaurant offers contemporary cuisine.

SWITZERLAND

Steigenberger Bellerive au Lac

Utoquai 47 ✉ 8008 15/25 VISA
– ☎ 0442 544 000 – bellerive@steigenberger.ch – Fax 0442 544 001
– www.zuerich.steigenberger.ch **B3**
51 rm – 310/450 CHF 430/490 CHF
Rest 53 CHF (lunch) and a la carte 54/127 CHF
◆ Traditional ◆ Stylish ◆
With its elegant décor in the style of the 1920s, this establishment stands on the lakeside. State-of-the-art design, comfort, and technical facilities in every room. Small, stylish restaurant with classic décor and beautifully upholstered seating.

Ascot

rm 15/30 VISA
Tessinerplatz 9 ✉ 8002 – ☎ 0442 081 414 – info@ascot.ch – Fax 0442 081 420
– www.ascot.ch **A3**
74 rm – 395/440 CHF 490/590 CHF
Rest ***Lawrence*** *(closed Saturday and Sunday)* 62 CHF (lunch) and a la carte 65/118 CHF
◆ Traditional ◆ Classic ◆
This stylishly decorated establishment offers rooms with furniture in either mahogany or limewashed oak. The Lawrence is decorated in Tudor style

Alden Hotel Splügenschloss

rest rm 20
Splügenstr. 2 ✉ 8002 – ☎ 0442 899 999 VISA
– welcome@alden.ch – Fax 0442 899 998 – www.alden.ch **A3**
10 rm – 700/1100 CHF 700/1100 CHF – 12 suites
Rest ***Gourmet*** *(closed Saturday and Sunday)* 68 CHF (lunch) and a la carte 83/150 CHF
Rest ***Bar / Bistro*** a la carte 56/102 CHF
◆ Grand Luxury ◆ Design ◆
Up-to-the-minute suites decorated in elegant designer style, behind a splendidly imposing late 19C façade. The tasteful formal restaurant serves contemporary dishes.

Inter-Continental Zurich

rm rm
Badenerstr. 420 ✉ 8040 – ☎ 0444 15/300 VISA
044 444 – zurich@interconti.com – Fax 0444 044 440
– www.intercontinental.com/zurich **A3**
364 rm – 300/370 CHF 300/370 CHF, 32 CHF
Rest ***Relais des Arts*** 45 CHF (lunch) and a la carte 57/93 CHF
◆ Business ◆ Functional ◆
Among the amenities of this hotel - as well as its comfortable and functional contemporary style rooms - is its accessibility to the airport and the motorway. Guests are invited to dine in the bright and elegant surroundings of the Relais des Arts.

Dolder Waldhaus

Zurich and lake, rest
Kurhausstr. 20 ✉ 8032 rm 15/30 VISA
– ☎ 0442 691 000 – reservations@dolderwaldhaus.ch – Fax 0442 691 001
– www.dolderwaldhaus.ch **B3**
70 rm – 240/310 CHF 370/460 CHF, 20 CHF
Rest a la carte 55/106 CHF
◆ Business ◆ Classic ◆
In a quiet location, this hotel offers rooms in modern style, all with balcony and fine views over city and lake, plus apartments for families or longer stays. There's a traditional atmosphere in the restaurant, which has a pleasant terrace.

Engimatt

rm rm 15/25 VISA
Engimattstr. 14 ✉ 8002 – ☎ 0442 841 616 – info@engimatt.ch
– Fax 0442 012 516 – www.engimatt.ch **A3**
74 rm – 230/340 CHF 295/390 CHF
Rest 43 CHF (lunch)/75 CHF and a la carte 45/90 CHF
◆ Business ◆ Modern ◆
Close to the city centre but nevertheless in an attractively leafy setting. Rooms solidly furnished in contemporary style, some with a tastefully rustic touch. The Orangerie restaurant is a modern interpretation of a winter garden in steel and glass.

SWITZERLAND

Mercure Hotel Stoller
🏠 ➙ ⨯rest 🖾 ⵵15/25 *VISA* 🐵 ⒜ ⓘ

Badenerstr. 357 ⊠ 8003 – ℰ 0444 054 747
– h5488@accor.com – Fax 0444 054 848 – www.mercure.com   **A3**
78 rm – ⴓ185/199 CHF ⴓⴓ185/199 CHF, ⌷ 17 CHF
Rest *Ratatouille* a la carte 41/101 CHF
♦ Chain hotel ♦ Functional ♦
On the edge of the city centre close to a tram stop. Rooms in similar style with furnishings in grey veneer. Quieter rooms with balcony to the rear. The two-room Ratatouille is furnished in dark wood: it opens up its street café in summer.

Greulich
🏠 ⅙ ➙rm 🖾 ⓣ ⵵20 🅿 *VISA* 🐵 ⒜ ⓘ

Herman Greulich-Str. 56 ⊠ 8004 – ℰ 0432 434 243 – mail@greulich.ch
– Fax 0432 434 200 – www.greulich.ch   **A3**
18 rm – ⴓ195 CHF ⴓⴓ275 CHF, ⌷ 20 CHF
Rest *(closed Sunday lunch)* 78 CHF and a la carte 73/111 CHF
♦ Business ♦ Modern ♦
Trim, modern, practically equipped garden rooms and mini-suites face a courtyard garden shaded by birches. Simple styling, warm colours, and parquet floors set the tone in the restaurant. Interesting Spanish-inspired cuisine.

Krone Unterstrass
🅰🅺rm ⅙rm ⨯rest 🖾 ⓣ ⵵15/75

Schaffhauserstr. 1 ⊠ 8006 – ℰ 0443 605 656   🅿 *VISA* 🐵 ⒜ ⓘ
– info@hotel-krone.ch – Fax 0443 605 600 – www.hotel-krone.ch   **A2**
57 rm – ⴓ170/195 CHF ⴓⴓ230/250 CHF, ⌷ 18 CHF
Rest a la carte 48/97 CHF
♦ Business ♦ Modern ♦
Just above the city centre, this establishment offers classically comfortable, newly refitted rooms in a tasteful, modern style. One of the restaurants boasts a splendid open fireplace.

Novotel Zürich City-West
🏠 🛦 🖵 ⅙rm ⅙rm ⵵15/120

Schiffbaustr. 13 ⊠ 8005 – ℰ 0442 762 222   🚗 *VISA* 🐵 ⒜ ⓘ
– H2731@accor.com – Fax 0442 762 323 – www.novotel.com   **A2**
142 rm ⌷ – ⴓ224/230 CHF ⴓⴓ249/255 CHF
Rest a la carte 40/101 CHF
♦ Chain hotel ♦ Modern ♦
This newly-built hotel with its cladding of black glass offers identical, contemporary style and reasonably spacious rooms featuring white built-in furniture.

Rigihof
🏠 ⅙rm ⅙rm 🖾 ⓣ ⵵20 🅿 *VISA* 🐵 ⒜ ⓘ

Universitätstr. 101 ⊠ 8006 – ℰ 0443 601 200 – info@hotel-rigihof.ch
– Fax 0443 601 207 – www.hotel-rigihof.ch   **B2**
66 rm ⌷ – ⴓ190/250 CHF ⴓⴓ215/360 CHF
Rest *Bauhaus* 42 CHF and a la carte 47/84 CHF
♦ Business ♦ Design ♦
Designed in timeless Bauhaus style, the hotel offers rooms that are linked in an artistic way to personalities associated with Zurich and are named after them. Bold lines and colours distinguish the Bauhaus restaurant.

Ibis
🏠 ⅙rm ⅙rm 🖾 🚗 *VISA* 🐵 ⒜ ⓘ

Schiffbaustr. 11 ⊠ 8005 – ℰ 0442 762 100 – h2942@accor.com
– Fax 0442 762 101 – www.ibishotel.com   **A2**
155 rm – ⴓ124/134 CHF ⴓⴓ124/134 CHF, ⌷ 14 CHF
Rest *(closed Saturday lunch and Sunday lunch)* a la carte 35/64 CHF
♦ Chain hotel ♦ Minimalist ♦
This hotel is on the site of the old shipbuilding sheds: practical rooms provide all the essentials for what is a very reasonable price.

Sonnenberg
≤ Zurich and lake, 🏠 ⅙ 🅿 *VISA* 🐵 ⒜ ⓘ

Hitziweg 15 ⊠ 8032 – ℰ 0442 669 797 – restaurant@sonnenberg-zh.ch
– Fax 0442 669 798 – www.sonnenberg-zh.ch   **B3**
Rest *(booking essential)* (veal and beef specialities) a la carte 76/141 CHF
♦ International ♦ Fashionable ♦
High up in the FIFA Building with a grandstand view of city, lake, and Alps. Classic French dishes served in the half-moon-shaped panoramic restaurant.

SWITZERLAND

XXX ✿

Rigiblick - Rest Spice (Eppisser) with rm ☜ ← Zurich, 🌴 🚃
Germaniastr. 99 ⊠ 8006 – ✆ 0432 551 570 ᘒ VISA ⑯ 🄰🄴 ⓪
– eppisser@restaurantrigiblick.ch – Fax 0432 551 580
– www.restaurantrigiblick.ch
closed Sunday and Monday **B2**
7 rm � – ♦380/750 CHF ♦♦380/750 CHF
Rest (booking essential) 54 CHF (lunch)/140 CHF and a la carte 98/125 CHF ⅋
Rest Bistro Quadrino a la carte 48/83 CHF
Spec. Wrap von Hummer mit gebratenem Scampo, Tomatenemulsion mit
Sambal verfeinert. Tom Ka Gai Nage mit Jakobsmuscheln unter der roten
Currykruste. Bengalisch gewürztes Lammrückenfilet auf Süsskartoffeln mit
"Spicy Joghurtsauce".
♦ Euro-asiatic ♦ Fashionable ♦
Straightforward, elegant design and an unsurpassed view epitomise Restaurant
Spice. Impressive Western and Asian cuisine. Ultra-modern apartment
studios. Trendy bistro with snack bar, lounge and wine display area open to
diners.

XX

Wirtschaft Flühgass ⟲20 P VISA ⑯ 🄰🄴
Zollikerstr. 214 ⊠ 8008 – ✆ 0443 811 215 – info@fluehgass.ch
– Fax 0444 227 532 – www.fluehgass.ch
closed 14 July - 13 August, 24 December - 2 January, Saturday (except dinner from
November - December) and Sunday **B3**
Rest (booking essential) 65 CHF/135 CHF and a la carte 57/119 CHF
♦ Contemporary ♦ Family ♦
The old 16C wine bar is now a congenial restaurant serving cuisine with a
traditional French flavour.

XX

Riesbächli ᘒ VISA ⑯ 🄰🄴 ⓪
Zollikerstr. 157 ⊠ 8008 – ✆ 0444 222 324 – Fax 0444 222 941
closed 22 July - 13 August, 25 December - 2 January, Saturday (except dinner from
November - March) and Sunday **B3**
Rest 110 CHF and a la carte 65/143 CHF ⅋
♦ International ♦ Rustic ♦
This traditional restaurant is divided up into three visually separate dining areas.
Remarkable choice of wines to go with a range of classic dishes.

XX

Casa Piccoli "Il Gattopardo" 🄰🄺 ↩ ℀ VISA ⑯ 🄰🄴 ⓪
Rotwandstr. 48 ⊠ 8004 – ✆ 0434 434 848 – Fax 0432 438 551
closed 18 July - 14 August, Saturday lunch and Sunday **A3**
Rest 45 CHF (lunch)/95 CHF and a la carte 60/119 CHF
♦ Italian ♦ Formal ♦
High quality classic Italian cuisine, served in an elegant atmosphere. Wine cellar
open to diners (groups).

XX

Lake Side ← Lake Zurich, 🌴 🄰🄺 ℀ ⟲600 VISA ⑯ 🄰🄴 ⓪
Bellerivestr. 170 ⊠ 8008 – ✆ 0443 858 600 – info@lake-side.ch
– Fax 0443 858 601 – www.lake-side.ch **B3**
Rest a la carte 60/119 CHF
♦ Contemporary ♦ Trendy ♦
Choose from contemporary cooking or sushi at this modern restaurant in
Seepark Zürichhorn. The large lakefront terrace is particularly appealing in
summer.

X ☻

Josef VISA ⑯ 🄰🄴 ⓪
Gasometerstr. 24 ⊠ 8005 – ✆ 0442 716 595 – welcome@josef.ch
– Fax 0444 405 564 – www.josef.ch
closed Christmas, New Year, Saturday lunch, Monday lunch
and Sunday **A2**
Rest 59 CHF and a la carte 56/64 CHF
♦ Contemporary ♦ Friendly ♦
This contemporary place with a relaxed atmosphere offers a convincing blend of
well-sourced modern cooking and helpful, personable service.

SWITZERLAND

X **Caduff's Wine Loft** $\overline{VISA}$ **M⊙** **AE** **①**
Kanzleistr. 126 ⊠ 8004 – 𝒞 0442 402 255 – caduff@wineloft.ch
– Fax 0442 402 256 – www.wineloft.ch   **A3**
Rest *(closed 24 December - 3 January, Saturday lunch and Sunday)* (booking essential) 52 CHF (lunch)/115 CHF and a la carte 50/122 CHF 🕮
♦ Contemporary ♦ Trendy ♦
This former wholesale flower market now serves tasty morsels at the long bar and well-sourced dishes accompanied by a fine wine from the famous cellars.

X **Zentraleck** $\overline{VISA}$ **M⊙** **AE** **①**
Zentralstr. 161 ⊠ 8003 – 𝒞 0444 610 800 – restaurant@zentraleck.ch
– Fax 0444 610 801 – www.zentraleck.ch
closed 23 July - 6 August, 1 to 8 January, Saturday and Sunday   **A3**
Rest 78 CHF and a la carte 61/101 CHF
♦ Contemporary ♦ Bistro ♦
Pale walls and wood floors both add to the pleasantly smart, up-to-date feel of the Zentraleck, where little pots of kitchen herbs decorate the tables. Modern menus.

X **Ciro** $\overline{\cdots}$ $\overline{VISA}$ **M⊙** **AE** **①**
Militärstr. 16 ⊠ 8004 – 𝒞 0442 417 841 – ciro@swissonline.ch
– Fax 0442 911 424   **A3**
Rest *(closed Sunday)* a la carte 48/78 CHF
♦ Italian ♦ Friendly ♦
In the welcoming interiors of this restaurant close to the station guests are served with a variety of Italian dishes and the wines to accompany them.

X **Blaue Ente** $\overline{\cdots}$ **⇔25** $\overline{VISA}$ **M⊙** **AE** **①**
Seefeldstr. 223 (mill Tiefenbrunnen) ⊠ 8008 – 𝒞 0443 886 840 – info@
blaue-ente.ch – Fax 0444 227 741 – www.blaue-ente.ch
closed 1 to 9 August   **B3**
Rest (booking essential) a la carte 55/119 CHF 🕮
♦ Contemporary ♦ Fashionable ♦
This trendy establishment with lots of glass, pipework, and gigantic gearwheels is housed in an old mill. Cheerful atmosphere and good, unfussy cooking in a modern style.

UNITED KINGDOM
UNITED KINGDOM

UNITED KINGDOM

PROFILE

- **AREA:**
  244 157 km²
  (94 269 sq mi).

- **POPULATION:**
  60 441 000 inhabitants
  (est. 2005), density =
  248 per km².

- **CAPITAL:**
  London (conurbation
  9 332 000 inhabitants).

- **CURRENCY:**
  Pound sterling (£); rate
  of exchange:
  £ 1 = € 1.46 =
  US$ 1.72
  (Nov 2005).

- **GOVERNMENT:**
  Constitutional
  parliamentary
  monarchy
  (since 1707). Member
  of European Union
  since 1973.

- **LANGUAGE:**
  English.

- **SPECIFIC PUBLIC
  HOLIDAYS:**
  Good Friday (Friday
  before Easter), first
  and last Monday in
  May, last Monday in
  August, Boxing Day
  (26 December).

- **LOCAL TIME:**
  GMT in winter and
  GMT + 1 hour in
  summer.

- **CLIMATE:**
  Temperate maritime
  with cool winters
  and mild summers
  (London: January:
  3°C, July: 17°C),
  rainfall evenly
  distributed
  throughout the year.

Glasgow Edinburgh

Birmingham
London

- **INTERNATIONAL
  DIALLING CODE:**
  00 44 followed by
  area or city code
  (London: **20**, Glasgow:
  141, etc.) and then the
  local number.

- **EMERGENCY:**
  Police, Fire Brigade,
  Ambulance: ☏ **999**.

- **ELECTRICITY:**
  240 volts AC, 50 Hz.
  3 flat pin plugs.

FORMALITIES

Travellers from the European Union (EU), Switzerland, Iceland, the main countries of North and South America and some Commonwealth countries need a national identity card or passport (except for Irish nationals; America: passport required) to visit United Kingdom for less than three months (tourism or business purpose). For visitors from other countries a visa may be required, in addition to a passport, especially for those wishing to stay for longer than three months. We advise you to check with your embassy before travelling.

Nationals of EU countries require a valid national driving licence. US citizens should hold a driving licence valid for 12 months. Insurance cover is compulsory and it is advisable to have an International Insurance Certificate (Green Card).

MAJOR NEWSPAPERS

The main national daily newspapers are *The Times*, *The Daily Telegraph*, *The Independent*, *The Guardian* and *The Financial Times*. *The Observer* is published on Sundays only and *The Evening Standard* is London's evening newspaper. In Scotland the major two newspapers are *The Herald* (Glasgow) and *The Scotsman* (Edinburgh).

HOTELS

◆ CATEGORIES

Accommodation ranges from luxurious 5-star and boutique hotels with a wide choice of amenities to elegant country houses set in splendid grounds offering all kinds of sports and recreation. There are comfortable business hotels and moderately priced establishments as well as a great selection of bed and breakfasts and guesthouses. Some restaurants and pubs also have rooms.

◆ PRICE RANGE

The price is per room. Special rates may be on offer at weekends or in quiet periods. There is very little difference between the cost of a single and a double room. A supplement is usually charged for single occupancy of a double room.

◆ TAX

Tax (VAT) and service charges are included in the room price.

◆ CHECK OUT TIME

Between 10.30am and noon. It is usually possible for luggage to be left with the concierge for collection later in the day.

◆ RESERVATIONS

You can book your accommodation by phone or Internet. Ask for written confirmation by fax or email. Some hotels may require a deposit which may be forfeited in the event of a late cancellation. A credit card number is usually required as a guarantee.

◆ TIPS FOR HANDLING LUGGAGE

It is usual to give a gratuity to luggage porters at the customer's discretion.

◆ BREAKFAST

Breakfast is often not included in the price of the room. It is served between 6.30-7am and 10am. A full cooked English breakfast is generally on offer. Continental breakfast and a self-service buffet with hot dishes are also available.

RESTAURANTS

In addition to the conventional **restaurants** serving international cuisine, there is a multitude of brasseries, ethnic eating places, pizzerias and steak houses. **Gastropubs**, which offer food of an excellent quality at reasonable prices in simple surroundings, have become increasingly popular. In pubs and wine bars you will find less elaborate dishes: pies, steaks, jacket potatoes, pasta dishes, ploughman's lunch (cheese, pickle, bread), sausages and mashed potatoes, stews and curries. Fish and chips shops are an institution: fish in a crisp fried batter and served with golden chipped potatoes.

◆ RESERVATIONS

Reservations can be made by phone or by Internet. For gourmet and smart restaurants, it is advisable to book well in advance. A telephone number is usually required and you may also be asked for a credit card number as a guarantee.

Some restaurants may impose a charge if you do not show up or if you do not give adequate notice in the event of a cancellation.

◆ THE BILL

The bill (check) usually includes an optional service charge (10-15%) which you may choose not to pay if you are not satisfied with the service. Credit cards are widely accepted. Some restaurants leave the total open so make sure you check before signing the voucher. Occasionally a cover charge is levied for bread and canapés which are offered at the start of the meal.

Breakfast	7am – 10am
Lunch	12.30pm – 2-3pm
Dinner	6.30pm – 10-11pm sometimes later

NB: Outside large towns, restaurants may close early. In the north of England and in Scotland, dinner is the term often used for the midday meal and tea for the evening meal.

LOCAL CUISINE

Although the United Kingdom is known for its cosmopolitan and fusion food, many British chefs have become very successful in recent years and modern British cuisine has become fashionable. However there are many regional dishes, all using fresh local products to best advantage, which reflect the nation's history.

The British are very fond of pies of all sorts. **Melton Mowbray pies** consist of succulent lean pork in jelly, with a little anchovy flavouring in a pastry case. Steak and kidney, steak and onion, chicken and mushroom or leek are some of the many varieties of pie baked in puff or shortcrust pastry. **Cornish pasty** is made with beef (skirt), turnip or swede, potatoes and onion baked in a pastry case, shaped like a half-moon, so that it could be carried down the mine to be eaten at midday; sometimes fruit was put at one end to provide a sweet. **Sherwood venison pie** is eaten hot or cold with redcurrant jelly. Game pies are very tasty. Cumberland sauce is not to be missed as an accompaniment to ham or game pies.

Roasted joints of meat are great favourites. The national dish is undoubtedly **roast beef and Yorkshire pudding** – a succulent batter pudding on which the juices of the roasting beef have been allowed to drip – served with horseradish sauce. Lamb is usually eaten with mint sauce, mutton with redcurrant jelly and pork with golden crackling and apple sauce. Other meat dishes include **Dorset jugged steak**, cooked with sausage meat and port; **stuffed chine of pork**, a piece of back of fat pig, stuffed with green herbs; **Welsh honey lamb** cooked in cider with thyme and garlic and basted with honey. **Aylesbury duck** is prepared with green peas. Rabbit is served with forcemeat balls. **Veal collops with orange** are said to have been a favourite dish of Oliver Cromwell. Stews and casseroles are wholesome dishes often served with dumplings: steak and onion, lamb and carrots and in particular, the tasty **Lancashire hotpot. Pigeon casserole** is flavoured with cider and orange.

Fish and seafood dishes include **Dover sole, 'Arnold Bennett omelette'** with haddock and cheese, **mussels in cider and mustard, samphire**, 'poor man's asparagus' eaten with melted butter, **spicy shrimp pie** cooked with wine, mace and cloves in a puff pastry case, **herrings** baked with mint, sage and pepper.

Baked crab and cockle pie is a Welsh dish and the local sea trout – **sewin** – is stuffed with herbs before cooking. **Char**, a freshwater fish, is either cooked straight from the lakes or potted. Whitstable and Colchester oysters, Cromer crabs, Manx kippers, cockles, scallops, potted shrimps in butter, fresh and potted mackerel, potted salmon are some of the local delicacies. **Fish and chips'** is a traditional dish which is popular all over the country.

Scotland is renowned for its beef and lamb, for venison and grouse in season and wild and farmed salmon. **Partan Bree**, a tasty crab soup, **Arbroath smokies**, kippers, mutton pies are some of the specialities. **Haggis** served with swede and potatoes – 'haggis, neeps and tatties' – is a tasty dish often accompanied with a dram of whisky. **Kedgeree** is made with salmon, haddock or other fish, rice, hard-boiled eggs and butter and is usually served at breakfast.

Cheese and biscuits are an essential part of a meal, which usually comes after the pudding or sweet course. There is an increasing variety of cheeses on offer as producers are encouraged to innovate. The traditional **Cheddar** is named after the caves in which it is ripened; the blue-veined **Stilton**, Red Leicester, sage Derby, Gloucester, Cheshire (white and blue vein), the delicate Wensleydale and Caerphilly are enjoyed nationwide.

You should always leave space for a pudding at the end of a meal. **Fruit pies and crumbles** – apple, apple and blackcurrant, gooseberry, plum, cherry, rhubarb – creamy rice puddings, jam roly-poly, spotted dick, steamed jam puddings are delicious with custard. **Trifle** laced with sherry, **bread and butter pudding** and **lemon meringue pie** are scrumptious. **Bakewell tart** is made of shortcrust pastry with an almond and jam filling. **Black caps** are large baked apples filled with brown sugar, citrus peel and raisins. **Devon junket** is laced with rum and brandy. **Cranachan** made with soft fruit and cream and **Atholl Brose**, a mixture of honey, oatmeal, malt whisky and cream are Scottish desserts.

Rich fruit cakes and sponge cakes are teatime treats. Buttery **scones** are served with strawberry jam and clotted cream. Regional specialities include **parkin**, a dark oatmeal cake made with cinnamon, ginger, nutmeg and treacle from Yorkshire; **Bucks cherry bumpers**, cherries in shortcrust pastry; **Goosnargh cakes**, **gingerbread** from the Lake District; Welsh **crempog**, small soft pancakes, eaten hot with butter, and **Bara brith**, a rich moist cake bread, full of raisins, currants, sultanas and citrus peel. **Pikelets** are a cross between a crumpet and a pancake. **Taunton cider cake** includes raisins and a large apple, and the cider is reduced to concentrate the apple flavour.

DRINK

♦ WINE

Wine is generally drunk with meals and the best vintages are available at a price throughout the country. The British have a reputation as serious wine drinkers as is evident from the large quantities imported from all over the world. The local wine industry has improved by leaps and bounds and there are notable wine makers particularly in the south of the country. White wines are often blended from one or more varieties of grape to produce light, dry, fruity wines similar to German wines; red wines are fairly light. A range of fruit-flavoured liqueurs is also available: sloe gin, ginger whisky, whisky mead, raspberry brandy, etc.

◆ BEER

However, the most popular alcoholic drink is **beer**, which can be divided into two principal types: **ales** and **lagers**. It can also be described as keg or cask; there are several different beer styles in Britain and Ireland. **Keg beer** is filtered, pasteurised and chilled and then packed into pressurised containers from which it gets its name. **Cask beer** or 'Real Ale' is not filtered, pasteurised or chilled and is served from casks using simple pumps. It is considered by some to be a more characterful, flavoursome and natural beer. **Bitter** is the most popular traditional beer in England and Wales. It is usually paler and drier than **Mild** with a high hop content and slightly bitter taste. **Mild**, which is largely found in Wales, the West Midlands and the North West of England, is a gentle, sweetish and full-flavoured beer. It is generally lower in alcohol and sometimes darker in colour, owing to the addition of caramel or the use of dark malt. **Stout** has a pronounced roast flavour with plenty of hop bitterness. The best dry stouts are brewed in Ireland and are instantly recognisable by their black colour and creamy head. Sweet stouts, including milk or cream stout are sweetened with sugar before being bottled. In addition there are Pale Ales, Brown Ales and Old Ales whilst the term Barley Wine is frequently used by English breweries to describe their strongest beer.

Although Ireland is most famous for its stouts, it also makes a range of beers which have been variously described as malty, buttery, rounded and fruity with a reddish tinge. In Scotland the beers produced are full bodied and malty.

◆ WHISKY

The term **whisky** is derived from the Scottish Gaelic *uisage beatha* and the Irish Gaelic *uisce beathadh*, both meaning 'water of life'. When spelt without an *e* it usually refers to **Scotch Whisky** which can be produced only in Scotland by the distillation of malted and unmalted barley, maize, rye and mixtures of two or more of these. It can be divided into 2 basic types: malt whisky and grain whisky. **Malt whisky** is produced from malted barley, traditionally dried over peat fires. After fermentation and two distilling processes using a pot still, the whisky is matured in oak, ideally sherry casks, for at least three years which affects both its colour and flavour. A single malt is the product of an individual distillery. All malts have a distinctive smell and intense flavour. Malt whiskies can be divided into 4 classic regions: the Lowlands, the Highlands, Campbeltown and the Isle of Islay. There are approximately 100 malt whisky distilleries in Scotland. Each distillery produces a completely individual whisky of great complexity. **Grain whisky** is made from a mixture of any malted or unmalted cereal such as maize or wheat and is distilled by a continuous process. It matures more quickly than malt whisky. Very little grain whisky is ever drunk unblended. **De Luxe whiskies** are special because of the ages and qualities of the malts and grain whiskies used in them. They usually include a higher proportion of malts than in most blends. **Irish whiskey** is traditionally made from cereals, distilled three times and matured for at least seven years. The different brands are as individual as straight malt and considered by some to be smoother in character.

♦ CIDER

Cider is said to have been brewed from apples since Celtic times. Only bitter apples are used for 'real' West Country cider which is dry in taste, flat and with an alcoholic content of 5.5-5.8%. Full-bodied draught cider is available in pubs. A sparkling cider is produced by fermenting the brew a second time in the bottle. There is also a small production of a strong cider brandy. Genuine perry is made from bitter perry pears.

LONDON

LONDON

Population (est. 2005): 2 914 000 (conurbation 9 332 000) – Altitude: sea level

P./Age Adams/HOA QUI

London is not only the capital of the United Kingdom, but also an international financial centre, a focus of fashion and entertainment, and an important centre for the arts. Before the Middle Ages, the City of London was already a busy commercial centre, while the royal palace and the abbey built by King Edward the Confessor marked the start of the City of Westminster. The differences between them are still evident: the City is the hub of trade and finance, while the West End is renowned for its elegant shops, theatres, clubs, parks, Buckingham Palace and the Houses of Parliament.

This great conurbation started as a Roman settlement on the north bank of the Thames, which evolved into the City of London, the famous square mile of banking houses and commerce. In the 12C London had replaced Winchester as the capital of England and by the 19C was the capital of a worldwide empire. It has grown, without much formal planning, by absorbing the surrounding villages but retained many green open spaces in its extensive royal parks, old commons, churchyards and municipal parks.

London is a great attraction for its tradition and its pageantry, its theatres and concerts, its great range of national and ethnic restaurants and its reputation for clubbing.

WHICH DISTRICT TO CHOOSE

For business visitors it may be best to choose a **hotel** near the City *Plan IX* **AE2** or Canary Wharf, whereas for tourists there is a selection of expensive hotels in the West End and cheaper hotels in the neighbouring suburbs. There are also **B&Bs (bed-and-breakfast)** addresses.

The widest range of choice of **restaurants** is to be found in the West End

(Soho *Plan II* **G1**, Covent Garden *Plan III* **K2**, South Kensington *Plan X* **AI2**) and Bloomsbury (Charlotte Street) but there are also good places on the South Bank *Plan III* **K3**. Smarter restaurants are in Mayfair *Plan II* **F1** and St James's *Plan II* **G2**.

If you are going out for a **drink** the West End, particularly Covent Garden, Soho and Shepherd Market, is well provided

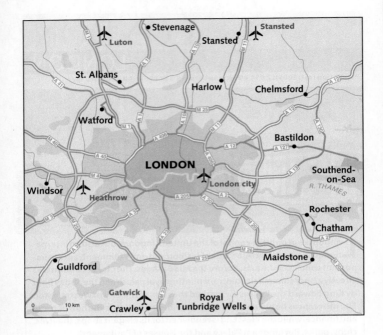

Map showing London and surrounding areas including Stevenage, Stansted, Luton, St. Albans, Harlow, Chelmsford, Watford, Bastildon, Windsor, Heathrow, London city, Southend-on-Sea, Rochester, Chatham, Guildford, Maidstone, Gatwick, Crawley, and Royal Tunbridge Wells.

with traditional pubs, wine bars and clubs; the City and Canary Wharf have many pubs and wine bars, although some are closed in the evenings. In Central London or the suburbs, there is a local pub on almost every corner.

PRACTICAL INFORMATION

ARRIVAL – DEPARTURE

Heathrow Airport – About 32 km (20 mi) west of London. ☎ 650 39 43 (flight information).

From the airport to Central London – By **rail**: **Heathrow Express** (15min) to Paddington Railway Station (5.10am-11.25pm); £14, return £26; ☎ 0845 600 1515; www.heathro wexpress.com. By **underground**: Piccadilly Line (50min) to Piccadilly Circus (Mon-Fri 5.15am-11.50am, Sun 7am-11.30pm); £3.80 (Zone 1-6 tic-ket); ☎ 020 7222 1234; www.tfl. gov.uk. By **bus**: at night N9 shuttles between Heathrow and Central London every 30min. By **taxi**: 40min

to 1hr (depending on traffic conditions), £55 approx.

Gatwick Airport – 48 km (30 mi) south of London. ☎ 01293 535353.

From the airport to Central London – By **rail**: Gatwick Express (30min) to Victoria Station (5am-11.45pm, every 15min); £14, return £25; ☎ 0845 600 1515; www.gatwickex press.com By **rail**: Southern Trains (40min) to Victoria Station (every 15min); £9; ☎ 0870 830 6000; www.southern-railway.com. By **rail**: Thameslink Rail (30min) to London Bridge or (40min) to King Cross (day time every 15min; at night every 1hr; £10; ☎ 0845 330 3660). By **coach**: National Express Speedlink (1hr 20min) to Victoria Coach

Station (7am-11.30pm); £6, return £11; ℰ 08705 757 747; www.nationalexpress.com/airport By **taxi**: 90min (subject to traffic conditions), £77 approx.

City Airport – About 13 km (6 mi) east of London. ℰ 020 7646 0000.

From the airport to Central London – By **bus**: Airport Shuttle (10min) to Canning Town and Canary Wharf and (25min) to Liverpool Street (6am-9pm); £3, £3.50, £6.50; ℰ 020 7222 1234; www.tfl.gov.uk; www.londoncit yairport.com By **rail**: Docklands Light railway (from 2006) to Bank Station on the underground. By **taxi**: 30min (depending on traffic), £30 approx.

Luton Airport – About 56 km (35 mi) northwest of London. ℰ 01582 405 100.

From the airport to Central London – By **rail**: Thameslink (40min) to Kings Cross Station (4.30am-1.30am, 1-3 times per hr); £10.40, return £10.60; ℰ 0845 330 6333; www.thameslink.co.uk By **coach**: Greenline (1hr) to Buckingham Palace Road (near Victoria Station) (4.30am-1.30am, 1-3 times per hr); £9, return £12; ℰ 0870 608 7261; www.greenline.co.uk

Stansted Airport – About 56 km (34 mi) northeast of London. ℰ 0870 000 0303, 01279 680 500.

From the airport to Central London – By **rail**: Stansted Express (45min) to Liverpool Street Station (5.30-0.30am, every 15min); £15; return £25; ℰ 0845 850 0150, www.stanstedexpress.com By **coach**: National Express (1hr 45min) to Victoria Coach Station (24hr service, every 15min); £10, return £15; ℰ 08705 757 747; www.nationalexpress.com/airport By **coach**: Terravision (1hr 15min) to Victoria and (1hr) to Liverpool Street (7.30-1am); £8.50, return £14; ℰ 020 7630 7196; www.terravision.it

Railway Stations – There are 8 London termini: **Charing Cross** *Plan III* **J2** (via London Bridge) Southeast England. **Euston** *Plan VI* **T1** North West England; North Wales. **King's Cross** *Plan VI* **U1** Thameslink to St Albans, Hatfield, Brighton; Northeast England; East Scotland; **Liverpool Street** East Anglia. **Marylebone** *Plan V* **Q1** Chiltern Lines to Warwick and Stratford. **Paddington** *Plan VIII* **AB1** Thames Valley; Cotswolds; West of England; South Wales. **St Pancras** *Plan VI* **T1** Nottingham; the Peak District. **Victoria** *Plan IV* **M2** Gatwick Express: Southern England. **Waterloo** *Plan III* **K3** Southwest England. National Rail Enquiry Line ℰ 08457 484 950; www.nationalrail.co.uk

TRANSPORT

♦ UNDERGROUND, DLR, BUS AND TRAMLINK

The underground network is divided into 6 concentric charging zones. The Docklands Light Railway, 5 lines east of Central London, is linked to the underground network. Single tickets can be bought in underground stations at automatic ticket vending machines or the ticket office; at DLR ticket machines; at bus stops at automatic ticket vending machines or from the bus driver. Day Travelcard (off-peak Zones 1 & 2) £5 approx.; 3-day Travelcard (off-peak Zones 1-6) £20 approx. Bus Saver (6 tickets) £6. ℰ 020 7222 1234; www.tfl.gov.uk

♦ TAXIS

Taxis are distinctive black cabs, with room for 4 passengers in the back and luggage beside the driver. They are numerous and can be hailed in the street, at a stand, at railway stations and at Heathrow Airport; they are occupied if the illuminated sign on the roof is not lit. Minimum charge £2; £4 for 1 mile, £6.40 for 2 miles, £11 for 4 miles, higher tariff 8pm-6am, at week ends and on public holidays. Tipping is not obligatory but 10% is usual. Tariff by negotiation for journeys outside Greater London. ℰ 02 7222 1234; www.tfl.gov.uk One Number Taxi bookings ℰ 871 871 8710 (+ £2 if booked by phone).

USEFUL ADDRESSES

◆ TOURIST INFORMATION

British Travel Centre, 1 Regent Street *Plan II* **G2**, SW1Y 4XT; Mon-Fri 9am (9.30 Tues)-6.30pm, Sat-Sun 10am-4pm (5pm Sat June-Sept); ℰ 020 8846 9000; Fax 020 7808 3801; www. visitbritain.com **City of London Information Centre** *Plan IX* **AE2**, St Paul's Churchyard, EC4; May-Oct daily 9.30am-5pm; otherwise Mon-Sat 9.30am-5pm (12.30pm Sat). ℰ 020 7332 1456/7; www.visitlondon.com; www.london.gov.uk **Southwark Information Centre**, Vinopolis *Plan IX* **AF3** 1 Bank End, SE1 9BU; all year, Tues-Sun, 10am-6pm; ℰ 020 7357 9168; www.visitsouthwark.com

◆ POST OFFICES

Mon-Fri 9am-5.30pm. Main Post Office, William IV Street, Mon-Fri 8.30am-6.30pm, Sat 9am-5.30pm. Stamps can be bought at post offices, newsagents and supermarkets. Currency exchange without commission.

◆ BANKS/CURRENCY EXCHANGE

Open generally Mon-Fri (except public holidays) 9.30am-5pm; some are also open on Saturday mornings. There are 24-hr cash machines (ATMs).

◆ EMERGENCY

ℰ **999** for Police, Fire Brigade, Ambulance.

EXPLORING LONDON

DIFFERENT FACETS OF THE CITY

It requires four to six days to visit the main sights and museums.

Museums and sights are usually open in summer from 10am to 5pm. Some places close on bank holidays.

London Pass – Free admission to museums, galleries, historic buildings and other attractions; discounts and enhancements; 1-day, 2-day, 3-day and 6-day passes (adult and child); www.leisurepassgroup.com

WESTMINSTER – Westminster Abbey *Plan IV* **O2**: masterpiece of Gothic architecture, the burial place of kings and queens and the setting for state occasions as well as daily worship. **Houses of Parliament** *Plan IV* **O2**: Royal palace, rebuilt after a fire in 1834 in Victorian Gothic style to contain the House of Commons and the House of Lords. **Whitehall** *Plan IV* **O2**: Broad street lined with government offices and the **Banqueting Hall** (1619).

MUSEUMS AND GALLERIES – **British Museum** *Plan VI* **T1**: Egyptian antiquities (Rosetta Stone), Oriental artefacts and Greek and Roman exhibits (Elgin marbles from the Parthenon, Roman Portland vase). **Victoria and Albert Museum** *Plan VII* **W3**: Treasures from the Middle Ages to the Renaissance: British works from 1500 to 20C; musical instruments; 18C French furniture. **Science Museum** *Plan VII* **W3**: Scientific activity of all kinds with practical applications. **National Gallery** *Plan II* **H2**: Major British and European artists, one of the world's finest collections of works of art. **Tate Britain** *Plan IV* **N3**: British School – Gainsborough, Turner, William Blake, Constable, Stubbs, the Pre-Raphaelites and a major collection of 20C work.

Tate Modern *Plan IX* **AE3**: handsome power station converted to display modern art.

ROYAL RESIDENCES – **Buckingham Palace** *Plan II* **F3**: the London home of the monarch set in own garden and flanked by St James's Park and Green Park. **Tower of London** *Plan IX* **AG3**: the Tower, where famous prisoners languished in fear of execution, now houses the Crown Jewels, guarded by Yeoman Wardens in Tudor costume. **Kensington Palace** *Plan VII* **V2**: a royal residence with State Apartments by Sir Christopher Wren, Colen Campbell and William Kent. **Clarence House** *Plan IV* **N1**: the residence of the Prince of Wales.

CITY OF LONDON – **St Paul's Cathedral** *Plan IX* **AE2**: Baroque masterpiece (1675-1708) by Sir Christopher Wren, setting for the funerals of Nelson, Wellington and Churchill and also daily worship; acoustic effect in the **Whispering Gallery** in the dome; many neighbouring churches also designed by Wren.

THE THAMES – Magnificent view of the river and Central London from the **London Eye** *Plan III* **K3**. River boat cruises from one the piers down stream past HMS Belfast to **Greenwich** (Cutty Sark, Observatory, Queen's House, National Maritime Museum) and on past the Dome to the **Thames Barrage** or upstream to **Kew** (Kew Gardens), **Richmond** (Marble Hill House, Ham House, Richmond Park) and **Hampton Court** (historic royal palace).

GOURMET TREATS

Afternoon tea, cucumber sandwiches, scones and clotted cream with jam, and cakes with Indian or China tea: *Fortnum & Masons*, 181 Picadilly; *Richoux*, 172 Piccadilly or 86 Old Brompton Road; most large hotels: some small bakeries and patisseries. **Lunch** in the distinctive ambiance of some museums, galleries and department stores: *V&A Museum* courtyard in summer; the smart frescoed restaurant at *Tate Britain* *Plan IV* **N3**, *National Portrait Gallery* *Plan III* **J2**, *Harvey Nichols* *Plan VII* **X3**, *Fortnum & Masons* *Plan II* **G2**, *Selfridges* *Plan II* **E1**. **Brunch**, a halfway meal between breakfast and lunch, and **tea dances**, afternoon tea with live music: some of the larger hotels. **Lunch or dinner cruise** on the Thames. A drink in a pub is a traditional way of starting or rounding off an evening.

SHOPPING

Shops are usually open Mon-Sat 10am to 6/6.30pm; Sun 11am-4pm; late night shopping until 8pm in Knightsbridge (Wed) and in West End (Thurs). Food shops often close later.

The main shopping locations are **Oxford Street** *Plan II* **F2**: department stores; **Regent Street** *Plan II* **G1**: smarter department stores; **Knightsbridge** *Plan VII* **X2**: smarter department stores (*Harvey Nichols, Harrods*); **Jermyn Street** *Plan II* **G2** and **Savile Row** *Plan II* **G1** men's outfitters and tailors. For luxury goods: **Bond Street** *Plan II* **F1**, **Jermyn Street**, **Burlington Arcade** *Plan II* **G2**, **Princes Arcade** *Plan II* **G2**, **Halkin Street** *Plan II* **E3**. Smaller specialist and trendy shops can be found in **Covent Garden, Neal's Yard** and **Seven Dials**. The main auction houses and art galleries are located in the **West End** (Bond Street, Cork Street and St James's).

MARKETS – **Portobello Road** *Plan XI* **AL2** (Sat) may be the best known street market but **Petticoat Lane** *Plan IX* **AG1** (Sun-Fri), **Brick Lane** *Plan I* **D2**, **Camden Passage** *Plan I* **C1** (Wed-Thu-Sat), **Charing Cross Collectors Market** *Plan III* **D2** (Sat) and **Greenwich Antiques Market** (Thu-Fri) provide a show and perhaps a bargain too.

WHAT TO BUY – Fashion: knitwear, tweeds, woollen garments; porcelain by Wedgwood, Royal Doulton, Minton, Royal Worcester, glassware by Dartington, marmalade, marmite, tea, whisky; books; art and antiques.

ENTERTAINMENT

Current events – plays, shows, films, concerts etc. – are listed in the following publications: *The London Planner* and *The London Guide* (www.visitlondon.com), both published monthly and available free of charge from Tourist Information Centres, *Welcome to London* (www.welcometolondon.com), *Time Out* (www.timeout.com) and *What's On?*, published weekly and on sale in street kiosks and newsagents. Theatre tickets can be obtained at the theatre, from agents (10% booking fee) or, for same day performances, from the Half-Price Ticket Booth in Leicester Square. Most of the numerous West End theatres are located in and around Shaftesbury Avenue.

Royal Opera House, Covent Garden *Plan III* **J2** – Opera and ballet

London Coliseum *Plan III* **J2** – Opera in English

Royal Albert Hall *Plan X* **AI1** – Venue for many events including the Henry Wood Promenade Concerts (mid-July to mid-September)

Royal Festival Hall *Plan III* **K3** – Home to the **London Philharmonic Orchestra**: concerts of orchestral and chamber music and organ recitals; also Queen Elizabeth Hall and Purcell Room

Barbican *Plan IX* **AF1** – Home to the **London Symphony Orchestra** and venue for visiting orchestras

Royal National Theatre *Plan IX* **AD3** – Three stages – **Olivier, Lyttleton** and **Cottesloe** – varied programme

Barbican Arts Centre *Plan IX* **AF1** – Varied programme of plays

NIGHTLIFE

The list of venues is so eclectic and fluid, including river boat parties,that it is best to consult the listings publications or their websites *(see Entertainment above).*

HOTEL – ALPHABETIC LIST

RESTAURANTS – ALPHABETIC ORDER

UNITED KINGDOM

2	MAYFAIR, SOHO AND ST. JAMES	7	HYDE PARK & KNIGHTSBRIDGE
3	STRAND & COVENT GARDEN AND LAMBETH	8	BAYSWATER & MAIDA VALE
4	BELGRAVIA AND VICTORIA	9	CITY OF LONDON & SOUTHWARK & TOWER HAM
5	REGENT'S PARK & MARYLEBONE	10	CHELSEA, SOUTH KENSINGTON AND EARL'S COURT
6	CAMDEN	11	KENSINGTON AND NORTH KENSINGTON

- Hotel
- Restaurant

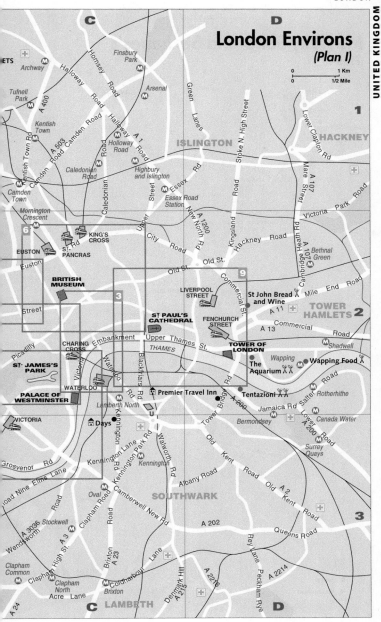

London Environs
(Plan I)

0   1 Km
0   1/2 Mile

C

D

ETS
Archway

Tufnell Park

Kentish Town

A 400

Kentish Town Rd

A 503

Camden Road

Camden Town

Mornington Crescent

EUSTON

St Pancras

KING'S CROSS

BRITISH MUSEUM

Street

Euston

CHARING CROSS

Picadilly

St-JAMES'S PARK

PALACE OF WESTMINSTER

VICTORIA

Grosvenor Rd

Crosvenor Rd

Nine Elms Lane

Road

A 3036

Wendsworth

Clapham Common

A 24

Clapham High St.

Clapham North

Acre Lane

Halloway Road

Horsey Road

Finsbury Park

Holloway Road

Caledonian Road

Camden Road

Highbury and Islington

Upper Street

Essex Road Station

City Road

A 1200

New North Rd

Old St.

Old St.

LIVERPOOL STREET

ST PAUL'S CATHEDRAL

FENCHURCH STREET

Upper Thames St.

THAMES

Embankment

Victoria

Waterloo

Blackfriars Rd

WATERLOO

Lambeth North

Kennington Lane

Kennington Park Rd

Kennington

Oval

Camberwell New Rd

Clapham Road

Coldharbour Lane

Brixton

Brixton

Denmark Hill

A 215

LAMBETH

C

Arsenal

ISLINGTON

Green Lanes

Essex Road

Kingsland Road

Hackney Road

A 107

Bethnal Green

A 107

Cambridge Heath Rd

Spoke N. High Street

Victoria Park Road

Lower Clapton Rd

Mare Street

A 107

HACKNEY

1

Commercial St.

St John Bread and Wine

Mile End Road

A 11

TOWER HAMLETS

2

Commercial Road

A 13

Shadwell

TOWER OF LONDON

Wapping

The Aquarium

Wapping Food

Tower Bridge Rd

A 200

Tentazioni

Jamaica Rd

Bermondsey

Salter Road

Rotherhithe

Lower Road

A 200

Canada Water

Surrey Quays

Premier Travel Inn

Days

Walworth Rd

Old Kent Road

Albany Road

SOUTHWARK

A 202

A 2

Old Kent Road

Rey Lane

Queens Road

A 2216

Peckham Rye

A 2214

3

D

817

UNITED KINGDOM

REGENT'S PARK AND
MARYLEBONE (Plan V)

CAVENDISH SQ.

Mayfair, Soho and St. James's
(Plan II)

HANOVER SQ.

MAYFAIR

Taman Gang

London Marriott Park Lane

Maze

Claridge's
Le Club at hush
Teca
Patterson's

Gordon Ramsay at Claridges

The Cafe

Le Gavroche

Umu
Westbury

GROSVENOR SQUARE

Connaught

The Square

Grosvenor House

Angela Hartnett at The Connaught

BERKELEY SQ.

Benares

Alloro

Nobu Berkeley

China Tang

The Greenhouse

Mirabelle

Dorchester
Grill Room

Tamarind

Flemings

HYDE PARK

London Hilton

Hilton London Green Park

Green Park

Windows

The Metropolitan

Park Lane

Nobu

Serpentine

Athenaeum

Road

Four Seasons

Rotten Row

APSLEY HOUSE WELLINGTON MUSEUM

GREEN PARK

The Carriage Road

Knightsbridge

Hyde Park Corner

Constitution Hill

BUCKINGHAM PALACE GARDENS

BUCKINGHAM PALACE

BELGRAVE SQ.

ROYAL MEWS

● Hotel
● Restaurant

0   200 m
0   200 yards

818

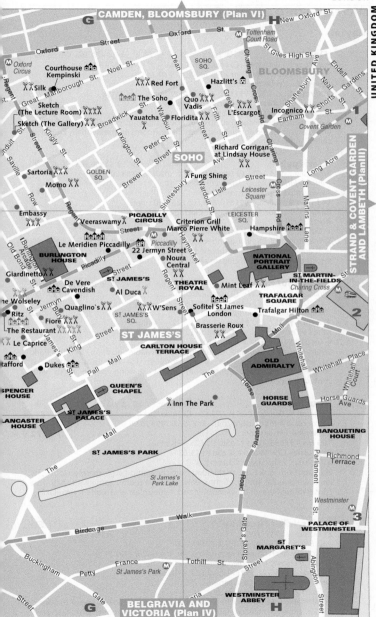

UNITED KINGDOM

MAYFAIR, SOHO & ST JAMES'S

Mayfair
Plan II

Dorchester
Park Lane ⊠ W1A 2HJ – Ⓜ Hyde Park Corner – ℰ (020) 7629 88 88
– info@thedorchester.com – Fax (020) 7409 01 14
– www.thedorchester.com
E2
200 rm – †£423/522 ††£522, ⊇ £26 – 49 suites
Rest see *Grill Room and China Tang* below
♦ Grand Luxury ♦ Classic ♦
A sumptuously decorated, luxury hotel offering every possible facility.
Impressive marbled and pillared promenade. Rooms quintessentially English in
style. Faultless service.

Claridge's
Brook St ⊠ W1A 2JQ – Ⓜ Bond Street – ℰ (020) 7629 88 60
– info@claridges.com – Fax (020) 7499 22 10
– www.maybournehotels.com
F1
143 rm – †£480/504 ††£610/633, ⊇ £25 – 60 suites
Rest see also *Gordon Ramsay at Claridge's* below
Rest £32/35
♦ Grand Luxury ♦ Art Deco ♦
The epitome of English grandeur, celebrated for its Art Deco. Exceptionally
well-appointed and sumptuous bedrooms, all with butler service. Magnificently
restored foyer. Relaxed, elegant restaurant.

Grosvenor House
Park Lane ⊠ W1K 7TN – Ⓜ Marble Arch
– ℰ (020) 7499 63 63 – Fax (020) 7493 85 12
– www.marriott.com/longh
E2
378 rm – †£257/280 ††£257/280, ⊇ £22 – 74 suites
Rest *La Terrazza* £26 and a la carte £27/41
♦ Grand Luxury ♦ Classic ♦
Over 70 years old and occupying an enviable position by the Park.
Edwardian-style décor. The Great Room, an ice rink in the 1920s, is
Europe's largest banqueting room. Bright, relaxing dining room with
contemporary feel.

Four Seasons
Hamilton Pl, Park Lane ⊠ W1A 1AZ – Ⓜ Hyde Park Corner – ℰ (020) 7499 08 88
– fsh.london@fourseasons.com – Fax (020) 7493 18 95
– www.fourseasons.com
F2
185 rm – †£393/428 ††£458, ⊇ £25 – 35 suites
Rest *Lanes* £29/36 and a la carte £43/63
♦ Grand Luxury ♦ Classic ♦
Set back from Park Lane so shielded from the traffic. Large, marbled lobby; its
lounge a popular spot for light meals. Spacious rooms, some with their own
conservatory. Restaurant's vivid blue and stained glass give modern yet relaxing,
feel.

Le Meridien Piccadilly
21 Piccadilly ⊠ W1J 0BH
– Ⓜ Piccadilly Circus – ℰ (020) 7734 80 00
– piccadilly.reservations@lemeridien.com – Fax (020) 7437 35 74
– www.piccadilly.lemeridien.com
G2
248 rm – †£164/212 ††£212, ⊇ £23 – 18 suites
Rest *Terrace* £23 and a la carte £37/55
♦ Grand Luxury ♦ Classic ♦
Comfortable international hotel, in a central location. Boasts one of the finest
leisure clubs in London. Individually decorated bedrooms with first class
facilities. Modern cuisine in comfortable surroundings.

London Hilton ⟨ London, 𝄞 ⚥ ⚅ 🅐🅒 ⅔rm ⚇ 🄰🄲 🏊1000 VISA ⓄⓈ ⒜Ⓔ ①
22 Park Lane ⊠ W1K 1BE – Ⓜ Hyde Park Corner
– ℰ (020) 7493 80 00 – reservations.parklane@hilton.com
– Fax (020) 7208 41 42 – www.hilton.co.uk/londonparklane **E-F2**
395 rm – ♦£200/394 ♦♦£247/488, ⌒ £22 – 55 suites
Rest see also **Windows** below
Rest Trader Vics, ℰ (020) 7208 41 13 (closed lunch Saturday and Sunday) £20 (lunch) and a la carte £34/50
Rest Park Brasserie £22 (lunch) and a la carte £28/43
♦ Business ♦ Classic ♦
This 28 storey tower is one of the city's tallest hotels, providing impressive views from the upper floors. Club floor bedrooms are particularly comfortable. Exotic Trader Vics with bamboo and plants. A harpist adds to the relaxed feel of Park Brasserie.

Connaught 𝄞 🅐🅒 ⚇ 🄰🄲 ⓣⓟ VISA ⓄⓈ ⒜Ⓔ ①
16 Carlos Pl ⊠ W1K 2AL – Ⓜ Bond Street – ℰ (020) 7499 70 70 – info@
the-connaught.co.uk – Fax (020) 7495 32 62 – www.maybournegroup.com
68 rm – ♦£352/458 ♦♦£500, ⌒ £27 – 24 suites **F1-2**
Rest see **Angela Hartnett at The Connaught** below
♦ Luxury ♦ Classic ♦
19C quintessentially English hotel with country house feel. The grand mahogany staircase leads up to antique furnished rooms. One of the capital's most exclusive addresses.

Park Lane 𝄞 ⚅ 🅐🅒 ⅔rm ⚇ 🄰🄲 ⓣⓟ 🏊500 ⓐ VISA ⓄⓈ ⒜Ⓔ ①
Piccadilly ⊠ W1J 7BX – Ⓜ Green Park – ℰ (020) 7499 63 21
– reservations.theparklane@sheraton.com – Fax (020) 7499 19 65
– www.sheraton.com/theparklane **F2**
285 rm – ♦£306 ♦♦£306, ⌒ £20 – 20 suites
Rest Citrus, ℰ (020) 7290 73 64 – a la carte £28/35
♦ Luxury ♦ Art Deco ♦
The history of the hotel is reflected in the elegant 'Palm Court' lounge and ballroom, both restored to their Art Deco origins. Bedrooms vary in shape and size. Summer pavement tables in restaurant opposite Green Park.

London Marriott Park Lane 𝄞 🄳 ⚅ 🅐🅒 ⅔ ⚇ 🄰🄲 🏊75
140 Park Lane ⊠ W1K 7AA – Ⓜ Marble Arch VISA ⓄⓈ ⒜Ⓔ ①
– ℰ (020) 7493 70 00 – mhrs.parklane@marriotthotels.com
– Fax (020) 7493 83 33 – www.marriotthotels.com/lonpl **E1**
148 rm – ♦£311/358 ♦♦£311/358, ⌒ £21 – 9 suites
Rest 140 Park Lane (bar lunch Saturday) £19 (lunch) and a la carte £27/35
♦ Luxury ♦ Design ♦
Superbly located 'boutique' style hotel at intersection of Park Lane and Oxford Street. Attractive basement health club. Spacious, well-equipped rooms with luxurious elements. Attractive restaurant overlooking Marble Arch.

Westbury 𝄞 ⚅ 🅐🅒 ⅔rm ⚇ 🏊120 VISA ⓄⓈ ⒜Ⓔ ①
Bond St ⊠ W1S 2YF – Ⓜ Bond Street – ℰ (020) 7629 77 55 – sales@
westburymayfair.com – Fax (020) 7495 11 63 – www.westburymayfair.com **F1**
233 rm – ♦£327/351 ♦♦£351, ⌒ £23 – 21 suites
Rest (closed Sunday and Saturday lunch) £25 and a la carte £40/51
♦ Business ♦ Modern ♦
Surrounded by London's most fashionable shops; the renowned Polo bar and lounge provide soothing sanctuary. Some suites have their own terrace. Bright, fresh restaurant enhanced by modern art.

The Metropolitan ⟨ 𝄞 🅐🅒 ⅔ ⚇ ⓐ VISA ⓄⓈ ⒜Ⓔ ①
Old Park Lane ⊠ W1Y 1LB – Ⓜ Hyde Park Corner – ℰ (020) 7447 10 00
– res.lon@metropolitan.como.bz – Fax (020) 7447 11 00
– www.metropolitan.como.bz **F2**
147 rm – ♦£376 ♦♦£376, ⌒ £24 – 3 suites – **Rest** see **Nobu** below
♦ Luxury ♦ Minimalist ♦
Minimalist interior and a voguish reputation make this the favoured hotel of pop stars and celebrities. Innovative design and fashionably attired staff set it apart.

UNITED KINGDOM

Athenaeum 55 VISA AE
116 Piccadilly ✉ W1J 7BS – Ⓜ Hyde Park Corner – ☎ (020) 7499 34 64
– info@athenaeumhotel.com – Fax (020) 7493 18 60
– www.athenaeumhotel.com **F2**
124 rm – †£323 ††£323, ☕ £21 – 33 suites
Rest *Bulloch's at 116* *(closed lunch Saturday and Sunday)* £15 (lunch) and a la carte approx. £54
◆ Luxury ◆ Classic ◆
Built in 1925 as a luxury apartment block. Comfortable bedrooms with video and CD players. Individually designed suites are in an adjacent Edwardian townhouse. Conservatory roofed dining room renowned for its mosaics and malt whiskies.

Hilton London Green Park 130 VISA AE
Half Moon St ✉ W1J 7BN – Ⓜ Green Park – ☎ (020) 7629 75 22
– reservations.greenpark@hilton.com – Fax (020) 7491 89 71
– www.hilton.co.uk **F2**
162 rm – †£182/245 ††£194/245, ☕ £20
Rest (dinner only) £24 and a la carte £24/36
◆ Business ◆ Functional ◆
A row of sympathetically adjoined townhouses, dating from the 1730s. Discreet marble lobby. Bedrooms share the same décor but vary in size and shape. Monet prints decorate light, airy dining room.

Flemings rm 55 VISA AE
Half Moon St ✉ W1J 7BH – Ⓜ Green Park – ☎ (020) 7499 29 64
– sales@flemings-mayfair.co.uk – Fax (020) 7491 88 66
– www.flemings-mayfair.co.uk **F2**
121 rm – †£205/247 ††£247, ☕ £18 – 10 suites
Rest *(closed Saturday lunch)* £25
◆ Traditional ◆ Classic ◆
A Georgian town house where the oil paintings and English furniture add to the charm. Apartments located in adjoining house, once home to noted polymath Henry Wagner. Candlelit basement restaurant with oil paintings.

Grill Room – at Dorchester H. VISA AE
Park Lane ✉ W1A 2HJ – Ⓜ Hyde Park Corner – ☎ (020) 7317 63 36
– Fax (020) 7317 64 64 **E2**
Rest £25 (lunch) and a la carte £35/58
◆ English ◆ Design ◆
Ornate Spanish influenced, baroque decoration with gilded ceiling, tapestries and highly polished oak tables. Formal and immaculate service. Traditional English cooking.

Le Gavroche (Roux) VISA AE
43 Upper Brook St ✉ W1K 7QR – Ⓜ Marble Arch – ☎ (020) 7408 08 81
– bookings@le-gavroche.com – Fax (020) 7491 43 87 – www.le-gavroche.co.uk
closed Christmas-New Year, Sunday, Saturday lunch and Bank Holidays
Rest (booking essential) £46 (lunch) and a la carte £60/117 **E1**
Spec. Foie gras chaud et pastilla de canard à la cannelle. Râble de lapin et galette au parmesan. Le palet au chocolat amer et praline croustillant.
◆ French ◆ Formal ◆
Long-standing, renowned restaurant with a clubby, formal atmosphere. Accomplished classical French cuisine, served by smartly attired and well-drilled staff.

Angela Hartnett at The Connaught VISA AE
16 Carlos Pl ✉ W1K 2AL – Ⓜ Bond Street – ☎ (020) 7592 12 22 – reservations@angelahartnett.com – Fax (020) 7592 12 23 – www.angelahartnett.com
Rest (booking essential) £30/70 **F2**
Spec. Mosaic of pressed tomatoes with feta cheese and balsamic vinegar. Roast rabbit, confit of shoulder and loin, girolles and truffle vinaigrette. Apricot soufflé, almond and amaretto ice cream.
◆ Italian influences ◆ Formal ◆
Refined Italian influenced cooking can be enjoyed in the elegantly panelled 'Menu'. Meanwhile, the more intimate 'Grill' offers a selection of traditional British favourites.

XXXX ⌖
Gordon Ramsay at Claridge's 🄰 ⅓ 𝗩𝗜𝗦𝗔 ⓄⒸ 🄰🄴

Brook St ⊠ W1A 2JQ – Ⓜ Bond Street
– ✆ (020) 7499 00 99 – reservations@gordonramsay.com
– Fax (020) 7499 30 99 – www.gordonramsay.com   F1
Rest (booking essential) £30/70 ⬡
Spec. Salad of crab and carrot à la Grecque, ginger and carrot vinaigrette. Pork
cheeks cooked in honey and cloves, spring vegetables, braising juices. Banana
and passion fruit parfait with coconut tuile.
♦ Modern ♦ Formal ♦
A thoroughly comfortable dining room with a charming and gracious
atmosphere. Serves classically-inspired food executed with a high degree of
finesse.

XXXX ⌖⌖
The Square (Howard) 🄰 ⅓ ⟷18 𝗩𝗜𝗦𝗔 ⓄⒸ 🄰🄴 Ⓞ

6-10 Bruton St ⊠ W1J 6PU – Ⓜ Green Park – ✆ (020) 7495 71 00
– info@squarerestaurant.com – Fax (020) 7495 71 50
– www.squarerestaurant.com
closed 24-26 December, 1 January and lunch Saturday, Sunday and Bank
Holidays   F1
Rest £30/60 ⬡
Spec. Lasagne of crab with shellfish and basil cappuccino. Langoustines with
parmesan gnocchi, wild mushrooms and truffle emulsion. Assiette of chocolate.
♦ Modern ♦ Formal ♦
Varnished wood and bold abstract canvases add an air of modernity. Extensive
menus offer French-influenced cooking of the highest order. Prompt and
efficient service.

XXXX ⌖
Sketch (The Lecture Room) 🄰 𝗩𝗜𝗦𝗔 ⓄⒸ 🄰🄴 Ⓞ

First Floor, 9 Conduit St ⊠ W1S 2XG – Ⓜ Oxford Street – ✆ (0870) 777 44 88
– Fax (0870) 777 44 00 – www.sketch.uk.com
closed 25 December, 1 January, Sunday, Monday, Saturday lunch and Bank
Holidays   G1
Rest (booking essential) £35 (lunch) and a la carte £39/90 ⬡
Spec. Langoustine four ways. Sea bass with apple purée, ratte potatoes and
sweet whisky sauce. Cumin roasted lamb with baby carrots, sweet onions and
watercress.
♦ French ♦ Design ♦
Stunning venue, combining art and food, creating an experience of true sensory
stimulation. Vibrant dining options: Lecture Room or Library. Highly original,
complex cooking.

XXXX
China Tang – at Dorchester H. 🄰 ⟷16 𝗩𝗜𝗦𝗔 ⓄⒸ 🄰🄴 Ⓞ

Park Lane ⊠ W1A 2HJ – Ⓜ Hyde Park Corner
– ✆ (020) 7629 99 88
– Fax (020) 7629 95 95
closed 25 December   E2
Rest a la carte £35/70
♦ Chinese ♦ Fashionable ♦
A striking mix of Art Deco, Oriental motifs, hand-painted fabrics, mirrors and
marbled table tops. Carefully prepared, traditional Cantonese dishes using
quality ingredients.

XXXX
Windows – at London Hilton H. ≤ London, 🄰 𝗩𝗜𝗦𝗔 ⓄⒸ 🄰🄴 Ⓞ

22 Park Lane ⊠ W1Y 1BE – Ⓜ Hyde Park Corner
– ✆ (020) 7208 40 21
– windows.parklane@hilton.com
– Fax (020) 7208 41 42
– www.hilton.co.uk/londonparklane
closed Saturday lunch and Sunday dinner   E-F2
Rest £40/60 and a la carte £37/65
♦ Modern ♦ Formal ♦
Enjoys some of the city's best views. The lunchtime buffet provides a popular
alternative to the international menu. Formal service and a busy adjoining piano
bar.

UNITED KINGDOM

XXX ✿ The Greenhouse
AC 🖐 🔄 12 VISA ⓜⓞ AE ⓞ

27a Hay's Mews ⊠ W1X 7RJ – ⓜ Hyde Park Corner – ℰ (020) 7499 33 31
– reservations@greenhouserestaurant.co.uk – Fax (020) 7499 53 68
– www.greenhouserestaurant.co.uk
closed Christmas-New Year, Sunday, Saturday lunch and
Bank Holidays **F2**
Rest £32/60 ☒

Spec. Seared foie gras, espresso syrup, amaretto foam. Quail galantine with plum carpaccio and microcress salad. Poached halibut, sweet pea sabayon and liquorice.

♦ Innovative ♦ Fashionable ♦

A pleasant courtyard, off a quiet mews, leads to this stylish, discreet restaurant where an elaborate, innovative blend of flavours is much in evidence on inventive menus.

XXX ✿ Mirabelle
🍴 AC 🔄 48 VISA ⓜⓞ AE ⓞ

56 Curzon St ⊠ W1J 8PA – ⓜ Green Park – ℰ (020) 7499 46 36
– sales@whitestarline.org.uk – Fax (020) 7499 54 49
– www.whitestarline.org.uk
closed 26 December and 1 January **F2**
Rest £21 (lunch) and a la carte £33/50 ☒

Spec. Omelette Arnold Bennett, Mornay sauce. Braised pig's trotter with morels and pomme purée, Périgueux sauce. Raspberry soufflé, Cardinal sauce.

♦ Modern ♦ Design ♦

As celebrated now as it was in the 1950s. Stylish bar with screens and mirrors, leather banquettes and rows of windows. Modern interpretation of some classic dishes.

XXX ✿ Maze
AC 🖐 🔄 10 VISA ⓜⓞ AE

10-13 Grosvenor Sq ⊠ W1K 6JP – ⓜ Bond Street – ℰ (020) 7107 00 00
– maze@gordonramsay.com – Fax (020) 7107 00 01
– www.gordonramsay.com **F1**
Rest a la carte £24/35

Spec. Wild sea trout with lime, peas, caper and raisin purée. Grilled spring lamb with cinnamon sweetbreads, lettuce with bacon and onion. Aged beef with foie gras, parsley, snail and garlic.

♦ Contemporary ♦ Fashionable ♦

Part of the Gordon Ramsay empire; a stylish, sleek restaurant. Kitchen eschews usual three-course menus by offering a number of small dishes of variety, precision and flair.

XXX Benares
AC 🔄 22 VISA ⓜⓞ AE ⓞ

12 Berkeley House, Berkeley Sq ⊠ W1J 6BS
– ⓜ Green Park – ℰ (020) 7629 88 86
– enquiries@benaresrestaurant.com – Fax (020) 7491 88 83
– www.benaresrestaurant.com
closed 25-26 December, 1 January, lunch Saturday and Sunday **F2**
Rest a la carte £30/44

♦ Indian ♦ Formal ♦

Indian restaurant where pools of water scattered with petals and candles compensate for lack of natural light. Original Indian dishes; particularly good value at lunch.

XXX Embassy
🍴 AC VISA ⓜⓞ AE

29 Old Burlington St ⊠ W1S 3AN – ⓜ Green Park – ℰ (020) 7851 09 56
– embassy@embassylondon.com – Fax (020) 7734 32 24
– www.embassylondon.com
closed 25 December, 1 January, Sunday, Monday and Saturday lunch
Rest £23 (lunch) and dinner a la carte £27/49 **G1-2**

♦ Modern ♦ Trendy ♦

Marble floors, ornate cornicing and a long bar create a characterful, moody dining room. Tables are smartly laid and menus offer accomplished, classic dishes.

XXX
£3£3

Tamarind
20 Queen St ⊠ W1J 5PR – Ⓜ Green Park – 𝒞 (020) 7629 35 61
– manager@tamarindrestaurant.com – Fax (020) 7499 50 34
– www.tamarindrestaurant.com
closed 25-26 December, 1 January and lunch Saturday and Bank Holidays   **F2**
Rest £19 (lunch) and a la carte £38/55
Spec. Ground lamb with cinnamon, red chillies and garlic. Grilled monkfish with coriander, mint and pickling spices. Chicken grilled in tandoor with tomatoes, ginger, honey and fenugreek.
♦ Indian ♦ Fashionable ♦
Gold coloured pillars add to the opulence of this basement room. Windows allow diners the chance to watch the kitchen prepare original and accomplished Indian dishes.

XXX

Sartoria
20 Savile Row ⊠ W1X 1AE – Ⓜ Green Park – 𝒞 (020) 7534 70 00
– sartoriareservations@conran-restaurants.co.uk – Fax (020) 7534 70 70
– www.conran.com
closed 25-27 December, Sunday, Saturday lunch and Bank Holidays   **G1**
Rest £22 and a la carte £30/43
♦ Italian ♦ Formal ♦
In the street renowned for English tailoring, a coolly sophisticated restaurant to suit those looking for classic Italian cooking with modern touches.

XX
£3

Umu
14-16 Bruton Pl ⊠ W1J 6LX – Ⓜ Bond Street – 𝒞 (020) 7499 88 81
– enquiries@umurestaurant.com – www.umurestaurant.com
closed between Christmas and New Year, Sunday and Bank Holidays   **F1**
Rest £22/60 and a la carte £50/70 ⅋
Spec. Sesame tofu with wasabi and nori seaweed. Eel kabayaki with kinone pepper. Sake flavoured soup with fish of the day.
♦ Japanese ♦ Fashionable ♦
Exclusive neighbourhood location: stylish, discreet interior with central sushi bar. Japanese dishes, specialising in Kyoto cuisine, employing highest quality ingredients.

XX

Giardinetto
39-40 Albermarle St ⊠ W1S 4TE – Ⓜ Green Park – 𝒞 (020) 7493 70 91
– info@giardinetto.co.uk – Fax (020) 7493 70 96
closed Saturday lunch   **G2**
Rest £22 (lunch) and a la carte £33/46
♦ Italian ♦ Cosy ♦
Manages to mix a smart, stylish interior with a neighbourhood intimacy. Three dining areas, front being largest. Genoese chef/owner conjures up well-presented Ligurian dishes.

XX

Patterson's
4 Mill St ⊠ W1S 2AX – Ⓜ Oxford Street – 𝒞 (020) 7499 13 08
– pattersonmayfair@btconnect.com – Fax (020) 7491 21 22
– www.pattersonsrestaurant.com
closed Sunday and Saturday lunch   **F1**
Rest £20/35
♦ Contemporary ♦ Intimate ♦
Stylish modern interior in black and white. Elegant tables and attentive service. Modern British cooking with concise wine list and sensible prices.

XX

Teca
54 Brooks Mews ⊠ W1Y 2NY – Ⓜ Bond Street – 𝒞 (020) 7495 47 74
– Fax (020) 7491 35 45
closed 1 week January, Sunday and Saturday lunch   **F1**
Rest £34 (dinner) and lunch a la carte £30/49
♦ Italian ♦ Trendy ♦
A glass-enclosed cellar is one of the features of this modern, slick Italian restaurant. Set price menu, with the emphasis on fresh, seasonal produce.

UNITED KINGDOM

XX **Alloro**   AC ⇔16 VISA ◑◯ AE ◑

19-20 Dover St ⊠ W1S 4LU – Ⓜ Green Park – ℰ (020) 7495 47 68
– Fax (020) 7629 53 48
closed 25 December-2 January, Saturday lunch, Sunday and
Bank Holidays   **F2**
Rest £26/36
• Italian • Fashionable •
One of the new breed of stylish Italian restaurants with contemporary art and
leather seating. A separate, bustling bar. Smoothly run with modern cooking.

XX **Le Club at hush**   ⌂ AC VISA ◑◯ AE ◑

8 Lancashire Court, Brook St ⊠ W1S 1EY – Ⓜ Bond Street – ℰ (020) 7659 15 00
– info@hush.co.uk – Fax (020) 7659 15 01 – www.hush.co.uk
closed 24-26 December, 31 December-3 January,
Sunday and Saturday lunch   **F1**
Rest (booking essential) £27 (lunch) and a la carte £30/50
Rest *Brasserie* a la carte approx. £32
• Modern • Fashionable •
Tucked away down a side street with a secluded courtyard terrace. Join the
fashionable set at the bar or settle down on the banquettes for modern,
satisfying food.

XX **Nobu** – at The Metropolitan H.   ≤ AC ⇔40 VISA ◑◯ AE ◑
ॐ
19 Old Park Lane ⊠ W1Y 4LB – Ⓜ Hyde Park Corner – ℰ (020) 7447 47 47
– confirmations@noburestaurants.com. – Fax (020) 7447 47 49
– www.noburestaurants.com
closed 25 December   **F2**
Rest (booking essential) £30/70 and a la carte £34/40
Spec. Yellowtail with jalapeño. Black cod with miso. Sashimi salad.
• Japanese • Fashionable •
Its celebrity clientele has made this one of the most glamorous spots. Staff are
fully conversant in the unique menu that adds South American influences to
Japanese cooking.

XX **Taman Gang**   AC VISA ◑◯ AE ◑

141 Park Lane ⊠ W1K 7AA – Ⓜ Marble Arch – ℰ (020) 7518 31 60
– info@tamangang.com – Fax (020) 7518 31 61 – www.tamangang.com   **E1**
Rest (dinner only and Sunday lunch) a la carte £26/87
• South-East Asian • Exotic •
Basement restaurant with largish bar and lounge area. Stylish but intimate décor.
Informal and intelligent service. Pan-Asian dishes presented in exciting modern
manner.

XX **Sketch (The Gallery)**   AC VISA ◑◯ AE ◑

9 Conduit St ⊠ W1S 2XG – Ⓜ Oxford Street – ℰ (0870) 777 44 88
– info@sketch.uk.com – Fax (0870) 777 44 00 – www.sketch.uk.com
closed 25 December, 1 January, Sunday and Bank Holidays   **G1**
Rest (booking essential) (dinner only) a la carte £30/48
• Modern • Trendy •
On the ground floor of the Sketch building: daytime video art gallery
metamorphoses into evening brasserie with ambient wall projections and light
menus with eclectic range.

XX **Nobu Berkeley**   AC ↤ VISA ◑◯ AE
ॐ
15 Berkeley St ⊠ W1J 8DY – Ⓜ Green Park – ℰ (020) 7290 92 22
– nobuberkeley@noburestaurants.com – Fax (020) 7290 92 23
– www.noburestaurants.com
closed Sunday and Bank Holidays   **F2**
Rest (bookings not accepted) (dinner only) a la carte £39/76
Spec. Crispy pork belly with spicy miso. Yellowtail sashimi with jalapeño. Rib-eye
anti-cucho.
• Japanese • Fashionable •
In a prime position off Berkeley Square: downstairs 'destination' bar and above,
a top quality, minimal restaurant. Innovative Japanese dishes with original
combinations.

XX **Momo**   🛱 🖭 𝑽𝑰𝑺𝑨 ◐◓ 𝔸𝔼 ⓪

25 Heddon St ⊠ *W1B 4BH –* Ⓜ *Oxford Circus –* ℰ *(020) 7434 40 40*
– info@momoresto.com – Fax (020) 7287 04 04 – www.momoresto.com
closed 24-26 and 31 December, 1 January and Sunday lunch   **G1**
Rest £14 (lunch) and a la carte £27/40
♦ Moroccan ♦ Exotic ♦
Elaborate adornment of rugs, drapes and ornaments mixed with Arabic music
lend an authentic feel to this busy Moroccan restaurant. Helpful service. Popular
basement bar.

X **Veeraswamy**   🖭 𝑽𝑰𝑺𝑨 ◐◓ 𝔸𝔼 ⓪

Victory House, 99 Regent St (entrance on Swallow St) ⊠ *W1B 4RS –* Ⓜ *Piccadilly
Circus –* ℰ *(020) 7734 14 01 – veeraswamy@realindianfood.com*
– Fax (020) 7439 84 34 – www.realindianfood.com   **G2**
Rest £18 (lunch) and a la carte £23/41
♦ Indian ♦ Design ♦
The country's oldest Indian restaurant boasts a new look with vivid coloured walls
and glass screens. The menu also combines the familiar with some modern twists.

X **The Cafe** – at Sotheby's   ⅃⅄ 𝑽𝑰𝑺𝑨 ◐◓ 𝔸𝔼 ⓪

34-35 New Bond St ⊠ *W1A 2AA –* Ⓜ *Bond Street –* ℰ *(020) 7293 50 77*
– Fax (020) 7293 59 20 – www.sothebys.com
*closed last 2 weeks August, 22 December-3 January, Saturday, Sunday and Bank
Holidays*   **F1**
Rest (booking essential) (lunch only) a la carte £20/31
♦ Modern ♦ Friendly ♦
A velvet rope separates this simple room from the main lobby of this famous
auction house. Pleasant service from staff in aprons. Menu is short but
well-chosen and light.

Soho   *Plan II*

🏨 **The Soho**   𝑘ᵢ 🔥 🖭 🖳 📞 𝗦𝗔100 𝑽𝑰𝑺𝑨 ◐◓ 𝔸𝔼

4 Richmond Mews ⊠ *W1D 3DH –* Ⓜ *Tottenham Court Road*
– ℰ *(020) 7559 30 00 – soho@firmdale.com – Fax (020) 7559 30 03*
– www.sohohotel.com   **G1**
83 rm – ✝£276 ✝✝£346, ☷ £19 – 2 suites
Rest *Refuel* £20 (lunch) and a la carte £27/35
♦ Luxury ♦ Stylish ♦
Opened in autumn 2004: stylish hotel with two screening rooms, comfy drawing
room and up-to-the-minute bedrooms, some vivid, others more muted, all
boasting hi-tec extras. Contemporary bar and restaurant.

🏨 **Hampshire**   🛱 𝑘ᵢ 🖭 ⅃⅄rm 🍽 🖳 📞 𝗦𝗔100 𝑽𝑰𝑺𝑨 ◐◓ ⓪

Leicester Sq ⊠ *WC2H 7LH –* Ⓜ *Leicester Square –* ℰ *(020) 7839 93 99*
– Fax (020) 7930 81 22 – www.radissonedwardian.com   **H2**
119 rm – ✝£309 ✝✝£405, ☷ £17 – 5 suites
Rest *The Apex* (dinner only) a la carte £25/45
♦ Luxury ♦ Classic ♦
The bright lights of the city are literally outside and many rooms overlook the
bustling Square. Inside it is tranquil and comfortable with well-appointed
bedrooms. Formal yet relaxing dining room with immaculately dressed tables.

🏨 **Courthouse Kempinski**   𝑘ᵢ 🍸 🔽 🔥 🖭 ⅃⅄rm 🖳

19-21 Great Marlborough St ⊠ *W1F 7HL*   📞 𝗦𝗔180 𝑽𝑰𝑺𝑨 ◐◓ 𝔸𝔼
– Ⓜ *Oxford Circus –* ℰ *(020) 7297 55 55 – info@courthouse-hotel.com*
– Fax (020) 7297 55 66 – www.courthouse-hotel.com   **G1**
107 rm – ✝£317 ✝✝£317, ☷ £23 – 5 suites
Rest see also *Silk* below
Rest *The Carnaby* a la carte approx. £23
♦ Business ♦ Classic ♦
Striking Grade II listed ex magistrates' court: interior fused imaginatively with
original features; for example, the bar incorporates three former cells. Ultra
stylish rooms. Informal Carnaby offers extensive French, modern and British
menu.

Hazlitt's without rest   AC ⬚ VISA ⬚ AE ①

6 Frith St ⊠ W1D 3JA – **Ⓜ** *Tottenham Court Road –* ℰ *(020) 7434 17 71*
– reservations @ hazlitts.co.uk – Fax (020) 7439 15 24
– www.hazlittshotel.com   **H1**
22 rm – †£206/240 ††£240 – 1 suite
♦ Townhouse ♦ Historic ♦
A row of three adjoining early 18C town houses and former home of the eponymous essayist. Individual and charming bedrooms, many with antique furniture and Victorian baths.

L'Escargot   AC ⬚60 VISA ⬚ AE ①

48 Greek St ⊠ W1D 5EF – **Ⓜ** *Tottenham Court Road –* ℰ *(020) 7437 26 79*
– sales @ whitestarline.org.uk – Fax (020) 7437 07 90
– www.whitestarline.org.uk   **H1**
Rest *(closed 25-26 December, 1 January, Sunday and Saturday lunch)* £18
(lunch) and a la carte £27/29
Rest *Picasso Room (closed August, Sunday, Monday and Saturday lunch)* 26/42
Spec. Escargots en coquille Bordelaise. Roast pork cutlet, stuffed pig's trotter and fondant potato. Hot chocolate fondant, iced crème fraîche.
♦ Modern ♦ Fashionable ♦
Soho institution. Ground Floor is chic, vibrant brasserie with early-evening buzz of theatre-goers. Finely judged modern dishes. Intimate and more formal upstairs Picasso Room famed for its limited edition art.

Quo Vadis   AC VISA ⬚ AE ①

26-29 Dean St ⊠ W1D 3LL – **Ⓜ** *Tottenham Court Road –* ℰ *(020) 7437 95 85*
– whitestarline @ org.uk – Fax (020) 7734 75 93 – www.whitestarline.org.uk
closed 24-25 December, 1 January, Sunday and Saturday lunch   **H1**
Rest £20 (lunch) and a la carte £22/36
♦ Italian ♦ Formal ♦
Stained glass windows and a neon sign hint at the smooth modernity of the interior. Modern artwork abounds. Contemporary cooking and a serious wine list.

Red Fort   AC VISA ⬚ AE

77 Dean St ⊠ W1D 3SH – **Ⓜ** *Tottenham Court Road –* ℰ *(020) 7437 25 25*
– info @ redfort.co.uk – Fax (020) 7434 07 21 – www.redfort.co.uk
closed lunch Saturday, Sunday and Bank Holidays   **G1**
Rest a la carte £26/46
♦ Indian ♦ Formal ♦
Smart, stylish restaurant with modern water feature and glass ceiling to rear. Seasonally changing menus of authentic dishes handed down over generations.

Richard Corrigan at Lindsay House   AC VISA ⬚ AE ①

21 Romilly St ⊠ W1D 5AF – **Ⓜ** *Leicester Square –* ℰ *(020) 7439 04 50*
– richardcorrigan @ lindsayhouse.co.uk – Fax (020) 7437 73 49
– www.lindsayhouse.co.uk
closed Christmas, Sunday, Saturday lunch and Bank Holidays   **H1**
Rest £27/52
Spec. Ravioli of chorizo and feta with onion and lime velouté. Tea roasted veal sweetbreads with cauliflower. Compote of rhubarb, mango, nutmeg and vanilla ice cream.
♦ Contemporary ♦ Intimate ♦
One rings the doorbell before being welcomed into this handsome 18C town house, retaining many original features. Skilled and individual cooking with a subtle Irish hint.

Floridita   AC ⬚8 VISA ⬚ AE ①

100 Wardour St ⊠ W1F 0TN – **Ⓜ** *Tottenham Court Road –* ℰ *(020) 7314 40 00*
– Fax (020) 7314 40 40 – www.floriditalondon.com
closed Sunday – **Rest** *(live music and dancing) (dinner only and lunch mid*   **G1**
November-December) a la carte £33/39
♦ Latin American ♦ Musical ♦
Buzzy destination where the Latino cuisine is a fiery accompaniment to the vivacious Cuban dancing. Slightly less frenetic upstairs in the Spanish tapas and cocktail bar.

XX **Silk** – at Courthouse Kempinski H.   AC VISA ᗌ AE
19-21 Great Marlborough St ⊠ W1F 7HL – ⓂOxford Circus – ℰ (020) 7297 55 55
– Fax (020) 7297 55 66 – www.courthouse-hotel.com
closed Sunday   G1
Rest (dinner only) £45 and a la carte £40/52
♦ International ♦ Formal ♦
Stunningly unique former courtroom with original panelling, court benches and glass roof. Menu follows the journey of the Silk Route with Asian, Indian and Italian influences.

X **Yauatcha**   AC ↔ VISA ᗌ AE
ॐ *15 Broadwick St ⊠ W1F 0DL – ⓂTottenham Court Road – ℰ (020) 7494 88 88*
– mail@yauatcha.com – Fax (020) 7494 88 89
closed 25-26 December   G1
Rest a la carte £18/46
Spec. Venison puff. Scallop shumai. Prawn and beancurd cheung fun.
♦ Chinese (Dim Sum) ♦ Fashionable ♦
Converted 1960s post office in heart of Soho. Below the smart, cool tea room is a spacious restaurant serving Chinese cuisine that's original, refined, authentic and flavoursome.

X **Fung Shing**   AC ⇄50 VISA ᗌ AE ⓞ
15 Lisle St ⊠ WC2H 7BE – ⓂLeicester Square – ℰ (020) 7437 15 39
– Fax (020) 7734 02 84 – www.fung.shing.co.uk
closed 24-26 December and lunch Bank Holidays   H1
Rest £17/35 and a la carte £13/24
♦ Chinese (Canton) ♦ Friendly ♦
A long-standing Chinese restaurant on the edge of Chinatown. Chatty and pleasant service. A mix of authentic, rustic dishes and the more adventurous chef's specials.

St James's   *Plan II*

🏚🏚 **The Ritz**   ᒥᓭ AC ↔ ⅏ ▦ ♨50 VISA ᗌ AE ⓞ
150 Piccadilly ⊠ W1J 9BR – ⓂGreen Park – ℰ (020) 7493 81 81 – enquire@
theritzlondon.com – Fax (020) 7493 26 87 – www.theritzlondon.com   G2
116 rm – ⁑£388 ⁑⁑£588, ⌕ £30 – 17 suites
Rest see *The Restaurant* below
♦ Grand Luxury ♦ Classic ♦
Opened 1906, a fine example of Louis XVI architecture and decoration. Elegant Palm Court famed for afternoon tea. Many of the lavishly appointed rooms overlook the park.

🏚🏚 **Sofitel St James London**   ᒥᓭ ♿ AC ↔ ▦ ♨180 VISA ᗌ AE ⓞ
6 Waterloo Pl ⊠ SW1Y 4AN – ⓂPiccadilly Circus – ℰ (020) 7747 22 00
– h3144@accor-hotels.com – Fax (020) 7747 22 10
– www.sofitelstjames.com   H2
179 rm – ⁑£350 ⁑⁑£350, ⌕ £21 – 7 suites
Rest see *Brasserie Roux* below
♦ Luxury ♦ Classic ♦
Grade II listed building in smart Pall Mall location. Classically English interiors include floral Rose Lounge and club-style St. James bar. Comfortable, well-fitted bedrooms.

🏚 **Stafford** ॐ   AC ⅏ ▦ ℭ ♨40 VISA ᗌ AE ⓞ
16-18 St James's Pl ⊠ SW1A 1NJ – ⓂGreen Park – ℰ (020) 7493 01 11
– info@thestaffordhotel.co.uk – Fax (020) 7493 71 21
– www.thestaffordhotel.co.uk   G2
75 rm – ⁑£252/293 ⁑⁑£323/393, ⌕ £20 – 6 suites
Rest *(closed lunch Saturday and Bank Holidays)* £30 (lunch) and a la carte £54/68
♦ Traditional ♦ Luxury ♦ Classic ♦
A genteel atmosphere prevails in this elegant and discreet country house in the city. Do not miss the famed American bar. Well-appointed rooms created from 18C stables. Refined, elegant, intimate dining room.

Dukes 🌳   🖾 🖾 ⅟rest 🛠 🖾 🕻 🖾50 *VISA* 🝇 🖾 ⓪
35 St James's Pl ✉ SW1A 1NY – ⓜ Green Park – ☏ (020) 7491 48 40
– bookings@dukeshotel.com – Fax (020) 7493 12 64
– www.dukeshotel.com   **G2**
82 rm – ❙£188/364 ❙❙£217/429, ☑ £20 – 7 suites
Rest a la carte £35/43
♦ Traditional ♦ Luxury ♦ Classic ♦
Privately owned, discreet and quiet hotel. Traditional bar, famous for its martinis and Cognac collection. Well-kept spacious rooms in a country house style. Refined dining.

Trafalgar Hilton   🖾 🖾 ⅟rm 🛠 🖾 🖾50 *VISA* 🝇 🖾 ⓪
2 Spring Gdns ✉ SW1A 2TS – ⓜ Charing Cross – ☏ (020) 7870 29 00
– sales.trafalgar@hilton.com – Fax (020) 7870 29 11
– www.thetrafalgar.com   **H2**
127 rm – ❙£340 ❙❙£398, ☑ £18 – 2 suites
Rest *Rockwell* *(closed Saturday lunch and Sunday)* £18/45 and a la carte £30/42
♦ Business ♦ Chain hotel ♦ Modern ♦
Enjoys a commanding position on the square of which the deluxe rooms, some split-level, have views. Bedrooms are in pastel shades with leather armchairs or stools; mod cons. Low-lit restaurant with open-plan kitchen.

De Vere Cavendish   🖾 🖾 ⅟rm 🛠 🕻 🖾100 🍽 *VISA* 🝇 🖾 ⓪
81 Jermyn St ✉ SW1Y 6JF – ⓜ Piccadilly Circus – ☏ (020) 7930 21 11
– cavendish.reservations@devere-hotels.com – Fax (020) 7839 21 25
– www.cavendish-london.co.uk   **G2**
227 rm – ❙£288 ❙❙£311, ☑ £20 – 3 suites
Rest a la carte £18/32
♦ Business ♦ Design ♦
Modern hotel in heart of Piccadilly. Contemporary, minimalist style of rooms with moody prints of London; top five floors offer far-reaching views over and beyond the city. Classic-styled restaurant overlooks Jermyn Street.

22 Jermyn Street   🖾 🛠 🖾 🕻 *VISA* 🝇 🖾 ⓪
22 Jermyn St ✉ SW1Y 6HL – ⓜ Piccadilly Circus – ☏ (020) 7734 23 53
– office@22jermyn.com – Fax (020) 7734 07 50
– www.22jermyn.com
closed 24-25 December   **G2**
5 rm – ❙£246 ❙❙£246 – 13 suites – ❙£346 ❙❙£393, ☑ £13
Rest (room service only)
♦ Townhouse ♦ Classic ♦
Discreet entrance amid famous shirt-makers' shops leads to this exclusive boutique hotel. Stylishly decorated bedrooms more than compensate for the lack of lounge space.

The Restaurant – at The Ritz H.   🍽 🖾 *VISA* 🝇 🖾 ⓪
150 Piccadilly ✉ W1V 9DG – ⓜ Green Park – ☏ (020) 7493 81 81
– Fax (020) 7493 26 87 – www.theritzlondon.com   **G2**
Rest *(dancing Friday and Saturday evenings)* £45/65 and a la carte £52/89
♦ Traditional ♦ Formal ♦
The height of opulence: magnificent Louis XVI décor with trompe l'oeil and ornate gilding. Delightful terrace over Green Park. Refined service, classic and modern menu.

The Wolseley   🖾 *VISA* 🝇 🖾 ⓪
160 Piccadilly ✉ W1J 9EB – ⓜ Green Park – ☏ (020) 7499 69 96
– Fax (020) 7499 68 88 – www.thewolseley.com
closed dinner 24-25 December, 1 January and August Bank Holiday   **G2**
Rest *(booking essential)* a la carte £28/54
♦ Modern ♦ Fashionable ♦
Has the feel of a grand European coffee house: pillars, high vaulted ceiling, mezzanine tables. Menus range from caviar to a hot dog. Also open for breakfasts and tea.

XXX **W'Sens**   AK ◇12 VISA ◑◯ AE

12 Waterloo Pl ⊠ SW1Y 4AU – ◍ Piccadilly Circus – ℰ (020) 7484 13 55
– info @ wsens.co.uk – Fax (020) 7484 13 66 – www.wsens.co.uk
closed Saturday lunch and Sunday   **G2**
Rest £23/30 and a la carte £27/50
♦ Inventive ♦ Trendy ♦
Impressive 19C façade; contrastingly cool interior: dive bar is a destination in its
own right and the wildly eclectic restaurant is matched by three intriguing menu
sections.

XXX **Fiore**   AK VISA ◑◯ AE ◑

33 St James's St ⊠ SW1A 1HD – ◍ Green Park – ℰ (020) 7930 71 00
– info @ fiore-restaurant.co.uk – Fax (020) 7930 40 70
closed 25 December and 1 January – **Rest** £22/45 and a la carte £26/37   **G2**
♦ Italian ♦ Formal ♦
Formal restaurant with affluent feel appropriate to its setting: full linen cover and
smart banquettes. Traditional Italian regional cooking with contemporary
embellishments.

XX **Le Caprice**   AK VISA ◑◯ AE ◑

Arlington House, Arlington St ⊠ SW1A 1RT – ◍ Green Park – ℰ (020) 7629 22 39
– Fax (020) 7493 90 40
closed 25-26 December, 1 January and August Bank Holiday   **G2**
Rest (Sunday brunch) a la carte £22/54
♦ Modern ♦ Fashionable ♦
Still attracting a fashionable clientele and as busy as ever. Dine at the bar or in the
smoothly run restaurant. Food combines timeless classics with modern dishes.

XX **Quaglino's**   AK ◇45 VISA ◑◯ AE ◑

16 Bury St ⊠ SW1Y 6AL – ◍ Green Park – ℰ (020) 7930 67 67 – Fax (020) 7839
28 66 – www.conran.com – closed 25 December and 1 January   **G2**
Rest (booking essential) £19 (lunch) and a la carte £22/38
♦ Modern ♦ Design ♦
Descend the sweeping staircase into the capacious room where a busy and
buzzy atmosphere prevails. Watch the chefs prepare everything from osso
bucco to fish and chips.

XX **Mint Leaf**   AK VISA ◑◯ AE ◑

Suffolk Pl ⊠ SW1Y 4HX – ◍ Piccadilly Circus – ℰ (020) 7930 90 20
– reservations @ mintleafrestaurant.com – Fax (020) 7930 62 05
– www.mintleafrestaurant.com
closed Bank Holidays and lunch Saturday and Sunday   **H2**
Rest a la carte £25/45
♦ Indian ♦ Design ♦
Basement restaurant in theatreland. Cavernous dining room incorporating busy,
trendy bar with unique cocktail list and loud music. Helpful service.
Contemporary Indian dishes.

XX **Criterion Grill Marco Pierre White**   AK VISA ◑◯ AE ◑

224 Piccadilly ⊠ W1J 9HP – ◍ Piccadilly Circus – ℰ (020) 7930 04 88 – sales @
whitestarline.org.uk – Fax (020) 7930 83 80 – www.whitestarline.org.uk
closed 24-26 December, 1 January and Sunday   **G-H2**
Rest £18 (lunch) and a la carte £27/56
♦ Modern ♦ Brasserie ♦
A stunning modern brasserie behind the revolving doors. Ornate gilding, columns
and mirrors aplenty. Bustling, characterful atmosphere, pre and post-theatre menus.

XX **Brasserie Roux**   AK VISA ◑◯ AE ◑
⊛
8 Pall Mall ⊠ SW1Y 5NG – ◍ Piccadilly Circus – ℰ (020) 7968 29 00
– h3144-fb4 @ accor-hotels.com – Fax (020) 7747 22 42   **H2**
Rest £25 and a la carte £23/32
♦ French ♦ Brasserie ♦
Informal, smart, classic brasserie style with large windows making the most of the
location. Large menu of French classics with many daily specials; comprehensive
wine list.

XX **Noura Central**   [AC] [VISA] [MO] [AE] [O]
22 Lower Regent St ⊠ SW1Y 4UJ – ⓜ Piccadilly Circus
– ℰ (020) 7839 20 20 – Fax (020) 7839 77 00
– www.noura.co.uk   G2
Rest £15/34 and a la carte £15/35
♦ Lebanese ♦ Exotic ♦
Eye-catching Lebanese façade, matched by sleek interior design. Buzzy
atmosphere enhanced by amplified background music. Large menus cover all
aspects of Lebanese cuisine.

X **Al Duca**   [AC] [VISA] [MO] [AE] [O]
😊 4-5 Duke of York St ⊠ SW1Y 6LA – ⓜ Piccadilly Circus – ℰ (020) 7839 30 90
– info @ alduca-restaurant.co.uk – Fax (020) 7839 40 50
– www.alduca-restaurant.co.uk
closed 23 December-4 January, Sunday and Bank Holidays   G2
Rest £21/24
♦ Italian ♦ Friendly ♦
Relaxed, modern, stylish restaurant. Friendly and approachable service of robust
and rustic Italian dishes. Set priced menu is good value.

X **Inn The Park**   ≼ 🍴 [VISA] [MO] [AE]
St James's Park ⊠ SW1A 2BJ – ⓜ Charing Cross – ℰ (020) 7451 99 99
– info @ innthepark.co.uk – Fax (020) 7451 99 98
– www.innthepark.co.uk
closed 25 December   H2
Rest a la carte £23/40
♦ Modern ♦ Design ♦
Eco-friendly restaurant with grass covered roof; pleasant views across park and
lakes. Super-heated dining terrace. Modern British menus of tasty, wholesome
dishes.

STRAND, COVENT GARDEN & LAMBETH

Strand and Covent Garden   *Plan III*

🏨🏨🏨 **Savoy**   ⅙ 🍸 ▣ [AC] ⅙rm ⅜ 🔲 ⚑500 ⌂ [VISA] [MO] [AE] [O]
Strand ⊠ WC2R 0EU – ⓜ Charing Cross – ℰ (020) 7836 43 43
– info @ the-savoy.co.uk – Fax (020) 7240 60 40
– www.savoy-group.co.uk   J2
236 rm – †£422/516 ††£539/656, ⌷ £25 – 27 suites
Rest see also **The Savoy Grill** below
Rest *Banquette* a la carte approx. £30
♦ Grand Luxury ♦ Art Deco ♦
Famous the world over, since 1889, as the epitome of English elegance and style.
Celebrated for its Art Deco features and luxurious bedrooms. Banquette is bright,
airy, upmarket American diner.

🏨🏨🏨 **Swissôtel The Howard**   ≼ [AC] ⅙ ⅜ 🔲 ⚑120 ⌂ [VISA] [MO] [AE] [O]
Temple Pl ⊠ WC2R 2PR – ⓜ Temple – ℰ (020) 7836 35 55
– reservations.london @ swissotel.com – Fax (020) 7379 45 47
– www.london.swissotel.com   K2
177 rm – †£358 ††£358, ⌷ £24 – 12 suites
Rest see **Jaan** below
♦ Luxury ♦ Modern ♦
Cool elegance is the order of the day at this handsomely appointed hotel.
Many of the comfortable rooms enjoy balcony views of the Thames. Attentive
service.

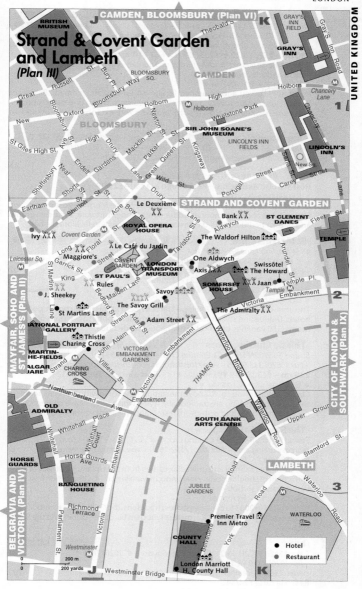

Strand & Covent Garden and Lambeth
(Plan III)

CAMDEN, BLOOMSBURY (Plan VI)

BRITISH MUSEUM

GRAY'S INN FIELD

GRAY'S INN

Theobald's

Chancery Lane

CAMDEN

Holborn

Holborn

Whetstone Park

BLOOMSBURY

SIR JOHN SOANE'S MUSEUM

LINCOLN'S INN FIELDS

LINCOLN'S INN

New Sq.

STRAND AND COVENT GARDEN

Le Deuxième

Bank

ST CLEMENT DANES

Aldwych

TEMPLE

Ivy

Covent Garden

ROYAL OPERA HOUSE

The Waldorf Hilton

Le Café du Jardin

Maggiore's

COVENT GARDEN

LONDON TRANSPORT MUSEUM

One Aldwych

Axis

Swissôtel The Howard

Leicester Sq.

ST PAUL'S

Jaan

Rules

SOMERSET HOUSE

J. Sheekey

Savoy

St Martins Lane

The Savoy Grill

The Admiralty

NATIONAL PORTRAIT GALLERY

Adam Street

ST MARTIN-IN-THE-FIELDS

Thistle Charing Cross

TRAFALGAR SQUARE

CHARING CROSS

VICTORIA EMBANKMENT GARDENS

THAMES

CITY OF LONDON & SOUTHWARK (Plan IX)

OLD ADMIRALTY

SOUTH BANK ARTS CENTRE

Waterloo Bridge

Upper Ground

HORSE GUARDS

Stamford St.

LAMBETH

BANQUETING HOUSE

JUBILEE GARDENS

WATERLOO

Richmond Terrace

Premier Travel Inn Metro

COUNTY HALL

London Marriott H. County Hall

Westminster Bridge

● Hotel
● Restaurant

0   200 m
0   200 yards

MAYFAIR, SOHO AND ST JAMES'S (Plan II)

BELGRAVIA AND VICTORIA (Plan IV)

The Waldorf Hilton

Aldwych ⊠ WC2B 4DD – Ⓜ Covent Garden
– ℰ (020) 7836 24 00 – waldorflondon@hilton.com – Fax (02) 7836 72 44
– www.hilton.co.uk/waldorf

K2

290 rm – ♦£233/329 ♦♦£233/329, ☲ £22 – 10 suites
Rest *Homage* (closed lunch Saturday and Sunday and Bank Holidays) £17
(lunch) and a la carte £26/38
♦ Luxury ♦ Modern ♦
Impressive curved and columned façade: an Edwardian landmark. Basement
leisure club. Ornate meeting rooms. Two bedroom styles: one contemporary,
one more traditional. Large, modish brasserie with extensive range of modern
menus.

One Aldwych

1 Aldwych ⊠ WC2B 4RH – Ⓜ Covent Garden – ℰ (020) 7300 10 00
– reservations@onealdwych.com – Fax (020) 7300 10 01
– www.onealdwych.com

K2

96 rm – ♦£370 ♦♦£476, ☲ £21 – 9 suites
Rest see also *Axis* below – **Rest** *Indigo* a la carte £29/38
♦ Luxury ♦ Stylish ♦
Decorative Edwardian building, former home to the Morning Post newspaper.
Now a stylish and contemporary address with modern artwork, a screening room
and hi-tech bedrooms. All-day restaurant looks down on fashionable bar.

St Martins Lane

45 St Martin's Lane ⊠ WC2N 4HX – Ⓜ Trafalgar Square
– ℰ (020) 7300 55 00 – sml@morganshotelgroup.com
– Fax (020) 7300 55 01 – www.morganshotelgroup.com

J2

202 rm – ♦£370 ♦♦£394, ☲ £21 – 2 suites
Rest *Asia de Cuba* a la carte £49/84
♦ Luxury ♦ Design ♦
The unmistakable hand of Philippe Starck evident at this most contemporary of
hotels. Unique and stylish, from the starkly modern lobby to the state-of-the-art
rooms. 350 varieties of rum at fashionable Asia de Cuba.

Thistle Charing Cross

Strand ⊠ WC2N 5HX – Ⓜ Charing Cross – ℰ (0870) 333 91 05
– Fax (0870) 333 92 05 – www.thistlehotels.com/thistle-charing-cross

J2

239 rm – ♦£305/349 ♦♦£349, ☲ £18 – **Rest** a la carte approx. £32
♦ Business ♦ Classic ♦
Classic Victorian hotel built above the station. In keeping with its origins, rooms in
the Buckingham wing are traditionally styled whilst others have contemporary
décor. Watch the world go by from restaurant's pleasant vantage point.

The Savoy Grill – at Savoy H.

Strand ⊠ WC2R 0EU – Ⓜ Charing Cross – ℰ (020) 7592 16 00 – savoygrill@
marcuswareing.com – Fax (020) 7592 16 01 – www.marcuswareing.com

J2

Rest £30/65
Spec. Smoked salmon and gravadlax carved from the trolley. Roast rack of lamb
with confit of shoulder, celery leaf gnocchi. Vanilla parfait with passion fruit curd,
blood orange sorbet.
♦ Modern ♦ Formal ♦
Redesigned in 2003 to conserve its best traditions, the Grill buzzes at midday and
in the evening. Formal service; menu of modern European dishes and the Savoy
classics.

Ivy

1 West St ⊠ WC2H 9NQ – Ⓜ Leicester Square – ℰ (020) 7836 47 51
– Fax (020) 7240 93 33
clodes 25-26 December, 1 January and August Bank Holiday

J2

Rest a la carte £24/54
♦ Modern ♦ Fashionable ♦
Wood panelling and stained glass combine with an unpretentious menu to
create a veritable institution. A favourite of 'celebrities', so securing a table can
be challenging.

XXX **Axis** – at One Aldwych H.　　　　　　　　AK *VISA* ●● AE ●
1 Aldwych ✉ WC2B 4RH – Ⓜ Covent Garden – ✆ (020) 7300 03 00 – axis @
onealdwych.com – Fax (020) 7300 03 01 – www.onealdwych.co.uk
closed 24 December-4 January, Easter, Sunday, Saturday lunch and Bank
Holidays　　　　　　　　　　　　　　　　　　　　　　　　　　K2
Rest (live jazz at dinner Tuesday and Wednesday) £20 (lunch) and a la carte
£24/40
♦ Modern ♦ Design ♦
Lower-level room overlooked by gallery bar. Muted tones, black leather chairs and
vast futuristic mural appeal to the fashion cognoscenti. Globally-influenced menu.

XXX **Jaan** – at Swissôtel The Howard　　　　　🚬 AK *VISA* ●● AE ●
Temple Pl ✉ WC2R 2PR – Ⓜ Temple – ✆ (020) 7300 17 00
– jaan.london @ swissotel.com – Fax (020) 7240 78 16
– www.swissotel-london.com
closed lunch Saturday and Sunday　　　　　　　　　　　　　　K2
Rest £33
♦ Innovative ♦ Design ♦
Bright room on the ground floor of the hotel with large windows overlooking an
attractive terrace. Original cooking - modern French with Cambodian flavours
and ingredients.

XX **J. Sheekey**　　　　　　　　　　　　　AK *VISA* ●● AE ●
28-32 St Martin's Court ✉ WC2N 4AL – Ⓜ Leicester Square – ✆ (020) 7240 25 65
– Fax (020) 7240 81 14
closed 25-26 December, 1 January and August Bank Holiday　　　　　J2
Rest (booking essential) a la carte £25/48
♦ Seafood ♦ Fashionable ♦
Festooned with photographs of actors and linked to the theatrical world since
opening in 1890. Wood panels and alcove tables add famed intimacy.
Accomplished seafood cooking.

XX **Rules**　　　　　　　　　　　　　　AK ⅙ *VISA* ●● AE ●
35 Maiden Lane ✉ WC2E 7LB – Ⓜ Leicester Square – ✆ (020) 7836 53 14
– info @ rules.co.uk – Fax (020) 7497 10 81
– www.rules.co.uk
closed 4 days Christmas　　　　　　　　　　　　　　　　　　J2
Rest (booking essential) a la carte £29/40
♦ English ♦ Formal ♦
London's oldest restaurant boasts a fine collection of antique cartoons, drawings
and paintings. Tradition continues in the menu, specialising in game from its
own estate.

XX **Maggiore's**　　　　　　　　　AK ⅙ ✿20 *VISA* ●● AE
33 King St ✉ WC2 8JD – Ⓜ Leicester Square – ✆ (020) 7379 96 96
– enquiries @ maggiores.uk.com – Fax (020) 7379 67 67
– www.maggiores.uk.com
closed 24-26 December and 1 January　　　　　　　　　　　　　J2
Rest £18 (lunch) and a la carte £32/43 ⊞
♦ Innovative ♦ Formal ♦
Walls covered with flowering branches create delightful woodland feel to rear
dining area with retractable glass roof. Seriously accomplished, original, rustic
French cooking.

XX **Adam Street**　　　　　　　　　　　AK *VISA* ●● AE ●
9 Adam St ✉ WC2N 6AA – Ⓜ Charing Cross – ✆ (020) 7379 80 00
– info @ adamstreet.co.uk – Fax (020) 7379 14 44
– www.adamstreet.co.uk
closed 25 December, Saturday, Sunday and Bank Holidays　　　　　J2
Rest (lunch only) £20 and a la carte £28/38
♦ Modern ♦ Formal ♦
Set in the striking vaults of a private members club just off the Strand. Sumptuous
suede banquettes and elegantly laid tables. Well executed classic and modern
English food.

XX **The Admiralty**　　　　　　　　　　　 4/ *VISA* ◐ AE ⑩
Somerset House, The Strand ⊠ *WC2R 1LA* – Ⓜ *Temple*
– 𝒞 *(020) 7845 46 46* – Fax *(020) 7845 46 58*
– *www.somerset-house.org.uk*
closed 23-26 December and dinner Sunday and Bank Holidays　　　**K2**
Rest a la carte £37/42
♦ French ♦ Brasserie ♦
Interconnecting rooms with bold colours and informal service contrast with its
setting within the restored Georgian splendour of Somerset House. 'Cuisine de
terroir'.

XX **Bank**　　　　　　　　　　　　　 AK *VISA* ◐ AE ⑩
1 Kingsway, Aldwych ⊠ *WC2B 6XF* – Ⓜ *Covent Garden* – 𝒞 *(020) 7379 97 97*
– *aldres@bankrestaurants.com* – Fax *(020) 7379 50 70*
– *www.bankrestaurants.com*
closed 25 December, 1-2 January and Sunday dinner　　　　**K2**
Rest £16 (lunch) and a la carte £24/45
♦ Modern ♦ Brasserie ♦
Ceiling decoration of hanging glass shards creates a high level of interest in this
bustling converted bank. Open-plan kitchen provides an extensive array of
modern dishes.

XX **Le Deuxième**　　　　　　　　　　　 AK *VISA* ◐ AE
65a Long Acre ⊠ *WC2E 9JH* – Ⓜ *Covent Garden* – 𝒞 *(020) 7379 00 33*
– Fax *(020) 7379 00 66* – *www.ledeuxieme.com*
closed 25-26 December　　　　　　　　　　**J1**
Rest £15 (lunch) and a la carte £24/30
♦ Modern ♦ Brasserie ♦
Caters well for theatregoers: opens early, closes late. Buzzy eatery, quietly
decorated in white with subtle lighting. Varied international menu: Japanese to
Mediterranean.

X **Le Café du Jardin**　　　　　　　　　 AK *VISA* ◐ AE ⑩
28 Wellington St ⊠ *WC2E 7BD* – Ⓜ *Covent Garden* – 𝒞 *(020) 7836 87 69*
– Fax *(020) 7836 41 23* – *www.lecafedujardin.com*
closed 25-26 December　　　　　　　　　　**J2**
Rest £15 (lunch) and a la carte £24/29 ⊛
♦ Modern ♦ Bistro ♦
Divided into two floors with the downstairs slightly more comfortable. Light and
contemporary interior with European-influenced cooking. Ideally placed for the
Opera House.

Lambeth　　　　　　　　　　　　　　　　　 *Plan III*

🏨 **London Marriott H. County Hall**　　 ⇐ ⊕ ℔ 🏠 ⃞ ⅃ AK 4/rm ℅
Westminster Bridge Rd ⊠ *SE1 7PB*　　　　 🛗70 *VISA* ◐ AE ⑩
– Ⓜ *Westminster* – 𝒞 *(020) 7928 52 00* – *salesadmin.countyhall@*
marriotthotels.co.uk – Fax *(020) 7928 53 00* – *www.marriott.com/lonch*　**K3**
195 rm – ✝£293 ✝✝£293, ⊑ £22 – 5 suites
Rest *County Hall* £27 and a la carte £26/51
♦ Luxury ♦ Classic ♦
Occupying the historic County Hall building. Many of the spacious and
comfortable bedrooms enjoy river and Parliament outlook. Impressive leisure
facilities. Famously impressive views from restaurant.

🏨 **Premier Travel Inn Metro**　　 ♿ AK rest 4/ ℅ *VISA* ◐ AE ⑩
Belvedere Rd ⊠ *SE1 7PB* – Ⓜ *Waterloo* – 𝒞 *(0870) 238 33 00*
– *london.county.hall.mti@whitbread.com* – Fax *(020) 7902 16 19*
– *www.travelinn.co.uk*　　　　　　　　　　**K3**
314 rm – ✝£87 ✝✝£90
Rest (grill rest) (dinner only)
♦ Chain hotel ♦ Functional ♦
Adjacent to the London Eye and within the County Hall building. Budget
accommodation in a central London location that is the envy of many, more
expensive, hotels.

BELGRAVIA & VICTORIA

Belgravia

Plan IV

The Berkeley ⊛ ⅃ᵶ ℅ ☒ ☒ ↤rm ℅ ☒ ⅍250 ⊛ *VISA* ◍ ᴁ ⓪
Wilton Pl ⊠ *SW1X 7RL* – ⓜ *Knightsbridge* – ℰ *(020) 7235 60 00*
– info@the-berkeley.co.uk – Fax (020) 7235 43 30
– www.the-berkeley.com
L1
189 rm – ✝£433/480 ✝✝£492/539, ⊑ £24 – 25 suites
Rest see also *Pétrus* below
Rest *Boxwood Café*, ℰ *(020) 7235 10 10* – £21 (lunch) and a la carte £28/36
♦ Grand Luxury ♦ Stylish ♦
A gracious and discreet hotel. Relax in the gilded and panelled Lutyens lounge or enjoy a swim in the roof-top pool with its retracting roof. Opulent bedrooms. Split-level basement restaurant, divided by bar with modern stylish décor; New York-style dining.

The Lanesborough ⅃ᵶ ⅊ ☒ ↤rm ☒ ⅍90 ℗ *VISA* ◍ ᴁ ⓪
Hyde Park Corner ⊠ *SW1X 7TA* – ⓜ *Hyde Park Corner* – ℰ *(020) 7259 55 99*
– info@lanesborough.com – Fax (020) 7259 56 06
– www.lanesborough.com
L1
86 rm – ✝£347/464 ✝✝£582, ⊑ £26 – 9 suites
Rest *The Conservatory* £24/48 and a la carte £57/78
♦ Grand Luxury ♦ Classic ♦
Converted in the 1990s from 18C St George's Hospital. A grand and traditional atmosphere prevails. Butler service offered. Regency-era decorated, lavishly appointed rooms. Ornate, glass-roofed dining room with palm trees and fountains.

The Halkin ☒ ℅ ☒ *VISA* ◍ ᴁ ⓪
5 Halkin St ⊠ *SW1X 7DJ* – ⓜ *Hyde Park Corner* – ℰ *(020) 7333 10 00*
– res@halkin.como.bz – Fax (020) 7333 11 00
– www.halkin.como.bz
closed 25-26 December and 1 January
L-M1
35 rm – ✝£388 ✝✝£388, ⊑ £23 – 6 suites
Rest see *Nahm* below
♦ Luxury ♦ Stylish ♦
One of London's first minimalist hotels. The cool, marbled reception and bar have an understated charm. Spacious rooms have every conceivable facility.

Sheraton Belgravia ⅊ ☒ ↤rm ℅ ⅍25 ℗ *VISA* ◍ ᴁ ⓪
20 Chesham Pl ⊠ *SW1X 8HQ* – ⓜ *Knightsbridge* – ℰ *(020) 7235 60 40*
– reservations.sheratonbelgravia@sheraton.com – Fax (020) 7259 62 43
– www.sheraton.com/belgravia
L2
82 rm – ✝£329 ✝✝£329, ⊑ £20 – 7 suites
Rest *The Dining Room* a la carte £26/33
♦ Business ♦ Classic ♦
Modern corporate hotel overlooking Chesham Place. Comfortable and well-equipped for the tourist and business traveller alike. A few minutes' walk from Harrods. Modern, international menus.

Diplomat without rest ℅ *VISA* ◍ ᴁ ⓪
2 Chesham St ⊠ *SW1X 8DT* – ⓜ *Sloane Square* – ℰ *(020) 7235 15 44*
– diplomat.hotel@btinternet.com – Fax (020) 7259 61 53
– www.btinternet.com/diplomat.hotel
L2
26 rm – ✝£90/115 ✝✝£150/175
♦ Traditional ♦ Classic ♦
Imposing Victorian corner house built in 1882 by Thomas Cubitt. Attractive glass-domed stairwell and sweeping staircase. Spacious and well-appointed bedrooms.

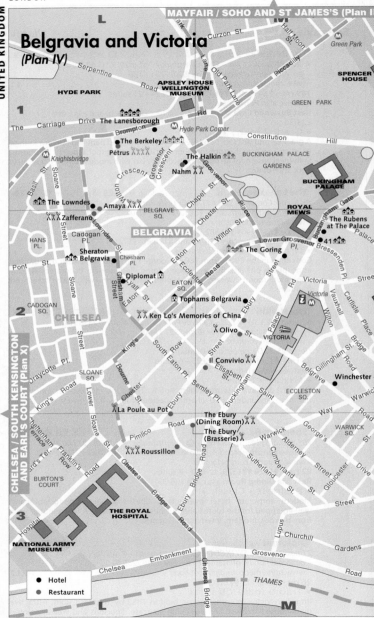

Belgravia and Victoria
(Plan IV)

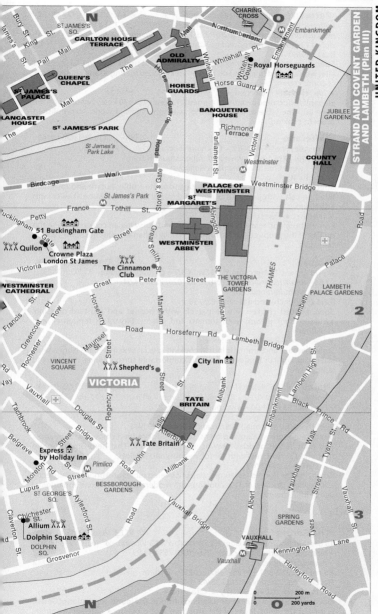

CHARING
CROSS

Embankment

Northumberland

Royal Horseguards

ST JAMES'S
SQ.

Bury St.

James's

King

St.

Pall Mall

CARLTON HOUSE
TERRACE

The Mall

QUEEN'S
CHAPEL

ST JAMES'S
PALACE

LANCASTER
HOUSE

The Mall

ST JAMES'S PARK

St James's
Park Lake

Birdcage

Walk

OLD
ADMIRALTY

Whitehall

Whitehall Pl.

Whitehall Court

HORSE
GUARDS

Horse Guard Av.

BANQUETING
HOUSE

Richmond
Terrace

Parliament St.

Victoria

Westminster

JUBILEE
GARDENS

COUNTY
HALL

Westminster Bridge

Horse Guards Road

St James's Park

France

Tothill

St.

Storey's Gate

Abingdon

PALACE OF
WESTMINSTER

THAMES

Buckingham

Petty

51 Buckingham Gate

Quilon

Gate

Crowne Plaza
London St James

Street

Great Smith St.

ST
MARGARET'S

WESTMINSTER
ABBEY

St.

THE VICTORIA
TOWER
GARDENS

LAMBETH
PALACE GARDENS

2

Victoria

Great

The Cinnamon
Club

Peter

Street

Millbank

WESTMINSTER
CATHEDRAL

Francis

St.

Greycoat

Pl.

Row

Rochester

Horseferry

Maunsel St.

Street

Road

Horseferry Rd

Lambeth Bridge

Embankment

Lambeth

Palace

Road

Lambeth High St.

VINCENT
SQUARE

Shepherd's

City Inn

Black

Vay

Rd

Vauxhall

Tachbrook

Belgrave

VICTORIA

Regency

Street

St.

Douglas St.

Millbank

TATE
BRITAIN

Prince

Rd

Vauxhall

Walk

Tyers

St.

Vauxhall

Street

Express
by Holiday Inn

Moreton

Rd

Pimlico

Road

Tate Britain

John

Islip St.

Millbank

BESSBOROUGH
GARDENS

Lupus

ST GEORGE'S
SQ.

Aylesford St.

Vauxhall Road

Vauxhall Bridge

Albert

Embankment

SPRING
GARDENS

Tyers St.

Vauxhall

3

Chichester
St.

Allium

Dolphin Square

DOLPHIN
SQ.

Grosvenor

VAUXHALL

Vauxhall

Kennington

Lane

Harleyford

Road

0   200 m
0   200 yards

UNITED KINGDOM

XXXX ✿

Pétrus (Wareing) – at The Berkeley H.   AC ⅃ ✿14 VISA OO AE ①
Wilton Pl ⊠ SW1X 7RL – Ⓜ Knightsbridge – ℰ (020) 7235 12 00 – petrus@
marcuswareing.com – Fax (020) 7235 12 66 – www.marcuswareing.com
closed 1 week Christmas, Sunday, Saturday lunch and Bank Holidays   **L1**
Rest £30/80 ⊛
Spec. Tuna Rossini with chicory salad, Madeira and truffle dressing. Glazed beef fillet with sautéed foie gras and braised leeks. Baked meringue and cherry sauce, coconut cream.
◆ Modern ◆ Formal ◆
Elegantly appointed restaurant named after one of the 40 Pétrus vintages on the wine list. One table in the kitchen to watch the chefs at work. Accomplished modern cooking.

XXX ✿

Zafferano   AC ⅃ ✿18 VISA OO AE ①
15 Lowndes St ⊠ SW1X 9EY – Ⓜ Knightsbridge – ℰ (020) 7235 58 00
– Fax (020) 7235 19 71 – www.zafferanorestaurant.com
closed 1 week Christmas and Bank Holidays   **L2**
Rest £30/40 ⊛
Spec. Slow baked onion with fonduta and white truffle. Potato and rosemary filled parcels with porcini mushrooms. Lobster and langoustine skewer with artichokes.
◆ Italian ◆ Fashionable ◆
Forever busy and relaxed. No frills, robust and gutsy Italian cooking, where the quality of the produce shines through. Wholly Italian wine list has some hidden treasures.

XXX ✿

Amaya   AC ✿14 VISA OO AE ①
Halkin Arcade, 19 Motcomb St ⊠ SW1X 8JT – Ⓜ Knightsbridge – ℰ (020) 7823
11 66 – info@realindianfood.com – Fax (020) 7259 64 64
– www.realindianfood.com   **L1**
Rest £19 (lunch) and a la carte £25/50
Spec. Minced chicken lettuce parcels with coconut and mustard dressing. Tandoori tiger prawns with tomato and ginger. Biryani of fenugreek and cauliflower.
◆ Indian ◆ Fashionable ◆
Light, piquant and aromatic Indian cooking specialising in kebabs from a tawa skillet, sigri grill or tandoor oven. Chic comfortable surroundings, modern and subtly exotic.

XX ✿

Nahm – at The Halkin H.   AC ✿30 VISA OO AE ①
5 Halkin St ⊠ SW1X 7DJ – Ⓜ Hyde Park Corner – ℰ (020) 7333 12 34
– Fax (020) 7333 11 00 – www.halkin.co.uk
closed lunch Saturday and Sunday and Bank Holidays   **L1**
Rest (booking essential) £26/50 and a la carte £31/41
Spec. Lemongrass salad of prawns, squid and shredded chicken with peanuts and mint. Relish of dried prawns with sweet pork, Thai herb omelette and turmeric. Curry of beef with santol, peanuts and shallots.
◆ Thai ◆ Design ◆
Brown marble floored restaurant with uncovered tables and understated decor. Menu offers the best of Thai cooking with modern interpretations and original use of ingredients.

Victoria   *Plan IV*

🏠

The Goring   ⌷ AC ▭ ⅍50 VISA OO AE ①
15 Beeston Pl, Grosvenor Gdns ⊠ SW1W 0JW – Ⓜ Victoria – ℰ (020) 7396 90 00
– reception@goringhotel.co.uk – Fax (020) 7834 43 93
– www.goringhotel.co.uk   **M2**
65 rm – ⸙£212/341 ⸙⸙£259/382, ⌷ £19 – 6 suites
Rest (closed Saturday lunch) £28/42 ⊛
◆ Traditional ◆ Luxury ◆ Classic ◆
Opened in 1910 as a quintessentially English hotel. The fourth generation of Goring is now at the helm. Many of the attractive rooms overlook a peaceful garden. Elegantly appointed restaurant provides memorable dining experience.

Crowne Plaza London St James

45 Buckingham Gate ✉ SW1E 6AF – Ⓜ St James's Park – ✆ (020) 7834 66 55 – sales@cplonsj.co.uk – Fax (020) 7630 75 87 – www.london.crowneplaza.com **N2**

323 rm – ♦£292 ♦♦£294, ☕ £16 – 19 suites

Rest see also ***Quilon*** below

Rest *Bistro 51* £15/19 and a la carte £21/40

♦ Luxury ♦ Classic ♦

Built in 1897 as serviced accommodation for visiting aristocrats. Behind the impressive Edwardian façade lies an equally elegant interior. Quietest rooms overlook courtyard. Bright and informal café-style restaurant.

Royal Horseguards

2 Whitehall Court ✉ SW1A 2EJ – Ⓜ Charing Cross – ✆ (020) 7839 34 00 – royalhorseguards@thistle.co.uk – Fax (020) 7925 22 63 – www.thistlehotels.com/royalhorseguards **O1**

276 rm – ♦£309 ♦♦£329/372, ☕ £18 – 4 suites

Rest *One Twenty One Two* *(closed lunch Saturday and Sunday)* £26 and a la carte £26/38

♦ Business ♦ Classic ♦

Imposing Grade I listed property in Whitehall overlooking the Thames and close to London Eye. Impressive meeting rooms. Some of the well-appointed bedrooms have river views. Stylish restaurant, sub-divided into intimate rooms.

51 Buckingham Gate without rest

51 Buckingham Gate ✉ SW1E 6AF – Ⓜ St James's Park – ✆ (020) 7769 77 66 – info@51-buckinghamgate.co.uk – Fax (020) 7828 59 09 – www.51-buckinghamgate.com **N2**

82 suites – ♦£382 ♦♦£999, ☕ £18

Rest see ***Quilon and Bank*** below

♦ Luxury ♦ Classic ♦

Canopied entrance leads to luxurious suites: every detail considered, every mod con provided. Colour schemes echoed in plants and paintings. Butler and nanny service.

41 without rest

41 Buckingham Palace Rd ✉ SW1W 0PS – Ⓜ Victoria – ✆ (020) 7300 00 41 – book41@rchmail.com – Fax (020) 7300 01 41 – www.41hotel.com **M2**

19 rm – ♦£346 ♦♦£346/370 – 1 suite

♦ Luxury ♦ Classic ♦

Discreet appearance; exudes exclusive air. Leather armchairs; bookcases line the walls. Intimate service. State-of-the-art rooms where hi-tech and fireplace merge appealingly.

The Rubens at The Palace

39 Buckingham Palace Rd ✉ SW1W 0PS – Ⓜ Victoria – ✆ (020) 7834 66 00 – bookrb@rchmail.com – Fax (020) 7828 54 01 – www.redcarnationhotels.com **M2**

170 rm – ♦£217/287 ♦♦£264/287, ☕ £15 – 2 suites

Rest *(closed lunch Saturday and Sunday)* (carvery) £20

♦ Traditional ♦ Classic ♦

Traditional hotel with an air of understated elegance. Tastefully furnished rooms: the Royal Wing, themed after Kings and Queens, features TVs in bathrooms. Smart carvery restaurant. Intimate, richly decorated Library restaurant has sumptuous armchairs.

Dolphin Square

Dolphin Square, Chichester St ✉ SW1V 3LX – Ⓜ Pimlico – ✆ (020) 7834 38 00 – reservations@dolphinsquarehotel.co.uk – Fax (020) 7798 87 35 – www.dolphinsquarehotel.co.uk **N3**

30 rm – ♦£195 ♦♦£195 – **118 suites** – ♦£215 ♦♦£450, ☕ £14

Rest see also ***Allium*** below

Rest *The Brasserie* £16 and a la carte £22/26

♦ Traditional ♦ Classic ♦

Built in 1935 and shared with residential apartments. Art Deco influence remains in the Clipper bar overlooking the leisure club. Spacious suites with contemporary styling. Brasserie overlooks the swimming pool.

City Inn　　　　　　　ଌ ఈ 📶 ⅍ ⅏150 *VISA* **◑⊙** 𝔸𝔼 ⓪
30 John Islip St ⊠ SW1P 4DD – ⓜ *Pimlico – ℰ (020) 7630 10 00*
– westminster.res@cityinn.com – Fax (020) 7233 75 75
– www.cityinn.com　　　　　　　　　　　　　　　**O2**
444 rm – †£264 ††£264, ⌑ £19 – 16 suites
Rest *City Cafe* £17 and a la carte £23/36
• Business • Functional •
Modern hotel five minutes' walk from Westminster Abbey and Tate Britain.
Well-appointed bedrooms with high-tech equipment and some with pleasant
views of London. Brasserie serving modern-style food next to a glass-covered
terrace with artwork feature.

Tophams Belgravia without rest　　　　 ⅍ ⅏30 *VISA* **◑⊙** 𝔸𝔼
28 Ebury St ⊠ SW1W 0LU – ⓜ *Victoria – ℰ (020) 7730 81 47*
– tophamsbelgravia@compuserve.com – Fax (020) 7823 59 66
– www.zolahotels.com　　　　　　　　　　　　　**M2**
37 rm – †£85/130 ††£100/150
• Traditional • Classic •
Five adjoining houses creating a hotel which has a certain traditional charm.
Cosy lounges, roaring fires and antique furniture aplenty. Individually decorated
bedrooms.

Winchester without rest　　　　　　　　　　　　 ⅍
17 Belgrave Rd ⊠ SW1V 1RB – ⓜ *Victoria – ℰ (020) 7828 29 72*
– winchesterhotel17@hotmail.com – Fax (020) 7828 51 91
– www.winchester-hotel.net　　　　　　　　　　　**M2**
18 rm – †£70/85 ††£85/140
• Traditional • Functional •
Behind the portico entrance one finds a friendly, well-kept private hotel. The
generally spacious rooms are pleasantly appointed. Comprehensive English
breakfast offered.

Express by Holiday Inn without rest　　 ఈ ⅍ ⅍ *VISA* **◑⊙** 𝔸𝔼 ⓪
106-110 Belgrave Rd ⊠ SW1V 2BJ – ⓜ *Pimlico – ℰ (020) 7630 88 88*
– info@hiexpressvictoria.co.uk – Fax (020) 7828 04 41
– www.hiexpressvictoria.co.uk　　　　　　　　　　**N3**
52 rm – †£119 ††£119
• Chain hotel • Functional •
Converted Georgian terraced houses a short walk from station. Despite
converted property's age, all rooms are stylish and modern with good range of facilities
including TV movies.

XXX　**Allium** – at Dolphin Square H.　　　　 📶 *VISA* **◑⊙** 𝔸𝔼 ⓪
Dolphin Square, Chichester St ⊠ SW1V 3LX – ⓜ *Pimlico – ℰ (020) 7798 68 88*
– info@allium.co.uk – Fax (020) 7798 56 85
– www.allium.co.uk
closed Monday and Saturday lunch　　　　　　　　**N3**
Rest £24/30 and a la carte £32/46
• Contemporary • Design •
A calm atmosphere prevails in this richly decorated room. Raised tables to rear
with sumptuous banquettes for more privacy. Interesting and assured modern
British cooking.

XXX　**The Cinnamon Club**　　　　　 📶 ⇔50 ℙ *VISA* **◑⊙** 𝔸𝔼 ⓪
Great Smith St ⊠ SW1P 3BU – ⓜ *St James's Park*
– ℰ (020) 7222 25 55
– info@cinnamonclub.com – Fax (020) 7222 13 33
– www.cinnamonclub.com
closed Saturday lunch, Sunday and Bank Holidays　　**N2**
Rest £22 (lunch) and a la carte £26/49
• Indian • Formal •
Housed in former Westminster Library: exterior has ornate detail, interior is
stylish and modern. Walls are lined with books. New wave Indian cooking with
plenty of choice.

XXX **Quilon** – at Crowne Plaza London St James H.　　　AC VISA MO AE ①
45 Buckingham Gate ⊠ SW1E 6AF – Ⓜ Victoria – ℰ (020) 7821 18 99
– Fax (020) 7828 58 02 – www.thequilonrestaurant.com
closed Sunday and Saturday lunch　　　　　　　　　　　　　**N2**
Rest £16 (lunch) and a la carte £18/36
♦ Indian ♦ Formal ♦
A selection of Eastern pictures adorn the walls in this smart, modern and busy restaurant. Specialising in progressive south coasta Indian cooking.

XXX **Shepherd's**　　　　　　　　　　　　　AC VISA MO AE ①
Marsham Court, Marsham St ⊠ SW1P 4LA – Ⓜ Pimlico – ℰ (020) 7834 95 52
– langansrestaurants.co.uk – Fax (020) 7233 60 47
– www.langansrestaurants.co.uk
closed Saturday, Sunday and Bank Holidays　　　　　　　**N2**
Rest (booking essential) £30
♦ English ♦ Formal ♦
A truly English restaurant where game and traditional puddings are a highlight. Popular with those from Westminster - the booths offer a degree of privacy.

XXX **Roussillon**　　　　　　　　　　　　　AC VISA MO AE
ॐ *16 St Barnabas St ⊠ SW1W 8PE – Ⓜ Sloane Square – ℰ (020) 7730 55 50*
– alexis@roussillon.co.uk – Fax (020) 7824 86 17
– www.roussillon.co.uk
closed 27 August-4 September, 25 December-3 January, Sunday and lunch
Saturday-Tuesday　　　　　　　　　　　　　　　　　　**L3**
Rest £30/45 ॐ
Spec. Chestnut and pheasant soup, ceps and marrow ravioli. Venison with pear, truffle and celeriac purée. Spicy soufflé of duck eggs with a maple infusion.
♦ French ♦ Neighbourhood ♦
Tucked away in a smart residential area. Cooking clearly focuses on the quality of the ingredients. Seasonal menu with inventive elements and a French base.

XX **The Ebury (Dining Room)**　　　　　　　AC VISA MO AE
1st Floor, 11 Pimlico Rd, ⊠ SW1W 8NA – Ⓜ Sloane Square
– ℰ (020) 7730 67 84 – info@theebury.co.uk – Fax (020) 7730 61 49
– www.theebury.co.uk
closed Christmas, Sunday and Monday　　　　　　　　　**M3**
Rest (dinner only) a la carte £25/34
♦ Modern ♦ Formal ♦
Mount the spiral stairs to the formal restaurant with tall windows overlooking the street. Open-plan kitchen provides set gastronomic-style menu using first-class ingredients.

XX **Il Convivio**　　　　　　　🛎 AC ⟷14 VISA MO AE ①
143 Ebury St ⊠ SW1W 9QN – Ⓜ Sloane Square – ℰ (020) 7730 40 99
– comments@etruscarestaurants.com – Fax (020) 7730 41 03
– www.etruscarestaurants.com
closed Sunday and Bank Holidays　　　　　　　　　　　**M2**
Rest £20/33
♦ Italian ♦ Design ♦
A retractable roof provides alfresco dining to part of this comfortable and modern restaurant. Contemporary and traditional Italian menu with home-made pasta specialities.

XX **Tate Britain**　　　　　　　　　　　　AC VISA MO AE ①
Tate Britain, Millbank ⊠ SW1P 4RG – Ⓜ Pimlico – ℰ (020) 7887 88 25
– tate.restaurant@tate.org.uk – Fax (020) 7887 89 02 – www.tate.org.uk
closed 24-26 December　　　　　　　　　　　　　　　　**N3**
Rest (booking essential) (lunch only) £27 ॐ
♦ English ♦ Brasserie ♦
Continue your appreciation of art when lunching in this basement room decorated with original Rex Whistler murals. Forever busy, it offers modern British fare.

XX **Ken Lo's Memories of China**   AC VISA ◍ AE ◐
65-69 Ebury St ⊠ SW1W 0NZ – Ⓜ Victoria – ℰ (020) 7730 77 34
– Fax (020) 7730 29 92
closed Sunday lunch   **M2**
Rest a la carte approx. £28
♦ Chinese ♦ Neighbourhood ♦
An air of tranquillity pervades this traditionally furnished room. Lattice screens add extra privacy. Extensive Chinese menu: bold flavours with a clean, fresh style.

X **The Ebury (Brasserie)**   AC VISA ◍ AE
Ground Floor, 11 Pimlico Rd, ⊠ SW1W 8NA – Ⓜ Sloane Square
– ℰ (020) 7730 67 84 – info@theebury.co.uk – Fax (020) 7730 61 49
– www.theebury.co.uk
closed 24-26 December and 1 January   **M3**
Rest £21/34
♦ Modern ♦ Pub ♦
Victorian corner pub restaurant with walnut bar, simple tables and large seafood bar. Friendly service. Wide-ranging menu from snacks to full meals.

X **Olivo**   AC VISA ◍ AE ◐
21 Eccleston St ⊠ SW1W 9LX – Ⓜ Victoria – ℰ (020) 7730 25 05
– maurosanna@oliveto.fsnet.co.uk – Fax (020) 7823 53 77
closed lunch Saturday and Sunday and Bank Holidays   **M2**
Rest £19 (lunch) and a la carte £27/31
♦ Italian ♦ Neighbourhood ♦
Rustic, informal Italian restaurant. Relaxed atmosphere provided by the friendly staff. Simple, non-fussy cuisine with emphasis on best available fresh produce.

X **La Poule au Pot**   ⌂ AC VISA ◍ AE ◐
231 Ebury St ⊠ SW1W 8UT – Ⓜ Sloane Square – ℰ (020) 7730 77 63
– Fax (020) 7259 96 51
closed 25 December   **L2**
Rest £17 (lunch) and a la carte £26/41
♦ French ♦ Bistro ♦
The subdued lighting and friendly informality make this one of London's more romantic restaurants. Classic French menu with extensive plats du jour.

REGENT'S PARK & MARYLEBONE   *Plan V*

🏨🏨🏨🏨 **Landmark London**   Ló 🏊 🗔 🕭 AC ↲rm ℀ 🖾 🔊350
222 Marylebone Rd ⊠ NW1 6JQ – Ⓜ Baker   ⌂ VISA ◍ AE ◐
Street – ℰ (020) 7631 80 00 – reservations@thelandmark.co.uk
– Fax (020) 7631 80 80 – www.landmarklondon.co.uk   **P-Q1**
290 rm – ♦£238/288 ♦♦£288, ⊇ £25 – 9 suites
Rest *Winter Garden* a la carte £36/55
♦ Grand Luxury ♦ Classic ♦
Imposing Victorian Gothic building with a vast glass enclosed atrium, overlooked by many of the modern, well-equipped bedrooms. Winter Garden popular for afternoon tea.

🏨🏨🏨 **Langham**   ◍ Ló 🏊 🗔 🕭 AC ↲rm ℀ 🖾 🔊250 VISA ◍ AE ◐
1c Portland Pl, Regent St ⊠ W1B 1JA – Ⓜ Oxford Circus – ℰ (020) 7636 10 00
– info@langhamhotels.com – Fax (020) 7323 23 40
– www.langhamlondon.com   **R2**
409 rm – ♦£220/257 ♦♦£320/364, ⊇ £23 – 20 suites
Rest *Memories* £24/45
♦ Luxury ♦ Classic ♦
Opposite the BBC, with Colonial inspired décor. Polo themed bar and barrel vaulted Palm Court. Concierge Club rooms offer superior comfort and butler service. Memories is a bright, elegant dining room.

The Cumberland   🕭 🎬 ↝ 🖵 ♨300 <u>VISA</u> ◍ AE ①

Great Cumberland Pl ⊠ W1A 4RF – **Ⓜ** *Marble Arch –* ℰ *(0870) 333 92 80*
– enquiries@thecumberland.co.uk – Fax (0870) 333 92 81
– www.guoman.com   **Q2**
1019 rm – ♥£140/315 ♥♥£150/315, ⌑ £17
Rest see *Rhodes W1* below
♦ Business ♦ Design ♦
Fully refurbished, conference oriented hotel whose vast lobby boasts modern art, sculpture and running water panels. Distinctive bedrooms with a host of impressive extras.

Hyatt Regency London-The Churchill   🕭 🔊 ℁ 🕭 🎬 ↝rm

30 Portman Sq ⊠ W1A 4ZX   ℁ 🖵 ♨ 🎬 AE ①
– **Ⓜ** *Marble Arch –* ℰ *(020) 7486 58 00 – london.churchill@hyattintl.com*
– Fax (020) 7486 12 55 – www.london-churchill.hyatt.com   **Q2**
405 rm – ♥£282 ♥♥£305, ⌑ £21 – 40 suites
Rest *The Montagu* a la carte £33/46
♦ Luxury ♦ Classic ♦
Modern property overlooking attractive square. Elegant marbled lobby. Cigar bar open until 2am for members. Well-appointed rooms have the international traveller in mind. Restaurant provides popular Sunday brunch entertainment.

Charlotte Street   🕭 🕭 🎬 ℁ 🖵 ♨ ♨65 <u>VISA</u> ◍ AE

15 Charlotte St ⊠ W1T 1RJ – **Ⓜ** *Goodge Street –* ℰ *(020) 7806 20 00*
– charlotte@firmdale.com – Fax (020) 7806 20 02
– www.charlottestreethotel.co.uk   **S2**
44 rm – ♥£230/240 ♥♥£335, ⌑ £19 – 8 suites
Rest see *Oscar* below
♦ Luxury ♦ Stylish ♦
Interior designed with a charming and understated English feel. Welcoming lobby laden with floral displays. Individually decorated rooms with CDs and mobile phones.

Sanderson   🗟 🕭 🎬 ↝rm ℁ 🖵 ♨ <u>VISA</u> ◍ AE ①

50 Berners St ⊠ W1T 3NG – **Ⓜ** *Oxford Circus –* ℰ *(020) 7300 14 00*
– sanderson@morganshotelgroup.com – Fax (020) 7300 14 01
– www.morganshotelgroup.com   **S2**
150 rm – ♥£376 ♥♥£376/750, ⌑ £25
Rest *Spoon+* a la carte £55/135
♦ Luxury ♦ Minimalist ♦
Designed by Philipe Starck: the height of contemporary design. Bar is the place to see and be seen. Bedrooms with minimalistic white décor have DVDs and striking bathrooms. Stylish Spoon+ allows diners to construct own dishes.

The Leonard   🕭 🎬 ↝ ℁ 🖵 ♨ <u>VISA</u> ◍ AE ①

15 Seymour St ⊠ W1H 7JW – **Ⓜ** *Marble Arch –* ℰ *(020) 7935 20 10*
– reservations@theleonard.com – Fax (020) 7935 67 00
– www.theleonard.com   **Q2**
24 rm – ♥£276 ♥♥£276, ⌑ £20 – 20 suites
Rest (room service only)
♦ Townhouse ♦ Classic ♦
Around the corner from Selfridges, an attractive Georgian townhouse: antiques and oil paintings abound. Informal, stylish café bar offers light snacks. Well-appointed rooms.

Radisson SAS Portman   🕭 🔊 ℁ 🕭 ↝rm ℁ 🖵 ♨

22 Portman Sq ⊠ W1H 7BG – **Ⓜ** *Marble Arch*   ♨650 <u>VISA</u> ◍ AE ①
– ℰ *(020) 7208 60 00 – sales.london@radissonsas.com*
– Fax (020) 7208 60 01 – www.radisson.com   **Q2**
265 rm – ♥£163/187 ♥♥£212/246, ⌑ £18 – 7 suites
Rest *Talavera (closed lunch Saturday, Sunday and Bank Holidays)* (buffet lunch) dinner a la carte £28/38
♦ Business ♦ Classic ♦
This modern, corporate hotel offers check-in for both British Midland and SAS airlines. Rooms in attached towers decorated in Scandinavian, Chinese and Italian styles. Restaurant renowned for its elaborate buffet lunch.

Montcalm

A/C rest 80 VISA MC AE

Great Cumberland Pl ✉ W1H 7TW – Ⓜ Marble Arch – ✆ (020) 7402 42 88
– montcalm@montcalm.co.uk – Fax (020) 7724 91 80
– www.montcalm.co.uk **Q2**

110 rm – £270/294 £294, ☕ £16 – 10 suites

Rest see ***The Crescent*** below

◆ Business ◆ Classic ◆

Named after the 18C French general, the Marquis de Montcalm. In a charming crescent a short walk from Hyde Park. Spacious bedrooms with a subtle oriental feel.

Durrants

A/C rest 55 VISA MC AE

26-32 St George St ✉ W1H 5BJ – Ⓜ Bond Street – ✆ (020) 7935 81 31
– enquiries@durrantshotel.co.uk – Fax (020) 7487 35 10
– www.durrantshotel.co.uk **R2**

88 rm – £99/145 £165, ☕ £14 – 4 suites

Rest £20/22 (lunch) and a la carte £28/39

◆ Traditional ◆ Classic ◆

First opened in 1790 and family owned since 1921. Traditionally English feel with the charm of a bygone era. Cosy wood panelled bar. Attractive rooms vary somewhat in size. Semi-private booths in quintessentially British dining room.

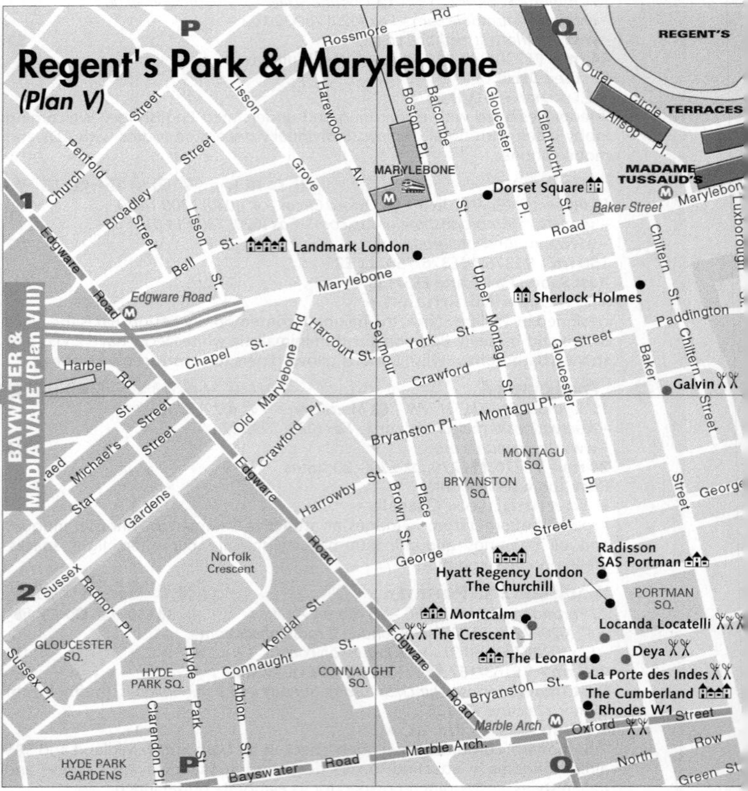

Dorset Square 🛏 🗚 ⚙ 📶 🕻 VISA 🐵 AE ①
39-40 Dorset Sq ⊠ NW1 6QN – Ⓜ Marylebone – ℰ (020) 7723 78 74
– reservations @dorsetsquare.co.uk – Fax (020) 7724 33 28
– www.dorsetsquare.co.uk –closed 25-26 December
Q1
37 rm – †£258/306 ††£306, ⊡ £14
Rest *The Potting Shed* (booking essential) £20/25 and a la carte £25/35
♦ Townhouse ♦ Classic ♦
Converted Regency townhouses in a charming square and the site of the original Lord's cricket ground. A relaxed country house in the city. Individually decorated rooms. The Potting Shed features modern cuisine and a set business menu.

Sherlock Holmes ℔ 🕭 🗚 ⇆ 📶 🔧45 VISA 🐵 AE ①
108 Baker St ⊠ W1U 6LJ – Ⓜ Baker Street – ℰ (020) 7486 61 61
– info @sherlockholmeshotel.com – Fax (020) 7958 52 11
– www.sherlockholmeshotel.com
Q1
116 rm – †£235 ††£235, ⊡ £17 – 3 suites – **Rest** £17 (lunch) and a la carte £25/44
♦ Business ♦ Modern ♦
A stylish building with a relaxed contemporary feel. Comfortable guests' lounge with Holmes pictures on the walls. Bedrooms welcoming and smart, some with wood floors. Brasserie style dining.

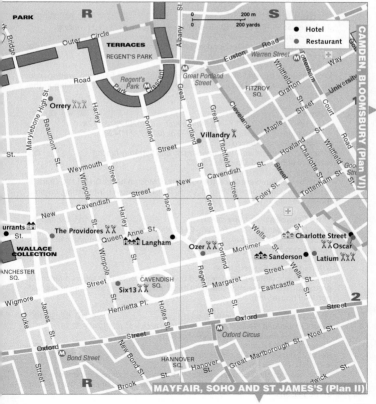

UNITED KINGDOM

XXX ⸙
Orrery
`VISA` `MC` `AE` `①`

55 Marylebone High St ⊠ W1U 5RB – **M** Regent's Park
– ℰ (020) 7616 80 00 – Fax (020) 7616 80 80 – www.orrery.co.uk
closed Christmas and New Year   **R1**
Rest (booking essential) £25 (lunch) and a la carte £37/54 ⅜
Spec. Langoustine and ceps, sherry jelly, shellfish velouté. Poached and roasted
pigeon, confit of leg, creamed spinach and date purée. Apricot soufflé, pistachio
ice cream.
♦ Contemporary ♦ Design ♦
Contemporary elegance: a smoothly run 1st floor restaurant in converted 19C
stables, with a Conran shop below. Accomplished modern British cooking.

XXX ⸙
Locanda Locatelli
`AC` `VISA` `MC` `AE` `①`

8 Seymour St ⊠ W1H 7JZ – **M** Marble Arch – ℰ (020) 7935 90 88 – info @
locandalocatelli.com – Fax (020) 7935 11 49 – www.locandalocatelli.com
closed Bank Holidays   **Q2**
Rest a la carte £33/52 ⅜
Spec. Roast rabbit wrapped in Parma ham with polenta. Scallops with saffron
vinaigrette. Tagliatelle with kid goat ragu.
♦ Italian ♦ Fashionable ♦
Very stylishly appointed restaurant with banquettes and cherry wood or glass
dividers which contribute to an intimate and relaxing ambience. Accomplished
Italian cooking.

XXX
Latium
`AC` `VISA` `MC` `AE`

21 Berners St ⊠ W1T 3LP – **M** Oxford Circus – ℰ (020) 7323 91 23 – info @
latiumrestaurant.com – Fax (020) 7323 32 05 – www.latiumrestaurant.com
closed Easter, 25 December, Sunday, Saturday lunch and Bank Holidays   **S2**
Rest £29
♦ Italian ♦ Neighbourhood ♦
Welcoming restaurant owned by affable chef. Smart feel with well-spaced
linen-clad tables, tiled floors and rural pictures. Italian country cooking in the
heart of town.

XX
Deya
`AC` `VISA` `MC` `AE`

34 Portman Sq ⊠ W1H 7BY – **M** Marble Arch – ℰ (020) 7224 00 28
– reservations @ deya-restaurant.co.uk – Fax (020) 7224 04 11
– www.deya-restaurant.co.uk
closed 25-26 December, 1 January, Sunday and Saturday lunch   **Q2**
Rest £20 (lunch) and a la carte £23/32
♦ Indian ♦ Fashionable ♦
Has its own pillared entrance, though part of Mostyn hotel. Grand 18C Grade II
listed room with ornate ceiling. Modern, stylish makeover. Interesting, original
Indian menus.

XX
The Crescent – at Montcalm H.
`AC` `VISA` `MC` `AE` `①`

Great Cumberland Pl ⊠ W1H 7TW – **M** Marble Arch – ℰ (020) 7402 42 88
– reservations @ montcalm.co.uk – Fax (020) 7724 91 80 – www.montcalm.co.uk
closed lunch Saturday and Sunday   **Q2**
Rest £26/30
♦ Modern ♦ Friendly ♦
Discreetly appointed room favoured by local residents. Best tables overlook a
pretty square. Frequently changing fixed price modern menu includes half
bottle of house wine.

XX
Rhodes W1 – at The Cumberland H.
`AC` `VISA` `MC` `AE` `①`

Great Cumberland Pl ⊠ W1A 4RF – **M** Marble Arch – ℰ (020) 7479 38 38
– rhodesw1 @ thecumberland.co.uk – Fax (020) 7479 38 88
– www.garyrhodes.com   **Q2**
Rest £22 (lunch) and a la carte £20/42
♦ English ♦ Brasserie ♦
In the heart of the Cumberland Hotel, a very stylish dining experience with
impressively high ceiling and classical Gary Rhodes dishes bringing out the best
of the seasons.

XX **Galvin** 　　　　　　　　　　　 AC VISA ⓪ AE

😊

66 Baker St ⊠ W14 7DH – Ⓜ Baker Street – ℰ (020) 7935 40 07 – info @
galvinbistrotdeluxe.co.uk – Fax (020) 7486 17 35 – www.galvinbistrotdeluxe.co.uk
closed 25-26 December and 1 January　　　　　　　　　　　　　　**Q1**
Rest £16 (lunch) and a la carte £20/32
♦ Modern ♦ Bistro ♦
A modern take on the classic Gallic bistro with ceiling fans, globe lights, rich
wood panelled walls and French influenced dishes where precision and good
value are paramount.

XX **Six13** 　　　　　　　　　　　　 AC VISA ⓪ AE ①

19 Wigmore St ⊠ W1H 9UA – Ⓜ Bond Street – ℰ (020) 7629 61 33
– jay @ six13.com – Fax (020) 7629 61 35 – www.six13.com
closed Jewish Holidays, Friday dinner and Saturday　　　　　　　**R2**
Rest £25 (lunch) and a la carte £29/41
♦ Kosher ♦ Friendly ♦
Stylish and immaculate with banquette seating. Strictly kosher menu supervised
by the Shama offering interesting cooking with a modern slant.

XX **Oscar** – at Charlotte Street H.　　　　 AC VISA ⓪ AE

15 Charlotte St ⊠ W1T 1RJ – Ⓜ Goodge Street – ℰ (020) 7907 40 05
– charlotte @ firmdale.com – Fax (020) 7806 20 02
– www.charlottestreethotel.co.uk – closed Sunday lunch　　　　**S2**
Rest (booking essential) a la carte £33/49
♦ Modern ♦ Trendy ♦
Adjacent to hotel lobby and dominated by a large, vivid mural of contemporary
London life. Sophisticated dishes served by attentive staff: oysters, wasabi and
soya dressing.

XX **The Providores** 　　　　　　 AC ♧ VISA ⓪ AE

109 Marylebone High St ⊠ W1U 4RX – Ⓜ Bond Street – ℰ (020) 7935 61 75
– anyone @ theprovidores.co.uk – Fax (020) 7935 68 77
– www.theprovidores.co.uk
closed 25-26 and 31 December and 1 January　　　　　　　　　**R2**
Rest a la carte £30/43
♦ Innovative ♦ Trendy ♦
Swish, stylish restaurant on first floor; unusual dishes with New World base and
fusion of Asian, Mediterranean influences. Tapas and light meals in downstairs
Tapa Room.

XX **La Porte des Indes** 　　　　 AC ♧14 VISA ⓪ AE ①

32 Bryanston St ⊠ W1H 7EG – Ⓜ Marble Arch – ℰ (020) 7224 00 55
– london.reservation @ laportedesindes.com – Fax (020) 7224 11 44
closed 25-27 December and Saturday lunch　　　　　　　　　　**Q2**
Rest a la carte £22/45
♦ Indian ♦ Exotic ♦
Don't be fooled by the discreet entrance: inside there is a spectacularly unrestrained
display of palm trees, murals and waterfalls. French influenced Indian cuisine.

XX **Rosmarino** 　　　　　　　　 ♫ AC VISA ⓪ AE

1 Blenheim Terrace ⊠ NW8 0EH – Ⓜ St John's Wood – ℰ (020) 7328 50 14
– Fax (020) 7625 26 39
closed Easter Monday, 25 December and 1 January　　　*Plan I* **B1-2**
Rest £25/30
♦ Italian ♦ Neighbourhood ♦
Modern, understated and relaxed. Friendly and approachable service of robust
and rustic Italian dishes. Set priced menu is carefully balanced.

XX **Ozer** 　　　　　　　　　　　 AC VISA ⓪ AE

4-5 Langham Pl, Regent St ⊠ W1B 3DG – Ⓜ Oxford Circus – ℰ (020) 7323 05 05
– info @ sofra.co.uk – Fax (020) 7323 01 11 – www.sofra.co.uk　　**S2**
Rest £17/22 and a la carte £17/35
♦ Turkish ♦ Design ♦
Behind the busy and vibrantly decorated bar you'll find a smart modern
restaurant. Lively atmosphere and efficient service of modern, light and aromatic
Turkish cooking.

UNITED KINGDOM

XX **Roka** 🔤 ⅙/⟶ 𝘝𝘐𝘚𝘈 ⚫⚫ 🄰🄴 ⓪
37 Charlotte St ⊠ *W1T 1RR* – 🄜 *Goodge Street* – 𝒞 *(020) 7580 64 64* – *info@*
rokarestaurant.com – *Fax (020) 7580 02 20* – *www.rokarestaurant.com*
closed Sunday lunch — Plan VI **T1**
Rest a la carte £36/79
♦ Japanese ♦ Fashionable ♦
Striking glass and steel frontage. Airy, atmospheric interior of teak, oak and paper
wall screens. Authentic, flavoursome Japanese cuisine with variety of grill dishes.

X **Villandry** 🔤 ⅙/⟶ 𝘝𝘐𝘚𝘈 ⚫⚫ 🄰🄴 ⓪
170 Great Portland St ⊠ *W1W 5QB* – 🄜 *Regent's Park* – 𝒞 *(020) 7631 31 31*
– *bookatable@villandry.com* – *Fax (020) 7631 30 30* – *www.villandry.com*
closed Sunday dinner and Bank Holidays **S1**
Rest a la carte £23/38
♦ Modern ♦ Rustic ♦
The senses are heightened by passing through the well-stocked deli to the dining
room behind. Bare walls, wooden tables and a menu offering simple, tasty dishes.

📠 **The Abbey Road** 🕾 𝘝𝘐𝘚𝘈 ⚫⚫ 🄰🄴
63 Abbey Rd ⊠ *NW8 0AE* – 🄜 *St John's Wood* – 𝒞 *(020) 7328 66 26*
– *theabbeyroadpub@btconnect.com* – *Fax (020) 7625 91 68*
closed 25 and 31 December — Plan I **B1**
Rest *(closed Monday lunch)* a la carte £20/25
♦ Modern ♦ Pub ♦
Grand Victorian pub appearance in bottle green. Busy bar at the front; main
dining room, in calm duck egg blue, to the rear. Modern menus boast a distinct
Mediterranean style.

CAMDEN

Bloomsbury Plan VI

🏠🏠🏠 **Russell** 🔤 ⅙/⟶rm ⚡ 🖂 🕻 🛗400 𝘝𝘐𝘚𝘈 ⚫⚫ 🄰🄴 ⓪
Russell Sq ⊠ *WC1B 5BE* – 🄜 *Russell Square* – 𝒞 *(020) 7837 64 70* – *sales.russell@*
principal-hotels.com – *Fax (020) 7837 28 57* – *www.principal-hotels.com*
371 rm – †£185 ††£215, ⌑ £20 – 2 suites **T1**
Rest a la carte approx. £31
♦ Business ♦ Classic ♦
An impressive Victorian building dominating Russell Square. Boasts many
original features including the imposing marbled lobby and staircase.
Traditional or modern rooms. Restaurant has noticeable feel of grandeur.

🏠🏠 **Covent Garden** ⌖ 🔤 ⚡ 🖂 🕻 🛗50 𝘝𝘐𝘚𝘈 ⚫⚫ 🄰🄴
10 Monmouth St ⊠ *WC2H 9HB* – 🄜 *Covent Garden* – 𝒞 *(020) 7806 10 00*
– *covent@firmdale.com* – *Fax (020) 7806 11 00*
– *www.coventgardenhotel.co.uk* **T1**
56 rm – †£246/300 ††£358, ⌑ £18 – 2 suites
Rest *Brasserie Max* (booking essential) a la carte £33/48
♦ Luxury ♦ Stylish ♦
Individually designed and stylish bedrooms, with CDs and VCRs discreetly
concealed. Boasts a very relaxing first floor oak-panelled drawing room with its
own honesty bar. Informal restaurant.

🏠🏠 **Marlborough** ⅙ 🔤 rest ⅙/⟶rm ⚡ 🖂 🕻 🛗250 𝘝𝘐𝘚𝘈 ⚫⚫ 🄰🄴 ⓪
9-14 Bloomsbury St ⊠ *WC1B 3QD* – 🄜 *Tottenham Court Road* – 𝒞 *(020)*
7636 56 01 – *resmarl@radisson.com* – *Fax (020) 7636 05 32*
– *www.radissonedwardian.com* **T1**
171 rm – †£172 ††£239, ⌑ £15 – 2 suites
Rest *Glass* (closed Saturday-Sunday) a la carte £25/30
♦ Business ♦ Classic ♦
A Victorian building around the corner from the British Museum. The lobby has
been restored to its original marbled splendour and the bedrooms offer good
comforts. Bright, breezy restaurant with suitably modish cooking.

🏠 **Mountbatten**   ᴸᵃ 🅺 ⇆rm ⅀ 🔲 ℃ ⅗90 𝗩𝗜𝗦𝗔 ⓂⓄ 🅰🅴 ⑩
20 Monmouth St ⊠ WC2H 9HD – Ⓜ Covent Garden – ℰ (020) 7836 43 00
– Fax (020) 7240 35 40 – www.radissonedwardian.com   **T1**
149 rm – ♦£241 ♦♦£297, ⊡ £15 – 2 suites
Rest *Dial* (closed lunch Friday-Sunday) a la carte £25/45
♦ Business ♦ Classic ♦
Photographs and memorabilia of the eponymous Lord Louis adorn the walls and
corridors. Ideally located in the heart of Covent Garden. Compact but
comfortable bedrooms. Bright, stylish restaurant.

🏠 **Myhotel Bloomsbury**   ᴸᵃ 🅺 ⇆ ⅀ 🔲 ℃ ⅗40 𝗩𝗜𝗦𝗔 ⓂⓄ 🅰🅴
11-13 Bayley St, Bedford Sq ⊠ WC1B 3HD – Ⓜ Tottenham Court Road
– ℰ (020) 7667 60 00 – res@myhotels.co.uk – Fax (020) 7667 60 01
– www.myhotels.com   **T1**
77 rm – ♦£155/230 ♦♦£340/360, ⊡ £18
Rest *Yo! Sushi* a la carte £18/23
♦ Business ♦ Minimalist ♦
The minimalist interior is designed on the principles of feng shui; even the
smaller bedrooms are stylish and uncluttered. Mybar is a fashionable meeting
point. Diners can enjoy Japanese food from conveyor belt.

🍴🍴🍴 **Pied à Terre** (Osborn)   🅺 ⇆ ⇅12 𝗩𝗜𝗦𝗔 ⓂⓄ 🅰🅴 ⑩
🌀🌀 *34 Charlotte St ⊠ W1T 2NH – Ⓜ Goodge Street – ℰ (020) 7636 11 78*
– p-a-t@dircon.co.uk – Fax (020) 7916 11 71 – www.pied.a.terre.co.uk   **T1**
closed 10 days Christmas, Saturday lunch, Sunday and Bank Holidays **– Rest** £29/60 ☕
Spec. Ceviche of scallops, avocado and crème fraîche, basil jelly. Assiette of rabbit
with pistachios, baby carrots and mustard sauce. Chocolate tart with stout ice
cream and macadamia mousse.
♦ Innovative ♦ Fashionable ♦
Understated, discreet exterior; intimate, stylish interior, incorporating sleek first
floor lounge. Elaborate yet refined modern cuisine complemented by accomplished service.

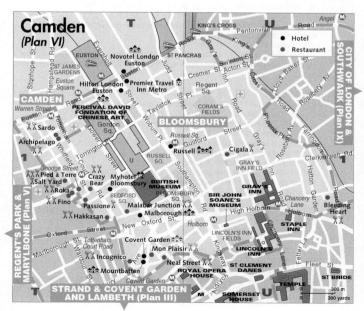

XX **Mon Plaisir**   VISA MC AE

21 Monmouth St ⊠ WC2H 9DD – Ⓜ *Covent Garden*
– ℰ (020) 7836 72 43 – eatafrog@mail.com – Fax (020) 7240 47 74
– www.monplaisir.co.uk closed Christmas, Saturday lunch, Sunday and Bank
Holidays   **T1**
Rest £16 (lunch) and a la carte £26/38
• French • Family •
London's oldest French restaurant and family-run for over fifty years.
Divided into four rooms, all with a different feel but all proudly Gallic in their
decoration.

XX **Incognico**   AK VISA MC AE ①

117 Shaftesbury Ave ⊠ WC2H 8AD – Ⓜ *Tottenham Court Road*
– ℰ (020) 7836 88 66 – Fax (020) 7240 95 25
closed 1 week Christmas, Sunday and Bank Holidays   **T1**
Rest a la carte £21/32
• Modern • Brasserie •
Opened in 2000 with its robust décor of wood panelling and brown leather
chairs. Downstairs bar has a window into the kitchen, from where French and
English classics derive.

XX **Neal Street**   VISA MC AE ①

26 Neal St ⊠ WC2H 9QT – Ⓜ *Covent Garden – ℰ (020) 7836 83 68*
– Fax (020) 7240 39 64 – www.carluccios.co.uk
closed 24 December-2 January, Sunday and Bank Holidays   **T1**
Rest £25 (lunch) and a la carte £28/45 ⌘
• Italian • Brasserie •
Light, bright and airy; tiled flooring and colourful pictures. Dishes range from
the simple to the more complex. Mushrooms a speciality. Has its own shop next
door.

XX **Sardo**   VISA MC AE ①

45 Grafton Way ⊠ W1T 5DQ – Ⓜ *Warren Street – ℰ (020) 7387 25 21*
– info@sardo-restaurant.com – Fax (020) 7387 25 59
– www.sardo-restaurant.com closed Saturday lunch and Sunday   **T1**
Rest a la carte £25/34
• Sardinian • Family •
Simple, stylish interior run in a very warm and welcoming manner with very
efficient service. Rustic Italian cooking with a Sardinian character and a modern
tone.

XX **Hakkasan**   AK rm VISA MC AE
£3
8 Hanway Pl ⊠ W1T 1HD – Ⓜ *Tottenham Court Road – ℰ (020) 7927 70 00*
– mail@hakkasan.com – Fax (020) 7907 18 89
closed 24-25 December   **T1**
Rest a la carte £29/78
Spec. Roast sesame chicken in Malay sauce. Stir-fry black pepper rib-eye beef.
Pan-fried silver cod in XO sauce.
• Chinese (Canton) • Fashionable •
A distinctive, modern interpretation of Cantonese cooking in an appropriately
contemporary and cavernous basement. The lively, bustling bar is an equally
popular nightspot.

XX **Fino**   VISA MC AE

33 Charlotte St (entrance on Rathbone St) ⊠ W1T 1RR – Ⓜ *Goodge Street*
– ℰ (020) 7813 80 10 – info@finorestaurant.com – Fax (020) 7813 80 11
– www.finorestaurant.com
closed 25 December, Sunday and Bank Holidays   **T1**
Rest a la carte £17/50
• Spanish • Fashionable •
Spanish-run basement bar with modern style décor and banquette seating.
Wide-ranging menu of authentic dishes; 2 set-price selections offering an
introduction to tapas.

XX **Crazy Bear** AK VISA ⓴ AE
26-28 Whitfield St ✉ W1T 2RG – Ⓜ Goodge Street
– ℰ (020) 7631 00 88 – enquiries @ crazybeargroup.co.uk
– Fax (020) 7631 11 88
– www.crazybeargroup.co.uk
closed 1 week Christmas, Saturday lunch and Sunday   T1
Rest a la carte £23/32
♦ South-East Asian ♦ Trendy ♦
Exotic destination: downstairs bar geared to fashionable set; ground floor dining room is art deco inspired. Asian flavoured menus, with predominance towards Thai dishes.

XX **Archipelago** ↤ VISA ⓴ AE ⓪
110 Whitfield St ✉ W1T 5ED – Ⓜ Goodge Street
– ℰ (020) 7383 33 46
– archipelago @ onetel.com
– Fax (020) 7383 71 81   T1
closed 25 December, Saturday lunch, Sunday and Bank Holiday Mondays
Rest a la carte £26/37
♦ Innovative ♦ Exotic ♦
Eccentric in both menu and décor and not for the faint hearted. Crammed with knick-knacks from cages to Buddhas. Menu an eclectic mix of influences from around the world.

XX **Malabar Junction** AK VISA ⓴ AE
107 Great Russell St ✉ WC1B 3NA – Ⓜ Tottenham Court Road
– ℰ (020) 7580 52 30
– malabarjunction @ hotmail.com
– Fax (020) 7436 99 42
closed 25-27 December   T1
Rest a la carte £15/24
♦ South Indian ♦ Friendly ♦
Specialising in dishes from southern India. Bright restaurant with a small fountain in the centre of the room below a large skylight. Helpful and attentive service.

X **Passione** VISA ⓴ AE ⓪
10 Charlotte St ✉ W1T 2LT – Ⓜ Goodge Street
– ℰ (020) 7636 28 33
– liz @ passione.co.uk – Fax (020) 7636 28 89
– www.passione.co.uk
closed Saturday lunch and Sunday   T1
Rest (booking essential) a la carte £41/46
♦ Italian ♦ Friendly ♦
Compact but light and airy. Modern Italian cooking served in informal surroundings, with friendly and affable service. Particularly busy at lunchtime.

X **Cigala** VISA ⓴ AE ⓪
54 Lamb's Conduit St ✉ WC1N 3LW – Ⓜ Holborn
– ℰ (020) 7405 17 17
– tasty @ cigala.co.uk – Fax (020) 7242 99 49
– www.cigala.co.uk
closed 25-26 December, 1 January and Easter Sunday   U1
Rest £18 (lunch) and a la carte £19/35
♦ Spanish ♦ Rustic ♦
Spanish restaurant on the corner of attractive street. Simply furnished with large windows and open-plan kitchen. Robust Iberian cooking. Informal tapas bar downstairs.

Salt Yard

🍴   😊

🄰🄲 *VISA* 🅼🄾 🄰🄴

54 Goodge St ⊠ W1T 4NA – 🄼 *Googe Street – ℰ (020) 7637 06 57*
– info @ saltyard.co.uk – Fax (020) 7580 74 35
– www.saltyard.co.uk
closed 2 weeks Christmas-New Year, Sunday, Saturday lunch and Bank
Holidays   **T1**
Rest a la carte £15/30
♦ Mediterranean ♦ Tapas bar ♦
Vogue destination with buzzy downstairs restaurant specialising in inexpensive
sharing plates of tasty Italian and Spanish dishes: try the freshly cut hams. Super
wine list.

Euston   *Plan VI*

Novotel London Euston

🏨   ≤ 🖪 𝔐 ♿ 🄰🄲 ↯rm ℀
     🅰450 *VISA* 🅼🄾 🄰🄴 ⓪

100-110 Euston Rd ⊠ NW1 2AJ – 🄼 *Euston*
– ℰ (020) 7666 90 00 – h5309 @ accor.com – Fax (020) 7666 90 01
– www.accorhotels.com   **T1**
311 rm – �£165 ♦♦£165, � £15 – 1 suite
Rest *(closed Saturday-Sunday)* £18 (lunch) and dinner a la carte
£24/32
♦ Business ♦ Chain hotel ♦ Functional ♦
Extensive conference facilities that include the redeveloped Shaw theatre.
Large marbled lobby. Modern bedrooms that offer views of London's
rooftops from the higher floors. Lobby-based restaurant and bar look
onto busy street.

Hilton London Euston

🏨   🖪 𝔐 ♿ 🄰🄲 ↯rm ℀ 🖾 📞
     🅰120 *VISA* 🅼🄾 🄰🄴 ⓪

17-18 Upper Woburn Pl ⊠ WC1H 0HT
– 🄼 *Euston – ℰ (020) 7943 45 00*
– euston.reservations @ hilton.com – Fax (020) 7943 45 01
– www.hilton.co.uk   **T1**
150 rm – ♦£217 ♦♦£264, � £16
Rest *Woburn Place* £20 (dinner) and a la carte £20/30
♦ Business ♦ Chain hotel ♦ Functional ♦
Nearby transport links make this a useful location. Scandinavian styled
bedrooms. Executive rooms are particularly well-equipped. Lighter fare in
Woburn Place conservatory.

Premier Travel Inn Metro

🏠   ♿ 🄰🄲 rest ↯rm ℀ *VISA* 🅼🄾 🄰🄴 ⓪

1 Dukes Rd ⊠ WC1H 9PJ – 🄼 *Euston – ℰ (0870) 238 33 01*
– Fax (020) 7554 34 19 – www.travelinn.co.uk
220 rm – ♦£75 ♦♦£75   **T1**
Rest (grill rest.)
♦ Chain hotel ♦ Functional ♦
Budget accommodation with clean and spacious bedrooms, all with a large
workspace. Double glazed but still ask for a quieter room at the back.

Hatton Garden   *Plan VI*

Bleeding Heart

🍴🍴

🌣 *VISA* 🅼🄾 🄰🄴 ⓪

Bleeding Heart Yard (off Greville St) ⊠ EC1N 8SJ – 🄼 *Farringdon*
– ℰ (020) 7242 82 38 – bookings @ bleedingheart.co.uk
– Fax (020) 7831 14 02
– www.bleedingheart.co.uk
closed 24 December-3 January, Saturday, Sunday and Bank Holidays   **U1**
Rest a la carte £25/36 🍷
♦ French ♦ Romantic ♦
Wood panelling, candlelight and a heart motif; a popular romantic dinner spot.
By contrast, a busy City restaurant at lunchtime. French influenced menu.
Weighty wine list.

HYDE PARK & KNIGHTSBRIDGE *Plan VII*

Mandarin Oriental Hyde Park
66 Knightsbridge ✉ SW1X 7LA – Ⓜ Knightsbridge – ✆ (020) 7235 20 00 – molon-reservations@mohg.com – Fax (020) 7235 20 01 – www.mandarinoriental.com
220 VISA MC AE DI
Y2-3

177 rm – 🚹£429/440 🚹🚹£646/705, ☕ £25 – 23 suites
Rest see also ***Foliage*** below
Rest *The Park* £31 (lunch) and a la carte £25/35

◆ Grand Luxury ◆ Classic ◆

Built in 1889 this classic hotel, with striking façade, remains one of London's grandest. Many of the luxurious bedrooms enjoy Park views. Immaculate and detailed service. Smart ambience in The Park.

Knightsbridge Green without rest
AC VISA MC AE DI
159 Knightsbridge ✉ SW1X 7PD – Ⓜ Knightsbridge – ✆ (020) 7584 62 74 – reservations@thekghotel.co.uk – Fax (020) 7225 16 35 – www.thekghotel.com
X3

16 rm – 🚹£118/170 🚹🚹£153/170, ☕ £12 – 12 suites

◆ Traditional ◆ Classic ◆

Privately owned hotel, boasting peaceful sitting room with writing desk. Breakfast - sausage and bacon from Harrods! - served in the generously proportioned bedrooms.

Foliage – at Mandarin Oriental Hyde Park H.
AC VISA MC AE DI
66 Knightsbridge ✉ SW1X 7LA – Ⓜ Knightsbridge – ✆ (020) 7201 37 23 – Fax (020) 7235 45 52
Y2-3

Rest £25 (lunch) and a la carte £48/50
Spec. Duo of foie gras with caramelised endive tarte Tatin. Roast turbot with pork, langoustine and horseradish cream. Pear and almond tart with malted milk ice cream.

◆ Inventive ◆ Formal ◆

Reached via a glass-enclosed walkway that houses the cellar. Hyde Park outside the window reflected in the foliage-themed décor. Gracious service, skilled modern cooking.

Zuma
AC VISA MC AE
5 Raphael St ✉ SW7 1DL – Ⓜ Knightsbridge – ✆ (020) 7584 10 10 – info@zumarestaurant.com – Fax (020) 7584 50 05 – www.zumarestaurant.com
X3

Rest a la carte £27/46

◆ Japanese ◆ Fashionable ◆

Strong modern feel with exposed pipes, modern lighting and granite flooring. A theatrical atmosphere around the Sushi bar and a varied and interesting modern Japanese menu.

Mr Chow
AC VISA MC AE DI
151 Knightsbridge ✉ SW1X 7PA – Ⓜ Knightsbridge – ✆ (020) 7589 73 47 – mrchow@aol.com – Fax (020) 7584 57 80 – www.mrchow.com
closed 24-26 December, 1 January and Easter Monday
X3

Rest £22 (lunch) and a la carte £44/51

◆ Chinese ◆ Friendly ◆

Cosmopolitan Chinese restaurant with branches in New York and L.A. Well established ambience. Walls covered with mirrors and modern art. House specialities worth opting for.

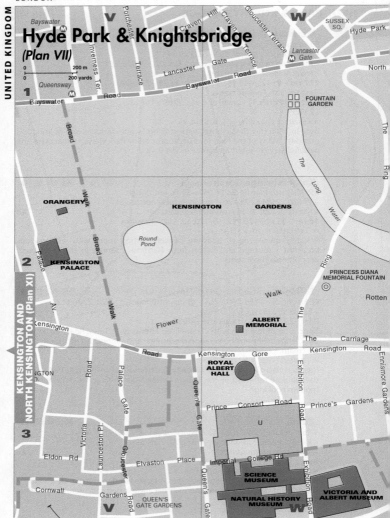

Hyde Park & Knightsbridge
(Plan VII)

Bayswater

SUSSEX SQ.

Hyde Park

Polchester

Craven Hill

Gloucester Terrace

Craven Terrace

Lancaster Gate

Inverness Ter.

Lancaster Gate

Terrace

North

The Ring

1 Queensway

Bayswater Road

Bayswater Road

☐☐ FOUNTAIN
☐☐ GARDEN

The Long Water

ORANGERY

KENSINGTON   GARDENS

Broad

Walk

Round Pond

The Ring

2 KENSINGTON PALACE

Palace

PRINCESS DIANA
MEMORIAL FOUNTAIN
◎

Walk

Rotten

Kensington

Flower

ALBERT
MEMORIAL

The

The Carriage

Av.

Walk

Road

Kensington   Gore

Kensington   Road

Ennismore Gardens

Road

ROYAL
ALBERT
HALL

Queen's Gate

Exhibition   Road

Prince's Gardens

JGTON
SQ.

Palace Gate

Prince   Consort   Road

Prince's Road

3

Victoria

Launceston Pl.

Gloucester

U

Imperial   College Rd

Exhibition   Road

Eldon Rd

Elvaston   Place

SCIENCE
MUSEUM

Cornwall

Gardens

QUEEN'S
GATE GARDENS

Queen's Gate

NATURAL HISTORY
MUSEUM

VICTORIA AND
ALBERT MUSEUM

UNITED KINGDOM

KENSINGTON AND
NORTH KENSINGTON (Plan XI)

0   200 m
0   200 yards

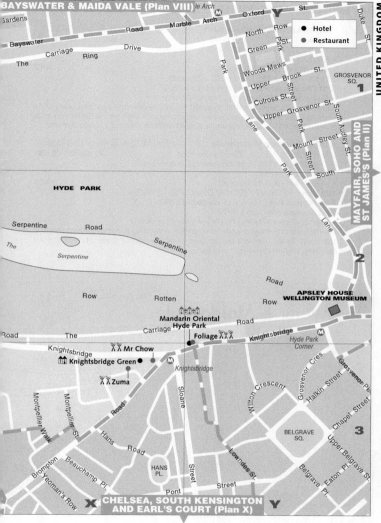

BAYSWATER & MAIDA VALE (Plan VIII)

le Arch

Gardens

Bayswater

The Carriage Ring Drive

Road

Marble Arch

Oxford St.

North Row

Green

Woods Mews

Upper Brook St.

Culross St.

Upper Grosvenor St.

Mount Street

Street

Park

South

Park

Lane

South Audley St.

GROSVENOR SQ.

1

2

MAYFAIR, SOHO AND ST JAMES'S (Plan II)

● Hotel
● Restaurant

HYDE PARK

Serpentine Road

The Serpentine

Serpentine

Row

Rotten

Road

Row

Park Lane

APSLEY HOUSE
WELLINGTON MUSEUM

Mandarin Oriental
Hyde Park

Foliage ✗✗✗

Road

Knightsbridge

Hyde Park Corner

Road

The Carriage

Knightsbridge ✗✗ Mr Chow

🏨 Knightsbridge Green ●

✗ ✗ Zuma

Knightsbridge

Sloane

Montpellier Walk

Montpellier St.

Hans Road

Beauchamp Pl.

Brompton

Yeoman's Row

HANS PL.

Street

Pont Street

Lowndes St.

Wilton Crescent

BELGRAVE SQ.

Grosvenor Cres.

Halkin Street

Chapel Street

Upper Belgrave St.

Belgrave Pl.

Eaton Pl.

Grosvenor Pl.

3

CHELSEA, SOUTH KENSINGTON
AND EARL'S COURT (Plan X)

X **Y**

BAYSWATER & MAIDA VALE

Plan VIII

Hilton London Paddington

£ 館 & AC 4rm ⅏ 🎮 📞
🛉 350 VISA ◉ AE ⓪

146 Praed St ✉ W2 1EE – Ⓜ Paddington
– 𝒞 (020) 7850 05 00 – paddington@hilton.com
– Fax (020) 7850 06 00
– www.hilton.co.uk/paddington

AB2

335 rm – 🛉£282 🛉🛉£282, ☑ £20 – 20 suites
Rest *The Brasserie* £15/30 and a la carte £20/51

♦ Business ♦ Chain hotel ♦ Modern ♦

Early Victorian railway hotel, sympathetically restored in contemporary style with Art Deco details. Co-ordinated bedrooms with high tech facilities continue the modern style. Contemporarily styled brasserie offering a modern menu.

Hilton London Metropole

≤ £ 館 🔲 & AC 4rm ⅏ 🎮 🛉 2000
P VISA ◉ AE ⓪

Edgware Rd ✉ W2 1JU – Ⓜ Edgware Road
– 𝒞 (020) 7402 41 41 – cbs-londonmet@hilton.com
– Fax (020) 7724 88 66
– www.hilton.co.uk/londonmet

AC1

1033 rm – 🛉£100/229 🛉🛉£100/229, ☑ £18 – 25 suites
Rest *Nippon Tuk* £14/35 and a la carte £32/43
Rest *Fiamma* a la carte £18/29

♦ Business ♦ Chain hotel ♦ Functional ♦

One of London's most popular convention venues by virtue of both its size and transport links. Well-appointed and modern rooms have state-of-the-art facilities. Vibrant restaurant and bar.

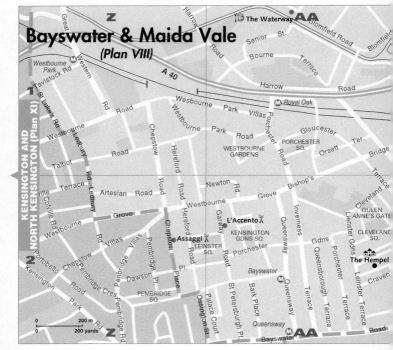

Royal Lancaster ≤ ⅚ 🅰🅒 ⅍ ⅏ 🄰🄼 🛗1200 🄿 *VISA* 🯃 🄰🄴 ①
Lancaster Terrace ⊠ *W2 2TY* – Ⓜ *Lancaster Gate* – 𝒞 *(020) 7262 67 37* – *sales @ royallancaster.com* – *Fax (020) 7724 31 91* – *www.royallancaster.com*   **AB2**
394 rm – ♥£290 ♥♥£378, ⊆ £18 – **22 suites** – **Rest** see *Island* and *Nipa* below
♦ Business ♦ Classic ♦
Imposing 1960s purpose-built hotel overlooking Hyde Park. Some of London's most extensive conference facilities. Well-equipped bedrooms are decorated in traditional style.

The Hempel ⨯ ⇌ ⅚ 🅰🅒 ⅍ 🄫 *VISA* 🯃 🄰🄴 ①
31-35 Craven Hill Gdns ⊠ *W2 3EA* – Ⓜ *Queensway* – 𝒞 *(020) 7298 90 00*
– *hotel@the-hempel.co.uk* – *Fax (020) 7402 46 66* – *www.the-hempel.co.uk*
37 rm – ♥£311 ♥♥£311, ⊆ £15 – **9 suites**   **AA2**
Rest *I-Thai* *(closed Sunday)* a la carte £32/42
♦ Luxury ♦ Minimalist ♦
A striking example of minimalist design. Individually appointed bedrooms are understated yet very comfortable. Relaxed ambience. Modern basement restaurant.

The Royal Park 🅰🅒 ⅍ *VISA* 🯃 🄰🄴 ①
3 Westbourne Terrace, Lancaster Gate ⊠ *W2 3UL* – Ⓜ *Lancaster Gate*
– 𝒞 *(020) 7479 66 00* – *info @ theroyalpark.com* – *Fax (020) 7479 66 01*
– *www.theroyalpark.com*   **AB2**
45 rm – ♥£141/223 ♥♥£176/247 – **3 suites** – **Rest** *(room service only)*
♦ Townhouse ♦ Modern ♦
Three superbly restored Grade II listed Victorian houses. Comfy, period styled drawing rooms exude townhouse style. A minimalist air pervades the understated bedrooms.

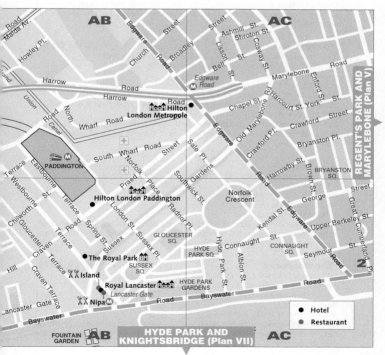

Colonnade Town House without rest   AC ♿ ⌘
2 Warrington Crescent ⊠ W9 1ER   📞 VISA ⑩ AE ⑩
– Ⓜ Warwick Avenue – ℰ (020) 7286 10 52
– rescolonnade@theetongroup.com – Fax (020) 7286 10 57
– www.theetoncollection.com   Plan XI **AM1**
43 rm – ✦£153/165 ✦✦£165/188, � £15
♦ Townhouse ♦ Classic ♦
Two Victorian townhouses with comfortable well-furnished communal rooms decorated with fresh flowers. Stylish and comfortable bedrooms with many extra touches.

%% **Island** – at Royal Lancaster H.   AC VISA ⑩ AE ⑩
Lancaster Terrace ⊠ W2 2TY – Ⓜ Lancaster Gate
– ℰ (020) 7551 60 70 – eat@islandrestaurant.co.uk – Fax (020) 7551 60 71
– www.islandrestaurant.co.uk   **AB2**
Rest £15 (lunch) and a la carte £25/35
♦ Modern ♦ Brasserie ♦
Modern, stylish restaurant with buzzy open kitchen. Full length windows allow good views of adjacent Hyde Park. Seasonally based, modern menus with wide range of dishes.

%% **Nipa** – at Royal Lancaster H.   AC P VISA ⑩ AE ⑩
Lancaster Terrace ⊠ W2 2TY – Ⓜ Lancaster Gate – ℰ (020) 7262 67 37
– Fax (020) 7724 31 91
closed Saturday lunch, Sunday and Bank Holidays   **AB2**
Rest £15 (lunch) and a la carte £29/42
♦ Thai ♦ Exotic ♦
On the 1st floor and overlooking Hyde Park. Authentic and ornately decorated restaurant offers subtly spiced Thai cuisine. Keen to please staff in traditional silk costumes.

% **Assaggi** (Sassu)   AC VISA ⑩ ⑩
🕸 39 Chepstow Pl (above Chepstow pub) ⊠ W2 4TS – Ⓜ Bayswater
– ℰ (020) 7792 55 01 – nipi@assaggi.demon.co.uk
– www.assaggi.com
closed 2 weeks Christmas and Sunday   **Z2**
Rest (booking essential) a la carte £37/39
Spec. Pecorino con carpegna & rucola. Tagliolini alle erbe. Fegato di vitello.
♦ Italian ♦ Rustic ♦
Polished wood flooring, tall windows and modern artwork provide the bright surroundings for this forever busy restaurant. Concise menu of robust Italian dishes.

% **L'Accento**   VISA ⑩ AE
😊 16 Garway Rd ⊠ W2 4NH – Ⓜ Bayswater – ℰ (020) 7243 22 01
– laccentorest@aol.com – Fax (020) 7243 22 01
closed 25-26 December and Sunday   **AA2**
Rest £19 and a la carte £26/31
♦ Italian ♦ Rustic ♦
Rustic surroundings and provincial, well priced, Italian cooking. Menu specialises in tasty pasta, made on the premises, and shellfish. Rear conservatory for the summer.

🏠 **The Waterway**   � AC VISA ⑩ AE
54 Formosa St ⊠ W9 2JU – Ⓜ Warwick Avenue – ℰ (020) 7266 35 57
– info@thewaterway.co.uk – Fax (020) 7266 35 47
– www.thewaterway.co.uk   **AA1**
Rest a la carte £19/27
♦ Modern ♦ Pub ♦
Pub with a thoroughly modern, metropolitan ambience. Spacious bar and large decked terrace overlooking canal. Concise, well-balanced menu served in open plan dining room.

CITY OF LONDON, SOUTHWARK & TOWER HAMLETS

City of London

Plan IX

Great Eastern
♨ & ẢC ↔rm 🖾 ♨250 *VISA* ◑◐ AE ◐

Liverpool St ⊠ EC2M 7QN – **Ⓜ** Liverpool Street – 𝒞 (020) 7618 50 00
– info@great-eastern-hotel.co.uk – Fax (020) 7618 50 01
– www.great-eastern-hotel.co.uk   **AG2**
264 rm – ♦£287/346 ♦♦£405 – 3 suites
Rest see also *Aurora* below
Rest *Fishmarket* (closed Saturday-Sunday) a la carte £31/49
Rest *Miyabi* (closed Easter, Christmas, Saturday and Sunday) (booking
essential) £18 (lunch) and a la carte £15/25
♦ Luxury ♦ Modern ♦
A contemporary and stylish interior hides behind the classic Victorian façade of
this railway hotel. Bright and spacious bedrooms with state-of-the-art facilities.
Fishmarket based within original hotel lobby. Miyabi is compact Japanese
restaurant.

Crowne Plaza London-The City
♨ 🐾 & ẢC ↔rm 🛠 🖾 ⓣ

19 New Bridge St ⊠ EC4V 6DB – **Ⓜ**
Blackfriars – 𝒞 (0870) 400 91 90 – loncy.info@ichotelsgroup.com   ♨180 *VISA* ◑◐ AE ◐
– Fax (020) 7438 80 80 – www.crowneplaza.com   **AD2**
201 rm – ♦£358 ♦♦£358, � £17 – 2 suites
Rest *Refettorio* (closed Sunday and Saturday lunch) a la carte £26/36
Rest *Benugo* a la carte £25/30
♦ Business ♦ Chain hotel ♦ Modern ♦
Art deco façade by the river; interior enhanced by funky chocolate, cream and
brown palette. Compact meeting room; well equipped fitness centre. Sizable,
stylish rooms. Modish Refettorio for Italian cuisine. Informal, all-day dining at
Benugo.

Threadneedles
& ẢC ↔ 🛠 🖾 ⓣ ♨35 *VISA* ◑◐ AE ◐

5 Threadneedle St ⊠ EC2R 8AY – **Ⓜ** Bank – 𝒞 (020) 7657 80 80
– resthreadneedles@theetongroup.com – Fax (020) 7657 81 00
– www.theetoncollection.com   **AF2**
68 rm – ♦£288/317 ♦♦£288/487, � £20 – 1 suite
Rest see *Bonds* below
♦ Business ♦ Modern ♦
A converted bank, dating from 1856, with a stunning stained-glass cupola in the
lounge. Rooms are very stylish and individual featuring CD players and Egyptian
cotton sheets.

The Chamberlain
& ẢC ↔ 🛠 🖾 ♨50 *VISA* ◑◐ AE ◐

130-135 Minories ⊠ EC3N 1NU – **Ⓜ** Aldgate – 𝒞 (020) 7680 15 00
– thechamberlain@fullers.co.uk – Fax (020) 7702 25 00
– www.thechamberlainhotel.com
closed Christmas   **AG2**
64 rm – ♦£195 ♦♦£195, � £13
Rest (in bar Saturday and Sunday) a la carte £11/20
♦ Business ♦ Functional ♦
Modern hotel aimed at business traveller, two minutes from the Tower of
London. Warmly decorated bedrooms with writing desks. All bathrooms have
inbuilt plasma TVs. Popular range of dishes.

Novotel London Tower Bridge
♨ 🐾 & ẢC rest ↔rm 🖾

10 Pepys St ⊠ EC3N 2NR – **Ⓜ** Tower Hill   ♨100 *VISA* ◑◐ AE ◐
– 𝒞 (020) 7265 60 00 – h3107@accor-hotels.com – Fax (020) 7265 60 60
– www.accorhotels.com   **AG2**
199 rm – ♦£175 ♦♦£195, � £14 – 4 suites
Rest *The Garden Brasserie* (buffet lunch) dinner a la carte £24/30
♦ Business ♦ Chain hotel ♦ Functional ♦
Modern, purpose-built hotel with carefully planned, comfortable bedrooms.
Useful City location and close to Tower of London which is visible from some of
the higher rooms. Informally styled brasserie.

City of London, Southwark & Tower Hamlets
(Plan IX)

AD

AE

Theobald's

Rosebery

Ave

John

Old

GRAY'S INN FIELD

GRAY'S INN

Gray's Inn

Clerkenwell

Road

Farringdon

Street

Aldersgate

St.

U

CHATERHOUSE

Rd

Leather

Lane

Hatton

Garden

Greville

St.

Street

Farringdon

Charterhouse Street

Long Lane

Barbican

BARBICAN
CENTRE

ST BARTHOLOMEW
THE GREAT

Aldersgate

MUSEUM
OF LONDON

Chancery

Lane

Holborn

Holborn

West Smithfield

Club Gascon ✗✗

Hosier Lane

London

STAPLE
INN

Furnival St.

Holborn

Holborn Viaduct

Snow Hill

CITY OF
LONDON

Street

Wood

Gresham

LINCOLN'S
INN FIELDS

LINCOLN'S
INN

Searle

Street

Carey

Street

Fetter Lane

New Fetter La.

New St.
Square

Shoe

Lane

Farringdon

St.

Old

Bailey

CITY
THAMESLINK

Newgate

Warwick Lane

St Paul's

Paternoster
Sq.

St.

New Change

St VEDAST

Cheapside

ST MARY-
LE-BOW

DR JOHNSON'S
HOUSE

Bouverie St.

Fleet

Street

ST MARTIN
LUDGATE

ST BRIDE

Paternoster ✗
Chop House

TEMPLE

Fleet

Street

Temple Ave.

Tudor
St.

New Bridge

St.

ST PAUL'S
CATHEDRAL

Cannon

Street

COLE ABBEY
PRESBYTERIAN

Victoria

Mansion
House

Crowne Plaza London-
The City

Queen

St.

BLACKFRIARS

ST JAMES
GARLICKHYTHE

Upper Thames

Temple
Place

Victoria

Embankment

Blackfriars

Bridge

THAMES

Millenium
Bridge

Southwark
bridge

✗ Souvlaki & Bar
(Bankside)

✗✗✗ Oxo Tower

Oxo Tower Brasserie

Blackfriars

Road

INTERNATIONAL
SHAKESPEARE
GLOBE CENTRE

SOUTH BANK
ARTS CENTRE

Upper

Ground

Street

✗ Tate Cafe (7th Floor)

TATE
MODERN

Southwark

Sumner

Street

Southwark Rose

Novotel London
City South

Stamford

Street

Hatfields

Express
by Holiday Inn

Great

Suffolk

Street

Bridge

BRAMAH MUSEUM
OF TEA AND COFFEE

Roupel

Street

Blackfriars

Lavington St.

SOUTHWARK

WATERLOO
EAST

Anchor and Hope

The Cut

Southwark

Union

Street

Baltic ✗✗

Street

Guildford

Southwark

NELSON
SQ.

Copperfield

Street

Redcross

Way

Surrey Row

Pocock

Street

Union

AD

AE

● Hotel

● Restaurant

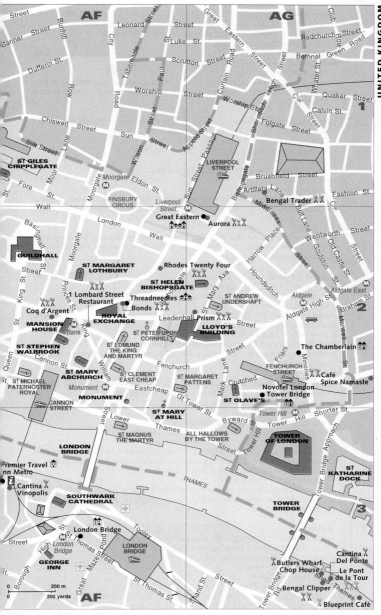

UNITED KINGDOM

XXX **Aurora** – at Great Eastern H.   A/C VISA ◍ AE ◍

Liverpool St ⊠ EC2M 7QN – Ⓜ *Liverpool Street –* ℰ *(020) 7618 70 00*
– restaurants @ great-eastern-hotel.co.uk – Fax (020) 7618 50 35
– www.great-eastern-hotel.co.uk
closed Saturday-Sunday   **AG2**
Rest £28 (lunch) and a la carte £34/53
• Modern • Formal •
Vast columns, ornate plasterwork and a striking glass dome feature in this imposing dining room. Polished and attentive service of an elaborate and modern menu.

XXX **Rhodes Twenty Four**   ⩽ London, A/C VISA ◍ AE ◍
✿
24th floor, Tower 42, 25 Old Broad St ⊠ EC2N 1HQ
– Ⓜ *Liverpool Street –* ℰ *(020) 7877 77 03*
– reservations @ rhodes24.co.uk – Fax (020) 7877 77 88
– www.rhodes24.co.uk
closed Christmas-New year, Saturday, Sunday and
Bank Holidays   **AF2**
Rest a la carte £27/33
Spec. Seared scallops with mashed potato and shallot mustard sauce. Truffled macaroni cheese with chestnut mushroom, watercress and rocket salad. Bread and butter pudding.
• English • Formal •
Modern restaurant on the 24th floor of the former Natwest building with panoramic views of the city. Modern, refined cooking of classic British recipes. Booking advised.

XXX **Coq d'Argent**   🍽 A/C VISA ◍ AE ◍

No 1 Poultry ⊠ EC2R 8EJ – Ⓜ *Bank –* ℰ *(020) 7395 50 00*
– coqdargent @ conran-restaurants.co.uk – Fax (020) 7395 50 50
– www.conran.com
closed Saturday lunch, Sunday dinner and Bank Holidays   **AF2**
Rest (booking essential) £27 (lunch) and a la carte £37/44
• French • Design •
Take the dedicated lift to the top of this modern office block. Tables on the rooftop terrace have city views; busy bar. Gallic menus highlighted by popular shellfish dishes.

XXX **1 Lombard Street Restaurant**   A/C ⊬ ⇔25 VISA ◍ AE ◍
✿
1 Lombard St ⊠ EC3V 9AA – Ⓜ *Bank –* ℰ *(020) 7929 66 11*
– hb @ 1lombardstreet.com – Fax (020) 7929 66 22
– www.1lombardstreet.com
closed Saturday, Sunday and Bank Holidays   **AF2**
Rest (booking essential at lunch) 39/45 and a la carte £53/62
Spec. Carpaccio of tuna with Oriental spices, ginger and lime vinaigrette. Beef tournedos with wild mushrooms, parsley purée and oxtail sauce. Feuillantine of apple, Guinness ice cream and glazed hazelnuts.
• Modern • Formal •
A haven of tranquillity behind the forever busy brasserie. Former bank provides the modern and very comfortable surroundings in which to savour the accomplished cuisine.

XXX **Prism**   A/C VISA ◍ AE ◍

147 Leadenhall ⊠ EC3V 4QT – Ⓜ *Aldgate –* ℰ *(020) 7256 38 75*
– Fax (020) 7256 38 76 – www.harveynichols.com
closed 23 December-2 January, Saturday,
Sunday and Bank Holidays   **AG2**
Rest a la carte £33/43
• Innovative • Trendy •
Enormous Corinthian pillars and a busy bar feature in this capacious and modern restaurant. Efficient service of an eclectic menu. Quieter tables in covered courtyard.

XXX **Bonds** – at Threadneedles H.   AC ⅘ VISA OO AE ①
5 Threadneedle St ⊠ EC2R 8AY – Ⓜ Bank – 𝒞 (020) 7657 80 88 – bonds@
theetongroup.com – Fax (020) 7657 80 89 – www.theetoncollection.com
closed 2 weeks Christmas-New Year, Sunday and Bank Holidays   **AF2**
Rest £20/25 and a la carte £30/48
♦ Modern ♦ Retro ♦
Modern interior juxtaposed with the grandeur of a listed city building. Vast
dining room with high ceiling and tall pillars. Attentive service of hearty,
contemporary food.

XX **Club Gascon** (Aussignac)   AC VISA OO AE
🥂 57 West Smithfield ⊠ EC1A 9DS – Ⓜ Barbican – 𝒞 (020) 7796 06 00
– Fax (020) 7796 06 01
closed 22-31 December, Sunday, Saturday lunch and Bank Holidays   **AE1**
Rest (booking essential) £38/60 and a la carte £33/79
Spec. Foie gras "Rose Sangria". Glazed black cod with almonds and smoked
grapes. Stew of "confit" snails, mousserons, Aligot and ventrèche.
♦ French ♦ Fashionable ♦
Intimate restaurant on the edge of Smithfield Market. Specialises in both the
food and wines of Southwest France. Renowned for its tapas-sized dishes.

X **Paternoster Chop House**   � AC ⅘ VISA OO AE ①
Warwick Court, Paternoster Square ⊠ EC4N 7DX – Ⓜ St Paul's
– 𝒞 (020) 7029 94 00 – Fax (020) 7029 94 09 – www.conran.com
closed 23 December-3 January, Saturday and Sunday   **AE2**
Rest a la carte £31/36
♦ English ♦ Brasserie ♦
A brasserie ambience holds sway, while there's a reassuringly resolute British
classic style to the food. Back to basics menu relies on seasonality and sourcing
of ingredients.

Southwark   *Plan IX*

Bermondsey

🏨 **London Bridge**   ℔ 🕭 AC ⅘rm 🍴 ▥ ♨100 VISA OO AE ①
8-18 London Bridge St ⊠ SE1 9SG – Ⓜ London Bridge – 𝒞 (020) 7855 22 00
– sales@london-bridge-hotel.co.uk – Fax (020) 7855 22 33
– www.londonbridgehotel.co.uk   **AF3**
135 rm – ♥£199 ♥♥£199, ⇆ £15 – 3 suites
Rest *Georgetown* £25/30 (lunch) and a la carte £19/29
♦ Business ♦ Classic ♦
In one of the oldest parts of London, independently owned with an ornate
façade dating from 1915. Modern interior with classically decorated bedrooms
and an impressive gym. Restaurant echoing the colonial style serving Malaysian
dishes.

XXX **Le Pont de la Tour**   ≤ � ⇄24 VISA OO AE ①
36d Shad Thames (Butlers Wharf) ⊠ SE1 2YE – Ⓜ London Bridge
– 𝒞 (020) 7403 84 03 – Fax (020) 7403 02 67 – www.conran.com   **AG3**
Rest £30 (lunch) and dinner a la carte £41/83 ⅋
♦ Modern ♦ Formal ♦
Elegant and stylish room commanding spectacular views of the Thames and
Tower Bridge. Formal and detailed service. Modern menu with an informal bar
attached.

XX **Bengal Clipper**   AC VISA OO AE
Cardamom Building, Shad Thames, Butlers Wharf ⊠ SE1 2YR – Ⓜ London Bridge
– 𝒞 (020) 7357 90 01 – mail@bengalclipper.co.uk – Fax (020) 7357 90 02
– www.bengalclipper.co.uk   **AG3**
Rest a la carte £17/27
♦ Indian ♦ Friendly ♦
Housed in a Thames-side converted warehouse, a smart Indian restaurant with
original brickwork and steel supports. Menu features Bengali and Goan dishes.
Evening pianist.

UNITED KINGDOM

XX **Tentazioni** *VISA* **CO** AE

2 Mill St, Lloyds Wharf ⊠ SE1 2BD – Ⓜ Bermondsey – ℰ (020) 7237 11 00
– tentazioni@aol.com – Fax (020) 7237 11 00 – www.tentazioni.co.uk
*closed 23 December-3 January, Easter, Sunday and lunch Saturday
and Monday* Plan I **D2**
Rest £19 (lunch) and a la carte £30/36
♦ Italian ♦ Rustic ♦
Former warehouse provides a bright and lively environment. Open staircase
between the two floors. Keenly run, with a menu offering simple, carefully
prepared Italian food.

X **Blueprint Café** ⪡ Tower Bridge, *VISA* **CO** AE ⓪

Design Museum, Shad Thames, Butlers Wharf ⊠ SE1 2YD – Ⓜ London Bridge
– ℰ (020) 7378 70 31 – Fax (020) 7357 88 10 – www.conran.com
closed 25-28 December, 1-2 January and Sunday dinner **AG3**
Rest a la carte £24/38
♦ Modern ♦ Design ♦
Above the Design Museum, with impressive views of the river and bridge: handy
binoculars on tables. Eager and energetic service, modern British menus: robust
and rustic.

X **Cantina Del Ponte** ⪡ 🕭 *VISA* **CO** AE ⓪

36c Shad Thames, Butlers Wharf ⊠ SE1 2YE – Ⓜ London Bridge – ℰ (020) 7403
54 03 – Fax (020) 7403 44 32 – www.conran.com
closed 25-26 December **AG3**
Rest a la carte £16/28
♦ Italian ♦ Bistro ♦
Quayside setting with a large canopied terrace. Terracotta flooring; modern
rustic style décor, simple and unfussy. Tasty, refreshing Mediterranean-
influenced cooking.

X **Butlers Wharf Chop House** ⪡ Tower Bridge, 🕭 *VISA* **CO** AE ⓪

36e Shad Thames, Butlers Wharf ⊠ SE1 2YE – Ⓜ London Bridge – ℰ (020) 7403
34 03 – Fax (020) 7403 34 14 – www.conran.com
closed 25-26 December, 1-3 January and Sunday dinner **AG3**
Rest £26 (lunch) and dinner a la carte £25/38
♦ English ♦ Rustic ♦
Book the terrace in summer and dine in the shadow of Tower Bridge. Rustic feel
to the interior, with obliging service. Menu focuses on traditional English dishes.

Rotherhithe

🏨 **Hilton London Docklands** ⪡ 🕭 ₤ᵴ 🀫 🖵 ₺ 🗚 ⇔rm 🚪 ₷Å350

265 Rotherhithe St, Nelson Dock ⊠ SE16 5HW **P** *VISA* **CO** AE ⓪
– ℰ (020) 7231 10 01 – sales-docklands@hilton.com – Fax (020) 7231 05 99
– www.hilton.co.uk/docklands
closed 22-30 December
361 rm – ✝£110/200 ✝✝£110/200 – 4 suites
Rest *Traders Bistro* (closed Sunday) (dinner only) £25
♦ Business ♦ Chain hotel ♦ Functional ♦
Redbrick group hotel with glass façade. River-taxi from the hotel's own pier.
Extensive leisure facilities. Standard size rooms with all mod cons. Eat on board
Traders Bistro, a reconstructed galleon moored in dry dock.

Southwark

🏨 **Novotel London City South** ₤ᵴ 🀫 ₺ 🗚 ⇔rm 🚪

53-61 Southwark Bridge Rd ⊠ SE1 9HH – Ⓜ ₷Å100 *VISA* **CO** AE ⓪
London Bridge – ℰ (020) 7089 04 00 – h3269@accor.com – Fax (020) 7089 04 10
– www.novotel.com **AE3**
178 rm – ✝£170/250 ✝✝£190/280, � £14 – 4 suites
Rest *The Garden Brasserie* a la carte £17/32
♦ Business ♦ Chain hotel ♦ Functional ♦
The new style of Novotel with good business facilities. Triple glazed bedrooms,
furnished in the Scandinavian style with keyboard and high speed internet.
Brasserie style dining room with windows all down one side.

UNITED KINGDOM

Premier Travel Inn Metro   ら ⇔rm ℅ *VISA* ⓄⒺ ⒶⒺ ⓄⒹ
Bankside, 34 Park St ⊠ *SE1 9EF –* Ⓜ *London Bridge –* ℰ *(0870) 700 14 56*
– Fax (0870) 700 14 57 – www.travelinn.co.uk   **AF3**
56 rm – ♦£83 ♦♦£85
Rest (grill rest)
♦ Chain hotel ♦ Functional ♦
A good value lodge with modern, well-equipped bedrooms which include a spacious desk area, ideal for the corporate and leisure traveller. Popular, tried-and-tested menus.

Express by Holiday Inn without rest   ら Ⓐ ⇔ ℅
103-109 Southwark St ⊠ *SE1 0JQ –* Ⓜ   Ⓟ *VISA* ⓄⒺ ⒶⒺ ⓄⒹ
Southwark – ℰ *(020) 7401 25 25 – stay@expresssouthwark.co.uk*
– Fax (020) 7401 33 22 – www.hiexpress.com/lon-southwark   **AE3**
88 rm – ♦£93/125 ♦♦£110/128
♦ Chain hotel ♦ Functional ♦
Useful location, just ten minutes from Waterloo. Purpose-built hotel with modern bedrooms in warm pastel shades. Fully equipped business centre.

Southwark Rose   ら Ⓐ ⇔ ℅ 🖭 ℅ 🍽80 Ⓟ *VISA* ⓄⒺ ⒶⒺ
43-47 Southwark Bridge Rd ⊠ *SE1 9HH –* Ⓜ *London Bridge –* ℰ *(020) 7015 14 80*
– info@southwarkrosehotel.co.uk – Fax (020) 7015 14 81
– www.southwarkrosehotel.co.uk   **AE3**
78 rm – ♦£115 ♦♦£115, ⌷ £10 – 6 suites
Rest (dinner only) a la carte £12/21
♦ Business ♦ Functional ♦
Purpose built budget hotel south of the City, near the Globe Theatre. Top floor breakfast room with bar. Uniform style, reasonably spacious bedrooms with writing desks.

XXX   **Oxo Tower**   ⩽ London Skyline and River Thames, �
(8th Floor) Oxo Tower Wharf, Barge House St,   Ⓐ *VISA* ⓄⒺ ⒶⒺ ⓄⒹ
⊠ *SE1 9PH –* Ⓜ *Southwark –* ℰ *(020) 7803 38 88*
– oxo.reservations@harveynichols.co.uk – Fax (020) 7803 38 38
– www.harveynichols.com
closed 25-26 December   **AD3**
Rest see also *Oxo Tower Brasserie* below
Rest £30 (lunch) and dinner a la carte £42/57 🕸
♦ Modern ♦ Formal ♦
Top of a converted factory, providing stunning views of the Thames and beyond. Stylish, minimalist interior with huge windows. Smooth service of modern cuisine.

XX   **Baltic**   *VISA* ⓄⒺ ⒶⒺ ⓄⒹ
74 Blackfriars Rd ⊠ *SE1 8HA –* Ⓜ *Southwark –* ℰ *(020) 7928 11 11*
– info@balticrestaurant.co.uk – Fax (020) 7928 84 87
– www.balticrestaurant.co.uk   **AD3**
Rest £14 (lunch) and a la carte £23/28
♦ Eastern European ♦ Brasserie ♦
Set in a Grade II listed 18C former coach house. Enjoy authentic and hearty east European and Baltic influenced food. Interesting vodka selection and live jazz on Sundays.

X   **Oxo Tower Brasserie**   ⩽ London Skyline and River Thames, �
(8th Floor) Oxo Tower Wharf, Barge House St   Ⓐ *VISA* ⓄⒺ ⒶⒺ ⓄⒹ
⊠ *SE1 9PH –* Ⓜ *Southwark –* ℰ *(020) 7803 38 88*
– oxo.reservations@harveynichols.co.uk – Fax (020) 7803 38 38
– www.harveynichols.com
closed 25-26 December   **AD3**
Rest £22 (lunch) and a la carte £30/41
♦ Modern ♦ Brasserie ♦
Same views but less formal than the restaurant. Open-plan kitchen, relaxed service, the modern menu is slightly lighter. In summer, try to secure a table on the terrace.

Cantina Vinopolis
AC VISA MO AE ①

No 1 Bank End ⊠ *SE1 9BU –* Ⓜ *London Bridge – ℰ (020) 7940 83 33*
– cantina @ vinopolis.co.uk – Fax (020) 7940 83 34
– www.cantinavinopolis.com
closed 24 December-2 January and Sunday dinner **AF3**
Rest £18 (lunch) and a la carte £20/28 ✿

♦ Modern ♦ Bistro ♦

Large, solid brick vaulted room under Victorian railway arches, with an adjacent wine museum. Modern menu with a huge selection of wines by the glass.

Tate Cafe (7th Floor)
≤ London Skyline and River Thames,

Tate Modern, Bankside ⊠ *SE1 9TG* ↳ VISA MO AE ①
– Ⓜ *Southwark – ℰ (020) 7401 50 20 – Fax (020) 7401 51 71*
– www.tate.org.uk
closed 24-26 December **AE3**
Rest (lunch only and dinner Friday-Saturday) a la carte £20/32

♦ Innovative ♦ Design ♦

Modernity to match the museum, with vast murals and huge windows affording stunning views. Canteen-style menu at a sensible price with obliging service.

Souvlaki & Bar (Bankside)
≤ 斎 AC VISA MO

Units 1-2, Riverside House, 2A Southwark Bridge Rd ⊠ *SE1 9HA – ℰ (020)*
7620 01 62 – Fax (020) 7620 02 62 – www.therealgreek.co.uk **AE3**
Rest a la carte £14/25

♦ Greek ♦ Bistro ♦

Overlooking the Thames, two minutes from Globe Theatre: a casual, modern restaurant with excellent value menus featuring totally authentic Greek dishes and beers.

Anchor and Hope
VISA MO

36 The Cut ⊠ *SE1 8LP –* Ⓜ *Southwark – ℰ (020) 7928 98 98*
– Fax (020) 7928 45 95
closed Christmas-New Year, last 2 weeks August, Sunday, Monday lunch and
Bank Holidays **AD3**
Rest (bookings not accepted) a la carte £20/30

♦ Modern ♦ Pub ♦

Close to Waterloo, the distinctive dark green exterior lures visitors in droves. Bare floorboards, simple wooden furniture. Seriously original cooking with rustic French base.

Tower Hamlets

Canary Wharf

Four Seasons
≤ ₤₅ 斎 ☒ ₺ AC ↳ 匣 ☎ 斿200 ㊒ VISA MO AE ①

Westferry Circus, ⊠ *E14 8RS –* Ⓜ *Canary Wharf (DLR) – ℰ (020) 7510 19 99*
– Fax (020) 7510 19 98 – www.fourseasons.com/canarywharf
128 rm – ✝£376 ✝✝£400, ⊃ £21 – 14 suites
Rest see **Quadrato** below

♦ Grand Luxury ♦ Classic ♦

Stylish hotel opened in 2000, with striking river and city views. Atrium lobby leading to modern bedrooms boasting every conceivable extra. Detailed service.

Marriott London West India Quay
₤₅ 斿 ₺ AC ↳ ✗ 匣

22 Hertsmere Rd, ⊠ *E14 4ED* 斿300 VISA MO AE ①
– Ⓜ *West India Quay (DLR) – ℰ (020) 7093 10 00 – reservations @ marriott.com*
– Fax (020) 7093 10 01 – www.marriott.co.uk/loncw
294 rm – ✝£274/327 ✝✝£274/327, ⊃ £18 – 7 suites
Rest *Curve* a la carte £21/40

♦ Business ♦ Modern ♦

Spacious, very well-equipped bedrooms, classic or modern, plus a 24-hour business centre in this glass-fronted high-rise hotel on the quay. Champagne and oyster bar and informal, American-style seafood inn serving fish from nearby Billingsgate market.

Circus Apartments without rest ⭑ 🕸 📺 🗚 ⅍ ⚡ 🖾 📞

39 Westferry Circus, ⊠ *E14 8RW* 🚗 ⅤⅠⅮ 🆆🅾 🗛🅴 🆀🄳

– 🅜 Canary Wharf (DLR) – 🖉 (020) 7719 70 00

– res@circusapartments.co.uk – Fax (020) 7719 70 01

– www.circusapartments.co.uk

45 suites – †£217 ††£240

♦ Business ♦ Modern ♦

Smart, contemporary, fully serviced apartment block close to Canary Wharf: rooms, comfortable and spacious, can be taken from one day to one year.

Plateau (Restaurant) 🗚 ⅤⅠⅮ 🆆🅾 🗛🅴 🆀🄳

Canada Place, Canada Square, ⊠ *E14 5ER Canary Wharf*

– 🅜 Canary Wharf (DLR) – 🖉 (020) 7715 71 00 – Fax (020) 7715 71 10

– www.conran.com

closed 25 December, 1 January, Saturday lunch and Sunday

Rest £25 (dinner) and a la carte £40/51

♦ Modern ♦ Design ♦

Fourth floor restaurant overlooking Canada Square and The Big Blue art installation. Glass-sided kitchen; well-spaced, uncluttered tables. Modern menus with classical base.

Ubon by Nobu ≤ River Thames and city skyline, 🗚

39 Westferry Circus, ⊠ *E14 8RR – 🅜 Canary* 🅿 ⅤⅠⅮ 🆆🅾 🗛🅴 🆀🄳

Wharf (DLR) – 🖉 (020) 7719 78 00 – ubon@noburestaurants.com

– Fax (020) 7719 78 01 – www.noburestaurants.com

closed Saturday lunch, Sunday and Bank Holidays

Rest £45/70

♦ Japanese ♦ Trendy ♦

Light, airy, open-plan restaurant, with floor to ceiling glass and great Thames views. Informal atmosphere. Large menu with wide selection of modern Japanese dishes.

Quadrato – at Four Seasons H. � 🗚 🅿 ⅤⅠⅮ 🆆🅾 🗛🅴 🆀🄳

Westferry Circus, ⊠ *E14 8RS – 🅜 Canary Wharf (DLR)*

– 🖉 (020) 7510 19 99 – Fax (020) 7510 19 98

– www.fourseasons.com/canarywharf

Rest £27/33 and a la carte £27/41

♦ Italian ♦ Design ♦

Striking, modern restaurant with terrace overlooking river. Sleek, stylish dining room with glass-fronted open-plan kitchen. Menu of northern Italian dishes; swift service.

Plateau (Grill) 🗚 ⅤⅠⅮ 🆆🅾 🗛🅴 🆀🄳

Canada Place, Canada Square, ⊠ *E14 5ER – 🅜 Canary Wharf (DLR)*

– 🖉 (020) 7715 71 00 – Fax (020) 7715 71 10

– www.conran.com

closed 25 December, 1 January and Sunday dinner

Rest £20/35 and a la carte £24/35

♦ Modern ♦ Design ♦

Situated on fourth floor of 21C building; adjacent to Plateau Restaurant, with simpler table settings. Classical dishes, with seasonal base, employing grill specialities.

The Gun 🌤 ⅤⅠⅮ 🆆🅾 🗛🅴

27 Coldharbour ⊠ *E14 9NS – 🅜 Blackwall (DLR)*

– 🖉 (020) 7515 52 22

– info@thegundocklands.com

– www.thegundocklands.com

closed 25-26 December and 1 January

Rest a la carte £20/33

♦ Modern ♦ Pub ♦

Restored historic pub with a terrace facing the Dome: tasty dishes, including Billingsgate market fish, balance bold simplicity and a bit of French finesse. Efficient service.

St Katherine's Dock

XX **The Aquarium**   ≤ 🛱 _VISA_ 🐵 🆎 ①
Ivory House ⊠ *E1W 1AT –* Ⓜ *Tower Hill –* ℰ *(020) 7480 61 16*
– info@theaquarium.co.uk – Fax (020) 7480 59 73
– www.theaquarium.co.uk
closed 2 weeks Christmas, Saturday lunch, Sunday and Monday dinner
and Bank Holidays   *Plan I* **D2**
Rest a la carte £30/70
◆ Seafood ◆ Bistro ◆
Seafood restaurant in a pleasant marina setting with views of the boats
from some tables. Simple, smart modern décor. Menu of market-fresh, seafood
dishes.

Spitalfields

XX **Bengal Trader**   _AK_ _VISA_ 🐵 🆎
44 Artillery Lane ⊠ *E1 7NA –* Ⓜ *Liverpool Street*
– ℰ *(020) 7375 00 72 – mail@bengalclipper.co.uk*
– Fax (020) 7247 10 02 – www.bengalclipper.co.uk   *Plan IX* **AG1**
Rest a la carte £13/25
◆ Indian ◆ Brasserie ◆
Contemporary Indian paintings feature in this stylish basement room beneath a
ground floor bar. Menu provides ample choice of Indian dishes.

X **St John Bread and Wine**   _AK_ _VISA_ 🐵 🆎
94-96 Commercial St ⊠ *E1 6LZ –* Ⓜ *Shoreditch*
– ℰ *(020) 7247 87 24 – Fax (020) 7247 89 24*
– www.stjohnbreadandwine.com
closed 24 December-2 January, Sunday dinner and Bank
Holiday Mondays   *Plan I* **D2**
Rest a la carte £25/29
◆ Innovative ◆ Bistro ◆
Very popular neighbourhood bakery providing wide variety of home-made
breads. Appealing, intimate dining section: all day menus that offer continually
changing dishes.

Wapping

X **Wapping Food**   🛱 **P** _VISA_ 🐵 🆎
Wapping Wall ⊠ *E1W 3ST –* Ⓜ *Wapping –* ℰ *(020) 7680 20 80*
– info@wapping-wpt.com – www.thewappingproject.com
closed 24 December-2 January and Sunday dinner   *Plan I* **D2**
Rest a la carte £26/42
◆ Modern ◆ Design ◆
Something a little unusual; a combination of restaurant and gallery in a
converted hydraulic power station. Enjoy the modern menu surrounded by
turbines and TV screens.

Whitechapel

XX **Cafe Spice Namaste**   _AK_ _VISA_ 🐵 🆎 ①
😊 *16 Prescot St,* ⊠ *E1 8AZ –* Ⓜ *Tower Hill –* ℰ *(020) 7488 92 42*
– info@cafespice.co.uk – Fax (020) 7481 05 08
– www.cafespice.co.uk
closed Christmas-New Year, Sunday and Bank Holidays   *Plan IX* **AG2**
Rest £30 and a la carte £17/29
◆ Indian ◆ Neighbourhood ◆
A riot of colour from the brightly painted walls to the flowing drapes.
Sweet-natured service adds to the engaging feel. Fragrant and competitively
priced Indian cooking.

CHELSEA, SOUTH KENSINGTON & EARL'S COURT

Chelsea

Plan X

Jumeirah Carlton Tower

Cadogan Pl ⊠ SW1X 9PY – Ⓜ

Knightsbridge – ℰ *(020) 7235 12 34 – jctinfo@jumeirah – Fax (020) 7235 91 29*
– www.jumeirah.com

AK1

190 rm – ✝£393 ✝✝£393, ⊑ £28 – 30 suites

Rest *Rib Room (closed Sunday lunch)* £28 (lunch) and a la carte £24/44

♦ Grand Luxury ♦ Classic ♦

Imposing international hotel overlooking a leafy square. Well-equipped roof-top health club has funky views. Generously proportioned rooms boast every conceivable facility. Rib Room restaurant has a clubby atmosphere.

Conrad London

Chelsea Harbour ⊠ SW10 0XG – ℰ *(020) 7823*
30 00 – lonch-rs@hilton.com – Fax (020) 7351 65 25
– www.conradlondon.com

AI3

160 suites – ✝£411 ✝✝£411, ⊑ £23 –**Rest** *Aquasia* a la carte £28/43

♦ Luxury ♦ Modern ♦

Modern, all-suite hotel within an exclusive marina and retail development. Many of the spacious and well-appointed rooms have balconies and views across the Thames.

Sheraton Park Tower

101 Knightsbridge ⊠ SW1X 7RN – Ⓜ

Knightsbridge – ℰ *(020) 7235 80 50 – central.london.reservations@*
sheraton.com – Fax (020) 7235 82 31
– www.luxurycollection.com/parktowerlondon

AK1

258 rm – ✝£447 ✝✝£517, ⊑ £22 – 22 suites –**Rest** see *One-O-One* below

♦ Luxury ♦ Business ♦

Built in the 1970s in a unique cylindrical shape. Well-equipped bedrooms are all identical in size. Top floor executive rooms have commanding views of Hyde Park and City.

Capital

22-24 Basil St ⊠ SW3 1AT – Ⓜ *Knightsbridge –* ℰ *(020) 7589 51 71*
– reservations@capitalhotel.co.uk – Fax (020) 7225 00 11
– www.capitalhotel.co.uk

AK1

49 rm – ✝£229/323 ✝✝£417/500, ⊑ £17

Rest see *The Capital Restaurant* below

♦ Luxury ♦ Traditional ♦ Classic ♦

Discreet and privately owned town house with distinct English charm. Individually decorated rooms with plenty of thoughtful touches.

Draycott

26 Cadogan Gdns ⊠ SW3 2RP – Ⓜ *Sloane Square –* ℰ *(020) 7730 64 66*
– reservations@draycotthotel.com – Fax (020) 7730 02 36
– www.draycotthotel.com

AK2

31 rm – ✝£141/229 ✝✝£376, ⊑ £19 – 4 suites –**Rest** (room service only)

♦ Townhouse ♦ Stylish ♦

Charmingly discreet 19C house in exclusive residential area. Elegant sitting room overlooks tranquil communal garden. Individually decorated rooms in a country house style.

The Cadogan

75 Sloane St ⊠ SW1X 9SG – Ⓜ *Knightsbridge –* ℰ *(020) 7235 71 41*
– reservations@cadogan.com – Fax (020) 7245 09 94
– www.thesteingroup.com/cadogan

AK1

61 rm – ✝£223/323 ✝✝£382, ⊑ £20 – 4 suites

Rest (dinner only in August) 18 (lunch) and a la carte £28/45

♦ Luxury ♦ Cosy ♦

An Edwardian town house, where Oscar Wilde was arrested; modernised and refurbished with a French accent. Contemporary drawing room. Stylish bedrooms; latest facilities. Discreet, stylish restaurant.

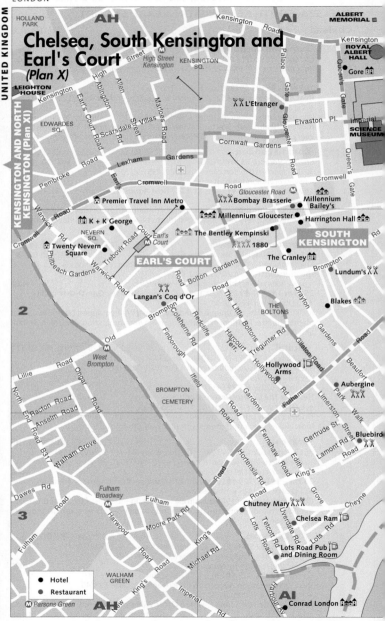

Chelsea, South Kensington and Earl's Court
(Plan X)

UNITED KINGDOM

KENSINGTON AND NORTH KENSINGTON (Plan XI)

HOLLAND PARK

AH

AI

ALBERT MEMORIAL

Kensington Road

LEIGHTON HOUSE

Kensington

High Street Kensington

KENSINGTON SQ.

Kensington Road

ROYAL ALBERT HALL

Queen's Gate

Gore

High Street

Abingdon Street

Allen Street

Marloes Road

Earl's Court Road

Scarsdale Villas

EDWARDES SQ.

Kensington

L'Etranger

Gate

Gloucester

Elvaston Pl.

Imperial

SCIENCE MUSEUM

Cornwall Gardens

Queen's Gate

Pembroke Road

Lexham Gardens

Cromwell

Road

Cromwell

Road

Gloucester Road

Bombay Brasserie

Millennium Bailey's

Warwick Rd

Earl's Court Road

Premier Travel Inn Metro

Millennium Gloucester

Harrington Hall

Cromwell

K + K George

Earl's Court

SOUTH KENSINGTON

Rd

NEVERN SQ.

Trebovir Road

The Bentley Kempinski

Twenty Nevern Square

Warwick Road

Earl's Court

EARL'S COURT

1880

The Cranley

Phillbeach Gardens

Bolton Gardens

Old Brompton

Lundum's

Langan's Coq d'Or

The Little Boltons

THE BOLTONS

Drayton Gardens

Blakes

2

Old Brompton Road

Coleherne Rd

Redcliffe

Harcourt Terr.

Tregunter Rd

Gilston Road

Road

Beaufort

Lillie Road

West Brompton

Finborough

Ifield

Hollywood Rd

Hollywood Arms

Fulham

Limerston Street

Aubergine

North End Road B317

Bracton Road

Anselm Road

BROMPTON CEMETERY

Gardens

Fernshaw Road

Edith Grove

Gertrude St.

Lamont Rd

Bluebird

Walham Grove

King's

Road

Dawes Rd

Fulham Broadway

Fulham

Hortensia Rd

Cheyne

3

Fulham Road

Moore Park Rd

King's

Road

Chutney Mary

Uverdale Rd

Lots Rd

Chelsea Ram

Michael Rd

Lots Road Pub and Dining Room

WALHAM GREEN

King's Road

Imperial

Harbour

AH

Parsons Green

New

Rd

AI

Conrad London

• Hotel
• Restaurant
Ⓜ Metro

872

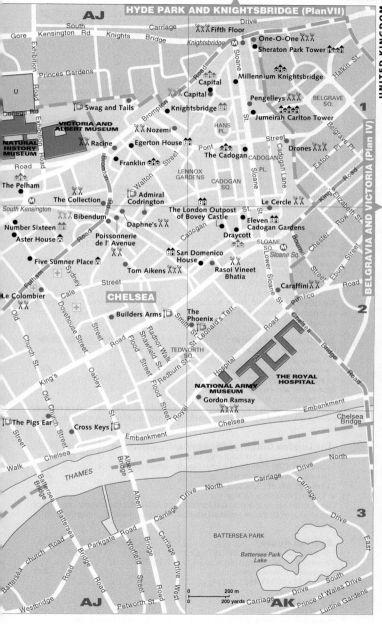

UNITED KINGDOM

Millennium Knightsbridge
🔥 🟰 🔊 🛁 📺 ♨ 120 VISA ⚫ AE ①
17-25 Sloane St ⊠ SW1X 9NU – Ⓜ *Knights-*
bridge – ℰ *(020) 7235 43 77 – reservations.knightsbridge@mill-cop.com*
– Fax (020) 7235 71 25 – www.millenniumhotels.com   **AK1**
218 rm – 👤£258/282 👤👤£282, � £18 – 4 suites
Rest *Mju (closed Saturday lunch and Sunday)* £20/38
♦ Business ♦ Modern ♦
Modern, corporate hotel in the heart of London's most fashionable shopping
district. Executive bedrooms are well-appointed and equipped with the latest
technology.

Franklin
🚿 🟰 🔊 rest ♨ 🕙 VISA ⚫ AE ①
22-28 Egerton Gdns ⊠ SW3 2DB – Ⓜ *South Kensington –* ℰ *(020) 7584 55 33*
– bookings@franklinhotel.co.uk – Fax (020) 7584 54 49
– www.franklinhotel.co.uk   **AJ1**
47 rm – 👤£135/247 👤👤£347/464, ⊊ £18
Rest a la carte £30/38
♦ Townhouse ♦ Classic ♦
Attractive Victorian town house in an exclusive residential area. Charming
drawing room overlooks a tranquil communal garden. Well-furnished rooms in
a country house style. Elegantly appointed dining room offering traditional
meals.

Knightsbridge
🔥 🟰 🔊 ♨ 📺 🕙 VISA ⚫ AE
10 Beaufort Gdns ⊠ SW3 1PT – Ⓜ *Knightsbridge –* ℰ *(020) 7584 63 00*
– knightsbridge@firmdale.com – Fax (020) 7584 63 55
– www.knightsbridgehotel.com   **AJ1**
44 rm – 👤£176/212 👤👤£306, ⊊ £15
Rest (room service only)
♦ Townhouse ♦ Stylish ♦
Attractively furnished town house with a very stylish, discreet feel. Every
bedroom is immaculately appointed and has an individuality of its own; fine
detailing throughout.

San Domenico House
🟰 🔊 rm ♨ 📺 VISA ⚫ AE ①
29-31 Draycott Pl ⊠ SW3 2SH – Ⓜ *Sloane Square –* ℰ *(020) 7581 57 57 – info@*
sandomenicohouse.com – Fax (020) 7584 13 48
– www.sandomenicohouse.com   **AK2**
18 rm – 👤£207 👤👤£329, ⊊ £11
Rest (room service only)
♦ Townhouse ♦ Classic ♦
Intimate and discreet Victorian town house with an attractive rooftop terrace.
Individually styled and generally spacious rooms with antique furniture and rich
fabrics.

The London Outpost of Bovey Castle without rest
🚿 🟰 🟰
69 Cadogan Gdns ⊠ SW3 2RB – Ⓜ *Sloane*   ♨ 🕙 VISA ⚫ AE ①
Square – ℰ *(020) 7589 73 33 – info@londonoutpost.co.uk – Fax (020) 7581 49 58*
– www.londonoutpost.co.uk   **AK2**
11 rm – 👤£200 👤👤£329, ⊊ £17
♦ Townhouse ♦ Cosy ♦
Classic town house in a most fashionable area. Relaxed and comfy lounges full of
English charm. Bedrooms, named after local artists and writers, full of thoughtful
touches.

Egerton House
🟰 🟰 ♨ VISA ⚫ AE ①
17-19 Egerton Terrace ⊠ SW3 2BX – Ⓜ *South Kensington –* ℰ *(020) 7589 24 12*
– bookings@egertonhousehotel.co.uk – Fax (020) 7584 65 40
– www.egertonhousehotel.co.uk   **AJ1**
29 rm – 👤£135/211 👤👤£170/294, ⊊ £17
Rest (room service only)
♦ Townhouse ♦ Classic ♦
Stylish redbrick Victorian town house close to the exclusive shops. Relaxed
drawing room. Antique furnished and individually decorated rooms.

Eleven Cadogan Gardens

11 Cadogan Gdns ⊠ SW3 2RJ – Ⓜ Sloane Square – ℰ (020) 7730 70 00
– reservations@number-eleven.co.uk – Fax (020) 7730 52 17
– www.number-eleven.co.uk

55 rm – †£182/229 ††£276/382, ⊑ £14 – 4 suites
Rest (residents only) a la carte £26/44   **AK2**

♦ Townhouse ♦ Classic ♦

Occupying four Victorian houses, one of London's first private town house hotels. Traditionally appointed bedrooms vary considerably in size. Genteel atmosphere. Light and airy basement dining room exclusively for residents.

Gordon Ramsay

68-69 Royal Hospital Rd ⊠ SW3 4HP – Ⓜ Sloane Square – ℰ (020) 7352 44 41
– reservations@gordonramsay.com – Fax (020) 7352 33 34
– www.gordonramsay.com

closed 2 weeks Christmas-New Year, Saturday and Sunday   **AK2**
Rest (booking essential) £40/70 🕮

Spec. Beef tartare with caviar, peppers and deep-fried onion rings. Roast pigeon with foie gras, braised cabbage and creamed potatoes. Chocolate cylinder with coffee granité and ginger mousse.

♦ Modern ♦ Formal ♦

Elegant and sophisticated room. The eponymous chef creates some of Britain's finest, classically inspired cooking. Detailed and attentive service. Book one month in advance.

The Capital Restaurant – at Capital H.

22-24 Basil St ⊠ SW3 1AT – Ⓜ Knightsbridge – ℰ (020) 7589 51 71
– caprest@capitalhotel.co.uk – Fax (020) 7225 00 11
– www.capitalhotel.co.uk   **AK1**
Rest (booking essential) £30/55 🕮

Spec. Langoustine with pork belly and sweet spice. Saddle of rabbit with calamari and tomato risotto. Coffee parfait with chocolate fondant.

♦ Modern ♦ Formal ♦

A hotel restaurant known for its understated elegance, discretion and graceful service. Cooking blends the innovative with the classic to create carefully crafted dishes.

Bibendum

Michelin House, 81 Fulham Rd ⊠ SW3 6RD – Ⓜ South Kensington
– ℰ (020) 7581 58 17 – manager@bibendum.co.uk – Fax (020) 7823 79 25
– www.bibendum.co.uk

closed 25-26 December and 1 January   **AJ2**
Rest £29 (lunch) and dinner a la carte £32/60 🕮

♦ Modern ♦ Design ♦

A fine example of Art Nouveau architecture; a London landmark. 1st floor restaurant with striking stained glass 'Michelin Man'. Attentive service of modern British cooking.

Tom Aikens

43 Elystan St ⊠ SW3 3NT – Ⓜ South Kensington – ℰ (020) 7584 20 03
– info@tomaikens.co.uk – Fax (020) 7584 20 01
– www.tomaikens.co.uk

closed last two weeks August, 2 weeks Christmas-New Year, Saturday and Sunday   **AJ2**
Rest £29/60 🕮

Spec. Ballottine of foie gras with apple jelly and foie gras mousse. Loin of lamb with fennel risotto, anchovy tart and almonds. Chocolate marquise with grapefruit and chocolate mousses.

♦ Innovative ♦ Fashionable ♦

Smart restaurant; minimalist style decor with chic tableware. Highly original menu of individual and inventive dishes; smooth service. Book one month in advance.

UNITED KINGDOM

UNITED KINGDOM

XXX ✿

Aubergine　　　　　　　　　　　　　🄰🄲 ⅙ VISA 🆗 🄰🄴 ①

11 Park Walk ⊠ SW10 0AJ – Ⓜ South Kensington – ℰ (020) 7352 34 49
– Fax (020) 7351 17 70　　　　　　　　　　　　　　　　　　**AI2**
closed 23 December -3 January, Sunday, Saturday lunch and Bank Holidays
Rest (booking essential) £34/60
Spec. Carpaccio of scallops, artichoke and truffle vinaigrette. Best end of lamb with garlic purée. Assiette of sorbets.
♦ Modern ♦ Formal ♦
Intimate, refined restaurant where the keen staff provide well drilled service. French influenced menu uses top quality ingredients with skill and flair. Extensive wine list.

XXX

One-O-One – at Sheraton Park Tower H.　　🄰🄲 VISA 🆗 🄰🄴 ①

William St ⊠ SW1X 7RN – Ⓜ Knightsbridge – ℰ (020) 7290 71 01
– Fax (020) 7235 61 96
– www.luxurycollection.com/parktowerlondon　　　　　　**AK1**
Rest £25 (lunch) and a la carte approx. £54
♦ Seafood ♦ Design ♦
Modern and very comfortable restaurant overlooking Knightsbridge decorated in cool blue tones. Predominantly seafood menu offers traditional and more adventurous dishes.

XXX

Drones　　　　　　　　　　　🄰🄲 ✦40 VISA 🆗 🄰🄴 ①

1 Pont St ⊠ SW1X 9EJ – Ⓜ Knightsbridge – ℰ (020) 7235 95 55
– sales@whitestarline.org.uk – Fax (020) 7235 95 66
– www.whitestarline.org.uk
closed 26 December, 1 January, Saturday lunch and Sunday dinner　**AK1**
Rest £18 (lunch) and a la carte £28/44
♦ Modern ♦ Formal ♦
Smart exterior with etched plate-glass window. U-shaped interior with moody film star photos on walls. French and classically inspired tone to dishes.

XXX

Fifth Floor – at Harvey Nichols　　　🄰🄲 VISA 🆗 🄰🄴 ①

Knightsbridge ⊠ SW1X 7RJ – Ⓜ Knightsbridge
– ℰ (020) 7235 52 50 – Fax (020) 7235 78 56
– www.harveynichols.com
closed Christmas, Sunday dinner and Monday　　　　　**AK1**
Rest £20/40 and a la carte £30/48 🍸
♦ Modern ♦ Fashionable ♦
On Harvey Nichols' top floor; elevated style sporting a pink-hued oval shaped interior with green frosted glass. Chic surroundings with food to match and smooth service.

XXX

Chutney Mary　　　　　　　　🄰🄲 VISA 🆗 🄰🄴 ①

535 King's Rd ⊠ SW10 0SZ – Ⓜ Fulham Broadway – ℰ (020) 7351 31 13
– chutneymary@realindianfood.com – Fax (020) 7351 76 94
– www.realindianfood　　　　　　　　　　　　　　**AI3**
Rest (dinner only and lunch Saturday and Sunday) £17 (lunch) and dinner a la carte £25/47
♦ Indian ♦ Exotic ♦
Soft lighting and sepia etchings hold sway at this forever popular restaurant. Extensive menu of specialities from all corners of India. Complementary wine list.

XX

Daphne's　　　　　　　　　🄰🄲 VISA 🆗 🄰🄴 ①

112 Draycott Ave ⊠ SW3 3AE – Ⓜ South Kensington – ℰ (020) 7589 42 57
– office@daphnes-restaurant.co.uk – Fax (020) 7225 27 66
– www.daphnes.co.uk
closed 25-26 December, 1 January and August Bank Holiday　　**AJ2**
Rest (booking essential) a la carte £27/43
♦ Italian ♦ Fashionable ♦
Positively buzzes in the evening, the Chelsea set gelling smoothly and seamlessly with the welcoming Tuscan interior ambience. A modern twist updates classic Italian dishes.

XX

£3

Rasoi Vineet Bhatia

10 Lincoln St ⊠ SW3 2TS – Ⓜ Sloane Square
– ℰ (020) 7225 18 81 – Fax (020) 7581 02 20
– www.vineetbhatia.com
closed Saturday lunch, Sunday and Bank Holidays
AK2
Rest £24 (lunch) and a la carte £46/61
Spec. Tandoori salmon, masala crab cake and spring onion khichdi. Grilled
spiced duck, tamarind chutney, crispy onion fritters. Chocolate and almond
samosa, Indian tea ice cream.

♦ Indian ♦ Neighbourhood ♦

Elegant mid-19C townhouse off Kings Road with L-shaped dining room and
attractive friezes. Seamlessly crafted mix of classic and contemporary Indian
flavour combinations.

XX

Racine

239 Brompton Rd ⊠ SW3 2EP – Ⓜ South Kensington – ℰ (020) 7584 44 77
– Fax (020) 7584 49 00
closed 25 December
AJ1
Rest £18 (lunch) and a la carte £25/38

♦ French ♦ Brasserie ♦

Dark leather banquettes, large mirrors and wood floors create the atmosphere
of a genuine Parisienne brasserie. Good value, well crafted, regional French
fare.

XX

Nozomi

15 Beauchamp Pl, ⊠ SW3 1NQ – Ⓜ Knightsbridge – ℰ (020) 7838 15 00
– Fax (020) 7838 10 01
closed 2 weeks January, 2 weeks August and Sunday
AJ1
Rest a la carte £27/42

♦ Japanese ♦ Minimalist ♦

DJ mixes lounge music at the front bar; up the stairs in the restaurant the feeling
is minimal with soft lighting. Innovative Japanese menus provide an interesting
choice.

XX

Bluebird

350 King's Rd ⊠ SW3 5UU – ℰ (020) 7559 10 00 – Fax (020) 7559 11 11
– www.conran.com
AI3
Rest a la carte £22/37

♦ Modern ♦ Design ♦

A foodstore, café and homeware shop also feature at this impressive skylit
restaurant. Much of the modern British food is cooked in wood-fired ovens. Lively
atmosphere.

XX

Poissonnerie de l'Avenue

82 Sloane Ave ⊠ SW3 3DZ – Ⓜ South Kensington – ℰ (020) 7589 24 57
– info@poissonnerie.co.uk – Fax (020) 7581 33 60
– www.poissonneriedel'avenue.co.uk
closed dinner 24 December, 25 December, Sunday and
Bank Holidays
AJ2
Rest £22 (lunch) and a la carte £25/36

♦ Seafood ♦ Formal ♦

Long-established and under the same ownership since 1965. Spacious and
traditional French restaurant offering an extensive seafood menu. An institution
favoured by locals.

XX

Le Cercle

1 Wilbraham Pl ⊠ SW1X 9AE – Ⓜ Sloane Square – ℰ (020) 7901 99 99
– info@lecercle.co.uk – Fax (020) 7901 91 11
closed Sunday-Monday
AK1-2
Rest £20 (lunch) and a la carte £12/48

♦ French ♦ Fashionable ♦

Discreetly signed basement restaurant down residential side street. High,
spacious room with chocolate banquettes. Tapas style French menus;
accomplished cooking.

UNITED KINGDOM

877

UNITED KINGDOM

XX **Le Colombier** 🛋 *VISA* **MO** **AE**
145 Dovehouse St ⊠ *SW3 6LB* – **M** *South Kensington* – ℰ *(020) 7351 11 55*
– Fax (020) 7351 51 24 **AJ2**
Rest £15 (lunch) and a la carte £27/34
♦ French ♦ Neighbourhood ♦
Proudly Gallic corner restaurant in an affluent residential area. Attractive enclosed terrace. Bright and cheerful surroundings and service of traditional French cooking.

XX **Caraffini** 🛋 *AC* *VISA* **MO** **AE**
61-63 Lower Sloane St ⊠ *SW1W 8DH* – **M** *Sloane Square* – ℰ *(020) 7259 02 35*
– info @ caraffini.co.uk – Fax (020) 7259 02 36 – www.caraffini.co.uk
closed 25 December, Easter, Sunday and Bank Holidays **AK2**
Rest a la carte £24/32
♦ Italian ♦ Friendly ♦
The omnipresent and ebullient owner oversees the friendly service in this attractive neighbourhood restaurant. Authentic and robust Italian cooking; informal atmosphere.

XX **The Collection** *AC* *VISA* **MO** **AE**
264 Brompton Rd ⊠ *SW3 2AS* – **M** *South Kensington* – ℰ *(020) 7225 12 12*
– office @ thecollection.co.uk – Fax (020) 7225 10 50 – www.the-collection.co.uk
closed 25-26 December, 1 January and Bank Holidays **AJ1**
Rest (dinner only) £40 and a la carte £29/41
♦ Modern ♦ Trendy ♦
Beyond the impressive catwalk entrance one will find a chic bar and a vast split level, lively restaurant. The eclectic and global modern menu is enjoyed by the young crowd.

î▯ **Admiral Codrington** *AC* *VISA* **MO** **AE**
17 Mossop St ⊠ *SW3 2LY* – **M** *South Kensington* – ℰ *(020) 7581 00 05*
– admiralcodrington @ longshotplc.com – Fax (020) 7589 24 52
– www.theadmiralcodrington.co.uk **AJ2**
Rest a la carte £20/35
♦ Modern ♦ Pub ♦
Aproned staff offer attentive, relaxed service in this busy gastropub. A retractable roof provides alfresco dining in the modern back room. Cosmopolitan menu of modern dishes.

î▯ **Chelsea Ram** *VISA* **MO**
32 Burnaby St ⊠ *SW10 0PL* – **M** *Fulham Broadway* – ℰ *(020) 7351 40 08*
– pint @ chelsearam.com – Fax (020) 7349 08 85 – www.chelsearam.com
Rest a la carte £18/21 **AI3**
♦ Modern ♦ Pub ♦
Wooden floors, modern artwork and books galore feature in this forever popular pub. Concise menu of modern British cooking with daily changing specials. Friendly atmosphere.

î▯ **Swag and Tails** *VISA* **MO** **AE**
10-11 Fairholt St ⊠ *SW7 1EG* – **M** *Knightsbridge* – ℰ *(020) 7584 69 26*
– theswag @ swagandtails.com – Fax (020) 7581 99 35 – www.swagandtails.com
closed Saturday, Sunday and Bank Holidays **AJ1**
Rest a la carte £24/32
♦ Modern ♦ Pub ♦
Attractive Victorian pub close to Harrods and the fashionable Knightsbridge shops. Polite and approachable service of a blackboard menu of light snacks and seasonal dishes.

î▯ **Builders Arms** *AC* *VISA* **MO**
13 Britten St ⊠ *SW3 3TY* – **M** *South Kensington* – ℰ *(020) 7349 90 40*
closed 25-26 December and 1 January **AJ2**
Rest a la carte £17/26
♦ Modern ♦ Pub ♦
Extremely busy modern 'gastropub' favoured by the locals. Eclectic menu of contemporary dishes with blackboard specials. Polite service from a young and eager team.

The Pig's Ear   ⅍ VISA ◍ AE

35 Old Church St ⊠ SW3 5BS – ℰ (020) 7352 29 08 – hello@thepigsear.co.uk
– Fax (020) 7352 93 21 – www.thepigsear.co.uk   **AJ3**
Rest a la carte £16/22
♦ Modern ♦ Pub ♦

Corner pub that gets very busy, particularly for downstairs bar dining. Upstairs,
more sedate wood panelled dining room. Both menus are rustic, robust and
seasonal in nature.

The Phoenix   ⽊ AC ⅍ VISA ◍

23 Smith St ⊠ SW3 4EE – ◍ Sloane Square – ℰ (020) 7730 91 82
– mail@geronimo-phoenix.fsnet.co.uk – www.geronimo-inns.co.uk
closed 25-26 December   **AK2**
Rest a la carte £15/28
♦ Modern ♦ Pub ♦

Tile-fronted pub with al fresco seating area, very popular in summer. Shabby chic
décor that's been modernised but feels retro. Modern British repertoire on
extensive menus.

Cross Keys   AC VISA ◍ AE

1 Lawrence St ⊠ SW3 5NB – ◍ South Kensington – ℰ (020) 7349 91 11
– cross-keys@fsmail.net – Fax (020) 7349 93 33 – www.thexkeys.co.uk
closed 23-28 December, and Bank Holidays   **AJ3**
Rest £25/28
♦ Modern ♦ Pub ♦

Hidden away near the Embankment, this 18C pub has period furniture and
impressive carved stone fireplaces. Interesting, modern menus include
blackboard of daily specials.

Lots Road Pub and Dining Room   AC VISA ◍

114 Lots Rd ⊠ SW10 0RJ – ◍ Gloucester Road – ℰ (020) 7352 66 45
– lotsroad@thespiritgroup.com – Fax (020) 7376 49 75
– www.thespiritgroup.com   **AI3**
Rest a la carte £18/26
♦ Modern ♦ Pub ♦

Traditional corner pub with an open-plan kitchen, flowers at each table and large
modern pictures on the walls. Contemporary menus change daily.

South Kensington   *Plan X*

The Bentley Kempinski   ⅃☞ ⽊ AC ⅍ ▥ ㏜80 VISA ◍ AE ①

27-33 Harrington Gdns ⊠ SW7 4JX – ◍ Gloucester Road – ℰ (020) 7244 55 55
– info@thebentley-hotel.com – Fax (020) 7244 55 66
– www.thebentley-hotel.com   **AI2**
52 rm – ♥£340 ♥♥£616, ⌸ £19 – 12 suites
Rest see also **1880** below
Rest *Peridot* (lunch only) £26
♦ Grand Luxury ♦ Classic ♦

A number of 19C houses have been joined to create this opulent, lavish, hidden
gem, decorated with marble, mosaics and ornate gold leaf. Bedrooms with
gorgeous silk fabrics. Airy, intimate Peridot offers brasserie menus.

Millennium Gloucester   ⅃☞ & ⽊ ⅍ ▥ ㏜500 ℗ VISA ◍ AE ①

4-18 Harrington Gdns ⊠ SW7 4LH – ◍ Gloucester Road – ℰ (020) 7373 60 30
– sales.gloucester@mill-cop.com – Fax (020) 7373 04 09
– www.millenniumhotels.com   **AI2**
604 rm – ♥£252 ♥♥£252, ⌸ £18 – 6 suites
Rest *Bugis Street* £16
Rest *South West 7* (dinner only) (buffet only) £21
♦ Luxury ♦ Classic ♦

A large international group hotel. Busy marbled lobby and vast conference
facilities. Smart and well-equipped bedrooms are generously sized, especially
the 'Club' rooms. Dinner or buffet at South West 7. Informal, compact Bugis
Street.

UNITED KINGDOM

The Pelham
15 Cromwell Pl ⊠ SW7 2LA – **M** South Kensington – ℰ (020) 7589 82 88
– pelham@firmdale.com – Fax (020) 7584 84 44
– www.pelhamhotel.co.uk **AJ1**
50 rm – †£176/212 ††£294, ⊇ £18 – 2 suites
Rest Kemps £18 (lunch) and a la carte £28/35
♦ Luxury ♦ Stylish ♦
Attractive Victorian town house with a discreet and comfortable feel. Wood panelled drawing room and individually decorated bedrooms with marble bathrooms. Detailed service. Warm basement dining room.

Blakes
33 Roland Gdns ⊠ SW7 3PF – **M** Gloucester Road – ℰ (020) 7370 67 01
– blakes@blakeshotels.com – Fax (020) 7373 04 42
– www.blakeshotels.com **AI2**
45 rm – †£153/200 ††£305/323, ⊇ £25 – 3 suites
Rest (closed 25-26 December and 1 January) a la carte £63/124
♦ Luxury ♦ Design ♦
Behind the Victorian façade lies one of London's first 'boutique' hotels. Dramatic, bold and eclectic décor, with oriental influences and antiques from around the globe. Fashionable restaurant with bamboo and black walls.

Harrington Hall
5-25 Harrington Gdns ⊠ SW7 4JW – **M** Gloucester Road – ℰ (020) 7396 96 96
– sales@harringtonhall.co.uk – Fax (020) 7396 90 90
– www.harringtonhall.co.uk **AI2**
200 rm – †£195 ††£195, ⊇ £16
Rest Wetherby's (closed lunch Saturday and Sunday) £19 and a la carte £22/36
♦ Business ♦ Functional ♦
A series of adjoined terraced houses, with an attractive period façade that belies the size. Tastefully furnished bedrooms, with an extensive array of facilities. Classically decorated dining room.

Millennium Bailey's
140 Gloucester Rd ⊠ SW7 4QH – **M** Gloucester Road – ℰ (020) 7373 60 00
– baileys@mill-cop.com – Fax (020) 7370 37 60
– www.millennium-hotels.com **AI1**
211 rm – †£188/264 ††£264, ⊇ £17
Rest Olives (dinner only) £20/25 and a la carte £26/35
♦ Business ♦ Classic ♦
Elegant lobby, restored to its origins dating from 1876, with elaborate plasterwork and a striking grand staircase. Victorian feel continues through into the bedrooms. Modern, pastel shaded restaurant.

Number Sixteen
16 Sumner Pl ⊠ SW7 3EG – **M** South Kensington – ℰ (020) 7589 52 32
– sixteen@firmdale.com – Fax (020) 7584 86 15
– www.numbersixteenhotel.co.uk **AJ2**
42 rm – †£112/200 ††£294, ⊇ £13
Rest (room service only)
♦ Townhouse ♦ Stylish ♦
Enticingly refurbished 19C town houses in smart area. Discreet entrance, comfy sitting room and charming breakfast terrace. Bedrooms in English country house style.

The Cranley
10 Bina Gdns ⊠ SW5 0LA – **M** Gloucester Road – ℰ (020) 7373 01 23 – info@thecranley.com – Fax (020) 7373 94 97 – www.thecranley.com **AI2**
38 rm – †£141 ††£164, ⊇ £10 – 1 suite
Rest (room service only)
♦ Townhouse ♦ Stylish ♦
Delightful Regency town house that artfully combines charm and period details with modern comforts and technology. Individually styled bedrooms; some with four-posters.

The Gore
🏨🏨   AC rest ↳rm 🕻 ♨70 VISA CO AE ①

190 Queen's Gate ⊠ SW7 5EX – Ⓜ *Gloucester Road* – ℰ *(020) 7584 66 01*
– *reservations@gorehotel.co.uk* – Fax *(020) 7589 81 27*
– *www.gorehotel.com*
49 rm – †£176/224 ††£329, ⊡ £17   **AI1**
Rest *Bistrot 190* (booking essential) £20/30 and a la carte £24/31
♦ Townhouse ♦ Personalised ♦
Opened its doors in 1892; has retained its individual charm. Richly decorated with antiques, rugs and over 4,000 pictures that cover every inch of wall. Bistrot 190 boasts French-inspired décor.

Aster House without rest
🏠   🚃 AC ↳ ℅ CO 🕻 VISA CO

3 Sumner Pl ⊠ SW7 3EE – Ⓜ *South Kensington* – ℰ *(020) 7581 58 88*
– *asterhouse@btinternet.com* – Fax *(020) 7584 49 25*
– *www.asterhouse.com*   **AJ2**
13 rm – †£106/153 ††£153/170
♦ Townhouse ♦ Cosy ♦
End of terrace Victorian house with a pretty little rear garden and first floor conservatory. Ground floor rooms available. A wholly non-smoking establishment.

Five Sumner Place without rest
🏠   ↳ ℅ VISA CO AE ①

5 Sumner Pl ⊠ SW7 3EE – Ⓜ *South Kensington* – ℰ *(020) 7584 75 86*
– *reservations@sumnerplace.com* – Fax *(020) 7823 99 62*
– *www.sumnerplace.com*   **AJ2**
13 rm – †£85 ††£150
♦ Townhouse ♦ Cosy ♦
Part of a striking white terrace built in 1848 in this fashionable part of town. Breakfast served in bright conservatory. Good sized bedrooms.

Premier Travel Inn Metro
🏠   ♿ ↳ ℅ VISA CO AE ①

11 Knaresborough Place ⊠ SW5 0TJ – Ⓜ *Earls Court*
– ℰ *(0870) 238 33 04* – Fax *(020) 7370 92 92*
– *www.travelinn.co.uk*   **AH1-2**
184 rm – †£75 ††£80
Rest (dinner only)
♦ Chain hotel ♦ Functional ♦
Lodge hotel providing clean, comfortable, well-priced accommodation for visitors to the museums who find themselves on a budget. Well situated for local restaurants.

1880 – at The Bentley Kempinski H.
ⅩⅩⅩⅩ   AC ↳ VISA CO AE ①

27-33 Harrington Gdns ⊠ SW7 4JX – Ⓜ *Gloucester Road*
– ℰ *(020) 7244 55 55* – *info@thebentley-hotel.com*
– Fax *(020) 7244 55 66*
– *www.thebentley-hotel.com*
closed Sunday and Monday   **AI2**
Rest (dinner only) £45
♦ Innovative ♦ Formal ♦
Luxurious, opulently decorated room in Bentley basement: silk panels, gold leaf, Italian marble, chandeliers. Choose à la carte or extensive "grazing" menu up to 10 courses.

Bombay Brasserie
ⅩⅩⅩ   AC VISA CO AE ①

Courtfield Rd ⊠ SW7 4QH – Ⓜ *Gloucester Road*
– ℰ *(020) 7370 40 40* – *bombay1brasserie@aol.com*
– Fax *(020) 7835 16 69*
– *www.bombaybrasserielondon.com*
closed 25-26 December   **AI1**
Rest (buffet lunch) £19 and dinner a la carte £28/36
♦ Indian ♦ Exotic ♦
Something of a London institution: an ever busy Indian restaurant with Raj-style décor. Ask to sit in the brighter plant-filled conservatory. Popular lunchtime buffet.

Lundum's 🎐 ⁂ VISA ⓒ AE ①
119 Old Brompton Rd ⊠ *SW7 3RN* – Ⓜ *Gloucester Road*
– ℰ *(020) 7373 77 74* – *Fax (020) 7373 44 72*
– *www.lundums.com*
closed Sunday dinner   **AI2**
Rest £19/25 and a la carte £27/49
♦ Modern Danish ♦ Family ♦
A family run Danish restaurant offering an authentic, traditional lunch with a
more expansive dinner menu. Comfortable room, with large windows.
Charming service.

L'Etranger ⁂ ✧12 VISA ⓒ AE
36 Gloucester Rd ⊠ *SW7 4QT* – Ⓜ *Gloucester Road* – ℰ *(020) 7584 11 18*
– *sasha@etranger.co.uk* – *Fax (020) 7584 88 86* – *www.etranger.co.uk*
closed lunch Saturday and Sunday   **AI1**
Rest (booking essential) £17 (lunch) and a la carte £31/54 ⸙
♦ French ♦ Neighbourhood ♦
Corner restaurant with mosaic entrance floor and bay window. Modern décor.
Tables extend into adjoining wine shop. French based cooking with Asian
influences.

Earl's Court *Plan X*

K + K George 🚗 ⁂ ⅋ 📧 📞 🏋30 ℗ VISA ⓒ AE ①
1-15 Templeton Pl ⊠ *SW5 9NB* – Ⓜ *Earl's Court* – ℰ *(020) 7598 87 00*
– *hotelgeorge@kkhotels.co.uk* – *Fax (020) 7370 22 85*
– *www.kkhotels.com*   **AH2**
154 rm – ☗£182 ☗☗£217
Rest (in bar) a la carte £18/29
♦ Business ♦ Modern ♦
Five converted 19C houses overlooking large rear garden. Scandinavian style to
rooms with low beds, white walls and light wood furniture. Breakfast room has
the garden view. Informal dining in the bar.

Twenty Nevern Square without rest ⅋ ⁑ 📧 ℗ VISA ⓒ AE
Nevern Sq ⊠ *SW5 9PD* – Ⓜ *Earl's Court* – ℰ *(020) 7565 95 55*
– *hotel@twentynevernsquare.co.uk* – *Fax (020) 7565 94 44*
– *www.twentynevernsquare.co.uk*   **AH2**
19 rm – ☗£79/99 ☗☗£95/109, � £9
♦ Townhouse ♦ Functional ♦
In an attractive Victorian garden square, an individually designed, privately
owned town house. Original pieces of furniture and some rooms with their own
terrace.

Langan's Coq d'Or ⁂ VISA ⓒ AE ①
254-260 Old Brompton Rd ⊠ *SW5 9HR* – Ⓜ *Earl's Court* – ℰ *(020) 7259 25 99*
– *admin@langansrestaurant.co.uk* – *Fax (020) 7370 77 35*
– *www.langansrestaurants.co.uk*
closed 25-26 December and 1 January   **AH2**
Rest £21
♦ Traditional ♦ Brasserie ♦
Classic, buzzy brasserie and excellent-value menu to match. Walls adorned with
pictures of celebrities: look out for more from the enclosed pavement terrace.
Smooth service.

Hollywood Arms ⁂ VISA ⓒ AE
45 Hollywood Rd ⊠ *SW10 9HX* – Ⓜ *Earl's Court* – ℰ *(020) 7349 78 40*
– *Fax (020) 7349 78 41*
closed 25 December   **AI2**
Rest a la carte £17/24
♦ Modern ♦ Pub ♦
Period pub in smart residential area with stylish interior furnished in rich
autumnal colours. Efficient service. Concise menu with Mediterranean
influences and flavours.

KENSINGTON & NORTH KENSINGTON

Kensington

Plan XI

Royal Garden ≤ 🏋 🏊 ♨ 🅰 ♿rm 🍴 🖭 🛗 550 🅿 VISA 🕦 AE ⊙

2-24 Kensington High St ⊠ W8 4PT – Ⓜ High Street Kensington
– ℰ (020) 7937 80 00 – sales@royalgarden.co.uk – Fax (020) 7361 19 91
– www.royalgardenhotel.co.uk
376 rm – ♦£317/388 ♦♦£388, � £18 – 20 suites   AM3
Rest see also **The Tenth** below
Rest *Park Terrace* a la carte £24/33
♦ Luxury ♦ Classic ♦
A tall, modern hotel with many of its rooms enjoying enviable views over the
adjacent Kensington Gardens. All the modern amenities and services, with
well-drilled staff. Bright, spacious, large-windowed restaurant.

The Milestone 🏋 🏊 🅰 ♿ 🖭 🕿 VISA 🕦 AE ⊙

1-2 Kensington Court ⊠ W8 5DL – Ⓜ High Street Kensington
– ℰ (020) 7917 10 00 – bookms@rchmail.com – Fax (020) 7917 10 10
– www.milestonehotel.com   AM3
52 rm – ♦£352/376 ♦♦£383/405, � £22 – 5 suites
Rest (booking essential to non-residents) £19 and a la carte
£28/50
♦ Luxury ♦ Stylish ♦
Elegant 'boutique' hotel with decorative Victorian façade and English feel.
Charming oak panelled lounge and snug bar. Meticulously decorated bedrooms
with period detail. Panelled dining room with charming little oratory for privacy
seekers.

Baglioni 🏛 🏋 🏊 🅰 ♿rm 🍴 🖭 🛗80 VISA 🕦 AE ⊙

60 Hyde Park Gate ⊠ SW7 5BB – Ⓜ High Street Kensington
– ℰ (020) 7368 57 00 – info@baglionihotellondon.com
– Fax (020) 7368 57 01
– www.baglionihotellondon.com   AM3
53 rm – ♦£352 ♦♦£423, � £25 – 15 suites
Rest *Brunello* £24 (lunch) and a la carte £47/72
♦ Luxury ♦ Stylish ♦
Opposite Kensington Palace: ornate interior, trendy basement bar. Impressively
high levels of service. Small gym/sauna. Superb rooms in cool shades boast
striking facilities. Restaurant specialises in rustic Italian cooking.

Hilton London Kensington 🏋 🏊 ♿ 🅰 ♿rm 🍴 🖭 🛗250

179-199 Holland Park Ave ⊠ W11 4UL   🅿 VISA 🕦 AE ⊙
– Ⓜ Holland Park – ℰ (020) 7603 33 55
– rm.kensington@hilton.com – Fax (020) 7602 93 97
– www.hilton.co.uk/kensington   AL2
602 rm – ♦£75/175 ♦♦£198, � £20
Rest £25 and a la carte £22/62
♦ Chain hotel ♦ Business ♦ Functional ♦
The executive bedrooms and the nearby exhibition centres make this a popular
business hotel. Equally useful spot for tourists; it has all the necessary amenities.
Warm, pastel coloured Imbue restaurant.

Hilton London Olympia 🏋 ♿ 🅰 ♿rm 🖭 🛗250

380 Kensington High St ⊠ W14 8NL   🅿 VISA 🕦 AE ⊙
– Ⓜ Kensington Olympia – ℰ (020) 7603 33 33 – Fax (020) 7603 48 46
– www.hilton.co.uk/olympia   AL3
395 rm – ♦£104/194 ♦♦£116/216, � £18 – 10 suites
Rest (bar lunch Saturday) £15/20 and a la carte
£18/32
♦ Chain hotel ♦ Business ♦ Functional ♦
Busy, corporate hotel, benefiting from being within walking distance of Olympia.
Bedrooms of a good size, with light wood furniture and fully tiled bathrooms.
Bright dining room with large windows.

UNITED KINGDOM

XXX **The Tenth** – at Royal Garden H.   ≤ Kensington Palace and Gardens,
2-24 Kensington High St   London skyline, 𝔸�ℂ 𝗣 𝘝𝘐𝘚𝘈 ⓩⓞ ᴬᴱ ⓞ
⊠ W8 4PT – Ⓜ High Street Kensington – ℰ (020) 7361 19 10
– tenthrestaurant@royalgardenhotel.co.uk – Fax (020) 7361 19 21
– www.royalgardenhotel.co.uk
closed Saturday lunch, Sunday and Bank Holidays   AM3
Rest £23 (lunch) and a la carte £34/47
♦ Modern ♦ Formal ♦
Named after the hotel's top floor where this stylish yet relaxed room is situated.
Commanding views of Kensington Palace and the Park. Well-structured service;
modern menu.

XXX **Belvedere**   🌂 🕭 𝔸ℂ ⇄70 𝘝𝘐𝘚𝘈 ⓩⓞ ᴬᴱ ⓞ
Holland House, off Abbotsbury Rd ⊠ W8 6LU – Ⓜ Holland Park – ℰ (020) 7602
12 38 – sales@whitestarline.org.uk – Fax (020) 7610 43 82
– www.whitestarline.org.uk
closed 26 December, 1 January and Sunday dinner   AL3
Rest £18/23 (lunch) and a la carte £26/36
♦ Modern ♦ Romantic ♦
Former 19C orangery in a delightful position in the middle of the Park. On two
floors with a bar and balcony terrace. Huge vases of flowers. Modern take on
classic dishes.

XX **Zaika**   𝔸ℂ 𝘝𝘐𝘚𝘈 ⓩⓞ ᴬᴱ ⓞ
1 Kensington High St ⊠ W8 5NP – Ⓜ High Street Kensington – ℰ (020)
7795 65 33 – info@zaika-restaurant.co.uk – Fax (020) 7937 88 54
– www.zaika-restaurant.co.uk
closed 25-26 December and Saturday lunch   AM3
Rest £18 (lunch) and a la carte £27/42
♦ Indian ♦ Exotic ♦
A converted bank, sympathetically restored, with original features and Indian
artefacts. Well organised service of modern Indian dishes.

XX **Clarke's**   𝔸ℂ ↵ 𝘝𝘐𝘚𝘈 ⓩⓞ ᴬᴱ ⓞ
124 Kensington Church St ⊠ W8 4BH – Ⓜ Notting Hill Gate
– ℰ (020) 7221 92 25 – restaurant@sallyclarke.com – Fax (020) 7229 45 64
– www.sallyclarke.com
closed 10 days Christmas-New Year, Monday dinner, Sunday and Bank
Holidays   AM2
Rest (set menu only at dinner) £44 (dinner) and lunch a la carte £27/32
♦ Modern ♦ Neighbourhood ♦
Open-plan kitchen, personally overseen by the owner, provides modern British
cooking. No choice, set menu at dinner. Comfortable and bright, with a
neighbourhood feel.

XX **Launceston Place**   𝔸ℂ 𝘝𝘐𝘚𝘈 ⓩⓞ ᴬᴱ ⓞ
1a Launceston Pl ⊠ W8 5RL – Ⓜ Gloucester Road – ℰ (020) 7937 69 12
– Fax (020) 7938 24 12   AM3
closed 24-28 December, 1 January, Saturday lunch and August Bank Holiday
Rest £19 (lunch) and a la carte £31/38
♦ English ♦ Neighbourhood ♦
Divided into a number of rooms, this corner restaurant is lent a bright feel
by its large windows and gilded mirrors. Chatty service and contemporary
cooking.

X **Kensington Place**   𝔸ℂ 𝘝𝘐𝘚𝘈 ⓩⓞ ᴬᴱ ⓞ
201 Kensington Church St ⊠ W8 7LX – Ⓜ Notting Hill Gate – ℰ (020) 7727 31 84
– kpr@egami.co.uk – Fax (020) 7229 20 25 – www.egami.co.uk
closed 24-26 December   AM2
Rest (booking essential) £19/25 and a la carte £29/46
♦ Modern ♦ Fashionable ♦
A cosmopolitan crowd still head for this establishment that set the trend for
large, bustling and informal restaurants. Professionally run with skilled modern
cooking.

Malabar VISA ⓜⒸ Æ

27 Uxbridge St ⊠ *W8 7TQ –* Ⓜ *Notting Hill Gate*
– ✆ *(020) 7727 88 00 – feedback@malabar-restaurant.co.uk*
– www.malabar-restaurant.co.uk
closed 1 week Christmas and last week August
Rest (booking essential) (buffet lunch Sunday) £21 and a la carte
£17/31

♦ Indian ♦ Neighbourhood ♦

Indian restaurant in a residential street. Three rooms with individual personalities and informal service. Extensive range of good value dishes, particularly vegetarian.

AM2

UNITED KINGDOM

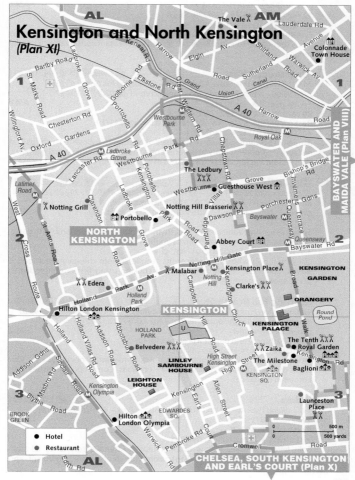

UNITED KINGDOM

The Portobello without rest 🖼 📞 **VISA** 💳 AE

22 Stanley Gdns ⊠ W11 2NG – Ⓜ Notting Hill Gate – ℰ (020) 7727 27 77
– info@portobello-hotel.co.uk – Fax (020) 7792 96 41
– www.portobello-hotel.co.uk
closed 24-29 December **AL2**
24 rm – ♦£130/160 ♦♦£170/285, ⊇ £13
♦ Townhouse ♦ Personalised ♦
An attractive Victorian town house in an elegant terrace. Original and theatrical décor. Circular beds, half-testers, Victorian baths: no two bedrooms are the same.

Abbey Court without rest 🔌 🍽 🖼 📞 **VISA** 💳 AE ①

20 Pembridge Gdns ⊠ W2 4DU – Ⓜ Notting Hill Gate – ℰ (020) 7221 75 18
– info@abbeycourthotel.co.uk – Fax (020) 7792 08 58
– www.abbeycourthotel.co.uk **AM2**
22 rm – ♦£99/125 ♦♦£130/279, ⊇ £8
♦ Townhouse ♦ Classic ♦
Five-storey Victorian town house with individually decorated bedrooms, with many thoughtful touches. Breakfast served in a pleasant conservatory. Friendly service.

🏠

Guesthouse West 🔌 🔌rm 🍽 🖼 📞 **VISA** 💳 AE

163-165 Westbourne Grove ⊠ W11 2RS – Ⓜ Notting Hill Gate – ℰ (020)
7792 98 00 – reception@guesthousewest.com – Fax (020) 7792 97 97
– www.guesthousewest.com **AM2**
20 rm – ♦£170/200 ♦♦£170/200, ⊇ £10
Rest *(closed lunch Monday-Wednesday)* a la carte £11/19
♦ Townhouse ♦ Stylish ♦
Attractive Edwardian house in the heart of Notting Hill, close to its shops and restaurants. Contemporary bedrooms boast the latest in audio visual gadgetry. Chic Parlour Bar for all-day light dishes in a tapas style.

XXX
🏵

The Ledbury 🍴 🔌 🔌 **VISA** 💳 AE ①

127 Ledbury Rd ⊠ W11 2AQ – Ⓜ Notting Hill Gate – ℰ (020) 7792 90 90 – info@
theledbury.com – Fax (020) 7792 91 91 – www.theledbury.com
closed 25-26 December, 1 January and August Bank Holiday **AM2**
Rest £25/45
Spec. Lasagne of rabbit and girolles, thyme velouté. Assiette of lamb with garlic, borlotti beans and rosemary. Vanilla yoghurt parfait.
♦ Modern ♦ Neighbourhood ♦
Converted pub whose cool décor fits seamlessly into the neighbourhood it serves. Confident, highly accomplished cooking using first-rate ingredients; portions are generous.

XX

Notting Hill Brasserie 🔌 🔄44 **VISA** 💳 AE

92 Kensington Park Rd ⊠ W11 2PN – Ⓜ Notting Hill Gate – ℰ (020) 7229 44 81
– enquiries@nottinghillbrasserie.com – Fax (020) 7221 12 46
closed Sunday dinner **AL2**
Rest £20 (lunch) and dinner a la carte £30/40
♦ Modern ♦ Neighbourhood ♦
Modern, comfortable restaurant with quiet, formal atmosphere set over four small rooms. Authentic African artwork on walls. Contemporary dishes with European influence.

XX

Edera 🔌 **VISA** 💳 AE

148 Holland Park Ave ⊠ W11 4UE – Ⓜ Holland Park – ℰ (020) 7221 60 90
– Fax (020) 7313 97 00 **AL2**
Rest a la carte £23/35
♦ Italian ♦ Neighbourhood ♦
Split level restaurant with 4 outdoor tables. Attentive service by all staff. Interesting menus of modern Italian cooking with some unusual ingredients and combinations.

✗ **Notting Grill** 🛧 _VISA_ **⦿◉** ㏂ ⓪

123A Clarendon Rd ⊠ W11 4JG – Ⓜ Holland Park
– ✆ (020) 7229 15 00 – nottinggrill@aol.com
– Fax (020) 7229 88 89
closed 24 December-3 January, 27-28 August and Monday lunch   **AL2**
Rest a la carte £23/39
♦ Beef specialities ♦ Neighbourhood ♦
Converted pub that retains a rustic feel, with bare brick walls and wooden tables.
Specialises in well sourced, quality meats.

LONDON AIRPORTS

Heathrow Airport West: 17 m. by A 4, M 4

🏨 **London Heathrow Marriott** ℔ 🕉 🖾 ₠ ㎴ ⅍rm ⅏ ▦ 🛁540
Bath Rd, Hayes ⊠ UB3 5AN 🅿 _VISA_ **⦿◉** ㏂ ⓪
– ✆ (020) 8990 11 00 – reservations.heathrow@mariotthotels.co.uk
– Fax (020) 8990 11 10
– www.marriott.co.uk/lhrhr
391 rm – ♦£163 ♦♦£163, ⌚ £14,95 – 2 suites
Rest _Tuscany_ (dinner only) a la carte £32/39
Rest _Allie's Grille_ a la carte £19/30
♦ Chain hotel ♦ Business ♦ Functional ♦
Built at the end of 20C, this modern, comfortable hotel is centred around a large
atrium, with comprehensive business facilities: there is an exclusive Executive
floor. Tuscany is bright and convivial. Grill favourites at Allie's.

🏨 **Crowne Plaza London Heathrow** ℔ 🕉 🖾 🎦 ㎴ ⅍rm ⅏
Stockley Rd, West Drayton ⊠ UB7 9NA 🛁200 🅿 _VISA_ **⦿◉** ㏂ ⓪
– ✆ (0870) 400 91 40 – reservations.cplhr@ichotelsgroup.com
– Fax (01895) 44 51 22
– www.crowneplaza.com/lon-heathrow
457 rm – ♦£229 ♦♦£229, ⌚ £18 – 1 suite
Rest see _Simply Nico Heathrow_ below
Rest _Concha Grill_ £19 (lunch) and dinner a la carte approx. £23
♦ Chain hotel ♦ Business ♦ Functional ♦
Extensive leisure, aromatherapy and beauty salons make this large hotel a
popular stop-over for travellers. Club bedrooms are particularly well-equipped.
Bright, breezy Concha Grill with juice bar.

🏨 **Radisson Edwardian** ℔ 🕉 ㎴ ⅍rm ▦ 🛁550 🅿 _VISA_ **⦿◉** ㏂ ⓪
140 Bath Rd, Hayes ⊠ UB3 5AW – ✆ (020) 8759 63 11
– resreh@radisson.com – Fax (020) 8759 45 59
– www.radissonedwardian.com
442 rm – ♦£186 ♦♦£237, ⌚ £15 – 17 suites
Rest _Henleys_ a la carte £22/37
Rest _Brasserie_ £18 (lunch) and a la carte £19/28
♦ Chain hotel ♦ Business ♦ Functional ♦
Capacious group hotel with a huge atrium over the leisure facilities. Plenty of
comfortable lounges, well-appointed bedrooms and attentive service. Henleys
boasts oil paintings and cocktail bar.

🏨 **Sheraton Skyline** ℔ 🖾 ₠ ⅍ ⅏ ▦ 🛁500 🅿 _VISA_ **⦿◉** ㏂ ⓪
Bath Rd, Hayes ⊠ UB3 5BP – ✆ (020) 8759 25 35
– res268skyline@sheraton.com – Fax (020) 8750 91 50
– www.sheraton.com/skyline
348 rm – ♦£209 ♦♦£209, ⌚ £17 – 2 suites
Rest _Sage_ a la carte £15/25
♦ Chain hotel ♦ Business ♦ Functional ♦
Well known for its unique indoor swimming pool surrounded by a tropical
garden which is overlooked by many of the bedrooms. Business centre available.
Classically decorated dining room.

UNITED KINGDOM

Hilton London Heathrow Airport ╚╗ 🕸 ▨ ⅙ 🅰🄲 ↔rm 🖾250
Terminal 4 ⊠ TW6 3AF – ℰ (020) 8759 77 55 🅿 VISA ⓜⓞ 🄰🄴 ①
– gm-heathrow@hilton.com – Fax (020) 8759 75 79
– www.hilton.com
390 rm – ♥£209 ♥♥£209/256, ⊑ £20 – 5 suites
Rest Brasserie (closed lunch Saturday and Sunday) (buffet lunch) £27/33
and dinner a la carte £25/51
Rest Zen Oriental £29 and a la carte £20/56
♦ Chain hotel ♦ Business ♦ Functional ♦
Group hotel with a striking modern exterior and linked to Terminal 4
by a covered walkway. Good sized bedrooms, with contemporary styled
suites. Spacious Brasserie in vast atrium. Zen Oriental offers formal Chinese
experience.

Holiday Inn Heathrow Ariel 🄰🄲 rest ↔rm 🖾 🖾55
118 Bath Rd, Hayes ⊠ UB3 5AJ – ℰ (0870) 4 00 🅿 VISA ⓜⓞ 🄰🄴 ①
90 40 – reservations-heathrow@ichotelsgroup.com
– Fax (020) 8564 92 65 – www.holiday-inn.com/hiheathrow
186 rm – ♥£59/184 ♥♥£59/184, ⊑ £15
Rest £20
♦ Chain hotel ♦ Business ♦ Functional ♦
Usefully located hotel in a cylindrical shape. Modern bedrooms with warm
colours. Third floor executive rooms particularly impressive. Conference rooms
available. Subtly-lit, relaxing restaurant.

Premier Travel Inn Metro ⅙ 🄰🄲 ↔rm 🖾30 🅿 VISA ⓜⓞ 🄰🄴 ①
15 Bath Rd ⊠ TW6 2AB – ℰ (0870) 6 07 50 75 – Fax (0870) 2 41 90 00
– www.travelinn.co.uk
590 rm – ♥£53 ♥♥£75
Rest
♦ Chain hotel ♦ Business ♦ Functional ♦
Well-priced Travel Inn with modern, wood-panelled exterior and huge atrium.
Well-equipped meeting rooms. Bedrooms are of good quality with triple glazing.
Bright, airy, informal grill restaurant.

XX **Simply Nico Heathrow** – at Crowne Plaza Heathrow H. 🄰🄲
Stockley Rd, West Drayton ⊠ UB7 9NA 🅿 VISA ⓜⓞ 🄰🄴 ①
– ℰ (01895) 43 75 64 – heathrow.simplynico@corushotels.com
– Fax (01895) 43 75 65 – www.simplyrestaurants.com
closed Sunday
Rest (dinner only) £20 and a la carte £29/44
♦ French ♦ Brasserie ♦
Located within the hotel but with its own personality. Mixes modern with
more classically French dishes. Professional service in comfortable
surroundings.

Gatwick Airport South: 28 m. by A 23 and M 23

Hilton London Gatwick Airport ╚╗ ⅙ 🄰🄲 ↔rm 🖾500
South Terminal ⊠ RH6 0LL – ℰ (01293) 🅿 VISA ⓜⓞ 🄰🄴 ①
51 80 80 – londongatwick@hilton.com – Fax (01293) 52 89 80
– www.hilton.com
791 rm – ♥£118/275 ♥♥£118/275, ⊑ £18
Rest £26 (dinner) and a la carte £23/32
♦ Chain hotel ♦ Business ♦ Functional ♦
Large, well-established hotel, popular with business travellers. Two ground floor
bars, lounge and leisure facilities. Older rooms co-ordinated, newer in minimalist
style. Restaurant enlivened by floral profusions.

Renaissance London Gatwick   *Lₒ 𝔖 ◰ & 瓯 ⋕rm 𝗦̂ 180*

Povey Cross Rd ⊠ RH6 0BE   **P VISA ◉ AE ①**
– ℰ (01293) 82 01 69
– Fax (01293) 82 02 59
252 rm – ♦£119/176 ♦♦£119/176, ⊆ £16 – 2 suites
Rest £20 (dinner) and a la carte £38/54
♦ Chain hotel ♦ Business ♦ Functional ♦
Large red-brick hotel. Good recreational facilities including indoor pool, solarium. Bedrooms are spacious and decorated in smart, chintzy style. Small brasserie area open all day serving popular meals.

Premier Travel Inn Metro   *& 瓯 rest ⋕rm P VISA ◉ AE ①*

Longbridge Way, Gatwick Airport (North Terminal) ⊠ RH6 0NX
– ℰ (0870) 2 38 33 05 – Fax (01293) 56 82 78
– www.travelinn.com
219 rm – ♦£55 ♦♦£60
Rest
♦ Chain hotel ♦ Business ♦ Functional ♦
Consistent standard of trim, simply fitted accommodation in contemporary style. Family rooms with sofa beds. Ideal for corporate or leisure travel.

Luton Airport North: 32m by M1 and A505

Express by Holiday Inn without rest   *& 瓯 ⋕ 𝗦̂ 50*

2 Percival Way (East : 2m by A505) ⊠ LU2 9GP   **P VISA ◉ AE ①**
– ℰ (0870) 4 44 89 20 – lutonairport@expressbyholidayinn.net
– Fax (0870) 4 44 89 30
147 rm – ♦£90 ♦♦£90
♦ Chain hotel ♦ Business ♦ Functional ♦
Purpose-built hotel handily placed beside the airport. Inclusive continental breakfasts, plus 24 hour snack menus. Rooms are modern and well-equipped.

Stansted Airport North: 37m by M11 and A120

Radisson SAS   *◉ Lₒ 𝔖 ◰ & 瓯 ⋕ ▤ ℰ̈ 𝗦̂ 400 P VISA ◉ AE ①*

Waltham Close ⊠ CM24 1PP – ℰ (01279) 66 10 12
– info.stansted@radissonsas.com – Fax (01279) 66 10 13
– www.stansted.radissonsas.com
484 rm – ♦£125 ♦♦£125, ⊆ £13 – 16 suites
Rest *New York Grill Bar* a la carte £23/31
Rest *Wine Tower* a la carte £11/13
Rest *Filini* a la carte £16/25
♦ Chain hotel ♦ Business ♦ Functional ♦
Impressive hotel just two minutes from main terminal; vast open atrium housing 40 foot wine cellar. Extensive meeting facilities. Very stylish bedrooms in three themes. Small, formal New York Grill Bar. Impressive Wine Tower. Filini for Italian dishes.

Hilton London Stansted Airport   *Lₒ 𝔖 ◰ & 瓯 rest ⋕rm*

Round Coppice Rd ⊠ CM24 1SF   **𝗦̂ 250 P VISA ◉ AE ①**
– ℰ (01279) 68 08 00 – reservations.stansted@hilton.com
– Fax (01279) 68 08 90
237 rm – ♦£90/146 ♦♦£90/146, ⊆ £18 – 2 suites
Rest a la carte £29/35
♦ Chain hotel ♦ Business ♦ Functional ♦
Bustling hotel whose facilities include leisure club, hairdressers and beauty salon. Modern rooms, with two of executive style. Transport can be arranged to and from terminal. Restaurant/bar has popular menu; sometimes carvery lunch as well.

UNITED KINGDOM

Express by Holiday Inn without rest   &. 1/2 ☉60 P ☉ AE ☉

Thremhall Ave. ✉ CM24 1PY
– ✆ (01279) 68 00 15
– stansted@kewgreen.co.uk
– Fax (01279) 68 08 38

183 rm – ♦£80 ♦♦£80

Adjacent to the airport and medium term parking facilities, so useful for leisure and business travellers. Functional rooms provide good value accommodation.

BIRMINGHAM

BIRMINGHAM

Population (est. 2005): 889 000 (conurbation 2 371 000) – Altitude: 98m

Duclerc/COLORISE

Birmingham, Britain's flourishing second city, is characterised by its cultural diversity and dynamic fusion of tradition and modernity. It takes pride in its manufacturing past while forging a new identity as a leader in leisure, entertainment, sport, commercial and industrial activities. The attractive squares adorned with modern sculpture and floral displays, the fine museums, theatres and art galleries, the profusion of shopping arcades and eating and drinking establishments as well as a thriving nightlife with one of the best club scenes, justify its designation as a World City.

The canals that weave their way through and beneath the city, played an essential role in the transport of products that made Birmingham a centre of trade and commerce. They are now the focal point for the cultural quarter and provide a pleasant waterfront setting for the many entertainment venues.

WHICH DISTRICT TO CHOOSE

Birmingham offers ample choice of **accommodation** in the city centre and surrounding area to suit every taste and budget. Luxury and boutique hotels are located around Broad Street *Plan II* **D2**, Wharfside Street *Plan II* **E2**, New Street *Plan II* **E2** and Church Street *Plan I* **A1**. For hotels with a country house ambience look on the outskirts. There are comfortable business hotels near the airport and the National Exhibition Centre (NEC).

The city's amazing diversity is reflected in the cosmopolitan array of places to eat (modern British, French, Italian, Irish, Japanese, Indian, Chinese, Thai, South American, Caribbean, Mediterranean). The Water's Edge *Plan II* **E1** and Brindley Place *Plan II* **D2** are the areas to explore for **cafés, gastro bars, brasseries** and **restaurants**. The city is famous for its Indian and Chinese restaurants. You may wish to visit Ladypool Road *Plan I* **B2** and Storey Lane *Plan I* **B2** at the heart of the Balti Triangle and the Arcadian Centre and the area around Hurst Street *Plan II* **F3** in the Chinese Quarter but there are some stylish ethnic establishments in the city centre.

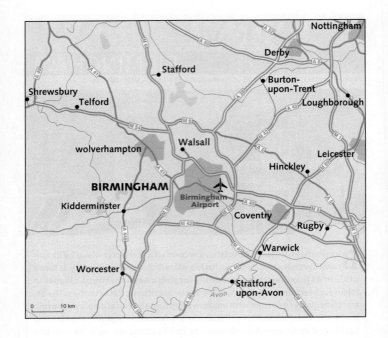

PRACTICAL INFORMATION

ARRIVAL – DEPARTURE

Birmingham International Airport – 13 km (8 mi) east of the city. ℰ 08707 335 511; www.bhx.co.uk

From the airport to the city centre – By **free Air-Rail** to Birmingham International Station: every 2min, time: 90sec; then frequent **trains** to New St Station, time: 10-20min. Fare: £2.70. ℰ 0845 748 4950. By **taxi**: Black cabs take up to 5 people with luggage. Credit cards are accepted. Fare: about £16. ℰ 0121 782 3744. By **bus**: local buses link the airport to the surrounding districts; all stop outside Terminal 2. Line 900 to Digbeth Coach Station (stop K), every 20-30min, time: 20min; fare: £2.70 single, £4.85 round trip.

ℰ 0870 608 2608; www.centro.org. uk; www.travelwm.co.uk

Railway Stations – Birmingham International Station (in the borough of Solihull, just east of the city) and New Street Station *Plan II* **E2** for mainline trains. www.nationalrail.co.uk

TRANSPORT

♦ BUSES AND METRO

The integrated public transport system is a convenient way to get about. £2.70 single ticket. **Day Centrocard** £5.60, off-peak weekly £8.10. Tickets can be purchased at rail stations, on buses, at the Centro Information Centre at New Street Station and at Travel WM Travelcard and Information Centres.

There is a good taxi service in the city. Allow £5-6 for a short journey. It is customary to add a tip (10%).

USEFUL ADDRESSES

♦ **TOURIST OFFICES**

Tourism Centre & Ticket Shop, The Rotunda, 150 New Street, Birmingham B2 4TA *Plan II* **F2** (open Mon-Sat 9.30am-5.30pm, Sun and Bank hols 10.30am-4.30pm); **Welcome Centre**, Junction of New Street and Corporation Street *Plan II* **E2** (open Mon-Sat 9am-6pm, Sun and Bank hols 10am-4pm). ✆ 0121 202 5099; www.beinbirmingham.com

♦ **POST OFFICES**

The main post offices are at 1 Pinfold St *Plan II* **E2**, 19 Union Passage *Plan II* **F2**. Open Mon-Fri 9.30am-5.30pm, Sat 9.30am-1.30pm.

♦ **BANKS/CURRENCY EXCHANGE**

Banks open Mon-Fri, 9.30am-4.30pm. Some offer a limited service on Saturday mornings. There are cash dispensers (ATM) all over the city that accept international credit cards (PIN required).

♦ **EMERGENCY**

Police, Fire Brigade and Ambulance Service ✆ **999**.

EXPLORING BIRMINGHAM

It is possible to visit the main sights and museums in two days.

Museums and other sights are usually open from 10am to 5pm. Some close on Mondays.

VISITING

Canal trips from Gas Street Basin *Plan II* **D3**, The International Convention Centre Quay *Plan II* **D2** and National Sea Life Centre *Plan II* **D2**.

The Wheel *Plan II* **D2** – Panoramic views of the city.

Birmingham Museum and Art Gallery *Plan II* **E2** – A fine building houses an outstanding collection of Pre-Raphaelite paintings as well as works of art by English and European masters.

Barber Institute of Fine Arts *Plan I* **A2** – An excellent collection of French, Italian, Flemish and English paintings as well as furniture and art objects.

St Philip's Cathedral *Plan II* **E2** – A Baroque cathedral (18C) adorned with splendid Pre-Raphaelite stained glass.

Thinktank *Plan I* **B2** – A museum devoted to scientific and technological invention.

Jewellery Quarter *Plan II* **D1** – A survival of early industrial Birmingham: visit the **Museum of the Jewellery Quarter** for the story of the area and for a demonstration of traditional skills and techniques as well as the Georgian **St Paul's Church**, the centrepiece St Paul's Square, the only remaining 18C square in the city.

Back-to-Backs *Plan II* **F3** – Discover the past way of life in an industrial town.

Soho House *Plan I* **A1** – The elegant Georgian home of the industrialist Matthew Boulton.

Aston Hall *Plan I* **B1** – A fine Jacobean house with original furnishings.

Bournville – *6km (4 mi) SW*. The planned estate was a progressive social achievement: workers' cottages, Rest House, school, Selly Manor. A visit to **Cadbury World** is a must for chocoholics.

SHOPPING

Birmingham is a shoppers' paradise. *The Pallasades*, New St, *Pavilion Central*, High St, *Arcadian Centre*, Pershore St, *Martineau Place*, near High St, and *The Mailbox*, Wharfside St are trendy shopping centres with designer shops, department stores, young fashions and accessories. The pedestrianised **Bullring** *Plan II* **F2** boasts the spectacular Selfridges store and other fashion shops. **The Burlington Arcade**, New Street *Plan II* **E2**, has a good selection of stylish shops. You will find that special gift or you may commission your own jewellery in silver, gold, platinum and diamonds in the numerous shops in the **'Golden Triangle'** bounded by Waterstone Lane and Vyse Street *Plan I* **A1**.

ANTIQUES – For arts and crafts visit **The Custard Gallery**, Gibb St (Urban Village, Fragile Design, Sarah Priesler), *Birmingham Antiques*, 68m Wyrley Road, *The Art Lounge*, 28-30 Wharfside Street, *Temple Gallery*, 5 Great Western Arcade and *Vesey Manor*, 62-64 Birmingham Road, Sutton Coldfield.

MARKETS – The Bullring area has a longstanding market tradition: **St Martin's Market** (Tue, Fri-Sat 9am-5pm), produce, clothing, antiques; **Indoor Market**, Edgbaston Street (Mon-Sat 9am-5.30pm); **Farmers' Market**, New St/Victoria Sq (first and third Wed of every month, 9am-5pm).

ENTERTAINMENT

Symphony Hall (ICC) *Plan II* **D2** – concerts of classical, folk, rock, pop, world music and stand-up comedy.

The Hippodrome *Plan II* **F3** – Ballet, opera, musicals and pantomimes.

Alexandra *Plan II* **E3** and **Repertory** *Plan II* **D3 Theatres** – Drama, musicals, comedies, dance.

NEC Arena – Pop and rock concerts, sporting events.

The Drum *Plan I* **A1** – African, Asian and Caribbean Arts and Culture: music, comedy, dance, drama.

Mac Midlands Arts Centre *Plan I* **B2** – Visual and performance arts.

NIGHTLIFE

Visit the Water's Edge and Brindley Place developments in the **Gas Street Basin** area *Plan I* **D2** and the **Jewellery Quarter** *Plan I* **A1** for trendy wine bars, café bars, restaurants and traditional English pubs. Some of the lively venues which attract a young crowd are: *The Jam House*, St Paul's Sq; *Dome II*, Horsefair, the largest discotheque in the city; *The Works* nightclub, Broad St; *The Canal Club*, Broad Street for dancing; *Mechu* and *Après*, 38-59 Summer Row for bars and clubs. **Starcity Entertainment Centre**, Watson Road, offers all kinds of entertainment: cinemas, restaurants, bowling, snow slope, casino.

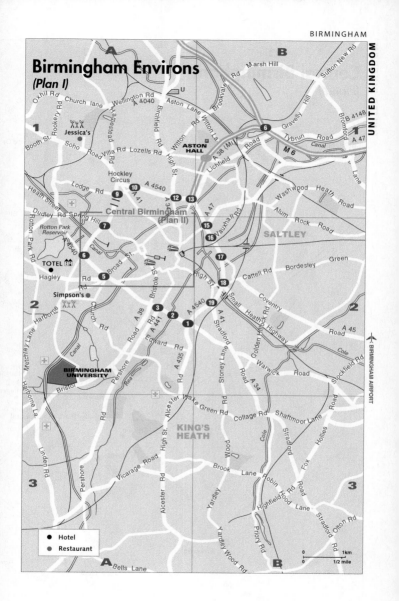

Central Birmingham
(Plan II)

C **D**

Rosebery St.
Camden
Spring
Eyre Street
Cope
Stour Street
Freeth Street

George St. West
Ellen St.
Hill
A 4540
Middleway King Edwards Rd
Saint
Marks
Crescent

Hingeston St.
Icknield
Street
Carver
Street
Camden
Summer Hill Rd
Summer Hill St.

Pitsford Street
Warstone Lane
Tenby Street
Albion Street
Legge Lane
A 457
Sand Pits Parade
St. Clement St.

BROOKFIELDS

Spencer Street
Wyse
Frederick
Vittoria
Street
Graham Street
Newhall Hill
George Street
Summer Row
Charlott

La Toque d'Or ⚔⚔

1

7 Spring Hill Circus

LADYWOOD

Ladywood
Ledseam
Street
Canal
Great Tindal St.
Browing St.
St. Vincent St. West
Gilby Rd
Ladywood
Morville St.
Ryland
Ruston St.

King
Vincent
Street
Saint
Sheepcote

NATIONAL
INDOOR
ARENA

INTERNATIONAL
CONVENTION
CENTRE

Edwards Rd
Cambridge
CENTENARY
SQUARE

SEA LIFE

Bank ⚔⚔

Brindley Place

Hyatt Regen
Broad
Bridge
**Zinc Bar
and Grill** ⚔⚔

2

6 Ladywood Circus

City Inn 🏨

Novotel 🏨

A 456
Broad Street
Berkley Street
Gas Street
Granville St.
Holliday

Duchess Road
Francis
A 4540 Middleway
Grosvenor Street West
Tennant
Bishopsgate St.
William St.
Canal

3

5 Fiveways

A 456
Hagley Road
Highfield
Harborne Rd
Frederick Road

4

B 4127
Bath
Wheeley's Lane
B 4127
Row

Rd

| ● | Hotel |
| ● | Restaurant |

C **D**

896

E

F

St. George's St.

Lane

Lancaster

mpton St.

Constitution

A 41

Henrietta Street

Lr. Loveday Street

Cliveland Street

Summer

Bagot Street

A 38

Street

Hill

St.

Shadwell St.

Princip St.

Canal

Street

Corporation

1

U

St. Northwood St.

Livery

Cox Street

Street

St Chads
Circus

St Chads

Ringway

Whittall

Lancaster
Circus

U

asan

ST PAUL'S
SQUARE

Ludgate

Livery

St.

St.

Steelhouse Lane

James Watt Queensway

Aston St.

Chapel St.

Jennen's Rd.

Street Newhall

Hill

Charles

Church

St.

Colmore
Circus

Newton St.

Express by
Holiday Inn

Metro Bar
and Grill

Great

Cornwall

Opus

St.

Hotel du Vin

Bull

Row

Masshouse
Circus

Street

Edmund

St.

ST PHILLIP'S
CATHEDRAL

Temple Row

St.

Dale End

Albert St. Queensway

Street

MUSEUM AND
ART GALLERY

Colmore

Corporation

2

Paradise

Copthorne

Circus

Waterloo

Victoria
Square

New

St.

H

The Burlington

Street

High St.

MOOR STATION

Moor St. Queensway

Park

Bordesley St.

owne Plaza
irmingham

Suffolk

Navigation

Hill

St Martin's Circus

Park St.

Street

NEW STATION

liday St.

Malmaison

Street

BULL RING
CENTRE

Allison Street

Paris

St.

Queensway

Pershore

Upper Dean St.

St.

Digbeth

Digbeth

mmercial St.

Severn

St.

Blucher St.

Gough St.

Holloway
Circus

Thorp St.

Street

Inge Street

Hurst

Street

Lower St.

Park St.

Head

B 4127

Holloway

Bow St.

Horse Fair

Moseley Street

Irving

Street

Bromsgrove

Lower Essex Street

South St.

LEE BANK

A 38 Street

Kent

Bishop St.

3

Cregoe

St.

Great

Colmore

Street

Bristol

Wrentham Street

Rea

St.

0   200 m
0   200 yards

E

F

897

Hyatt Regency
≤ ⊛ ⅃₆ ⅋ ⊠ & ⅏ ⅋rm ⅋ ⊡ ☜ ⅍200
2 Bridge St ⊠ B1 2ZJ – ✆ (0121) 643 12 34
– birmingham @ hyattintl.com – Fax (0121) 616 23 23   ⊗ VISA ◯⊙ AE ⓪
– www.birmingham.regency.hyatt.com   **D2**
315 rm – †£99/169 ††£99/169 , ⊊ £15 – 4 suites
Rest *Aria* £17 and a la carte £29/34

♦ Luxury ♦ Modern ♦

Striking mirrored exterior. Glass enclosed lifts offer panoramic views. Sizeable rooms with floor to ceiling windows. Covered link with International Convention Centre. Contemporary style restaurant in central atrium; modish cooking.

Malmaison
⅃₆ ⅏ & ⅏ ⅋ ⅋ ⊡ ⅍45 VISA ◯⊙ AE ⓪
Mailbox, 1 Wharfside St ⊠ B1 1RD – ✆ (0121) 246 50 00 – birmingham @
malmaison.com – Fax (0121) 246 50 02 – www.malmaison.com   **E2**
184 rm – †£140 ††£140, ⊊ £14 – 5 suites
Rest *Brasserie* a la carte £22/37

♦ Luxury ♦ Stylish ♦

Stylish, modern boutique hotel, forms centrepiece of Mailbox development. Stylish bar. Spacious contemporary bedrooms with every modern facility; superb petit spa. Brasserie serving contemporary French influenced cooking at reasonable prices.

Hotel du Vin
⊞ ⅃₆ ⅏ & ⅏ ⅋rest ⅋ ⊡ ☜ ⅍85 VISA ◯⊙ AE ⓪
25 Church St ⊠ B3 2NR – ✆ (0121) 200 06 00 – info @
birmingham.hotelduvin.com – Fax (0121) 236 08 89 – www.hotelduvin.com
66 rm – †£130 ††£130, ⊊ £15   **E2**
Rest *Bistro* £15 (lunch) and a la carte £31/34 ⅋

♦ Business ♦ Design ♦

Former 19C eye hospital in heart of shopping centre; has relaxed, individual, boutique style. Low lighting in rooms of muted tones: Egyptian cotton and superb bathrooms. Champagne in "bubble lounge"; Parisian style brasserie.

The Burlington
⅃₆ ⅏ & ⅏ ⅋ ⊡ ⅍400 VISA ◯⊙ AE ⓪
Burlington Arcade, 126 New St ⊠ B2 4JQ – ✆ (0121) 643 91 91 – mail @
burlingtonhotel.com – Fax (0121) 643 50 75 – www.macdonaldhotels.co.uk
closed 25-26 December   **E2**
110 rm – †£155 ††£155, ⊊ £15 – 2 suites
Rest *Berlioz* £23 and a la carte £25/35

♦ Traditional ♦ Classic ♦

Approached by a period arcade. Restored Victorian former railway hotel retains much of its original charm. Period décor to bedrooms yet with fax, modem and voice mail. Elegant dining room: ornate ceiling, chandeliers and vast mirrors.

Crowne Plaza Birmingham
⅃₆ ⅏ ⊠ & ⅏ ⅋rm ⊡ ☜ ⅍150
Central Sq ⊠ B1 1HH – ✆ (0870) 400 91 50   ⊗ VISA ◯⊙ AE ⓪
– reservations.bhamcity @ ichotelsgroup.com – Fax (0121) 643 90 18
– www.crowneplaza.com   **E2**
281 rm ⊊ – †£159/179 ††£179 – 3 suites
Rest £16 /19 and a la carte £22/30

♦ Business ♦ Functional ♦

Ideal for both corporate and leisure guests. Extensive leisure facilities include children's pool. Well-equipped bedrooms with air-conditioning and triple glazing. Conservatory restaurant with views across city.

Copthorne
⅃₆ ⅏ ⊠ & ⅏ rest ⅋ ⅋ ⊡ ⅍250 P VISA ◯⊙ AE ⓪
Paradise Circus ⊠ B3 3HJ – ✆ (0121) 200 27 27 – reservations.birmingham @
mill-cop.com – Fax (0121) 200 11 97 – www.copthornehotels.com   **E2**
209 rm – †£165 ††£185, ⊊ £16 – 3 suites
Rest *Goldsmiths* (closed Sunday) (dinner only) £25 /35 and a la carte £26/36
Rest *Goldies* £11 /19 and a la carte £21/34

♦ Business ♦ Functional ♦

Overlooking Centenary Square. Corporate hotel with extensive leisure club and cardiovascular gym. Cricket themed bar. Connoisseur rooms offer additional comforts. Flambé dishes offered in intimate Goldsmiths. Goldies is all-day relaxed brasserie.

City Inn
🛜 ℔ ⅊ 🅰🅲 ↤rm ❄ 🆂🅰🆅 ⅍100 **VISA** 🆎 ①

1 Brunswick Sq, Brindley Pl ⊠ *B1 2HW*
– ℰ *(0121) 643 10 03*
– *birmingham.reservations @ cityinn.com*
– *Fax (0121) 643 10 05*
– *www.cityinn.com*
closed 26-28 December

D2

238 rm – †£149 ††£149, � £11
Rest *City Café* £13 /17 and a la carte £19/32

♦ Chain hotel ♦ Business ♦ Functional ♦

In heart of vibrant Brindley Place; the spacious atrium with bright rugs and blond wood sets the tone for equally stylish rooms. Corporate friendly with many meeting rooms. Eat in restaurant, terrace or bar.

TOTEL without rest
↤ **P** **VISA** 🆎 ①

19 Portland Rd, Edgbaston ⊠ *B16 9HN* – ℰ *(0121) 454 52 82*
– *info @ totaluk.com*
– *Fax (0121) 456 46 68*
– *www.toteluk.com*
closed 25 December

Plan I **A2**

9 suites ⊔ – †£65 ††£95

♦ Business ♦ Design ♦

19C house converted into comfortable, spacious fully-serviced apartments, individually styled with modern facilities. Friendly service. Continental breakfast served in room.

Novotel
℔ 🐾 ℥ ↤ 🆂🅰🆅 ⅍300 🚗 **VISA** 🆎 ①

70 Broad St ⊠ *B1 2HT* – ℰ *(0121) 643 20 00*
– *hlo77 @ accor.com*
– *Fax (0121) 643 97 96*
– *www.novotel.com*

D3

148 rm ⊔ – †£158/165 ††£165
Rest £15 and a la carte £17/24

♦ Chain hotel ♦ Business ♦ Functional ♦

Well located for the increasingly popular Brindleyplace development. Underground parking. Modern, well-kept, branded bedrooms suitable for families. Modern, open-plan restaurant.

Express by Holiday Inn without rest
℥ 🅰🅲 ↤ ⅍30 🚗 **VISA** 🆎 ①

65 Lionel St ⊠ *B11JE* – ℰ *(0121) 200 19 00*
– *ebhi-bhamcity @ btconnect.com*
– *Fax (0121) 200 19 10*
– *www.hiexpress.co.uk*

E2

120 rm – †£55/95 ††£55/95

♦ Chain hotel ♦ Functional ♦

Well-kept, well-managed hotel situated in a handy location for visitors to the city centre. Tidy, comfortable accommodation to suit tourists or business travellers alike.

Simpsons (Antona) with rm
🛜 🚲 🅰🅲 rest ↤ ⊕18 **P** **VISA** 🆎 🆎

😋

20 Highfield Rd, Edgbaston ⊠ *B15 3DX* – ℰ *(0121) 454 34 34*
– *info @ simpsonsrestaurant.co.uk*
– *Fax (0121) 454 33 99*
– *www.simpsonsrestaurant.co.uk*
closed 27-28 August and 25-26 December

Plan I **A2**

4 rm – †£140/190 ††£140/190
Rest £20 /30 and a la carte £38/54

Spec. Torte of smoked salmon, crab and creamed guacamole. Fillet of Aberdeenshire beef cooked on the bone, red wine shallot sauce. Black forest cake, cherry sorbet.

♦ Innovative ♦ Fashionable ♦

Restored Georgian residence; its interior a careful blend of Victorian features and contemporary style. Refined, classically based cooking. Elegant bedrooms.

UNITED KINGDOM

Jessica's (Purnell) 🕸

£₃

1 Montague Rd ⊠ B16 9HU – ℰ (0121) 455 09 99 – Fax (0121) 455 82 22
– www.jessicasrestaurant.co.uk
closed last 2 weeks July, 1 week Easter, 24 December-2 January, Saturday lunch,
Sunday and Monday *Plan I* **A1**
Rest £24 /33
Spec. Salted Cornish cod with smoked black olives and frozen passion fruit.
Gressingham duck in two ways. Chocolate soufflé with compote of strawberry.
♦ Innovative ♦ Formal ♦
Georgian 'outbuilding' and conservatory offering excellently presented, highly
original French influenced modern British cooking sourced from quality Midland
suppliers.

Paris

109-111 Wharfside St, The Mailbox, ⊠ B1 1RF – ℰ (0121) 632 14 88
– paris.restaurant @ virgin.net – Fax (0121) 632 14 89
– www.restaurantparis.co.uk
closed Sunday and Monday **E3**
Rest £22 (lunch) and a la carte £40/53
♦ Modern ♦ Formal ♦
Located in fashionable Mailbox area and painted in a deep chocolate brown
palette with stylish tan leather chairs. Fine dining, with chef's gourmand menu
also available.

Opus

54 Cornwall St ⊠ B3 2DE – ℰ (0121) 200 23 23 – restaurant @
opusrestaurant.co.uk – Fax (0121) 200 20 90 – www.opusrestaurant.co.uk
closed last week July, first week August, 1 week Christmas, Sunday, Saturday
lunch and Bank Holidays **E2**
Rest £15/18 (lunch) and a la carte £25/35
♦ Modern ♦ Design ♦
Restaurant of floor-to-ceiling glass in evolving area of city. Seafood and shellfish
bar for diners on the move. Assured cooking underpins modern menus with
traditional base.

Lasan

3-4 Dakota Buildings, James St ⊠ B3 1SD – ℰ (0121) 212 36 64
– info @ lasan.co.uk – Fax (0121) 212 36 65 – www.lasan.co.uk
closed 25-26 December and Sunday **E1**
Rest (dinner only) a la carte £14/19
♦ Indian ♦ Design ♦
Jewellery quarter restaurant of sophistication and style; good quality
ingredients allow the clarity of the spices to shine through in this well-run Indian
establishment.

Bank

4 Brindley Place ⊠ B1 2JB – ℰ (0121) 633 44 66 – birmres @ bankrestaurants.com
– Fax (0121) 633 44 65 – www.bankrestaurants.com
closed 1-2 January, August Bank Holiday and dinner
Bank Holiday Mondays **D2**
Rest £15 (lunch) and a la carte £30/48
♦ Modern ♦ Brasserie ♦
Capacious, modern and busy bar-restaurant where chefs can be watched
through a glass wall preparing the tasty modern dishes. Pleasant terrace area.

La Toque d'Or

27 Warstone Lane, Hockley ⊠ B18 6JQ – ℰ (0121) 233 36 55
– didier @ latoquedor.co.uk – Fax (0121) 233 36 55 – www.latoquedor.co.uk
closed Easter, 2 weeks August, 1 week Christmas, Sunday, Monday
and Saturday lunch **D1**
Rest (booking essential) £20 /25
♦ French ♦ Cosy ♦
A different type of gem in the Jewellery Quarter. Personally run former rolling
mill: bare brick and stained glass. Well-judged seasonal menu bears classic
French hallmarks.

XX **Metro Bar and Grill** [AC] [VISA] [MO] [AE]
73 Cornwall St ⊠ B3 2DF – ℰ (0121) 200 19 11 – Fax (0121) 200 16 11
– www.metrobarandgrill.co.uk
closed 25 December-1 January, Sunday and Bank Holidays **E2**
Rest (booking essential) a la carte £21/29
♦ Modern ♦ Brasserie ♦
Gleaming chrome and mirrors in a bright, contemporary basement restaurant.
Modern cooking with rotisserie specialities. Spacious, ever-lively bar serves
lighter meals.

XX **Zinc Bar and Grill** [🍴] [AC] [⬧40] [VISA] [MO] [AE] [O]
Regency Wharf, Broad St, ⊠ B1 2DS – ℰ (0121) 200 06 20 – zinc-birmingham @
conran-restaurants.co.uk – Fax (0121) 200 06 30 – www.conran.com
closed 25-26 December and Sunday dinner **D2**
Rest a la carte £17/32
♦ Modern ♦ Brasserie ♦
Purpose-built restaurant in lively pub and club area of city. Spiral staircase leads
to dining area, including terrace overlooking canal. Modern, classically toned,
dishes.

at Birmingham Airport

 Novotel Birmingham Airport [&] [⅓] [📺] [⬧35] [VISA] [MO] [AE] [O]
Passenger Terminal ⊠ B26 3QL – ℰ (0121) 782 70 00 – h1158 @ accor.com
– Fax (0121) 782 04 45 – www.novotel.com
195 rm – †£125 ††£125, ⊇ £13
Rest (bar lunch Saturday, Sunday and Bank Holidays) £17 /23 and a la carte
£17/29
♦ Chain hotel ♦ Business ♦ Functional ♦
Opposite main terminal building: modern hotel benefits from sound proofed
doors and double glazing. Mini bars and power showers provided in spacious
rooms with sofa beds. Open-plan garden brasserie.

at National Exhibition Centre

 Crowne Plaza [£ɜ] [🐾] [&] [AC] [⅓] [%] [📺] [⬧200] [P] [VISA] [MO] [AE] [O]
Pendigo Way ⊠ B40 1PS – ℰ (0870) 400 91 60 – necroomsales @
ichotelsgroup.com – Fax (0121) 781 43 21
– www.birminghamnec.crowneplaza.com
242 rm – †£89 ††£89, ⊇ £16
Rest (closed Saturday lunch) a la carte £21/36
♦ Business ♦ Modern ♦
Modern hotel adjacent to NEC. Small terrace area overlooks lake. Extensive
conference facilities. State-of-the-art bedrooms with a host of extras. Basement
dining room: food with a Yorkshire twist.

 Express by Holiday Inn without rest [&] [⅓] [⬧100] [P]
Bickenhill Parkway, Bickenhill, ⊠ B1 1QA Birmingham – ℰ (0121) 782 32 22
– exhi-nec @ foremosthotels.co.uk – Fax (0121) 780 42 24 – www.exhi-nec.co.uk
179 rm – †£115 ††£115
♦ Chain hotel ♦ Functional ♦
Handy for the NEC and airport. Modern budget hotel ideal for the corporate
traveller. Extensive cold buffet breakfast included.

EDINBURGH

EDINBURGH

Population (2001): 430 082 (conurbation 452 194) – Altitude: 50m

J. Fuste Raga / HOA QUI

Set on a series of volcanic hills, Edinburgh, the capital of Scotland, is re-nowned for its cool elegance and sophistication. The Old Town, huddled on the ridge running down from Castle Rock contrasts with the New, with its elegant Georgian streets and squares. The numerous monuments, evidence of its rich historical past, the outstanding museum collections, its colour-ful traditions and its perennial zest for enjoyment are all reasons to visit this beautiful city. The Edinburgh Festival confirms its status as a cultural capital. The historic opening of the Scottish Parliament in 1999 has further enhanced the city's prestige.

The Castle Rock had been a secure refuge for generations and in the 11C it was chosen as the site for a residence by Malcolm Canmore and his Queen Margaret. Their son, David I, favoured the site by founding the Abbey of the Holy Rood. During the reign of the early Stuarts Edinburgh gradually assumed the roles of royal residence, seat of government and capital of Scotland. With the Union of the Crowns (1603) and subsequent departure of James VI of Scotland (James I of England) for London, Edinburgh lost most of its pageantry, cultural activity and in 1707, with the Union of the Parliaments, its parliament.

WHICH DISTRICT TO CHOOSE

There are several classic **hotels** with impressive amenities around Princes St *Plan II* **G2**, North Bridge *Plan II* **G2** and near Charlotte Square *Plan II* **F2**. Comfortable hotels and guest hous-es with good facilities are located in the New Town, Calton Hill *Plan II* **G2**, around Lauriston Place *Plan II* **G3**, Shandwick Place *Plan II* **F2** and near Ocean Drive *Plan I* **C1** in Leith.

Restaurants of some of the large hotels and museums in the city cen-tre are famous for their imaginative cooking. There are pleasant eater-ies and pubs serving good food in Princes St, along the Royal Mile and in neighbouring streets, as well as around Rose St *Plan II* **F2**. Leith is a trendy area with many eating places.

PRACTICAL INFORMATION

ARRIVAL – DEPARTURE

Edinburgh International Airport – 12 km (8 mi) west of the city. ℰ 0870 040 0007; www.edinburghairport.com

From the airport to the city centre – By **bus**: Airlink services (line 100) every 10min to Waverley Bridge. Time: 35min. Fare: £3 one-way, £5 round trip. By **taxi**: time 25min. Fare: about £16.

Railway Stations – Waverley Station, Princes St *Plan II* **G2** and **Haymarket Station**, Haymarket Terrace *Plan II* **E2** for mainline trains. ℰ 08457 484 950; www.nationalrail.co.uk

TRANSPORT

◆ BUSES

An efficient bus service operates in the city. A single ticket costs £1. Make sure you have the right money. **Daysaver** tickets £2.50 (£2 after 9.30am and all day Sat-Sun).

◆ TAXIS

Metered taxis may be hailed from taxi ranks, outside rail and bus stations and at the airport. You can also order a taxi by phone: *Citycabs Edinburgh Ltd* ℰ 0131 228 1211; *Computer Cabs* ℰ 0131 228 2555.

USEFUL ADDRESSES

◆ TOURIST OFFICES

Edinburgh & Scotland Information Centre, 3 Princes Street, Edinburgh EH2 2QP ℰ 0845 22 55 121; *Plan II* **G2**. **Edinburgh Airport**, Tourist Information Desk; www.edinburgh.org

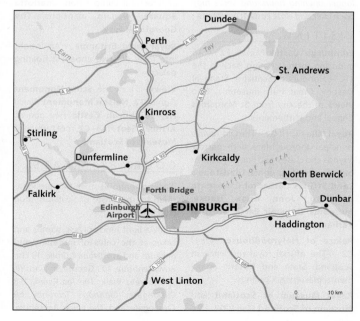

◆ POST OFFICES

Opening times Mon-Fri 9am-5.30pm, Sat 9am-noon. Main post offices are at 8-10 St James' Centre *Plan II* **G1** and 40 Frederick St *Plan II* **F2**.

◆ BANKS/CURRENCY EXCHANGE

Opening times, Mon-Fri 9.30am to 4-5.30pm; some banks open on Sat 9.30am to 12.30pm but offer a limited service. Cash machines (ATM) are available all over the city. There are foreign exchange offices in the city centre, at post offices, at the airport and train stations, in some stores and at the main tourist office.

◆ PHARMACIES

Pharmacies open Mon-Fri, 9.30am-5.30pm, Sat, 9.30am-12.30pm. Boots, 48 Shandwick Place *Plan II* **F2** opens longer hours and on Sunday. There is also a list of pharmacies which open in rotation on Sundays displayed in the window of pharmacies.

BUSY PERIODS

It may be difficult to find a room when special events are held in the city:

Edinburgh International Festival: 3 weeks in August.

Royal Highland Show: late June.

Hogmanay: late December-1 January.

EXPLORING EDINBURGH

It is possible to visit the main sights and museums in Edinburgh in two days.

Museums and sights are usually open daily 9.30-10am to 5pm. Some may have longer opening hours and some may open later and close early at weekends.

VISITING

Edinburgh Castle *Plan II* **F2** – An imposing fortress dating back to the 11C – Honours of Scotland, Stone of Destiny, Great Hall, museums. Fine **views** of the city from St Margaret's Chapel and battlements.

Royal Mile *Plan II* **G2** – The Old Town's principal thoroughfare with narrow 'wynds and closes' and lined by a number of interesting sights: **Gladstone's Land**, **St Giles' Cathedral**, **Canongate Tolbooth**, **John Knox House**, **museums**, **Dynamic Earth**, **Scottish Parliament**.

Palace of Holyroodhouse *Plan I* **C2** – The official royal residence in Scotland: State and historic apartments, plasterwork ceilings.

Royal Museum of Scotland and **Museum of Scotland** *Plan II* **G2** – An enlightening presentation of the comprehensive art collections and of the history of Scotland.

New Town *Plan II* **F2** – An harmonious architectural composition: **Charlotte Square**, elegant mansions, **The Georgian House**.

Royal Yacht Britannia – An insight into royal lifestyle aboard a floating palace.

Views – From the **Scott Monument** *Plan II* **G2**, **Nelson Monument** *Plan II* **H2**, **Edinburgh Castle** *(see above)*, **Arthur's Seat** *Plan I* **C2**, roof terrace of **Museum of Scotland**.

GOURMET TREATS

Places offering Scottish fare are identified by the 'Taste of Scotland' logo (stockpot).

Enjoy a light lunch or tea, scones and cakes at the cafés of museums and galleries and at *Valvona & Crolla*, 19 Elm Row; *Centrotre*, 103 George St; *Vincaffe*, 11 Multrees Walk; *The Tea Room*, 158 Canongate; *Clarinda's Tearoom*, 69 Canongate and *The Laigh Bakehouse*,

17a Hanover St are all well worth a visit. *The Oyster Bar* at the Café Royal, Register Place is a stylish place. You can book whisky tastings at *The Scotch Malt Whisky Society Ltd*, 87 Giles St, Leith.

SHOPPING

Stores are usually open Mon-Sat, 9-10am to 5.30-6.30pm. Some shops open Sun, 11am to 4.30-5.30pm.

DESIGNER SHOPS, BOUTIQUES AND FASHION OUTLETS – For designer shops visit **The Walk**, off St Andrews Square *Plan II* **G1**, **William Street** *Plan II* **E2** and **Victoria St** *Plan II* **G2**. **Princes Street** *Plan II* **G2** is lined with quality stores such as *Jenners, House of Fraser* and trendy shops are located in **George Street** *Plan II* **G2** and **Rose St** *Plan II* **F2**.

SPECIALIST SHOPS – Tweed, tartan, cashmere, wool garments: *Romanes Paterson*, 62 Princes St; *Kinloch Anderson*, Commercial/Dock St, Leith; *The Cashmere Store*, 2 Saint Giles St, *Ragamuffin*, Canongate and *Troon*, 1 York Place. Crystal: *Edinburgh Crystal Visitor Centre*, Eastfield, Penicuik. Fossils and minerals: *Mr Wood's Fossils*, 5 Cowgatehead, Grassmarket. Jewellery: *Scottish Gems*, 24 High St; *The Tappit Hen*, 89 High St. Crafts: *The Ceramic Experience*, Hopetoun St. There are specialist food shops along the Royal Mile and *Baxters* is at Ocean Terminal in Leith. Malt whisky: *Royal Mile Whiskies*, 379 High St.

ANTIQUE SHOPS – Explore the area around the **Royal Mile, Victoria St** and **Grassmarket** in the Old Town and in **Dundas** *Plan II* **G1** and **Thistle Streets** *Plan II* **G2**. Also visit *Georgian Antiques*, 10 Pattison St, Leith Links.

MARKETS – **Leith Market**, Commercial Quay, Ocean Drive *Plan I* **C1**, Leith – food, art, fashion, flowers – open Sat 9am-5.30pm; Sun 10am-4pm. **Farmers' Market**, Castle Terrace: open Sat 9am-2pm.

WHAT TO BUY – Edinburgh crystal, ceramics, tartan, knitwear, malt whisky, smoked fish, shortbread, oatcakes, marmalade and jams, Dundee cake, crafts and jewellery.

ENTERTAINMENT

For listings consult the fortnightly magazine, The List. The Edinburgh pages of the weekly *Time Out* give useful information.

Usher Hall *Plan II* **F2** – Concerts.

Royal Lyceum Theatre *Plan II* **F2** – Scottish drama and dance.

Edinburgh Playhouse *Plan II* **H1** – Musicals.

King's Theatre *Plan II* **F3** and **Edinburgh Festival Theatre** *Plan II* **H3** – Plays, ballet, opera.

Traverse Theatre *Plan II* **F2** – Experimental theatre.

CornExchange, 11 Newmarket Rd – Live music.

Assembly Rooms *Plan II* **G2** – Ceilidhs.

NIGHTLIFE

Edinburgh **pubs** have a great atmosphere: *Abbotsford*, 3-5 Rose St *Plan II* **F2**; *Deacon Brodie* and *Ensign Ewart*, Lawnmarket; *Greyfriars Bobby*, 34 Candlemaker Row; *Bow Bar*, 80 West Row; *Oxford Bar*, 8 Young St; *Halfway House*, Fishmarket Close. Pubs in Grassmarket *Plan II* **G2** are popular with students and there are fashionable pubs and wine bars on the quayside at Leith. For live music, go to *Bannerman's*, 212 Cowgate; *Whistle Binkies*, 6 Niddry St; *Bongo Club*, 37 Holyrood Rd. A young and trendy crowd flocks to *Po Na Na*, 43b Frederick St; *The City Club*, 1a Market St; *The Subway*, 69 Cowgate; *The Vaults*, 15-17 Niddry St. Jazz fans will enjoy *Henry's Jazz Cellar*, 8 Morrison St. The *George Inter-Continental Hotel*, 19-21 George St and *Thistle Hotel*, 107 Leith St organise Scottish evenings.

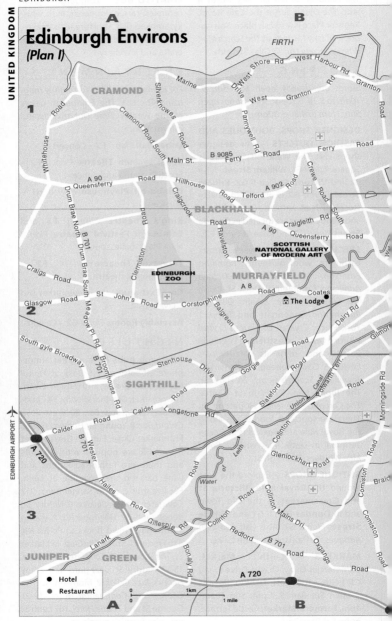

Edinburgh Environs
(Plan I)

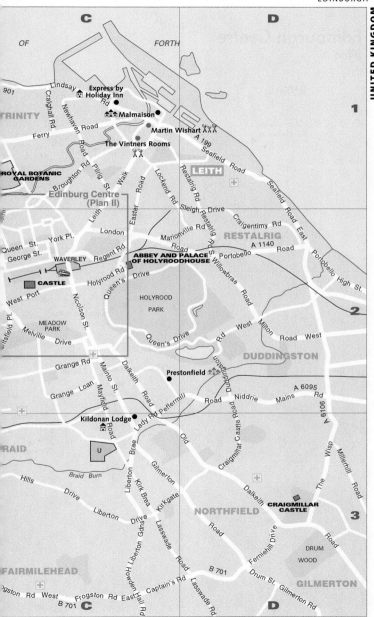

Edinburgh Centre
(Plan II)

E F

1

Channings
Channings

Bank Road
Comely
Orchard
Brae
Comely Bank Avenue
Dean Park Cres.
Dean
St.
Raeburn Pl.
Hamilton Pl.
St Stephen Street
Henderson Row
Brandon
Royal Circus
Howe St.
Gloucester
Great
Ro
Christopher North House
Queensferry
Water of Leith

Moray Pl.
Heriot
QUEEN STREET GARDENS

Belford
Road
Belford
Road
Rothesay Pl.
Walker St.
Palmerston
Place
The Bonham
Queensferry Street
Randolph Crescent
Ainslie Pl.
Queen
THE GEORGIAN HOUSE
CHARLOTTE SQ.
George
Frederick
Street
Oloroso
The Roxburghe
Princes

2

Clarendon
Caledonian Hilton
William Street
Shandwick Pl.
PRINCES STREE
GARDENS
CASTLE
Castle Terrace
Johnsto
West
Lothian

Haymarket Ter.
West Maitland St.
Morrison
Morrison Link
Gardner's Crescent
Sheraton Grand
Santini
Grill Room
Street
Atrium
Spittal St.
Bread St.
West
Novotel Edinburgh Centre
Lauriston
Edinburgh City

3

Dalry
Road
West
Dundee Street
Approach
Fountainbridge
Canal
Viewforth
Gilmore
Place
Leven St.
Home St.
Melville

Union
Granville Terr.
Viewforth
Brunsfield Pl.
Warrender Pa
Warrender
Pa

0 300 m
0 300 yards

E F

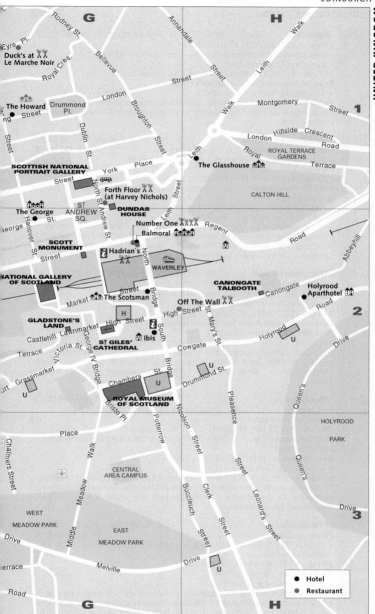

EDINBURGH CENTRE *Plan II*

UNITED KINGDOM

Balmoral 🏰 🏠 ☐ & 🅰 ↩ ✗ ▨ ⚓350 🚬 🆅🆂🅰 🆖🆂 🅰🅴 ⓪
1 Princes St ⊠ EH2 2EQ – ℰ (0131) 556 24 14
– reservations @ thebalmoralhotel.com – Fax (0131) 557 87 40
– www.roccofortehotels.com **G2**
167 rm – ♦£270/470 ♦♦£320/470, ☲ £19 – 21 suites
Rest see *Number One* and *Hadrian's* below
♦ Grand Luxury ♦ Classic ♦
Richly furnished rooms in grand baronial style complemented by contemporary
furnishings in the Palm Court exemplify this de luxe Edwardian railway hotel and
city landmark.

Caledonian Hilton 🏰 🏠 ☐ & 🅰 ↩rm ▨ ⚓250
Princes St, ⊠ EH1 2AB – ℰ (0131) 222 88 88 **P** 🆅🆂🅰 🆖🆂 🅰🅴 ⓪
– guest.caledonian @ hilton.com – Fax (0131) 222 88 89
– www.hilton.co.uk **F2**
238 rm – ♦£150/245 ♦♦£180/275, ☲ £20 – 13 suites
Rest *The Pompadour* (closed Saturday lunch, Sunday and Monday) £17 (lunch)
and a la carte £34/44
Rest *Chisholms* £20 (dinner) and a la carte £23/33
♦ Grand Luxury ♦ Classic ♦
A city landmark, affectionately known locally as "The Cally". Overlooked by the
castle, with handsomely appointed rooms and wood-panelled halls behind an
imposing 19C façade. The Pompadour boasts elegant dining. Informal
Chisholms serves popular brasserie fare.

Sheraton Grand 🕙 🏰 🏠 ☐ & 🅰 ↩rm ✗ ▨ 🕻 ⚓500
1 Festival Sq ⊠ EH3 9SR – ℰ (0131) 229 91 31 **P** 🆅🆂🅰 🆖🆂 🅰🅴 ⓪
– grandedinburgh.sheraton @ sheraton.com – Fax (0131) 229 96 31
– www.sheraton.com/grandedinburgh **F2**
244 rm – ♦£225 ♦♦£265, ☲ £17 – 16 suites
Rest see also *Grill Room* and *Santini* below
Rest *Terrace* (buffet only)£20/21
♦ Grand Luxury ♦ Business ♦ Modern ♦
A modern, centrally located and smartly run hotel. A popular choice for the
working traveller, as it boasts Europe's most advanced urban spa. Comfy,
well-kept rooms. Glass expanse of Terrace restaurant overlooks Festival
Square.

The George ↩rm ✗ ▨ ⚓200 🆅🆂🅰 🆖🆂 🅰🅴 ⓪
19-21 George St ⊠ EH2 2PB – ℰ (0131) 225 12 51 – Fax (0131) 226 56 44
– www.principal-hotels.com **G2**
192 rm – ♦£134/184 ♦♦£149/199, ☲ £16 – 3 suites
Rest *Le Chambertin* , ℰ (0131) 240 71 78 (closed Saturday lunch and Sunday)
a la carte £29/42
Rest *Carvers* , ℰ (0131) 459 23 05 – a la carte £17/29
♦ Luxury ♦ Classic ♦
An established classic that makes the most of Robert Adam's listed 18C design.
Welcoming marble-floored lobby, convivial Clans bar and well-proportioned
bedrooms. Le Chambertin is light, spacious and stylish. Carvers is set in
magnificent glass-domed room.

Prestonfield 🐌 ← 🚗 🖉 🖼 & 🅰 rest ↩ ▨ 🕻 ⚓900
Prestonfield Rd ⊠ EH16 5UT **P** 🆅🆂🅰 🆖🆂 🅰🅴 ⓪
– ℰ (0131) 225 78 00 – reservations @ prestonfield.com – Fax (0131) 220 43 92
– www.prestonfield.com *Plan I* **C2**
20 rm ☲ – ♦£195 ♦♦£255/295 – 2 suites
Rest *Rhubarb* a la carte £32/49
♦ Traditional ♦ Stylish ♦
Superbly preserved interior, tapestries and paintings in the main part of this
elegant country house, built in 1687 with modern additions. Set in parkland
below Arthur's Seat. Two-roomed, period-furnished 18C dining room with fine
views of the grounds.

The Howard
↳rest 🖼 🔧30 🅿 *VISA* 🐵 🖭 ①

34 Great King St ⊠ *EH3 6QH –* ℰ *(0131) 557 35 00 – reserve@thehoward.com*
– Fax (0131) 557 65 15 – www.thehoward.com
closed Christmas G1
13 rm ⊊ – †£145/210 ††£240/275 – 4 suites
Rest *The Atholl* (booking essential for non-residents) £33
♦ Townhouse ♦ Stylish ♦
Crystal chandeliers, antiques, richly furnished rooms and the relaxing opulence of the drawing room set off a fine Georgian interior. An inviting "boutique" hotel. Elegant, linen-clad tables for sumptuous dining.

The Scotsman
🕮 ⅃ふ 🕅 🖸 & ↳rm 🖼 🕻 🔧80 🅿 *VISA* 🐵 🖭 ①

20 North Bridge ⊠ *EH1 1YT –* ℰ *(0131) 556 55 65*
– reservations@thescotsmanhotelgroup.co.uk – Fax (0131) 652 36 52
– www.thescotsmanhotel.co.uk G2
57 rm – †£295 ††£295, ⊊ £18 – 12 suites
Rest *Vermilion* *(closed Monday and Tuesday)* (dinner only) £35 /50 and a la carte £32/45
Rest *North Bridge Brasserie* a la carte £18/32
♦ Luxury ♦ Classic ♦
Imposing former offices of "The Scotsman" newspaper, with marble reception hall and historic prints. Notably impressive leisure facilities. Well-equipped modern bedrooms. Vibrant, richly red Vermilion. North Bridge Brasserie boasts original marble pillars.

Channings
🚙 ↳ 🔧35 *VISA* 🐵 🖭 ①

15 South Learmonth Gdns ⊠ *EH4 1EZ –* ℰ *(0131) 623 93 02 – reserve@*
channings.co.uk – Fax (0131) 623 93 06 – www.channings.co.uk E1
43 rm ⊊ – †£135/160 ††£175/185 – 3 suites
Rest see *Channings* below
♦ Townhouse ♦ Stylish ♦
Sensitively refurbished rooms and fire-lit lounges blend an easy country house elegance with original Edwardian character. Individually appointed bedrooms.

The Bonham
& ↳ ℅ 🖼 🔧50 🅿 *VISA* 🐵 🖭 ①

35 Drumsheugh Gdns ⊠ *EH3 7RN –* ℰ *(0131) 623 93 01 – reserve@*
thebonham.com – Fax (0131) 623 93 06 – www.thebonham.com E2
46 rm ⊊ – †£145/165 ††£195 – 2 suites
Rest £16 (lunch) and dinner a la carte £29/33
♦ Townhouse ♦ Stylish ♦
A striking synthesis of Victorian architecture, eclectic fittings and bold, rich colours of a contemporary décor. Numerous pictures by "up-and-coming" local artists. Chic dining room with massive mirrors and "catwalk" in spotlights.

The Glasshouse without rest
← 🚙 & 🔠 ↳ ℅

2 Greenside Pl ⊠ *EH1 3AA* 🔧70 *VISA* 🐵 🖭 ①
– ℰ *(0131) 525 82 00 – resglasshouse@theetongroup.com*
– Fax (0131) 525 82 05 – www.theetoncollection.com H1
65 rm – †£230 ††£270 , ⊊ £17
♦ Business ♦ Modern ♦
Glass themes dominate the discreet style. Modern bedrooms, with floor to ceiling windows, have views of spacious roof garden or the city below. Breakfast room to the rear.

The Roxburghe
⅃ふ 🕅 🔠 & 🔠 rest ↳ 🕻 🔧350 *VISA* 🐵 🖭 ①

38 Charlotte Sq ⊠ *EH2 4HG –* ℰ *(0131) 240 55 00 – roxburghe@csmm.co.uk*
– Fax (0131) 240 55 55 – www.macdonaldhotels.co.uk/roxburghe F2
197 rm ⊊ – †£65/210 ††£90/290 – 1 suite
Rest *The Melrose* *(closed Saturday lunch)* £19 /24 and a la carte £19/29
♦ Business ♦ Classic ♦
Attentive service, understated period-inspired charm and individuality in the British style. Part modern, part Georgian but roomy throughout; welcoming bar. Restaurant reflects the grandeur of architect Robert Adam's exterior.

UNITED KINGDOM

UNITED KINGDOM

Holyrood Aparthotel without rest
1 Nether Bakehouse (via Gentles entry)
⊠ EH8 8PE – ℰ (0131) 524 32 00
– mail@holyroodaparthotel.com – Fax (0131) 524 32 10
– www.holyroodaparthotel.com **H2**
41 suites – ♦£100 ♦♦£300
♦ Business ♦ Modern ♦
These two-bedroomed apartments are neat and up-to-date with well-stocked kitchens. Located in a booming area of the city, not far from the Palace of Holyrood.

Christopher North House
6 Gloucester Pl ⊠ EH3 6EF – ℰ (0131) 225 27 20
– reservations@christophernorth.co.uk – Fax (0131) 220 47 06
– www.christophernorth.co.uk **F1**
32 rm ⊑ – ♦£98/140 ♦♦£140/240
Rest (dinner only) a la carte £16/26
♦ Townhouse ♦ Classic ♦
Georgian house on cobbled street in quiet residential area; a chintzy feel overlays the contemporary interior. Eclectically styled bedrooms feature homely extra touches. Classic Scottish cooking in formally styled dining room.

Novotel Edinburgh Centre
80 Lauriston Pl ⊠ EH3 9DE
– ℰ (0131) 656 35 00 – h3271@accor.com – Fax (0131) 656 35 10
– www.novotel.com **F3**
180 rm – ♦£85 ♦♦£169, ⊑ £12
Rest (bar lunch) £19 (dinner) and dinner a la carte £24/32
♦ Chain hotel ♦ Business ♦ Functional ♦
21C hotel in a smart, contemporary style. Well-equipped leisure club. Modern bedrooms: two top-floor suites have private balconies, while 40 rooms look towards the castle. Informal dining room, open 18 hours a day.

Clarendon without rest
25 Shandwick Pl ⊠ EH2 4RG – ℰ (0131) 229 14 67 – res@clarendonhoteledi.com
– Fax (0131) 229 75 49 – www.clarendonhoteledi.com **F2**
66 rm ⊑ – ♦£70/120 ♦♦£90/160
♦ Business ♦ Modern ♦
Two minutes' walk from Princes Street, and completely refurbished in 2004, this smart hotel boasts bright, vivid colours, a cosy, contemporary bar and well-presented rooms.

Edinburgh City
79 Lauriston Pl ⊠ EH3 9HZ – ℰ (0131) 622 79 79
– reservations@bestwesternedinburghcity.co.uk – Fax (0131) 622 79 00
– www.edinburghcity.co.uk
closed 24-27 December **F3**
51 rm – ♦£70/160 ♦♦£95/190, ⊑ £7 – 1 suite
Rest (bar lunch) dinner a la carte £20/29
♦ Business ♦ Functional ♦
Tidily run hotel, converted from Scotland's first maternity hospital, an easy stroll from the centre. A listed Victorian building, it boasts bright, good-sized bedrooms. Smart, comfortable restaurant.

The Lodge
6 Hampton Terrace, West Coates ⊠ EH16 5PE – ℰ (0131) 337 36 82
– info@thelodgehotel.co.uk – Fax (0131) 313 17 00
– www.thelodgehotel.co.uk *Plan I* **B2**
10 rm ⊑ – ♦£60/95 ♦♦£80/135
Rest (booking essential) (dinner only) a la carte £23/35
♦ Family ♦ Classic ♦
A converted Georgian manse, family owned and immaculately kept. Individually designed bedrooms and lounge decorated with taste and care; close to Murrayfield rugby stadium.

Kildonan Lodge without rest ⚤ ⌖ 📞 **P** **VISA** **MO** **AE**
27 Craigmillar Park ✉ *EH16 5PE* – ✆ *(0131) 667 27 93*
– info@kildonanlodgehotel.co.uk – Fax (0131) 667 97 77
– www.kildonanlodgehotel.co.uk
closed 23-26 December   *Plan I* **C3**
12 rm ⌣ – †£56/89 ††£70/145
♦ Family ♦ Cosy ♦
Privately managed, with a cosy, firelit drawing room which feels true to the
Lodge's origins as a 19C family house. One room has a four-poster bed and a fine
bay window.

Ibis without rest ⎷ ⚤ 🖭 **VISA** **MO** **AE** **①**
6 Hunter Sq ✉ *EH1 1QW* – ✆ *(0131) 240 70 00*
– h2039@accor.com – Fax (0131) 240 70 07
– www.accorhotels.com   **G2**
99 rm – †£55/77 ††£55/77, ⌣ £5
♦ Chain hotel ♦ Business ♦ Functional ♦
Interior design reflects the group's ethos - compact and functional, yet
comfortable. A super position just off the High Street will appeal to tourists
throughout the year.

XXXX **Number One** – at Balmoral H. **AC** **VISA** **MO** **AE** **①**
☺ *1 Princes St* ✉ *EH2 2EQ* – ✆ *(0131) 622 88 31 – Fax (0131) 557 87 40*
– www.roccofortehotels.com
closed first 2 weeks January   **G2**
Rest (dinner only) a la carte £46/62
Spec. Isle of Skye crab with melon, cucumber and tomato jus. Roast fillet of beef,
onion purée, girolles and Madeira jus. Raspberry soufflé with raspberry sorbet in
dark chocolate.
♦ Modern ♦ Formal ♦
Edinburgh's nonpareil for polished fine dining and immaculate service; spacious
basement setting. Original dishes with a well-balanced flair showcase Scottish
produce.

XXX **Oloroso** ⬉ 🍴 **AC** ⇕14 **VISA** **MO** **AE**
33 Castle St ✉ *EH2 3DN* – ✆ *(0131) 226 76 14*
– info@oloroso.co.uk
– Fax (0131) 226 76 08 – www.oloroso.co.uk   **F2**
Rest a la carte £26/35
♦ Innovative ♦ Design ♦
Modish third floor restaurant in heart of city. Busy, atmospheric bar. Lovely
terrace with good castle views to the west. Stylish, modern cooking with Asian
influence.

XXX **Grill Room** – at Sheraton Grand H. **AC** ⚤ **P** **VISA** **MO** **AE** **①**
1 Festival Sq ✉ *EH3 9SR* – ✆ *(0131) 221 64 22 – Fax (0131) 229 62 54*
– www.sheraton.com/grandedinburgh
closed Saturday lunch, Sunday and Monday   **F2**
Rest a la carte £29/47
♦ Modern ♦ Formal ♦
Ornate ceilings, wood panels and modern glass make an ideal setting for
imaginative, well presented cooking. Local ingredients with a few European and
Pacific Rim elements.

XXX **Santini** – at Sheraton Grand H. **AC** **P** **VISA** **MO** **AE** **①**
8 Conference Sq ✉ *EH3 8AN* – ✆ *(0131) 221 77 88 – Fax (0131) 221 77 89*
– www.sheraton.com/grandedinburgh
closed Saturday lunch and Sunday   **F2**
Rest a la carte £27/38
♦ Italian ♦ Formal ♦
The personal touch is predominant in this stylish restaurant appealingly situated
under a superb spa. Charming service heightens the enjoyment of tasty, modern
Italian food.

UNITED KINGDOM

XX **Off The Wall** VISA ◯◯ AE
105 High St ⊠ EH1 1SG – ℰ (0131) 558 14 97 – otwedinburgh@aol.com
– www.off-the-wall.co.uk
closed 25-26 December, 1-2 January, Monday lunch January-May
and Sunday except during Edinburgh Festival **G-H2**
Rest £17/20 (lunch) and dinner a la carte £37/42
♦ Scottish ♦ Formal ♦
Located on the Royal Mile, though hidden on first floor away from bustling crowds. Vividly coloured dining room. Modern menus underpinned by a seasonal Scottish base.

XX **Channings** – at Channings H. 🔒 ⇐ VISA ◯◯ AE ◯
12-16 South Learmonth Gdns ⊠ EH4 1EZ – ℰ (0131) 623 93 02
– Fax (0131) 623 93 06 – www.channings.co.uk
closed Sunday **E1**
Rest £16 (lunch) and a la carte £28/33
♦ Mediterranean ♦ Fashionable ♦
A warm, contemporary design doesn't detract from the formal ambience pervading this basement restaurant in which classic Gallic flavours hold sway.

XX **Forth Floor (at Harvey Nichols)** ⇐ Castle and city skyline, 🔒
30-34 St Andrew Sq ⊠ EH2 2AD AC VISA ◯◯ AE ◯
– ℰ (0131) 524 83 50 – Fax (0131) 524 83 51
– www.harveynichols.com
closed 25 December, 1 January and dinner Sunday-Monday **G1**
Rest £14 /25 and a la carte £22/38
♦ Modern ♦ Brasserie ♦
Stylish restaurant with delightful outside terrace affording views over the city. Half the room in informal brasserie-style and the other more formal. Modern, Scottish menus.

XX **Atrium** AC VISA ◯◯ AE ◯
😊 *10 Cambridge St ⊠ EH1 2ED – ℰ (0131) 228 88 82*
– eat@atriumrestaurant.co.uk – Fax (0131) 228 88 08
– www.atriumrestaurant.co.uk
closed 25-26 December, 1-2 January, Sunday and Saturday lunch
except during Edinburgh Festival **F2**
Rest £18 /25 and a la carte £31/41 🍴
♦ Modern ♦ Design ♦
Located inside the Traverse Theatre, an adventurous repertoire enjoyed on tables made of wooden railway sleepers. Twisted copper lamps subtly light the ultra-modern interior.

XX **Duck's at Le Marche Noir** ⇐ ⟷24 VISA ◯◯ AE ◯
2-4 Eyre Pl ⊠ EH3 5EP – ℰ (0131) 558 16 08 – enquiries@ducks.co.uk
– Fax (0131) 556 07 98 – www.ducks.co.uk
closed 25-26 December and lunch Saturday-Monday **G1**
Rest a la carte £26/37
♦ Innovative ♦ Bistro ♦
Confident, inventive cuisine with a modern, discreetly French character, served with friendly efficiency in bistro-style surroundings - intimate and very personally run.

XX **Hadrian's** – at Balmoral H. AC VISA ◯◯ AE ◯
2 North Bridge ⊠ EH1 1TR – ℰ (0131) 557 50 00 – Fax (0131) 557 37 47
– www.roccofortehotels.com **G2**
Rest £15 /19 and a la carte £19/29
♦ Modern ♦ Brasserie ♦
Drawing on light, clean-lined styling, reminiscent of Art Deco, and a "British new wave" approach; an extensive range of contemporary brasserie classics and smart service.

LEITH

Malmaison

🏠 ☆ ᴅ ⇔rm ⅍ ⚘70 🅿 VISA ⦿ AE ⓪

1 Tower Pl ⊠ EH6 7DB – ℰ (0131) 468 50 00 – edinburgh @ malmaison.com
– Fax (0131) 468 50 02 – www.malmaison.com
C1
95 rm – ✝£135 ✝✝£135, � £13 – 5 suites
Rest *Brasserie* £15 /14 and a la carte £22/36

♦ Business ♦ Stylish ♦

Imposing quayside sailors' mission converted in strikingly elegant style.
Good-sized rooms, thoughtfully appointed, combine more traditional comfort
with up-to-date overtones. Sophisticated brasserie with finely wrought iron.

Express by Holiday Inn without rest

ᴅ ⇔ ⚲ ⚘25

Britannia Way, Ocean Drive ⊠ EH6 6JJ
🅿 VISA ⦿ AE ⓪
– ℰ (0131) 555 44 22 – info @ hiex-edinburgh.com – Fax (0131) 555 46 46
– www.hiex-edinburgh.com
C1
145 rm – ✝£95 ✝✝£95

♦ Business ♦ Chain hotel ♦ Functional ♦

Modern, purpose-built hotel offering trim, bright, reasonably-priced
accommodation. Convenient for Leith centre restaurants and a short walk from
the Ocean Terminal.

Martin Wishart

⇔ VISA ⦿ AE

54 The Shore ⊠ EH6 6RA – ℰ (0131) 553 35 57 – info @ martin-wishart.co.uk
– Fax (0131) 467 70 91 – www.martin-wishart.co.uk
closed 25-26 December, 1 January, 1 week February, Sunday, Monday and
Saturday lunch
C1
Rest (booking essential) £21 (lunch) and a la carte £47/52
Spec. Lobster and smoked haddock soufflé. Roast halibut, glazed pig's trotter
and braised endive. Caramel mousseline, chocolate croustillant and milk sorbet.

♦ Innovative ♦ Formal ♦

Simply decorated dockside conversion with a growing reputation. Modern
French-accented menus characterised by clear, intelligently combined flavours.

The Vintners Rooms

⇔ VISA ⦿ AE

The Vaults, 87 Giles St ⊠ EH6 6BZ – ℰ (0131) 554 67 67
– enquiries @ thevintnersrooms.com – Fax (0131) 555 56 53
– www.thevintnersrooms.com
closed 1-15 January, Sunday dinner and Monday
C1
Rest £18 (lunch) and a la carte £33/38

♦ Mediterranean ♦ Rustic ♦

Atmospheric 18C bonded spirits warehouse with high ceilings, stone floor,
rug-covered walls and candlelit side-room with ornate plasterwork.
French/Mediterranean cooking.

GLASGOW

Population (est. 2005): 616 000 (conurbation 1 228 000) – Altitude: 8m

AGE Atlantide SNC/HOA QUI

The dynamic image which Glasgow has projected in recent years is in sharp contrast to its robust reputation as a populous, industrial city and major port. It is now enjoying a growing popularity as a cultural centre and evidence of a resolutely modern outlook is to be found in the eye-catching buildings on the banks of the Clyde which punctuate the Glasgow skyline. There is much animation in the city centre with the smart shopping centres and numerous places to eat and drink and have a good time.

St Mungo became its first bishop in the mid-6C and later its patron saint. In the 17C Glasgow – always a radical city – became the centre of the Protestant cause. By the 18C the city was rich from trade in textiles, sugar and tobacco, her wealth increasing in the 19C through banking, shipbuilding and heavy industry.

The arts prospered amid the wealth as the rich merchants proved to be enlightened patrons. In the late 19C a progressive outlook was fostered by the Glasgow Boys and a pioneer modern movement led by Charles Rennie Mackintosh, who was responsible for a renewal in fine and applied arts. Today the realism and radicalism of contemporary Glasgow artists are acclaimed. Glasgow is the home of Scottish Opera, Scottish ballet and several notable art collections.

WHICH DISTRICT TO CHOOSE

You will find luxury **accommodation** from 5-star hotels to stylish, boutique hotels around George Square *Plan II* **E2** and Argyle St *Plan II* **C2** in the city centre and around Great Western Road *Plan I* **A1** in the fashionable West End. For good accommodation at reasonable prices in a central loca-tion look around Sauchiehall St *Plan II* **C1**, Renfrew St *Plan II* **D1** and Hope St *Plan II* **D2**. There are comfortable business hotels near Central Station *Plan II* **D2**, near Finnieston Quay *Plan I* **A2** and along the riverside near the Scottish Exhibition and Conference Centre.

There is a fine selection of quality **restaurants** along Bath Street *Plan II* **D2** and in the parallel West Regent *Plan II* **D2**, West George *Plan II* **D2** and St Vincent streets *Plan II* **D2** as well as Albion St *Plan II* **E3** and Candleriggs *Plan II* **E3**. Tucked behind Byres Lane *Plan I* **A1** are cobblestone lanes with lively bistros and cafés. Some of the best restaurants and pubs are in charming Ashton Lane *Plan I* **A1**. For Glasgow's thriving pavement café culture, explore Merchant Square *Plan II* **E3**, Candleriggs *Plan II* **E3**, Royal Exchange Square *Plan II* **D2** in The Merchant City.

PRACTICAL INFORMATION

ARRIVAL – DEPARTURE

Glasgow International Airport – 13 km (8mi) west of the city centre. ℰ 0870 040 0008; www.baa.co.uk/lasgow

Prestwick International Airport – 48km (30mi) southwest of the city. ℰ 01292 511 000 (outside the UK), 0871 223 0700 (inside the UK); www.gpia.co.uk

From Glasgow airport to the city centre – By **taxi**: about £18-20. By **bus**: No 905 and 950 from the front of the terminal building to stops close to Central Station, Queen Street Station and Buchanan Bus Station. City bus stops have an airport logo on them. Mon-Fri 6am-midnight, every 10min at peak times and 15-30min the rest of the day; Sat-Sun every 15-30min. Fare £3.30 single, £5 round trip. ℰ 0870 550 5050; www.travellinescotland.co.uk; www,citylink.co.uk

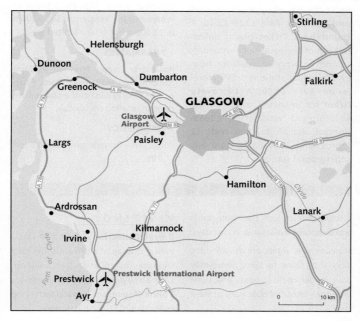

From Prestwick Airport to the city centre – By **rail** via Paisley Gilmour St Station: every 30 min (hourly on Sun). Time 45min. Fare: 50% reduction on standard rail fare for air passengers. By **bus** to Buchanan Bus Station via Kilmarnock: every 30min at peak times. Time 50min. £7, return £12. ℰ 0870 608 2608; www.travellines cotland.co.uk

Railway Stations – Central Station *Plan II* **D2** – Services from the south and England. **Queen Street Station** *Plan II* **E2** – Trains from Edinburgh and the north. ℰ 08457 484 950; www. nationalrail.co.uk

TRANSPORT

◆ UNDERGROUND AND BUS

Glasgow and its environs have a very comprehensive public transport network. A **FirstDay** ticket for First Day services is available from bus drivers on the day of travel and is valid until midnight. Fare £2.20-£2.50. A **Roundabout Ticket** giving unlimited use of the local rail and underground network is available from any staffed rail stations or SPT Travel Centre. Fare £4.50. A **Discovery Ticket** for unlimited travel on the underground valid after 9.30am Mon-Sat and all day Sun costs £2 approx. and is available from any underground station.

◆ TAXIS

Metered taxis can be picked up at taxi ranks in the town centre, outside the main rail and bus stations, at the airport or can be ordered by phone. Additional charges are levied for luggage, night travel and extra passengers. Many taxis accept credit cards.

USEFUL ADDRESSES

◆ TOURIST OFFICES

Glasgow TIC, 11 George Square, Glasgow G2 1DY *Plan II* **E2**. ℰ 0141 204 4400. **Glasgow Airport TIC**, International Arrivals Hall, Glasgow. ℰ 0141 848 4400; www.seeglasgow.com

◆ POST OFFICES

The main post office at 47 St Vincent St *Plan II* **D2** is open Mon-Fri, 8.30am-5.30pm and Sat, 9am-5.30pm.

◆ BANKS/CURRENCY EXCHANGE

Opening times, Mon-Fri 9.30am to 4pm; some banks open on Sat, 9.30am to 12.30pm but offer a limited service.

◆ PHARMACIES

Pharmacies open Mon-Fri, 9.30am-5.30pm, Sat, 9.30am-12.30pm. Pharmacies display a list of the pharmacies open in rotation on Sunday.

◆ EMERGENCY

Police, Fire Brigade and Ambulance: ℰ **999**.

EXPLORING GLASGOW

It is possible to visit the main sights and museums in Glasgow in two days.

Museums and sights are usually open daily 9.30-10am to 5pm. Some may have longer opening hours and some may open later and close early at week ends.

VISITING

Burrell Collection *Plan I* **A3** – A fascinating display of a private collector's treasures in an attractive building. Later stroll down to the 18C mansion, **Pollok House**, set in parkland – fine collection of Spanish paintings.

Glasgow Cathedral *Plan II* **F2** – A magnificent medieval building marking the birthplace of the city. View from the Necropolis. Proceed to Cathedral Square with its original buildings and visit **Provand's Lordship**.

George Square *Plan II* **E2** – A splendid Victorian square lined with ornate buildings: **City Chambers**, **Merchants' House**, Post Office.

Glasgow University district *Plan I* **A1** – Grand university buildings. Do not miss the **Art Gallery and Museum Kelvingrove** (British and European paintings, arms and armour), the **Hunterian Museum and Art Gallery** (Whistler collection, Scottish paintings) and the **Mackintosh Wing** (interiors, furnishings, drawings, watercolours).

Museum of Transport *Plan I* **A1** – A comprehensive collection of trams and trolley buses, Scottish-built cars, fire vehicles and bicycles as well as model ships illustrating Scottish shipbuilding.

Gallery of Modern Art *Plan II* **E2** – A great 18C mansion houses a collection of contemporary art from around the world.

Glasgow Science Centre *Plan I* **A2** – Explore the wonders of science and technology in three sleek modern buildings on the river bank.

Tenement House *Plan II* **C1** – A piece of social history. Life in a tenement house in the early 20C.

Mackintosh Trail – *Ticket for bus travel and admission from SPT travel centres, tourist offices and participating sights.* A must for Mackintosh fans: **The Glasgow School of Art** *Plan II* **D1**, **The Lighthouse** *Plan II* **D2**, **Queen's Cross Church** *Plan II* **D2**, **Mackintosh Wing** *(see above)*, **Scotland Street School Museum** *Plan I* **A2**, **The Willow Tea Rooms**

(*Sauchiehall Street*) *Plan II* **C1**, **House for an Art Lover** and **Hill House** in Helensburgh.

Boat trip along the Firth of Clyde starting from Waverley Terminal, Anderston Quay *Plan II* **C3** and from Broomielaw *Plan II* **D3** to Braehead with commentary on the history of the Clyde.

GOURMET TREATS

Establishments which offer the best Scottish fare are identified by a 'stockpot' sign. Take a break at the delightful *Willow Tea Rooms* at 217 Sauchiehall Street and 97 Buchanan Street which serve breakfast, light meals and afternoon tea.

SHOPPING

Stores are usually open Mon-Sat, 9-10am to 5.30-6.30pm. Some shops open Sun, 11am to 4.30-5.30pm.

LUXURY SHOPS, BOUTIQUES – **Sauchiehall** *Plan II* **D1** and **Argyle** *Plan II* **D2 Streets** are pedestrian shopping precincts. Exclusive shops and elegant malls line **Buchanan St** (*St Enoch Centre, Buchanan Galleries* and *Princes Square*) *Plan II* **D2**. Stylish shops are to be found in **John Street** *Plan II* **E2** and **Ingram Street** *Plan II* **E2** in the Merchant City. The **Braehead** shopping centre, Kings Inch Road, has a huge number of shops.

SCOTTISH CRAFTS AND GIFTS – *Mackintosh Shop* at Glasgow School of Art. *Hutchesons' Hall shop*, 158 Ingram St. *Form, The Lighthouse Shop*, 11 Mitchell Lane. For handcrafted jewellery, go to *Orro*, 12 Wilson St; *Nancy Smillie Shop & Gallery*, 53 Creswell St; *Starry, Starry Night*, 21 Downside Lane.

ANTIQUES – Take time to browse at *DeCourcy Arcade*, 5-12 Creswell St; *Victorian Village*, 93 West Regent St; *Tim Wright Antiques*, 147 Bath St.

MARKETS – The Barras *Plan II* **F3** is a lively flea market, full of local colour. Open Sat-Sun, 10am-5pm.

WHAT TO BUY – Tartans, knitwear, Scottish crafts, shortbread and cakes, marmalade and jams, whisky, Mackintosh-inspired jewellery and other gifts.

ENTERTAINMENT

For listings of what's on in Glasgow consult the daily papers, The Herald and The Evening Times or the fortnightly magazine The List. The Glasgow pages of the weekly Time Out also give useful information.

Glasgow Royal Concert Hall *Plan II* **D2** – Concerts.

Royal Scottish Academy of Music and Drama *Plan II* **D1** – National Conservatoire and performing arts centre.

Theatre Royal *Plan II* **D2** – Performances of Scottish Opera and Scottish Ballet.

Scottish Exhibition and Conference Centre *Plan I* **A2** – Live music, pop and rock concerts.

St Andrews in the Square *Plan II* **E3** – Folk and traditional Scottish music.

Centre for Contemporary Arts *Plan II* **C1** – Live music and cutting-edge theatre.

Mitchell Theatre *Plan II* **C2** – Drama and live music.

King's Theatre *Plan II* **D2** – Musicals, dance, drama.

Citizens' Theatre *Plan I* **B2**, **Tron Theatre** *Plan II* **E3**, **Tramway Theatre** *Plan I* **A2** – Experimental drama.

NIGHTLIFE

The lively atmosphere of **Glasgow pubs** is famous. Visit *Rab-Ha's*, 83 Hutchenson St;*Times Square*, St Enoch's Square, *Bonhams*, 194 Byres Rd and *Dows*, 9 Dundas St. Pubs with folk music include *Scotia Bar* and *Clutha Vaults*, both in Stockwell St (112 and 167); *Molly Malone's*, 224 Hope St.

For **live music and nightclubs**, a trendy crowd frequents *Archaos*, 25-37 Queen St; *Sub Club*, 22 Jamaica St; *The Tunnel*, 38 Mitchell St; while a young crowd dances the night away at *The Arches*, 253 Argyle St; *Barrowlands*, 244 Gallowgate; *The Garage*, 490 Sauchiehall St; and *The Carling Academy*, 121 Eglinton Rd. *The Riverside Club*, 33 Fox St and *Park Bar*, 1202 Argyle St have folk evenings at weekends.

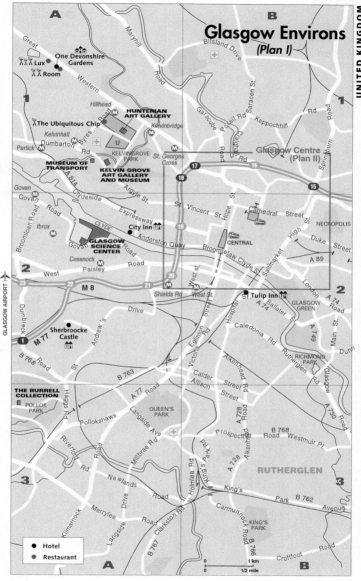

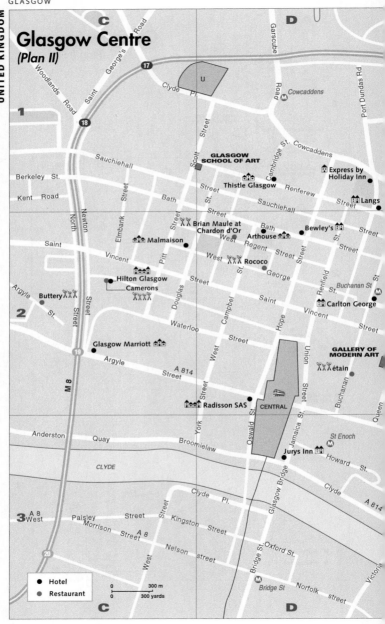

Glasgow Centre
(Plan II)

UNITED KINGDOM

GLASGOW SCHOOL OF ART

Express by Holiday Inn

Thistle Glasgow

Langs

Brian Maule at Chardon d'Or

Bewley's

Malmaison

Arthouse

Rococo

Buttery

Hilton Glasgow

Camerons

Carlton George

Glasgow Marriott

GALLERY OF MODERN ART

étain

Radisson SAS

CENTRAL

Jurys Inn

CLYDE

● Hotel
● Restaurant

| 0 | | 300 m |
| 0 | | 300 yards |

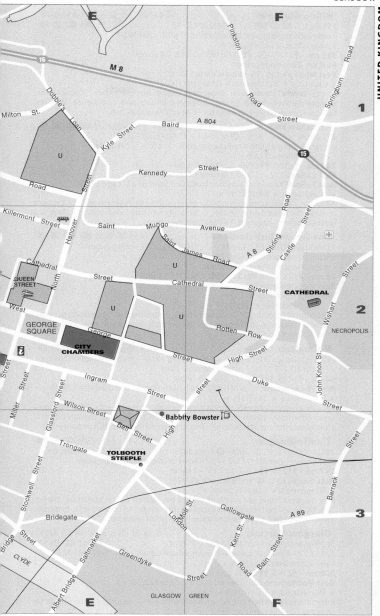

Hilton Glasgow
🛏🛏🛏🛏 ≼ ⅙ ⋔ ☒ & ᵐ ⅘ ℀ ♨1000 ⬤

1 William St ⊠ G3 8HT – 𝒞 (0141) 204 55 55
– reservations.glasgow@hilton.com – Fax (0141) 204 50 04
– www.hilton.co.uk/glasgow
315 rm – †£170/190 ††£170/190, ⌷ £18 – 4 suites
Rest see *Camerons* below
Rest *Minsky's* £19 /25 and a la carte £27/37

C2

♦ Luxury ♦ Business ♦ Modern ♦

A city centre tower with impressive views on every side. Comfortable, comprehensively fitted rooms. Extensive leisure and conference facilities. Spacious, modern Minsky's has the style of a New York deli.

Radisson SAS
🛏🛏🛏 ⅙ ⋔ ☒ & ᵐ ⅘rm ℀ ℃ ♨800 🅿 𝘝𝘐𝘚𝘈 ⓒⓒ 🄰🄴 ⓪

301 Argyle St ⊠ G2 8DL – Ⓜ St Enoch – 𝒞 (0141) 204 33 33
– reservations.glasgow@radissonsas.com – Fax (0141) 204 33 44
– www.radissonsas.com
246 rm – †£190 ††£190, ⌷ £14 – 1 suite
Rest *Collage* £12 /15 and a la carte £21/35
Rest *TaPaell'Ya* (closed Saturday lunch and Sunday) a la carte £17/27

D2

♦ Business ♦ Modern ♦

A stunning, angular, modish exterior greets visitors to this consummate, modern commercial hotel. Large, stylish, eclectically furnished bedrooms. Collage is a bright modern restaurant. Ta Paell'Ya serves tapas.

One Devonshire Gardens
🛏🛏 ⅙ ⅘ ℃ ♨50 𝘝𝘐𝘚𝘈 ⓒⓒ 🄰🄴 ⓪

1 Devonshire Gdns ⊠ G12 0UX – 𝒞 (0141) 339 20 01 – reservations@
onedevonshiregardens.com – Fax (0141) 337 16 63
– www.onedevonshiregardens.com
32 rm – †£135/495 ††£135/495, ⌷ £17 – 3 suites
Rest see also *Room* below
Rest *No.5* (dinner only) £39

Plan I **A1**

♦ Townhouse ♦ Stylish ♦

Collection of adjoining 19C houses in terrace, furnished with attention to detail. Elegantly convivial drawing room, comfortable bedrooms and unobtrusive service. Smart No.5.

Malmaison
🛏🛏 ⅙ & ⅘rm ♨25 𝘝𝘐𝘚𝘈 ⓒⓒ 🄰🄴 ⓪

278 West George St ⊠ G2 4LL – 𝒞 (0141) 572 10 00 – glasgow@malmaison.com
– Fax (0141) 572 10 02 – www.malmaison.com
64 rm – †£135 ††£135, ⌷ £13 – 8 suites
Rest *The Brasserie*, 𝒞 (0141) 572 10 01 – £15 (lunch) and a la carte £25/40

C2

♦ Business ♦ Stylish ♦

Visually arresting former Masonic chapel. Comfortable, well-proportioned rooms seem effortlessly stylish with bold patterns and colours and thoughtful extra attentions. Informal Brasserie with French themed menu and Champagne bar.

Thistle Glasgow
🛏🛏 ⅙ ⋔ ☒ ᵐ ♨1300 𝘝𝘐𝘚𝘈 ⓒⓒ 🄰🄴 ⓪

36 Cambridge St ⊠ G2 3HN – Ⓜ Cowcaddens – 𝒞 (0141) 332 33 11 – glasgow@
thistle.co.uk – Fax (0141) 332 40 50 – www.thistlehotels.com/glasgow
297 rm – †£210 ††£210, ⌷ £13 – 3 suites
Rest *Gengis* £11 /18 and a la carte £17/24

D1

♦ Business ♦ Functional ♦

Purpose-built hotel just north of the centre, geared to the corporate market. Smartly-appointed rooms and excellent inter-city road connections. Extensive meeting facilities. Grills meet tandoori in themed restaurant.

Glasgow Marriott
🛏🛏 ≼ ⅙ ⋔ ☒ & ᵐ ⅘ ℀ ⊠ ♨600

500 Argyle St, Anderston ⊠ G3 8RR – 𝒞 (0141)
226 55 77 – frontdesk.glasgow@marriotthotels.co.uk – Fax (0141) 221 92 02
– www.marriott.co.uk/gladt
300 rm – †£145 ††£185, ⌷ £15
Rest *Mediterrano* £21 (dinner) and a la carte £22/30

🅿 𝘝𝘐𝘚𝘈 ⓒⓒ 🄰🄴 ⓪

C2

♦ Business ♦ Functional ♦

Internationally owned city centre hotel with every necessary convenience for working travellers and an extensive lounge and café-bar. Upper floors have views of the city. Strong Mediterranean feel infuses restaurant.

Arthouse
⭐ Ⓐ rest ⧗rm ⚐70 VISA ⓂⓄ AE

129 Bath St ⊠ G2 2SZ – Ⓜ Buchanan St – ℰ (0141) 221 67 89 – info @
arthousehotel.com – Fax (0141) 221 67 77 – www.arthousehotel.com
60 rm – ♦£115 ♦♦£125/155, ☑ £15   **D2**
Rest Grill £13 /17 and a la carte £24/33

◆ **Business** ◆ **Stylish** ◆

Near Mackintosh's School of Art, an early 20C building decorated with a daring modern palette: striking colour schemes and lighting in the spacious, elegantly fitted rooms. Basement grill restaurant, plus seafood and Teppan-Yaki bar.

Carlton George
⭐ Ⓐ ⧗ ⚐ Ⓒ VISA ⓂⓄ AE

44 West George St ⊠ G2 1DH – Ⓜ Buchanan St – ℰ (0141) 353 63 73
– salesgeorge@ carltonhotels.co.uk – Fax (0141) 353 62 63
– www.carltonhotels.co.uk   **D2**
64 rm – ♦£165/185 ♦♦£165/185, ☑ £14
Rest Windows £16 (lunch) and a la carte £22/30

◆ **Business** ◆ **Classic** ◆

A quiet oasis away from the city bustle. Attractive tartan decorated bedrooms bestow warm tidings. Comfortable 7th floor business lounge. An overall traditional ambience. Ask for restaurant table with excellent view across city's rooftops.

Langs
⅃⅃ ⭐rm Ⓐ rest ⧗ VISA ⓂⓄ AE Ⓓ

2 Port Dundas Pl ⊠ G2 3LD – Ⓜ Buchanan St – ℰ (0141) 333 15 00
– reservations @ langshotel.co.uk – Fax (0141) 333 57 00
– www.langshotels.co.uk
closed 24-26 December   **D1**
100 rm – ♦£100/110 ♦♦£210 , ☑ £12
Rest Aurora (dinner only) a la carte £17/32
Rest Oshi £14 (lunch) and a la carte £16/27

◆ **Business** ◆ **Stylish** ◆

Opposite the Royal Concert Hall. Themed loft suites and stylish Japanese or Californian inspired rooms, all with CD players and computer game systems. Cool and contemporary. Scottish ingredients to fore at Aurora. Stunning water feature enhances Oshi.

Sherbrooke Castle
⇌ Ⓐ rest ⧗ Ⓒ ⚐300 Ⓟ VISA ⓂⓄ AE Ⓓ

11 Sherbrooke Ave, Pollokshields ⊠ G41 4PG – ℰ (0141) 427 42 27 – mail @
sherbrooke.co.uk – Fax (0141) 427 56 85 – www.sherbrooke.co.uk   Plan I **A2**
16 rm ☑ – ♦£75/140 ♦♦£95/160 – 2 suites
Rest Morrisons a la carte £15/35

◆ **Castle** ◆ **Classic** ◆

Late 19C baronial Romanticism given free rein inside and out. The hall is richly furnished and imposing; rooms in the old castle have a comfortable country house refinement. Panelled Victorian dining room with open fire.

City Inn
≤ 🚗 ⭐ Ⓐ ⧗rm Ⓒ Ⓔ ⚐50 Ⓟ VISA ⓂⓄ AE Ⓓ

Finnieston Quay ⊠ G3 8HN – ℰ (0141) 240 10 02 – glasgow.reservations @
cityinn.com – Fax (0141) 248 27 54 – www.cityinn.com   Plan I **A2**
164 rm – ♦£129 ♦♦£129, ☑ £13
Rest City Cafe £15 /17 and a la carte £18/34

◆ **Chain hotel** ◆ **Business** ◆ **Functional** ◆

Quayside location and views of the Clyde. Well priced hotel with a "business-friendly" ethos; neatly maintained modern rooms with sofas and en suite power showers. Restaurant fronts waterside terrace.

Jurys Inn
⭐ Ⓐ ⧗rm Ⓒ Ⓒ ⚐100 VISA ⓂⓄ AE Ⓓ

80 Jamaica St ⊠ G1 4QE – Ⓜ St Enoch – ℰ (0141) 314 48 00 – jurysinnglasgow @
jurysdoyle.com – Fax (0141) 314 48 88 – www.jurysdoyle.com
closed 24-26 December   **D3**
321 rm – ♦£79/89 ♦♦£79/89, ☑ £10
Rest £24 (dinner) and a la carte £19/29

◆ **Chain hotel** ◆ **Business** ◆ **Functional** ◆

Attractive modern hotel on the riverside with excellent access to main shopping areas. Spacious interior with all day coffee bar. Good value, up-to-date, comfy bedrooms. Informal eatery serves breakfast as well as eclectic range of dinners.

UNITED KINGDOM

Bewley's
    ⟦icons: 🅰️C rest ⟵rm 🍴 ☎ VISA ⓪ ☒ ⓪⟧

110 Bath St ⊠ *G2 2EN* – 🚇 *Buchanan St* – ℰ *(0141) 353 08 00* – *gla @ bewleyshotels.com* – *Fax (0141) 353 09 00* – *www.bewleyshotels.com*
closed 25-27 December   **D2**
103 rm – ♦£69 ♦♦£69/99, ⊊ £7
Rest *Loop* a la carte £18/25
• Business • Functional •

A well-run group hotel, relaxed but professional in approach, in the middle of Glasgow's shopping streets. Upper rooms boast rooftop views and duplex apartments. People-watch from glass-walled eatery.

Tulip Inn
    ⟦icons: ♦₅ & 🅰️C rest ⟵ 🖭 ☎ ♨180 🅿️ VISA ⓪ ☒ ⓪⟧

80 Ballater St ⊠ *G5 0TW* – 🚇 *Bridge St* – ℰ *(0141) 429 42 33* – *info @ tulipinnglasgow.co.uk* – *Fax (0141) 429 42 44*
– www.tulipinnglasgow.co.uk   *Plan I* **B2**
114 rm – ♦£60/85 ♦♦£60/85, ⊊ £8
Rest *Bibo Bar and Bistro* (dinner only) a la carte £18/22
• Chain hotel • Business • Functional •

Sensibly priced hotel appealing to cost-conscious business travellers. Good access to motorway and city centre. Bedrooms have working space and most modern conveniences. Informal, bright eatery serves a varied menu.

Express by Holiday Inn without rest
    ⟦icons: & ⟵ ☎ VISA ⓪ ☒ ⓪⟧

Theatreland, 165 West Nile St ⊠ *G1 2RL* – 🚇 *Cowcaddens* – ℰ *(0141) 331 68 00*
– express @ higlasgow.com – *Fax (0141) 331 68 28*
– www.hiexpressglasgow.co.uk
closed 25-26 December   **D1**
88 rm ⊊ – ♦£75/89 ♦♦£75/89
• Chain hotel • Functional •

Modern accommodation - simple and well arranged with adequate amenities. Equally suitable for business travel or leisure tourism.

Camerons – at Hilton Glasgow H.
    ⟦icons: 🅰️C ⟵ 🅿️ VISA ⓪ ☒ ⓪⟧

1 William St ⊠ *G3 8HT* – ℰ *(0141) 204 55 11* – *Fax (0141) 204 50 04*
– www.hilton.co.uk/glasgow
closed Saturday lunch, Sunday and Bank Holidays   **C2**
Rest £20 (lunch) and dinner a la carte £30/45
• Modern • Formal •

Carefully prepared and full-flavoured modern cuisine with strong Scottish character. Very formal, neo-classical styling and smart staff have advanced its local reputation.

Buttery
    ⟦icons: ⟵ 🅿️ VISA ⓪ ☒⟧

652 Argyle St ⊠ *G3 8UF* – ℰ *(0141) 221 81 88* – *ia.fleming @ btopenworld.com*
– Fax (0141) 204 46 39
closed first week January, Sunday, Monday and Saturday lunch   **C2**
Rest £38 and lunch a la carte £24/28
• Modern • Formal •

Established, comfortable restaurant away from the bright lights; red velour and ageing bric-a-brac reveal its past as a pub. Ambitiously composed modern Scottish repertoire.

étain
    ⟦icons: 🅰️C VISA ⓪ ☒⟧

The Glass House, Springfield Court ⊠ *G1 3JN* – 🚇 *St Enoch*
– ℰ (0141) 225 56 30 – etain @ conran.com – Fax (0141) 225 56 40
– www.conran.com
closed 25 December,1 January, Saturday lunch and Sunday dinner   **D2**
Rest £29 /32
• Modern • Brasserie •

Comfortable, contemporary restaurant in unusual glass extension to Princes Square Centre. Well-sourced Scottish ingredients prepared in a modern, interesting way.

XXX **Rococo**　　　　　　　　　　　　　　　AC VISA ⓜ AE ①

202 West George St ⊠ G2 2NR – ⓜ Buchanan St – ℰ (0141) 221 50 04
– info@rococoglasgow.co.uk – Fax (0141) 221 50 06
– www.rococoglasgow.co.uk
closed 26 December and 1 January　　　　　　　　　　　　　　　D2
Rest £18 /37 and lunch a la carte £32/43 ⅋

♦ Contemporary ♦ Design ♦

In style, more like studied avant-garde: stark, white-walled cellar with vibrant modern art and high-backed leather chairs. Accomplished, fully flavoured contemporary menu.

XXX **Lux**　　　　　　　　　　AC ⅋ P VISA ⓜ AE ①

1051 Great Western Rd ⊠ G12 0XP – ℰ (0141) 576 75 76 – luxstazione@
btconnect.com – Fax (0141) 576 01 62 – www.lux.5pm.co.uk
closed 25-26 December, 1-2 January and Sunday　　　　　　*Plan I* **A1**
Rest (dinner only) £30 /34

♦ Modern ♦ Design ♦

19C railway station converted with clean-lined elegance: dark wood, subtle lighting and vivid blue banquettes. Fine service and flavourful, well-prepared modern menus.

XX **Brian Maule at Chardon d'Or**　　　　⅋ VISA ⓜ AE

176 West Regent St ⊠ G2 4RL – ⓜ Buchanan St – ℰ (0141) 248 38 01
– info@brianmaule.com – Fax (0141) 248 39 01
– www.brianmaule.com
closed 2 weeks January, 2 weeks summer, 25-26 December, Saturday lunch,
Sunday and Bank Holidays　　　　　　　　　　　　　　　D2
Rest £19 (lunch) and a la carte £29/40

♦ Modern ♦ Brasserie ♦

Large pillared Georgian building. Airy interior with ornate carved ceiling and hung with modern art. Modern dishes with fine Scottish produce; substantial wine list.

XX **Room**　　　　　　　　　　⅋ ⬡16 VISA ⓜ AE ①

1 Devonshire Gdns ⊠ G12 0UX – ℰ (0141) 339 20 01
– glasgow.reservations@roomrestaurants.com – Fax (0141) 337 16 63
– www.roomrestaurants.com　　　　　　　　　　*Plan I* **A1**
Rest £13 /19 and a la carte approx. £28

♦ Contemporary ♦ Design ♦

Victorian façade hides trendy interior with cool, comfy bar and stylish eating area with bold colour schemes and modern art. Good value dishes are exciting and original.

X **The Ubiquitous Chip**　　　　　　　AC VISA ⓜ AE ①

12 Ashton Lane ⊠ G12 8SJ, off Byres Rd – ⓜ Kelvinhall – ℰ (0141) 334 50 07
– mail@ubiquitouschip.co.uk – Fax (0141) 337 13 02
– www.ubiquitouschip.co.uk
closed 25 December and 1 January　　　　　　　　*Plan I* **A1**
Rest £23 /39 and a la carte £17/29 ⅋

♦ Traditional ♦ Bistro ♦

A long-standing favourite, "The Chip" mixes Scottish and fusion styles. Well known for its glass-roofed courtyard, with a more formal but equally lively warehouse interior.

🍺 **Babbity Bowster**　　　　　　　　🍴 VISA ⓜ AE ①

16-18 Blackfriars St ⊠ G1 1PE – ℰ (0141) 552 50 55 – fraser@babbity.com
– Fax (0141) 552 77 74 – www.babbity.com
closed 25 December　　　　　　　　　　　　　　　E3
Rest a la carte £13/26

♦ Traditional ♦ Pub ♦

Well regarded pub of Georgian origins with columned façade. Paradoxically simple ambience: gingham-clothed tables, hearty Scottish dishes, slightly more formal in evenings.

at Glasgow Airport West : 8m by M8

Ramada
♿ AC rest ⅙ 🏛30 P VISA MC AE ⓓ

Marchburn Drive ✉ PA3 2SJ – ✆ (0141) 840 22 00 – sales.glasgowairport@ramadajarvis.co.uk – Fax (0141) 889 68 30 – www.ramadajarvis.co.uk

108 rm – †£85 ††£85, ☕ £12

Rest *Bagio* a la carte £20/26

♦ Chain hotel ♦ Business ♦ Functional ♦

Within walking distance of the terminal building and with facilities for long-term parking; modern style throughout, with well-equipped, generously proportioned bedrooms. Casual Mediterranean eatery: emphasis on pizzas and pastas.

Express by Holiday Inn
♿ AC rest ⅙ ✆ 🏛75 P VISA MC AE ⓓ

St Andrews Drive ✉ PA3 2TJ – ✆ (0141) 842 11 00 – info@hiex-glasgow.com – Fax (0141) 842 11 22 – www.hiex-glasgow.com

143 rm – †£99/109 ††£99/109

Rest (dinner only) a la carte £16/22

♦ Chain hotel ♦ Functional ♦

Ideal for both business travellers and families. Spacious, carefully designed, bright and modern bedrooms with plenty of work space. Complimentary continental breakfast. Traditional and busy buffet-style restaurant.

Dear Reader

Welcome to the 25th edition of the 'Main Cities of Europe' guide, newly remodelled in order to make it even more useful and user-friendly for our readers.

The new guide is aimed primarily at the international businessman who regularly travels throughout Europe but it is equally ideal for those wishing to discover the delights of some of Europe's most romantic and culturally stimulating cities for a weekend break or special occasion.

Entry in the Michelin Guide is completely free of charge and it continues to be compiled by our professionaly trained teams of full-time inspectors from across Europe who make their assessments anonymously in order to ensure complete impartiality and independence. Their mission is to check the quality and consistency of the amenities and services provided by the hotels and restaurants throughout the year and our listings are updated annually in order to ensure the most up-to-date information.

Most of the establishments featured have been hand-picked from our other national guides and therefore our European selection is, effectively, a best-of-the-best listing.

In addition to the new user-friendly layout the new guide contains key thematic words which succinctly convey the style of the establishment; practical and cultural information on each country and each city; suggestions on what to see, where to shop and where to spend the evening.

Thank you for your support and please continue to send us your comments. We hope you will enjoy travelling with the 'Main Cities of Europe' guide 2006.

Consult the Michelin Guide at **www.ViaMichelin.com** and write to us at:
themichelinguide-europe@uk.michelin.com

Contents